Television Network Prime-Time Programming

Television Network Prime-Time Programming, 1948–1988

by

Mitchell E. Shapiro

McFarland & Company, Inc., Publishers
Jefferson, North Carolina, and London

British Library Cataloguing-in-Publication data available

Library of Congress Cataloguing-in-Publication Data

Shapiro, Mitchell E., 1953–
 Television network prime-time programming, 1948–1988.

 Includes index.
 1. Television programs – United States – Chronology.
I. Title.
PN1992.3.U5S54   1989   791.45′0236′0973   89-45006

ISBN 0-89950-412-4 (lib. bdg. : 50# alk. paper) ∞

Manufactured in the United States of America.

McFarland & Company, Inc., Publishers
 Box 611, Jefferson, North Carolina 28640

To my family

Table of Contents

Acknowledgments

I wish to express my gratitude and sincere appreciation to the numerous people, too many to name here, who have offered encouragement and have provided inspiration to me throughout my personal and professional life.

I would especially like to thank the faculty, staff and students in the School of Communication at the University of Miami for their support. They are all a constant source of enjoyment to me.

I would also like to thank the people at McFarland & Company for their assistance and support.

Finally, I would like to express my most heartfelt thanks to my family for always being there.

Introduction

This book is designed to be a comprehensive chronicle of network prime-time television programming. Beginning with September 1948 and continuing to the fall of 1988, this work provides month-by-month prime-time schedules for all national broadcasting networks; a detailed listing of all network programming moves, including series premieres, cancellations, and time slot moves; and a yearly recap of key programming moves.

This book is organized into seven chapters, each representing a different night of the week. Each chapter consists of individual month-by-month prime-time schedules for each network beginning with September 1948, followed by a detailed chronological listing of every one of that network's series and programming moves (series premieres, series cancellations, and time slot moves). At the end of each chapter is the summary of key programming moves for each television season since 1948.

The information contained within this book has been compiled by the author in part from personal observations. In addition, several sources were used in compiling the program listing information. These sources include *TV Guide,* television listings from Miami *Herald* and Chicago *Tribune,* and the following encyclopedias: *The Complete Directory to Prime Time Network TV Shows: 1946–1984* by Tim Brooks and Earle Marsh, *The Complete Encyclopedia of Television Programs: 1947–1976* by Vincent Terrace, and *Total Television: A Comprehensive Guide to Programming from 1948 to 1984* by Alex McNeil.

How to Use This Book

The month-by-month program schedules and the detailed listings of all network programming moves are organized by individual network for each night of the week. For instance, there is a separate month-by-month schedule and detailed listing for ABC-Monday, ABC-Tuesday, CBS-Tuesday, NBC-Wednesday, and so on.

On the month-by-month schedules (the chart, or grid, pages), series are blocked in by time period (all times are based on the Eastern Time zone). Capital letters signify the series' debut. When there is an asterisk at the end of a series block it signifies that the series was cancelled at that time and no longer appeared on a regular basis.

See "How to Use the Schedule Grids" beginning on page xix.

The detailed listings of all programming moves (the strictly columnar pages) contain the following information:

Network: the network involved in the specific programming move is shown in the "running head" at the very top of each page.

Date of the action: the month and year (e.g., "8/48") that the specific programming move occurred.

Time: the time in the evening (Eastern Time zone) that the program began.

Title: the specific title of the series.

Length: the length, in minutes, is given in parentheses for all episodes that are other than 30 minutes long.

Type: the program type of the series is shown in a two-letter code (after a dash) at the end of each title. The following abbreviations are used:

AA	Adventure Anthology	DA	Dramatic Anthology
AD	Adventure	DB	Debate
CA	Comedy Anthology	DD	Docudrama
CD	Crime Drama	DN	Dance
CK	Cooking	DO	Documentary
CO	Comedy-Drama	DR	Drama
CR	Courtroom Reenactment	DS	Discussion
CV	Comedy Variety	FA	Science Fiction Anthology
CY	Comedy	FI	Film

FS	Fashion	QU	Quiz/Audience Participation
FY	Fantasy	RA	Crime Anthology
HS	Home Shopping	RD	Religious Drama
IF	Information	RE	Religion
IN	Inventions	RO	Rodeo
IS	Instruction	SA	Suspense Anthology
IV	Interview	SC	Situation Comedy
KA	Children's Anthology	SD	Spy Drama
KV	Children's	SF	Science Fiction
LD	Lawyer Drama	SH	Sports Highlights
MA	Mystery Anthology	SI	Science
MC	Musical Comedy	SL	Serialized Drama
MD	Medical Drama	SN	Sports News
ME	Medical Anthology	SP	Sporting Event
MO	Medical Documentary	ST	Sports Talk
MR	Military Reenactments	TA	Talent
MU	Music	TK	Talk
MV	Musical Variety	TR	Travel
MY	Mystery	UD	Musical Drama
NA	News Analysis	VS	Various/Miscellaneous
ND	Newspaper Drama	VY	Variety
NM	Newsmagazine	WA	Western Anthology
NW	News	WD	War Drama
OA	Occult Anthology	WE	Western
PA	Public Affairs	WL	Wildlife
PO	Political		

Action: the specific move that was made by the network. The following moves are included:

d — Debut — when a series first appears

c — Cancelled — when a series last appears

m — Moved — when a series is moved to or from a different time slot or night of the week

s — Start — used for movie slots, regularly scheduled sporting events, and newscasts, when they first appear

f — Finish — used for movies, sporting events, and news, when they last appear

* — Used to designate summer replacement series;

— Used to designate that a series was still occupying that specific time slot at the beginning of the 1988–1989 television season.

From/To: when a series was moved (i.e., an "m" appears in the **Action** column), this tells from ("Fr:") where or to ("To:") where and when it was moved. In this column at the right, the following abbreviations are used:

f	Friday
m	Monday
n	Sunday
r	Thursday

s	Saturday
t	Tuesday
w	Wednesday

Several examples, designed to help the reader use and understand the information in the charts detailing all programming moves, are presented below:

This example is from a page headed *"Tuesday ABC Schedule"*:

Date	Time	Title (min. if not 30) — Type	Action	From/To
9/53	9:00	Danny Thomas Show — SC	d	

In this example, we see that the program involved is *The Danny Thomas Show*. This series consists of 30 minute episodes, as signified by the absence of a length indication in parentheses after the title, and is a situation comedy, as shown by the "SC" abbreviation at the end of the title. The programming move (the *Action*) is the series debut, represented by the symbol "d." The date of the programming move *(Date)* is September, 1953, and the program occupies the *Time* slot beginning at 9:00 p.m. Eastern Time.

This example is from a page headed *"Tuesday CBS Schedule"*:

Date	Time	Title (min. if not 30) — Type	Action	From/To
7/85	8:30	Alice — SC	c	

In this example, the program involved is *Alice,* it is 30 minutes long (i.e., there is no parenthesized note to the contrary) and it is a situation comedy on the CBS network. It occupied the time slot beginning at 8:30 p.m. Eastern Time, and was cancelled (as signified by the "c" under the *Action* column) in July, 1985.

Note that the two examples so far involved a debut and a cancellation, so there is no information in the *From* and *To* columns (because there was no "move").

This example is from a page headed *"Tuesday CBS Schedule"*:

Date	Time	Title (min. if not 30) — Type	Action	From/To
9/87	8:00	Houston Knights (60) — CD	m	Fr:t-9

In this example, we see that the program involved is *Houston Knights,* a 60-minute crime drama (represented by the abbreviation "CD") on CBS. We can see that the program begins at 8:00 p.m. (Eastern Time). We see that there is an "m" under the action column. This means that the programming move involves the series *moving* to or from this time period, which means there will be an entry under the *"From/To"* column. In this example, there is a "Fr:t-9" entry under that column, which is to be read as "moved from the 9:00 p.m. slot on Tuesday" (and into the 8:00 p.m. slot on Tuesday).

This example is from a page headed *"Monday NBC Schedule"*:

Date	Time	Title (min. if not 30) — Type	Action	From/To
6/81	9:00	Flamingo Road (60) — SL	m	To:t-10-11/81

In this example, the program *Flamingo Road,* a 60-minute serialized drama ("SL") on NBC, moved (an "m" under *Action*) to a new slot. That is, in June 1981 this series was moved *out* of its 9:00 p.m. slot on Monday; and in November 1981 is was moved *into* the 10:00 p.m. slot on Tuesday (i.e., "t-10-11/81").

How to Use
the Schedule Grids

As stated in the previous section, the month-by-month program schedule grids are organized by individual network for each night of the week. All prime-time television series are blocked in by time period (all times are based on Eastern Standard Time). Capital letters signify the series' debut. An asterisk at the end of a series block signifies that the series was cancelled at that time.

When the title of the series is presented in ordinary capitals and lower-case letters, it signifies that the series was moved into that time slot after airing previously in a different time slot. If one wanted to find out what time slot a series previously occupied, one would simply refer to the monthly listing chart immediately following the program schedule grid. For example, on page 6, one can see that *Colt .45* was moved into the 9:00–9:30 time slot on Sunday in October 1958. To find out where *Colt .45* aired previously, refer to the chronological chart immediately following the program grid, look up 10/58 (which can be found on page 24), and discover that *Colt .45* was moved from the 8:30–9:00 slot on Friday, which it last occupied in April 1958.

Also in reference to the previous example, one can see that *Colt .45* occupied the 9:00–9:30 slot on Sunday (see pages 6 and 7) until September 1959. Since there is no asterisk listed at that time, it means that *Colt .45* was then moved into another time slot. To find out where it was moved, follow the same procedure described in the previous example: refer to the chart immediately following the schedule grid, look up 9/59 (page 24), and notice that *Colt .45* was moved into the 7:00–7:30 slot on Sunday.

One can also use the schedule grids to determine exactly what series occupied a specific time slot at any point in time between 1948 and 1988. For example if one wanted to know what series occupied the 8:00–9:00 slot on ABC's Sunday night schedule in September 1978, you would turn to the schedule grid for ABC in the Sunday chapter, look up 9/78, look at the 8:00–9:00 slot and discover that *Battlestar Galactica* occupied that slot at that time (see page 13). If, instead of September 1978, one were interested in what series occupied the 8:00–9:00 in January 1979, follow the procedure just described. In this case, there is no series title listed on the grid for the 8:00–9:00 slot (see page 14). Instead, there is a blank box with an arrow at the top. This signifies that the series that is occupying this slot is the same series listed for this slot on the previous page. In this case we see that it is *Battlestar Galactica.*

When no series occupies a time slot, the grid is marked with cross-hatching.

Summer replacement series are not depicted on the schedule grids if the series they replaced was continuing in the time slot.

Sunday Night
September 1948 – August 1988

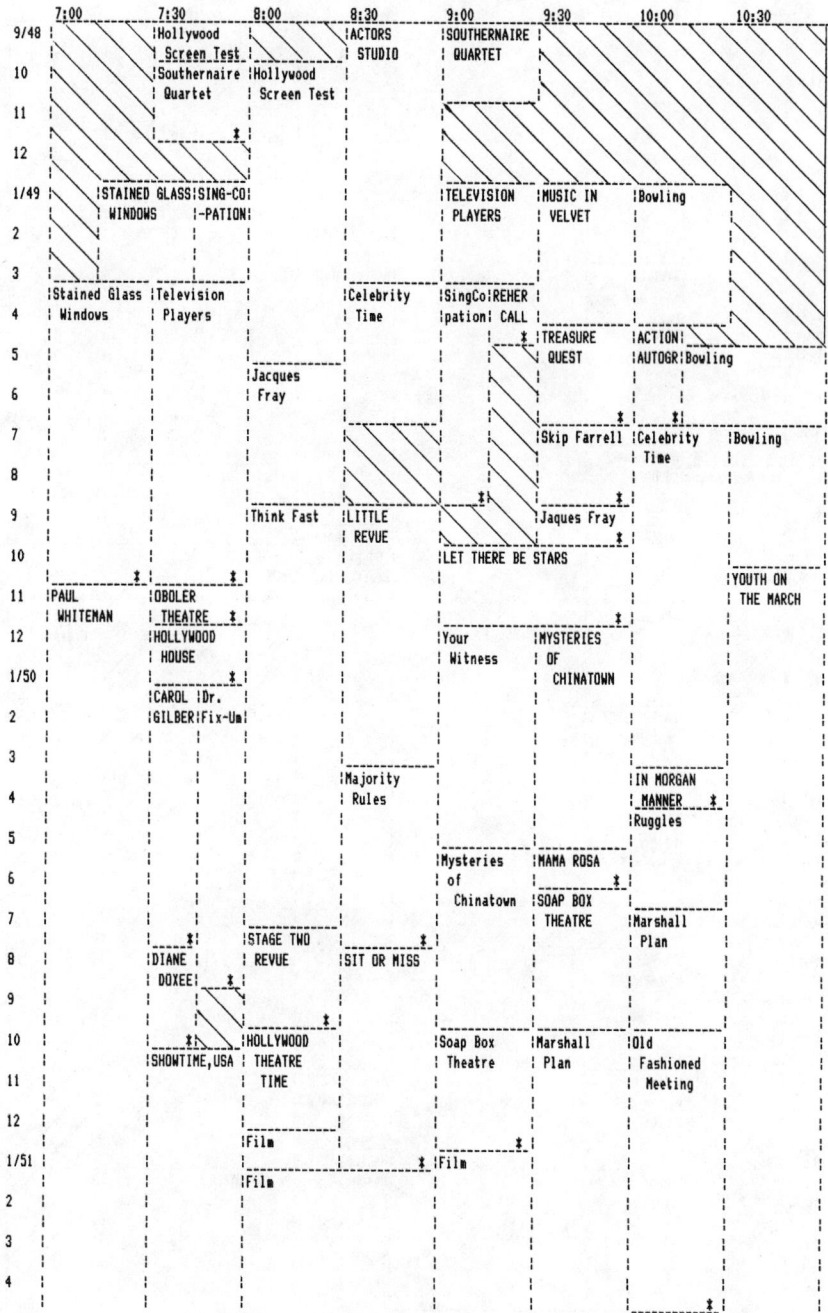

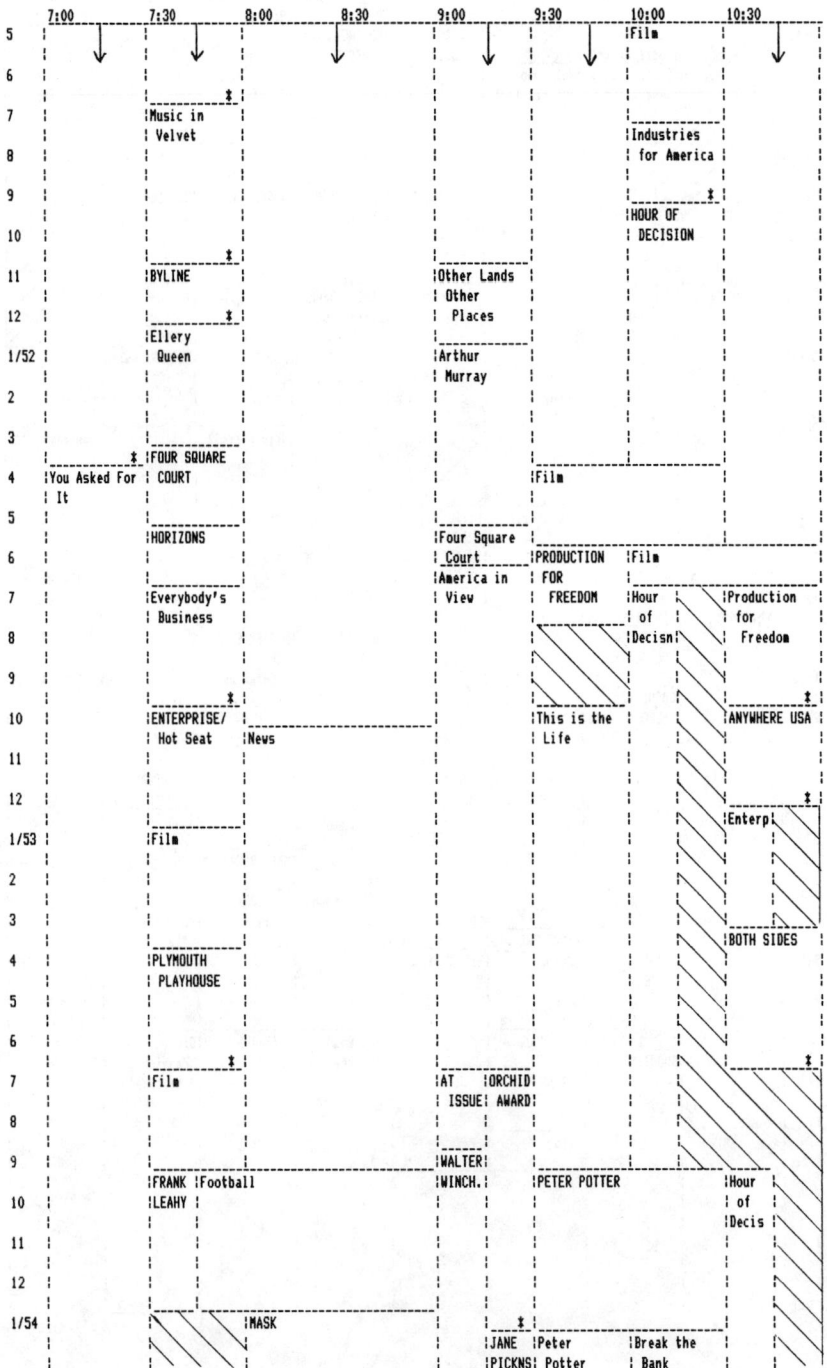

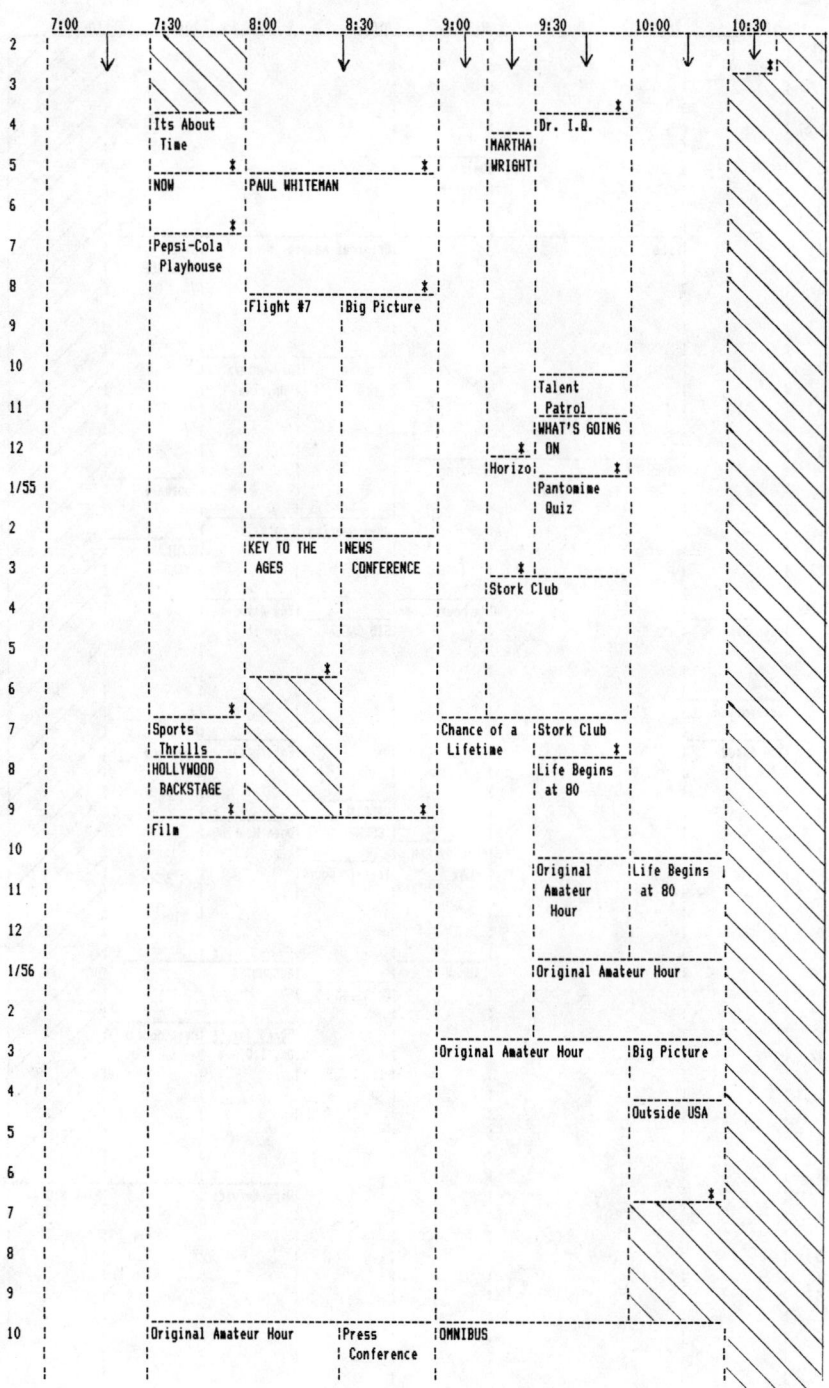

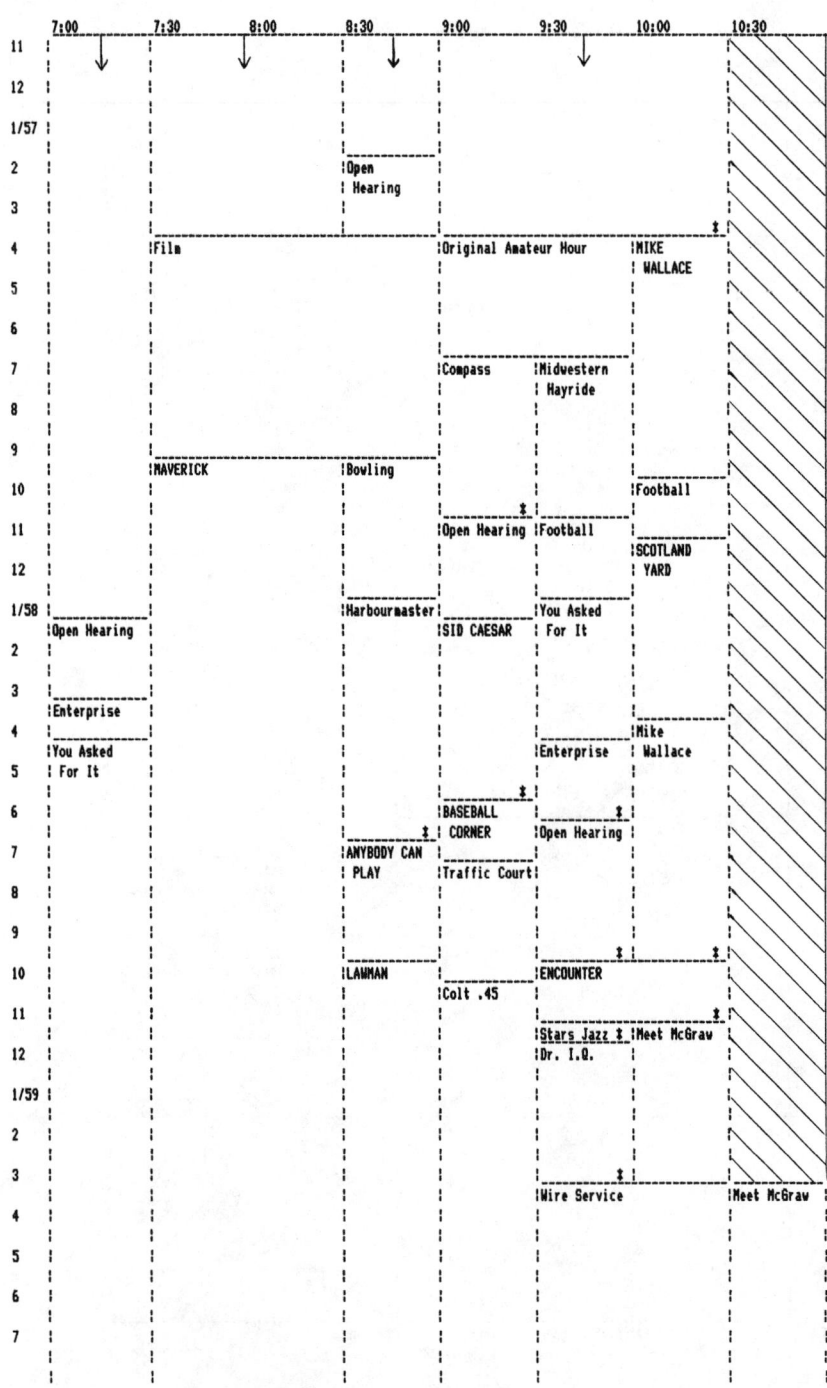

	7:00	7:30	8:00	8:30	9:00	9:30	10:00	10:30
8								
9								
10	Colt .45				REBEL	ALASKANS		DICK CLARK
11								
12								21 Beacon
1/60								Street
2								
3								
4	Broken Arrow							Johnny Staccato
5								
6								
7								
8								
9								
10	Walt Disney					ISLANDERS		Walter Winchell
11								
12								WINSTON CHURCHILL
1/61								
2								
3								
4						ASPHALT JUNGLE		
5								
6								
7								EDITORS CHOICE
8								
9								
10	Maverick	FOLLOW THE SUN			BUS STOP		Adventures in Paradise	
11								
12								
1/62								
2								
3								
4				Film				Lawman

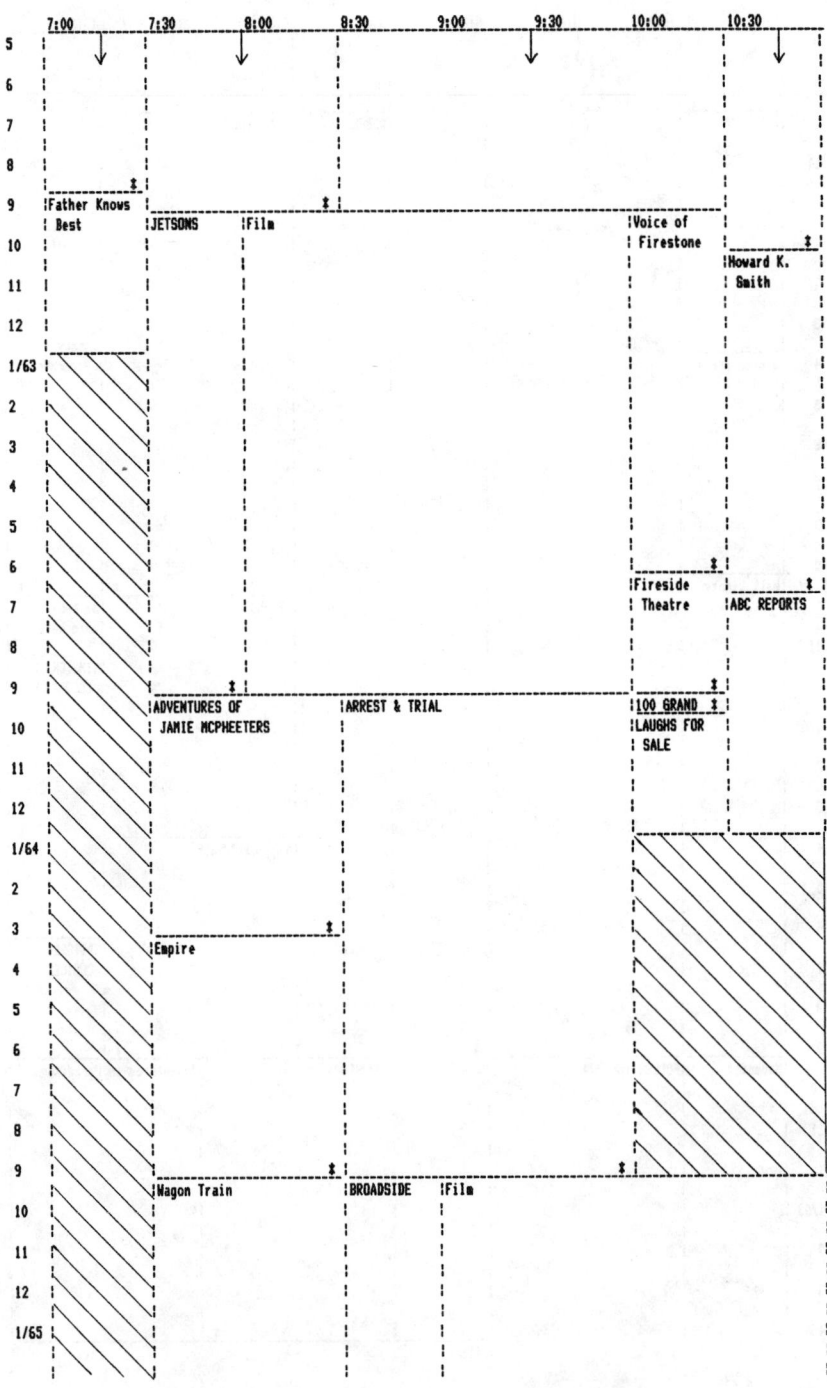

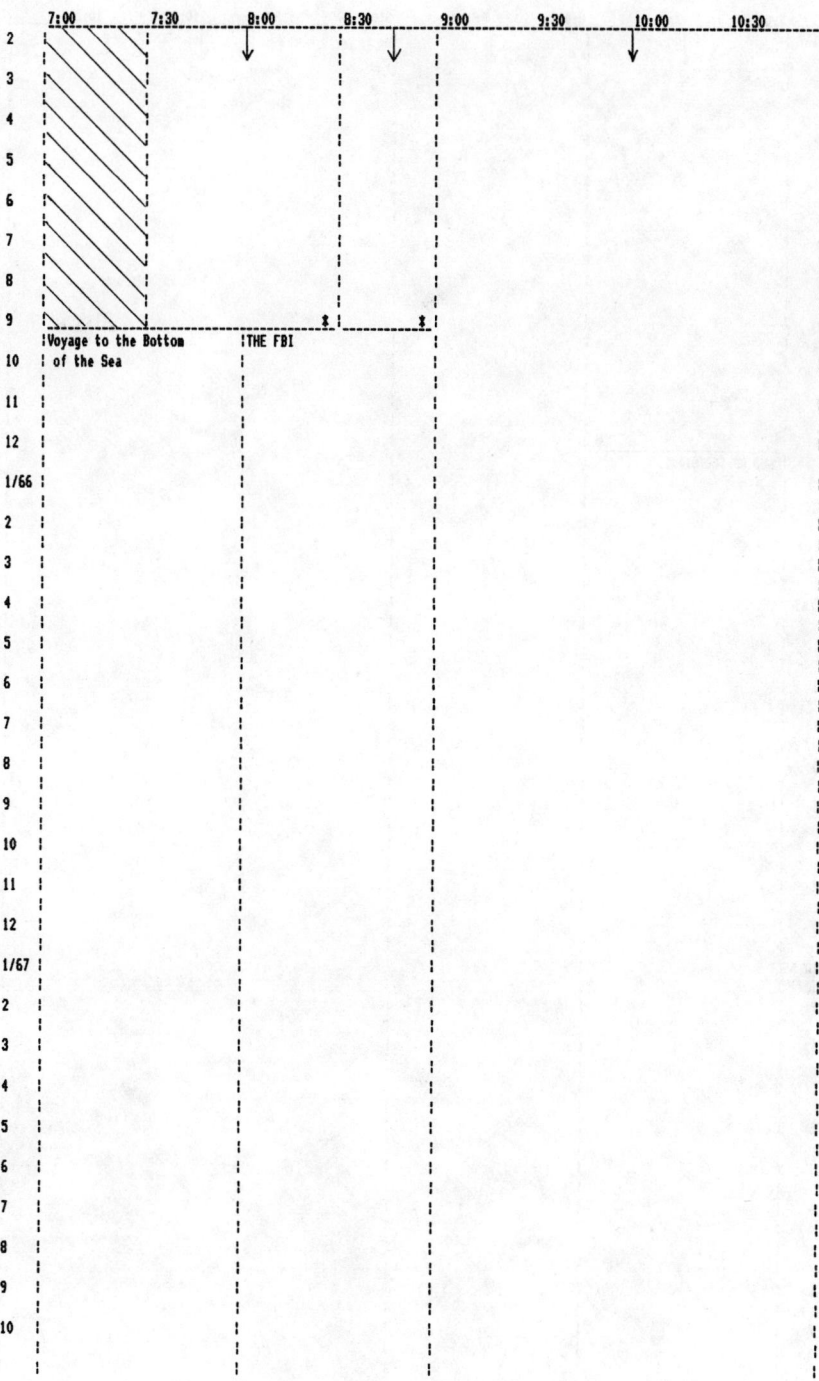

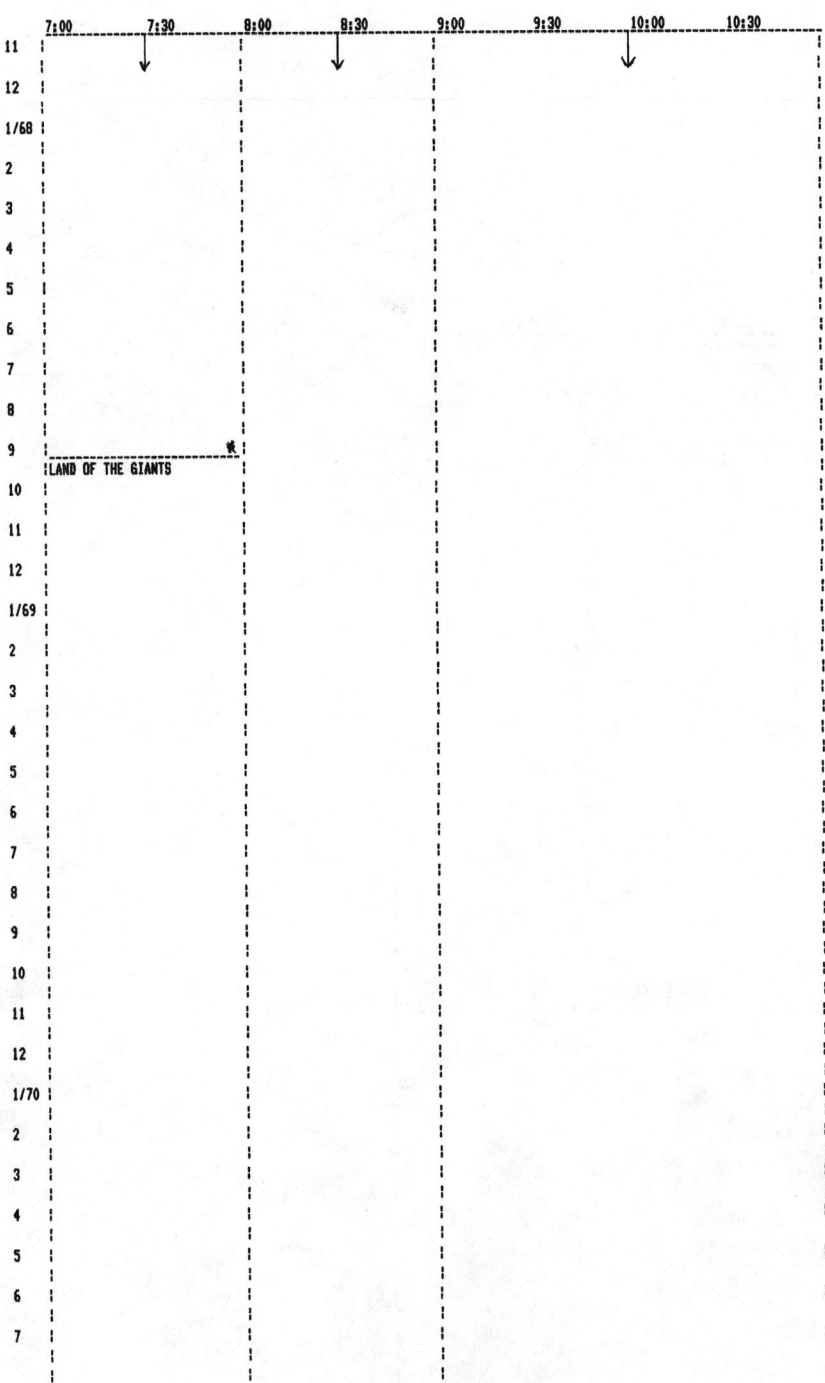

LAND OF THE GIANTS

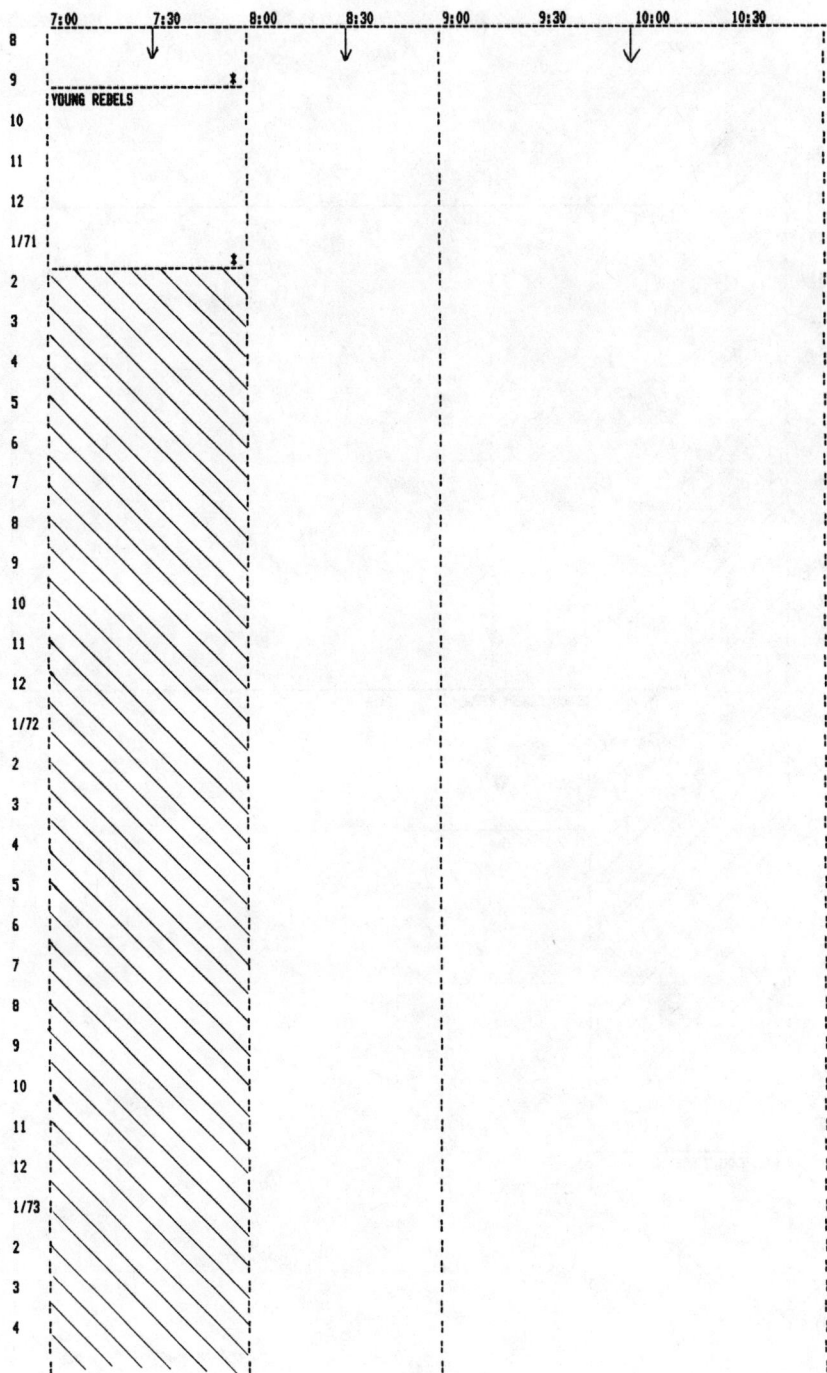

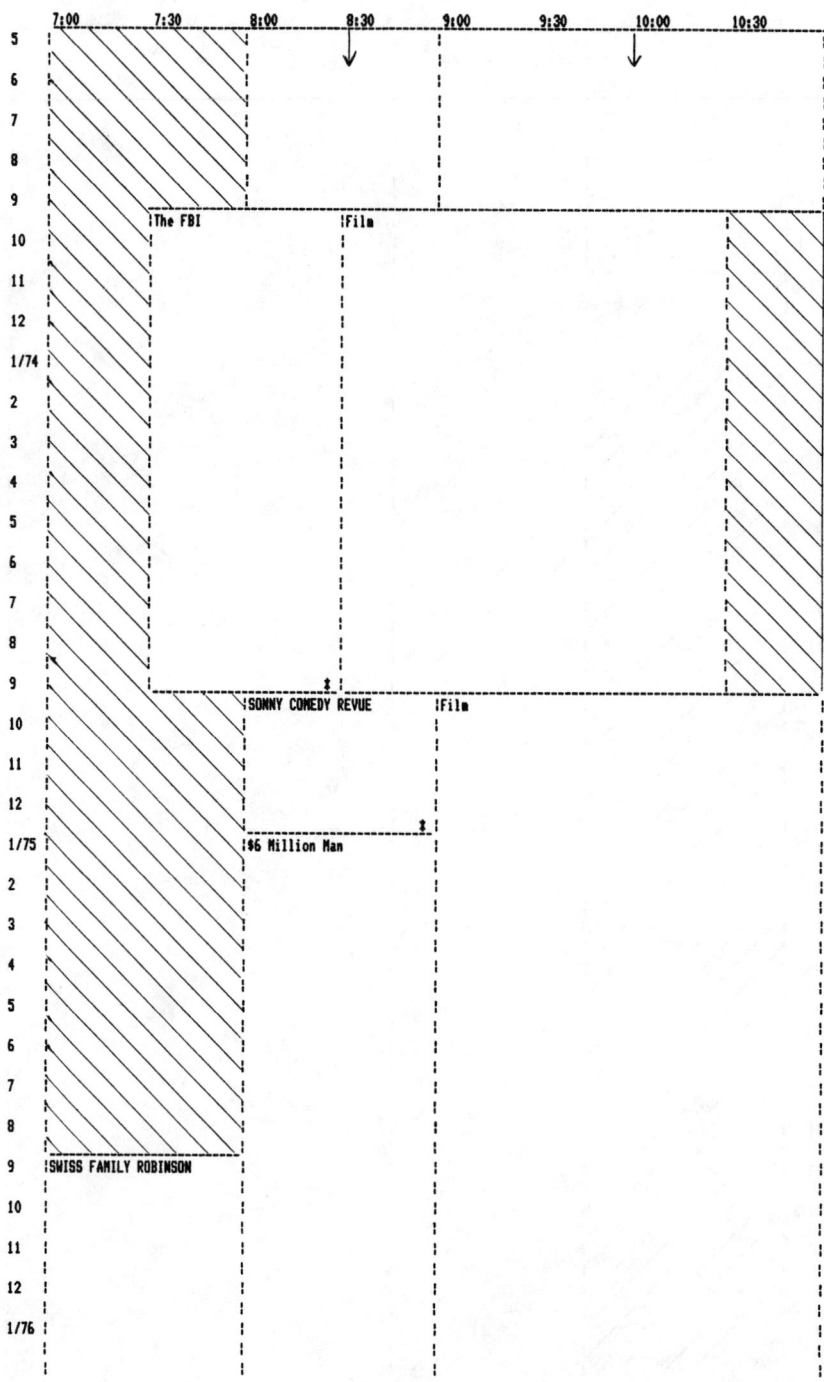

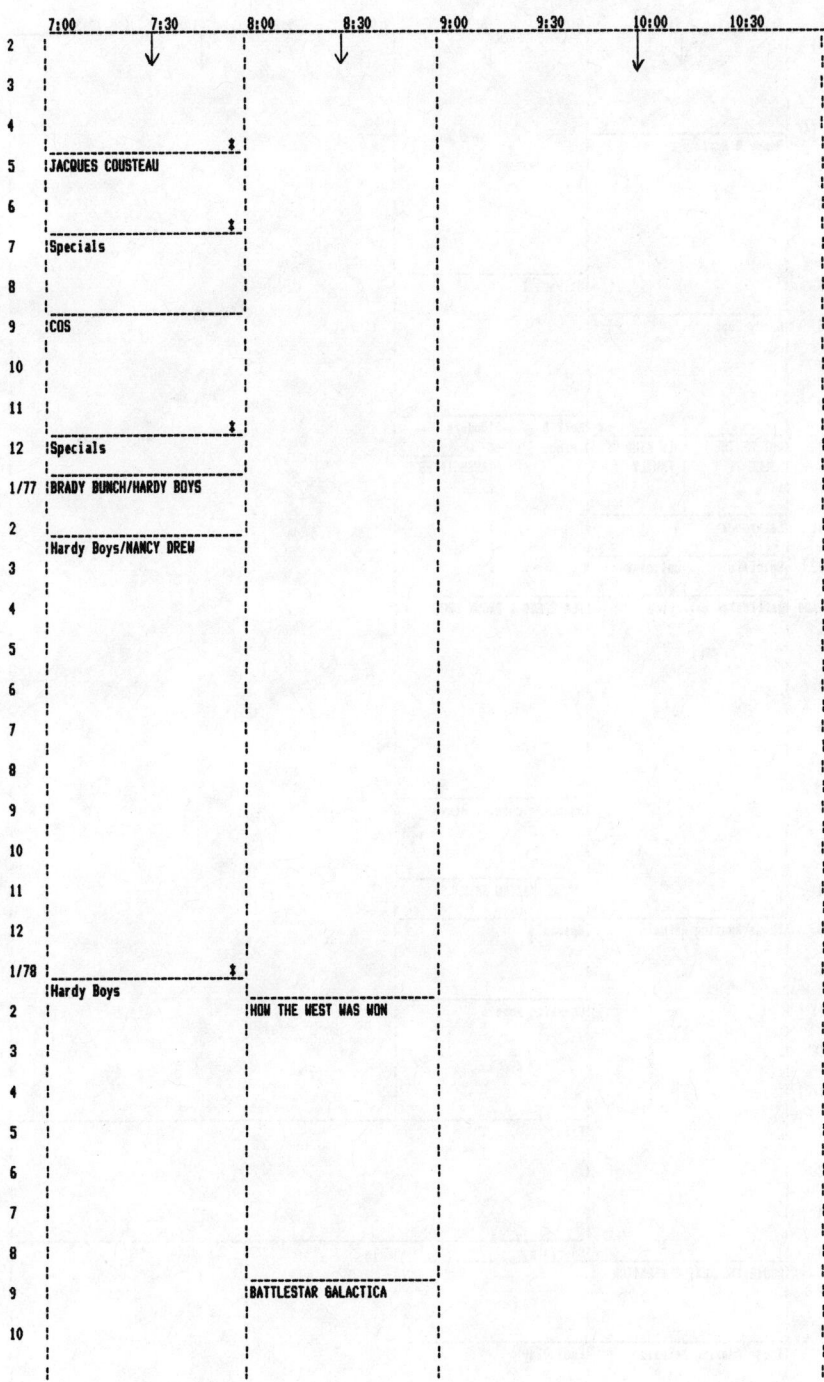

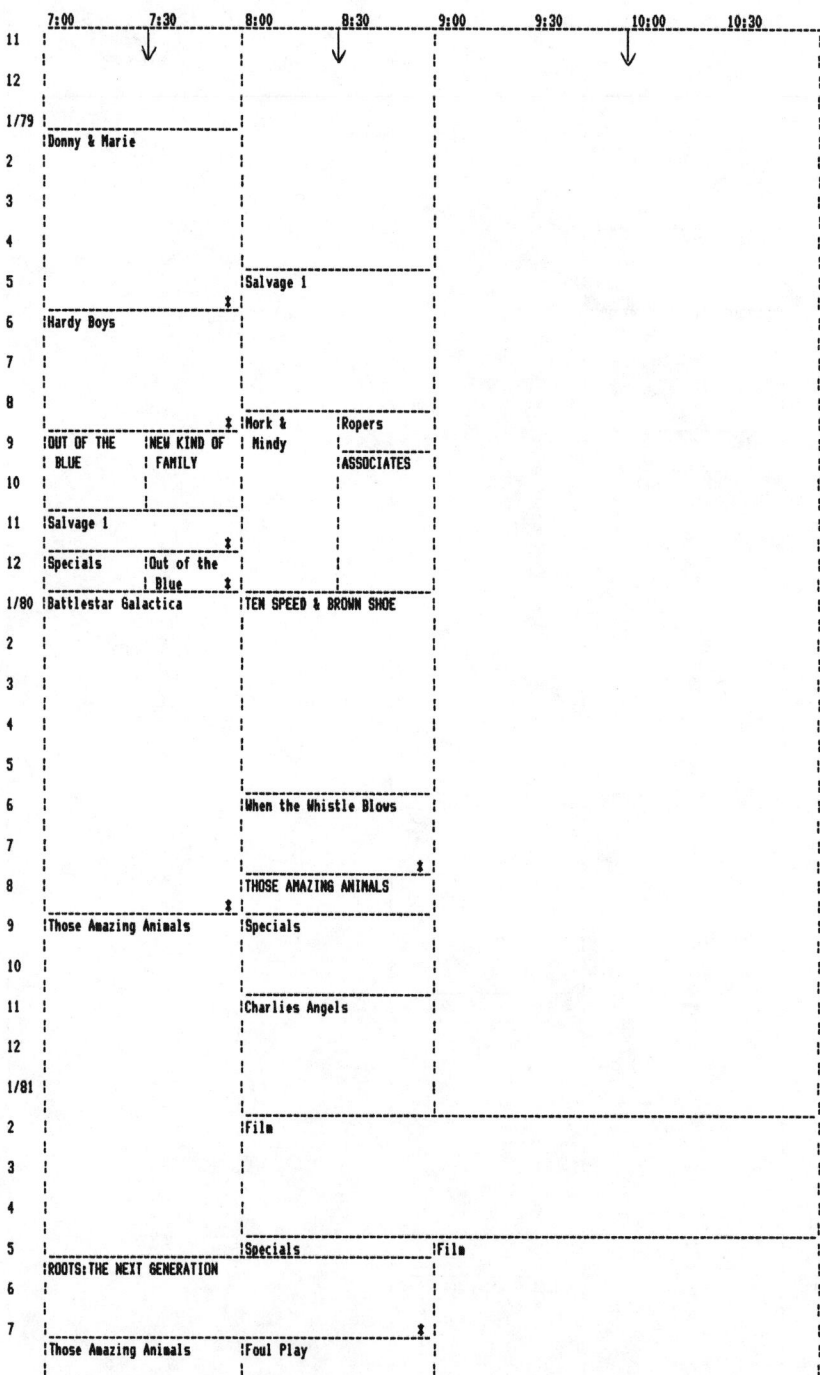

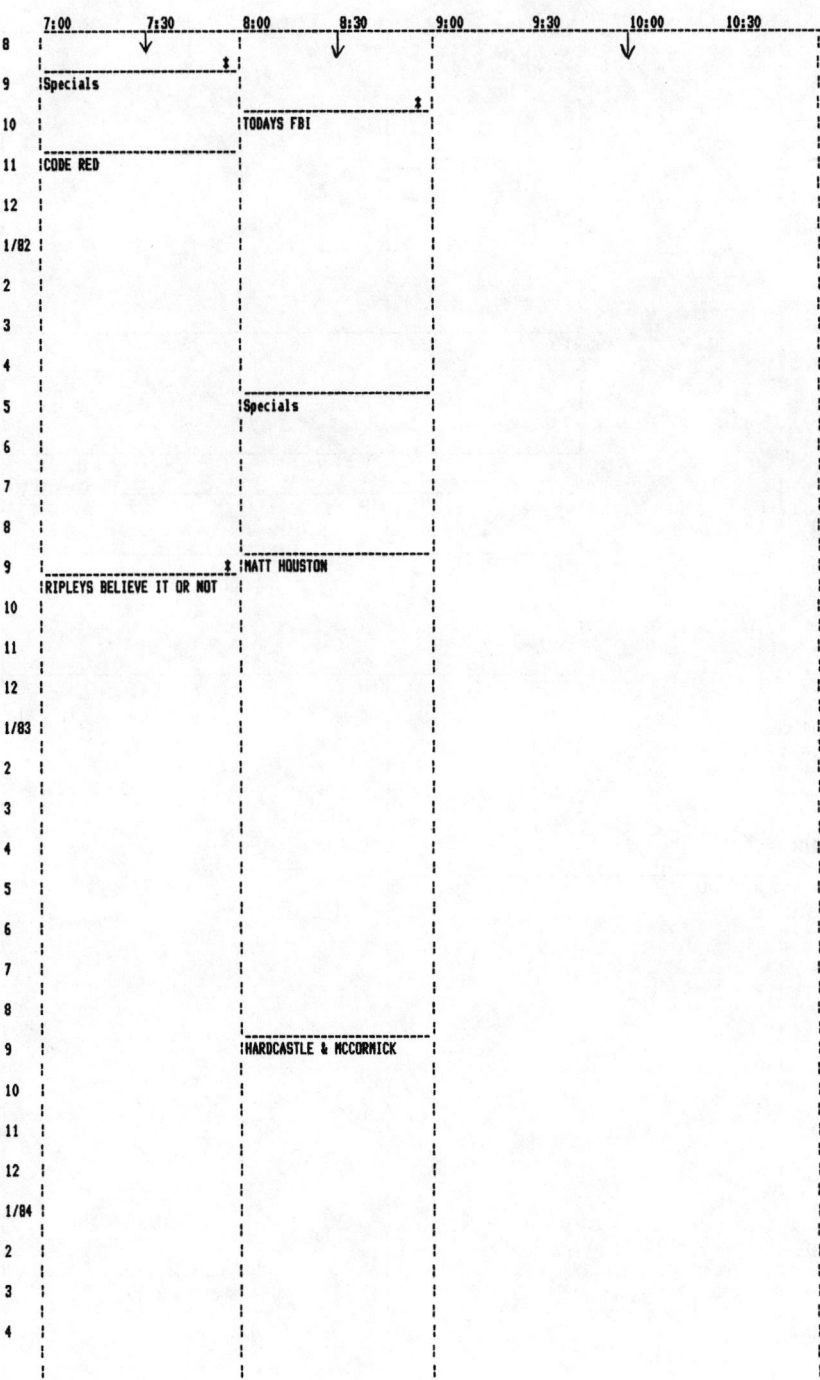

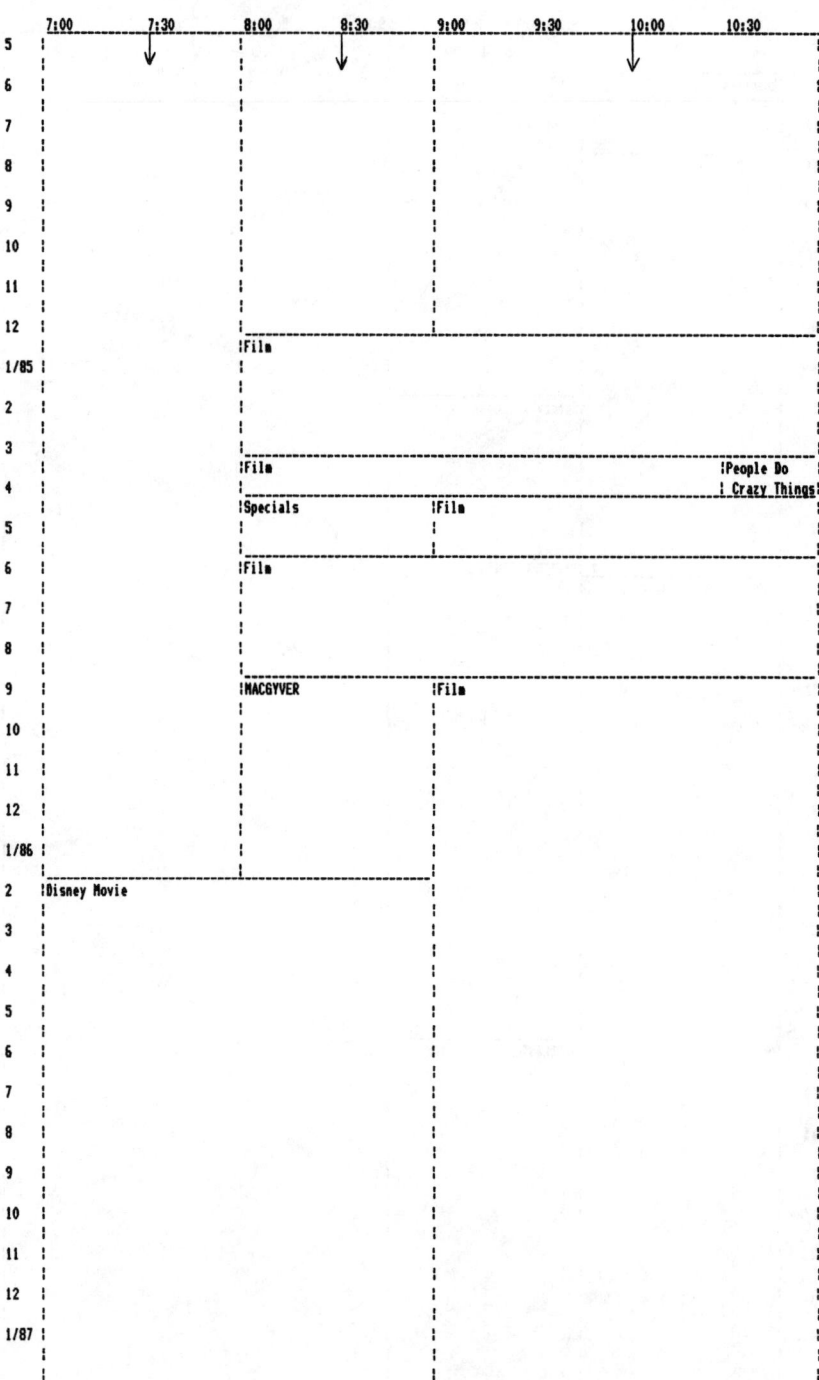

	7:00	7:30	8:00	8:30	9:00	9:30	10:00	10:30
5								
6								
7								
8								
9								
10								
11								
12			Film					
1/85								
2								
3								
			Film					People Do
4								Crazy Things
			Specials		Film			
5								
6			Film					
7								
8								
9			MACGYVER		Film			
10								
11								
12								
1/86								
2	Disney Movie							
3								
4								
5								
6								
7								
8								
9								
10								
11								
12								
1/87								

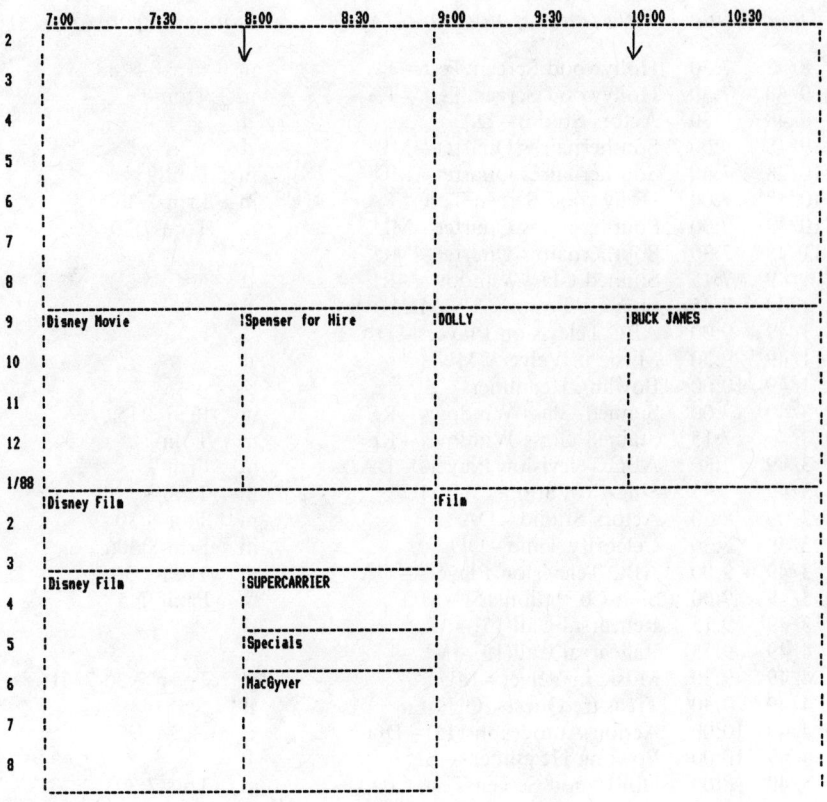

Date	Time	Title (min. if not 30) – Type	Action	From/To
8/48	7:30	Hollywood Screen Test – TA	m	Fr:r-8-5/48
9/48	7:30	Hollywood Screen Test – TA	m	To:n-8
9/48	8:30	Actors Studio – DA	d	
9/48	9:00	Southernaires Quartet – MU	d	
10/48	7:30	Southernaires Quartet – MU	m	Fr:n-9
10/48	8:00	Hollywood Screen Test – TA	m	Fr:n-7:30
10/48	9:00	Southernaires Quartet – MU	m	To:n-7:30
11/48	7:30	Southernaires Quartet – MU	c	
1/49	7:15	Stained Glass Windows – RE	d	
1/49	7:45	Sing-Co-Pation(15) – MU	d	
1/49	9:00	ABC Television Players – DA	d	
1/49	9:30	Music in Velvet – MU	d	
1/49	10:00	Bowling Headliners – SP	s	
3/49	7:00	Stained Glass Windows – RE	m	Fr:n-7:15
3/49	7:15	Stained Glass Windows – RE	m	To:n-7
3/49	7:30	ABC Television Players – DA	m	Fr:n-9
3/49	7:45	Sing-Co-Pation(15) – MU	m	To:n-9
3/49	8:30	Actors Studio – DA	m	To:r-8:30
3/49	8:30	Celebrity Time – QU	m	Fr:n-8:30(c)
3/49	9:00	ABC Television Players – DA	m	To:n-7:30
3/49	9:00	Sing-Co-Pation(15) – MU	m	Fr:n-7:45
3/49	9:15	Rehearsal Call(15) – VY	d	
4/49	9:15	Rehearsal Call(15) – VY	c	
4/49	9:30	Music in Velvet – MU	m	To: n-7:30-7/51
4/49	9:30	Treasure Quest – QU	d	
4/49	10:00	Action Autographs(15) – DO	d	
4/49	10:00	Bowling Headliners – SP	f	
5/49	8:00	Hollywood Screen Test – TA	m	To:s-7:30
5/49	8:00	Jacques Fray Music Room – TA	m	Fr:s-8
5/49	10:15	Bowling Headliners(45) – SP	s	
6/49	8:30	Celebrity Time – QU	m	To:n-10
6/49	9:30	Treasure Quest – QU	c	
6/49	10:00	Action Autographs(15) – DO	c	
6/49	10:15	Bowling Headliners(45) – SP	f	
7/49	9:30	Skip Farrell – MU	m	Fr:m-9
7/49	10:00	Celebrity Time – QU	m	Fr:n-8:30
7/49	10:30	Bowling Headliners – SP	s	
8/49	8:00	Jacques Fray Music Room – TA	m	To:n-9:30
8/49	9:00	Sing-Co-Pation(15) – MU	c	
8/49	9:30	Skip Farrell – MU	c	
9/49	8:00	Think Fast – QU	m	Fr:f-8
9/49	8:30	Little Revue – MU	d	
9/49	9:30	Jacques Fray Music Room – TA	m	Fr:n-8
10/49	7:00	Stained Glass Windows – RE	c	
10/49	7:30	ABC Television Players – DA	c	
10/49	9:00	Let There Be Stars(60) – MV	d	
10/49	9:30	Jacques Fray Music Room – TA	c	
10/49	10:30	Bowling Headliners – SP	f	
10/49	10:30	Youth on the March – RE	d	

Date	Time	Title (min. if not 30) — Type	Action	From/To
11/49	7:00	Paul Whiteman's Goodyear Revue — MV	d	
11/49	7:30	Oboler Comedy Theatre — CA	d	
11/49	7:30	Oboler Comedy Theatre — CA	c	
11/49	9:00	Let There Be Stars(60) — MV	c	
12/49	7:30	Hollywood House — VY	d	
12/49	9:00	Your Witness — CR	m	Fr:m-8-10/49
12/49	9:30	Mysteries of Chinatown — CD	d	
1/50	7:30	Carolyn Gilbert(15) — MU	d	
1/50	7:30	Hollywood House — VY	c	
1/50	7:45	Dr. Fix-Um(15) — IF	m	Fr:t-9:30-6/49
3/50	8:30	Little Revue — MU	m	To:f-9:30
3/50	8:30	Majority Rules — QU	m	Fr:f-9:30
3/50	10:00	Celebrity Time — QU	m	To:n-10(c)
3/50	10:00	In the Morgan Manner — MV	d	
4/50	10:00	In the Morgan Manner — MV	c	
4/50	10:00	Ruggles — SC	m	Fr:f-8:30
5/50	9:00	Mysteries of Chinatown — CD	m	Fr:n-9:30
5/50	9:00	Your Witness — CR	m	To:w-9-8/50
5/50	9:30	Mama Rosa — SC	d	
5/50	9:30	Mysteries of Chinatown — CD	m	To:n-9
6/50	9:30	Mama Rosa — SC	c	
6/50	9:30	Soap Box Theatre — DA	d	
6/50	10:00	Ruggles — SC	m	To:r-9:30
7/50	7:00	Think Fast — QU	m*	Fr:n-8
7/50	7:30	Carolyn Gilbert(15) — MU	c	
7/50	8:00	Stage Two Revue — MV	d	
7/50	8:00	Think Fast — QU	m	To:n-7
7/50	8:30	Majority Rules — QU	c	
7/50	10:00	Marshall Plan in Action — DO	m	Fr:s-9
8/50	7:30	Diane Doxee — MU	d	
8/50	7:45	Dr. Fix-Um(15) — IF	c	
8/50	8:30	Sit Or Miss — QU	d	
9/50	7:30	Diane Doxee — MU	c	
9/50	8:00	Stage Two Revue — MV	c	
9/50	9:00	Mysteries of Chinatown — CD	m	To:m-8:30
10/50	7:00	Think Fast — QU	c*	
10/50	7:30	Showtime, USA — VY	d	
10/50	8:00	Hollywood Theatre Time — VS	d	
10/50	9:00	Soap Box Theatre — DA	m	Fr:n-9:30
10/50	9:30	Marshall Plan in Action — DO	m	Fr:n-10
10/50	9:30	Soap Box Theatre — DA	m	To:n-9
10/50	10:00	Marshall Plan in Action — DO	m	To:n-9:30
10/50	10:00	Old Fashioned Meeting — RE	d	
12/50	8:00	Hollywood Theatre Time — VS	m	To:s-7
12/50	8:00	Film — FI	s	
12/50	9:00	Soap Box Theatre — DA	c	
1/51	8:00	Film — FI	f	
1/51	8:00	Film(60) — FI	s	
1/51	8:30	Sit Or Miss — QU	c	

Date	Time	Title (min. if not 30) — Type	Action	From/To
1/51	9:00	Film — FI	s	
4/51	10:00	Old Fashioned Meeting — RE	c	
5/51	10:00	Film — FI	s	
6/51	7:30	Showtime, USA — VY	c	
7/51	7:30	Music in Velvet — MU	m	Fr:n-9:30-4/49
7/51	10:00	Industries for America — DO	m	Fr:r-10
7/51	10:00	Film — FI	f	
7/51	10:30	Everybody's Business — DO	d*	
8/51	10:30	Everybody's Businees — DO	m*	To:n-7:30-7/52
9/51	10:00	Hour of Decision — RE	d	
9/51	10:00	Industries for America — DO	m	To:f-10:30
10/51	7:30	Music in Velvet — MU	c	
10/51	9:00	Film — FI	f	
11/51	7:30	Byline — DR	d	
11/51	9:00	Other Lands, Other Places — TR	m	Fr:t-8:45-9/51
12/51	7:30	Adventures of Ellery Queen — CD	m	Fr:r-9(d)
12/51	7:30	Byline — DR	c	
12/51	9:00	Other Lands, Other Places — TR	c	
1/52	9:00	Arthur Murray Party — MV	m	Fr:w-9
3/52	7:00	Paul Whiteman's Goodyear Revue — MV	c	
3/52	7:30	Adventures of Ellery Queen — CD	m	To:w-9
3/52	7:30	Four Square Court — DS	d	
3/52	9:30	Marshall Plan in Action — DO	m	To:t-8
3/52	10:00	Hour of Decision — RE	m	To:n-10-7/52
4/52	7:00	You Asked for It — NM	m	Fr:m-9
4/52	9:30	Film(60) — FI	s	
5/52	7:30	Four Square Court — DS	m	To:n-9
5/52	7:30	Horizons — DS	d	
5/52	9:00	Arthur Murray Party — MV	m	To:f-8-7/52(c)
5/52	9:00	Four Square Court — DS	m	Fr:n-7:30
5/52	9:30	Film(60) — FI	f	
5/52	10:30	Youth on the March — RE	m	To:n-10:30-10/52(d)
6/52	7:30	Horizons — DS	m	To:n-9:15-12/54
6/52	9:00	America in View — TR	m	Fr:s-10:45-3/52
6/52	9:00	Four Square Court — DS	c	
6/52	9:30	Production for Freedom — DO	d	
6/52	10:00	Film(60) — FI	s	
6/52	10:00	Film(60) — FI	f	
7/52	7:30	Everybody's Business — DO	m	Fr:n-10:30-8/51
7/52	9:30	Production for Freedom — DO	m	To:n-10:30
7/52	10:00	Hour of Decision(15) — RE	m	Fr:n-10-3/52
7/52	10:30	Production for Freedom — DO	m	Fr:n-9:30
9/52	7:30	Everybody's Business — DO	c	
9/52	10:30	Production for Freedom — DO	c	
10/52	7:30	Enterprise — DO	d	
10/52	7:30	Hot Seat — IV	m	Fr:f-8-7/52
10/52	8:00	Film(60) — FI	f	
10/52	8:00	News(60) — NW	s	
10/52	9:30	This Is the Life — RD	m	Fr:f-8(d)

Date	Time	Title (min. if not 30) – Type	Action	From/To
10/52	10:30	Anywhere, USA – DD	d	
11/52	7:30	Hot Seat – IV	m	To:m-8:30
12/52	7:30	Enterprise – DO	m	To:n-10:30
12/52	10:30	Anywhere, USA – DD	c	
12/52	10:30	Enterprise(15) – DO	m	Fr:n-7:30
1/53	7:30	Film – FI	s	
3/53	7:30	Film – FI	f	
3/53	10:30	Both Sides – DB	d	
3/53	10:30	Enterprise(15) – DO	m	To:s-8-1/54
4/53	7:30	Plymouth Playhouse – VS	d	
6/53	7:30	Plymouth Playhouse – VS	c	
6/53	9:00	America in View – TR	m	To:w-8-10/53
6/53	10:30	Both Sides – DB	c	
7/53	7:30	Film – FI	s	
7/53	9:00	At Issue(15) – IV	d	
7/53	9:15	Orchid Award(15) – MV	d	
8/53	9:00	At Issue(15) – IV	m	To:w-8-10/53
9/53	7:30	Film – FI	f	
9/53	7:30	Frank Leahy(15) – ST	d	
9/53	7:45	Football(75) – SP	s	
9/53	8:00	News(60) – NW	f	
9/53	9:00	Walter Winchell(15) – NA	d	
9/53	9:30	Peter Potter(60) – DS	d	
9/53	9:30	This Is the Life – RD	m	To:m-10
9/53	10:00	Hour of Decision(15) – RE	m	To:n-10:30
9/53	10:30	Hour of Decision(15) – RE	m	Fr:n-10
12/53	7:30	Frank Leahy(15) – ST	c	
12/53	7:45	Football(75) – SP	f	
1/54	8:00	The Mask(60) – CD	d	
1/54	9:15	Jane Pickens(15) – MU	d	
1/54	9:15	Orchid Award(15) – MV	c	
1/54	9:30	Peter Potter(60) – DS	m	To:n-9:30
1/54	9:30	Peter Potter – DS	m	Fr:n-9:30
1/54	10:00	Break the Bank – QU	m	Fr:t-8:30-9/53(n)
2/54	10:30	Hour of Decision(15) – RE	c	
3/54	9:30	Peter Potter – DS	c	
4/54	7:30	It's About Time – QU	m	Fr:r-8
4/54	9:15	Jane Pickens(15) – MU	m	To:n-9:15-7/54
4/54	9:15	Martha Wright(15) – MU	d	
4/54	9:30	Doctor I.Q. – QU	m	Fr:m-8:30
5/54	7:30	It's About Time – QU	c	
5/54	7:30	Now – DO	d	
5/54	8:00	The Mask(60) – CD	c	
5/54	8:00	On the Boardwalk with Paul Whiteman (60) – VY	d	
6/54	7:30	Now – DO	c	
7/54	7:30	Pepsi-Cola Playhouse – DA	m	Fr:f-8:30
7/54	9:00	On the Line with Considine(15) – IV	m*	Fr:t-10:30-1/54(n)
7/54	9:15	Jane Pickens(15) – MU	m*	Fr:n-9:15-4/54
8/54	8:00	Flight #7 – TR	m	Fr:m-7:30

Date	Time	Title (min. if not 30) — Type	Action	From/To
8/54	8:00	On the Boardwalk with Paul Whiteman(60) — VY	c	
8/54	8:30	Big Picture — DO	m	Fr:w-9
8/54	9:00	On the Line with Considine(15) — IV	c*	
9/54	9:15	Jane Pickens(15) — MU	c*	
10/54	9:30	Doctor I.Q. — QU	m	To:n-9:30-12/58
10/54	9:30	Talent Patrol — TA	m	Fr:w-7:30
11/54	9:30	Talent Patrol — TA	m	To:m-8
11/54	9:30	What's Going On? — QU	d	
12/54	9:15	Horizons(15) — DS	m	Fr:n-7:30-6/52
12/54	9:15	Martha Wright(15) — MU	c	
12/54	9:30	What's Going On? — QU	c	
1/55	9:30	Pantomime Quiz — QU	m	Fr:f-8-8/54(c)
2/55	8:00	Flight #7 — TR	m	To:s-7-6/55
2/55	8:00	Key to the Ages — DS	d	
2/55	8:30	Big Picture — DO	m	To:s-7:30
2/55	8:30	President Eisenhower's News Conference — IF	d	
3/55	9:15	Horizons(15) — DS	c	
3/55	9:15	Stork Club(45) — TK	m	Fr:s-10
3/55	9:30	Pantomime Quiz — QU	m	To:f-8-7/55(c)
5/55	8:00	Key to the Ages — DS	c	
6/55	7:30	Pepsi-Cola Playhouse — DA	c	
6/55	9:00	Walter Winchell(15) — NA	m	To:n-10:30-10/60
6/55	9:15	Stork Club(45) — TK	m	To:n-9:30
7/55	7:30	Greatest Sports Thrills — SH	s	
7/55	7:30	Greatest Sports Thrills — SH	f	
7/55	9:00	Chance of a Lifetime — TA	m	Fr:f-10(d)
7/55	9:30	Stork Club — TK	m	Fr:n-9:15
7/55	9:30	Stork Club — TK	c	
8/55	7:30	Hollywood Backstage — IF	d	
8/55	9:30	Life Begins at Eighty — DS	m	Fr:n-9:30(d)
9/55	7:30	Hollywood Backstage — IF	c	
9/55	7:30	Film(90) — FI	s	
9/55	8:30	President Eisenhower's News Conference — IF	c	
10/55	9:30	Life Begins at Eighty — DS	m	To:n-10
10/55	9:30	Original Amateur Hour — TA	m	Fr:s-8:30-9/54(n)
10/55	10:00	Break the Bank — QU	m	To:w-9:30
10/55	10:00	Life Begins at Eighty — DS	m	Fr:n-9:30
12/55	9:30	Original Amateur Hour — TA	m	To:n-9:30
12/55	10:00	Life Begins at Eighty — DS	m	To:s-10
1/56	9:30	Original Amateur Hour(60) — TA	m	Fr:n-9:30
2/56	9:00	Chance of a Lifetime — TA	m	To:s-10
2/56	9:30	Original Amateur Hour(60) — TA	m	To:n-9
3/56	9:00	Original Amateur Hour(60) — TA	m	Fr:n-9:30
3/56	10:00	Big Picture — DO	m	Fr:m-10-1/56
4/56	10:00	Big Picture — DO	m	To:t-10-6/56
4/56	10:00	Outside USA — DO	m	Fr:m-10
6/56	10:00	Outside USA — DO	c	

Date	Time	Title (min. if not 30) — Type	Action	From/To
9/56	7:30	Film(90) — FI	f	
9/56	9:00	Original Amateur Hour(60) — TA	m	To:n-7:30
10/56	7:30	Original Amateur Hour(60) — TA	m	Fr:n-9
10/56	8:30	Press Conference — IV	m	Fr:w-8(n)
10/56	9:00	Omnibus(90) — VS	d	
1/57	8:30	Press Conference — IV	m	To:m-9-4/57
2/57	8:30	Open Hearing — PA	m	Fr:r-9-7/54
3/57	7:30	Original Amateur Hour(60) — TA	m	To:n-9
3/57	8:30	Open Hearing — PA	m	To:n-9-11/57
3/57	9:00	Omnibus(90) — VS	c	
4/57	7:30	Film(90) — FI	s	
4/57	9:00	Original Amateur Hour(60) — TA	m	Fr:n-7:30
4/57	10:00	Mike Wallace Interviews — IV	d	
6/57	9:00	Original Amateur Hour(60) — TA	m	To:m-10(n)
7/57	9:00	Compass — TR	m	Fr:r-9:30
7/57	9:30	Midwestern Hayride — MV	m	Fr:w-10:30-6/56(n)
9/57	7:30	Maverick(60) — WE	d	
9/57	7:30	Film(90) — FI	f	
9/57	8:30	National Bowling Champions — SP	s	
9/57	10:00	Mike Wallace Interviews — IV	m	To:s-10
10/57	9:00	Compass — TR	c	
10/57	9:30	Midwestern Hayride — MV	m	To:s-10-6/58
10/57	10:00	Football — SP	s	
11/57	9:00	Open Hearing — PA	m	Fr:n-8:30
11/57	9:30	Football — SP	s	
11/57	10:00	Football — SP	f	
11/57	10:00	Scotland Yard — RA	d	
12/57	8:30	National Bowling Champions — SP	f	
12/57	9:30	Football — SP	f	
1/58	7:00	Open Hearing — PA	m	Fr:n-9
1/58	7:00	You Asked for It — NM	m	To:n-9:30
1/58	8:30	Harbourmaster — AD	m	Fr:r-8(c)
1/58	9:00	Open Hearing — PA	m	To:n-7
1/58	9:00	Sid Caesar Invites You — CV	d	
1/58	9:30	You Asked for It — NM	m	Fr:n-7
3/58	7:00	Enterprise — DO	m	Fr:f-9-10/57
3/58	7:00	Open Hearing — PA	m	To:n-9:30-6/58
3/58	10:00	Scotland Yard — RA	m	To:w-9:30-5/58
4/58	7:00	Enterprise — DO	m	To:n-9:30
4/58	7:00	You Asked for It — NM	m	Fr:n-9:30
4/58	9:30	Enterprise — DO	m	Fr:n-7
4/58	9:30	You Asked for It — NM	m	To:n-7
4/58	10:00	Mike Wallace Interviews — IV	m	Fr:s-10
5/58	9:00	Sid Caesar Invites You — CV	c	
6/58	8:30	Harbourmaster — AD	c	
6/58	9:00	Baseball Corner — ST	d	
6/58	9:30	Enterprise — DO	c	
6/58	9:30	Open Hearing — PA	m	Fr:n-7-3/58
7/58	8:30	Anybody Can Play — QU	d	
7/58	9:00	Baseball Corner — ST	m	To:w-9:30

Date	Time	Title (min. if not 30) — Type	Action	From/To
7/58	9:00	Traffic Court — CR	m	Fr:w-9:30
9/58	8:30	Anybody Can Play — QU	m	To:m-9:30
9/58	9:30	Open Hearing — PA	c	
9/58	10:00	Mike Wallace Interviews — IV	c	
10/58	8:30	The Lawman — WE	d	
10/58	9:00	Colt .45 — WE	m	Fr:f-8:30-4/58
10/58	9:00	Traffic Court — CR	m	To:r-10
10/58	9:30	Encounter(60) — DA	d	
11/58	9:30	Encounter(60) — DA	c	
11/58	9:30	Stars of Jazz — MU	m	Fr:r-10
11/58	9:30	Stars of Jazz — MU	c	
11/58	10:00	Meet McGraw — CD	m	Fr:t-9-6/58(n)
12/58	9:30	Doctor I.Q. — QU	m	Fr:n-9:30-10/54
2/59	10:00	Meet McGraw — CD	m	To:n-10:30
2/59	10:30	Meet McGraw — CD	m	Fr:n-10
3/59	9:30	Doctor I.Q. — QU	c	
3/59	9:30	Wire Service(60) — ND	m	Fr:m-7:30-9/57
9/59	7:00	You Asked for It — NM	c	
9/59	9:00	Colt .45 — WE	m	To:n-7
9/59	9:30	Wire Service(60) — ND	c	
9/59	10:30	Dick Clark's World of Talent — TA	d	
9/59	10:30	Meet McGraw — CD	m	To:r-9:30
10/59	7:00	Colt .45 — WE	m	Fr:n-9
10/59	9:00	The Rebel — WE	d	
10/59	9:30	The Alaskans(60) — AD	d	
12/59	10:30	Dick Clark's World of Talent — TA	c	
12/59	10:30	21 Beacon Street — CD	m	Fr:r-9:30-9/59(n)
3/60	7:00	Colt .45 — WE	m	To:t-9:30
3/60	10:30	Johnny Staccato — CD	m	Fr:r-8:30(n)
3/60	10:30	21 Beacon Street — CD	c	
4/60	7:00	Broken Arrow — WE	m	Fr:t-9-9/58
9/60	7:00	Broken Arrow — WE	c	
9/60	7:00	Walt Disney — KV	m	Fr:f-7:30
9/60	9:30	The Alaskans(60) — AD	c	
9/60	10:30	Johnny Staccato — CD	c	
10/60	9:30	The Islanders(60) — AD	d	
10/60	10:30	Walter Winchell — NA	m	Fr:n-9-6/55
11/60	10:30	Walter Winchell — NA	c	
11/60	10:30	Winston Churchill — DO	d	
3/61	9:30	The Islanders(60) — AD	c	
4/61	9:30	Asphalt Jungle(60) — CD	d	
6/61	10:30	Editor's Choice — NA	d	
6/61	10:30	Winston Churchill — DO	m	To:f-7:30-12/62
9/61	7:00	Maverick — WE	m	Fr:n-7:30
9/61	7:00	Walt Disney — KV	m	To:n-7:30(n)
9/61	7:30	Follow the Sun(60) — AD	d	
9/61	7:30	Maverick(60) — WE	m	To:n-7
9/61	9:00	The Rebel — WE	m	To:w-8:30-6/62(n)
9/61	9:30	Asphalt Jungle(60) — CD	c	
9/61	10:30	Editor's Choice — NA	c	

Date	Time	Title (min. if not 30) — Type	Action	From/To
10/61	9:00	Bus Stop(60) — DR	d	
10/61	10:00	Adventures in Paradise(60) — AD	m	Fr:m-9:30
3/62	9:00	Bus Stop(60) — DR	c	
4/62	8:30	The Lawman — WE	m	To:n-10:30
4/62	8:30	Film(120) — FI	s	
4/62	10:00	Adventures in Paradise(60) — AD	c	
4/62	10:30	The Lawman — WE	m	Fr:n-8:30
8/62	7:00	Maverick — WE	c	
9/62	7:00	Father Knows Best — SC	m	Fr:m-8:30(c)
9/62	7:30	Follow the Sun(60) — AD	c	
9/62	7:30	Jetsons — KV	d	
9/62	8:00	Film(120) — FI	s	
9/62	8:30	Film(120) — FI	f	
9/62	10:00	Voice of Firestone — MU	m	Fr:m-9-6/59
10/62	10:30	Howard K. Smith — NA	m	Fr:w-7:30
10/62	10:30	The Lawman — WE	c	
12/62	7:00	Father Knows Best — SC	m	To:f-8
6/63	10:00	Fireside Theatre — DA	m	Fr:r-10:30-5/58(n)
6/63	10:00	Voice of Firestone — MU	c	
6/63	10:30	Howard K. Smith — NA	c	
7/63	10:30	ABC News Reports — DO	d	
9/63	7:30	Jetsons — KV	c	
9/63	7:30	Travels of Jaimie McPheeters(60) — WE	d	
9/63	8:00	Film(120) — FI	f	
9/63	8:30	Arrest and Trial(90) — CD	d	
9/63	10:00	Fireside Theatre — DA	c	
9/63	10:00	100 Grand — QU	d	
9/63	10:00	100 Grand — QU	c	
10/63	10:00	Laughs for Sale — CY	d	
12/63	10:00	Laughs for Sale — CY	c	
12/63	10:30	ABC News Reports — DO	m	To:r-10:30
3/64	7:30	Empire(60) — WE	m	Fr:t-8:30-9/63(n)
3/64	7:30	Travels of Jaimie McPheeters(60) — WE	c	
9/64	7:30	Empire(60) — WE	c	
9/64	7:30	Wagon Train(60) — WE	m	Fr:m-8:30
9/64	8:30	Arrest and Trial(90) — CD	c	
9/64	8:30	Broadside — SC	d	
9/64	9:00	Film(120) — FI	s	
9/65	7:00	Voyage to the Bottom of the Sea (60) — SF	m	Fr:m-7:30
9/65	7:30	Wagon Train(60) — WE	c	
9/65	8:00	The F.B.I.(60) — CD	d	
9/65	8:30	Broadside — SC	c	
8/66	8:00	Preview Tonight(60) — DA	d*	
9/66	8:00	Preview Tonight(60) — DA	c*	
9/68	7:00	Land of the Giants(60) — SF	d	
9/68	7:00	Voyage to the Bottom of the Sea (60) — SF	c	

Date	Time	Title (min. if not 30) – Type	Action	From/To
9/70	7:00	Land of the Giants(60) – SF	c	
9/70	7:00	Young Rebels(60) – AD	d	
1/71	7:00	Young Rebels(60) – AD	c	
9/73	7:30	The F.B.I.(60) – CD	m	Fr:n-8
9/73	8:00	The F.B.I.(60) – CD	m	To:n-7:30
9/73	8:30	Film(120) – FI	s	
9/73	9:00	Film(120) – FI	f	
9/74	7:30	The F.B.I.(60) – CD	c	
9/74	8:00	Sonny Comedy Revue(60) – CV	d	
9/74	8:30	Film(120) – FI	f	
9/74	9:00	Film(120) – FI	s	
12/74	8:00	Sonny Comedy Revue(60) – CV	c	
1/75	8:00	Six Million Dollar Man(60) – AD	m	Fr:f-9
9/75	7:00	Swiss Family Robinson(60) – AD	d	
4/76	7:00	Swiss Family Robinson(60) – AD	c	
5/76	7:00	Undersea World of Jacques Cousteau(60) – DO	d	
6/76	7:00	Undersea World of Jacques Cousteau(60) – DO	c	
9/76	7:00	Cos(60) – CV	d	
11/76	7:00	Cos(60) – CV	c	
1/77	7:00	Brady Bunch Hour(60) – CV	d	
1/77	7:00	Hardy Boys Mysteries(60) – MY	d	
2/77	7:00	Brady Bunch Hour(60) – CV	m	To:m-8
2/77	7:00	Nancy Drew Mysteries(60) – MY	d	
1/78	7:00	Nancy Drew Mysteries(60) – MY	c	
1/78	8:00	Six Million Dollar Man(60) – AD	m	To:m-8
2/78	8:00	How the West Was Won(60) – WE	d	
6/78	8:00	Lucan(60) – AD	m*	Fr:m-8-1/78
7/78	8:00	Lucan(60) – AD	m*	To:m-8-11/78
8/78	8:00	How the West Was Won(60) – WE	m	To:m-9
9/78	8:00	Battlestar Galactica(60) – SF	d	
1/79	7:00	Donny and Marie(60) – MV	m	Fr:f-8
1/79	7:00	Hardy Boys Mysteries(60) – MY	m	To:n-7-6/79
3/79	7:00	Friends(60) – CO	d*	
4/79	7:00	Friends(60) – CO	c*	
4/79	8:00	Battlestar Galactica(60) – SF	m	To:s-8-6/79
5/79	7:00	Donny and Marie(60) – MV	c	
5/79	8:00	Salvage 1(60) – AD	m	Fr:m-8
6/79	7:00	Hardy Boys Mysteries(60) – MY	m	Fr:n-7-1/79
8/79	7:00	Hardy Boys Mysteries(60) – MY	c	
8/79	8:00	Mork & Mindy – SC	m	Fr:r-8
8/79	8:00	Salvage 1(60) – AD	m	To:n-7-11/79
8/79	8:30	Ropers – SC	m	Fr:t-10-4/79
9/79	7:00	Out of the Blue – SC	d	
9/79	7:30	A New Kind of Family – SC	d	
9/79	8:30	Associates – SC	d	
9/79	8:30	Ropers – SC	m	To:s-8
10/79	7:00	Out of the Blue – SC	m	To:n-7:30-12/79
10/79	7:30	A New Kind of Family – SC	m	To:s-8:30-12/79

Date	Time	Title (min. if not 30) — Type	Action	From/To
10/79	8:30	Associates — SC	m	To:r-9:30-3/80
11/79	7:00	Salvage 1(60) — AD	m	Fr:n-8-8/79
11/79	7:00	Salvage 1(60) — AD	c	
12/79	7:30	Out of the Blue — SC	m	Fr:n-7-10/79
12/79	7:30	Out of the Blue — SC	c	
12/79	8:00	Mork & Mindy — SC	m	To:r-8
1/80	7:00	Battlestar Galactica(60) — SF	m	To:s-8-8/79
1/80	8:00	Tenspeed and Brown Shoe(60) — CD	d	
5/80	8:00	Tenspeed and Brown Shoe(60) — CD	m	To:f-10
6/80	8:00	When the Whistle Blows(60) — SC	m	Fr:s-10
7/80	8:00	When the Whistle Blows(60) — SC	c	
8/80	7:00	Battlestar Galactica(60) — SF	c	
8/80	8:00	Those Amazing Animals(60) — WL	d	
8/80	8:00	Those Amazing Animals(60) — WL	m	To:n-7
9/80	7:00	Those Amazing Animals(60) — WL	m	Fr:n-8
11/80	8:00	Charlie's Angels(60) — CD	m	Fr:w-9
1/81	8:00	Charlie's Angels(60) — CD	m	To:s-8
1/81	9:00	Film(120) — FI	f	
2/81	8:00	Film(180) — FI	s	
4/81	8:00	Film(180) — FI	f	
5/81	7:00	Roots: The Next Generation(120) — DR	d	
5/81	7:00	Those Amazing Animals(60) — WL	m	To:n-7-7/81
5/81	9:00	Film(120) — FI	s	
7/81	7:00	Roots: The Next Generation(120) — DR	c	
7/81	7:00	Those Amazing Animals(60) — WL	m	Fr:n-7-5/81
7/81	8:00	Foul Play(60) — CD	m	Fr:m-10-3/81
8/81	7:00	Those Amazing Animals(60) — WL	c	
9/81	8:00	Foul Play(60) — CD	c	
10/81	8:00	Today's FBI(60) — CD	d	
11/81	7:00	Code Red(60) — AD	d	
4/82	7:00	Inside America(60) — NM	d*	
4/82	7:00	Inside America(60) — NM	c*	
4/82	8:00	Today's FBI(60) — CD	m	To:m-8
5/82	7:00	Counterattack: Crime in America (60) — IF	d*	
5/82	7:00	Counterattack: Crime in America (60) — IF	c*	
9/82	7:00	Code Red(60) — AD	c	
9/82	7:00	Ripley's Believe It or Not(60) — VY	d	
9/82	8:00	Matt Houston(60) — CD	d	
8/83	8:00	Matt Houston(60) — CD	m	To:f-10
9/83	8:00	Hardcastle & McCormick(60) — CD	d	
12/84	8:00	Hardcastle & McCormick(60) — CD	m	To:m-8
12/84	8:00	Film(180) — FI	s	
12/84	9:00	Film(120) — FI	f	
3/85	8:00	Film(180) — FI	f	
3/85	8:00	Film(150) — FI	s	
3/85	10:30	People Do the Craziest Things — CY	m	Fr:r-8-9/84

Date	Time	Title (min. if not 30) — Type	Action	From/To
4/85	8:00	Film(150) — FI	f	
4/85	9:00	Film(120) — FI	s	
4/85	10:30	People Do the Craziest Things — CY	m	To:f-9:30
5/85	9:00	Film(120) — FI	f	
6/85	8:00	Film(180) — FI	s	
8/85	8:00	Film(180) — FI	f	
9/85	8:00	MacGyver(60) — SD	d	
9/85	9:00	Film(120) — FI	s	
1/86	7:00	Ripley's Believe It or Not(60) — VY	m	To:r-8
1/86	8:00	MacGyver(60) — SD	m	To:w-8
2/86	7:00	Disney Movie(120) — FI	s	
8/87	7:00	Disney Movie(120) — FI	f	
8/87	9:00	Film(120) — FI	f	
9/87	7:00	Disney Movie(60) — FI	s	
9/87	8:00	Spenser for Hire(60) — CD	m	Fr:t-8
9/87	9:00	Dolly(60) — VY	d	
9/87	10:00	Buck James(60) — DR	d	
1/88	7:00	Disney Movie(60) — FI	f	
1/88	7:00	Disney Movie(120) — FI	s	
1/88	8:00	Spenser for Hire(60) — CD	m	To:s-10
1/88	9:00	Dolly(60) — VY	m	To:s-8
1/88	9:00	Film(120) — FI	s#	
1/88	10:00	Buck James(60) — DR	m	To:r-10-3/88
3/88	7:00	Disney Movie(120) — FI	f	
3/88	7:00	Disney Movie(60) — FI	s	
3/88	8:00	Supercarrier(60) — AD	d	
4/88	8:00	Supercarrier(60) — AD	m	To:s-8-7/88
6/88	8:00	MacGyver(60) — SD	m	Fr:m-8
8/88	7:00	Disney Movie(60) — FI	f	
8/88	8:00	MacGyver(60) — SD	m	To:m-8

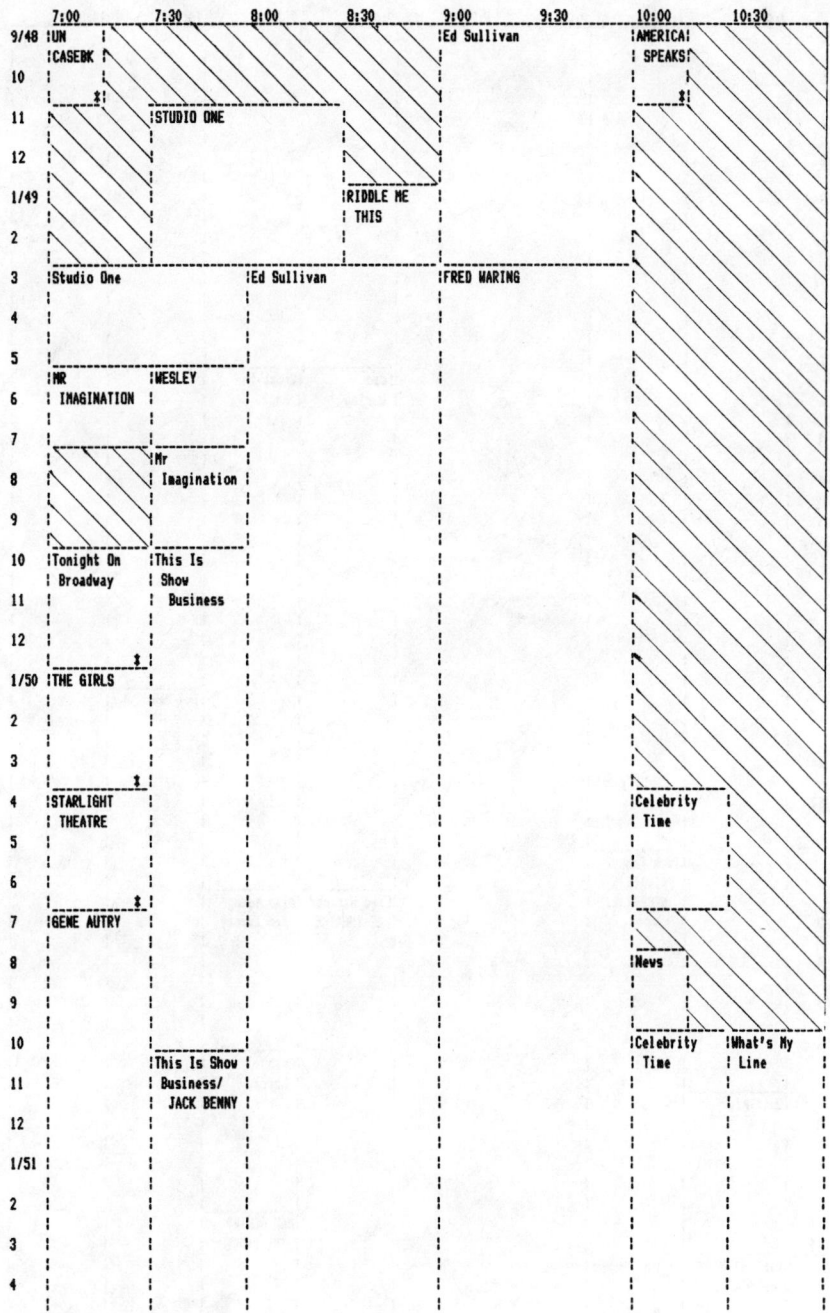

	7:00	7:30	8:00	8:30	9:00	9:30	10:00	10:30
5								
6								
7								
8								
9								
10								
11								
12								
1/52								
2					Fred Waring	Break the Bank		
3								
4								
5								
6								
7								
8								
9							The Web	
10								
11								
12								
1/53		Jack Benny/ PRIVATE SECRETARY						
2								
3					Fred Waring/ GE THEATRE	Alan Young/ Ken Murray		
4								
5								
6						Arthur Murray		
7	Quiz Kids							
8								
9								
10						MAN BEHIND THE BADGE		
11	LIFE WITH FATHER							
12								
1/54								

	7:00	7:30	8:00	8:30	9:00	9:30	10:00	10:30
2								
3	↓	↓		↓	↓	↓	↓	↓
4								
5								
6	EARN YOUR VACATION				GE Theatre			
7								
8								
9								
10	LASSIE						FATHER	
11						HONESTLY CELESTE	KNOWS BEST	
12								
1/55						STAGE 7		
2								
3								
4							APPOINTMENT WITH	
5							ADVENTURE	
6								
7								
8								
9								
10						ALFRED HITCHCOCK PRESENTS		
11								
12								
1/56								
2								
3								
4							$64,000	
5							CHALLENGE	
6								
7								
8								
9								
10								

	7:00	7:30	8:00	8:30	9:00	9:30	10:00	10:30
11								
12								
1/57								
2								
3								
4		Jack Benny/ CHAMPION						
5								
6		Jack Benny						
7								
8								
9								
10		Jack Benny/ BACHELOR FATHER						
11								
12								
1/58								
2								
3								
4								
5								
6								
7								
8								
9								
10							$64,000 Question	
11							Keep Talking	
12								
1/59								
2							Richard Diamond	
3								
4								
5								
6								
7		Suspicion/ Thats My Boy						

	7:00	7:30	8:00	8:30	9:00	9:30	10:00	10:30
8								
9								
10		DENNIS THE MENACE					George Gobel/ Jack Benny	
11								
12								
1/60								
2								
3								
4								
5								
6								
7							LUCY IN CONNECTICUT	
8								
9								
10						Jack Benny	Candid Camera	
11								
12								
1/61								
2								
3								
4								
5								
6								
7								
8								
9								
10								
11								
12								
1/62								
2								
3								
4								

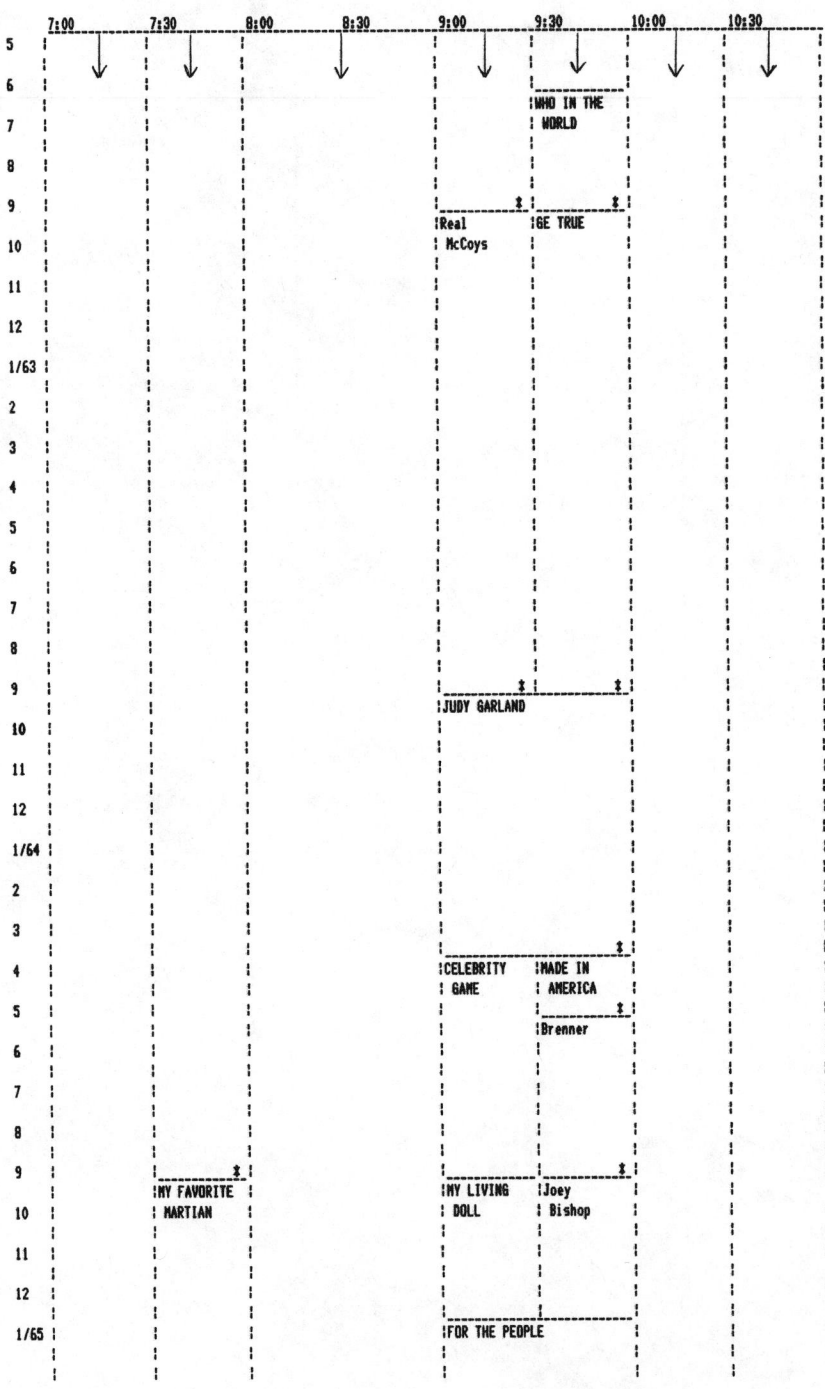

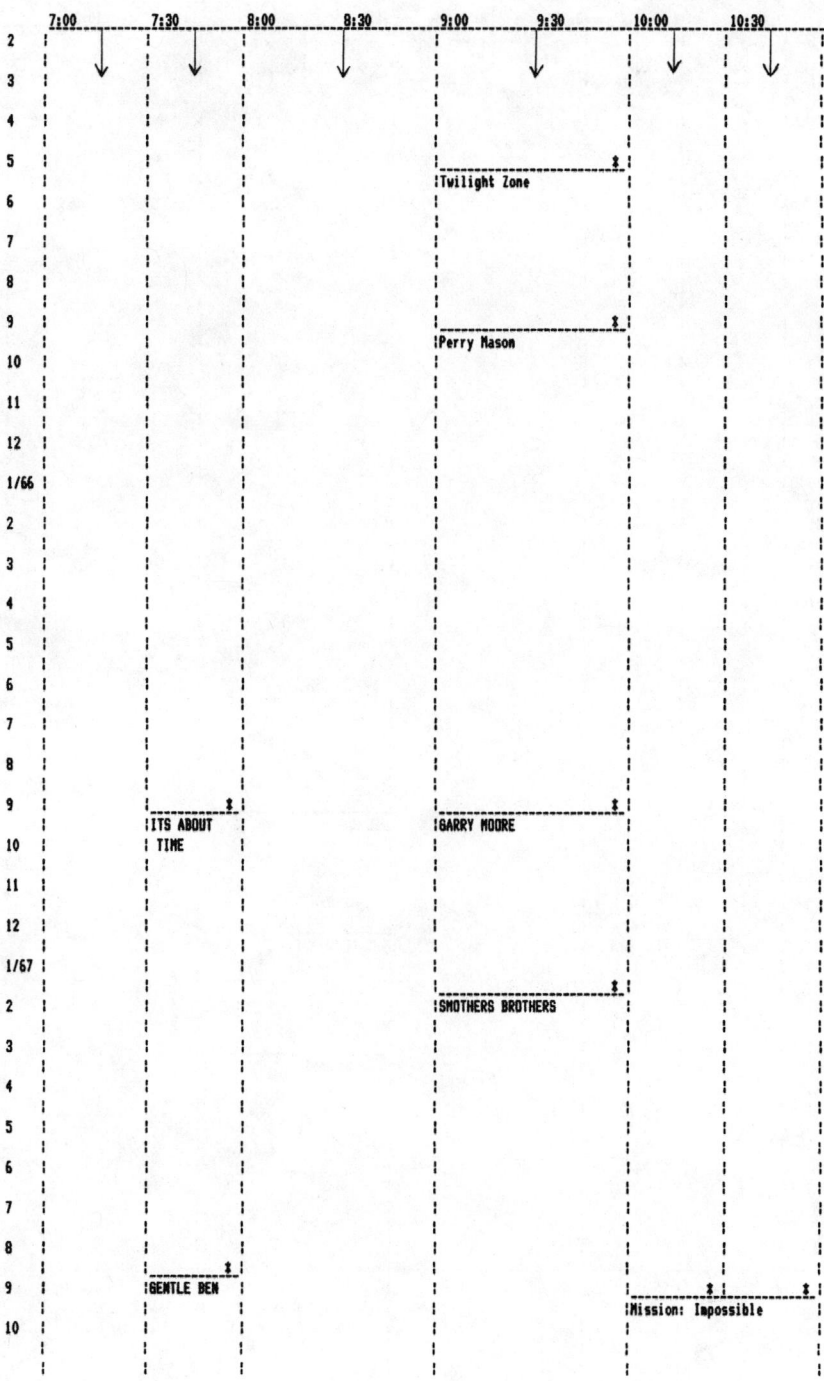

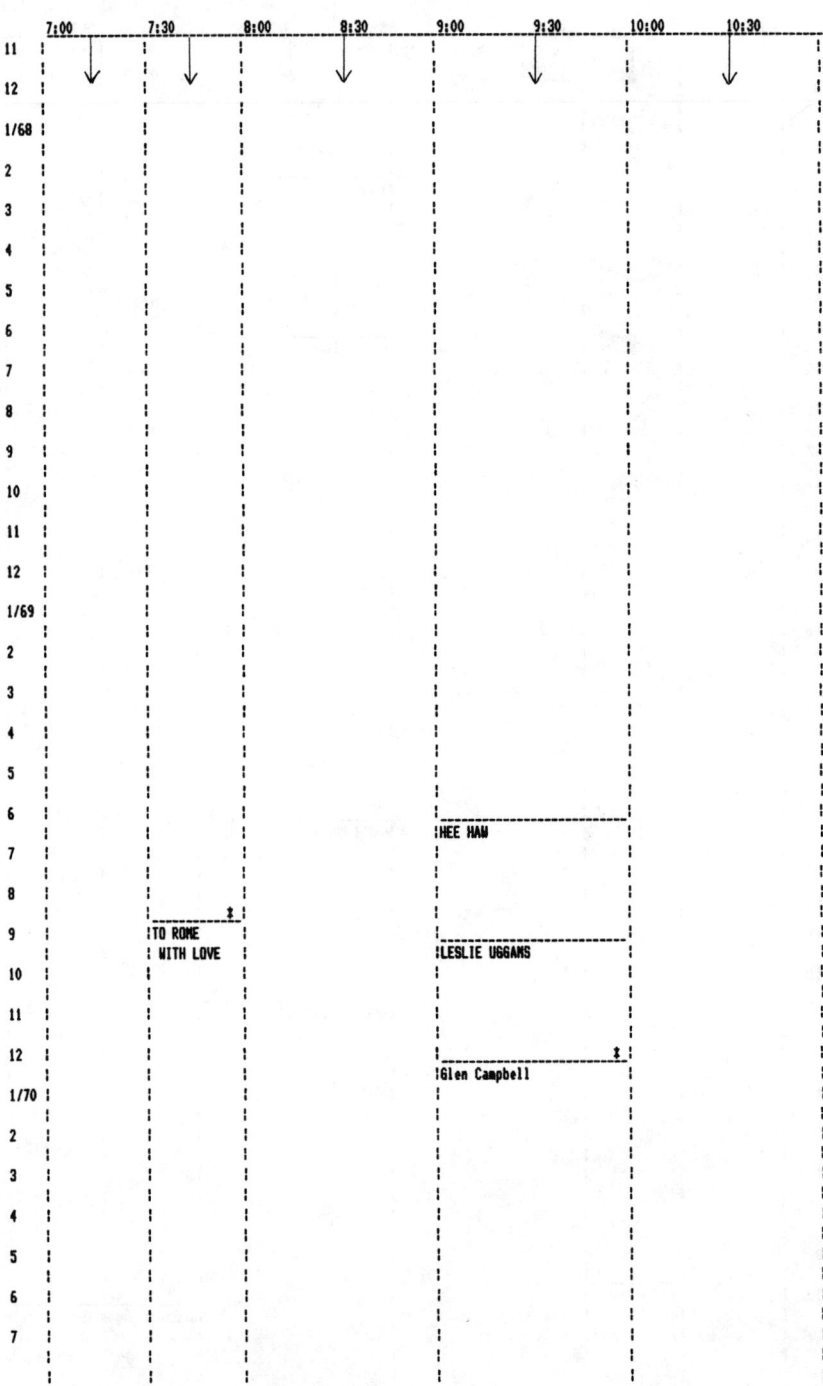

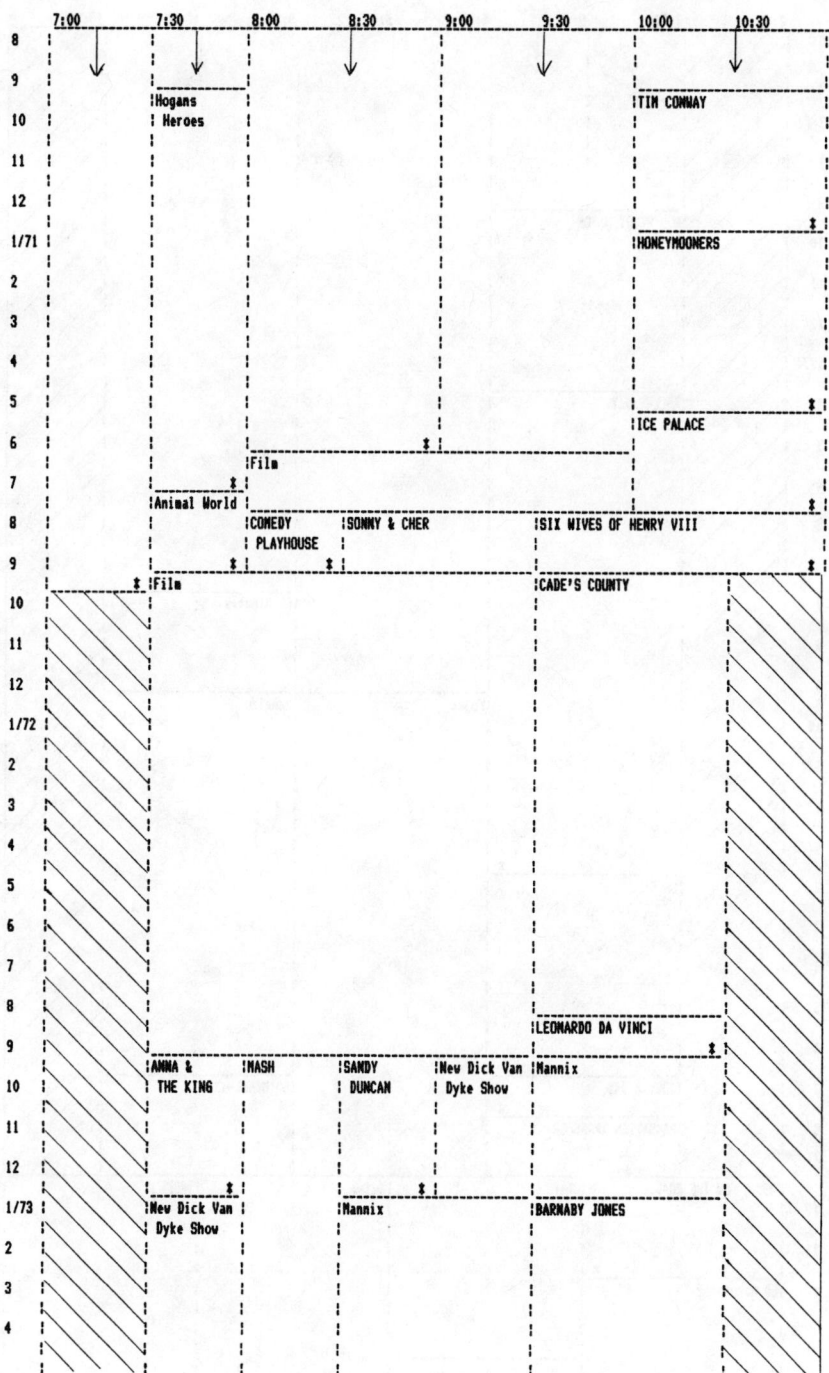

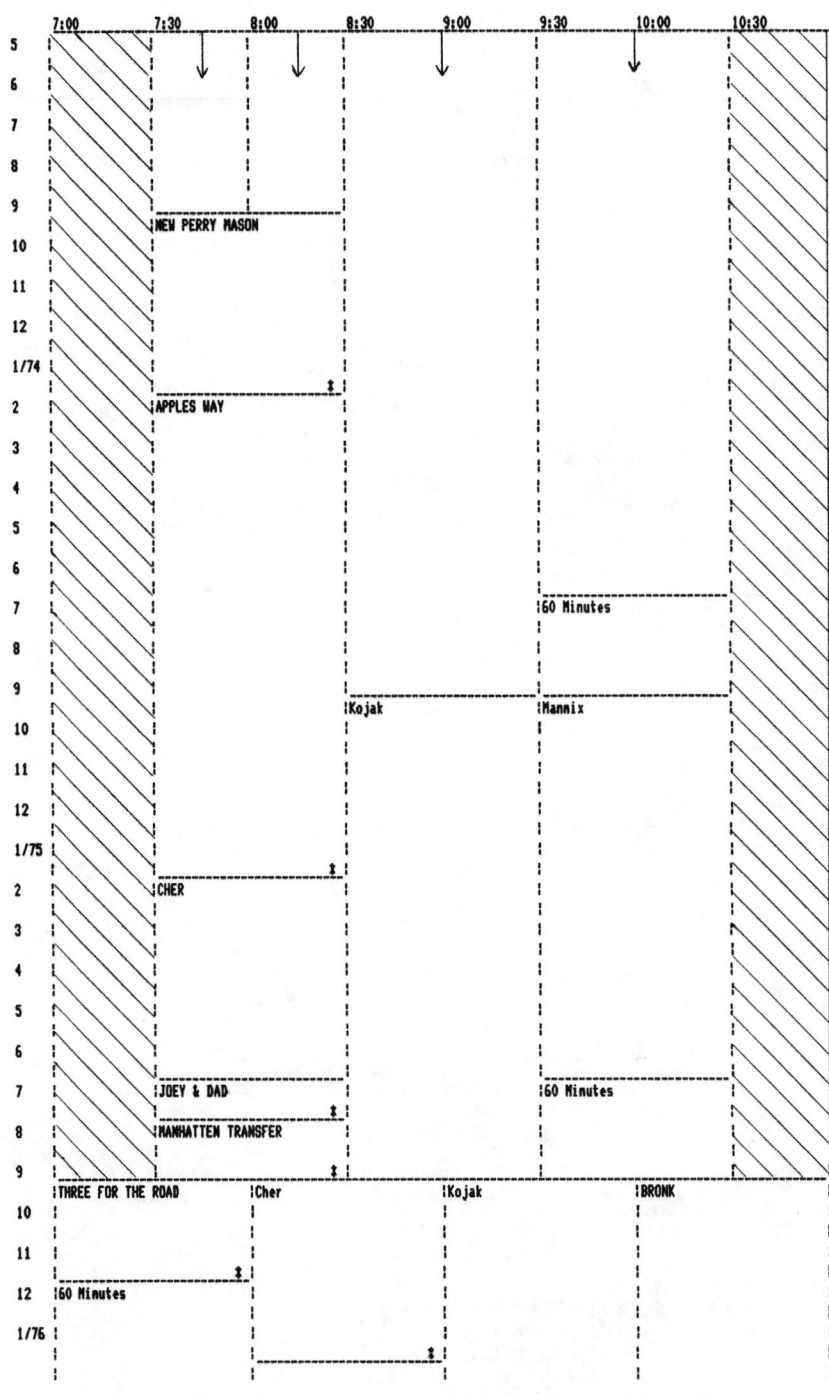

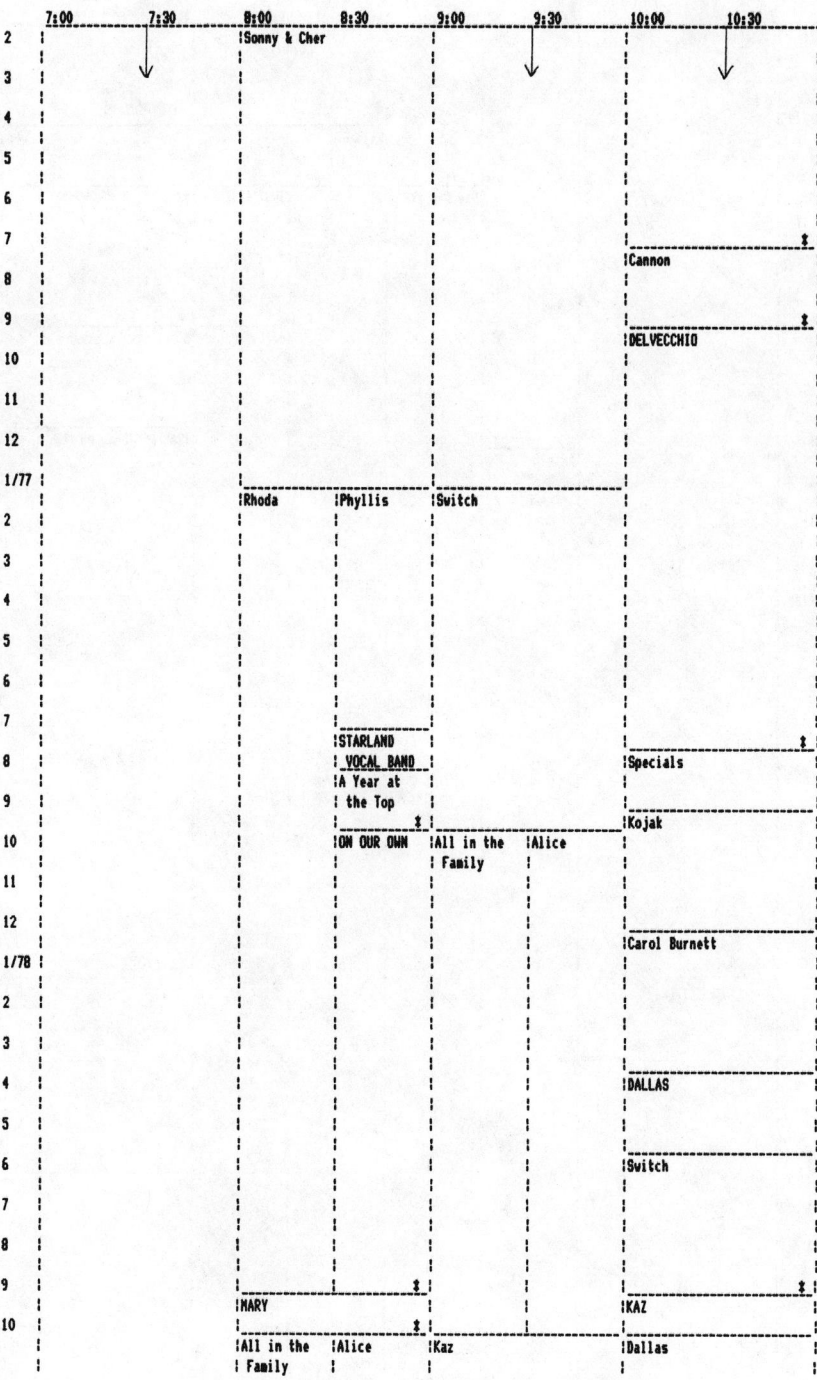

	7:00	7:30	8:00	8:30	9:00	9:30	10:00	10:30
11								
12		↓		↓		↓		↓
1/79					Film			
2								
3				One Day at a Time	Alice	JUST FRIENDS	MARY TYLER MOORE	
4								
5								
6								
7						Jeffersons	Moses the Lawgiver	
8							Kaz	
9			ARCHIE				TRAPPER JOHN, MD	
10			BUNKER'S					
11			PLACE					
12								
1/80								
2								
3								
4								
5								
6								
7								
8								
9								
10								
11								
12								
1/81								
2								
3								
4								
5								
6								
7								

	7:00	7:30	8:00	8:30	9:00	9:30	10:00	10:30
8								
9								
10								
11								
12								
1/82								
2								
3								
4								
5								
6								
7								
8								
9				GLORIA	Jeffersons	One Day at		
10						a Time		
11								
12								
1/83								
2								
3						Newhart		
4			GOODNIGHT					
			BEANTOWN	Newhart		Alice		
5								
			A.Bunker					
6			Alice	One Day at		Newhart		
7				a Time				
8								
						Goodnight		
9						Beantown		
10								
11								
12								
1/84						Alice		
2			FOUR					
			SEASONS					
3			MAGGIE	Four				
			BRIGGS	Seasons				
4								
			Aftermash					

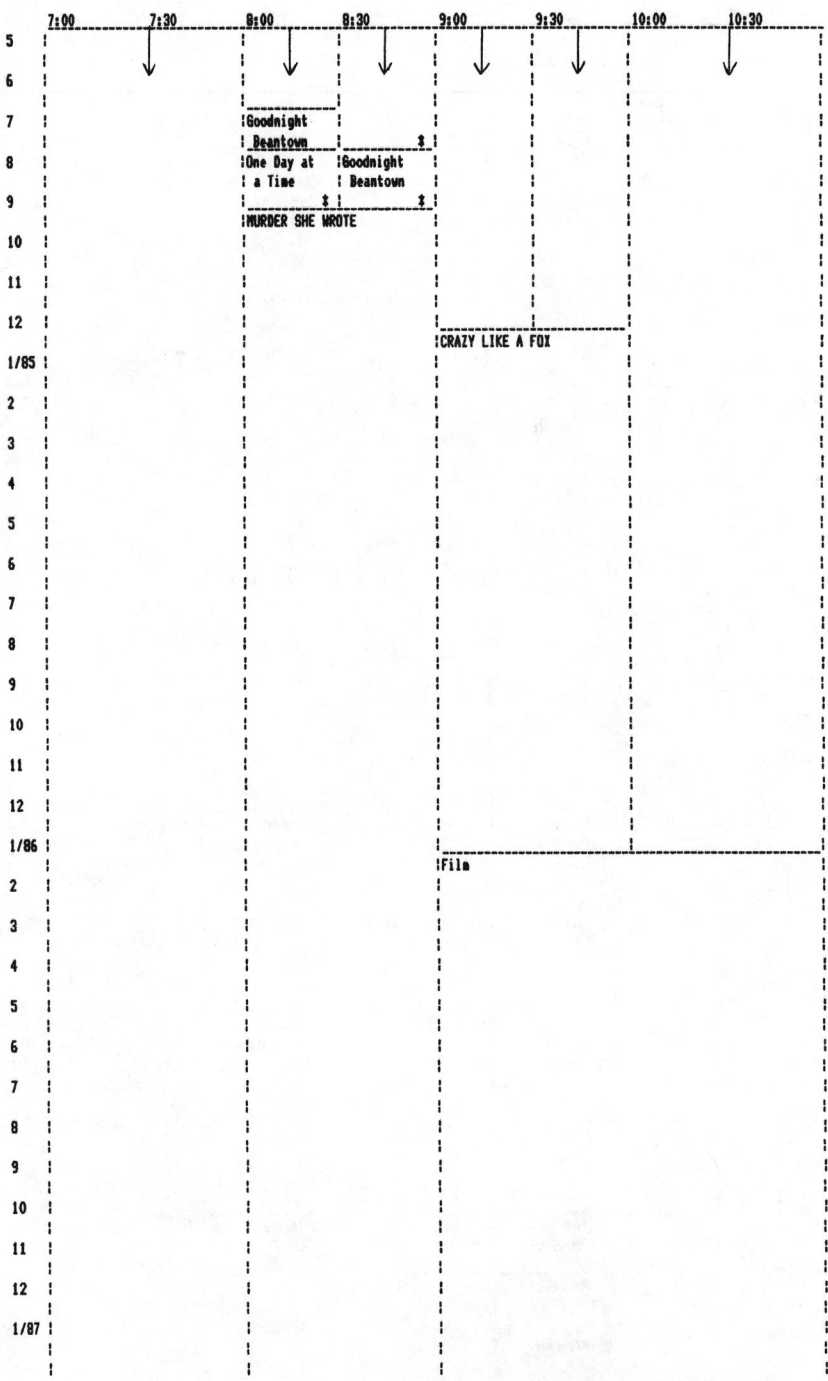

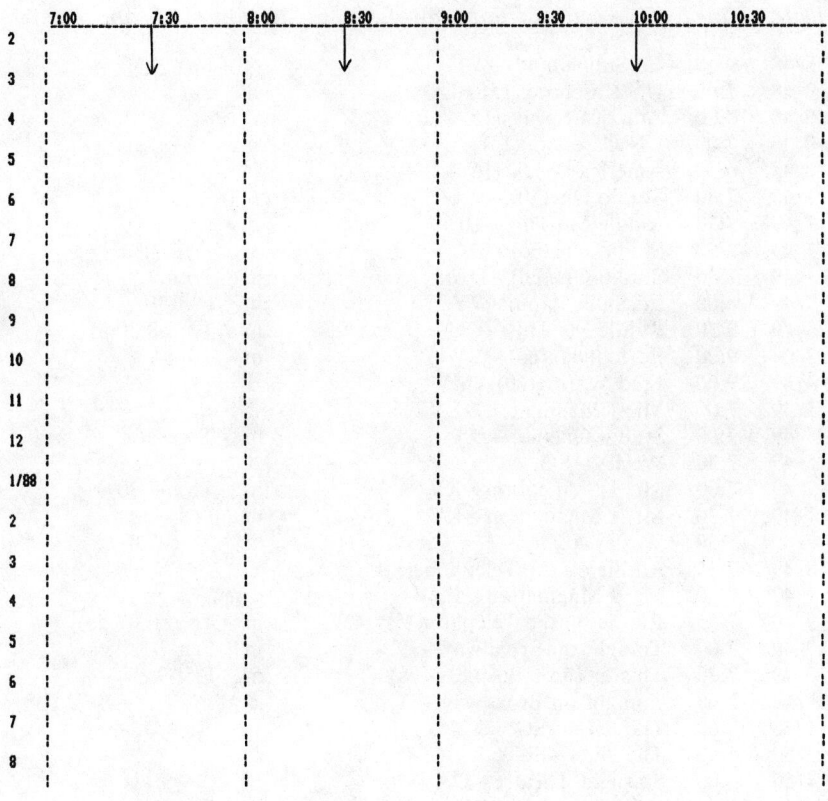

Date	Time	Title (min. if not 30) — Type	Action	From/To
8/48	9:00	Ed Sullivan(60) — VY	m	Fr:n-9:30
9/48	7:00	UN Casebook(15) — DO	d	
9/48	10:00	America Speaks(15) — IF	d	
10/48	7:00	UN Casebook(15) — DO	c	
10/48	10:00	America Speaks(15) — IF	c	
11/48	7:30	Studio One(60) — DA	d	
1/49	8:30	Riddle Me This — QU	d	
3/49	7:00	Studio One(60) — DA	m	Fr:n-7:30
3/49	7:30	Studio One(60) — DA	m	To:n-7
3/49	8:00	Ed Sullivan(60) — VY	m	Fr:n-9
3/49	8:30	Riddle Me This — QU	m	To:n-8:30(a)
3/49	9:00	Ed Sullivan(60) — VY	m	To:n-8
4/49	9:00	Fred Waring(60) — MV	d	
5/49	7:00	Mr. I Magination — KV	d	
5/49	7:00	Studio One(60) — DA	m	To:w-10
5/49	7:30	Wesley — SC	d	
7/49	7:00	Mr. I Magination — KV	m	To:n-7:30
7/49	7:30	Mr. I Magination — KV	m	Fr:n-7
7/49	7:30	Wesley — SC	m	To:t-9:30
8/49	7:55	Ruthie on the Telephone(5) — CY	d	
9/49	7:30	Mr. I Magination — KV	c	
9/49	7:55	Ruthie on the Telephone(5) — CV	m	To:mtrs-7:55
10/49	7:00	Tonight on Broadway — IV	m	Fr:t-7-5/48
10/49	7:30	This Is Show Business — VY	m	Fr:f-9
12/49	7:00	Tonight on Broadway — IV	c	
1/50	7:00	The Girls — SC	d	
3/50	7:00	The Girls — SC	c	
4/50	7:00	Starlight Theatre — DA	d	
4/50	10:00	Celebrity Time — QU	m	Fr:n-10(a)
6/50	7:00	Starlight Theatre — DA	m	To:m-8
6/50	10:00	Celebrity Time — QU	m	To:n-10-10/50
7/50	7:00	Gene Autry — WE	d	
7/50	7:30	By Popular Demand — VY	d*	
8/50	7:30	By Popular Demand — VY	m*	To:f-10
8/50	10:00	News(15) — NW	s	
9/50	10:00	News(15) — NW	f	
10/50	7:30	Jack Benny — CY	d	
10/50	10:00	Celebrity Time — QU	m	Fr:n-10-6/50
10/50	10:30	What's My Line — QU	m	Fr:w-9
7/51	7:30	Go Lucky — QU	d*	
7/51	9:00	G.E. Guest House(60) — QU	d*	
8/51	9:00	G.E. Guest House(60) — QU	c*	
9/51	7:30	Go Lucky — QU	c*	
1/52	9:00	Fred Waring(60) — MV	m	To:n-9
1/52	9:00	Fred Waring — MV	m	Fr:n-9
1/52	9:30	Break the Bank — QU	m	Fr:w-10(n)
6/52	9:00	Information Please — QU	d*	
7/52	7:30	Your Lucky Clue — QU	d*	
8/52	7:30	Your Lucky Clue — QU	c*	
9/52	9:00	Information Please — QU	c*	

Date	Time	Title (min. if not 30) — Type	Action	From/To
9/52	10:00	Celebrity Time — QU	c	
9/52	10:00	The Web — DA	m	Fr:w-9:30-7/52
1/53	7:30	This Is Show Business — VY	m	To:s-9
2/53	7:30	Private Secretary — SC	d	
2/53	9:00	General Electric Theater — DA	d	
2/53	9:30	Alan Young — CV	m	Fr:r-9-3/52
2/53	9:30	Break the Bank — QU	m	To:t-8:30-6/53(n)
2/53	9:30	Ken Murray — VY	m	Fr:s-8-6/52
6/53	7:30	Private Secretary — SC	m	To:s-10:30(n)
6/53	7:30	Your Play Time — DA	d*	
6/53	9:30	Alan Young — CV	c	
6/53	9:30	Arthur Murray Party — MV	m	Fr:n-10-4/53(d)
6/53	9:30	Ken Murray — VY	c	
7/53	7:00	Gene Autry — WE	m	To:t-8
7/53	7:00	Quiz Kids — QU	m	Fr:s-10
9/53	7:30	Private Secretary — SC	m	Fr:s-10:30(n)
9/53	7:30	Your Play Time — DA	m*	To:n-7:30-6/54
10/53	9:30	Arthur Murray Party — MV	m	To:m-7:30(n)
10/53	9:30	Man Behind the Badge — RA	d	
11/53	7:00	Life with Father — SC	d	
11/53	7:00	Quiz Kids — QU	m	To:r-10:30-1/56
5/54	7:00	Earn Your Vacation — QU	d	
5/54	7:00	Life with Father — SC	m	To:t-10-8/54
5/54	9:00	Fred Waring — MV	c	
6/54	7:30	Private Secretary — SC	m	To:s-10:30(n)
6/54	7:30	Your Play Time — DA	m*	Fr:n-7:30-9/53
9/54	7:00	Earn Your Vacation — QU	c	
9/54	7:00	Lassie — AD	d	
9/54	7:30	Private Secretary — SC	m	Fr:s-10:30(n)
9/54	7:30	Your Play Time — DA	m*	To:s-10:30-6/55(n)
9/54	10:00	The Web — DA	m	To:n-10-7/57(n)
10/54	9:30	Honestly Celeste — SC	d	
10/54	9:30	Man Behind the Badge — RA	c	
10/54	10:00	Father Knows Best — SC	d	
12/54	9:30	Honestly Celeste — SC	c	
12/54	9:30	Stage 7 — DA	d	
3/55	10:00	Father Knows Best — SC	m	To:w-8:30-8/55(n)
4/55	10:00	Appointment with Adventure — AA	d	
6/55	7:00	Pride of the Family — SC	m*	Fr:f-9-9/54(a)
7/55	7:00	It's Magic — VY	d*	
7/55	7:00	Pride of the Family — SC	c*	
9/55	7:00	It's Magic — VY	c*	
9/55	9:30	Stage 7 — DA	c	
10/55	9:30	Alfred Hitchcock Presents — SA	d	
4/56	10:00	Appointment with Adventure — AA	c	
4/56	10:00	$64,000 Challenge — QU	d	
3/57	7:30	Marge & Gower Champion — SC	d*	
3/57	7:30	Private Secretary — SC	m	To:t-8:30
6/57	7:30	Marge & Gower Champion — SC	c*	
6/57	7:30	My Favorite Husband — SC	m*	Fr:t-10:30-12/55

Date	Time	Title (min. if not 30) — Type	Action	From/To
9/57	7:30	Bachelor Father — SC	d	
9/57	7:30	My Favorite Husband — SC	c*	
6/58	7:30	Brothers — SC	m*	Fr:t-8:30-3/57
9/58	7:30	Brothers — SC	c*	
9/58	10:00	$64,000 Challenge — QU	c	
9/58	10:00	$64,000 Question — QU	m	Fr:t-10-6/58
11/58	10:00	Keep Talking — QU	m	Fr:t-8
11/58	10:00	$64,000 Question — QU	c	
2/59	10:00	Keep Talking — QU	m	To:w-8
2/59	10:00	Richard Diamond, Pvt. Detective — CD	m	Fr:r-8-9/58
6/59	7:30	Bachelor Father — SC	m	To:r-9(n)
6/59	7:30	Jack Benny — CY	m	To:n-10-10/59
6/59	7:30	Suspicion(60) — SA	m	Fr:m-10-9/58
6/59	7:30	That's My Boy — SC	m	Fr:s-10-1/55
9/59	7:30	Suspicion(60) — SA	c	
9/59	7:30	That's My Boy — SC	c	
9/59	10:00	Richard Diamond, Pvt. Detective — CD	m	To:m-7:30(n)
10/59	7:30	Dennis the Menace — SC	d	
10/59	10:00	George Gobel — CV	m	Fr:t-8-3/59(n)
10/59	10:00	Jack Benny — CY	m	Fr:n-7:30-6/59
6/60	10:00	George Gobel — CV	c	
6/60	10:00	Jack Benny — CY	m	To:n-9:30-10/60
7/60	10:00	Lucy in Connecticut — SC	d	
9/60	9:30	Alfred Hitchcock Presents — SA	m	To:t-8:30(n)
9/60	10:00	Lucy in Connecticut — SC	c	
10/60	9:30	Jack Benny — CY	m	Fr:n-10-6/60
10/60	10:00	Candid Camera — CY	m	Fr:w-10-7/53(n)
6/61	9:30	Holiday Lodge — SC	d*	
10/61	9:30	Holiday Lodge — SC	c*	
6/62	9:30	Jack Benny — CY	m	To:t-9:30-9/62
6/62	9:30	Who in the World — IV	d	
9/62	9:00	General Electric Theater — DA	c	
9/62	9:00	Real McCoys — SC	m	Fr:r-8:30(a)
9/62	9:30	General Electric True — DA	d	
9/62	9:30	Who in the World — IV	c	
9/63	7:30	Dennis the Menace — SC	c	
9/63	7:30	My Favorite Martian — SC	d	
9/63	9:00	Judy Garland(60) — MV	d	
9/63	9:00	Real McCoys — SC	c	
9/63	9:30	General Electric True — DA	c	
3/64	9:00	Judy Garland(60) — MV	c	
4/64	9:00	Celebrity Game — QU	d	
4/64	9:30	Made in America — QU	d	
5/64	9:30	Brenner — CD	m	Fr:r-9-9/62
5/64	9:30	Made in America — QU	c	
9/64	9:00	Celebrity Game — QU	m	To:r-9:30-4/65
9/64	9:00	My Living Doll — SC	d	
9/64	9:30	Brenner — CD	c	

Date	Time	Title (min. if not 30) – Type	Action	From/To
9/64	9:30	Joey Bishop–SC	m	Fr:s-8:30(n)
12/64	9:00	My Living Doll–SC	m	To:w-8
12/64	9:30	Joey Bishop–SC	m	To:t-8
1/65	9:00	For the People(60)–CD	d	
5/65	9:00	For the People(60)–CD	c	
5/65	9:00	Twilight Zone(60)–FA	m	Fr:f-9:30-9/64
9/65	9:00	Perry Mason(60)–LD	m	Fr:r-8
9/65	9:00	Twilight Zone(60)–FA	c	
9/66	7:30	It's About Time–SC	d	
9/66	7:30	My Favorite Martian–SC	c	
9/66	9:00	Garry Moore(60)–VY	d	
9/66	9:00	Perry Mason(60)–LD	c	
1/67	9:00	Garry Moore(60)–VY	c	
2/67	9:00	Smothers Brothers Comedy Hour (60)–CV	d	
7/67	9:00	Our Place(60)–MV	d*	
8/67	7:30	It's About Time–SC	c	
9/67	7:30	Gentle Ben–AD	d	
9/67	9:00	Our Place(60)–MV	c*	
9/67	10:00	Candid Camera–CY	c	
9/67	10:00	Mission: Impossible(60)–SD	m	Fr:s-8:30
9/67	10:30	What's My Line–QU	c	
6/68	9:00	Summer Smothers Brothers Show (60)–CV	d*	
9/68	9:00	Summer Smothers Brothers Show (60)–CV	c*	
6/69	9:00	Hee Haw(60)–VY	d	
6/69	9:00	Smothers Brothers Comedy Hour (60)–CV	m	To:w-10-7/70(a)
8/69	7:30	Gentle Ben–AD	c	
9/69	7:30	To Rome with Love–SC	d	
9/69	9:00	Hee Haw(60)–VY	m	To:w-7:30-12/69
9/69	9:00	Leslie Uggams(60)–MV	d	
12/69	9:00	Glen Campbell Goodtime Hour (60)–MV	m	Fr:w-7:30
12/69	9:00	Leslie Uggams(60)–MV	c	
7/70	9:00	Comedy Tonight(60)–CV	d*	
8/70	9:00	Comedy Tonight(60)–CV	c*	
9/70	7:30	Hogan's Heroes–SC	m	Fr:f-8:30
9/70	7:30	To Rome with Love–SC	m	To:t-9:30
9/70	10:00	Mission: Impossible(60)–SD	m	To:s-7:30
9/70	10:00	Tim Conway Comedy Hour (60)–CV	d	
12/70	10:00	Tim Conway Comedy Hour(60) –CV	c	
1/71	10:00	Honeymooners(60)–SC	d	
5/71	10:00	Honeymooners(60)–SC	c	
5/71	10:00	Ice Palace(60)–MV	d	
6/71	8:00	Ed Sullivan(60)–VY	c	
6/71	8:00	Film(120)–FI	s	

Date	Time	Title (min. if not 30) — Type	Action	From/To
6/71	9:00	Glen Campbell Goodtime Hour(60) — MV	m	To:t-7:30-9/71
7/71	7:30	Animal World — WL	m	Fr:r-7:30-9/70(a)
7/71	7:30	Hogan's Heroes — SC	c	
7/71	8:00	Film(120) — FI	f	
7/71	10:00	Ice Palace(60) — MV	c	
8/71	8:00	Comedy Playhouse — CA	d	
8/71	8:30	Sonny and Cher Comedy Hour(60) — MV	d	
8/71	9:30	Six Wives of Henry VIII(90) — DR	d	
9/71	7:00	Lassie — AD	c	
9/71	7:30	Animal World — WL	c	
9/71	7:30	Film(120) — FI	s	
9/71	8:00	Comedy Playhouse — CA	c	
9/71	8:30	Sonny and Cher Hour(60) — MV	m	To:m-10-12/71
9/71	9:30	Cade's County(60) — CD	d	
9/71	9:30	Six Wives of Henry VIII(90) — DR	c	
8/72	9:30	Cade's County(60) — CD	m	To:m-10
8/72	9:30	Life of Leonardo da Vinci(60) — DR	d	
9/72	7:30	Anna and the King — SC	d	
9/72	7:30	Film(120) — FI	f	
9/72	8:00	M*A*S*H — SC	d	
9/72	8:30	Sandy Duncan — SC	d	
9/72	9:00	New Dick Van Dyke Show — SC	m	Fr:s-9
9/72	9:30	Life of Leonardo da Vinci(60) — DR	c	
9/72	9:30	Mannix(60) — CD	m	Fr:w-10
12/72	7:30	Anna and the King — SC	c	
12/72	8:30	Sandy Duncan — SC	c	
12/72	9:00	New Dick Van Dyke Show — SC	m	To:n-7:30
12/72	9:30	Mannix(60) — CD	m	To:n-8:30
1/73	7:30	New Dick Van Dyke Show — SC	m	Fr:n-9
1/73	8:30	Mannix(60) — CD	m	Fr:n-9:30
1/73	9:30	Barnaby Jones(60) — CD	d	
9/73	7:30	New Dick Van Dyke Show — SC	m	To:m-9:30
9/73	7:30	New Perry Mason(60) — LD	d	
9/73	8:00	M*A*S*H — SC	m	To:s-8:30
1/74	7:30	New Perry Mason(60) — LD	c	
2/74	7:30	Apple's Way(60) — DR	d	
6/74	9:30	Barnaby Jones(60) — CD	m	To:t-10
7/74	9:30	60 Minutes(60) — NM	m	Fr:f-8-9/73
9/74	8:30	Kojak(60) — CD	m	Fr:w-10
9/74	8:30	Mannix(60) — CD	m	To:n-9:30
9/74	9:30	Mannix(60) — CD	m	Fr:n-8:30
9/74	9:30	60 Minutes(60) — NM	m	To:n-9:30-7/75
1/75	7:30	Apple's Way(60) — DR	c	
2/75	7:30	Cher(60) — MV	d	
6/75	7:30	Cher(60) — MV	m	To:n-8-9/75
6/75	9:30	Mannix(60) — CD	m	To:w-10
7/75	7:30	Joey & Dad(60) — MV	d	
7/75	7:30	Joey & Dad(60) — MV	c	

Date	Time	Title (min. if not 30) — Type	Action	From/To
7/75	9:30	60 Minutes(60) — NM	m	Fr:n-9:30-9/74
8/75	7:30	Manhattan Transfer(60) — MV	d	
8/75	7:30	Manhattan Transfer(60) — MV	c	
9/75	7:00	Three for the Road(60) — AD	d	
9/75	8:00	Cher(60) — MV	m	Fr:n-7:30-6/75
9/75	8:30	Kojak(60) — CD	m	To:n-9
9/75	9:00	Kojak(60) — CD	m	Fr:n-8:30
9/75	9:30	60 Minutes(60) — NM	m	To:n-7-12/75
9/75	10:00	Bronk(60) — CD	d	
11/75	7:00	Three for the Road(60) — AD	c	
12/75	7:00	60 Minutes(60) — NM	m#	Fr:n-9:30-9/75
1/76	8:00	Cher(60) — MV	c	
2/76	8:00	Sonny and Cher Comedy Hour(60) — MV	m	Fr:w-8-5/74
7/76	10:00	Bronk(60) — CD	c	
7/76	10:00	Cannon(60) — CD	m	Fr:w-9
8/76	8:00	Johnny Cash(60) — MV	d*	
9/76	8:00	Johnny Cash(60) — MV	c*	
9/76	10:00	Cannon(60) — CD	c	
9/76	10:00	Delvecchio(60) — CD	d	
1/77	8:00	Rhoda — SC	m	Fr:m-8
1/77	8:00	Sonny and Cher Comedy Hour(60) — MV	m	To:f-9
1/77	8:30	Phyllis — SC	m	Fr:m-8:30
1/77	9:00	Kojak(60) — CD	m	To:m-10
1/77	9:00	Switch(60) — CD	m	Fr:t-10
7/77	8:30	Phyllis — SC	m	To:t-8:30
7/77	8:30	Starland Vocal Band — VY	d	
7/77	10:00	Delvecchio(60) — CD	c	
8/77	8:30	Starland Vocal Band — VY	m	To:f-8:30
8/77	8:30	A Year at the Top — SC	m	Fr:f-8
9/77	8:30	A Year at the Top — SC	c	
9/77	9:00	Switch(60) — CD	m	To:m-10-12/77
9/77	10:00	Kojak(60) — CD	m	Fr:m-10
10/77	8:30	On Our Own — SC	d	
10/77	9:00	All in the Family — SC	m	Fr:s-9
10/77	9:30	Alice — SC	m	Fr:s-9:30
12/77	10:00	Carol Burnett(60) — CV	m	Fr:s-10
12/77	10:00	Kojak(60) — CD	m	To:s-10
3/78	10:00	Carol Burnett(60) — CV	m	To:w-8-6/78
4/78	10:00	Dallas(60) — SL	d	
5/78	10:00	Dallas(60) — SL	m	To:s-10-9/78
6/78	10:00	Switch(60) — CD	m	Fr:m-10-1/78
9/78	8:00	Mary(60) — CV	d	
9/78	8:00	Rhoda — SC	m	To:s-8
9/78	8:30	On Our Own — SC	c	
9/78	10:00	Kaz(60) — LD	d	
9/78	10:00	Switch(60) — CD	c	
10/78	8:00	All in the Family — SC	m	Fr:n-9
10/78	8:00	Mary(60) — CV	c	

Date	Time	Title (min. if not 30) — Type	Action	From/To
10/78	8:30	Alice — SC	m	Fr:n-9:30
10/78	9:00	All in the Family — SC	m	To:n-8
10/78	9:00	Kaz(60) — LD	m	Fr:n-10
10/78	9:30	Alice — SC	m	To:n-8:30
10/78	10:00	Dallas(60) — SL	m	Fr:s-10
10/78	10:00	Kaz(60) — LD	m	To:n-9
1/79	9:00	Kaz(60) — LD	m	To:w-10
1/79	9:00	Film(120) — FI	s	
1/79	10:00	Dallas(60) — SL	m	To:f-10
2/79	8:30	Alice — SC	m	To:n-9
2/79	9:00	Film(120) — FI	f	
3/79	8:30	One Day at a Time — SC	m	Fr:w-9
3/79	9:00	Alice — SC	m	Fr:n-8:30
3/79	9:30	Stockard Channing in Just Friends — SC	d	
3/79	10:00	Mary Tyler Moore(60) — CV	d	
6/79	9:30	Jeffersons — SC	m	Fr:w-8
6/79	9:30	Stockard Channing in Just Friends — SC	m	To:s-8:30
6/79	10:00	Mary Tyler Moore(60) — CV	c	
6/79	10:00	Moses — the Lawgiver(60) — RD	m	Fr:s-10-8/75
7/79	10:00	Kaz(60) — LD	m	Fr:w-10-4/79
7/79	10:00	Moses — the Lawgiver(60) — RD	c	
8/79	10:00	Kaz(60) — LD	c	
9/79	8:00	All in the Family — SC	c	
9/79	8:00	Archie Bunker's Place — SC	d	
9/79	10:00	Trapper John, MD(60) — MD	d	
9/82	8:30	Gloria — SC	d	
9/82	8:30	One Day at a Time — SC	m	To:n-9:30
9/82	9:00	Alice — SC	m	To:w-9
9/82	9:00	Jeffersons — SC	m	Fr:n-9:30
9/82	9:30	Jeffersons — SC	m	To:n-9
9/82	9:30	One Day at a Time — SC	m	Fr:n-8:30
3/83	8:00	Archie Bunker's Place — SC	m	To:m-8
3/83	9:30	Newhart — SC	m	Fr:m-9:30
3/83	9:30	One Day at a Time — SC	m	To:m-9:30
4/83	8:00	Goodnight Beantown — SC	d	
4/83	8:30	Gloria — SC	m	To:w-8:30-6/83
4/83	8:30	Newhart — SC	m	Fr:n-9:30
4/83	9:30	Alice — SC	m	Fr:m-9
4/83	9:30	Newhart — SC	m	To:n-8:30
5/83	8:00	Archie Bunker's Place — SC	m	Fr:m-8
5/83	8:00	Archie Bunker's Place — SC	m	To:w-8
5/83	8:00	Goodnight Beantown — SC	m	To:n-9:30-8/83
5/83	8:30	Newhart — SC	m	To:n-9:30-7/83
5/83	9:30	Alice — SC	m	To:n-8
6/83	8:00	Alice — SC	m	Fr:n-9:30
6/83	8:30	One Day at a Time — SC	m	Fr:m-9:30
7/83	9:30	Newhart — SC	m	Fr:n-8:30
8/83	9:30	Goodnight Beantown — SC	m	Fr:n-8-5/83

Date	Time	Title (min. if not 30) — Type	Action	From/To
8/83	9:30	Newhart — SC	m	To:m-9:30
1/84	8:00	Alice — SC	m	To:n-9:30
1/84	8:00	Four Seasons — SC	d	
1/84	9:30	Alice — SC	m	Fr:n-8
1/84	9:30	Goodnight Beantown — SC	m	To:n-8-7/84
2/84	8:00	Four Seasons — SC	m	To:n-8:30
2/84	8:30	One Day at a Time — SC	m	To:w-8
3/84	8:00	Suzanne Pleshette Is Maggie Briggs — SC	d	
3/84	8:30	Four Seasons — SC	m	Fr:n-8
4/84	8:00	Aftermash — SC	m	Fr:m-9
4/84	8:00	Suzanne Pleshette Is Maggie Briggs — SC	c	
6/84	8:00	Aftermash — SC	m	To:t-8
7/84	8:00	Goodnight Beantown — SC	m	Fr:n-9:30-1/84
7/84	8:00	Goodnight Beantown — SC	m	To:n-8:30
7/84	8:30	Four Seasons — SC	c	
8/84	8:00	One Day at a Time — SC	m	Fr:m-9
8/84	8:30	Goodnight Beantown — SC	m	Fr:n-8
9/84	8:00	Murder, She Wrote(60) — MY	d#	
9/84	8:00	One Day at a Time — SC	c	
9/84	8:30	Goodnight Beantown — SC	c	
12/84	9:00	Jeffersons — SC	m	To:t-8
12/84	9:00	Crazy Like a Fox(60) — CO	d	
12/84	9:30	Alice — SC	m	To:t-8:30
1/86	9:00	Crazy Like a Fox(60) — CO	m	To:w-9
1/86	9:00	Film(120) — FI	s#	
1/86	10:00	Trapper John, MD(60) — MD	m	To:t-8

	7:00	7:30	8:00	8:30	9:00	9:30	10:00	10:30
9/48			Author Meets the Critics	Meet the Press				
10	Mary Kay & Johnny	WELCOME ABOARD	Critics		PHILCO TV PALYHOUSE			
11								
12								Who Said That
1/49							Girl About Town	
2		HARTMANS		LAMBS GAMBOL				
3			Lambs Gambol	Author Meets the Critics				
4								
5	Broadway Spotlight	Candid Camera	Leave It to the Girls					
6							Garroway at Large	
7		SUNDAY DATE	Broadway Spotlight	MEREDITH WILSON				
8				Leave It to the Girls				
9								
10	Leave It to the Girls	ALDRICH FAMILY	Perry Como	Colgate Theatre				
11								
12								
1/50								
2								
3								ANSWER YES OR NO
4								
5								
6			SAMMY KAYE					
7								
8			BATTLE REPORT	SPOTLIGHT ON SPORTS				
9			COLGATE COMEDY HOUR					
10								TAKE A CHANCE
11								
12								
1/51								
2								
3								
4								

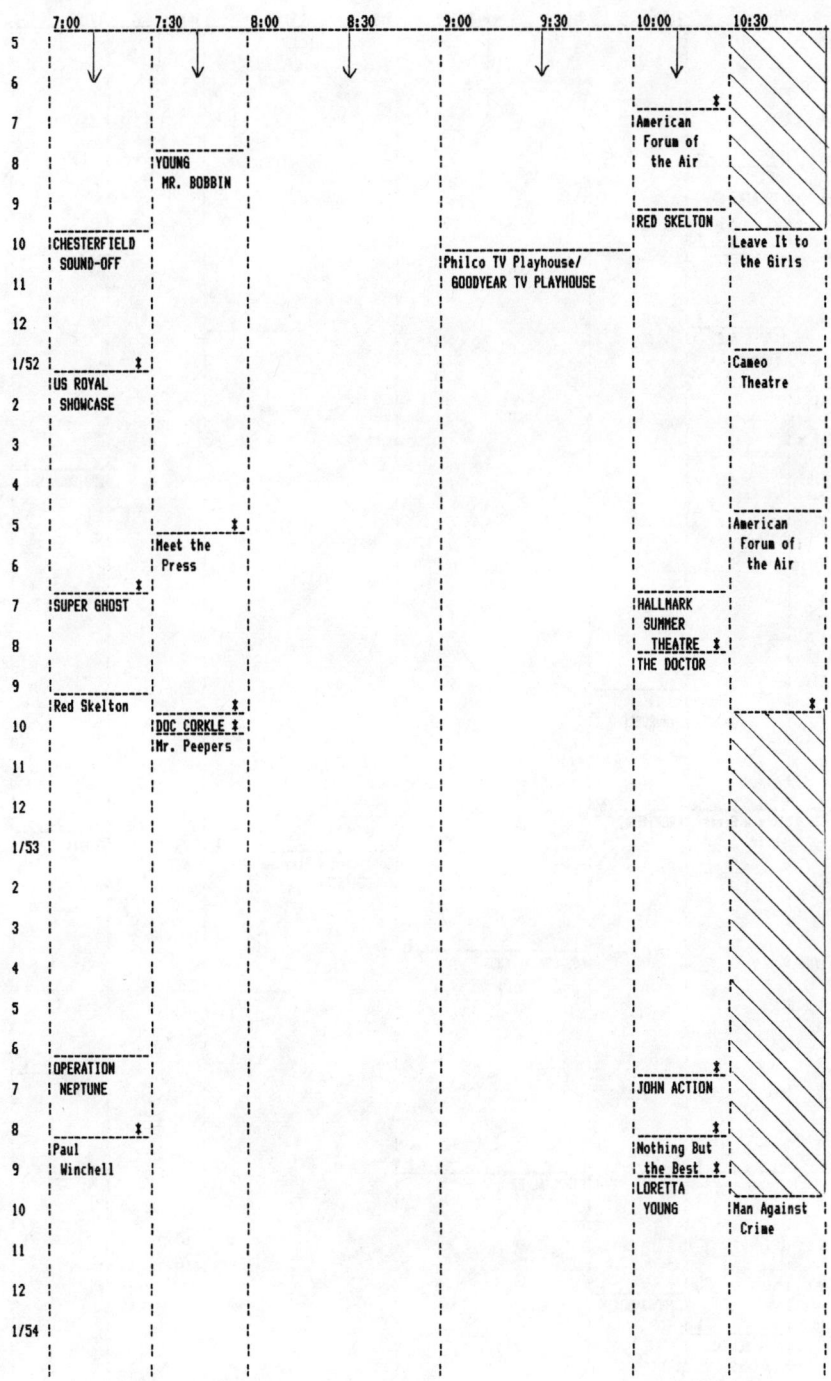

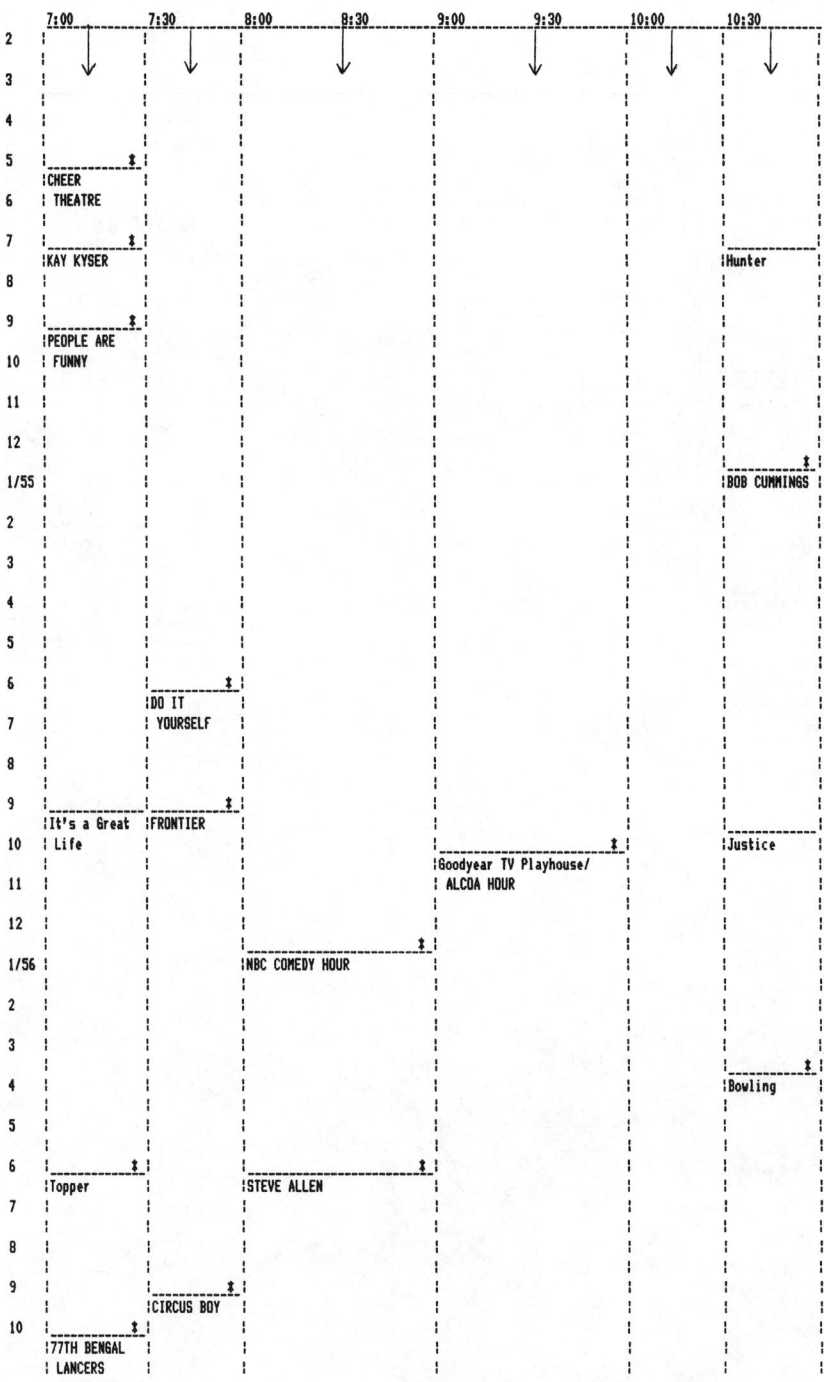

	7:00	7:30	8:00	8:30	9:00	9:30	10:00	10:30
2								
3								
4								
5	CHEER							
6	THEATRE							
7	KAY KYSER							Hunter
8								
9	PEOPLE ARE							
10	FUNNY							
11								
12								
1/55								BOB CUMMINGS
2								
3								
4								
5								
6		DO IT						
7		YOURSELF						
8								
9	It's a Great	FRONTIER						
10	Life				Goodyear TV Playhouse/			Justice
11					ALCOA HOUR			
12								
1/56			NBC COMEDY HOUR					
2								
3								
4								Bowling
5								
6	Topper		STEVE ALLEN					
7								
8								
9		CIRCUS BOY						
10	77TH BENGAL							
	LANCERS							

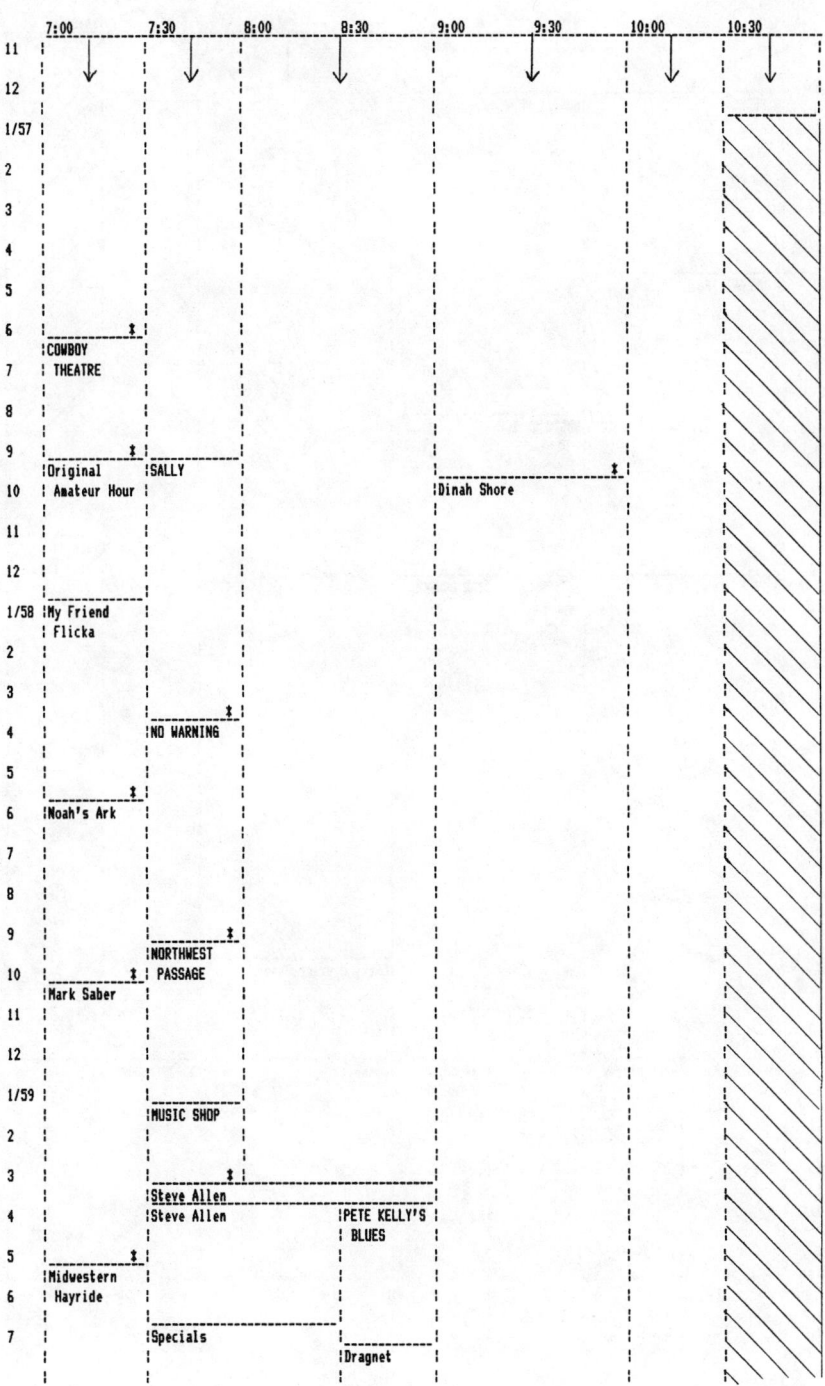

	7:00	7:30	8:00	8:30	9:00	9:30	10:00	10:30
11								
12								
1/57								
2								
3								
4								
5								
6	COWBOY							
7	THEATRE							
8								
9	Original	SALLY						
10	Amateur Hour			Dinah Shore				
11								
12								
1/58	My Friend							
	Flicka							
2								
3								
4		NO WARNING						
5								
6	Noah's Ark							
7								
8								
9		NORTHWEST						
10	Mark Saber	PASSAGE						
11								
12								
1/59		MUSIC SHOP						
2								
3		Steve Allen						
4		Steve Allen		PETE KELLY'S				
				BLUES				
5								
6	Midwestern							
	Hayride							
7		Specials		Dragnet				

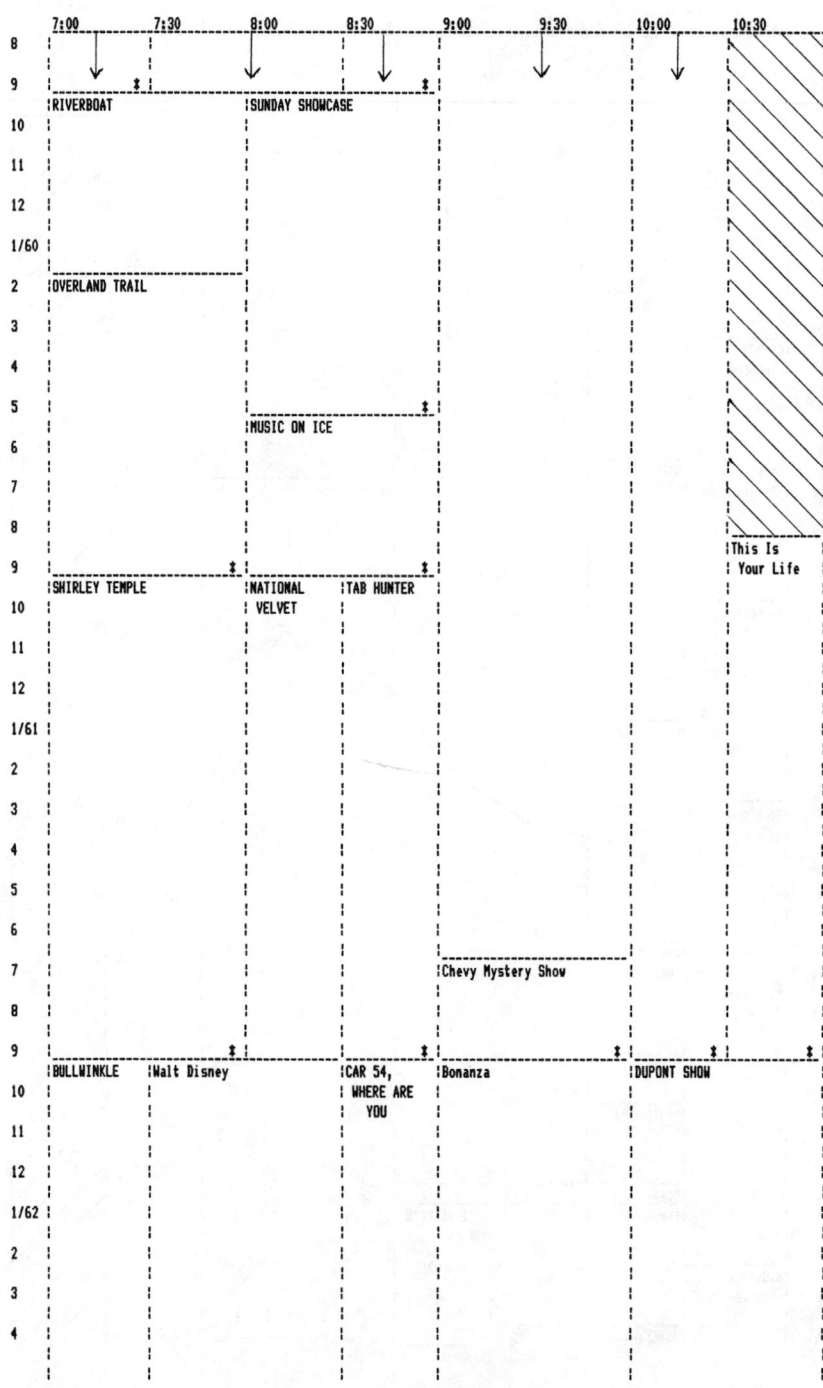

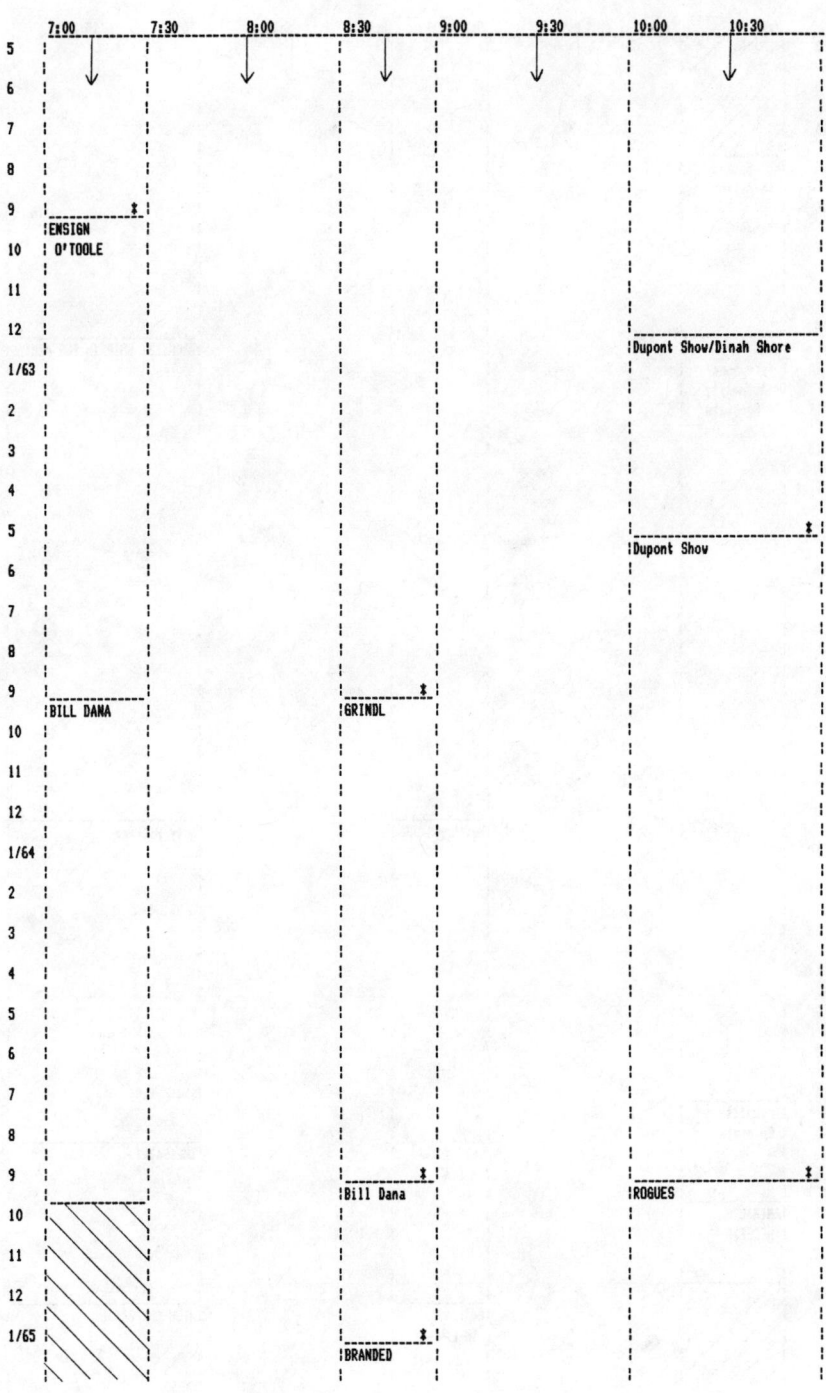

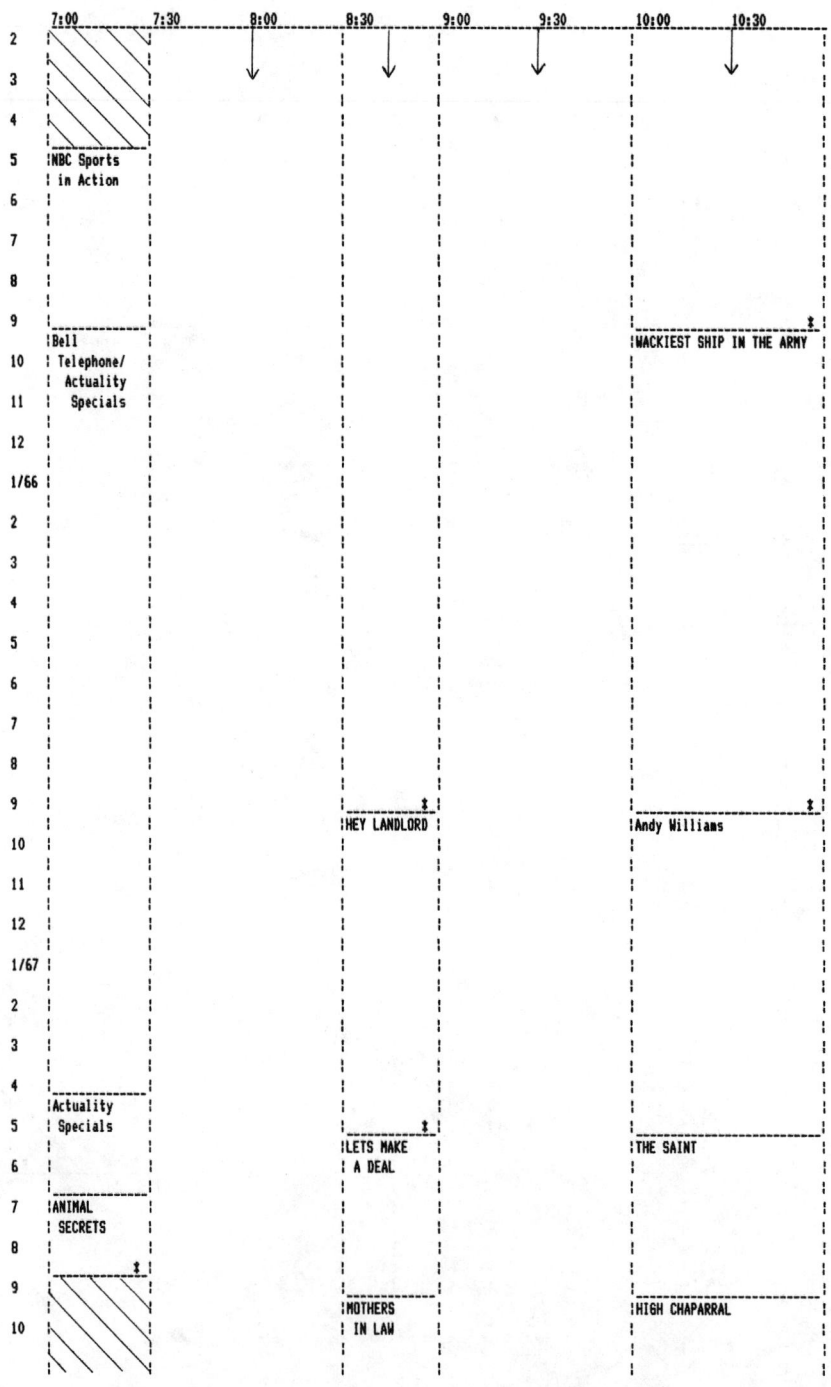

	7:00	7:30	8:00	8:30	9:00	9:30	10:00	10:30
2								
3	NBC Sports							
4	in Action							
5								
6								
7								
8								
9	Bell						WACKIEST SHIP IN THE ARMY	
10	Telephone/							
11	Actuality Specials							
12								
1/66								
2								
3								
4								
5								
6								
7								
8								
9			HEY LANDLORD				Andy Williams	
10								
11								
12								
1/67								
2								
3								
4	Actuality							
5	Specials		LETS MAKE				THE SAINT	
6			A DEAL					
7	ANIMAL							
8	SECRETS							
9			MOTHERS				HIGH CHAPARRAL	
10			IN LAW					

	7:00	7:30	8:00	8:30	9:00	9:30	10:00	10:30
11								
12								
1/68	WILD KINGDOM							
2								
3								
4								
5								
6								
	Flipper							
7								
8								
9								
	HUCK FINN					PHYLLIS DILLER		
10								
11								
12								
1/69						MY FRIEND TONY		
2								
3								
4								
5								
6								
7								
8								
9								
	Wild Kingdom		BILL COSBY			LAWYERS/NEW DOCTORS/		
10							PROTECTORS	
11								
12								
1/70								
2								
3								
4								
5								
6								
7								

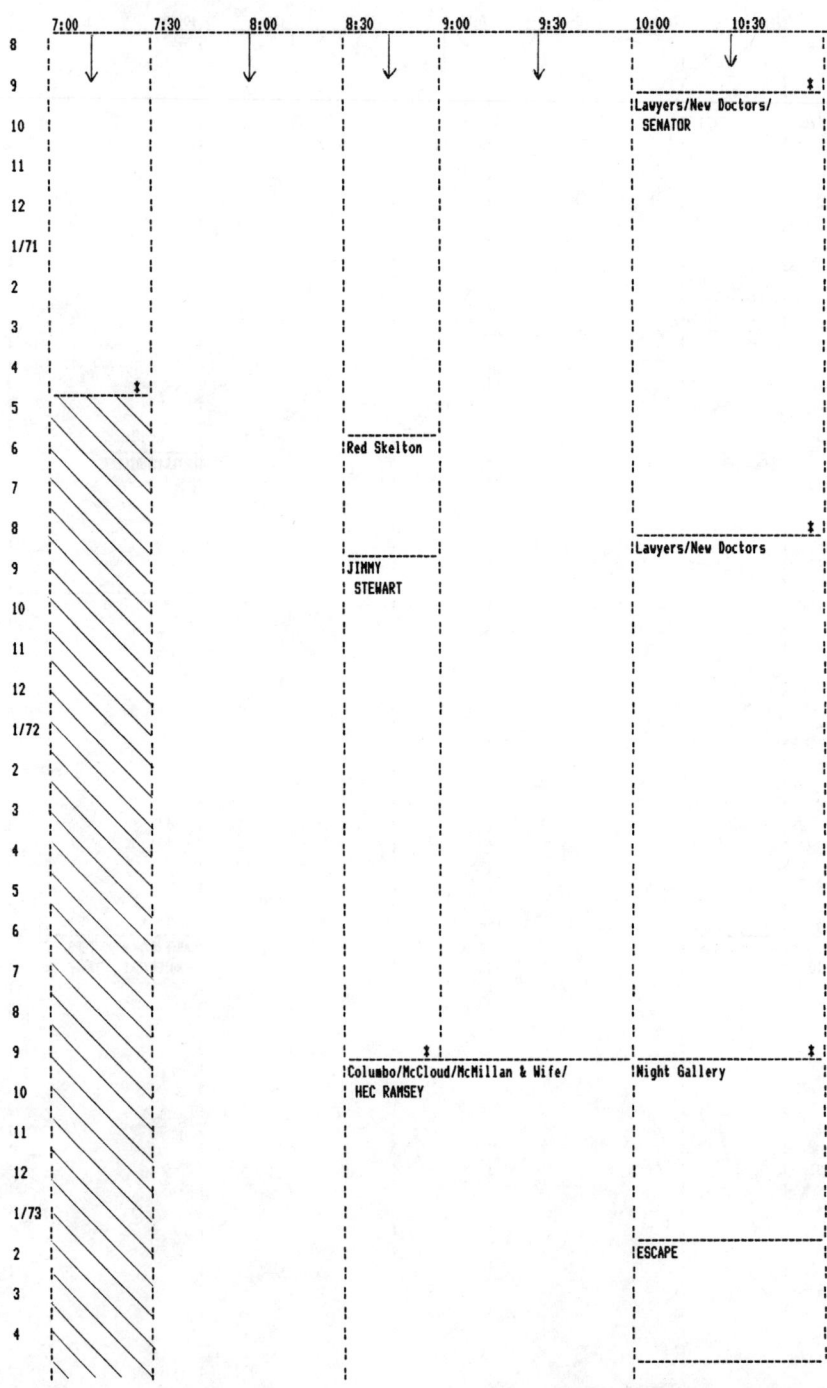

	7:00	7:30	8:00	8:30	9:00	9:30	10:00	10:30

Lavyers/Nev Doctors/ SENATOR

Red Skelton

JIMMY STEWART

Lavyers/Nev Doctors

Columbo/McCloud/McMillan & Wife/ HEC RAMSEY

Night Gallery

ESCAPE

8 9 10 11 12 1/71 2 3 4 5 6 7 8 9 10 11 12 1/72 2 3 4 5 6 7 8 9 10 11 12 1/73 2 3 4

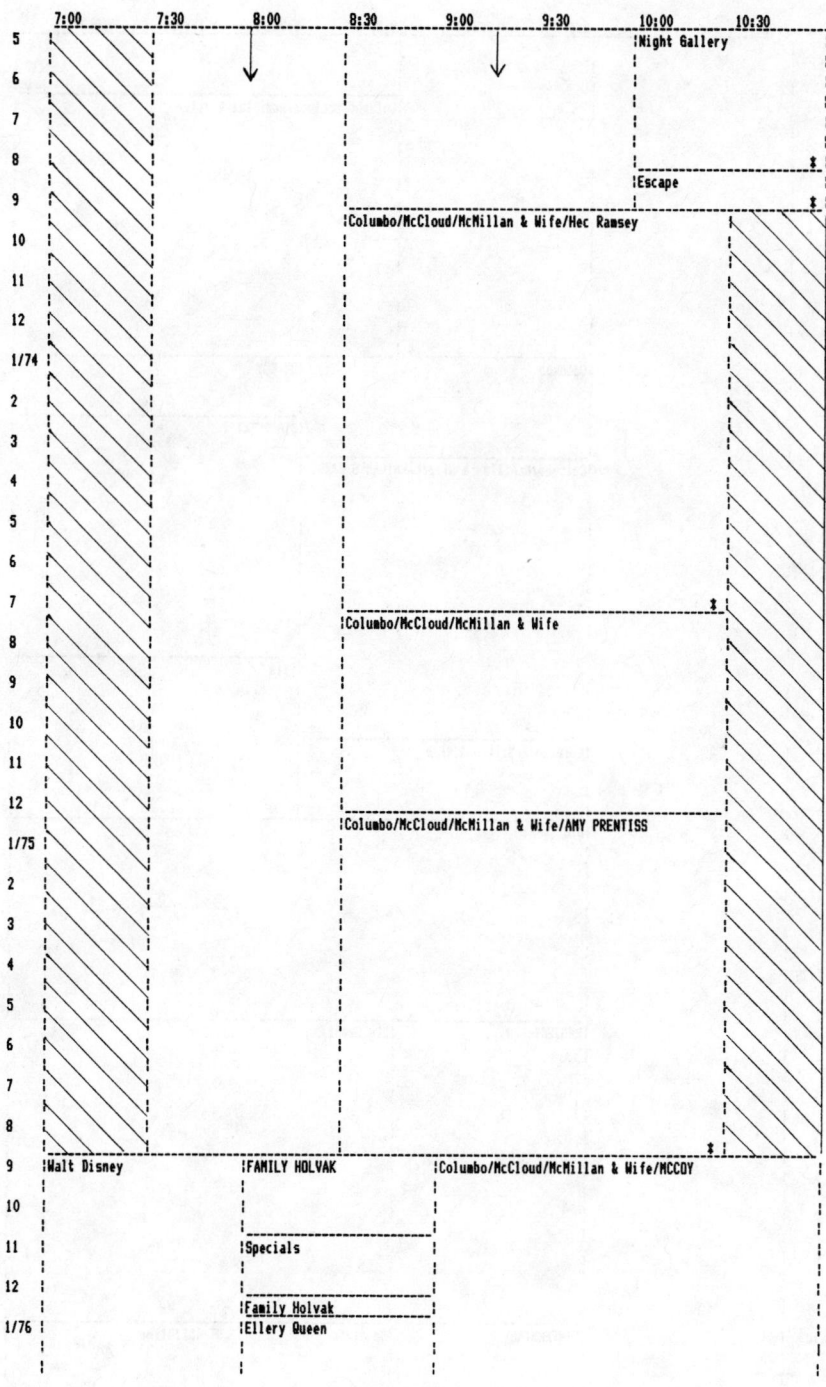

	7:00	7:30	8:00	8:30	9:00	9:30	10:00	10:30

Night Gallery

Escape

Columbo/McCloud/McMillan & Wife/Hec Ramsey

Columbo/McCloud/McMillan & Wife

Columbo/McCloud/McMillan & Wife/AMY PRENTISS

Walt Disney

FAMILY HOLVAK

Columbo/McCloud/McMillan & Wife/MCCOY

Specials

Family Holvak

Ellery Queen

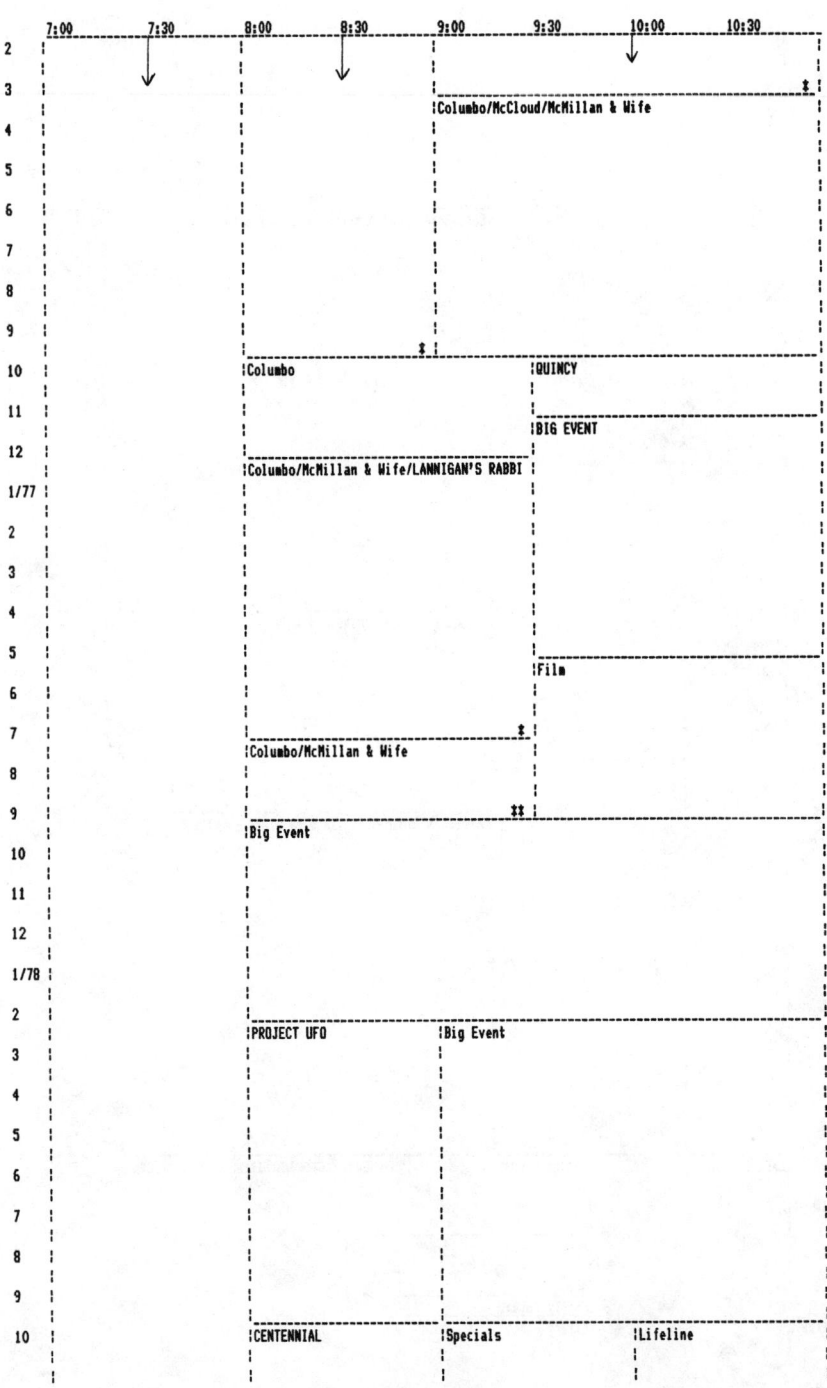

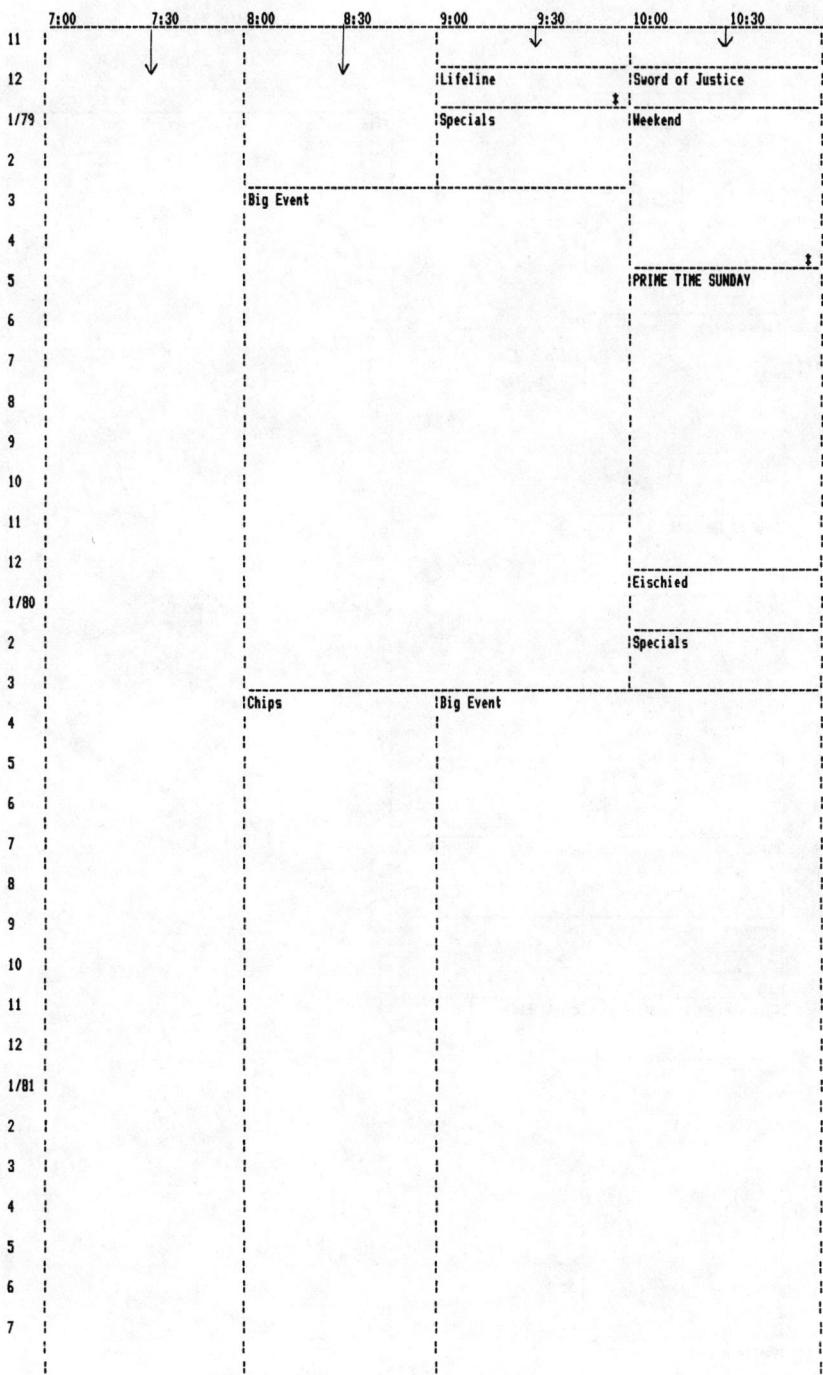

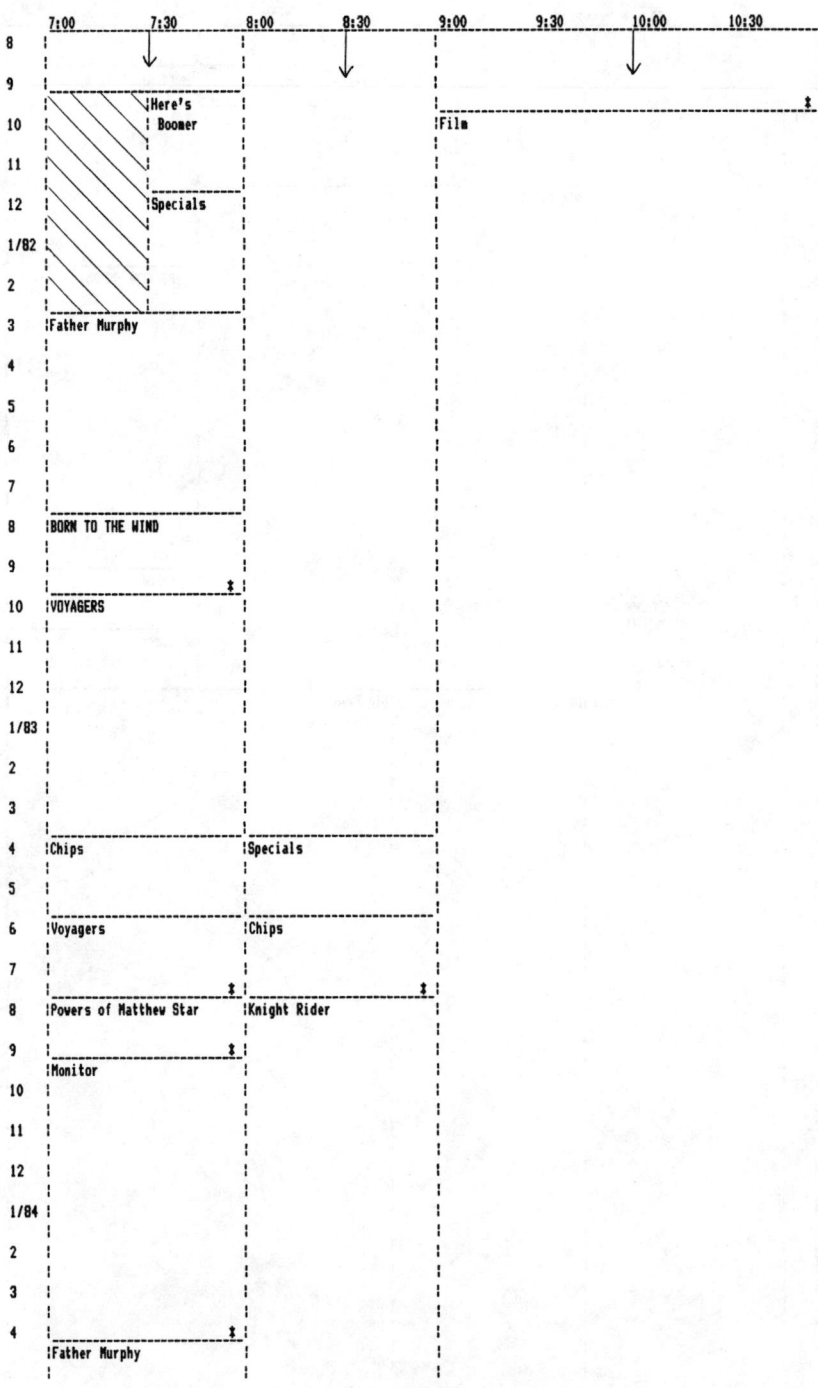

```
        7:00      7:30      8:00      8:30      9:00      9:30      10:00     10:30
5  :                 |                 |                           |
6  :                 v                 v                           v
   :_____:
7  :SUMMER SUNDAY           :
8  :                        :
9  :_____:
   :Silver    :PUNKY        :
10 : Spoons   : BREWSTER    :
11 :          :             :
12 :          :             :
1/85:         :             :
2  :          :             :
3  :          :             :
4  :          :             :
5  :          :             :
6  :Punky     :Silver       :
   : Brewster : Spoons      :
7  :          :             :
8  :          :        :OCEAN QUEST            :
9  :          :        :_____:
   :          :        :AMAZING   :ALFRED      :
10 :          :        : STORIES  : HITCHCOCK  :
   :          :        :          : PRESENTS   :
11 :          :        :          :            :
12 :          :        :          :            :
1/86:         :        :          :            :
2  :          :        :          :            :
3  :          :        :          :            :
4  :_____:Specials :          :            :
   :FATHERS&SONS :Fathers &        :            :
5  :Silver    : Sons   :           :
   : Spoons   :Punky   :
6  :          : Brewster:
7  :          :        :DALTONS: CODE OF VENGEANCE :
8  :          :        :                          :
9  :_____:   :    :Easy Street :Valerie      :
   :OUR HOUSE          :            :
10 :                   :            :
11 :                   :_____:
   :                   :Valerie   :Easy Street    :
12 :                   :          :               :
1/87:                  :_____:
   :                   :Easy Street :Valerie      :
```

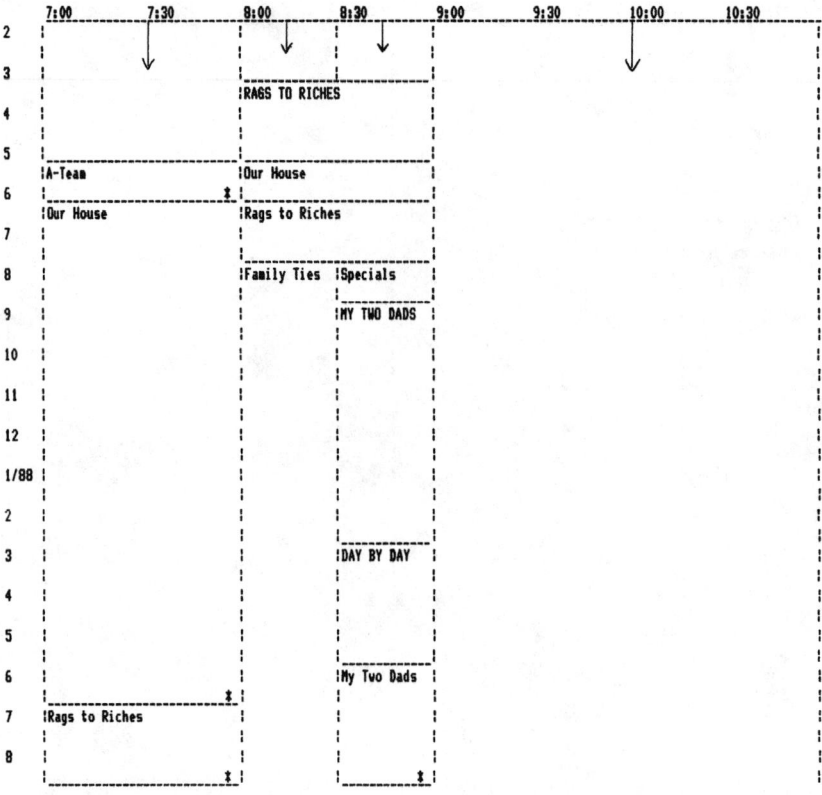

	7:00	7:30	8:00	8:30	9:00	9:30	10:00	10:30
2								
3			RAGS TO RICHES					
4								
5	A-Team		Our House					
6	Our House		Rags to Riches					
7								
8			Family Ties	Specials				
9				MY TWO DADS				
10								
11								
12								
1/88								
2								
3				DAY BY DAY				
4								
5								
6				My Two Dads				
7	Rags to Riches							
8								

Date	Time	Title (min. if not 30) — Type	Action	From/To
4/48	8:00	Author Meets the Critics — DS	d	
9/48	8:30	Meet the Press — IV	m	Fr:r-8-12/47
10/48	7:00	Mary Kay and Johnny — SC	m	Fr:t-7:15-8/48(d)
10/48	7:30	Welcome Aboard — MV	d	
10/48	9:00	Philco TV Playhouse(60) — DA	d	
1/49	10:30	Who Said That? — QU	m	Fr:m-10
2/49	7:00	Mary Kay and Johnny — SC	m	To:w-9(c)
2/49	7:30	The Hartmans — SC	d	
2/49	7:30	Welcome Aboard — MV	c	
2/49	8:30	Lamb's Gambol — MV	d	
2/49	8:30	Meet the Press — IV	m	To:w-10
2/49	10:00	Girl About Town — MU	m	Fr:w-8
3/49	8:00	Author Meets the Critics — DS	m	To:n-8:30
3/49	8:00	Lamb's Gambol — MV	m	Fr:n-8:30
3/49	8:30	Author Meets the Critics — DS	m	Fr:n-8
3/49	8:30	Lamb's Gambol — MV	m	To:n-8
3/49	10:30	Who Said That? — QU	m	To:s-9
4/49	9:00	NBC Repertory Theatre(60) — DA	d*	
5/49	7:00	Broadway Spotlight — VY	m	Fr:w-8
5/49	7:30	Candid Camera — CY	m	Fr:f-8-12/48(a)
5/49	7:30	The Hartmans — SC	c	
5/49	8:00	Lamb's Gambol — MV	c	
5/49	8:00	Leave It to the Girls — DS	m	Fr:w-8
6/49	10:00	Girl About Town — MU	c	
7/49	7:00	Broadway Spotlight — VY	m	To:n-7:30
7/49	7:30	Broadway Spotlight — VY	m	Fr:n-7
7/49	7:30	Candid Camera — CY	m	To:r-9
7/49	8:30	Author Meets the Critics — DS	m	To:m-7:30-10/49(a)
7/49	8:30	Meredith Wilson — MU	d	
7/49	9:00	NBC Repertory Theatre(60) — DA	c*	
7/49	10:00	Garroway at Large — VY	m	Fr:s-10
8/49	7:15	Sunday Date(15) — MU	d	
8/49	8:00	Leave It to the Girls — DS	m	To:n-8:30
8/49	8:30	Leave It to the Girls — DS	m	Fr:n-8
8/49	8:30	Meredith Wilson — MU	c	
9/49	7:30	Broadway Spotlight — VY	c	
10/49	7:00	Leave It to the Girls — DS	m	Fr:n-8:30
10/49	7:15	Sunday Date(15) — MU	c	
10/49	7:30	Aldrich Family — SC	d	
10/49	8:00	Perry Como — MV	m	Fr:f-7-1/49
10/49	8:30	Colgate Theatre — DA	m	Fr:m-9
10/49	8:30	Leave It to the Girls — DS	m	To:n-7
4/50	10:30	Answer Yes or No — QU	d	
6/50	8:00	Perry Como — MV	m	To:mwf-7:45-10/50 (c)
6/50	8:00	Sammy Kaye — MV	d	
7/50	7:30	Watch the World — DO	d*	
7/50	8:00	Sammy Kaye — MV	m	To:s-7-7/51(c)
7/50	8:30	Colgate Theatre — DA	c	
7/50	9:00	Masterpiece Playhouse(60) — DA	d*	

Date	Time	Title (min. if not 30) — Type	Action	From/To
7/50	10:00	Lights, Camera, Action — TA	d*	
7/50	10:30	Answer Yes or No — QU	c	
8/50	7:30	Watch the World — DO	c*	
8/50	8:00	Battle Report — DO	d	
8/50	8:30	Spotlight on Sports — ST	d	
8/50	10:00	Lights, Camera, Action — TA	c*	
9/50	8:00	Battle Report — DO	m	To:f-9:30-6/51
9/50	8:00	Colgate Comedy Hour(60) — CV	d	
9/50	8:30	Spotlight on Sports — ST	c	
9/50	9:00	Masterpiece Playhouse(60) — DA	c*	
10/50	10:30	Take a Chance — QU	d	
12/50	10:30	Take a Chance — QU	c	
6/51	10:00	Garroway at Large — VY	c	
7/51	7:30	Aldrich Family — SC	m	To:f-9:30-9/51
7/51	8:00	American Inventory — DD	d*	
7/51	8:30	TV Recital Hall — MU	d*	
7/51	10:00	American Forum of the Air — DS	m	Fr:s-7-9/50
8/51	7:30	Young Mr. Bobbin — SC	d	
8/51	8:00	American Inventory — DD	m*	To:s-7:30-6/52
8/51	8:30	TV Recital Hall — MU	m*	To:m-9-8/54
9/51	7:00	Leave It to the Girls — DS	m	To:n-10:30
9/51	10:00	American Forum of the Air — DS	m	To:n-10:30-5/52
9/51	10:00	Red Skelton — CV	m	
10/51	7:00	Chesterfield Sound Off Time — CV	d	
10/51	9:00	Goodyear TV Playhouse(60) — DA	d	
10/51	10:30	Leave It to the Girls — DS	m	Fr:n-7
12/51	10:30	Leave It to the Girls — DS	m	To:s-7:30-10/53(a)
1/52	7:00	Chesterfield Sound Off Time — CV	c	
1/52	7:00	U.S. Royal Showcase — CV	d	
1/52	10:30	Cameo Theatre — DA	m	Fr:m-8-8/51
4/52	10:30	Cameo Theatre — DA	m	To:n-10-7/55
5/52	7:30	Meet the Press — IV	m	Fr:s-var-2/50
5/52	7:30	Young Mr. Bobbin — SC	c	
5/52	10:30	American Forum of the Air — DS	m	Fr:n-10-9/51
6/52	7:00	U.S. Royal Showcase — CV	c	
6/52	8:00	Big Payoff(60) — QU	d*	
6/52	10:00	Red Skelton — CV	m	To:n-7-9/52
7/52	7:00	Super Ghost — QU	d	
7/52	10:00	Hallmark Summer Theatre — DA	d	
8/52	10:00	The Doctor — ME	d	
8/52	10:00	Hallmark Summer Theatre — DA	c	
9/52	7:00	Red Skelton — CV	m	Fr:n-10-6/52
9/52	7:00	Super Ghost — QU	m	To:n-7:30-7/53
9/52	7:30	Meet the Press — IV	c	
9/52	8:00	Big Payoff(60) — QU	m*	To:n-8-6/53
9/52	10:30	American Forum of the Air — DS	c	
10/52	7:30	Doc Corkle — SC	d	
10/52	7:30	Doc Corkle — SC	c	
10/52	7:30	Mr. Peepers — SC	m	Fr:r-9:30
6/53	7:00	Operation Neptune — SF	d	

Date	Time	Title (min. if not 30) — Type	Action	From/To
6/53	7:00	Red Skelton—CV	m	To:t-8:30-9/53(c)
6/53	8:00	Big Payoff(60)—QU	m*	Fr:n-8-9/52
6/53	10:00	The Doctor—ME	c	
7/53	7:30	Super Ghost—QU	m*	Fr:n-7-9/52
7/53	10:00	Wonderful John Action—DR	d	
8/53	7:00	Operation Neptune—SF	c	
8/53	7:00	Paul Winchell-Jerry Mahoney Show —CV	m	Fr:m-8-6/53
8/53	10:00	Nothing but the Best—MV	m	Fr:t-9
8/53	10:00	Wonderful John Action—DR	c	
9/53	7:30	Super Ghost—QU	c*	
9/53	8:00	Big Payoff(60)—QU	c*	
9/53	10:00	Loretta Young—DA	d	
9/53	10:00	Nothing but the Best—MV	c	
10/53	10:30	Man Against Crime—CD	m	Fr:f-8:30(c)
5/54	7:00	Cheer Television Theatre—DA	d	
5/54	7:00	Paul Winchell-Jerry Mahoney Show —CV	c	
7/54	7:00	Cheer Television Show—DA	c	
7/54	7:00	Kay Kyser's Kollege of Musical Knowledge—QU	d	
7/54	10:00	Dollar a Second—QU	m*	Fr:m-8(d)
7/54	10:30	The Hunter—SD	m	Fr:w-9:30-9/52(c)
7/54	10:30	Man Against Crime—CD	m	To:n-10-7/56
8/54	10:00	Dollar a Second—QU	m*	To:f-9-10/54(a)
9/54	7:00	Kay Kyser's Kollege of Musical Knowledge—QU	c	
9/54	7:00	People Are Funny—QU	d	
12/54	10:30	The Hunter—SD	c	
1/55	10:30	Bob Cummings—SC	d	
6/55	7:30	Do It Yourself—IF	d	
6/55	7:30	Mr. Peepers—SC	c	
7/55	10:00	Cameo Theatre—DA	m*	Fr:n-10:30-4/52
8/55	10:00	Cameo Theatre—DA	c	
9/55	7:00	It's a Great Life—SC	m	Fr:t-10:30
9/55	7:00	People Are Funny—QU	m	To:s-9
9/55	7:30	Do It Yourself—IF	c	
9/55	7:30	Frontier—WA	d	
9/55	10:30	Bob Cummings—SC	m	To:r-8(c)
10/55	9:00	Alcoa Hour(60)—DA	d	
10/55	9:00	Philco TV Playhouse(60)—DA	c	
10/55	10:30	Justice—LD	m	Fr:r-8:30-6/55
12/55	8:00	Colgate Comedy Hour(60)—CV	c	
1/56	8:00	NBC Comedy Hour(60)—CV	d	
3/56	10:30	Justice—LD	c	
4/56	10:30	National Bowling Champions—SP	s	
6/56	7:00	It's a Great Life—SC	c	
6/56	7:00	Topper—SC	m	Fr:m-7:30-3/56(a)
6/56	8:00	NBC Comedy Hour(60)—CV	c	
6/56	8:00	Steve Allen(60)—CV	d	

Date	Time	Title (min. if not 30) – Type	Action	From/To
7/56	10:00	Man Against Crime – CD	m*	Fr:n-10:30-7/54
8/56	10:00	Man Against Crime – CD	c*	
9/56	7:30	Circus Boy – AD	d	
9/56	7:30	Frontier – WA	c	
10/56	7:00	Tales of the 77th Bengal Lancers – AD	d	
10/56	7:00	Topper – SC	c	
12/56	10:30	National Bowling Champions – SP	f	
6/57	7:00	Cowboy Theatre – WA	d	
6/57	7:00	Tales of the 77th Bengal Lancers – AD	c	
7/57	10:00	The Web – DA	m*	Fr:n-10-9/54(c)
9/57	7:00	Cowboy Theatre – WA	c	
9/57	7:00	Original Amateur Hour – TA	m	Fr:m-10
9/57	7:30	Circus Boy – AD	m	To:r-7:30(a)
9/57	7:30	Sally – SC	d	
9/57	9:00	Alcoa Hour(60) – DA	c	
9/57	9:00	Goodyear TV Playhouse(60) – DA	m	To:m-9:30
10/57	9:00	Dinah Shore Chevy Show(60) – MV	m	Fr:f-10-6/57
10/57	10:00	The Web – DA	c*	
12/57	7:00	Original Amateur Hour – TA	m	To:s-10-2/58
1/58	7:00	My Friend Flicka – AD	m	Fr:w-7:30-8/57(c)
3/58	7:30	Sally – SC	c	
4/58	7:30	No Warning – DA	d	
5/58	7:00	My Friend Flicka – AD	c	
6/58	7:00	Noah's Ark – MD	m	Fr:t-8:30-2/57
6/58	9:00	Chevy Show(60) – MV	d*	
7/58	8:00	Steve Lawrence-Eydie Gorme Show (60) – MV	d*	
7/58	10:00	Decision – DA	d*	
8/58	8:00	Steve Lawrence-Eydie Gorme Show (60) – MV	c*	
9/58	7:30	No Warning – DA	c	
9/58	7:30	Northwest Passage – AD	d	
9/58	9:00	Chevy Show(60) – MV	m*	To:n-9-6/59
9/58	10:00	Decision – DA	c*	
10/58	7:00	Mark Saber – CD	m	Fr:f-7:30-12/57
10/58	7:00	Noah's Ark – MD	c	
1/59	7:30	Music Shop – MV	d	
1/59	7:30	Northwest Passage – AD	m	To:f-7:30
3/59	7:30	Music Shop – MV	c	
3/59	7:30	Steve Allen(90) – CV	m	Fr:n-8
3/59	7:30	Steve Allen(90) – CV	m	To:n-7:30
3/59	8:00	Steve Allen(60) – CV	m	To:n-7:30
4/59	7:30	Steve Allen(60) – CV	m	Fr:n-7:30
4/59	8:30	Pete Kelly's Blues – DR	d	
5/59	7:00	Mark Saber – CD	c	
5/59	7:00	Midwestern Hayride – MV	m	Fr:s-10-9/58(a)
6/59	7:30	Steve Allen(60) – CV	m	To:m-10-9/59
6/59	9:00	Chevy Show(60) – MV	m*	Fr:n-9-9/58

Date	Time	Title (min. if not 30) — Type	Action	From/To
7/59	8:30	Dragnet — CD	m	Fr:t-7:30
7/59	8:30	Pete Kelly's Blues — DR	m	To:f-7:30
9/59	7:00	Midwestern Hayride — MV	c	
9/59	7:00	Riverboat(60) — AD	d	
9/59	8:00	Sunday Showcase(60) — VY	d	
9/59	8:30	Dragnet — CD	c	
9/59	9:00	Chevy Show(60) — MV	c*	
1/60	7:00	Riverboat(60) — AD	m	To:m-7:30
2/60	7:00	The Overland Trail(60) — WE	d	
5/60	8:00	Music on Ice(60) — MV	d	
5/60	8:00	Sunday Showcase(60) — VY	c	
5/60	9:00	Chevy Mystery Show(60) — MA	d*	
9/60	7:00	The Overland Trail(60) — WE	c	
9/60	7:00	Shirley Temple's Storybook(60) — KV	d	
9/60	8:00	Music on Ice(60) — MV	c	
9/60	8:00	National Velvet — AD	d	
9/60	8:30	Tab Hunter — SC	d	
9/60	9:00	Chevy Mystery Show(60) — MA	m*	To:n-9-7/61
9/60	10:30	This Is Your Life — TK	m	Fr:w-10
6/61	9:00	Dinah Shore Chevy Show(60) — MV	m	To:f-9:30-10/61
7/61	9:00	Chevy Mystery Show(60) — MA	m	Fr:n-9-9/60
9/61	7:00	Bullwinkle Show — KV	d	
9/61	7:00	Shirley Temple's Storybook(60) — KV	c	
9/61	7:30	Walt Disney(60) — KV	m	Fr:n-7(a)
9/61	8:00	National Velvet — AD	m	To:m-8
9/61	8:30	Car 54, Where Are You? — SC	d	
9/61	8:30	Tab Hunter — SC	c	
9/61	9:00	Bonanza(60) — WE	m	Fr:s-7:30
9/61	9:00	Chevy Mystery Show(60) — MA	c	
9/61	10:00	DuPont Show of the Week(60) — VS	d	
9/61	10:00	Loretta Young — DA	c	
9/61	10:30	This Is Your Life — TK	c	
6/62	8:30	Adventures of Sir Francis Drake — AD	d*	
9/62	7:00	Bullwinkle Show — KV	c	
9/62	7:00	Ensign O'Toole — SC	d	
9/62	8:30	Adventures of Sir Francis Drake — AD	c*	
12/62	10:00	Dinah Shore Chevy Show(60) — MV	m	Fr:f-9:30-6/62
5/63	10:00	Dinah Shore Chevy Show(60) — MV	c	
9/63	7:00	Bill Dana — SC	d	
9/63	7:00	Ensign O'Toole — SC	m	To:r-9-3/64(a)
9/63	8:30	Car 54, Where Are You? — SC	c	
9/63	8:30	Grindl — SC	d	
3/64	10:00	Humble Report(60) — DO	d*	
5/64	10:00	Humble Report(60) — DO	c*	
9/64	7:00	Bill Dana — SC	m	To:n-8:30
9/64	8:30	Bill Dana — SC	m	Fr:n-7
9/64	8:30	Grindl — SC	c	
9/64	10:00	DuPont Show of the Week(60) — VS	c	

Date	Time	Title (min. if not 30) — Type	Action	From/To
9/64	10:00	The Rogues(60) — CO	d	
1/65	8:30	Bill Dana — SC	c	
1/65	8:30	Branded — WE	d	
5/65	7:00	NBC Sports in Action — SH	s	
7/65	8:30	Buckskin — WE	m*	Fr:m-7:30-9/59
8/65	8:30	Buckskin — WE	c*	
9/65	7:00	Bell Telephone Hour — MU	m	Fr:t-10-5/65
9/65	7:00	NBC Sports in Action — SH	f	
9/65	10:00	The Rogues(60) — CO	c	
9/65	10:00	Wackiest Ship in the Army(06) — CO	d	
10/65	7:00	Actuality Specials — DO	m	Fr:m-10-9/62
9/66	8:30	Branded — WE	c	
9/66	8:30	Hey Landlord — SC	d	
9/66	10:00	Andy Williams(60) — MV	m	Fr:m-9-5/66
9/66	10:00	Wackiest Ship in the Army(60) — CO	c	
4/67	7:00	Bell Telephone Hour — MU	m	To:f-10-9/67
5/67	8:30	Hey Landlord — SC	c	
5/67	8:30	Let's Make a Deal — QU	d	
5/67	10:00	Andy Williams(60) — MV	m	To:s-7:30-9/69
5/67	10:00	The Saint(60) — MY	d	
6/67	7:00	Actuality Specials — DO	m	To:f-10-9/67
7/67	7:00	Animal Secrets — WL	d	
8/67	7:00	Animal Secrets — WL	c	
9/67	8:30	Let's Make a Deal — QU	m	To:f-9-2/69(a)
9/67	8:30	Mothers-in-Law — SC	d	
9/67	10:00	High Chaparral(60) — WE	d	
9/67	10:00	The Saint(60) — MY	m	To:s-7:30-2/68
1/68	7:00	Wild Kingdom — WL	d	
6/68	7:00	Flipper — AD	m	Fr:s-7:30-9/67
6/68	7:00	Wild Kingdom — WL	m	To:n-7-9/69
9/68	7:00	Flipper — AD	c	
9/68	7:00	New Adventures of Huck Finn — AD	d	
9/68	10:00	Beautiful Phyllis Diller Show(60) — CV	d	
9/68	10:00	High Chaparral(60) — WE	m	To:f-7:30
12/68	10:00	Beautiful Phyllis Diller Show(60) — CV	c	
1/69	10:00	My Friend Tony(60) — CD	d	
9/69	7:00	New Adventures of Huck Finn — AD	c	
9/69	7:00	Wild Kingdom — WL	m	Fr:n-7-6/68
9/69	8:30	Bill Cosby — SC	d	
9/69	8:30	Mothers-in-Law — SC	c	
9/69	10:00	The Lawyers(60) — LD	d	
9/69	10:00	My Friend Tony(60) — CD	c	
9/69	10:00	The New Doctors(60) — MD	d	
9/69	10:00	The Protectors(60) — CD	d	
9/70	10:00	The Protectors(60) — CD	c	
9/70	10:00	The Senator(60) — DR	d	
4/71	7:00	Wild Kingdom — WL	c	
5/71	8:30	Bill Cosby — SC	m	To:t-7:30

Date	Time	Title (min. if not 30) — Type	Action	From/To
6/71	8:30	Red Skelton — CV	m	Fr:m-7:30-3/71
8/71	8:30	Red Skelton — CV	c	
8/71	10:00	The Senator(60) — DR	c	
9/71	8:30	Jimmy Stewart — SC	d	
8/72	10:00	The Lawyers(60) — LD	c	
9/72	8:30	Columbo(90) — CD	m	Fr:w-8:30
9/72	8:30	Jimmy Stewart — SC	c	
9/72	8:30	McCloud(90) — CD	m	Fr:w-8:30
9/72	8:30	McMillan and Wife(90) — CD	m	Fr:w-8:30
9/72	9:00	Bonanza(60) — WE	m	To:t-8
9/72	10:00	The New Doctors(60) — MD	m	To:t-9
9/72	10:00	Night Gallery — SA	m	Fr:w-10
10/72	8:30	Hec Ramsey(90) — WE	d	
1/73	10:00	Night Gallery — SA	m	To:n-10-5/73
2/73	10:00	Escape — AA	d	
4/73	10:00	Escape — AA	m	To:n-10-8/73
5/73	10:00	Night Gallery — SA	m	Fr:n-10-1/73
8/73	10:00	Escape — AA	m	Fr:n-10-4/73
8/73	10:00	Night Gallery — SA	c	
9/73	8:30	Columbo(90) — CD	m	To:n-8:30
9/73	8:30	Columbo(120) — CD	m	Fr:n-8:30
9/73	8:30	McMillan and Wife(90) — CD	m	To:n-8:30
9/73	8:30	McMillan and Wife(120) — CD	m	Fr:n-8:30
9/73	8:30	McCloud(90) — CD	m	To:n-8:30
9/73	8:30	McCloud(120) — CD	m	Fr:n-8:30
9/73	8:30	Hec Ramsey(90) — WE	m	To:n-8:30
9/73	8:30	Hec Ramsey(120) — WE	m	Fr:n-8:30
9/73	10:00	Escape — AA	c	
7/74	8:30	Hec Ramsey(90) — WE	c	
12/74	8:30	Amy Prentiss(120) — CD	d	
7/75	8:30	Amy Prentiss(120) — CD	c	
7/75	8:30	McMillan and Wife(120) — CD	m	To:n-9-9/75
8/75	7:30	Walt Disney(60) — KV	m	To:n-7
8/75	8:30	Columbo(120) — CD	m	To:n-9
8/75	8:30	McCloud(120) — CD	m	To:n-9
9/75	7:00	Walt Disney(60) — KV	m	Fr:n-7:30
9/75	8:00	Family Holvak(60) — DR	d	
9/75	9:00	Columbo(120) — CD	m	Fr:n-8:30
9/75	9:00	McCloud(120) — CD	m	Fr:n-8:30
9/75	9:00	McMillan and Wife(120) — CD	m	Fr:n-8:30-7/75
10/75	8:00	Family Holvak(60) — DR	m	To:m-8
10/75	9:00	McCoy(120) — CD	d	
12/75	8:00	Family Holvak(60) — DR	m	Fr:m-8-10/75
12/75	8:00	Family Holvak(60) — DR	m	To:t-8-5/77(c)
1/76	8:00	Adventures of Ellery Queen(60) — CD	m	Fr:r-9
3/76	9:00	McCoy(120) — CD	c	
8/76	9:00	McCloud(120) — CD	m	To:n-var-10/76
8/76	9:00	McMillan and Wife(120) — CD	m	To:n-8-12/76
9/76	8:00	Adventures of Ellery Queen(60) — CD	c	

Date	Time	Title (min. if not 30) – Type	Action	From/To
9/76	9:00	Columbo(120) – CD	m	To:n-8
10/76	8:00	Columbo(90) – CD	m	Fr:n-9
10/76	9:30	Quincy, M.E.(90) – CD	d	
11/76	9:30	Big Event(90) – VS	d	
11/76	9:30	Quincy, M.E.(90) – CD	m	To:f-10-2/77
12/76	8:00	Lanigan's Rabbi(90) – CD	d	
12/76	8:00	McMillan and Wife(90) – CD	m	Fr:n-9-8/76
5/77	9:30	Film(90) – FI	s	
5/77	9:30	Big Event(90) – VS	m	To:n-8-9/77
7/77	8:00	Lanigan's Rabbi(90) – CD	c	
8/77	8:00	McMillan and Wife(90) – CD	c	
8/77	var	McCloud(90) – CD	c	
9/77	8:00	Columbo(90) – CD	c	
9/77	8:00	Big Event(180) – VS	m	Fr:n-9:30-5/77
9/77	9:30	Film(90) – FI	f	
2/78	8:00	Project UFO(60) – DR	d	
2/78	8:00	Big Event(180) – VS	m	To:n-9
2/78	9:00	Big Event(120) – VS	m	Fr:n-8
9/78	8:00	Project UFO(60) – DR	m	To:r-8
9/78	9:00	Big Event(120) – VS	m	To:n-8-3/79
10/78	8:00	Centennial(60) – DR	d	
10/78	10:00	Lifeline(60) – MO	m	Fr:r-10
11/78	10:00	Lifeline(60) – MO	m	To:n-9
12/78	9:00	Lifeline(60) – MO	m	Fr:n-10
12/78	9:00	Lifeline(60) – MO	c	
12/78	10:00	Sword of Justice(60) – AD	m	Fr:s-10-10/78
12/78	10:00	Sword of Justice(60) – AD	m	To:s-9-7/79
1/79	10:00	Weekend(60) – NM	m	Fr:s-10
2/79	8:00	Centennial(60) – DR	m	To:s-var-9/80
3/79	8:00	Big Event(120) – VS	m	Fr:n-9
4/79	10:00	Weekend(60) – NM	c	
5/79	10:00	Prime Time Sunday(60) – NM	d	
12/79	10:00	Eischied(60) – CD	m	Fr:f-10
12/79	10:00	Prime Time Sunday(60) – NM	m	To:s-10
1/80	10:00	Eischied(60) – CD	m	To:f-10-6/83
3/80	8:00	Chips(60) – CD	m	Fr:s-8
3/80	8:00	Big Event(120) – VS	m	To:n-9
3/80	9:00	Big Event(120) – VS	m	Fr:n-8
9/81	7:00	Walt Disney(60) – KV	m	To:s-8(c)
9/81	7:30	Here's Boomer – AD	m	Fr:f-8-8/80
9/81	9:00	Big Event(120) – VS	c	
10/81	9:00	Film(120) – FI	s#	
11/81	7:30	Here's Boomer – AD	m	To:s-8-7/82
3/82	7:00	Father Murphy(60) – DR	m	Fr:t-8
7/82	7:00	Father Murphy(60) – DR	m	To:t-8
8/82	7:00	Born to the Wind(60) – AD	d	
9/82	7:00	Born to the Wind(60) – AD	c	
10/82	7:00	Voyagers(60) – SF	d	
3/83	7:00	Voyagers(60) – SF	m	To:n-7-6/83
3/83	8:00	Chips(60) – CD	m	To:n-7

Date	Time	Title (min. if not 30) — Type	Action	From/To
4/83	7:00	Chips(60) — CD	m	Fr:n-8
5/83	7:00	Chips(60) — CD	m	To:n-8
5/83	8:00	Chips(60) — CD	m	Fr:n-7
6/83	7:00	Voyagers(60) — SF	m	Fr:n-7-3/83
7/83	7:00	Voyagers(60) — SF	c	
7/83	8:00	Chips(60) — CD	c	
8/83	7:00	Powers of Matthew Star(60) — SF	m	Fr:f-8
8/83	8:00	Knight Rider(60) — AD	m	Fr:f-9
9/83	7:00	Monitor(60) — NM	m	Fr:s-10
9/83	7:00	Powers of Matthew Star(60) — SF	c	
4/84	7:00	Father Murphy(60) — DR	m	Fr:t-8
4/84	7:00	Monitor(60) — NM	c	
6/84	7:00	Father Murphy(60) — DR	c	
7/84	7:00	Summer Sunday, USA(60) — NM	d	
9/84	7:00	Silver Spoons — SC	m	Fr:s-8:30
9/84	7:00	Summer Sunday, USA(60) — NM	c	
9/84	7:30	Punky Brewster — SC	d	
5/85	7:00	Silver Spoons — SC	m	To:n-7:30
5/85	7:30	Punky Brewster — SC	m	To:n-7
6/85	7:00	Punky Brewster — SC	m	Fr:n-7:30
6/85	7:30	Silver Spoons — SC	m	Fr:n-7
8/85	8:00	Knight Rider(60) — AD	m	To:f-8
8/85	8:00	Ocean Quest(60) — DO	d	
9/85	8:00	Amazing Stories — DA	d	
9/85	8:00	Ocean Quest(60) — DO	c	
9/85	8:30	Alfred Hitchcock Presents — SA	d	
3/86	7:30	Silver Spoons — SC	m	To:n-7-5/86
4/86	7:00	Punky Brewster — SC	m	To:n-7:30
4/86	7:00	Fathers and Sons — SC	d	
4/86	7:00	Fathers and Sons — SC	m	To:n-7:30
4/86	7:30	Fathers and Sons — SC	m	Fr:n-7
5/86	7:00	Silver Spoons — SC	m	Fr:n-7:30-3/86
5/86	7:30	Punky Brewster — SC	m	Fr:n-7
5/86	7:30	Fathers and Sons — SC	c	
6/86	8:00	Amazing Stories — DA	m	To:m-8:30
6/86	8:30	Alfred Hitchcock Presents — SA	c	
7/86	8:00	Daltons: Code of Vengeance(60) — CD	d	
8/86	8:00	Daltons: Code of Vengeance(60) — CD	c	
9/86	7:00	Silver Spoons — SC	c	
9/86	7:00	Our House(60) — DR	d	
9/86	7:30	Punky Brewster — SC	c	
9/86	8:00	Easy Street — SC	m	Fr:s-9:30
9/86	8:30	Valerie — SC	m	Fr:m-8
11/86	8:00	Valerie — SC	m	Fr:n-8:30
11/86	8:00	Easy Street — SC	m	To:n-8:30
11/86	8:30	Valerie — SC	m	To:n-8
11/86	8:30	Easy Street — SC	m	Fr:n-8
1/87	8:00	Valerie — SC	m	To:n-8:30

Date	Time	Title (min. if not 30) — Type	Action	From/To
1/87	8:00	Easy Street — SC	m	Fr:n-8:30
1/87	8:30	Valerie — SC	m	Fr:n-8
1/87	8:30	Easy Street — SC	m	To:n-8
3/87	8:00	Rags to Riches(60) — CO	d	
3/87	8:00	Easy Street — SC	m	To:t-9:30
3/87	8:30	Valerie — SC	m	To:m-8:30
5/87	7:00	A-Team(60) — AD	m	Fr:f-8-12/86
5/87	7:00	Our House(60) — DR	m	To:n-8
5/87	8:00	Rags to Riches(60) — CO	m	To:n-8-7/87
5/87	8:00	Our House(60) — DR	m	Fr:n-7
6/87	7:00	A-Team(60) — AD	c	
6/87	7:00	Our House(60) — DR	m	Fr:n-8
6/87	8:00	Our House(60) — DR	m	To:n-7
7/87	8:00	Rags to Riches(60) — CO	m	Fr:n-8-5/87
7/87	8:00	Rags to Riches(60) — CO	m	To:f-8
8/87	8:00	Family Ties — SC	m#	Fr:r-8:30
9/87	8:30	My Two Dads — SC	d	
2/88	8:30	My Two Dads — SC	m	To:n-8:30-6/88
3/88	8:30	Day by Day — SC	d	
5/88	8:30	Day by Day — SC	m	To:n-8:30-9/88
6/88	7:00	Our House(60) — DR	c	
6/88	8:30	My Two Dads — SC	m	Fr:n-8:30-2/88
7/88	7:00	Rags to Riches(60) — CO	m	Fr:f-8-1/88
8/88	7:00	Rags to Riches(60) — CO	c	
8/88	8:30	My Two Dads — SC	c	

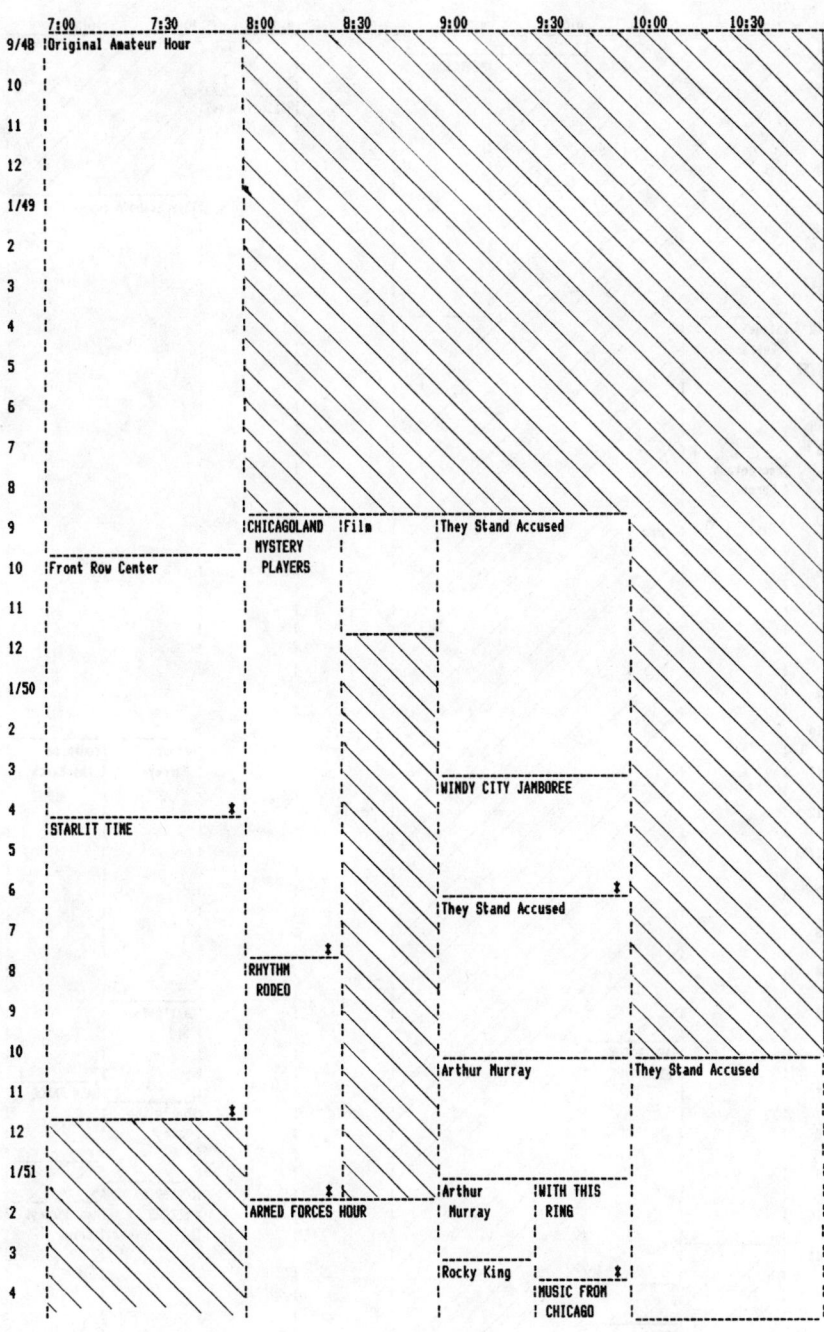

```
        7:00      7:30      8:00      8:30      9:00      9:30      10:00     10:30
9/48  :Original Amateur Hour

10    :

11    :

12    :

1/49  :

2     :

3     :

4     :

5     :

6     :

7     :

8     :

9     :              :CHICAGOLAND :Film    :They Stand Accused
                     : MYSTERY
10    :Front Row Center  : PLAYERS

11    :

12    :

1/50  :

2     :

3     :                             :WINDY CITY JAMBOREE

4     :
      :STARLIT TINE
5     :

6     :                             :They Stand Accused

7     :

8     :              :RHYTHM
                     : RODEO
9     :

10    :                             :Arthur Murray      :They Stand Accused

11    :

12    :

1/51  :

2     :              :ARMED FORCES HOUR  :Arthur   :WITH THIS
                                          : Murray  : RING
3     :                             :Rocky King
                                                   :MUSIC FROM
4     :                                            : CHICAGO
```

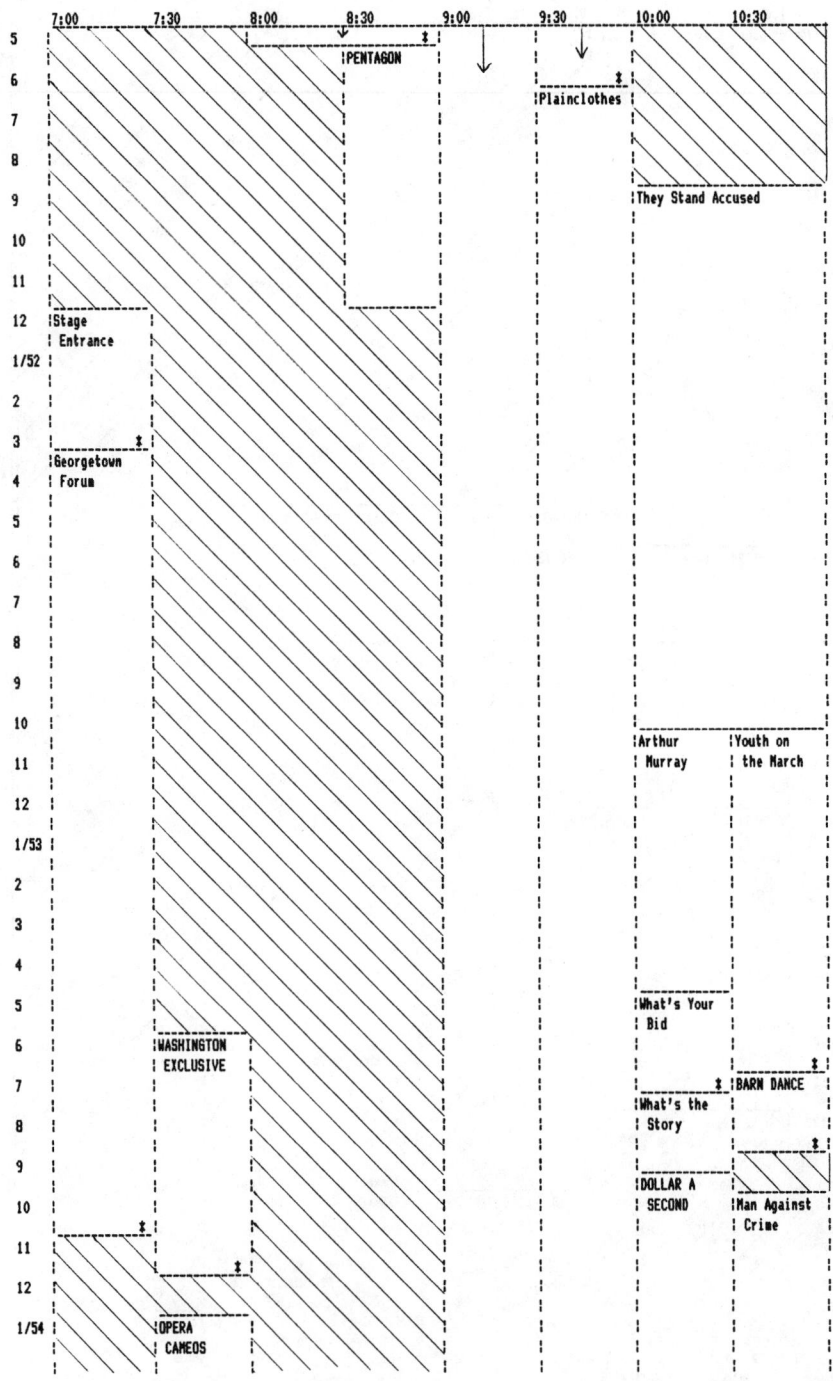

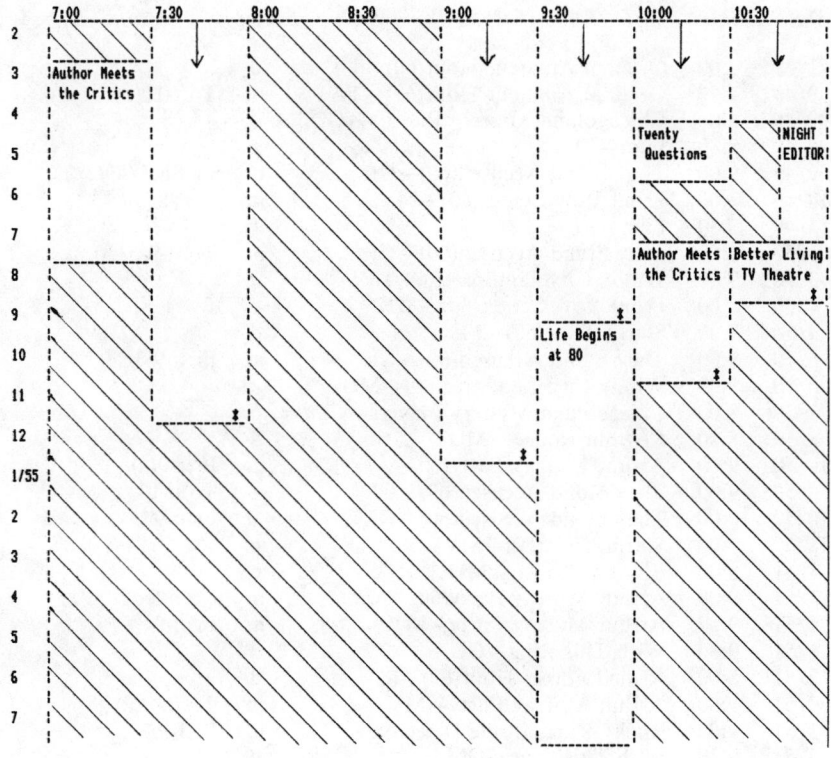

Date	Time	Title (min. if not 30) — Type	Action	From/To
1/48	7:00	Original Amateur Hour(60) — TA	d	
9/49	7:00	Original Amateur Hour(60) — TA	m	To:t-10(n)
9/49	8:00	Chicagoland Mystery Players — CD	d	
9/49	8:30	Film — FI	s	
9/49	9:00	They Stand Accused(60) — CR	m	Fr:t-8-5/49(c)
10/49	7:00	Front Row Center(60) — MV	m	Fr:f-8
11/49	8:30	Film — FI	f	
3/50	9:00	They Stand Accused(60) — CR	m	To:n-9-6/50
3/50	9:00	Windy City Jamboree(60) — MU	d	
4/50	7:00	Front Row Center(60) — MV	c	
4/50	7:00	Starlit Time(60) — MV	d	
6/50	9:00	They Stand Accused(60) — CR	m	Fr:n-9-3/50
6/50	9:00	Windy City Jamboree(60) — MU	c	
7/50	8:00	Chicagoland Mystery Players — CD	c	
8/50	8:00	Rhythm Rodeo — MU	d	
10/50	9:00	Arthur Murray Party(60) — MV	m	Fr:r-9(a)
10/50	9:00	They Stand Accused(60) — CR	m	To:n-10
10/50	10:00	They Stand Accused(60) — CR	m	Fr:n-9
11/50	7:00	Starlit Time(60) — MV	c	
1/51	8:00	Rhythm Rodeo — MU	c	
1/51	9:00	Arthur Murray Party(60) — MV	m	To:n-9
1/51	9:00	Arthur Murray Party — MV	m	Fr:n-9
1/51	9:30	With This Ring — QU	d	
2/51	8:00	Armed Forces Hour(60) — MV	d	
3/51	9:00	Arthur Murray Party — MV	m	To:m-9(a)
3/51	9:00	Rocky King, Inside Detective — CD	m	Fr:f-9:30
3/51	9:30	With This Ring — QU	c	
4/51	9:30	Music from Chicago — MU	d	
4/51	10:00	They Stand Accused(60) — CR	m	To:s-9
5/51	8:00	Armed Forces Hour(60) — MV	c	
5/51	8:30	Pentagon — IV	d	
6/51	9:30	Music from Chicago — MU	c	
6/51	9:30	The Plainclothesman — CD	m	Fr:w-9:30
9/51	10:00	They Stand Accused(60) — CR	m	Fr:t-10
11/51	8:30	Pentagon — IV	m	To:m-8
12/51	7:00	Stage Entrance — IV	m	Fr:m-8
3/52	7:00	Georgetown University Forum — DS	m	Fr:r-8-11/51
3/52	7:00	Stage Entrance — IV	c	
10/52	10:00	Arthur Murray Party — MV	m	Fr:f-8-8/52(c)
10/52	10:00	They Stand Accused(60) — CR	m	To:r-8-9/54
10/52	10:30	Youth on the March — RE	m	Fr:n-10:30-5/52(a)
4/53	10:00	Arthur Murray Party — MV	m	To:n-9:30-6/53(c)
5/53	10:00	What's Your Bid — HS	m	Fr:s-7:30(a)
6/53	7:30	Washington Exclusive — DS	d	
6/53	10:30	Youth on the March — RE	c	
7/53	10:00	What's the Story? — QU	m	Fr:w-7:30
7/53	10:00	What's Your Bid — HS	c	
7/53	10:30	Old American Barn Dance — MU	d	
8/53	10:30	Old American Barn Dance — MU	c	
9/53	10:00	Dollar a Second — QU	d	

Date	Time	Title (min. if not 30) — Type	Action	From/To
9/53	10:00	What's the Story? — QU	m	To:r-9
10/53	7:00	Georgetown University Forum — DS	c	
10/53	10:30	Man Against Crime — CD	s	
11/53	7:30	Washington Exclusive — DS	c	
1/54	7:30	Opera Cameos — MU	d	
3/54	7:00	Author Meets the Critics — DS	m	Fr:w-9:30-10/53
4/54	10:00	Dollar a Second — QU	m	To:m-8
4/54	10:00	Twenty Questions — QU	m	Fr:m-8
4/54	10:30	Man Against Crime — CD	f	
4/54	10:45	Night Editor(15) — DA	d	
5/54	10:00	Twenty Questions — QU	m	To:t-8:30-7/54(a)
7/54	7:00	Author Meets the Critics — DS	m	To:n-10
7/54	10:00	Author Meets the Critics — DS	m	Fr:n-7
7/54	10:30	Better Living TV Theatre — DO	m	Fr:w-10:30
7/54	10:45	Night Editor(15) — DA	m	To:w-10:30
8/54	10:30	Better Living TV Theatre — DO	c	
9/54	9:30	Life Begins at Eighty — DS	m	Fr:f-9-6/54
9/54	9:30	The Plainclothesman — CD	c	
10/54	10:00	Author Meets the Critics — DS	c	
11/54	7:30	Opera Cameos — MU	c	
12/54	9:00	Rocky King, Inside Detective — CD	c	
7/55	9:30	Life Begins at Eighty — DS	m	To:n-9:30(a)

```
      7:00       7:30    8:00      8:30      9:00      9:30      10:00     10:30
4/87 :21 JUMP STREET     :MARRIED  :TRACEY   :MR.      :DUET     :
   :                     : WITH    : ULLMAN  : PRESIDENT:         :
 5 :                     : CHILDREN :                              :
   :                     :         :Duet     :         :Tracey    :
 6 :                     :         :         :         : Ullman   :
 7 :                     :         :         :         :          :
 8 :                     :         :         :         :          :
 9 :                     :         :         :         :          :
10 :                     :         :         :         :          :
   :                     :Werewolf :Married  :Tracey   :Duet      :
11 :                     :         : With    : Ullman  :          :
   :                     :         : Children:         :          :
12 :                     :         :         :         :          :
1/88:                    :         :         :         :          :
 2 :                     :         :         :         :          :
 3 :                     :         :         :         :          :
   :                     :         :         :GARRY    :Tracey    :
 4 :                     :MOST WANTED:        : SHANDLING:Ullman    :
 5 :                     :         :         :         :          :
 6 :                     :         :         :         :          :
 7 :                     :         :         :         :          :
   :                     :         :         :         :Tracey    :Duet
 8 :                     :         :         :         : Ullman   :
```

Date	Time	Title (min. if not 30) – Type	Action	From/To
4/87	7:00	21 Jump Street(60) – CD	d#	
4/87	8:00	Married with Children – SC	d	
4/87	8:30	Tracey Ullman – CY	d	
4/87	9:00	Mr. President – SC	d	
4/87	9:30	Duet – SC	d	
5/87	8:30	Tracey Ullman – CY	m	To:n-9:30
5/87	8:30	Duet – SC	m	Fr:n-9:30
5/87	9:30	Tracey Ullman – CY	m	Fr:n-8:30
5/87	9:30	Duet – SC	m	To:n-8:30
9/87	8:30	Duet – SC	m	To:s-9:30
10/87	8:00	Married with Children – SC	m	To:n-8:30
10/87	8:00	Werewolf – AD	m	Fr:s-8
10/87	8:30	Married with Children – SC	m#	Fr:n-8
10/87	9:00	Tracey Ullman – CY	m	Fr:n-9:30
10/87	9:00	Mr. President – SC	m	To:s-8
10/87	9:30	Tracey Ullman – CY	m	To:n-9
10/87	9:30	Duet – SC	m	Fr:s-9:30
3/88	8:00	Werewolf – AD	m	To:s-9
3/88	9:00	Tracey Ullman – CY	m	To:n-10
3/88	9:00	Garry Shandling – SC	d#	
3/88	10:00	Tracey Ullman – CY	m	Fr:n-9
4/88	8:00	Most Wanted – DD	d#	
7/88	9:30	Tracey Ullman – CY	m#	Fr:n-10
7/88	9:30	Duet – SC	m	To:n-10
7/88	10:00	Tracey Ullman – CY	m	To:n-9:30
7/88	10:00	Duet – SC	m#	Fr:n-9:30

Sunday Programming Moves Summary

1948-49

ABC. *Series Premieres:* Actor's Studio; Action Autographs; Music in Velvet; Rehearsal Call; Sing-Co-Pation; Southernaire Quartet; Stained Glass Windows; Television Players; Treasure Quest.

CBS. *Series Premieres:* America Speaks; Fred Waring; Mr. Imagination; Riddle Me This; Studio One; UN Casebook; Wesley. *Key Programming Moves:* ED SULLIVAN SHOW (TOAST OF THE TOWN) is moved into the 8-9 slot, which it occupied until 6/71; STUDIO ONE debuts; it is eventually moved to Monday where it stayed until 9/58; FRED WARING SHOW debuts; it stays on the air until 5/54.

NBC. *Series Premieres:* Hartmans; Lambs Gambol; Meredith Wilson; Philco TV Playhouse; Sunday Date; Welcome Aboard. *Key Programming Moves:* PHILCO TV PLAYHOUSE debuts; it stays on the air until 10/55.

DuMont. *Key Programming Moves:* ORIGINAL AMATEUR HOUR transfers to NBC, as was the case with most programs on DuMont that were competitive; eventually ran on all four networks; was on the air until 9/60.

1949-50

ABC. *Series Premieres:* Carolyn Gilbert; Diane Doxee; Hollywood House; In the Morgan Manner; Let There Be Stars; Mama Rosa; Mysteries of Chinatown; Oboler Theatre; Paul Whiteman; Sit or Miss; Soap Box Theatre; Stage Two Revue; Youth on the March.

CBS. *Series Premieres:* Gene Autry; The Girls; Starlight Theatre. *Key Programming Moves:* GENE AUTRY SHOW debuts; it stays on the air until 8/56.

NBC. *Series Premieres:* Aldrich Family; Answer Yes or No; Battle Report; Sammy Kaye; Spotlight on Sports. *Key Programming Moves:* ALDRICH FAMILY debuts; it is adapted from the successful radio series of the same name.

DuMont. *Series Premieres:* Chicagoland Mystery Players; Rhythm Rodeo; Starlit Time; Windy City Jamboree. *Key Programming Moves:* Expands programming from one to three hours.

1950–51

ABC. *Series Premieres:* Hollywood Theatre Time; Showtime, USA.

CBS. *Series Premieres:* Jack Benny. *Key Programming Moves:* JACK BENNY debuts; the successful radio series moves to television; stayed in 7:30–8 slot until 6/59; stayed on air until 9/65; WHAT'S MY LINE is moved into 10:30–11 slot where it stayed until 9/67.

NBC. *Series Premieres:* Colgate Comedy Hour; Take a Chance; Young Mr. Bobbin. *Key Programming Moves:* COLGATE COMEDY HOUR debuts; it stays in 8–9 slot to compete with ED SULLIVAN SHOW until its cancellation in 12/55.

DuMont. *Series Premieres:* Armed Forces Hour; Music from Chicago; Pentagon; With This Ring.

1951–52

ABC. *Series Premieres:* Byline; Four Square Court; Horizons; Hour of Decision; Production for Freedom. *Key Programming Moves:* YOU ASKED FOR IT moved from Monday to Sunday 7–7:30, where it stayed until 9/59.

CBS. *Key Programming Moves:* FRED WARING SHOW is cut back to 30 minutes; BREAK THE BANK is moved into 9:30–10 slot, establishing a 90 minute block of quiz shows.

NBC. *Series Premieres:* Chesterfield Sound-Off; Goodyear TV Playhouse; Hallmark Summer Theatre; Red Skelton; Super Ghost; US Royal Showcase. *Key Programming Moves:* GOODYEAR TV PLAYHOUSE debuts, alternating with PHILCO TV PLAYHOUSE; it stays in time slot until 9/57; RED SKELTON SHOW debuts; series switched to CBS in 9/53, where it stayed until 6/70; it then returned to NBC for one final year.

1952–53

ABC. *Series Premieres:* Anywhere, USA; At Issue; Both Sides; Enterprise; Orchid Award; Plymouth Playhouse. *Key Programming Moves:* ABC tried 60-minute newscast in prime time (8–9); it was not successful and was discontinued after one year.

CBS. *Series Premieres:* General Electric Threatre; Private Secretary. *Key Programming Moves:* PRIVATE SECRETARY debuts, alternating with JACK BENNY SHOW until 3/57; GENERAL ELECTRIC THEATRE debuts, alternating with FRED WARING SHOW until 5/54; continues in 9–9:30 slot until 9/62.

NBC. *Series Premieres:* Doc Corkle; The Doctor; John Action; Operation Neptune. *Key Programming Moves:* RED SKELTON SHOW moved into 7–7:30 slot; MR. PEEPERS moved into 7:30–8 slot.

DuMont. *Series Premieres:* Barn Dance; Washington Exclusive.

1953–54

ABC. *Series Premieres:* Jane Pickens; Martha Wright; Mask; Now; Paul Whiteman; Peter Potter; Walter Winchell. *Key Programming Moves:* BREAK THE BANK picked up after NBC dropped it.

CBS. *Series Premieres:* Earn Your Vacation; Life with Father; Man Behind the Badge. *Key Programming Moves:* EARN YOUR VACATION, a summer replacement series, debuts with a young Johnny Carson as emcee; the series didn't catch on but the host did.

NBC. *Series Premieres:* Cheer Theatre; Kay Kyser; Loretta Young. *Key Programming Moves:* LORETTA YOUNG SHOW debuts; stays on air until 9/61.

DuMont. *Series Premieres:* Dollar a Second; Night Editor; Opera Cameos. *Key Programming Moves:* DOLLAR A SECOND debuts; it is picked up by NBC at the end of the season, where it stays on the air until 9/57.

1954–55

ABC. *Series Premieres:* Hollywood Backstage; Key to the Ages; News Conference; What's Going On.

CBS. *Series Premieres:* Appointment with Adventure; Father Knows Best; Honestly Celeste; Lassie; Stage 7. *Key Programming Moves:* LASSIE debuts; it stays on the air until 9/71; FATHER KNOWS BEST debuts; has runs on CBS, NBC and ABC; it lasts until 4/63; Ronald Reagan takes over as host of GENERAL ELECTRIC THEATRE; he stays with the series until the end in 1962.

NBC. *Series Premieres:* Bob Cummings; Do It Yourself; People Are Funny. *Key Programming Moves:* PEOPLE ARE FUNNY debuts, it stays on the air until 4/61; PHILCO TV PLAYHOUSE is cancelled.

DuMont. *Key Programming Moves:* Stops programming on Sunday evenings permanently.

1955-56

CBS. *Series Premieres:* Alfred Hitchcock Presents; $64,000 Challenge. *Key Programming Moves:* ALFRED HITCHCOCK PRESENTS debuts; it stays in 9:30-10 slot until 9/60, after which it alternated between CBS and NBC until 9/65; $64,000 CHALLENGE debuts; spin-off from top-rated $64,000 QUESTION.

NBC. *Series Premieres:* Alcoa Hour; Frontier; NBC Comedy Hour; Steve Allen. *Key Programming Moves:* STEVE ALLEN SHOW debuts; it is placed opposite CBS' ED SULLIVAN SHOW, where it stayed until 3/59.

1956-57

ABC. *Series Premieres:* Mike Wallace; Omnibus. *Key Programming Moves:* OMNIBUS debuts in prime time; hailed as one of the greatest series ever in the history of television, this afternoon series was given a shot at prime time; it lasted only six months in prime time.

CBS. *Series Premieres:* Marge & Gower Champion.

NBC. *Series Premieres:* Circus Boy; Cowboy Theatre; 77th Bengal Lancers.

1957-58

ABC. *Series Premieres:* Anybody Can Play; Baseball Corner; Maverick; Scotland Yard; Sid Caesar. *Key Programming Moves:* MAVERICK debuts; it becomes one of the few hit series on ABC; stays on Sunday until 7/62.

CBS. *Series Premieres:* Bachelor Father. *Key Programming Moves:* BACHELOR FATHER debuts; eventually has runs on NBC and ABC; lasts until 9/62; $64,000 CHALLENGE is cancelled.

NBC. *Series Premieres:* No Warning; Sally. *Key Programming Moves:* DINAH SHORE SHOW is moved into the 9-10 slot where it stays until 6/61.

1958-59

ABC. *Series Premieres:* Encounter; Lawman. *Key Programming Moves:* LAWMAN debuts; stays on the air until 10/62; YOU ASKED FOR IT is cancelled.

CBS. *Key Programming Moves:* $64,000 QUESTION is moved into 10-10:30 slot (replacing $64,000 CHALLENGE); series is cancelled two months later.

NBC. *Series Premieres:* Music Shop; Northwest Passage; Pete Kelly's Blues. *Key Programming Moves:* DRAGNET is cancelled.

1959–60

ABC. *Series Premieres:* Alaskans; Dick Clark; The Rebel.

CBS. *Series Premieres:* Dennis the Menace; Lucy in Connecticut. *Key Programming Moves:* DENNIS THE MENACE debuts; it runs until 9/63; LUCY IN CONNECTICUT debuts; this summer replacement series consisted of reruns of episodes from I LOVE LUCY.

NBC. *Series Premieres:* Music on Ice; Overland Trail; Riverboat; Sunday Showcase.

1960–61

ABC. *Series Premieres:* Asphalt Jungle; Editor's Choice; Islanders; Winston Churchill.

CBS. *Key Programming Moves:* CANDID CAMERA is moved into 10–10:30 slot, where it stayed until 9/67.

NBC. *Series Premieres:* National Velvet; Shirley Temple; Tab Hunter. *Key Programming Moves:* THIS IS YOUR LIFE is moved into 10:30–11 slot; series is cancelled at the end of the season.

1961–62

ABC. *Series Premieres:* Bus Stop; Follow the Sun. *Key Programming Moves:* MAVERICK is cancelled; LAWMAN is cancelled.

CBS. *Series Premieres:* Who in the World. *Key Programming Moves:* GENERAL ELECTRIC THEATRE is cancelled.

NBC. *Series Premieres:* Bullwinkle; Car 54, Where Are You?; DuPont Show. *Key Programming Moves:* WALT DISNEY is picked up from ABC; series stayed on NBC Sunday night until 9/81; BONANZA is moved into 9–10 slot; series became the highest rated series on television between 1964–1966; it stayed in this time slot until 9/72.

1962–63

ABC. *Series Premieres:* ABC Reports; Jetsons. *Key Programming Moves:* VOICE OF FIRESTONE is cancelled.

CBS. *Series Premieres:* GE True. *Key Programming Moves:* THE REAL McCOYS is moved into 9–9:30 slot; series is cancelled at the end of the season.

NBC. *Series Premieres:* Ensign O'Toole. *Key Programming Moves:* DINAH SHORE SHOW is cancelled.

1963–64

ABC. *Series Premieres:* Adventures of Jamie McPheeters; Arrest & Trial; Laughs for Sale; 100 Grand. *Key Programming Moves:* In January, ABC cut back to 2½ hours of programming (7:30–10) for the rest of the season.

CBS. *Series Premieres:* Celebrity Game; Judy Garland; Made in America. *Key Programming Moves:* DENNIS THE MENACE is cancelled.

NBC. *Series Premieres:* Bill Dana; Grindl.

1964–65

ABC. *Series Premieres:* Broadside. *Key Programming Moves:* WAGON TRAIN is moved into 7:30–8:30 slot after seven years on the air; it is cancelled at the end of the season; ABC started airing theatrical films on Sunday on a regular basis, a practice that has continued to 1988 and is still going.

CBS. *Series Premieres:* For the People; My Favorite Martian; My Living Doll. *Key Programming Moves:* TWILIGHT ZONE is moved to Sunday and is cancelled at the end of the season.

NBC. *Series Premieres:* Branded; The Rogues.

1965–66

ABC. *Series Premieres:* The FBI. *Key Programming Moves:* THE FBI debuts; it stays on Sundays until 9/74; VOYAGE TO THE BOTTOM OF THE SEA is moved to Sundays at 7–8.

CBS. *Key Programming Moves:* PERRY MASON is moved to Sunday after eight years on the air; it is cancelled at the end of the season.

NBC. *Series Premieres:* Wackiest Ship in the Army.

1966–67

CBS. *Series Premieres:* Garry Moore; It's About Time; Smothers Brothers Comedy Hour. *Key Programming Moves:* GARRY MOORE SHOW debuts; CBS attempts to repeat the success of his previous series of the same name; this one lasts only four months; SMOTHERS BROTHERS COMEDY HOUR debuts replacing GARRY MOORE SHOW; the series becomes a hit, though it also becomes highly controversial because of its anti-war sentiments; the controversy eventually brings about the series' demise; CANDID CAMERA and WHAT'S MY LINE ae cancelled after seven years together in the 10–11 slot.

NBC. *Series Premieres:* Animal Secrets; Hey Landlord; Let's Make a Deal; The Saint. *Key Programming Moves:* THE ANDY WILLIAMS SHOW is moved to Sunday where it stays for only eight months.

1967–68

ABC. *Key Programming Moves:* VOYAGE TO THE BOTTOM OF THE SEA is cancelled.

CBS. *Series Premieres:* Gentle Ben. *Key Programming Moves:* MISSION IMPOSSIBLE is moved into 10–11 slot where it stayed for three years.

NBC. *Series Premieres:* High Chaparral; Mothers-in-Law; Wild Kingdom. *Key Programming Moves:* FLIPPER is cancelled.

1968–69

ABC. *Series Premieres:* Land of the Giants.

CBS. *Series Premieres:* Hee Haw. *Key Programming Moves:* HEE HAW debuts in 6/69 as the replacement for SMOTHERS BROTHERS COMEDY HOUR; it stays on CBS for two years and then went into syndication where it has been ever since.

NBC. *Series Premieres:* Huck Finn; My Friend Tony; Phyllis Diller.

1969–70

CBS. *Series Premieres:* Leslie Uggams; To Rome with Love. *Key Programming Moves:* GLEN CAMPBELL SHOW is moved into 9–10 slot where it succeeds for almost two seasons; MISSION IMPOSSIBLE is moved to Saturday at the end of the season.

NBC. *Series Premieres:* Bill Cosby; The Lawyers; The New Doctors; The Protectors. *Key Programming Moves:* THE LAWYERS, THE NEW DOCTORS and THE PROTECTORS all debut as rotating series under the title "THE BOLD ONES."

1970–71

ABC. *Series Premieres:* Young Rebels.

CBS. *Series Premieres:* Comedy Playhouse; Honeymooners; Ice Palace; Six Wives of Henry VIII; Sonny & Cher; Tim Conway. *Key Programming Moves:* SONNY & CHER SHOW debuts as a summer replacement series; it appears on the CBS schedule off and on over the next seven years; A revival of THE HONEYMOONERS debuts; it does not catch on and is cancelled in five months; THE ED SULLIVAN SHOW is cancelled after 23 years; HOGAN'S HEROES is moved to Sunday; it is cancelled at the end of the season.

NBC. *Series Premieres:* The Senator. *Key Programming Moves:* THE SENATOR debuts as one of the rotating series under THE BOLD ONES' umbrella; it is cancelled at the end of the season despite much critical acclaim.

1971–72

CBS. *Series Premieres:* Cade's County; Leonardo da Vinci. *Key Programming Moves:* CBS schedules theatrical films from 7:30–9:30; it abandons the practice at the end of the season.

NBC. *Series Premieres:* Jimmy Stewart. *Key Programming Moves:* After 11 seasons on Sunday, BONANZA is moved to Tuesdays at the end of the season.

1972–73

CBS. *Series Premieres:* Anna & the King; Barnaby Jones; M*A*S*H; Sandy Duncan. *Key Programming Moves:* M*A*S*H debuts, beginning an 11 year run on CBS; BARNABY JONES debuts; it is later moved to Saturdays; MANNIX is moved to Sunday night.

NBC. *Series Premieres:* Escape; Hec Ramsey. *Key Programming Moves:* NBC MYSTERY MOVIE is moved to Sunday, it is the umbrella title for rotating series: COLUMBO, McMILLAN & WIFE, McCLOUD and HEC RAMSEY.

1973-74

ABC. *Key Programming Moves:* THE FBI and SUNDAY NIGHT MOVIE are moved up 30 minutes to 7:30 and 8:30, respectively.

CBS. *Series Premieres:* Apple's Way; New Perry Mason. *Key Programming Moves:* In an attempt to revive the success of the earlier version, THE NEW PERRY MASON debuts; it is cancelled four months later.

NBC. *Key Programming Moves:* NBC MYSTERY MOVIE expands from 90 minutes to two hours.

1974-75

ABC. *Series Premieres:* Sonny Comedy Revue. *Key Programming Moves:* In January, $6 MILLION MAN is moved to Sunday.

CBS. *Series Premieres:* Cher; Joey & Dad; Manhatten Transfer. *Key Programming Moves:* KOJAK is moved to Sunday; MANNIX is moved to Wednesday in July, just prior to its cancellation in August.

NBC. *Series Premieres:* Amy Prentiss.

1975-76

ABC. *Series Premieres:* Jacques Cousteau; Swiss Family Robinson.

CBS. *Series Premieres:* Bronk; Three for the Road. *Key Programming Moves:* 60 MINUTES is moved into 7-8 slot where it becomes an enormous ratings success; it continues in this slot to the present time; CANNON is moved into the 10-11 slot in the summer and is then cancelled.

NBC. *Series Premieres:* Family Holvak; McCoy.

1976-77

ABC. *Series Premieres:* Brady Bunch Hour; Cos; Hardy Boys; Nancy Drew.

CBS. *Series Premieres:* Delvecchio; Starland Vocal Band. *Key Programming Moves:* RHODA and PHYLLIS are moved to Sunday.

NBC. *Series Premieres:* Big Event; Lannigan's Rabbi; Quincy. *Key Programming Moves:* QUINCY debuts; after a two month stint it moves to Friday and continues on different nights for the next seven years; THE BIG EVENT debuts; NBC tried to schedule block-buster events, specials and films under this title; the concept was continued at various times for five years; COLUMBO is cancelled; McMILLAN & WIFE is cancelled.

1977-78

ABC. *Series Premieres:* How the West Was Won.

CBS. *Series Premieres:* Dallas; On Our Own. *Key Programming Moves:* ALL IN THE FAMILY is moved to Sunday, 9-9:30 and ALICE is moved to the 9:30-10 slot, setting up a two hour block of situation comedies which will last for six years; DALLAS debuts as a limited series; combining serialized and episodic forms, it begins the era of "prime time soap operas"; DALLAS was extremely successful and has continued on CBS for the next 11 years, with no end in sight.

NBC. *Series Premieres:* Project UFO. *Key Programming Moves:* THE BIG EVENT expands from 90 minutes to three hours; it is cut back to two hours in 2/78.

1978-79

ABC. *Series Premieres:* Battlestar Galactica. *Key Programming Moves:* DONNY & MARIE is moved to Sunday, 7-8 in January; it is cancelled five months later; THE HARDY BOYS is cancelled.

CBS. *Series Premieres:* Just Friends; Kaz; Mary; Mary Tyler Moore. *Key Programming Moves:* MARY debuts; CBS attempts a variety series with Mary Tyler Moore; it fails and is cancelled after one month; CBS tries the variety form again, later in the season with THE MARY TYLER MOORE SHOW; it fares slightly better this time, lasting three months before cancellation; ALL IN THE FAMILY is cancelled at the end of the season; the series is resurrected as ARCHIE BUNKER'S PLACE the following year; ONE DAY AT A TIME is moved to Sunday, 8:30-9; THE JEFFERSONS is moved to Sunday, 9:30-10.

NBC. *Series Premieres:* Centennial; Prime Time Sunday. *Key Programming Moves:* NBC tries its hand at newsmagazines, first with WEEKEND, then with PRIME TIME SUNDAY; neither really catch on with the audience.

1979-80

ABC. *Series Premieres:* The Associates; A New Kind of Family; Out of the Blue; Ten Speed & Brown Shoe; Those Amazing Animals. *Key Programming Moves:* MORK & MINDY is moved from its successful Thursday night slot to anchor ABC's Sunday night schedule; the experiment fails and MORK & MINDY is returned to its original time slot but never regains the ratings success it had before the move.

CBS. *Series Premieres:* Archie Bunker's Place; Trapper John, MD. *Key Programming Moves:* TRAPPER JOHN, MD debuts; a spin-off from M*A*S*H, it begins a successful eight year run.

NBC. *Key Programming Moves:* CHIPS moved into 8–9 slot in 3/80.

1980–81

ABC. *Series Premieres:* Roots: The Next Generation. *Key Programming Moves:* ROOTS: THE NEXT GENERATION, a sequel to the block-buster mini-series ROOTS, airs from May to July.

1981–82

ABC. *Series Premieres:* Code Red; Today's FBI. *Key Programming Moves:* TODAY'S FBI debuts; an attempt to duplicate the success of the original, THE FBI, the series lasts only one season.

NBC. *Series Premieres:* Born to the Wind. *Key Programming Moves:* NBC schedules movies in the 9–11 slot.

1982–83

ABC. *Series Premieres:* Matt Houston; Ripley's Believe It or Not. *Key Programming Moves:* RIPLEY'S BELIEVE IT OR NOT debuts; it occupies the 7–8 slot for the next three years.

CBS. *Series Premieres:* Gloria; Goodnight, Beantown. *Key Programming Moves:* GLORIA debuts; the fifth spin-off series from ALL IN THE FAMILY; scheduled after ARCHIE BUNKER'S PLACE, it lasts only one season.

NBC. *Series Premieres:* Voyagers. *Key Programming Moves:* CHIPS is cancelled after a six year run.

1983–84

ABC. *Series Premieres:* Hardcastle & McCormick.

CBS. *Series Premieres:* Four Seasons; Maggie Briggs. *Key Programming Moves:* ONE DAY AT A TIME is cancelled after ten years on CBS.

NBC. *Series Premieres:* Summer Sunday. *Key Programming Moves:* NBC goes head-to-head with CBS' 60 MINUTES by scheduling MONITOR in the 7–8 slot; it doesn't succeed and is cancelled in 4/84; NBC tries to tackle

60 MINUTES again, this time with SUMMER SUNDAY; it also fails to make a dent in CBS' ratings.

1984-85

CBS. *Series Premieres:* Crazy Like a Fox; Murder, She Wrote. *Key Programming Moves:* MURDER, SHE WROTE debuts in the 8-9 slot; CBS breaks up its two-hour block of situation comedies for the first time in seven years.

NBC. *Series Premieres:* Ocean Quest; Punky Brewster. *Key Programming Moves:* After having failed to compete with CBS in the 7-8 slot with a newsmagazine, NBC counterprograms with SILVER SPOONS and PUNKY BREWSTER, situation comedies geared toward children.

1985-86

ABC. *Series Premieres:* MacGyver.

CBS. *Key Programming Moves:* In January, CBS began airing made-for-tv films on a regular weekly basis in the 9-11 slot; all three networks now have films in this time slot.

NBC. *Series Premieres:* Alfred Hitchcock Presents; Amazing Stories; Daltons: Code of Vengeance; Fathers and Sons. *Key Programming Moves:* NBC tried to resurrect the anthology form with AMAZING STORIES and ALFRED HITCHCOCK PRESENTS; both series were gone by the season's end.

1986-87

NBC. *Series Premieres:* Our House; Rags to Riches. *Key Programming Moves:* Now that CBS has abandoned them, NBC starts to schedule situation comedies in the 8-9 slot; they worked fairly well.

Fox. *Series Premieres:* Duet; Married with Children; Mr. President; Tracey Ullman Show; 21 Jump Street. *Key Programming Moves:* The Fox Broadcasting Company begins operation as the "fourth network"; starting modestly by first offering programs on Sunday nights, Fox does get off the ground; 21 JUMP STREET debuts; the series airs in the 7-8 slot and attracts a fairly respectable audience, consisting mainly of kids and teenagers; THE TRACEY ULLMAN SHOW debuts; while it is hailed by critics as "innovative" it performs modestly for its stations.

1987–88

ABC. *Series Premieres:* Buck James; Dolly; Supercarrier. *Key Programming Moves:* ABC schedules weekly series (DOLLY and BUCK JAMES) in the 9–11 slot for the first time since 1964; by January they were back to scheduling films in this slot; In an attempt to revive the variety form, which was once so successful, DOLLY debuts; it does not catch on with the audience.

NBC. *Series Premieres:* Day by Day; My Two Dads.

Fox. *Series Premieres:* Garry Shandling; Most Wanted. *Key Programming Moves:* MOST WANTED debuts; focusing on unsolved crimes, this series becomes the most successful program on the Fox network; NBC imitates the form with UNSOLVED MYSTERIES; THE GARRY SHANDLING SHOW debuts after two successful seasons on cable television's Showtime network; critics praise the show as "new and refreshing."

Monday Night
September 1948 – August 1988

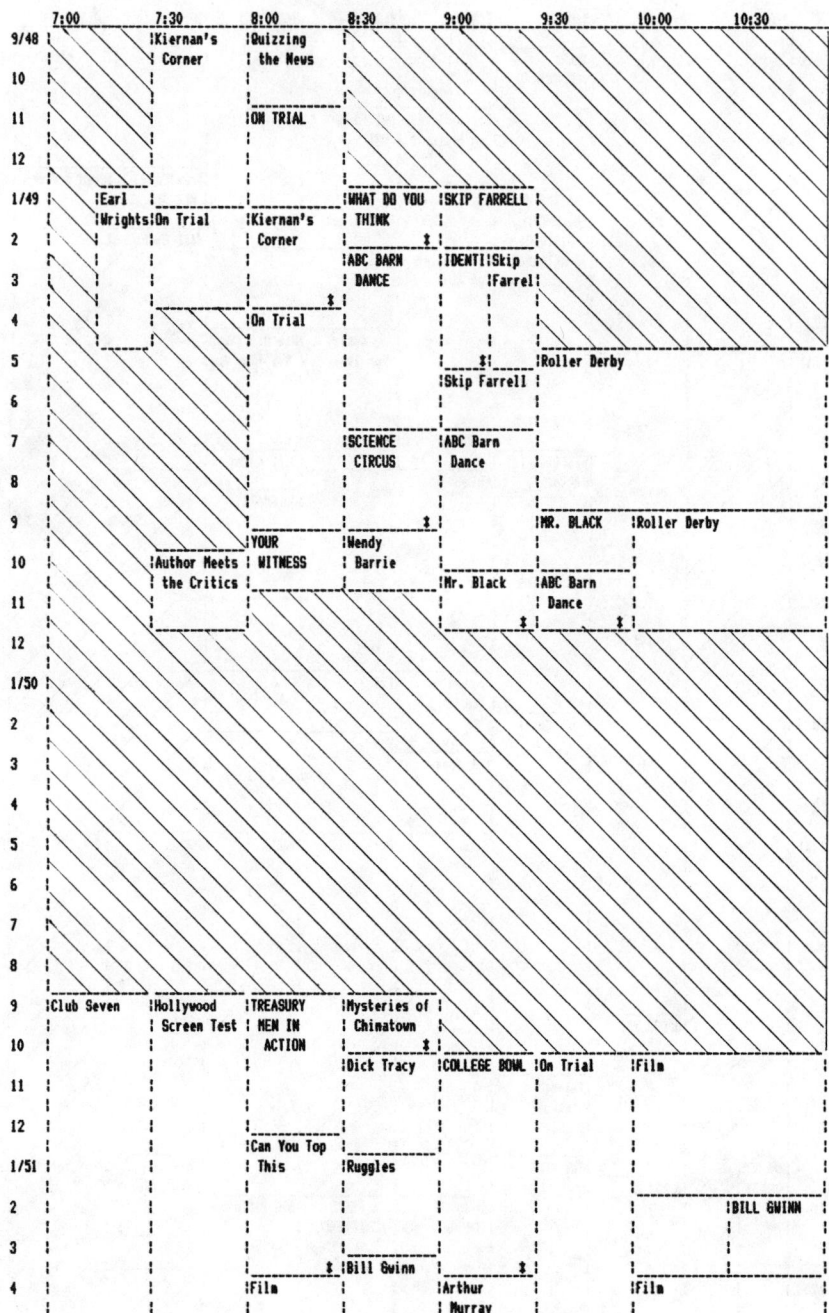

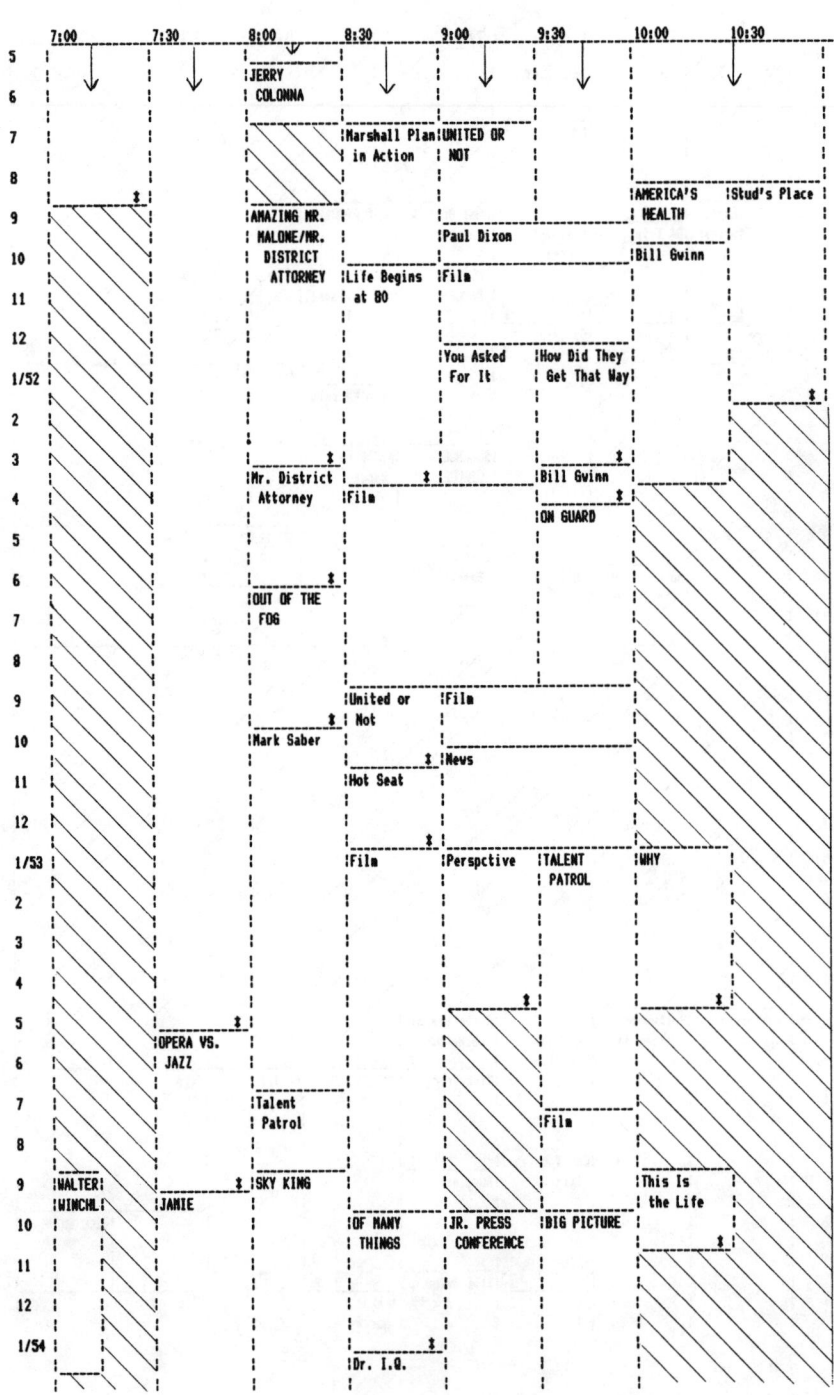

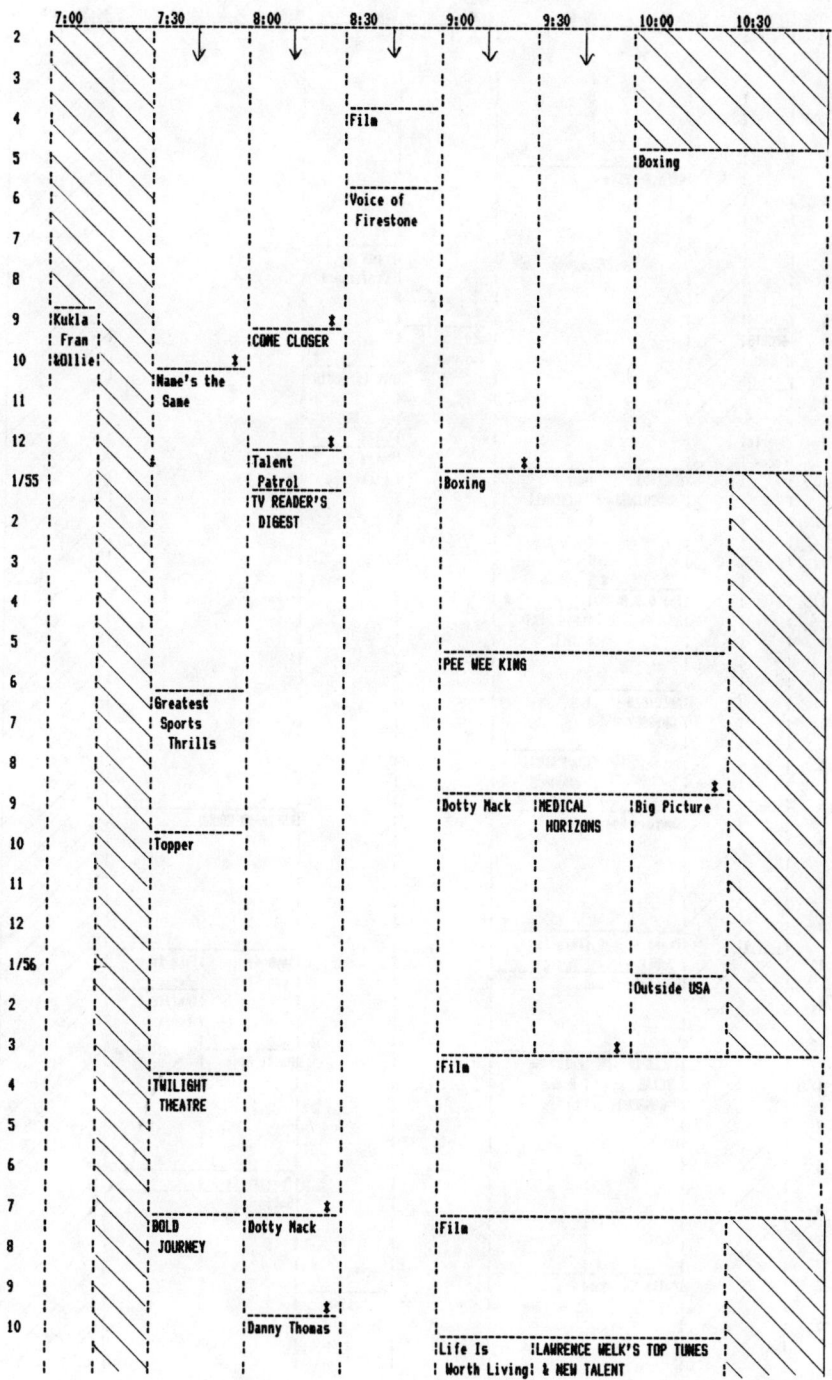

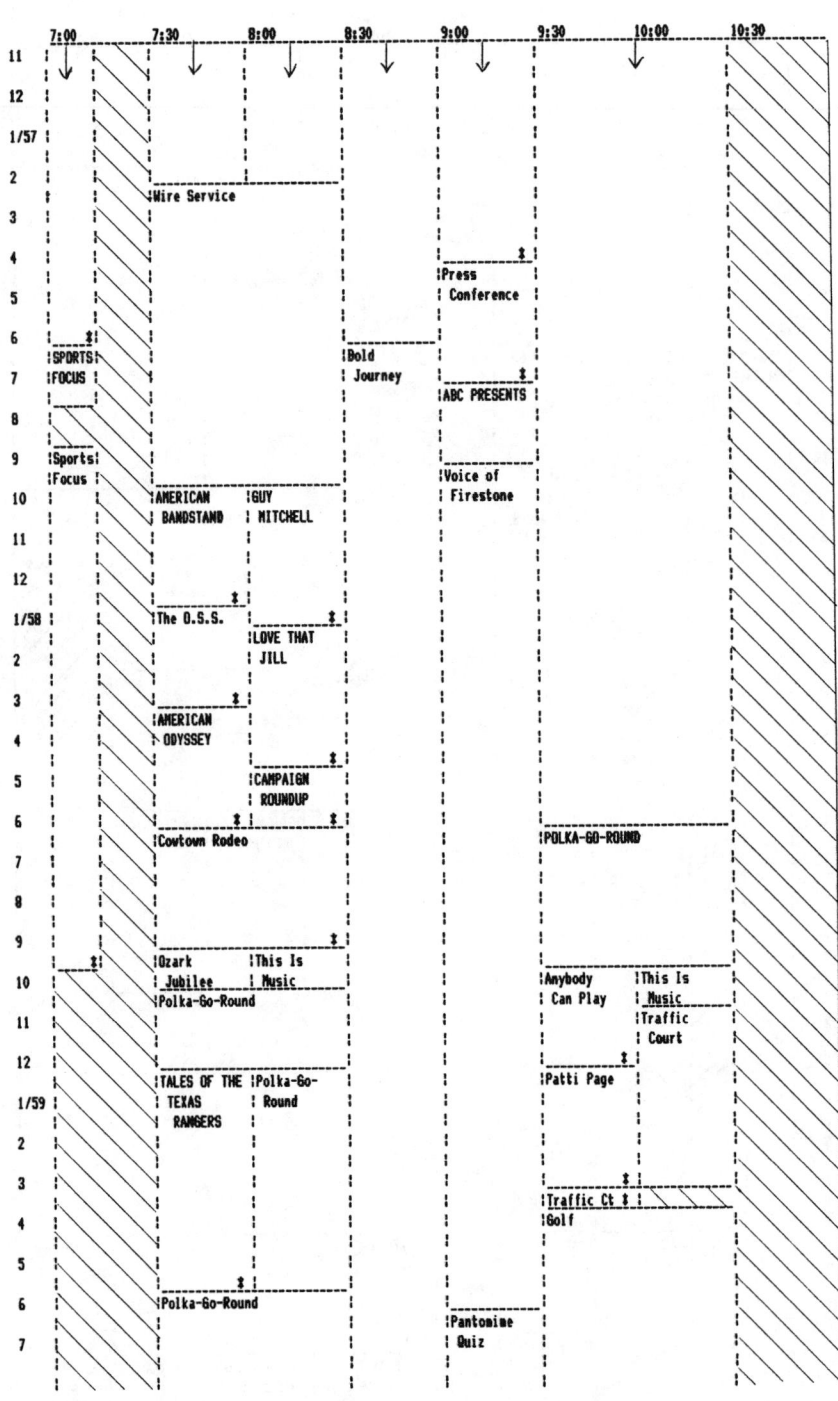

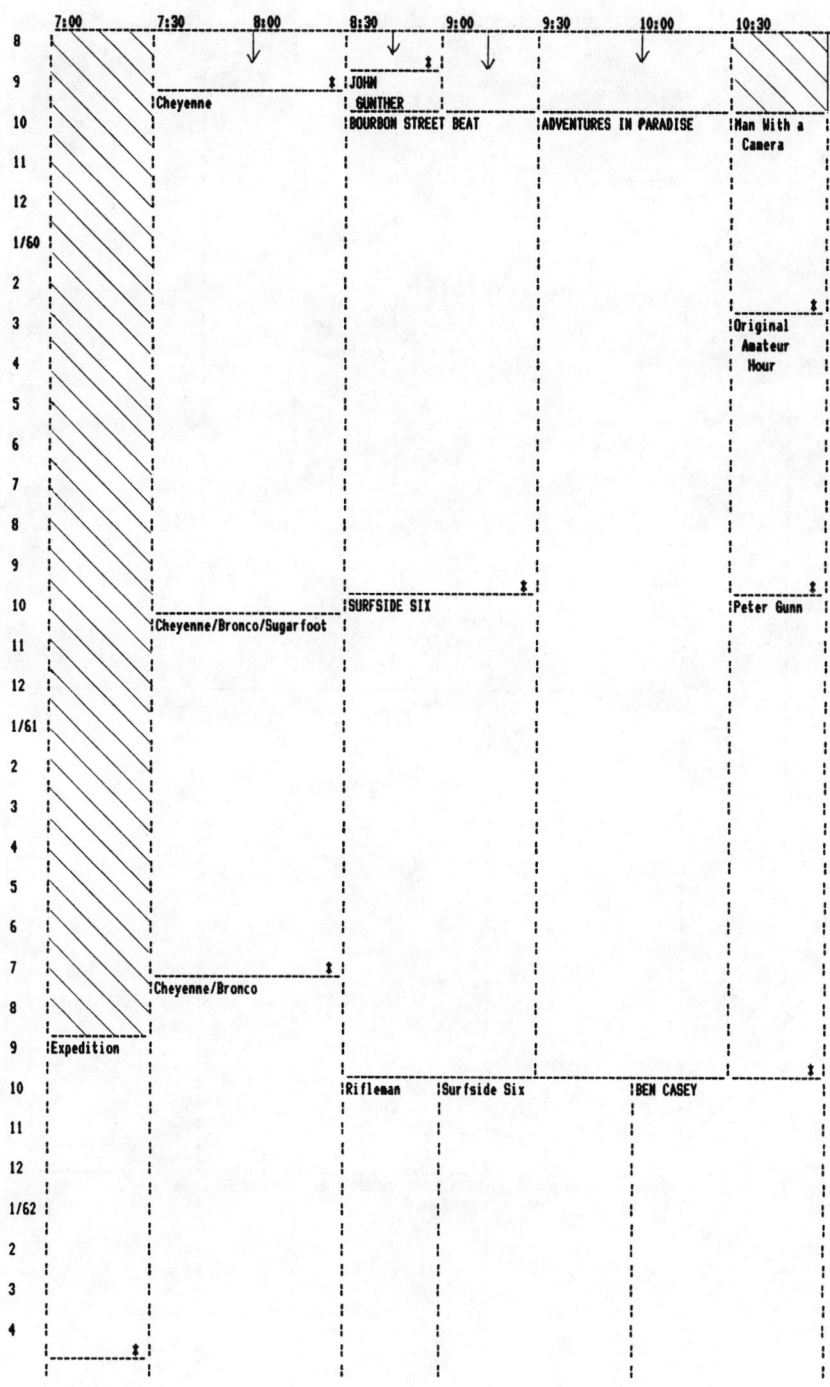

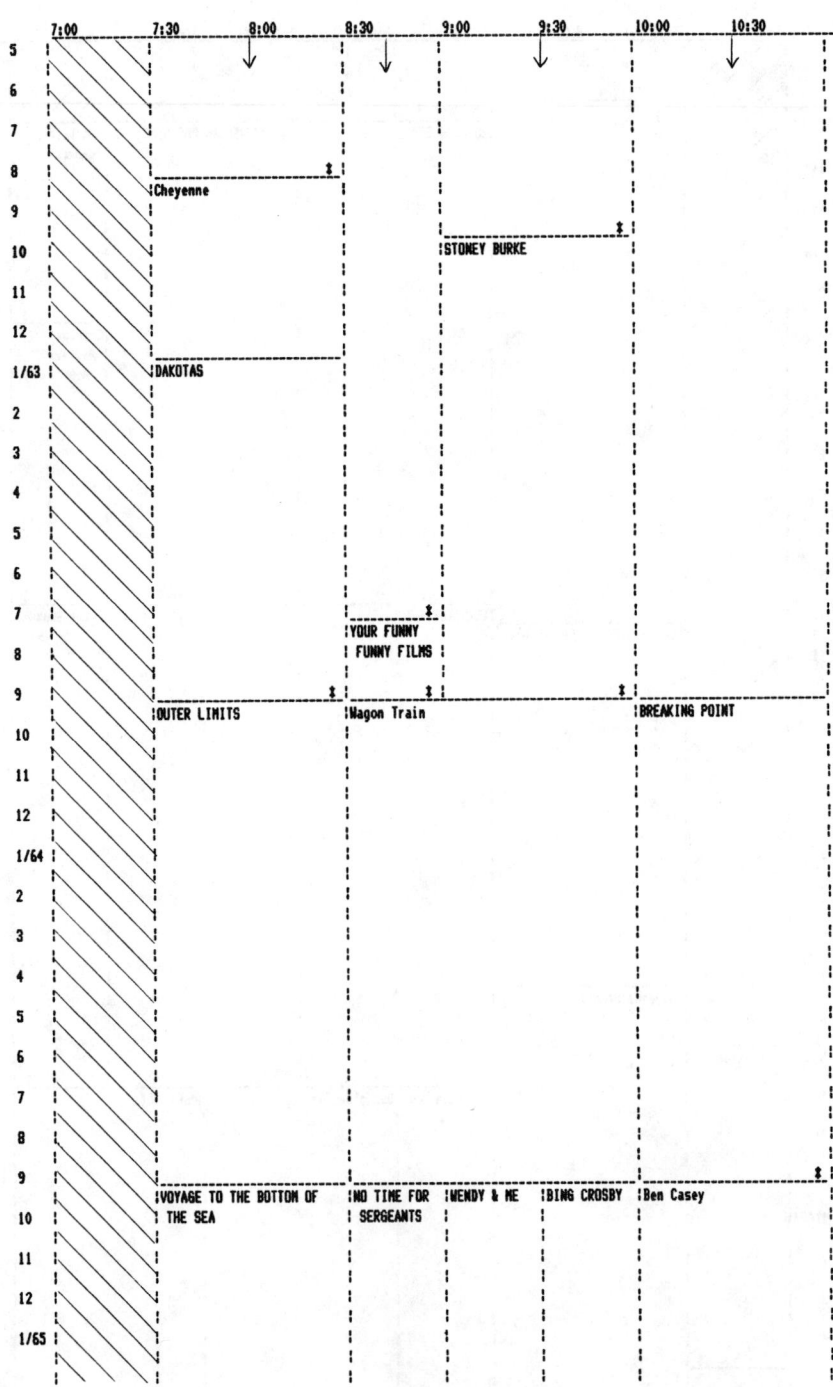

	7:00	7:30	8:00	8:30	9:00	9:30	10:00	10:30

Cheyenne

STONEY BURKE

DAKOTAS

YOUR FUNNY
FUNNY FILMS

OUTER LIMITS   Wagon Train   BREAKING POINT

VOYAGE TO THE BOTTOM OF   NO TIME FOR   WENDY & ME   BING CROSBY   Ben Casey
THE SEA   SERGEANTS

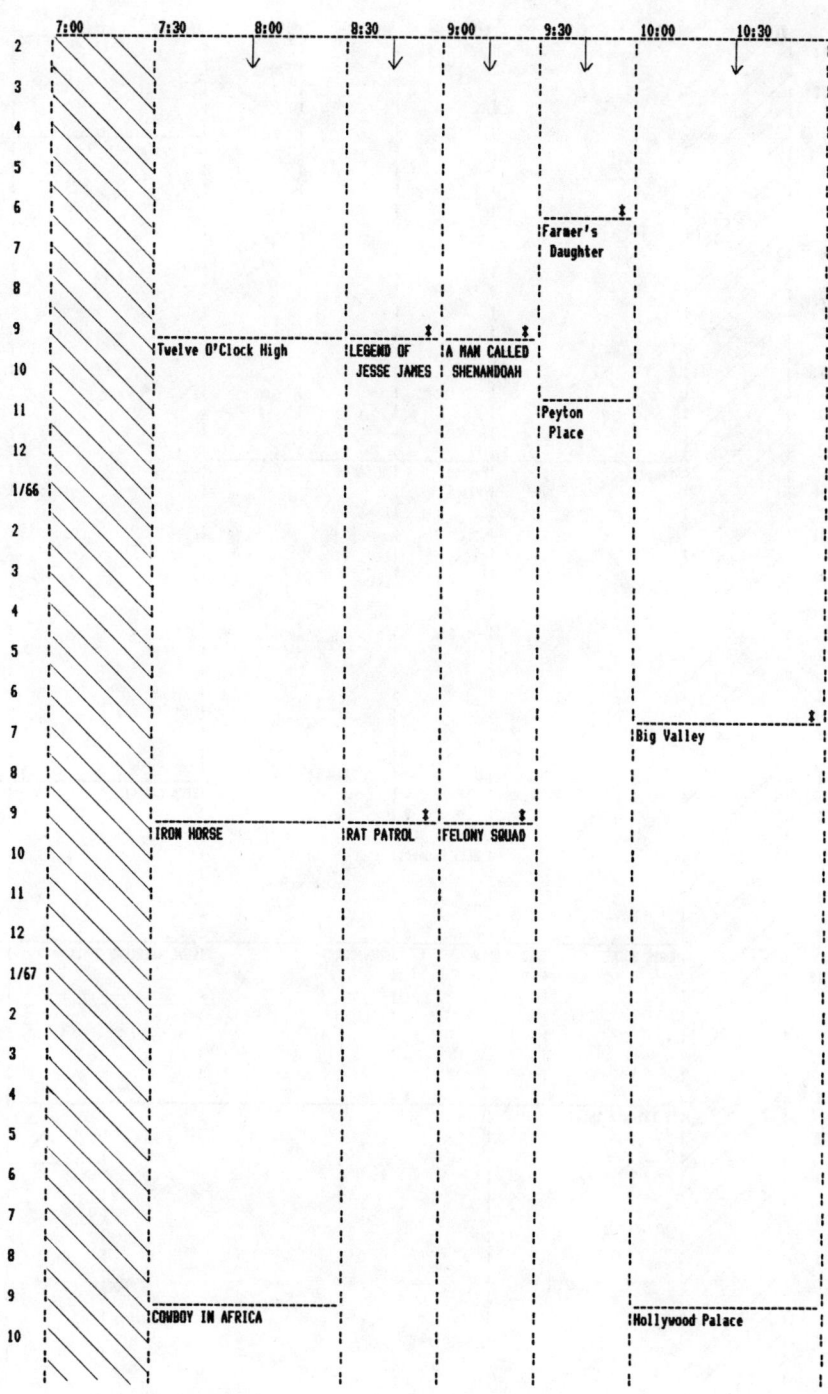

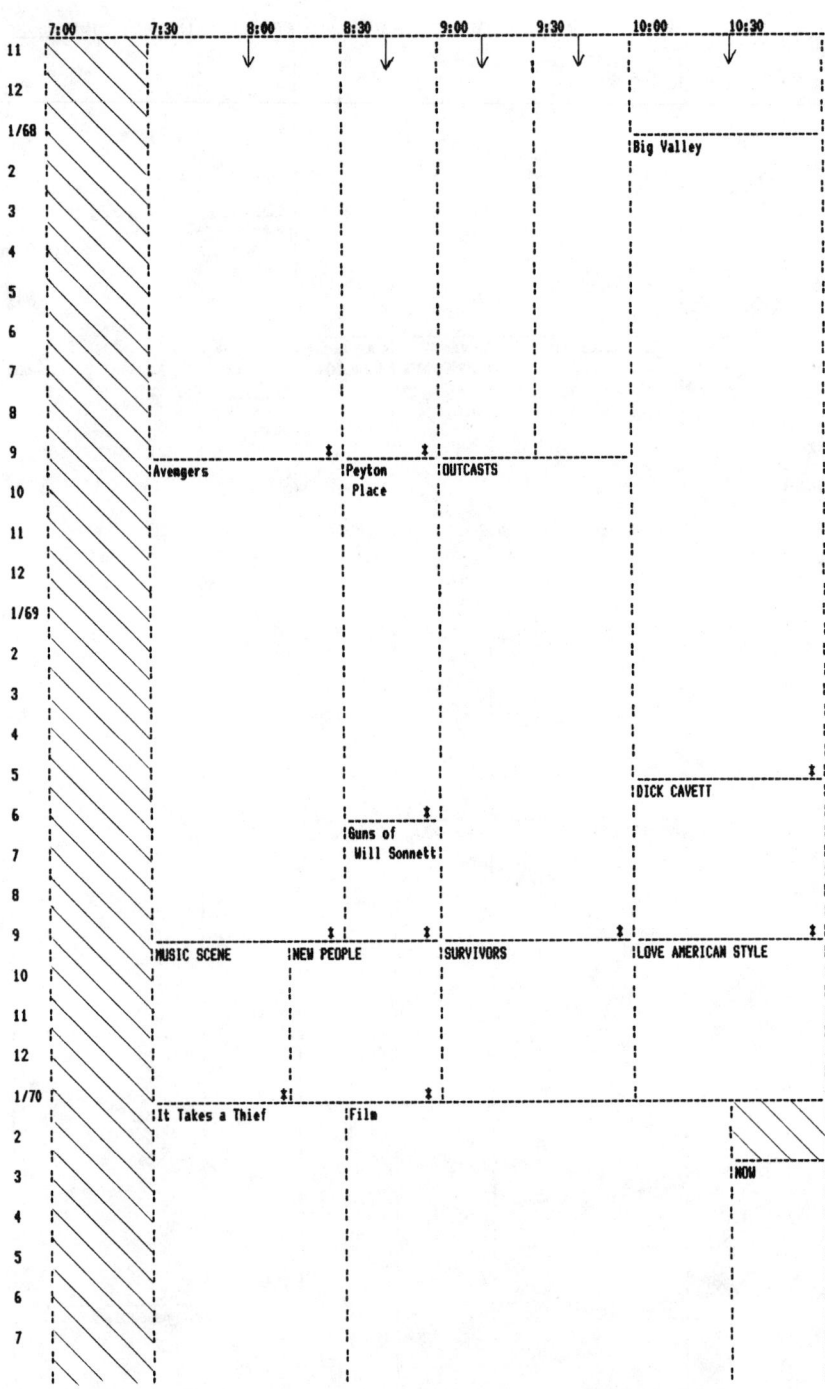

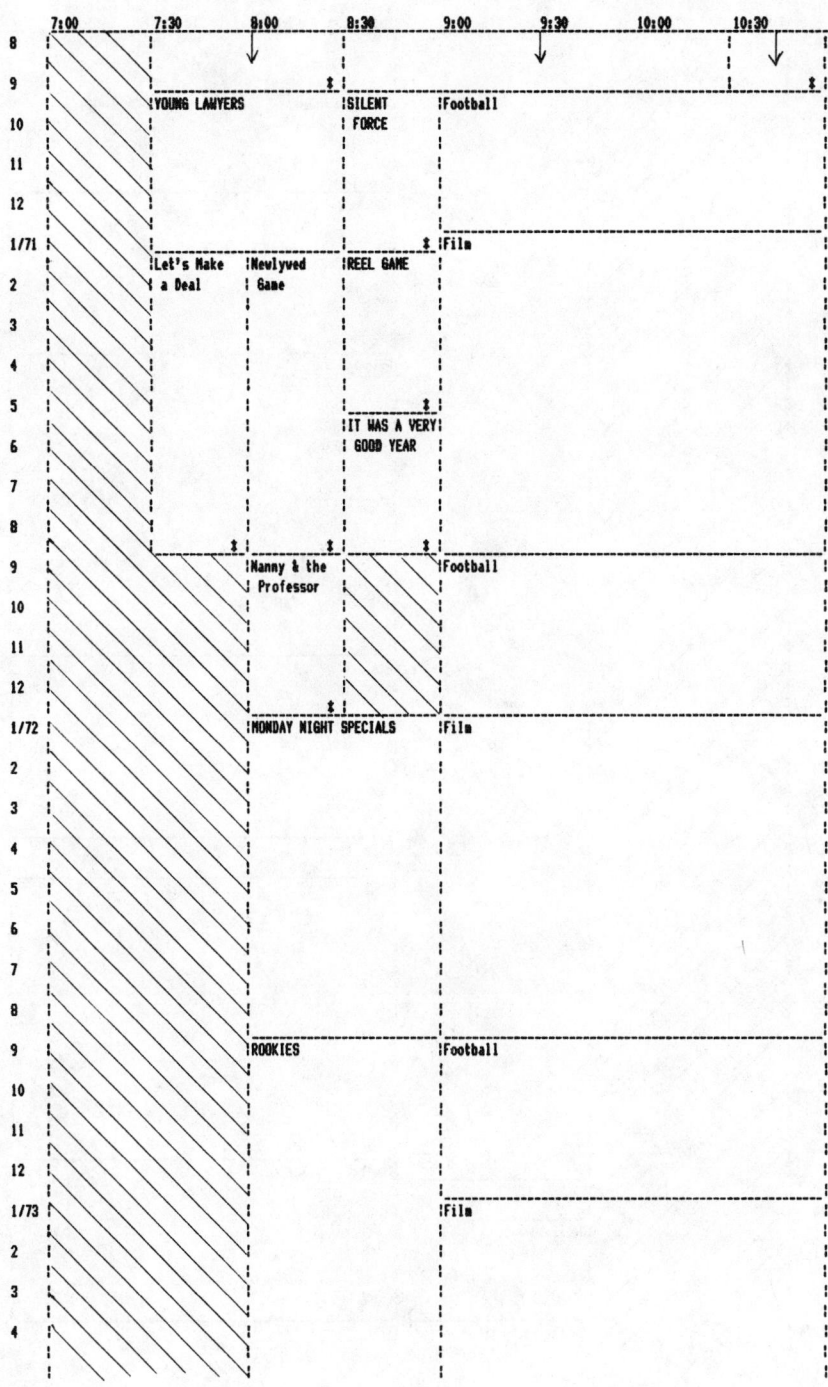

	7:00	7:30	8:00	8:30	9:00	9:30	10:00	10:30
8								
9		YOUNG LAWYERS		SILENT	Football			
10				FORCE				
11								
12								
1/71		Let's Make	Newlywed	REEL GAME	Film			
2		a Deal	Game					
3								
4								
5				IT WAS A VERY				
6				GOOD YEAR				
7								
8								
9			Nanny & the		Football			
10			Professor					
11								
12								
1/72			MONDAY NIGHT SPECIALS		Film			
2								
3								
4								
5								
6								
7								
8								
9			ROOKIES		Football			
10								
11								
12								
1/73					Film			
2								
3								
4								

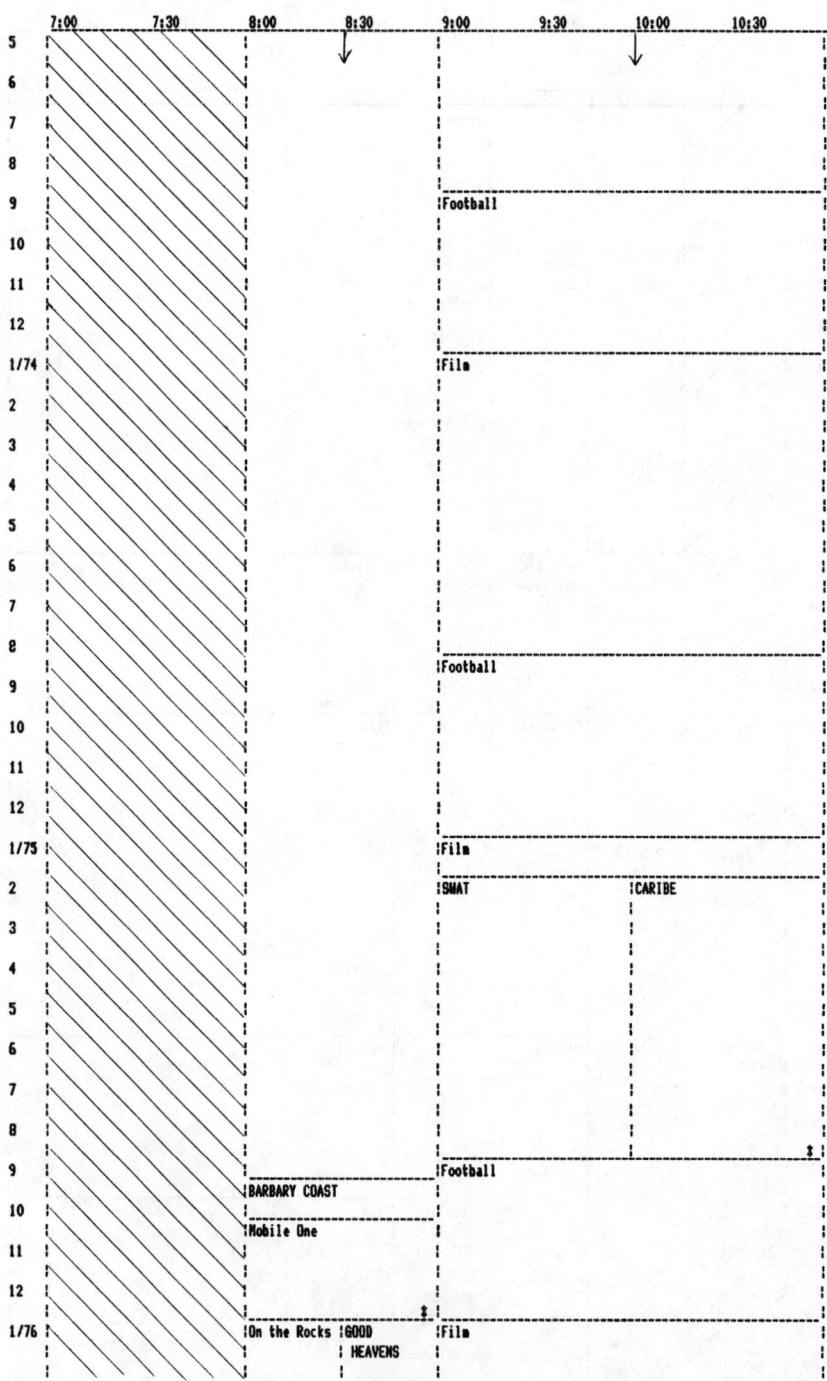

	7:00	7:30	8:00	8:30	9:00	9:30	10:00	10:30
2								
3								
4				Baseball				
5			VIVA VALDEZ					
6								
7								
8								
9			CAPTAIN & TENNILLE		Football			
10								
11								
12								
1/77					Film			
2								
3			Brady Bunch Hour		Most Wanted		FEATHER & FATHER GANG	
4			COMEDY SPECIAL	Baseball				
5								
6								
7								
8								
9			SAN PEDRO BEACH BUMS		Football			
10								
11								
12			LUCAN					
1/78			$6 Million Man		Film			
2								
3								
4			Sugar Time	Baseball				
5								
6								
7								
8								
9			Welcome Back Kotter	Operation Petticoat	Football			
10								

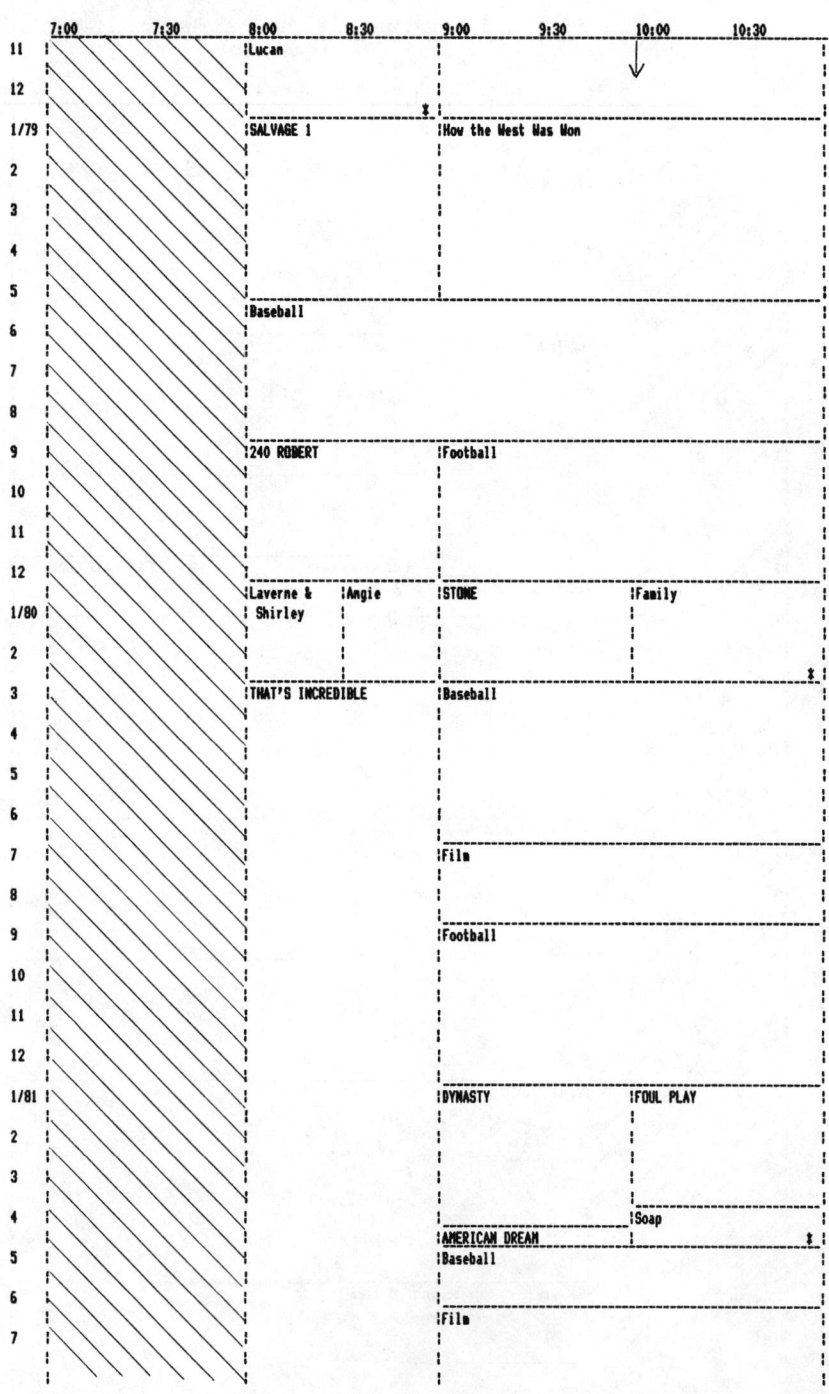

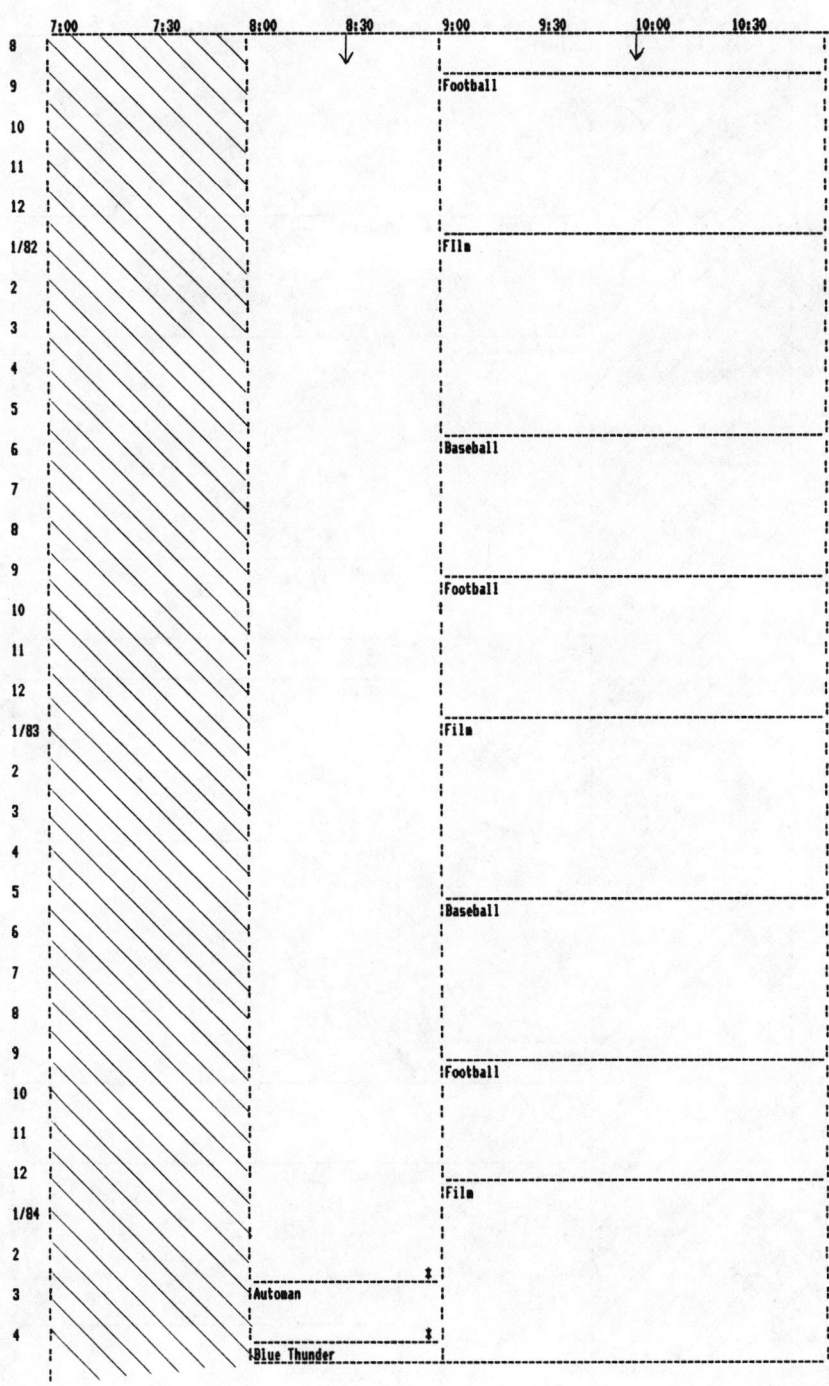

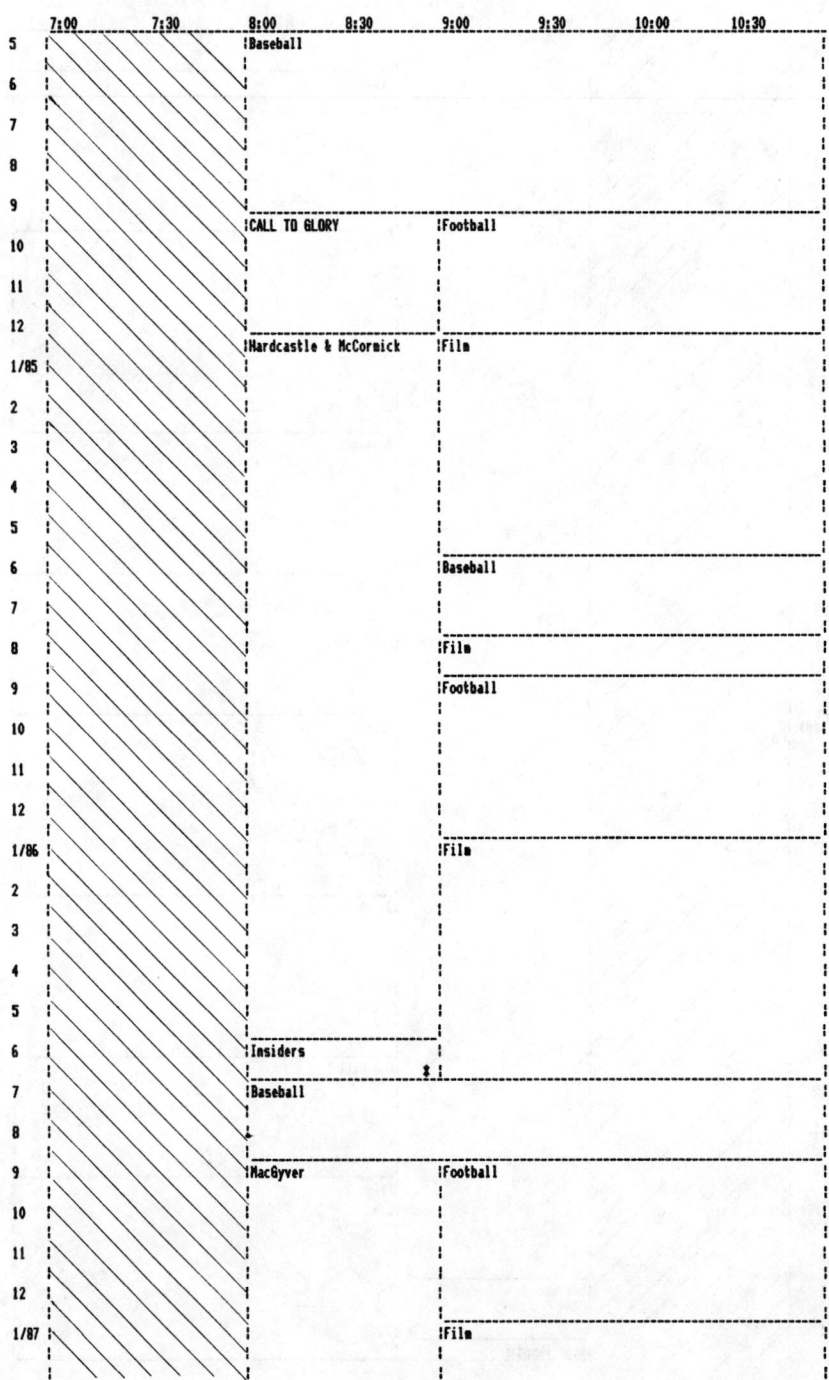

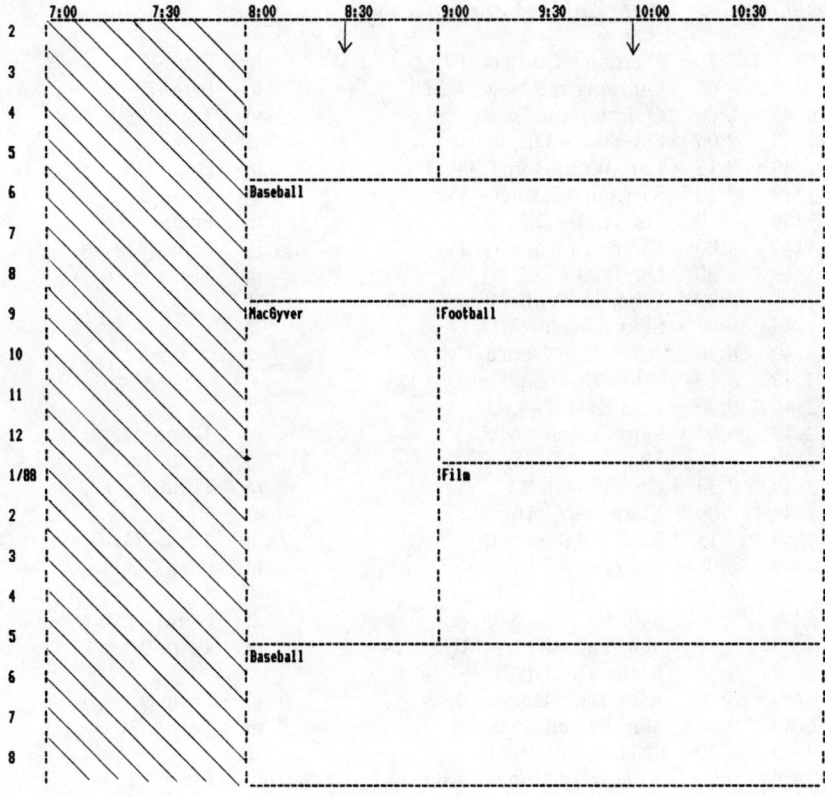

Date	Time	Title (min. if not 30) — Type	Action	From/To
9/48	7:30	Kiernan's Corner — IV	m	Fr:m-8
9/48	8:00	Quizzing the News — QU	m	Fr:m-7:30
10/48	8:00	Quizzing the News — QU	m	To:w-8:30
11/48	8:00	On Trial — DB	d	
1/49	7:15	Earl Wrightson(15) — MU	m	Fr:s-7:45
1/49	7:30	Kiernan's Corner — IV	m	To:m-8
1/49	7:30	On Trial — DB	m	Fr:m-8
1/49	8:00	Kiernan's Corner — IV	m	Fr:m-7:30
1/49	8:00	On Trial — DB	m	To:m-7:30
1/49	8:30	What Do You Think? — DS	d	
1/49	9:00	Skip Farrell — MU	d	
2/49	8:30	ABC Barn Dance — MU	d	
2/49	8:30	What Do You Think? — DS	c	
2/49	9:00	Identify(15) — QU	d	
2/49	9:00	Skip Farrell — MU	m	To:m-9:15
2/49	9:15	Skip Farrell(15) — MU	m	Fr:m-9
3/49	7:30	On Trial — DB	m	To:m-8
3/49	8:00	Kiernan's Corner — IV	c	
4/49	7:15	Earl Wrightson(15) — MU	m	To:w-7:45-9/49(c)
4/49	8:00	On Trial — DB	m	Fr:m-7:30
5/49	9:00	Identify(15) — QU	c	
5/49	9:00	Skip Farrell — MU	m	Fr:m-9:15
5/49	9:15	Skip Farrell(15) — MU	m	To:m-9
5/49	9:30	Roller Derby(90) — SP	s	
6/49	8:30	ABC Barn Dance — MU	m	To:m-9
6/49	9:00	Skip Farrell — MU	m	To:n-9:30
7/49	8:30	Science Circus — IS	d	
7/49	9:00	ABC Barn Dance — MU	m	Fr:m-8:30
8/49	9:30	Roller Derby(90) — SP	f	
9/49	8:00	Your Witness — CR	d	
9/49	8:00	On Trial — DB	m	To:w-8-2/50
9/49	8:30	Science Circus — IS	c	
9/49	8:30	Wendy Barrie — IV	m	Fr:w-7-7/49(d)
9/49	9:30	Mr. Black — MA	d	
9/49	10:00	Roller Derby(60) — SP	s	
10/49	7:30	Author Meets the Critics — DS	m	Fr:n-8:30-7/49(n)
10/49	8:00	Your Witness — CR	m	To:n-9-12/49
10/49	8:30	Wendy Barrie — IV	m	To:w-8
10/49	9:00	ABC Barn Dance — MU	m	To:m-9:30
10/49	9:00	Mr. Black — MA	m	Fr:m-9:30
10/49	9:30	ABC Barn Dance — MU	m	Fr:m-9
10/49	9:30	Mr. Black — MA	m	To:m-9
11/49	7:30	Author Meets the Critics — DS	m	To:w-9
11/49	9:00	Mr. Black — MA	c	
11/49	9:30	ABC Barn Dance — MU	c	
11/49	10:00	Roller Derby(60) — SP	f	
9/50	7:00	Club Seven — MV	m	Fr:r-10:30-3/49
9/50	7:30	Hollywood Screen Test — TA	m	Fr:s-7:30
9/50	8:00	Treasury Men in Action — CD	d	
9/50	8:30	Mysteries of Chinatown — CD	m	Fr:n-9

Date	Time	Title (min. if not 30) — Type	Action	From/To
10/50	8:30	Dick Tracy — CD	m	Fr:w-8:30
10/50	8:30	Mysteries of Chinatown — CD	c	
10/50	9:00	College Bowl — MC	d	
10/50	9:30	On Trial — DB	m	Fr:w-8
10/50	10:00	Film(60) — FI	s	
11/50	9:15	Manhattan Maharaja(15) — VY	d	
12/50	7:00	Andy and Della Russell(5) — MU	d	
12/50	8:00	Can You Top This? — CY	m	Fr:t-9:30
12/50	8:00	Treasury Men in Action — CD	m	To:r-8:30-4/51(n)
12/50	8:30	Dick Tracy — CD	m	To:t-8
1/51	8:30	Ruggles — SC	m	Fr:r-9:30-8/50
1/51	10:00	Film(60) — FI	f	
2/51	9:15	Manhattan Maharaja(15) — VY	c	
2/51	10:30	Bill Gwinn — QU	d	
3/51	8:00	Can You Top This? — CY	c	
3/51	8:30	Bill Gwinn — QU	m	Fr:m-10:30
3/51	8:30	Ruggles — SC	m	To:w-8
3/51	9:00	College Bowl — MC	c	
3/51	10:30	Bill Gwinn — QU	m	To:m-8:30
4/51	8:00	Film — FI	s	
4/51	9:00	Arthur Murray Party — MV	m	Fr:n-9(d)
4/51	10:00	Film(60) — FI	s	
5/51	8:00	Jerry Colonna — CV	d	
5/51	8:00	Film — FI	f	
6/51	7:00	Andy and Della Russell(5) — MU	c	
6/51	8:00	Jerry Colonna — CV	m	To:f-8
6/51	8:30	Bill Gwinn — QU	m	To:w-9
6/51	9:00	Arthur Murray Party — MV	m	To:w-9-9/51
7/51	8:30	Marshall Plan in Action — DO	m	Fr:f-10
7/51	9:00	United or Not — IV	d	
8/51	7:00	Club Seven — MV	c	
8/51	10:00	America's Health — DO	d	
8/51	10:00	Film(60) — FI	f	
8/51	10:30	Stud's Place — VY	m	Fr:f-10:30
9/51	8:00	Amazing Mr. Malone — CD	d	
9/51	9:00	Paul Dixon(60) — VY	m	Fr:w-8
9/51	9:00	United or Not — IV	m	To:t-9
9/51	9:30	On Trial — DB	m	To:t-9:30
9/51	10:00	America's Health — DO	m	To:s-9:30
10/51	8:00	Mr. District Attorney — CD	d	
10/51	8:30	Life Begins at Eighty — DS	m	Fr:t-9:30
10/51	8:30	Marshall Plan in Action — DO	m	To:t-8-4/52
10/51	9:00	Film(60) — FI	s	
10/51	9:00	Paul Dixon(60) — VY	m	To:r-10
10/51	10:00	Bill Gwinn — QU	m	Fr:w-9
12/51	9:00	Film(60) — FI	f	
12/51	9:00	You Asked for It — NM	m	Fr:f-8:30(d)
1/52	9:30	How Did They Get That Way — DS	m	Fr:t-8:30
1/52	10:30	Stud's Place — VY	c	
3/52	8:00	Amazing Mr. Malone — CD	c	

Date	Time	Title (min. if not 30) — Type	Action	From/To
3/52	8:30	Life Begins at Eighty — DS	m	To:f-8:30(d)
3/52	9:00	You Asked for It — NM	m	To:n-7
3/52	9:30	Bill Gwinn — QU	m	Fr:m-10
3/52	9:30	How Did They Get That Way — DS	c	
3/52	10:00	Bill Gwinn — QU	m	To:m-9:30
4/52	8:30	Film(60) — FI	s	
4/52	9:30	Bill Gwinn — QU	c	
4/52	9:30	On Guard — DO	d	
6/52	8:00	Mr. District Attorney — CD	c	
6/52	8:00	Out of the Fog — DR	d	
8/52	8:30	Film(60) — FI	f	
8/52	9:30	On Guard — DO	m	To:r-9:30
9/52	8:00	Out of the Fog — DR	c	
9/52	8:30	United or Not — IV	m	Fr:t-8:30
9/52	9:00	Film(60) — FI	s	
10/52	8:00	Mark Saber — CD	m	Fr:w-9:30-6/52
10/52	8:30	United or Not — IV	c	
10/52	9:00	Film(60) — FI	f	
10/52	9:00	News(60) — NW	s	
11/52	8:30	Hot Seat — IV	m	Fr:n-7:30
12/52	8:30	Hot Seat — IV	c	
12/52	9:00	News(60) — NW	f	
1/53	8:30	Film — FI	s	
1/53	9:00	Perspective — DS	m	Fr:r-9
1/53	9:30	Talent Patrol — TA	d	
1/53	10:00	Why? — QU	d	
4/53	9:00	Perspective — DS	c	
4/53	10:00	Why? — QU	c	
5/53	7:30	Hollywood Screen Test — TA	c	
5/53	7:30	Opera vs. Jazz — MU	d	
6/53	8:00	Mark Saber — CD	m	To:w-7:30-10/53
7/53	8:00	Talent Patrol — TA	m	Fr:m-9:30
7/53	9:30	Film — FI	s	
7/53	9:30	Talent Patrol — TA	m	To:m-8
8/53	8:00	Talent Patrol — TA	m	To:w-8
9/53	7:00	Walter Winchell(15) — NA	d	
9/53	7:30	Jamie — SC	d	
9/53	7:30	Opera vs. Jazz — MU	c	
9/53	8:00	Sky King — AD	d	
9/53	8:30	Film — FI	f	
9/53	9:30	Film — FI	f	
9/53	10:00	This Is the Life — RD	m	Fr:n-9:30
10/53	8:30	Of Many Things — DS	d	
10/53	9:00	Junior Press Conference — IV	d	
10/53	9:30	Big Picture — DO	d	
10/53	10:00	This Is the Life — RD	c	
1/54	7:00	Walter Winchell(15) — NA	m	To:n-9
1/54	8:30	Doctor IQ — QU	m	Fr:r-9
1/54	8:30	Of Many Things — DS	c	
3/54	8:30	Doctor IQ — QU	m	To:n-9:30

Date	Time	Title (min. if not 30) — Type	Action	From/To
4/54	8:30	Film — FI	s	
5/54	8:30	Film — FI	f	
5/54	9:30	Boxing(60) — SP	s	
6/54	7:30	Flight #7 — TR	d*	
6/54	8:30	Voice of Firestone — MU	m	Fr:m-8:30(n)
8/54	7:30	Flight #7 — TR	m*	To:n-8
8/54	7:30	U.S. Highway 1954 — TR	d*	
9/54	7:00	Kukla, Fran & Ollie(15) — KV	m	Fr:m-f-7-6/52(n)
9/54	7:30	U.S. Highway 1954 — TR	c*	
9/54	8:00	Come Closer — QU	d	
9/54	8:00	Sky King — AD	c	
10/54	7:30	Jamie — SC	c	
10/54	7:30	The Name's the Same — QU	m	Fr:t-10:30-8/54
12/54	8:00	Come Closer — QU	c	
12/54	8:00	Talent Patrol — TA	m	Fr:n-9:30
12/54	9:00	Junior Press Conference — IV	c	
12/54	9:30	Big Picture — DO	m	To:n-8:30
12/54	9:30	Boxing(60) — SP	f	
1/55	8:00	TV Reader's Digest — DA	d	
1/55	8:00	Talent Patrol — TA	m	To:r-8
1/55	9:00	Boxing(90) — SP	s	
5/55	9:00	Boxing(90) — SP	f	
5/55	9:00	Pee Wee King(90) — MV	d	
6/55	7:30	Greatest Sports Thrills — SH	m	Fr:s-8:30-9/54
6/55	7:30	The Name's the Same — QU	m	To:t-10
7/55	7:00	Soupy Sales(15) — KV	d*	
8/55	7:00	Soupy Sales(15) — KV	c*	
9/55	7:30	Greatest Sports Thrills — SH	m	To:r-10-11/55
9/55	9:00	Dotty Mack — MU	m	Fr:t-9:30
9/55	9:00	Pee Wee King(90) — MV	c	
9/55	9:30	Medical Horizons — PA	d	
9/55	10:00	Big Picture — DO	m	Fr:t-8:30
10/55	7:30	Topper — SC	m	Fr:f-8:30(c)
1/56	10:00	Big Picture — DO	m	To:n-10-3/56
1/56	10:00	Outside, USA — DO	m	Fr:t-10
3/56	7:30	Topper — SC	m	To:n-7-6/56(n)
3/56	9:00	Dotty Mack — MU	m	To:r-10
3/56	9:00	Film(120) — FI	s	
3/56	9:30	Medical Horizons — PA	c	
3/56	10:00	Outside, USA — DO	m	To:n-10
4/56	7:30	Twilight Theater — DA	d	
7/56	7:00	Jack Drees(15) — SN	d*	
7/56	7:30	Bold Journey — TR	d	
7/56	7:30	Twilight Theater — DA	m	To:w-7:30-7/58(c)
7/56	8:00	Dotty Mack — MU	m	Fr:r-10
7/56	8:00	TV Reader's Digest — DA	c	
7/56	9:00	Film(120) — FI	f	
7/56	9:00	Film(90) — FI	s	
8/56	7:00	Jack Drees(15) — SN	c*	
9/56	8:00	Dotty Mack — MU	c	

Date	Time	Title (min. if not 30) — Type	Action	From/To
10/56	8:00	Danny Thomas — SC	m	Fr:t-9-6/56
10/56	9:00	Life Is Worth Living — RE	m	Fr:r-8-4/56
10/56	9:00	Film(90) — FI	f	
10/56	9:30	Lawrence Welk's Top Tunes & New Talent(60) — TA	d	
2/57	7:30	Bold Journey — TR	m	To:r-9:30
2/57	7:30	Wire Service(60) — ND	m	Fr:r-9
2/57	8:00	Danny Thomas — SC	m	To:r-9
4/57	9:00	Life Is Worth Living — RE	c	
4/57	9:00	Press Conference — IV	m	Fr:n-8:30-12/56
6/57	7:00	Sports Focus(15) — SN	d	
6/57	7:00	Kukla, Fran & Ollie(15) — KV	c	
6/57	8:30	Bold Journey — TR	m	Fr:r-9:30
6/57	8:30	Voice of Firestone — MU	m	To:m-9-9/57
7/57	7:00	Sports Focus(15) — SN	m	To:m-f-7-9/57
7/57	9:00	ABC Presents — DO	d	
7/57	9:00	Press Conference — IV	c	
9/57	7:00	Sports Focus(15) — SN	m	Fr:m-f-7-7/57
9/57	7:30	Wire Service(60) — ND	m	To:n-9:30-2/59
9/57	9:00	ABC Presents — DO	m	To:r-8
9/57	9:00	Voice of Firestone — MU	m	Fr:m-8:30-6/57
10/57	7:30	American Bandstand — MU	d	
10/57	8:00	Guy Mitchell — MV	d	
12/57	7:30	American Bandstand — MU	c	
1/58	7:30	O.S.S. — WD	m	Fr:r-9:30
1/58	8:00	Guy Mitchell — MV	c	
1/58	8:00	Love That Jill — SC	d	
3/58	7:30	American Odyssey — DO	d	
3/58	7:30	O.S.S. — WD	c	
4/58	8:00	Love That Jill — SC	c	
5/58	8:00	Campaign Roundup — NA	d	
6/58	7:30	American Odyssey — DO	c	
6/58	7:30	Cowtown Rodeo(60) — RO	m	Fr:r-8-9/57
6/58	8:00	Campaign Roundup — NA	c	
6/58	9:00	Stars of Jazz — MU	m*	Fr:f-8:30
6/58	9:30	Lawrence Welk's Top Tunes & New Talent(60) — TA	m	To:w-7:30-9/58
6/58	9:30	Polka-Go-Round(60) — MU	d	
9/58	7:00	Sports Focus(15) — SN	c	
9/58	7:30	Cowtown Rodeo(60) — RO	c	
9/58	7:30	Ozark Jubilee(60) — MU	s	
9/58	7:30	This Is Music — MU	m	Fr:f-8:30
9/58	9:00	Stars of Jazz — MU	m*	To:r-10
9/58	9:30	Polka-Go-Round(60) — MU	m	To:m-7:30
9/58	10:30	News(15) — NW	s	
10/58	7:30	Ozark Jubilee(60) — MU	f	
10/58	7:30	Polka-Go-Round(60) — MU	m	Fr:m-9:30
10/58	7:30	This Is Music — MU	m	To:m-10
10/58	9:30	Anybody Can Play — QU	m	Fr:n-8:30
10/58	10:00	This Is Music — MU	m	Fr:m-7:30

Date	Time	Title (min. if not 30) — Type	Action	From/To
10/58	10:00	This Is Music — MU	m	To:r-10
11/58	10:00	Traffic Court — CR	m	Fr:r-10
11/58	10:00	Traffic Court — CR	m	To:m-10-3/59
12/58	7:30	Polka-Go-Round(60) — MU	m	To:m-8
12/58	7:30	Tales of the Texas Rangers — WE	d	
12/58	8:00	Polka-Go-Round — MU	m	Fr:m-7:30
12/58	9:30	Anybody Can Play — QU	c	
12/58	10:00	Patti Page Olds Show — MV	m	Fr:w-9:30
3/59	9:30	This Is Music — MU	m*	Fr:r-10
3/59	9:30	This Is Music — MU	m*	To:r-10
3/59	10:00	Patti Page Olds Show — MV	c	
3/59	10:00	Traffic Court — CR	m	Fr:m-10-11/58
3/59	10:00	Traffic Court — CR	c	
4/59	9:30	Top Pro Golf(60) — SP	s	
5/59	7:30	Tales of the Texas Rangers — WE	c	
5/59	8:00	Polka-Go-Round — MU	m	To:m-7:30
5/59	10:30	News(15) — NW	f	
6/59	7:30	Polka-Go-Round(60) — MU	m	Fr:m-8
6/59	9:00	Pantomime Quiz — QU	m	Fr:t-9:30-9/58
6/59	9:00	Voice of Firestone — MU	m	To:n-10-9/62
8/59	8:30	Bold Journey — TR	c	
9/59	7:30	Cheyenne(60) — WE	m	Fr:t-7:30
9/59	7:30	Polka-Go-Round(60) — MU	c	
9/59	8:30	John Gunther's High Road — TR	d	
9/59	8:30	John Gunther's High Road — TR	m	To:s-8
9/59	9:00	Pantomime Quiz — QU	m	To:m-10:30-9/62(c)
9/59	9:30	Top Pro Golf(60) — SP	f	
10/59	8:30	Bourbon Street Beat(60) — CD	d	
10/59	9:30	Adventures in Paradise(60) — AD	d	
10/59	10:30	Man with a Camera — DR	m	Fr:f-9-3/59
2/60	10:30	Man with a Camera — DR	c	
3/60	10:30	Original Amateur Hour — TA	m	Fr:f-10:30-10/59(c)
9/60	8:30	Bourbon Street Beat(60) — CD	c	
9/60	10:30	Original Amateur Hour — TA	c	
10/60	7:30	Bronco(60) — WE	m	Fr:t-7:30
10/60	7:30	Sugarfoot(60) — WE	m	Fr:t-7:30
10/60	8:30	Surfside Six(60) — CD	d	
10/60	10:30	Peter Gunn — CD	m	Fr:m-9(n)
7/61	7:30	Sugarfoot(60) — WE	c	
9/61	7:00	Expedition — WL	m	Fr:t-7-6/61
9/61	8:30	Surfside Six(60) — CD	m	To:m-9
9/61	9:30	Adventures in Paradise(60) — AD	m	To:n-10
9/61	10:30	Peter Gunn — CD	c	
10/61	8:30	Rifleman — WE	m	Fr:t-8
10/61	9:00	Surfside Six(60) — CD	m	Fr:m-8:30
10/61	10:00	Ben Casey(60) — MD	d	
4/62	7:00	Expedition — WL	c	
7/62	8:30	Law of the Plainsman — WE	m*	Fr:r-7:30-9/60(n)
8/62	7:30	Bronco(60) — WE	c	
9/62	8:30	Law of the Plainsman — WE	c*	

Date	Time	Title (min. if not 30) – Type	Action	From/To
9/62	9:00	Surfside Six(60) – CD	c	
10/62	9:00	Stoney Burke(60) – WE	d	
12/62	7:30	Cheyenne(60) – WE	m	To:f-7:30-4/63
1/63	7:30	Dakotas(60) – WE	d	
7/63	8:30	Rifleman – WE	c	
7/63	8:30	Your Funny, Funny Films – CY	d	
9/63	7:30	Dakotas(60) – WE	c	
9/63	7:30	Outer Limits(60) – FA	d	
9/63	8:30	Wagon Train(90) – WE	m	Fr:w-7:30
9/63	8:30	Your Funny, Funny Films – CY	c	
9/63	9:00	Stoney Burke(60) – WE	c	
9/63	10:00	Ben Casey(60) – MD	m	To:w-9
9/63	10:00	Breaking Point(60) – MD	d	
9/64	7:30	Outer Limits(60) – FA	m	To:s-7:30
9/64	7:30	Voyage to the Bottom of the Sea (60) – SF	d	
9/64	8:30	No Time for Sergeants – SC	d	
9/64	8:30	Wagon Train(90) – WE	m	To:n-7:30
9/64	9:00	Wendy and Me – SC	d	
9/64	9:30	Bing Crosby – SC	d	
9/64	10:00	Ben Casey(60) – MD	m	Fr:w-9
9/64	10:00	Breaking Point(60) – MD	c	
6/65	9:30	Bing Crosby – SC	c	
6/65	9:30	Farmer's Daughter – SC	m	Fr:f-8
9/65	7:30	Twelve O'Clock High(60) – WD	m	Fr:f-10
9/65	7:30	Voyage to the Bottom of the Sea (60) – SF	m	To:n-7
9/65	8:30	Legend of Jesse James – WE	d	
9/65	8:30	No Time for Sergeants – SC	c	
9/65	9:00	A Man Called Shenandoah – WE	d	
9/65	9:00	Wendy and Me – SC	c	
10/65	9:30	Farmer's Daughter – SC	m	To:f-9:30
11/65	9:30	Peyton Place – SL	m	Fr:trf-9:30
6/66	10:00	Ben Casey(60) – MD	c	
7/66	10:00	Big Valley(60) – WE	m	Fr:w-9
9/66	7:30	Iron Horse(60) – WE	d	
9/66	7:30	Twelve O'Clock High(60) – WD	m	To:f-10
9/66	8:30	Legend of Jesse James – WE	c	
9/66	8:30	Rat Patrol – WD	d	
9/66	9:00	Felony Squad – CD	d	
9/66	9:00	A Man Called Shenandoah – WE	c	
9/67	7:30	Cowboy in Africa(60) – AD	d	
9/67	7:30	Iron Horse(60) – WE	m	To:s-9:30
9/67	10:00	Hollywood Palace(60) – VY	m	Fr:s-9:30-5/67
9/67	10:00	Big Valley(60) – WE	m	To:m-10-1/68
1/68	10:00	Hollywood Palace(60) – VY	m	To:s-9:30
1/68	10:00	Big Valley(60) – WE	m	Fr:m-10-9/67
9/68	7:30	Avengers(60) – SD	m	Fr:w-7:30
9/68	7:30	Cowboy in Africa(60) – AD	c	
9/68	8:30	Peyton Place – SL	m	Fr:mr-9:30

Date	*Time*	*Title (min. if not 30) — Type*	*Action*	*From/To*
9/68	8:30	Rat Patrol — WD	c	
9/68	9:00	Felony Squad — CD	m	To:f-8:30
9/68	9:00	Outcasts(60) — WE	d	
9/68	9:30	Peyton Place — SL	m	To:m-8:30
5/69	10:00	Big Valley(60) — WE	c	
5/69	10:00	Dick Cavett(60) — TK	d	
6/69	8:30	Guns of Will Sonnett — WE	m	Fr:f-9:30
6/69	8:30	Peyton Place — SL	c	
9/69	7:30	Avengers(60) — SD	c	
9/69	7:30	Music Scene(45) — MU	d	
9/69	8:15	The New People(45) — DR	d	
9/69	8:30	Guns of Will Sonnett — WE	c	
9/69	9:00	Outcasts(60) — WE	c	
9/69	9:00	Survivors(60) — DR	d	
9/69	10:00	Dick Cavett(60) — TK	c	
9/69	10:00	Love, American Style(60) — CA	d	
1/70	7:30	It Takes a Thief(60) — SD	m	Fr:r-10
1/70	7:30	Music Scene(45) — MU	c	
1/70	8:15	The New People(45) — DR	c	
1/70	8:30	Film(120) — FI	s	
1/70	9:00	Survivors(60) — DR	m	To:r-10-6/70
1/70	10:00	Love, American Style(60) — CA	m	To:f-10
3/70	10:30	Now — DO	d	
9/70	7:30	It Takes a Thief(60) — SD	c	
9/70	7:30	Young Lawyers(60) — LD	d	
9/70	8:30	Silent Force — CD	d	
9/70	8:30	Film(120) — FI	f	
9/70	9:00	Football(120) — SP	s#	
9/70	10:30	Now — DO	c	
1/71	7:30	Let's Make a Deal — QU	m	Fr:s-7:30
1/71	7:30	Young Lawyers(60) — LD	m	To:w-10
1/71	8:00	Newlywed Game — QU	m	Fr:s-8
1/71	8:30	Reel Game — QU	d	
1/71	8:30	Silent Force — CD	c	
1/71	9:00	Film(120) — FI	s	
5/71	8:30	It Was a Very Good Year — DO	d	
5/71	8:30	Reel Game — QU	c	
8/71	7:30	Let's Make a Deal — QU	c	
8/71	8:00	Newlywed Game — QU	c	
8/71	8:30	It Was a Very Good Year — DO	c	
9/71	8:00	Nanny and the Professor — SC	m	Fr:f-8
12/71	8:00	Nanny and the Professor — SC	c	
1/72	8:00	Monday Night Special(60) — VS	d	
8/72	8:00	Monday Night Special(60) — VS	c	
9/72	8:00	Rookies(60) — CD	d	
2/75	9:00	Film(120) — FI	f	
2/75	9:00	S.W.A.T.(60) — CD	d	
2/75	10:00	Caribe(60) — CD	d	
8/75	9:00	S.W.A.T.(60) — CD	m	To:s-9
8/75	10:00	Caribe(60) — CD	c	

Date	Time	Title (min. if not 30) — Type	Action	From/To
9/75	8:00	Barbary Coast(60) — WE	d	
9/75	8:00	Rookies(60) — CD	m	To:t-9
10/75	8:00	Barbary Coast(60) — WE	m	To:f-8
10/75	8:00	Mobile One(60) — AD	m	Fr:f-8
12/75	8:00	Mobile One(60) — AD	c	
1/76	8:00	On the Rocks — SC	m	Fr:r-8:30
1/76	8:30	Good Heavens — SC	d	
1/76	9:00	Film(120) — FI	s	
4/76	8:30	Baseball(150) — SP	s#	
4/76	8:30	Good Heavens — SC	m	To:s-8
4/76	9:00	Film(120) — FI	f	
5/76	8:00	On the Rocks — SC	c	
5/76	8:00	Viva Valdez — SC	d	
9/76	8:00	Captain & Tennille(60) — MV	d	
9/76	8:00	Viva Valdez — SC	c	
1/77	9:00	Film(120) — FI	s	
2/77	9:00	Film(120) — FI	f	
3/77	8:00	Brady Bunch Hour(60) — CV	m	Fr:n-7
3/77	8:00	Captain & Tennille(60) — MV	c	
3/77	9:00	Most Wanted(60) — CD	m	Fr:s-10
3/77	10:00	Feather and Father Gang(60) — CD	d	
4/77	8:00	Brady Bunch Hour(60) — CV	m	To:w-8
4/77	9:00	Most Wanted(60) — CD	c	
4/77	10:00	Feather and Father Gang(60) — CD	m	To:s-10
5/77	8:00	ABC Monday Night Comedy Special — CY	d	
9/77	8:00	ABC Monday Night Comedy Special — CY	c	
9/77	8:00	San Pedro Beach Bums(60) — SC	d	
12/77	8:00	Lucan(60) — AD	d	
12/77	8:00	San Pedro Beach Bums(60) — SC	c	
1/78	8:00	Lucan(60) — AD	m	To:n-8-6/78
1/78	8:00	Six Million Dollar Man(60) — AD	m	Fr:n-8
1/78	9:00	Film(120) — FI	s	
3/78	8:00	Six Million Dollar Man(60) — AD	c	
3/78	9:00	Film(120) — FI	f	
4/78	8:00	Sugar Time — SC	m	Fr:s-8:30-9/77
5/78	8:00	Sugar Time — SC	c	
9/78	8:00	Welcome Back, Kotter — SC	m	Fr:r-8
9/78	8:30	Operation Petticoat — SC	m	Fr:f-8:30
10/78	8:00	Welcome Back, Kotter — SC	m	To:s-8
10/78	8:30	Operation Petticoat — SC	m	To:f-8-6/79
11/78	8:00	Lucan(60) — AD	m	Fr:n-8-7/78
12/78	8:00	Lucan(60) — AD	c	
1/79	8:00	Salvage 1(60) — AD	d	
1/79	9:00	How the West Was Won(120) — WE	m	Fr:n-8-8/78
4/79	9:00	How the West Was Won(120) — WE	c	
5/79	8:00	Salvage 1(60) — AD	m	To:n-8
9/79	8:00	240-Robert(60) — AD	d	
12/79	8:00	Laverne & Shirley — SC	m	Fr:r-8

Date	Time	Title (min. if not 30) – Type	Action	From/To
12/79	8:00	240-Robert(60) – AD	m	To:s-8-5/80
12/79	8:30	Angie – SC	m	Fr:t-8:30
12/79	9:00	Stone(60) – CD	d	
12/79	10:00	Family(60) – DR	m	Fr:r-10-5/79
2/80	8:00	Laverne & Shirley – SC	m	To:t-8:30
2/80	8:30	Angie – SC	m	To:s-8-4/80
2/80	9:00	Stone(60) – CD	m	To:m-10
2/80	10:00	Family(60) – DR	m	To:m-9
3/80	8:00	That's Incredible(60) – NM	d	
3/80	9:00	Family(60) – DR	m	Fr:m-10
3/80	9:00	Family(60) – DR	c	
3/80	10:00	Stone(60) – CD	m	Fr:m-9
3/80	10:00	Stone(60) – CD	c	
7/80	9:00	Film(120) – FI	s	
8/80	9:00	Film(120) – FI	f	
1/81	9:00	Dynasty(60) – SL	d	
1/81	10:00	Foul Play(60) – CD	d	
3/81	10:00	Foul Play(60) – CD	m	To:n-8-7/81
4/81	9:00	American Dream(60) – DR	d	
4/81	9:00	American Dream(60) – DR	m	To:w-9
4/81	9:00	Dynasty(60) – SL	m	To:w-10-7/81
4/81	10:00	Soap(60) – SC	m	Fr:w-9:30-1/81
4/81	10:00	Soap(60) – SC	c	
6/81	8:00	Breaking Away(60) – AD	m*	Fr:s-8
6/81	9:00	Film(120) – FI	s	
7/81	8:00	Breaking Away(60) – AD	c*	
8/81	9:00	Film(120) – FI	f	
1/82	9:00	Film(120) – FI	s	
4/82	8:00	Today's FBI(60) – CD	m*	Fr:n-8
5/82	8:00	Today's FBI(60) – CD	m*	To:s-8
5/82	9:00	Film(120) – FI	f	
6/82	8:00	Best of the West – SC	m*	Fr:f-9-2/82
8/82	8:00	Best of the West – SC	c*	
1/83	9:00	Film(120) – FI	s	
5/83	9:00	Film(120) – FI	f	
12/83	9:00	Film(120) – FI	s	
2/84	8:00	That's Incredible(60) – NM	c	
3/84	8:00	Automan(60) – SF	m	Fr:r-8-1/84
4/84	8:00	Automan(60) – SF	c	
4/84	8:00	Blue Thunder(60) – CD	m	Fr:f-9
4/84	8:00	Blue Thunder(60) – CD	m	To:f-9
5/84	9:00	Film(120) – FI	f	
8/84	8:00	Call to Glory(60) – DR	d	
12/84	8:00	Call to Glory(60) – DR	m	To:t-10
12/84	8:00	Hardcastle & McCormick(60) – CD	m	Fr:n-8
12/84	9:00	Film(120) – FI	s	
5/85	9:00	Film(120) – FI	f	
8/85	9:00	Film(120) – FI	s	
8/85	9:00	Film(120) – FI	f	
1/86	9:00	Film(120) – FI	s	

Date	Time	Title (min. if not 30) — Type	Action	From/To
5/86	8:00	Hardcastle & McCormick(60)—CD	m	To:w-9
6/86	8:00	Insiders(60)—CD	m	Fr:w-8-1/86
6/86	8:00	Insiders(60)—CD	c	
6/86	9:00	Film(120)—FI	f	
9/86	8:00	MacGyver(60)—SD	m	Fr:w-9
12/86	9:00	Film(120)—FI	s	
5/87	8:00	MacGyver(60)—SD	m	To:w-9
5/87	9:00	Film(120)—FI	f	
9/87	8:00	MacGyver(60)—SD	m	Fr:w-9
1/88	9:00	Film(120)—FI	s	
5/88	8:00	MacGyver(60)—SD	m	To:n-8
5/88	9:00	Film(120)—FI	f	

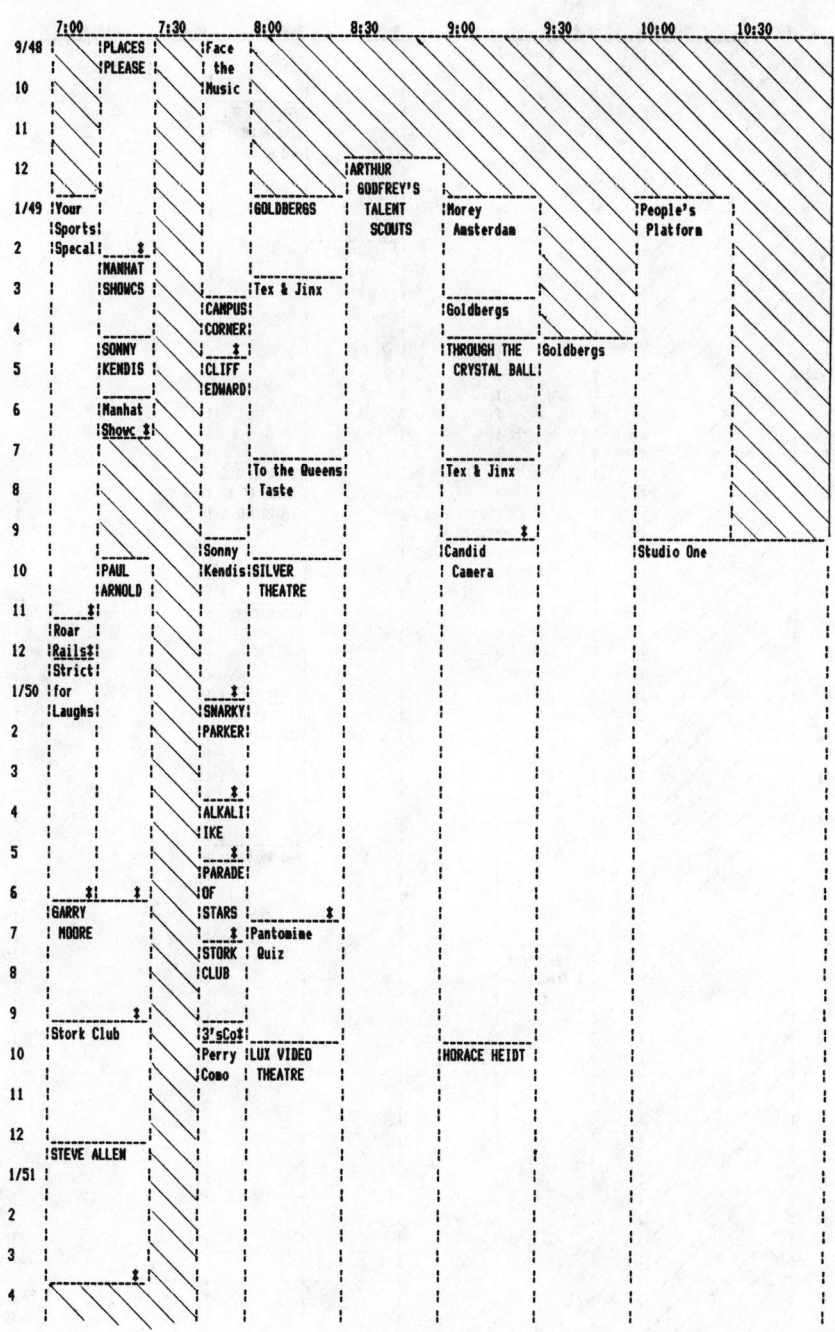

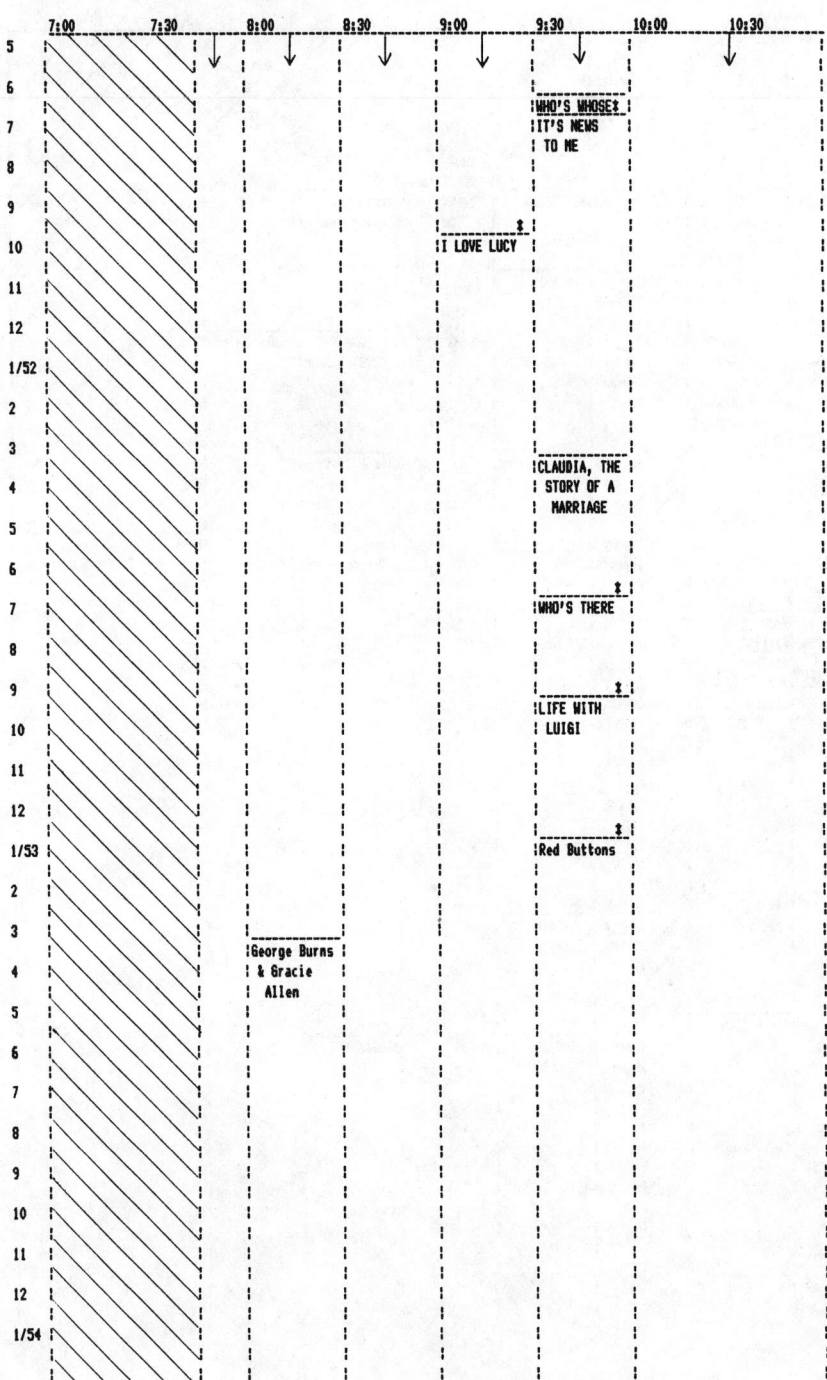

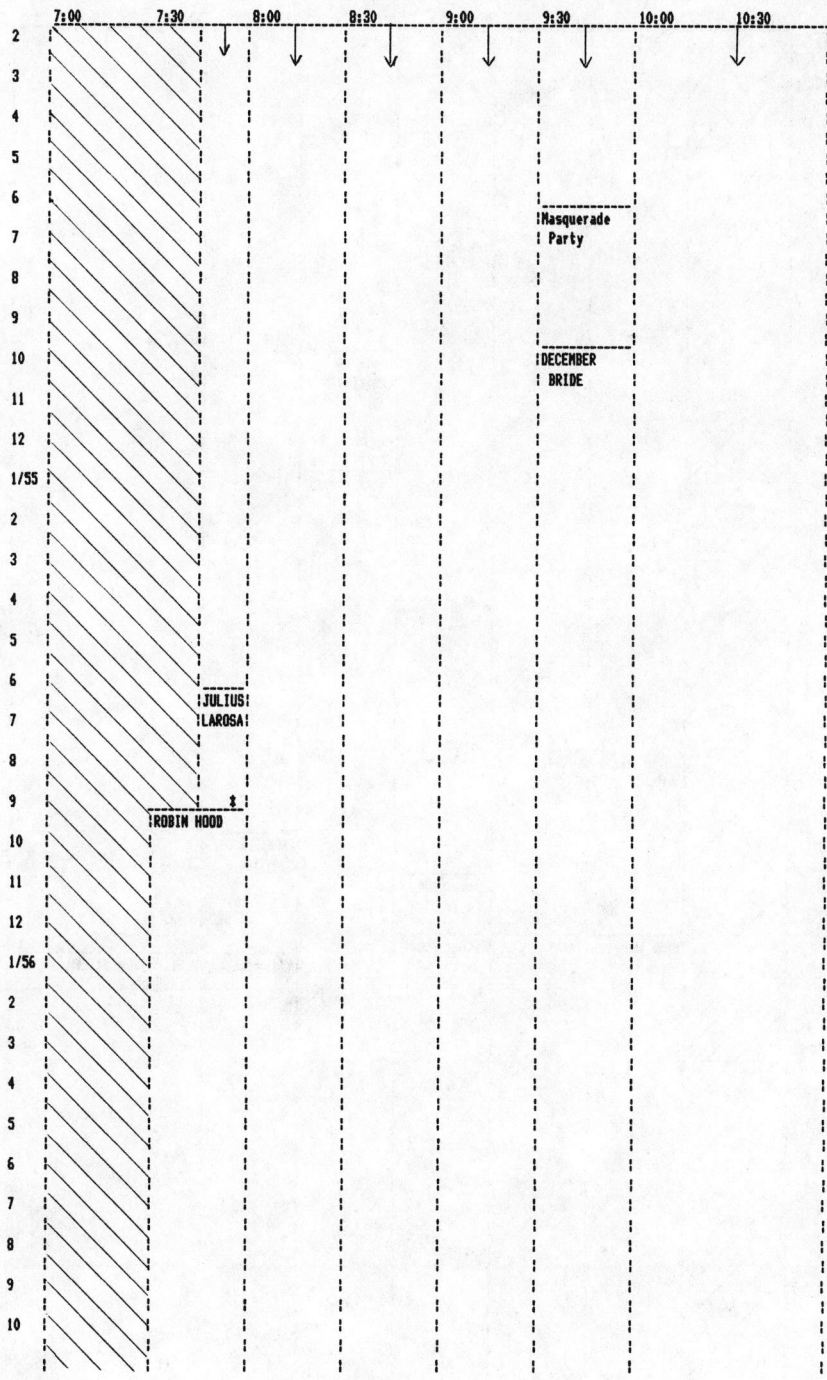

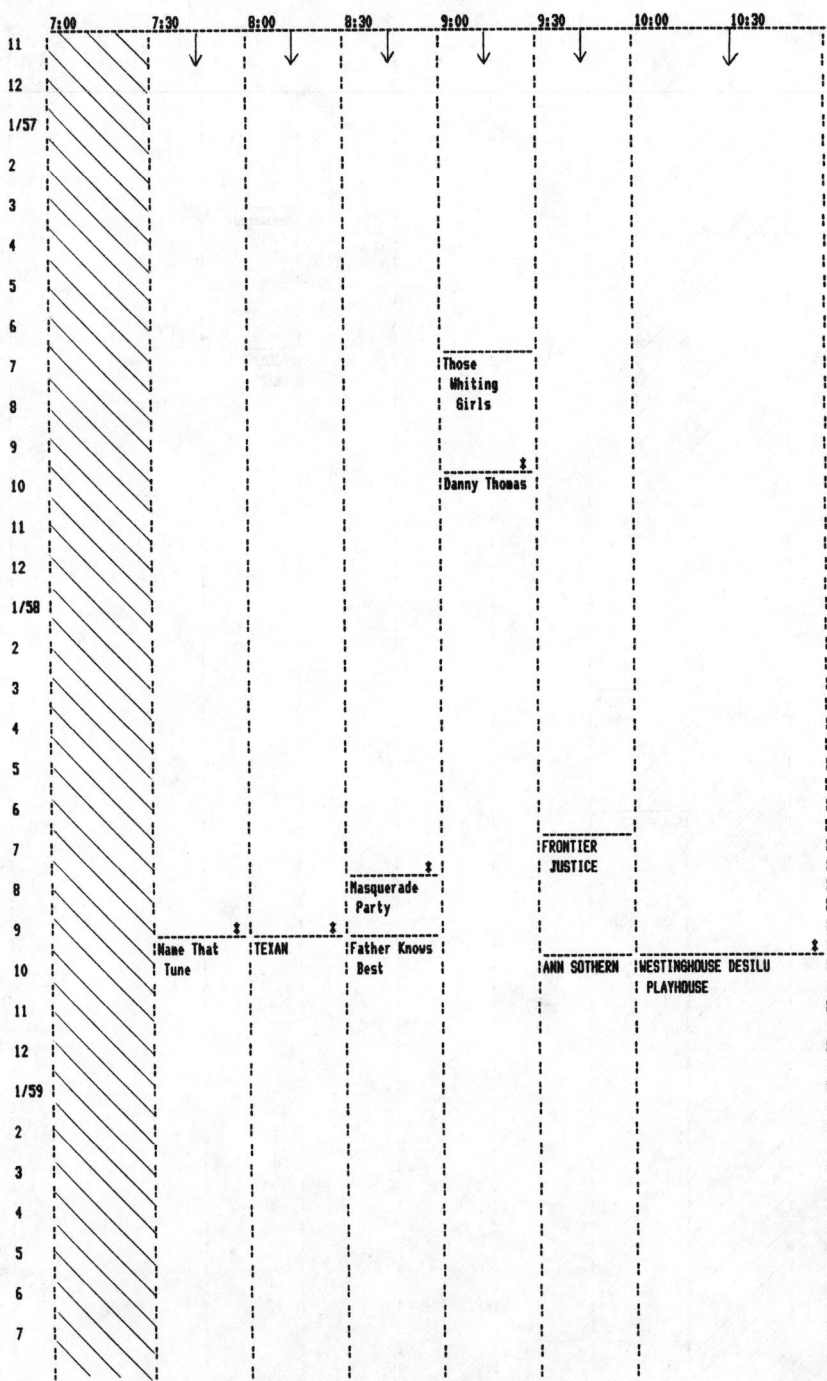

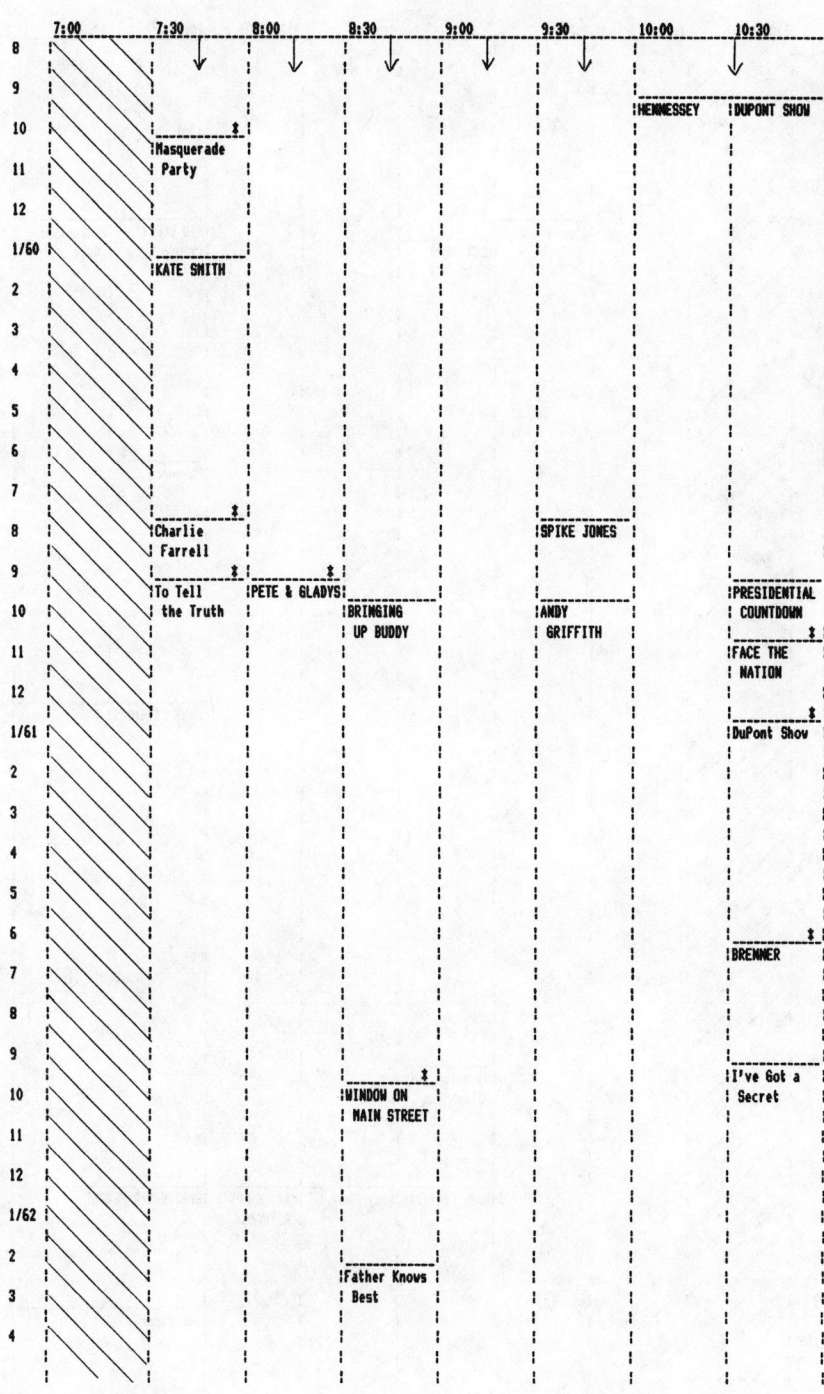

	7:00	7:30	8:00	8:30	9:00	9:30	10:00	10:30
8		↓	↓	↓	↓	↓	↓	
9							HENNESSEY	DUPONT SHOW
10		Masquerade						
11		Party						
12								
1/60		KATE SMITH						
2								
3								
4								
5								
6								
7								
8		Charlie				SPIKE JONES		
		Farrell						
9		To Tell	PETE & GLADYS					PRESIDENTIAL
10		the Truth		BRINGING		ANDY		COUNTDOWN
11				UP BUDDY		GRIFFITH		FACE THE
								NATION
12								
1/61								DuPont Show
2								
3								
4								
5								
6								BRENNER
7								
8								
9								I've Got a
10				WINDOW ON				Secret
11				MAIN STREET				
12								
1/62								
2								
3				Father Knows				
				Best				
4								

	7:00	7:30	8:00	8:30	9:00	9:30	10:00	10:30
5			↓	↓	↓	↓	↓	↓	↓
6								
7								
8								
9			I've Got a				NEW LORETTA	Pantomime
10			Secret	LUCY SHOW			YOUNG SHOW	Quiz
11								
12								
1/63								
2								
3								
4							Password	
5								
6								
7								
8								
9							EAST SIDE/WEST SIDE	
10								
11								
12								
1/64								
2								
3								
4								
5								
6				Vacation				
7				Playhouse				
8								
9				Andy Griffith	Lucy Show	MANY HAPPY	SLATTERY'S PEOPLE	
10						RETURNS		
11								
12							CBS Reports	
1/65								

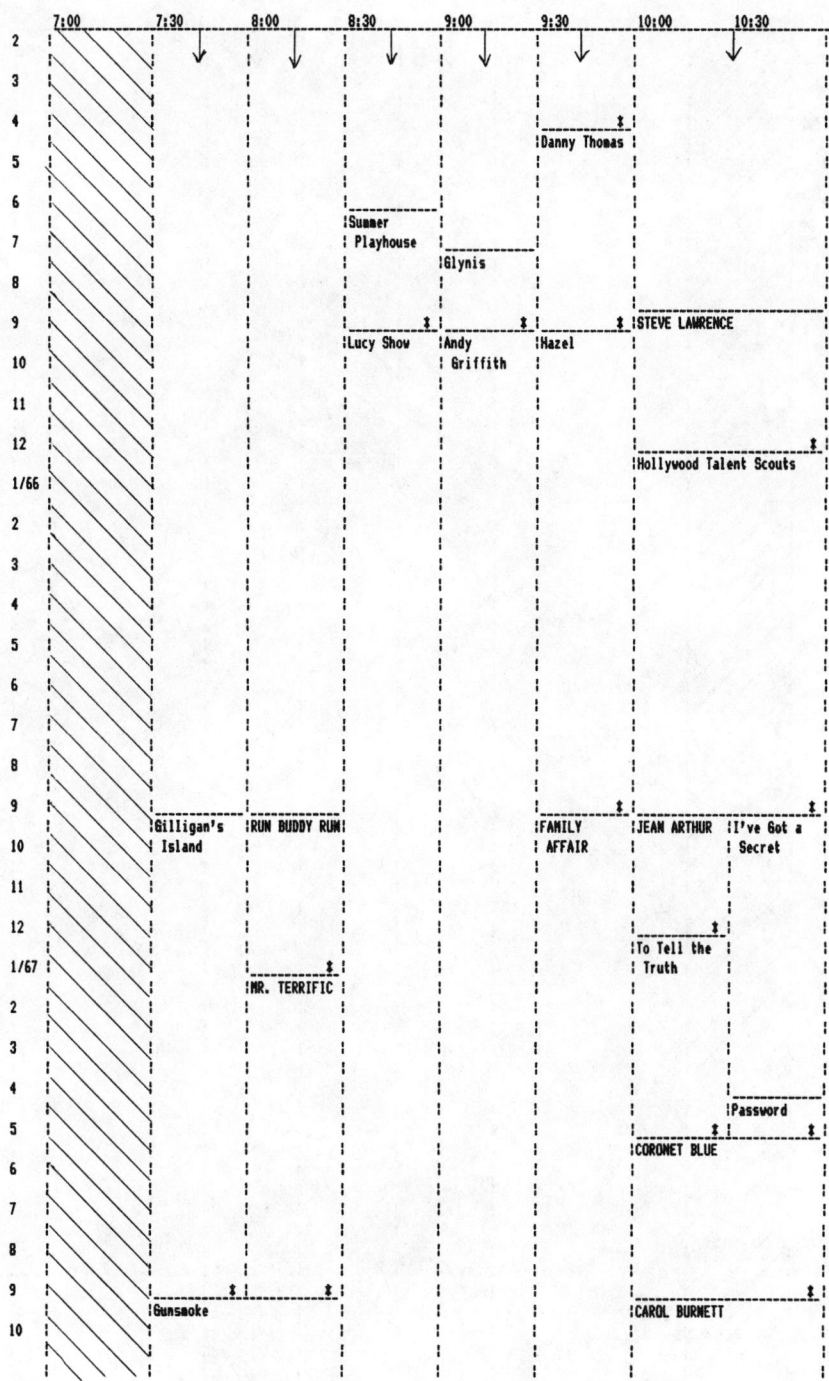

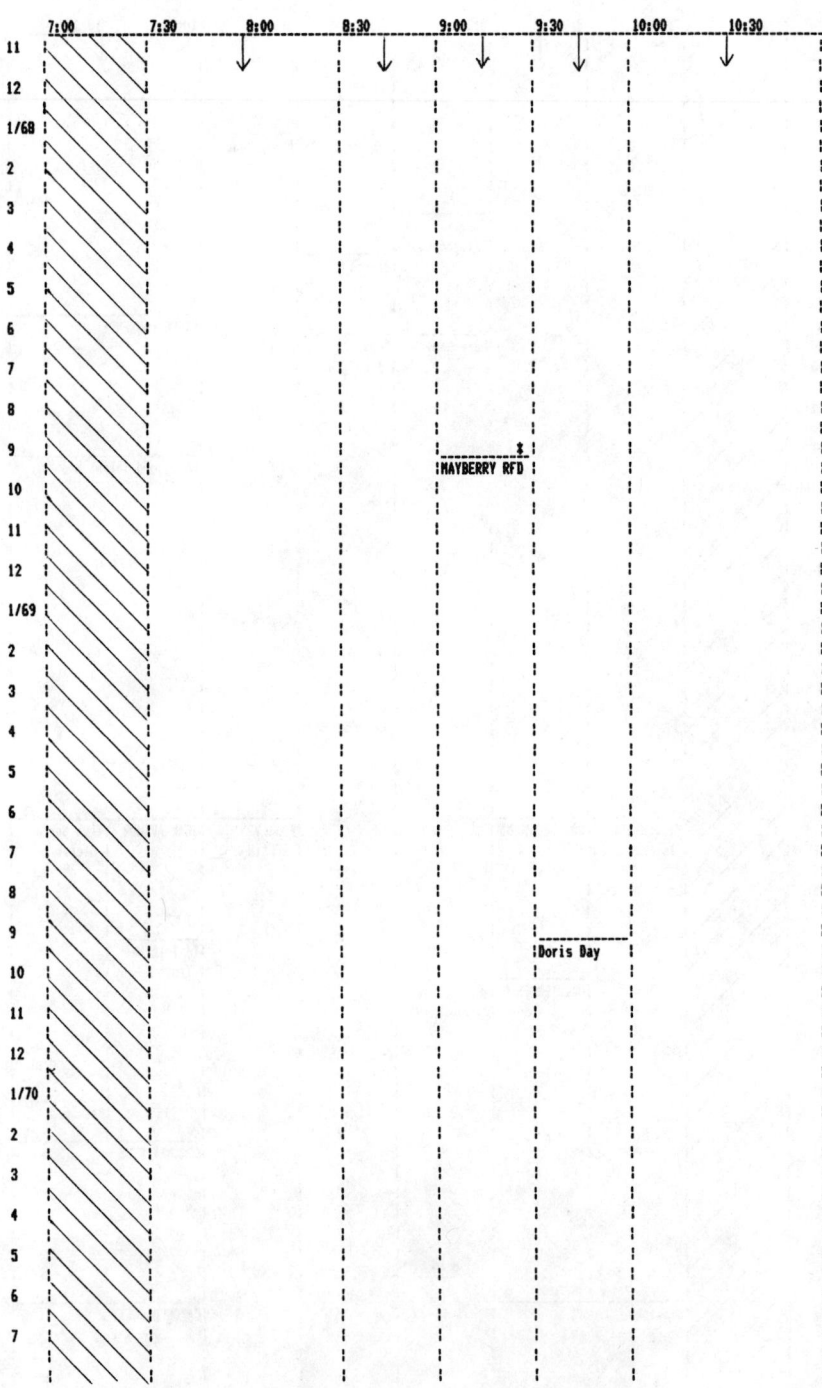

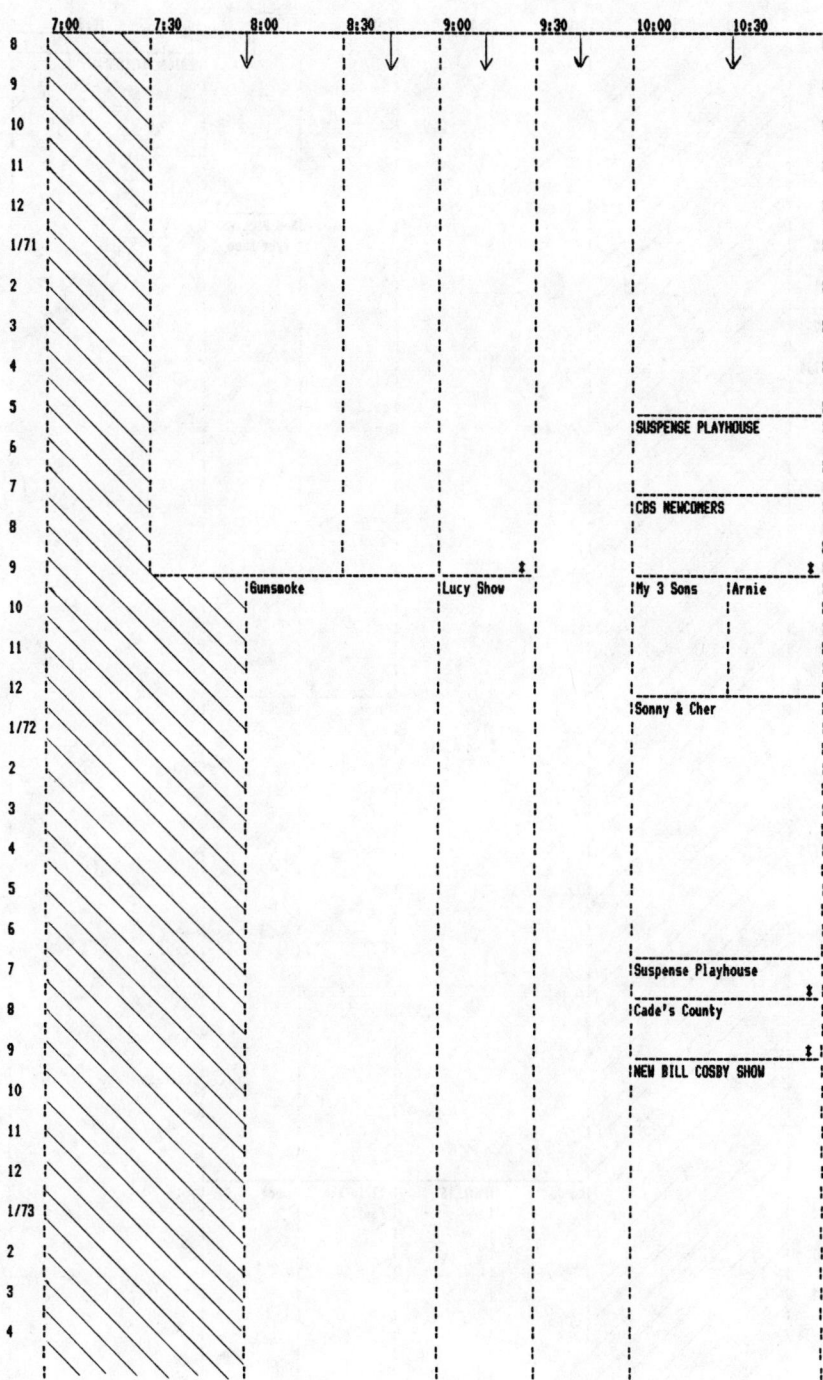

	7:00	7:30	8:00	8:30	9:00	9:30	10:00	10:30
			Gunsmoke		Lucy Show		My 3 Sons	Arnie
							Sonny & Cher	
							Suspense Playhouse	
							Cade's County	
							NEW BILL COSBY SHOW	
							SUSPENSE PLAYHOUSE	
							CBS NEWCOMERS	

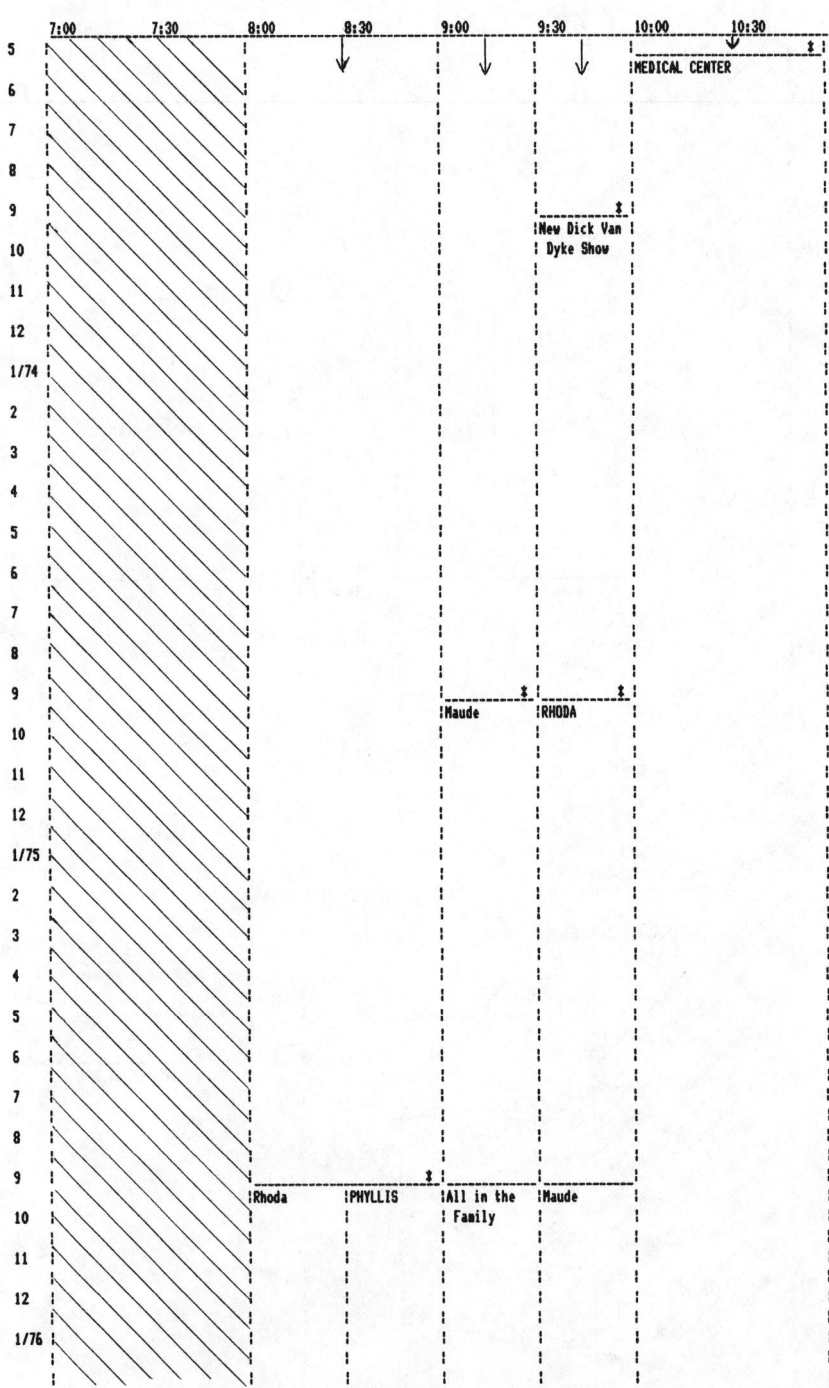

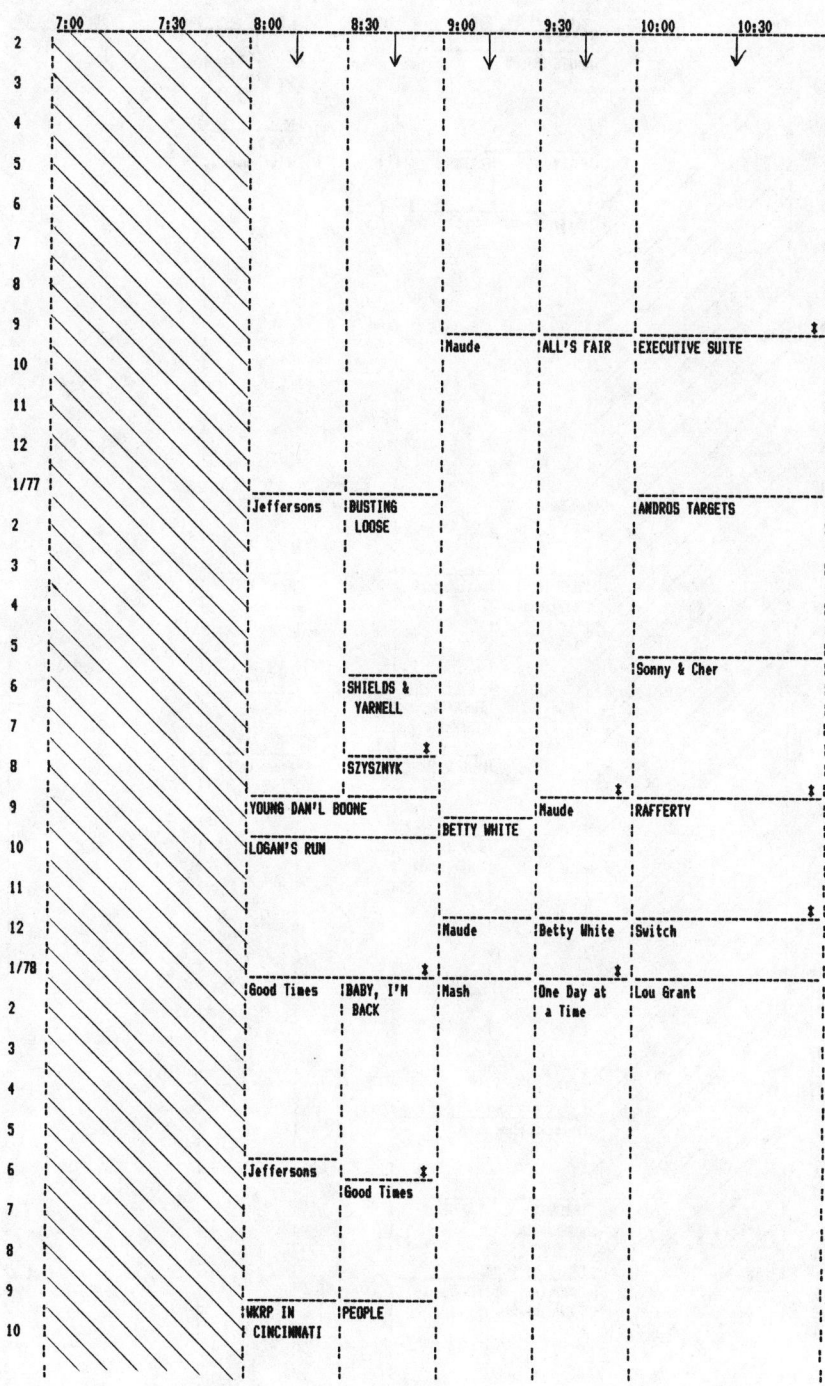

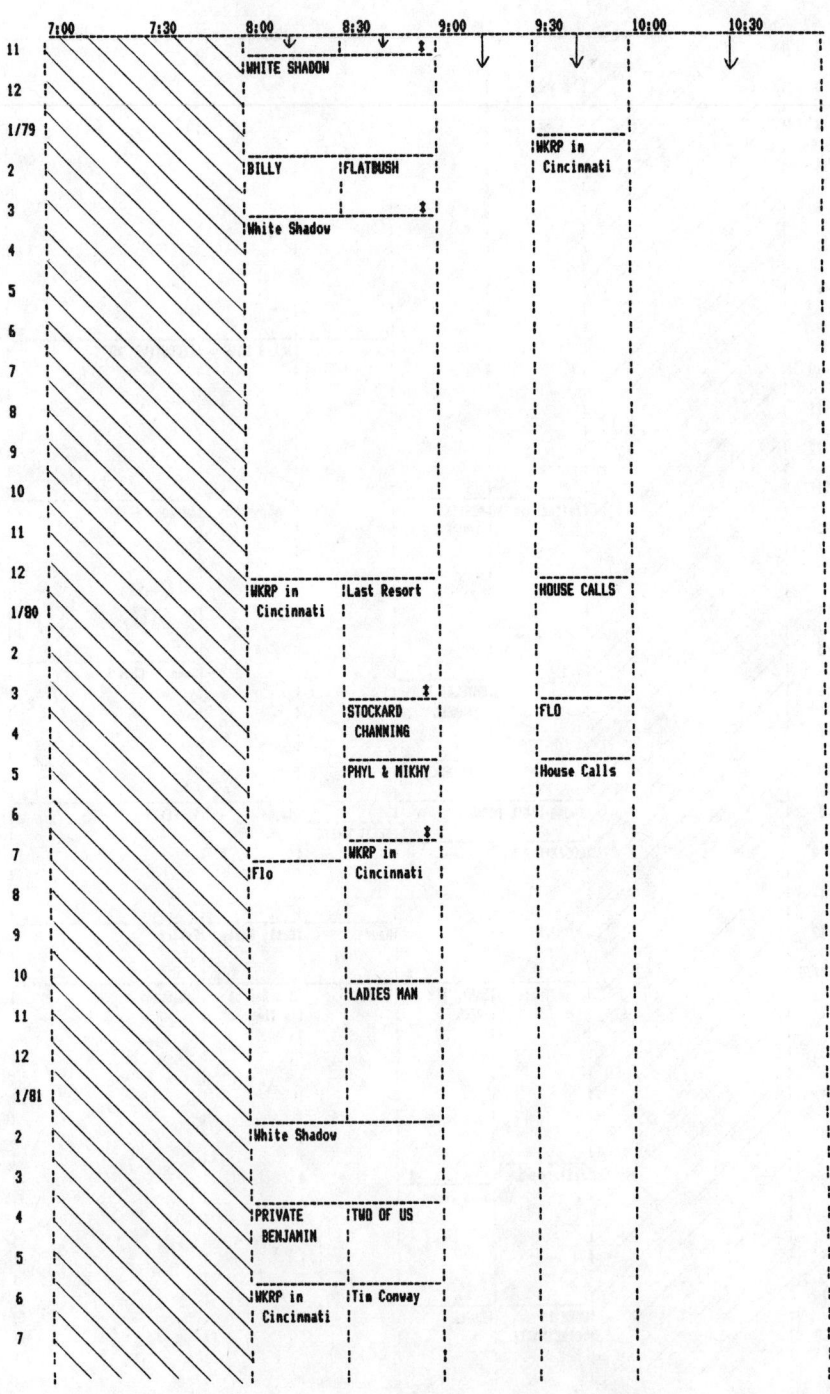

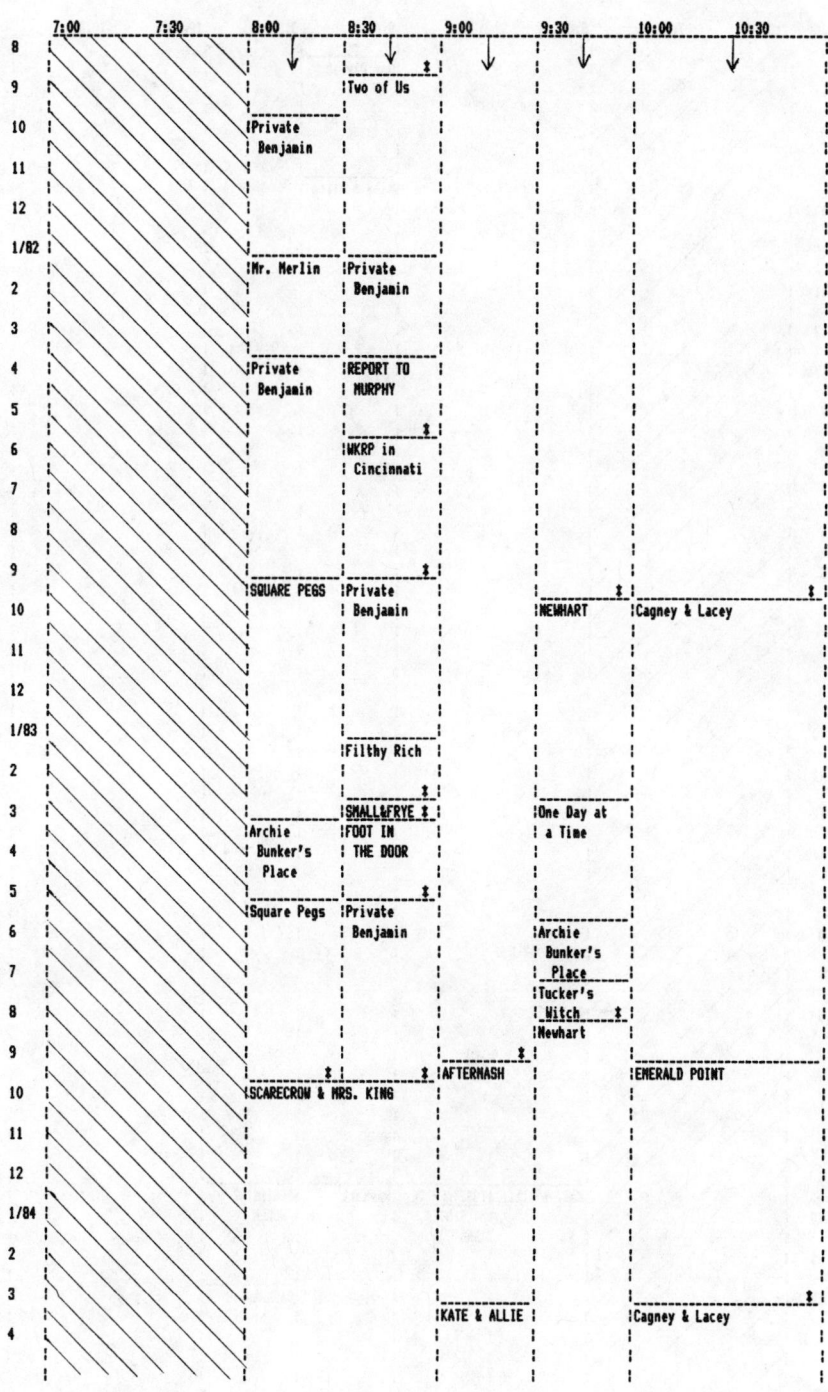

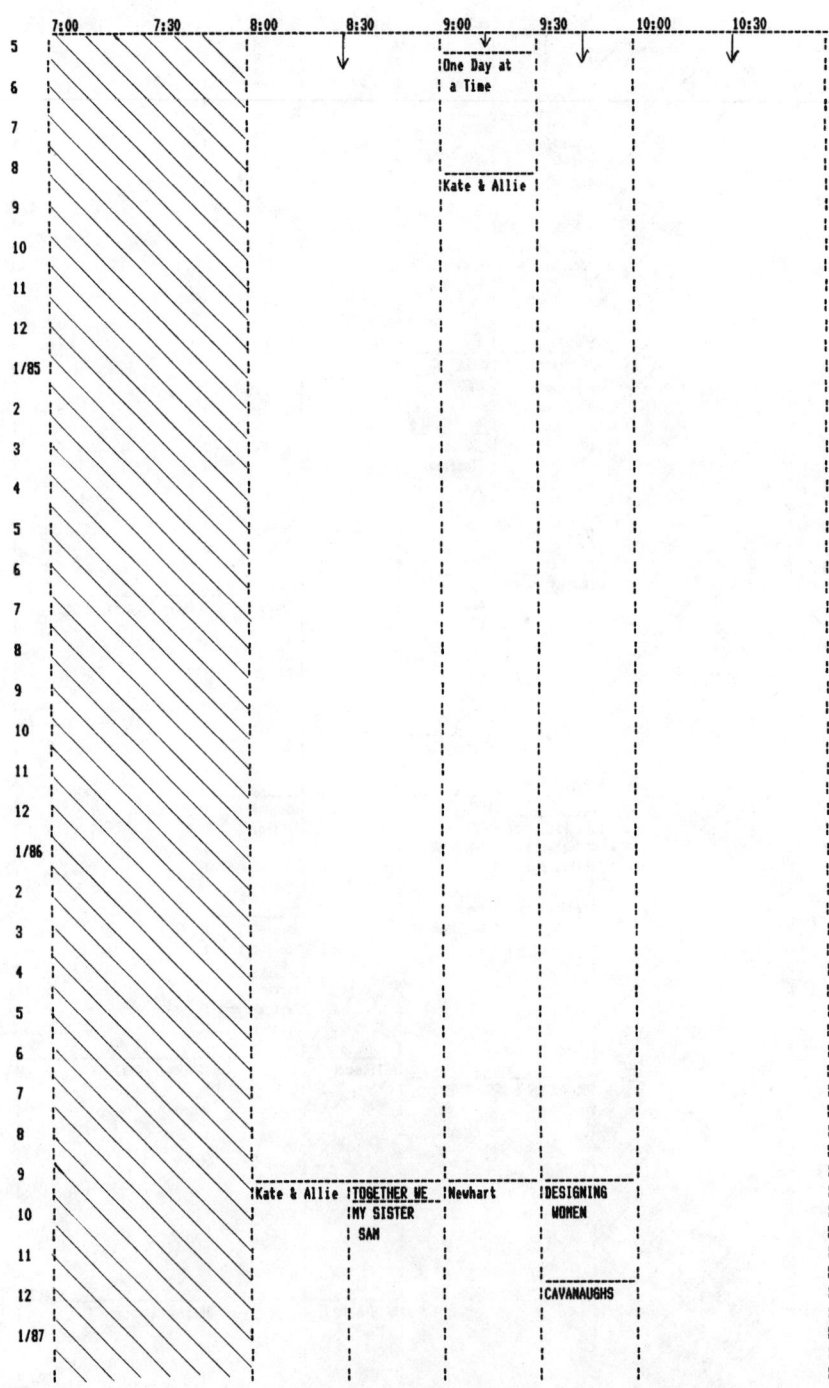

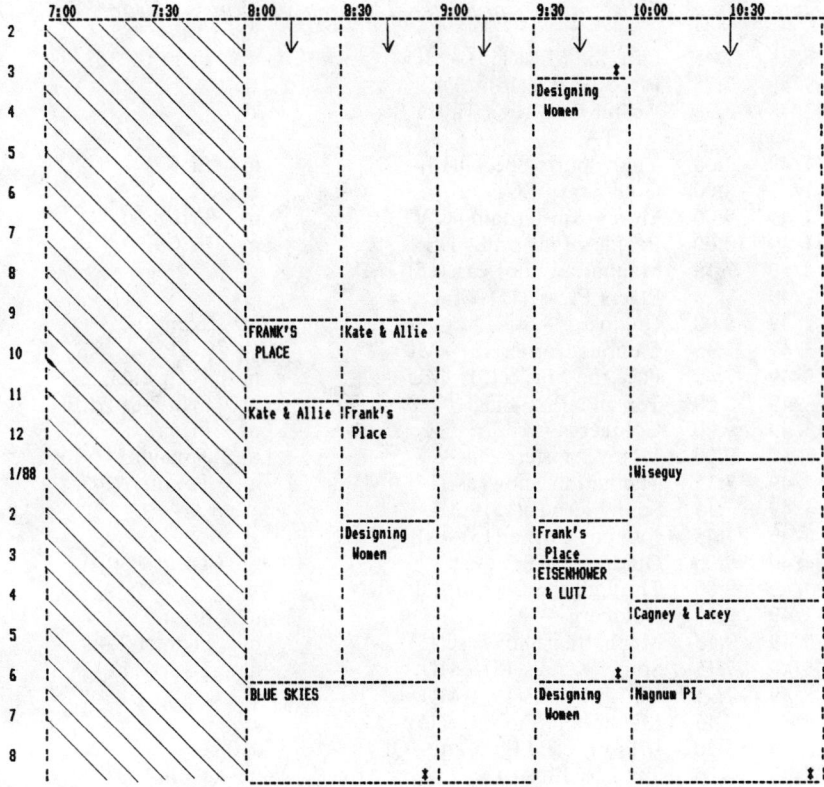

Date	Time	Title (min. if not 30) — Type	Action	From/To
8/48	7:45	Face the Music(15) — MU	m	Fr:m-f-7:15
9/48	7:15	Places Please(15) — TA	d	
12/48	8:30	Arthur Godfrey's Talent Scouts — TA	d	
1/49	7:00	Your Sports Special(15) — SN	m	Fr:f-7
1/49	8:00	Goldbergs — SC	d	
1/49	9:00	Morey Amsterdam — CV	m	Fr:f-8:30
1/49	10:00	People's Platform — DS	m	Fr:t-9:30
2/49	7:15	Manhattan Showcase(15) — MV	d	
2/49	7:15	Places Please(15) — TA	c	
2/49	8:00	Goldbergs — SC	m	To:m-9
3/49	7:45	Campus Corner(15) — MU	d	
3/49	7:45	Face the Music(15) — MU	m	To:tr-7:45
3/49	8:00	Tex and Jinx — TK	m	Fr:n-8-8/47(n)
3/49	9:00	Goldbergs — SC	m	Fr:m-8
3/49	9:00	Morey Amsterdam — CV	m	To:r-9(d)
4/49	7:15	Manhattan Showcase(15) — MV	m	To:mtrf-7:45
4/49	7:15	Sonny Kendis(15) — MU	d	
4/49	7:45	Campus Corner(15) — MU	c	
4/49	9:00	Goldbergs — SC	m	To:m-9:30
4/49	9:00	Through the Crystal Ball — DN	d	
4/49	9:30	Goldbergs — SC	m	Fr:m-9
5/49	7:15	Manhattan Showcase(15) — MV	m	Fr:mtrf-7:45
5/49	7:15	Sonny Kendis(15) — MU	m	To:tr-7:45
5/49	7:45	Cliff Edwards(15) — MU	d	
6/49	7:15	Manhattan Showcase(15) — MV	c	
6/49	8:30	It Pays to Be Ignorant — QU	d*	
7/49	8:00	Tex and Jinx — TK	m	To:m-9
7/49	8:00	To the Queen's Taste — CK	m	Fr:r-9:30
7/49	9:00	Tex and Jinx — TK	m	Fr:m-8
7/49	9:00	Through the Crystal Ball — DN	c	
9/49	7:45	Cliff Edwards(15) — MU	c	
9/49	7:45	Sonny Kendis(10) — MU	m	Fr:tr-7:45
9/49	7:55	Ruthie on the Telephone(5) — CY	d	
9/49	8:00	To the Queen's Taste — CK	m	To:r-7
9/49	8:30	It Pays to Be Ignorant — QU	m*	To:r-8-7/51(n)
9/49	9:00	Candid Camera — CY	m	Fr:r-9(n)
9/49	9:00	Tex and Jinx — TK	c	
9/49	10:00	People's Platform — DS	m	To:f-10
9/49	10:00	Studio One(60) — DA	m	Fr:w-10
10/49	7:15	Paul Arnold(15) — MU	d	
10/49	8:00	Silver Theater — DA	d	
11/49	7:00	Roar of the Rails(15) — AD	m	Fr:t-7-12/48
11/49	7:00	Your Sports Special(15) — SN	c	
11/49	7:55	Herb Shriner(5) — CV	d	
11/49	7:55	Ruthie on the Telephone(5) — CY	c	
12/49	7:00	Roar of the Rails(15) — AD	c	
12/49	7:00	Strictly for Laughs(15) — MU	m	Fr:twf-7
1/50	7:45	Life with Snarky Parker(15) — KV	d	
1/50	7:45	Sonny Kendis(10) — MU	c	

Date	Time	Title (min. if not 30) — Type	Action	From/To
2/50	7:55	Herb Shriner(5) — CV	c	
3/50	7:45	Life with Snarky Parker(15) — KV	c	
4/50	7:45	Alkali Ike(15) — CY	d	
5/50	7:45	Alkali Ike(15) — CY	c	
5/50	7:45	Popsicle Parade of Stars(15) — VY	d	
6/50	7:00	Garry Moore — VY	d	
6/50	7:00	Strictly for Laughs(15) — MU	c	
6/50	7:15	Paul Arnold(15) — MU	c	
6/50	8:00	Silver Theater — DA	c	
7/50	7:45	Popsicle Parade of Stars(15) — VY	c	
7/50	7:45	Stork Club(15) — TK	d	
7/50	8:00	Pantomime Quiz — QU	m	Fr:m-9:30
7/50	8:30	Prize Performance — TA	d*	
7/50	9:30	Pantomime Quiz — QU	d*	
7/50	9:30	Pantomime Quiz — QU	m*	To:m-8
8/50	8:30	Prize Performance — TA	m*	To:t-10
8/50	9:30	We Take Your Word — QU	m*	Fr:f-8
9/50	7:00	Garry Moore — VY	c	
9/50	7:00	Stork Club — TK	m	Fr:mwf-7:45
9/50	7:45	Stork Club(15) — TK	m	To:m-f-7
9/50	7:45	Three's Company(15) — MU	m	Fr:tr-7:45
9/50	7:45	Three's Company(15) — MU	c	
9/50	8:00	Pantomime Quiz — QU	m	To:m-8-7/51
9/50	9:00	Candid Camera — CY	m	To:w-10-7/53(n)
9/50	9:30	We Take Your Word — QU	m	To:t-10:30
10/50	7:45	Perry Como(15) — MV	m	Fr:n-8-6/50(n)
10/50	8:00	Lux Video Theatre — DA	d	
10/50	9:00	Horace Heidt — TA	d	
12/50	7:00	Steve Allen — CV	d	
12/50	7:00	Stork Club — TK	m	To:trs-7:45
3/51	7:00	Steve Allen — CV	c	
6/51	9:30	Goldbergs — SC	m	To:mwf-7:15-2/52 (n)
6/51	9:30	Who's Whose — QU	d	
6/51	9:30	Who's Whose — QU	c	
7/51	7:45	TV's Top Tunes(15) — MU	d*	
7/51	8:00	Pantomime Quiz — QU	m*	Fr:m-8-9/50
7/51	9:30	It's News to Me — QU	d	
8/51	7:45	TV's Top Tunes(15) — MU	m*	To:mwf-7:45-6/53
8/51	8:00	Pantomime Quiz — QU	m*	To:w-10:30-1/52(n)
9/51	9:00	Horace Heidt — TA	c	
10/51	9:00	I Love Lucy — SC	d	
3/52	9:30	Claudia, the Story of a Marriage — DR	d	
3/52	9:30	It's News to Me — QU	m	To:f-9:30
6/52	9:00	My Little Margie — SC	d*	
6/52	9:30	Claudia, the Story of a Marriage — DR	c	
7/52	7:45	Eddy Arnold(15) — MV	d*	
7/52	9:30	Who's There — QU	d	

Date	Time	Title (min. if not 30) — Type	Action	From/To
8/52	7:45	Eddy Arnold(15) — MV	m*	To:tr-7:30-7/53(n)
9/52	9:00	My Little Margie — SC	m*	To:s-7:30(n)
9/52	9:30	Life with Luigi — SC	d	
9/52	9:30	Who's There — QU	c	
12/52	9:30	Life with Luigi — SC	c	
1/53	9:30	Red Buttons — CV	m	Fr:t-8:30
3/53	8:00	George Burns & Gracie Allen — SC	m	Fr:r-8
3/53	8:00	Lux Video Theatre — DA	m	To:r-9
6/53	7:45	TV's Top Tunes(15) — MU	m*	Fr:mwf-7:45-8/51
6/53	9:30	Masquerade Party — QU	m*	Fr:m-8-8/52(n)
7/53	9:00	Racket Squad — CD	m*	Fr:r-10:30
8/53	7:45	TV's Top Tunes(15) — MU	m*	To:mwf-7:45-6/54
9/53	9:00	Racket Squad — CD	c*	
9/53	9:30	Masquerade Party — QU	m*	To:m-9:30-6/54
6/54	7:45	TV's Top Tunes(15) — MU	m*	Fr:mwf-7:45-8/53
6/54	9:30	Masquerade Party — QU	m	Fr:m-9:30-9/53
6/54	9:30	Red Buttons — CV	m	To:f-8-10/54(n)
7/54	9:00	Public Defender — LD	m*	Fr:r-10
8/54	7:45	TV's Top Tunes(15) — MU	m*	To:s-10-7/55
9/54	9:00	Public Defender — LD	m*	To:r-10
9/54	9:30	Masquerade Party — QU	m	To:w-9(a)
10/54	9:30	December Bride — SC	d	
6/55	7:45	Julius LaRosa(15) — MU	d	
6/55	7:45	Perry Como(15) — MV	m	To:s-8-9/55(n)
6/55	9:30	Ethel and Albert — SC	m*	Fr:s-7:30-12/54(n)
7/55	9:00	Those Whiting Girls — SC	d*	
9/55	7:30	Adventures of Robin Hood — AD	d	
9/55	7:45	Julius LaRosa(15) — MU	c	
9/55	9:00	Those Whiting Girls — SC	m*	To:m-9-7/57
9/55	9:30	Ethel and Albert — SC	m*	To:f-10(a)
7/56	9:00	Charlie Farrell — SC	d*	
7/56	9:30	Vic Damone — MV	d*	
9/56	9:00	Charlie Farrell — SC	m*	To:m-8-7/57(n)
9/56	9:30	Vic Damone — MV	m*	To:w-8-7/57
6/57	9:00	I Love Lucy — SC	m	To:w-7:30-9/57
7/57	9:00	Those Whiting Girls — SC	m	Fr:m-9-9/55
7/57	9:30	Richard Diamond, Pvt. Detective — CD	d*	
9/57	9:00	Those Whiting Girls — SC	c	
9/57	9:30	Richard Diamond, Pvt. Detective — CD	m*	To:r-8-1/58
10/57	9:00	Danny Thomas — SC	m	Fr:r-9-7/57(a)
6/58	9:30	December Bride — SC	m	To:r-8-10/58
7/58	8:30	Arthur Godfrey's Talent Scouts — TA	c	
7/58	9:00	I Love Lucy — SC	m*	Fr:w-7:30-5/58
7/58	9:00	Frontier Justice — WA	d	
8/58	8:30	Masquerade Party — QU	m	Fr:w-8-9/57(n)
9/58	7:30	Adventures of Robin Hood — AD	c	
9/58	7:30	Name That Tune — QU	m	Fr:t-7:30
9/58	8:00	George Burns & Gracie Allen — SC	c	

Date	Time	Title (min. if not 30) – Type	Action	From/To
9/58	8:00	The Texan – WE	d	
9/58	8:30	Father Knows Best – SC	m	Fr:w-8:30(n)
9/58	8:30	Masquerade Party – QU	m	To:r-10:30(n)
9/58	9:00	I Love Lucy – SC	m*	To:r-7:30
9/58	9:30	Frontier Justice – WA	m	To:m-9-7/59
9/58	10:00	Studio One(60) – DA	c	
10/58	9:30	Ann Sothern – SC	d	
10/58	10:00	Westinghouse Desilu Playhouse(60) – DA	d	
7/59	9:00	Frontier Justice – WA	m*	Fr:m-9:30-9/58
7/59	9:30	Joseph Cotten – DA	m*	Fr:s-10:30-8/58(n)
9/59	9:00	Frontier Justice – WA	m*	To:r-8:30-8/61
9/59	9:30	Joseph Cotten – DA	c*	
9/59	10:00	Hennesey – SC	d	
9/59	10:00	Westinghouse Desilu Playhouse(60) – DA	m	To:f-9
9/59	10:30	DuPont Show with June Allyson – DA	d	
10/59	7:30	Masquerade Party – QU	m	Fr:r-10:30(n)
10/59	7:30	Name that Tune – QU	c	
1/60	7:30	Kate Smith – MV	d	
1/60	7:30	Masquerade Party – QU	m	To:f-9:30(n)
7/60	7:30	Kate Smith – MV	c	
7/60	9:30	Ann Sothern – SC	m	To:r-9:30-10/60
8/60	7:30	Charlie Farrell – SC	m	Fr:m-8-9/57(n)
8/60	9:00	Celebrity Talent Scouts – TA	d*	
8/60	9:30	Spike Jones – CV	d	
8/60	10:00	New Comedy Showcase – CA	d*	
9/60	7:30	Charlie Farrell – SC	c	
9/60	7:30	To Tell the Truth – QU	m	Fr:r-10:30
9/60	8:00	Pete and Gladys – SC	d	
9/60	8:00	The Texan – WE	c	
9/60	8:30	Father Knows Best – SC	m	To:t-8
9/60	9:00	Celebrity Talent Scouts – TA	c*	
9/60	9:30	Spike Jones – CV	m	To:m-9-7/61
9/60	10:00	New Comedy Showcase – CA	c*	
9/60	10:30	DuPont Show with June Allyson – DA	m	To:r-10:30
9/60	10:30	Presidential Countdown – PO	d	
10/60	8:30	Bringing Up Buddy – SC	d	
10/60	9:30	Andy Griffith – SC	d	
10/60	10:30	Presidential Countdown – PO	c	
11/60	10:30	Face the Nation – IV	d	
12/60	10:30	Face the Nation – IV	c	
1/61	10:30	DuPont Show with June Allyson – DA	m	Fr:r-10:30
6/61	10:30	Brenner – CD	d	
6/61	10:30	DuPont Show with June Allyson – DA	c	
7/61	9:00	Spike Jones – CV	m*	Fr:m-9:30-9/60

Date	Time	Title (min. if not 30) — Type	Action	From/To
7/61	9:30	Ann Sothern — SC	m*	Fr:r-7:30-3/61
7/61	10:00	Glenn Miller Time — MU	d*	
9/61	8:30	Bringing Up Buddy — SC	c	
9/61	9:00	Spike Jones — CV	c*	
9/61	9:30	Ann Sothern — SC	c*	
9/61	10:00	Glenn Miller Time — MU	c*	
9/61	10:30	Brenner — CD	m	To:r-9-6/62
9/61	10:30	I've Got a Secret — QU	m	Fr:w-9:30
10/61	8:30	Window on Main Street — SC	d	
2/62	8:30	Father Knows Best — SC	m	Fr:w-8
2/62	8:30	Window on Main Street — SC	m	To:w-8
7/62	9:00	Lucy-Desi Comedy Hour(60) — SC	d*	
9/62	8:00	I've Got a Secret — QU	m	Fr:m-10:30
9/62	8:00	Pete and Gladys — SC	c	
9/62	8:30	Father Knows Best — SC	m	To:n-7(a)
9/62	9:00	Lucy-Desi Comedy Hour(60) — SC	m*	To:s-7:30-6/63
9/62	10:00	Hennesey — SC	c	
9/62	10:00	New Loretta Young Show — DR	d	
9/62	10:30	I've Got a Secret — QU	m	To:m-8
9/62	10:30	Pantomime Quiz — QU	m	Fr:m-9-9/59(a)
10/62	8:30	Lucy Show — SC	d	
3/63	10:00	New Loretta Young Show — DR	c	
3/63	10:00	Password — QU	m	Fr:t-8-9/62
7/63	8:30	Vacation Playhouse — VS	d*	
7/63	9:00	Comedy Hour Special(60) — CV	d*	
9/63	8:30	Vacation Playhouse — VS	m*	To:m-8:30-6/64
9/63	9:00	Comedy Hour Special(60) — CV	c*	
9/63	10:00	East Side/West Side(60) — DR	d	
9/63	10:00	Password — QU	m	To:r-7:30
9/63	10:30	Pantomime Quiz — QU	c	
6/64	8:30	Lucy Show — SC	m	To:m-9-9/64
6/64	8:30	Vacation Playhouse — VS	m	Fr:m-8:30-9/63
9/64	8:30	Andy Griffith — SC	m	Fr:m-9:30
9/64	8:30	Vacation Playhouse — VS	m	To:f-9:30-6/65
9/64	9:00	Danny Thomas — SC	m	To:m-9:30-4/65
9/64	9:00	Lucy Show — SC	m	Fr:m-8:30-6/64
9/64	9:30	Andy Griffith — SC	m	To:m-8:30
9/64	9:30	Many Happy Returns — SC	d	
9/64	10:00	East Side/West Side(60) — DR	c	
9/64	10:00	Slattery's People(60) — DR	d	
12/64	10:00	CBS Reports(60) — DO	m	Fr:w-7:30
12/64	10:00	Slattery's People(60) — DR	m	To:f-10
4/65	9:30	Danny Thomas — SC	m	Fr:m-9-9/64
4/65	9:30	Many Happy Returns — SC	c	
6/65	8:30	Andy Griffith — SC	m	To:m-9-9/65
6/65	8:30	Summer Playhouse — VS	m	Fr:s-9:30-9/64
7/65	9:00	Glynis — SC	m	Fr:w-8:30-12/63
7/65	9:00	Lucy Show — SC	m	To:m-8:30-9/65
8/65	10:00	CBS Reports(60) — DO	m	To:t-10
9/65	8:30	Lucy Show — SC	m	Fr:m-9-7/65

Date	*Time*	*Title (min. if not 30) – Type*	*Action*	*From/To*
9/65	8:30	Summer Playhouse – VS	c	
9/65	9:00	Andy Griffith – SC	m	Fr:m-8:30-6/65
9/65	9:00	Glynis – SC	c	
9/65	9:30	Danny Thomas – SC	c	
9/65	9:30	Hazel – SC	m	Fr:r-9:30(n)
9/65	10:00	Steve Lawrence(60) – MV	d	
12/65	10:00	Hollywood Talent Scouts(60) – VY	m	Fr:t-8:30-9/65
12/65	10:00	Steve Lawrence(60) – MV	c	
7/66	8:30	Vacation Playhouse – VS	m*	Fr:f-9:30-9/65
9/66	7:30	Gilligan's Island – SC	m	Fr:r-8
9/66	7:30	To Tell the Truth – QU	m	To:m-10-12/66
9/66	8:00	I've Got a Secret – QU	m	To:m-10:30
9/66	8:00	Run Buddy Run – SC	d	
9/66	8:30	Vacation Playhouse – VS	m*	To:m-8:30-7/67
9/66	9:30	Family Affair – SC	d	
9/66	9:30	Hazel – SC	c	
9/66	10:00	Hollywood Talent Scouts(60) – VY	c	
9/66	10:00	Jean Arthur – SC	d	
9/66	10:30	I've Got a Secret – QU	m	Fr:m-8
12/66	10:00	Jean Arthur – SC	c	
12/66	10:00	To Tell the Truth – QU	m	Fr:m-7:30-9/66
1/67	8:00	Mr. Terrific – SC	d	
1/67	8:00	Run Buddy Run – SC	c	
4/67	10:30	I've Got a Secret – QU	m	To:t-8-6/76
4/67	10:30	Password – QU	m	Fr:r-9-9/65
5/67	10:00	Coronet Blue(60) – MY	d	
5/67	10:00	To Tell the Truth – QU	c	
5/67	10:30	Password – QU	c	
7/67	8:30	Vacation Playhouse – VS	m*	Fr:m-8:30-9/66
8/67	8:30	Vacation Playhouse – VS	c*	
9/67	7:30	Gilligan's Island – SC	c	
9/67	7:30	Gunsmoke(60) – WE	m	Fr:s-10
9/67	8:00	Mr. Terrific – SC	c	
9/67	10:00	Carol Burnett(60) – CV	d	
9/67	10:00	Coronet Blue(60) – MY	c	
7/68	10:00	Premiere(60) – DA	d*	
9/68	9:00	Andy Griffith – SC	c	
9/68	9:00	Mayberry RFD – SC	d	
9/68	10:00	Premiere(60) – DA	c*	
6/69	10:00	Jimmie Rodgers(60) – MV	d*	
9/69	9:30	Doris Day – SC	m	Fr:t-9:30
9/69	9:30	Family Affair – SC	m	To:r-7:30
9/69	10:00	Jimmie Rodgers(60) – MV	c*	
7/70	10:00	Wild Wild West(60) – WE	m*	Fr:f-7:30-9/69
9/70	10:00	Wild Wild West(60) – WE	c*	
5/71	10:00	Carol Burnett(60) – CV	m	To:w-8-9/71
5/71	10:00	Suspense Playhouse(60) – SA	d	
7/71	10:00	CBS Newcomers(60) – VY	c	
7/71	10:00	Suspense Playhouse(60) – SA	m	To:m-10-7/72
9/71	7:30	Gunsmoke(60) – WE	m	To:m-8

Date	Time	Title (min. if not 30) – Type	Action	From/To
9/71	8:00	Gunsmoke(60) – WE	m	Fr:m-7:30
9/71	8:30	Lucy Show – SC	m	To:m-9
9/71	9:00	Lucy Show – SC	m	Fr:m-8:30
9/71	9:00	Mayberry RFD – SC	c	
9/71	10:00	CBS Newcomers(60) – VY	c	
9/71	10:00	My Three Sons – SC	m	Fr:s-8:30
9/71	10:30	Arnie – SC	m	Fr:s-9
12/71	10:00	My Three Sons – SC	m	To:r-8:30
12/71	10:00	Sonny and Cher Comedy Hour(60) – MV	m	Fr:n-8:30-9/71
12/71	10:30	Arnie – SC	m	To:s-9:30
6/72	10:00	Sonny and Cher Comedy Hour(60) – MV	m	To:f-8-9/72
7/72	10:00	Suspense Playhouse(60) – SA	m	Fr:m-10-7/71
7/72	10:00	Suspense Playhouse(60) – SA	c	
8/72	10:00	Cade's County(60) – CD	m	Fr:n-9:30
9/72	10:00	Cade's County(60) – CD	c	
9/72	10:00	New Bill Cosby Show(60) – CV	d	
5/73	10:00	Medical Center(60) – MD	m	Fr:w-9
5/73	10:00	New Bill Cosby Show(60) – CV	c	
9/73	9:30	Doris Day – SC	c	
9/73	9:30	New Dick Van Dyke Show – SC	m	Fr:n-7:30
9/74	9:00	Lucy Show – SC	c	
9/74	9:00	Maude – SC	m	Fr:t-8
9/74	9:30	New Dick Van Dyke Show – SC	c	
9/74	9:30	Rhoda – SC	d	
9/75	8:00	Gunsmoke(60) – WE	c	
9/75	8:00	Rhoda – SC	m	Fr:m-9:30
9/75	8:30	Phyllis – SC	d	
9/75	9:00	All in the Family – SC	m	Fr:s-8
9/75	9:00	Maude – SC	m	To:m-9:30
9/75	9:30	Maude – SC	m	Fr:m-9
9/75	9:30	Rhoda – SC	m	To:m-8
9/76	9:00	All in the Family – SC	m	To:w-9
9/76	9:00	Maude – SC	m	Fr:m-9:30
9/76	9:30	All's Fair – SC	d	
9/76	9:30	Maude – SC	m	To:m-9
9/76	10:00	Executive Suite(60) – DR	d	
9/76	10:00	Medical Center(60) – MD	c	
1/77	8:00	Jeffersons – SC	m	Fr:w-8:30
1/77	8:00	Rhoda – SC	m	To:n-8
1/77	8:30	Busting Loose – SC	d	
1/77	8:30	Phyllis – SC	m	To:n-8:30
1/77	10:00	Andros Targets(60) – ND	d	
1/77	10:00	Executive Suite(60) – DR	m	To:f-10
1/77	10:00	Kojak(60) – CD	m	Fr:n-9
5/77	8:30	Busting Loose – SC	m	To:w-8:30
5/77	10:00	Andros Targets(60) – ND	m	To:s-10-7/77
5/77	10:00	Sonny and Cher Comedy Hour(60) – MV	m	Fr:f-9-3/77

Date	Time	Title (min. if not 30) — Type	Action	From/To
6/77	8:30	Shields and Yarnell — VY	d	
7/77	8:30	Shields and Yarnell — VY	c	
8/77	8:00	Jeffersons — SC	m	To:s-9
8/77	8:30	Szysznyk — SC	d	
8/77	8:30	Szysznyk — SC	m	To:w-8:30-12/77
8/77	9:30	All's Fair — SC	c	
8/77	10:00	Sonny and Cher Comedy Hour(60) — MV	c	
9/77	8:00	Young Dan'l Boone(60) — AD	d	
9/77	8:00	Young Dan'l Boone(60) — AD	m	To:t-8
9/77	9:00	Betty White — SC	d	
9/77	9:00	Maude — SC	m	To:m-9:30
9/77	9:30	Maude — SC	m	Fr:m-9
9/77	10:00	Kojak(60) — CD	m	To:n-10
9/77	10:00	Rafferty(60) — MD	d	
10/77	8:00	Logan's Run(60) — SF	d	
11/77	9:00	Betty White — SC	m	To:m-9:30
11/77	9:30	Maude — SC	m	To:m-9
11/77	10:00	Rafferty(60) — MD	c	
12/77	9:00	Maude — SC	m	Fr:m-9:30
12/77	9:30	Betty White — SC	m	Fr:m-9
12/77	10:00	Switch(60) — CD	m	Fr:n-9-9/77
1/78	8:00	Good Times — SC	m	Fr:w-8
1/78	8:00	Logan's Run(60) — SF	c	
1/78	8:30	Baby, I'm Back — SC	d	
1/78	9:00	M*A*S*H — SC	m	Fr:t-9
1/78	9:00	Maude — SC	m	To:s-9:30
1/78	9:30	Betty White — SC	c	
1/78	9:30	One Day at a Time — SC	m	Fr:t-9:30
1/78	10:00	Lou Grant(60) — ND	m	Fr:t-10
1/78	10:00	Switch(60) — CD	m	To:n-10-6/78
5/78	8:00	Good Times — SC	m	To:m-8:30
6/78	8:00	Jeffersons — SC	m	Fr:s-8
6/78	8:30	Baby, I'm Back — SC	c	
6/78	8:30	Good Times — SC	m	Fr:m-8
9/78	8:00	Jeffersons — SC	m	To:w-8
9/78	8:00	WKRP in Cincinnati — SC	d	
9/78	8:30	Good Times — SC	m	To:s-8:30
9/78	8:30	People — NM	d	
11/78	8:00	WKRP in Cincinnati — SC	m	To:m-9:30-1/79
11/78	8:00	White Shadow(60) — DR	d	
11/78	8:30	People — NM	c	
1/79	8:00	White Shadow(60) — DR	m	To:s-8
1/79	9:30	One Day at a Time — SC	m	To:w-9
1/79	9:30	WKRP in Cincinnati — SC	m	Fr:m-8-11/78
2/79	8:00	Billy — SC	d	
2/79	8:30	Flatbush — SC	d	
3/79	8:00	Billy — SC	m	To:s-8:30
3/79	8:00	White Shadow(60) — DR	m	Fr:s-8
3/79	8:30	Flatbush — SC	c	

Date	Time	Title (min. if not 30) – Type	Action	From/To
12/79	8:00	WKRP in Cincinnati – SC	m	Fr:m-9:30
12/79	8:00	White Shadow(60) – DR	m	To:t-8
12/79	8:30	Last Resort – SC	m	Fr:w-8-10/79
12/79	9:30	House Calls – SC	d	
12/79	9:30	WKRP in Cincinnati – SC	m	To:m-8
3/80	8:30	Last Resort – SC	c	
3/80	8:30	Stockard Channing – SC	d	
3/80	9:30	Flo – SC	d	
3/80	9:30	House Calls – SC	m	To:m-9:30-5/80
4/80	8:30	Stockard Channing – SC	m	To:s-8:30-6/80
4/80	9:30	Flo – SC	m	To:m-8-7/80
5/80	8:30	Phyl & Mikhy – SC	d	
5/80	9:30	House Calls – SC	m	Fr:m-9:30-3/80
6/80	8:30	Phyl & Mikhy – SC	c	
7/80	8:00	Flo – SC	m	Fr:m-9:30-4/80
7/80	8:00	WKRP in Cincinnati – SC	m	To:m-8:30
7/80	8:30	WKRP in Cincinnati – SC	m	Fr:m-8
10/80	8:30	Ladies Man – SC	d	
10/80	8:30	WKRP in Cincinnati – SC	m	To:s-8
1/81	8:00	Flo – SC	m	To:s-9
1/81	8:30	Ladies Man – SC	m	To:s-9:30
2/81	8:00	White Shadow(60) – DR	m	Fr:t-8
3/81	8:00	White Shadow(60) – DR	m	To:w-8-6/81
4/81	8:00	Private Benjamin – SC	d	
4/81	8:30	The Two of Us – SC	d	
5/81	8:00	Private Benjamin – SC	m	To:m-8-10/81
5/81	8:30	The Two of Us – SC	m	To:m-8:30-9/81
6/81	8:00	WKRP in Cincinnati – SC	m	Fr:s-8
6/81	8:30	Tim Conway – CV	m	Fr:m-8:30-3/81
8/81	8:30	Tim Conway – CV	c	
9/81	8:00	WKRP in Cincinnati – SC	m	To:w-8:30
9/81	8:30	The Two of Us – SC	m	Fr:m-8:30-5/81
10/81	8:00	Private Benjamin – SC	m	Fr:m-8-5/81
1/82	8:00	Mr. Merlin – SC	m	Fr:w-8
1/82	8:00	Private Benjamin – SC	m	To:m-8:30
1/82	8:30	Private Benjamin – SC	m	Fr:m-8
1/82	8:30	The Two of Us – SC	m	To:w-8:30
3/82	8:00	Mr. Merlin – SC	m	To:w-8-7/82
3/82	8:30	Private Benjamin – SC	m	To:m-8
4/82	8:00	Private Benjamin – SC	m	Fr:m-8:30
4/82	8:30	Report to Murphy – SC	d	
4/82	9:30	Making the Grade – SC	d*	
5/82	8:30	Report to Murphy – SC	c	
5/82	9:30	Making the Grade – SC	c*	
6/82	8:30	WKRP in Cincinnati – SC	m	Fr:w-9-4/82
8/82	9:30	Filthy Rich – SC	d*	
8/82	9:30	Filthy Rich – SC	m*	To:w-9:30-10/82
9/82	8:00	Private Benjamin – SC	m	To:m-8:30
9/82	8:00	Square Pegs – SC	d	
9/82	8:30	Private Benjamin – SC	m	Fr:m-8

Date	Time	Title (min. if not 30) – Type	Action	From/To
9/82	8:30	WKRP in Cincinnati – SC	c	
9/82	9:30	House Calls – SC	c	
9/82	10:00	Lou Grant(60) – ND	c	
10/82	9:30	Newhart – SC	d	
10/82	10:00	Cagney & Lacey(60) – CD	m	Fr:r-9-4/82
1/83	8:30	Filthy Rich – SC	m	Fr:w-9:30-11/82
1/83	8:30	Private Benjamin – SC	m	To:m-8:30-5/83
2/83	8:30	Filthy Rich – SC	c	
2/83	9:30	Newhart – SC	m	To:n-9:30
3/83	8:00	Archie Bunker's Place – SC	m	Fr:n-8
3/83	8:00	Square Pegs – SC	m	To:w-8:30
3/83	8:30	Foot in the Door – SC	d	
3/83	8:30	Small & Frye – SC	d	
3/83	8:30	Small & Frye – SC	c	
3/83	9:00	Alice – SC	m	Fr:w-9-11/82
3/83	9:30	One Day at a Time – SC	m	Fr:n-9:30
4/83	9:00	Alice – SC	m	To:n-9:30
5/83	8:00	Archie Bunker's Place – SC	m	To:n-8
5/83	8:00	Square Pegs – SC	m	Fr:w-8:30
5/83	8:30	Foot in the Door – SC	c	
5/83	8:30	Private Benjamin – SC	m	Fr:m-8:30-1/83
5/83	9:30	One Day at a Time – SC	m	To:n-8:30
6/83	9:30	Archie Bunker's Place – SC	s	
7/83	9:00	Tucker's Witch(60) – CD	m	Fr:r-10
7/83	9:30	Archie Bunker's Place – SC	f	
8/83	9:00	Tucker's Witch(60) – CD	c	
8/83	9:30	Newhart – SC	m	Fr:n-9:30
9/83	8:00	Square Pegs – SC	c	
9/83	8:30	Private Benjamin – SC	c	
9/83	9:00	Aftermash – SC	d	
9/83	9:00	M*A*S*H – SC	c	
9/83	10:00	Cagney & Lacey(60) – CD	m	To:m-10-3/84
9/83	10:00	Emerald Point, N.A.S.(60) – SL	d	
10/83	8:00	Scarecrow and Mrs. King(60) – AD	d	
3/84	9:00	Aftermash – SC	m	To:n-8
3/84	9:00	Kate & Allie – SC	d	
3/84	10:00	Cagney & Lacey(60) – CD	m	Fr:m-10-9/83
3/84	10:00	Emerald Point, N.A.S.(60) – SL	c	
5/84	9:00	One Day at a Time – SC	m	Fr:w-8
5/84	9:00	Kate & Allie – SC	m	To:m-9-8/84
8/84	9:00	One Day at a Time – SC	m	To:n-8
8/84	9:00	Kate & Allie – SC	m	Fr:m-9-5/84
9/86	8:00	Scarecrow & Mrs. King(60) – AD	m	To:f-8
9/86	8:00	Kate & Allie – SC	m	Fr:m-9
9/86	8:30	Together We Stand – SC	d	
9/86	8:30	Together We Stand – SC	m	To:w-8
9/86	9:00	Kate & Allie – SC	m	To:m-8
9/86	9:00	Newhart – SC	m	Fr:m-9:30
9/86	9:30	Newhart – SC	m	To:m-9
9/86	9:30	Designing Women – SC	d	

Date	Time	Title (min. if not 30) — Type	Action	From/To
10/86	8:30	My Sister Sam — SC	d	
11/86	9:30	Designing Women — SC	m	To:r-9:30
12/86	9:30	Cavanaughs — SC	d	
3/87	9:30	Cavanaughs — SC	c	
3/87	9:30	Designing Women — SC	m	Fr:r-9:30-1/87
4/87	10:00	West 57th(60) — NM	m*	Fr:w-10-7/86
4/87	10:00	West 57th(60) — NM	m*	To:t-8
8/87	8:30	My Sister Sam — SC	m	To:s-8:30
9/87	8:00	Kate & Allie — SC	m	To:m-8:30
9/87	8:00	Frank's Place — SC	d	
9/87	8:30	Kate & Allie — SC	m	Fr:m-8
11/87	8:00	Kate & Allie — SC	m	Fr:m-8:30
11/87	8:00	Frank's Place — SC	m	To:m-8:30
11/87	8:30	Kate & Allie — SC	m	To:m-8
11/87	8:30	Frank's Place — SC	m	Fr:m-8
12/87	10:00	Cagney & Lacey(60) — CD	m	To:t-10
1/88	10:00	Wiseguy(60) — CD	m	Fr:r-9-11/87
2/88	8:30	Frank's Place — SC	m	To:m-9:30
2/88	8:30	Designing Women — SC	m	Fr:m-9:30
2/88	9:30	Frank's Place — SC	m	Fr:m-8:30
2/88	9:30	Designing Women — SC	m	To:m-8:30
3/88	9:30	Eisenhower & Lutz — SC	d	
3/88	9:30	Frank's Place — SC	m	To:t-9:30
4/88	10:00	Wiseguy(60) — CD	m	To:w-10-6/88
4/88	10:00	Cagney & Lacey(60) — CD	m	Fr:t-10
6/88	8:00	Kate & Allie — SC	m	To:s-8
6/88	8:00	Blue Skies(60) — DR	d	
6/88	8:30	Designing Women — SC	m	To:m-9:30
6/88	9:30	Eisenhower & Lutz — SC	c	
6/88	9:30	Designing Women — SC	m#	Fr:m-8:30
6/88	10:00	Magnum, PI(60) — CD	m	Fr:w-9-2/88
6/88	10:00	Cagney & Lacey(60) — CD	m	To:r-10
8/88	8:00	Blue Skies(60) — DR	c	
8/88	9:00	Newhart — SC	m	To:m-8
8/88	10:00	Magnum, PI(60) — CD	c	

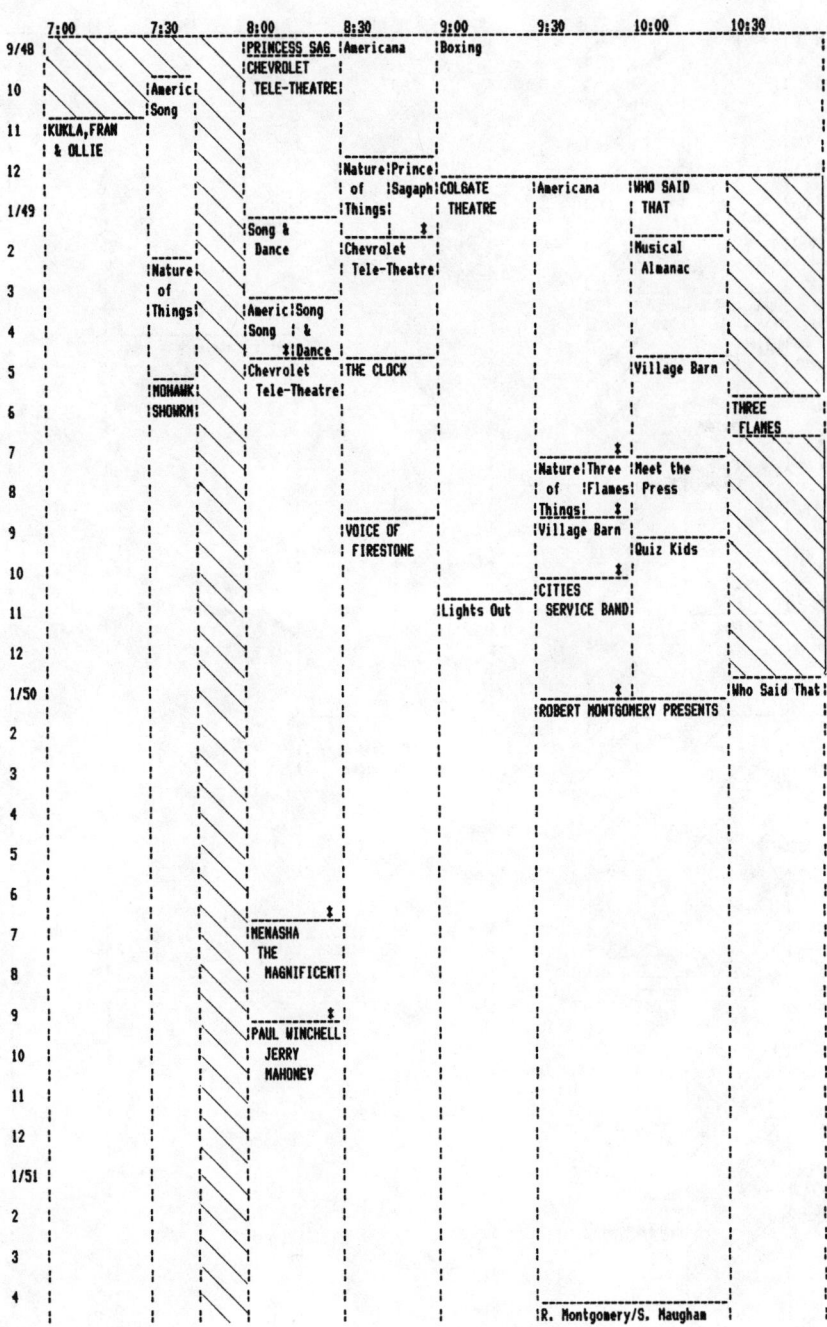

	7:00	7:30	8:00	8:30	9:00	9:30	10:00	10:30
9/48			PRINCESS SAG	Americana	Boxing			
			CHEVROLET					
10		Americ	TELE-THEATRE					
		Song						
11	KUKLA,FRAN							
	& OLLIE							
12				Nature Prince				
				of Sagaph	COLGATE	Americana	WHO SAID	
1/49				Things	THEATRE		THAT	
2			Song &				Musical	
		Nature	Dance	Chevrolet			Almanac	
3		of		Tele-Theatre				
		Things	Americ Song					
4			Song &					
			Dance					
5			Chevrolet	THE CLOCK			Village Barn	
		MOHAWK	Tele-Theatre					
6		SHOWRM						THREE
								FLAMES
7								
						Nature Three	Meet the	
8						of Flames	Press	
						Things		
9				VOICE OF		Village Barn		
				FIRESTONE			Quiz Kids	
10						CITIES		
11					Lights Out	SERVICE BAND		
12								
1/50								Who Said That
						ROBERT MONTGOMERY PRESENTS		
2								
3								
4								
5								
6								
7			MENASHA					
			THE					
8			MAGNIFICENT					
9								
			PAUL WINCHELL					
10			JERRY					
			MAHONEY					
11								
12								
1/51								
2								
3								
4						R. Montgomery/S. Maugham		

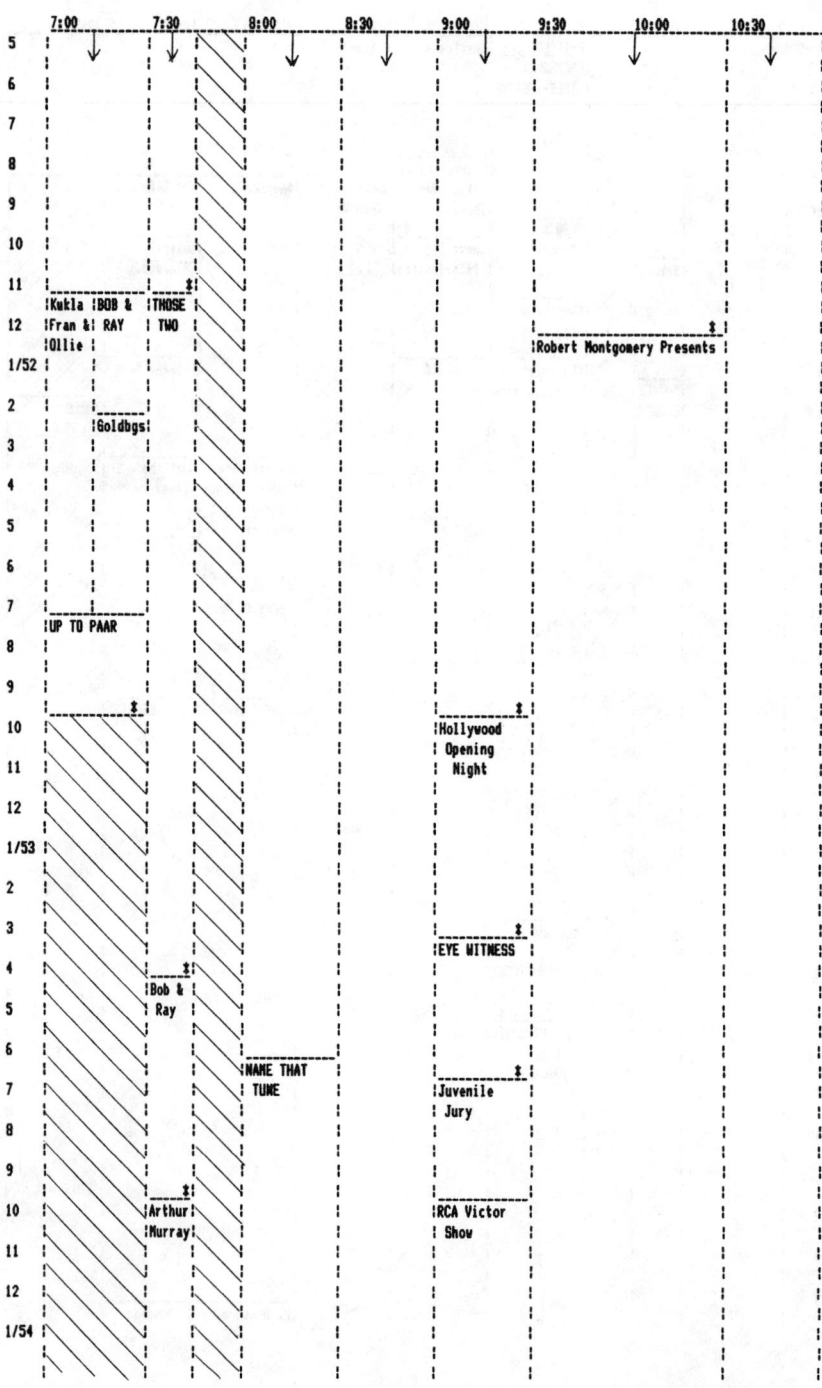

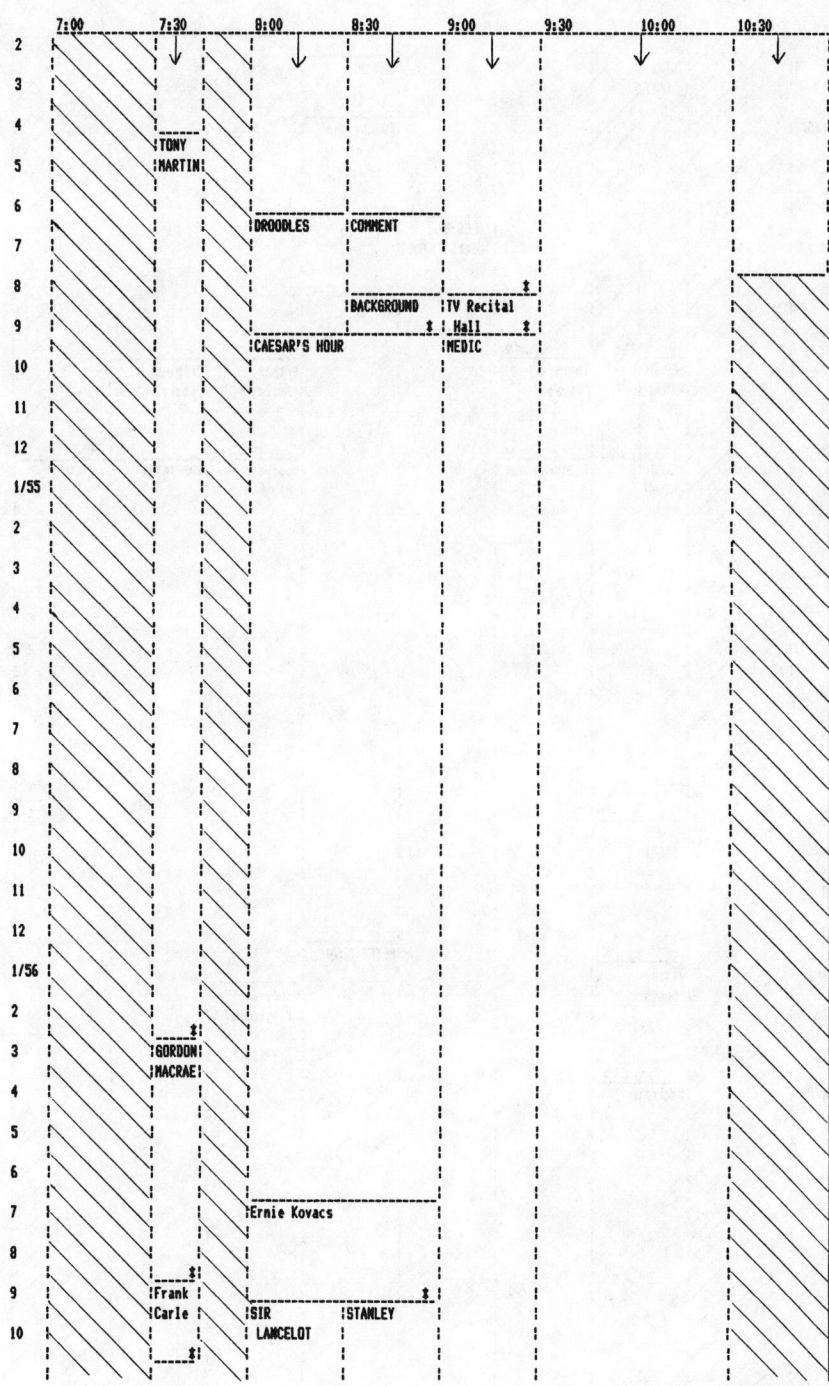

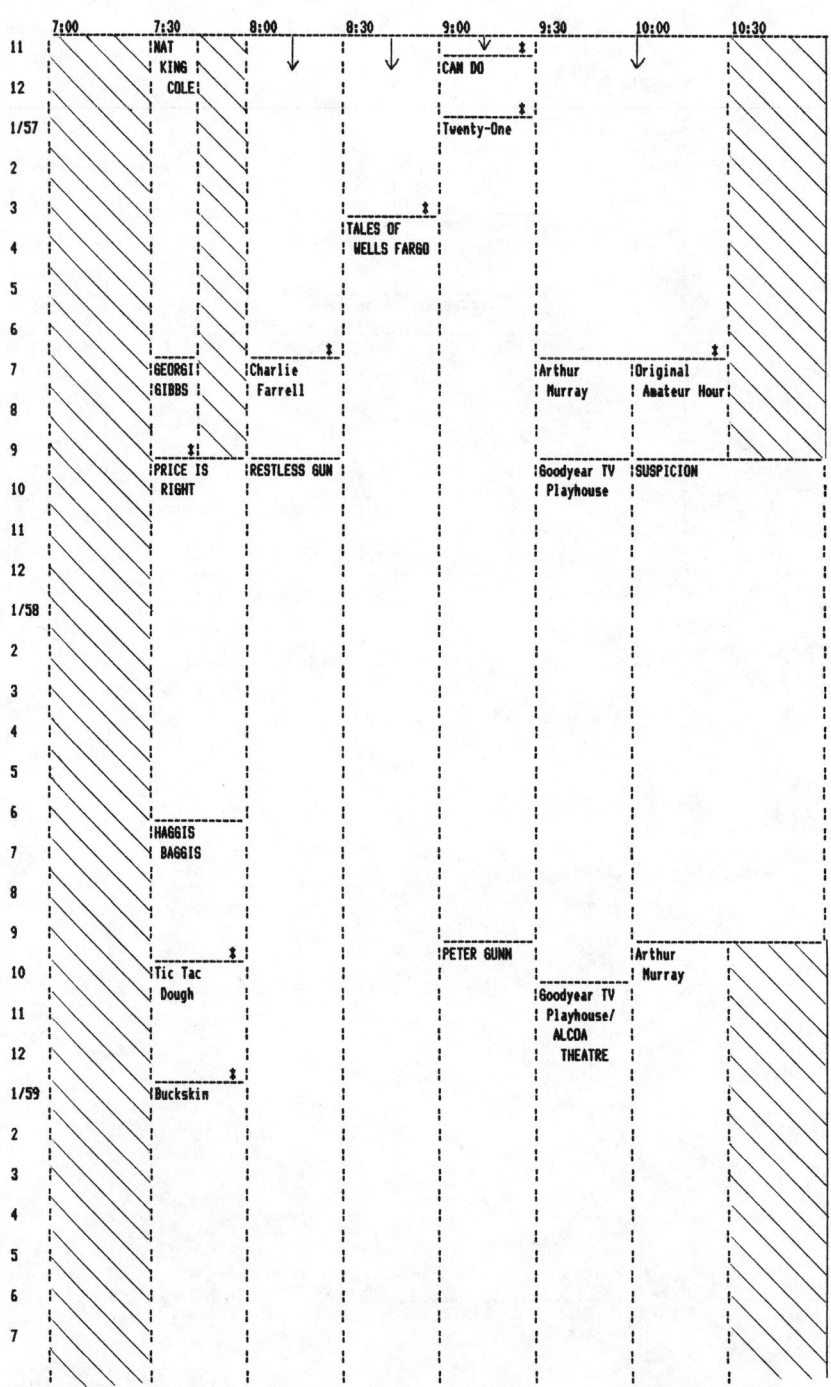

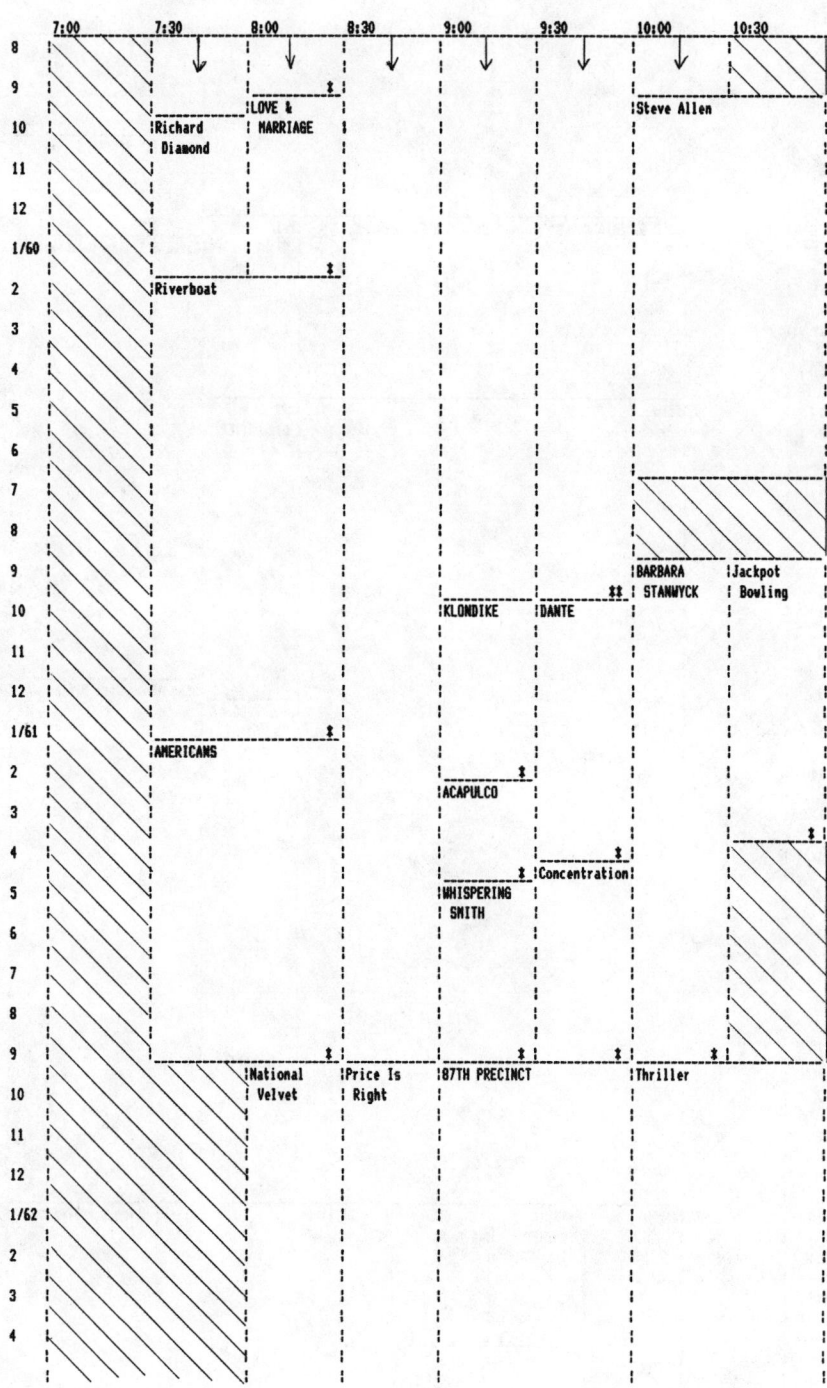

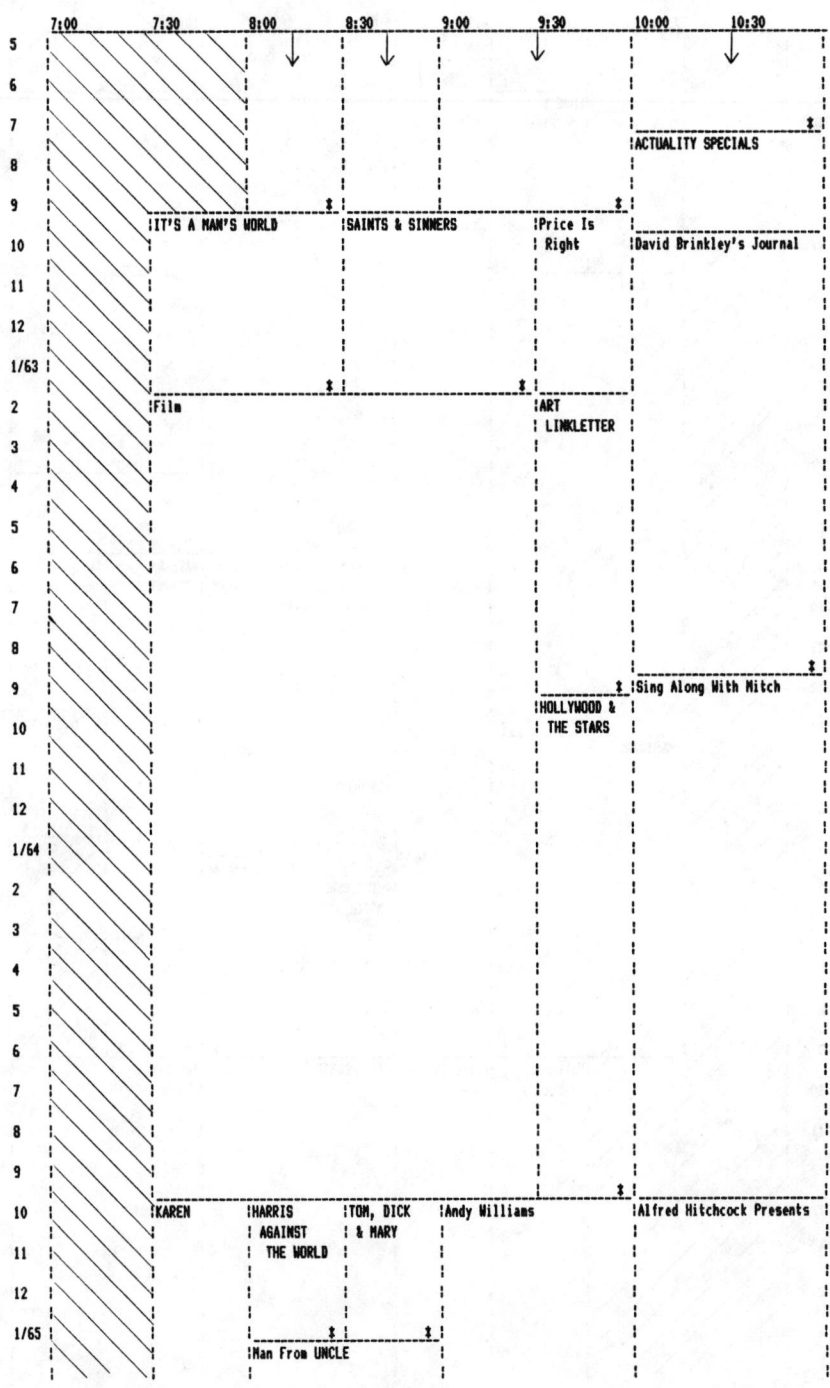

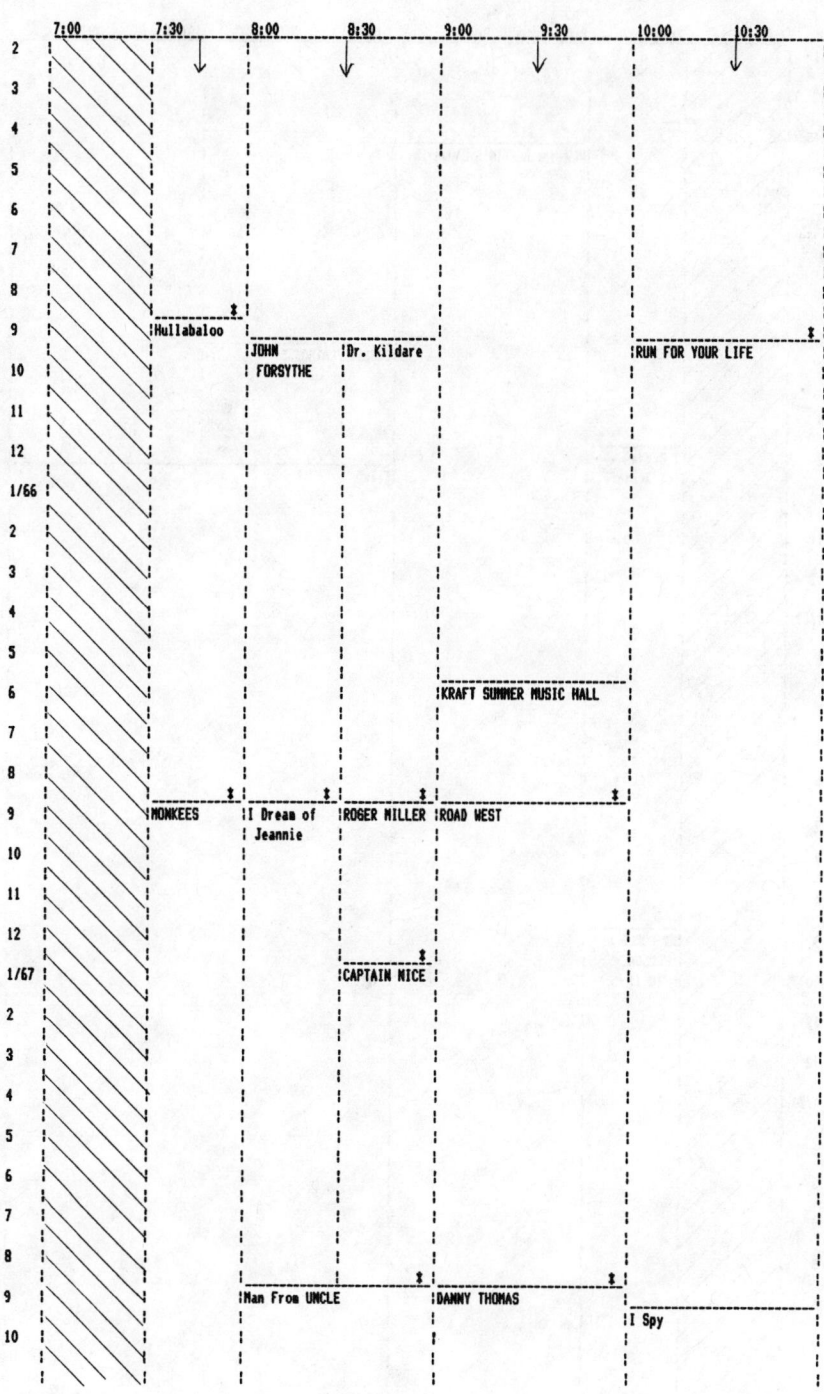

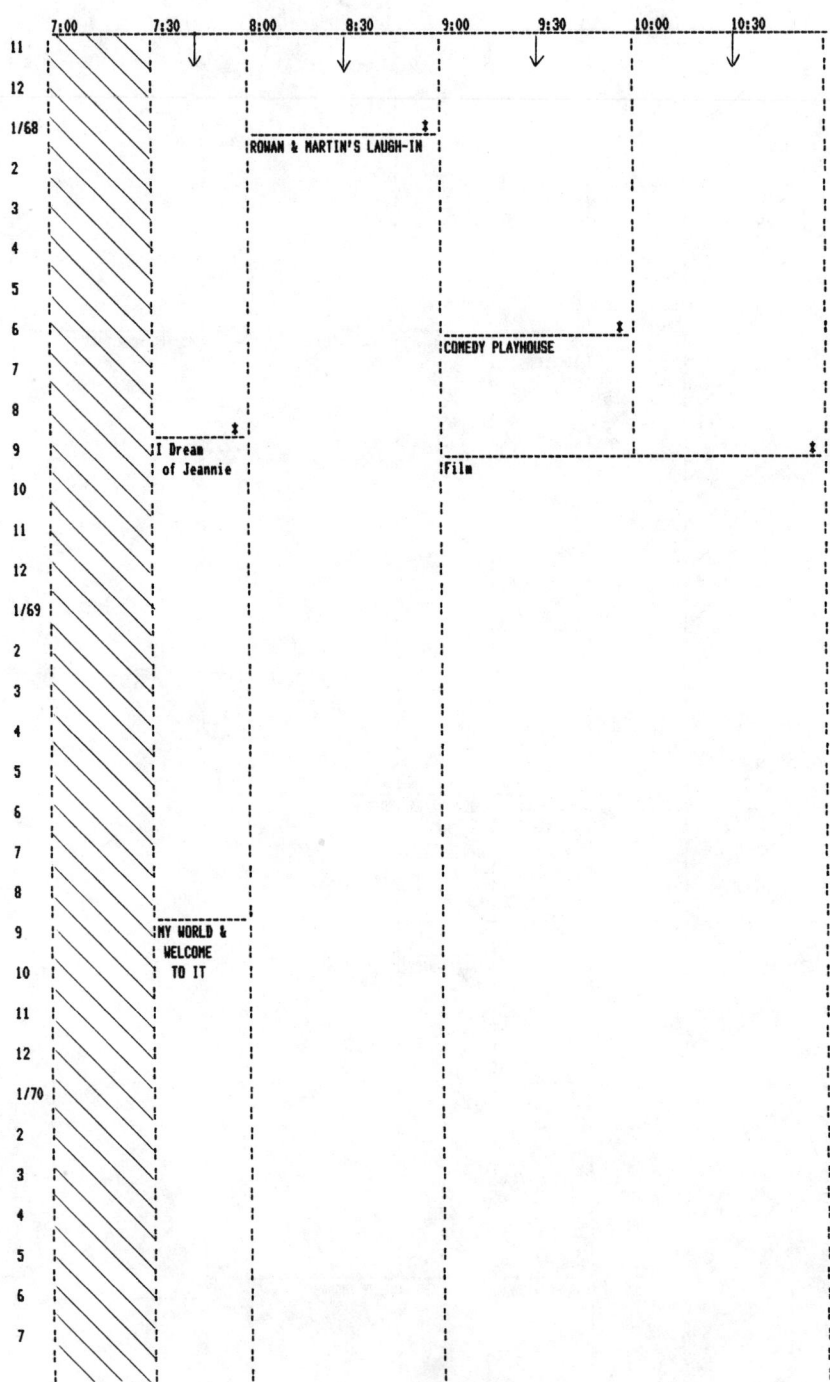

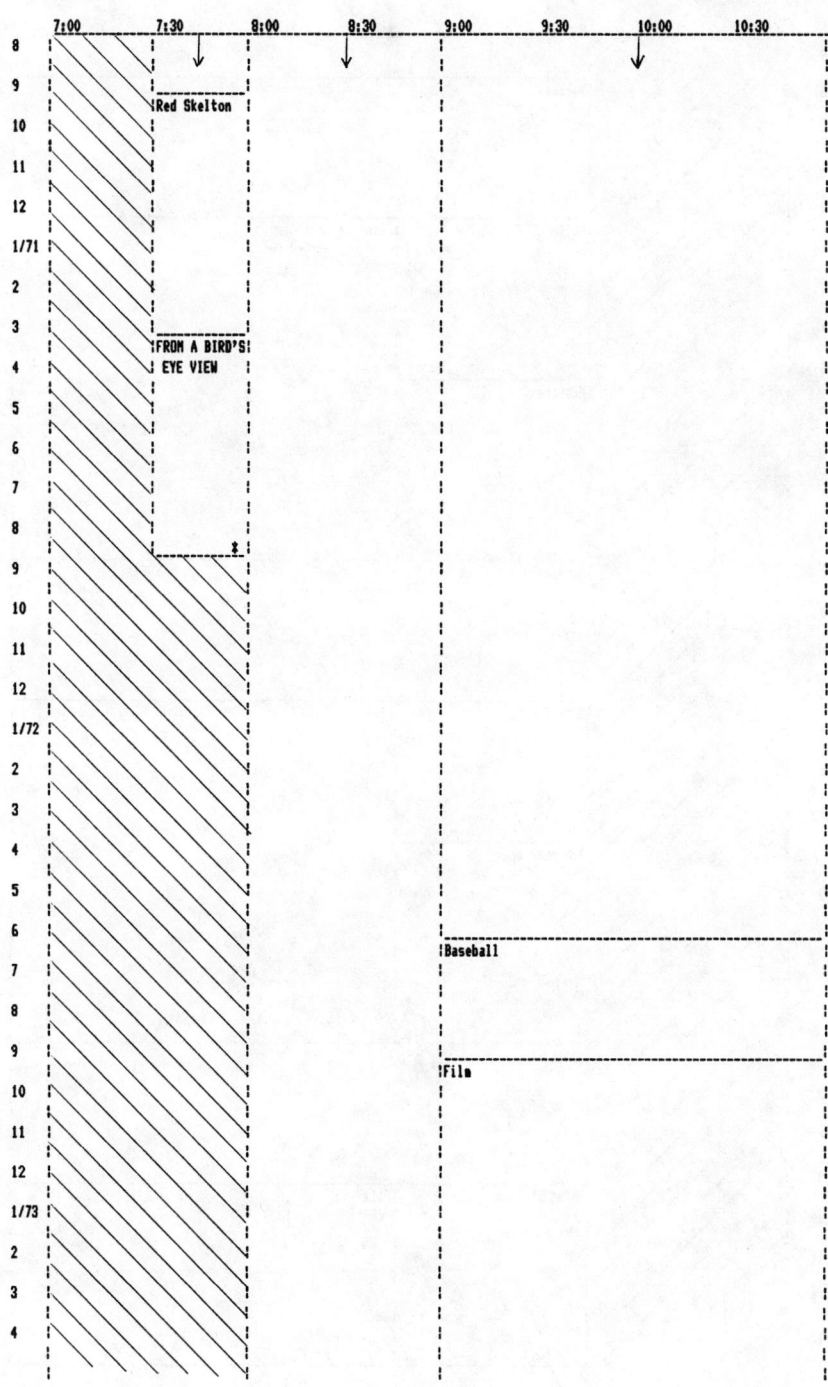

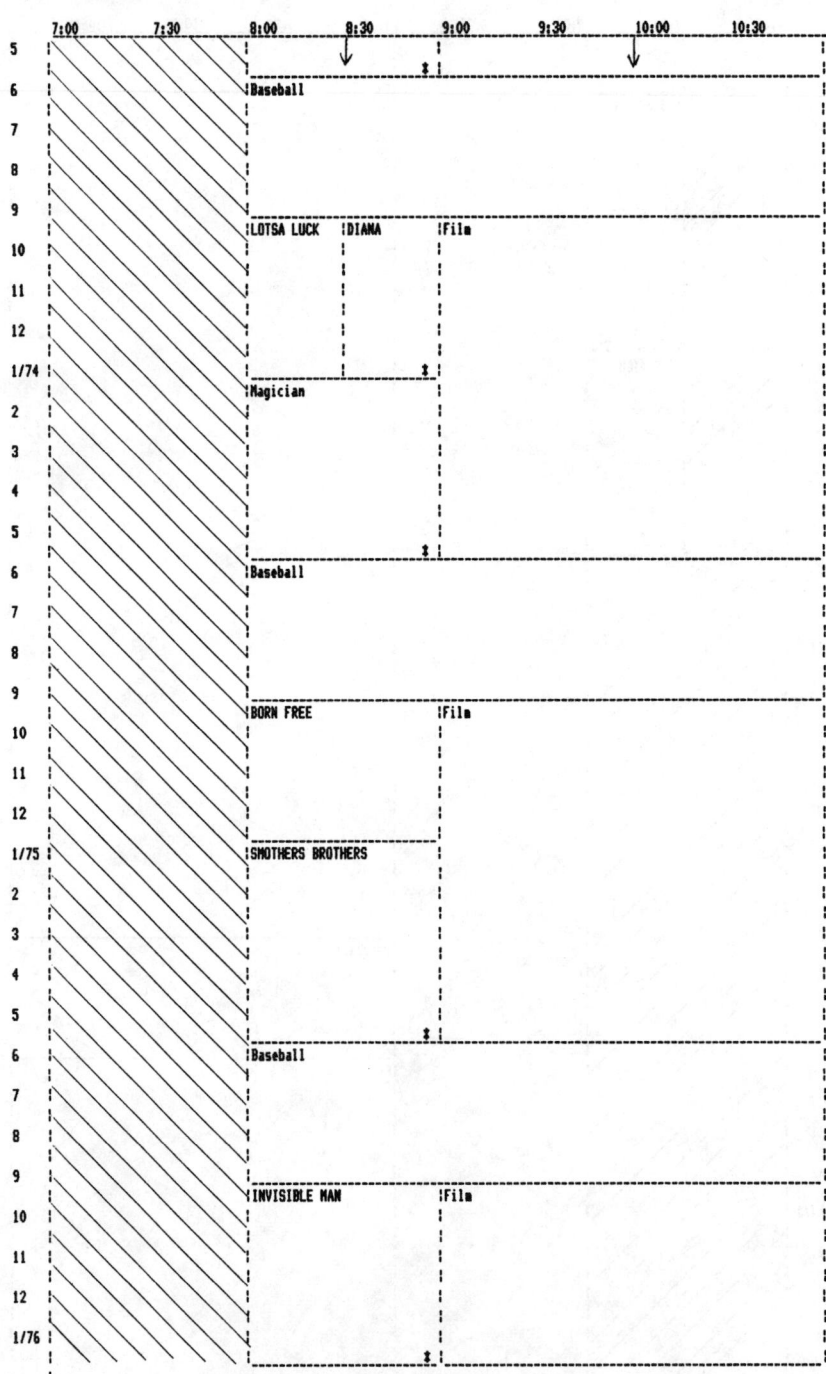

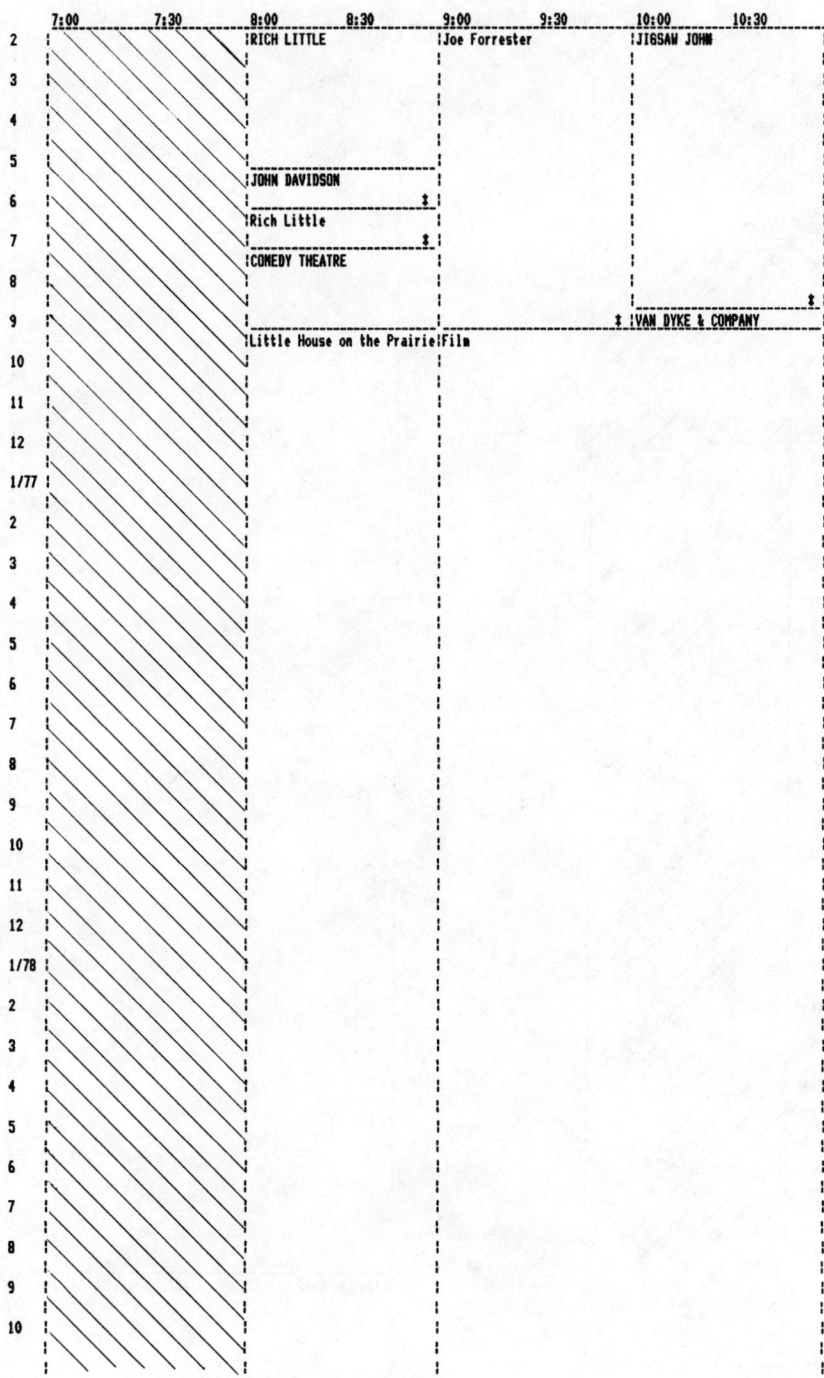

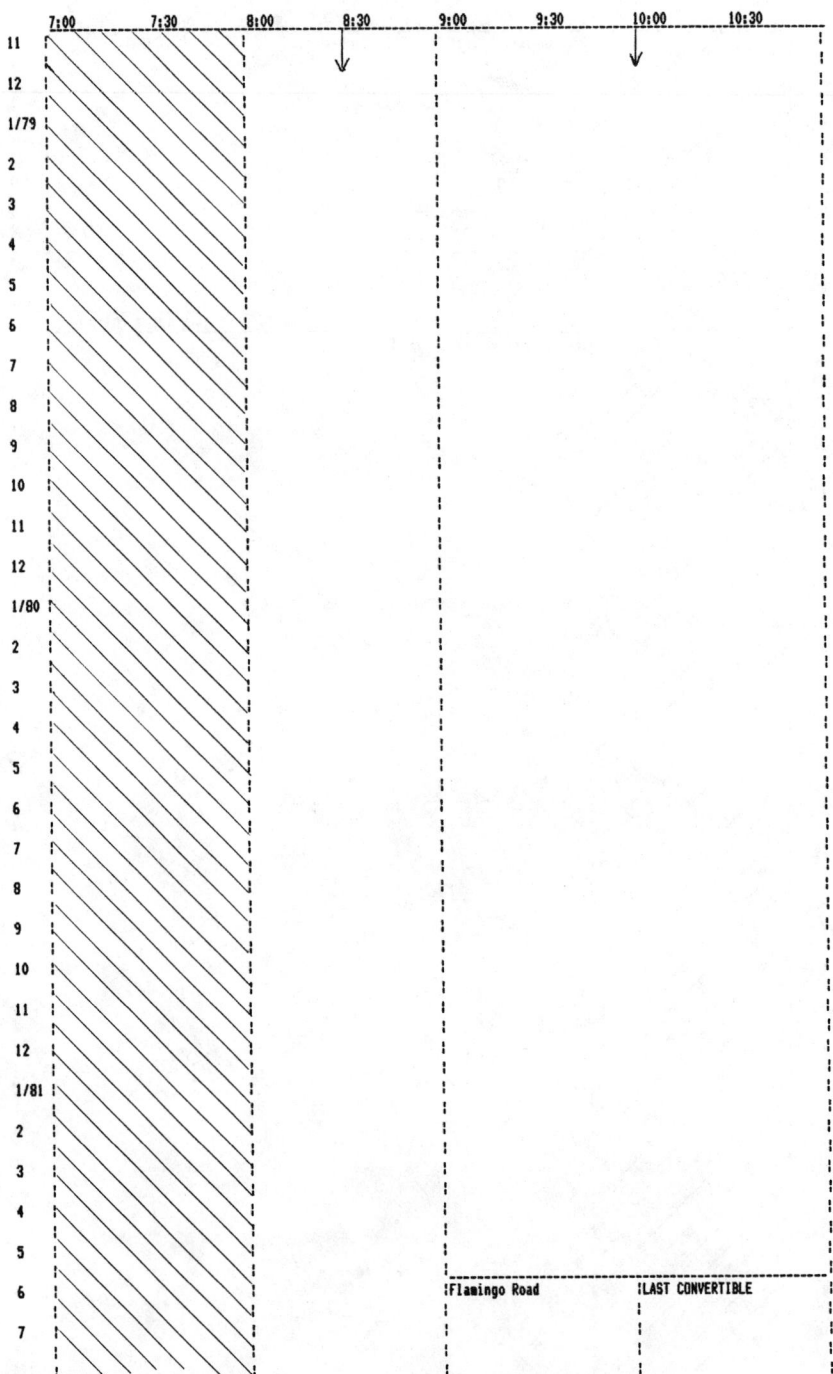

Flamingo Road

LAST CONVERTIBLE

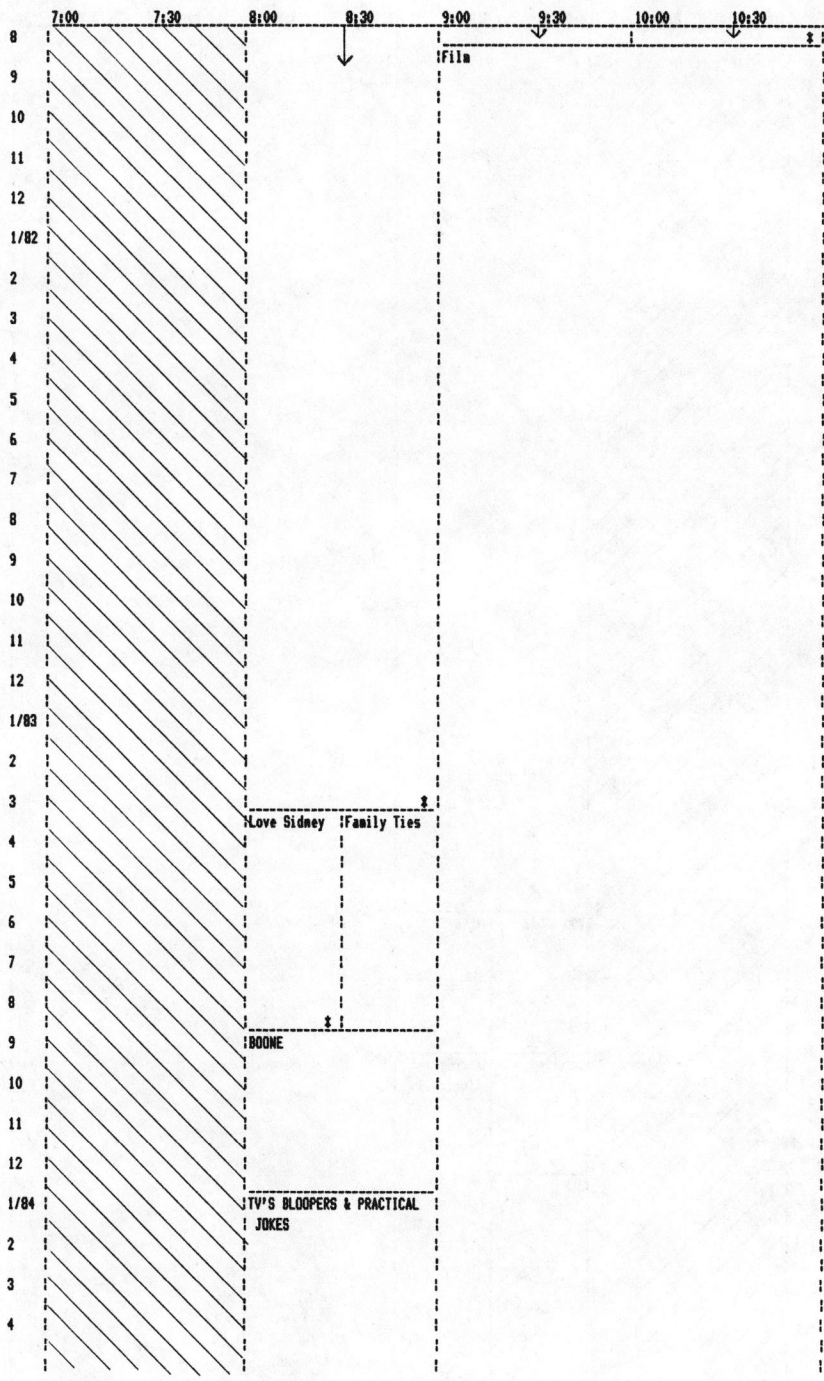

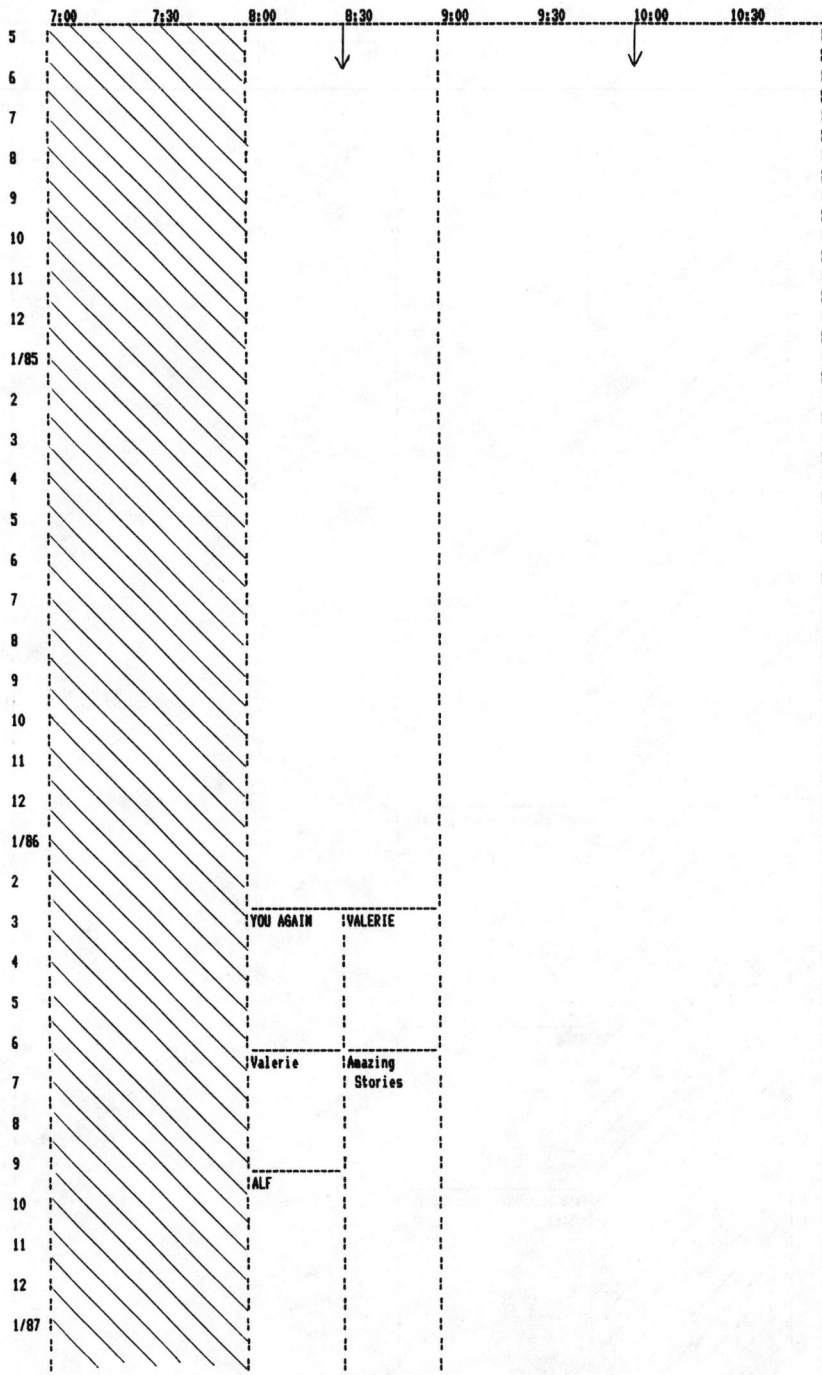

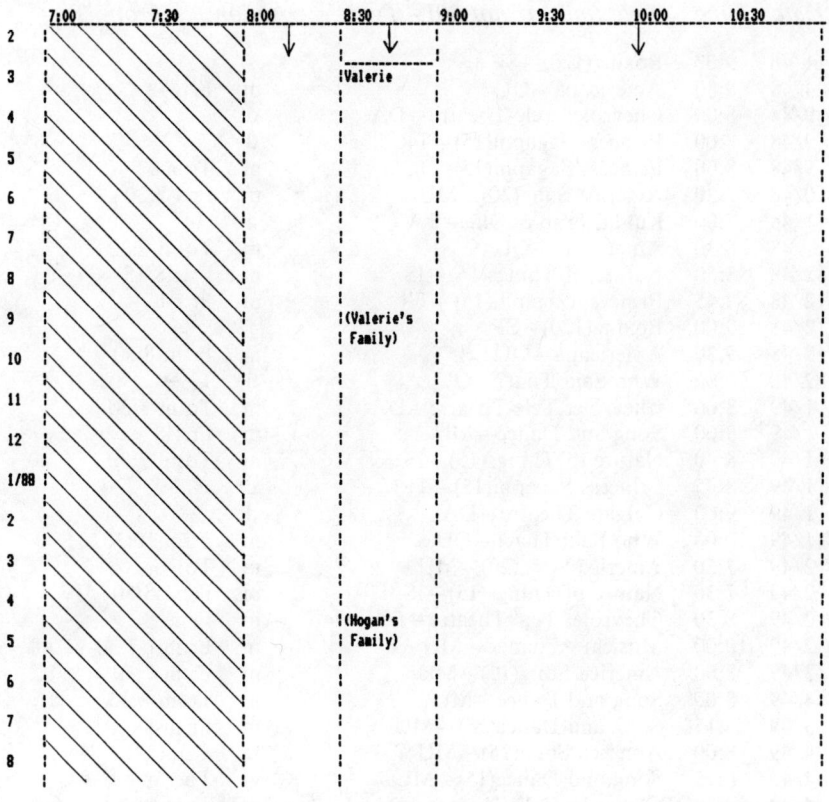

Date	Time	Title (min. if not 30) — Type	Action	From/To
11/46	9:00	Boxing(120) — SP	s	
4/48	8:30	Americana — QU	m	Fr:w-8
9/48	8:00	Chevrolet Tele-Theatre — DA	d	
9/48	8:00	Princess Sagaphi(15) — TR	d	
9/48	8:00	Princess Sagaphi(15) — TR	m	To:r-8
10/48	7:30	America Song(20) — MU	m	Fr:t-7:30
11/48	7:00	Kukla, Fran & Ollie — KV	d	
11/48	8:30	Americana — QU	m	To:m-9:30
12/48	8:30	Nature of Things(15) — IS	m	Fr:r-8:15
12/48	8:45	Princess Sagaphi(15) — TR	m	Fr:r-8
12/48	9:00	Boxing(120) — SP	f	
12/48	9:30	Americana — QU	m	Fr:m-8:30
12/48	10:00	Who Said That? — QU	d	
1/49	8:00	Chevrolet Tele-Theatre — DA	m	To:m-8:30
1/49	8:00	Song and Dance — MU	m	Fr:f-8
1/49	8:30	Nature of Things(15) — IS	m	To:m-7:30
1/49	8:45	Princess Sagaphi(15) — TR	c	
1/49	9:00	Colgate Theatre — DA	d	
1/49	10:00	Who Said That? — QU	m	To:n-10:30
2/49	7:30	America Song(20) — MU	m	To:var
2/49	7:30	Nature of Things(15) — IS	m	Fr:m-8:30
2/49	8:30	Chevrolet Tele-Theatre — DA	m	Fr:m-8
2/49	10:00	Musical Almanac — MU	m	Fr:m-r-7:30-12/48
3/49	8:00	America Song(15) — MU	m	Fr:m-7:30
3/49	8:00	Song and Dance — MU	m	To:m-8:15
3/49	8:15	Song and Dance(15) — MU	m	Fr:m-8
4/49	8:00	America Song(15) — MU	c	
4/49	8:15	Song and Dance(15) — MU	m	To:var
4/49	8:30	Chevrolet Tele-Theatre — DA	m	To:m-8
4/49	10:00	Musical Almanac — MU	c	
5/49	7:30	Mohawk Showroom(15) — MU	d	
5/49	7:30	Nature of Things(15) — IS	m	To:m-9:30-7/49
5/49	8:00	Chevrolet Tele-Theatre — DA	m	Fr:m-8:30
5/49	8:30	The Clock — SA	d	
5/49	10:00	Village Barn — MV	m	Fr:w-8:30
6/49	7:00	Judy Splinters(15) — KV	d*	
6/49	7:15	Mary Kay and Johnny(15) — SC	m*	Fr:w-9(c)
6/49	10:30	Three Flames — MU	d	
6/49	10:30	Three Flames — MU	m	To:m-9:45
7/49	8:00	Academy Theatre — DA	d*	
7/49	9:30	Americana — QU	c	
7/49	9:30	Nature of Things(15) — IS	m	Fr:m-var-5/49
7/49	9:45	Three Flames(15) — MU	m	Fr:m-10:30
7/49	10:00	Meet the Press — IV	m	Fr:w-10
7/49	10:00	Village Barn — MV	m	To:r-10
8/49	7:00	Judy Splinters(15) — KV	c*	
8/49	7:15	Mary Kay and Johnny(15) — SC	m*	To:r-8:30
8/49	7:30	Capitol Capers(15) — MU	d*	
8/49	8:30	Black Robe(var) — CR	m*	Fr:w-8:30
8/49	8:30	The Clock — SA	m	To:w-8:30

Date	Time	Title (min. if not 30) — Type	Action	From/To
8/49	9:30	Nature of Things(15) — IS	m	To:s-7:30
8/49	9:45	Three Flames(15) — MU	c	
9/49	7:30	Capitol Capers(15) — MU	c*	
9/49	8:00	Academy Theatre — DA	c*	
9/49	8:30	Voice of Firestone — MU	d	
9/49	9:30	Village Barn — MV	m	Fr:r-10
9/49	10:00	Meet the Press — IV	m	To:s-var
9/49	10:00	Quiz Kids — QU	m	Fr:w-8
10/49	8:30	Black Robe(var) — CR	m*	To:s-10
10/49	9:00	Colgate Theatre — DA	m	To:n-8:30
10/49	9:30	Cities Service Band of America — MU	d	
10/49	9:30	Village Barn — MV	c	
11/49	9:00	Lights Out — SA	m	Fr:t-9-8/49
1/50	9:30	Cities Service Band of America — MU	c	
1/50	9:30	Robert Montgomery Presents(60) — DA	d	
1/50	10:00	Quiz Kids — QU	m	To:f-8
1/50	10:30	Who Said That? — QU	m	Fr:s-9
6/50	8:00	Chevrolet Tele-Theatre — DA	c	
6/50	9:30	Lewisohn Stadium Concert(60) — MU	d*	
7/50	7:00	Ransom Sherman — CV	d*	
7/50	7:30	Wendy Barrie(15) — IV	m*	Fr:tr-7:30
7/50	8:00	Menasha the Magnificent — SC	d	
7/50	9:00	Your Hit Parade — MU	d*	
8/50	7:00	Ransom Sherman — CV	c*	
8/50	7:30	Wendy Barrie(15) — IV	m*	To:w-8:15
8/50	9:00	Your Hit Parade — MU	m*	To:s-10:30-10/50
8/50	9:30	Lewisohn Stadium Concert(60) — MU	c*	
9/50	8:00	Menasha the Magnificent — SC	c	
9/50	8:00	Paul Winchell-Jerry Mahoney — CV	d	
4/51	9:30	Somerset Maugham TV Theatre(60) — DA	m	Fr:w-9(c)
6/51	8:00	Cameo Theatre — DA	m*	Fr:w-8:30-9/50
7/51	7:00	Ernie in Kovacsland — CV	d*	
7/51	7:30	Songs at Twilight(15) — MU	d*	
8/51	7:00	Ernie in Kovacsland — CV	c*	
8/51	7:30	Songs at Twilight(15) — MU	c*	
8/51	8:00	Cameo Theatre — DA	m*	To:n-10-1/52
11/51	7:00	Kukla, Fran & Ollie — KV	m	To:m-f-7
11/51	7:00	Kukla, Fran & Ollie(15) — KV	m	Fr:m-f-7
11/51	7:15	Bob and Ray(15) — CV	d	
11/51	7:30	Mohawk Showroom(15) — MU	c	
11/51	7:30	Those Two(15) — SC	d	
12/51	9:30	Somerset Maugham TV Theatre(60) — DA	c	
2/52	7:15	Bob and Ray(15) — CV	m	To:tr-7:15

Date	Time	Title (min. if not 30) — Type	Action	From/To
2/52	7:15	Goldbergs(15) — SC	m	Fr:m-9:30-6/51(c)
7/52	7:00	Kukla, Fran & Ollie(15) — KV	m	To:m-f-7-9/54(a)
7/52	7:00	Up to Paar — QU	d	
7/52	7:15	Goldbergs(15) — SC	m	To:f-8-7/53
7/52	8:00	Masquerade Party — QU	d*	
8/52	8:00	Masquerade Party — QU	m*	To:m-9:30-6/53(c)
8/52	8:00	Quiz Kids — QU	m*	Fr:f-8-10/51
9/52	7:00	Up to Paar — QU	c	
9/52	8:00	Quiz Kids — QU	m*	To:s-10-1/53(c)
9/52	9:00	Lights Out — SA	c	
10/52	9:00	Hollywood Opening Night — DA	m	Fr:f-10:30-3/52(c)
3/53	9:00	Eye Witness — DA	d	
3/53	9:00	Hollywood Opening Night — DA	c	
4/53	7:30	Bob and Ray(15) — CV	m	Fr:tr-7:15-5/52
4/53	7:30	Those Two(15) — SC	c	
6/53	8:00	Name That Tune — QU	d	
6/53	8:00	Paul Winchell-Jerry Mahoney — CV	m	To:n-7-8/53
6/53	9:00	Eye Witness — DA	c	
7/53	9:00	Juvenile Jury — QU	m	Fr:w-8-10/52
9/53	7:30	Bob and Ray(15) — CV	c	
9/53	9:00	Juvenile Jury — QU	m	To:t-8:30-6/54(c)
10/53	7:30	Arthur Murray Party(15) — MV	m	Fr:n-9:30(c)
10/53	9:00	RCA Victor Show — VS	m	Fr:f-8-6/53
4/54	7:30	Arthur Murray Party(15) — MV	m	To:t-8:30-6/54
4/54	7:30	Tony Martin(15) — MU	d	
6/54	8:00	Droodles — QU	d	
6/54	8:00	Name That Tune — QU	m	To:r-10:30-9/54(c)
6/54	8:30	Comment — PA	d	
6/54	8:30	Voice of Firestone — MU	m	To:m-8:30(a)
7/54	10:30	Who Said That? — QU	m	To:w-9-2/55(a)
8/54	8:30	Background — DO	d	
8/54	8:30	Comment — PA	m	To:f-10:45-1/58
8/54	9:00	RCA Victor Show — VS	c	
8/54	9:00	TV Recital Hall — MU	m	Fr:n-8:30-8/51
9/54	8:00	Caesar's Hour(60) — CV	d	
9/54	8:00	Droodles — QU	m	To:f-8
9/54	8:30	Background — DO	c	
9/54	9:00	Medic — MD	d	
9/54	9:00	TV Recital Hall — MU	c	
6/55	7:30	Matt Dennis(15) — MU	d*	
7/55	8:00	Caesar Presents(60) — CV	d*	
8/55	7:30	Matt Dennis(15) — MU	c*	
9/55	8:00	Caesar Presents(60) — CV	c*	
2/56	7:30	Tony Martin(15) — MU	c	
3/56	7:30	Gordon MacRae(15) — MU	d	
6/56	8:00	Caesar's Hour(60) — CV	m	To:s-9-9/56
7/56	8:00	Ernie Kovacs(60) — CV	m	Fr:t-8-4/53(c)
8/56	7:30	Gordon MacRae(15) — MU	c	
9/56	7:30	Frankie Carle(15) — MU	m	Fr:t-7:30
9/56	8:00	Adventures of Sir Lancelot — AD	d	

Date	Time	Title (min. if not 30) — Type	Action	From/To
9/56	8:00	Ernie Kovacs(60) — CV	c	
9/56	8:30	Stanley — SC	d	
10/56	7:30	Frankie Carle(15) — MU	c	
11/56	7:30	Nat King Cole(15) — MV	d	
11/56	9:00	Can Do — QU	d	
11/56	9:00	Medic — MD	c	
12/56	9:00	Can Do — QU	c	
1/57	9:00	Twenty-One — QU	m	Fr:w-10:30
3/57	8:30	Stanley — SC	c	
3/57	8:30	Tales of Wells Fargo — WE	d	
6/57	7:30	Nat King Cole(15) — MV	m	To:t-10
6/57	8:00	Adventures of Sir Lancelot — AD	c	
6/57	9:30	Robert Montgomery Presents(60) — DA	c	
7/57	7:30	Georgia Gibbs(15) — MU	d	
7/57	8:00	Charlie Farrell — SC	m	Fr:m-9-9/56(c)
7/57	8:30	Action Tonight — DA	d*	
7/57	9:30	Arthur Murray Party — MV	m	Fr:t-8
7/57	10:00	Original Amateur Hour — TA	m	Fr:n-9(a)
9/57	7:30	Georgia Gibbs(15) — MU	c	
9/57	7:30	The Price Is Right — QU	d	
9/57	8:00	Charlie Farrell — SC	m	To:m-7:30-8/60(c)
9/57	8:00	Restless Gun — WE	d	
9/57	8:30	Action Tonight — DA	c*	
9/57	9:30	Arthur Murray Party — MV	m	To:m-10-9/58
9/57	9:30	Goodyear TV Playhouse — DA	m	Fr:n-9
9/57	10:00	Original Amateur Hour — TA	m	To:n-7
9/57	10:00	Suspicion(60) — SA	d	
10/57	9:30	Alcoa Theatre — DA	d	
6/58	7:30	Haggis Baggis — QU	d	
6/58	7:30	The Price Is Right — QU	m	To:r-10
9/58	7:30	Haggis Baggis — QU	c	
9/58	9:00	Peter Gunn — CD	d	
9/58	9:00	Twenty-One — QU	m	To:r-8:30
9/58	10:00	Arthur Murray Party — MV	m	Fr:m-9:30-9/57
9/58	10:00	Suspicion(60) — SA	m	To:n-7:30-6/59
10/58	7:30	Tic Tac Dough — QU	m	Fr:r-7:30
12/58	7:30	Tic Tac Dough — QU	c	
1/59	7:30	Buckskin — WE	m	Fr:f-7:30
9/59	7:30	Buckskin — WE	m	To:n-8:30-7/65
9/59	8:00	Love & Marriage — SC	d	
9/59	8:00	Restless Gun — WE	c	
9/59	10:00	Arthur Murray Party — MV	m	To:t-9
9/59	10:00	Steve Allen(60) — CV	m	Fr:n-7:30-6/59
10/59	7:30	Richard Diamond, Pvt. Detective — CD	m	Fr:n-10(c)
1/60	7:30	Richard Diamond, Pvt. Detective — CD	m	To:t-9-6/60
1/60	8:00	Love & Marriage — SC	c	
2/60	7:30	Riverboat(60) — AD	m	Fr:n-7

Date	Time	Title (min. if not 30) – Type	Action	From/To
6/60	10:00	Steve Allen(60) – CV	m	To:w-7:30-9/61(a)
9/60	9:00	Peter Gunn – CD	m	To:m-10:30(a)
9/60	9:30	Alcoa Theatre – DA	c	
9/60	9:30	Goodyear TV Playhouse – DA	c	
9/60	10:00	Barbara Stanwyck – DA	d	
9/60	10:30	Jackpot Bowling Starring Milton Berle – QU	m	Fr:f-10:45-6/60
10/60	9:00	Klondike – AD	d	
10/60	9:30	Dante – MY	d	
1/61	7:30	The Americans(60) – WD	d	
1/61	7:30	Riverboat(60) – AD	c	
2/61	9:00	Acapulco – AD	d	
2/61	9:00	Klondike – AD	c	
3/61	10:30	Jackpot Bowling Starring Milton Berle – QU	c	
4/61	9:00	Acapulco – AD	c	
4/61	9:30	Concentration – QU	m	Fr:r-8:30-11/58
4/61	9:30	Dante – MY	c	
5/61	9:00	Whispering Smith – WE	d	
9/61	7:30	The Americans(60) – WD	c	
9/61	8:00	National Velvet – AD	m	Fr:n-8
9/61	8:30	The Price Is Right – QU	m	Fr:w-8:30
9/61	8:30	Tales of Wells Fargo – WE	m	To:s-7:30
9/61	9:00	87th Precinct(60) – CD	d	
9/61	9:00	Whispering Smith – WE	c	
9/61	9:30	Concentration – QU	c	
9/61	10:00	Barbara Stanwyck – DA	c	
9/61	10:00	Thriller(60) – SA	m	Fr:t-9
7/62	10:00	Actuality Specials(60) – DO	d	
7/62	10:00	Thriller(60) – SA	c	
9/62	7:30	It's a Man's World(60) – SC	d	
9/62	8:00	National Velvet – AD	c	
9/62	8:30	The Price Is Right – QU	m	To:m-9:30
9/62	8:30	Saints and Sinners(60) – ND	d	
9/62	9:00	87th Precinct(60) – CD	c	
9/62	9:30	The Price Is Right – QU	m	Fr:m-8:30
9/62	10:00	Actuality Specials(60) – DO	m	To:n-7-10/65
10/62	10:00	David Brinkley's Journal(60) – DO	m	Fr:w-10:30
1/63	7:30	It's a Man's World(60) – SC	c	
1/63	8:30	Saints and Sinners(60) – ND	c	
1/63	9:30	The Price Is Right – QU	m	To:f-9:30
2/63	7:30	Film(120) – FI	s	
2/63	9:30	Art Linkletter – QU	d	
8/63	10:00	David Brinkley's Journal(60) – DO	c	
9/63	9:30	Art Linkletter – QU	c	
9/63	9:30	Hollywood and the Stars – DO	d	
9/63	10:00	Sing Along with Mitch(60) – MV	m	Fr:f-8:30
9/64	7:30	Film(120) – FI	f	
9/64	9:30	Hollywood and the Stars – DO	c	
9/64	10:00	Sing Along with Mitch(60) – MV	m	To:f-8:30-4/66

Date	Time	Title (min. if not 30) — Type	Action	From/To
10/64	7:30	Karen — SC	d	
10/64	8:00	Harris Against the World — SC	d	
10/64	8:30	Tom, Dick and Mary — SC	d	
10/64	9:00	Andy Williams(60) — MV	m	Fr:t-10-5/64
10/64	10:00	Alfred Hitchcock Presents(60) — SA	m	Fr:f-10(c)
1/65	8:00	Harris Against the World — SC	c	
1/65	8:00	Man from U.N.C.L.E.(60) — SD	m	Fr:t-8:30
1/65	8:30	Tom, Dick and Mary — SC	c	
8/65	7:30	Karen — SC	c	
9/65	7:30	Hullabaloo — MU	m	Fr:t-10
9/65	8:00	John Forsythe — SC	d	
9/65	8:00	Man from U.N.C.L.E.(60) — SD	m	To:f-10
9/65	8:30	Dr. Kildare — MD	m	Fr:r-8:30
9/65	10:00	Alfred Hitchcock Presents(60) — SA	c	
9/65	10:00	Run for Your Life(60) — AD	d	
5/66	9:00	Andy Williams(60) — MV	m	To:n-10-9/66
6/66	9:00	Kraft Summer Music Hall(60) — VY	d	
8/66	7:30	Hullabaloo — MU	c	
8/66	8:00	John Forsythe — SC	c	
8/66	8:30	Dr. Kildare — MD	c	
8/66	9:00	Kraft Summer Music Hall(60) — VY	c	
9/66	7:30	Monkees — SC	d	
9/66	8:00	I Dream of Jeannie — SC	m	Fr:s-9
9/66	8:30	Roger Miller — MV	d	
9/66	9:00	The Road West(60) — WE	d	
12/66	8:30	Roger Miller — MV	c	
1/67	8:30	Captain Nice — SC	d	
8/67	8:00	I Dream of Jeannie — SC	m	To:t-7:30
8/67	8:30	Captain Nice — SC	c	
8/67	9:00	The Road West(60) — WE	c	
9/67	8:00	Man from U.N.C.L.E.(60) — SD	m	Fr:f-8:30
9/67	9:00	Danny Thomas Hour(60) — VS	d	
9/67	10:00	I Spy(60) — SD	m	Fr:w-10
9/67	10:00	Run for Your Life(60) — AD	m	To:w-10
1/68	8:00	Man from U.N.C.L.E.(60) — SD	c	
1/68	8:00	Rowan & Martin's Laugh-In(60) — CV	d	
6/68	8:00	The Champion(60) — AD	d*	
6/68	9:00	NBC Comedy Playhouse(60) — CA	d	
6/68	9:00	Danny Thomas Hour(60) — VS	c	
8/68	7:30	Monkees — SC	c	
9/68	7:30	I Dream of Jeannie — SC	m	Fr:t-7:30
9/68	8:00	The Champion(60) — AD	c*	
9/68	9:00	Film(120) — FI	s	
9/68	9:00	NBC Comedy Playhouse(60) — CA	m	To:s-7:30-8/70
9/68	10:00	I Spy(60) — SD	c	
7/69	8:00	Monday Theatre(60) — VS	d*	
8/69	7:30	I Dream of Jeannie — SC	m	To:t-7:30
9/69	7:30	My World and Welcome to It — SC	d	
9/69	8:00	Monday Theatre(60) — VS	m*	To:m-8-7/70

Date	Time	Title (min. if not 30) — Type	Action	From/To
7/70	8:00	Monday Theatre(60) — VS	m*	Fr:m-8-9/69
8/70	8:00	Monday Theatre(60) — VS	c*	
9/70	7:30	My World and Welcome to It — SC	m	To:r-8-6/72(c)
9/70	7:30	Red Skelton — CV	m	Fr:t-8:30-6/70(c)
3/71	7:30	From a Bird's Eye View — SC	d	
3/71	7:30	Red Skelton — CV	m	To:n-8:30-6/71
6/71	8:00	NBC Comedy Theatre(60) — CA	d*	
8/71	7:30	From a Bird's Eye View — SC	c	
8/71	8:00	NBC Comedy Theatre(60) — CA	m*	To:s-8-7/72
6/72	8:00	Baseball(180) — SP	s	
5/73	8:00	Rowan & Martin's Laugh-In(60) — CV	c	
9/73	8:00	Lotsa Luck — SC	d	
9/73	8:30	Diana — SC	d	
1/74	8:00	Lotsa Luck — SC	m	To:f-8:30
1/74	8:00	The Magician(60) — AD	m	Fr:t-9
1/74	8:30	Diana — SC	c	
5/74	8:00	The Magician(60) — AD	c	
9/74	8:00	Born Free(60) — AD	d	
12/74	8:00	Born Free(60) — AD	c	
1/75	8:00	Smothers Brothers Comedy Hour (60) — CV	d	
5/75	8:00	Smothers Brothers Comedy Hour (60) — CV	c	
9/75	8:00	Baseball(180) — SP	f	
9/75	8:00	Invisible Man(60) — SF	d	
1/76	8:00	Invisible Man(60) — SF	c	
1/76	9:00	Film(120) — FI	f	
2/76	8:00	Rich Little(60) — CV	d	
2/76	9:00	Joe Forrester(60) — CD	m	Fr:t-10
2/76	10:00	Jigsaw John(60) — CD	d	
5/76	8:00	John Davidson(60) — MV	d	
5/76	8:00	Rich Little(60) — CV	m	To:m-8-6/76
6/76	8:00	John Davidson(60) — MV	c	
6/76	8:00	Rich Little(60) — CV	m	Fr:m-8-5/76
7/76	8:00	Comedy Theatre(60) — CA	d	
7/76	8:00	Rich Little(60) — CV	c	
9/76	8:00	Comedy Theatre(60) — CA	m	To:r-8:30-5/79
9/76	8:00	Little House on the Prairie(60) — DR	m	Fr:w-8
9/76	9:00	Joe Forrester(60) — CD	c	
9/76	9:00	Film(120) — FI	s	
9/76	10:00	Jigsaw John(60) — CD	c	
9/76	10:00	Van Dyke and Company(60) — CV	d	
9/76	10:00	Van Dyke and Company(60) — CV	m	To:r-10
4/78	8:00	Roller Girls — SC	d*	
4/78	8:30	Joe & Valerie — SC	d*	
5/78	8:00	Roller Girls — SC	m*	To:w-8
5/78	8:30	Joe & Valerie — SC	m*	To:w-8:30
5/81	9:00	Film(120) — FI	f	
6/81	9:00	Flamingo Road(60) — SL	m	Fr:t-10-3/81

Date	Time	Title (min. if not 30) — Type	Action	From/To
6/81	10:00	Last Convertible(60) — DR	d	
8/81	9:00	Flamingo Road(60) — SL	m	To:t-10-11/81
8/81	9:00	Film(120) — FI	s#	
8/81	10:00	Last Convertible(60) — DR	c	
3/83	8:00	Little House on the Prairie(60) — DR	c	
3/83	8:00	Love, Sidney — SC	m	Fr:s-9:30-12/82
3/83	8:30	Family Ties — SC	m	Fr:w-9:30
8/83	8:00	Love, Sidney — SC	c	
8/83	8:30	Family Ties — SC	m	To:w-8:30
9/83	8:00	Boone(60) — DR	d	
12/83	8:00	Boone(60) — DR	m	To:s-10-7/84
1/84	8:00	TV's Bloopers & Practical Jokes (60) — CY	d	
2/86	8:00	TV's Bloopers & Practical Jokes (60) — CY	m	To:f-8-5/88
3/86	8:00	You Again — SC	d	
3/86	8:30	Valerie — SC	d	
6/86	8:00	You Again — SC	m	To:w-9:30
6/86	8:00	Valerie — SC	m	Fr:m-8:30
6/86	8:30	Amazing Stories — DA	m	Fr:n-8
6/86	8:30	Valerie — SC	m	To:m-8
9/86	8:00	Valerie — SC	m	To:n-8:30
9/86	8:00	ALF — SC	d#	
2/87	8:30	Amazing Stories — DA	m	To:f-8:30
3/87	8:30	Valerie — Sc	m#	Fr:n-8:30

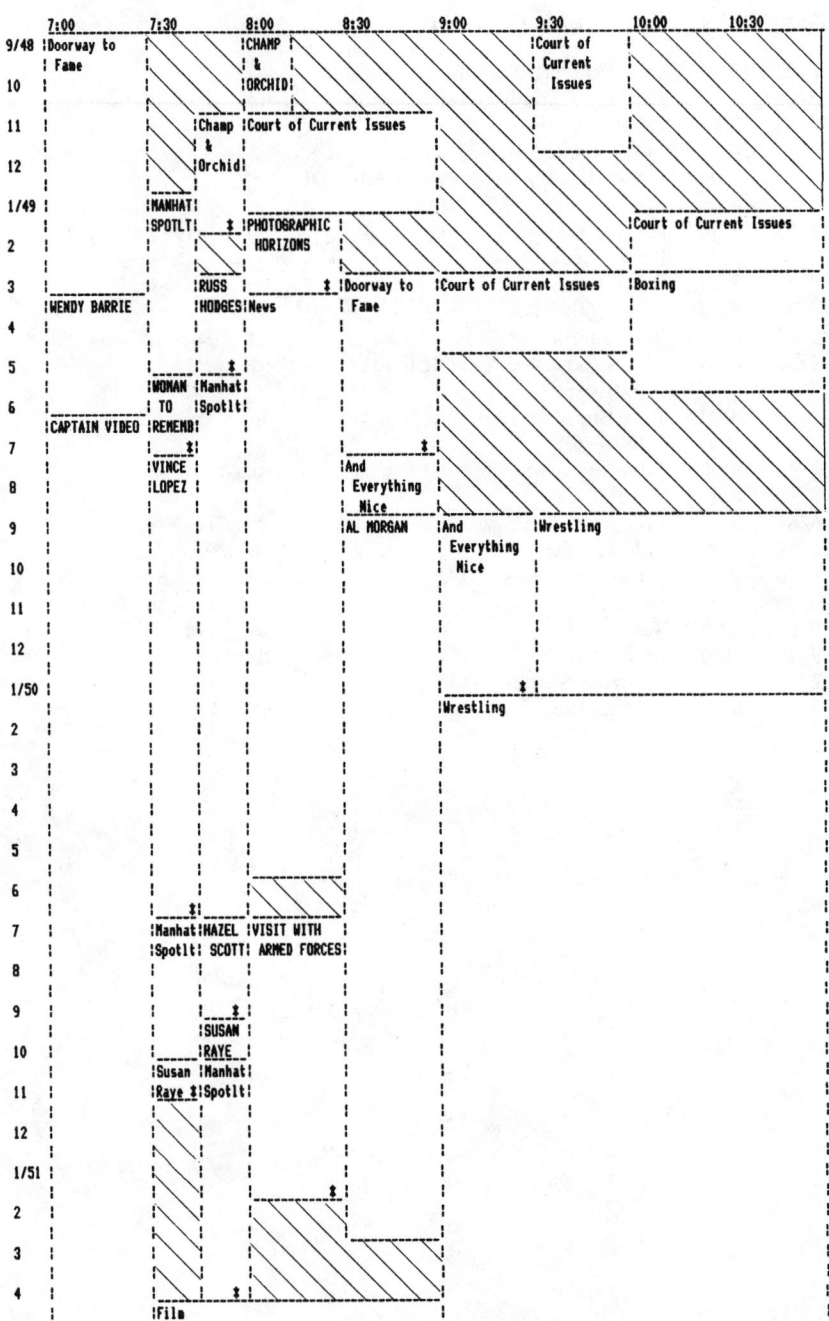

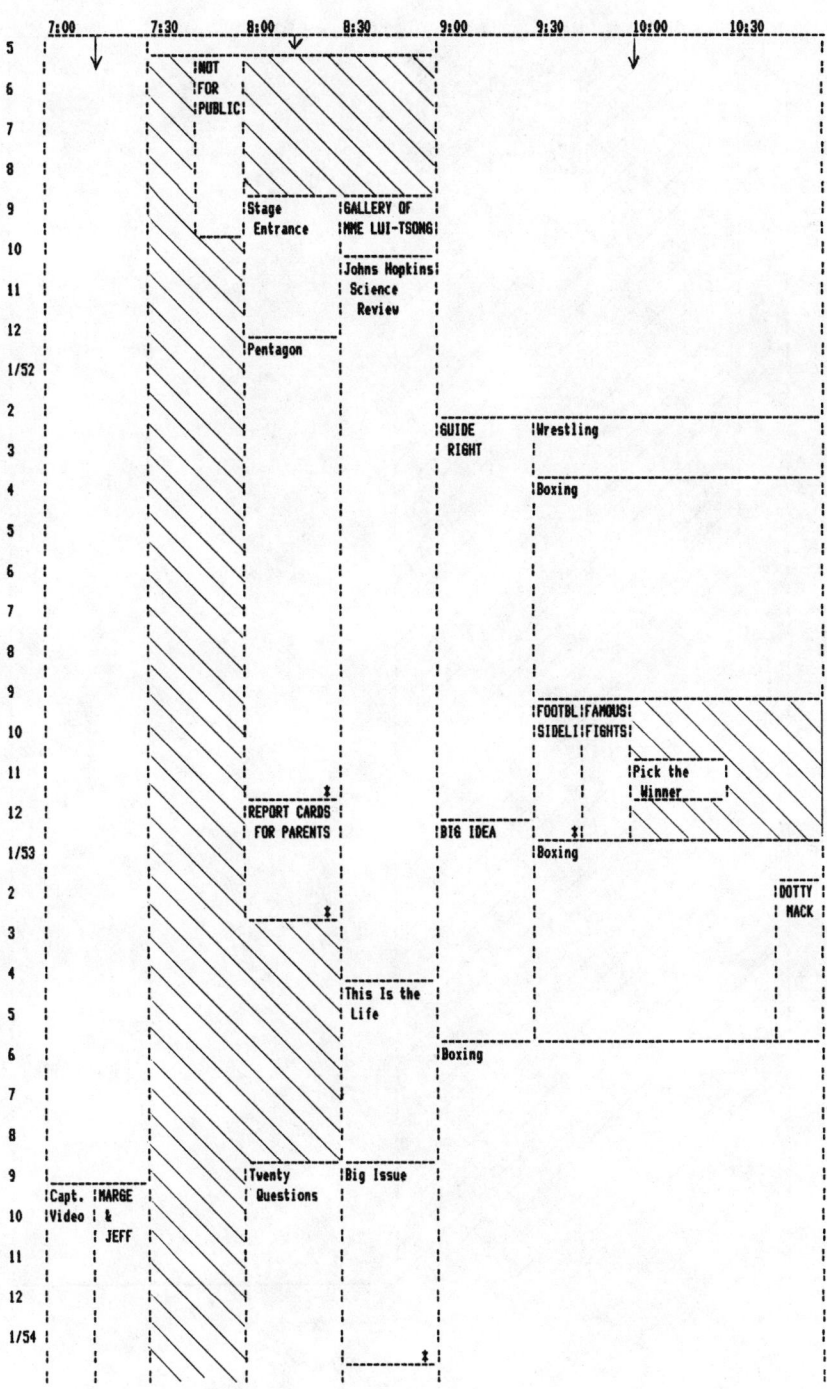

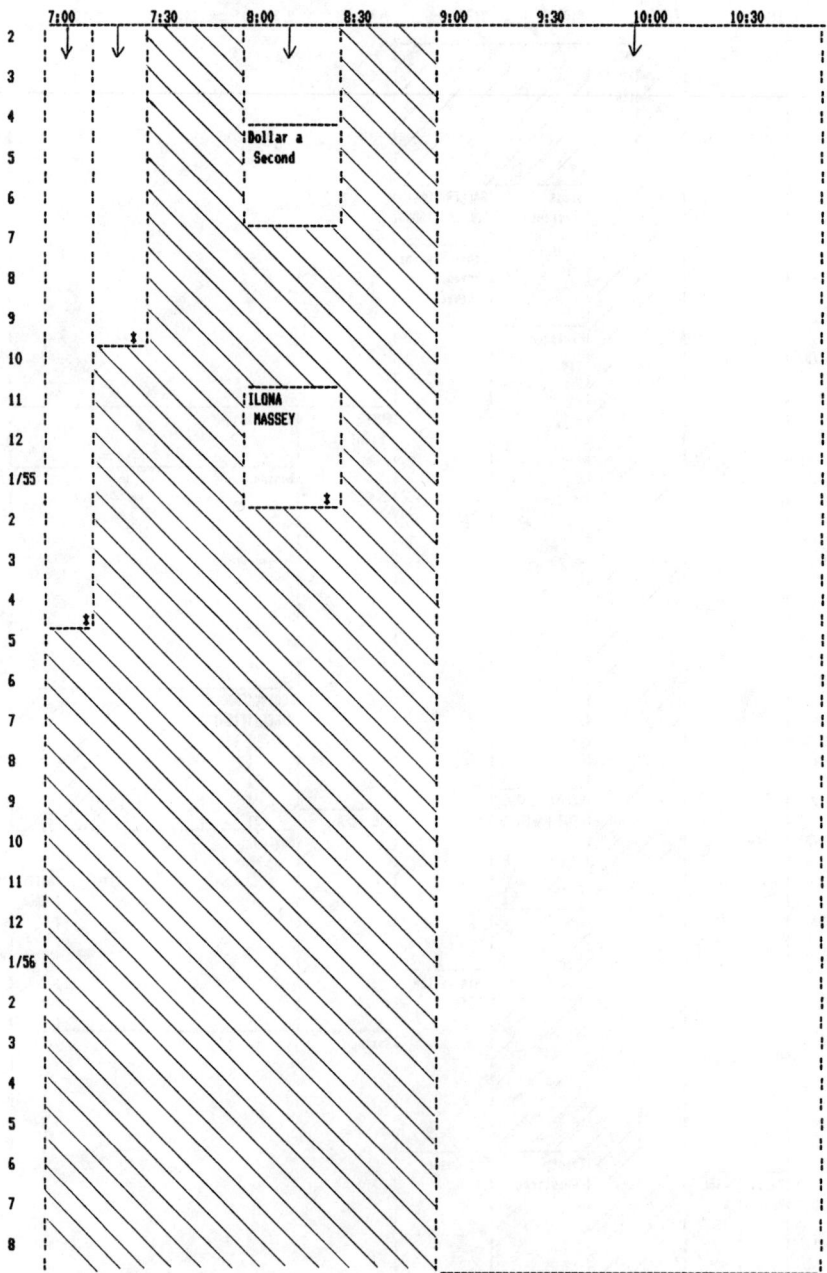

Date	*Time*	*Title (min. if not 30) — Type*	*Action*	*From/To*
1/48	7:00	Doorway to Fame — TA	m	Fr:f-7:30
7/48	9:30	Court of Current Issues — DB	m	Fr:t-8
9/48	8:00	Champagne & Orchids(15) — MU	d	
11/48	7:45	Champagne & Orchids(15) — MU	m	Fr:m-8
11/48	8:00	Champagne & Orchids(15) — MU	m	To:m-7:45
11/48	8:00	Court of Current Issues(60) — DB	m	Fr:m-9:30
11/48	9:30	Court of Current Issues — DB	m	To:m-8
1/49	7:30	Manhattan Spotlight(15) — IV	d	
1/49	7:45	Champagne & Orchids(15) — MU	c	
1/49	8:00	Court of Current Issues(60) — DB	m	To:m-10
1/49	8:00	Photographic Horizons — IS	d	
1/49	10:00	Court of Current Issues(60) — DB	m	Fr:m-8
2/49	10:00	Court of Current Issues(60) — DB	m	To:m-9
3/49	7:00	Doorway to Fame — TA	m	To:m-8:30
3/49	7:00	Wendy Barrie — IV	d	
3/49	7:45	Russ Hodges(15) — SN	d	
3/49	8:00	News — NW	s	
3/49	8:00	Photographic Horizons — IS	c	
3/49	8:30	Doorway to Fame — TA	m	Fr:m-7
3/49	9:00	Court of Current Issues(60) — DB	m	Fr:m-10
3/49	10:00	Boxing(60) — SP	s	
4/49	9:00	Court of Current Issues(60) — DB	m	To:w-9
5/49	7:30	A Woman to Remember(15) — SL	d	
5/49	7:30	Manhattan Spotlight(15) — IV	m	To:m-7:45
5/49	7:45	Russ Hodges(15) — SN	c	
5/49	7:45	Manhattan Spotlight(15) — IV	m	Fr:m-7:30
5/49	10:00	Boxing(60) — SP	f	
6/49	7:00	Captain Video & Video Rangers — KV	d	
6/49	7:00	Wendy Barrie — IV	m	To:w-7
7/49	7:30	Vincent Lopez(15) — MV	d	
7/49	7:30	A Woman to Remember(15) — SL	c	
7/49	8:30	And Everything Nice — FS	m	Fr:t-7
7/49	8:30	Doorway to Fame — TA	c	
8/49	8:30	And Everything Nice — FS	m	To:m-9
9/49	8:30	Al Morgan — MU	d	
9/49	9:00	And Everything Nice — FS	m	Fr:m-8:30
9/49	9:30	Wrestling(90) — SP	s	
1/50	9:00	And Everything Nice — FS	c	
1/50	9:00	Wrestling(120) — SP	s	
1/50	9:30	Wrestling(90) — SP	f	
5/50	8:00	News — NW	f	
6/50	7:30	Vincent Lopez(15) — MV	c	
6/50	7:45	Manhattan Spotlight(15) — IV	m	To:m-7:30
7/50	7:30	Manhattan Spotlight(15) — IV	m	Fr:m-7:45
7/50	7:45	Hazel Scott(15) — MU	d	
7/50	8:00	Visit with the Armed Forces — DO	d	
9/50	7:45	Hazel Scott(15) — MU	c	
9/50	7:45	Susan Raye(15) — MU	d	
10/50	7:30	Susan Raye(15) — MU	m	Fr:m-7:45

Date	Time	Title (min. if not 30) — Type	Action	From/To
10/50	7:30	Manhattan Spotlight(15) — IV	m	To:m-7:45
10/50	7:45	Susan Raye(15) — MU	m	To:m-7:30
10/50	7:45	Manhattan Spotlight(15) — IV	m	Fr:m-7:30
11/50	7:30	Susan Raye(15) — MU	c	
1/51	8:00	Visit with the Armed Forces — DO	c	
2/51	8:30	Al Morgan — MU	m	To:r-8-5/51
4/51	7:30	Film(90) — FI	s	
4/51	7:45	Manhattan Spotlight(15) — IV	c	
5/51	7:30	Film(90) — FI	f	
5/51	7:45	Not for Publication(15) — ND	d	
9/51	7:45	Not for Publication(15) — ND	m	To:f-8:30-12/51
9/51	8:00	Stage Entrance — IV	m	Fr:w-7:45
9/51	8:30	Gallery of Mme. Lui-Tsong — CD	d	
10/51	8:30	Gallery of Mme. Lui-Tsong — CD	m	To:w-9
10/51	8:30	Johns Hopkins Science Review — IF	m	Fr:t-8:30
12/51	8:00	Pentagon — IV	m	Fr:n-8:30
12/51	8:00	Stage Entrance — IV	m	To:n-7
2/52	9:00	Guide Right — VY	d	
2/52	9:00	Wrestling(120) — SP	f	
2/52	9:30	Wrestling(90) — SP	s	
3/52	9:30	Wrestling(90) — SP	f	
4/52	9:30	Boxing(90) — SP	s	
9/52	9:30	Football Sidelines(15) — SH	d	
9/52	9:30	Boxing(90) — SP	f	
9/52	9:45	Famous Fights(15) — SH	d	
11/52	8:00	Pentagon — IV	c	
11/52	10:00	Pick the Winner — PO	m	Fr:r-9
11/52	10:00	Pick the Winner — PO	m	To:w-7:30-9/56(c)
12/52	8:00	Report Card for Parents — DS	d	
12/52	9:00	Big Idea — IN	d	
12/52	9:00	Guide Right — VY	m	To:r-8
12/52	9:30	Football Sidelines(15) — SH	c	
12/52	9:45	Famous Fights(15) — SH	m	To:w-10:45-7/57(a)
1/53	9:30	Boxing(90) — SP	s	
2/53	8:00	Report Card for Parents — DS	c	
2/53	10:45	Dotty Mack(15) — MU	d	
4/53	8:30	Johns Hopkins Science Review — IF	m	To:w-8
4/53	8:30	This Is the Life — RD	s	
5/53	9:00	Big Idea — In	m	To:r-10
5/53	9:30	Boxing(90) — SP	f	
6/53	9:00	Boxing(120) — SP	s	
6/53	10:45	Dotty Mack(15) — MU	m	To:t-9
8/53	8:30	This Is the Life — RD	f	
9/53	7:00	Captain Video & Video Rangers — KV	m	To:m-f-7
9/53	7:00	Captain Video & Video Rangers (15) — KV	m	Fr:m-f-7
9/53	7:15	Marge and Jeff(15) — SC	d	
9/53	8:00	Twenty Questions — QU	m	Fr:f-10
9/53	8:30	Big Issue — PA	m	Fr:t-8:30-6/53

Date	Time	Title (min. if not 30) — Type	Action	From/To
1/54	8:30	Big Issue — PA	c	
4/54	8:00	Dollar a Second — QU	m	Fr:n-10
4/54	8:00	Twenty Questions — QU	m	To:n-10
6/54	8:00	Dollar a Second — QU	m	To:n-10(n)
9/54	7:15	Marge and Jeff(15) — SC	c	
11/54	8:00	Ilona Massey — MU	d	
1/55	8:00	Ilona Massey — MU	c	
4/55	7:00	Captain Video & Video Rangers (15) — KV	c	
8/56	9:00	Boxing(120) — SP	f	

Monday Programming
Moves Summary

1948–49

ABC. *Series Premieres:* ABC Barn Dance; Identify; On Trial; Science Circus; Skip Farrell; What Do You Think.

CBS. *Series Premieres:* Arthur Godfrey's Talent Scouts; Campus Corner; Cliff Edwards; The Goldbergs; Manhattan Showcase; Places Please; Sonny Kendis; Through the Crystal Ball. *Key Programming Moves:* THE GOLDBERGS debuts; this was one of the long-running radio situation comedies that made a successful transition to television; ARTHUR GODFREY'S TALENT SCOUTS debuts in the 8:30–9 slot; it was to occupy this time slot for the next 10 years.

NBC. *Series Premieres:* Chevrolet Tele-Theatre; The Clock; Colgate Theatre; Kukla, Fran & Ollie; Mohawk Showroom; Princess Sagaphi; Three Flames; Who Said That. *Key Programming Moves:* KUKLA, FRAN & OLLIE debuts; this children's program aired every Monday through Friday for 10 years.

DuMont. *Series Premieres:* Captain Video & His Video Rangers; Champagne & Orchids; Manhattan Spotlight; Photographic Horizons; Russ Hodges; Vincent Lopez; Wendy Barrie; A Woman to Remember. *Key Programming Moves:* CAPTAIN VIDEO & HIS VIDEO RANGERS debuts; this series was the longest running series that the DuMont network ever had, lasting over six years.

1949–50

ABC. *Series Premieres:* Mr. Black; Your Witness. *Key Programming Moves:* In November, ABC suspended programming on Monday night for the rest of the season.

CBS. *Series Premieres:* Alkali Ike; Garry Moore Show; Life with

Snarky Parker; Parade of Stars; Paul Arnold Show; Silver Theatre; Stork Club. *Key Programming Moves:* STUDIO ONE was moved into 10–11 slot where it stayed until 9/58.

NBC. *Series Premieres:* Cities Service Band of America; Menasha the Magnificent; Robert Montgomery Presents; Voice of Firestone. *Key Programming Moves:* VOICE OF FIRESTONE debuts in 8:30–9 slot where it stays for the next five years; in 6/54 it switched to ABC, occupying the same time slot until 6/59; ROBERT MONTGOMERY PRESENTS debuts; it is one of the most successful anthology drama series, lasting until 6/57.

DuMont: *Series Premieres:* Al Morgan Show; Hazel Scott Show; Visit with the Armed Forces. *Key Programming Moves:* DuMont schedules professional wrestling in prime time, where it becomes a staple of the network's Monday night schedule until 4/52.

1950–51

ABC. *Series Premieres:* America's Health; Bill Gwinn Show; College Bowl; Jerry Colonna Show; Treasury Men in Action; United or Not. *Key Programming Moves:* ABC resumes Monday night programming with a lineup that is uneventful.

CBS. *Series Premieres:* Horace Heidt Show; It's News to Me; Lux Video Theatre; Steve Allen Show; Who's Whose. *Key Programming Moves:* LUX VIDEO THEATRE debuts; this dramatic anthology series lasted until 9/57; THE PERRY COMO SHOW is moved into 7:45–8 slot, where it stayed in this slot until 6/55; it then moved to NBC, expanded to 60 minutes and lasted eight more years.

NBC. *Series Premieres:* Paul Winchell & Jerry Mahoney Show.

DuMont: *Series Premieres:* Not for Publication; Susan Raye Show.

1951–52

ABC. *Series Premieres:* Amazing Mr. Malone; Mr. District Attorney; On Guard; Out of the Blue. *Key Programming Moves:* ABC stops programming the 7–7:30 slot; in April, they discontinue programming 10–11, as well, leaving it with only 2½ hours of programming (7:30–10).

CBS. *Series Premieres:* Claudia, the Story of a Marriage; I Love Lucy; Who's There. *Key Programming Moves:* I LOVE LUCY debuts; this series is one of the most successful in the history of television; the first regular prime time series to film its episodes for subsequent re-use; I LOVE LUCY is the classic situation comedy, the one whose form all others are derived from; I LOVE LUCY, and later, THE LUCY SHOW anchored CBS' successful Monday night lineup for most of the next 23 years; ARTHUR GODFREY'S TALENT SCOUTS becomes the #1 rated series on television with an average weekly rating of 53.8.

NBC. *Series Premieres:* Bob & Ray; Those Two; Up to Paar. *Key Programming Moves:* KUKLA, FRAN & OLLIE is cut back to 15 minutes in 11/51; it leaves NBC in 7/52; LIGHTS OUT is cancelled.

DuMont: *Series Premieres:* The Gallery of Madame Lui-Tsong; Guide Right.

1952-53

ABC. *Series Premieres:* Opera vs. Jazz; Talent Patrol; Why.

CBS. *Series Premieres:* Life with Luigi. *Key Programming Moves:* I LOVE LUCY becomes the #1 rated series on television, with an average weekly rating of 67.3 (the highest ever recorded for a series); the success of CBS' Monday night lineup is such that it renders the other networks' programming moves useless; THE GEORGE BURNS & GRACIE ALLEN SHOW is moved into the 8-8:30 slot which it occupies until 9/58.

NBC. *Series Premieres:* Eye Witness; Name That Tune.

DuMont. *Series Premieres:* Big Idea; Dotty Mack Show; Famous Fights; Football Sidelines; Report Card for Parents.

1953-54

ABC. *Series Premieres:* Big Picture; Jamie; Jr. Press Conference; Of Many Things; Sky King; Walter Winchell. *Key Programming Moves:* VOICE OF FIRESTONE is picked up for NBC; it lasts until 6/59.

CBS. *Key Programming Moves:* I LOVE LUCY is again the #1 rated series on television, anchoring CBS' dominant Monday night lineup.

NBC. *Series Premieres:* Background; Comment; Droodles; Tony Martin Show.

DuMont: *Series Premieres:* Marge & Jeff. *Key Programming Moves:* CAPTAIN VIDEO & HIS VIDEO RANGERS is cut back to 15 minutes; DuMont is floundering; by July they only had programming in the 7-7:30 slot and Boxing from 9-11.

1954-55

ABC. *Series Premieres:* Come Closer; Pee Wee King Show; TV Reader's Digest. *Key Programming Moves:* KUKLA, FRAN & OLLIE moved to ABC; it lasts until 6/57.

CBS. *Series Premieres:* December Bride; Julius LaRosa Show. *Key Programming Moves:* DECEMBER BRIDE debuts in the 9:30–10 slot, taking advantage of the I LOVE LUCY lead-in; it stays on Monday until 7/58; I LOVE LUCY is the #1 rated series on television for the third consecutive year.

NBC. *Series Premieres:* Caesar's Hour; Medic. *Key Programming Moves:* CAESAR'S HOUR debuts; NBC tries to counter the strength of CBS but doesn't have much success.

DuMont: *Series Premieres:* Ilona Massey Show. *Key Programming Moves:* CAPTAIN VIDEO & HIS VIDEO RANGERS is cancelled in 4/55; Du-Mont is left with Boxing as its only Monday night programming.

1955–56

ABC. *Series Premieres:* Bold Journey; Medical Horizons; Twilight Theatre.

CBS. *Series Premieres:* Adventures of Robin Hood. *Key Programming Moves:* I LOVE LUCY is unseated as the #1 rated series by CBS' $64,000 QUESTION (seen on Tuesday), but CBS' Monday night lineup is as strong as ever, placing two programs (I LOVE LUCY and DECEMBER BRIDE) in the top six.

NBC. *Series Premieres:* Gordon MacRae Show.

DuMont. *Key Programming Moves:* DuMont ceases programming at the end of the season.

1956–57

ABC. *Series Premieres:* ABC Presents; Lawrence Welk's Top Tunes and New Talent; Sports Focus.

CBS. *Key Programming Moves:* For the fourth time in five years I LOVE LUCY is the #1 series on television; despite its success I LOVE LUCY stopped producing new episodes at the end of the season.

NBC. *Series Premieres:* Can Do; Georgia Gibbs Show; Nat King Cole; Sir Lancelot; Stanley; Tales of Wells Fargo. *Key Programming Moves:* TALES OF WELLS FARGO debuts in 8:30–9 slot; it stays in this slot until 9/61; ROBERT MONTGOMERY PRESENTS is cancelled in 6/57.

1957–58

ABC. *Series Premieres:* American Bandstand; American Odyssey; Campaign Roundup; Guy Mitchell Show; Love That Jill; Polka-Go-Round.

Key Programming Moves: After a successful run on daytime television, AMERICAN BANDSTAND debuts in prime time; it lasts only three months (though it has continued successfully on weekends into the 1980s).

CBS. *Series Premieres:* Frontier Justice. *Key Programming Moves:* THE DANNY THOMAS SHOW is picked up from ABC and placed in the 9-9:30 slot (which was previously occupied by I LOVE LUCY); it lasts in this slot until 9/64; CBS cancelled four of its long-running Monday night series (ADVENTURES OF ROBIN HOOD, GEORGE BURNS & GRACIE ALLEN SHOW, ARTHUR GODFREY'S TALENT SCOUTS, STUDIO ONE) and moved a fifth (DECEMBER BRIDE) at the end of the season; this was the break-up of one of the most successful nights of programming in the history of television.

NBC. *Series Premieres:* Haggis Baggis; The Price Is Right; Restless Gun; Suspicion. *Key Programming Moves:* RESTLESS GUN debuts; this was one of the many series riding the new popularity of the western format.

1958-59

ABC. *Series Premieres:* John Gunther; Tales of the Texas Rangers.

CBS. *Series Premieres:* Ann Sothern Show; The Texan; Westinghouse Desilu Playhouse. *Key Programming Moves:* FATHER KNOWS BEST is picked up from NBC and moved into the 8:30-9 slot; it stayed there for the next two years; Situation comedies are still the anchor of CBS' Monday night lineup with FATHER KNOWS BEST, THE DANNY THOMAS SHOW, and THE ANN SOTHERN SHOW.

NBC. *Series Premieres:* Alcoa Theatre; Peter Gunn. *Key Programming Moves:* RESTLESS GUN is cancelled.

1959-60

ABC. *Series Premieres:* Adventures in Paradise; Bourbon Street Beat. *Key Programming Moves:* CHEYENNE is moved to Monday, where it continued until 12/63; ADVENTURES IN PARADISE debuts; it lasted until 4/62.

CBS. *Series Premieres:* DuPont Show; Hennesey; Kate Smith Show; Spike Jones Show. *Key Programming Moves:* HENNESEY debuts in the 10-10:30 slot; it lasts for three years; At the end of the season, FATHER KNOWS BEST is moved to Tuesday and THE ANN SOTHERN SHOW is moved to Thursday.

NBC. *Series Premieres:* Love & Marriage. *Key Programming Moves:* GOODYEAR TV PLAYHOUSE is cancelled at the end of the season.

1960-61

ABC. *Series Premieres:* Surfside Six. *Key Programming Moves:* PETER GUNN is picked up from NBC; it is cancelled at the end of the season.

CBS. *Series Premieres:* Andy Griffith Show; Brenner; Bringing Up Buddy; Face the Nation; Pete & Gladys; Presidential Countdown. *Key Programming Moves:* THE ANDY GRIFFITH SHOW debuts; it begins a highly successful seven year Monday night run; TO TELL THE TRUTH is moved into the 7:30-8 slot, which it occupies until 9/66.

NBC. *Series Premieres:* Acapulco; Americans; Barbara Stanwyck Show; Dante; Klondike; Whispering Smith. *Key Programming Moves:* TALES OF WELLS FARGO is moved to Saturday at the end of the season.

1961-62

ABC. *Series Premieres:* Ben Casey. *Key Programming Moves:* BEN CASEY debuts; it begins a five year run; THE RIFLEMAN is moved to Monday night; SURFSIDE SIX is moved to Monday night and is cancelled at the end of the season.

CBS. *Series Premieres:* Window on Main Street. *Key Programming Moves:* CBS regains its stranglehold on Monday night with THE ANDY GRIFFITH SHOW, THE DANNY THOMAS SHOW and TO TELL THE TRUTH as its anchors; HENNESEY is cancelled at the end of the season.

NBC. *Series Premieres:* Actuality Specials; 87th Precinct. *Key Programming Moves:* NBC has an entirely different Monday night lineup from the previous season, though none of the new moves pan out; at the end of the season they change the entire lineup again.

1962-63

ABC. *Series Premieres:* Dakotas; Stoney Burke; Your Funny Funny Films. *Key Programming Moves:* CHEYENNE is moved out of the 7:30-8:30 slot in December; BEN CASEY is moved to Wednesday night at the end of the season.

CBS. *Series Premieres:* The Lucy Show; The New Loretta Young Show. *Key Programming Moves:* After five years, Lucille Ball returns in a weekly series as THE LUCY SHOW debuts; joining an already strong Monday night lineup; it stays on the air until 9/74; I'VE GOT A SECRET moves into the 8-8:30 slot, where it stays for the next four years.

NBC. *Series Premieres:* Art Linkletter Show; It's a Man's World;

Saints and Sinners. *Key Programming Moves:* NBC turns to theatrical films in place of weekly series in January and continues the practice until the end of the 1963–64 season.

1963–64

ABC. *Series Premieres:* Breaking Point; Outer Limits. *Key Programming Moves:* WAGON TRAIN is moved to Monday nights and is expanded to 90 minutes; at the end of the season it is cut back to 60 minutes and moved to Sunday.

CBS. *Series Premieres:* East Side / West Side. *Key Programming Moves:* EAST SIDE/WEST SIDE debuts; starring George C. Scott and Cicely Tyson, this series about a New York City social worker was praised by critics, but was not very successful with audiences or advertisers; it was cancelled at the end of the season. THE DANNY THOMAS SHOW is taken off the air at the end of the season but is not cancelled.

NBC. *Series Premieres:* Hollywood and the Stars.

1964–65

ABC. *Series Premieres:* Bing Crosby Show; No Time for Sergeants; Voyage to the Bottom of the Sea; Wendy & Me. *Key Programming Moves:* ABC tries an entirely different lineup from the previous season; VOYAGE TO THE BOTTOM OF THE SEA debuts; it is moved to Sunday at the end of the season; ABC brings George Burns back to weekly television in WENDY & ME; it is cancelled at the end of the season; BEN CASEY is moved back to the Monday 10–11 slot.

CBS. *Series Premieres:* Many Happy Returns; Slattery's People. *Key Programming Moves:* THE ANDY GRIFFITH SHOW is moved to 8:30 and THE LUCY SHOW is moved to 9; THE DANNY THOMAS SHOW is brought back in April; it is finally cancelled at the end of the season; CBS tries serious programming again in the 10–11 slot; first with SLATTERY'S PEOPLE, then with CBS REPORTS; neither works.

NBC. *Series Premieres:* Harris Against the World; Karen; Tom, Dick & Mary. *Key Programming Moves:* NBC tries an experiment called 90 BRISTOL COURT from 7:30-9; it consisted of three different series who's plots were connected in that all characters in all series lived in the same apartment house; the experiment didn't fare too well – all three series were gone by season's end.

1965-66

ABC. *Series Premieres:* A Man Called Shenandoah; Legend of Jesse James. *Key Programming Moves:* PEYTON PLACE is moved to Monday 9:30-10; it continues in this slot until 9/68; BEN CASEY is cancelled in 6/66; BIG VALLEY is moved into its time slot.

CBS. *Series Premieres:* Steve Lawrence Show. *Key Programming Moves:* THE LUCY SHOW and THE ANDY GRIFFITH SHOW switch time slots; TO TELL THE TRUTH and I'VE GOT A SECRET are moved at the end of the season to the 10-11 slot.

NBC. *Series Premieres:* John Forsythe Show; Kraft Summer Music Hall; Run for Your Life. *Key Programming Moves:* HULLABALOO is moved to Monday 7:30-8; it is cancelled at the end of the season; DR. KILDARE is moved to Monday (and Tuesday) after four years on Thursday; it is cancelled at the end of the season; RUN FOR YOUR LIFE debuts, beginning a three year run.

1966-67

ABC. *Series Premieres:* Felony Squad; Iron Horse; Rat Patrol. *Key Programming Moves:* FELONY SQUAD debuts; it lasts until 1/69.

CBS. *Series Premieres:* Coronet Blue; Family Affair; Jean Arthur Show; Mr. Terrific; Run Buddy Run. *Key Programming Moves:* GILLIGAN'S ISLAND is moved to Monday 7:30-8; it is cancelled at the end of the season; FAMILY AFFAIR debuts, beginning a five year run; CBS discontinues airing prime-time quiz shows as TO TELL THE TRUTH is cancelled after 11 years and I'VE GOT A SECRET and PASSWORD are taken off the air.

NBC. *Series Premieres:* Captain Nice; The Monkees; The Road West; Roger Miller Show. *Key Programming Moves:* THE MONKEES debuts; this series played off the popularity of the revolution of rock and roll music; the group portrayed in the series actually released records (though the NBC orchestra played the instruments), some of which made the popular music charts; I DREAM OF JEANNIE is moved to Monday 8-8:30; at the end of the season it is moved to Tuesday.

1967-68

ABC. *Series Premieres:* Cowboy in Africa.

CBS. *Series Premieres:* Carol Burnett Show. *Key Programming Moves:* THE CAROL BURNETT SHOW debuts; it begins a highly successful 12 year run on CBS; GUNSMOKE is moved to Monday after 12 years on

Saturday; it lasts for another eight years on Monday; THE ANDY GRIFFITH SHOW becomes the #1 rated series on television; it is discontinued at the end of the season because the star chose to leave the series.

NBC. *Series Premieres:* Comedy Playhouse; Danny Thomas Show; Rowan & Martin's Laugh-In. *Key Programming Moves:* ROWAN & MARTIN'S LAUGH-IN debuts in January, replacing the cancelled MAN FROM U.N.C.L.E.; LAUGH-IN was a highly innovative departure from the traditional comedy-variety form; it had a very successful five year run; I SPY is moved to Monday night and is cancelled at the end of the season; THE MONKEES is cancelled at the end of the season.

1968-69

ABC. *Series Premieres:* Dick Cavett Show; The Outcasts. *Key Programming Moves:* THE BIG VALLEY is cancelled in May; PEYTON PLACE is cancelled in June.

CBS. *Series Premieres:* Mayberry, RFD. *Key Programming Moves:* MAYBERRY, RFD debuts; this series was a situational spin-off from THE ANDY GRIFFITH SHOW; while this series maintained most of the flavor and supporting cast of its predecessor, it was never quite as popular with audiences.

NBC. *Key Programming Moves:* ROWAN & MARTIN'S LAUGH-IN becomes the #1 rated series on television; for the first time, NBC seriously challenged CBS for ratings supremacy on Monday night; NBC begins airing motion pictures in the 9–11 slot, a practice it would continue, off and on, to the present time.

1969-70

ABC. *Series Premieres:* Love, American Style; Music Scene; New People; Now; The Survivors. *Key Programming Moves:* ABC introduces an entire lineup of new series; by January, they abandon the lineup; ABC tries an experiment with MUSIC SCENE and NEW PEOPLE — both are 45 minutes long; both are cancelled four months later; LOVE, AMERICAN STYLE, a comedy anthology series, debuts; it lasts for five years; In January, ABC begins offering theatrical films on a regular basis each Monday; it has continued this practice, off and on, to the present time; IT TAKES A THIEF is cancelled at the end of the season.

CBS. *Key Programming Moves:* THE DORIS DAY SHOW moves into the 9:30-10 time slot.

NBC. *Series Premieres:* My World & Welcome to It. *Key Programming*

Moves: ROWAN & MARTIN'S LAUGH-IN is again the #1 rated series on television.

1970–71

ABC. *Series Premieres:* It Was a Very Good Year; Reel Game; Silent Force; Young Lawyers. *Key Programming Moves:* ABC introduces NFL'S MONDAY NIGHT FOOTBALL, bringing live professional football to weekly prime-time for the first time; the experiment is a huge success.

CBS. *Series Premieres:* CBS Newcomers; Suspense Playhouse. *Key Programming Moves:* THE CAROL BURNETT SHOW is moved to Wednesday at the end of the season; MAYBERRY, RFD is cancelled at the end of the season.

NBC. *Series Premieres:* From a Bird's Eye View.

1971–72

ABC. *Series Premieres:* Monday Night Specials. *Key Programming Moves:* ABC cuts back to three hours or programming (as does CBS and NBC) to accommodate the FCC's new Prime Time Access Rule, which limited networks to three hours of programming in prime time (instead of the previous 3½ hours).

NBC. *Key Programming Moves:* NBC begins offering live Major League Baseball in prime time during the summer months.

1972–73

ABC. *Series Premieres:* The Rookies. *Key Programming Moves:* THE ROOKIES debuts; it lasts for four years.

CBS. *Series Premieres:* The New Bill Cosby Show. *Key Programming Moves:* MEDICAL CENTER moves to Monday in May; THE DORIS DAY SHOW is cancelled at the end of the season.

NBC. *Key Programming Moves:* ROWAN & MARTIN'S LAUGH-IN is cancelled in May.

1973–74

CBS. *Key Programming Moves:* THE LUCY SHOW is cancelled at the end of the season.

NBC. *Series Premieres:* Diana; Lotsa Luck.

1974-75

ABC. *Series Premieres:* Caribe; S.W.A.T.

CBS. *Series Premieres:* Rhoda. *Key Programming Moves:* RHODA debuts; the first of three spin-offs from THE MARY TYLER MOORE SHOW; it lasts for four years; GUNSMOKE is cancelled at the end of the season, ending a successful 20 year run.

NBC. *Series Premieres:* Born Free; Smothers Brothers Show. *Key Programming Moves:* THE SMOTHERS BROTHERS SHOW debuts; it is unable to duplicate the popularity and success of its earlier version on CBS; this attempt was cancelled after five months.

1975-76

ABC. *Series Premieres:* Barbary Coast; Good Heavens; Viva Valdez.

CBS. *Series Premieres:* Phyllis. *Key Programming Moves:* CBS schedules a two hour comedy block from 8-10; ALL IN THE FAMILY is moved to Monday; it is the highest rated series on television for an unprecedented fifth consecutive year; MEDICAL CENTER is cancelled at the end of the season.

NBC. *Series Premieres:* Comedy Theatre; Invisible Man; Jigsaw John; John Davidson Show; Rich Little Show. *Key Programming Moves:* NBC tries airing weekly series from 9-11 in place of movies in January; at season's end they return to movies.

1976-77

ABC. *Series Premieres:* The Captain & Tennille Show; Comedy Special; Feather and Father Gang. *Key Programming Moves:* In April, ABC begins regular coverage of live Major League Baseball in prime time.

CBS. Series Premieres: All's Fair; Andros Targets; Busting Loose; Executive Suite; Shields and Yarnell Show; Szysznyk. *Key Programming Moves:* THE SONNY AND CHER SHOW is moved to Monday in May; it is cancelled at the end of the season.

NBC. *Series Premieres:* Van Dyke & Company. *Key Programming Moves:* LITTLE HOUSE ON THE PRAIRIE is moved to Monday, 8-9; it continues in this time slot for the next seven years.

1977-78

ABC. *Series Premieres:* Lucan; San Pedro Beach Bums. *Key Programming Moves:* In January, $6 MILLION MAN is moved to Monday; it is cancelled two months later.

CBS. *Series Premieres:* Baby, I'm Back; Betty White Show; Logan's Run; Rafferty; Young Dan'l Boone. *Key Programming Moves:* In January, M*A*S*H is moved to Monday, 9-9:30; it continues in this slot until 9/83; Also in January, ONE DAY AT A TIME is moved to Monday, 9:30-10, and LOU GRANT is moved into the 10-11 slot.

1978-79

ABC. *Series Premieres:* Salvage 1.

CBS. *Series Premieres:* Billy; Flatbush; People; WKRP in Cincinnati; The White Shadow. *Key Programming Moves:* WKRP IN CINCINNATI debuts; it stays on the air until 9/82; PEOPLE debuts; this series attempted to be the video version of the highly popular magazine; it wasn't, and was cancelled after only two months; In January, ONE DAY AT A TIME is moved to Wednesday.

1979-80

ABC. *Series Premieres:* Stone; That's Incredible; 240-Robert. *Key Programming Moves:* FAMILY is moved to Monday in December; it is cancelled in February; THAT'S INCREDIBLE debuts; this "info-tainment" program closely resembled an earlier series — YOU ASKED FOR IT — and the current NBC series, REAL PEOPLE; it stayed on the air until 2/84.

CBS. *Series Premieres:* Flo; House Calls; Phyl & Mikhy; Stockard Channing Show. *Key Programming Moves:* HOUSE CALLS debuts; it stays on the air for the next three years.

1980-81

ABC. *Series Premieres:* American Dream; Dynasty; Foul Play. *Key Programming Moves:* DYNASTY debuts in January, 1981; one of the "prime time soaps" introduced because of the success of CBS' DALLAS; in April, DYNASTY was moved to Wednesday, where it became a hit in its own right.

CBS. *Series Premieres:* Ladies Man; Private Benjamin; The Two of Us.

NBC. *Series Premieres:* The Last Convertible. *Key Programming Moves:* NBC tries airing weekly series in the 9–11 slot during the summer; by season's end they returned to movies.

1981–82

CBS. *Series Premieres:* Report to Murphy. *Key Programming Moves:* WKRP IN CINCINNATI, HOUSE CALLS, and LOU GRANT were all cancelled at the end of the season.

1982–83

CBS. *Series Premieres:* Foot in the Door; Newhart; Small & Frye; Square Pegs. *Key Programming Moves:* NEWHART debuts; this series becomes part of CBS' Monday night lineup, and continues to the present time; CAGNEY & LACEY is moved into the 10–11 slot; it is moved out of this slot at season's end, only to return the following season; M*A*S*H leaves the air at the end of the season, after 11 successful years.

NBC. *Key Programming Moves:* LITTLE HOUSE ON THE PRAIRIE is cancelled in March, after nine years on the air.

1983–84

ABC. *Key Programming Moves:* THAT'S INCREDIBLE is cancelled in 2/84.

CBS. *Series Premieres:* Aftermash; Emerald Point; Kate & Allie; Scarecrow & Mrs. King. *Key Programming Moves:* SCARECROW & MRS. KING debuts; series lasts on CBS for over four years; AFTERMASH debuts; in an attempt to continue the success established by M*A*S*H, this spin-off was placed in the 9–9:30 slot, previously occupied by M*A*S*H; the new series never caught on and was gone by season's end; KATE & ALLIE debuts in 3/84; series has continued on CBS to the present time. In March, CAGNEY & LACEY is returned to Monday, where it continued until 12/87.

NBC. *Series Premieres:* Boone; TV's Bloopers & Practical Jokes.

1984–85

ABC. *Series Premieres:* Call to Glory. *Key Programming Moves:* CALL TO GLORY debuts after enormous publicity push during Summer

Olympics; the series attracted large audiences in the first few weeks, but lost it in big chunks in subsequent weeks.

1985-86

NBC. *Series Premieres:* Valerie; You Again. *Key Programming Moves:* VALERIE debuts; series will undergo name and cast changes in subsequent years (VALERIE'S FAMILY, HOGAN'S FAMILY); through these changes, series has continued to capture audiences.

1986-87

CBS. *Series Premieres:* Cavanaughs; Designing Women; My Sister Sam; Together We Stand. *Key Programming Moves:* DESIGNING WOMEN debuts.

NBC. *Series Premieres:* ALF. *Key Programming Moves:* ALF debuts, becoming a strong lead-in for NBC on Monday nights; continues in 8-8:30 time slot to the present time.

1987-88

CBS. *Series Premieres:* Blue Skies; Eisenhower & Lutz; Frank's Place. *Key Programming Moves:* MAGNUM, P.I. is moved into 10-11 slot in June; it is cancelled at the end of the season, after an eight year run.

Tuesday Night

September 1948 – August 1988

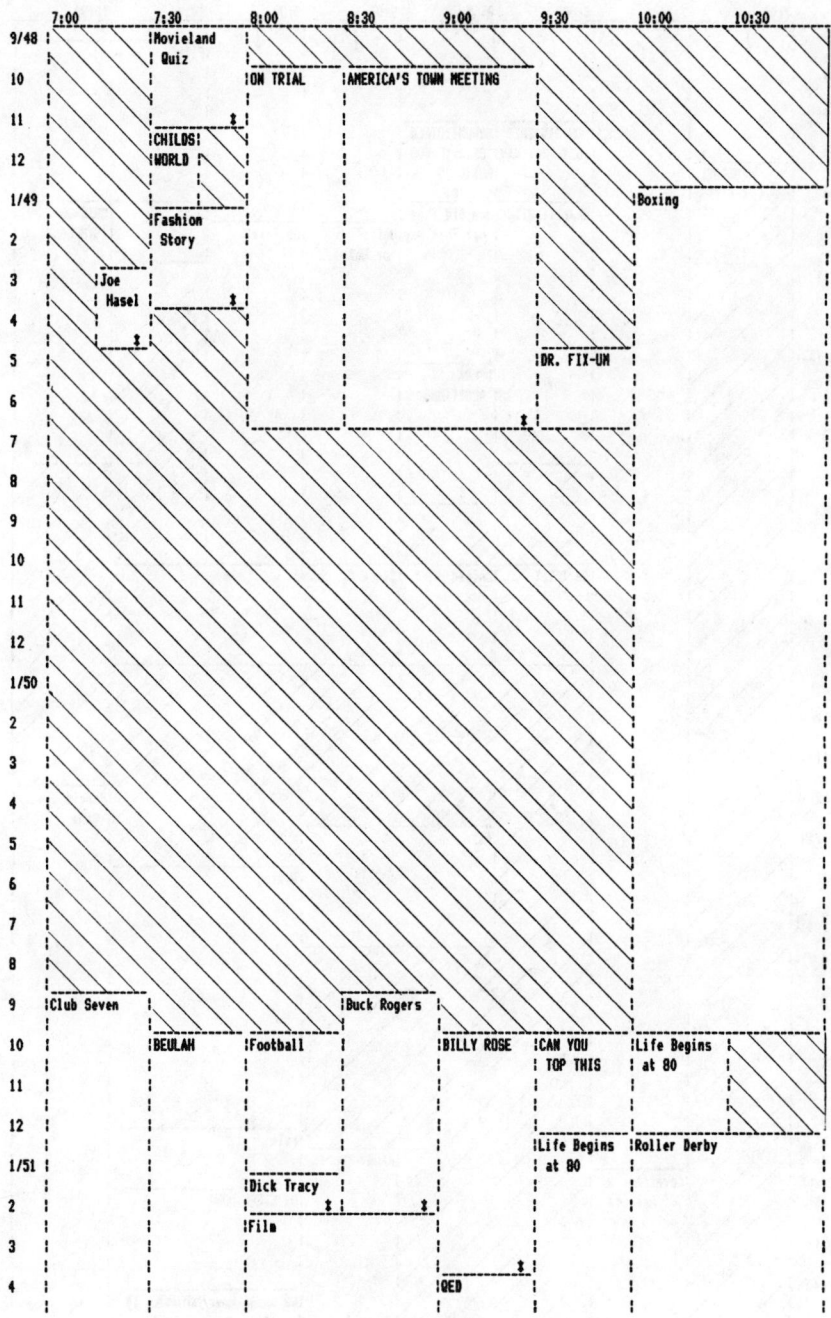

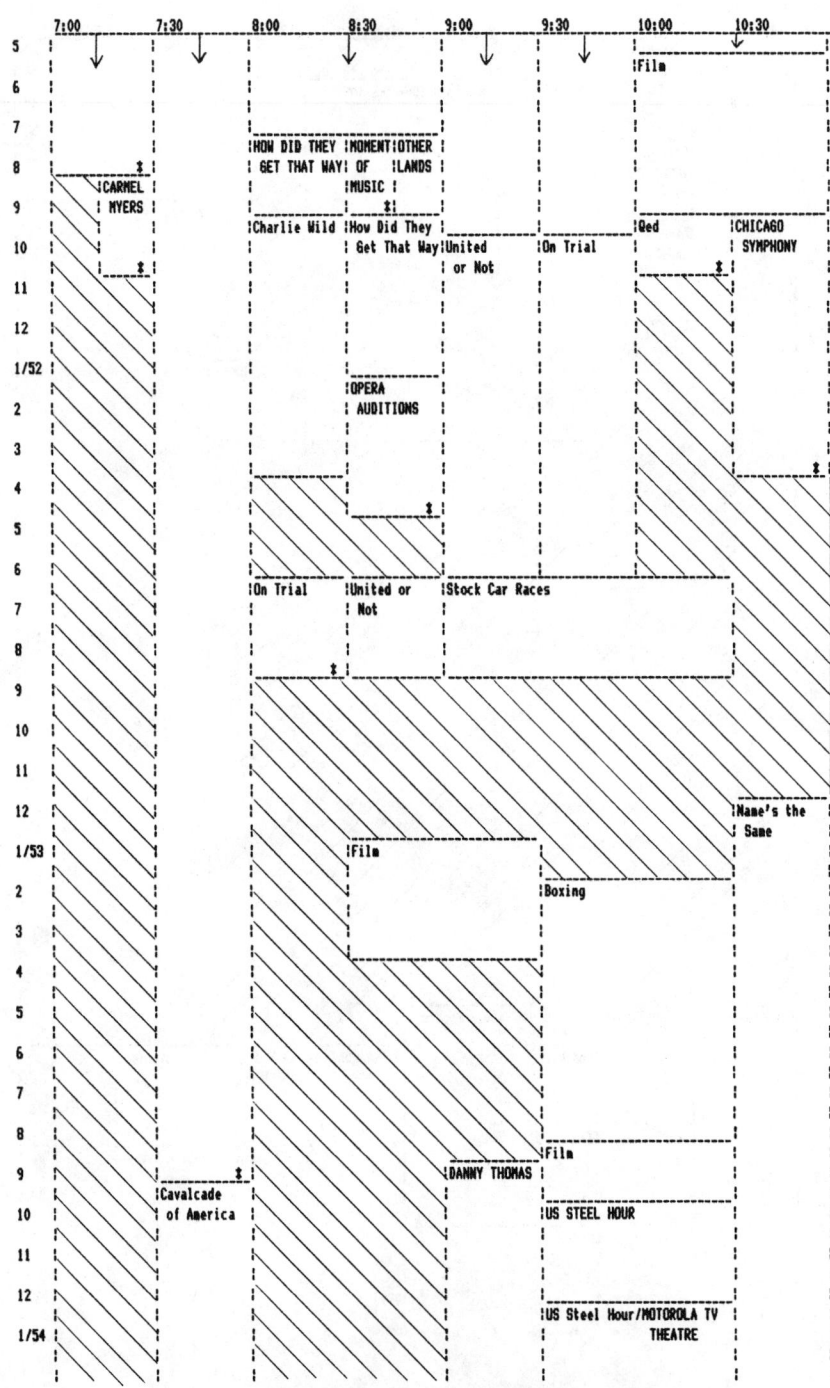

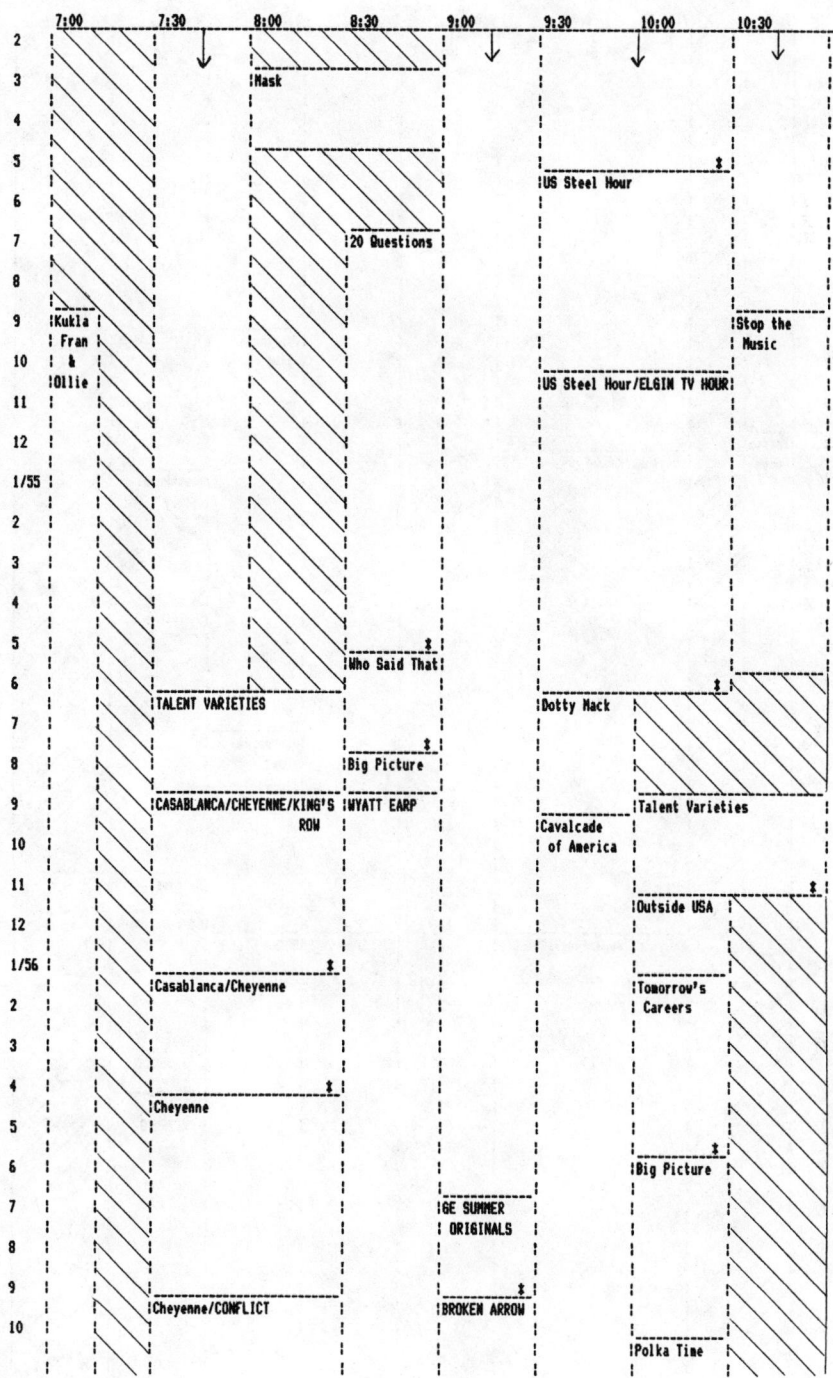

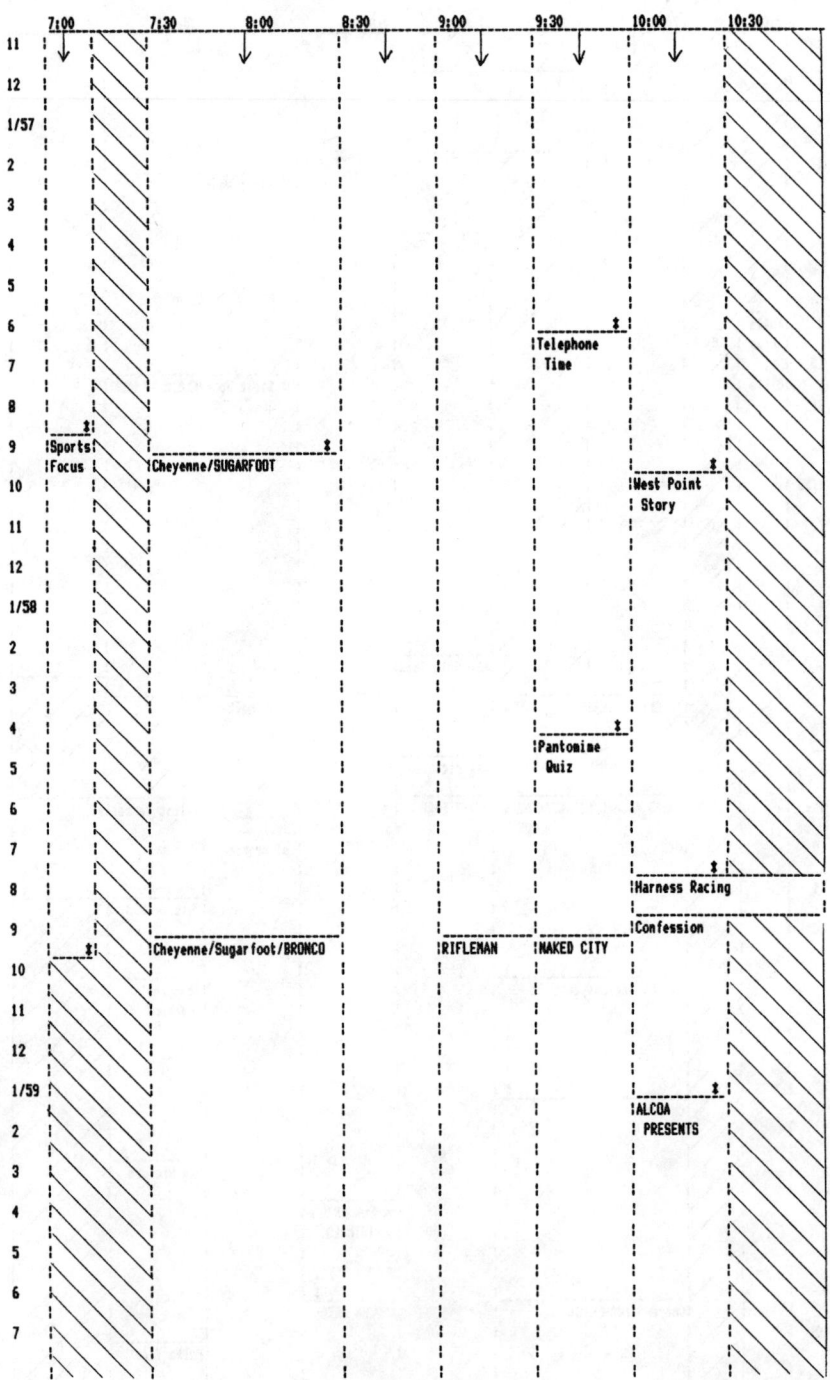

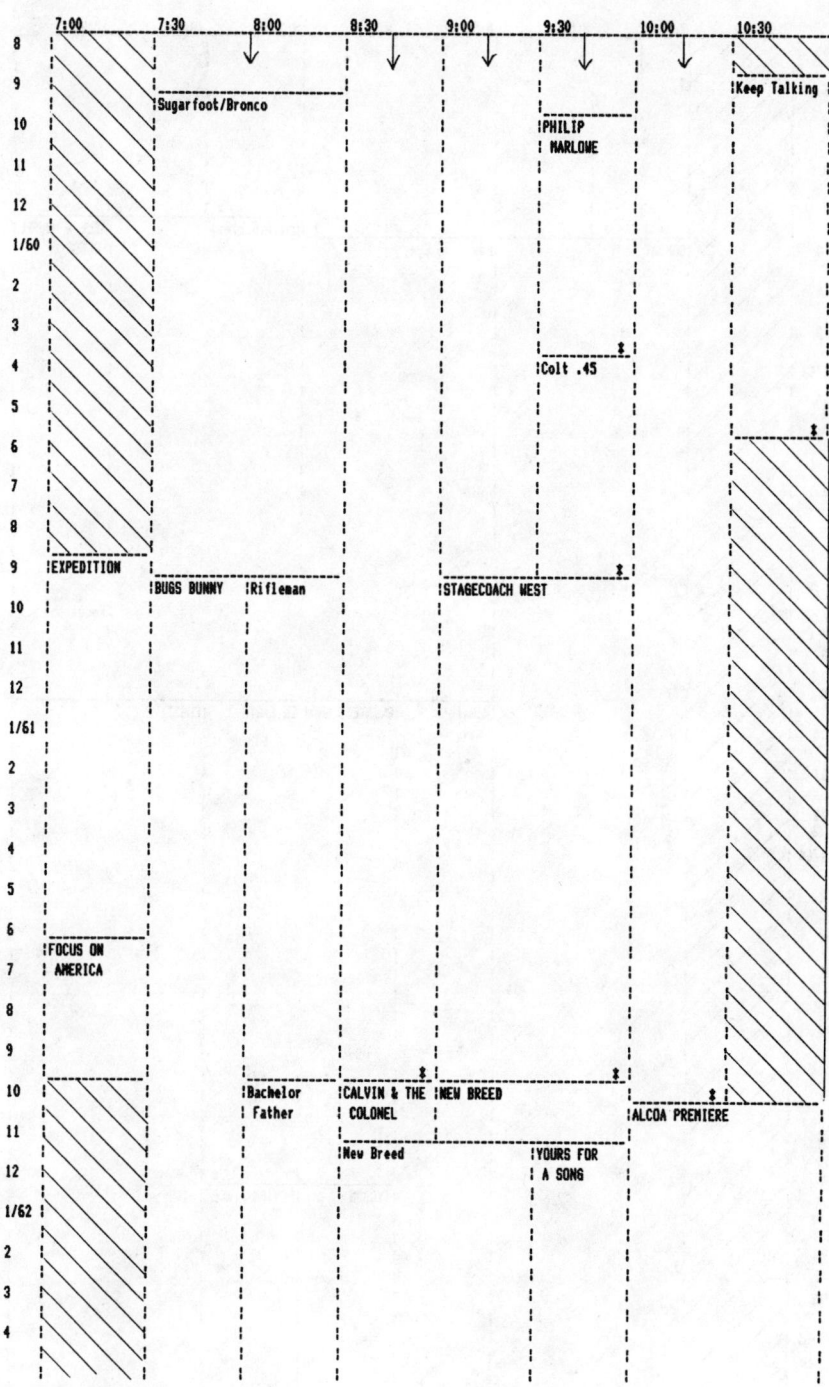

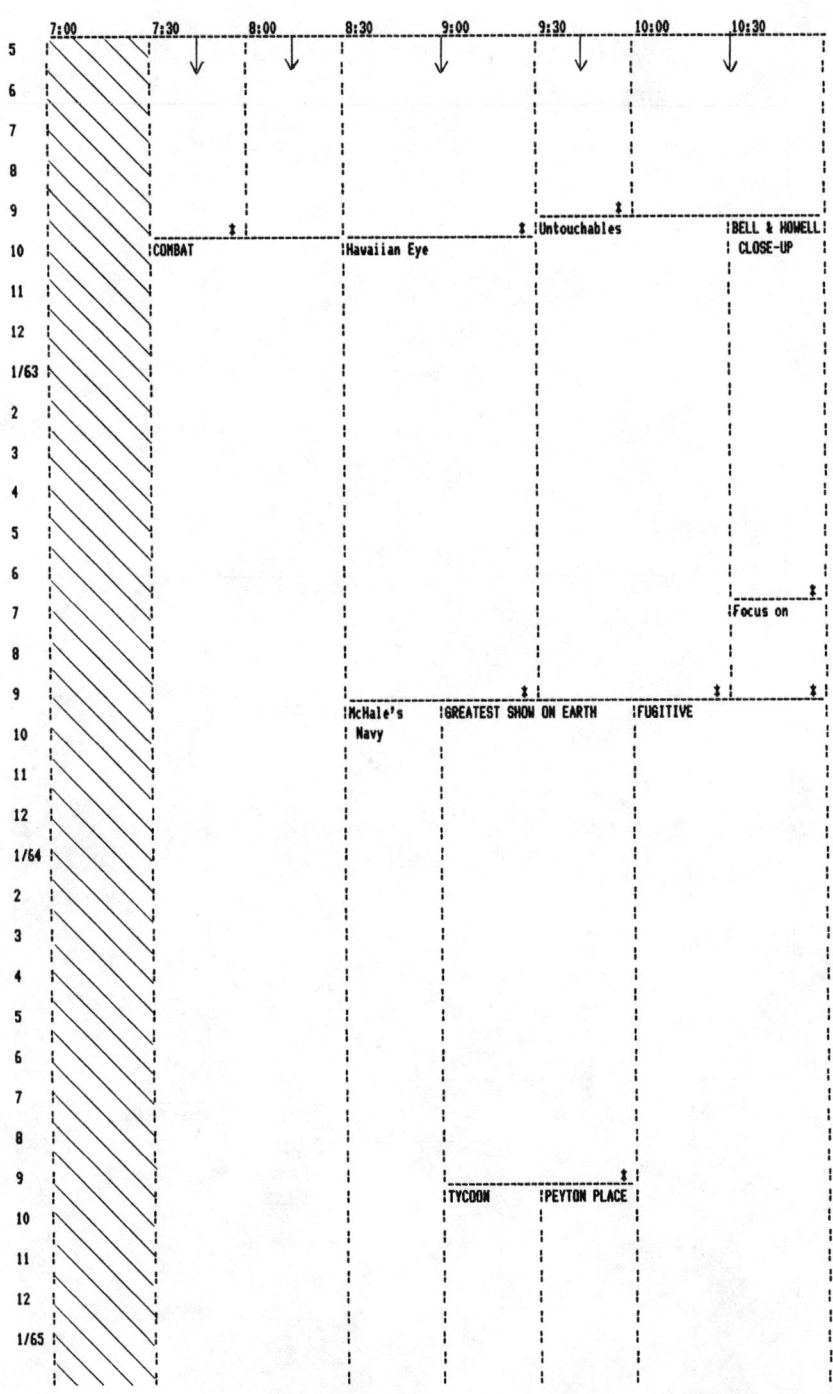

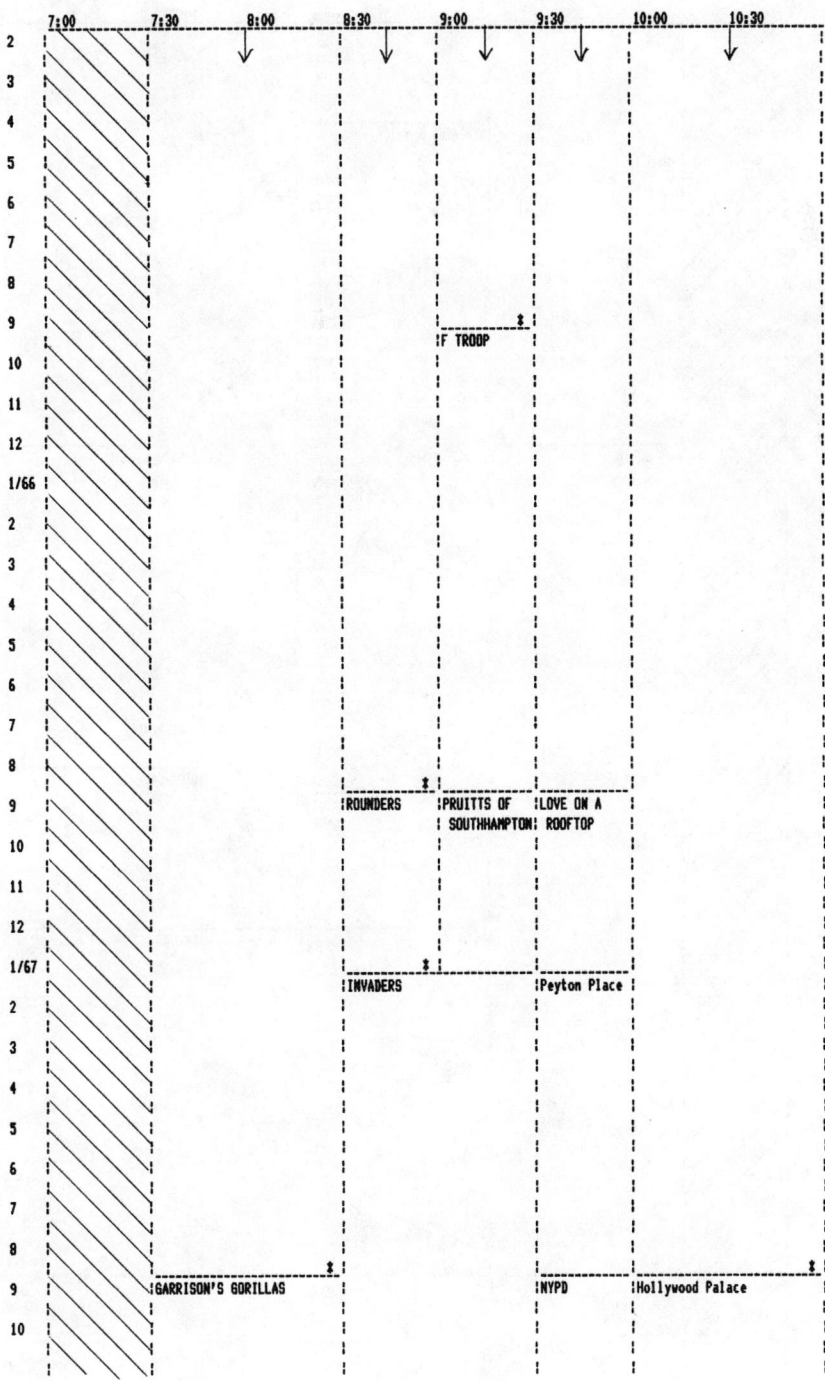

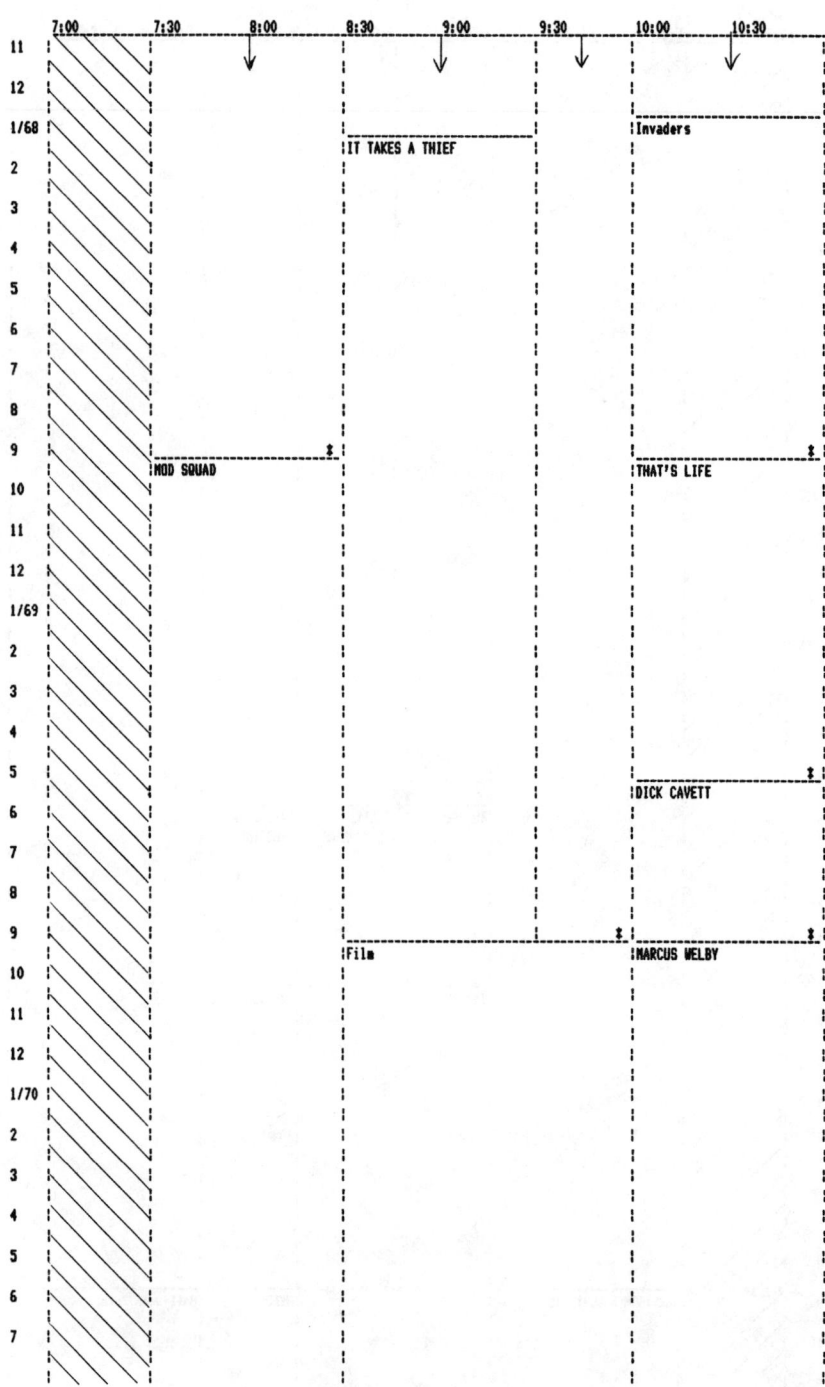

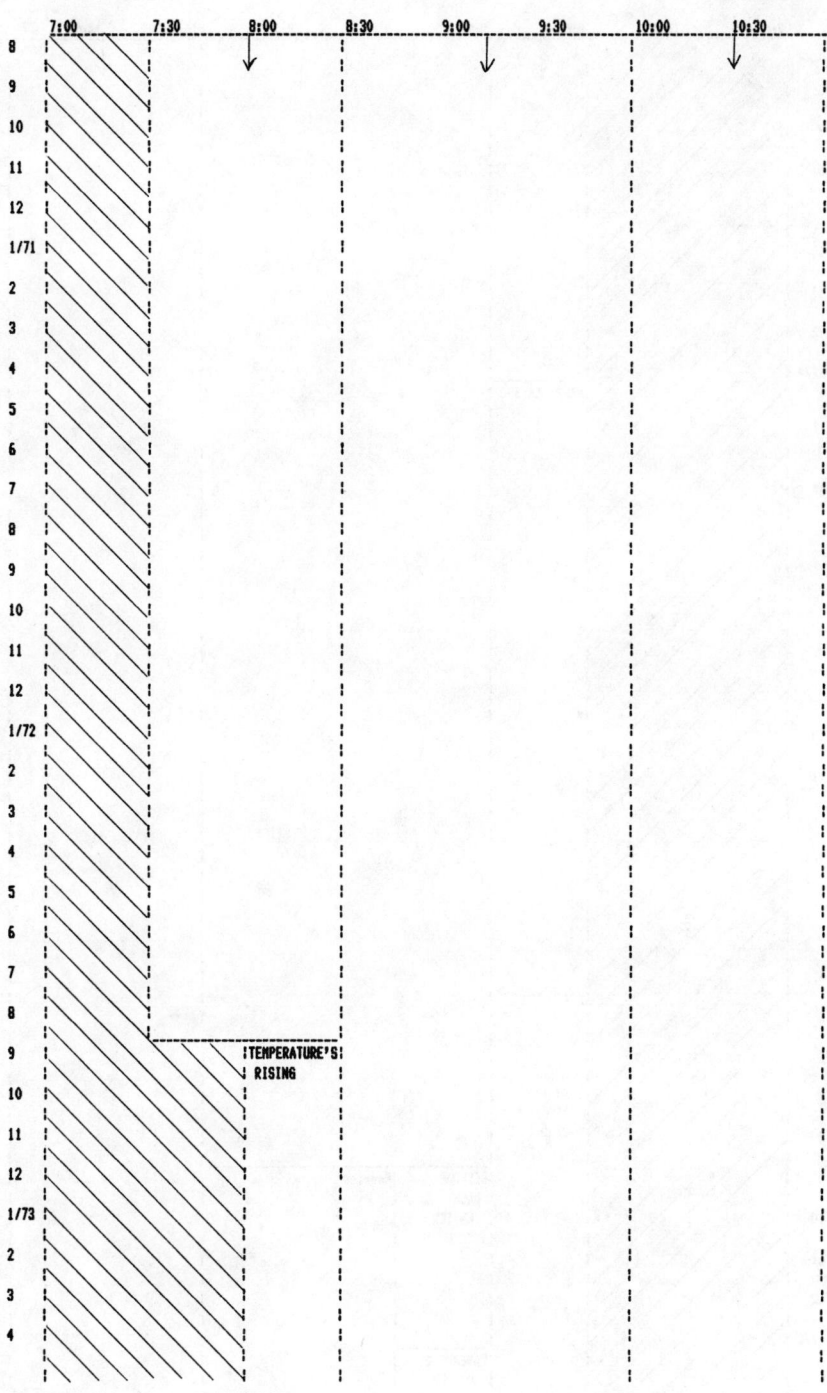

TEMPERATURE'S
RISING

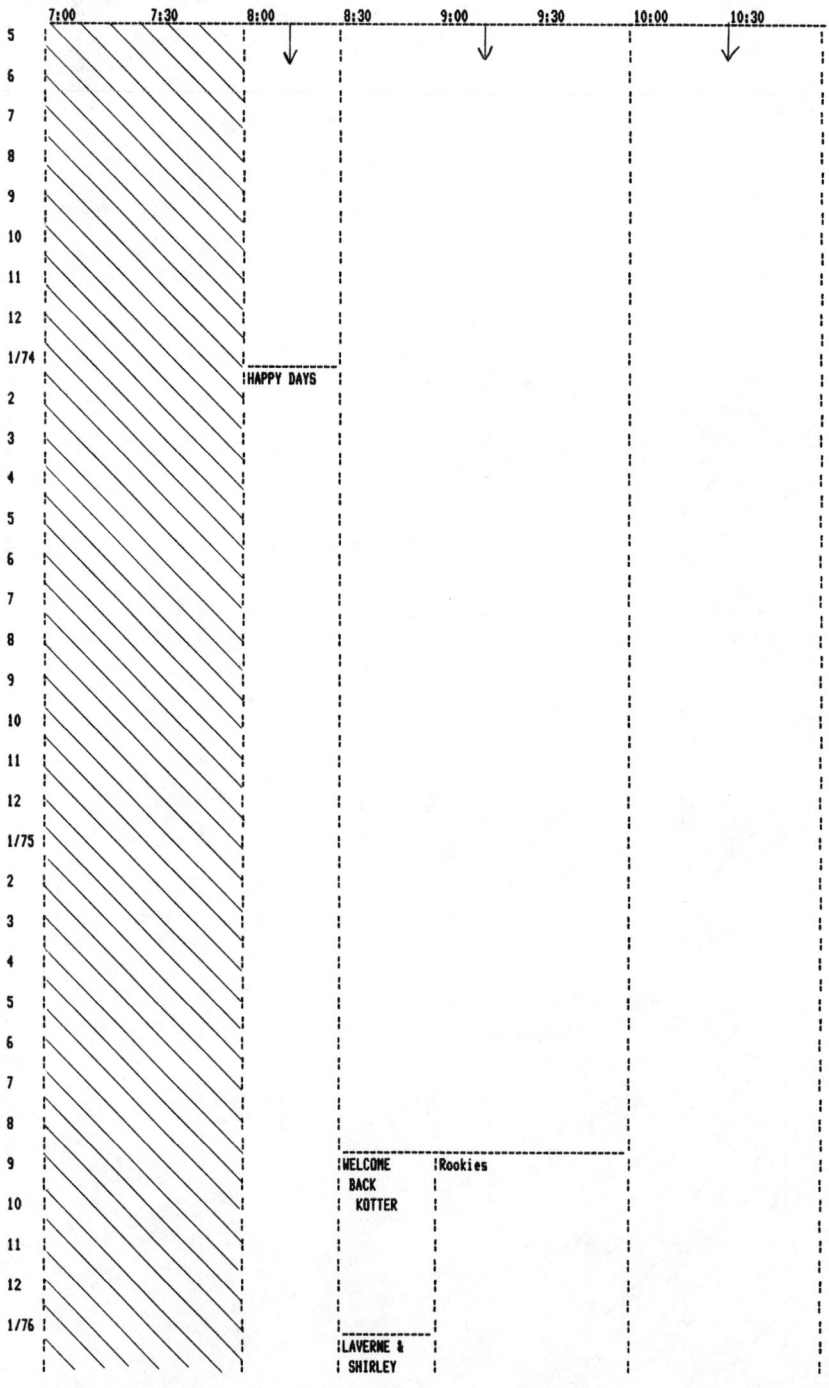

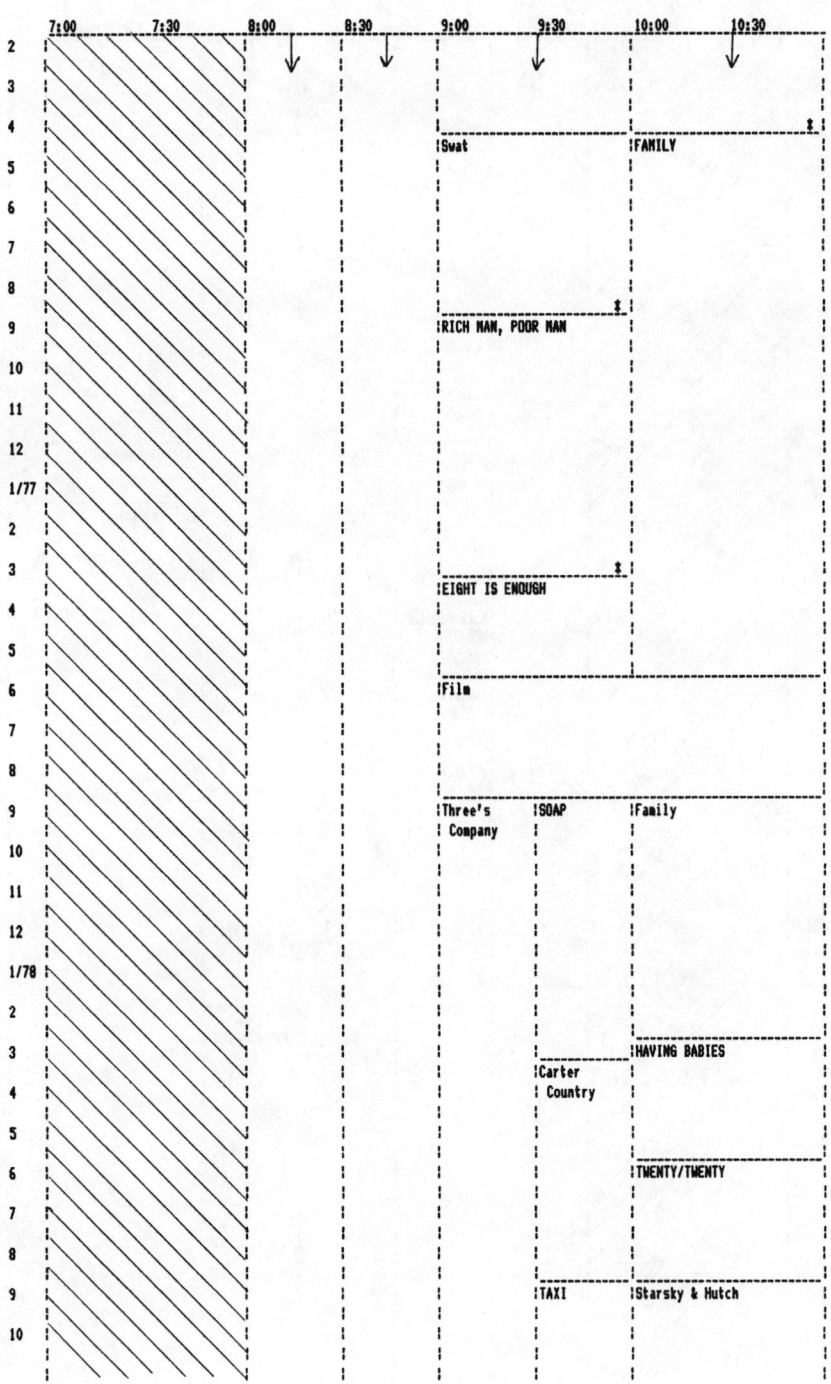

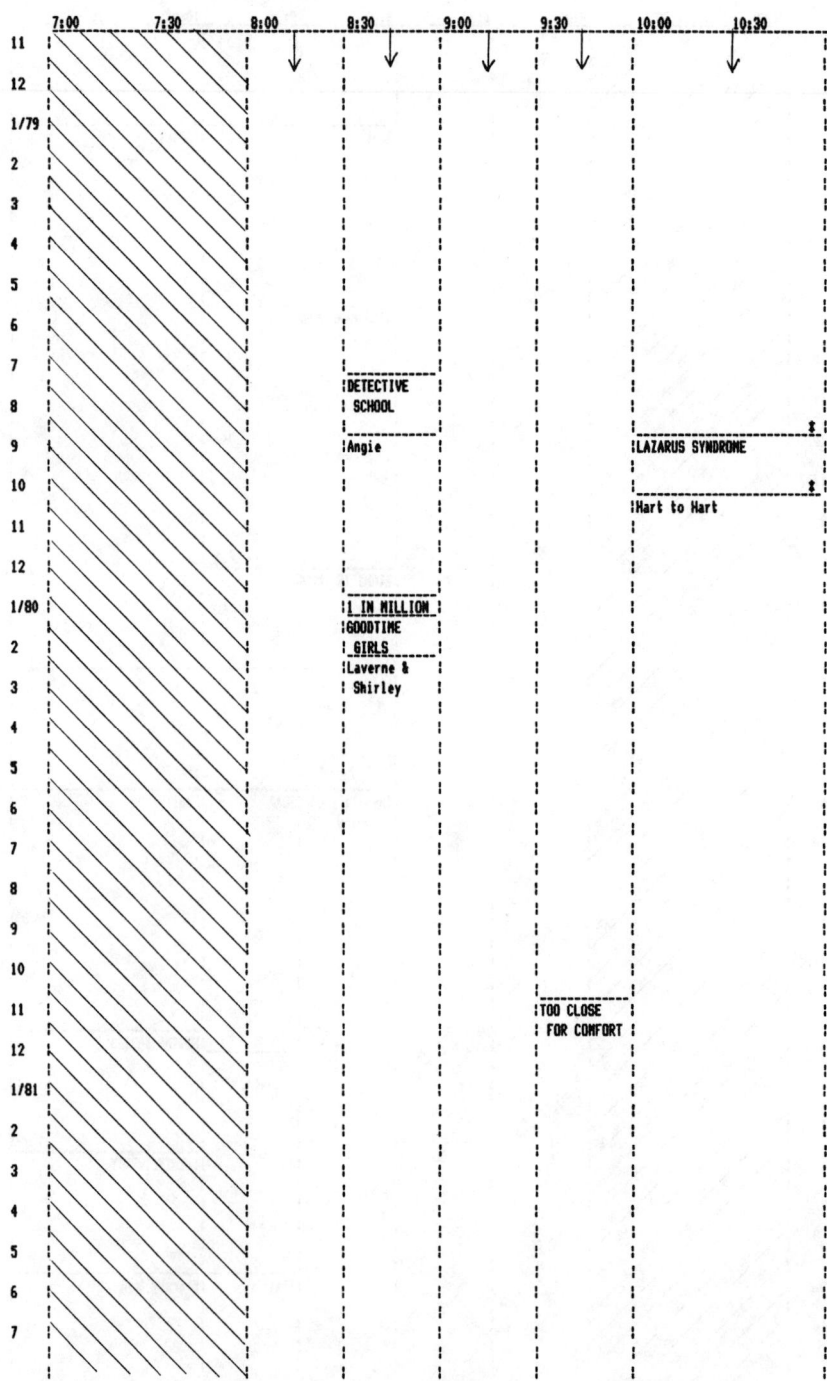

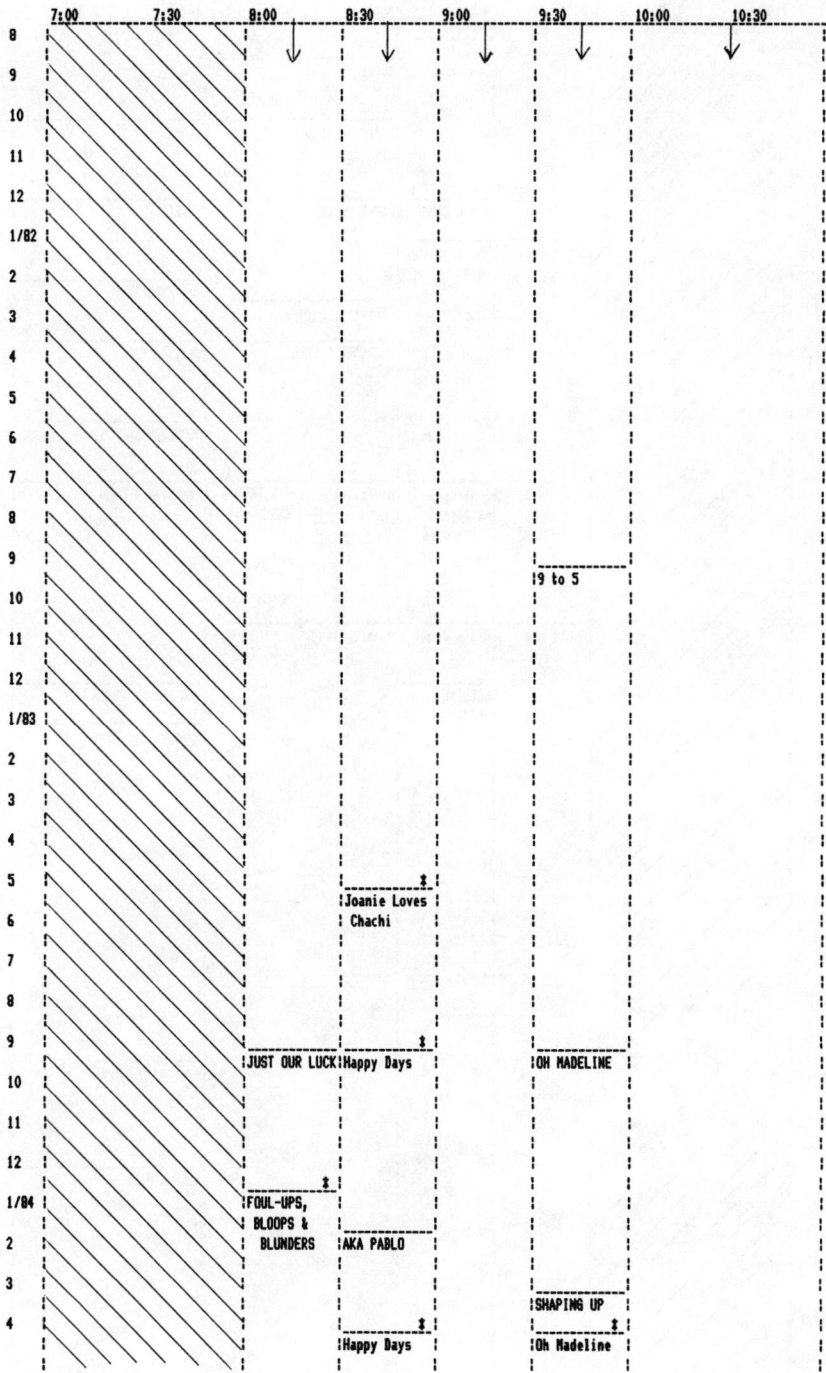

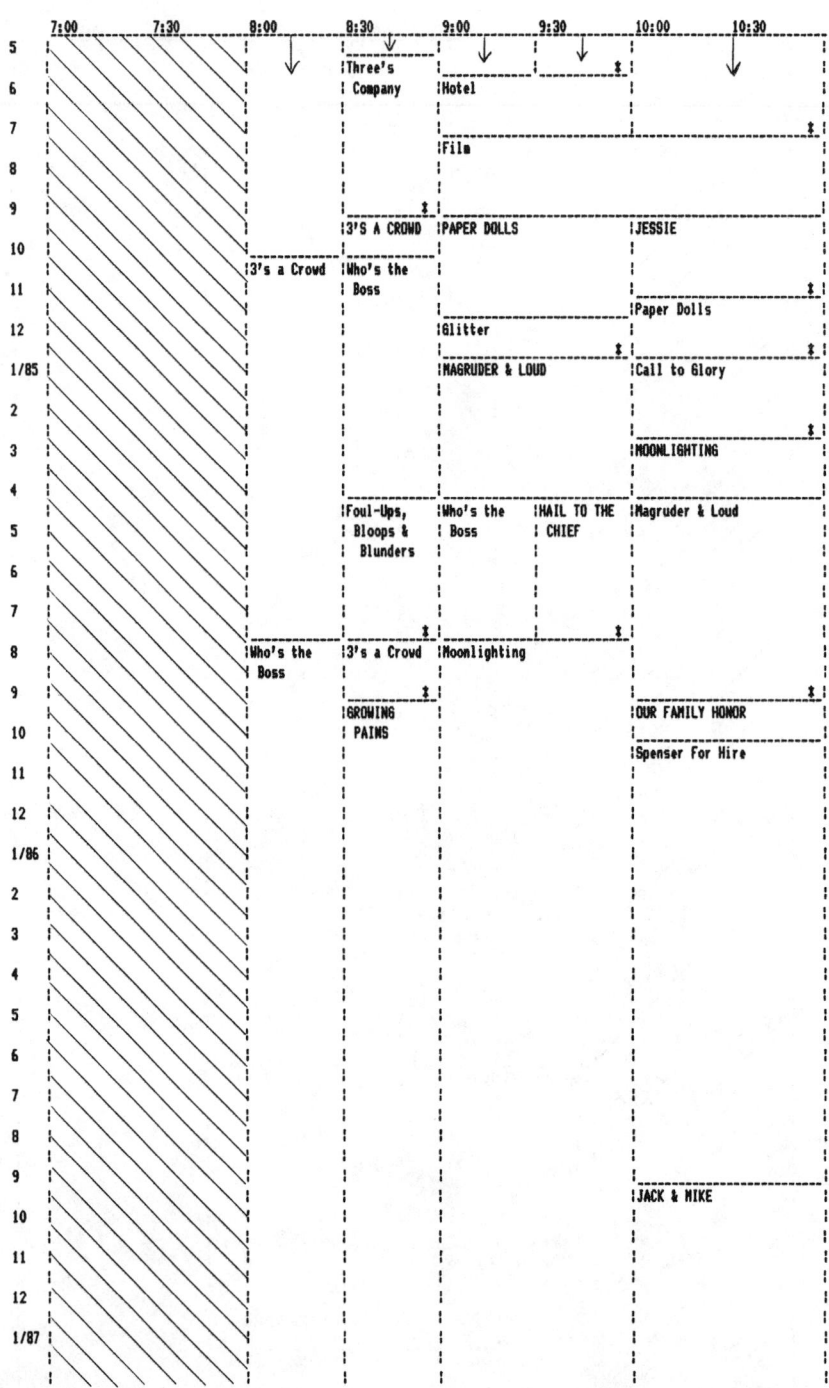

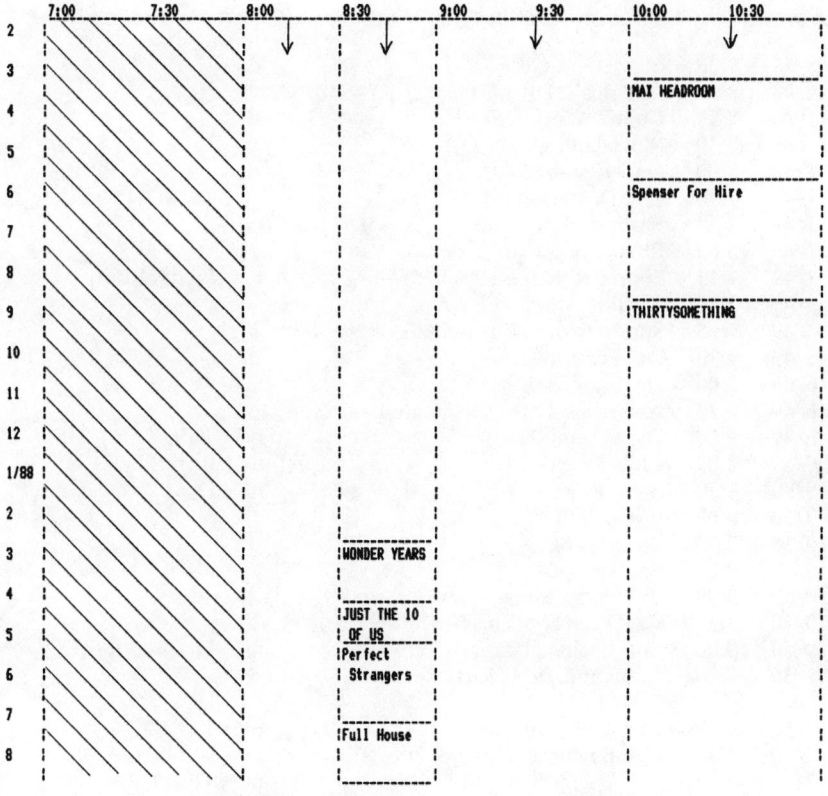

Date	Time	Title (min. if not 30) — Type	Action	From/To
8/48	7:30	Movieland Quiz — QU	d	
10/48	8:30	America's Town Meeting(60) — DB	d	
11/48	7:30	Child's World(15) — KV	d	
11/48	7:30	Movieland Quiz — QU	c	
11/48	8:00	On Trial — DB	d	
1/49	7:30	Child's World(15) — KV	m	To:w-7:15
1/49	7:30	Fashion Story — FS	m	Fr:r-8
1/49	10:00	Boxing(60) — SP	s	
3/49	7:15	Sports with Joe Hasel(15) — SN	m	Fr:f-9:30
3/49	7:30	Fashion Story — FS	c	
4/49	7:15	Sports with Joe Hasel(15) — SN	c	
5/49	9:30	Dr. Fix-um — IF	d	
6/49	8:00	On Trial — DB	m	To:w-8
6/49	8:30	America's Town Meeting(60) — DB	c	
6/49	9:30	Dr. Fix-um — IF	m	To:n-7:45-1/50
9/50	7:00	Club Seven — MV	m	Fr:r-10:30-3/49
9/50	8:30	Buck Rogers — SF	m	Fr:s-7
9/50	10:00	Boxing(60) — SP	f	
10/50	7:30	Beulah — SC	d	
10/50	8:00	Football — SP	s	
10/50	9:00	Billy Rose Show — DA	d	
10/50	9:30	Can You Top This? — CY	d	
10/50	10:00	Life Begins at Eighty — DS	m	Fr:f-9-8/50(n)
12/50	7:00	Andy and Della Russell Show(5) — MU	d	
12/50	9:30	Can You Top This? — CY	m	To:m-8
12/50	9:30	Life Begins at Eighty — DS	m	Fr:t-10
12/50	10:00	Life Begins at Eighty — DS	m	To:t-9:30
12/50	10:00	Roller Derby(60) — SP	s	
1/51	8:00	Dick Tracy — CD	m	Fr:m-8:30
1/51	8:00	Football — SP	f	
2/51	8:00	Dick Tracy — CD	c	
2/51	8:00	Film(60) — FI	s	
2/51	8:30	Buck Rogers — SF	c	
3/51	9:00	Billy Rose Show — DA	c	
4/51	9:00	Q.E.D. — QU	d	
5/51	10:00	Film(60) — FI	s	
5/51	10:00	Roller Derby(60) — SP	f	
6/51	7:00	Andy and Della Russell Show(5) — MU	c	
7/51	8:00	How Did They Get That Way — DS	d	
7/51	8:00	Film(60) — FI	f	
7/51	8:30	Moments of Music(15) — MU	d	
7/51	8:45	Other Lands, Other Places(15) — TR	d	
8/51	7:00	Club Seven — MV	c	
8/51	7:15	Carmel Myers Show(15) — IV	d	
9/51	8:00	Charlie Wild, Pvt. Detective — CD	m	Fr:w-9-6/51(c)
9/51	8:00	How Did They Get That Way — DS	m	To:t-8:30
9/51	8:30	How Did They Get That Way — DS	m	Fr:t-8
9/51	8:30	Moments of Music(15) — MU	c	

Date	Time	Title (min. if not 30) — Type	Action	From/To
9/51	8:45	Other Lands, Other Places(15) — TR	m	To:n-9-11/51
9/51	9:00	Q.E.D. — QU	m	To:t-10
9/51	9:30	Life Begins at Eighty — DS	m	To:m-8:30
9/51	10:00	Film(60) — FI	f	
9/51	10:00	Q.E.D. — QU	m	Fr:t-9
9/51	10:30	Chicago Symphony Chamber Orchestra — MU	d	
10/51	7:15	Carmel Myers Show(15) — IV	m	To:r-10:45
10/51	9:00	United or Not — IV	m	Fr:m-9
10/51	9:30	On Trial — DB	m	Fr:m-9:30
10/51	10:00	Q.E.D. — QU	c	
1/52	8:30	How Did They Get That Way — DS	m	To:m-9:30
1/52	8:30	Metropolitan Opera Auditions of the Air — TA	d	
3/52	8:00	Charlie Wild, Pvt. Detective — CD	m	To:r-10(d)
3/52	10:30	Chicago Symphony Chamber Orchestra — MU	c	
4/52	8:30	Metropolitan Opera Auditions of the Air — TA	c	
6/52	8:00	On Trial — DB	m	Fr:t-9:30
6/52	8:30	United or Not — IV	m	Fr:t-9
6/52	9:00	Stock Car Races(90) — SP	s	
6/52	9:00	United or Not — IV	m	To:t-8:30
6/52	9:30	On Trial — DB	m	To:t-8
8/52	8:00	On Trial — DB	c	
8/52	8:30	United or Not — IV	m	To:m-8:30
8/52	9:00	Stock Car Races(90) — SP	f	
12/52	10:30	Name's the Same — QU	m	Fr:w-7:30
1/53	8:30	Film(60) — FI	s	
2/53	9:30	Boxing(60) — SP	s	
3/53	8:30	Film(60) — FI	f	
8/53	9:00	Film(90) — FI	s	
8/53	9:30	Boxing(60) — SP	f	
9/53	7:30	Beulah — SC	c	
9/53	7:30	Cavalcade of America — DA	m	Fr:w-8:30-6/53(n)
9/53	9:00	Film(90) — FI	f	
9/53	9:00	Danny Thomas Show — SC	d	
10/53	9:30	U.S. Steel Hour(60) — DA	d	
12/53	9:30	Motorola TV Theater(60) — DA	d	
3/54	8:00	Mask(60) — CD	s	
4/54	8:00	Mask(60) — CD	f	
5/54	9:30	Motorola TV Theater(60) — DA	c	
6/54	7:30	Men of Tomorrow — DO	d*	
6/54	9:30	Center Stage(60) — DA	d*	
7/54	8:30	Twenty Questions — QU	m	Fr:n-10-5/54(d)
8/54	10:30	Name's the Same — QU	m	To:m-7:30-10/54
9/54	7:00	Kukla, Fran & Ollie(15) — KV	m	Fr:m-f-7-6/52(n)
9/54	7:30	Men of Tomorrow — DO	c*	
9/54	9:30	Center Stage(60) — DA	c*	
9/54	10:30	Stop the Music — QU	m	Fr:r-8-4/52

Date	Time	Title (min. if not 30) — Type	Action	From/To
10/54	9:30	Elgin TV Hour(60) — DA	d	
5/55	8:30	Twenty Questions — QU	c	
5/55	8:30	Who Said That? — QU	m	Fr:w-9
5/55	10:30	Stop the Music — QU	m	To:r-8:30-9/55
6/55	7:30	Cavalcade of America — DA	m	To:t-9:30-9/55
6/55	7:30	Talent Varieties(60) — VY	d	
6/55	9:30	Dotty Mack Show — MU	m	Fr:s-8
6/55	9:30	Elgin TV Hour(60) — DA	c	
6/55	9:30	U.S. Steel Hour(60) — DA	m	To:w-10(c)
7/55	7:00	Soupy Sales(15) — KV	d*	
7/55	8:30	Who Said That? — QU	c	
8/55	7:00	Soupy Sales(15) — KV	c*	
8/55	8:30	Big Picture — DO	m	Fr:s-7:30-6/55
8/55	8:30	Big Picture — DO	m	To:m-10
9/55	7:30	Casablanca(60) — MY	d	
9/55	7:30	Cheyenne(60) — WE	d	
9/55	7:30	King's Row(60) — DR	d	
9/55	7:30	Talent Varieties(60) — VY	m	To:t-10
9/55	8:30	Life and Legend of Wyatt Earp — WE	d	
9/55	9:30	Cavalcade of America — DA	m	Fr:t-7:30-6/55
9/55	9:30	Dotty Mack Show — MU	m	To:m-9
9/55	10:00	Talent Varieties(60) — VY	m	Fr:t-7:30
11/55	10:00	Outside USA — DO	m	Fr:r-10
11/55	10:00	Talent Varieties(60) — VY	c	
1/56	7:30	King's Row(60) — DR	c	
1/56	10:00	Outside USA — DO	m	To:m-10
1/56	10:00	Tomorrow's Careers — IF	m	Fr:s-10
4/56	7:30	Casablanca(60) — MV	c	
5/56	10:00	Tomorrow's Careers — IF	c	
6/56	9:00	Danny Thomas Show — SC	m	To:m-8-10/56
6/56	10:00	Big Picture — DO	m	Fr:n-10-4/56
7/56	7:00	Jack Drees Sports Show(15) — SN	d*	
7/56	9:00	General Electric Summer Originals — DA	d	
8/56	7:00	Jack Drees Sports Show(15) — SN	c*	
9/56	7:30	Conflict(60) — DA	d	
9/56	9:00	Broken Arrow — WE	d	
9/56	9:00	General Electric Summer Originals — DA	c	
10/56	10:00	Big Picture — DO	m	To:r-8-7/57
10/56	10:00	Polka Time — MU	m	Fr:f-10
6/57	7:00	Sports Focus(15) — SN	d*	
6/57	9:30	Cavalcade of America — DA	c	
6/57	9:30	Telephone Time — DA	m	Fr:r-10
7/57	7:00	Sports Focus(15) — SN	m*	To:m-f-7-9/57
8/57	7:00	Kukla, Fran & Ollie(15) — KV	c	
9/57	7:00	Sports Focus(15) — SN	m	Fr:m-f-7-7/57
9/57	7:30	Conflict(60) — DA	c	
9/57	7:30	Sugarfoot(60) — WE	d	

Date	Time	Title (min. if not 30) — Type	Action	From/To
9/57	10:00	Polka Time — MU	c	
10/57	10:00	West Point Story — MR	m	Fr:f-8(c)
4/58	9:30	Pantomime Quiz — QU	m	Fr:f-10:30-9/57(c)
4/58	9:30	Telephone Time — DA	c	
7/58	10:00	West Point Story — MR	c	
8/58	10:00	Harness Racing — SP	s	
8/58	10:00	Harness Racing — SP	f	
9/58	7:00	Sports Focus(15) — SN	c	
9/58	7:30	Bronco(60) — WE	d	
9/58	9:00	Broken Arrow — WE	m	To:n-7-4/60
9/58	9:00	Rifleman — WE	d	
9/58	9:30	Naked City — CD	d	
9/58	9:30	Pantomime Quiz — QU	m	To:m-9-6/59
9/58	10:00	Confession — IV	m	Fr:r-10
9/58	10:30	News(15) — NW	s	
1/59	10:00	Alcoa Presents — OA	d	
1/59	10:00	Confession — IV	c	
5/59	10:30	News(15) — NW	f	
9/59	7:30	Cheyenne(60) — WE	m	To:m-7:30
9/59	9:30	Naked City — CD	m	To:w-10-10/60
9/59	10:30	Keep Talking — QU	m	Fr:w-8(c)
10/59	9:30	Philip Marlowe — CD	d	
3/60	9:30	Philip Marlowe — CD	c	
4/60	9:30	Colt .45 — WE	m	Fr:n-7
5/60	10:30	Keep Talking — QU	c	
9/60	7:00	Expedition — WL	d	
9/60	7:30	Bronco(60) — WE	m	To:m-7:30
9/60	7:30	Bugs Bunny Show — KV	d	
9/60	7:30	Sugarfoot(60) — WE	m	To:m-7:30
9/60	8:00	Rifleman — WE	m	Fr:t-9
9/60	9:00	Rifleman — WE	m	To:t-8
9/60	9:30	Colt .45 — WE	c	
10/60	9:00	Stagecoach West(60) — WE	d	
6/61	7:00	Expedition — WL	m	To:m-7-9/61
6/61	7:00	Focus on America — DO	d	
9/61	7:00	Focus on America — DO	m	To:w-8-7/62
9/61	8:00	Rifleman — WE	m	To:m-8:30
9/61	8:30	Life and Legend of Wyatt Earp — WE	c	
9/61	9:00	Stagecoach West(60) — WE	c	
10/61	8:00	Bachelor Father — SC	m	Fr:r-9(n)
10/61	8:30	Calvin and the Colonel — KV	d	
10/61	9:00	New Breed(60) — CD	d	
10/61	10:00	Alcoa Premiere(60) — DA	d	
10/61	10:00	Alcoa Presents — OA	c	
11/61	8:30	Calvin and the Colonel — KV	m	To:s-7:30-1/62
11/61	8:30	New Breed(60) — CD	m	Fr:t-9
11/61	9:00	New Breed(60) — CD	m	To:t-8:30
11/61	9:30	Yours for a Song — QU	d	
9/62	7:30	Bugs Bunny Show — KV	c	

Date	Time	Title (min. if not 30) — Type	Action	From/To
9/62	8:00	Bachelor Father — SC	c	
9/62	8:30	New Breed(60) — CD	c	
9/62	9:30	Untouchables(60) — CD	m	Fr:r-10
9/62	9:30	Yours for a Song — QU	c	
9/62	10:00	Alcoa Premiere(60) — DA	m	To:r-10
9/62	10:30	Bell and Howell Closeup — DO	d	
10/62	7:30	Combat(60) — WD	d	
10/62	8:30	Hawaiian Eye(60) — CD	m	Fr:w-9
6/63	10:30	Bell and Howell Closeup — DO	c	
7/63	10:30	Focus on America — DO	m	Fr:w-8-9/62
9/63	8:30	Hawaiian Eye(60) — CD	c	
9/63	8:30	McHale's Navy — SC	m	Fr:r-9:30
9/63	9:00	Greatest Show on Earth(60) — DR	d	
9/63	9:30	Untouchables(60) — CD	c	
9/63	10:00	Fugitive(60) — DR	d	
9/63	10:30	Focus on America — DO	c	
9/64	9:00	Greatest Show on Earth(60) — DR	c	
9/64	9:00	Tycoon — SC	d	
9/64	9:30	Peyton Place — SL	d	
9/65	9:00	F Troop — SC	d	
9/65	9:00	Tycoon — SC	c	
8/66	8:30	McHale's Navy — SC	c	
8/66	9:00	F Troop — SC	m	To:r-8
8/66	9:30	Peyton Place — SL	m	To:mw-9:30
9/66	8:30	Rounders — WE	d	
9/66	9:00	Pruitts of Southampton — SC	d	
9/66	9:30	Love on a Rooftop — SC	d	
1/67	8:30	Invaders(60) — SF	d	
1/67	8:30	Rounders — WE	c	
1/67	9:00	Pruitts of Southampton — SC	m	To:f-9:30
1/67	9:30	Love on a Rooftop — SC	m	To:r-9
1/67	9:30	Peyton Place — SL	m	Fr:mw-9:30
8/67	7:30	Combat(60) — WD	c	
8/67	9:30	Peyton Place — SL	m	To:mr-9:30
8/67	10:00	Fugitive(60) — DR	c	
9/67	7:30	Garrison's Gorillas(60) — WD	d	
9/67	9:30	N.Y.P.D. — CD	d	
9/67	10:00	Hollywood Palace(60) — VY	s	
12/67	10:00	Hollywood Palace(60) — VY	f	
1/68	8:30	Invaders(60) — SF	m	To:t-10
1/68	8:30	It Takes a Thief(60) — SD	d	
1/68	10:00	Invaders(60) — SF	m	Fr:t-8:30
9/68	7:30	Garrison's Gorillas(60) — WD	c	
9/68	7:30	Mod Squad(60) — CD	d	
9/68	10:00	Invaders(60) — SF	c	
9/68	10:00	That's Life(60) — CY	d	
5/69	10:00	Dick Cavett(60) — TK	d	
5/69	10:00	That's Life(60) — CY	c	
9/69	8:30	It Takes a Thief(60) — SD	m	To:r-10
9/69	8:30	Film(90) — FI	s	

Date	Time	Title (min. if not 30) – Type	Action	From/To
9/69	9:30	N.Y.P.D. – CD	c	
9/69	10:00	Dick Cavett(60) – TK	c	
9/69	10:00	Marcus Welby, M.D.(60) – MD	d	
8/72	7:30	Mod Squad(60) – CD	m	To:r-8
9/72	8:00	Temperature's Rising – SC	d	
1/74	8:00	Happy Days – SC	d	
1/74	8:00	Temperature's Rising – SC	m	To:r-8-7/74
8/75	8:30	Film(90) – FI	f	
9/75	8:30	Welcome Back, Kotter – SC	d	
9/75	9:00	Rookies(60) – CD	m	Fr:m-8
1/76	8:30	Laverne & Shirley – SC	d	
1/76	8:30	Welcome Back, Kotter – SC	m	To:r-8
3/76	10:00	Marcus Welby, M.D.(60) – MD	c	
4/76	9:00	Rookies(60) – CD	c	
4/76	9:00	S.W.A.T.(60) – CD	m	Fr:s-9
4/76	10:00	Family(60) – DR	d	
8/76	9:00	S.W.A.T.(60) – CD	c	
9/76	9:00	Rich Man, Poor Man – Book 2(60) – SL	d	
3/77	9:00	Eight Is Enough(60) – CO	d	
3/77	9:00	Rich Man, Poor Man – Bk 2(60) – SL	c	
5/77	9:00	Eight Is Enough(60) – CO	m	To:w-8-8/77
6/77	???	Film(120) – FI	s	
6/77	10:00	Family(60) – DR	m	To:t-10-9/77
8/77	???	Film(120) – FI	f	
9/77	9:00	Three's Company – SC	m	Fr:r-9:30
9/77	9:30	Soap – SC	d	
9/77	10:00	Family(60) – DR	m	Fr:t-10-6/77
2/78	10:00	Family(60) – DR	m	To:r-10-9/78
3/78	9:30	Carter Country – SC	m	Fr:r-9:30
3/78	9:30	Soap – SC	m	To:r-9:30-9/78
3/78	10:00	Having Babies(60) – MD	d	
5/78	10:00	Having Babies(60) – MD	m	To:t-10-6/79
6/78	10:00	20/20(60) – NM	d	
8/78	9:30	Carter Country – SC	m	To:s-8
8/78	10:00	20/20(60) – NM	m	To:var
9/78	9:30	Taxi – SC	d	
9/78	10:00	Starsky and Hutch(60) – CD	m	Fr:w-10
3/79	10:00	Ropers – SC	d*	
3/79	10:30	13 Queens Boulevard – SC	d*	
4/79	10:00	Ropers – SC	m*	To:n-8:30-8/79
4/79	10:30	13 Queens Boulevard – SC	c*	To:t-10-7/79
6/79	10:00	Having Babies(60) – MD	m	Fr:t-10-4/78
6/79	10:00	Having Babies(60) – MD	c	
7/79	8:30	Detective School – SC	d	
7/79	8:30	Laverne & Shirley – SC	m	To:r-8
8/79	8:30	Detective School – SC	m	To:s-8:30
8/79	10:00	Starsky and Hutch(60) – CD	c	
9/79	8:30	Angie – SC	m	Fr:r-8:30
9/79	10:00	Lazarus Syndrome(60) – MD	d	

Date	Time	Title (min. if not 30) — Type	Action	From/To
10/79	10:00	Hart to Hart(60) — AD	m	Fr:s-10
10/79	10:00	Lazarus Syndrome(60) — MD	c	
1/80	8:30	Angie — SC	m	To:m-8:30
1/80	8:30	Goodtime Girls — SC	d	
1/80	8:30	One in a Million — SC	d	
1/80	8:30	One in a Million — SC	m	To:s-8
2/80	8:30	Goodtime Girls — SC	m	To:s-8:30-4/80
2/80	8:30	Laverne & Shirley — SC	m	Fr:m-8
10/80	9:30	Taxi — SC	m	To:w-9
11/80	9:30	Too Close for Comfort — SC	d	
7/81	9:30	It's a Living — SC	m*	Fr:r-9:30-1/81
8/81	9:30	It's a Living — SC	m*	To:f-8:30
3/82	8:30	Joanie Loves Chachi — SC	d*	
4/82	8:30	Joanie Loves Chachi — SC	m*	To:r-8-9/82
9/82	9:30	9 to 5 — SC	m	Fr:r-9-4/82
9/82	9:30	Too Close for Comfort — SC	m	To:r-9
5/83	8:30	Joanie Loves Chachi — SC	m	Fr:r-8-12/82
5/83	8:30	Laverne & Shirley — SC	c	
9/83	8:00	Happy Days — SC	m	To:t-8:30
9/83	8:00	Just Our Luck — SC	d	
9/83	8:30	Happy Days — SC	m	Fr:t-8
9/83	8:30	Joanie Loves Chachi — SC	c	
9/83	9:30	9 to 5 — SC	m	To:r-9
9/83	9:30	Oh Madeline — SC	d	
12/83	8:00	Just Our Luck — SC	c	
1/84	8:00	Foul-Ups, Bleeps & Blunders — CY	d	
1/84	8:30	Happy Days — SC	m	To:t-8:30-4/84
2/84	8:30	A.K.A. Pablo — SC	d	
3/84	9:30	Shaping Up — SC	d	
3/84	9:30	Oh Madeline — SC	m	To:t-9:30-4/84
4/84	8:30	A.K.A. Pablo — SC	c	
4/84	8:30	Happy Days — SC	m	Fr:t-8:30-1/84
4/84	9:30	Shaping Up — SC	c	
4/84	9:30	Oh Madeline — SC	m	Fr:t-9:30-3/84
5/84	8:30	Happy Days — SC	m	To:r-8
5/84	8:30	Three's Company — SC	m	Fr:t-9
5/84	9:00	Three's Company — SC	m	To:t-8:30
5/84	9:30	Oh Madeline — SC	c	
6/84	9:00	Hotel(60) — DR	m	Fr:w-10
7/84	9:00	Hotel(60) — DR	m	To:w-10
7/84	9:00	Film(120) — FI	s	
7/84	10:00	Hart to Hart(60) — AD	c	
9/84	8:30	Three's a Crowd — SC	d	
9/84	8:30	Three's Company — SC	c	
9/84	9:00	Paper Dolls(60) — DR	d	
9/84	9:00	Film(120) — FI	f	
9/84	10:00	Jessie(60) — CD	d	
10/84	8:00	Foul-Ups, Bleeps & Blunders — CY	m	To:t-8:30-4/85
10/84	8:00	Three's a Crowd — SC	m	Fr:t-8:30
10/84	8:30	Who's the Boss — SC	m	Fr:r-8:30

Date	Time	Title (min. if not 30) – Type	Action	From/To
10/84	8:30	Three's a Crowd – SC	m	To:t-8
11/84	9:00	Paper Dolls(60) – DR	m	To:t-10
11/84	10:00	Jessie(60) – CD	c	
11/84	10:00	Paper Dolls(60) – DR	m	Fr:t-9
12/84	9:00	Glitter(60) – DR	m	Fr:r-9
12/84	9:00	Glitter(60) – DR	c	
12/84	10:00	Paper Dolls(60) – DR	c	
1/85	9:00	Magruder & Loud(60) – CD	d	
1/85	10:00	Call to Glory(60) – DR	m	Fr:m-8
2/85	10:00	Call to Glory(60) – DR	c	
3/85	10:00	Moonlighting(60) – CD	d	
4/85	8:30	Who's the Boss – SC	m	To:t-9
4/85	8:30	Foul Ups, Bloops & Blunders – CY	m	Fr:t-8-10/84
4/85	9:00	Magruder & Loud(60) – CD	m	To:t-10
4/85	9:00	Who's the Boss – SC	m	Fr:t-8:30
4/85	9:30	Hail to the Chief – SC	d	
4/85	10:00	Magruder & Loud(60) – CD	m	Fr:t-9
4/85	10:00	Moonlighting(60) – CD	m	To:t-9-8/85
7/85	8:00	Three's a Crowd – SC	m	To:t-8:30
7/85	8:30	Foul Ups, Bloops & Blunders – CY	c	
7/85	9:00	Who's the Boss – SC	m	To:t-8
7/85	9:30	Hail to the Chief – SC	c	
8/85	8:00	Who's the Boss – SC	m#	Fr:t-9
8/85	8:30	Three's a Crowd – SC	m	Fr:t-8
8/85	9:00	Moonlighting(60) – CD	m#	Fr:t-10-4/85
9/85	8:30	Three's a Crowd – SC	c	
9/85	8:30	Growing Pains – SC	d	
9/85	10:00	Our Family Honor(60) – DR	d	
9/85	10:00	Magruder & Loud(60) – CD	c	
10/85	10:00	Our Family Honor(60) – DR	m	To:f-10
10/85	10:00	Spenser for Hire(60) – CD	m	Fr:f-10
3/86	8:30	Perfect Strangers – SC	d*	
4/86	8:30	Perfect Strangers – SC	m*	To:w-8-8/86
9/86	10:00	Jack & Mike(60) – DR	d	
9/86	10:00	Spenser for Hire(60) – CD	m	To:s-10
3/87	10:00	Jack & Mike(60) – DR	m	To:r-9
3/87	10:00	Max Headroom(60) – DR	d	
5/87	10:00	Max Headroom(60) – DR	m	To:f-9-8/87
6/87	10:00	Spenser for Hire(60) – CD	m	Fr:s-10
8/87	10:00	Spenser for Hire(60) – CD	m	To:n-8
9/87	10:00	Thirtysomething(60) – DR	d#	
2/88	8:30	Growing Pains – SC	m	To:w-8
3/88	8:30	Wonder Years – SC	d	
4/88	8:30	Wonder Years – SC	m	To:w-9-9/88
4/88	8:30	Just the 10 of Us – SC	d	
5/88	8:30	Just the 10 of Us – SC	m	To:f-9:30-9/88
5/88	8:30	Perfect Strangers – SC	s	
7/88	8:30	Full House – SC	s	
7/88	8:30	Perfect Strangers – SC	f	
8/88	8:30	Full House – SC	f	

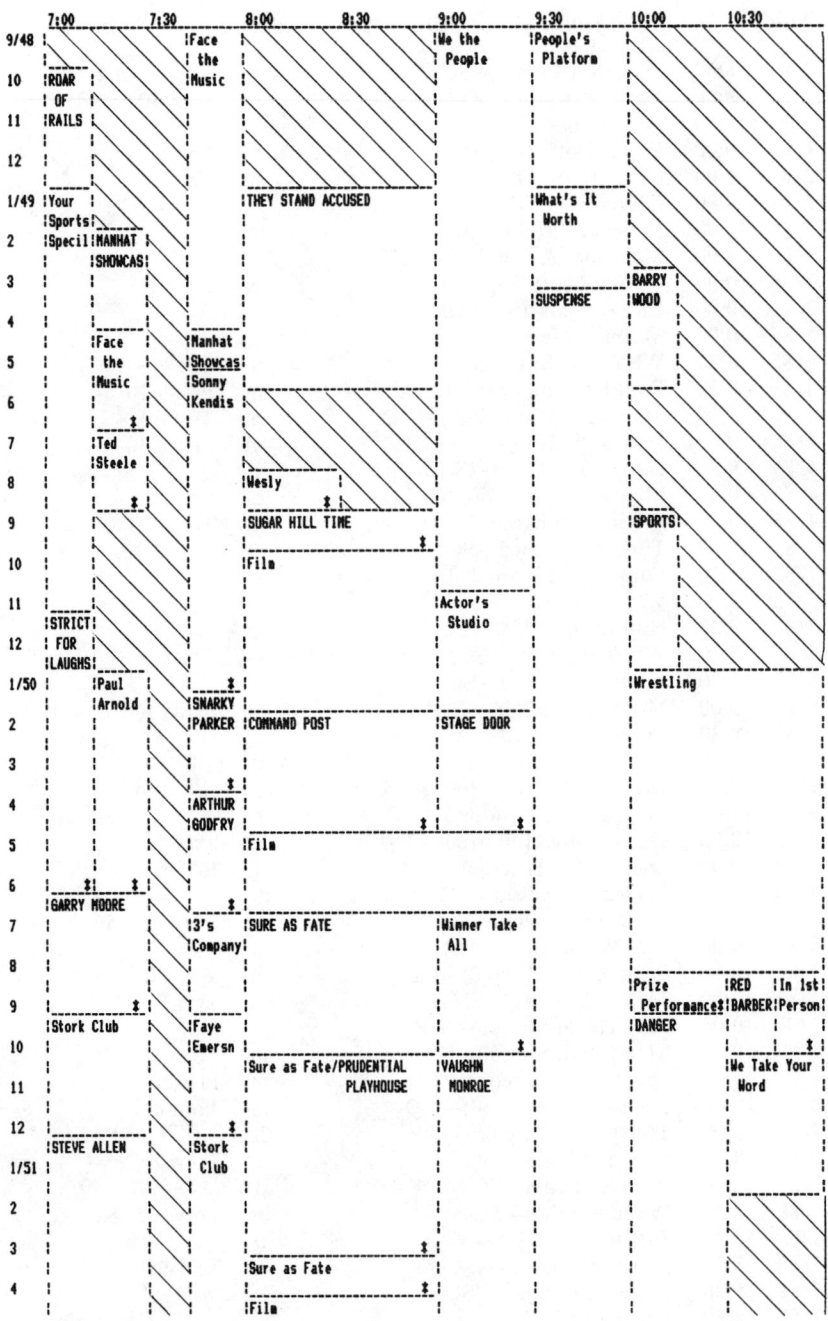

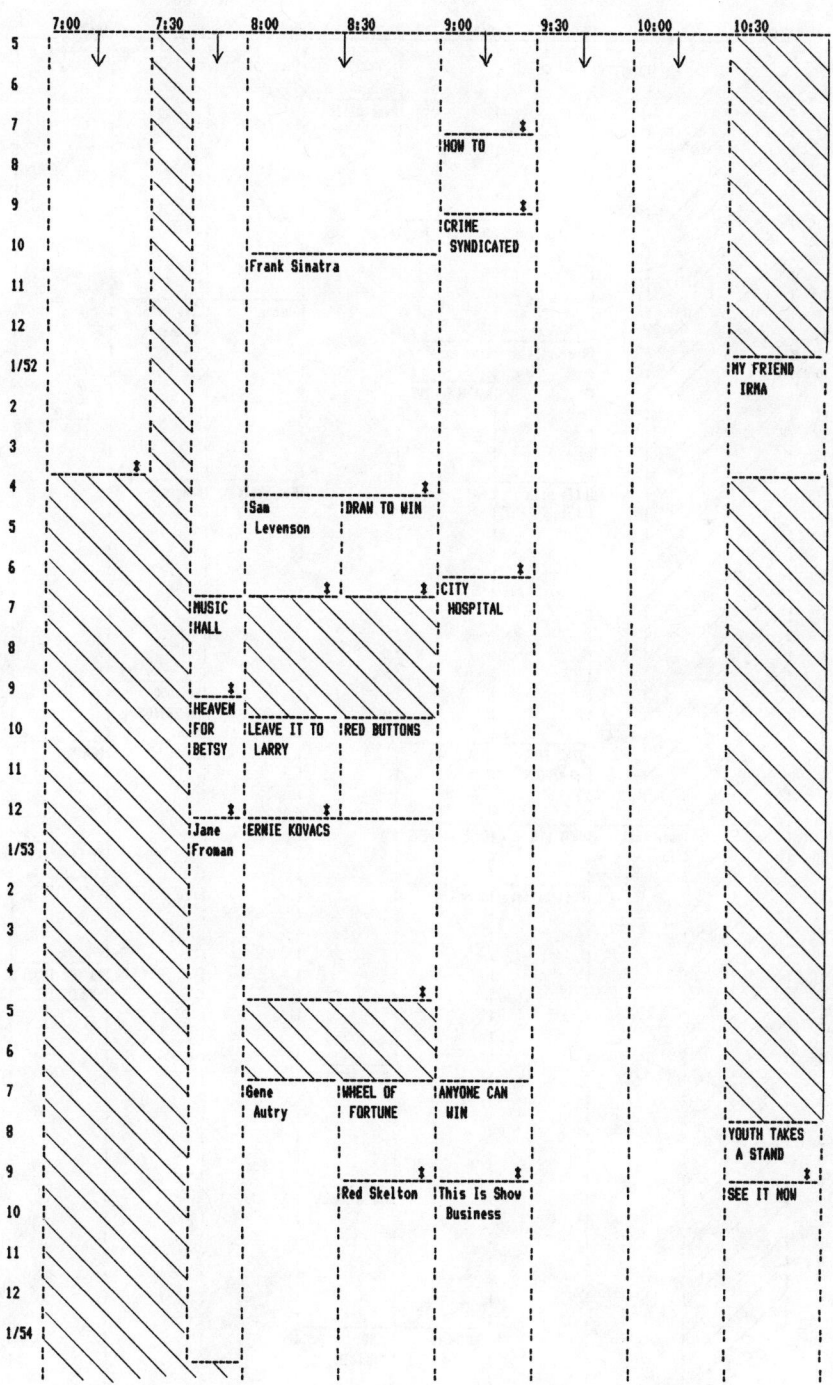

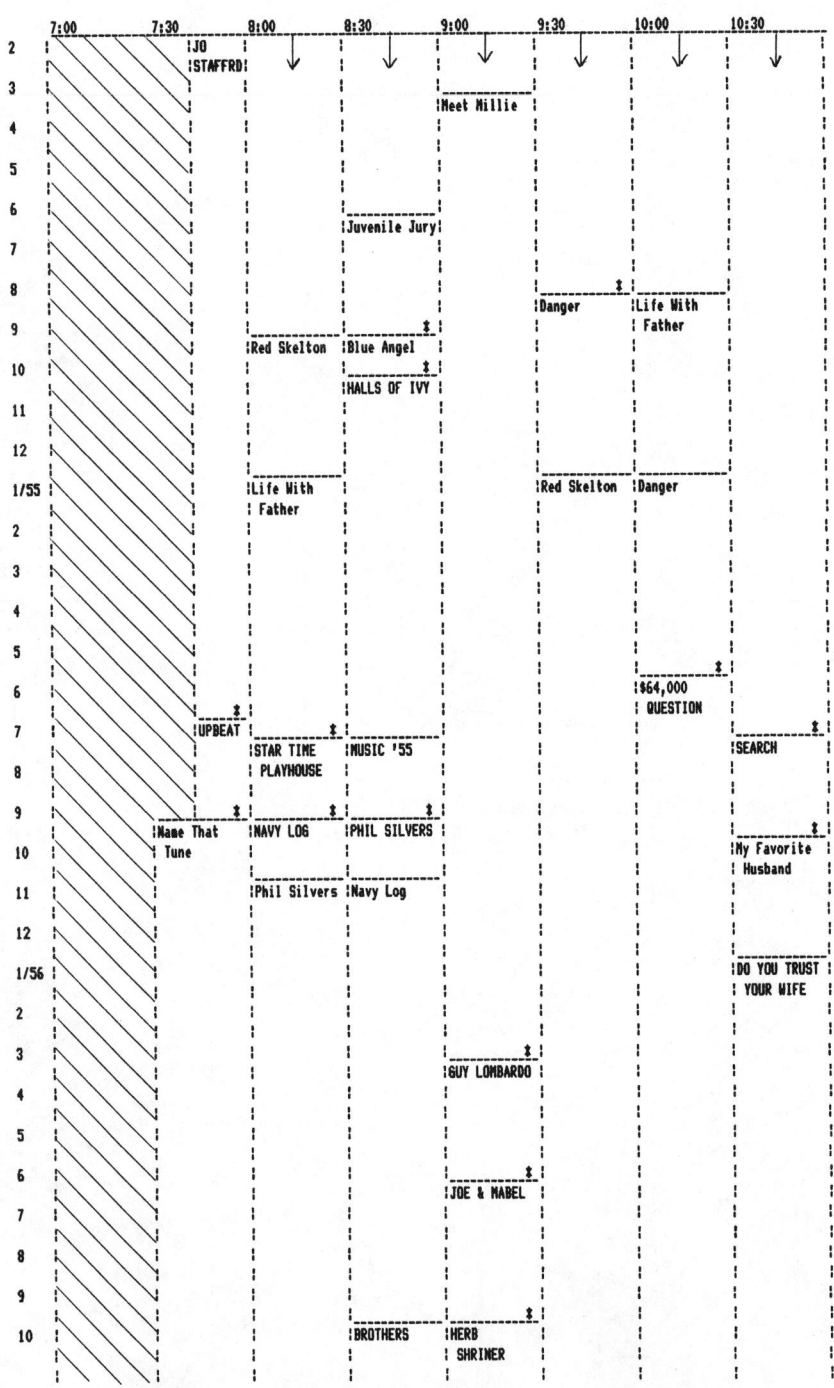

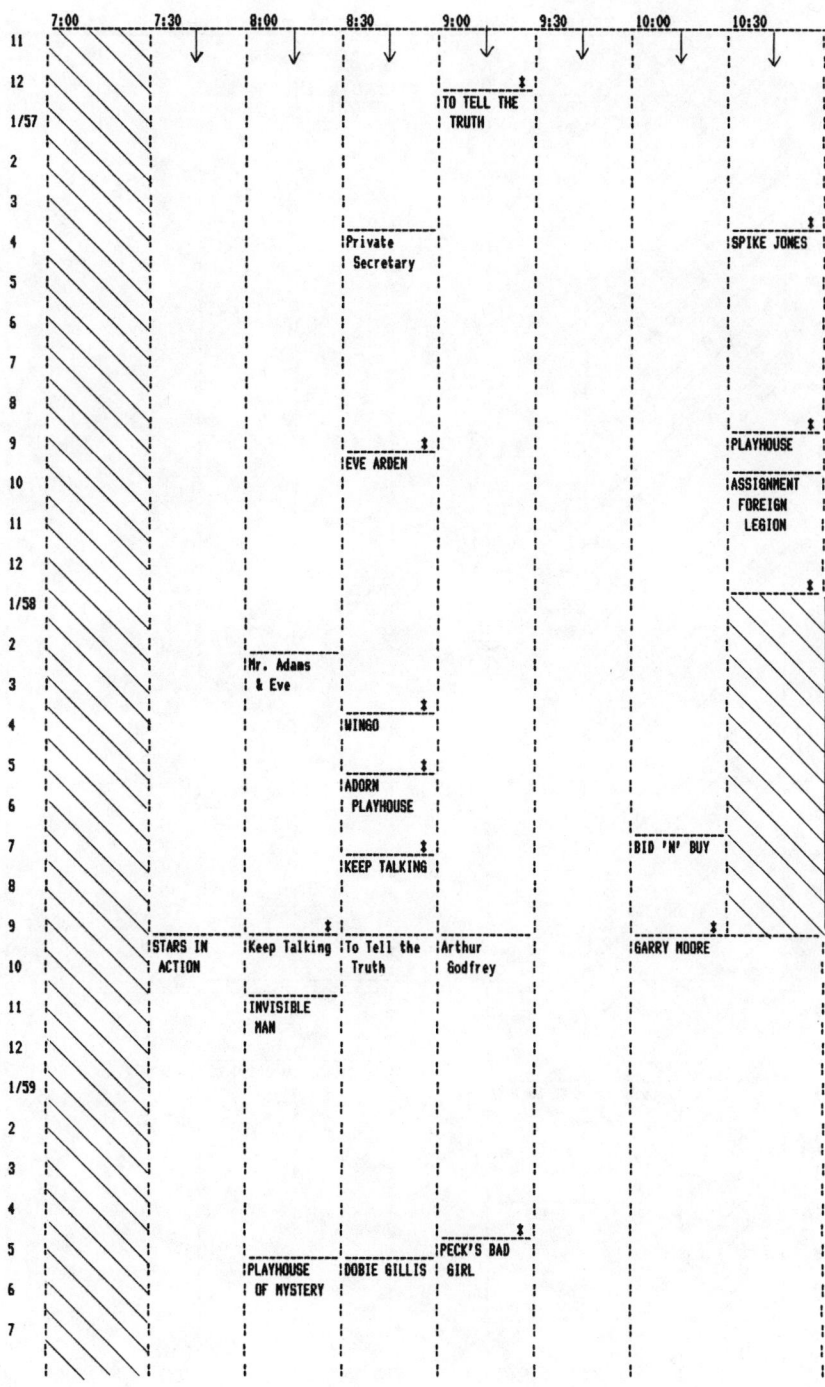

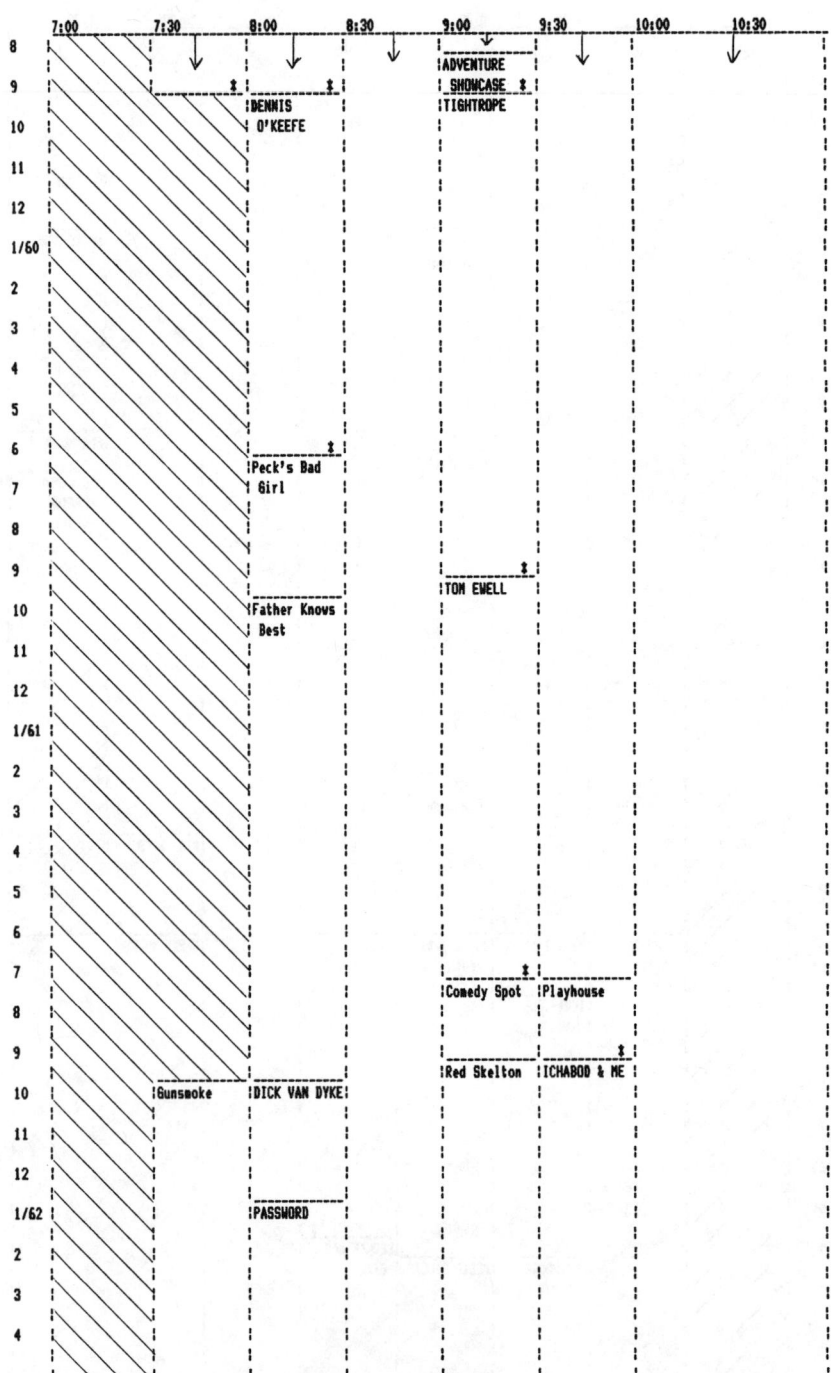

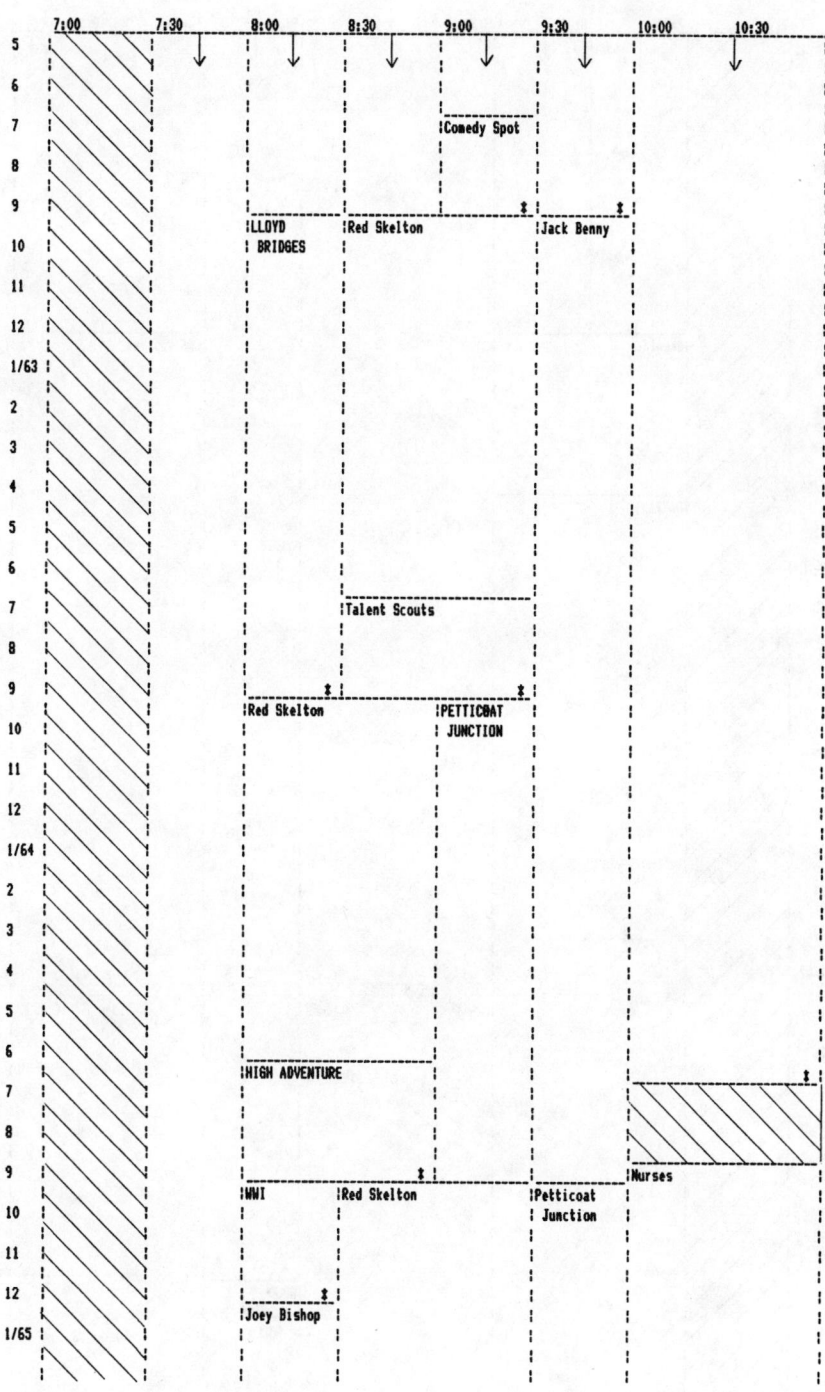

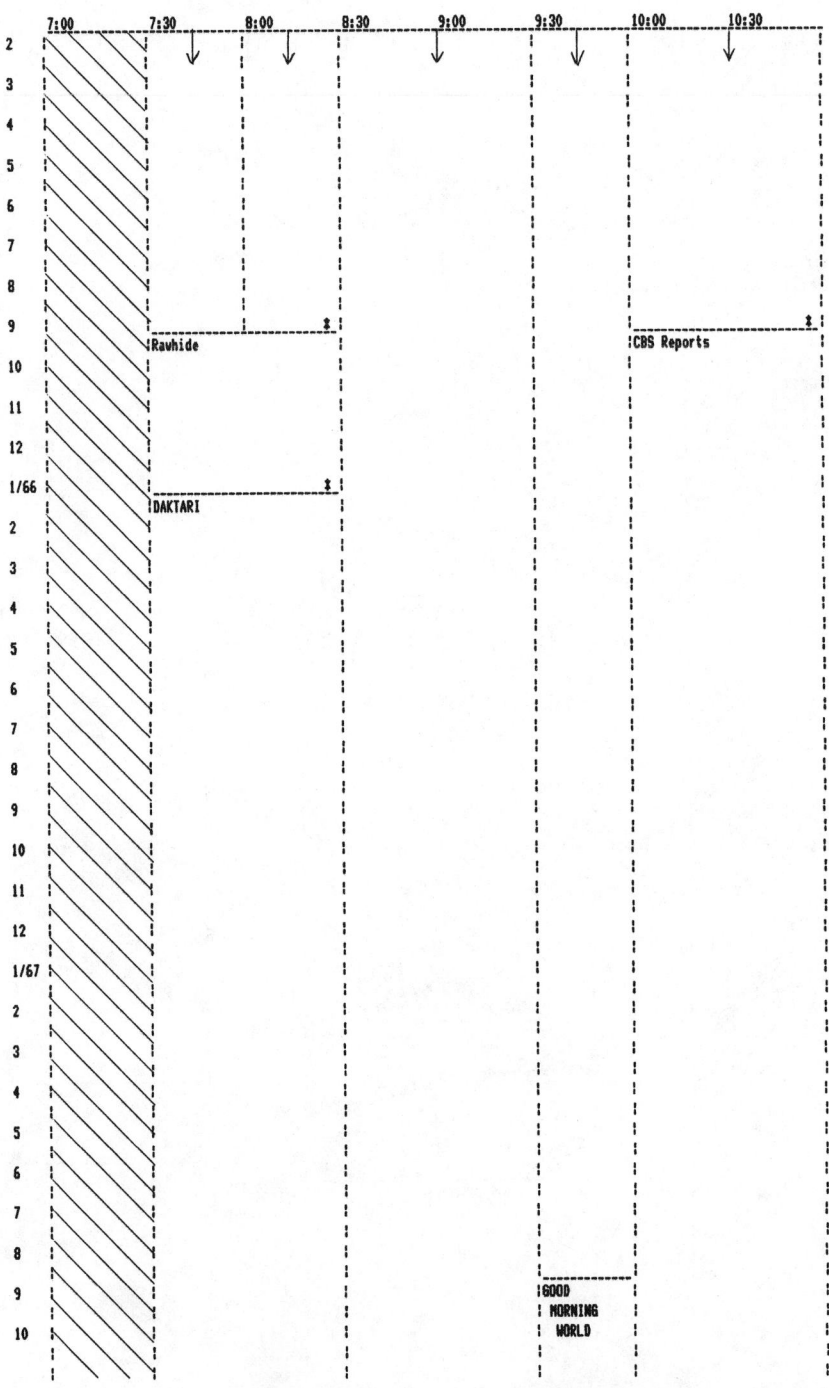

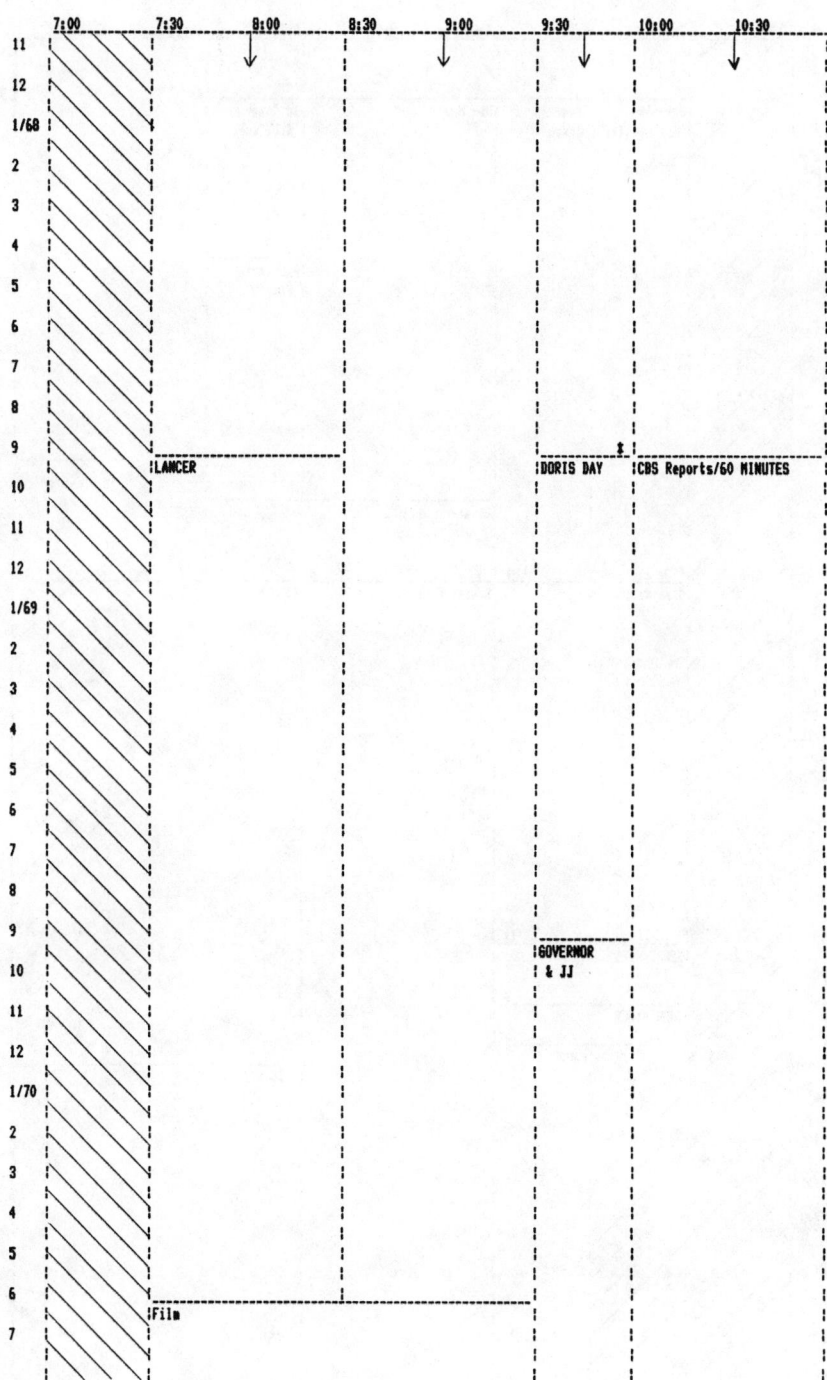

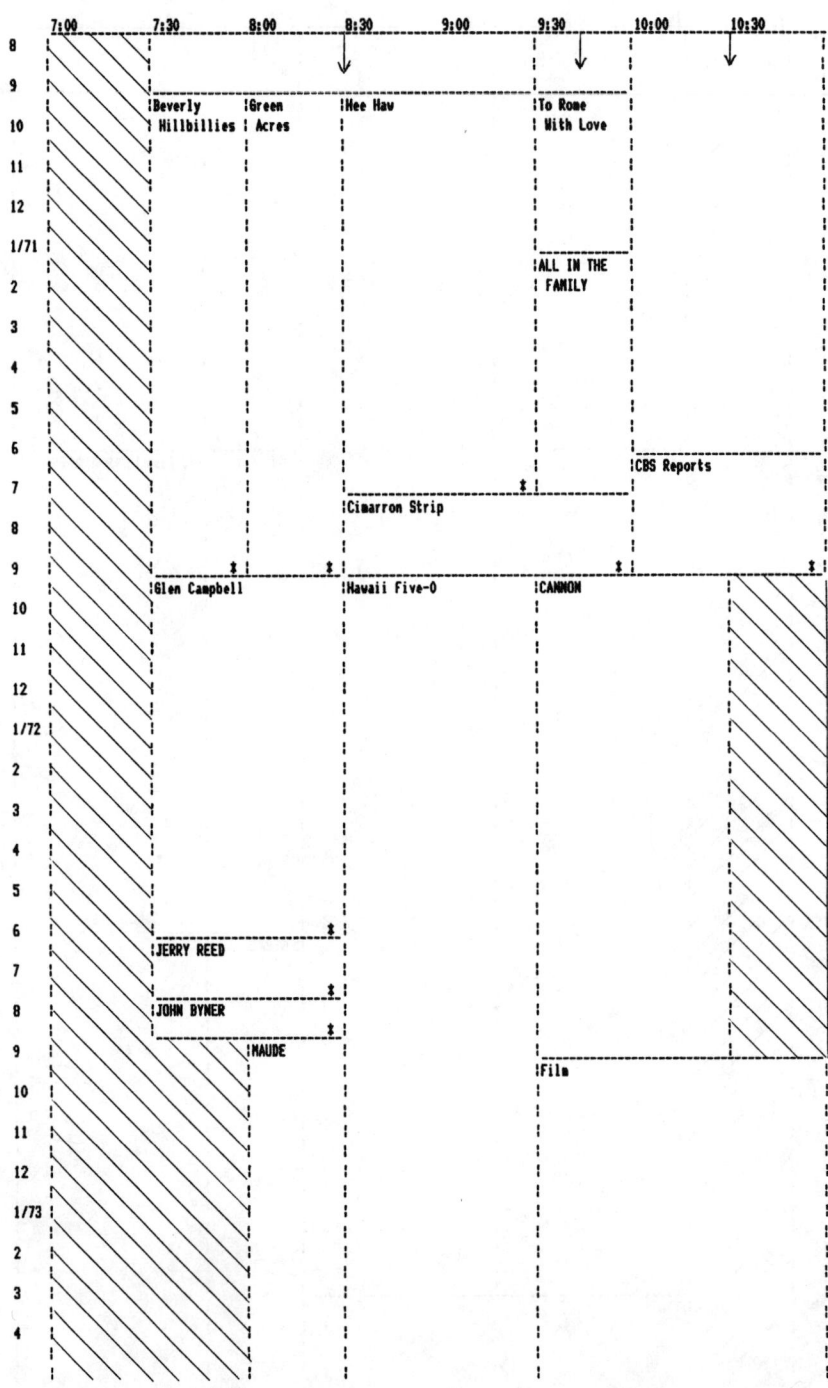

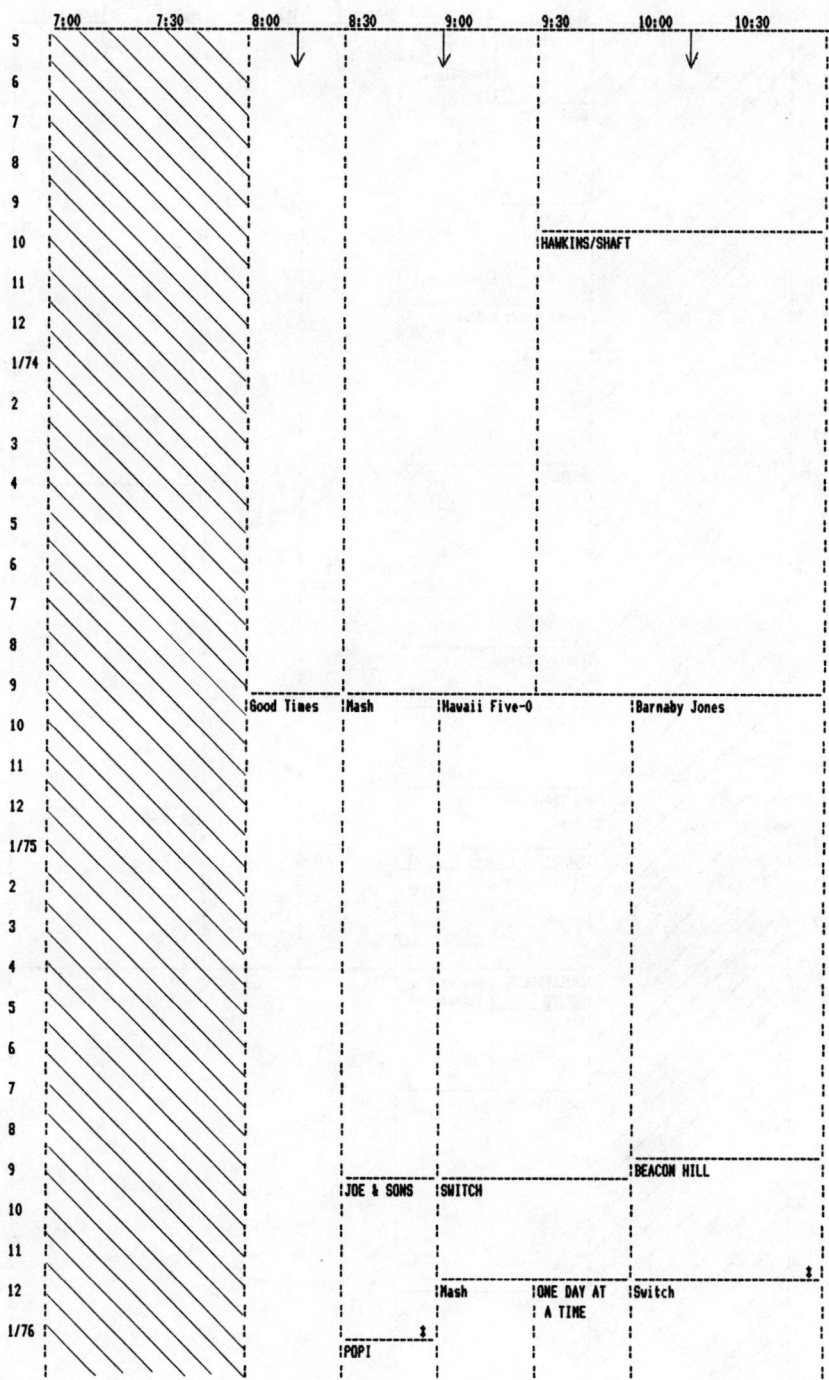

	7:00	7:30	8:00	8:30	9:00	9:30	10:00	10:30
5				↓	↓		↓	
6								
7								
8								
9								
10						HAWKINS/SHAFT		
11								
12								
1/74								
2								
3								
4								
5								
6								
7								
8								
9			Good Times	Mash	Hawaii Five-O		Barnaby Jones	
10								
11								
12								
1/75								
2								
3								
4								
5								
6								
7								
8								
9							BEACON HILL	
10				JOE & SONS	SWITCH			
11								
12					Mash	ONE DAY AT A TIME	Switch	
1/76				POPI				

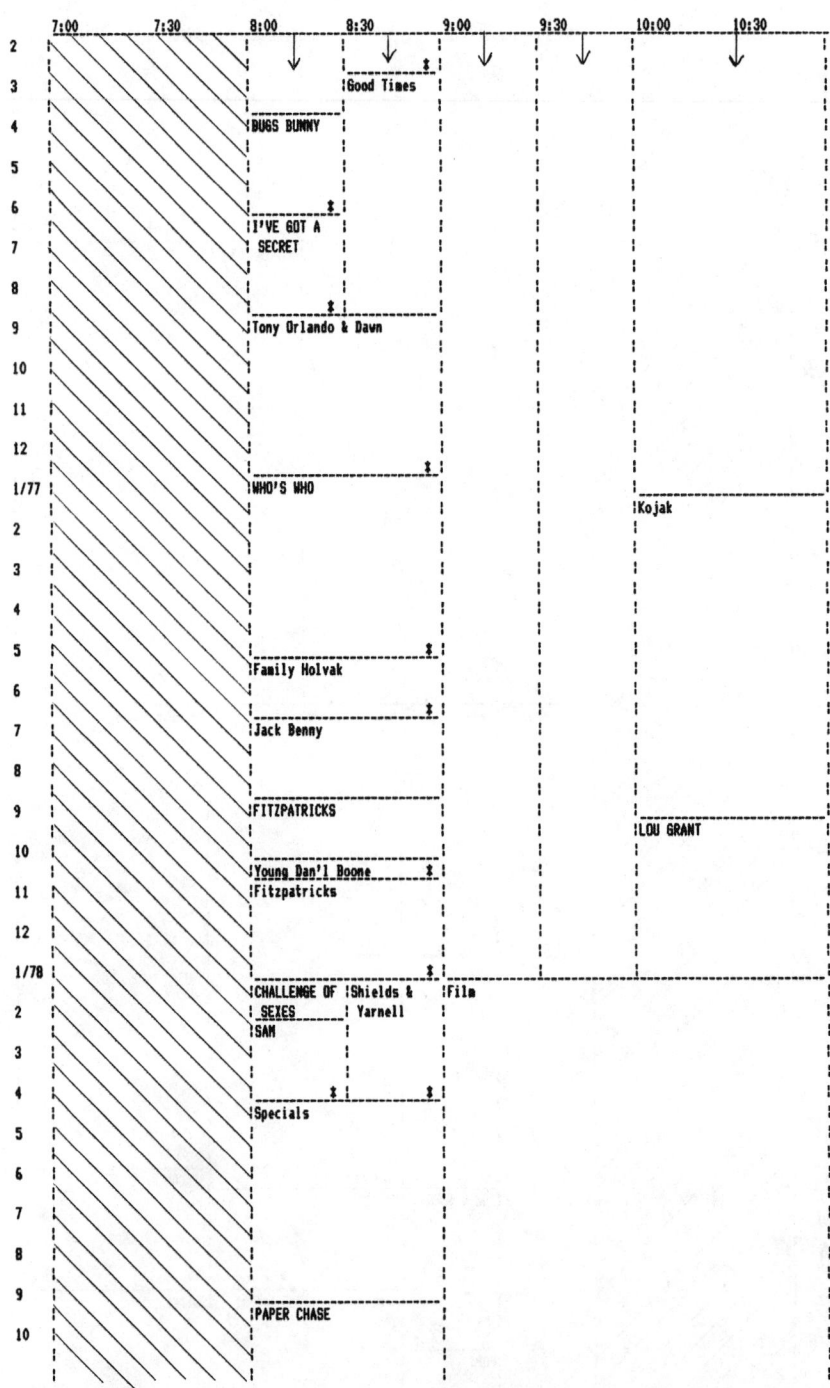

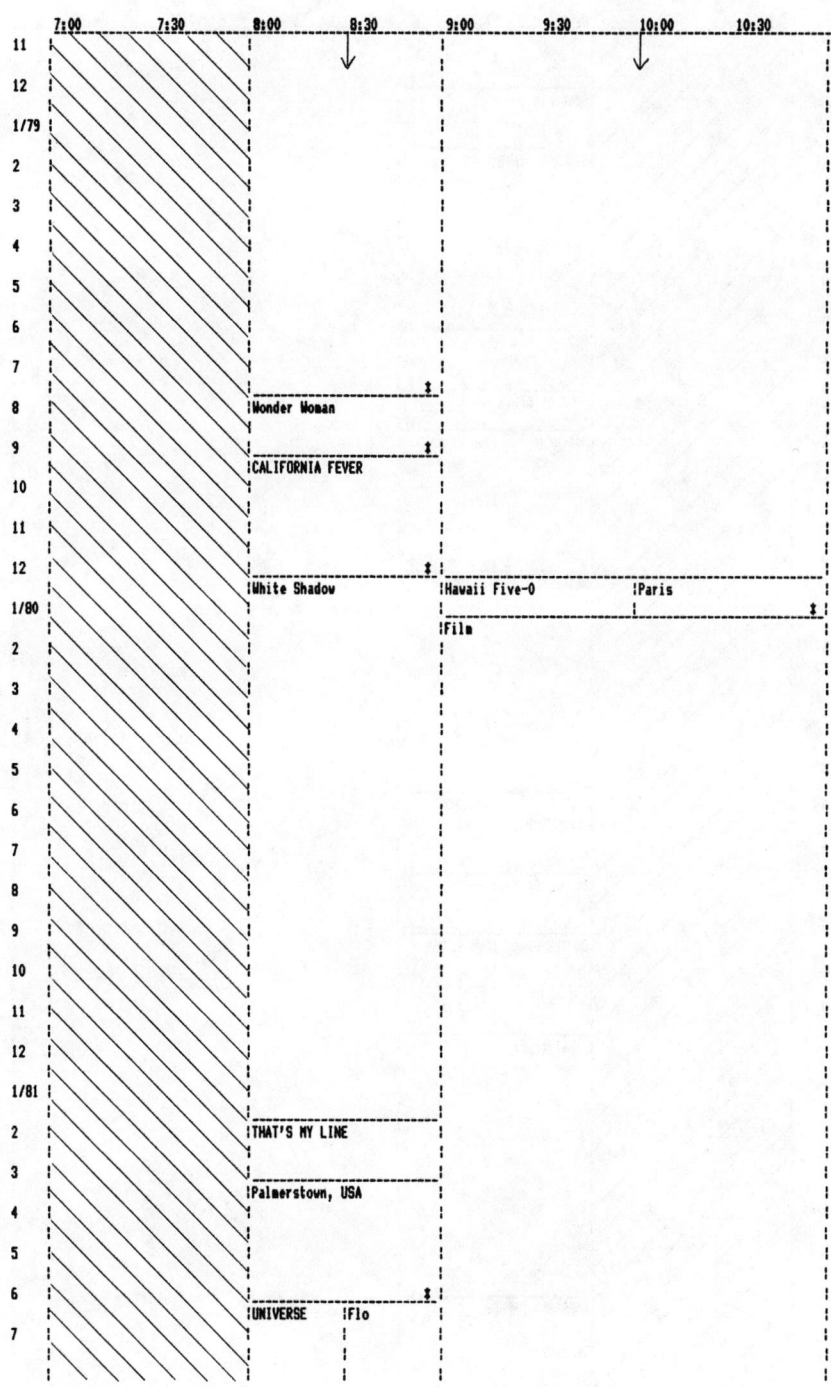

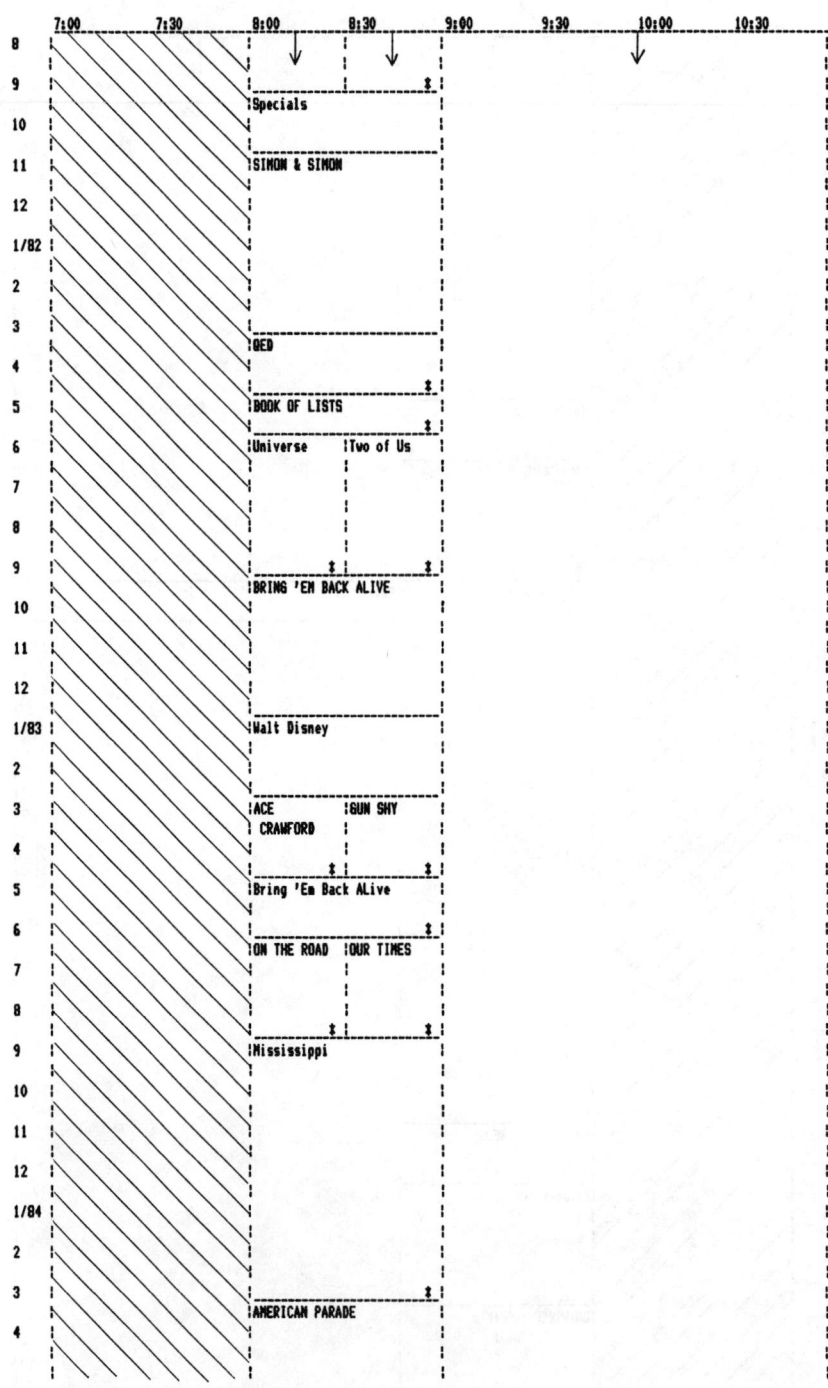

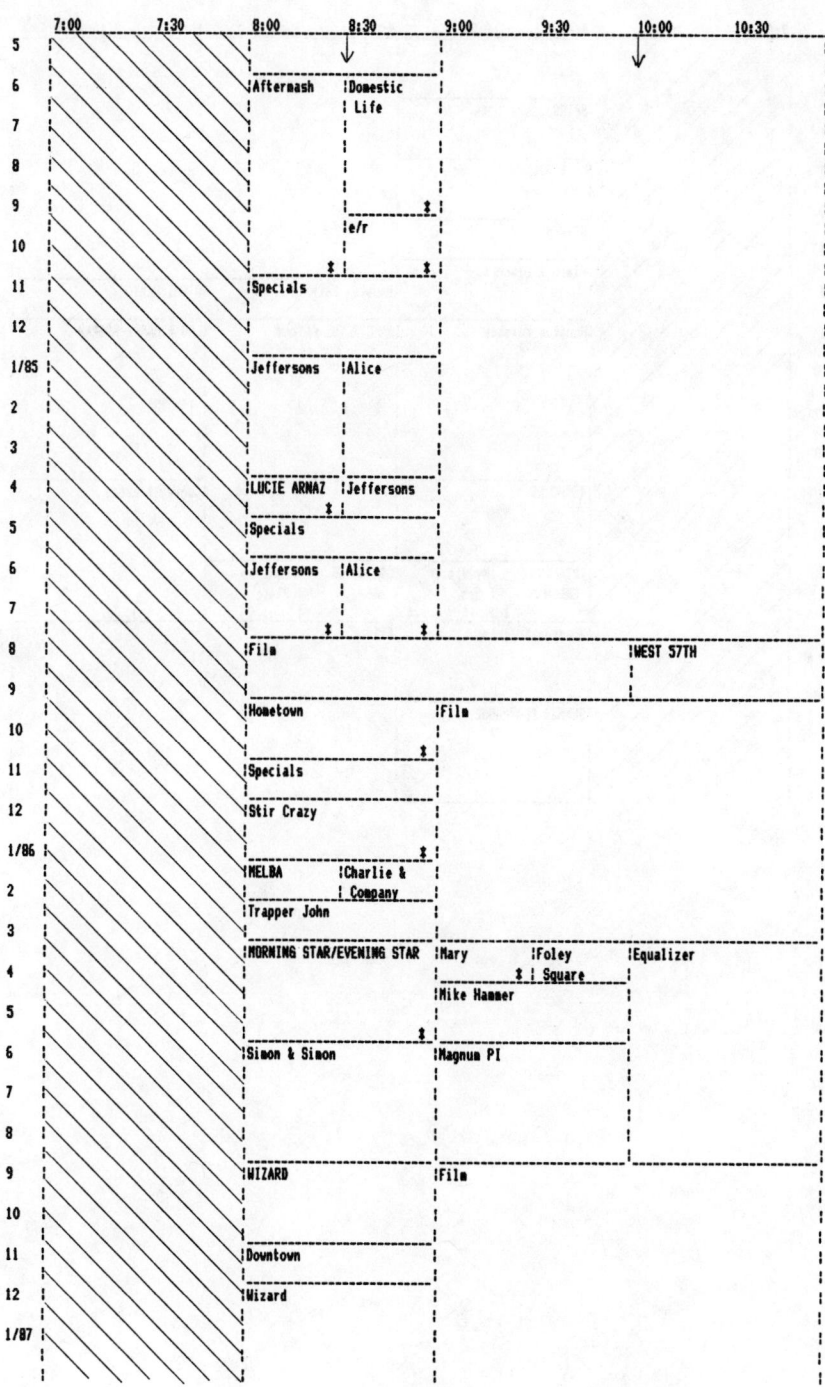

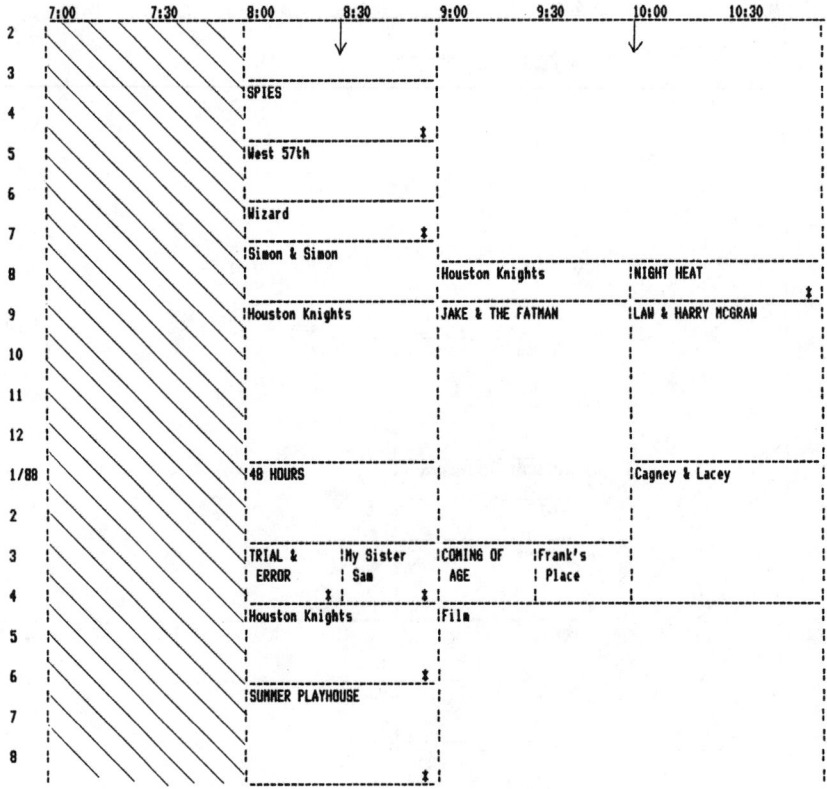

Date	Time	Title (min. if not 30) — Type	Action	From/To
6/48	9:00	We, the People — IV	d	
8/48	7:45	Face the Music(15) — MU	m	Fr:m-f-7:15
8/48	9:30	People's Platform — DS	d	
10/48	7:00	Roar of the Rails(15) — AD	d	
12/48	7:00	Roar of the Rails(15) — AD	m	To:m-7-10/49
12/48	9:30	People's Platform — DS	m	To:m-var
1/49	7:00	Your Sports Special(15) — SN	m	Fr:f-7
1/49	8:00	They Stand Accused(60) — LD	d	
1/49	9:30	What's It Worth — QU	m	Fr:f-8:30
2/49	7:15	Manhattan Showcase(15) — MV	d	
3/49	9:30	Suspense — SA	d	
3/49	9:30	What's It Worth — QU	m	To:w-8:30-10/52(d)
3/49	10:00	Backstage with Barry Wood(15) — VY	d	
4/49	7:15	Face the Music(15) — MU	m	Fr:tr-7:45
4/49	7:15	Manhattan Showcase(15) — MV	m	To:mtrf-7:45
4/49	7:45	Face the Music(15) — MU	m	To:tr-7:15
4/49	7:45	Manhattan Showcase(15) — MV	m	Fr:var-7:15
5/49	7:45	Manhattan Showcase(15) — MV	m	To:mwr-7:15
5/49	7:45	Sonny Kendis Show(15) — MU	m	Fr:mw-7:15
5/49	8:00	They Stand Accused(60) — LD	m	To:n-9-9/49(d)
5/49	10:00	Backstage with Barry Wood(15) — VY	c	
6/49	7:15	Face the Music(15) — MU	c	
7/49	7:15	Ted Steele(15) — MU	m	Fr:t-9(d)
7/49	9:30	Wesley — SC	m*	Fr:n-7:30
8/49	7:15	Ted Steele(15) — MU	c	
8/49	7:55	Ruthie on the Telephone(5) — CY	d	
8/49	8:00	Wesley — SC	m	Fr:t-9:30
8/49	8:00	Wesley — SC	c	
8/49	9:30	Wesley — SC	m*	To:t-8
9/49	8:00	Sugar Hill Times(60) — MV	d	
9/49	8:00	Sugar Hill Times(60) — MV	c	
9/49	10:00	This Week in Sports(15) — SN	d	
10/49	8:00	Film(60) — FI	s	
10/49	9:00	We, the People — IV	m	To:f-8:30(n)
11/49	7:00	Strictly for Laughs(15) — MU	d	
11/49	7:00	Your Sports Special(15) — SN	c	
11/49	7:55	Herb Shriner(5) — CV	d	
11/49	7:55	Ruthie on the Telephone(5) — CY	c	
11/49	9:00	Actors Studio — DA	m	Fr:w-8(a)
12/49	10:00	This Week in Sports(15) — SN	c	
1/50	7:15	Paul Arnold(15) — MU	m	Fr:mwrf-7:15
1/50	7:45	Life with Snarky Parker(15) — KV	d	
1/50	7:45	Sonny Kendis Show(15) — MU	c	
1/50	8:00	Film(60) — FI	f	
1/50	9:00	Actors Studio — DA	m	To:f-9
1/50	10:00	Wrestling(60) — SP	s	
2/50	7:55	Herb Shriner(5) — CV	c	
2/50	8:00	Command Post(60) — IS	d	

Date	Time	Title (min. if not 30) — Type	Action	From/To
2/50	9:00	Stage Door — DR	d	
3/50	7:45	Life with Snarky Parker(15) — KV	c	
4/50	7:45	Arthur Godfrey and His Ukulele (15) — IS	d	
4/50	8:00	Command Post(60) — IS	c	
4/50	9:00	Stage Door — DR	c	
5/50	8:00	Film(90) — FI	s	
6/50	7:00	Garry Moore Show — VY	d	
6/50	7:00	Strictly for Laughs(15) — MU	c	
6/50	7:15	Paul Arnold(15) — MU	c	
6/50	7:45	Arthur Godfrey and His Ukulele (15) — IS	c	
6/50	8:00	Film(90) — FI	f	
7/50	7:45	Three's Company(15) — MU	m	Fr:wr-7:45
7/50	8:00	Sure as Fate(60) — DA	d	
7/50	9:00	Winner Take All — QU	m	Fr:r-9:45
7/50	9:30	Web — DA	d*	
8/50	9:30	Web — DA	m*	To:w-9:30
8/50	10:00	Prize Performance — TA	m	Fr:m-8:30
8/50	10:00	Wrestling(60) — SP	f	
9/50	7:00	Garry Moore Show — VY	c	
9/50	7:00	Stork Club — TK	m	Fr:mwf-7:45
9/50	7:45	Faye Emerson(15) — IV	m	Fr:w-8
9/50	7:45	Three's Company(15) — MU	m	To:mwf-7:45
9/50	10:00	Danger — DA	d	
9/50	10:00	Prize Performance — TA	c	
9/50	10:30	Red Barber's Corner(15) — ST	d	
9/50	10:45	In the First Person(15) — IV	m	Fr:n-9:15
10/50	8:00	Prudential Family Playhouse(60) — DA	d	
10/50	9:00	Vaughn Monroe — MV	d	
10/50	9:00	Winner Take All — QU	c	
10/50	10:30	Red Barber's Corner(15) — ST	m	To:w-10:45-12/54
10/50	10:30	We Take Your Word — QU	m	Fr:m-9:30
10/50	10:45	In the First Person(15) — IV	c	
12/50	7:00	Steve Allen Show — CV	d	
12/50	7:00	Stork Club — TK	m	To:trs-7:45
12/50	7:45	Faye Emerson(15) — IV	c	
12/50	7:45	Stork Club(15) — TK	m	Fr:m-f-7
1/51	10:30	We Take Your Word — QU	m	To:f-10:30-3/51
3/51	8:00	Prudential Family Playhouse(60) — DA	c	
4/51	8:00	Film(60) — FI	s	
4/51	8:00	Sure as Fate(60) — DA	c	
7/51	9:00	How To — IF	d	
7/51	9:00	Vaughn Monroe — MV	c	
9/51	9:00	Crime Syndicated — RA	d	
9/51	9:00	How To — IF	c	
10/51	8:00	Frank Sinatra(60) — MV	m	Fr:s-9-6/51
10/51	8:00	Film(60) — FI	f	

Date	Time	Title (min. if not 30) — Type	Action	From/To
1/52	10:30	My Friend Irma — SC	d	
3/52	7:00	Steve Allen Show — CV	c	
3/52	10:30	My Friend Irma — SC	m	To:f-8:30
4/52	8:00	Frank Sinatra(60) — MV	c	
4/52	8:00	Sam Levenson — CY	m	Fr:s-7-6/51
4/52	8:30	Draw to Win — QU	d	
6/52	7:45	Stork Club(15) — TK	m	To:s-7
6/52	8:00	Sam Levenson — CY	c	
6/52	8:30	Draw to Win — QU	c	
6/52	9:00	City Hospital — MD	d	
7/52	7:45	Music Hall(15) — MU	d	
9/52	7:45	Heaven for Betsy(15) — SC	d	
9/52	7:45	Music Hall(15) — MU	c	
10/52	8:00	Leave It to Larry — SC	d	
10/52	8:30	Red Buttons — CV	d	
12/52	7:45	Heaven for Betsy(15) — SC	c	
12/52	7:45	Jane Froman's U.S.A. Canteen(15) — MV	m	Fr:s-9
12/52	8:00	Ernie Kovacs(60) — CV	d	
12/52	8:00	Leave It to Larry — SC	c	
12/52	8:30	Red Buttons — CV	m	To:m-9:30
4/53	8:00	Ernie Kovacs(60) — CV	c	
6/53	9:00	City Hospital — MD	m	To:r-10:30
6/53	9:00	Crime Syndicated — RA	c	
7/53	7:45	Summertime U.S.A.(15) — MU	d*	
7/53	8:00	Gene Autry — WE	m	Fr:n-7
7/53	8:30	Wheel of Fortune — QU	d	
7/53	9:00	Anyone Can Win — QU	d	
8/53	7:45	Summertime U.S.A.(15) — MU	c*	
8/53	10:30	Youth Takes a Stand — DS	d	
9/53	8:30	Red Skelton — CV	m	Fr:n-7-6/53(n)
9/53	8:30	Wheel of Fortune — QU	c	
9/53	9:00	Anyone Can Win — QU	c	
9/53	9:00	This Is Show Business — VY	m	Fr:s-9-6/53
9/53	10:30	See It Now — DO	d	
9/53	10:30	Youth Takes a Stand — DS	c	
1/54	7:45	Jane Froman's U.S.A. Canteen(15) — MV	m	To:r-7:45
2/54	7:45	Jo Stafford(15) — MU	d	
3/54	9:00	Meet Millie — SC	m	Fr:s-7
3/54	9:00	This Is Show Business — VY	m	To:t-8:30-6/56(n)
6/54	8:30	Juvenile Jury — QU	m	Fr:m-9-9/53(n)
6/54	8:30	Red Skelton — CV	m	To:w-8
7/54	7:45	Summer Holiday(15) — MU	s*	
7/54	10:30	Blue Angel — VY	d*	
8/54	7:45	Summer Holiday(15) — MU	f*	
8/54	9:30	Danger — DA	m	Fr:t-10
8/54	9:30	Suspense — DA	c	
8/54	10:00	Danger — DA	m	To:t-9:30
8/54	10:00	Life with Father — SC	m	Fr:n-7-5/54

Date	Time	Title (min. if not 30) — Type	Action	From/To
8/54	10:30	Blue Angel — VY	m*	To:t-8:30
9/54	8:00	Gene Autry — WE	m	To:s-7
9/54	8:00	Red Skelton — CV	m	Fr:w-8
9/54	8:30	Blue Angel — VY	m	Fr:t-10:30
9/54	8:30	Juvenile Jury — QU	c	
10/54	8:30	Blue Angel — VY	c	
10/54	8:30	Halls of Ivy — SC	d	
12/54	8:00	Red Skelton — CV	m	To:t-9:30
12/54	9:30	Danger — DA	m	To:t-10
12/54	10:00	Life with Father — SC	m	To:t-8
1/55	8:00	Life with Father — SC	m	Fr:t-10
1/55	9:30	Red Skelton — CV	m	Fr:t-8
1/55	10:00	Danger — DA	m	Fr:t-9:30
5/55	10:00	Danger — DA	c	
6/55	7:45	Jo Stafford(15) — MU	c	
6/55	9:30	Spotlight Playhouse — DA	d*	
6/55	10:00	$64,000 Question — QU	d	
7/55	7:45	Upbeat(15) — MU	d	
7/55	8:00	Life with Father — SC	c	
7/55	8:00	Star Time Playhouse — DA	d	
7/55	8:30	Halls of Ivy — SC	m	To:r-10:30
7/55	8:30	Music 55 — MU	d	
7/55	10:30	Search — DO	d	
7/55	10:30	See It Now — DO	c	
9/55	7:30	Name That Tune — QU	m	Fr:r-10:30-3/55
9/55	7:45	Upbeat(15) — MU	c	
9/55	8:00	Navy Log — MR	d	
9/55	8:00	Star Time Playhouse — DA	c	
9/55	8:30	Music 55 — MU	c	
9/55	8:30	Phil Silvers Show — SC	d	
9/55	9:30	Spotlight Playhouse — DA	m*	To:t-9:30-6/56
9/55	10:30	Search — DO	c	
10/55	8:00	Navy Log — MR	m	To:t-8:30
10/55	8:30	Phil Silvers Show — SC	m	To:t-8
10/55	10:30	My Favorite Husband — SC	m	Fr:s-9:30-6/55
11/55	8:00	Phil Silvers Show — SC	m	Fr:t-8:30
11/55	8:30	Navy Log — MR	m	Fr:t-8
12/55	10:30	My Favorite Husband — SC	m	To:n-7:30-6/57
1/56	10:30	Do You Trust Your Wife? — QU	d	
3/56	9:00	Guy Lombardo's Diamond Jubilee — MV	d	
3/56	9:00	Meet Millie — SC	c	
6/56	9:00	Guy Lombardo's Diamond Jubilee — MV	c	
6/56	9:00	Joe & Mabel — SC	d	
6/56	9:30	Spotlight Playhouse — DA	m*	Fr:t-9:30-9/55
9/56	8:30	Navy Log — MR	m	To:w-8:30
9/56	9:00	Joe & Mabel — SC	c	
9/56	9:30	Spotlight Playhouse — DA	m*	To:t-9:30-6/57
10/56	8:30	Brothers — SC	d	

Date	Time	Title (min. if not 30) — Type	Action	From/To
10/56	9:00	Herb Shriner — CV	d	
12/56	9:00	Herb Shriner — CV	c	
12/56	9:00	To Tell the Truth — QU	d	
3/57	8:30	Brothers — SC	m	To:n-7:30-6/58
3/57	10:30	Do You Trust Your Wife? — QU	c	
4/57	8:30	Private Secretary — SC	m	Fr:n-7:30
4/57	10:30	Spike Jones Show — CV	d	
6/57	9:30	Spotlight Playhouse — DA	m*	Fr:t-9:30-9/56
8/57	10:30	Spike Jones Show — CV	c	
9/57	8:30	Eve Arden Show — SC	d	
9/57	8:30	Private Secretary — SC	c	
9/57	9:30	Spotlight Playhouse — DA	m*	To:t-9:30-6/58
9/57	10:30	Playhouse — DA	d	
9/57	10:30	Playhouse — DA	m	To:wr-7:30-7/59
10/57	10:30	Assignment Foreign Legion — AA	d	
12/57	10:30	Assignment Foreign Legion — AA	c	
2/58	8:00	Mr. Adams and Eve — SC	m	Fr:f-9
2/58	8:00	Phil Silvers Show — SC	m	To:f-9
3/58	8:30	Eve Arden Show — SC	c	
4/58	8:30	Wingo — QU	d	
5/58	8:30	Adorn Playhouse — DA	d	
5/58	8:30	Wingo — QU	c	
6/58	9:30	Spotlight Playhouse — DA	m*	Fr:t-9:30-9/57
6/58	10:00	$64,000 Question — QU	m	To:n-10-9/58
7/58	8:30	Adorn Playhouse — DA	c	
7/58	8:30	Keep Talking — QU	d	
7/58	10:00	Bid 'n' Buy — QU	d	
9/58	7:30	Name That Tune — QU	m	To:m-7:30
9/58	7:30	Stars in Action — DA	d	
9/58	8:00	Keep Talking — QU	m	Fr:t-8:30
9/58	8:00	Mr. Adams and Eve — SC	c	
9/58	8:30	Keep Talking — QU	m	To:t-8
9/58	8:30	To Tell the Truth — QU	m	Fr:t-9
9/58	9:00	Arthur Godfrey and His Friends — MV	m	Fr:w-8-6/57
9/58	9:00	To Tell the Truth — QU	m	To:t-8:30
9/58	9:30	Spotlight Playhouse — DA	m*	To:t-9:30-6/59
9/58	10:00	Bid 'n' Buy — QU	c	
9/58	10:00	Garry Moore Show(60) — VY	d	
10/58	8:00	Keep Talking — QU	m	To:n-10
11/58	8:00	Invisible Man — AD	d	
4/59	9:00	Arthur Godfrey and His Friends — MV	c	
5/59	8:00	Invisible Man — AD	m	To:r-7:30
5/59	8:00	Playhouse of Mystery — DA	d	
5/59	9:00	Peck's Bad Girl — SC	d	
6/59	9:30	Spotlight Playhouse — DA	m*	Fr:t-9:30-9/58
7/59	10:00	Andy Williams Show(60) — MV	m*	Fr:r-9-9/58(a)
8/59	9:00	Adventure Showcase — AA	d	
8/59	9:00	Peck's Bad Girl — SC	m	To:t-8-6/60

Date	Time	Title (min. if not 30) – Type	Action	From/To
9/59	7:30	Stars in Action – DA	c	
9/59	8:00	Dennis O'Keefe Show – SC	d	
9/59	8:00	Playhouse of Mystery – DA	c	
9/59	8:30	Many Loves of Dobie Gillis – SC	d	
9/59	8:30	To Tell the Truth – QU	m	To:r-7:30
9/59	9:00	Adventure Showcase – AA	c	
9/59	9:00	Tightrope – CD	d	
9/59	9:30	Spotlight Playhouse – DA	c*	
9/59	10:00	Andy Williams Show(60) – MV	m*	To:r-10-9/62(n)
6/60	8:00	Dennis O'Keefe Show – SC	c	
6/60	8:00	Peck's Bad Girl – SC	m	Fr:t-9-8/59
6/60	9:30	Comedy Spot – CA	d*	
7/60	10:00	Diagnosis:Unknown(60) – CD	d*	
9/60	8:00	Peck's Bad Girl – SC	m	To:r-9:30
9/60	9:00	Tightrope – CD	c	
9/60	9:00	Tom Ewell Show – SC	d	
9/60	9:30	Comedy Spot – CA	m*	To:t-9-7/61
9/60	10:00	Diagnosis:Unknown(60) – CD	c*	
10/60	8:00	Father Knows Best – SC	m	Fr:m-8:30
6/61	9:30	Red Skelton – CV	m	To:t-9-9/61
7/61	9:00	Comedy Spot – CA	m	Fr:t-9:30
7/61	9:00	Tom Ewell Show – SC	c	
7/61	9:30	Playhouse 90(90) – DA	m*	Fr:r-9:30-1/60
9/61	8:00	Father Knows Best – SC	m	To:w-8
9/61	9:00	Comedy Spot – CA	m	To:t-9-7/62
9/61	9:00	Red Skelton – CV	m	Fr:t-9:30-6/61
9/61	9:30	Ichabod and Me – SC	d	
9/61	9:30	Playhouse 90(90) – DA	c*	
10/61	7:30	Gunsmoke – WE	s	
10/61	8:00	Dick Van Dyke Show – SC	d	
12/61	8:00	Dick Van Dyke Show – SC	m	To:w-9:30
1/62	8:00	Password – QU	d	
6/62	9:00	Red Skelton – CV	m	To:t-8:30-9/62
7/62	9:00	Comedy Spot – CA	m	Fr:t-9-9/61
7/62	10:00	Talent Scouts(60) – TA	d*	
9/62	8:00	Lloyd Bridges Show – DA	d	
9/62	8:00	Password – QU	m	To:m-10-3/63
9/62	8:30	Many Loves of Dobie Gillis – SC	m	To:w-8:30
9/62	8:30	Red Skelton(60) – CV	m	Fr:t-9-6/62
9/62	9:00	Comedy Spot – CA	c	
9/62	9:30	Ichabod and Me – SC	c	
9/62	9:30	Jack Benny – CY	m	Fr:n-9:30-6/62
9/62	10:00	Talent Scouts(60) – TA	m*	To:t-8:30-7/63
6/63	8:30	Red Skelton(60) – CV	m	To:t-8-9/63
6/63	9:30	Picture This – QU	d*	
6/63	10:00	Keefe Brasselle(60) – MV	d*	
7/63	8:30	Talent Scouts(60) – TA	m	Fr:t-10-9/62
9/63	8:00	Lloyd Bridges Show – DA	c	
9/63	8:00	Red Skelton(60) – CV	m	Fr:t-8:30-6/63
9/63	8:30	Talent Scouts(60) – TA	c	

Date	Time	Title (min. if not 30) — Type	Action	From/To
9/63	9:00	Petticoat Junction—SC	d	
9/63	9:30	Picture This—QU	c*	
9/63	10:00	Keefe Brasselle(60)—MV	c*	
6/64	8:00	High Adventure w/ Lowell Thomas (60)—TR	d	
6/64	8:00	Red Skelton(60)—CV	m	To:t-8:30-9/64
6/64	10:00	Garry Moore Show(60)—VY	c	
9/64	8:00	High Adventure w/ Lowell Thomas (60)—TR	c	
9/64	8:00	World War I—DO	d	
9/64	8:30	Red Skelton(60)—CV	m	Fr:t-8-6/64
9/64	9:00	Petticoat Junction—SC	m	To:t-9:30
9/64	9:30	Jack Benny—CY	m	To:f-9:30
9/64	9:30	Petticoat Junction—SC	m	Fr:t-9
9/64	10:00	Nurses(60)—MD	m	Fr:r-10
12/64	8:00	Joey Bishop—SC	m	Fr:n-9:30
12/64	8:00	World War I—DO	c	
6/65	8:30	Hollywood Talent Scouts(60)—VY	d*	
9/65	7:30	Gunsmoke—WE	f	
9/65	7:30	Rawhide(60)—WE	m	Fr:f-7:30
9/65	8:00	Joey Bishop—SC	c	
9/65	8:30	Hollywood Talent Scouts(60)—VY	m*	To:m-10-12/65
9/65	10:00	CBS Reports(60)—DO	m	Fr:m-10
9/65	10:00	Nurses(60)—MD	c	
1/66	7:30	Daktari(60)—AD	d	
1/66	7:30	Rawhide(60)—WE	c	
7/66	8:30	Hippodrome(60)—VY	d*	
9/66	8:30	Hippodrome(60)—VY	c*	
7/67	8:30	Spotlight(60)—CV	d*	
8/67	8:30	Spotlight(60)—CV	c*	
8/67	9:30	Petticoat Junction—SC	m	To:s-9:30
9/67	9:30	Good Morning World—SC	d	
6/68	8:30	Showtime(60)—VY	d*	
6/68	7:30	Daktari(60)—AD	m	To:w-7:30
9/68	7:30	Lancer(60)—WE	d	
9/68	8:30	Showtime(60)—VY	c*	
9/68	9:30	Doris Day—SC	d	
9/68	9:30	Good Morning World—SC	c	
9/68	10:00	60 Minutes(60)—NM	d	
7/69	8:30	Liberace Show(60)—MV	d*	
9/69	8:30	Liberace Show(60)—MV	c*	
9/69	9:30	Doris Day—SC	m	To:m-9:30
9/69	9:30	Governor & J.J.—SC	d	
6/70	7:30	Lancer(60)—WE	m	To:r-8-5/71
6/70	7:30	Film(120)—FI	s	
6/70	8:30	Red Skelton(60)—CV	m	To:m-7:30-9/70(n)
9/70	7:30	Beverly Hillbillies—SC	m	Fr:w-8:30
9/70	7:30	Film(120)—FI	f	
9/70	8:00	Green Acres—SC	m	Fr:s-9
9/70	8:30	Hee Haw(60)—VY	m	Fr:w-7:30-6/70

Date	Time	Title (min. if not 30) — Type	Action	From/To
9/70	9:30	Governor & J.J. — SC	m	To:w-8:30
9/70	9:30	To Rome with Love — SC	m	Fr:n-7:30
1/71	9:30	All in the Family — SC	d	
1/71	9:30	To Rome with Love — SC	m	To:w-8:30
6/71	10:00	60 Minutes(60) — NM	m	To:f-8-6/73
7/71	8:30	Cimarron Strip(90) — WE	m	Fr:r-7:30-9/68
7/71	8:30	Hee Haw(60) — VY	c	
7/71	9:30	All in the Family — SC	m	To:s-8-9/71
9/71	7:30	Beverly Hillbillies — SC	c	
9/71	7:30	Glen Campbell Goodtime Hour(60) — MV	m	Fr:n-9-6/71
9/71	8:00	Green Acres — SC	c	
9/71	8:30	Cimarron Strip(90) — WE	c	
9/71	8:30	Hawaii Five-O(60) — CD	m	Fr:w-10
9/71	9:30	Cannon(60) — CD	d	
9/71	10:00	CBS Reports(60) — DO	c	
6/72	7:30	Glen Campbell Goodtime Hour(60) — MV	c	
6/72	7:30	Jerry Reed(60) — CV	d	
7/72	7:30	Jerry Reed(60) — CV	c	
8/72	7:30	John Byner Comedy Hour(60) — CV	d	
8/72	7:30	John Byner Comedy Hour(60) — CV	c	
9/72	8:00	Maude — SC	d	
9/72	9:30	Cannon(60) — CD	m	To:w-10
9/72	9:30	Film(90) — FI	s	
9/73	9:30	Film(90) — FI	f	
10/73	9:30	Hawkins(90) — LD	d	
10/73	9:30	Shaft(90) — CD	d	
9/74	8:00	Good Times — SC	m	Fr:f-8:30
9/74	8:00	Maude — SC	m	To:m-9
9/74	8:30	Hawaii Five-O(60) — CD	m	To:t-9
9/74	8:30	M*A*S*H — SC	m	Fr:s-8:30
9/74	9:00	Hawaii Five-O(60) — CD	m	Fr:t-8:30
9/74	9:30	Hawkins(90) — LD	c	
9/74	9:30	Shaft(90) — CD	c	
9/74	10:00	Barnaby Jones(60) — CD	m	Fr:s-10
8/75	10:00	Barnaby Jones(60) — CD	m	To:f-10
9/75	8:30	Joe and Sons — SC	d	
9/75	8:30	M*A*S*H — SC	m	To:f-8:30
9/75	9:00	Hawaii Five-O(60) — CD	m	To:f-9
9/75	9:00	Switch(60) — CD	d	
9/75	10:00	Beacon Hill(60) — DR	d	
11/75	9:00	Switch(60) — CD	m	To:t-10
11/75	10:00	Beacon Hill(60) — DR	c	
12/75	9:00	M*A*S*H — SC	m	Fr:f-8:30
12/75	9:30	One Day at a Time — SC	d	
12/75	10:00	Switch(60) — CD	m	Fr:t-9
1/76	8:30	Joe and Sons — SC	c	
1/76	8:30	Popi — SC	d	
2/76	8:30	Popi — SC	c	

Date	Time	Title (min. if not 30) — Type	Action	From/To
3/76	8:00	Good Times — SC	m	To:t-8:30
3/76	8:30	Good Times — SC	m	Fr:t-8
4/76	8:00	Bugs Bunny/Roadrunner Show — KV	d	
6/76	8:00	Bugs Bunny/Roadrunner Show — KV	c	
6/76	8:00	I've Got a Secret — QU	d	
8/76	8:00	I've Got a Secret — QU	c	
8/76	8:30	Good Times — SC	m	To:w-8
9/76	8:00	Tony Orlando and Dawn(60) — MV	m	Fr:w-8-6/76
12/76	8:00	Tony Orlando and Dawn(60) — MV	c	
1/77	8:00	Who's Who(60) — NM	d	
1/77	10:00	Switch(60) — CD	m	To:n-9
1/77	10:00	Kojak(60) — CD	m	Fr:n-9
5/77	8:00	Family Holvak(60) — DR	m	Fr:n-8-12/75(n)
5/77	8:00	Who's Who(60) — NM	c	
6/77	8:00	Family Holvak(60) — DR	c	
7/77	8:00	Jack Benny(60) — CY	s	
8/77	8:00	Jack Benny(60) — CY	f	
9/77	8:00	Fitzpatricks(60) — DR	d	
9/77	8:00	Fitzpatricks(60) — DR	m	To:t-8-11/77
9/77	10:00	Lou Grant(60) — ND	d	
9/77	10:00	Kojak(60) — CD	m	To:n-10
10/77	8:00	Young Dan'l Boone(60) — AD	m	Fr:m-8
10/77	8:00	Young Dan'l Boone(60) — AD	c	
11/77	8:00	Fitzpatricks(60) — DR	m	Fr:t-8-9/77
1/78	8:00	Celebrity Challenge of the Sexes — QU	d	
1/78	8:00	Fitzpatricks(60) — DR	c	
1/78	8:30	Shields and Yarnell — VY	m	Fr:m-8:30-7/77
1/78	9:00	M*A*S*H — SC	m	To:m-9
1/78	9:00	Film(120) — FI	s	
1/78	9:30	One Day at a Time — SC	m	To:m-9:30
1/78	10:00	Lou Grant(60) — ND	m	To:m-10
2/78	8:00	Celebrity Challenge of the Sexes — QU	c	
3/78	8:00	Sam — CD	d	
4/78	8:00	Sam — CD	c	
4/78	8:30	Shields and Yarnell — VY	c	
9/78	8:00	Paper Chase(60) — DR	d	
7/79	8:00	Paper Chase(60) — DR	c	
8/79	8:00	Wonder Woman(60) — AD	m	Fr:f-8-2/79
9/79	8:00	California Fever(60) — AD	d	
9/79	8:00	Wonder Woman(60) — AD	c	
11/79	9:00	Film(120) — FI	f	
12/79	8:00	California Fever(60) — AD	c	
12/79	8:00	White Shadow(60) — DR	m	Fr:m-8
12/79	9:00	Hawaii Five-O(60) — CD	m	Fr:r-9
12/79	10:00	Paris(60) — CD	m	Fr:s-10
1/80	9:00	Hawaii Five-O(60) — CD	m	To:s-9-3/80

Date	Time	Title (min. if not 30) — Type	Action	From/To
1/80	10:00	Paris(60) — CD	c	
2/80	9:00	Film(120) — FI	s	
1/81	8:00	White Shadow(60) — DR	m	To:m-8
2/81	8:00	That's My Line(60) — CV	d	
3/81	8:00	Palmerstown, U.S.A.(60) — DR	m	Fr:r-8-5/80
3/81	8:00	That's My Line(60) — CV	m	To:s-9
6/81	8:00	Palmerstown, U.S.A.(60) — DR	c	
6/81	8:00	Universe — SI	m	Fr:s-8-8/80
6/81	8:30	Flo — SC	m	Fr:s-8:30
9/81	8:00	Universe — SI	m	To:t-8-6/82
9/81	8:30	Flo — SC	c	
11/81	8:00	Simon & Simon(60) — CD	d	
3/82	8:00	Q.E.D.(60) — AD	d	
3/82	8:00	Simon & Simon(60) — CD	m	To:r-9
4/82	8:00	Q.E.D.(60) — AD	c	
5/82	8:00	Book of Lists(60) — VY	d	
5/82	8:00	Book of Lists(60) — VY	c	
6/82	8:00	Universe — SI	m	Fr:t-8:30-9/81
6/82	8:30	Two of Us — SC	m	Fr:w-8:30-2/82
9/82	8:00	Bring 'Em Back Alive(60) — AD	d	
9/82	8:00	Universe — SI	c	
9/82	8:30	Two of Us — SC	c	
12/82	8:00	Bring 'Em Back Alive(60) — AD	m	To:s-8
1/83	8:00	Walt Disney(60) — KV	m	Fr:s-8
2/83	8:00	Walt Disney(60) — KV	m	To:s-8-7/83
3/83	8:00	Ace Crawford, Private Eye — SC	d	
3/83	8:30	Gun Shy — SC	d	
4/83	8:00	Ace Crawford, Private Eye — SC	c	
4/83	8:30	Gun Shy — SC	c	
5/83	8:00	Bring 'Em Back Alive(60) — AD	m	Fr:s-8-2/83
6/83	8:00	Bring 'Em Back Alive(60) — AD	c	
6/83	8:00	On the Road with Charles Kuralt — NM	d	
6/83	8:30	Our Times with Bill Moyers — DO	d	
8/83	8:00	On the Road with Charles Kuralt — NM	c	
8/83	8:30	Our Times with Bill Moyers — DO	c	
9/83	8:00	Mississippi(60) — LD	m	Fr:f-10-5/83
3/84	8:00	American Parade(60) — NM	d	
3/84	8:00	Mississippi(60) — LD	c	
5/84	8:00	American Parade(60) — NM	m	To:w-8
6/84	8:00	Aftermash — SC	m	Fr:n-8
6/84	8:30	Domestic Life — SC	m	Fr:w-8-2/84
9/84	8:30	Domestic Life — SC	c	
9/84	8:30	E/R — SC	d	
10/84	8:00	Aftermash — SC	c	
10/84	8:30	E/R — SC	m	To:w-8:30
1/85	8:00	Jeffersons — SC	m	Fr:n-9
1/85	8:30	Alice — SC	m	Fr:n-9:30
3/85	8:00	Jeffersons — SC	m	To:t-8:30

Date	Time	Title (min. if not 30) — Type	Action	From/To
3/85	8:30	Alice — SC	m	To:t-8:30-6/85
4/85	8:00	Lucie Arnaz — SC	d	
4/85	8:00	Lucie Arnaz — SC	c	
4/85	8:30	Jeffersons — SC	m	Fr:t-8
4/85	8:30	Jeffersons — SC	m	To:t-8-6/85
6/85	8:00	Jeffersons — SC	m	Fr:t-8:30-4/85
6/85	8:30	Alice — SC	m	Fr:t-8:30-3/85
7/85	8:00	Jeffersons — SC	c	
7/85	8:30	Alice — SC	c	
7/85	9:00	Film(120) — FI	f	
8/85	8:00	Film(120 — FI	s	
8/85	10:00	West 57th(60) — NM	d	
9/85	8:00	Hometown(60) — CD	m	Fr:r-10
9/85	8:00	Film(120) — FI	f	
9/85	9:00	Film(120) — FI	s	
9/85	10:00	West 57th(60) — NM	m	To:w-8-4/86
10/85	8:00	Hometown(60) — CD	c	
12/85	8:00	Stir Crazy(60) — CO	m	Fr:w-8-10/85
1/86	8:00	Stir Crazy(60) — CO	c	
1/86	8:00	Melba — SC	d	
1/86	8:30	Charlie & Company — SC	m	Fr:w-9
2/86	8:00	Trapper John, MD(60) — MD	m	Fr:n-10
2/86	8:00	Melba — SC	m	To:s-8-8/86
2/86	8:30	Charlie & Company — SC	m	To:f-8-4/86
3/86	8:00	Trapper John, MD(60) — MD	m	To:r-9-6/86
3/86	8:00	Morning Star/Evening Star(60) — DR	d	
3/86	9:00	Mary — SC	m	Fr:w-8
3/86	9:00	Film(120) — FI	f	
3/86	9:30	Foley Square — SC	m	Fr:w-8:30
3/86	10:00	Equalizer(60) — CD	m	Fr:w-10
4/86	9:00	Mickey Spillane's Mike Hammer (60) — CD	m	Fr:s-10-7/85
4/86	9:00	Mary — SC	c	
4/86	9:30	Foley Square — SC	m	To:w-8-6/86
5/86	8:00	Morning Star/Evening Star(60) — DR	c	
5/86	9:00	Mickey Spillane's Mike Hammer (60) — CD	m	To:s-9-9/86
6/86	8:00	Simon & Simon(60) — CD	m	Fr:r-8
6/86	9:00	Magnum, P.I.(60) — CD	m	Fr:s-10
8/86	8:00	Simon & Simon(60) — CD	m	To:r-8
8/86	9:00	Magnum, P.I.(60) — CD	m	To:w-9
8/86	10:00	Equalizer(60) — CD	m	To:w-10
9/86	8:00	Wizard(60) — AD	d	
9/86	9:00	Film(120) — FI	s	
10/86	8:00	Wizard(60) — AD	m	To:s-8
11/86	8:00	Downtown(60) — CD	m	Fr:s-8
11/86	8:00	Downtown(60) — CD	m	To:s-8
12/86	8:00	Wizard(60) — AD	m	Fr:s-8

Date	Time	Title (min. if not 30) – Type	Action	From/To
3/87	8:00	Wizard(60) – AD	m	To:r-8
3/87	8:00	Spies(60) – SD	d	
4/87	8:00	Spies(60) – SD	c	
5/87	8:00	West 57th(60) – NM	m	Fr:m-10
6/87	8:00	West 57th(60) – NM	m	To:s-10
6/87	8:00	Wizard(60) – AD	m	Fr:r-8
7/87	8:00	Wizard(60) – AD	c	
7/87	8:00	Simon & Simon(60) – CD	m	Fr:r-9
7/87	9:00	Film(120) – FI	f	
8/87	8:00	Simon & Simon(60) – CD	c	
8/87	9:00	Houston Knights(60) – CD	m	Fr:w-10-4/87
8/87	9:00	Houston Knights(60) – CD	m	To:t-8
8/87	10:00	Night Heat(60) – CD	d	
8/87	10:00	Night Heat(60) – CD	c	
9/87	8:00	Houston Knights(60) – CD	m	Fr:t-9
9/87	9:00	Jake & the Fatman(60) – CD	d	
9/87	10:00	Law & Harry McGraw(60) – CD	d	
12/87	8:00	Houston Knights(60) – CD	m	To:s-9
12/87	10:00	Law & Harry McGraw(60) – CD	m	To:w-8
1/88	8:00	48 Hours(60) – DO	d	
1/88	10:00	Cagney & Lacey(60) – CD	m	Fr:m-10
2/88	8:00	48 Hours(60) – DO	m	To:r-8
2/88	9:00	Jake & the Fatman(60) – CD	m	To:w-9
3/88	8:00	Trial & Error – SC	d	
3/88	8:30	My Sister Sam – SC	m	Fr:s-8-11/87
3/88	9:00	Coming of Age – SC	d	
3/88	9:30	Frank's Place – SC	m	Fr:m-9:30
4/88	8:00	Houston Knights(60) – CD	m	Fr:s-9-2/88
4/88	8:00	Trial & Error – SC	c	
4/88	8:30	My Sister Sam – SC	c	
4/88	9:00	Coming of Age – SC	m	To:m-8:30-9/88
4/88	9:00	Film(120) – FI	s#	
4/88	9:30	Frank's Place – SC	m	To:s-8:30-7/88
4/88	10:00	Cagney & Lacey(60) – CD	m	To:m-10
6/88	8:00	Houston Knights(60) – CD	c	
6/88	8:00	Summer Playhouse(60) – VS	d*	
8/88	8:00	Summer Playhouse(60) – VS	c*	

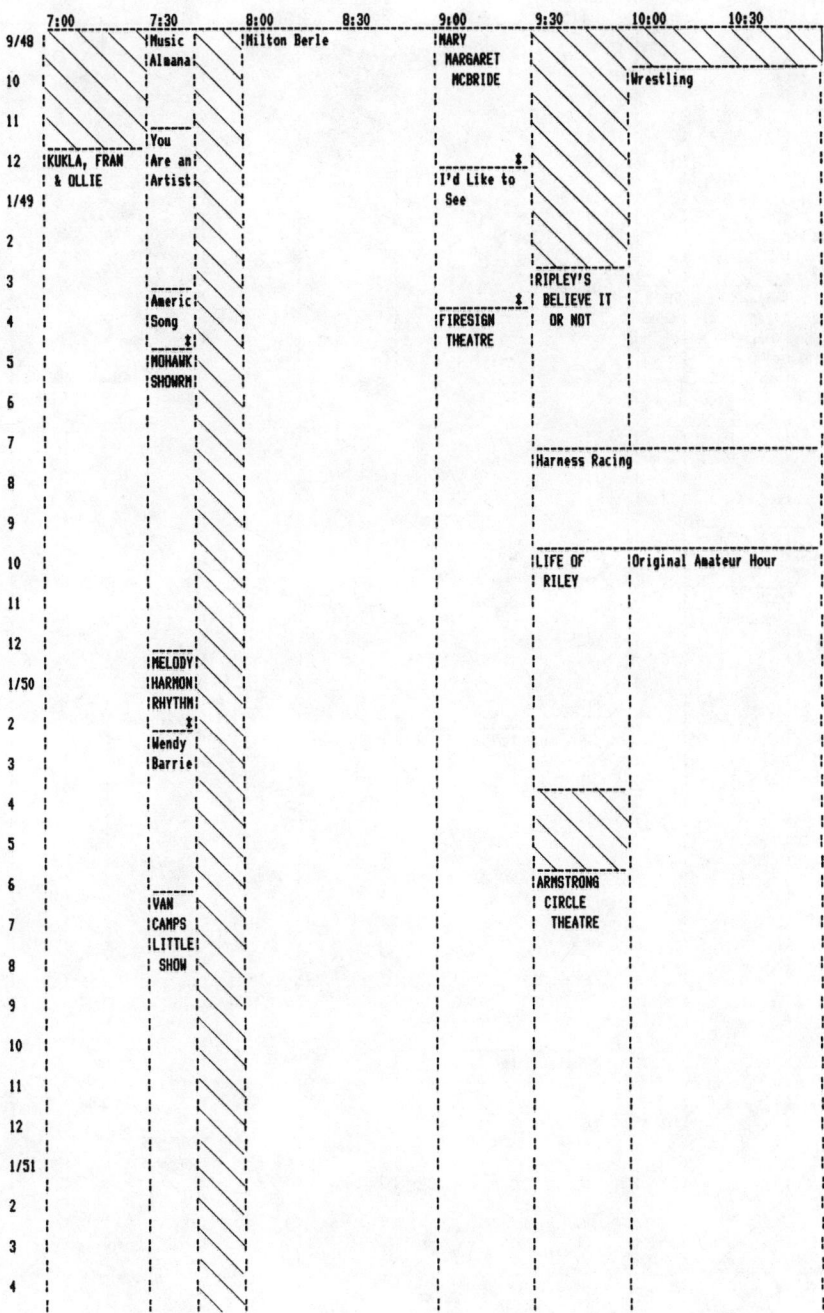

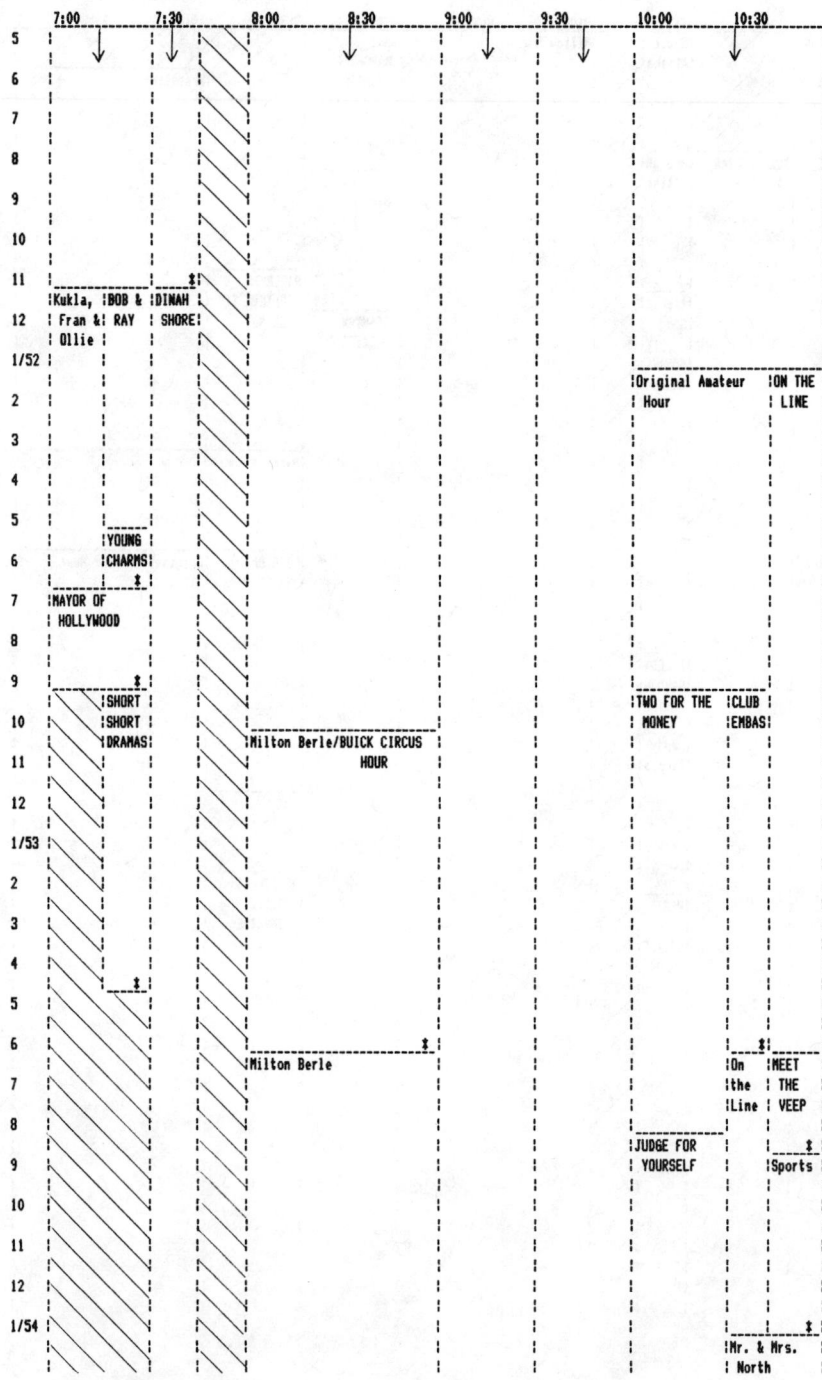

```
        7:00      7:30      8:00      8:30      9:00      9:30     10:00     10:30
 5
 6
 7
 8
 9
10
11
        Kukla, BOB & DINAH
12      Fran & RAY  SHORE
        Ollie
1/52
                                                                   Original Amateur   ON THE
 2                                                                 Hour                LINE
 3
 4
 5
                  YOUNG
 6                CHARMS
 7      MAYOR OF
        HOLLYWOOD
 8
 9
                  SHORT                                            TWO FOR THE  CLUB
10                SHORT                                            MONEY        EMBAS
                  DRAMAS         Milton Berle/BUICK CIRCUS
11                                        HOUR
12
1/53
 2
 3
 4
 5
 6
                                Milton Berle                                    On    MEET
 7                                                                              the   THE
                                                                                Line  VEEP
 8
                                                                   JUDGE FOR
 9                                                                 YOURSELF           Sports
10
11
12
1/54
                                                                                      Mr. & Mrs.
                                                                                      North
```

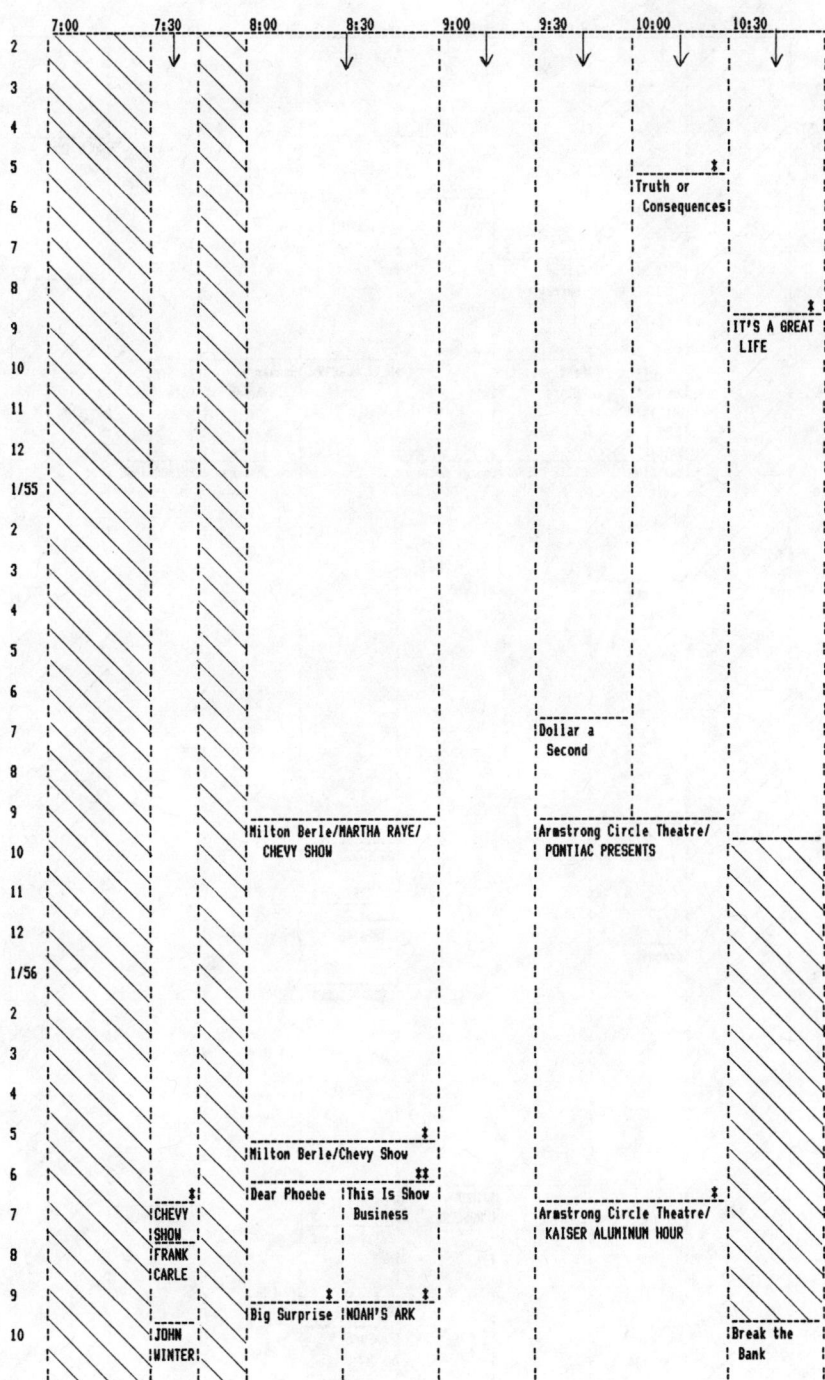

	7:00	7:30	8:00	8:30	9:00	9:30	10:00	10:30
2								
3								
4								
5							Truth or	
6							Consequences	
7								
8								
9								IT'S A GREAT
10								LIFE
11								
12								
1/55								
2								
3								
4								
5								
6								
7					Dollar a			
8					Second			
9								
10			Milton Berle/MARTHA RAYE/ CHEVY SHOW			Armstrong Circle Theatre/ PONTIAC PRESENTS		
11								
12								
1/56								
2								
3								
4								
5								
6			Milton Berle/Chevy Show					
7		CHEVY	Dear Phoebe	This Is Show Business		Armstrong Circle Theatre/ KAISER ALUMINUM HOUR		
8		SHOW FRANK CARLE						
9			Big Surprise	NOAH'S ARK				
10		JOHN WINTER						Break the Bank

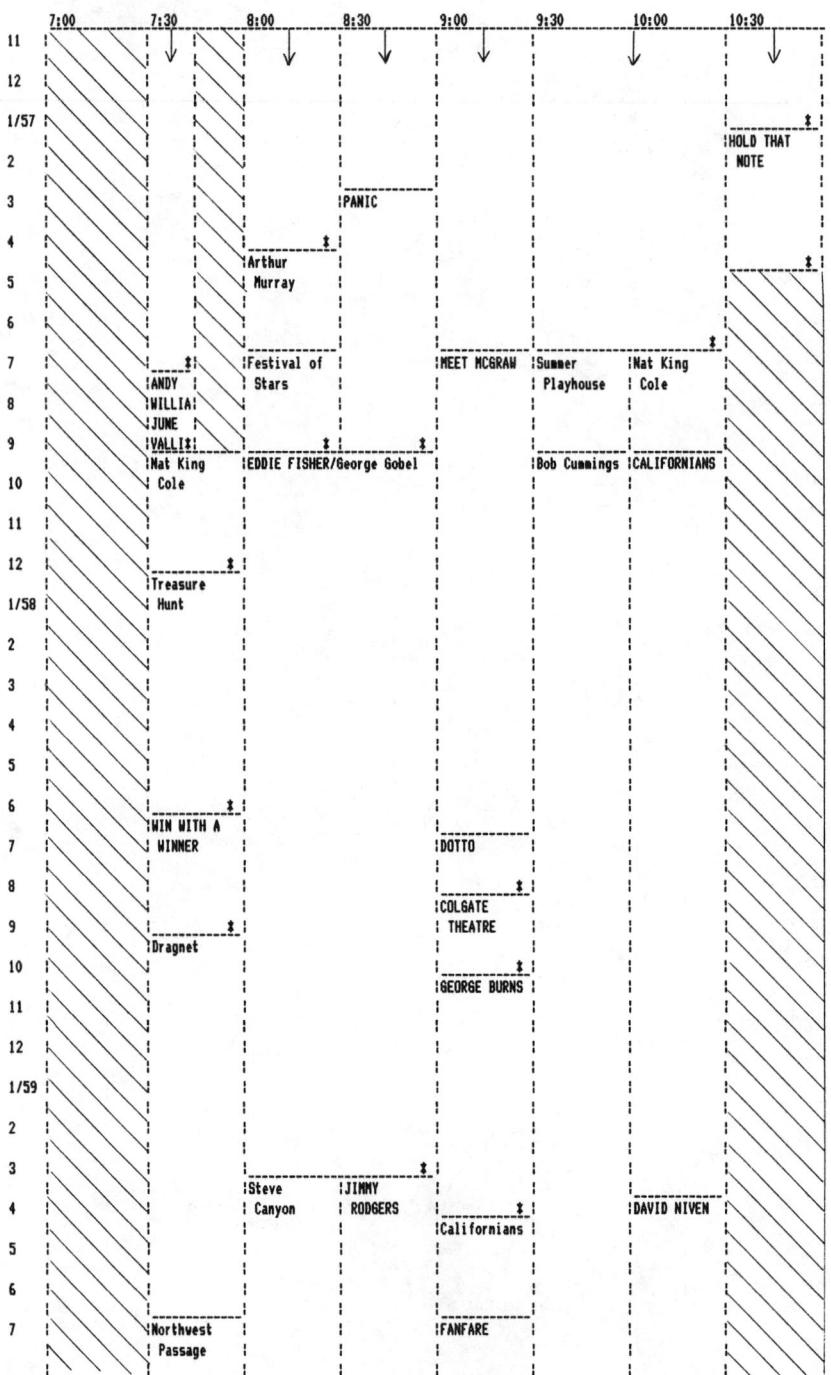

	7:00	7:30	8:00	8:30	9:00	9:30	10:00	10:30
8								
9		LARAMIE		FIBBER MCGEE	Arthur			
10				& MOLLY	Murray	STARTIME		
11								
12								
1/60				Startime		Arthur	M Squad	
2						Murray		
3								
4								
5								
6				NBC	Richard			
7				PLAYHOUSE	Diamond			
8								
9				Alfred	THRILLER			
10				Hitchcock				
11				Presents				
12								
1/61								
2								
3								
4								
5								
6								
7							PUREX SUMMER SPECIALS	
8								
9								
10					DICK POWELL		CAIN'S HUNDRED	
11								
12								
1/62								
2								
3								
4								

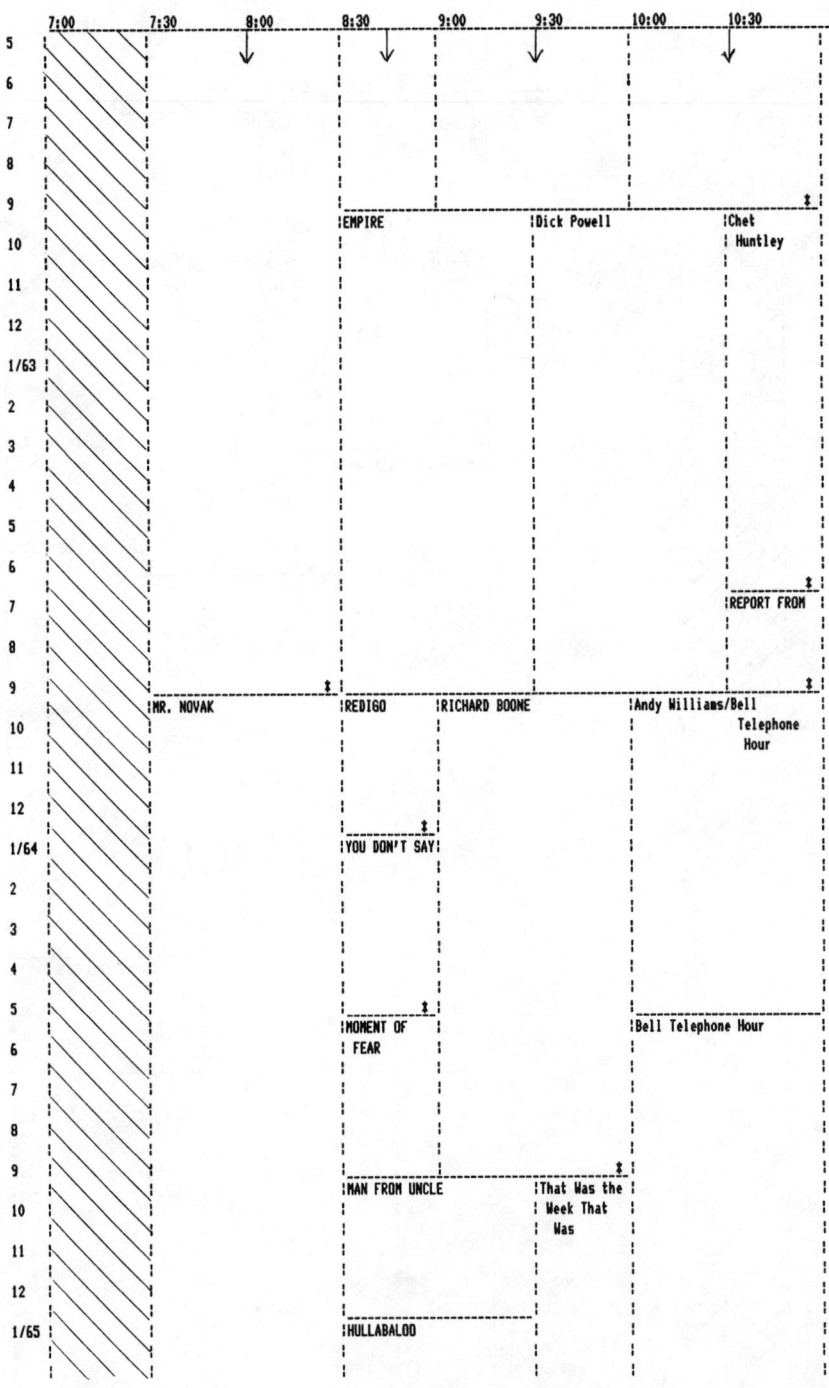

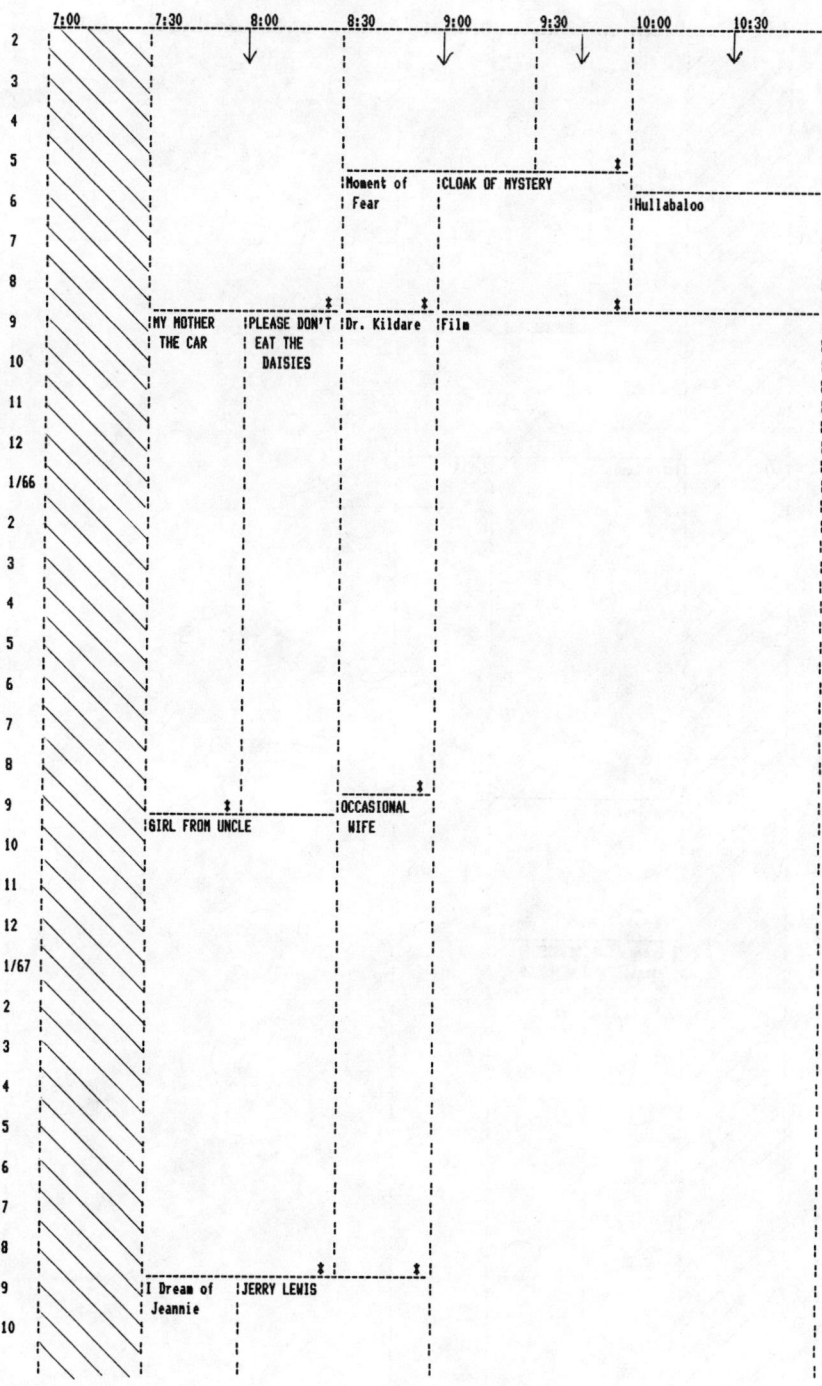

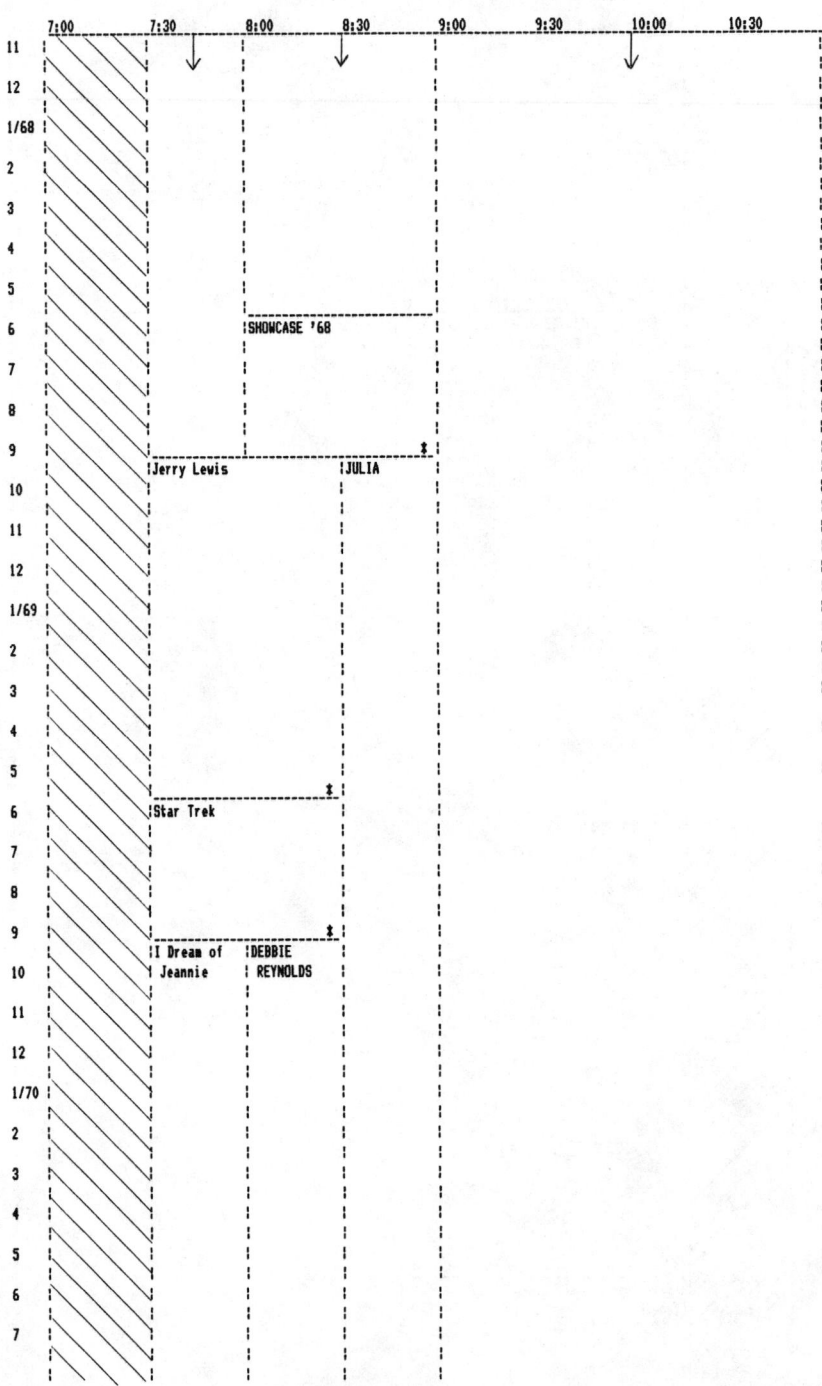

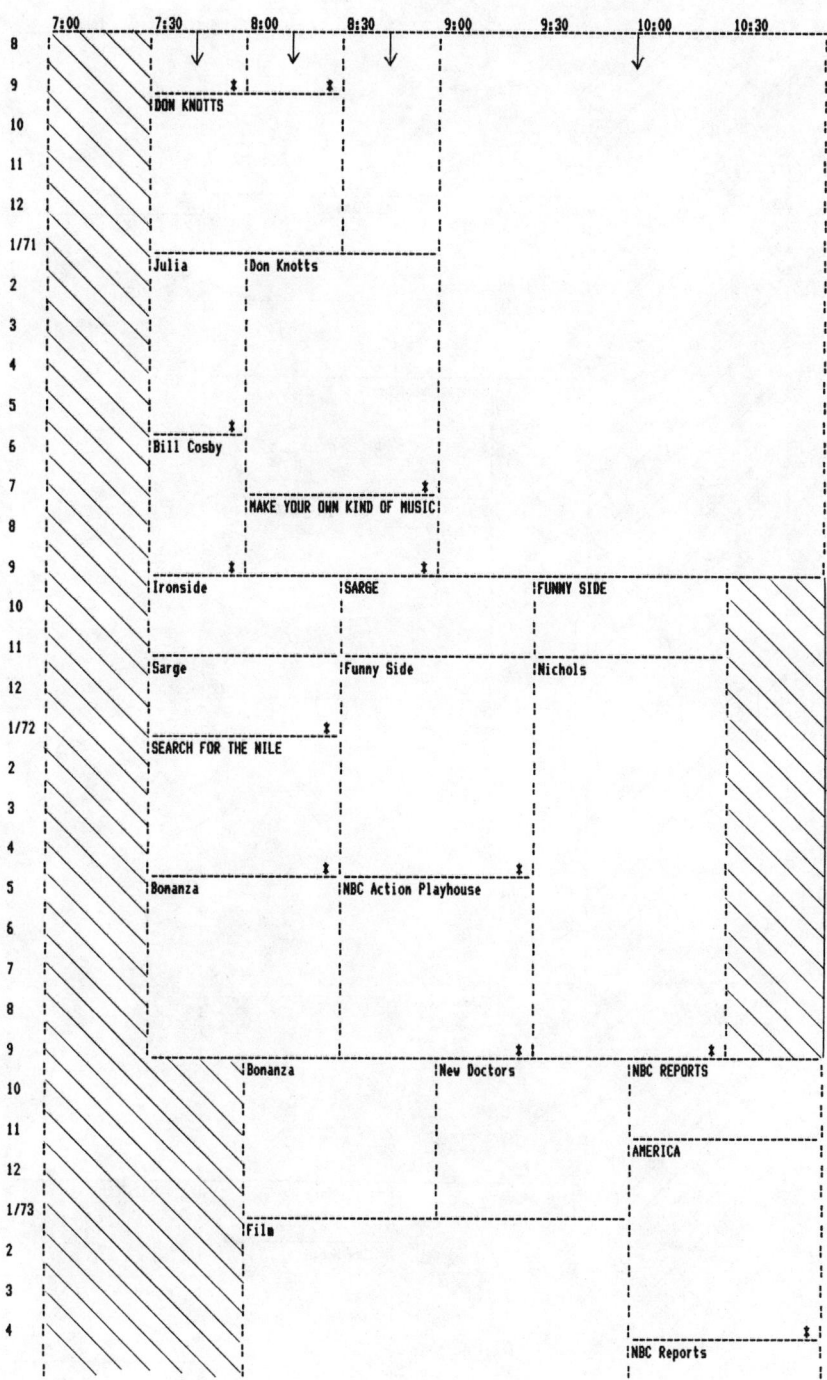

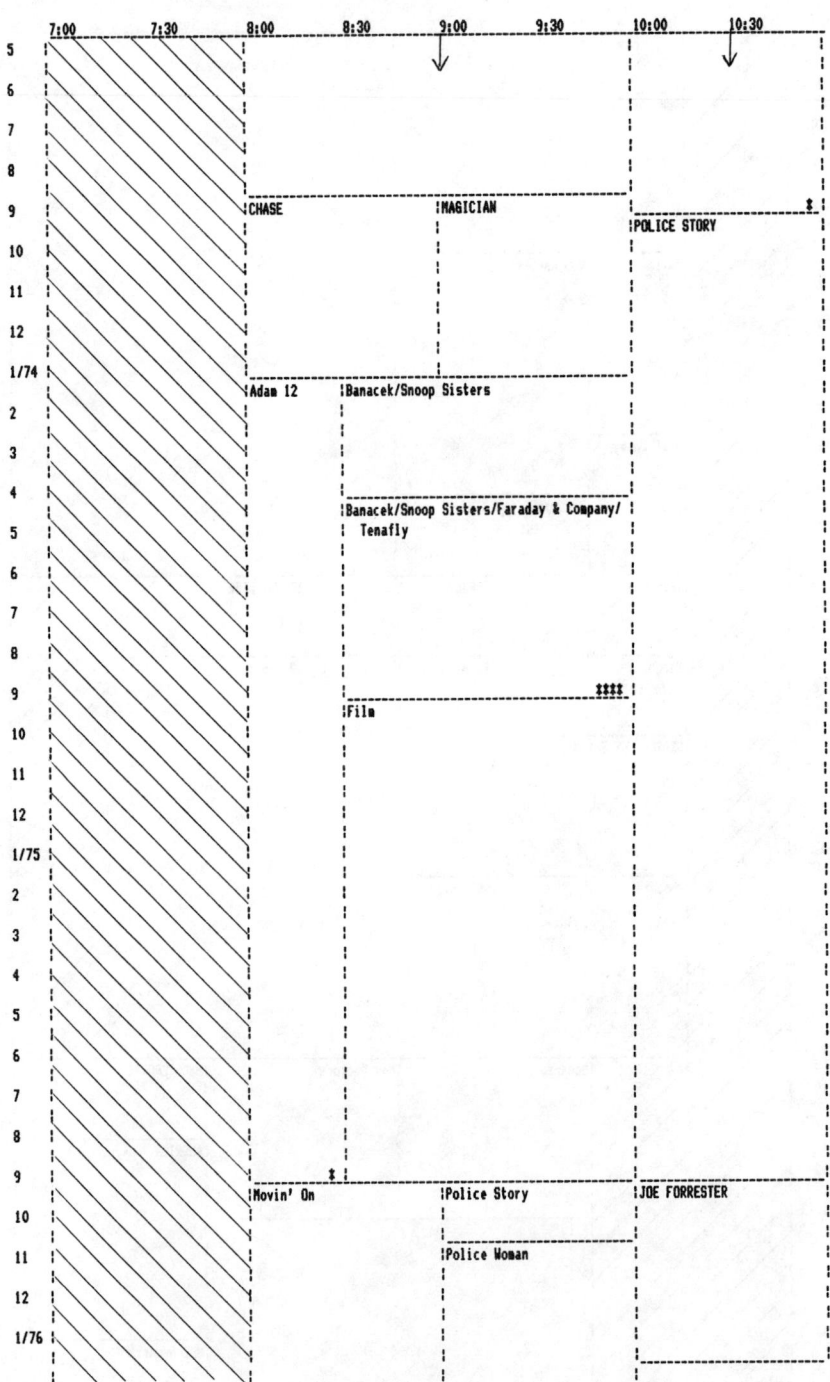

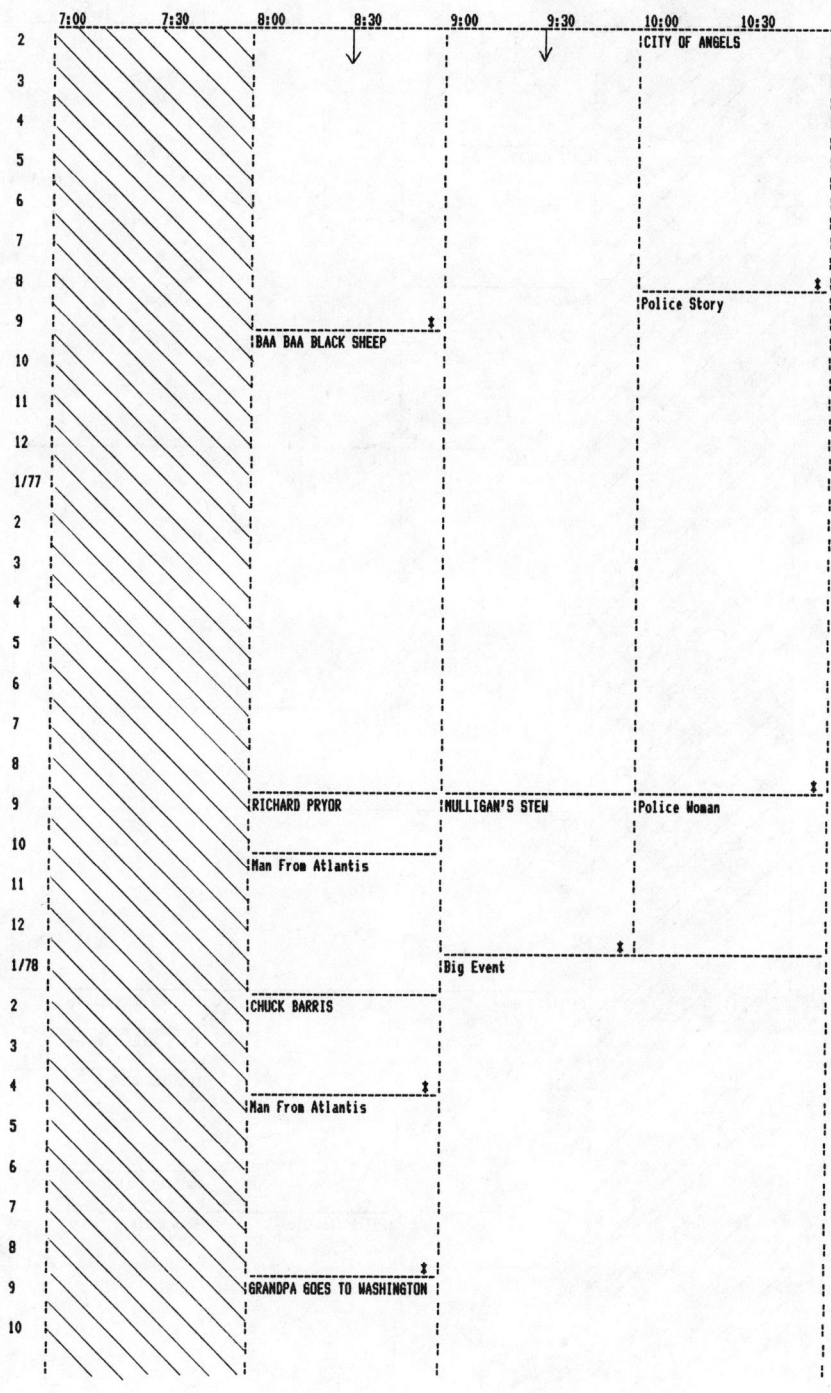

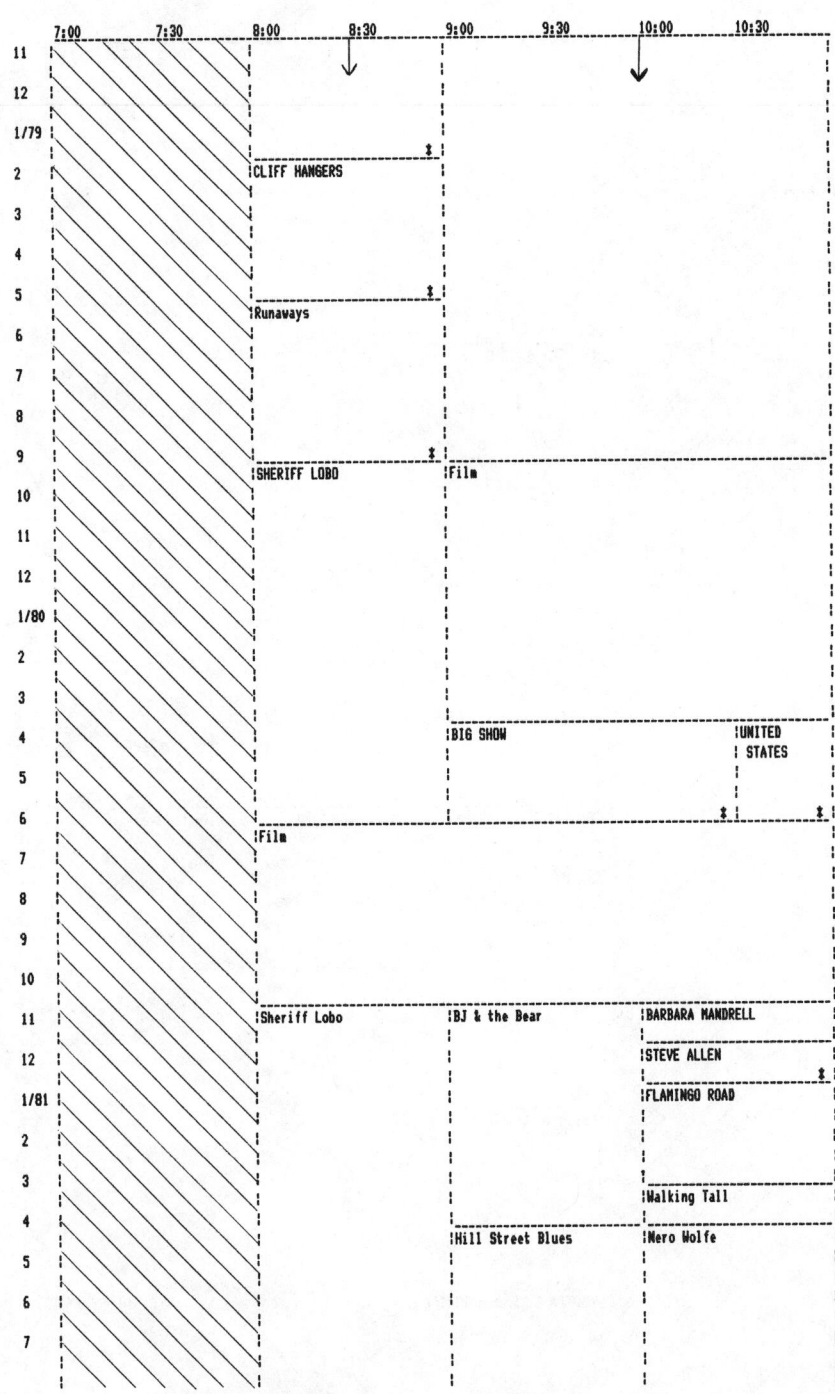

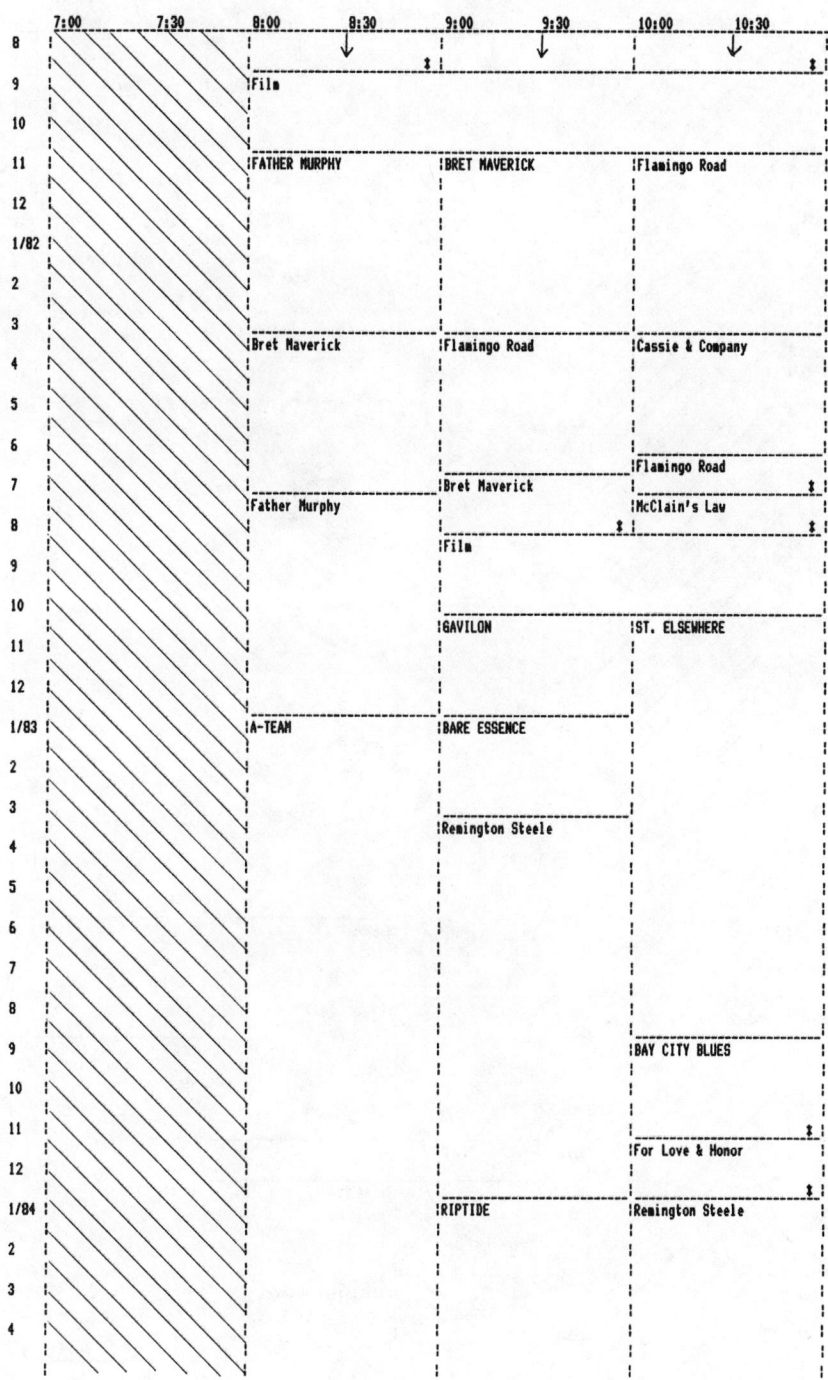

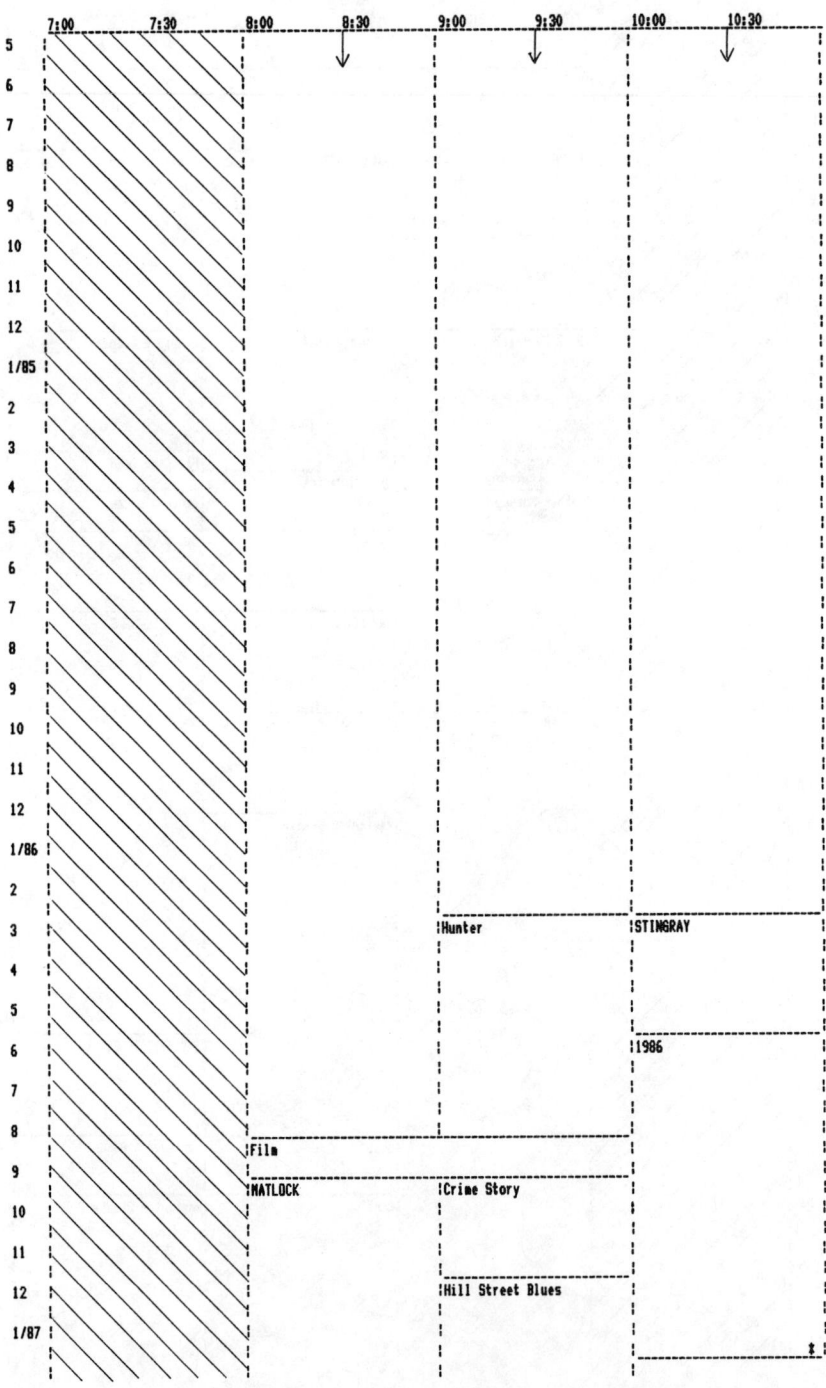

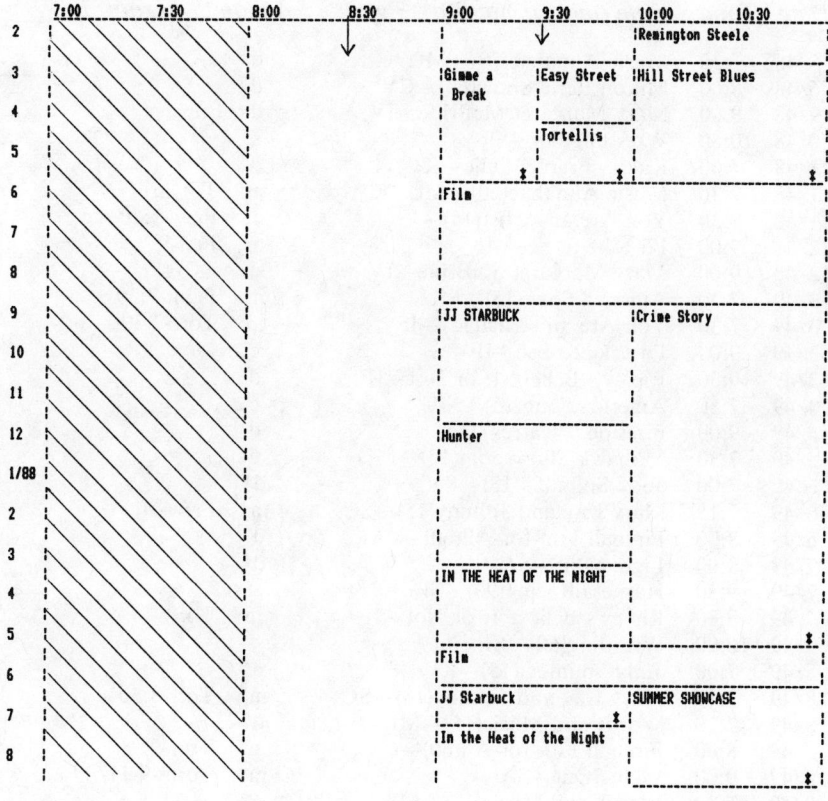

Date	Time	Title (min. if not 30) — Type	Action	From/To
5/48	7:30	Music Almanac(20) — MU	d	
6/48	8:00	Milton Berle Show(60) — CV	d	
9/48	9:00	Mary Margaret McBride — IV	d	
10/48	10:00	Wrestling(60) — SP	s	
11/48	7:00	Kukla, Fran & Ollie — KV	d	
11/48	7:30	Music Almanac(20) — MU	m	To:var
11/48	7:30	You Are an Artist(15) — IS	m	Fr:w-7:30
12/48	9:00	I'd Like to See — IF	m	Fr:f-9
12/48	9:00	Mary Margaret McBride — IV	c	
3/49	7:30	America Song(15) — MU	m	Fr:m-7:30
3/49	7:30	You Are an Artist(15) — IS	m	To:r-7:30
3/49	9:00	I'd Like to See — IF	c	
3/49	9:30	Ripley's Believe It or Not — IF	d	
4/49	7:30	America Song(15) — MU	c	
4/49	9:00	Fireside Theatre — DA	d	
5/49	7:30	Mohawk Showroom(15) — MU	d	
6/49	7:00	Judy Splinters(15) — KV	d*	
6/49	7:15	Mary Kay and Johnny(15) — SC	m*	Fr:w-9(c)
6/49	8:00	Fireball Fun-for-All(60) — CV	d*	
7/49	9:00	Lights Out — SA	d*	
7/49	9:30	Harness Racing(90) — SP	s	
7/49	9:30	Ripley's Believe It or Not — IF	m	To:w-10
7/49	10:00	Wrestling(60) — SP	f	
8/49	7:00	Judy Splinters(15) — KV	c*	
8/49	7:15	Mary Kay and Johnny(15) — SC	m*	To:r-8:30
8/49	7:30	Words and Music(15) — MU	d*	
8/49	8:00	Fireball Fun-for-All(60) — CV	m*	To:r-9
8/49	9:00	Lights Out — SA	m*	To:m-9-11/49
9/49	7:30	Words and Music(15) — MU	c*	
9/49	9:30	Harness Racing(90) — SP	f	
10/49	9:30	Life of Riley — SC	d	
10/49	10:00	Original Amateur Hour(60) — TA	m	Fr:n-7(d)
12/49	7:30	Melody, Harmony & Rhythm(15) — MU	d	
12/49	7:30	Mohawk Showroom(15) — MU	m	To:mwf-7:30
2/50	7:30	Melody, Harmony & Rhythm(15) — MU	c	
2/50	7:30	Wendy Barrie Show(15) — IV	m	Fr:r-9(a)
3/50	9:30	Life of Riley — SC	m	To:f-8:30-1/53
6/50	7:30	Van Camp's Little Show(15) — MU	d	
6/50	7:30	Wendy Barrie Show(15) — IV	m	To:mwf-7:30
6/50	8:00	Film(60) — FI	s*	
6/50	9:30	Armstrong Circle Theatre — DA	d	
7/50	7:00	Ransom Sherman Show — CV	d*	
7/50	9:00	Rendezvous with Music — MU	d*	
8/50	7:00	Ransom Sherman Show — CV	c*	
8/50	9:00	Rendezvous with Music — MU	c*	
9/50	8:00	Film(60) — FI	f*	
7/51	7:00	Ernie in Kovacsland — CV	d*	

Date	Time	Title (min. if not 30) — Type	Action	From/To
7/51	7:30	Songs at Twilight(15) — MU	d*	
7/51	9:00	Fireside Arena Theatre — DA	d*	
8/51	7:00	Ernie in Kovacsland — CV	c*	
8/51	7:30	Songs at Twilight(15) — MU	c*	
8/51	9:00	Fireside Arena Theatre — DA	c*	
11/51	7:00	Kukla, Fran & Ollie — KV	m	To:m-f-7
11/51	7:00	Kukla, Fran & Ollie(15) — KV	m	Fr:m-f-7
11/51	7:15	Bob and Ray(15) — CV	d	
11/51	7:30	Dinah Shore Show(15) — MU	d	
11/51	7:30	Van Camp's Little Show(15) — MU	c	
1/52	10:00	Original Amateur Hour(60) — TA	m	To:t-10
1/52	10:00	Original Amateur Hour(45) — TA	m	Fr:t-10
1/52	10:45	On the Line with Considine(15) — IV	d	
5/52	7:15	Bob and Ray(15) — CV	m	To:m-7:30-4/53
5/52	7:15	Those Endearing Young Charms (15) — SC	d	
6/52	7:00	Kukla, Fran & Ollie(15) — KV	m	To:m-f-7-9/54(a)
6/52	7:15	Those Endearing Young Charms (15) — SC	c	
6/52	8:00	Midwestern Hayride(60) — MV	m*	Fr:s-9-9/51
7/52	7:00	Mayor of Hollywood — VY	d	
7/52	7:30	Liberace Show(15) — MV	d*	
7/52	9:00	Boss Lady — SC	d*	
8/52	7:30	Liberace Show(15) — MV	c*	
9/52	7:00	Mayor of Hollywood — VY	c	
9/52	7:15	Short Short Dramas(15) — DA	d	
9/52	8:00	Midwestern Hayride(60) — MV	m*	To:t-8-6/54
9/52	9:00	Boss Lady — SC	c*	
9/52	10:00	Original Amateur Hour(45) — TA	m	To:s-8:30-4/53
9/52	10:00	Two for the Money — QU	d	
9/52	10:30	Club Embassy(15) — VY	d	
10/52	8:00	Buick Circus Hour(60) — UD	d	
4/53	7:15	Short Short Dramas(15) — DA	c	
6/53	8:00	Buick Circus Hour(60) — UD	c	
6/53	8:00	Revlon Mirror Theatre — DA	d*	
6/53	8:30	Break the Bank — QU	m*	Fr:n-9:30-2/53(c)
6/53	9:30	This Is Your Life — IV	s*	Fr:w-10
6/53	10:30	Club Embassy(15) — VY	c	
6/53	10:30	On the Line with Considine(15) — IV	m	Fr:t-10:45
6/53	10:45	Meet the Veep(15) — DS	d	
6/53	10:45	On the Line with Considine(15) — IV	m	To:t-10:30
7/53	7:30	Eddy Arnold(15) — MV	m*	Fr:mwf-7:45-8/52(c)
7/53	9:00	Nothing but the Best — MV	d*	
8/53	9:00	Nothing but the Best — MV	m*	To:n-10
8/53	9:30	This Is Your Life — IV	f*	
8/53	10:00	Judge for Yourself — QU	d	
8/53	10:00	Two for the Money — QU	m	To:s-9
8/53	10:45	Meet the Veep(15) — DS	c	
9/53	8:00	Revlon Mirror Theatre — DA	m*	To:s-10:30(c)
9/53	8:30	Break the Bank — QU	m*	To:n-10-1/54(a)

Date	Time	Title (min. if not 30) — Type	Action	From/To
9/53	10:45	It Happened in Sports(15) — ST	m	Fr:f-10:45
10/53	7:30	Eddy Arnold(15) — MV	c*	
1/54	10:30	Mr. & Mrs. North — MY	m	Fr:f-10-9/53(c)
1/54	10:30	On the Line with Considine(15) — IV	m	To:n-9-7/54
1/54	10:45	It Happened in Sports(15) — ST	c	
5/54	10:00	Judge for Yourself — QU	c	
5/54	10:00	Truth or Consequences — QU	m	Fr:r-10
6/54	7:30	World of Mr. Sweeney(15) — SC	d*	
6/54	8:00	Midwestern Hayride — MV	m*	Fr:t-8-9/52
6/54	8:30	Arthur Murray Party — MV	m*	Fr:m-7:30-4/54
6/54	9:30	Top Plays of 1954 — DA	d*	
7/54	9:00	Summer Playhouse — VS	d*	
8/54	7:30	Vaughn Monroe(15) — MV	d*	
8/54	7:30	World of Mr. Sweeney(15) — SC	c*	
8/54	9:00	Summer Playhouse — VS	m*	To:t-9:30-7/57
8/54	9:30	Top Plays of 1954 — DA	c*	
8/54	10:30	Mr. & Mrs. North — MY	c	
9/54	7:30	Vaughn Monroe(15) — MV	m*	To:tr-7:30-7/55
9/54	8:00	Midwestern Hayride — MV	m*	To:f-8-5/55
9/54	8:30	Arthur Murray Party — MV	m*	To:t-8:30-6/55
9/54	10:30	It's a Great Life — SC	d	
6/55	8:00	Place the Face — QU	m*	Fr:s-8-12/54
6/55	8:30	Arthur Murray Party — MV	m*	Fr:t-8:30-9/54
6/55	9:30	Armstrong Circle Theatre — DA	m	To:t-9:30-9/55
7/55	7:30	Vaughn Monroe(15) — MV	m*	Fr:tr-7:30-9/54
7/55	9:00	Clorets Summer Theater — DA	d*	
7/55	9:30	Dollar a Second — QU	m	Fr:f-9(a)
8/55	9:00	Clorets Summer Theater — DA	c*	
8/55	9:30	Dollar a Second — QU	m	To:f-9(a)
9/55	7:30	Vaughn Monroe(15) — MV	c*	
9/55	8:00	Chevy Show(60) — VY	d	
9/55	8:00	Martha Raye Show(60) — CV	d	
9/55	8:00	Place the Face — QU	c*	
9/55	8:30	Arthur Murray Party — MV	m*	To:r-10-4/56(c)
9/55	9:30	Armstrong Circle Theatre(60) — DA	m	Fr:t-9:30-6/55
9/55	9:30	Pontiac Presents Playwrights 56(60) — DA	d	
9/55	10:00	Truth or Consequences — QU	m	To:f-8
9/55	10:30	It's a Great Life — SC	m	To:n-7
5/56	8:00	Martha Raye Show(60) — CV	c	
6/56	7:30	Dinah Shore Show(15) — MU	c	
6/56	8:00	Chevy Show(60) — VY	c	
6/56	8:00	Dear Phoebe — SC	m	Fr:f-9:30-9/55
6/56	8:00	Milton Berle Show(60) — CV	c	
6/56	8:30	This Is Show Business — VY	m	Fr:t-9-3/54(c)
6/56	9:30	Pontiac Presents Playwrights 56(60) — DA	c	
7/56	7:30	Chevrolet on Broadway(15) — MV	d	
7/56	7:30	Chevrolet on Broadway(15) — MV	m	To:r-7:30
7/56	9:00	Sneak Preview — VS	d*	

Date	Time	Title (min. if not 30) – Type	Action	From/To
7/56	9:30	Kaiser Aluminum Hour(60) – DA	d	
8/56	7:30	Golden Touch of Frankie Carle(15) – MU	d	
8/56	9:00	Sneak Preview – VS	c*	
9/56	7:30	Golden Touch of Frankie Carle(15) – MU	m	To:m-7:30
9/56	8:00	Big Surprise – QU	m	Fr:s-7:30-6/56
9/56	8:00	Dear Phoebe – SC	c	
9/56	8:30	Noah's Ark – MD	d	
9/56	8:30	This Is Show Business – VY	c	
10/56	7:30	Jonathan Winters(15) – CV	d	
10/56	10:30	Break the Bank – QU	m	Fr:w-9:30
1/57	10:30	Break the Bank – QU	c	
1/57	10:30	Hold That Note – QU	d	
2/57	8:30	Noah's Ark – MD	m	To:n-7-6/58
3/57	8:30	Panic – DA	d	
4/57	8:00	Arthur Murray Party – MV	m	Fr:r-10-9/56(c)
4/57	8:00	Big Surprise – QU	c	
4/57	10:30	Hold That Note – QU	c	
6/57	7:30	Jonathan Winters(15) – CV	c	
6/57	8:00	Arthur Murray Party – MV	m	To:m-9:30
6/57	9:00	Fireside Theatre – DA	m	To:r-10:30-9/57
6/57	9:30	Armstrong Circle Theatre(60) – DA	m	To:w-10-10/57(c)
6/57	9:30	Kaiser Aluminum Hour(60) – DA	c	
7/57	7:30	Andy Williams and June Valli(15) – MU	d	
7/57	8:00	Festival of Stars – DA	m	Fr:s-9:30-9/56
7/57	9:00	Meet McGraw – CD	d	
7/57	9:30	Summer Playhouse – VS	m	Fr:t-9-8/54
7/57	10:00	Nat King Cole Show – MV	m	Fr:m-7:30
9/57	7:30	Andy Williams and June Valli(15) – MU	c	
9/57	7:30	Nat King Cole Show – MV	m	Fr:t-10
9/57	8:00	Eddie Fisher Show(60) – MV	d	
9/57	8:00	Festival of Stars – DA	c	
9/57	8:00	George Gobel(60) – CV	m	Fr:s-10-6/57
9/57	8:30	Panic – DA	c	
9/57	9:30	Bob Cummings Show – SC	m	Fr:r-8(c)
9/57	9:30	Summer Playhouse – VS	m	To:s-9:30-7/64(c)
9/57	10:00	Californians – WE	d	
9/57	10:00	Nat King Cole Show – MV	m	To:t-7:30
12/57	7:30	Nat King Cole Show – MV	c	
12/57	7:30	Treasure Hunt – QU	m	Fr:f-9-5/57(a)
6/58	7:30	Treasure Hunt – QU	c	
6/58	7:30	Win with a Winner – QU	d	
6/58	8:00	Investigator(60) – CD	d*	
6/58	9:00	Meet McGraw – CD	m	To:n-10-11/58
7/58	9:00	Dotto – QU	d	
8/58	9:00	Colgate Theatre – DA	d	
8/58	9:00	Dotto – QU	c	

Date	Time	Title (min. if not 30) — Type	Action	From/To
9/58	7:30	Win with a Winner — QU	c	
9/58	7:30	Dragnet — CD	m	Fr:r-8:30
9/58	8:00	Investigator(60) — CD	c*	
10/58	9:00	Colgate Theatre — DA	c	
10/58	9:00	George Burns — SC	d	
3/59	8:00	Eddie Fisher Show(60) — MV	c	
3/59	8:00	George Gobel(60) — CV	m	To:n-10-10/59(c)
3/59	8:00	Steve Canyon — AD	m	Fr:r-8
3/59	8:30	Jimmie Rodgers — MV	d	
3/59	10:00	Californians — WE	m	To:t-9
4/59	9:00	Californians — WE	m	Fr:t-10
4/59	9:00	George Burns — SC	c	
4/59	10:00	David Niven Show — DA	d	
6/59	7:30	Dragnet — CD	m	To:n-8:30
6/59	9:00	Californians — WE	m	To:r-7:30
7/59	7:30	Northwest Passage — AD	m	Fr:f-7:30
7/59	9:00	Fanfare — DA	d	
9/59	7:30	Laramie(60) — WE	d	
9/59	7:30	Northwest Passage — AD	c	
9/59	8:00	Steve Canyon — AD	m	To:r-7:30-4/60(a)
9/59	8:30	Fibber McGee and Molly — SC	d	
9/59	8:30	Jimmie Rodgers — MV	d	
9/59	9:00	Arthur Murray Party — MV	m	Fr:m-10
9/59	9:00	Fanfare — DA	c	
9/59	9:30	Bob Cummings Show — SC	c	
9/59	10:00	David Niven Show — DA	c	
10/59	9:30	Startime(60) — VY	d	
1/60	8:30	Fibber McGee and Molly — SC	c	
1/60	8:30	Startime(60) — VY	m	Fr:t-9:30
1/60	9:00	Arthur Murray Party — MV	m	To:t-9:30
1/60	9:30	Arthur Murray Party — MV	m	Fr:t-9
1/60	9:30	Startime(60) — VY	m	To:t-8:30
1/60	10:00	M Squad — CD	m	Fr:f-9:30
5/60	8:30	Startime(60) — VY	c	
6/60	8:30	NBC Playhouse — DA	d	
6/60	9:00	Richard Diamond, Pvt. Detective — CD	m	Fr:m-7:30-1/60
9/60	8:30	Alfred Hitchcock Presents — SA	m	Fr:n-9:30(c)
9/60	8:30	NBC Playhouse — DA	c	
9/60	9:00	Richard Diamond, Pvt. Detective — CD	c	
9/60	9:00	Thriller(60) — SA	d	
9/60	9:30	Arthur Murray Party — MV	c	
9/60	10:00	M Squad — CD	c	
7/61	10:00	Purex Summer Specials(60) — VS	d	
9/61	9:00	Dick Powell Show(60) — DA	d	
9/61	9:00	Thriller(60) — SA	m	To:m-10
9/61	10:00	Cain's Hundred(60) — CD	d	
9/61	10:00	Purex Summer Specials(60) — VS	m	To:f-9:30-7/62
9/62	8:30	Alfred Hitchcock Presents — SA	m	To:r-10(c)

Date	Time	Title (min. if not 30) — Type	Action	From/To
9/62	8:30	Empire(60) — WE	d	
9/62	9:00	Dick Powell Show(60) — DA	m	To:t-9:30
9/62	9:30	Dick Powell Show(60) — DA	m	Fr:t-9
9/62	10:00	Cain's Hundred(60) — CD	c	
9/62	10:30	Chet Huntley Reporting — DO	m	Fr:f-10:30
6/63	10:30	Chet Huntley Reporting — DO	c	
7/63	10:30	Report from... — TR	d	
9/63	7:30	Laramie(60) — WE	c	
9/63	7:30	Mr. Novak(60) — DR	d	
9/63	8:30	Empire(60) — WE	m	To:n-7:30-3/64(a)
9/63	8:30	Redigo — WE	d	
9/63	9:00	Richard Boone(60) — DA	d	
9/63	9:30	Dick Powell Show(60) — DA	c	
9/63	10:00	Andy Williams Show(60) — MV	m	Fr:r-10-6/63
9/63	10:30	Report from... — TR	c	
10/63	10:00	Bell Telephone Hour(60) — MU	m	Fr:f-9:30-4/62
12/63	8:30	Redigo — WE	c	
1/64	8:30	You Don't Say — QU	d	
5/64	8:30	Moment of Fear — DA	d	
5/64	8:30	You Don't Say — QU	c	
5/64	10:00	Andy Williams Show(60) — MV	m	To:m-9-10/64
9/64	8:30	Man from U.N.C.L.E.(60) — SD	d	
9/64	8:30	Moment of Fear — DA	m	To:t-8:30-5/65
9/64	9:00	Richard Boone(60) — DA	c	
9/64	9:30	That Was the Week That Was — CY	m	Fr:f-9:30-7/64
12/64	8:30	Man from U.N.C.L.E.(60) — SD	m	To:m-8
1/65	8:30	Hullabaloo(60) — MU	d	
5/65	8:30	Hullabaloo(60) — MU	m	To:t-10
5/65	8:30	Moment of Fear — DA	m	Fr:t-8:30-9/64
5/65	9:00	Cloak of Mystery(60) — DA	d	
5/65	9:30	That Was the Week That Was — CY	c	
5/65	10:00	Bell Telephone Hour(60) — MU	m	To:f-10-9/67
6/65	10:00	Hullabaloo(60) — MU	m	Fr:t-8:30
8/65	7:30	Mr. Novak(60) — DR	c	
8/65	8:30	Moment of Fear — DA	c	
8/65	9:00	Cloak of Mystery(60) — DA	c	
8/65	10:00	Hullabaloo(60) — MU	m	To:m-7:30
9/65	7:30	My Mother the Car — SC	d	
9/65	8:00	Please Don't Eat the Daisies — SC	d	
9/65	8:30	Dr. Kildare — MD	m	Fr:r-8:30
9/65	9:00	Film(120) — FI	s	
8/66	8:30	Dr. Kildare — MD	c	
9/66	7:30	Girl from U.N.C.L.E.(60) — SD	d	
9/66	7:30	My Mother the Car — SC	c	
9/66	8:00	Please Don't Eat the Daisies — SC	m	To:s-8
9/66	8:30	Occasional Wife — SC	d	
8/67	7:30	Girl from U.N.C.L.E.(60) — SD	c	
8/67	8:30	Occasional Wife — SC	c	
9/67	7:30	I Dream of Jeannie — SC	m	Fr:m-8
9/67	8:00	Jerry Lewis(60) — CV	d	

Date	Time	Title (min. if not 30) – Type	Action	From/To
5/68	8:00	Jerry Lewis(60) – CV	m	To:t-7:30-9/68
6/68	8:00	Showcase '68(60) – VY	d	
9/68	7:30	I Dream of Jeannie – SC	m	To:m-7:30
9/68	7:30	Jerry Lewis(60) – CV	m	Fr:t-8-5/68
9/68	8:00	Showcase '68(60) – VY	c	
9/68	8:30	Julia – SC	d	
5/69	7:30	Jerry Lewis(60) – CV	c	
6/69	7:30	Star Trek(60) – SF	m	Fr:f-10-4/69
9/69	7:30	I Dream of Jeannie – SC	m	Fr:m-7:30
9/69	7:30	Star Trek(60) – SF	c	
9/69	8:00	Debbie Reynolds Show – SC	d	
9/70	7:30	Don Knotts Show(60) – CV	d	
9/70	7:30	I Dream of Jeannie – SC	c	
9/70	8:00	Debbie Reynolds Show – SC	c	
1/71	7:30	Don Knotts Show(60) – CV	m	To:t-8
1/71	7:30	Julia – SC	m	Fr:t-8:30
1/71	8:00	Don Knotts Show(60) – CV	m	Fr:t-7:30
1/71	8:30	Julia – SC	m	To:t-7:30
5/71	7:30	Julia – SC	c	
6/71	7:30	Bill Cosby Show – SC	m	Fr:n-8:30
7/71	8:00	Don Knotts Show(60) – CV	c	
7/71	8:00	Make Your Own Kind of Music (60) – MV	d	
9/71	7:30	Bill Cosby Show – SC	c	
9/71	7:30	Ironside(60) – CD	m	Fr:r-8:30
9/71	8:00	Make Your Own Kind of Music (60) – MV	c	
9/71	8:30	Sarge(60) – DR	d	
9/71	9:00	Film(120) – FI	f	
9/71	9:30	Funny Side(60) – CV	d	
11/71	7:30	Ironside(60) – CD	m	To:r-9
11/71	7:30	Sarge(60) – DR	m	Fr:t-8:30
11/71	8:30	Funny Side(60) – CV	m	Fr:t-9:30
11/71	8:30	Sarge(60) – DR	m	To:t-7:30
11/71	9:30	Funny Side(60) – CV	m	To:t-8:30
11/71	9:30	Nichols(60) – WE	m	Fr:r-9
1/72	7:30	Sarge(60) – DR	c	
1/72	7:30	Search for the Nile(60) – DR	d	
4/72	7:30	Search for the Nile(60) – DR	c	
4/72	8:30	Funny Side(60) – CV	c	
5/72	7:30	Bonanza(60) – WE	m	Fr:n-9
5/72	8:30	NBC Action Playhouse(60) – DA	m	Fr:r-7:30-9/71
9/72	7:30	Bonanza(60) – WE	m	To:t-8
9/72	8:00	Bonanza(60) – WE	m	Fr:t-7:30
9/72	8:30	NBC Action Playhouse(60) – DA	c	
9/72	9:00	New Doctors(60) – MD	m	Fr:n-10
9/72	9:30	Nichols(60) – WE	c	
9/72	10:00	NBC Reports(60) – DO	d	
11/72	10:00	America(60) – DO	d	
11/72	10:00	NBC Reports(60) – DO	m	To:t-10-4/73

Date	Time	Title (min. if not 30) – Type	Action	From/To
1/73	8:00	Bonanza(60) – WE	c	
1/73	8:00	Film(120) – FI	s	
1/73	9:00	New Doctors(60) – MD	m	To:f-10-5/73
4/73	10:00	America(60) – DO	c	
4/73	10:00	NBC Reports(60) – DO	m	Fr:t-10-11/72
8/73	8:00	Film(120) – FI	f	
9/73	8:00	Chase(60) – CD	d	
9/73	9:00	Magician(60) – AD	d	
9/73	10:00	NBC Reports(60) – DO	c	
10/73	10:00	Police Story(60) – RA	d	
1/74	8:00	Adam 12 – CD	m	Fr:w-8
1/74	8:00	Chase(60) – CD	m	To:w-8
1/74	8:30	Banacek(90) – CD	m	Fr:w-8:30
1/74	8:30	Snoop Sisters(90) – CD	m	Fr:w-8:30
1/74	9:00	Magician(60) – AD	m	To:m-8
4/74	8:30	Faraday and Company(90) – CD	m	Fr:w-8:30-1/74
4/74	8:30	Tenafly(90) – CD	m	Fr:w-8:30-1/74
9/74	8:30	Banacek(90) – CD	c	
9/74	8:30	Faraday and Company(90) – CD	c	
9/74	8:30	Film(90) – FI	s	
9/74	8:30	Snoop Sisters(90) – CD	c	
9/74	8:30	Tenafly(90) – CD	c	
8/75	8:00	Adam 12 – CD	c	
9/75	8:00	Movin' On(60) – AD	m	Fr:r-10-5/75
9/75	8:30	Film(90) – FI	f	
9/75	9:00	Police Story(60) – RA	m	Fr:t-10
9/75	10:00	Joe Forrester(60) – CD	d	
9/75	10:00	Police Story(60) – RA	m	To:t-9
10/75	9:00	Police Story(60) – RA	m	To:f-10
11/75	9:00	Police Woman(60) – CD	m	Fr:f-10
1/76	10:00	Joe Forrester(60) – CD	m	To:m-9
2/76	10:00	City of Angels(60) – CD	d	
8/76	10:00	City of Angels(60) – CD	c	
8/76	10:00	Police Story(60) – RA	m	Fr:f-10
9/76	8:00	Baa Baa Black Sheep(60) – WD	d	
9/76	8:00	Movin' On(60) – AD	c	
8/77	8:00	Baa Baa Black Sheep(60) – WD	m	To:w-9-12/77
8/77	9:00	Police Woman(60) – CD	m	To:t-10
8/77	10:00	Police Story(60) – RA	c	
9/77	8:00	Richard Pryor Show(60) – CV	d	
9/77	9:00	Mulligan's Stew(60) – CO	d	
9/77	10:00	Police Woman(60) – CD	m	Fr:t-9
10/77	8:00	Man from Atlantis(60) – AD	m	Fr:r-9
10/77	8:00	Richard Pryor Show(60) – CV	m	To:r-9
12/77	9:00	Mulligan's Stew(60) – CO	c	
12/77	10:00	Police Woman(60) – CD	m	To:w-10
1/78	8:00	Man from Atlantis(60) – AD	m	To:t-8-4/78
1/78	9:00	Big Event(120) – VS	s	
2/78	8:00	Chuck Barris Rah Rah Show(60) – CV	d	

Date	Time	Title (min. if not 30) – Type	Action	From/To
4/78	8:00	Chuck Barris Rah Rah Show(60) – CV	c	
4/78	8:00	Man from Atlantis(60) – AD	m	Fr:t-8-1/78
8/78	8:00	Man from Atlantis(60) – AD	c	
9/78	8:00	Grandpa Goes to Washington(60) – CO	d	
1/79	8:00	Grandpa Goes to Washington(60) – CO	c	
2/79	8:00	Cliff Hangers(60) – SL	d	
5/79	8:00	Cliff Hangers(60) – SL	c	
5/79	8:00	Runaways(60) – DR	m	Fr:r-10-8/78
9/79	8:00	Misadventures of Sheriff Lobo(60) – CO	d	
9/79	8:00	Runaways(60) – DR	c	
9/79	9:00	Big Event(120) – VS	f	
9/79	9:00	Film(120) – FI	s	
2/80	9:00	Film(120) – FI	f	
3/80	9:00	Big Show(90) – VY	d	
4/80	10:30	United States – SC	d	
6/80	8:00	Misadventures of Sheriff Lobo(60) – CO	m	To:t-8-11/80
6/80	8:00	Film(180) – FI	s	
6/80	9:00	Big Show(90) – VY	c	
6/80	10:30	United States – SC	c	
9/80	8:00	Film(180) – FI	f	
11/80	8:00	Misadventures of Sheriff Lobo(60) – CO	m	Fr:t-8-6/80
11/80	9:00	B.J. and the Bear(60) – AD	m	Fr:s-8-8/80
11/80	10:00	Barbara Mandrell & Mandrell Sisters(60) – MV	d	
11/80	10:00	Barbara Mandrell & Mandrell (60) – MV	m	To:s-8
12/80	10:00	Steve Allen Comedy Hour(60) – CV	d	
12/80	10:00	Steve Allen Comedy Hour(60) – CV	c	
1/81	10:00	Flamingo Road(60) – SL	d	
3/81	10:00	Flamingo Road(60) – SL	m	To:m-9-6/81
3/81	10:00	Walking Tall(60) – CD	m	Fr:s-9
4/81	9:00	B.J. and the Bear(60) – AD	m	To:s-9
4/81	9:00	Hill Street Blues(60) – CD	m	Fr:s-10
4/81	10:00	Nero Wolfe(60) – CD	m	Fr:f-9
4/81	10:00	Walking Tall(60) – CD	m	To:s-10
8/81	8:00	Misadventures of Sheriff Lobo(60) – CO	c	
8/81	9:00	Hill Street Blues(60) – CD	m	To:r-10-10/81
8/81	10:00	Nero Wolfe(60) – CD	c	
9/81	8:00	Film(180) – FI	s	
10/81	8:00	Film(180) – FI	f	
11/81	8:00	Father Murphy(60) – DR	d	
11/81	9:00	Bret Maverick(60) – WE	d	
11/81	10:00	Flamingo Road(60) – SL	m	Fr:m-9-8/81

Date	Time	Title (min. if not 30) — Type	Action	From/To
3/82	8:00	Bret Maverick(60) — WE	m	Fr:t-9
3/82	8:00	Father Murphy(60) — DR	m	To:n-7
3/82	9:00	Bret Maverick(60) — WE	m	To:t-8
3/82	9:00	Flamingo Road(60) — SL	m	Fr:t-10
3/82	10:00	Cassie & Company(60) — CD	m	Fr:f-10
3/82	10:00	Flamingo Road(60) — SL	m	To:t-9
6/82	9:00	Flamingo Road(60) — SL	m	To:t-10
6/82	10:00	Cassie & Company(60) — CD	m	To:f-10
6/82	10:00	Flamingo Road(60) — SL	m	Fr:t-9
7/82	8:00	Bret Maverick(60) — WE	m	To:t-9
7/82	8:00	Father Murphy(60) — DR	m	Fr:n-7
7/82	9:00	Bret Maverick(60) — WE	m	Fr:t-8
7/82	10:00	Flamingo Road(60) — SL	c	
7/82	10:00	McClain's Law(60) — CD	m	Fr:f-10
8/82	9:00	Bret Maverick(60) — WE	c	
8/82	9:00	Film(120) — FI	s	
8/82	10:00	McClain's Law(60) — CD	c	
10/82	9:00	Gavilon(60) — AD	d	
10/82	9:00	Film(120) — FI	f	
10/82	10:00	St. Elsewhere(60) — MD	d	
12/82	8:00	Father Murphy(60) — DR	m	To:n-7
12/82	9:00	Gavilon(60) — AD	m	To:f-10-3/83
1/83	8:00	A-Team(60) — AD	d	
1/83	9:00	Bare Essence(60) — SL	d	
3/83	9:00	Bare Essence(60) — SL	m	To:f-10
3/83	9:00	Remington Steele(60) — CD	m	Fr:f-10
8/83	10:00	St. Elsewhere(60) — MD	m	To:w-10
9/83	10:00	Bay City Blues(60) — DR	d	
11/83	10:00	Bay City Blues(60) — DR	c	
12/83	9:00	Remington Steele(60) — CD	m	To:t-10
12/83	10:00	For Love and Honor(60) — DR	m	Fr:f-10
12/83	10:00	For Love and Honor(60) — DR	c	
1/84	9:00	Riptide(60) — CD	d	
1/84	10:00	Remington Steele(60) — CD	m	Fr:t-9
2/86	9:00	Riptide(60) — CD	m	To:f-8
2/86	10:00	Remington Steele(60) — CD	m	To:s-10
3/86	9:00	Hunter(60) — CD	m	Fr:s-10
3/86	10:00	Stingray(60) — CD	d	
5/86	10:00	Stingray(60) — CD	m	To:f-10
6/86	10:00	1986(60) — NM	d	
8/86	8:00	A-Team(60) — AD	m	To:f-8
8/86	8:00	Film(120) — FI	s	
8/86	9:00	Hunter(60) — CD	m	To:s-10
9/86	8:00	Matlock(60) — LD	d#	
9/86	8:00	Film(120) — FI	f	
9/86	9:00	Crime Story(60) — CD	m	Fr:f-10
11/86	9:00	Crime Story(60) — CD	m	To:f-10
12/86	9:00	Hill Street Blues(60) — CD	m	Fr:r-10
1/87	10:00	1986(60) — NM	c	
2/87	9:00	Hill Street Blues(60) — CD	m	To:t-10

Date	Time	Title (min. if not 30) — Type	Action	From/To
2/87	10:00	Remington Steele(60) — CD	m	Fr:s-10-7/86
2/87	10:00	Remington Steele(60) — CD	c	
3/87	9:00	Gimme a Break — SC	m	Fr:w-9
3/87	9:30	Easy Street — SC	m	Fr:n-8
3/87	10:00	Hill Street Blues(60) — CD	m	Fr:t-9
4/87	9:30	Easy Street — SC	m	To:w-9:30
4/87	9:30	Tortellis — SC	m	Fr:w-9:30
5/87	9:00	Gimme a Break — SC	c	
5/87	9:30	Tortellis — SC	c	
5/87	10:00	Hill Street Blues(60) — CD	c	
6/87	9:00	Film(120) — FI	s	
8/87	9:00	Film(120) — FI	f	
9/87	9:00	JJ Starbuck(60) — CD	d	
9/87	10:00	Crime Story(60) — CD	m	Fr:f-10
11/87	9:00	JJ Starbuck(60) — CD	m	To:s-10
12/87	9:00	Hunter(60) — CD	m	Fr:s-10
3/88	9:00	In the Heat of the Night(60) — CD	d	
3/88	9:00	Hunter(60) — CD	m	To:s-10
5/88	9:00	In the Heat of the Night(60) — CD	m	To:t-9-7/88
5/88	9:00	Film(120) — FI	s	
5/88	10:00	Crime Story(60) — CD	c	
6/88	9:00	Film(120) — FI	f	
6/88	9:00	JJ Starbuck(60) — CD	m	Fr:s-10-2/88
6/88	10:00	Summer Showcase(60) — VS	d*	
7/88	9:00	In the Heat of the Night(60) — CD	m#	Fr:t-9-5/88
7/88	9:00	JJ Starbuck(60) — CD	c	
8/88	10:00	Summer Showcase(60) — VS	c*	

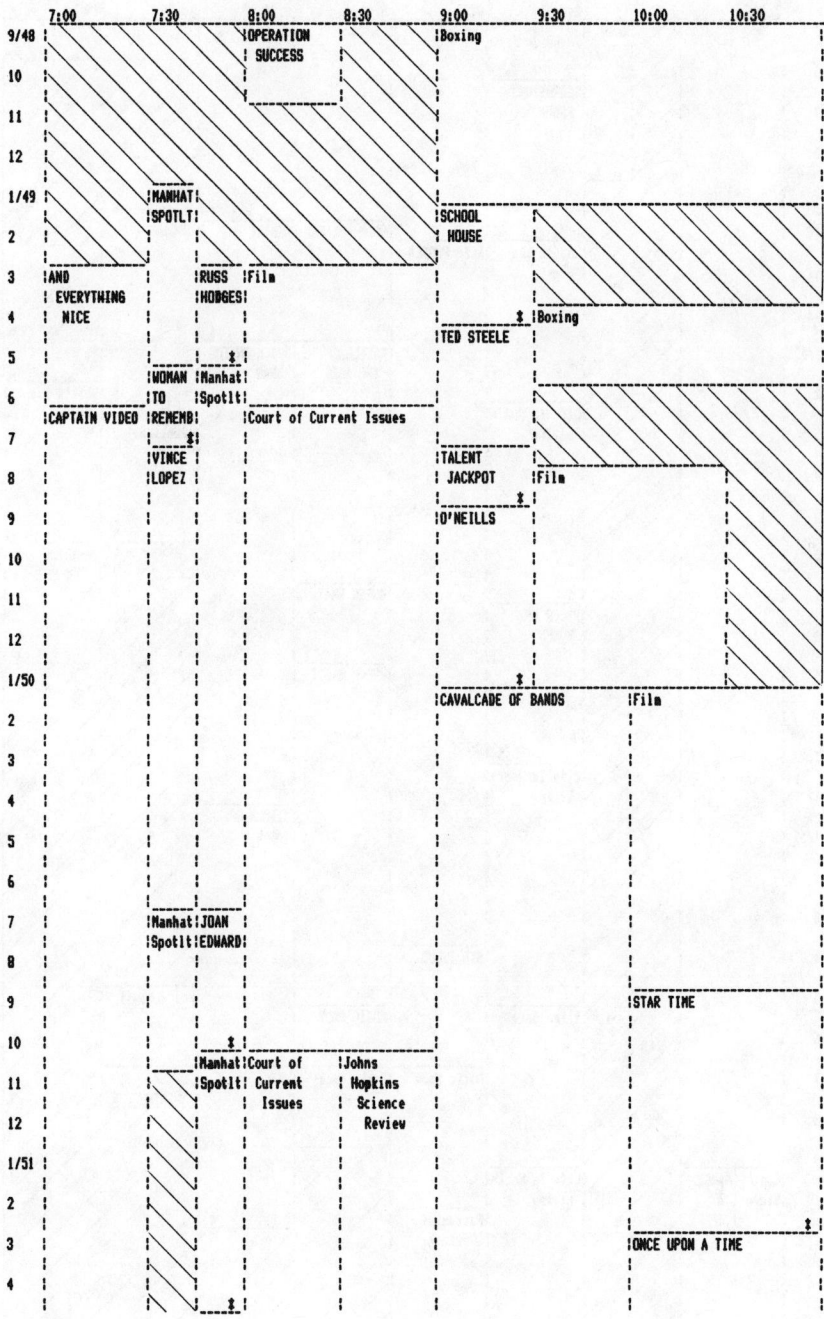

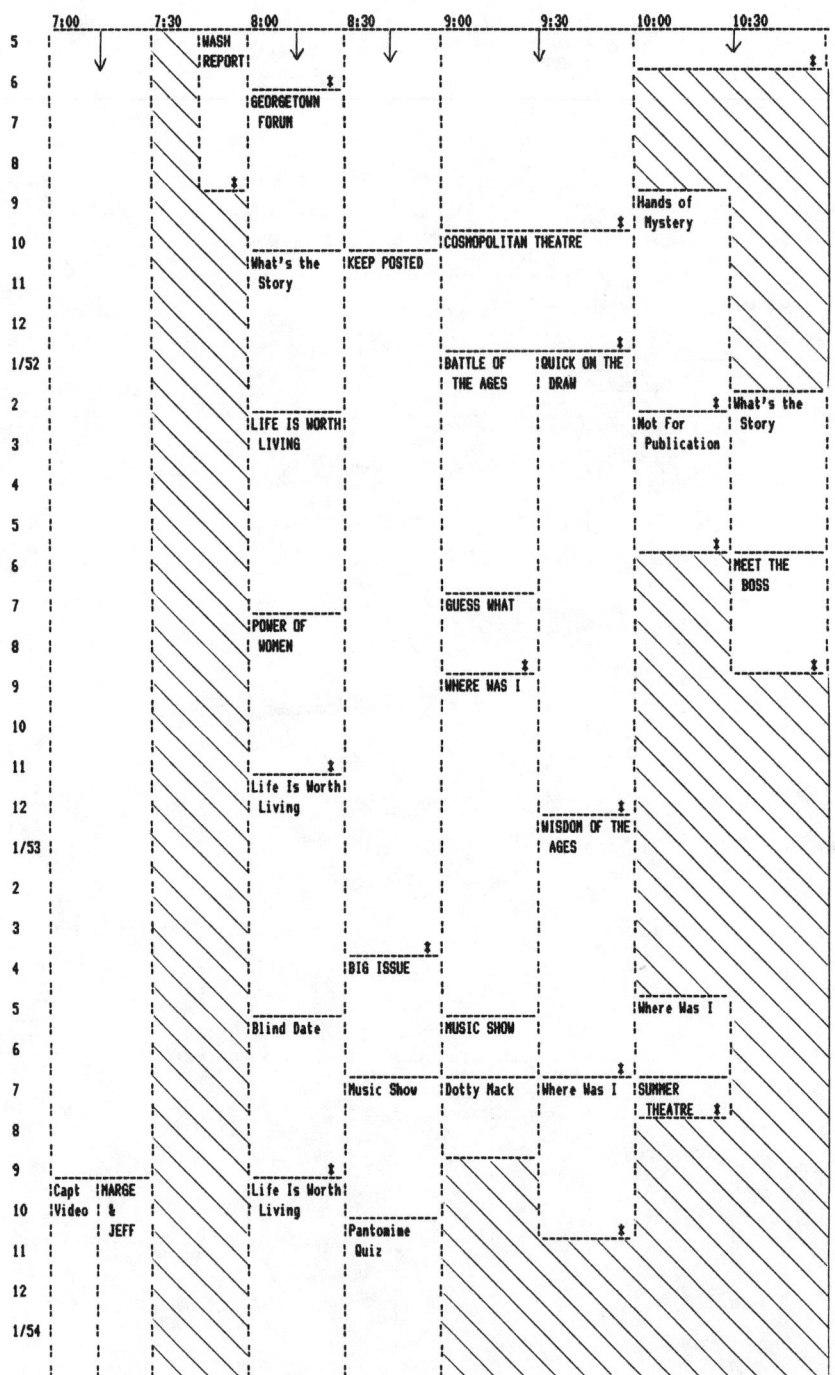

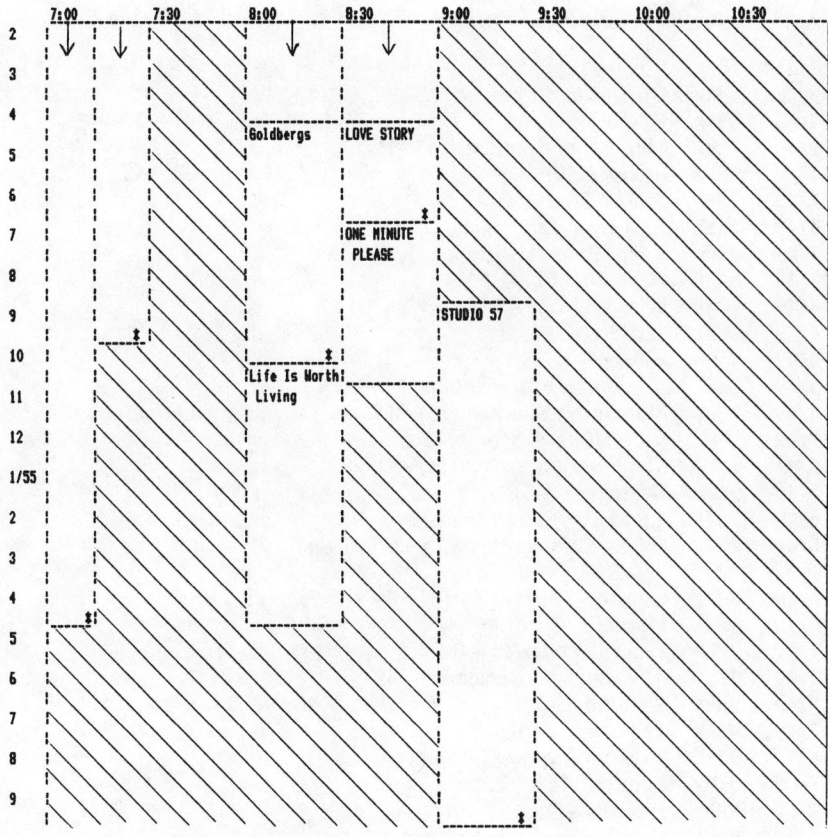

Date	Time	Title (min. if not 30) — Type	Action	From/To
7/48	9:00	Boxing(120) — SP	s	
9/48	8:00	Operation Success — IF	d	
10/48	8:00	Operation Success — IF	m	To:r-8-1/49
1/49	7:30	Manhattan Spotlight(15) — IV	d	
1/49	9:00	Boxing(120) — SP	f	
1/49	9:00	School House — CV	d	
3/49	7:00	And Everything Nice — FS	d	
3/49	7:45	Russ Hodges' Scoreboard(15) — SN	d	
3/49	8:00	Film(60) — FI	s	
4/49	9:00	School House — CV	c	
4/49	9:00	Ted Steele — MU	d	
4/49	9:30	Boxing(90) — SP	s	
5/49	7:30	A Woman to Remember(15) — SL	d	
5/49	7:30	Manhattan Spotlight(15) — IV	m	To:t-7:45
5/49	7:45	Russ Hodges' Scoreboard(15) — SN	c	
5/49	7:45	Manhattan Spotlight(15) — IV	m	Fr:t-7:30
5/49	9:30	Boxing(90) — SP	f	
6/49	7:00	And Everything Nice — FS	m	To:m-8:30
6/49	7:00	Captain Video & His Video Rangers — KV	d	
6/49	8:00	Court of Current Issues(60) — DB	m	Fr:w-9
6/49	8:00	Film(60) — FI	f	
7/49	7:30	Vincent Lopez(15) — MV	d	
7/49	7:30	A Woman to Remember(15) — SL	c	
7/49	9:00	Talent Jackpot — TA	d	
7/49	9:00	Ted Steele — MU	m	To:twr-7:15(c)
8/49	9:00	Talent Jackpot — TA	c	
8/49	9:30	Film(60) — FI	s	
9/49	9:00	O'Neills — DR	d	
1/50	9:00	Cavalcade of Bands(60) — MV	d	
1/50	9:00	O'Neills — DR	c	
1/50	9:30	Film(60) — FI	f	
1/50	10:00	Film(60) — FI	s	
6/50	7:30	Vincent Lopez(15) — MV	m	To:s-8
6/50	7:45	Manhattan Spotlight(15) — IV	m	To:t-7:30
7/50	7:30	Manhattan Spotlight(15) — IV	m	Fr:t-7:45
7/50	7:45	Joan Edwards(15) — MU	d	
8/50	10:00	Film(60) — FI	f	
9/50	10:00	Star Time(60) — MV	d	
10/50	7:30	Manhattan Spotlight(15) — IV	m	To:t-7:45
10/50	7:45	Joan Edwards(15) — MU	c	
10/50	7:45	Manhattan Spotlight(15) — IV	m	Fr:t-7:30
10/50	8:00	Court of Current Issues(60) — DB	m	To:t-8
10/50	8:00	Court of Current Issues — DB	m	Fr:t-8
10/50	8:30	Johns Hopkins Science Review — IF	m	Fr:f-9-5/49(c)
2/51	10:00	Star Time(60) — MV	c	
3/51	10:00	Once Upon a Time(60) — MU	d	
4/51	7:45	Manhattan Spotlight(15) — IV	c	
5/51	7:45	Washington Report(15) — DS	d	
5/51	10:00	Once Upon a Time(60) — MU	c	

Date	Time	Title (min. if not 30) — Type	Action	From/To
6/51	8:00	Court of Current Issues — DB	c	
7/51	8:00	Georgetown University Forum — DS	d	
8/51	7:45	Washington Report(15) — DS	c	
9/51	9:00	Cavalcade of Bands(60) — MV	c	
9/51	10:00	Hands of Mystery — SA	m	Fr:f-9
10/51	8:00	Georgetown University Forum — DS	m	To:r-8
10/51	8:00	What's the Story? — QU	m	Fr:w-9
10/51	8:30	Johns Hopkins Science Review — IF	m	To:m-8:30
10/51	8:30	Keep Posted — PA	d	
10/51	9:00	Cosmopolitan Theater(60) — DA	d	
12/51	9:00	Cosmopolitan Theater(60) — DA	c	
1/52	9:00	Battle of the Ages — TA	d	
1/52	9:30	Quick on the Draw — QU	d	
2/52	8:00	Life Is Worth Living — RE	d	
2/52	8:00	What's the Story? — QU	m	To:t-10:30
2/52	10:00	Hands of Mystery — SA	c	
2/52	10:30	What's the Story? — QU	m	Fr:t-8
3/52	10:00	Not for Publication — ND	m	Fr:f-8:30
5/52	8:00	Life Is Worth Living — RE	m	To:t-8-11/52
5/52	10:00	Not for Publication — ND	c	
5/52	10:30	What's the Story? — QU	m	To:r-9:30
6/52	9:00	Battle of the Ages — TA	m	To:s-10:30-9/52(c)
6/52	10:30	Meet the Boss — IV	d	
7/52	8:00	Power of Women — DS	d	
7/52	9:00	Guess What — QU	d	
8/52	9:00	Guess What — QU	c	
8/52	10:30	Meet the Boss — IV	c	
9/52	9:00	Where Was I? — QU	d	
11/52	8:00	Power of Women — DS	c	
11/52	8:00	Life Is Worth Living — RE	m	Fr:t-8-5/52
12/52	9:30	Quick on the Draw — QU	c	
12/52	9:30	Wisdom of the Ages — DS	d	
3/53	8:30	Keep Posted — PA	c	
4/53	8:30	Big Issue — PA	d	
5/53	8:00	Blind Date — QU	m	Fr:s-9-7/52(n)
5/53	8:00	Life Is Worth Living — RE	m	To:t-8-9/53
5/53	9:00	Music Show — MU	d	
5/53	9:00	Where Was I? — QU	m	To:t-10
5/53	10:00	Where Was I? — QU	m	Fr:t-9
6/53	8:30	Big Issue — PA	m	To:m-8:30-9/53
6/53	9:00	Music Show — MU	m	To:t-8:30
6/53	9:30	Wisdom of the Ages — DS	c	
6/53	10:00	Where Was I? — QU	m	To:t-9:30
7/53	8:30	Music Show — MU	m	Fr:t-9
7/53	9:00	Dotty Mack Show — MU	m	Fr:m-10:45
7/53	9:30	Where Was I? — QU	m	Fr:t-10
7/53	10:00	Summer Night Theatre — VS	d	
7/53	10:00	Summer Night Theatre — VS	c	
8/53	9:00	Dotty Mack Show — MU	m	To:r-9:30(a)

Date	Time	Title (min. if not 30) — Type	Action	From/To
9/53	7:00	Captain Video & His Video Rangers — KV	m	To:m-7
9/53	7:00	Captain Video & His Video Rangers (15) — KV	m	Fr:t-7
9/53	7:15	Marge and Jeff(15) — SC	d	
9/53	8:00	Blind Date — QU	c	
9/53	8:00	Life Is Worth Living — RE	m	Fr:t-8-5/53
10/53	8:30	Music Show — MU	m	To:w-10:30
10/53	8:30	Pantomime Quiz — QU	m	Fr:f-8-8/53(c)
10/53	9:30	Where Was I? — QU	c	
4/54	8:00	Goldbergs — SC	m	Fr:f-8-9/53(n)
4/54	8:00	Life Is Worth Living — RE	m	To:t-8-10/54
4/54	8:30	Love Story — DA	d	
4/54	8:30	Pantomime Quiz — QU	m	To:f-8-7/54(c)
6/54	8:30	Love Story — DA	c	
7/54	8:30	One Minute Please — QU	d	
9/54	7:15	Marge and Jeff(15) — SC	c	
9/54	9:00	Studio 57 — DA	d	
10/54	8:00	Goldbergs — SC	c	
10/54	8:00	Life Is Worth Living — RE	m	Fr:t-8-4/54
10/54	8:30	One Minute Please — QU	m	To:f-9:30
4/55	7:00	Captain Video & His Video Rangers (15) — KV	c	
4/55	8:00	Life Is Worth Living — RE	m	To:r-8-10/55(abc)
9/55	9:00	Studio 57 — DA	c	

Tuesday Programming
Moves Summary

1948–49

ABC. *Series Premieres:* America's Town Meeting; Child's World; Dr. Fix-Um; On Trial. *Key Programming Moves:* At the end of June, ABC discontinues programming on Tuesday night, except for live boxing; it doesn't resume Tuesday night programming until 9/50.

CBS. *Series Premieres:* Barry Wood Show; Manhattan Showcase; Roar of the Rails; Suspense; They Stand Accused. *Key Programming Moves:* SUSPENSE debuts in 9:30–10 slot, where it stays until 8/54.

NBC. *Series Premieres:* Fireside Theatre; Kukla, Fran & Ollie; Mary Margaret McBride; Mohawk Showroom; Ripley's Believe It or Not. *Key Programming Moves:* TEXACO STAR THEATRE (THE MILTON BERLE SHOW) occupies the 8–9 slot; it is the most dominant program on television; in fact, many movie theatres closed on Tuesday nights because so many people were staying home to watch Uncle Miltie; FIRESIDE THEATRE debuts in April, following TEXACO STAR THEATRE; it stays in that slot until 6/57.

DuMont. *Series Premieres:* And Everything Nice; Captain Video & His Video Rangers; Manhattan Spotlight; Operation Success; Russ Hodges; School House; Talent Jackpot; Ted Steele Show; A Woman to Remember.

1949–50

CBS. *Series Premieres:* Arthur Godfrey & His Ukulele; Command Post; Garry Moore Show; Life with Snarky Parker; Red Barber Show; Stage Door; Strictly for Laughs; Sugar Hill Time; Sure as Fate. *Key Programming Moves:* Due to the success of his program, ARTHUR GODFREY'S TALENT SCOUTS, CBS tried giving him another series, ARTHUR GODFREY

& HIS UKULELE, where Mr. Godfrey instructed the audience on playing the ukulele; it lasted only two months.

NBC. *Series Premieres:* Armstrong Circle Theatre; Life of Riley; Melody, Harmony & Rhythm; Van Camp's Little Show. *Key Programming Moves:* ARMSTRONG CIRCLE THEATRE, one of the more successful dramatic anthology series, debuts; it runs on NBC until 6/57, then it continued on CBS until 8/63; LIFE OF RILEY debuts, with Jackie Gleason starring; it lasted one season, but was resurrected in 1953, with William Bendix; the latter version lasted eight years; Although no official ratings were conducted until the following year, it is widely believed that TEXACO STAR THEATRE was still the most popular program on television; THE ORIGINAL AMATEUR HOUR is moved into the 10–11 slot, where it stays until 9/52.

DuMont: *Series Premieres:* Cavalcade of Bands; Joan Edwards Show; The O'Neills. *Key Programming Moves:* CAVALCADE OF BANDS debuts; it lasts for almost two years, a long time for a DuMont series.

1950–51

ABC. *Series Premieres:* Beulah; Billy Rose Show; Can You Top This; Carmel Myers Show; How Did They Get That Way; Moment of Music; Other Lands, Other Places; QED. *Key Programming Moves:* ABC resumes Tuesday night programming at the beginning of the season; BEULAH debuts; based on the popular radio series, it lasts until 9/53.

CBS. *Series Premieres:* Danger; How To; Prudential Playhouse; Steve Allen Show; Vaughn Monroe Show. *Key Programming Moves:* DANGER debuts; this critically acclaimed dramatic anthology series lasted until 5/55.

NBC. *Key Programming Moves:* A.C. Nielsen begins a regular ratings service for prime time television; Milton Berle's TEXACO STAR THEATRE is the #1 rated series on television; it anchors a very strong Tuesday night lineup for NBC.

DuMont: *Series Premieres:* Georgetown University Forum; Once Upon a Time; Star Time; Washington Report. *Key Programming Moves:* COURT OF CURRENT ISSUES is cut back from 60 minutes to 30 minutes in October; it is later cancelled at the end of the season.

1951–52

ABC. *Series Premieres:* Chicago Symphony; Opera Auditions. *Key Programming Moves:* In June, ABC cuts back to only 90 minutes of Tuesday night regular series programming; it cuts back further, to one program (BEULAH) at season's end.

CBS. *Series Premieres:* City Hospital; Crime Syndicated; Draw to Win; Music Hall; My Friend Irma. *Key Programming Moves:* During the summer months, CBS discontinues programming the 8-9 slot, opposite Milton Berle; it resumes programming this slot the following season.

NBC. *Series Premieres:* Bob & Ray; Dinah Shore Show; Mayor of Hollywood; On the Line; Young Charms. *Key Programming Moves:* THE DINAH SHORE SHOW debuts in 11/51; this 15 minute series airs until the end of the '56–'57 season, at which time it is expanded to one hour, and runs until 5/63; TEXACO STAR THEATRE is the #2 rated series on television.

DuMont: *Series Premieres:* Battle of the Ages; Cosmopolitan Theatre; Guess What; Keep Posted; Life Is Worth Living; Meet the Boss; Power of Women; Quick on the Draw. *Key Programming Moves:* DuMont schedules aggressively on Tuesday night, for the first time, though most of their offerings last for only a few months; KEEP POSTED, a public affairs program, debuts; it lasts for about 1½ years, a long time by DuMont standards.

1952–53

ABC. *Key Programming Moves:* ABC offers very little Tuesday night prime time fare in 1952–53; until December, only BEULAH, 7:30–8 was on the air; by season's end, BEULAH was cancelled, but boxing was added to the schedule.

CBS. *Series Premieres:* Anyone Can Win; Ernie Kovacs Show; Heaven for Betsy; Leave It to Larry; Red Buttons Show; Wheel of Fortune; Youth Takes a Stand. *Key Programming Moves:* THE ERNIE KOVACS SHOW debuts in December, opposite Milton Berle; while this series lasted only five months, it was one of the most innovative comedy variety programs of all time; the combination of being opposite the highly popular Berle and being ahead of its time precluded Kovacs' series from generating a large enough audience to continue; CBS discontinues programming the 8-9 slot after THE ERNIE KOVACS SHOW is cancelled and doesn't resume filling that slot until July.

NBC. *Series Premieres:* Buick Circus Hour; Club Embassy; Judge for Yourself; Meet the Veep; Short Short Dramas; Two for the Money. *Key Programming Moves:* BUICK CIRCUS HOUR debuts; it aired every fourth week in the 8-9 slot occupied by TEXACO STAR THEATRE; it is cancelled in 6/53.

DuMont: *Series Premieres:* Big Issue; The Music Show; Summer Theatre; Where Was I; Wisdom of the Ages.

1953–54

ABC. *Series Premieres:* Danny Thomas Show; Motorola TV Theatre; U.S. Steel Hour. *Key Programming Moves:* ABC begins offering regular series throughout the season; by season's end, they had a full schedule again; THE DANNY THOMAS SHOW debuts; it becomes a hit, something ABC had never experienced on Tuesdays; it stays on ABC until 7/57, when it was picked up by CBS; THE U.S. STEEL HOUR debuts; this dramatic anthology series was one of the most highly acclaimed series in the history of television; it stayed on ABC until 6/55, then CBS picked it up and it continued until 6/63. CAVALCADE OF AMERICA is picked up from NBC; it lasts on ABC until 6/57.

CBS. *Series Premieres:* Jo Stafford Show; See It Now. *Key Programming Moves:* SEE IT NOW debuts; this documentary series, produced by CBS News and featuring Edward R. Murrow, became a major force in America, tackling controversial issues like nuclear weapons, McCarthyism, and cigarette smoking; it lasted almost two years; SUSPENSE is cancelled at the end of the season.

DuMont: *Series Premieres:* Love Story; Marge and Jeff; One Minute Please. *Key Programming Moves:* DuMont cuts back to 90 minutes of programming; In April, DuMont resurrects THE GOLDBERGS; it lasts only until season's end.

1954–55

ABC. *Series Premieres:* Elgin TV Hour; Talent Varieties. *Key Programming Moves:* THE U.S. STEEL HOUR leaves ABC in June; it is picked up by CBS.

CBS. *Series Premieres:* Halls of Ivy; Music '55; Search; $64,000 Question; Star Time Playhouse; Upbeat. *Key Programming Moves:* DANGER is cancelled in June; $64,000 QUESTION, the first of the big-money quiz programs, debuts in June; it will become one of the most successful series on the air; it will also spawn a number of imitators; this series is most responsible for the "quiz show wave" on prime time television; SEE IT NOW is cancelled in July; LIFE WITH FATHER is moved to Tuesday in January; it is cancelled in July; THE RED SKELTON SHOW is moved to Tuesday, where it stays until 6/70.

NBC. *Series Premieres:* It's a Great Life.

DuMont. *Series Premieres:* Studio 57. *Key Programming Moves:* DuMont ceases Tuesday night programming at the end of the season.

1955-56

ABC. *Series Premieres:* Casablanca; Cheyenne; GE Summer Originals; King's Row; Life and Legend of Wyatt Earp. *Key Programming Moves:* CHEYENNE debuts; initially it rotated with two other series (CASABLANCA and KING'S ROW) under the title WARNER BROTHER PRESENTS; CHEYENNE stayed on Tuesday for three years, then switched to Monday, and eventually to Friday; in all it lasted for eight years; LIFE AND LEGEND OF WYATT EARP debuts in the 8:30–9 slot, where it stayed until its cancellation in 9/61; CAVALCADE OF AMERICA is moved to 9:30, where it continued for almost two years; THE DANNY THOMAS SHOW leaves ABC for CBS in June.

CBS. *Series Premieres:* Do You Trust Your Wife; Guy Lombardo Show; Joe & Mabel; Navy Log; Phil Silvers Show. *Key Programming Moves:* THE PHIL SILVERS SHOW debuts; it lasts for four years; $64,000 QUESTION becomes the #1 rated series on television; NAME THAT TUNE is moved to Tuesday, 7:30–8; it stays in this slot for the next three years.

NBC. *Series Premieres:* Chevy Show; Golden Touch of Frankie Carle; Kaiser Aluminum Hour; Martha Raye Show; Pontiac Presents. *Key Programming Moves:* TEXACO STAR THEATRE begins a rotating schedule (with THE MARTHA RAYE SHOW and THE CHEVY SHOW); this highly successful, long-running series is finally cancelled in 6/56.

1956-57

ABC. *Series Premieres:* Broken Arrow; Conflict. *Key Programming Moves:* BROKEN ARROW debuts; it lasts for four years; CAVALCADE OF AMERICA is cancelled in 6/57.

CBS. *Series Premieres:* Brothers; Herb Shriner Show; Spike Jones Show; To Tell the Truth. *Key Programming Moves:* TO TELL THE TRUTH debuts in December; it lasts 11 years on CBS.

NBC. *Series Premieres:* Andy Williams and June Valli Show; Hold That Note; Jonathan Winters Show; Meet McGraw; Noah's Ark; Panic. *Key Programming Moves:* After eight years on Tuesday, FIRESIDE THEATRE moves to Thursday at the end of the season.

1957-58

ABC. *Series Premieres:* Sugarfoot. *Key Programming Moves:* BROKEN ARROW is taken off at the end of the season; it eventually returns on Sunday in 4/60.

CBS. *Series Premieres:* Adorn Playhouse; Assignment Foreign Legion; Bid 'n' Buy; Eve Arden Show; Keep Talking; Playhouse; Wingo. *Key Programming Moves:* $64,000 QUESTION is moved to Sunday and NAME THAT TUNE is moved to Monday at the end of the season; THE PHIL SILVERS SHOW is moved to Friday in February.

NBC. *Series Premieres:* The Californians; Colgate Theatre; Dotto; Eddie Fisher Show; Win with a Winner. *Key Programming Moves:* DOTTO debuts in July; while this series only lasted for two months, it was important in that it was from this quiz program that an unhappy contestant blew the whistle on quiz shows by announcing that it was "rigged"; a major scandal ensued, including a Congressional investigation; early in the following season, most quiz shows were gone from prime time television; also, as a result of the quiz scandal, the networks took much of the control of program production away from the advertisers.

1958–59

ABC. *Series Premieres:* Alcoa Presents; Bronco; Naked City; Rifleman. *Key Programming Moves:* THE RIFLEMAN debuts, beginning a five year run on ABC; CHEYENNE is moved to Monday at the end of the season.

CBS. *Series Premieres:* Adventure Showcase; Garry Moore Show; Invisible Man; Many Loves of Dobie Gillis; Peck's Bad Girl; Playhouse of Mystery; Stars in Action. *Key Programming Moves:* THE GARRY MOORE SHOW debuts in the 10–11 slot, which it occupied for five years; ARTHUR GODFREY AND HIS FRIENDS, cut back to 30 minutes, is moved to Tuesday, after eight years on Monday; it is cancelled in 4/59; TO TELL THE TRUTH is moved to Monday in 5/59; THE MANY LOVES OF DOBIE GILLIS debuts in 5/59; it stayed in the same time slot until 9/62.

NBC. *Series Premieres:* David Niven Show; Fanfare; George Burns Show; Jimmy Rodgers Show. *Key Programming Moves:* THE BOB CUMMINGS SHOW is cancelled at the end of the season.

1959–60

ABC. *Series Premieres:* Philip Marlowe.

CBS. *Series Premieres:* Dennis O'Keefe Show; Tightrope.

NBC. *Series Premieres:* Fibber McGee and Molly; Laramie; NBC Playhouse; Startime. *Key Programming Moves:* LARAMIE debuts in the 7:30–8:30 slot; it stays there for the next four years; In an attempt to revive the successful radio series, FIBBER McGEE AND MOLLY debuts; it is cancelled after four months.

1960–61

ABC. *Series Premieres:* Bugs Bunny; Expedition; Focus on America; Stagecoach West. *Key Programming Moves:* THE RIFLEMAN is moved to Monday at the end of the season; After six years, THE LIFE AND LEGEND OF WYATT EARP is cancelled at the end of the season.

CBS. *Series Premieres:* Tom Ewell Show.

NBC. *Series Premieres:* Purex Summer Specials; Thriller. *Key Programming Moves:* NBC offers only 2½ hours (7:30–10) of programming on Tuesday evenings; in July it returns to 3½ hours of programming; ALFRED HITCHCOCK PRESENTS is picked up from CBS and scheduled in the 8:30–9 slot, where it stays for two years.

1961–62

ABC. *Series Premieres:* Alcoa Premiere; Calvin and the Colonel; The New Breed; Yours for a Song. *Key Programming Moves:* BACHELOR FATHER is picked up from NBC; it is cancelled at the end of the season.

CBS. *Series Premieres:* Dick Van Dyke Show; Ichabod & Me; Password. *Key Programming Moves:* THE DICK VAN DYKE SHOW debuts; in January it is moved to Wednesday, where it became one of the most successful situation comedies of all time; it eventually ran for five years; After expanding the #1 rated GUNSMOKE to 60 minutes, CBS began airing reruns of the series on Tuesday in the 7:30–8 slot; it continued this practice for four years; THE MANY LOVES OF DOBIE GILLIS is moved to Wednesday at the end of the season.

NBC. *Series Premieres:* Cain's Hundred; Dick Powell Show. *Key Programming Moves:* At the end of the season, ALFRED HITCHCOCK PRESENTS is picked up by CBS for the second time.

1962–63

ABC. *Series Premieres:* Bell & Howell Close-Up; Combat. *Key Programming Moves:* COMBAT debuts; this war drama lasts for five years; HAWAIIAN EYE and THE UNTOUCHABLES are both moved to Tuesday; both are cancelled at the end of the season.

CBS. *Series Premieres:* Lloyd Bridges Show. *Key Programming Moves:* THE RED SKELTON SHOW is expanded to one hour; After 12 years on Sunday, THE JACK BENNY SHOW is moved to Tuesday.

NBC. *Series Premieres:* Empire; Report from. . . . *Key Programming Moves:* LARAMIE is cancelled at the end of the season.

1963-64

ABC. *Series Premieres:* The Fugitive; The Greatest Show on Earth. *Key Programming Moves:* THE FUGITIVE debuts in the 10-11 slot; it stayed in this slot until the end of its run in 8/67; McHALE'S NAVY is moved to Tuesday, 8:30-9, where it stayed until 8/66.

CBS. *Series Premieres:* High Adventure; Petticoat Junction. *Key Programming Moves:* PETTICOAT JUNCTION debuts; it runs until 9/70; THE GARRY MOORE SHOW is cancelled in June; THE JACK BENNY SHOW is picked up by NBC at the end of the season.

NBC. *Series Premieres:* Mr. Novak; Moment of Fear; Redigo; Richard Boone Show; You Don't Say. *Key Programming Moves:* NBC offers an entirely different Tuesday lineup from the previous season; it doesn't fare too well.

1964-65

ABC. *Series Premieres:* Peyton Place; The Tycoon. *Key Programming Moves:* PEYTON PLACE debuts on Tuesday and Thursday; this series became the most successful prime time soap opera in the history of television, running for five years.

CBS. *Series Premieres:* World War One.

NBC. *Series Premieres:* Cloak of Mystery; Hullabaloo; Man from U.N.C.L.E. *Key Programming Moves:* Capitalizing on the success of the James Bond phenomenon, NBC offers up THE MAN FOR U.N.C.L.E., which made its debut in September; in January, it was moved to Monday; NBC also capitalized on the growing popularity of rock music by offering HULLABALOO; THAT WAS THE WEEK THAT WAS was cancelled in 5/65.

1965-66

ABC. *Series Premieres:* F Troop. *Key Programming Moves:* McHALE'S NAVY is cancelled at the end of the season.

CBS. *Series Premieres:* Daktari. *Key Programming Moves:* RAWHIDE is moved to Tuesday; it is cancelled in January; CBS REPORTS is scheduled in the 10-11 slot, where it continued until 9/71; DAKTARI debuts; this adventure series lasts for 3½ years.

NBC. *Series Premieres:* My Mother, the Car; Please Don't Eat the Daisies. *Key Programming Moves:* NBC begins airing theatrical motion pictures in the 9-11 slot, a practice it continues until 9/71; DR. KILDARE is cancelled at the end of the season.

1966-67

ABC. *Series Premieres:* The Invaders; Love on a Rooftop; The Pruitts of Southampton; The Rounders. *Key Programming Moves:* COMBAT and THE FUGITIVE were cancelled at the end of the season.

NBC. *Series Premieres:* Girl from U.N.C.L.E.; Occasional Wife. *Key Programming Moves:* THE GIRL FROM U.N.C.L.E. debuts; it is a spin-off from THE MAN FROM U.N.C.L.E.; it never catches on and is cancelled at the end of the season.

1967-68

ABC. *Series Premieres:* Garrison's Gorillas; It Takes a Thief; N.Y.P.D. *Key Programming Moves:* IT TAKES A THIEF debuts in January; series is popular at first, but gradually loses its audience.

CBS. *Series Premieres:* Good Morning World.

NBC. *Series Premieres:* Jerry Lewis Show; Showcase '68. *Key Programming Moves:* I DREAM OF JEANNIE is moved to Tuesday, 7:30-8.

1968-69

ABC. *Series Premieres:* Dick Cavett Show; Mod Squad; That's Life. *Key Programming Moves:* THE MOD SQUAD debuts; series lasts for five years.

CBS. *Series Premieres:* Doris Day Show; Lancer; 60 Minutes. *Key Programming Moves:* THE DORIS DAY SHOW debuts; it is moved to Monday at the end of the season, where it has a successful four year run; 60 MINUTES debuts; this newsmagazine series alternated with CBS REPORTS for three years; it was eventually placed in the 7-8 slot on Sunday, where it became a tremendous ratings success; it continues to occupy the 7-8 slot on Sunday to the present time.

NBC. *Series Premieres:* Julia. *Key Programming Moves:* JULIA debuts; this was one of the first series that featured a black actress in a leading role; it lasted until 5/71; STAR TREK is moved to Tuesday in June, and is cancelled at the end of the season.

1969-70

ABC. *Series Premieres:* Marcus Welby, MD. *Key Programming Moves:* MARCUS WELBY, MD debuts; this series becomes the most successful series that ABC ever had to that time; it occupied the 10–11 slot during its entire run, until 4/76; ABC began airing made-for-tv films in the 8:30–10 slot, which it continued until 8/75.

CBS. *Series Premieres:* Governor & J.J. *Key Programming Moves:* THE RED SKELTON SHOW is cancelled by CBS in June; it was out of the Tuesday night lineup for the first time since the 1953–54 season; NBC subsequently picked it up.

NBC. *Series Premieres:* Debbie Reynolds Show. *Key Programming Moves:* I DREAM OF JEANNIE is cancelled after a five year run.

1970–71

ABC. *Key Programming Moves:* MARCUS WELBY, MD becomes the first ABC series to be the highest rated series on television.

CBS. *Series Premieres:* All in the Family. *Key Programming Moves:* BEVERLY HILLBILLIES, GREEN ACRES and HEE HAW are moved to Tuesday; all are cancelled at the end of the season; ALL IN THE FAMILY debuts in January; it is moved to Saturday in July, and becomes one of the most successful and important series in the history of television; ALL IN THE FAMILY elevated the status of the situation comedy form; it broke many taboos, made liberal use of language, and dealt with serious issues; it's characters had histories, and many millions of Americans followed their lives and stories every week for eight years; 60 MINUTES is moved to Sunday in June; CBS REPORTS is discontinued as a regular series at the end of the season.

NBC. *Series Premieres:* Don Knotts Show; Make Your Own Kind of Music. *Key Programming Moves:* JULIA is cancelled in 5/71; NBC stops airing films at the end of the season and returns to weekly series.

1971–72

ABC. *Key Programming Moves:* THE MOD SQUAD is moved to Thursday at the end of the season.

CBS. *Series Premieres:* Cannon; Jerry Reed Show; John Byner Show. *Key Programming Moves:* HAWAII FIVE-O is moved to Tuesday, where it stayed for the next five years; CANNON debuts; it is moved to Wednesday at the end of the season; it stays on the air for five years; CBS does not offer programming in the 10:30–11 slot during the 1971–72 season.

NBC. *Series Premieres:* Funny Side; Sarge; Search for the Nile. *Key Programming Moves:* NBC offers an entirely different Tuesday lineup from the previous season; two months into the season the entire lineup is altered again; In May, reruns of BONANZA are aired Tuesday, 7:30–8:30, in addition to new episodes airing on Sundays.

1972–73

ABC. *Series Premieres:* Temperature's Rising. *Key Programming Moves:* In compliance with the FCC's new Prime Time Access Rule, ABC (as well as, CBS and NBC) cuts prime time programming back to three hours (8–11).

CBS. *Series Premieres:* Maude. *Key Programming Moves:* CBS also cuts back to three hours of prime time programming; MAUDE debuts; the first of five spin-offs from ALL IN THE FAMILY, this series follows in the tradition of the original, with episodes high on quality and controversy; the series stays on CBS for six years.

NBC. *Series Premieres:* America; NBC Reports. *Key Programming Moves:* NBC also cuts back to three hours of prime time programming; BONANZA is moved from Sunday to Tuesday; it is cancelled in 1/73.

1973–74

ABC. *Series Premieres:* Happy Days. *Key Programming Moves:* HAPPY DAYS debuts in January in the 8–8:30 slot, which it occupied until 9/83; this series formed the foundation for ABC's strong Tuesday night lineup for the rest of the 1970s.

CBS. *Series Premieres:* Hawkins; Shaft. *Key Programming Moves:* MAUDE is moved to Monday at the end of the season.

NBC. *Series Premieres:* Chase; The Magician; Police Story. *Key Programming Moves:* POLICE STORY debuts; this series resurrected the anthology form; it lasted until 8/77; In January, ADAM 12 is moved into the 8–8:30 slot.

1974–75

ABC. *Key Programming Moves:* ABC discontinues its Tuesday night made-for-tv movies at the end of the season.

CBS. *Key Programming Moves:* CBS moves GOOD TIMES, M*A*S*H, and BARNABY JONES to Tuesday; of these, only GOOD TIMES continues on Tuesday during the following season; HAWAII FIVE-O is moved to Friday at the end of the season.

NBC. *Key Programming Moves:* ADAM 12 is cancelled at the end of the season after seven years on NBC.

1975-76

ABC. *Series Premieres:* Family; Laverne & Shirley; Welcome Back Kotter. *Key Programming Moves:* WELCOME BACK KOTTER debuts; in January, it is moved to Thursday; LAVERNE & SHIRLEY debuts in January; this spin-off from HAPPY DAYS is scheduled right after the original; LAVERNE & SHIRLEY will occupy this slot (8:30-9) for most of the next seven years; MARCUS WELBY, MD is cancelled in April, after a seven year run.

CBS. *Series Premieres:* Beacon Hill; Bugs Bunny; I've Got a Secret; Joe & Sons; One Day at a Time; Popi; Switch. *Key Programming Moves:* ONE DAY AT A TIME debuts in December, beginning a highly successful 10 year run; M*A*S*H is moved back to Tuesday in December.

NBC. *Series Premieres:* City of Angels; Joe Forrester. *Key Programming Moves:* In November, POLICE WOMAN is moved to Tuesday, 9-10.

1976-77

ABC. *Series Premieres:* Eight Is Enough; Rich Man, Poor Man. *Key Programming Moves:* HAPPY DAYS becomes the higest rated series on television; LAVERNE & SHIRLEY is rated #2; RICH MAN, POOR MAN debuts; this limited series was extremely successful; it was one of the earliest "miniseries"; based on its success, many others followed, including a sequel (RICH MAN, POOR MAN—BOOK 2).

CBS. *Series Premieres:* Who's Who. *Key Programming Moves:* In January, KOJAK is moved to Tuesday for the rest of the season.

NBC. *Series Premieres:* Baa Baa Black Sheep. *Key Programming Moves:* POLICE STORY is cancelled at the end of the season.

1977-78

ABC. *Series Premieres:* Having Babies; Soap; 20/20. *Key Programming Moves:* THREE'S COMPANY is moved to Tuesday, 9-9:30; ABC's Tuesday night lineup has the three highest rated series on television— LAVERNE & SHIRLEY, HAPPY DAYS, and THREE'S COMPANY; SOAP debuts; this series was a comedic parody of soap operas; it lasted four years; 20/20 debuts in June; this was ABC's most successful newsmagazine; it was moved to Thursday at the end of the season, and is still on the air.

CBS. *Series Premieres:* Challenge of the Sexes; Fitzpatricks; Lou Grant; Sam. *Key Programming Moves:* LOU GRANT debuts; after a short stint on Tuesday, it is moved to Monday, where it lasted for five years;

In January, M*A*S*H and ONE DAY AT A TIME are moved to other nights; CBS fills the vacated 9–11 slot with films; it has continued this practice, off and on, to the present time; In April, CBS ceased airing regular series in the 8–9 slot, opposite HAPPY DAYS and LAVERNE & SHIRLEY; instead they aired specials for the rest of the season.

NBC. *Series Premieres:* Chuck Barris Rah Rah Show; Mulligan's Stew; Richard Pryor Show. *Key Programming Moves:* In January, NBC schedules THE BIG EVENT on Tuesday, in addition to its Sunday airing.

1978–79

ABC. *Series Premieres:* Detective School; Taxi. *Key Programming Moves:* TAXI debuts in the 9:30–10 slot, completing a two-hour block of situation comedies; LAVERNE & SHIRLEY and THREE'S COMPANY are the two highest rated series on television; HAPPY DAYS is sixth, and TAXI is tenth; STARSKY & HUTCH is moved to Tuesday, and is cancelled at the end of the season; LAVERNE & SHIRLEY is moved to Thursday, 8–8:30 in July.

CBS. *Series Premieres:* Paper Chase.

NBC. *Series Premieres:* Cliff Hangers; Grandpa Goes to Washington. *Key Programming Moves:* CLIFF HANGERS debuts in February; series was comprised of three separate serialized storylines that ended each week with a "cliff-hanger"; it was cancelled four months later.

1979–80

ABC. *Series Premieres:* Goodtime Girls; Lazarus Syndrome; One in a Million. *Key Programming Moves:* ANGIE is moved into LAVERNE & SHIRLEY's former slot; in February, LAVERNE & SHIRLEY is returned to its original 8:30–9 Tuesday slot, though it never did recapture its audience; HART TO HART is moved into the 10–11 slot in October, where it stays until 7/84.

CBS. *Series Premieres:* California Fever.

NBC. *Series Premieres:* Big Show; Misadventures of Sheriff Lobo; United States. *Key Programming Moves:* NBC's BIG EVENT simply becomes a film slot in 1979–80; UNITED STATES debuts; this series was touted to be the next "mega-hit" prior to its debut, but the 10:30–11 time slot and the lackluster scripts and acting insured that it wouldn't be; it lasted less than three months.

1980-81

ABC. *Series Premieres:* Too Close for Comfort. *Key Programming Moves:* In November, TAXI is moved to Wednesday; it is replaced with TOO CLOSE FOR COMFORT.

CBS. *Series Premieres:* That's My Line; Universe. *Key Programming Moves:* UNIVERSE debuts; this science series marked Walter Cronkite's return to television (he had recently retired as CBS' nightly news anchorman); the series aired for two summers.

NBC. *Series Premieres:* Barbara Mandrell & Mandrell Sisters; Flamingo Road; Steve Allen Show. *Key Programming Moves:* In November, NBC returned to programming regular series on Tuesday night; BARBARA MANDRELL & MANDRELL SISTERS debuts; this attempt at reviving the variety form was fairly successful; while the series was moved out of Tuesday night after only one month, it lasted for two years, which was longer than any variety series in many years; HILL STREET BLUES is moved to Tuesday for the rest of the season.

1981-82

CBS. *Series Premieres:* Book of Lists; QED; Simon & Simon. *Key Programming Moves:* SIMON & SIMON debuts; series has been on and off CBS' schedule until 8/88.

NBC. *Series Premieres:* Bret Maverick; Father Murphy.

1982-83

ABC. *Key Programming Moves:* LAVERNE & SHIRLEY is cancelled in 5/83.

CBS. *Series Premieres:* Ace Crawford; Bring 'Em Back Alive; Gun Shy; On the Road; Our Times. *Key Programming Moves:* ON THE ROAD debuts as a summer series, based on Charles Kuralt's features for the CBS EVENING NEWS; it is not continued beyond the summer.

NBC. *Series Premieres:* A-Team; Bare Essence; Gavilon; St. Elsewhere. *Key Programming Moves:* ST. ELSEWHERE debuts; this series was the second from the makers of HILL STREET BLUES; it is highly praised by the critics, but is only marginally successful with audiences; it does manage to stay on the air until 8/88; THE A-TEAM debuts; this action-adventure series is a surprising success; it is panned by critics and parent groups as "too violent" but manages to attract a sizable audience until 6/87.

1983–84

ABC. *Series Premieres:* AKA Pablo; Foul-Ups, Bloops & Blunders; Just Our Luck; Oh Madeline; Shaping Up. *Key Programming Moves:* HAPPY DAYS is moved to Thursday in May; it is subsequently cancelled in July; THREE'S COMPANY and HART TO HART are cancelled at the end of the season.
CBS. *Series Premieres:* American Parade.
NBC. *Series Premieres:* Bay City Blues; Riptide.

1984–85

ABC. *Series Premieres:* Hail to the Chief; Jessie; Magruder & Loud; Moonlighting; Paper Dolls; Three's a Crowd. *Key Programming Moves:* THREE'S A CROWD debuts; this spin-off from THREE'S COMPANY doesn't live up to expectations and is cancelled at the end of the season; WHO'S THE BOSS is moved to Tuesday, where it continues to air to the present; MOONLIGHTING debuts in March as a limited series; it is very successful and returns the following season in the 9–10 slot, where it has stayed to the present time.
CBS. *Series Premieres:* Lucie Arnaz Show; West 57th. *Key Programming Moves:* THE JEFFERSONS and ALICE are cancelled in July.

1985–86

ABC. *Series Premieres:* Growing Pains; Our Family Honor. *Key Programming Moves:* GROWING PAINS debuts; it becomes a top 10 hit, and continues to the present time.
CBS. *Series Premieres:* Melba; Morning Star/Evening Star.
NBC. *Series Premieres:* 1986; Stingray. *Key Programming Moves:* THE A-TEAM is moved to Friday at the end of the season.

1986–87

ABC. *Series Premieres:* Jack & Mike; Max Headroom.
CBS. *Series Premieres:* Night Heat; Spies; Wizard.
NBC. *Series Premieres:* Matlock. *Key Programming Moves:* MATLOCK debuts; Andy Griffith returns to weekly television in this courtroom series; the series continues to the present time; HILL STREET BLUES is moved to Tuesday and is cancelled in 5/87.

1987–88

ABC. *Series Premieres:* Just the 10 of Us; Thirtysomething; The Wonder Years. *Key Programming Moves:* THIRTYSOMETHING debuts; this series about "yuppies" won the Emmy award as the best dramatic series on television; THE WONDER YEARS debuts as a limited series in March; this series won the Emmy award for the best comedy series, and will return as a regular series.

CBS. *Series Premieres:* Coming of Age; 48 Hours; Jake & the Fatman; Law & Harry McGraw; Summer Playhouse; Trial & Error. *Key Programming Moves:* 48 HOURS debuts; this series, produced by CBS NEWS and anchored by Dan Rather, is an hour-long cinema-verite look at a single topic.

NBC. *Series Premieres:* In the Heat of the Night; JJ Starbuck; Summer Showcase. *Key Programming Moves:* IN THE HEAT OF THE NIGHT debuts in March; it marks Carroll O'Connor's return to weekly television; the series catches on and is renewed for the following season.

Wednesday Night
September 1948 – August 1988

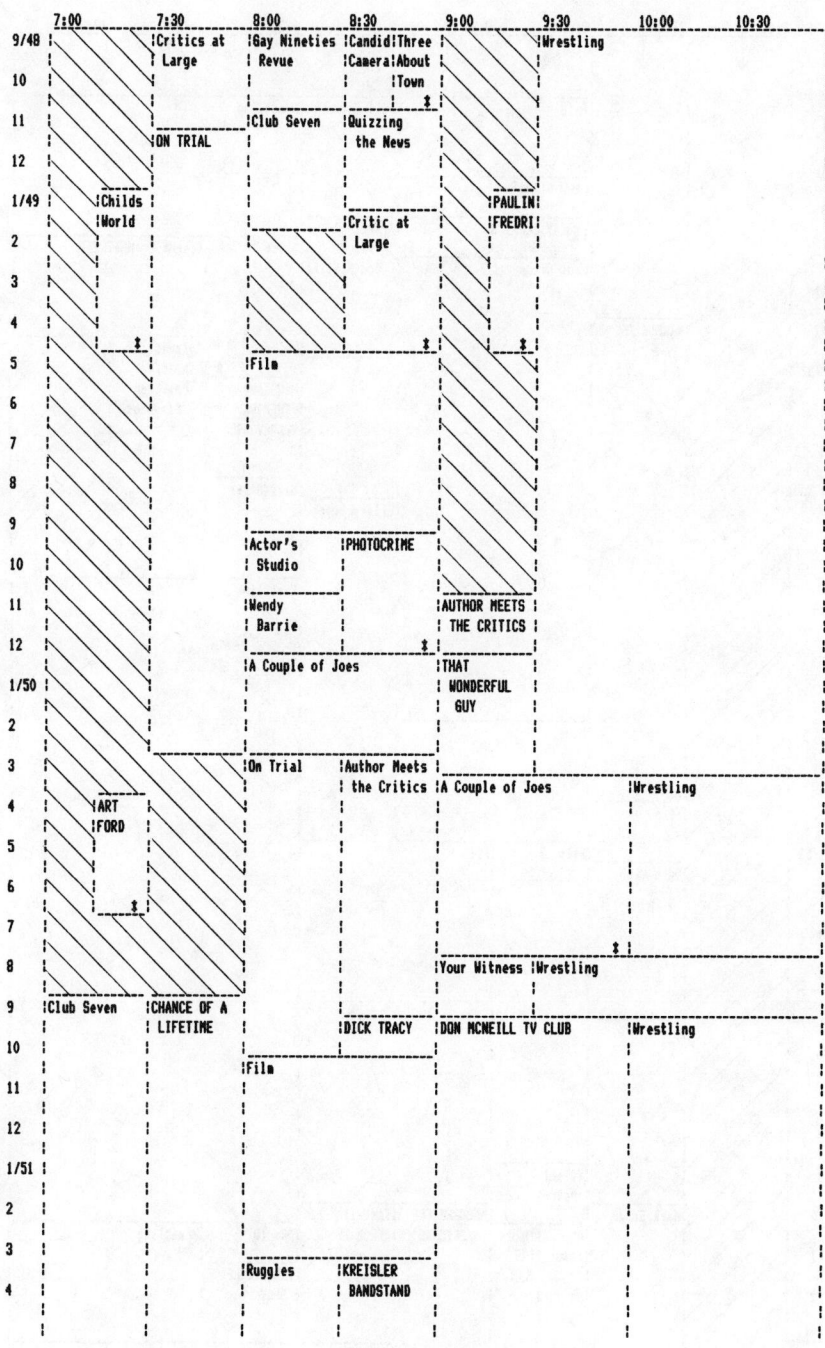

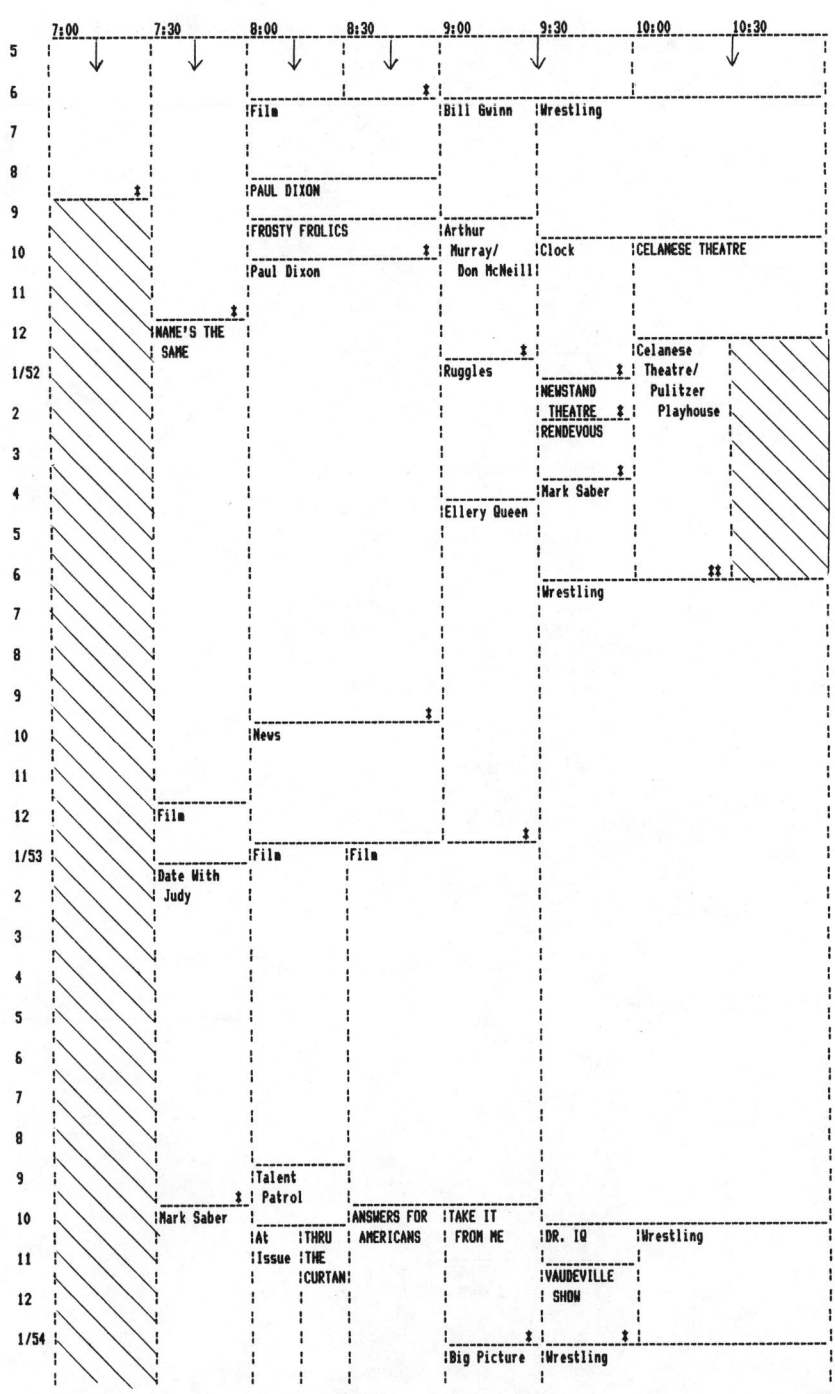

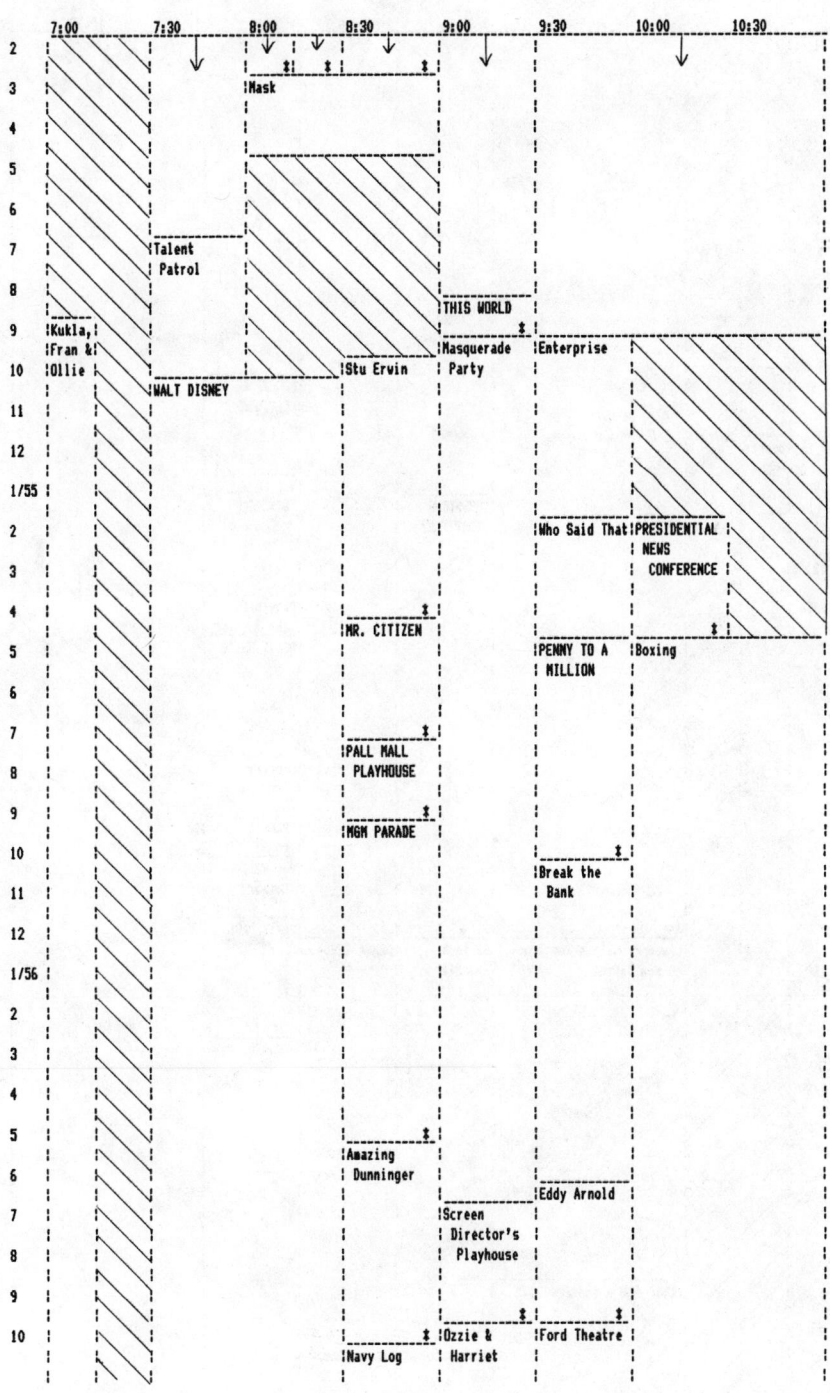

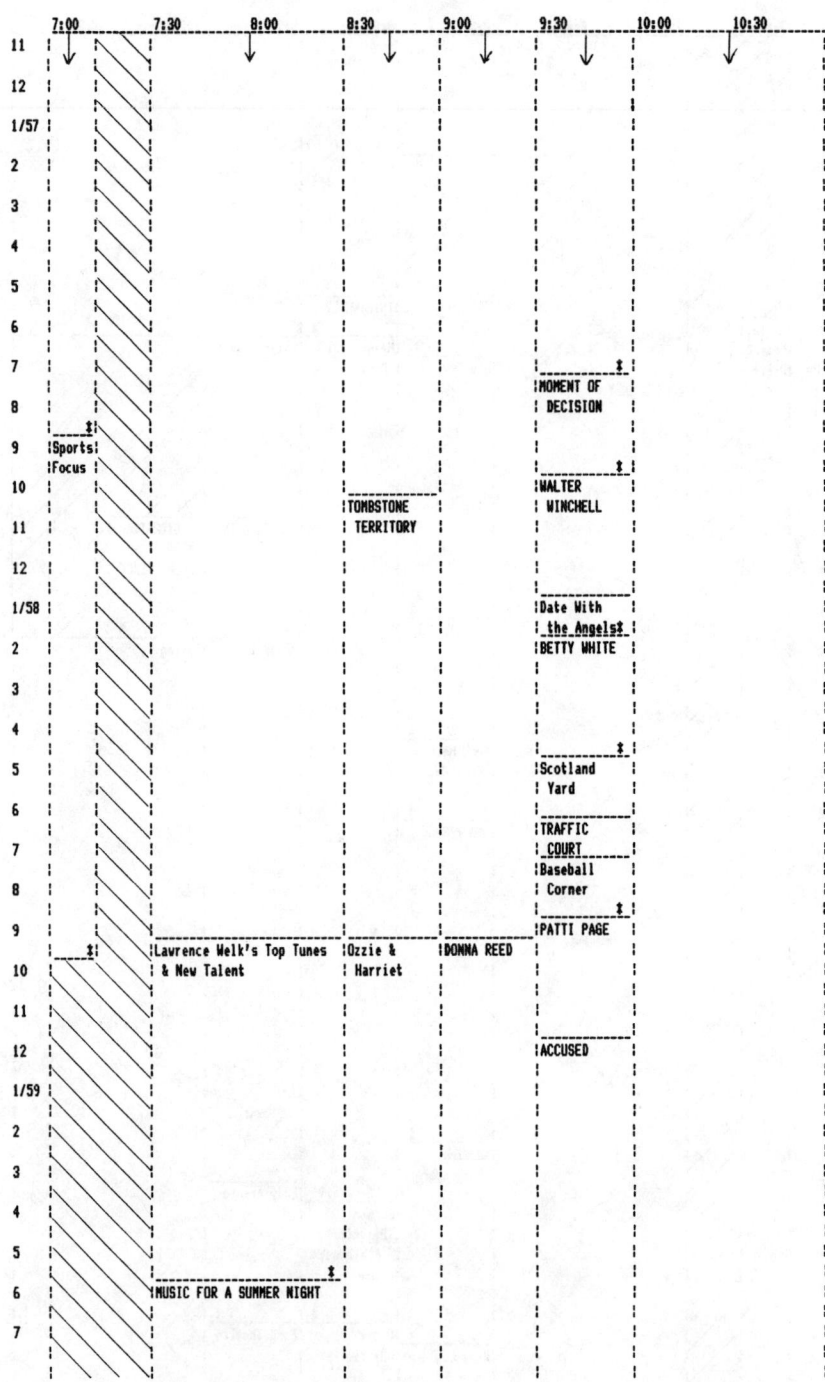

	7:00	7:30	8:00	8:30	9:00	9:30	10:00	10:30
11								
12								
1/57								
2								
3								
4								
5								
6								
7								
8						MOMENT OF DECISION		
9	Sports Focus							
10				TOMBSTONE TERRITORY		WALTER WINCHELL		
11								
12								
1/58						Date With the Angels / BETTY WHITE		
2								
3								
4								
5						Scotland Yard		
6						TRAFFIC COURT		
7						Baseball Corner		
8								
9						PATTI PAGE		
10		Lawrence Welk's Top Tunes & New Talent		Ozzie & Harriet	DONNA REED			
11								
12						ACCUSED		
1/59								
2								
3								
4								
5								
6		MUSIC FOR A SUMMER NIGHT						
7								

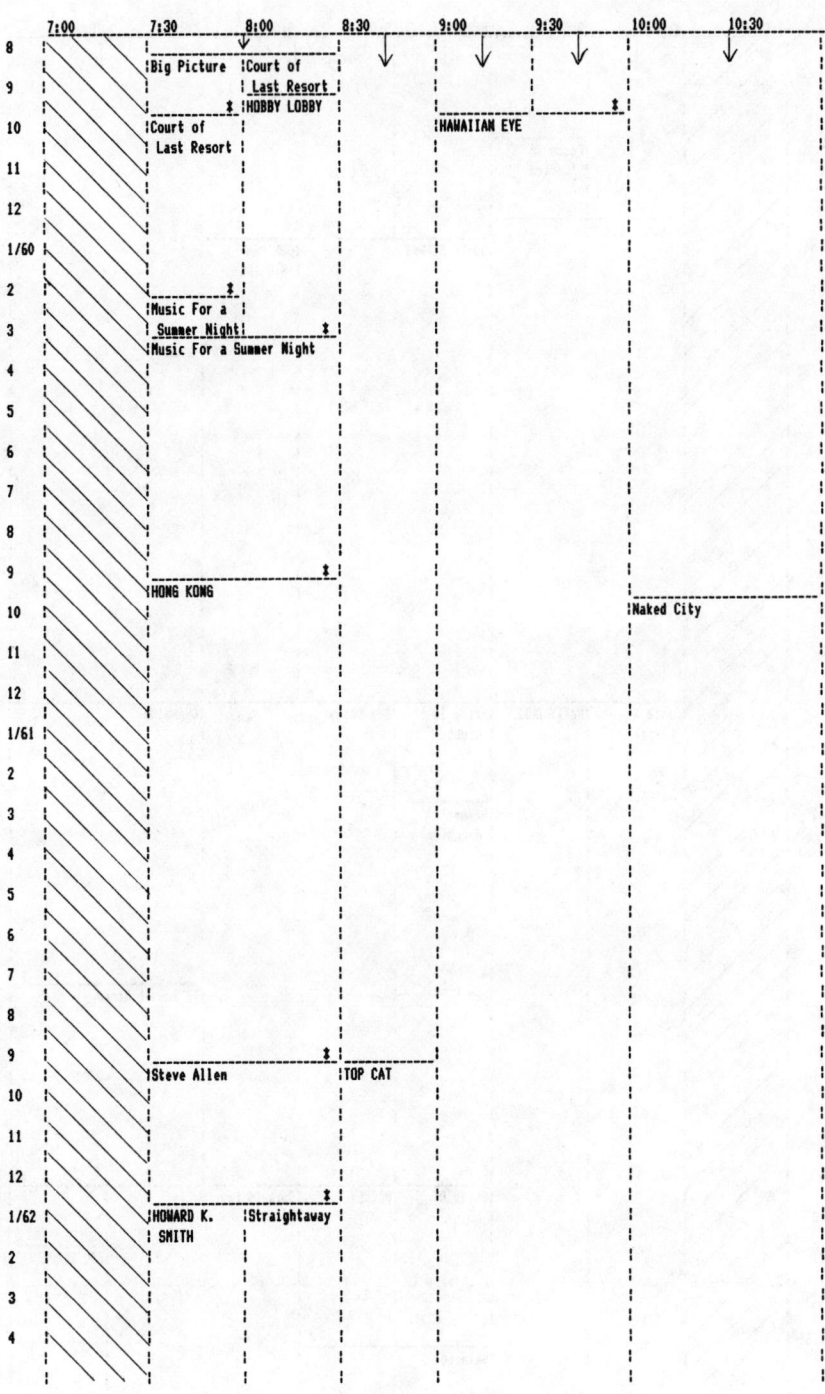

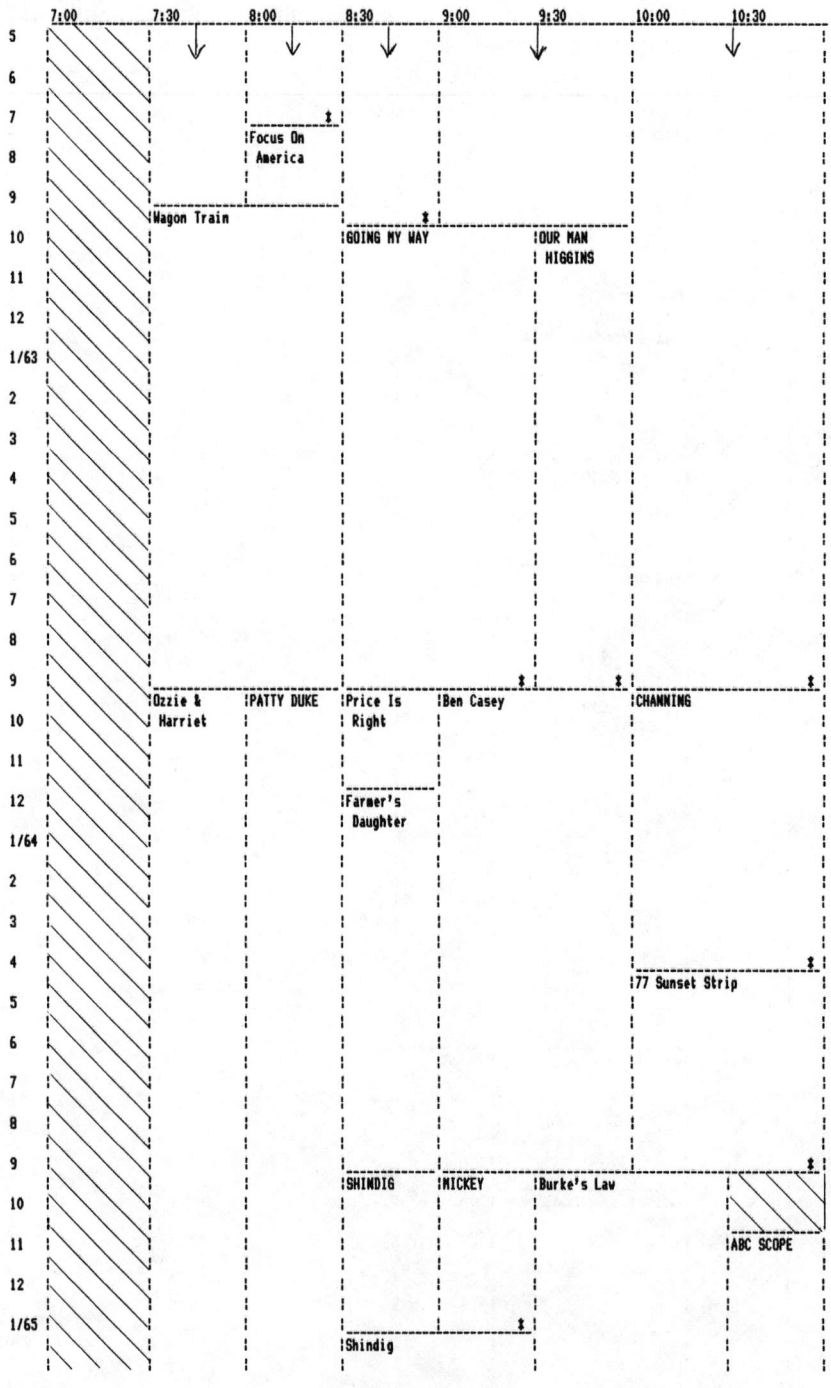

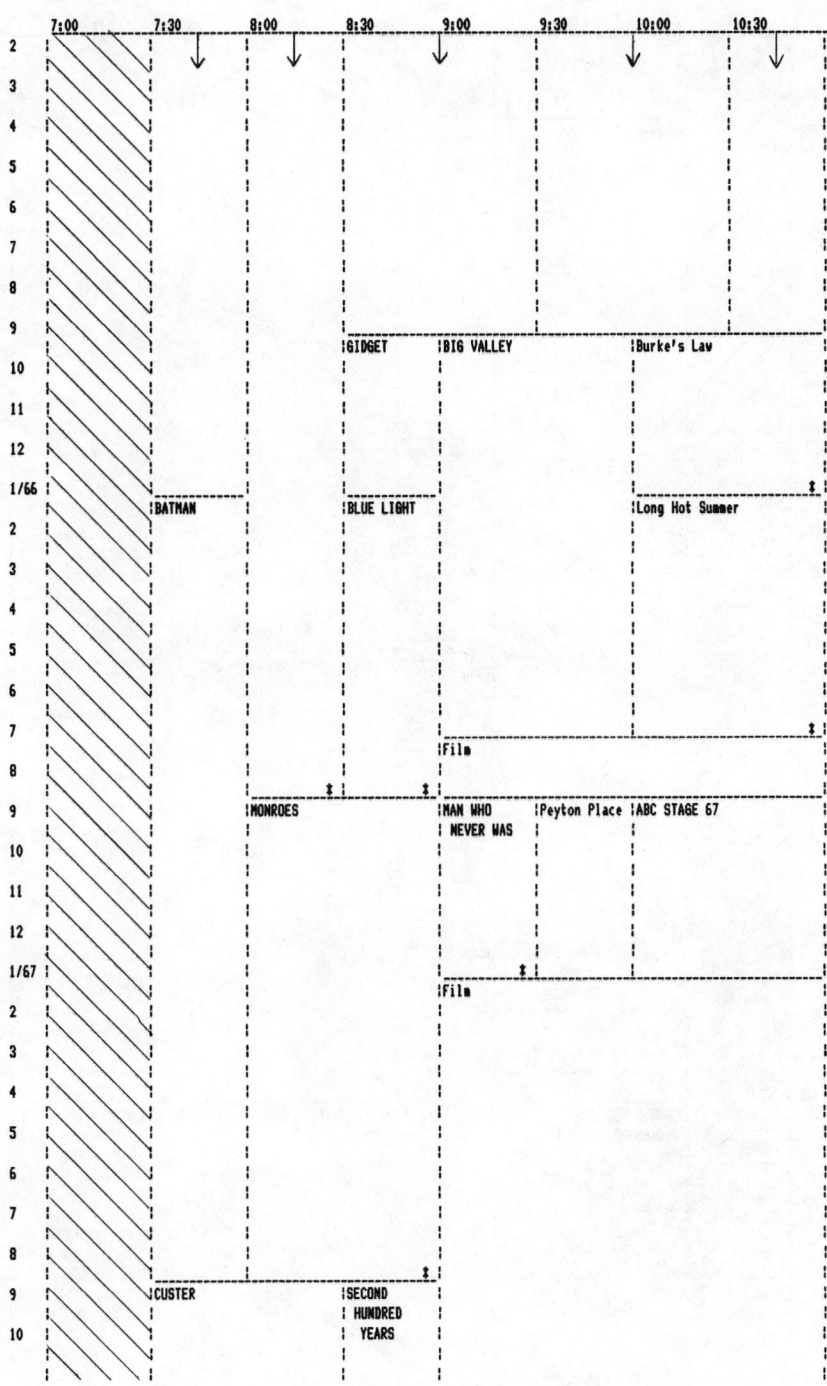

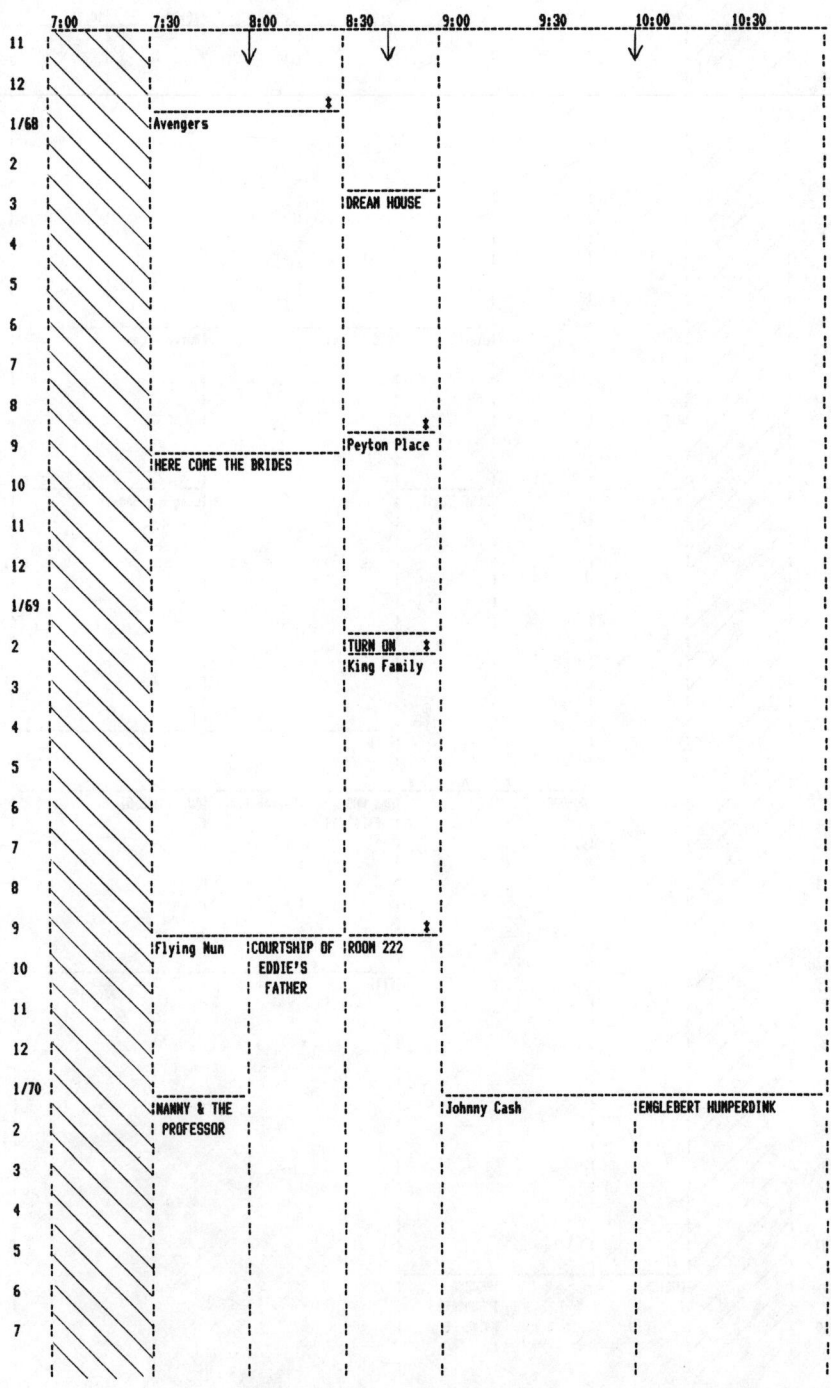

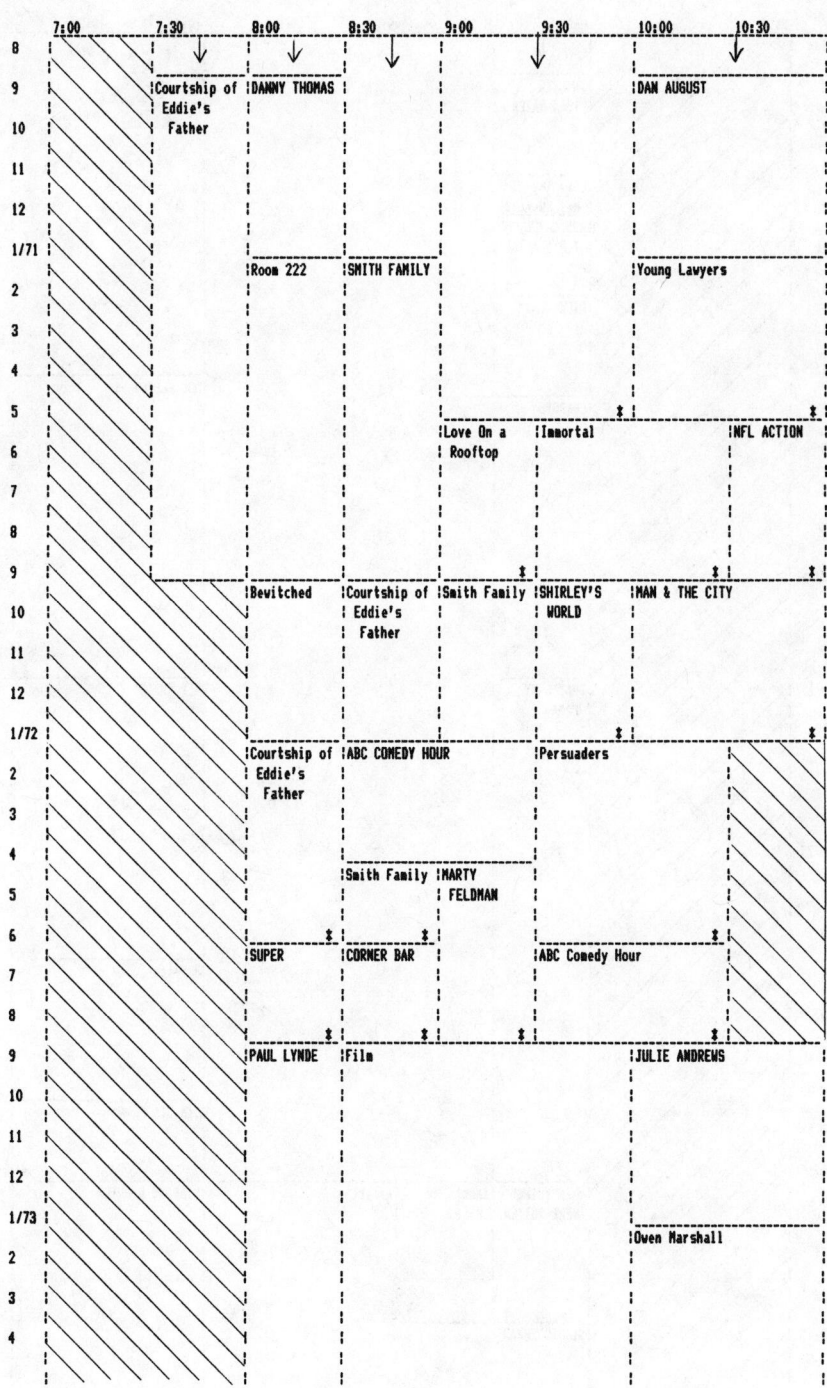

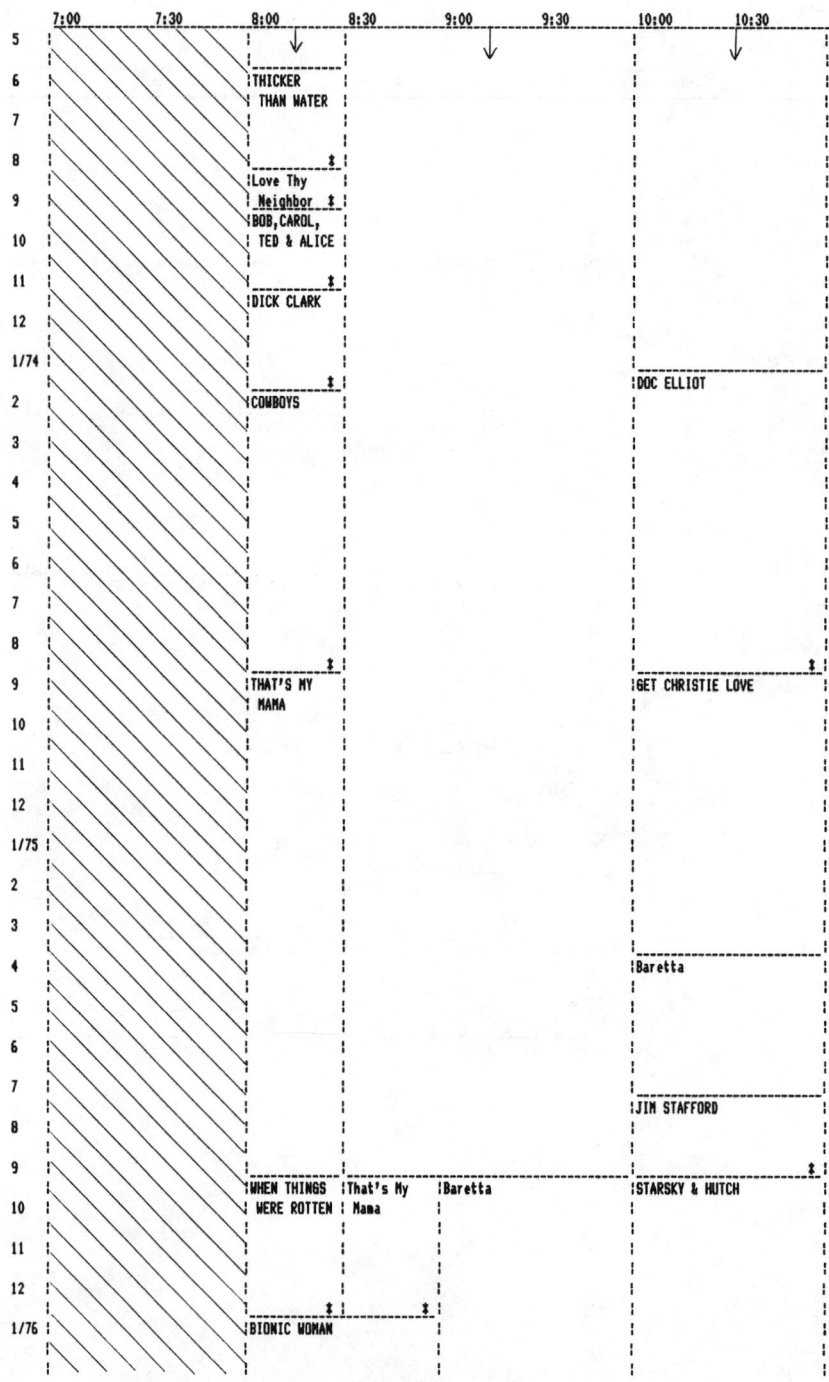

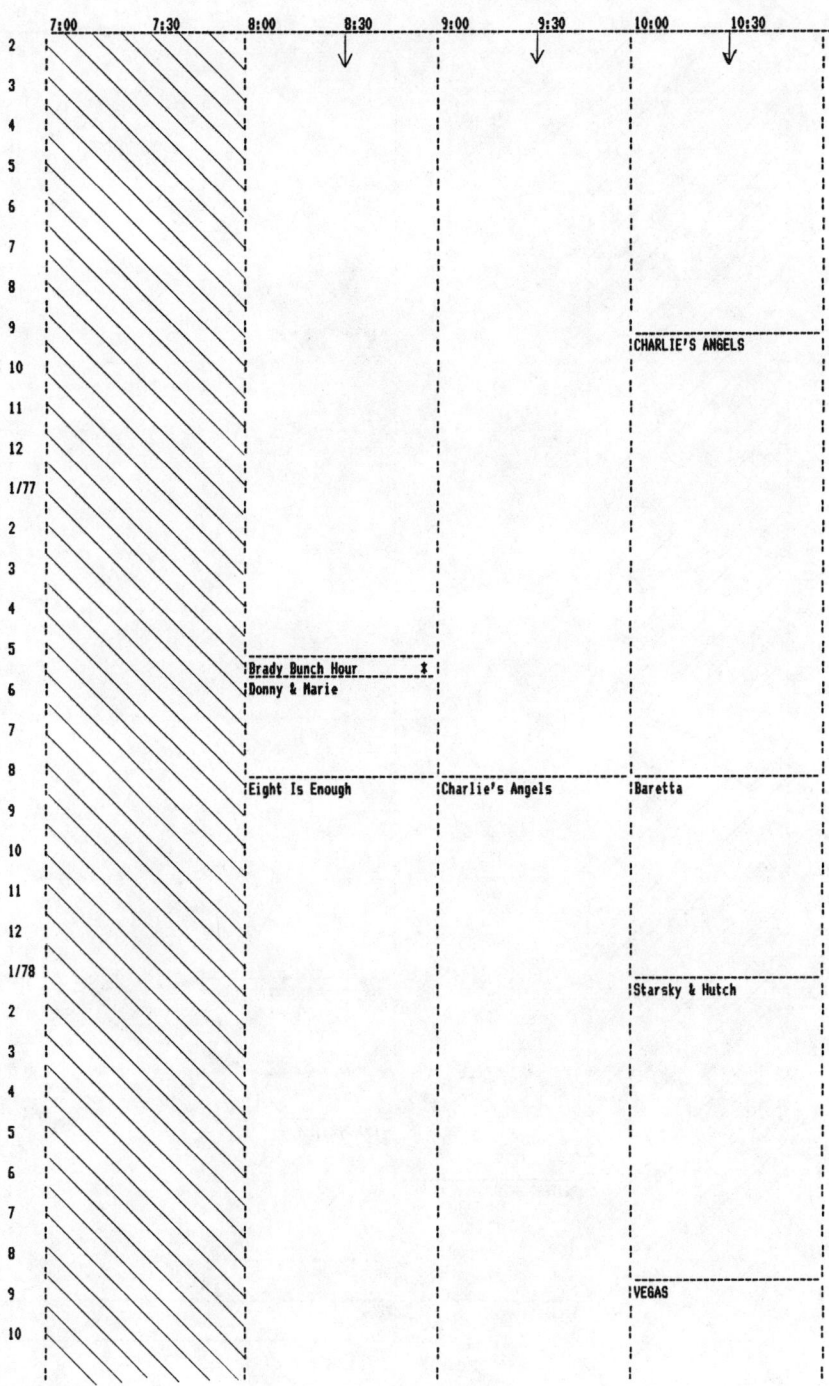

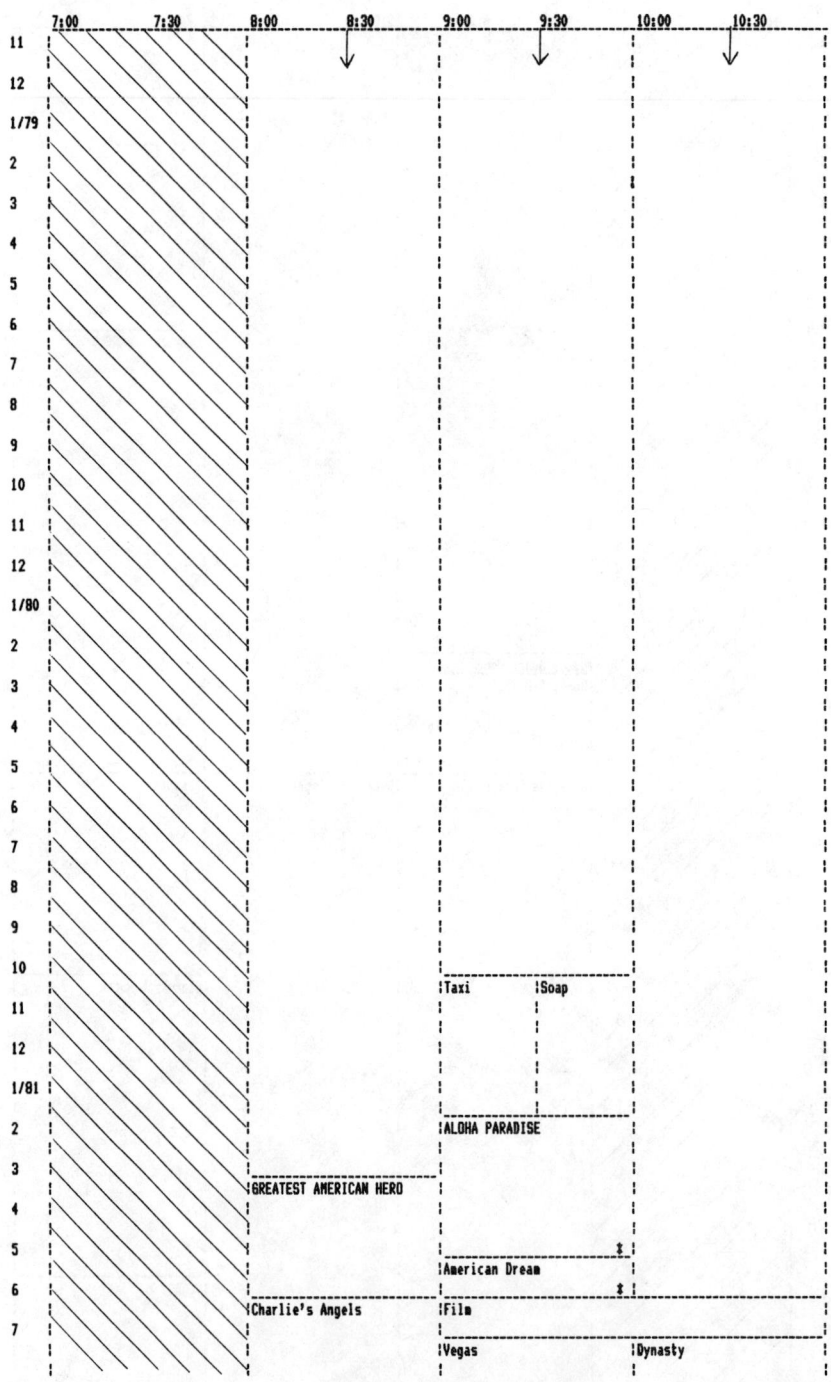

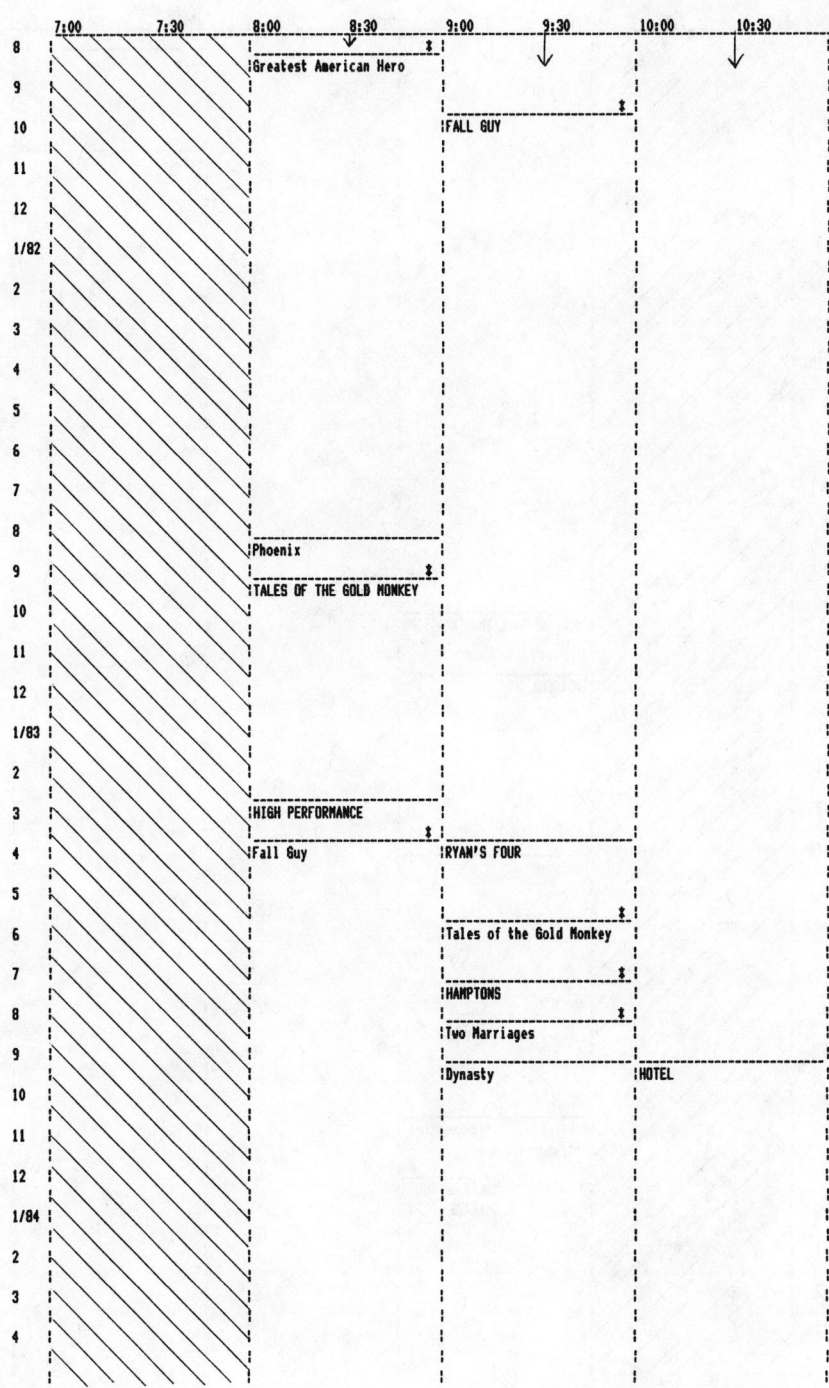

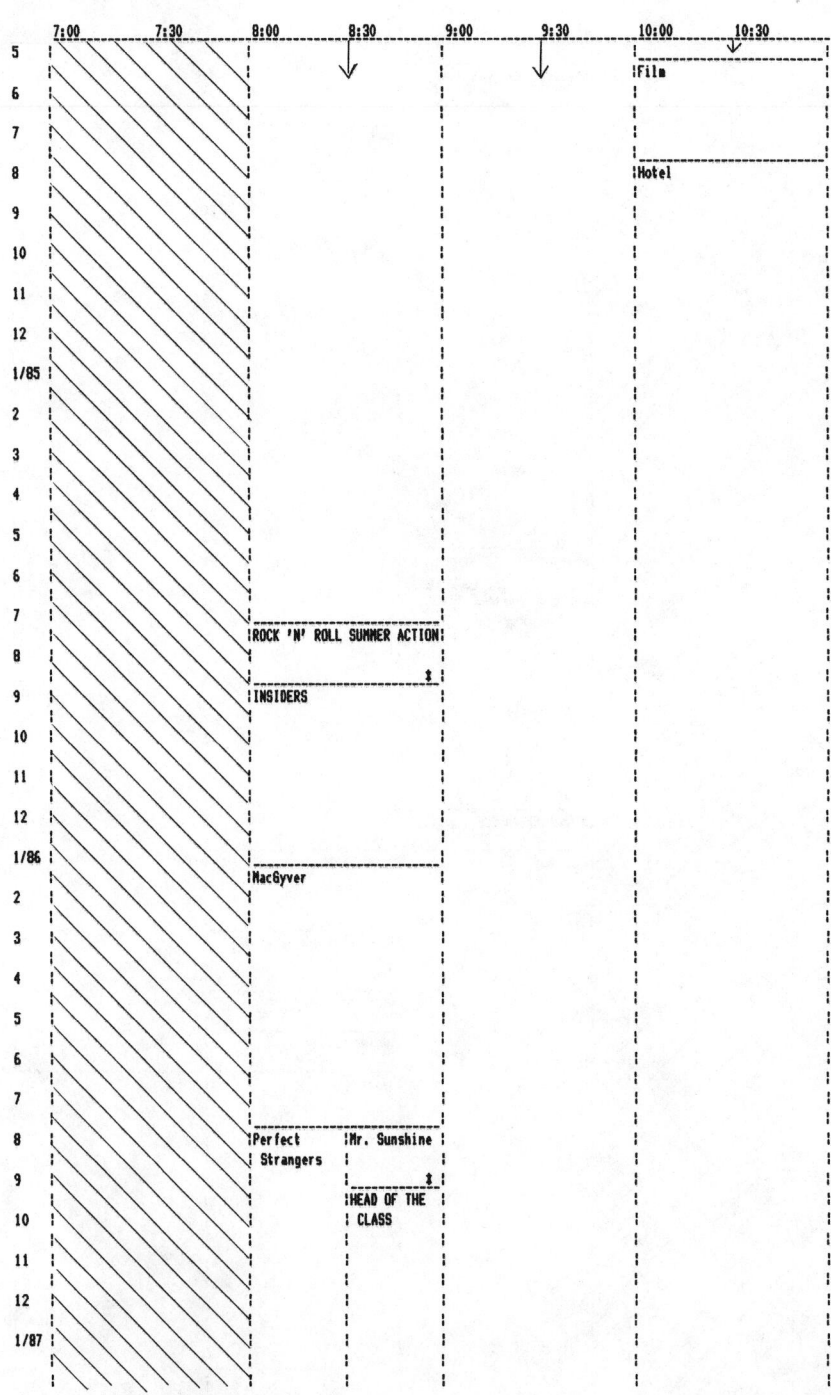

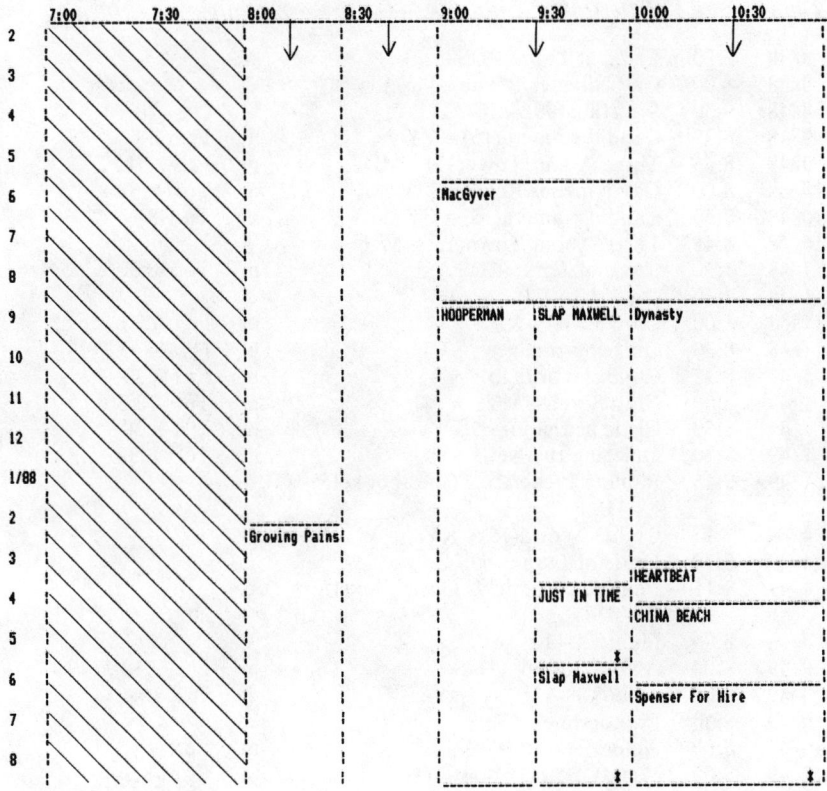

Date	Time	Title (min. if not 30) — Type	Action	From/To
8/48	7:30	Critic at Large—DS	d	
8/48	8:00	Gay Nineties Revue—MV	d	
8/48	9:30	Wrestling(90)—SP	s	
9/48	8:30	Candid Camera(15)—CY	m	Fr:n-8
9/48	8:45	Three About Town(15)—MU	m	Fr:w-7:15
10/48	8:00	Gay Nineties Revue—MV	m	To:f-8:30
10/48	8:30	Candid Camera(15)—CY	m	To:f-8
10/48	8:45	Three About Town(15)—MU	c	
11/48	7:30	Critic at Large—DS	m	To:r-8:30
11/48	7:30	On Trial—DB	d	
11/48	8:00	Club Seven—MV	m	Fr:r-8:30
11/48	8:30	Quizzing the News—QU	m	Fr:m-8
1/49	7:15	Child's World(15)—KV	m	Fr:t-7:30
1/49	8:00	Club Seven—MV	m	To:r-10:30
1/49	8:30	Critic at Large—DS	m	Fr:r-8:30
1/49	8:30	Quizzing the News—QU	m	To:s-8:30
1/49	9:15	Pauline Frederick's Guestbook(15)—IV	d	
4/49	7:15	Child's World(15)—KV	c	
4/49	8:30	Critic at Large—DS	c	
4/49	9:15	Pauline Frederick's Guestbook(15)—IV	c	
5/49	8:00	Film(60)—FI	s	
9/49	8:00	Actors Studio—DA	m	Fr:r-9:30-5/49
9/49	8:00	Film(60)—FI	f	
9/49	8:30	Photocrime—CD	d	
10/49	8:00	Actors Studio—DA	m	To:t-9
11/49	8:00	Wendy Barrie Show—IV	m	Fr:m-8:30
11/49	9:00	Author Meets the Critics—DS	m	Fr:m-7:30
12/49	8:00	A Couple of Joes(60)—VY	d	
12/49	8:00	Wendy Barrie Show—IV	m	To:r-9
12/49	8:30	Photocrime—CD	c	
12/49	9:00	Author Meets the Critics—DS	m	To:r-9:30
12/49	9:00	That Wonderful Guy—SC	d	
2/50	7:30	On Trial—DB	m	To:w-8
2/50	8:00	A Couple of Joes(60)—VY	m	To:w-9
3/50	8:00	On Trial—DB	m	Fr:var
3/50	8:30	Author Meets the Critics—DS	m	Fr:r-9:30
3/50	9:00	A Couple of Joes(60)—VY	m	Fr:w-8
3/50	9:00	That Wonderful Guy—SC	m	To:f-8:30
3/50	9:30	Wrestling(90)—SP	f	
3/50	10:00	Wrestling(60)—SP	s	
4/50	7:15	Art Ford on Broadway(15)—IV	d	
6/50	7:15	Art Ford on Broadway(15)—IV	c	
7/50	9:00	A Couple of Joes(60)—VY	c	
7/50	10:00	Wrestling(60)—SP	f	
8/50	9:00	Your Witness—CR	m	Fr:n-9-5/50
8/50	9:30	Wrestling(90)—SP	s	
9/50	7:00	Club Seven—MV	m	Fr:r-10:30-3/49
9/50	7:30	Chance of a Lifetime—QU	d	

Date	Time	Title (min. if not 30) — Type	Action	From/To
9/50	8:00	On Trial — DB	m	To:m-9:30
9/50	8:30	Author Meets the Critics — DS	m	To:r-10:30-3/52(d)
9/50	8:30	Dick Tracy — CD	d	
9/50	9:00	Don McNeill TV Club(60) — VY	d	
9/50	9:00	Your Witness — CR	c	
9/50	9:30	Wrestling(90) — SP	f	
9/50	10:00	Wrestling(60) — SP	s	
10/50	8:00	Film(60) — FI	s	
10/50	8:30	Dick Tracy — CD	m	To:m-8:30
12/50	7:00	Andy and Della Russell(5) — MU	d	
3/51	8:00	Film(60) — FI	f	
3/51	8:00	Ruggles — SC	m	Fr:m-8:30
3/51	8:30	Kreisler Bandstand — MU	d	
6/51	7:00	Andy and Della Russell(5) — MU	c	
6/51	8:00	Film(60) — FI	s	
6/51	8:00	Ruggles — SC	m	To:f-8:30
6/51	8:30	Kreisler Bandstand — MU	c	
6/51	9:00	Bill Gwinn Show — QU	m	Fr:m-8:30
6/51	9:00	Don McNeill TV Club(60) — VY	m	To:w-9-9/51
6/51	9:30	Wrestling(90) — SP	s	
6/51	10:00	Wrestling(60) — SP	f	
8/51	7:00	Club Seven — MV	c	
8/51	8:00	Film(60) — FI	f	
8/51	8:00	Paul Dixon(60) — VY	d	
9/51	8:00	Frosty Frolics(60) — MV	d	
9/51	8:00	Paul Dixon(60) — VY	m	To:m-9
9/51	9:00	Arthur Murray Party — MV	m	Fr:m-9-6/51
9/51	9:00	Bill Gwinn Show — QU	m	To:m-10
9/51	9:00	Don McNeill TV Club — VY	m	Fr:w-9-6/51
9/51	9:30	Wrestling(90) — SP	f	
10/51	8:00	Frosty Frolics(60) — MV	c	
10/51	8:00	Paul Dixon(60) — VY	m	Fr:m-9
10/51	9:30	Clock — SA	m	Fr:f-8:30-8/51(n)
10/51	10:00	Celanese Theatre(60) — DA	d	
11/51	7:30	Chance of a Lifetime — QU	c	
12/51	7:30	Name's the Same — QU	d	
12/51	9:00	Arthur Murray Party — MV	m	To:n-9
12/51	9:00	Don McNeill TV Club — VY	c	
12/51	10:00	Celanese Theatre(60) — DA	m	To:w-10
12/51	10:00	Celanese Theatre — DA	m	Fr:w-10
12/51	10:00	Pulitzer Prize Playhouse — DA	m	Fr:f-9-6/51
1/52	9:00	Ruggles — SC	m	Fr:f-8:30-9/51
1/52	9:30	Clock — SA	c	
1/52	9:30	Newsstand Theatre — DA	d	
2/52	9:30	Newsstand Theatre — DA	c	
2/52	9:30	Rendezvous — SD	d	
3/52	9:30	Rendezvous — SD	c	
4/52	9:00	Adventures of Ellery Queen — CD	m	Fr:n-7:30
4/52	9:00	Ruggles — SC	m	To:r-8
4/52	9:30	Mark Saber — CD	m	Fr:f-8

Date	Time	Title (min. if not 30) – Type	Action	From/To
6/52	9:30	Mark Saber – CD	m	To:m-8-10/52
6/52	9:30	Wrestling(90) – SP	s	
6/52	10:00	Celanese Theatre – DA	c	
6/52	10:00	Pulitzer Prize Playhouse – DA	c	
9/52	8:00	Paul Dixon(60) – VY	c	
10/52	8:00	News(60) – NW	s	
11/52	7:30	Name's the Same – QU	m	To:t-10:30
12/52	7:30	Film – FI	s	
12/52	8:00	News(60) – NW	f	
12/52	9:00	Adventures of Ellery Queen – CD	c	
1/53	7:30	Film – FI	f	
1/53	7:30	A Date with Judy – SC	m	Fr:r-8
1/53	8:00	Film – FI	s	
1/53	8:30	Film(60) – FI	s	
8/53	8:00	Film – FI	f	
9/53	7:30	A Date with Judy – SC	c	
9/53	8:00	Talent Patrol – TA	m	Fr:m-8
9/53	8:30	Film(60) – FI	f	
10/53	7:30	Mark Saber – CD	m	Fr:m-8-6/53
10/53	8:00	At Issue(15) – IV	m	Fr:n-9-8/53
10/53	8:00	Talent Patrol – TA	m	To:s-8
10/53	8:15	Through the Curtain(15) – DS	d	
10/53	8:30	Answers for Americans – DS	d	
10/53	9:00	Take It from Me – SC	d	
10/53	9:30	Doctor I.Q. – QU	d	
10/53	9:30	Wrestling(90) – SP	f	
10/53	10:00	Wrestling(60) – SP	s	
11/53	9:30	Doctor I.Q. – QU	m	To:r-9
12/53	9:30	Vaudeville Show – MV	d	
1/54	9:00	Big Picture – DO	m	Fr:m-9:30
1/54	9:00	Take It from Me – SC	c	
1/54	9:30	Vaudeville Show – MV	c	
1/54	9:30	Wrestling(90) – SP	s	
1/54	10:00	Wrestling(60) – SP	f	
2/54	8:00	At Issue(15) – IV	c	
2/54	8:15	Through the Curtain(15) – DS	c	
2/54	8:30	Answers for Americans – DS	c	
3/54	8:00	Mask(60) – CD	s	
4/54	8:00	Mask(60) – CD	f	
6/54	7:30	Mark Saber – CD	m	To:f-9:30-12/55
7/54	7:30	Talent Patrol – TA	m	Fr:r-8
8/54	9:00	Big Picture – DO	m	To:n-8:30
8/54	9:00	This World – 1954 – DO	d	
9/54	7:00	Kukla, Fran & Ollie(15) – KV	m	Fr:m-f-7-6/52(n)
9/54	9:00	Masquerade Party – QU	m	Fr:m-9:30(c)
9/54	9:00	This World – 1954 – DO	c	
9/54	9:30	Wrestling(90) – SP	f	
10/54	7:30	Talent Patrol – TA	m	To:n-9:30
10/54	7:30	Walt Disney(60) – VS	d	
10/54	8:30	Stu Erwin – SC	m	Fr:f-7:30

Date	Time	Title (min. if not 30) — Type	Action	From/To
10/54	9:30	Enterprise — DO	m	Fr:s-8
1/55	9:30	Enterprise — DO	m	To:r-8:30-7/57
2/55	9:30	Who Said That? — QU	m	Fr:m-10:30-7/54(n)
2/55	10:00	President Eisenhower's News Conference — IV	d	
4/55	8:30	Mr. Citizen — DA	d	
4/55	8:30	Stu Erwin — SC	c	
4/55	9:30	Who Said That? — QU	m	To:t-8:30
5/55	9:30	Penny to a Million — QU	d	
5/55	10:00	President Eisenhower's News Conference — IV	c	
6/55	10:00	Boxing(60) — SP	s	
7/55	7:00	Soupy Sales(15) — KV	d*	
7/55	8:30	Mr. Citizen — DA	c	
7/55	8:30	Pall Mall Playhouse — WA	d	
8/55	7:00	Soupy Sales(15) — KV	c*	
9/55	8:30	MGM Parade — DO	d	
9/55	8:30	Pall Mall Playhouse — WA	c	
10/55	9:30	Break the Bank — QU	m	Fr:n-10
10/55	9:30	Penny to a Million — QU	c	
5/56	8:30	Amazing Dunninger — QU	m	Fr:s-8:30-9/55
5/56	8:30	MGM Parade — DO	c	
6/56	9:00	Masquerade Party — QU	m	To:s-10
6/56	9:30	Break the Bank — QU	m	To:t-10:30-10/56(n)
6/56	9:30	Eddy Arnold — MV	m	Fr:r-8
7/56	7:00	Jack Drees Sports(15) — SN	d*	
7/56	9:00	Screen Director's Playhouse — VS	m	Fr:w-8(n)
8/56	7:00	Jack Drees Sports(15) — SN	c*	
9/56	9:00	Screen Director's Playhouse — VS	c	
9/56	9:30	Eddy Arnold — MV	c	
10/56	8:30	Amazing Dunninger — QU	c	
10/56	8:30	Navy Log — DA	m	Fr:t-8:30(c)
10/56	9:00	Adventures of Ozzie & Harriet — SC	m	Fr:t-8-6/56
10/56	9:30	Ford Theatre — DA	m	Fr:r-9:30(n)
6/57	7:00	Sports Focus(15) — SN	d*	
7/57	7:00	Sports Focus(15) — SN	m*	To:m-f-7-9/57
7/57	9:30	Ford Theatre — DA	c	
7/57	9:30	Moment of Decision — DA	d	
7/57	10:45	Famous Fights(15) — SH	m	Fr:m-9:45-12/52(d)
8/57	7:00	Kukla, Fran & Ollie(15) — KV	c	
9/57	7:00	Sports Focus(15) — SN	m	Fr:m-f-7-7/57
9/57	9:30	Moment of Decision — DA	c	
10/57	8:30	Navy Log — DA	m	To:r-10
10/57	8:30	Tombstone Territory — WE	d	
10/57	9:30	Walter Winchell File — RA	d	
12/57	9:30	Walter Winchell File — RA	m	To:f-10
12/57	10:45	Famous Fights(15) — SH	c	
1/58	9:30	Date with the Angels — SC	m	Fr:f-9:30
1/58	9:30	Date with the Angels — SC	c	
2/58	9:30	Betty White Show — CV	d	

Date	Time	Title (min. if not 30) — Type	Action	From/To
4/58	9:30	Betty White Show — CV	c	
5/58	9:30	Scotland Yard — RA	m	Fr:n-10-3/58
6/58	9:30	Scotland Yard — RA	m	To:r-10-8/58
6/58	9:30	Traffic Court — CR	d	
7/58	9:30	Baseball Corner — ST	m	Fr:n-9
7/58	9:30	Traffic Court — CR	m	To:n-9
8/58	9:30	Baseball Corner — ST	c	
9/58	7:00	Sports Focus(15) — SN	c	
9/58	7:30	Lawrence Welk's Top Tunes and New Talent(60) — TA	m	Fr:m-9:30-6/58
9/58	7:30	Walt Disney(60) — VS	m	To:f-8
9/58	8:30	Adventures of Ozzie & Harriet — SC	m	Fr:w-9
9/58	8:30	Tombstone Territory — WE	m	To:f-9-3/59
9/58	9:00	Adventures of Ozzie & Harriet — SC	m	To:w-8:30
9/58	9:00	Donna Reed Show — SC	d	
9/58	9:30	Patti Page Olds Show — MV	d	
9/58	10:45	News(15) — NW	s	
11/58	9:30	Patti Page Olds Show — MV	m	To:m-10
12/58	9:30	Accused — CR	d	
5/59	7:30	Lawrence Welk's Top Tunes and New Talent(60) — TA	c	
5/59	10:45	News(15) — NW	f	
6/59	7:30	Music for a Summer Night(60) — MU	d	
8/59	7:30	Big Picture — DO	m	Fr:s-10
8/59	7:30	Music for a Summer Night(60) — MU	m	To:w-7:30-2/60
8/59	8:00	Court of Last Resort — CD	m	Fr:f-8-4/58
9/59	7:30	Big Picture — DO	c	
9/59	8:00	Court of Last Resort — CD	m	To:w-7:30
9/59	8:00	Hobby Lobby — CY	d	
9/59	9:00	Donna Reed Show — SC	m	To:r-8
9/59	9:30	Accused — CR	c	
10/59	7:30	Court of Last Resort — CD	m	Fr:w-8
10/59	9:00	Hawaiian Eye(60) — CD	d	
2/60	7:30	Court of Last Resort — CD	c	
2/60	7:30	Music for a Summer Night — MU	m	Fr:w-7:30-8/59
3/60	7:30	Music for a Summer Night — MU	m	To:w-7:30
3/60	7:30	Music for a Summer Night(60) — MU	m	Fr:w-7:30
3/60	8:00	Hobby Lobby — CY	c	
9/60	7:30	Hong Kong(60) — AD	d	
9/60	7:30	Music for a Summer Night(60) — MU	c	
9/60	10:00	Boxing(60) — SP	f	
10/60	10:00	Naked City(60) — CD	m	Fr:t-9:30-9/59
9/61	7:30	Hong Kong(60) — AD	c	
9/61	7:30	Steve Allen(60) — CV	m	Fr:m-10-6/60(n)
9/61	8:30	Adventures of Ozzie & Harriet — SC	m	To:r-7:30
9/61	8:30	Top Cat — KV	d	

Date	Time	Title (min. if not 30) — Type	Action	From/To
12/61	7:30	Steve Allen(60) — CV	c	
1/62	7:30	Howard K. Smith — NA	d	
1/62	8:00	Straightaway — AD	m	Fr:f-7:30
7/62	8:00	Focus on America — DO	m	Fr:t-7-9/61
7/62	8:00	Straightaway — AD	c	
9/62	7:30	Howard K. Smith — NA	m	To:n-10:30
9/62	7:30	Wagon Train(60) — WE	m	Fr:w-7:30(n)
9/62	8:00	Focus on America — DO	m	To:t-10:30-7/63
9/62	8:30	Top Cat — KV	c	
9/62	9:00	Hawaiian Eye(60) — CD	m	To:t-8:30
10/62	8:30	Going My Way(60) — CO	d	
10/62	9:30	Our Man Higgins — SC	d	
9/63	7:30	Adventures of Ozzie & Harriet — SC	m	Fr:r-7:30
9/63	7:30	Wagon Train(60) — WE	m	To:m-8:30
9/63	8:00	Patty Duke Show — SC	d	
9/63	8:30	Going My Way(60) — CO	c	
9/63	8:30	Price Is Right — QU	m	Fr:f-9:30(n)
9/63	9:00	Ben Casey(60) — MD	m	Fr:m-10
9/63	9:30	Our Man Higgins — SC	c	
9/63	10:00	Channing(60) — DR	d	
9/63	10:00	Naked City(60) — CD	c	
11/63	8:30	Price Is Right — QU	m	To:f-9:30
12/63	8:30	Farmer's Daughter — SC	m	Fr:f-9:30
4/64	10:00	Channing(60) — DR	c	
4/64	10:00	77 Sunset Strip(60) — CD	m	Fr:f-7:30-2/64
9/64	8:30	Farmer's Daughter — SC	m	To:f-8
9/64	8:30	Shindig — MU	d	
9/64	9:00	Ben Casey(60) — MD	m	To:m-10
9/64	9:00	Mickey — SC	d	
9/64	9:30	Burke's Law(60) — CD	m	Fr:f-8:30
9/64	10:00	77 Sunset Strip(60) — CD	c	
11/64	10:30	ABC Scope — DO	d	
1/65	8:30	Shindig — MU	m	To:w-8:30
1/65	8:30	Shindig(60) — MU	m	Fr:w-8:30
1/65	9:00	Mickey — SC	c	
9/65	8:30	Gidget — SC	d	
9/65	8:30	Shindig(60) — MU	m	To:rs-7:30
9/65	9:00	Big Valley(60) — WE	d	
9/65	9:30	Burke's Law(60) — CD	m	To:w-10
9/65	10:00	Burke's Law(60) — CD	m	Fr:w-9:30
9/65	10:30	ABC Scope — DO	m	To:s-10:30
1/66	7:30	Adventures of Ozzie & Harriet — SC	m	To:s-7:30
1/66	7:30	Batman — AD	d	
1/66	8:30	Blue Light — SD	d	
1/66	8:30	Gidget — SC	m	To:r-8
1/66	10:00	Burke's Law(60) — CD	c	
1/66	10:00	Long Hot Summer(60) — DR	m	Fr:r-10
7/66	9:00	Big Valley(60) — WE	m	To:m-10
7/66	9:00	Film(120) — FI	s	
7/66	10:00	Long Hot Summer(60) — DR	c	

Date	Time	Title (min. if not 30) — Type	Action	From/To
8/66	8:00	Patty Duke Show — SC	c	
8/66	8:30	Blue Light — SD	c	
8/66	9:00	Film(120) — FI	f	
9/66	8:00	Monroes(60) — WE	d	
9/66	9:00	Man Who Never Was — SD	d	
9/66	9:30	Peyton Place — SL	m	Fr:mtr-9:30
9/66	10:00	ABC Stage 67(60) — VS	d	
1/67	9:00	Man Who Never Was — SD	c	
1/67	9:00	Film(120) — FI	s	
1/67	9:30	Peyton Place — SL	m	To:mt-9:30
1/67	10:00	ABC Stage 67(60) — VS	m	To:r-10
8/67	7:30	Batman — AD	m	To:r-7:30
8/67	8:00	Monroes(60) — WE	c	
9/67	7:30	Custer(60) — WE	d	
9/67	8:30	Second Hundred Years — SC	d	
12/67	7:30	Custer(60) — WE	c	
1/68	7:30	Avengers(60) — SD	m	Fr:f-10-9/67
2/68	8:30	Second Hundred Years — SC	m	To:r-7:30
3/68	8:30	Dream House — QU	d	
8/68	8:30	Dream House — QU	c	
9/68	7:30	Avengers(60) — SD	m	To:m-7:30
9/68	7:30	Here Come the Brides(60) — CO	d	
9/68	8:30	Peyton Place — SL	m	Fr:mr-9:30
1/69	8:30	Peyton Place — SL	m	To:m-9
2/69	8:30	King Family — MV	m	Fr:s-8-1/66
2/69	8:30	Turn-On — CV	d	
2/69	8:30	Turn-On — CV	c	
9/69	7:30	Flying Nun — SC	m	Fr:r-7:30
9/69	7:30	Here Come the Brides(60) — CO	m	To:f-9
9/69	8:00	Courtship of Eddie's Father — SC	d	
9/69	8:30	King Family — MV	c	
9/69	8:30	Room 222 — SC	d	
1/70	7:30	Flying Nun — SC	m	To:f-7:30
1/70	7:30	Nanny and the Professor — SC	d	
1/70	9:00	Johnny Cash(60) — MV	m	Fr:s-9:30-9/69
1/70	9:00	Film(120) — FI	f	
1/70	10:00	Engelbert Humperdinck(60) — MV	d	
7/70	9:00	Johnny Cash Presents the Everly Brothers(60) — MV	d*	
8/70	7:30	Nanny and the Professor — SC	m	To:f-8
8/70	10:00	Engelbert Humperdinck(60) — MV	m	To:s-9:30
9/70	7:30	Courtship of Eddie's Father — SC	m	Fr:w-8
9/70	8:00	Courtship of Eddie's Father — SC	m	To:w-7:30
9/70	8:00	Danny Thomas Show — SC	d	
9/70	9:00	Johnny Cash Presents the Everly Brothers(60) — MV	c*	
9/70	10:00	Dan August(60) — CD	d	
1/71	8:00	Danny Thomas Show — SC	m	To:r-9
1/71	8:00	Room 222 — SC	m	Fr:w-8:30
1/71	8:30	Room 222 — SC	m	To:w-8

Date	Time	Title (min. if not 30) — Type	Action	From/To
1/71	8:30	Smith Family — DR	d	
1/71	10:00	Dan August(60) — CD	m	To:r-9:30
1/71	10:00	Young Lawyers(60) — LD	m	Fr:m-7:30
5/71	9:00	Johnny Cash(60) — MV	c	
5/71	9:00	Love on a Rooftop — SC	m	Fr:r-9:30-8/67
5/71	9:30	Immortal(60) — AD	m	Fr:r-10-1/71
5/71	10:00	Young Lawyers(60) — LD	c	
5/71	10:30	NFL Action — SH	d	
9/71	7:30	Courtship of Eddie's Father — SC	m	To:w-8:30
9/71	8:00	Bewitched — SC	m	Fr:r-8:30
9/71	8:00	Room 222 — SC	m	To:f-9
9/71	8:30	Courtship of Eddie's Father — SC	m	Fr:w-7:30
9/71	8:30	Smith Family — DR	m	To:w-9
9/71	9:00	Love on a Rooftop — SC	c	
9/71	9:00	Smith Family — DR	m	Fr:w-8:30
9/71	9:30	Immortal(60) — AD	c	
9/71	9:30	Shirley's World — SC	d	
9/71	10:00	Man and the City(60) — DR	d	
9/71	10:30	NFL Action — SH	c	
1/72	8:00	Bewitched — SC	m	To:s-8
1/72	8:00	Courtship of Eddie's Father — SC	m	Fr:w-8:30
1/72	8:30	ABC Comedy Hour(60) — CV	d	
1/72	8:30	Courtship of Eddie's Father — SC	m	To:w-8
1/72	9:00	Smith Family — DR	m	To:w-8:30-4/72
1/72	9:30	Persuaders(60) — AD	m	Fr:s-10
1/72	9:30	Shirley's World — SC	c	
1/72	10:00	Man and the City(60) — DR	c	
4/72	8:30	ABC Comedy Hour(60) — CV	m	To:w-9:30-6/72
4/72	8:30	Smith Family — DR	m	Fr:w-9-1/72
4/72	9:00	Marty Feldman Comedy Machine — CV	d	
6/72	8:00	Courtship of Eddie's Father — SC	c	
6/72	8:00	Super — SC	d	
6/72	8:30	Corner Bar — SC	d	
6/72	8:30	Smith Family — DR	c	
6/72	9:30	ABC Comedy Hour(60) — CV	m	Fr:w-8:30-4/72
6/72	9:30	Persuaders(60) — AD	c	
8/72	8:00	Super — SC	c	
8/72	8:30	Corner Bar — SC	m	To:f-9:30-8/73
8/72	9:00	Marty Feldman Comedy Machine — CV	c	
8/72	9:30	ABC Comedy Hour(60) — CV	c	
9/72	8:00	Paul Lynde — SC	d	
9/72	8:30	Film(90) — FI	s	
9/72	10:00	Julie Andrews Hour(60) — MV	d	
1/73	10:00	Julie Andrews Hour(60) — MV	m	To:s-9
1/73	10:00	Owen Marshall, Counselor at Law (60) — LD	m	Fr:r-10
5/73	8:00	Paul Lynde — SC	m	To:s-8:30
6/73	8:00	Thicker Than Water — SC	d	

Date	Time	Title (min. if not 30) — Type	Action	From/To
8/73	8:00	Love Thy Neighbor — SC	m	Fr:f-9:30
8/73	8:00	Thicker Than Water — SC	c	
9/73	8:00	Bob & Carol & Ted & Alice — SC	d	
9/73	8:00	Love Thy Neighbor — SC	c	
11/73	8:00	Bob & Carol & Ted & Alice — SC	c	
11/73	8:00	Dick Clark Presents the Rock & Roll Years — MU	d	
1/74	8:00	Dick Clark Presents the Rock & Roll Years — MU	c	
1/74	10:00	Doc Elliot(60) — MD	d	
1/74	10:00	Owen Marshall, Counselor at Law (60) — LD	m	To:s-10
2/74	8:00	Cowboys — WE	d	
8/74	8:00	Cowboys — WE	c	
8/74	10:00	Doc Elliot(60) — MD	c	
9/74	8:00	That's My Mama — SC	d	
9/74	10:00	Get Christie Love(60) — CD	d	
3/75	10:00	Get Christie Love(60) — CD	m	To:f-10
4/75	10:00	Baretta(60) — CD	m	Fr:f-10
7/75	10:00	Baretta(60) — CD	m	To:w-9-9/75
7/75	10:00	Jim Stafford Show(60) — CV	d	
9/75	8:00	That's My Mama — SC	m	To:w-8:30
9/75	8:00	When Things Were Rotten — SC	d	
9/75	8:30	Film(90) — FI	f	
9/75	8:30	That's My Mama — SC	m	Fr:w-8
9/75	9:00	Baretta(60) — CD	m	Fr:w-10-7/75
9/75	10:00	Jim Stafford Show(60) — CV	c	
9/75	10:00	Starsky and Hutch(60) — CD	d	
12/75	8:00	When Things Were Rotten — SC	c	
12/75	8:30	That's My Mama — SC	c	
1/76	8:00	Bionic Woman(60) — AD	d	
9/76	10:00	Charlie's Angels(60) — CD	d	
9/76	10:00	Starsky and Hutch(60) — CD	m	To:s-9
5/77	8:00	Bionic Woman(60) — AD	m	To:s-8-9/77(n)
5/77	8:00	Brady Bunch Hour(60) — CV	m	Fr:m-8
5/77	8:00	Brady Bunch Hour(60) — CV	c	
6/77	8:00	Donny and Marie(60) — MV	m	Fr:f-8
8/77	8:00	Donny and Marie(60) — MV	m	To:f-8
8/77	8:00	Eight Is Enough(60) — CO	m	Fr:t-9-5/77
8/77	9:00	Baretta(60) — CD	m	To:w-10
8/77	9:00	Charlie's Angels(60) — CD	m	Fr:w-10
8/77	10:00	Baretta(60) — CD	m	Fr:w-9
8/77	10:00	Charlie's Angels(60) — CD	m	To:w-9
1/78	10:00	Baretta(60) — CD	m	To:r-10
1/78	10:00	Starsky and Hutch(60) — CD	m	Fr:s-9
8/78	10:00	Starsky and Hutch(60) — CD	m	To:t-10
9/78	10:00	Vegas(60) — CD	d	
10/80	9:00	Charlie's Angels(60) — CD	m	To:n-8
10/80	9:00	Taxi — SC	m	Fr:t-9:30
10/80	9:30	Soap — SC	m	Fr:r-9:30-3/80

Date	Time	Title (min. if not 30) — Type	Action	From/To
1/81	9:00	Taxi — SC	m	To:r-9:30
1/81	9:30	Soap — SC	m	To:m-10-4/81
2/81	9:00	Aloha Paradise(60) — CO	d	
3/81	8:00	Eight Is Enough(60) — CO	m	To:s-8
3/81	8:00	Greatest American Hero(60) — AD	d	
5/81	9:00	American Dream(60) — DR	m	Fr:m-9
5/81	9:00	Aloha Paradise(60) — CO	c	
6/81	8:00	Charlie's Angels(60) — CD	m*	Fr:s-8-2/81
6/81	8:00	Greatest American Hero(60) — AD	m	To:w-8-8/81
6/81	9:00	American Dream(60) — DR	c	
6/81	9:00	Film(120) — FI	s	
6/81	10:00	Vegas(60) — CD	m	To:w-9-8/81
7/81	9:00	Film(120) — FI	f	
7/81	9:00	Vegas(60) — CD	m	Fr:w-10-6/81
7/81	10:00	Dynasty(60) — SL	m	Fr:m-9-4/81
8/81	8:00	Charlie's Angels(60) — CD	c*	
8/81	8:00	Greatest American Hero(60) — AD	m	Fr:w-8-6/81
9/81	9:00	Vegas(60) — CD	c	
10/81	9:00	Fall Guy(60) — AD	d	
8/82	8:00	Greatest American Hero(60) — AD	m	To:f-9
8/82	8:00	Phoenix(60) — SF	m	Fr:f-9-4/82
9/82	8:00	Phoenix(60) — SF	c	
9/82	8:00	Tales of the Gold Monkey(60) — AD	d	
2/83	8:00	Tales of the Gold Monkey(60) — AD	m	To:f-10
3/83	8:00	High Performance(60) — AD	d	
3/83	8:00	High Performance(60) — AD	c	
3/83	9:00	Fall Guy(60) — AD	m	To:w-8
4/83	8:00	Fall Guy(60) — AD	m	Fr:w-9
4/83	9:00	Ryan's Four(60) — MD	d	
5/83	9:00	Ryan's Four(60) — MD	c	
6/83	9:00	Tales of the Gold Monkey(60) — AD	m	Fr:f-10-4/83
7/83	9:00	Hamptons(60) — DR	d	
7/83	9:00	Tales of the Gold Monkey(60) — AD	c	
8/83	9:00	Hamptons(60) — DR	c	
8/83	9:00	Two Marriages(60) — DR	d	
9/83	9:00	Dynasty(60) — SL	m	Fr:w-10
9/83	9:00	Two Marriages(60) — DR	m	To:r-8-3/84
9/83	10:00	Dynasty(60) — SL	m	To:w-9
9/83	10:00	Hotel(60) — DR	d	
5/84	9:00	Film(120) — FI	s*	
5/84	10:00	Hotel(60) — DR	m	To:t-9
7/84	9:00	Film(120) — FI	f*	
8/84	10:00	Hotel(60) — DR	m	Fr:t-9
7/85	8:00	Rock 'n' Roll Summer Action(60) — MU	d	
7/85	8:00	Fall Guy(60) — AD	m	To:r-8-9/85
8/85	8:00	Rock 'n' Roll Summer Action(60) — MU	c	
9/85	8:00	Insiders(60) — CD	d	
1/86	8:00	MacGyver(60) — SD	m	Fr:n-8

Date	Time	Title (min. if not 30) — Type	Action	From/To
1/86	8:00	Insiders(60) — CD	m	To:m-8-6/86
6/86	9:00	Hardcastle & McCormick(60) — CD	m*	Fr:m-8
7/86	8:00	MacGyver(60) — SD	m	To:w-9
7/86	9:00	Hardcastle & McCormick(60) — CD	c*	
8/86	8:00	Perfect Strangers — SC	m	Fr:t-8:30-4/86
8/86	8:30	Mr. Sunshine — SC	m	Fr:f-9
8/86	9:00	MacGyver(60) — SD	m*	Fr:w-8
8/86	9:00	MacGyver(60) — SD	m*	To:m-8
9/86	8:30	Mr. Sunshine — SC	c	
9/86	8:30	Head of the Class — SC	d#	
3/87	8:30	Harry — SC	d*	
3/87	8:30	Harry — SC	c*	
4/87	10:00	Mariah(60) — DR	d*	
5/87	9:00	Dynasty(60) — SL	m	To:w-10-9/87
5/87	10:00	Mariah(60) — DR	c*	
6/87	9:00	MacGyver(60) — SD	m	Fr:m-8
8/87	9:00	MacGyver(60) — SD	m	To:m-8
8/87	10:00	Hotel(60) — DR	m	To:s-10
9/87	9:00	Hooperman — SC	d	
9/87	9:30	Slap Maxwell — SC	d	
9/87	10:00	Dynasty(60) — SL	m	Fr:w-9
2/88	8:00	Perfect Strangers — SC	m	To:f-8
2/88	8:00	Growing Pains — SC	m#	Fr:t-8:30
3/88	9:30	Slap Maxwell — SC	m	To:f-9:30
3/88	10:00	Heartbeat(60) — DR	d	
3/88	10:00	Dynasty(60) — SL	m	To:r-9
4/88	9:30	Just in Time — SC	d	
4/88	10:00	China Beach(60) — DR	d	
4/88	10:00	Heartbeat(60) — DR	m	To:r-10-9/88
5/88	9:30	Just in Time — SC	c	
6/88	9:30	Slap Maxwell — SC	m	Fr:f-9:30
6/88	10:00	Spenser for Hire(60) — CD	m	Fr:s-10
6/88	10:00	China Beach(60) — DR	m	To:w-10-9/88
8/88	9:00	Hooperman — SC	m	To:w-9:30
8/88	9:30	Slap Maxwell — SC	c	
8/88	10:00	Spenser for Hire(60) — CD	c	

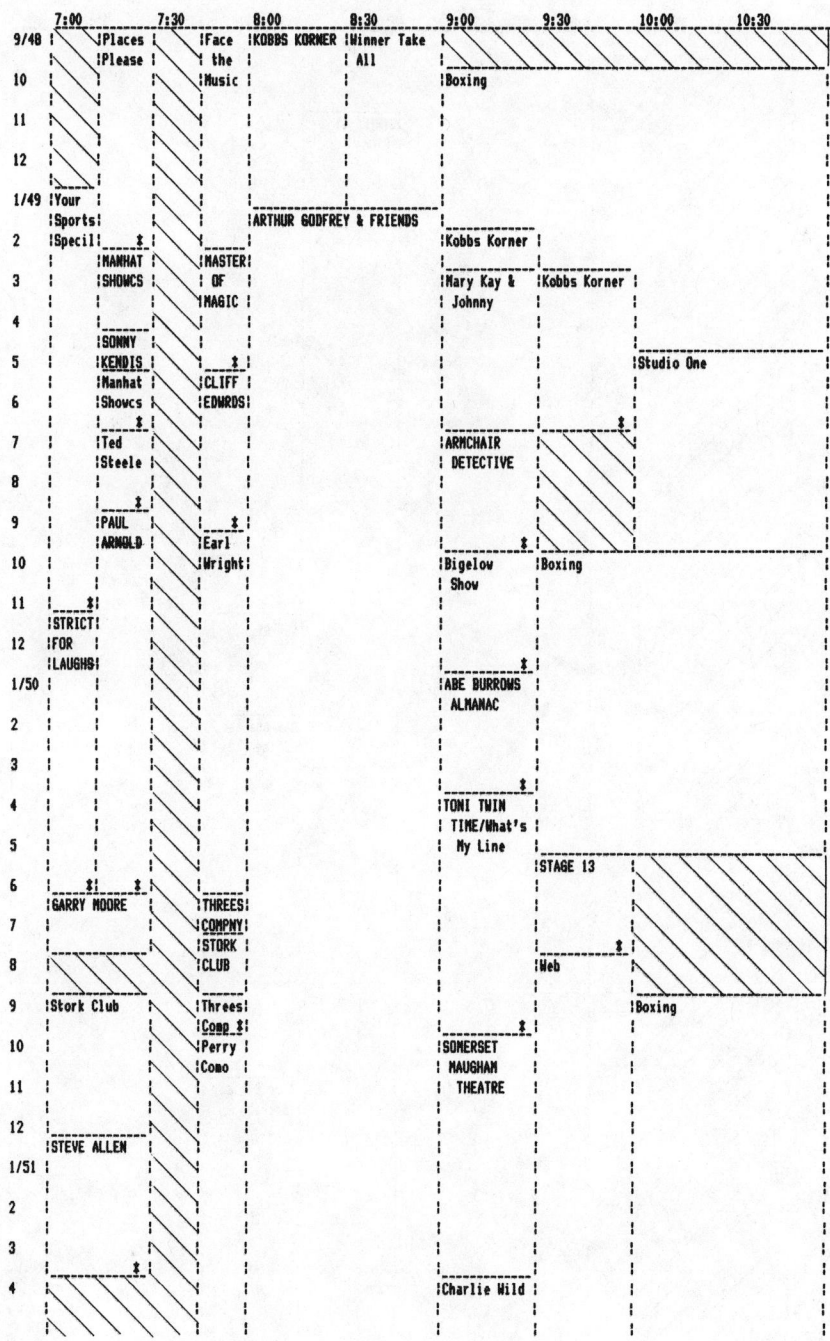

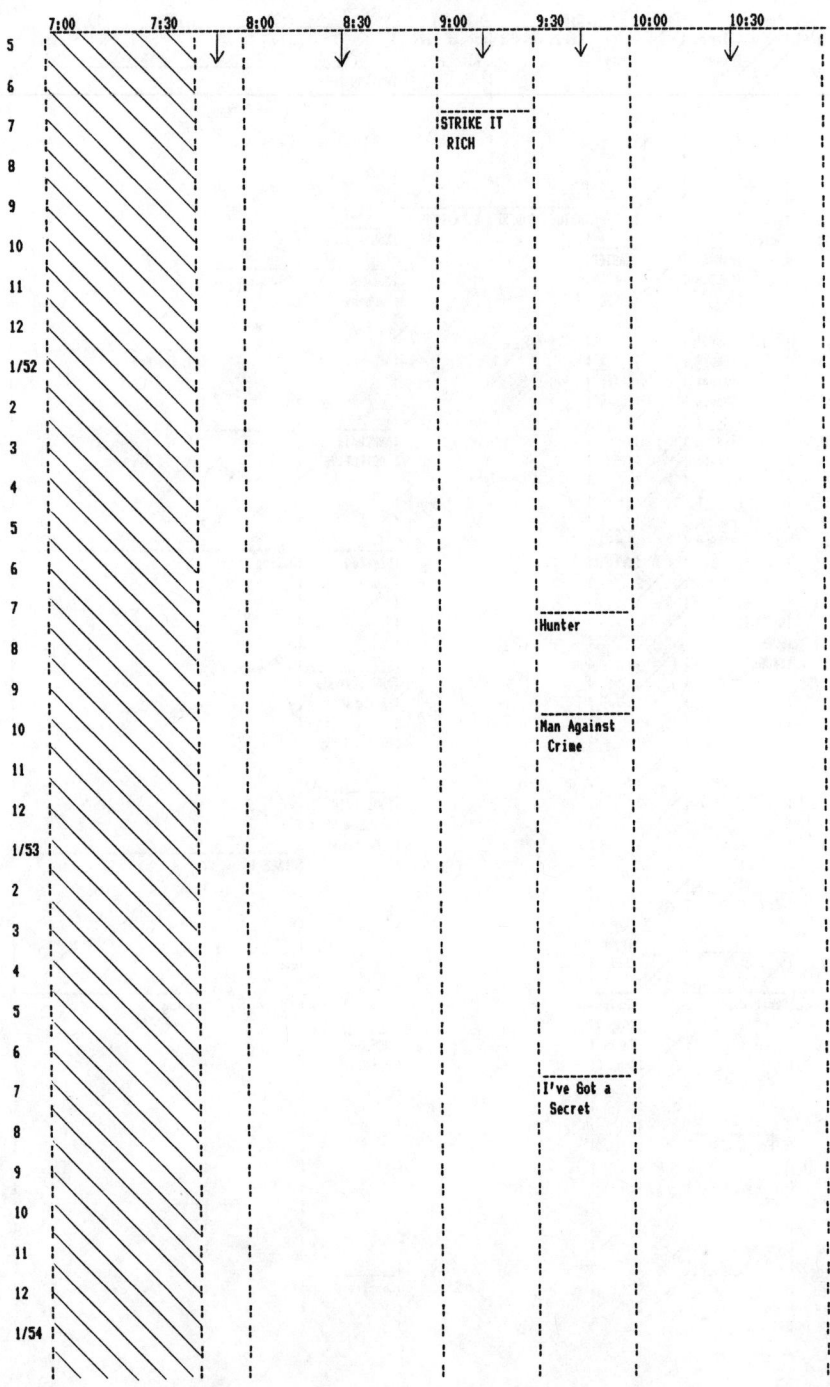

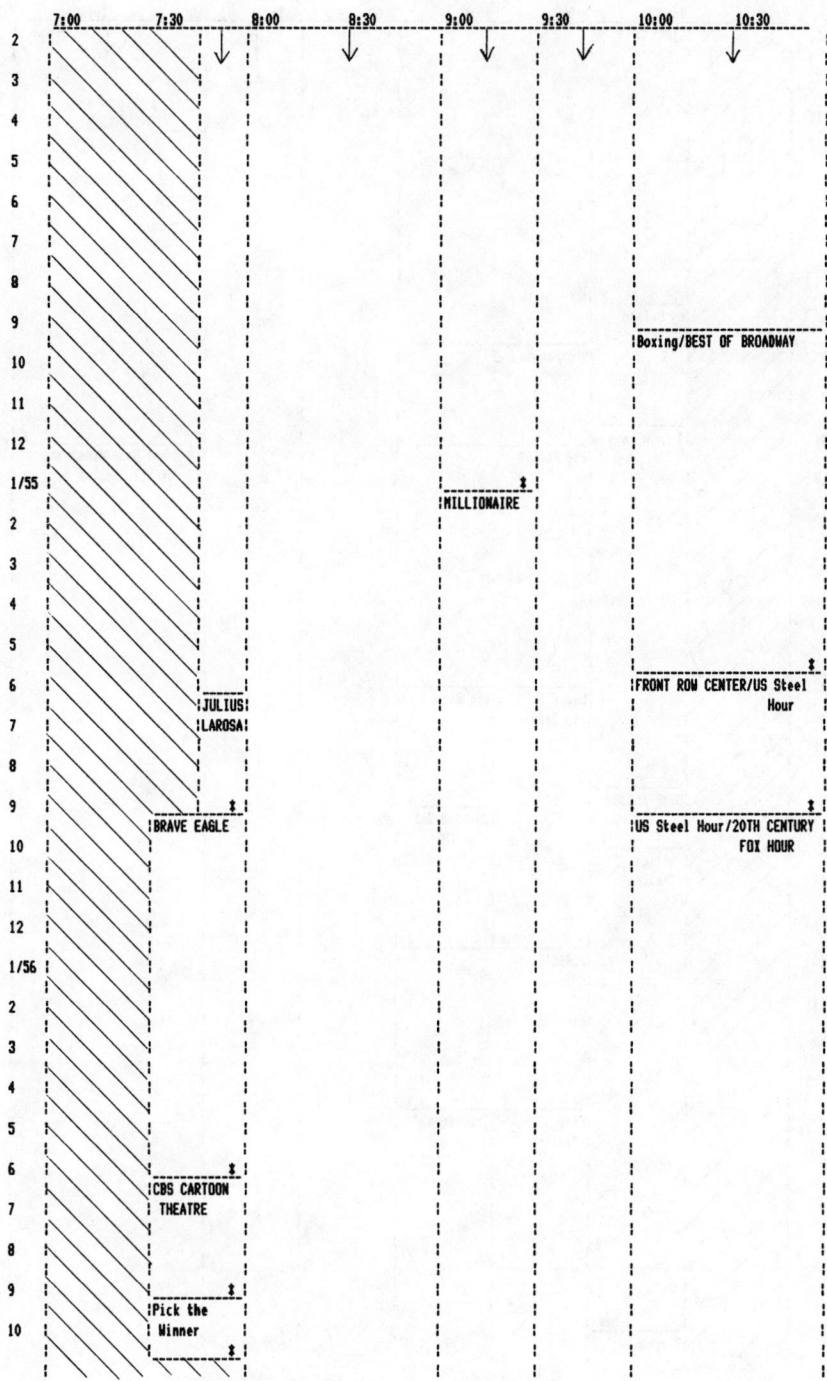

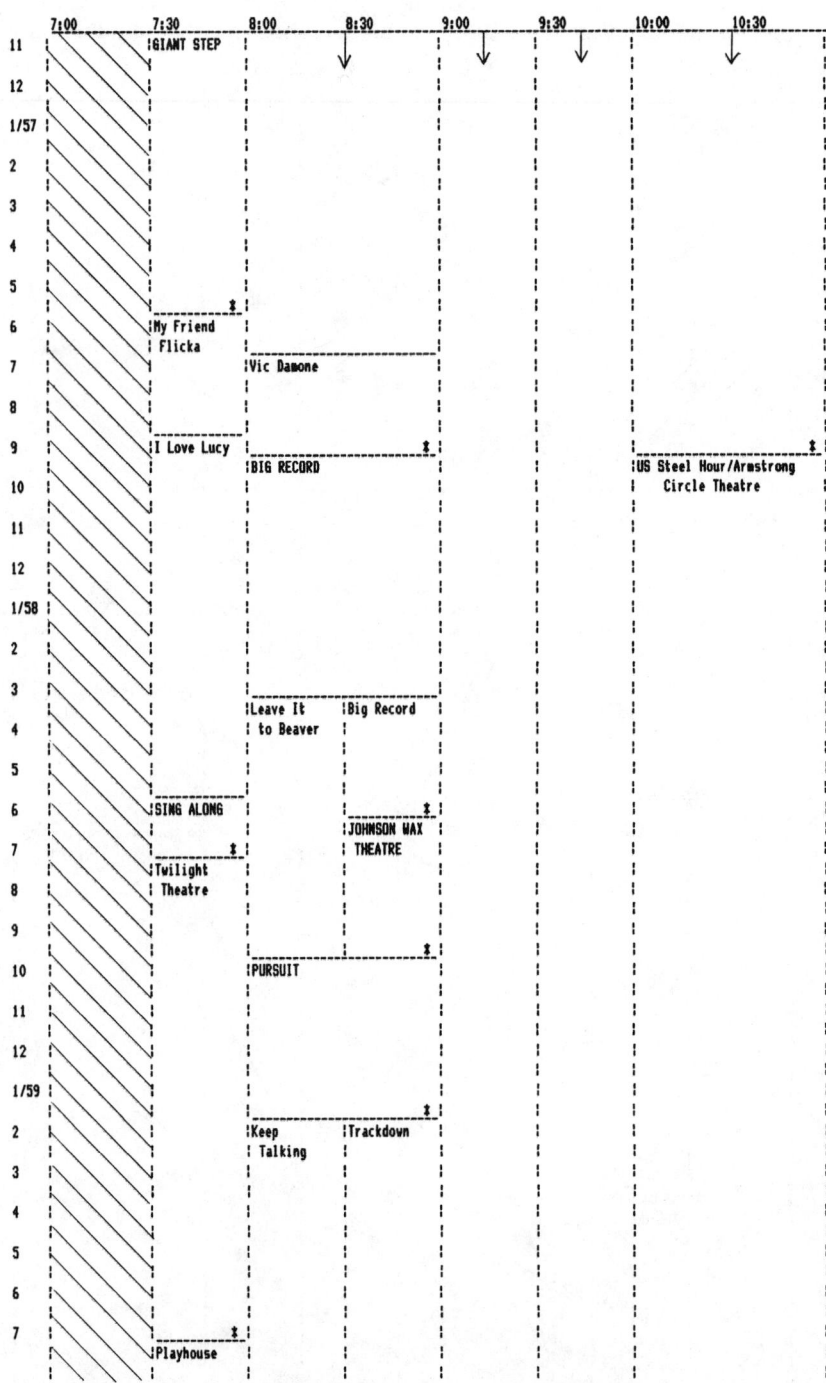

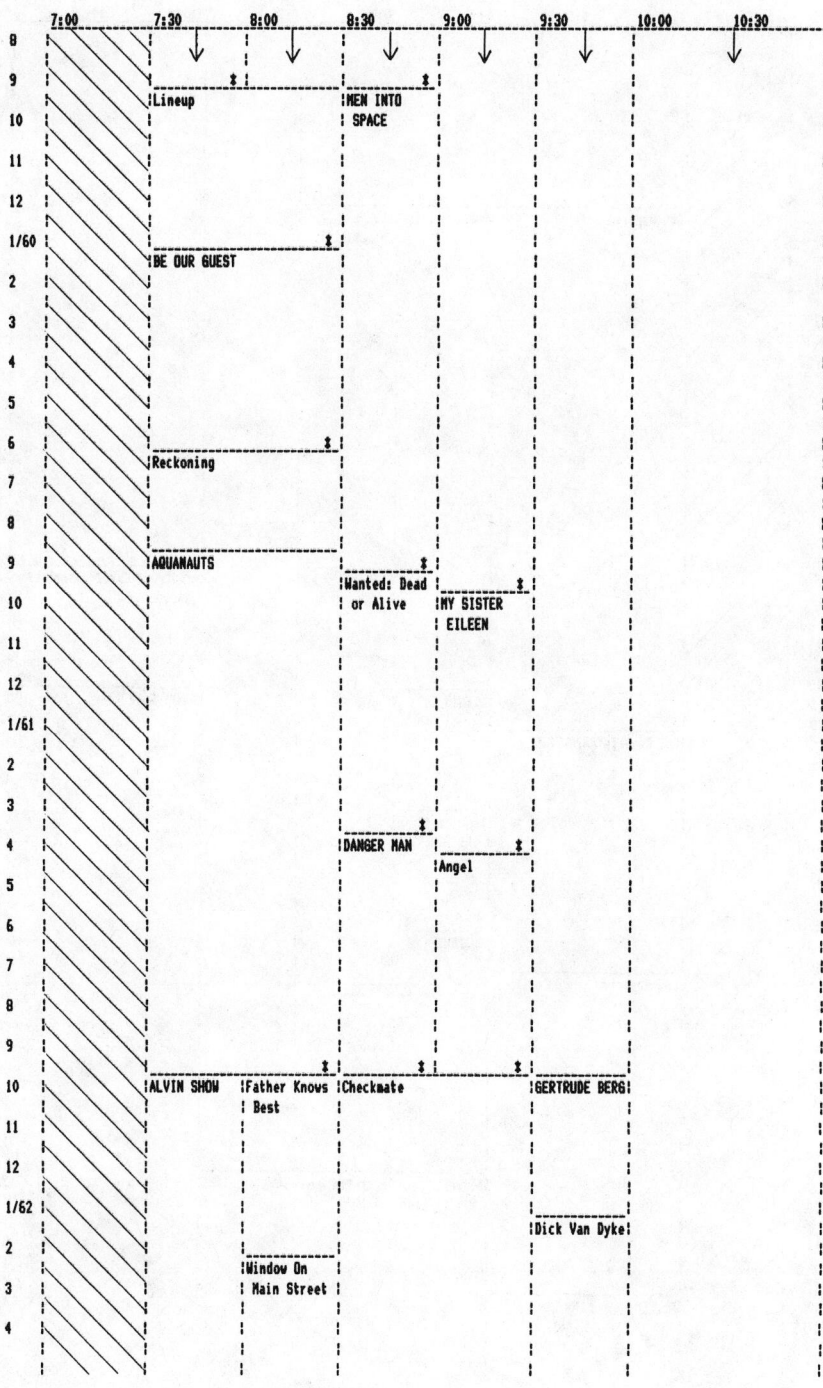

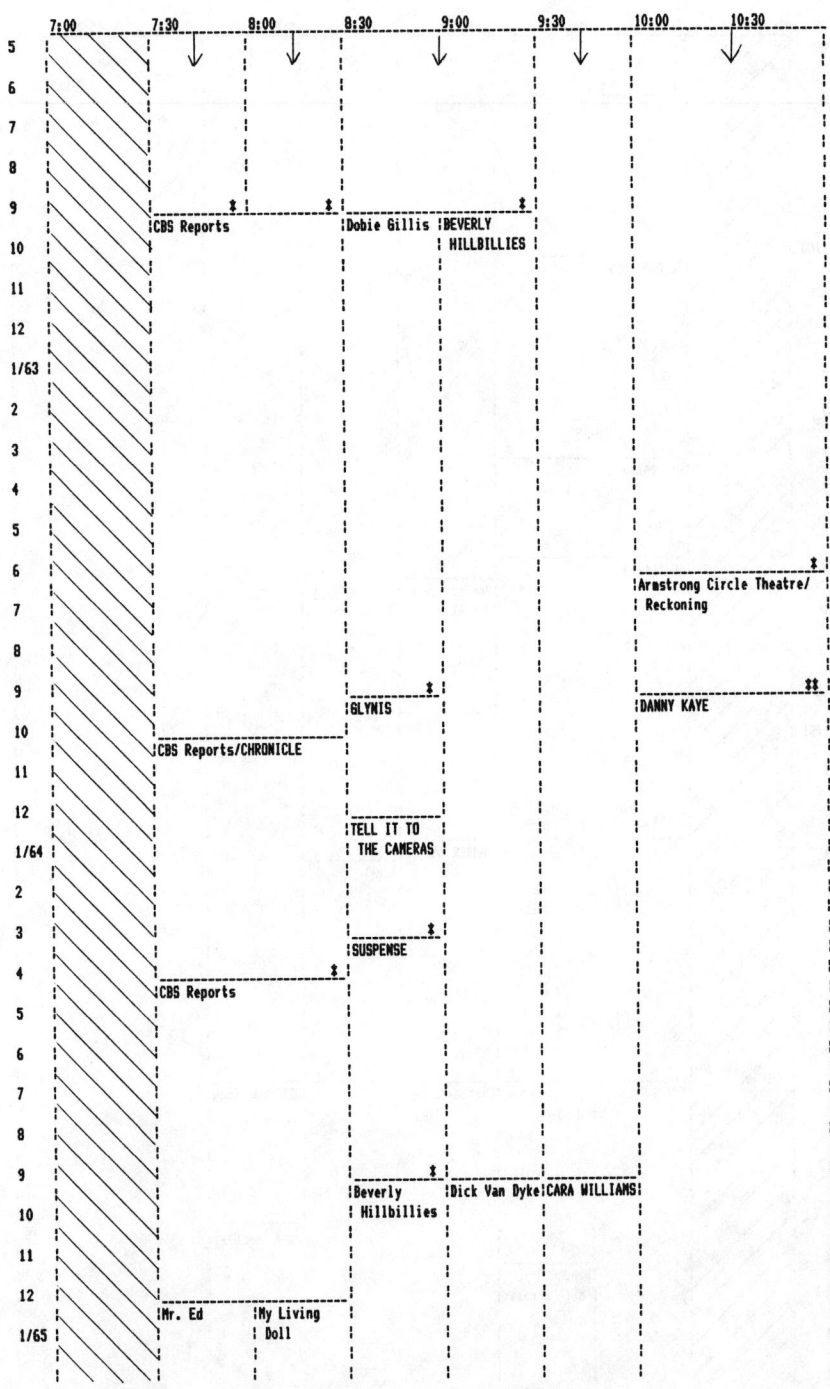

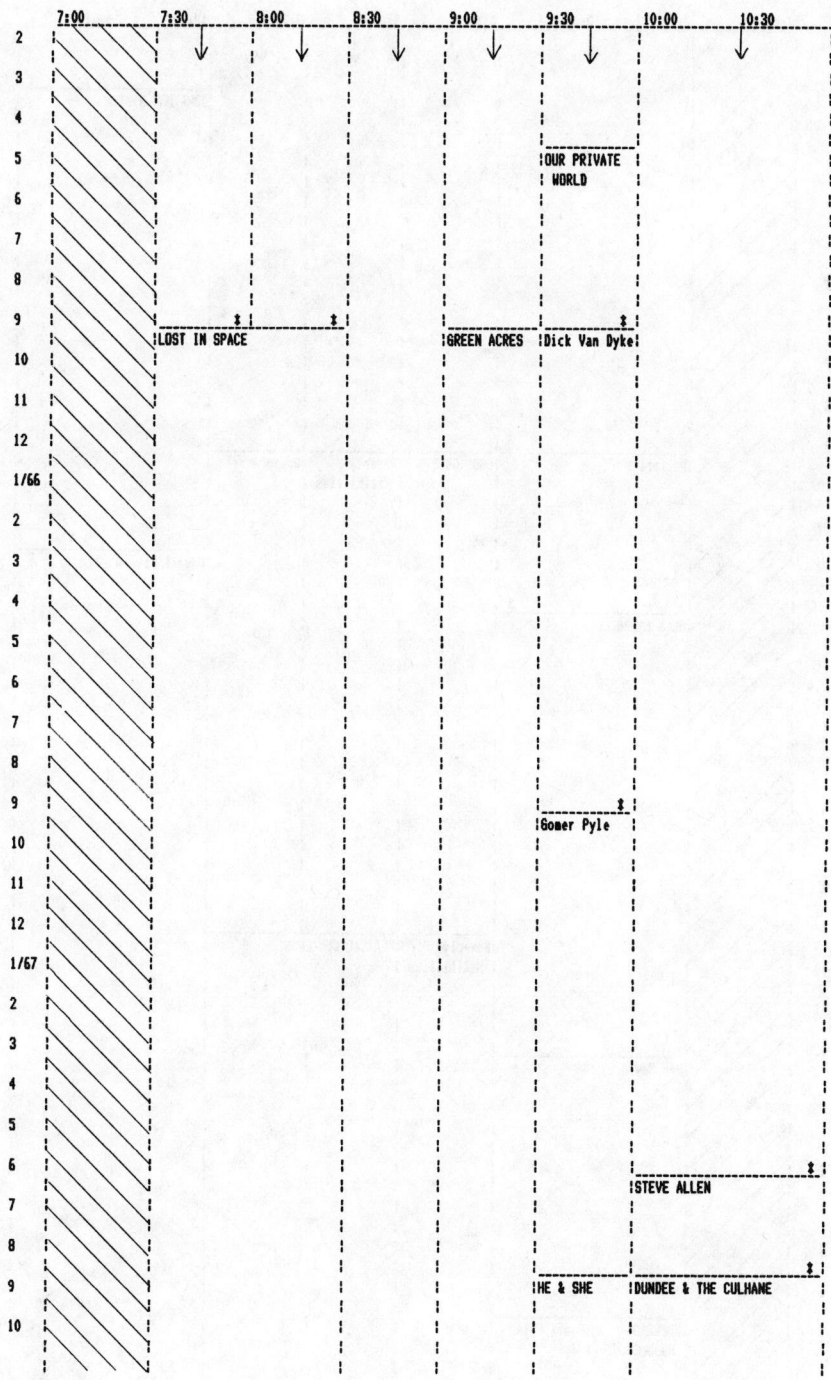

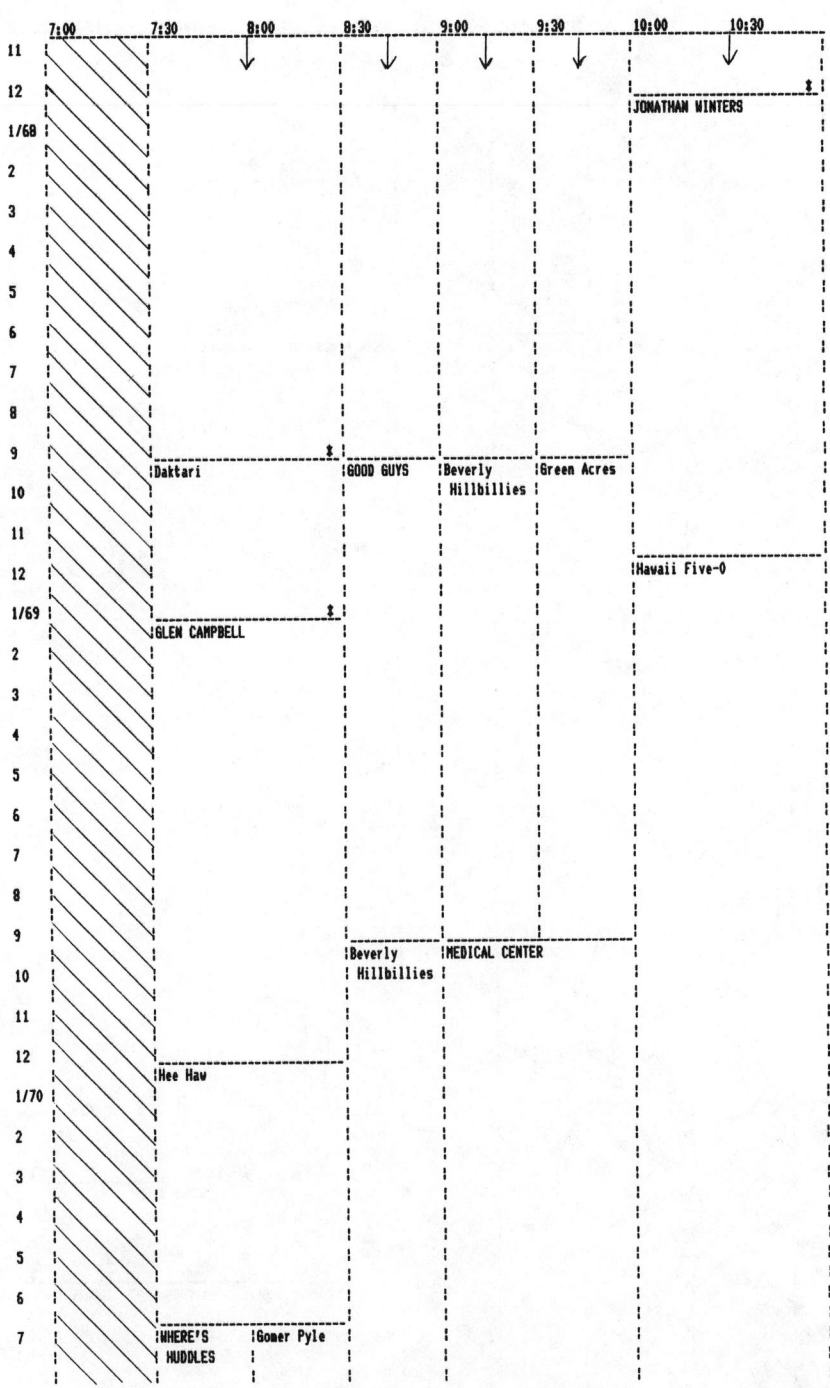

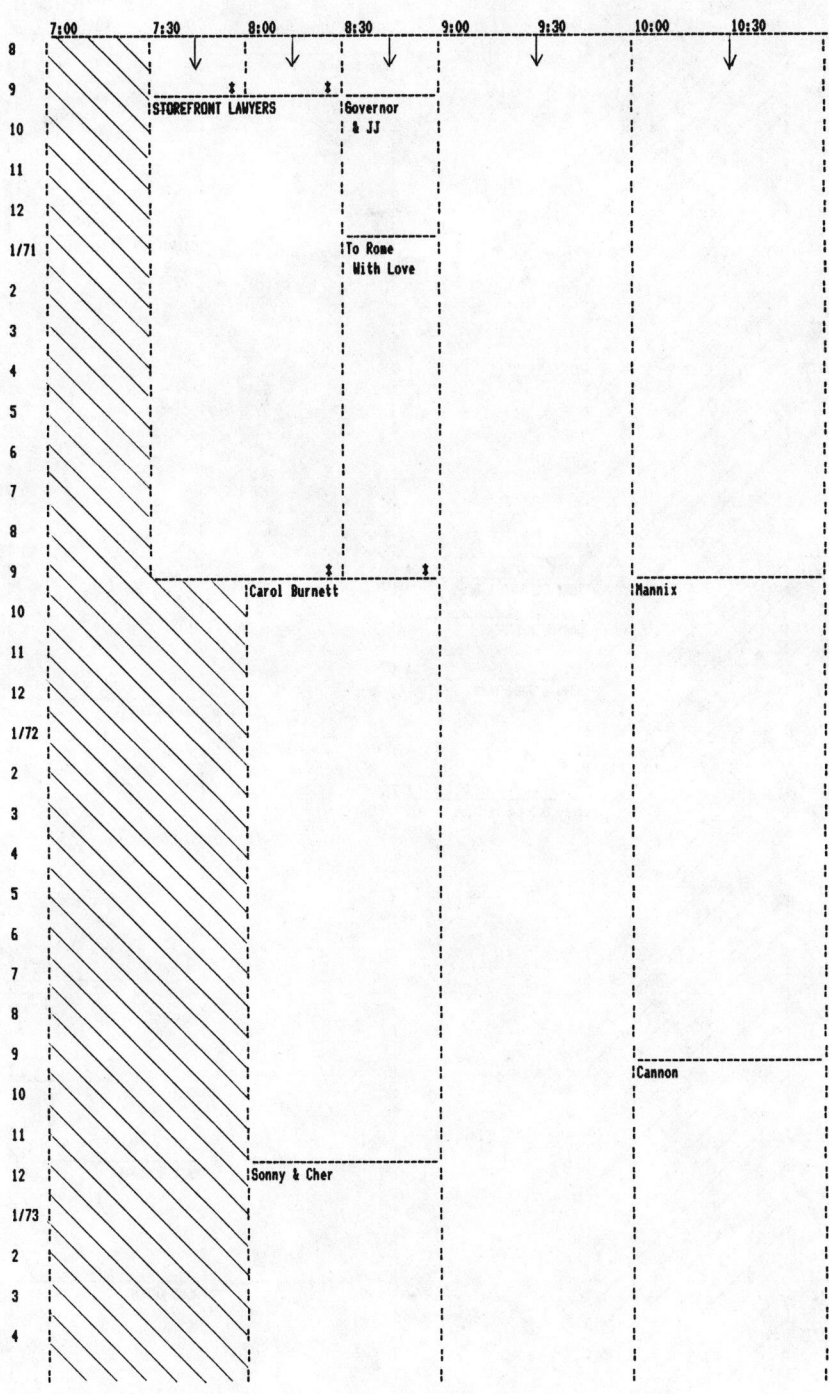

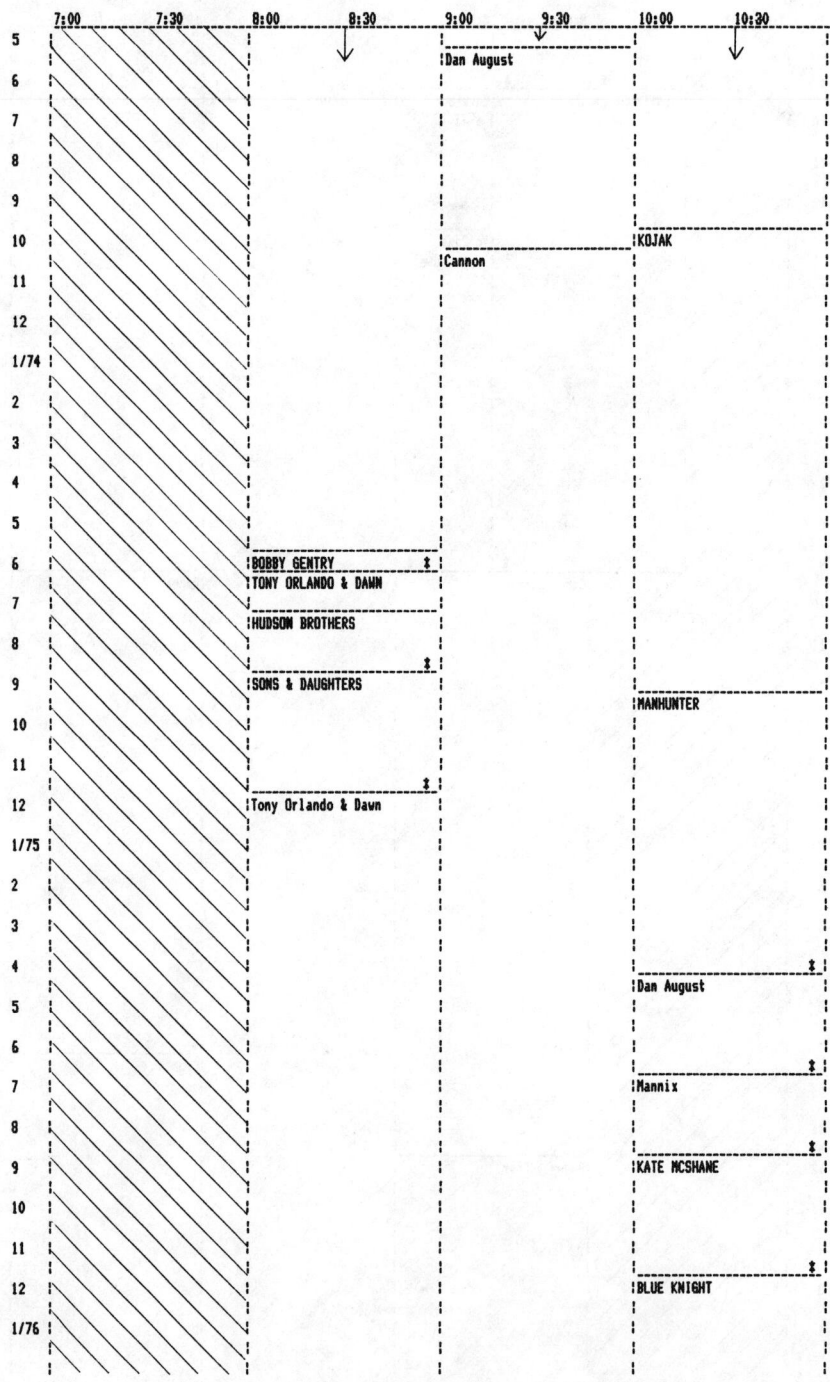

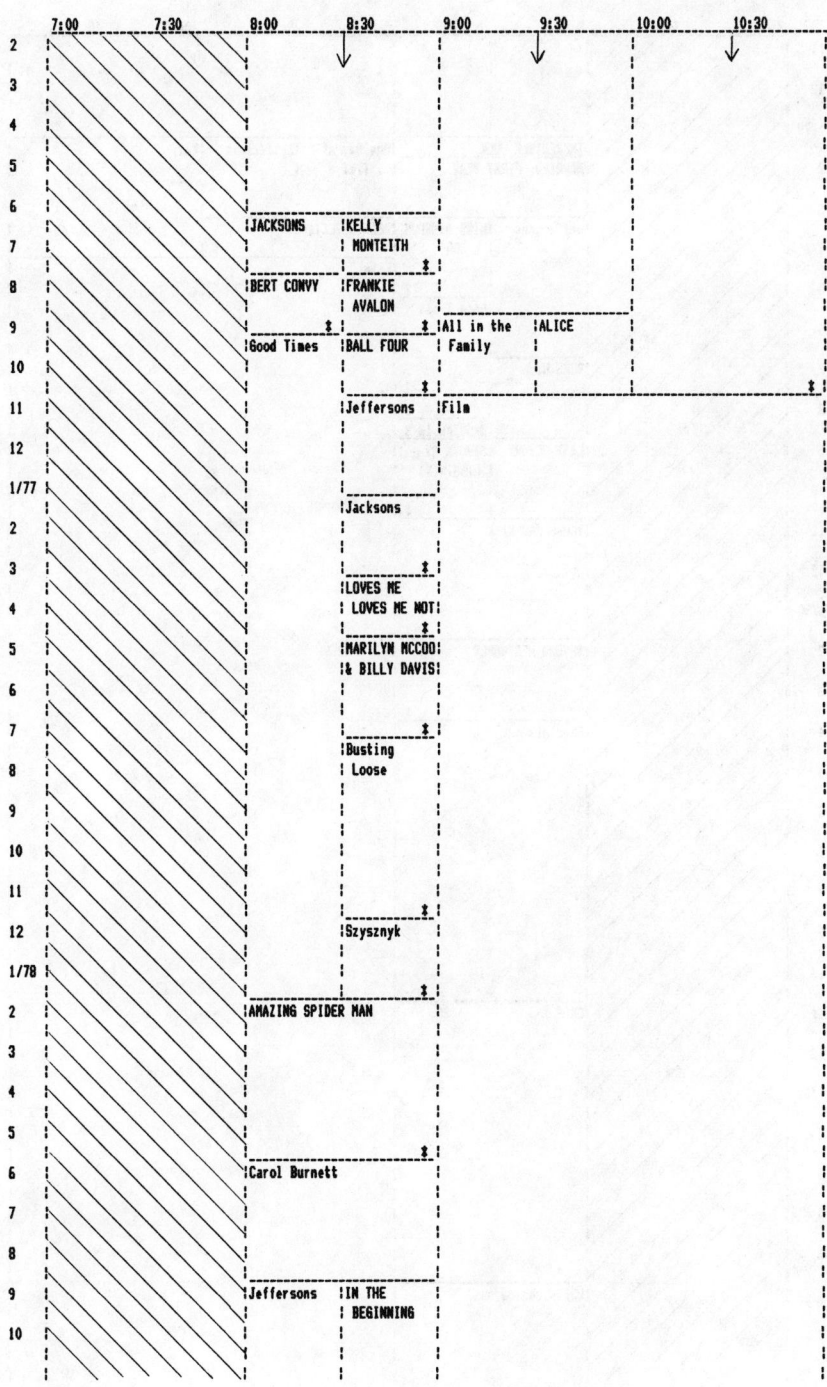

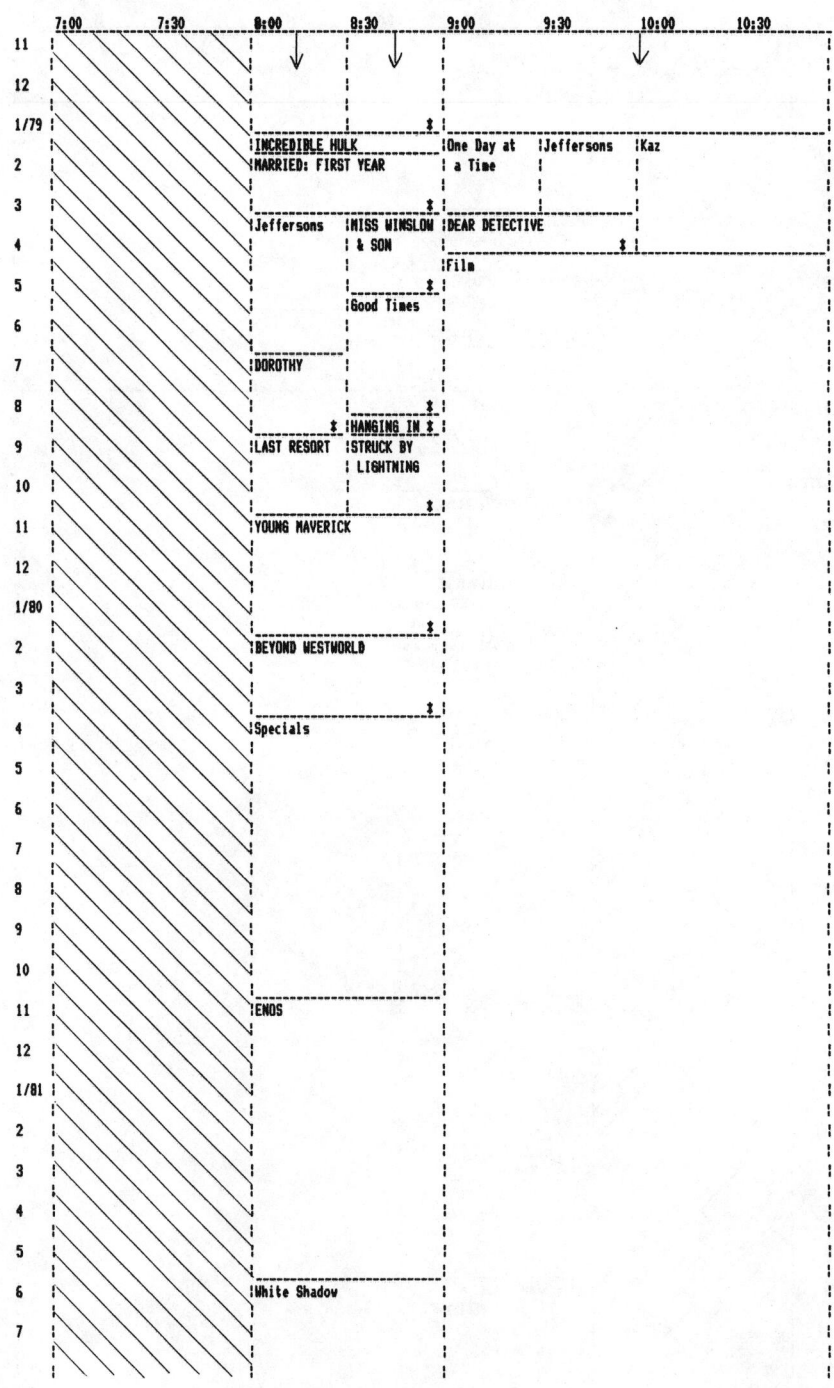

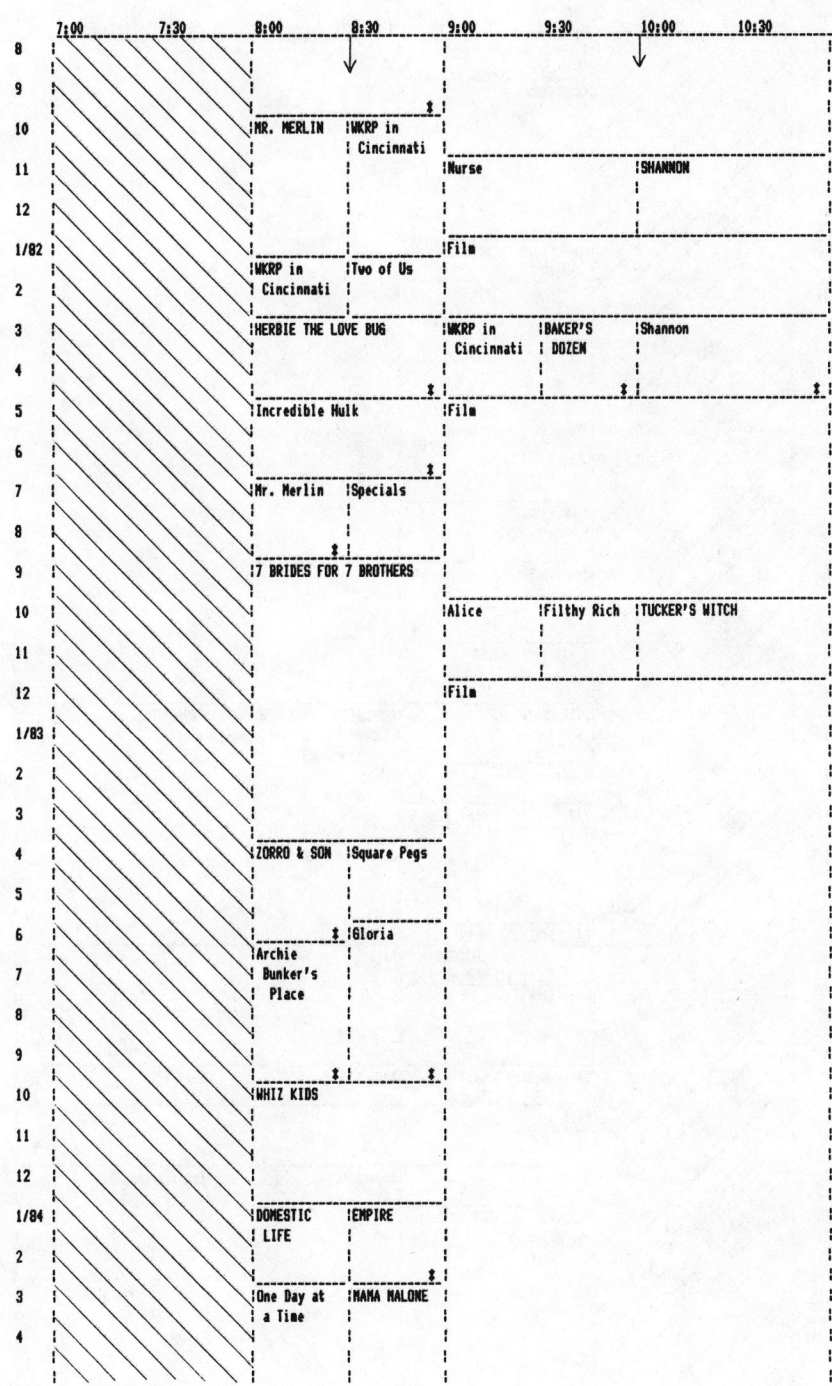

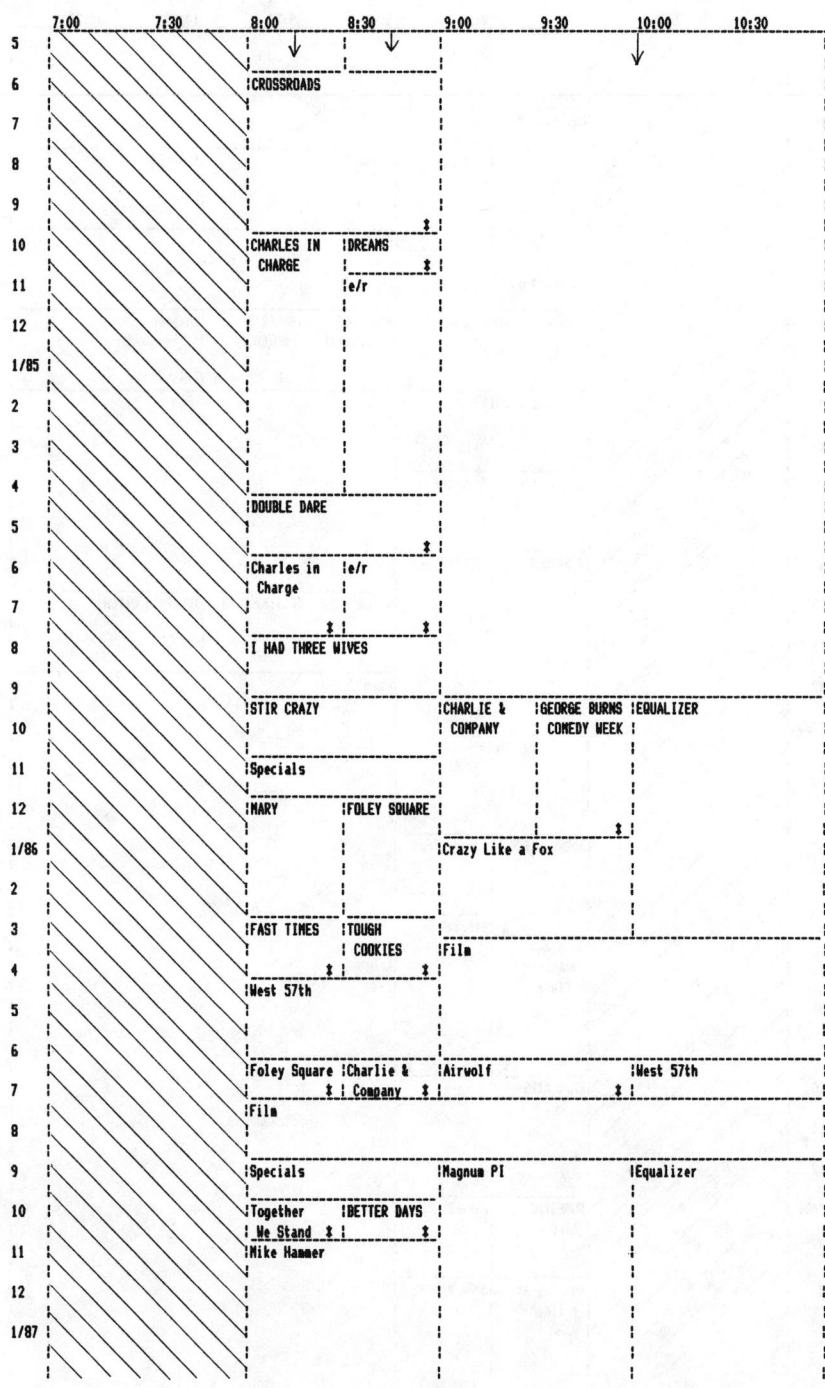

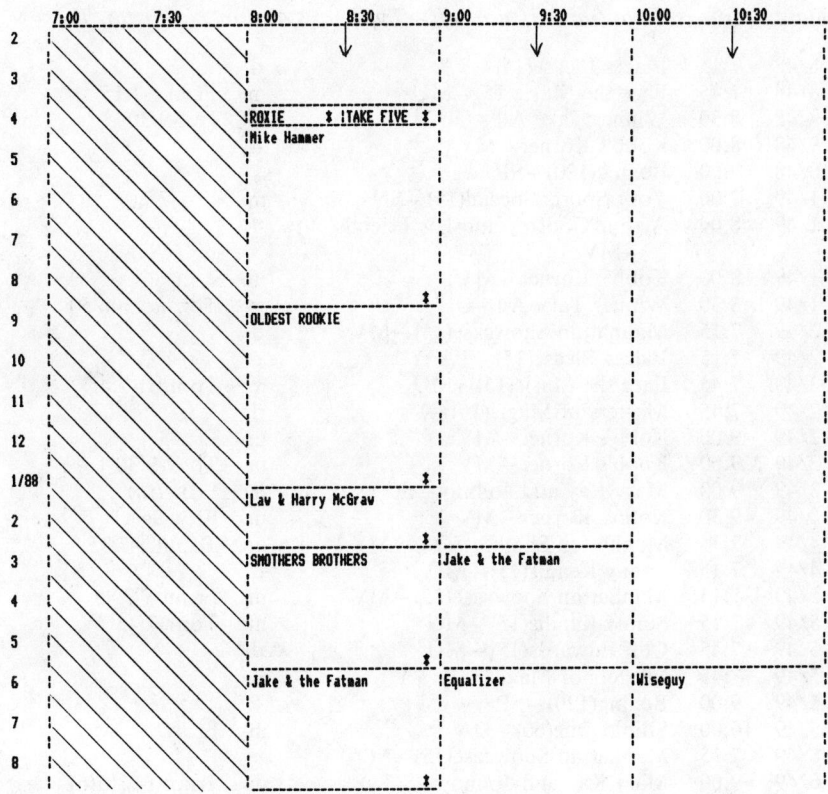

Date	Time	Title (min. if not 30) — Type	Action	From/To
8/48	7:15	Places Please(15) — TA	d	
8/48	7:45	Face the Music(15) — MU	m	Fr:m-f-7:15
8/48	8:30	Winner Take All — QU	m	Fr:r-9:30
9/48	8:00	Kobb's Korner — MV	d	
10/48	9:00	Boxing(120) — SP	s	
1/49	7:00	Your Sports Special(15) — SN	m	Fr:f-7
1/49	8:00	Arthur Godfrey and His Friends(60) — MV	d	
1/49	8:00	Kobb's Korner — MV	m	To:r-8
1/49	8:30	Winner Take All — QU	m	To:r-9:45-4/50
2/49	7:15	Manhattan Showcase(15) — MV	d	
2/49	7:15	Places Please(15) — TA	c	
2/49	7:45	Face the Music(15) — MU	m	To:mtrf-7:45
2/49	7:45	Masters of Magic(15) — VY	d	
2/49	9:00	Kobb's Korner — MV	m	Fr:r-8
2/49	9:00	Kobb's Korner — MV	m	To:w-9:30
3/49	9:00	Mary Kay and Johnny — SC	m	Fr:n-7(n)
3/49	9:30	Kobb's Korner — MV	m	Fr:w-9
4/49	7:15	Manhattan Showcase(15) — MV	m	To:mtrf-7:15
4/49	7:15	Sonny Kendis(15) — MU	d	
5/49	7:15	Manhattan Showcase(15) — MV	m	Fr:mtrf-7:45
5/49	7:15	Sonny Kendis(15) — MU	m	To:tr-7:45
5/49	7:45	Cliff Edwards(15) — MU	d	
5/49	7:45	Masters of Magic(15) — VY	c	
5/49	9:00	Boxing(120) — SP	f	
5/49	10:00	Studio One(60) — DA	m	Fr:n-7
6/49	7:15	Manhattan Showcase(15) — MV	c	
6/49	9:00	Mary Kay and Johnny — SC	m	To:m-f-7:15(n)
6/49	9:30	Kobb's Korner — MV	c	
7/49	7:15	Ted Steele(15) — MU	m	Fr:t-9
7/49	9:00	Armchair Detective — CD	d	
8/49	7:15	Ted Steele(15) — MU	c	
9/49	7:15	Paul Arnold(15) — MU	d	
9/49	7:45	Cliff Edwards(15) — MU	c	
9/49	9:00	Armchair Detective — CD	c	
9/49	10:00	Studio One(60) — DA	m	To:m-10
9/49	7:45	Earl Wrightson Show(15) — MU	m	Fr:m-7:15-4/49(a)
10/49	9:00	Bigelow Show — VY	m	Fr:r-9:30-7/49(n)
10/49	9:30	Boxing(90) — SP	s	
11/49	7:00	Strictly for Laughs(15) — MU	d	
11/49	7:00	Your Sports Special(15) — SN	c	
12/49	9:00	Bigelow Show — VY	c	
1/50	9:00	Abe Burrows' Almanac — CV	d	
3/50	9:00	Abe Burrows' Almanac — CV	c	
4/50	9:00	Toni Twin Time — VY	d	
4/50	9:00	What's My Line — QU	m	Fr:r-8
5/50	9:30	Boxing(90) — SP	f	
5/50	9:30	Stage 13 — DA	d	
6/50	7:00	Garry Moore Show — VY	d	
6/50	7:00	Strictly for Laughs(15) — MU	c	

Date	Time	Title (min. if not 30) — Type	Action	From/To
6/50	7:15	Paul Arnold(15)—MU	c	
6/50	7:45	Earl Wrightson Show(15)—MU	m	To:r-10:30-8/51(a)
6/50	7:45	Three's Company(15)—MU	d	
7/50	7:00	Garry Moore Show—VY	m	To:mtrf-7
7/50	7:45	Stork Club(15)—TK	d	
7/50	7:45	Three's Company(15)—MU	m	To:tr-7:45
7/50	9:30	Stage 13—DA	c	
8/50	8:00	Garry Moore Show(60)—VY	d*	
8/50	9:30	Web—DA	m	Fr:t-9:30
9/50	7:00	Stork Club—TK	m	Fr:mwf-7:45
9/50	7:45	Stork Club(15)—TK	m	To:m-f-7
9/50	7:45	Three's Company(15)—MU	m	Fr:tr-7:45
9/50	7:45	Three's Company(15)—MU	c	
9/50	8:00	Garry Moore Show(60)—VY	c*	
9/50	9:00	Toni Twin Time—VY	c	
9/50	9:00	What's My Line—QU	m	To:n-10:30
9/50	10:00	Boxing(60)—SP	s	
10/50	7:45	Perry Como(15)—MV	m	Fr:n-8-6/50(n)
10/50	9:00	Somerset Maugham TV Theatre —DA	d	
12/50	7:00	Steve Allen—CV	d	
12/50	7:00	Stork Club—TK	m	To:trs-7:45
3/51	7:00	Steve Allen—CV	c	
3/51	9:00	Somerset Maugham TV Theatre —DA	m	To:m-9:30(n)
4/51	9:00	Charlie Wild, Pvt. Detective—CD	m	Fr:f-9
6/51	9:00	Charlie Wild, Pvt. Detective—CD	m	To:t-8-9/51(a)
6/51	10:45	Sports Spot(15)—ST	d	
7/51	7:45	TV's Top Tunes(15)—MU	d*	
7/51	9:00	Strike It Rich—QU	d	
8/51	7:45	TV's Top Tunes(15)—MU	m*	To:mwf-7:45-6/53
7/52	7:45	Eddy Arnold(15)—MV	d*	
7/52	9:30	Hunter—SD	m	Fr:r-9
7/52	9:30	Web—DA	m	To:n-10
8/52	7:45	Eddy Arnold(15)—MV	m*	To:tr-7:30-7/53(n)
9/52	9:30	Hunter—SD	m	To:n-10:30-7/54(n)
10/52	9:30	Man Against Crime—CD	m	Fr:r-9-6/52
6/53	7:45	TV's Top Tunes(15)—MU	m*	Fr:mwf-7:45-8/51
6/53	9:30	Man Against Crime—CD	m	To:f-8:30
7/53	9:30	I've Got a Secret—QU	m	Fr:r-10:30
8/53	7:45	TV's Top Tunes(15)—MU	m*	To:mwf-7:45-6/54
6/54	7:45	TV's Top Tunes(15)—MU	m*	Fr:mwf-7:45-8/53
7/54	8:00	Red Skelton(60)—CV	m*	Fr:t-8:30
8/54	7:45	TV's Top Tunes(15)—MU	m*	To:s-10-7/55
9/54	8:00	Red Skelton(60)—CV	m*	To:t-8
9/54	10:00	Best of Broadway(60)—VS	d	
11/54	10:45	Sports Spot(15)—ST	c	
12/54	10:45	Red Barber's Corner(15)—ST	m	Fr:t-10:30-10/50
1/55	9:00	Millionaire—DA	d	
1/55	9:00	Strike It Rich—QU	c	

Date	Time	Title (min. if not 30) — Type	Action	From/To
5/55	10:00	Best of Broadway(60) — VS	c	
5/55	10:00	Boxing(60) — SP	f	
5/55	10:45	Red Barber's Corner(15) — ST	m	To:f-10:45(n)
6/55	7:45	Julius La Rosa(15) — MU	d	
6/55	7:45	Perry Como(15) — MV	m	To:s-9-9/55
6/55	10:00	Front Row Center(60) — DA	d	
7/55	8:00	Frankie Laine(60) — MV	d*	
7/55	10:00	U.S. Steel Hour(60) — DA	m	Fr:t-9:30(a)
9/55	7:30	Brave Eagle — WE	d	
9/55	7:45	Julius La Rosa(15) — MU	c	
9/55	8:00	Frankie Laine(60) — MV	m*	To:w-8-8/56
9/55	10:00	Front Row Center(60) — DA	c	
10/55	10:00	20th Century Fox Hour(60) — DA	d	
6/56	7:30	Brave Eagle — WE	c	
6/56	7:30	CBS Cartoon Theatre — KV	d	
8/56	8:00	Frankie Laine(60) — MV	m*	Fr:w-8-9/55
9/56	7:30	CBS Cartoon Theatre — KV	c	
9/56	7:30	Pick the Winner — PO	m	Fr:m-10-11/52(d)
9/56	8:00	Frankie Laine(60) — MV	c*	
10/56	7:30	Pick the Winner — PO	c	
11/56	7:30	Giant Step — QU	d	
5/57	7:30	Giant Step — QU	c	
6/57	7:30	My Friend Flicka — AD	m	Fr:s-7-3/57
6/57	8:00	Arthur Godfrey and His Friends (60) — MV	m	To:t-9-9/58
7/57	8:00	Vic Damone(60) — MV	m	Fr:m-9:30-9/56
8/57	7:30	My Friend Flicka — AD	m	To:n-7-1/58(n)
9/57	7:30	I Love Lucy — SC	m	Fr:m-9-6/57
9/57	8:00	Big Record(60) — MU	d	
9/57	8:00	Vic Damone(60) — MV	c	
9/57	10:00	20th Century Fox Hour(60) — DA	c	
10/57	10:00	Armstrong Circle Theatre(60) — DA	m	Fr:t-9:30-6/57(n)
3/58	8:00	Big Record(60) — MU	m	To:w-8:30
3/58	8:00	Leave It to Beaver — SC	m	Fr:f-7:30
3/58	8:30	Big Record — MU	m	Fr:w-8
5/58	7:30	I Love Lucy — SC	m	To:m-9-7/58
6/58	7:30	Sing Along — MU	d	
6/58	8:30	Big Record — MU	c	
6/58	8:30	Johnson's Wax Theatre — DA	d	
7/58	7:30	Sing Along — MU	c	
7/58	7:30	Twilight Theatre — DA	m	Fr:m-7:30-7/56(a)
9/58	8:00	Leave It to Beaver — SC	m	To:r-7:30(a)
9/58	8:30	Johnson's Wax Theatre — DA	c	
10/58	8:00	Pursuit(60) — DA	d	
1/59	8:00	Pursuit(60) — DA	c	
2/59	8:00	Keep Talking — QU	m	Fr:n-10
2/59	8:30	Trackdown — WE	m	Fr:f-8
7/59	7:30	Playhouse — DA	m	Fr:t-10:30-9/57
7/59	7:30	Twilight Theatre — DA	c	
9/59	7:30	Lineup(60) — CD	m	Fr:f-10

Date	Time	Title (min. if not 30) — Type	Action	From/To
9/59	7:30	Playhouse — DA	c	
9/59	8:00	Keep Talking — QU	m	To:t-10:30(a)
9/59	8:30	Men into Space — SF	d	
9/59	8:30	Trackdown — WE	c	
1/60	7:30	Be Our Guest(60) — MV	d	
1/60	7:30	Lineup(60) — CD	c	
6/60	7:30	Be Our Guest(60) — MV	c	
6/60	7:30	Reckoning(60) — DA	m	Fr:s-7:30-9/59
8/60	7:30	Reckoning(60) — DA	m	To:w-10-6/63
9/60	7:30	Aquanauts(60) — AD	d	
9/60	8:30	Men into Space — SF	c	
9/60	8:30	Wanted: Dead or Alive — WE	m	Fr:s-8:30
9/60	9:00	Millionaire — DA	c	
10/60	9:00	My Sister Eileen — SC	d	
3/61	8:30	Wanted: Dead or Alive — WE	c	
4/61	8:30	Danger Man — SD	d	
4/61	9:00	Angel — SC	m	Fr:r-8
4/61	9:00	My Sister Eileen — SC	c	
9/61	7:30	Aquanauts(60) — AD	c	
9/61	8:30	Danger Man — SD	c	
9/61	9:00	Angel — SC	c	
9/61	9:30	I've Got a Secret — QU	m	To:m-10:30
10/61	7:30	Alvin Show — KV	d	
10/61	8:00	Father Knows Best — SC	m	Fr:t-8
10/61	8:30	Checkmate(60) — CD	m	Fr:s-8:30
10/61	9:30	Gertrude Berg — SC	d	
1/62	9:30	Dick Van Dyke Show — SC	m	Fr:t-8
1/62	9:30	Gertrude Berg — SC	m	To:r-9:30
2/62	8:00	Father Knows Best — SC	m	To:m-8:30
2/62	8:00	Window on Main Street — SC	m	Fr:m-8:30
9/62	7:30	Alvin Show — KV	c	
9/62	7:30	CBS Reports(60) — DO	m	Fr:r-10
9/62	8:00	Window on Main Street — SC	c	
9/62	8:30	Checkmate(60) — CD	c	
9/62	8:30	Many Loves of Dobie Gillis — SC	m	Fr:t-8:30
9/62	9:00	Beverly Hillbillies — SC	d	
6/63	10:00	Reckoning(60) — DA	m	Fr:w-7:30-8/60
6/63	10:00	U.S. Steel Hour(60) — DA	c	
8/63	10:00	Armstrong Circle Theatre(60) — DA	c	
9/63	8:30	Glynis — SC	d	
9/63	8:30	Many Loves of Dobie Gillis — SC	c	
9/63	10:00	Danny Kaye(60) — MV	d	
9/63	10:00	Reckoning(60) — DA	c	
10/63	7:30	Chronicle(60) — DO	d	
12/63	8:30	Glynis — SC	m	To:m-9-7/65
12/63	8:30	Tell It to the Camera — IV	d	
3/64	8:30	Suspense — SA	d	
3/64	8:30	Tell It to the Camera — IV	c	
4/64	7:30	Chronicle(60) — DO	c	
7/64	10:00	On Broadway Tonight(60) — TA	d*	

Date	Time	Title (min. if not 30) — Type	Action	From/To
9/64	8:30	Beverly Hillbillies — SC	m	Fr:w-9
9/64	8:30	Suspense — SA	c	
9/64	9:00	Beverly Hillbillies — SC	m	To:w-8:30
9/64	9:00	Dick Van Dyke Show — SC	m	Fr:w-9:30
9/64	9:30	Cara Williams — SC	d	
9/64	9:30	Dick Van Dyke Show — SC	m	To:w-9
9/64	10:00	On Broadway Tonight(60) — TA	m*	To:f-8:30-1/65
12/64	7:30	CBS Reports(60) — DO	m	To:m-10
12/64	7:30	Mr. Ed — SC	m	Fr:r-7:30-3/63
12/64	8:00	My Living Doll — SC	m	Fr:n-9
4/65	9:30	Cara Williams — SC	m	To:f-8:30
5/65	9:30	Our Private World — SL	d	
6/65	10:00	Lucy-Desi Comedy Hour(60) — SC	m*	Fr:s-7:30-9/64
9/65	7:30	Lost in Space(60) — SF	d	
9/65	7:30	Mr. Ed — SC	c	
9/65	8:00	My Living Doll — SC	c	
9/65	9:00	Dick Van Dyke Show — SC	m	To:w-9:30
9/65	9:00	Green Acres — SC	d	
9/65	9:30	Dick Van Dyke Show — SC	m	Fr:w-9
9/65	9:30	Our Private World — SL	c	
9/65	10:00	Lucy-Desi Comedy Hour(60) — SC	m*	To:r-7:30-6/67
6/66	10:00	John Gary(60) — MV	d*	
9/66	9:30	Dick Van Dyke Show — SC	c	
9/66	9:30	Gomer Pyle, U.S.M.C. — SC	m	Fr:f-9
9/66	10:00	John Gary(60) — MV	c*	
6/67	10:00	Danny Kaye(60) — MV	c	
6/67	10:00	Steve Allen Comedy Hour(60) — CV	d	
8/67	9:30	Gomer Pyle, U.S.M.C. — SC	m	To:f-8:30
8/67	10:00	Steve Allen Comedy Hour(60) — CV	c	
9/67	9:30	He & She — SC	d	
9/67	10:00	Dundee and the Culhane(60) — WE	d	
12/67	10:00	Dundee and the Culhane(60) — WE	c	
12/67	10:00	Jonathan Winters(60) — CV	d	
5/68	10:00	Dom DeLuise Show(60) — CV	d*	
9/68	7:30	Daktari(60) — AD	m	Fr:t-7:30
9/68	7:30	Lost in Space(60) — SF	c	
9/68	8:30	Beverly Hillbillies — SC	m	To:w-9
9/68	8:30	Good Guys — SC	d	
9/68	9:00	Beverly Hillbillies — SC	m	Fr:w-8:30
9/68	9:00	Green Acres — SC	m	To:w-9:30
9/68	9:30	Green Acres — SC	m	Fr:w-9
9/68	9:30	He & She — SC	m	To:f-8-6/70
9/68	10:00	Dom DeLuise Show(60) — CV	c*	
12/68	10:00	Hawaii Five-O(60) — CD	m	Fr:r-8
12/68	10:00	Jonathan Winters(60) — CV	m	To:r-8
1/69	7:30	Daktari(60) — AD	c	
1/69	7:30	Glen Campbell Goodtime Hour(60) — MV	d	
6/69	7:30	Tarzan(60) — AD	m*	Fr:f-7:30-9/68
9/69	7:30	Tarzan(60) — AD	c*	

Date	Time	Title (min. if not 30) — Type	Action	From/To
9/69	8:30	Beverly Hillbillies—SC	m	Fr:w-9
9/69	8:30	Good Guys—SC	m	To:f-8
9/69	9:00	Beverly Hillbillies—SC	m	To:w-8:30
9/69	9:00	Medical Center(60)—MD	d	
9/69	9:30	Green Acres—SC	m	To:s-9
12/69	7:30	Glen Campbell Goodtime Hour(60)—MV	m	To:n-9
12/69	7:30	Hee Haw(60)—VY	m	Fr:n-9-9/69
6/70	7:30	Hee Haw(60)—VY	m	To:t-8:30-9/70
7/70	7:30	Where's Huddles—KV	d	
7/70	8:00	Gomer Pyle, U.S.M.C.—SC	m	Fr:f-8:30-9/69
7/70	10:00	Smothers Brothers Comedy Hour (60)—CV	m*	Fr:n-9
9/70	7:30	Storefront Lawyers(60)—LD	d	
9/70	7:30	Where's Huddles—KV	c	
9/70	8:00	Gomer Pyle, U.S.M.C.—SC	c	
9/70	8:30	Beverly Hillbillies—SC	m	To:t-7:30
9/70	8:30	Governor & J.J.—SC	m	Fr:t-9:30
9/70	10:00	Smothers Brothers Comedy Hour (60)—CV	c*	
12/70	8:30	Governor & J.J.—SC	m	To:f-10:30-6/72
1/71	8:30	To Rome with Love—SC	m	Fr:t-9:30
9/71	7:30	Storefront Lawyers(60)—LD	c	
9/71	8:00	Carol Burnett(60)—CV	m	Fr:m-10-5/71
9/71	8:30	To Rome with Love—SC	c	
9/71	10:00	Hawaii Five-O(60)—CD	m	To:t-8:30
9/71	10:00	Mannix(60)—CD	m	Fr:s-10
6/72	8:00	Melba Moore—Clifton Davis(60)—MV	d*	
7/72	8:00	David Steinberg Show(60)—CV	d*	
7/72	8:00	Melba Moore—Clifton Davis(60)—MV	c*	
8/72	8:00	David Steinberg Show(60)—CV	c*	
9/72	10:00	Cannon(60)—CD	m	Fr:t-9:30
9/72	10:00	Mannix(60)—CD	m	To:n-9:30
11/72	8:00	Carol Burnett(60)—CV	m	To:s-10
12/72	8:00	Sonny and Cher Comedy Hour(60)—MV	m	Fr:f-8
5/73	9:00	Dan August(60)—CD	m	Fr:r-9:30-8/71(a)
5/73	9:00	Medical Center(60)—MD	m	To:m-10
9/73	10:00	Cannon(60)—CD	m	To:w-9
10/73	9:00	Cannon(60)—CD	m	Fr:w-10
10/73	9:00	Dan August(60)—CD	m	To:w-10-4/75
10/73	10:00	Kojak(60)—CD	d	
5/74	8:00	Sonny and Cher Comedy Hour(60)—MV	m	To:n-8-2/76
6/74	8:00	Bobbie Gentry Show(60)—MV	d	
6/74	8:00	Bobbie Gentry Show(60)—MV	c	
7/74	8:00	Hudson Brothers(60)—VY	d	
7/74	8:00	Tony Orlando and Dawn(60)—MV	d	

Date	Time	Title (min. if not 30) — Type	Action	From/To
7/74	8:00	Tony Orlando and Dawn(60) — MV	m	To:w-8-12/74
8/74	8:00	Hudson Brothers(60) — VY	c	
9/74	8:00	Sons and Daughters(60) — DR	d	
9/74	10:00	Kojak(60) — CD	m	To:n-8:30
9/74	10:00	Manhunter(60) — CD	d	
11/74	8:00	Sons and Daughters(60) — DR	c	
12/74	8:00	Tony Orlando and Dawn(60) — MV	m	Fr:w-8-7/74
4/75	10:00	Dan August(60) — CD	m	Fr:w-9-10/73
4/75	10:00	Manhunter(60) — CD	c	
6/75	10:00	Dan August(60) — CD	c	
7/75	10:00	Mannix(60) — CD	m	Fr:n-9:30
8/75	10:00	Mannix(60) — CD	c	
9/75	10:00	Kate McShane(60) — LD	d	
11/75	10:00	Kate McShane(60) — LD	c	
12/75	10:00	Blue Knight(60) — CD	d	
6/76	8:00	Jacksons — MV	d	
6/76	8:00	Tony Orlando and Dawn(60) — MV	m	To:t-8-9/76
6/76	8:30	Kelly Monteith — CV	d	
7/76	8:00	Jacksons — MV	m	To:w-8:30-1/77
7/76	8:30	Kelly Monteith — CV	c	
8/76	8:00	Bert Convy Show — MV	d	
8/76	8:30	Easy Does It Starring Frankie Avalon — MV	d	
8/76	9:00	Cannon(60) — CD	m	To:n-10
9/76	8:00	Good Times — SC	m	Fr:t-8:30
9/76	8:00	Bert Convy Show — MV	c	
9/76	8:30	Ball Four — SC	d	
9/76	8:30	Easy Does It Starring Frankie Avalon — MV	c	
9/76	9:00	All in the Family — SC	m	Fr:m-9
9/76	9:30	Alice — SC	d	
10/76	8:30	Ball Four — SC	c	
10/76	9:00	All in the Family — SC	m	To:s-9
10/76	9:30	Alice — SC	m	To:s-9:30
10/76	10:00	Blue Knight(60) — CD	c	
11/76	8:30	Jeffersons — SC	m	Fr:s-8
11/76	9:00	Film(120) — FI	s	
1/77	8:30	Jacksons — MV	m	Fr:w-8-7/76
1/77	8:30	Jeffersons — SC	m	To:m-8
3/77	8:30	Jacksons — MV	c	
3/77	8:30	Loves Me, Loves Me Not — SC	d	
4/77	8:30	Loves Me, Loves Me Not — SC	c	
5/77	8:30	Marilyn McCoo and Billy Davis, Jr. — MV	d	
7/77	8:30	Busting Loose — SC	m	Fr:m-8:30
7/77	8:30	Marilyn McCoo and Billy Davis, Jr. — MV	c	
11/77	8:30	Busting Loose — SC	c	
12/77	8:30	Szysznyk — SC	m	Fr:m-8:30-8/77
1/78	8:00	Good Times — SC	m	To:m-8

Date	Time	Title (min. if not 30) – Type	Action	From/To
1/78	8:30	Szysznyk – SC	c	
2/78	8:00	Amazing Spider-Man(60) – AD	d	
5/78	8:00	Amazing Spider-Man(60) – AD	c	
6/78	8:00	Carol Burnett(60) – CV	m	Fr:n-10-3/78
8/78	8:00	Carol Burnett(60) – CV	m	To:s-8-8/79(a)
9/78	8:00	Jeffersons – SC	m	Fr:m-8
9/78	8:30	In the Beginning – SC	d	
1/79	8:00	Incredible Hulk(60) – AD	m	Fr:f-9
1/79	8:00	Incredible Hulk(60) – AD	m	To:f-8
1/79	8:00	Jeffersons – SC	m	To:w-9:30
1/79	8:30	In the Beginning – SC	c	
1/79	9:00	Film(120) – FI	f	
1/79	9:00	One Day at a Time – SC	m	Fr:m-9:30
1/79	9:30	Jeffersons – SC	m	Fr:w-8
1/79	10:00	Kaz(60) – CD	m	Fr:n-9
2/79	8:00	Married: The First Year(60) – DR	d	
3/79	8:00	Jeffersons – SC	m	Fr:w-9:30
3/79	8:00	Married: The First Year(60) – DR	c	
3/79	8:30	Miss Winslow and Son – SC	d	
3/79	9:00	Dear Detective(60) – CD	d	
3/79	9:00	One Day at a Time – SC	m	To:n-8:30
3/79	9:30	Jeffersons – SC	m	To:w-8
4/79	9:00	Dear Detective(60) – CD	c	
4/79	9:00	Film(120) – FI	s	
4/79	10:00	Kaz(60) – CD	m	To:n-10-7/79
5/79	8:30	Good Times – SC	m	Fr:s-8:30-12/78
5/79	8:30	Miss Winslow and Son – SC	c	
6/79	8:00	Jeffersons – SC	m	To:n-9:30
7/79	8:00	Dorothy – SC	d	
8/79	8:00	Dorothy – SC	c	
8/79	8:30	Good Times – SC	c	
8/79	8:30	Hanging In – SC	d	
8/79	8:30	Hanging In – SC	c	
9/79	8:00	Last Resort – SC	d	
9/79	8:30	Struck by Lightning – SC	d	
10/79	8:00	Last Resort – SC	m	To:m-8:30-12/79
10/79	8:30	Struck by Lightning – SC	c	
11/79	8:00	Young Maverick(60) – WE	d	
1/80	8:00	Young Maverick(60) – WE	c	
2/80	8:00	Beyond Westworld(60) – SF	d	
3/80	8:00	Beyond Westworld(60) – SF	c	
11/80	8:00	Enos(60) – CO	d	
5/81	8:00	Enos(60) – CO	m	To:s-8
6/81	8:00	White Shadow(60) – DR	m	Fr:m-8-3/81
9/81	8:00	White Shadow(60) – DR	c	
10/81	8:00	Mr. Merlin – SC	d	
10/81	8:30	WKRP in Cincinnati – SC	m	Fr:m-8
10/81	9:00	Film(120) – FI	f	
11/81	9:00	Nurse(60) – MD	m	Fr:r-9
11/81	10:00	Shannon(60) – CD	d	

Date	Time	Title (min. if not 30) — Type	Action	From/To
12/81	9:00	Nurse(60) — MD	m	To:r-10
12/81	10:00	Shannon(60) — CD	m	To:w-10-3/82
1/82	8:00	Mr. Merlin — SC	m	To:m-8
1/82	8:00	WKRP in Cincinnati — SC	m	Fr:w-8:30
1/82	8:30	Two of Us — SC	m	Fr:m-8:30
1/82	8:30	WKRP in Cincinnati — SC	m	To:w-8
1/82	9:00	Film(120) — FI	s	
2/82	8:00	WKRP in Cincinnati — SC	m	To:w-9
2/82	8:30	Two of Us — SC	m	To:t-8:30-6/82
2/82	9:00	Film(120) — FI	f	
3/82	8:00	Herbie the Love Bug(60) — SC	d	
3/82	9:00	WKRP in Cincinnati — SC	m	Fr:w-8
3/82	9:30	Baker's Dozen — SC	d	
3/82	10:00	Shannon(60) — CD	m	Fr:w-10-12/81
4/82	8:00	Herbie the Love Bug(60) — SC	c	
4/82	9:00	WKRP in Cincinnati — SC	m	To:m-8:30-6/82
4/82	9:30	Baker's Dozen — SC	c	
4/82	10:00	Shannon(60) — CD	c	
5/82	8:00	Incredible Hulk(60) — AD	m	Fr:f-8-11/81
5/82	9:00	Film(120) — FI	s	
6/82	8:00	Incredible Hulk(60) — AD	c	
7/82	8:00	Mr. Merlin — SC	m	Fr:m-8-3/82
8/82	8:00	Mr. Merlin — SC	c	
9/82	8:00	Seven Brides for Seven Brothers (60) — AD	d	
9/82	9:00	Film(120) — FI	f	
10/82	9:00	Alice — SC	m	Fr:n-9
10/82	9:30	Filthy Rich — SC	m	Fr:m-9:30-8/82
10/82	10:00	Tucker's Witch(60) — CD	d	
11/82	9:00	Alice — SC	m	To:m-9-3/83
11/82	9:30	Filthy Rich — SC	m	To:m-8:30-1/83
11/82	10:00	Tucker's Witch(60) — CD	m	To:r-10-3/83
12/82	9:00	Film(120) — FI	s	
3/83	8:00	Seven Brides for Seven Brothers (60) — AD	m	To:s-8-6/83
4/83	8:00	Zorro and Son — SC	d	
4/83	8:30	Square Pegs — SC	m	Fr:m-8
5/83	8:30	Square Pegs — SC	m	To:m-8
6/83	8:00	Archie Bunker's Place — SC	m	Fr:n-8
6/83	8:00	Zorro and Son — SC	c	
6/83	8:30	Gloria — SC	m	Fr:n-8:30-4/83
9/83	8:00	Archie Bunker's Place — SC	c	
9/83	8:30	Gloria — SC	c	
10/83	8:00	Whiz Kids(60) — CD	d	
12/83	8:00	Whiz Kids(60) — CD	m	To:s-8
1/84	8:00	Domestic Life — SC	d	
1/84	8:30	Empire — SC	d	
2/84	8:00	Domestic Life — SC	m	To:t-8:30-6/84
2/84	8:30	Empire — SC	c	
3/84	8:00	One Day at a Time — SC	m	Fr:n-8:30

Date	Time	Title (min. if not 30) — Type	Action	From/To
3/84	8:30	Mama Malone—SC	d	
5/84	8:00	One Day at a Time—SC	m	To:m-9
5/84	8:30	Mama Malone—SC	m	To:s-8-6/84
6/84	8:00	Crossroads(60)—NM	d	
9/84	8:00	Crossroads(60)—NM	c	
10/84	8:00	Charles in Charge—SC	d	
10/84	8:30	Dreams—SC	d	
10/84	8:30	Dreams—SC	c	
11/84	8:30	E/R—SC	m	Fr:t-8:30
4/85	8:00	Charles in Charge—SC	m	To:s-8
4/85	8:00	Double Dare(60)—AD	d	
4/85	8:30	E/R—SC	m	To:s-8:30
5/85	8:00	Double Dare(60)—AD	c	
6/85	8:00	Charles in Charge—SC	m	Fr:s-8-4/85
6/85	8:00	I Had Three Wives(60)—CD	d	
6/85	8:30	E/R—SC	m	Fr:s-8:30-4/85
7/85	8:00	Charles in Charge—SC	c	
7/85	8:30	E/R—SC	c	
9/85	8:00	I Had Three Wives(60)—CD	m	To:f-8
9/85	8:00	Stir Crazy(60)—CO	d	
9/85	9:00	Charlie & Company—SC	d	
9/85	9:00	Film(120)—FI	f	
9/85	9:30	George Burns' Comedy Week—CA	d	
9/85	10:00	Equalizer(60)—CD	d	
10/85	8:00	Stir Crazy(60)—CO	m	To:t-8-12/85
12/85	8:00	Mary—SC	d	
12/85	8:30	Foley Square—SC	d	
12/85	9:00	Charlie & Company—SC	m	To:t-8:30
12/85	9:30	George Burns' Comedy Week—CA	c	
1/86	9:00	Crazy Like a Fox(60)—CO	m	Fr:n-9
2/86	8:00	Mary—SC	m	To:t-9
2/86	8:30	Foley Square—SC	m	To:t-9:30
3/86	8:00	Fast Times—SC	d	
3/86	8:30	Tough Cookies—SC	d	
3/86	9:00	Crazy Like a Fox(60)—CO	m	To:s-8
3/86	9:00	Film(120)—FI	s	
3/86	10:00	Equalizer(60)—CD	m	To:t-10
4/86	8:00	Fast Times—SC	c	
4/86	8:00	West 57th(60)—NM	m	Fr:t-10-9/85
4/86	8:30	Tough Cookies—SC	c	
6/86	8:00	West 57th(60)—NM	m	To:w-10
6/86	8:00	Foley Square—SC	m	Fr:t-9:30-4/86
6/86	8:30	Charlie & Company—SC	m	Fr:f-8
6/86	9:00	Airwolf(60)—SD	m	Fr:s-9
6/86	9:00	Film(120)—FI	f	
6/86	10:00	West 57th(60)—NM	m	Fr:w-8
7/86	8:00	Foley Square—SC	c	
7/86	8:00	Film(180)—FI	s	
7/86	8:30	Charlie & Company—SC	c	
7/86	9:00	Airwolf(60)—SD	c	

Date	Time	Title (min. if not 30) — Type	Action	From/To
7/86	10:00	West 57th(60) — NM	m	To:m-10-4/87
8/86	8:00	Film(180) — FI	f	
9/86	9:00	Magnum, P.I.(60) — CD	m	Fr:t-9
9/86	10:00	Equalizer(60) — CD	m	Fr:t-10
10/86	8:00	Together We Stand — SC	m	Fr:m-8:30
10/86	8:00	Together We Stand — SC	c	
10/86	8:30	Better Days — SC	d	
10/86	8:30	Better Days — SC	c	
11/86	8:00	Mickey Spillane's Mike Hammer (60) — CD	m	Fr:s-9
3/87	8:00	Mickey Spillane's Mike Hammer (60) — CD	m	To:s-8
3/87	10:00	Houston Knights(60) — CD	d*	
4/87	8:00	Roxie — SC	d	
4/87	8:00	Roxie — SC	c	
4/87	8:00	Mickey Spillane's Mike Hammer (60) — CD	m	Fr:s-8
4/87	8:30	Take Five — SC	d	
4/87	8:30	Take Five — SC	c	
4/87	10:00	Houston Knights(60) — CD	m*	To:t-9-8/87
6/87	9:00	Shell Game(60) — CD	m*	Fr:r-8-2/87
6/87	9:00	Shell Game(60) — CD	c*	
8/87	8:00	Mickey Spillane's Mike Hammer (60) — CD	c	
9/87	8:00	Oldest Rookie(60) — CD	d	
1/88	8:00	Oldest Rookie(60) — CD	c	
1/88	8:00	Law & Harry McGraw(60) — CD	m	Fr:t-10
2/88	8:00	Law & Harry McGraw(60) — CD	c	
2/88	9:00	Magnum, P.I.(60) — CD	m	To:m-10-6/88
3/88	8:00	Smothers Brothers(60) — CV	d	
3/88	9:00	Jake & the Fatman(60) — CD	m	Fr:t-9
5/88	8:00	Smothers Brothers(60) — CV	c	
5/88	9:00	Jake & the Fatman(60) — CD	m	To:w-8
5/88	10:00	Equalizer(60) — CD	m	To:w-9
6/88	8:00	Jake & the Fatman(60) — CD	m	Fr:w-9
6/88	9:00	Equalizer(60) — CD	m#	Fr:w-10
6/88	10:00	Wiseguy(60) — CD	m#	Fr:m-10-4/88
8/88	8:00	Jake & the Fatman(60) — CD	c	

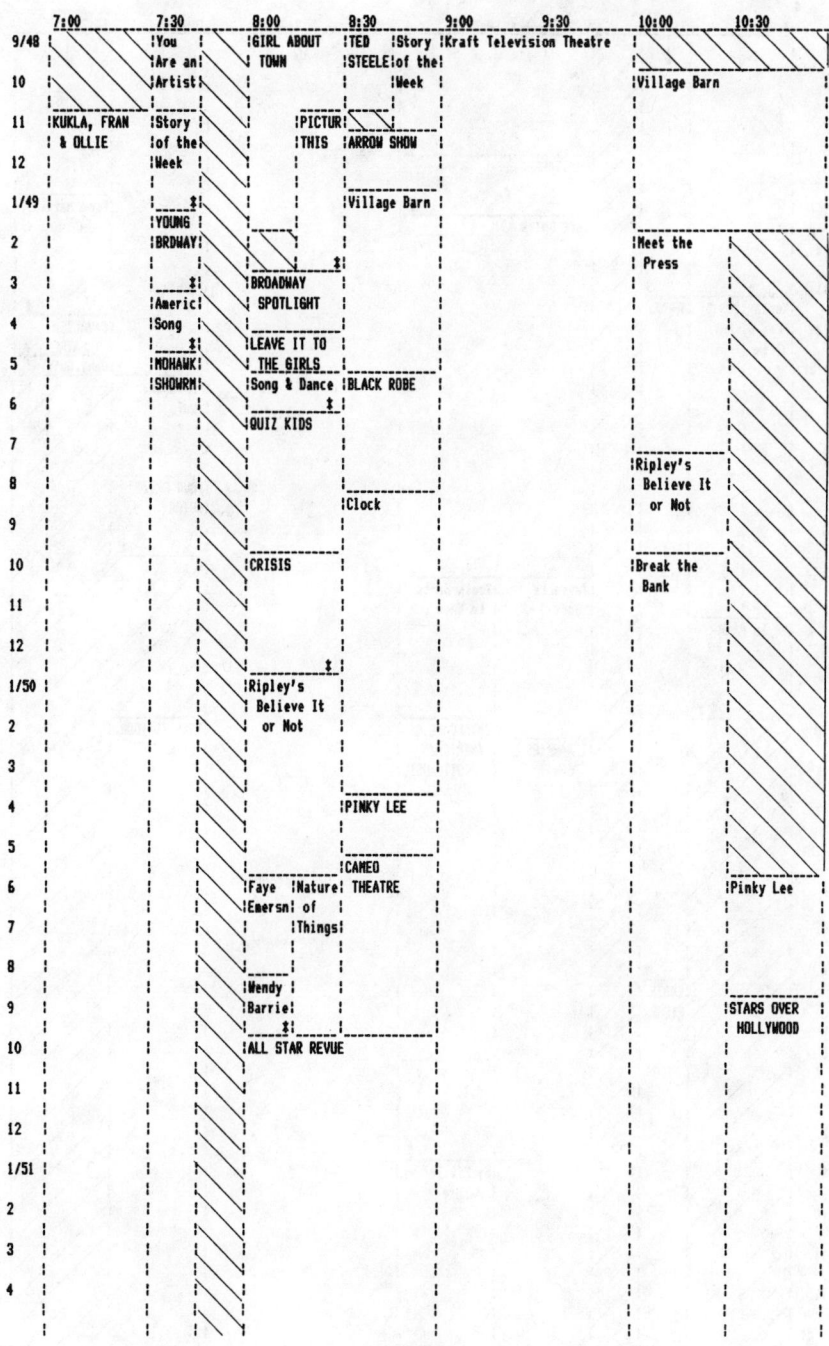

	7:00	7:30	8:00	8:30	9:00	9:30	10:00	10:30
9/48		You Are an Artist	GIRL ABOUT TOWN	TED STEELE	Story of the Week	Kraft Television Theatre		
10							Village Barn	
11	KUKLA, FRAN & OLLIE	Story of the Week		PICTUR THIS	ARROW SHOW			
12								
1/49		YOUNG BRDWAY		Village Barn				
2							Meet the Press	
3		Americ Song	BROADWAY SPOTLIGHT					
4								
5		MOHAWK SHOWRM	LEAVE IT TO THE GIRLS					
6			Song & Dance	BLACK ROBE				
7			QUIZ KIDS					
8							Ripley's Believe It or Not	
9				Clock				
10			CRISIS				Break the Bank	
11								
12								
1/50			Ripley's Believe It or Not					
2								
3								
4				PINKY LEE				
5								
6			Faye Emersn	CAMEO Nature THEATRE of				Pinky Lee
7				Things				
8			Wendy Barrie					
9							STARS OVER HOLLYWOOD	
10			ALL STAR REVUE					
11								
12								
1/51								
2								
3								
4								

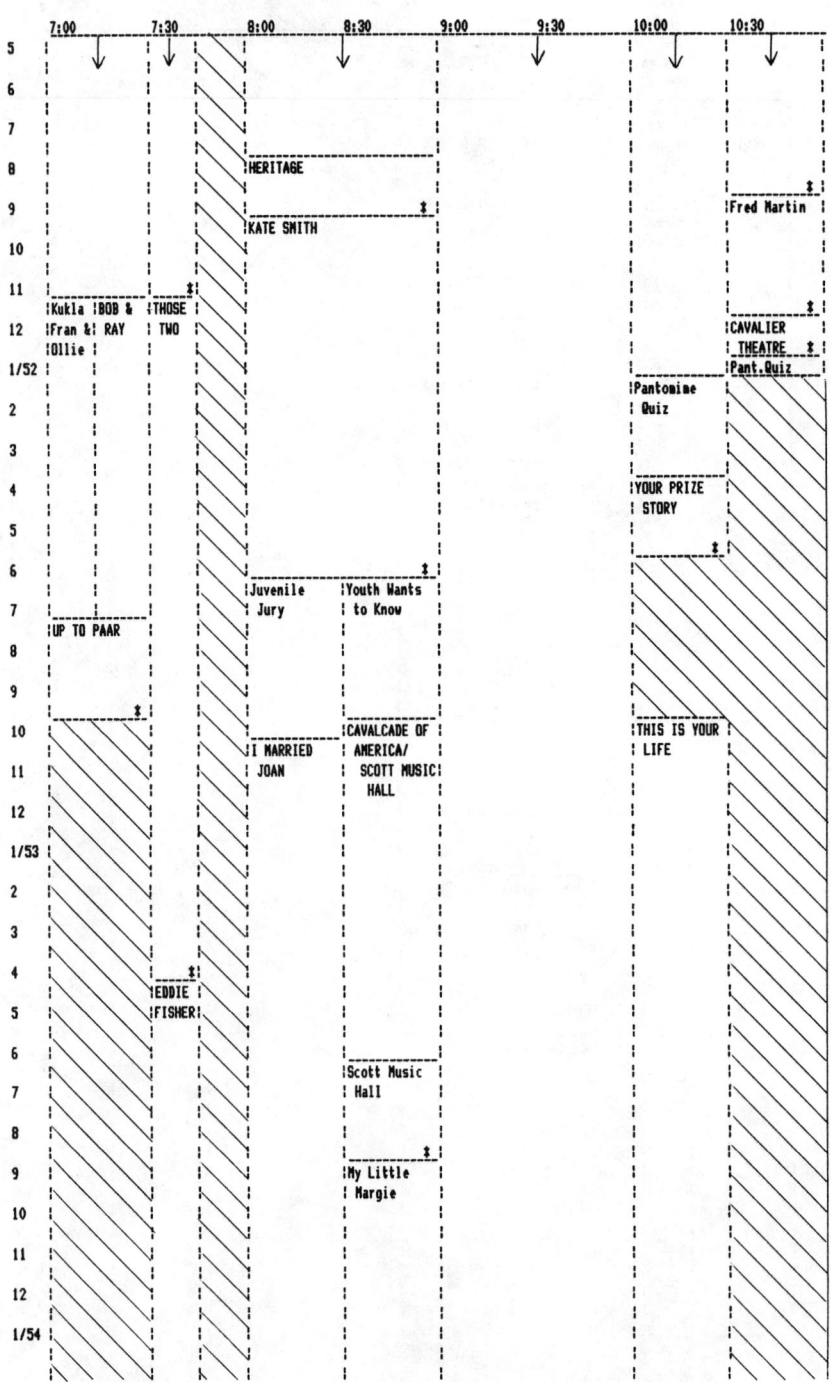

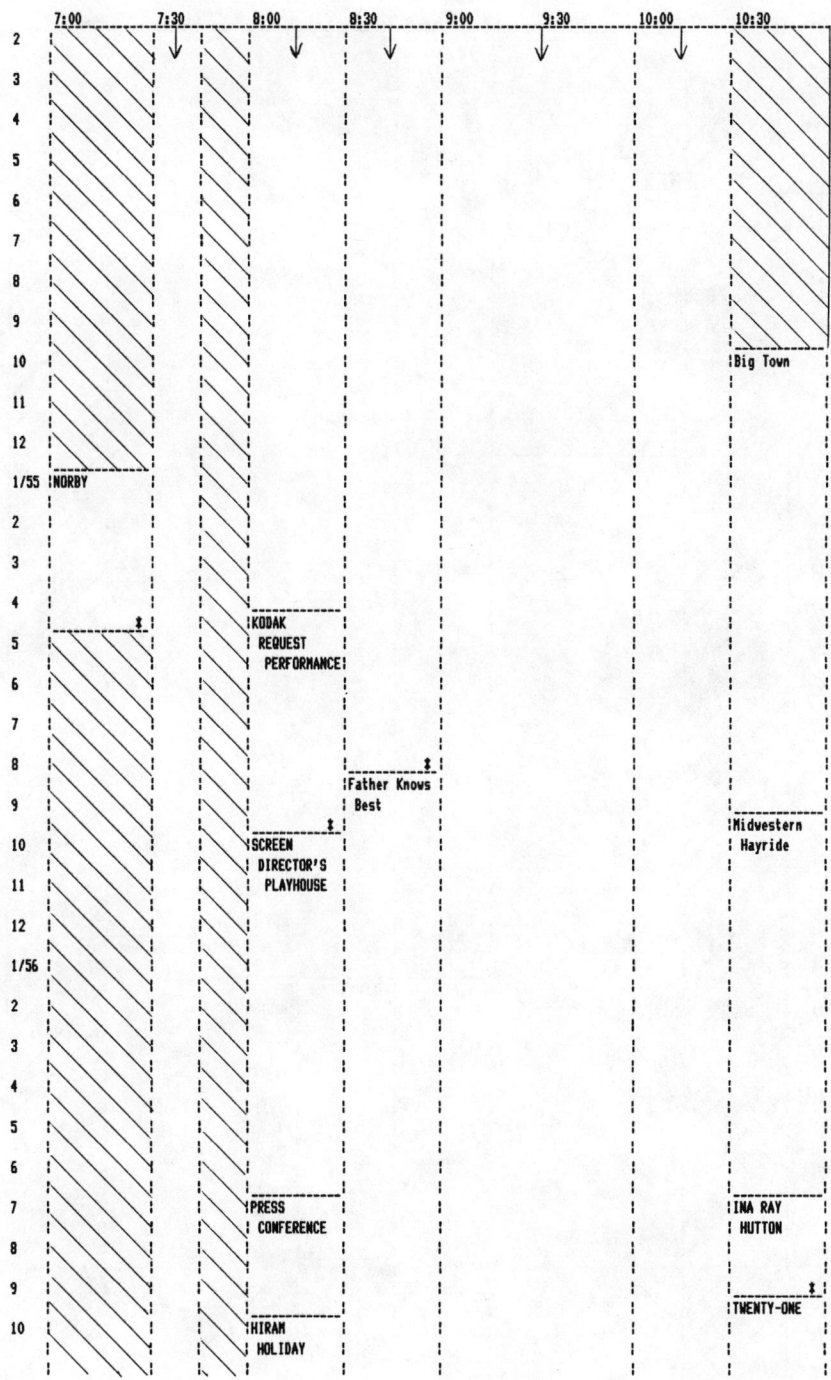

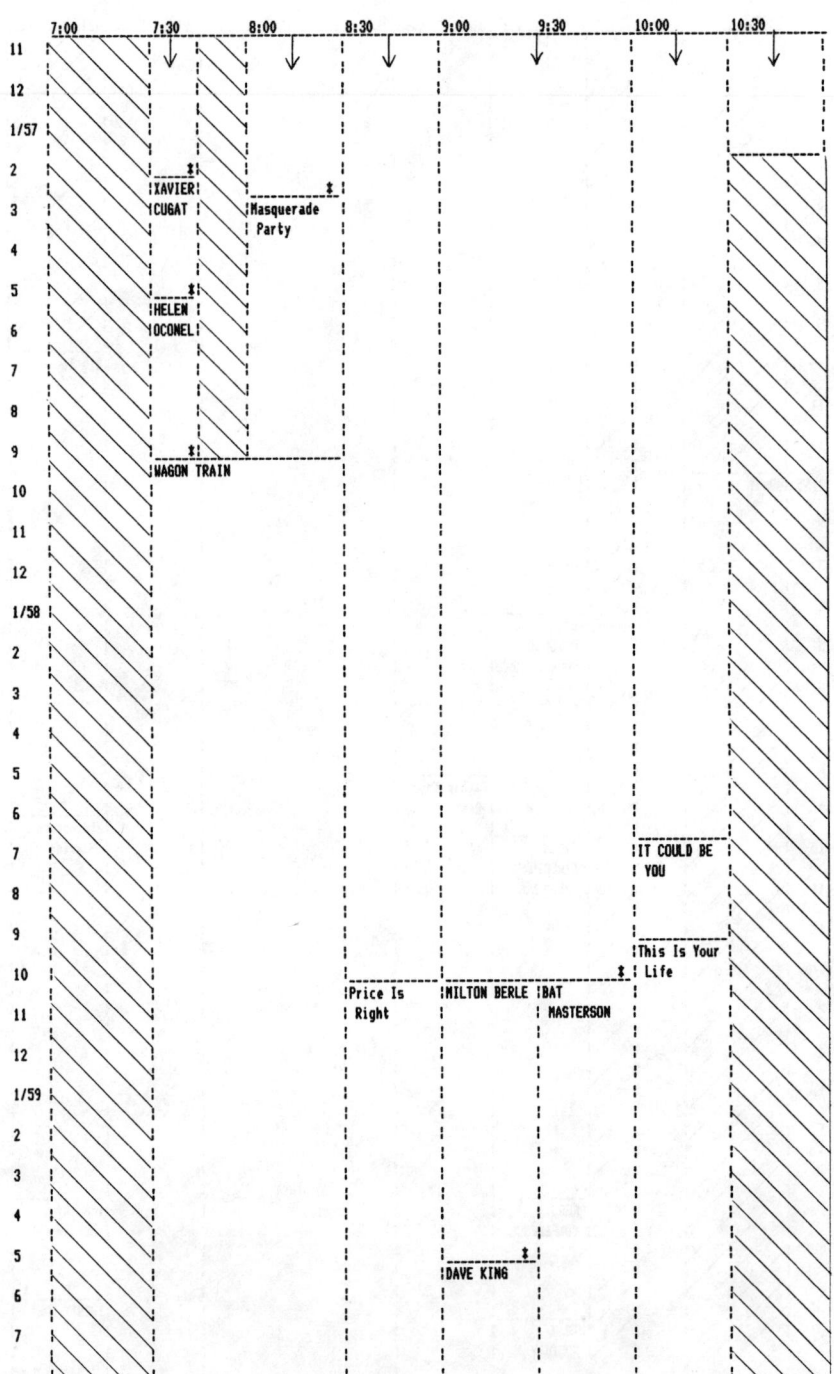

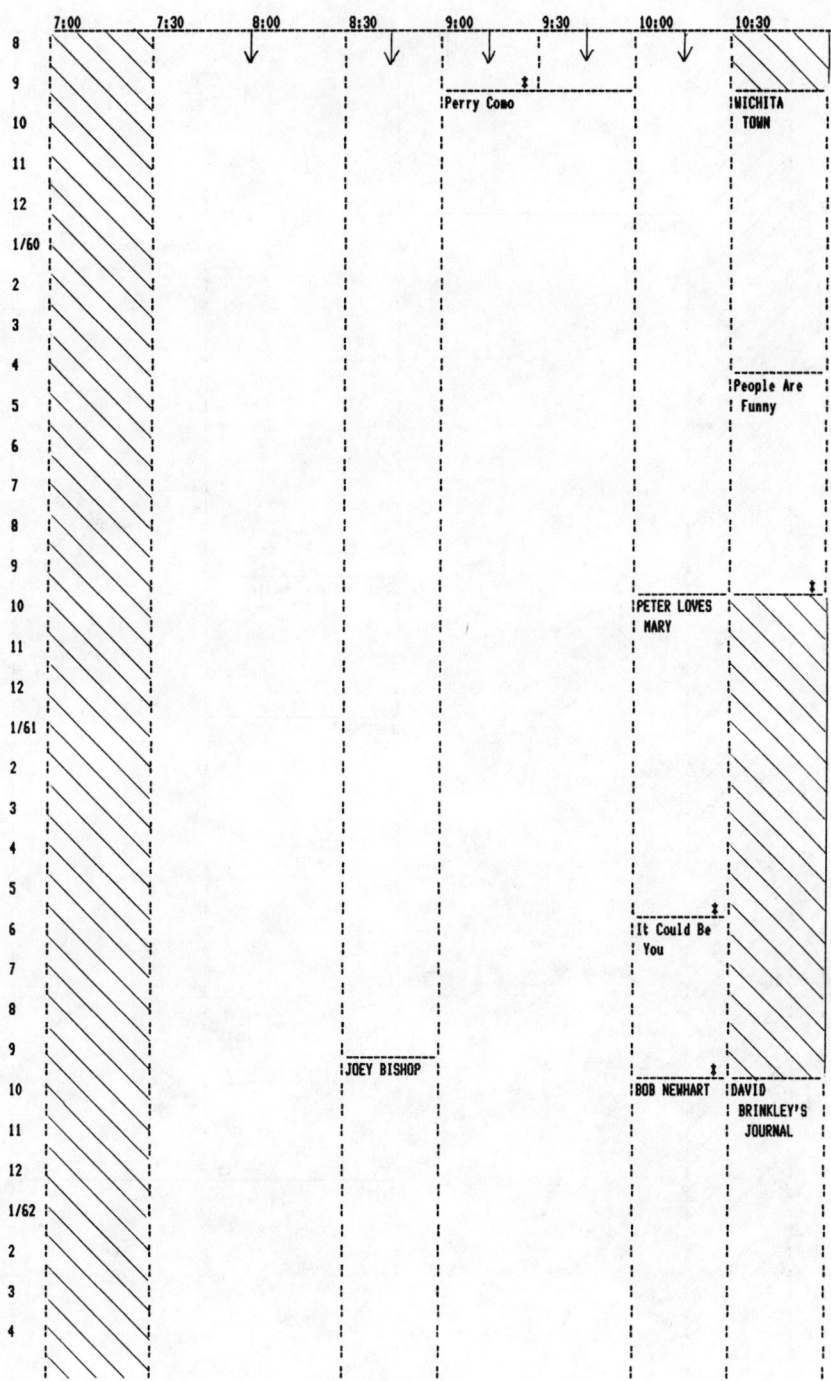

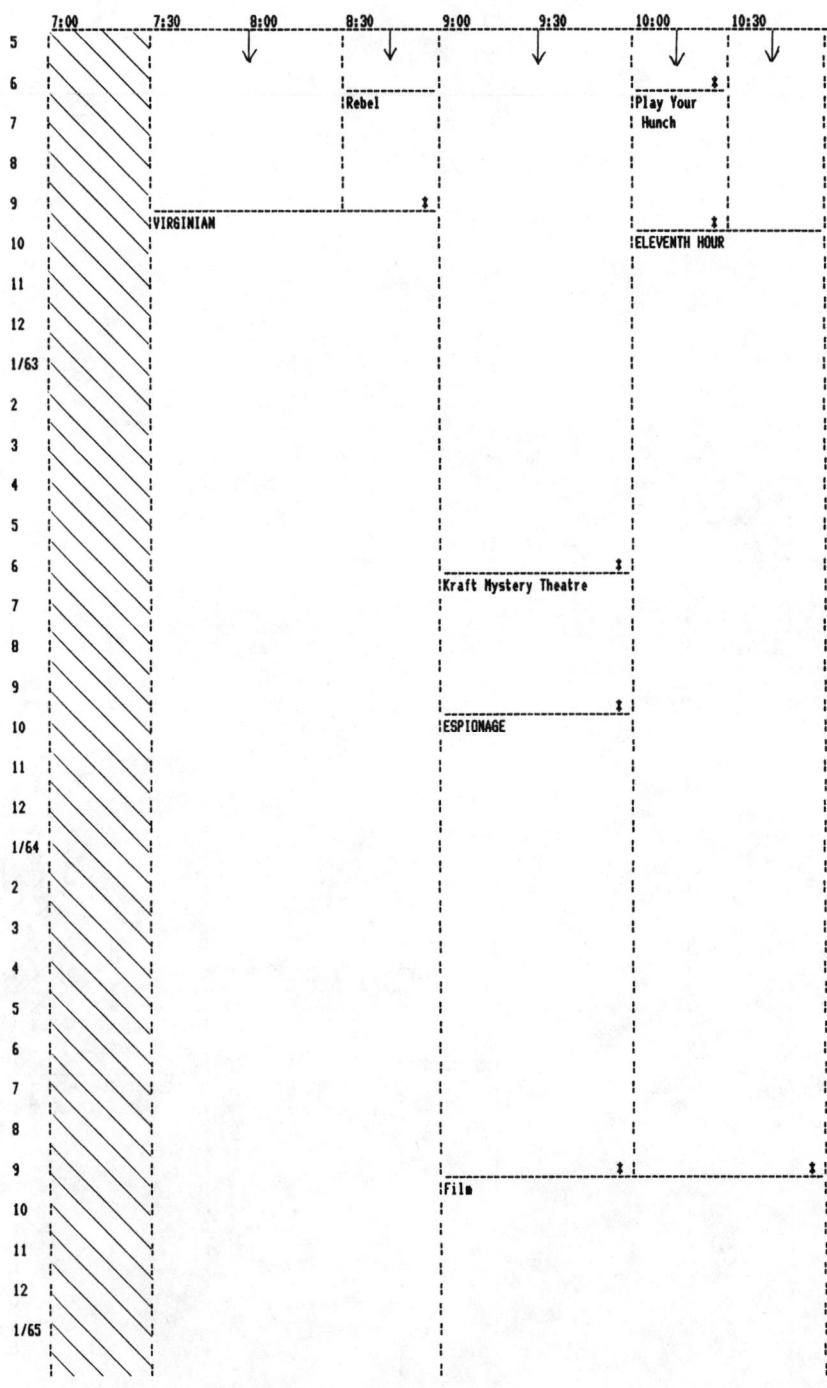

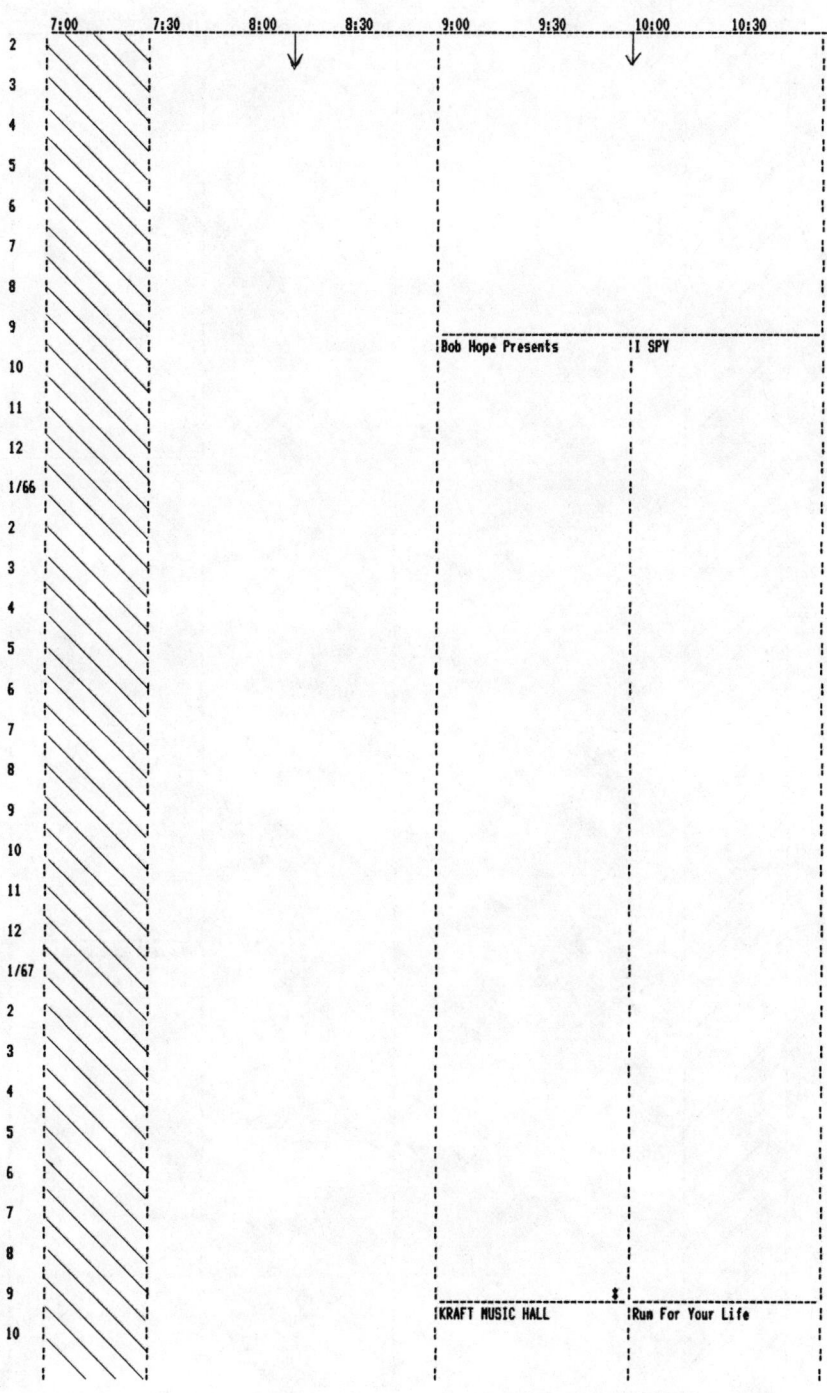

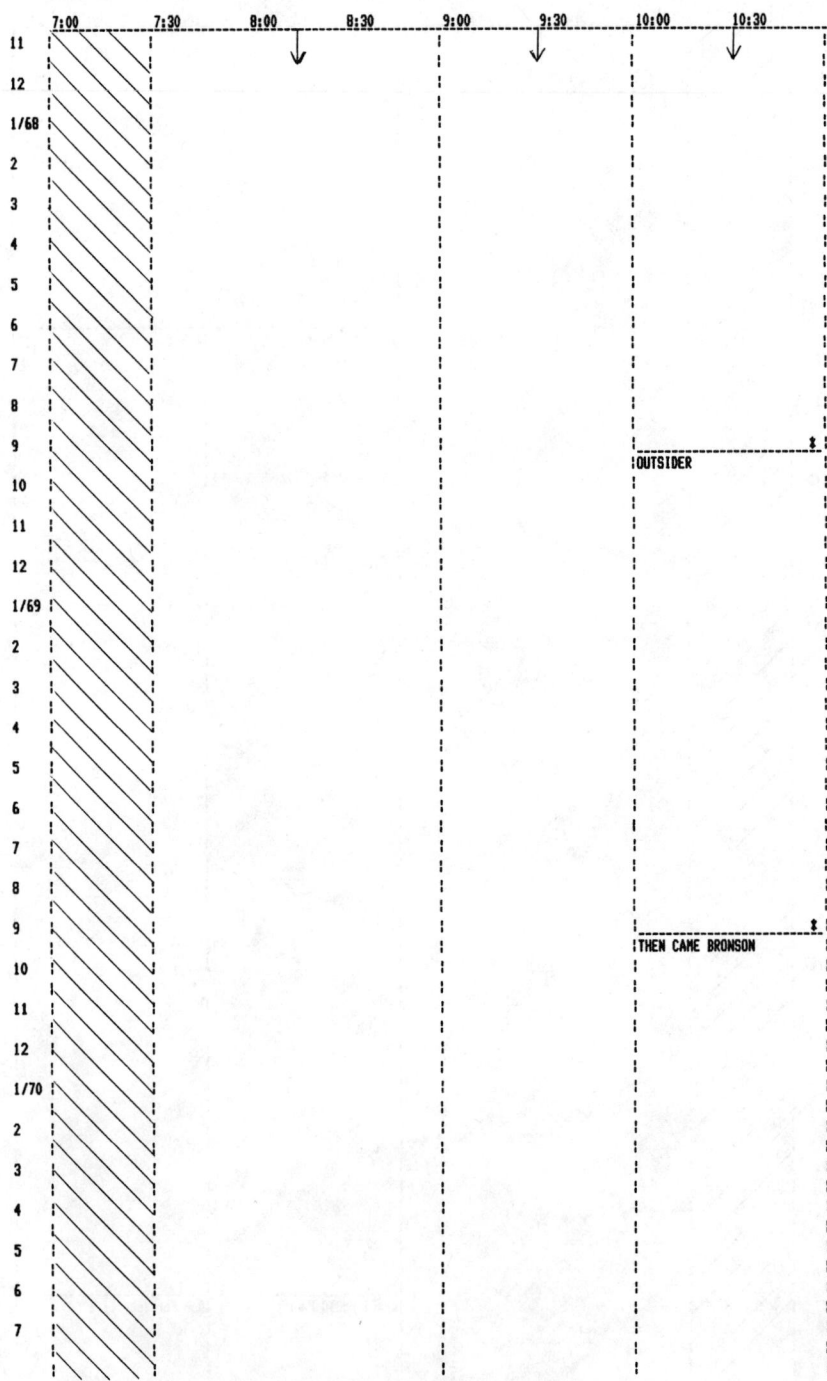

	7:00	7:30	8:00	8:30	9:00	9:30	10:00	10:30
11								
12								
1/68								
2								
3								
4								
5								
6								
7								
8								
9							OUTSIDER	
10								
11								
12								
1/69								
2								
3								
4								
5								
6								
7								
8								
9							THEN CAME BRONSON	
10								
11								
12								
1/70								
2								
3								
4								
5								
6								
7								

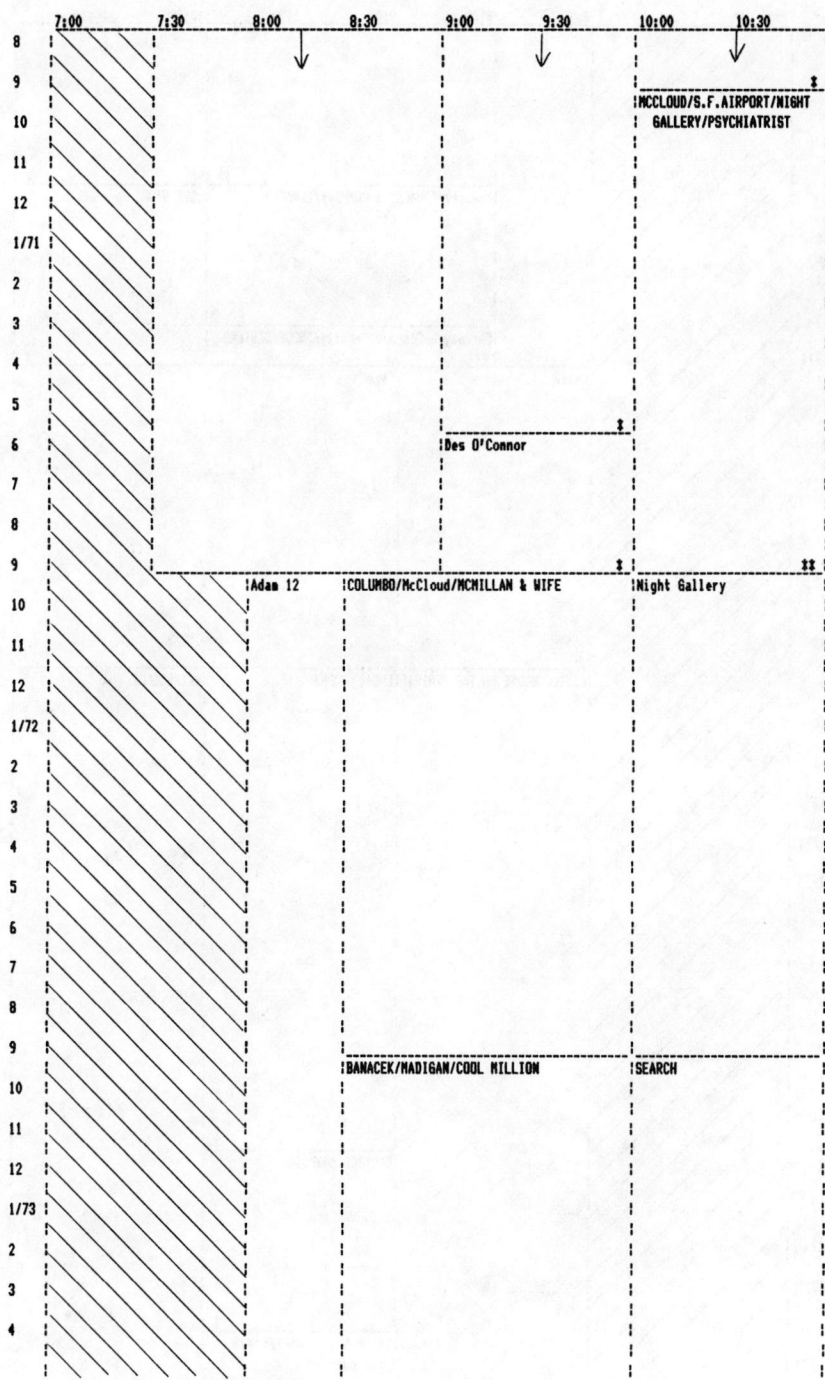

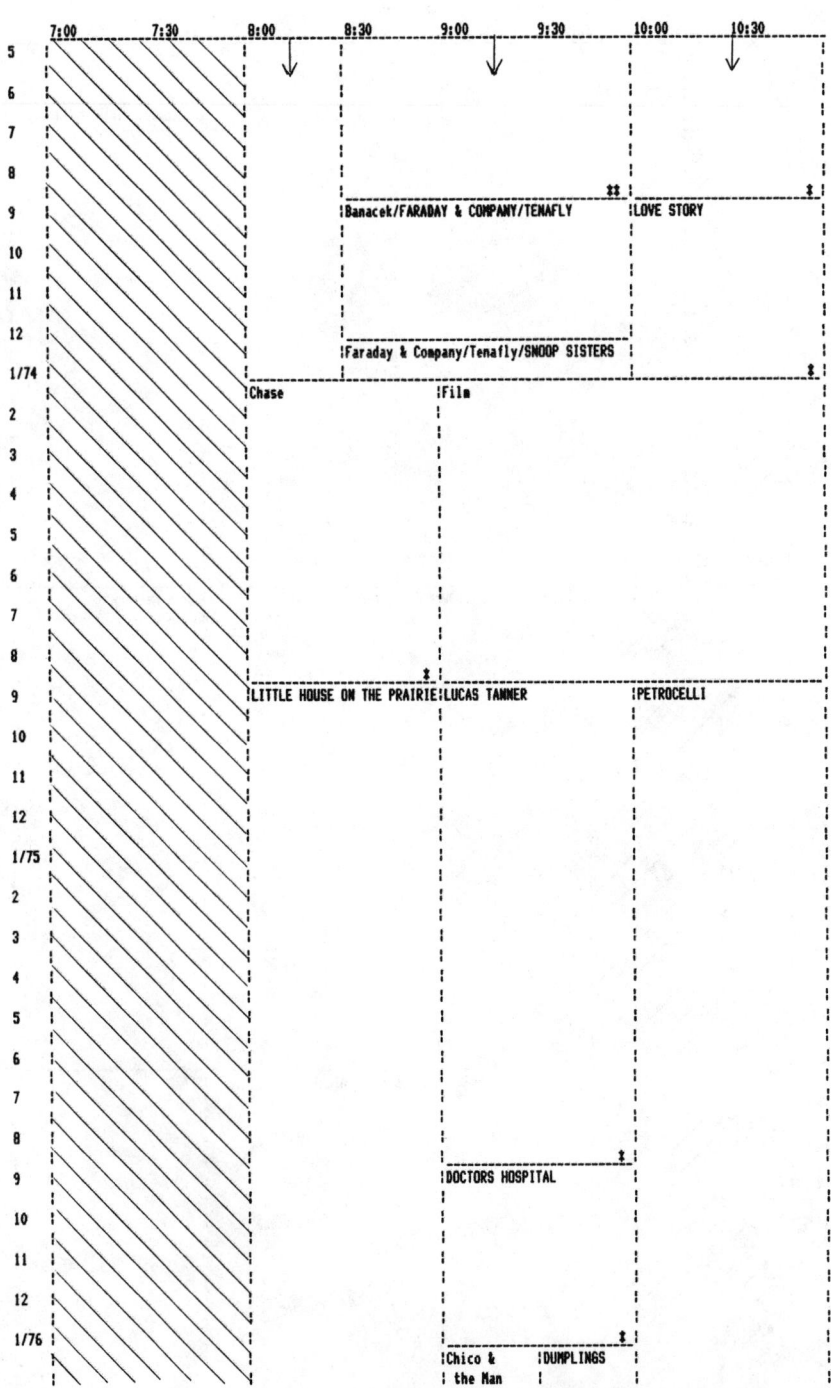

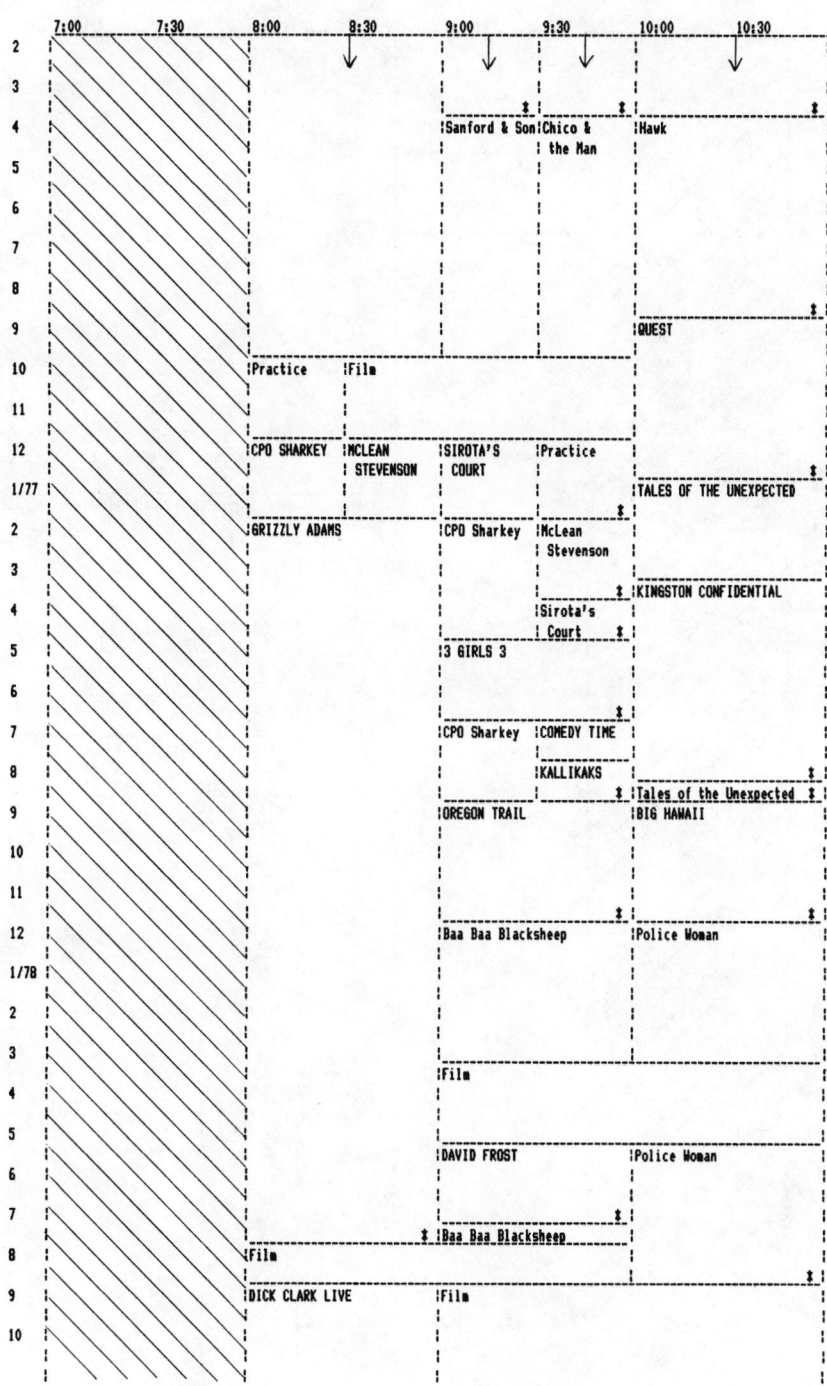

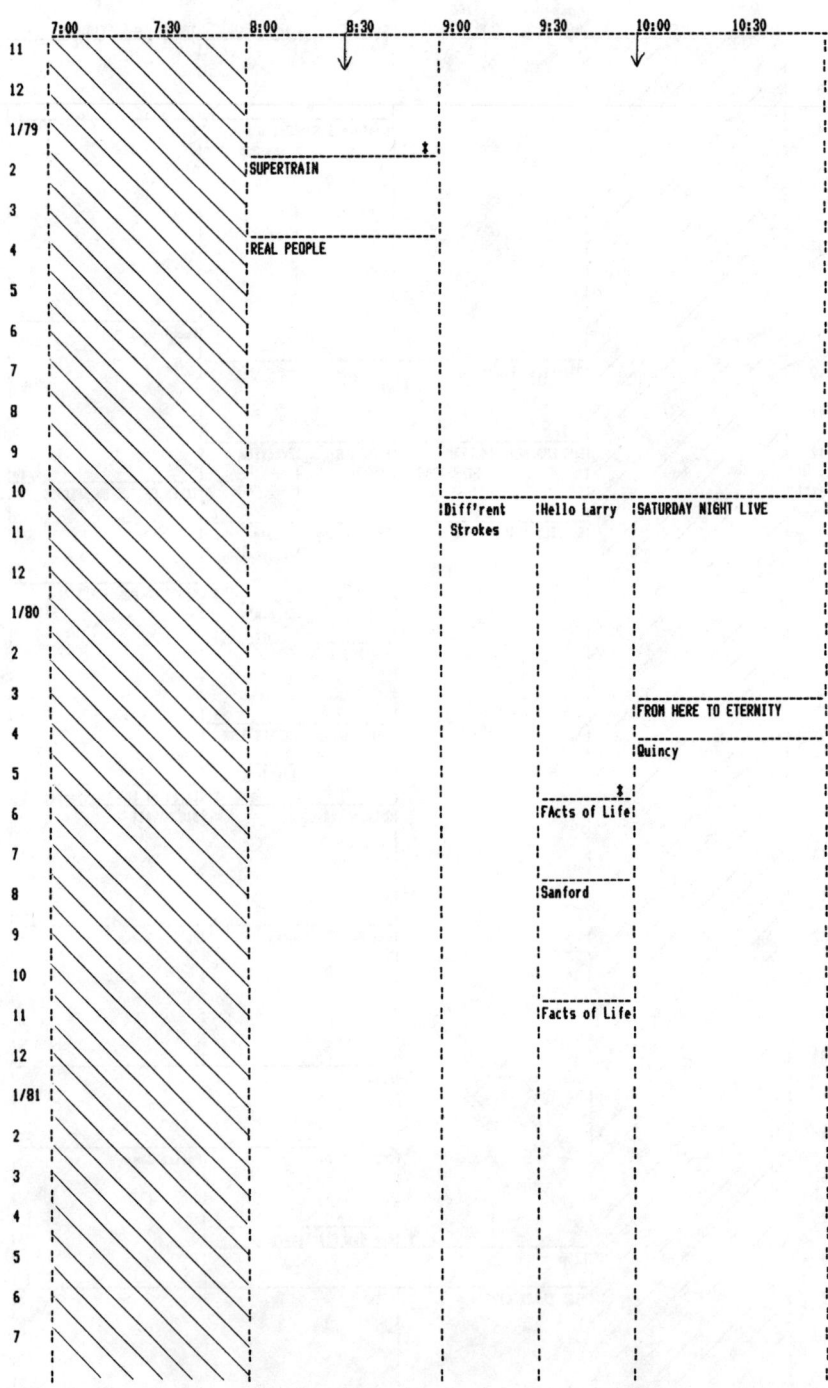

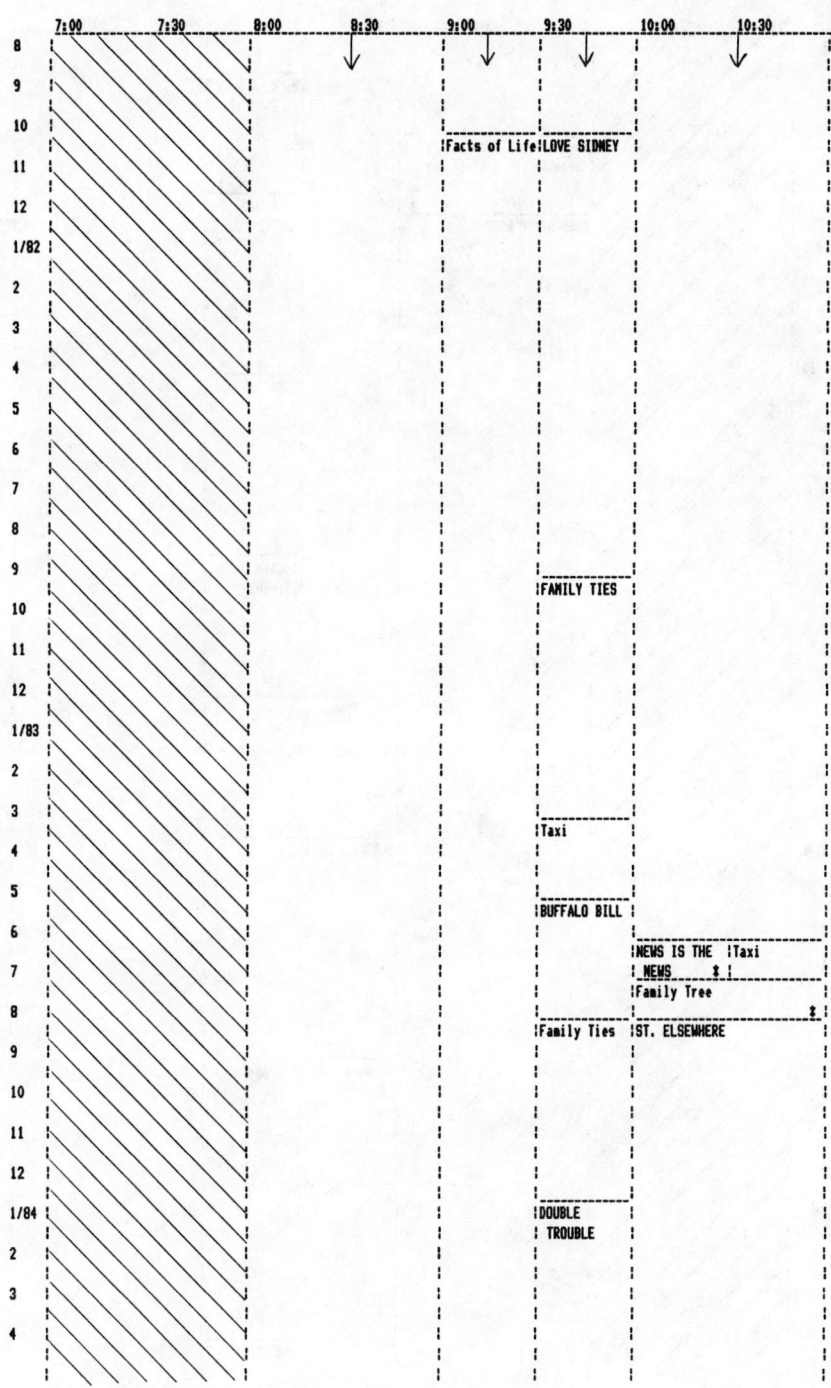

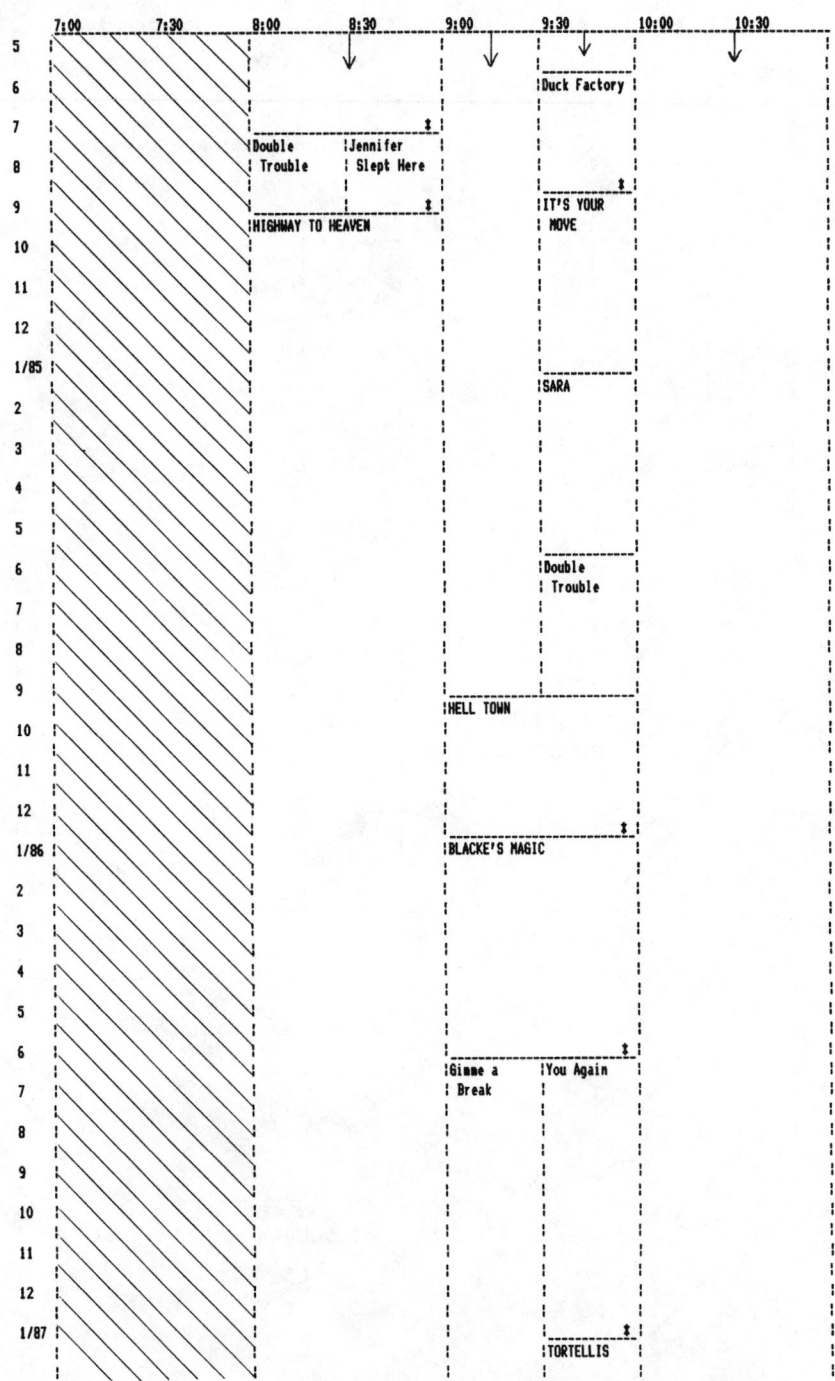

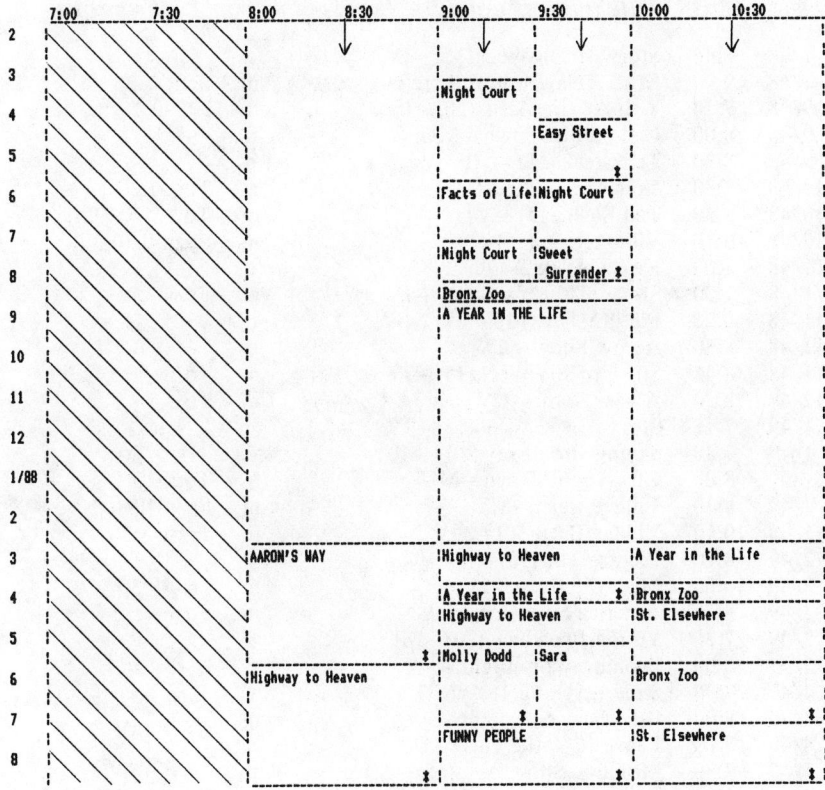

	7:00	7:30	8:00	8:30	9:00	9:30	10:00	10:30
2				↓	↓	↓		↓
3					Night Court			
4						Easy Street		
5								
6					Facts of Life	Night Court		
7					Night Court	Sweet		
8						Surrender		
					Bronx Zoo			
9					A YEAR IN THE LIFE			
10								
11								
12								
1/88								
2								
3			AARON'S WAY		Highway to Heaven		A Year in the Life	
4					A Year in the Life		Bronx Zoo	
					Highway to Heaven		St. Elsewhere	
5					Molly Dodd	Sara		
6			Highway to Heaven				Bronx Zoo	
7					FUNNY PEOPLE		St. Elsewhere	
8								

Date	Time	Title (min. if not 30) — Type	Action	From/To
1/48	8:45	Story of the Week(15)—IV	d	
1/48	9:00	Kraft Television Theatre(60)—DA	m	Fr:w-7:30
9/48	7:30	You Are an Artist(20)—IS	m	Fr:r-9
9/48	8:00	Girl About Town—MU	d	
9/48	8:30	Ted Steele(15)—MU	d	
10/48	7:30	You Are an Artist(20)—IS	m	To:t-7:30
10/48	8:30	Ted Steele(15)—MU	m	To:t-9-4/49(d)
10/48	10:10	Village Barn(50)—MV	m	Fr:m-9:10
11/48	7:00	Kukla, Fran & Ollie—KV	d	
11/48	7:30	Story of the Week(15)—IV	m	Fr:w-8:45
11/48	8:20	Picture This(10)—KV	d	
11/48	8:30	Arrow Show—CV	d	
11/48	8:45	Story of the Week(15)—IV	m	To:w-7:15
12/48	8:30	Arrow Show—CV	m	To:r-8
1/49	7:15	Story of the Week(15)—IV	c	
1/49	7:30	Young Broadway(20)—MU	d	
1/49	8:00	Girl About Town—MU	m	To:n-10
1/49	8:30	Village Barn—MV	m	Fr:w-10:10
1/49	10:10	Village Barn(50)—MV	m	To:w-8:30
2/49	8:20	Picture This(10)—KV	c	
2/49	10:00	Meet the Press—IV	m	Fr:n-8:30
3/49	7:30	America Song(15)—MU	m	Fr:m-7:30
3/49	7:30	Young Broadway(20)—MU	c	
3/49	8:00	Broadway Spotlight—VY	d	
4/49	7:30	America Song(15)—MU	c	
4/49	8:00	Broadway Spotlight—VY	m	To:n-7
4/49	8:00	Leave It to the Girls—DS	d	
5/49	7:30	Mohawk Showroom(15)—MU	d	
5/49	8:00	Leave It to the Girls—DS	m	To:n-8
5/49	8:00	Song and Dance—MU	m	Fr:m-8:15
5/49	8:30	Black Robe—CR	d	
5/49	8:30	Village Barn—MV	m	To:m-10
6/49	7:00	Judy Splinters(15)—KV	d*	
6/49	7:15	Mary Kay and Johnny(15)—SC	m*	Fr:w-9(c)
6/49	8:00	Quiz Kids—QU	d	
6/49	8:00	Song and Dance—MU	c	
7/49	10:00	Meet the Press—IV	m	To:m-10
7/49	10:00	Ripley's Believe It or Not—VY	m	Fr:t-9:30
8/49	7:00	Judy Splinters(15)—KV	c*	
8/49	7:15	Mary Kay and Johnny(15)—SC	m*	To:r-8:30
8/49	7:30	Capitol Capers(15)—MU	d*	
8/49	8:30	Black Robe—CR	m	To:m-var
8/49	8:30	Clock—SA	m	Fr:m-8:30
9/49	7:30	Capitol Capers(15)—MU	c*	
9/49	8:00	Quiz Kids—QU	m	To:m-10
9/49	10:00	Ripley's Believe It or Not—VY	m	To:var
10/49	8:00	Crisis—DR	d	
10/49	10:00	Break the Bank—QU	m	Fr:f-9(a)
12/49	8:00	Crisis—DR	c	
1/50	8:00	Ripley's Believe It or Not—VY	m	Fr:var-11/49

Date	Time	Title (min. if not 30) — Type	Action	From/To
3/50	8:30	Clock — SA	m	To:f-9:30
4/50	8:30	Pinky Lee — SC	d	
5/50	8:00	Ripley's Believe It or Not — VY	m	To:r-8
5/50	8:30	Cameo Theatre — DA	d	
5/50	8:30	Pinky Lee — SC	m	To:w-10:30
6/50	8:00	Faye Emerson Show(15) — IV	m	Fr:s-10:30
6/50	8:15	Nature of Things(15) — IS	m	Fr:s-7:30-2/50
6/50	10:30	Pinky Lee — SC	m	Fr:w-8:30
7/50	7:00	Ransom Sherman — CV	d*	
8/50	7:00	Ransom Sherman — CV	c*	
8/50	7:30	Wendy Barrie Show(15) — IV	m	Fr:tr-7:30
8/50	8:00	Faye Emerson Show(15) — IV	m	To:trs-7:45
8/50	10:30	Pinky Lee — SC	m	To:r-8:30-10/50
9/50	7:30	Wendy Barrie Show(15) — IV	c	
9/50	8:15	Nature of Things(15) — IS	m	To:f-10:45-6/51
9/50	8:30	Cameo Theatre — DA	m	To:m-8-6/51
9/50	10:30	Stars Over Hollywood — VS	d	
10/50	8:00	All Star Revue(60) — CV	d	
7/51	7:00	Ernie in Kovacsland — CV	d*	
7/51	7:30	Songs at Twilight(15) — MU	d*	
7/51	8:00	All Star Revue(60) — CV	m	To:s-8-9/51
8/51	7:00	Ernie in Kovacsland — CV	c*	
8/51	7:30	Songs at Twilight(15) — MU	c*	
8/51	8:00	Heritage(60) — MU	d	
8/51	10:30	Stars Over Hollywood — VS	c	
9/51	8:00	Heritage(60) — MU	c	
9/51	8:00	Kate Smith Evening Hour(60) — MV	d	
9/51	10:30	Freddy Martin — MV	m	Fr:r-10
11/51	7:00	Kukla, Fran & Ollie — KV	m	To:m-f-7
11/51	7:00	Kukla, Fran & Ollie(15) — KV	m	Fr:m-f-7
11/51	7:15	Bob and Ray(15) — CV	d	
11/51	7:30	Mohawk Showroom(15) — MU	c	
11/51	7:30	Those Two(15) — SC	d	
11/51	10:30	Freddy Martin — MV	c	
12/51	10:30	Cavalier Theatre — DA	d	
12/51	10:30	Cavalier Theatre — DA	c	
1/52	10:00	Break the Bank — QU	m	To:n-9:30(c)
1/52	10:00	Pantomime Quiz — QU	m	Fr:w-10:30
1/52	10:30	Pantomime Quiz — QU	m	Fr:m-8-8/51(c)
1/52	10:30	Pantomime Quiz — QU	m	To:w-10
2/52	7:15	Bob and Ray(15) — CV	m	To:tr-7:15
2/52	7:15	Goldbergs(15) — SC	m	Fr:m-9:30-6/51(c)
3/52	10:00	Pantomime Quiz — QU	m	To:f-8:30-7/52
4/52	10:00	Your Prize Story — DA	d	
5/52	10:00	Your Prize Story — DA	c	
6/52	7:00	Kukla, Fran & Ollie(15) — KV	m	To:m-f-7-9/54(a)
6/52	8:00	Juvenile Jury — QU	m	Fr:t-8:30-9/51
6/52	8:00	Kate Smith Evening Hour(60) — MV	c	
6/52	8:30	Youth Wants to Know — DS	m	Fr:s-7-10/51
7/52	7:00	Up to Paar — QU	d	

Date	Time	Title (min. if not 30) – Type	Action	From/To
7/52	7:15	Goldbergs(15) – SC	m	To:f-8-7/53
9/52	7:00	Up to Paar – QU	c	
9/52	8:30	Youth Wants to Know – DS	m	To:s-7:30-7/54
10/52	8:00	I Married Joan – SC	d	
10/52	8:00	Juvenile Jury – QU	m	To:m-9-6/53
10/52	8:30	Cavalcade of America – DA	d	
10/52	8:30	Scott Music Hall – MV	d	
10/52	10:00	This Is Your Life – IV	d	
4/53	7:30	Coke Time with Eddie Fisher(15) – MU	d	
4/53	7:30	Those Two(15) – SC	c	
6/53	8:30	Cavalcade of America – DA	m	To:t-7:30-9/53(a)
7/53	10:00	Candid Camera – CY	m*	Fr:m-9-9/50(c)
7/53	10:00	Candid Camera – CY	m*	To:n-10-10/60(c)
8/53	8:30	Scott Music Hall – MV	c	
9/53	8:30	My Little Margie – SC	m	Fr:r-10-7/53(c)
6/54	7:30	World of Mr. Sweeney(15) – SC	d*	
8/54	7:30	World of Mr. Sweeney(15) – SC	c*	
10/54	10:30	Big Town – ND	m	Fr:f-8-7/53(d)
1/55	7:00	Norby – SC	d	
4/55	7:00	Norby – SC	c	
4/55	8:00	I Married Joan – SC	c	
4/55	8:00	Kodak Request Performance – DA	d	
6/55	7:30	Matt Dennis(15) – MU	d*	
8/55	7:30	Matt Dennis(15) – MU	c*	
8/55	8:30	Father Knows Best – SC	m	Fr:n-10-3/55(c)
8/55	8:30	My Little Margie – SC	c	
9/55	8:00	Kodak Request Performance – DA	c	
9/55	10:30	Big Town – ND	m	To:t-10:30
9/55	10:30	Midwestern Hayride – MV	m	Fr:f-8
10/55	8:00	Screen Director's Playhouse – VS	d	
6/56	7:30	Jaye P. Morgan(15) – MU	d*	
6/56	8:00	Screen Director's Playhouse – VS	m	To:w-9(a)
6/56	10:30	Midwestern Hayride – MV	m	To:n-9:30-7/57(a)
7/56	8:00	Press Conference – IV	d	
7/56	10:30	Ina Ray Hutton Show – MV	d	
8/56	7:30	Jaye P. Morgan(15) – MU	c*	
9/56	8:00	Press Conference – IV	m	To:n-8:30
9/56	10:30	Ina Ray Hutton Show – MV	c	
9/56	10:30	Twenty-One – QU	d	
10/56	8:00	Adventures of Hiram Holiday – SC	d	
1/57	10:30	Twenty-One – QU	m	To:m-9
2/57	7:30	Coke Time with Eddie Fisher(15) – MU	c	
2/57	7:30	Xavier Cugat(15) – MU	d	
2/57	8:00	Adventures of Hiram Holiday – SC	c	
3/57	8:00	Masquerade Party – QU	m	Fr:s-10-12/56(a)
5/57	7:30	Helen O'Connell(15) – MU	d	
5/57	7:30	Xavier Cugat(15) – MU	c	
9/57	7:30	Helen O'Connell(15) – MU	c	

Date	Time	Title (min. if not 30) — Type	Action	From/To
9/57	7:30	Wagon Train(60) — WE	d	
9/57	8:00	Masquerade Party — QU	m	To:m-8:30-8/58(c)
6/58	10:00	This Is Your Life — IV	m	To:w-10-9/58
7/58	10:00	It Could Be You — QU	d	
9/58	8:30	Father Knows Best — SC	m	To:m-8:30(c)
9/58	8:30	Price Is Right — QU	m	Fr:r-10
9/58	10:00	It Could Be You — QU	m	To:r-8:30-11/58
9/58	10:00	This Is Your Life — IV	m	Fr:w-9:30-6/58
10/58	9:00	Kraft Television Theatre(60) — DA	c	
10/58	9:00	Milton Berle — CV	d	
10/58	9:30	Bat Masterson — WE	d	
5/59	9:00	Kraft Music Hall Presents Dave King — VY	d	
5/59	9:00	Milton Berle — CV	c	
9/59	9:00	Kraft Music Hall Presents Dave King — VY	c	
9/59	9:00	Perry Como(60) — MV	m	Fr:s-8-6/59
9/59	9:30	Bat Masterson — WE	m	To:r-8
9/59	10:30	Wichita Town — WE	d	
4/60	10:30	People Are Funny — QU	m	Fr:f-7:30
4/60	10:30	Wichita Town — WE	m	To:f-8:30-6/60
6/60	9:00	Happy — SC	d*	
6/60	9:30	Tate — WE	d*	
9/60	9:00	Happy — SC	m*	To:f-7:30-1/61
9/60	9:30	Tate — WE	c*	
9/60	10:00	This Is Your Life — IV	m	To:n-10:30
9/60	10:30	People Are Funny — QU	c	
10/60	10:00	Peter Loves Mary — SC	d	
5/61	10:00	Peter Loves Mary — SC	c	
6/61	9:00	Kraft Mystery Theatre(60) — MA	d*	
6/61	10:00	It Could Be You — QU	m	Fr:s-10:30-1/60
9/61	8:30	Joey Bishop Show — SC	d	
9/61	8:30	Price Is Right — QU	m	To:m-8:30
9/61	9:00	Kraft Mystery Theatre(60) — MA	m*	To:w-9-6/62
9/61	10:00	It Could Be You — QU	c	
10/61	10:00	Bob Newhart Show — CV	d	
10/61	10:30	David Brinkley's Journal — DO	d	
6/62	8:30	Joey Bishop Show — SC	m	To:s-8:30-9/62
6/62	8:30	Rebel — WE	m	Fr:n-9-9/61(a)
6/62	9:00	Kraft Mystery Theatre(60) — MA	m*	Fr:w-9-9/61
6/62	10:00	Bob Newhart Show — CV	c	
6/62	10:00	Play Your Hunch — QU	m	Fr:f-9-9/60
9/62	7:30	Virginian(90) — WE	d	
9/62	7:30	Wagon Train(60) — WE	m	To:w-7:30(a)
9/62	8:30	Rebel — WE	c	
9/62	9:00	Kraft Mystery Theatre(60) — MA	m*	To:w-9-6/63
9/62	10:00	Play Your Hunch — QU	c	
9/62	10:30	David Brinkley's Journal — DO	m	To:m-10
10/62	10:00	Eleventh Hour(60) — MD	d	
6/63	9:00	Kraft Mystery Theatre(60) — MA	m	Fr:w-9-9/62

Date	Time	Title (min. if not 30) — Type	Action	From/To
6/63	9:00	Perry Como(60) — MV	c	
9/63	9:00	Kraft Mystery Theatre(60) — MA	c	
10/63	9:00	Espionage(60) — SD	d	
9/64	9:00	Espionage(60) — SD	c	
9/64	9:00	Film(120) — FI	s	
9/64	10:00	Eleventh Hour(60) — MD	c	
9/65	9:00	Bob Hope Presents the Chrysler Theater(60) — DA	m	Fr:f-8:30
9/65	9:00	Film(120) — FI	f	
9/65	10:00	I Spy(60) — SD	d	
9/67	9:00	Bob Hope Presents the Chrysler Theater(60) — DA	c	
9/67	9:00	Kraft Music Hall(60) — MV	d	
9/67	10:00	I Spy(60) — SD	m	To:m-10
9/67	10:00	Run for Your Life(60) — AD	m	Fr:m-10
9/68	10:00	Outsider(60) — CD	d	
9/68	10:00	Run for Your Life(60) — AD	c	
5/69	9:00	Kraft Music Hall Presents Sandler & Young(60) — VY	d*	
8/69	9:00	Kraft Music Hall Presents Sandler & Young(60) — VY	c*	
9/69	10:00	Outsider(60) — CD	c	
9/69	10:00	Then Came Bronson(60) — AD	d	
5/70	9:00	Kraft Music Hall Presents Des O'Connor(60) — VY	d*	
9/70	9:00	Kraft Music Hall Presents Des O'Connor(60) — VY	m*	To:w-9-6/71
9/70	10:00	McCloud(60) — CD	d	
9/70	10:00	Night Gallery(60) — SA	d	
9/70	10:00	Psychiatrist(60) — MD	d	
9/70	10:00	San Francisco International Airport (60) — DR	d	
9/70	10:00	Then Came Bronson(60) — AD	c	
5/71	9:00	Kraft Music Hall(60) — MV	c	
6/71	9:00	Kraft Music Hall Presents Des O'Connor(60) — VY	m	Fr:w-9-9/70
9/71	7:30	Virginian(90) — WE	c	
9/71	8:00	Adam 12 — CD	m	Fr:r-9:30
9/71	8:30	Columbo(90) — CD	d	
9/71	8:30	McCloud(90) — CD	m	Fr:w-9
9/71	8:30	McMillan and Wife(90) — CD	d	
9/71	9:00	Kraft Music Hall Presents Des O'Connor(60) — VY	c	
9/71	10:00	McCloud(60) — CD	m	To:w-8:30
9/71	10:00	Psychiatrist(60) — MD	c	
9/71	10:00	San Francisco International Airport (60) — DR	c	
8/72	8:30	McCloud(90) — CD	m	To:n-8:30
8/72	8:30	McMillan and Wife(90) — CD	m	To:n-8:30
9/72	8:30	Banacek(90) — CD	d	

Date	Time	Title (min. if not 30) — Type	Action	From/To
9/72	8:30	Columbo(90) — CD	m	To:n-8:30
9/72	8:30	Madigan(90) — CD	d	
9/72	10:00	Night Gallery(60) — SA	m	To:n-10
9/72	10:00	Search(60) — AD	d	
10/72	8:30	Cool Million(90) — CD	d	
7/73	8:30	Cool Million(90) — CD	c	
8/73	8:30	Madigan(90) — CD	c	
8/73	10:00	Search(60) — AD	c	
9/73	8:30	Faraday and Company(90) — CD	d	
9/73	10:00	Love Story(60) — DA	d	
10/73	8:30	Tenafly(90) — CD	d	
12/73	8:30	Banacek(90) — CD	m	To:t-8:30
12/73	8:30	Snoop Sisters(90) — CD	d	
12/73	8:30	Snoop Sisters(90) — CD	m	To:t-8:30
1/74	8:00	Adam 12 — CD	m	To:t-8
1/74	8:00	Chase(60) — CD	m	Fr:t-8
1/74	8:30	Faraday and Company(90) — CD	m	To:t-8:30-4/74
1/74	8:30	Tenafly(90) — CD	m	To:t-8:30-4/74
1/74	9:00	Film(120) — FI	s	
1/74	10:00	Love Story(60) — DA	c	
8/74	8:00	Chase(60) — CD	c	
8/74	9:00	Film(120) — FI	f	
9/74	8:00	Little House on the Prairie(60) — DR	d	
9/74	9:00	Lucas Tanner(60) — DR	d	
9/74	10:00	Petrocelli(60) — LD	d	
8/75	9:00	Lucas Tanner(60) — DR	c	
9/75	9:00	Doctors' Hospital(60) — MD	d	
1/76	9:00	Chico and the Man — SC	m	Fr:f-8:30
1/76	9:00	Doctors' Hospital(60) — MD	c	
1/76	9:30	Dumplings — SC	d	
3/76	9:00	Chico and the Man — SC	m	To:w-9:30
3/76	9:30	Dumplings — SC	c	
3/76	10:00	Petrocelli(60) — LD	c	
4/76	9:00	Sanford and Son — SC	s	
4/76	9:30	Chico and the Man — SC	m	Fr:w-9
4/76	10:00	Hawk(60) — CD	m	Fr:r-10-12/66(a)
8/76	9:00	Sanford and Son — SC	f	
8/76	9:30	Chico and the Man — SC	m	To:f-8:30
8/76	10:00	Hawk(60) — CD	c	
9/76	8:00	Little House on the Prairie(60) — DR	m	To:m-8
9/76	8:30	Film(90) — FI	s	
9/76	10:00	Quest(60) — WE	d	
10/76	8:00	Practice — SC	m	Fr:f-8:30-7/76
11/76	8:00	Practice — SC	m	To:w-9:30
11/76	8:30	Film(90) — FI	f	
12/76	8:00	C.P.O. Sharkey — SC	d	
12/76	8:30	McLean Stevenson — SC	d	
12/76	9:00	Sirota's Court — SC	d	
12/76	9:30	Practice — SC	m	Fr:w-8
12/76	10:00	Quest(60) — WE	c	

Date	Time	Title (min. if not 30) – Type	Action	From/To
1/77	8:00	C.P.O. Sharkey – SC	m	To:w-9
1/77	8:30	McLean Stevenson – SC	m	To:w-9:30
1/77	9:00	Sirota's Court – SC	m	To:w-9:30-4/77
1/77	9:30	Practice – SC	c	
1/77	10:00	Tales of the Unexpected(60) – SA	d	
2/77	8:00	Life and Times of Grizzly Adams (60) – AD	d	
2/77	9:00	C.P.O. Sharkey – SC	m	Fr:w-8
2/77	9:30	McLean Stevenson – SC	m	Fr:w-8:30
3/77	9:30	McLean Stevenson – SC	c	
3/77	10:00	Kingston: Confidential(60) – ND	d	
3/77	10:00	Tales of the Unexpected(60) – SA	m	To:w-10-8/77
4/77	9:00	C.P.O. Sharkey – SC	m	To:w-9-7/77
4/77	9:30	Sirota's Court – SC	m	Fr:w-9-1/77
4/77	9:30	Sirota's Court – SC	c	
5/77	9:00	3 Girls 3(60) – VY	d	
6/77	9:00	3 Girls 3(60) – VY	c	
7/77	9:00	C.P.O. Sharkey – SC	m	Fr:w-9-4/77
7/77	9:30	Comedy Time – CA	d	
7/77	9:30	Comedy Time – CA	m	To:r-8
8/77	9:00	C.P.O. Sharkey – SC	m	To:f-8:30-10/77
8/77	9:30	Kallikaks – SC	d	
8/77	9:30	Kallikaks – SC	c	
8/77	10:00	Kingston: Confidential(60) – ND	c	
8/77	10:00	Tales of the Unexpected(60) – SA	m	Fr:w-10-3/77
8/77	10:00	Tales of the Unexpected(60) – SA	c	
9/77	9:00	Oregon Trail(60) – WE	d	
9/77	10:00	Big Hawaii(60) – AD	d	
11/77	9:00	Oregon Trail(60) – WE	c	
11/77	10:00	Big Hawaii(60) – AD	c	
12/77	9:00	Baa Baa Black Sheep(60) – WD	m	Fr:t-8-8/77
12/77	10:00	Police Woman(60) – CD	m	Fr:t-10
3/78	9:00	Baa Baa Black Sheep(60) – WD	m	To:r-9
3/78	9:00	Film(120) – FI	s	
3/78	10:00	Police Woman(60) – CD	m	To:r-10
5/78	8:00	Roller Girls – SC	m*	Fr:m-8
5/78	8:00	Roller Girls – SC	c*	
5/78	8:30	Joe & Valerie – SC	m*	Fr:m-8:30
5/78	8:30	Joe & Valerie – SC	m*	To:f-8:30-1/79
5/78	9:00	Headliners with David Frost(60) – IV	d	
5/78	9:00	Film(120) – FI	f	
5/78	10:00	Police Woman(60) – CD	m	Fr:r-10
7/78	8:00	Life and Times of Grizzly Adams (60) – AD	c	
7/78	9:00	Baa Baa Black Sheep(60) – WD	m	Fr:r-9-4/78
7/78	9:00	Baa Baa Black Sheep(60) – WD	m	To:f-8
7/78	9:00	Headliners with David Frost(60) – IV	c	
8/78	8:00	Film(120) – FI	s	

Date	Time	Title (min. if not 30) — Type	Action	From/To
8/78	10:00	Police Woman(60) — CD	c	
9/78	8:00	Dick Clark's Live Wednesday(60) — VY	d	
9/78	8:00	Film(120) — FI	f	
9/78	9:00	Film(120) — FI	s	
1/79	8:00	Dick Clark's Live Wednesday(60) — VY	c	
2/79	8:00	Supertrain(60) — DA	d	
3/79	8:00	Supertrain(60) — DA	m	To:s-10
4/79	8:00	Real People(60) — NM	d	
6/79	8:00	Laugh-In(60) — CV	d*	
7/79	8:00	Laugh-In(60) — CV	c*	
10/79	9:00	Diff'rent Strokes — SC	m	Fr:f-8
10/79	9:00	Film(120) — FI	f	
10/79	9:30	Hello Larry — SC	m	Fr:f-8:30
10/79	10:00	NBC's Saturday Night Live(60) — CV	d	
3/80	10:00	From Here to Eternity(60) — WD	d	
3/80	10:00	NBC's Saturday Night Live(60) — CV	m	To:f-10
4/80	10:00	From Here to Eternity(60) — WD	m	To:var-8/80
4/80	10:00	Quincy, M.E.(60) — CD	m	Fr:r-9
5/80	9:30	Hello Larry — SC	c	
6/80	9:30	Facts of Life — SC	m	Fr:f-8:30
7/80	9:30	Facts of Life — SC	m	To:f-8:30
8/80	9:30	Sanford — SC	m	Fr:s-9
10/80	9:30	Sanford — SC	m	To:f-8:30-1/81
11/80	9:30	Facts of Life — SC	m	Fr:f-8:30
12/80	10:00	Number 96(60) — DR	d*	
12/80	10:00	Number 96(60) — DR	m*	To:r-10
10/81	9:00	Diff'rent Strokes — SC	m	To:r-9
10/81	9:00	Facts of Life — SC	m	Fr:w-9:30
10/81	9:30	Facts of Life — SC	m	To:w-9
10/81	9:30	Love, Sidney — SC	d	
4/82	9:30	Teachers Only — SC	d*	
6/82	9:30	Teachers Only — SC	m*	To:r-9:30-9/82
9/82	9:30	Family Ties — SC	d	
9/82	9:30	Love, Sidney — SC	m	To:s-9:30
3/83	9:30	Family Ties — SC	m	To:m-8:30
3/83	9:30	Taxi — SC	m	Fr:s-9:30
5/83	9:30	Buffalo Bill — SC	d	
5/83	9:30	Taxi — SC	m	To:w-10:30
6/83	10:00	News Is the News — CV	d	
6/83	10:00	Quincy, M.E.(60) — CD	m	To:s-9
6/83	10:30	Taxi — SC	m	Fr:w-9:30
7/83	10:00	Family Tree(60) — DR	m	Fr:s-10-2/83
7/83	10:00	News Is the News — CV	c	
7/83	10:30	Taxi — SC	c	
8/83	9:30	Buffalo Bill — SC	m	To:r-9:30-12/83
8/83	9:30	Family Ties — SC	m	Fr:m-8:30

Date	Time	Title (min. if not 30) – Type	Action	From/To
8/83	10:00	Family Tree(60) – DR	c	
8/83	10:00	St. Elsewhere(60) – MD	m	Fr:t-10
12/83	9:30	Family Ties – SC	m	To:r-8:30
1/84	9:30	Double Trouble – SC	d	
5/84	9:30	Double Trouble – SC	m	To:w-8-7/84
6/84	9:30	Duck Factory – SC	m	Fr:r-9:30
7/84	8:00	Double Trouble – SC	m	Fr:w-9:30-5/84
7/84	8:00	Real People(60) – NM	c	
7/84	8:30	Jennifer Slept Here – SC	m	Fr:s-8:30-5/84
8/84	9:30	Duck Factory – SC	c	
9/84	8:00	Double Trouble – SC	m	To:s-8:30-12/84
9/84	8:00	Highway to Heaven(60) – DR	d	
9/84	8:30	Jennifer Slept Here – SC	c	
9/84	9:30	It's Your Move – SC	d	
1/85	9:30	It's Your Move – SC	m	To:s-9:30
1/85	9:30	Sara – SC	d	
5/85	9:30	Sara – SC	m	To:w-9:30-5/88
6/85	9:30	Double Trouble – SC	m	Fr:s-8:30
8/85	9:00	Facts of Life – SC	m	To:s-8:30
9/85	9:00	Hell Town(60) – DR	d	
9/85	9:30	Double Trouble – SC	c	
12/85	9:00	Hell Town(60) – DR	c	
1/86	9:00	Blacke's Magic(60) – CD	d	
6/86	9:00	Blacke's Magic(60) – CD	c	
6/86	9:00	Gimme a Break – SC	m	Fr:s-8
6/86	9:30	You Again – SC	m	Fr:m-8
1/87	9:30	You Again – SC	c	
1/87	9:30	Tortellis – SC	d	
3/87	9:00	Night Court – SC	m	Fr:r-9:30
3/87	9:00	Gimme a Break – SC	m	To:t-9
3/87	10:00	Bronx Zoo(60) – DR	d*	
4/87	9:30	Easy Street – SC	m	Fr:t-9:30
4/87	9:30	Tortellis – SC	m	To:t-9:30
5/87	9:00	Night Court – SC	m	To:w-9:30
5/87	9:30	Easy Street – SC	c	
5/87	10:00	Bronx Zoo(60) – DR	m*	To:w-9-8/87
6/87	9:00	Facts of Life – SC	m	Fr:s-8
6/87	9:30	Night Court – SC	m	Fr:w-9
7/87	9:00	Facts of Life – SC	m	To:s-8
7/87	9:00	Night Court – SC	m	Fr:w-9:30
7/87	9:30	Sweet Surrender – SC	m	Fr:s-8:30-5/87
7/87	9:30	Night Court – SC	m	To:w-9
8/87	9:00	Bronx Zoo(60) – DR	m	Fr:w-9-5/87
8/87	9:00	Bronx Zoo(60) – DR	m	To:w-10-4/88
8/87	9:00	Night Court – SC	m	To:r-9:30
8/87	9:30	Sweet Surrender – SC	c	
9/87	9:00	A Year in the Life(60) – DR	d	
2/88	8:00	Highway to Heaven(60) – DR	m	To:w-9
2/88	9:00	A Year in the Life(60) – DR	m	To:w-10
2/88	10:00	St. Elsewhere(60) – MD	m	To:w-10-4/88

Date	Time	Title (min. if not 30) — Type	Action	From/To
3/88	8:00	Aaron's Way(60) — DR	d	
3/88	9:00	Highway to Heaven(60) — DR	m	Fr:w-8
3/88	9:00	Highway to Heaven(60) — DR	m	To:w-9-4/88
3/88	10:00	A Year in the Life(60) — DR	m	Fr:w-9
3/88	10:00	A Year in the Life(60) — DR	m	To:w-9
4/88	9:00	A Year in the Life(60) — DR	m	Fr:w-10
4/88	9:00	A Year in the Life(60) — DR	c	
4/88	9:00	Highway to Heaven(60) — DR	m	Fr:w-9-3/88
4/88	10:00	St. Elsewhere(60) — MD	m	Fr:w-10-2/88
4/88	10:00	Bronx Zoo(60) — DR	m	Fr:w-9-8/87
4/88	10:00	Bronx Zoo(60) — DR	m	To:w-10-6/88
5/88	8:00	Aaron's Way(60) — DR	c	
5/88	9:00	Highway to Heaven(60) — DR	m	To:w-8
5/88	9:00	Days & Nights of Molly Dodd — SC	m	Fr:r-9:30
5/88	9:30	Sara — SC	m	Fr:w-9:30-5/85
5/88	10:00	St. Elsewhere(60) — MD	m	To:w-10-7/88
6/88	8:00	Highway to Heaven(60) — DR	m	Fr:w-9
6/88	8:00	Highway to Heaven(60) — DR	c	
6/88	10:00	Bronx Zoo(60) — DR	m	Fr:w-10-4/88
7/88	9:00	Funny People(60) — CY	d	
7/88	9:00	Days & Nights of Molly Dodd — SC	c	
7/88	9:30	Sara — SC	c	
7/88	10:00	St. Elsewhere(60) — MD	m	Fr:w-10-5/88
7/88	10:00	Bronx Zoo(60) — DR	c	
8/88	9:00	Funny People(60) — CY	c	
8/88	10:00	St. Elsewhere(60) — MD	c	

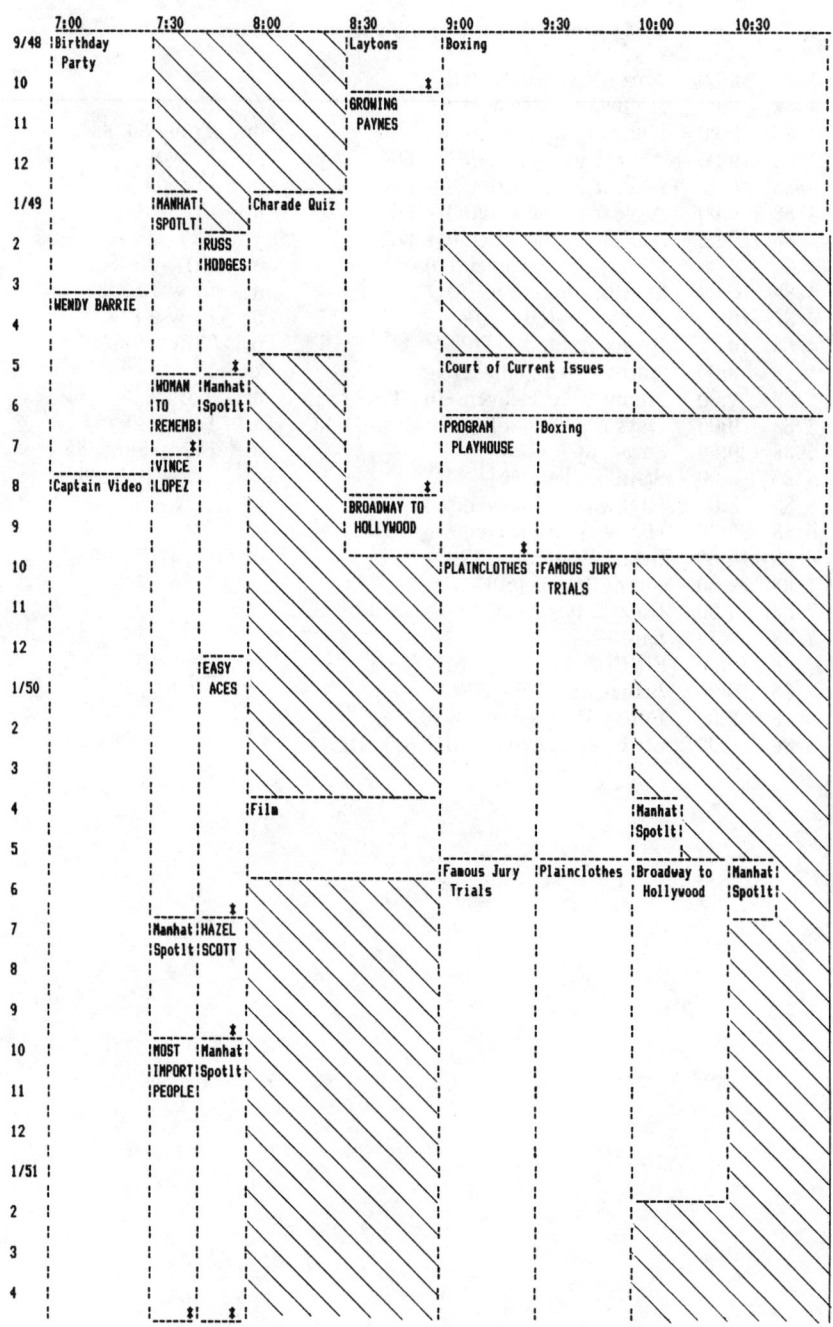

	7:00	7:30	8:00	8:30	9:00	9:30	10:00	10:30
9/48	Birthday Party			Laytons	Boxing			
10								
11				GROWING PAYNES				
12								
1/49		MANHAT SPOTLT	Charade Quiz					
2		RUSS HODGES						
3								
4	WENDY BARRIE							
5					Court of Current Issues			
6		WOMAN TO REMEMB	Manhat Spotlt					
7		VINCE LOPEZ			PROGRAM PLAYHOUSE	Boxing		
8	Captain Video			BROADWAY TO HOLLYWOOD				
9								
10					PLAINCLOTHES	FAMOUS JURY TRIALS		
11								
12			EASY ACES					
1/50								
2								
3								
4			Film				Manhat Spotlt	
5					Famous Jury Trials	Plainclothes	Broadway to Hollywood	Manhat Spotlt
6								
7		Manhat Spotlt	HAZEL SCOTT					
8								
9								
10		MOST IMPORT PEOPLE	Manhat Spotlt					
11								
12								
1/51								
2								
3								
4								

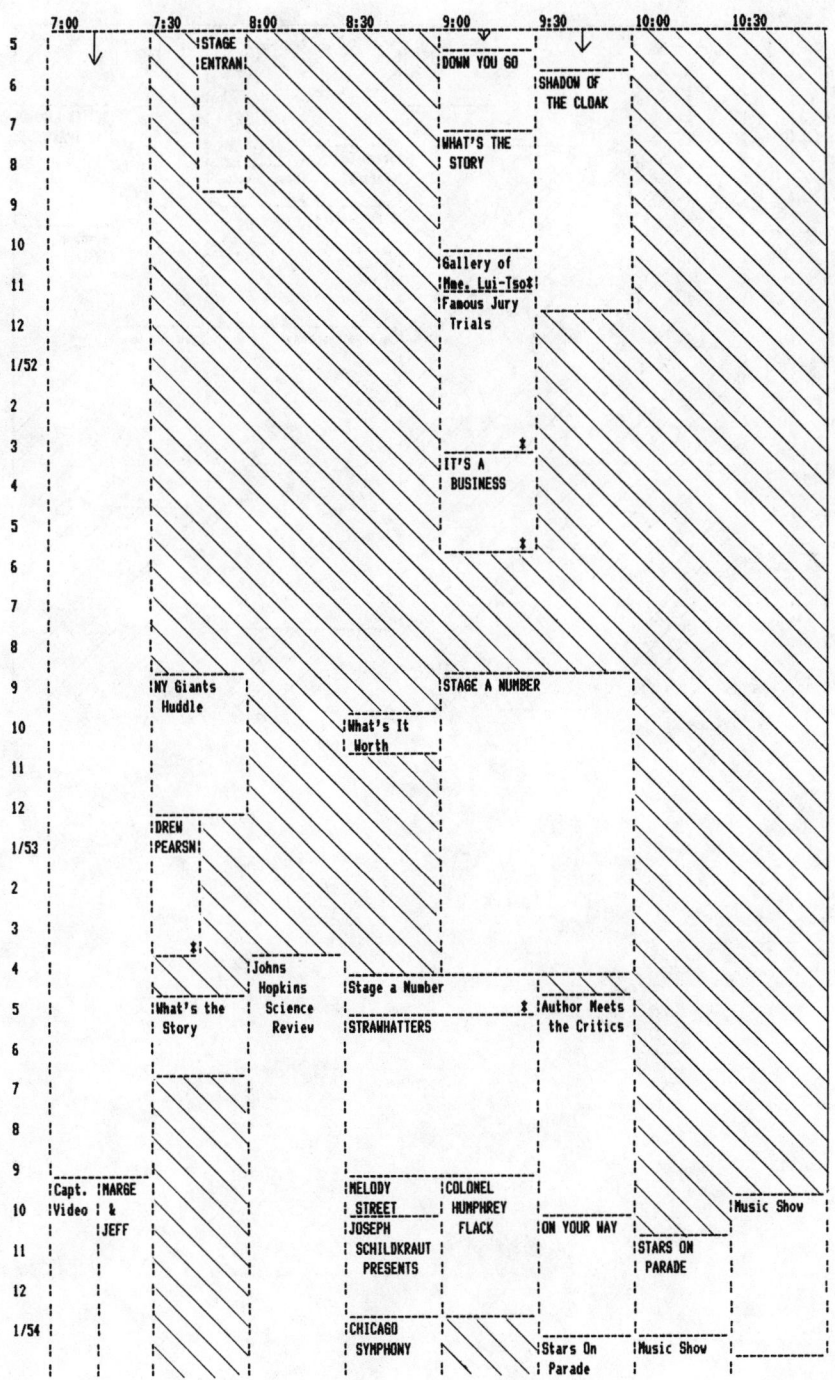

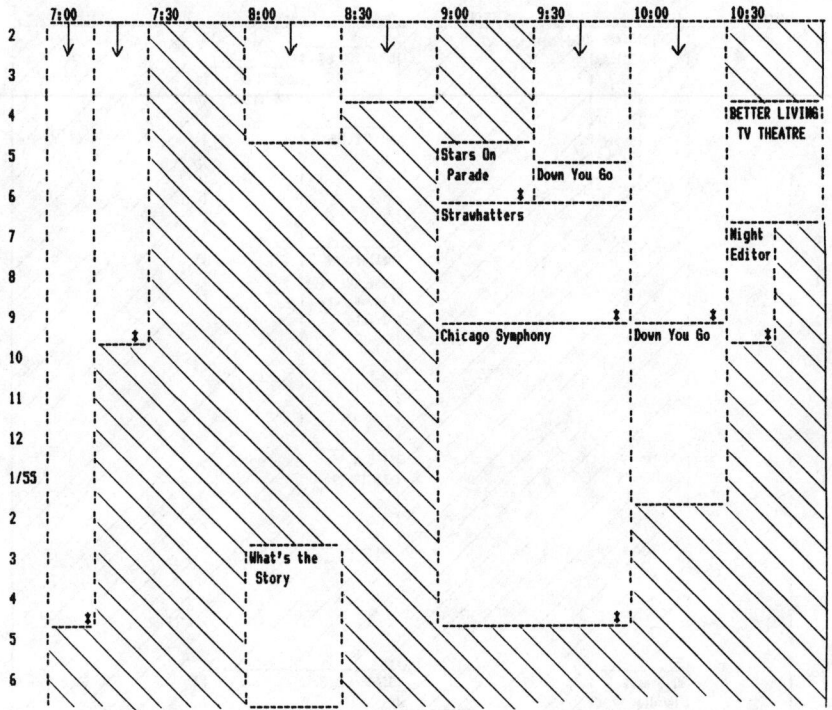

	7:00	7:30	8:00	8:30	9:00	9:30	10:00	10:30

Stars On Parade

Down You Go

Stravhatters

Chicago Symphony

Down You Go

BETTER LIVING TV THEATRE

Night Editor

What's the Story

Date	Time	Title (min. if not 30) — Type	Action	From/To
7/48	9:00	Boxing(120) — SP	s	
8/48	8:30	Laytons — SC	d	
9/48	7:00	Birthday Party — KV	m	Fr:r-7
10/48	8:30	Growing Paynes — SC	d	
10/48	8:30	Laytons — SC	c	
1/49	7:30	Manhattan Spotlight(15) — IV	d	
1/49	8:00	Charade Quiz — QU	m	Fr:r-8:30
1/49	9:00	Boxing(120) — SP	f	
3/49	7:00	Birthday Party — KV	m	To:r-7-5/49
3/49	7:00	Wendy Barrie Show — IV	d	
3/49	7:45	Russ Hodges' Scoreboard(15) — SN	d	
4/49	8:00	Charade Quiz — QU	m	To:r-8:30
5/49	7:30	A Woman to Remember(15) — SL	d	
5/49	7:30	Manhattan Spotlight(15) — IV	m	To:w-7:45
5/49	7:45	Russ Hodges' Scoreboard(15) — SN	c	
5/49	7:45	Manhattan Spotlight(15) — IV	m	Fr:w-7:30
5/49	9:00	Court of Current Issues(60) — DB	m	Fr:m-9
6/49	9:00	Court of Current Issues(60) — DB	m	To:t-8
6/49	9:00	Program Playhouse — VS	d	
6/49	9:30	Boxing(90) — SP	s	
7/49	7:00	Wendy Barrie Show — IV	m	To:m-8:30-9/49(a)
7/49	7:30	Vincent Lopez(15) — MV	d	
7/49	7:30	A Woman to Remember(15) — SL	c	
8/49	7:00	Captain Video and His Video Rangers — KV	m	Fr:mtrf-7
8/49	8:30	Broadway to Hollywood — Headline Clues — QU	d	
8/49	8:30	Growing Paynes — SC	c	
9/49	8:30	Broadway to Hollywood — Headline Clues — QU	m	To:f-8:30
9/49	9:00	Program Playhouse — VS	c	
9/49	9:30	Boxing(90) — SP	f	
10/49	9:00	Plainclothesman — CD	d	
10/49	9:30	Famous Jury Trials — CR	d	
12/49	7:45	Easy Aces(15) — CY	d	
12/49	7:45	Manhattan Spotlight(15) — IV	m	To:w-7:30-7/50
4/50	8:00	Film(60) — FI	s	
4/50	10:00	Manhattan Spotlight(15) — IV	s	
5/50	8:00	Film(60) — FI	f	
5/50	9:00	Famous Jury Trials — CR	m	Fr:w-9:30
5/50	9:00	Plainclothesman — CD	m	To:w-9:30
5/50	9:30	Famous Jury Trials — CR	m	To:w-9
5/50	9:30	Plainclothesman — CD	m	Fr:w-9
5/50	10:00	Broadway to Hollywood — Headline Clues — QU	m	Fr:f-8:30
5/50	10:00	Manhattan Spotlight(15) — IV	f	
5/50	10:30	Manhattan Spotlight(15) — IV	s	
6/50	7:30	Vincent Lopez(15) — MV	m	To:s-8
6/50	7:45	Easy Aces(15) — CY	c	
6/50	10:30	Manhattan Spotlight(15) — IV	f	

Date	Time	Title (min. if not 30) — Type	Action	From/To
7/50	7:30	Manhattan Spotlight(15) — IV	m	Fr:w-7:45-12/49
7/50	7:45	Hazel Scott(15) — MU	d	
9/50	7:30	Manhattan Spotlight(15) — IV	m	To:w-7:45
9/50	7:45	Hazel Scott(15) — MU	c	
10/50	7:30	Most Important People(15) — MV	d	
10/50	7:45	Manhattan Spotlight(15) — IV	m	Fr:w-7:30
1/51	10:00	Broadway to Hollywood — Headline Clues — QU	m	To:r-8:30
4/51	7:30	Most Important People(15) — MV	c	
4/51	7:45	Manhattan Spotlight(15) — IV	c	
5/51	7:45	Stage Entrance(15) — IV	d	
5/51	9:00	Down You Go — QU	d	
5/51	9:00	Famous Jury Trials — CR	m	To:w-9-11/51
5/51	9:30	Plainclothesman — CD	m	To:n-9:30
6/51	9:30	Shadow of the Cloak — SD	d	
7/51	9:00	Down You Go — QU	m	To:r-9
7/51	9:00	What's the Story — QU	d	
8/51	7:45	Stage Entrance(15) — IV	m	To:m-8
10/51	9:00	Gallery of Mme. Lui-Tsong — CD	m	Fr:m-8:30
10/51	9:00	What's the Story — QU	m	To:t-8
11/51	9:00	Famous Jury Trials — CR	m	Fr:w-9-5/51
11/51	9:00	Gallery of Mme. Lui-Tsong — CD	c	
11/51	9:30	Shadow of the Cloak — SD	m	To:r-9
3/52	9:00	Famous Jury Trials — CR	c	
3/52	9:00	It's a Business? — SC	d	
5/52	9:00	It's a Business? — SC	c	
9/52	7:30	New York Giants Quarterback Huddle — ST	m	Fr:f-8:30-12/50(a)
9/52	9:00	Stage a Number(60) — TA	d	
10/52	8:30	What's It Worth — QU	m	Fr:t-9:30-3/49(c)
10/52	8:30	What's It Worth — QU	m	To:r-9
12/52	7:30	Drew Pearson(15) — NA	d	
12/52	7:30	New York Giants Quarterback Huddle — ST	m	To:r-8-10/53
3/53	7:30	Drew Pearson(15) — NA	c	
4/53	8:00	Johns Hopkins Science Review — IF	m	Fr:m-8:30
4/53	8:30	Stage a Number(60) — TA	m	Fr:w-9
4/53	9:00	Stage a Number(60) — TA	m	To:w-8:30
5/53	7:30	What's the Story — QU	m	Fr:r-9:30
5/53	8:30	Stage a Number(60) — TA	c	
5/53	8:30	Strawhatters(60) — VY	d	
5/53	9:30	Author Meets the Critics — DS	m	Fr:r-10
6/53	7:30	What's the Story — QU	m	To:n-10
9/53	7:00	Captain Video and His Video Rangers — KV	m	To:m-f-7
9/53	7:00	Captain Video and His Video Rangers(15) — KV	m	Fr:m-f-7
9/53	7:15	Marge and Jeff(15) — SC	d	
9/53	8:30	Melody Street — MU	d	
9/53	8:30	Strawhatters(60) — VY	m	To:w-9-6/54

Date	Time	Title (min. if not 30) — Type	Action	From/To
9/53	9:00	Colonel Humphrey Flack — SC	d	
10/53	8:30	Joseph Schildkraut Presents — DA	d	
10/53	8:30	Melody Street — MU	m	To:f-8:30
10/53	9:30	Author Meets the Critics — DS	m	To:n-7-3/54
10/53	9:30	On Your Way — TA	d	
10/53	10:30	Music Show — MU	m	Fr:t-8:30
11/53	10:00	Stars on Parade — MV	d	
12/53	8:30	Joseph Schildkraut Presents — DA	m	To:r-8
12/53	9:00	Colonel Humphrey Flack — SC	m	To:s-10
1/54	8:30	Chicago Symphony — MU	d	
1/54	9:30	On Your Way — TA	m	To:s-7(a)
1/54	9:30	Stars on Parade — MV	m	Fr:w-10
1/54	10:00	Music Show — MU	m	Fr:w-10:30
1/54	10:00	Stars on Parade — MV	m	To:w-9:30
1/54	10:30	Music Show — MU	m	To:w-10
3/54	8:30	Chicago Symphony — MU	m	To:w-9-9/54
4/54	8:00	Johns Hopkins Science Review — IF	m	To:r-9
4/54	10:30	Better Living TV Theatre — DS	d	
5/54	9:00	Stars on Parade — MV	m	Fr:w-9:30
5/54	9:30	Down You Go — QU	m	Fr:f-10:30
5/54	9:30	Stars on Parade — MV	m	To:w-9
6/54	9:00	Stars on Parade — MV	c	
6/54	9:00	Strawhatters(60) — VY	m	Fr:w-8:30
6/54	9:30	Down You Go — QU	m	To:w-10-9/54
6/54	10:30	Better Living TV Theatre — DS	m	To:n-10:30
7/54	10:30	Night Editor(15) — DA	m	Fr:n-10:45
9/54	7:15	Marge and Jeff(15) — SC	c	
9/54	9:00	Chicago Symphony(60) — MU	m	Fr:w-8:30-3/54
9/54	9:00	Strawhatters(60) — VY	c	
9/54	10:00	Down You Go — QU	m	Fr:w-9:30-6/54
9/54	10:00	Music Show — MU	c	
9/54	10:30	Night Editor(15) — DA	c	
1/55	10:00	Down You Go — QU	m	To:f-10:30
3/55	8:00	What's the Story — QU	m	Fr:r-9
4/55	7:00	Captain Video and His Video Rangers(15) — KV	c	
4/55	9:00	Chicago Symphony(60) — MU	c	
6/55	8:00	What's the Story — QU	m	To:f-7:30

Wednesday Programming
Moves Summary

1948-49

ABC. *Series Premieres:* On Trial; Pauline Fredricks.

CBS. *Series Premieres:* Armchair Detective; Arthur Godfrey and His Friends; Cliff Edwards; Kobb's Korner; Manhattan Showcase; Master of Magic; Sonny Kendis. *Key Programming Moves:* Arthur Godfrey's second series, ARTHUR GODFREY AND HIS FRIENDS debuts in 1/49, one month after the debut of ARTHUR GODFREY'S TALENT SCOUTS; this series stays in the 8–9 slot until 6/57; it was then taken off the air and resurrected in 9/58 for another seven months.

NBC. *Series Premieres:* Arrow Show; Black Robe; Broadway Spotlight; Girl About Town; Kukla, Fran & Ollie; Leave It to the Girls; Mohawk Showroom; Picture This; Quiz Kids; Ted Steele Show; Young Broadway. *Key Programming Moves:* THE QUIZ KIDS debuts in 3/49; at the end of the season it was moved to Mondays; this quiz series, originally on radio, retained its popularity when it was moved to television; it stayed on NBC until 9/52; it was then picked up by CBS and continued until 9/56; KRAFT TELEVISION THEATRE, originally starting in 5/47, anchors NBC's Wednesday night lineup; it occupied the 9–10 slot until 10/58.

DuMont: *Series Premieres:* Broadway to Hollywood; Growing Paynes; Manhattan Spotlight; Program Playhouse; Russ Hodges; Vincent Lopez; Wendy Barrie Show; A Woman to Remember.

1949-50

ABC. *Series Premieres:* Art Ford; Author Meets the Critics; Photocrime; That Wonderful Guy.

CBS. *Series Premieres:* Abe Burrow's Almanac; Garry Moore Show; Paul Arnold Show; Stage 13; Stork Club; Strictly for Laughs; Three's

Company; Toni Twin Time. *Key Programming Moves:* THE WEB is moved to Wednesday, 9:30–10; it stays in this slot until 7/52.

NBC. *Series Premieres:* Cameo Theatre; Crisis; Pinky Lee. *Key Programming Moves:* BREAK THE BANK is moved to Wednesday, 10–10:30; it stays in this slot until 1/52.

DuMont: *Series Premieres:* Easy Aces; Famous Jury Trials; Hazel Scott; The Plainclothesman. *Key Programming Moves:* THE PLAINCLOTHESMAN debuts; this series was shot in the first person (from the point-of-view of the lead character, who was never seen on camera); this series was one of the most successful on the DuMont network, lasting until 9/54.

1950–51

ABC. *Series Premieres:* Chance of a Lifetime; Dick Tracy; Don McNeill TV Club; Kreisler Bandstand; Paul Dixon Show.

CBS. *Series Premieres:* Somerset Maugham Theatre; Steve Allen Show; Strike It Rich. *Key Programming Moves:* Boxing is scheduled in the 10–11 slot, where it stays until 5/55; STRIKE IT RICH debuts in the 9–9:30 slot in July; it stays in this slot until its cancellation in 1/55.

NBC. *Series Premieres:* All Star Revue; Heritage; Stars Over Hollywood.

DuMont. *Series Premieres:* Down You Go; Most Important People; Shadow of the Cloak; Stage Entrance; What's the Story. *Key Programming Moves:* By 1/51, DuMont had cut back Wednesday night programming to two hours (7–8 and 9–10); by season's end it was reduced further to 90 minutes (7–7:30 and 9–10).

1951–52

ABC. *Series Premieres:* Celanese Theatre; Frosty Frolics; Name's the Same; Newstand Theatre; Rendevous. *Key Programming Moves:* ABC discontinues programming the 7–7:30 slot.

CBS. *Key Programming Moves:* THE WEB is moved to Sunday in 7/52; ARTHUR GODFREY AND HIS FRIENDS is the sixth highest rated series on television, achieving the highest average rating (43.3) of any Wednesday night series up to its time.

NBC. *Series Premieres:* Bob & Ray; Cavalier Theatre; Kate Smith Show; Those Two; Up to Paar; Your Prize Story. *Key Programming Moves:* NBC goes head-to-head with CBS' ARTHUR GODFREY AND HIS FRIENDS in the 8–9 slot with THE KATE SMITH SHOW; by June THE KATE SMITH SHOW was cancelled.

DuMont. *Series Premieres:* It's a Business. *Key Programming Moves:* In November, DuMont was programming only the 7–7:30 and 9–9:30 time slots on Wednesday; in June, they ceased programming the 9–9:30 slot altogether.

1952–53

ABC. *Key Programming Moves:* ABC's Wednesday night schedule was dominated by wrestling and films, instead of weekly series; it fared very poorly.

CBS. *Key Programming Moves:* In July, I'VE GOT A SECRET is moved into the 9:30–10 slot, where it stayed until 9/61; ARTHUR GODFREY AND HIS FRIENDS is the #3 rated series on television, surpassing its previous high rating.

NBC. *Series Premieres:* Cavalcade of America; Coke Time with Eddie Fisher; I Married Joan; Scott Music Hall; This Is Your Life. *Key Programming Moves:* I MARRIED JOAN debuts in the 8–8:30 slot, where it continues until its cancellation in 4/55; THIS IS YOUR LIFE debuts in the 10–10:30 slot; this testimonial series continues in this slot until 9/60; COKE TIME WITH EDDIE FISHER debuts in the 7:30–7:45 slot, where it stays until 2/57.

DuMont. *Series Premieres:* Drew Pearson; Stage a Number; Strawhatters. *Key Programming Moves:* DuMont increases its offerings on Wednesday; by May, it was again airing programming from 7–10.

1953–54

ABC. *Series Premieres:* Answers for Americans; Dr. I.Q.; Take It from Me; This World; Through the Curtain; Vaudeville Show. *Key Programming Moves:* ABC returns to programming regular weekly series; they fare better than the films of the previous season, but still fare poorly compared to CBS and NBC.

NBC. *Key Programming Moves:* MY LITTLE MARGIE is moved to Wednesday, 8:30–9, forming a fairly strong sitcom block (with I MARRIED JOAN) from 8–9.

DuMont. *Series Premieres:* Better Living TV Theatre; Chicago Symphony; Colonel Humphrey Flack; Joseph Schildkraut Presents; Marge & Jeff; Melody Street; On Your Way; Stars on Parade. *Key Programming Moves:* DuMont is struggling and by May they had stopped programming from 7:30–9.

1954–55

ABC. *Series Premieres:* Disneyland; Mr. Citizen; Pall Mall Playhouse; Penny to a Million; Presidential News Conference. *Key Programming Moves:* DISNEYLAND debuts; it is the sixth highest rates series on television; it lasts on Wednesday until 9/58; ABC begins airing boxing in the 10–11 slot when CBS stops airing it in May; ABC continues to air boxing on Wednesday until 9/60.

CBS. *Series Premieres:* Best of Broadway; Front Row Center; Julius LaRosa Show; The Millionaire. *Key Programming Moves:* THE MILLIONAIRE debuts in the 9–9:30 slot, replacing STRIKE IT RICH; it stays in this slot until its cancellation in 9/60; CBS moves U.S. STEEL HOUR into the 10–11 slot, previously occupied by boxing; it continues in this slot until its cancellation in 6/63.

NBC. *Series Premieres:* Kodak Request Performance; Norby. *Key Programming Moves:* I MARRIED JOAN is cancelled in 4/55; MY LITTLE MARGIE is cancelled at the end of the season.

DuMont. *Key Programming Moves:* DuMont ceases programming Wednesday night in 6/55.

1955–56

ABC. *Series Premieres:* MGM Parade. *Key Programming Moves:* DISNEYLAND is the fourth highest rated series on television.

CBS. *Series Premieres:* Brave Eagle; CBS Cartoon Theatre; 20th Century Fox Hour. *Key Programming Moves:* THE MILLIONAIRE and I'VE GOT A SECRET are both ranked in the top ten (at numbers 9 and 10, respectively); THE 20TH CENTURY FOX HOUR debuts, alternating with U.S. STEEL HOUR in the 10–11 slot.

NBC. *Series Premieres:* Ina Ray Hutton; Press Conference; Screen Director's Playhouse. *Key Programming Moves:* FATHER KNOWS BEST is moved into the 8:30–9 slot, where it stays for the next three years.

1956–57

ABC. *Series Premieres:* Moment of Decision. *Key Programming Moves:* THE ADVENTURES OF OZZIE & HARRIET is moved into the 9–9:30 slot; it stays on Wednesday until 9/61.

CBS. *Series Premieres:* Giant Step. *Key Programming Moves:* After nine successful seasons, ARTHUR GODFREY AND HIS FRIENDS is taken off the air in 6/57; it returned in a 30 minute version in 1958 on Tuesday nights.

NBC. *Series Premieres:* Adventures of Hiram Holiday; Helen O'Connell; Twenty-One; Xavier Cugat. *Key Programming Moves:* COKE TIME WITH EDDIE FISHER is cancelled in 2/57, after a four year run.

1957–58

ABC. *Series Premieres:* Betty White Show; Tombstone Territory; Traffic Court; Walter Winchell. *Key Programming Moves:* DISNEYLAND is moved to Friday at the end of the season.

CBS. *Series Premieres:* Big Record; Johnson Wax Theatre; Sing Along. *Key Programming Moves:* Reruns of I LOVE LUCY are aired in the 7:30–8 slot; I'VE GOT A SECRET is the #5 rated series on television.

NBC. *Series Premieres:* It Could Be You; Wagon Train. *Key Programming Moves:* WAGON TRAIN debuts in the 7:30–8:30 slot, where it stays until 9/62; FATHER KNOWS BEST is picked up by CBS and is moved to Monday at the end of the season; KRAFT TELEVISION THEATRE is cancelled at the end of the season, ending 11 years on NBC.

1958–59

ABC. *Series Premieres:* Accused; Donna Reed Show; Music for a Summer Night; Patti Page. *Key Programming Moves:* THE DONNA REED SHOW debuts, beginning an eight year run on ABC; it is moved to Thursday at the end of the season.

CBS. *Series Premieres:* Pursuit.

NBC. *Series Premieres:* Bat Masterson; Dave King Show; Milton Berle Show. *Key Programming Moves:* WAGON TRAIN is the #2 rated series on television; Uncle Miltie returns to weekly television as THE MILTON BERLE SHOW debuts; it doesn't catch on with the audience, and is cancelled in May; BAT MASTERSON debuts; it is moved to Thursday at the end of the season; THE PRICE IS RIGHT is moved into the 8:30–9 slot, where it stayed for the next three years.

1959–60

ABC. *Series Premieres:* Hawaiian Eye; Hobby Lobby. *Key Programming Moves:* HAWAIIAN EYE debuts in the 9–10 slot; it enjoys a four year run on ABC; ABC stops airing boxing in the 10–11 slot at the end of the season.

CBS. *Series Premieres:* Be Our Guest; Men into Space. *Key Program-

ming Moves: After almost six years, THE MILLIONAIRE is cancelled at the end of the season.

NBC. *Series Premieres:* Wichita Town. *Key Programming Moves:* WAGON TRAIN (#2) and THE PRICE IS RIGHT (#8) are among the highest rated series on television; THE PERRY COMO SHOW is moved to Wednesday in the 9–10 slot; it stays in this slot until its cancellation in 6/63; THIS IS YOUR LIFE is moved to Sunday at the end of the season; PEOPLE ARE FUNNY is moved to Wednesday in April, it is cancelled at the end of the season, after a six year run on NBC.

1960–61

ABC. *Series Premieres:* Hong Kong. *Key Programming Moves:* THE ADVENTURES OF OZZIE & HARRIET is moved to Thursday at the end of the season; NAKED CITY is moved into the 10–11 slot, marking the first time ABC scheduled a regular weekly series in this slot in almost 10 years.

CBS. *Series Premieres:* Aquanauts; Danger Man; My Sister Eileen. *Key Programming Moves:* After eight years in the 9:30–10 slot on Wednesday, I'VE GOT A SECRET is moved to Monday, where it will continue for another six years.

NBC. *Series Premieres:* Peter Loves Mary. *Key Programming Moves:* WAGON TRAIN is the second highest rated series on television for the third consecutive year; THE PRICE IS RIGHT is moved to Monday at the end of the season; NBC discontinues programming the 10:30–11 slot; it will resume programming this slot the following season.

1961–62

ABC. *Series Premieres:* Howard K. Smith; Top Cat. *Key Programming Moves:* HAWAIIAN EYE is moved to Tuesday at the end of the season.

CBS. *Series Premieres:* Alvin Show; Gertrude Berg Show. *Key Programming Moves:* CBS brings back the star of the successful series THE GOLDBERGS, Gertrude Berg, to weekly television in THE GERTRUDE BERG SHOW; it is cancelled before the end of the season; FATHER KNOWS BEST is moved to Wednesday; in February it is moved to Monday, and is replaced by another Robert Young series, WINDOW ON MAIN STREET, which is cancelled at the end of the season; THE DICK VAN DYKE SHOW is moved to Wednesday in January, where it would stay until its end in 9/66.

NBC. *Series Premieres:* Bob Newhart Show; David Brinkley's Journal; Joey Bishop Show. *Key Programming Moves:* WAGON TRAIN becomes the highest rated series on television; at the end of the season it was picked up by ABC.

1962-63

ABC. *Series Premieres:* Going My Way; Our Man Higgins. *Key Programming Moves:* ABC picks up WAGON TRAIN, the #1 rated series on television for the 1961-62 season; it is scheduled in its familiar 7:30-8:30 slot; at the end of the season, it is moved to Monday and is expanded to 90 minutes; while the series continued to be moderately successful, it would never again achieve the success it had while on NBC; NAKED CITY is cancelled at the end of the season.

CBS. *Series Premieres:* Beverly Hillbillies. *Key Programming Moves:* THE BEVERLY HILLBILLIES debuts, beginning a highly successful 10 year run on CBS; it becomes the #1 rated series on television in its initial season; it also becomes a strong anchor for CBS' Wednesday night lineup; it produces a wave of imitators—situation comedies, often described as "mindless"—that lasted until the end of the decade; CBS REPORTS is moved into the 7:30-8:30 lead-off slot; it stays there for over two years; U.S. STEEL HOUR and ARMSTRONG CIRCLE THEATRE are cancelled at the end of the season.

NBC. *Series Premieres:* Eleventh Hour; The Virginian. *Key Programming Moves:* THE VIRGINIAN, a 90 minute western, debuts in the 7:30-9 slot, taking the place of the recently departed WAGON TRAIN; it stayed in this slot until 9/71; THE PERRY COMO SHOW is cancelled in 6/63, after an eight year run.

1963-64

ABC. *Series Premieres:* Channing; Patty Duke Show. *Key Programming Moves:* THE ADVENTURES OF OZZIE & HARRIET returns to Wednesday and is placed in the 7:30-8 time slot, which it occupies for the next three years; THE PATTY DUKE SHOW debuts; it has a successful four year run on ABC in the 8-8:30 slot; BEN CASEY is moved to Wednesday; it is returned to its Monday night slot at the end of the season; 77 SUNSET STRIP is moved to Wednesday in 4/64; it is cancelled at the end of the season.

CBS. *Series Premieres:* Chronicle; Danny Kaye Show; Glynis; Suspense; Tell It to the Cameras. *Key Programming Moves:* THE BEVERLY HILLBILLIES is the #1 rated series on television for the second consecutive year; THE DICK VAN DYKE SHOW is rated #3; THE DANNY KAYE SHOW debuts in the 10-11 slot; it lasts for four years.

NBC. *Series Premieres:* Espionage.

1964-65

ABC. *Series Premieres:* ABC Scope; Mickey; Shindig. *Key Programming Moves:* SHINDIG debuts; this was ABC's entry into the rock 'n' roll music trend; in January, the series expanded to one hour; at the end of the season it was moved to Thursday and Saturday.

CBS. *Series Premieres:* Cara Williams Show; Our Private World. *Key Programming Moves:* In December, CBS REPORTS is moved to Monday; it is replaced by two of the "mindless" situation comedies, MR. ED and MY LIVING DOLL; both are cancelled at the end of the season.

NBC. *Key Programming Moves:* NBC scheduled motion pictures in the 9-11 slot; at the end of the season, they discontinued this and returned to airing weekly series.

1965-66

ABC. *Series Premieres:* Batman, Big Valley; Blue Light; Gidget. *Key Programming Moves:* THE BIG VALLEY debuts; in July it is moved to Monday where it would stay for the duration of its four year run; THE ADVENTURES OF OZZIE & HARRIET is moved to Saturday in 1/66; BATMAN debuts in January; ABC scheduled this series on Wednesday and Thursday evenings; Thursday's episode was the conclusion to Wednesday's episode; THE PATTY DUKE SHOW is cancelled at the end of the season.

CBS. *Series Premieres:* Green Acres; Lost in Space. *Key Programming Moves:* GREEN ACRES debuts; hammocked between THE BEVERLY HILLBILLIES and THE DICK VAN DYKE SHOW, it performs well; it continued on Wednesday until 9/69; THE DICK VAN DYKE SHOW leaves the air at the end of the season; the series was still highly popular, but the star of the series was tired of doing weekly television and did not return to the series.

NBC. *Series Premieres:* I Spy. *Key Programming Moves:* I SPY debuts; this series was one of the first dramatic series to feature a black actor (Bill Cosby) in a starring role; it lasted for three years.

1966-67

ABC. *Series Premieres:* ABC Stage 67; The Man Who Never Was; The Monroes. *Key Programming Moves:* At the end of the season, BATMAN moved to Thursdays, airing only once a week; In January, ABC scheduled motion pictures in the 9-11 slot, a practice it continued for the next three years.

CBS. *Series Premieres:* Steve Allen Show. *Key Programming Moves:* GOMER PYLE, U.S.M.C. is moved into the 9:30–10 slot; at the end of the season it is moved back to Friday; THE DANNY KAYE SHOW is cancelled in 6/67.

NBC. *Key Programming Moves:* I SPY is moved to Monday at the end of the season.

1967–68

ABC. *Series Premieres:* Custer; Dream House; Second Hundred Years.

CBS. *Series Premieres:* Dundee and the Culhane; He & She; Jonathan Winters Show.

NBC. *Series Premieres:* Kraft Music Hall. *Key Programming Moves:* KRAFT MUSIC HALL debuts in the 9–10 slot; it lasts until 5/71; RUN FOR YOUR LIFE is moved to Wednesday; it is cancelled at the end of the season.

1968–69

ABC. *Series Premieres:* Here Come the Brides; Turn On. *Key Programming Moves:* TURN ON debuts and is cancelled on the same night, February 5, 1969; this "series" was an attempt to capitalize on the success of ROWAN & MARTIN'S LAUGH-IN, as it was produced by the same man, George Schlatter; TURN ON was so bad that many affiliates refused to carry any more episodes; as a result, ABC cancelled it after only one airing.

CBS. *Series Premieres:* Glen Campbell Goodtime Hour; The Good Guys. *Key Programming Moves:* In December, HAWAII FIVE-O is moved into the 10–11 slot, where it stayed until 9/71; GREEN ACRES is moved to Saturday at the end of the season.

NBC. *Series Premieres:* The Outsider.

1969–70

ABC. *Series Premieres:* Courtship of Eddie's Father; Engelbert Humperdinck Show; Nanny & the Professor; Room 222. *Key Programming Moves:* ABC schedules a 90 minute block (7:30–9) of situation comedies; it continues this for the next two years; ROOM 222 debuts, beginning a successful five year run.

CBS. *Series Premieres:* Medical Center; Where's Huddles. *Key Programming Moves:* MEDICAL CENTER debuts in the 9–10 slot, where it stays until 5/73; GOMER PYLE, U.S.M.C. is moved to Wednesday in 7/70, and is cancelled at the end of the season; After eight years on Wednesday, THE BEVERLY HILLBILLIES is moved to Tuesday at the end of the season.

NBC. *Series Premieres:* Then Came Bronson.

1970–71

ABC. *Series Premieres:* Dan August; Danny Thomas Show; NFL Action; The Smith Family. *Key Programming Moves:* ABC brings Danny Thomas back to weekly television in THE DANNY THOMAS SHOW; in 1/71 it moves to Thursday; it doesn't catch on and is cancelled at the end of the season. ROOM 222 is moved to Friday at the end of the season.

CBS. *Series Premieres:* Storefront Lawyers. *Key Programming Moves:* HAWAII FIVE-O is moved to Tuesday at the end of the season.

NBC. *Series Premieres:* McCloud; Night Gallery; The Psychiatrist; San Francisco International Airport. *Key Programming Moves:* NBC schedules four rotating series under the title "FOUR IN ONE," which made its debut at the beginning of the season; Two of the series, McCLOUD and NIGHT GALLERY continued after the season.

1971–72

ABC. *Series Premieres:* ABC Comedy Hour; Corner Bar; Man & the City; Marty Feldman Show; Shirley's World; The Super. *Key Programming Moves:* All three networks cut back to three hours of prime time programming because of the FCC's new Prime Time Access Rule; ABC juggles its lineup continually this season; at season's end, the entire lineup is cancelled.

CBS. *Key Programming Moves:* THE CAROL BURNETT SHOW and MANNIX are moved to Wednesday; MANNIX is moved to Sunday at the end of the season.

NBC. *Series Premieres:* Columbo; McMillan & Wife. *Key Programming Moves:* ADAM 12 is moved to Wednesday, 8–8:30, where it stays until 1/74; COLUMBO and McMILLAN & WIFE debut and McCLOUD is expanded to 90 minutes, as NBC schedules all three series in a rotating format under the title, "NBC MYSTERY MOVIE"; NIGHT GALLERY airs as a weekly series.

1972–73

ABC. *Series Premieres:* Julie Andrews Show; Paul Lynde Show; Thicker Than Water. *Key Programming Moves:* ABC schedules films in the 8:30-10 slot; it continues this practice for the next three years.

CBS. *Key Programming Moves:* CANNON is moved to Wednesday, where it stays for the next four years; THE CAROL BURNETT SHOW is moved to Saturday in December; THE SONNY AND CHER SHOW replaces it in the 8-9 slot; MEDICAL CENTER is moved to Monday in 5/73.

NBC. *Series Premieres:* Banacek; Cool Million; Madigan; Search. *Key Programming Moves:* NBC offers three new rotating series in the 8:30-10 slot, BANACEK, COOL MILLION and MADIGAN; only BANACEK continues at the end of the season.

1973-74

ABC. *Series Premieres:* Bob, Carol, Ted & Alice; The Cowboys; Dick Clark; Doc Elliott.

CBS. *Series Premieres:* Bobby Gentry Show; Hudson Brothers Show; Kojak; Tony Orlando & Dawn. *Key Programming Moves:* KOJAK debuts; series lasts for five years; at season's end it moves to Sunday; THE SONNY & CHER SHOW leaves the air in 5/74; it returns in 2/76, on Sunday evening.

NBC. *Series Premieres:* Faraday & Company; Love Story; Snoop Sisters; Tenafly. *Key Programming Moves:* In January, NBC overhauls its entire Wednesday night lineup; ADAM 12 is moved to Tuesday, and films are scheduled in the 9-11 slot.

1974-75

ABC. *Series Premieres:* Get Christie Love; Jim Stafford Show; That's My Mama. *Key Programming Moves:* BARETTA is moved to Wednesday night in 4/75; ABC discontinues airing films in the 8:30-10 slot at the end of the season.

CBS. *Series Premieres:* Manhunter; Sons & Daughters. *Key Programming Moves:* MANNIX is moved to Wednesday in July; it is cancelled at the end of the season.

NBC. *Series Premieres:* Little House on the Prairie; Lucas Tanner; Petrocelli. *Key Programming Moves:* NBC offers an entirely new Wednesday night lineup; LITTLE HOUSE ON THE PRAIRIE debuts, beginning a 10 year run on NBC.

1975-76

ABC. *Series Premieres:* Bionic Woman; Starsky and Hutch; When Things Were Rotten. *Key Programming Moves:* STARSKY AND HUTCH debuts in the 10–11 slot; it is moved to Saturday at the end of the season; THE BIONIC WOMAN debuts in January; this successful spin-off from $6 MILLION MAN stays on the air until 9/78.

CBS. *Series Premieres:* Bert Convy Show; The Blue Knight; Frankie Avalon; The Jacksons; Kate McShane; Kelly Monteith Show. *Key Programming Moves:* CANNON is moved to Sunday at the end of the season.

NBC. *Series Premieres:* Doctor's Hospital; The Dumplings. *Key Programming Moves:* LITTLE HOUSE ON THE PRAIRIE is moved to Monday at the end of the season; SANFORD AND SON and CHICO AND THE MAN are moved to Wednesday; at the end of the season, CHICO AND THE MAN is moved back to Friday, SANFORD AND SON is cancelled.

1976-77

ABC. *Series Premieres:* Charlie's Angels. *Key Programming Moves:* CHARLIE'S ANGELS debuts; this series begins a trend called "jiggle" programming—shows that have pretty young women running around scantily attired—causing citizen groups to complain; however, the series is very popular with the audience and stays on the air until 8/81; THE BIONIC WOMAN leaves the air in 5/77; it returns the next season on Saturday.

CBS. *Series Premieres:* Alice; Ball Four; Loves Me, Loves Me Not; Marilyn McCoo & Billy Davis Show. *Key Programming Moves:* CBS schedules two situation comedies in the 8–9 slot (GOOD TIMES and BALL FOUR); this slot had been occupied by variety series for the previous five years; ALICE debuts; it is moved to Saturday in 11/76; In November, CBS replaces weekly series with films in the 9–11 slot.

NBC. *Series Premieres:* Comedy Time; CPO Sharkey; Kallikaks; Kingston Confidential; Life and Times of Grizzly Adams; McLean Stevenson Show; Quest; Tales of the Unexpected; 3 Girls 3. *Key Programming Moves:* NBC constantly juggles its Wednesday schedule during the 1976–77 season; none of their combinations works well.

1977-78

ABC. *Key Programming Moves:* BARETTA is moved to Thursday in 2/78; it is replaced with STARSKY & HUTCH, which is later moved to Tuesday.

CBS. *Series Premieres:* Amazing Spider Man. *Key Programming Moves:* GOOD TIMES is moved to Monday in 1/78.

NBC. *Series Premieres:* Big Hawaii; David Frost Show; Oregon Trail. *Key Programming Moves:* POLICE WOMAN is moved to Wednesday; it is cancelled at the end of the season.

1978–79

ABC. *Series Premieres:* Vega$. *Key Programming Moves:* VEGA$ debuts in the 10–11 slot, where it stays until 6/81.

CBS. *Series Premieres:* Dear Detective; Dorothy; Hanging In; In the Beginning; Incredible Hulk; Married: the First Year; Miss Winslow & Son. *Key Programming Moves:* CBS constantly rearranged its schedule during this season, with nothing clicking with the audience; In January, CBS stopped airing films in favor of regular series; by April they were back to airing films.

NBC. *Series Premieres:* Dick Clark Live; Real People; Supertrain. *Key Programming Moves:* NBC offers DICK CLARK LIVE in the 8–9 slot, an attempt at a live variety series (a la THE ED SULLIVAN SHOW); it only lasted until January; SUPERTRAIN debuts in the 8–9 slot in February; this very expensive series never caught on with the audience; it was one of the most expensive mistakes in television history; REAL PEOPLE debuts in the 8–9 slot in April; this "info-tainment" magazine program catches on with the audience and stays on the air until 7/84; its success starts a mini-wave of info-tainment series on all three networks.

1979–80

CBS. *Series Premieres:* Beyond Westworld; Last Resort; Struck by Lightning; Young Maverick. *Key Programming Moves:* CBS tries several different series in the 8–9 time slot, though none of them seem to work; in April, they resort to airing specials in this slot for the duration of the season.

NBC. *Series Premieres:* Best of Saturday Night Live; From Here to Eternity. *Key Programming Moves:* DIFF'RENT STROKES is moved to Wednesday in the 9–9:30 slot; it stays here until 10/81; NBC airs highlights from its late-night weekend series SATURDAY NIGHT LIVE in the 10–11 slot until 3/80; QUINCY is moved into the 10–11 slot in April, where it stays until 6/83.

1980–81

ABC. *Series Premieres:* Aloha Paradise; Greatest American Hero. *Key Programming Moves:* CHARLIE'S ANGELS is moved to the 8–9 slot on Sunday as part of ABC's strategy to lead-off each night with a top series; the move, as well as all of ABC's other leading-off moves, fails; the series is returned to Wednesday, but the audience doesn't and it is cancelled at the end of the season; DYNASTY is moved to Wednesday in July; it stays on this night until 8/88; VEGA$ is cancelled at the end of the season.
CBS. *Series Premieres:* Enos.
NBC. *Key Programming Moves:* THE FACTS OF LIFE is moved to Wednesday, where it stays until 8/85.

1981–82

ABC. *Series Premieres:* The Fall Guy.
CBS. *Series Premieres:* Baker's Dozen; Herbie, the Love Bug; Mr. Merlin; Shannon. *Key Programming Moves:* CBS shuffles its Wednesday schedule repeatedly during the season, though nothing seems to do work for them.
NBC. *Series Premieres:* Love Sidney.

1982–83

ABC. *Series Premieres:* The Hamptons; High Performance; Ryan's Four; Tales of the Gold Monkey.
CBS. *Series Premieres:* Seven Brides for Seven Brothers; Tucker's Witch; Zorro & Son. *Key Programming Moves:* ARCHIE BUNKER'S PLACE is moved to Wednesday in June; it is cancelled at the end of the season.
NBC. *Series Premieres:* Buffalo Bill; Family Ties; News Is the News. *Key Programming Moves:* FAMILY TIES debuts; the series became one of the more successful series in NBC history; it has a six year run on NBC; QUINCY is moved to Saturday in June.

1983–84

ABC. *Series Premieres:* Hotel. *Key Programming Moves:* HOTEL debuts in the 10–11 slot, which it occupied until 9/87.
CBS. *Series Premieres:* Crossroads; Domestic Life; Empire; Mama Malone; Whiz Kids. *Key Programming Moves:* CBS tries several new series in the 8–9 slot; none of them catches on with the audience.

NBC. *Series Premieres:* Double Trouble; St. Elsewhere. *Key Programming Moves:* ST. ELSEWHERE debuts in the 10–11 slot, which it occupied, except for several months, until its cancellation in 8/88; this series was produced by the makers of HILL STREET BLUES, and followed the same formula as its predecessor.

1984–85

ABC. *Series Premieres:* Rock 'n' Roll Summer Action.

CBS. *Series Premieres:* Charles in Charge; Double Dare; Dreams; I Had Three Wives. *Key Programming Moves:* For the fourth consecutive year, CBS constantly shuffled its Wednesday lineup; still nothing worked.

NBC. *Series Premieres:* Highway to Heaven; It's Your Move; Sara. *Key Programming Moves:* HIGHWAY TO HEAVEN debuts; NBC again has a successful series starring Michael Landon; it lasts until 8/88; THE FACTS OF LIFE is moved to Saturday at the end of the season.

1985–86

ABC. *Series Premieres:* The Insiders. *Key Programming Moves:* PERFECT STRANGERS is moved to Wednesday in 8/86.

CBS. *Series Premieres:* Charlie & Company; The Equalizer; Fast Times; Foley Square; George Burns' Comedy Week; Mary; Stir Crazy; Tough Cookies. *Key Programming Moves:* CBS' Wednesday lineup is again constantly in transition; Mary Tyler Moore's new series MARY debuts in December; it is cancelled by season's end; THE EQUALIZER debuts; this series is the one bright spot on CBS' Wednesday schedule, but in March it is moved to Tuesday.

NBC. *Series Premieres:* Blacke's Magic; Hell Town.

1986–87

ABC. *Series Premieres:* Head of the Class. *Key Programming Moves:* HEAD OF THE CLASS debuts in the 8:30–9 slot; series continues in this slot to the present time; HOTEL is moved to Saturday at the end of the season.

CBS. *Series Premieres:* Better Days; Roxie; Take Five. *Key Programming Moves:* MAGNUM P.I. is moved to the 9–10 slot, and THE EQUALIZER is returned to Wednesday, 10–11; these moves provided some stability on CBS' Wednesday schedule for the first time in the 1980s.

NBC. *Series Premieres:* The Tortellis. *Key Programming Moves:* In January, NBC starts shuffling its 9–10 lineup, constantly changing one sitcom for another; none seem to perform well against CBS' MAGNUM P.I. and ABC's DYNASTY.

1987–88

ABC. *Series Premieres:* China Beach; Heartbeat; Hooperman; Just in Time; Slap Maxwell Story. *Key Programming Moves:* HOOPERMAN debuts; this series, starring John Ritter, is part of the new wave of "dramedies" — situation comedies that also have heavy doses of drama; the series is a small hit and was renewed for the next season; In February, PERFECT STRANGERS moved to Friday, and GROWING PAINS moved into Wednesday's lead-off slot; SPENSER FOR HIRE is cancelled at the end of the season.

CBS. *Series Premieres:* The Oldest Rookie; Smothers Brothers Show. *Key Programming Moves:* THE SMOTHERS BROTHERS SHOW returns to CBS in March, after 20 years; it was a modest showing, but is off the air by June.

NBC. *Series Premieres:* Aaron's Way; Funny People; A Year in the Life. *Key Programming Moves:* HIGHWAY TO HEAVEN and ST. ELSE-WHERE, two of NBC's long-running series, are cancelled at the end of the season.

Thursday Night
September 1948 — August 1988

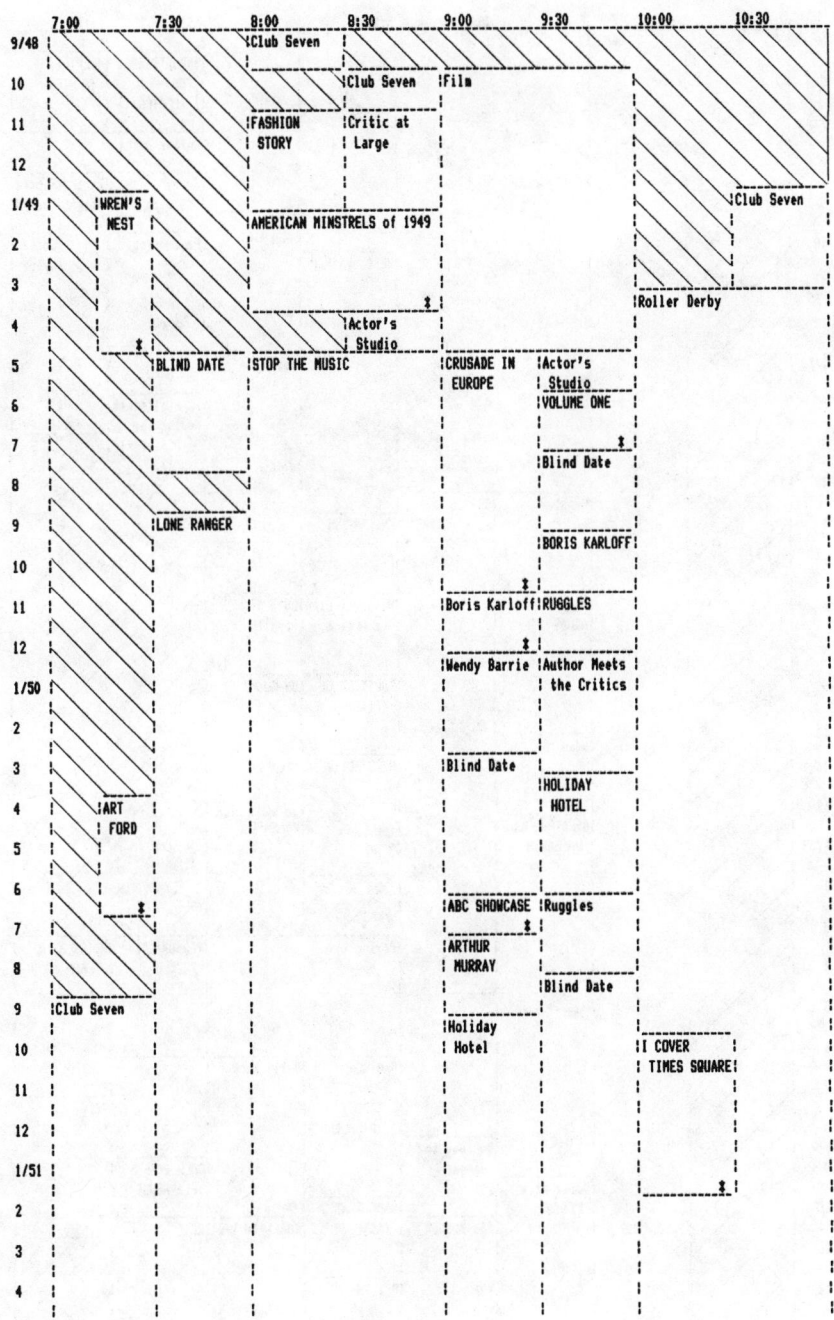

	7:00	7:30	8:00	8:30	9:00	9:30	10:00	10:30
5	↓	↓		↓	↓	↓		
6							INDUSTRIES FOR AMERICA	AMERICA IN VIEW
7								
							Roller Derby	
8								
9							Jerry Colonna	Earl Wright / Sports Camera
						Film		
10							Paul Dixon	Carmel Myers
					HERB SHRINER			
11								
12								
1/52						Boxing		
2							Americ Health	Indust for Americ
3								
4								
			Ruggles	CHANCE OF A LIFETIME	MR. ARSENIC			
5								
6								
7			A DATE WITH JUDY		Marshall Plan in Action	DO'S & DON'TS		
8								
9					POLITICS ON TRIAL	On Guard		
10								
			News					
11					PERSPECTIVE			
12								
			GREATEST MAN ON EARTH			VALENTINO		
1/53								
2								
			Film					
3								
					Boxing		PERSONALITY PUZZLE	QUICK AS A FLASH
4								
5								
6								
					MADISON SQUARE GARDEN HIGHLIGHTS	Dotty Mack		
7								
8								Film
				Doorway to Danger				
9							GOLD SEAL PLAYHOUSE	
			Quick As a Flash					
10					BACK THAT FACT			
				RAY BOLGER		KRAFT TV THEATRE		
11								
12					Dr. IQ			
1/54								
					Talent Patrol			

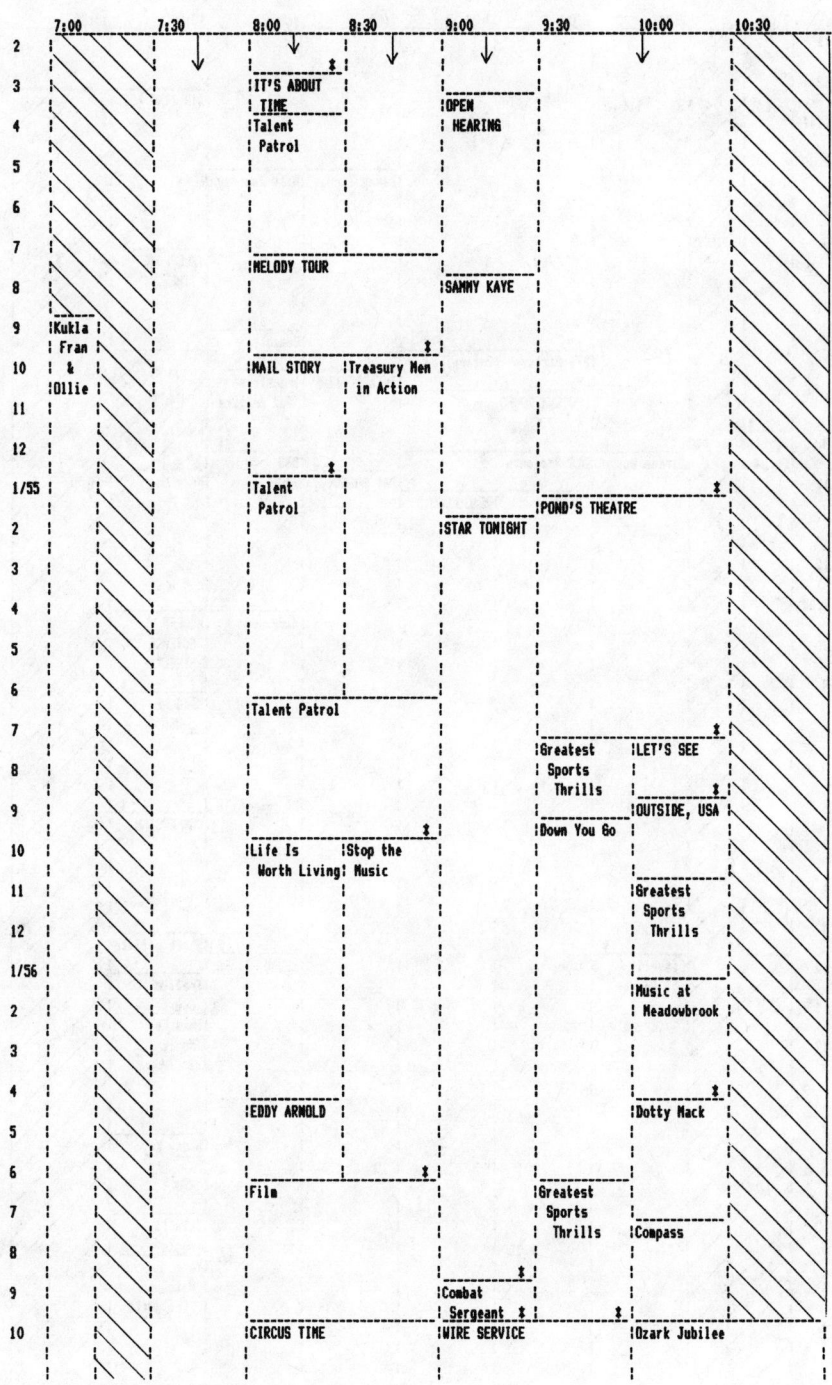

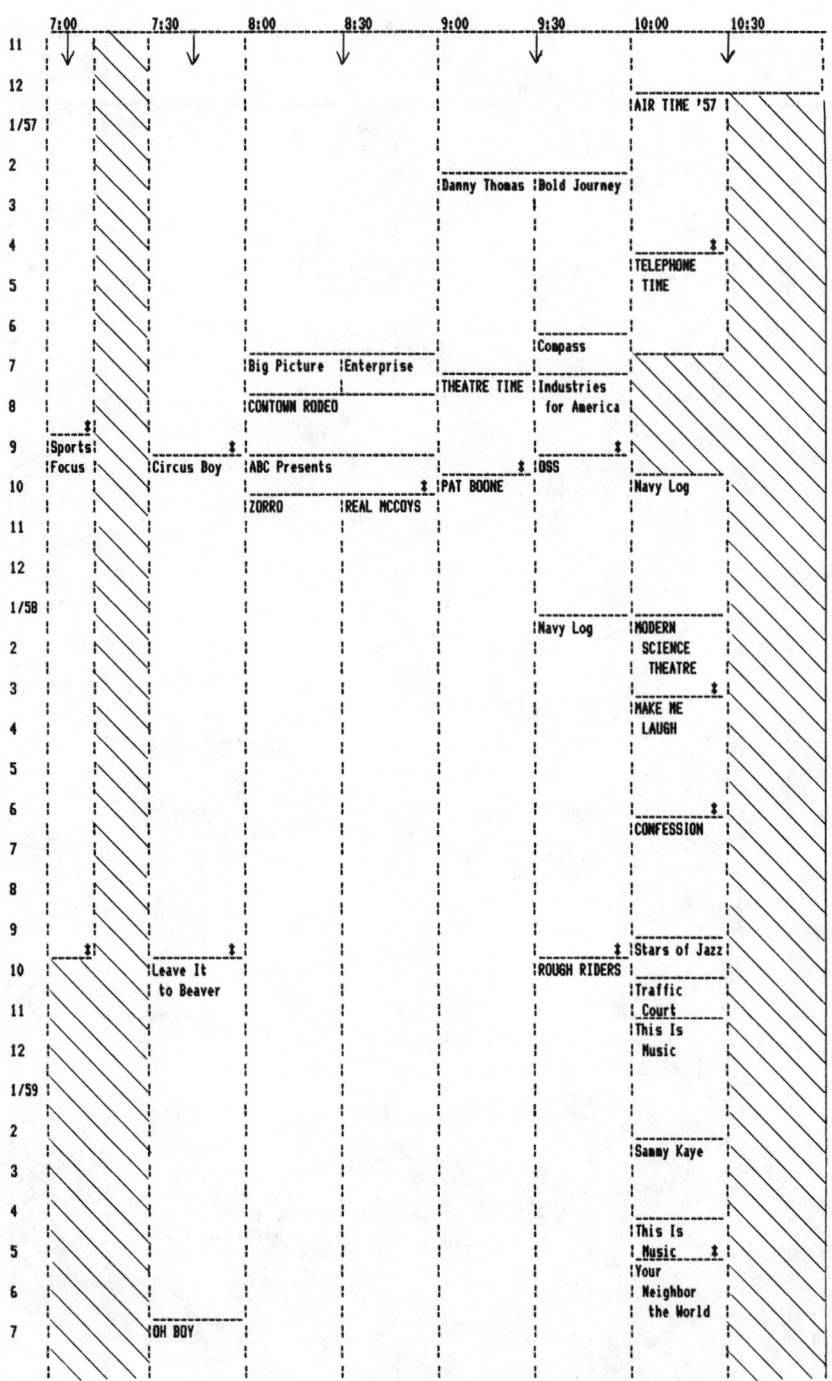

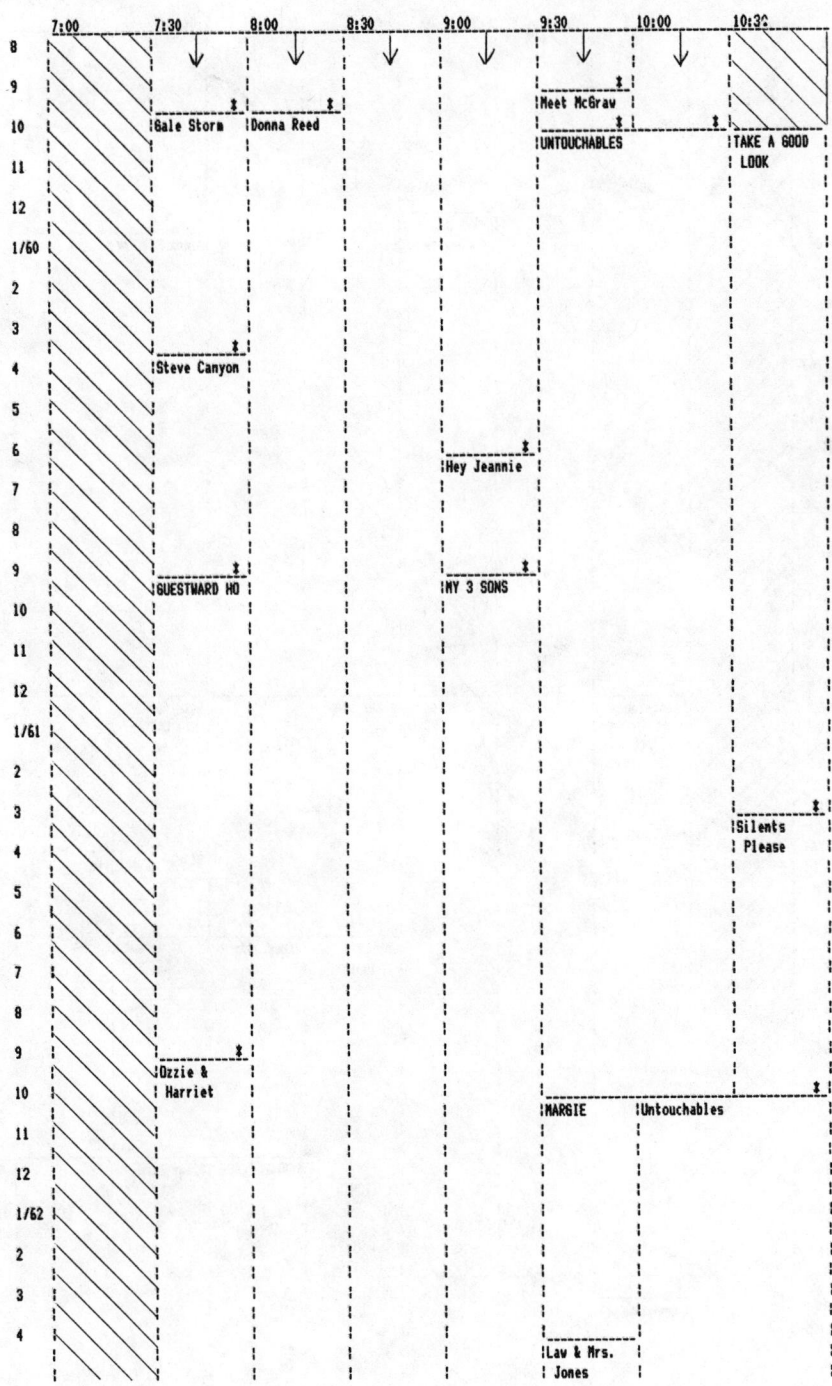

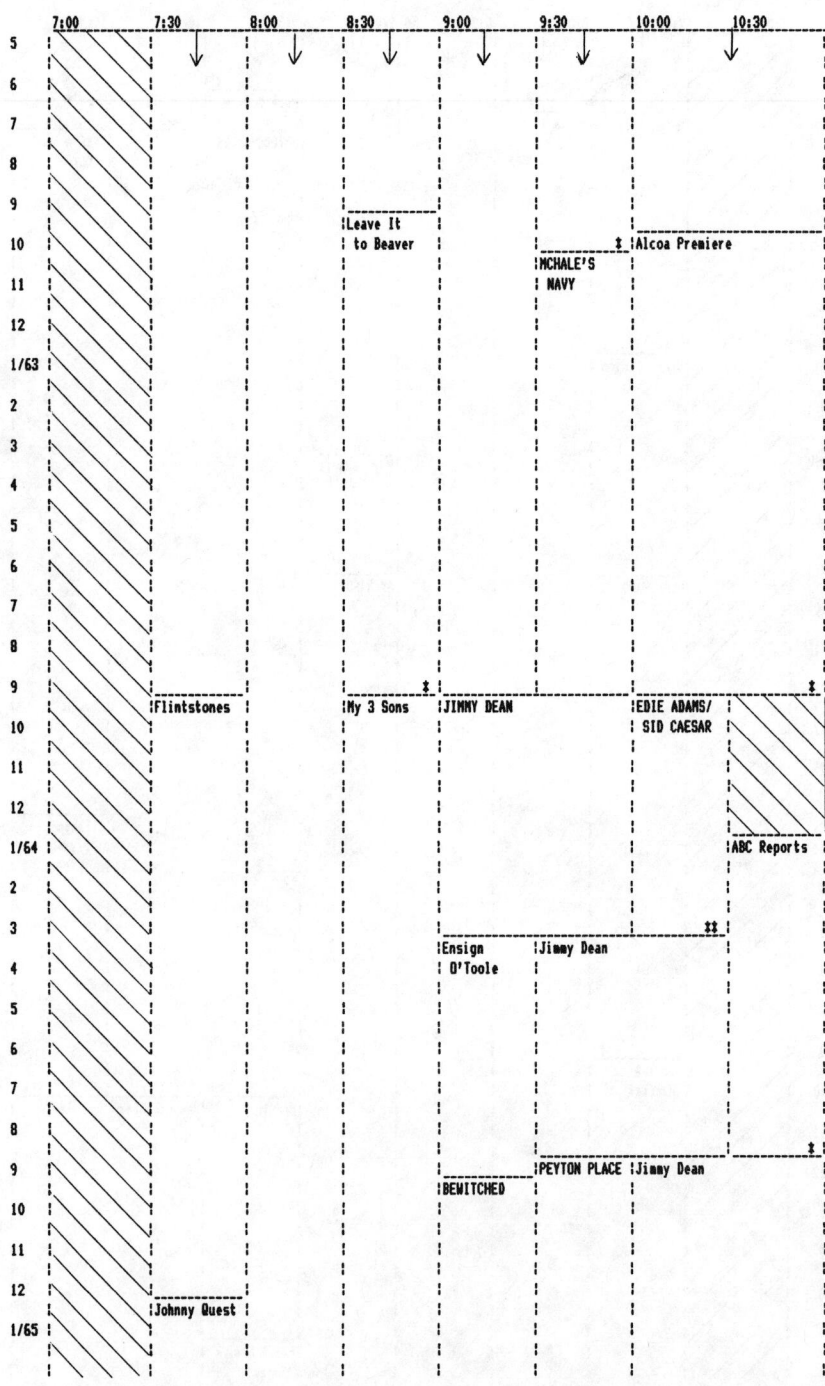

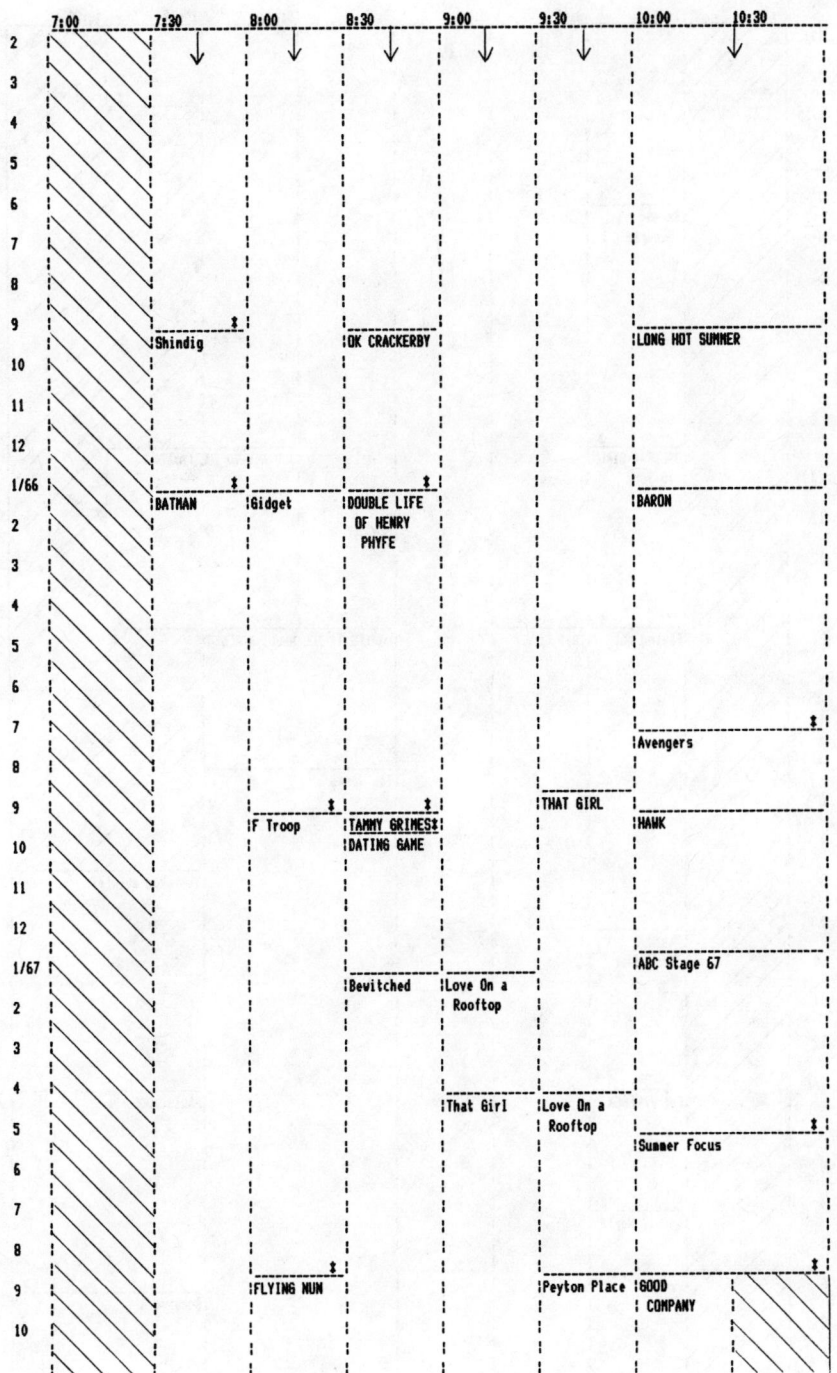

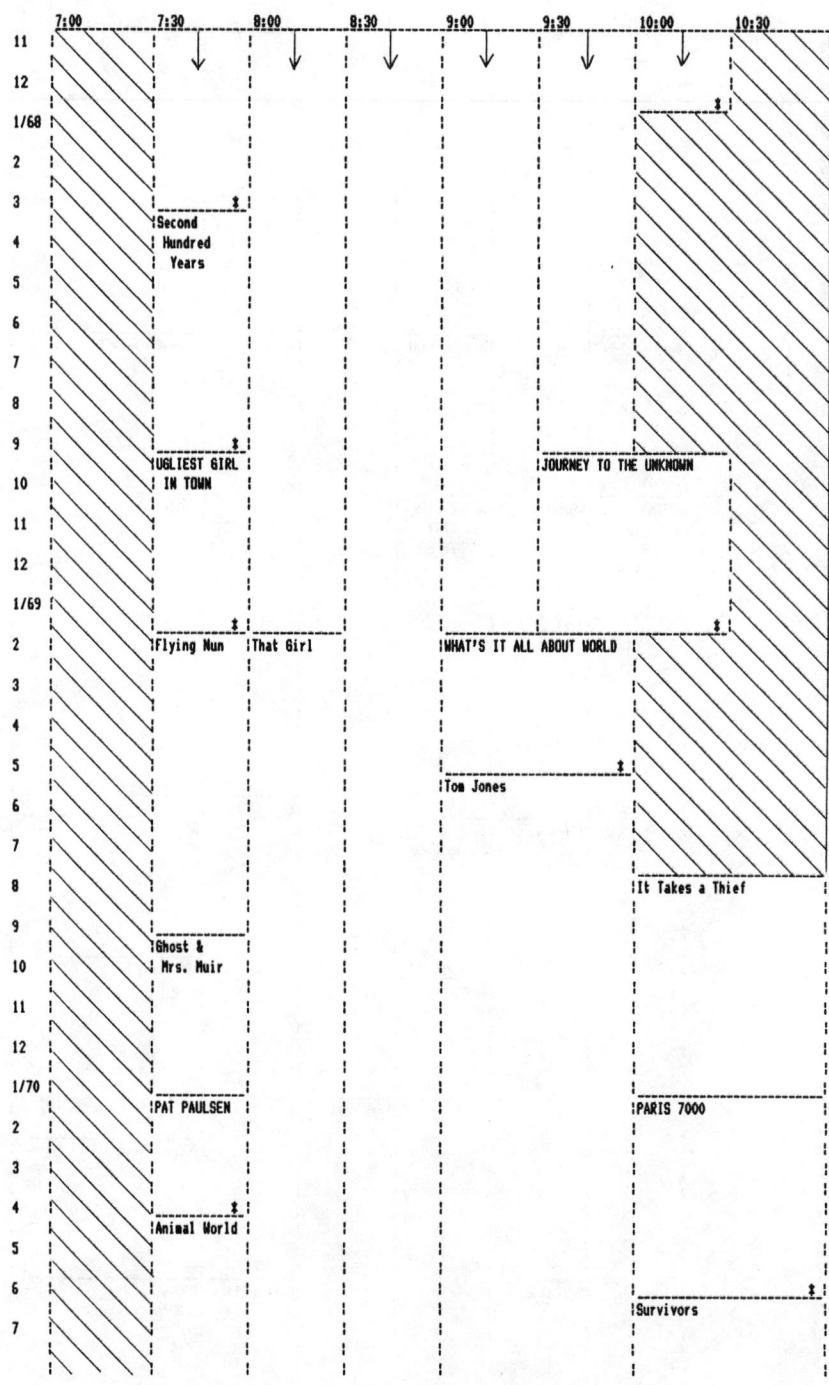

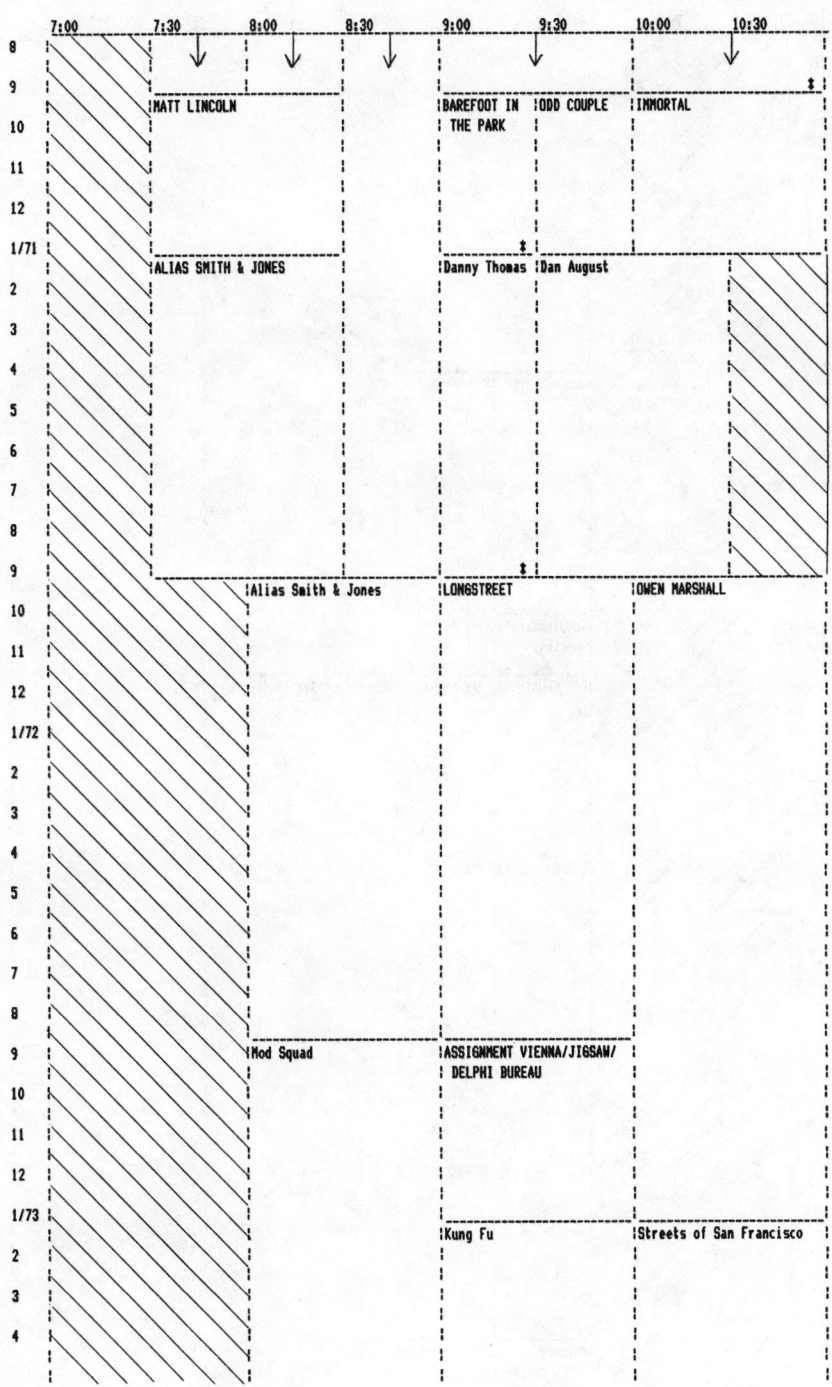

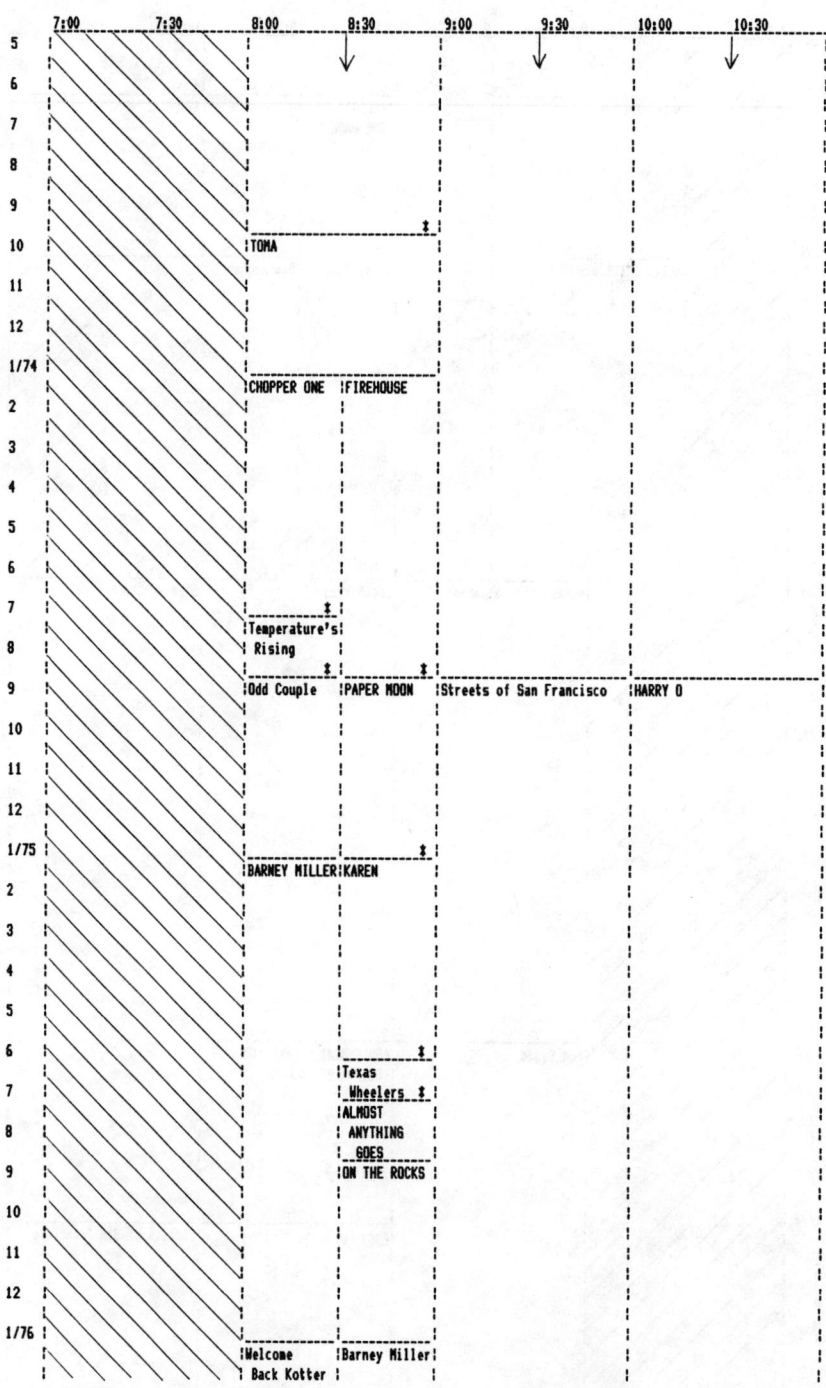

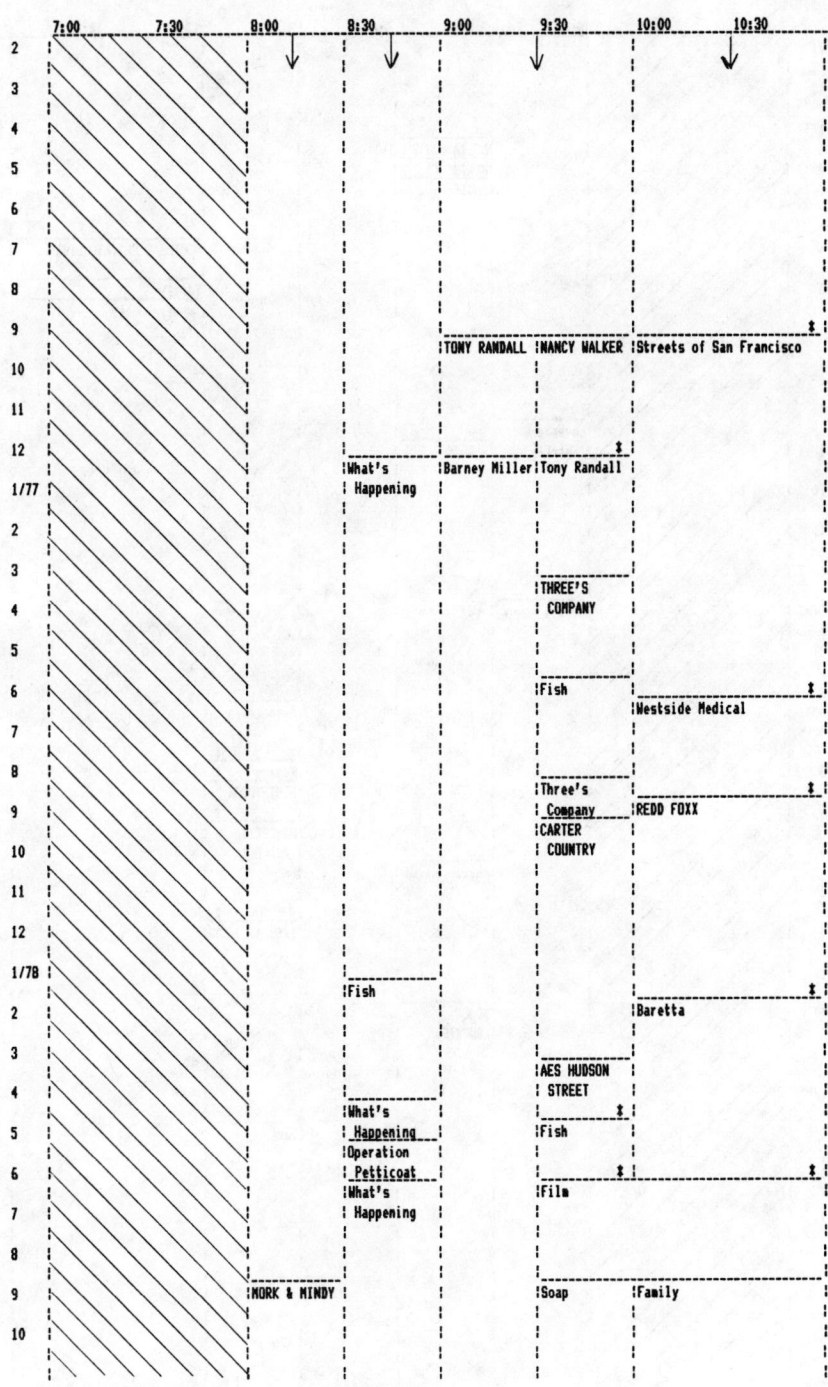

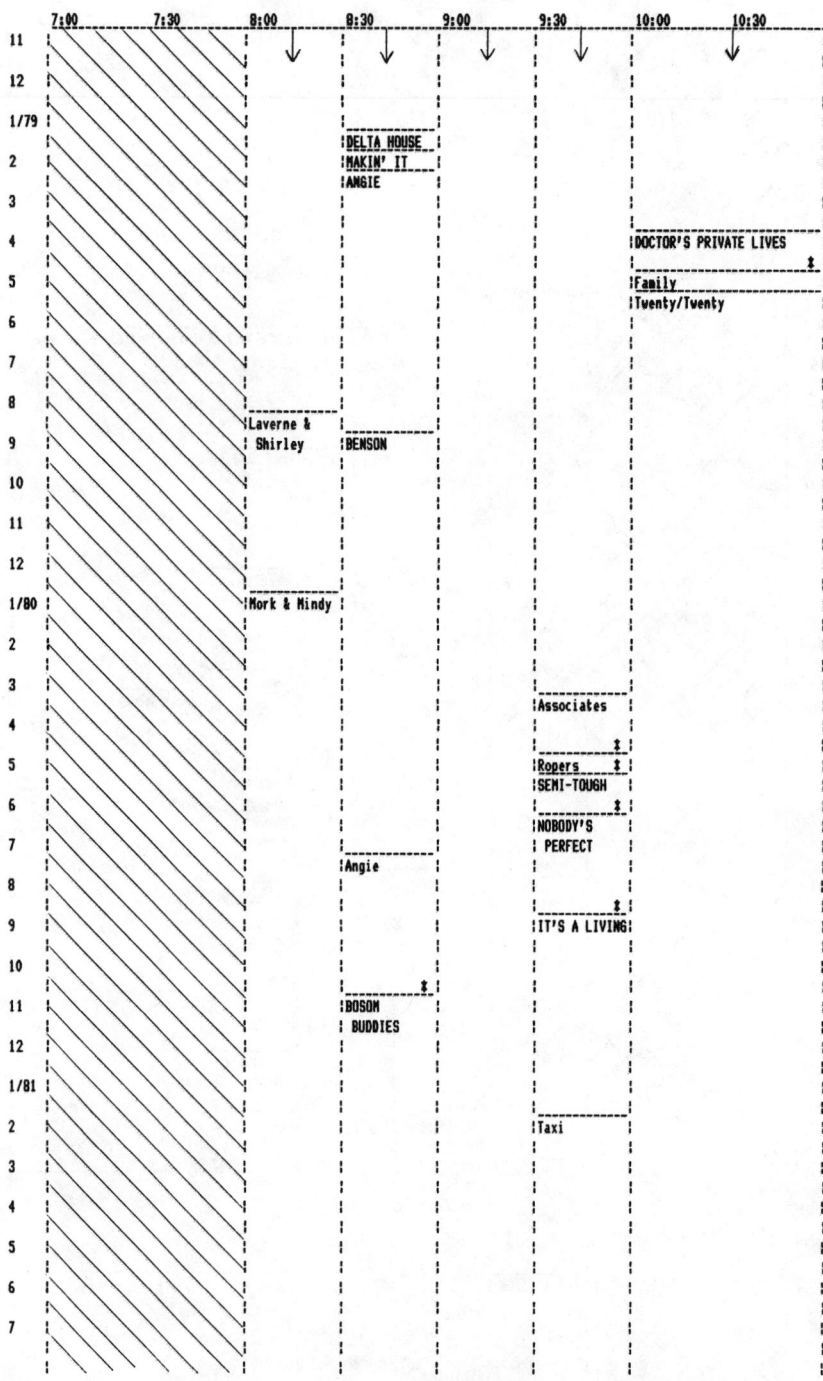

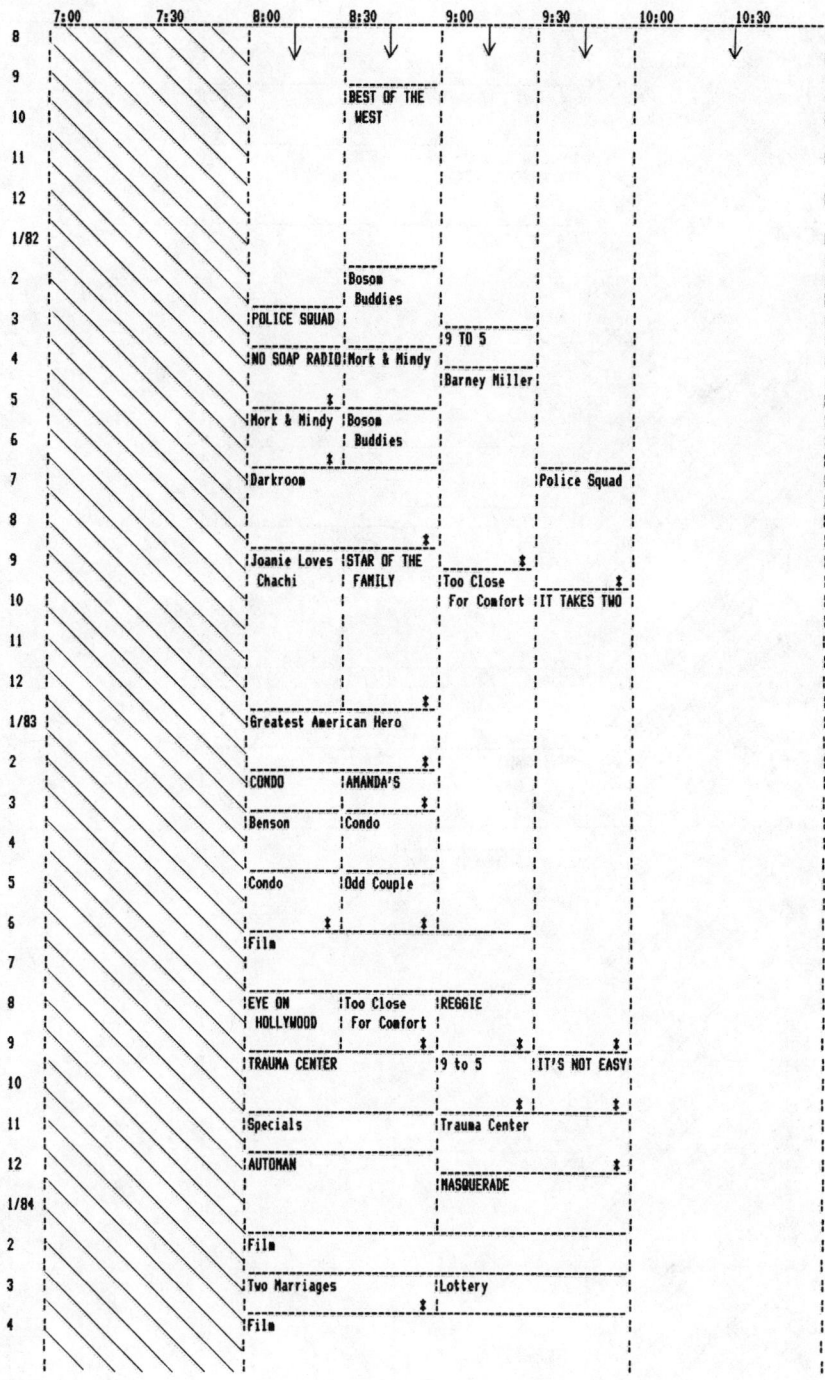

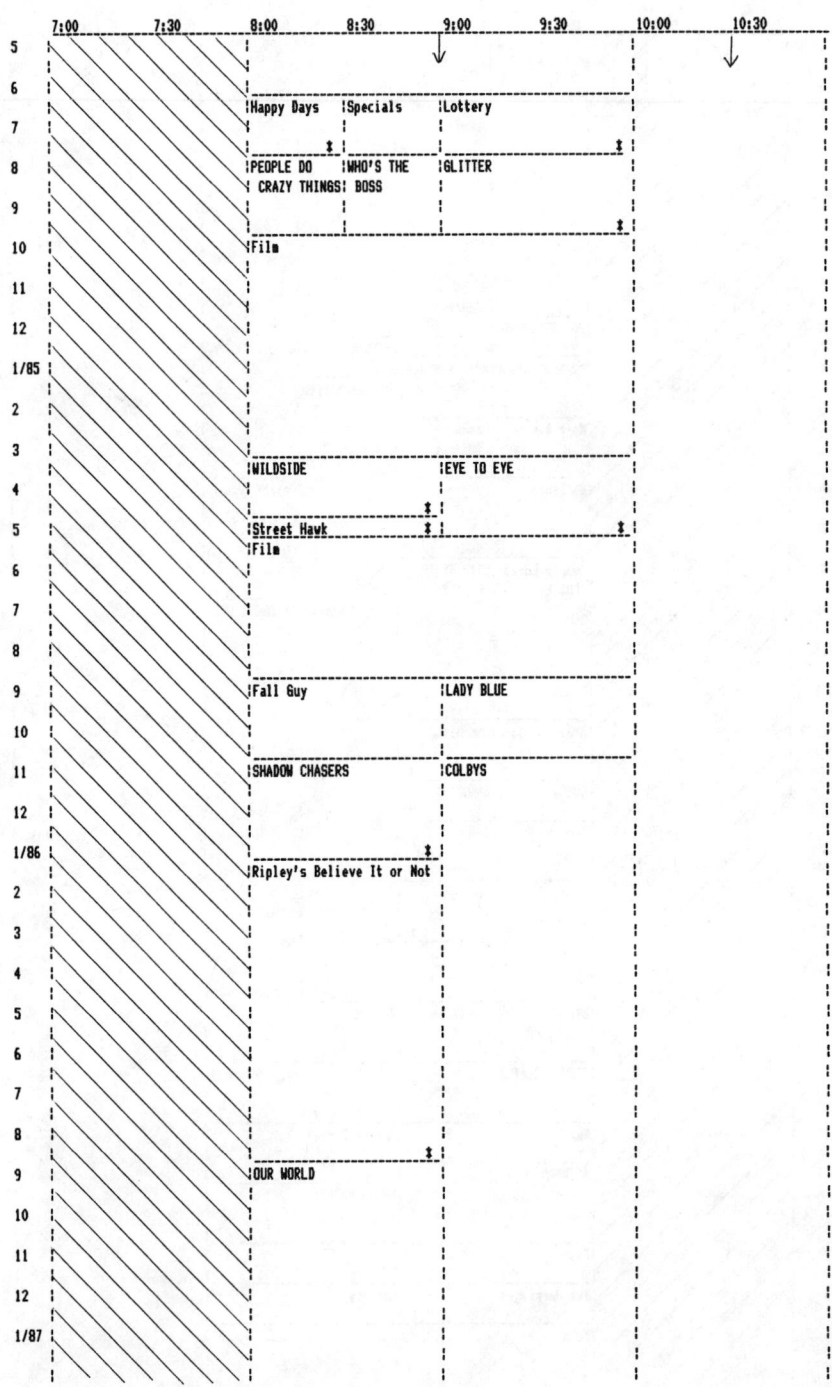

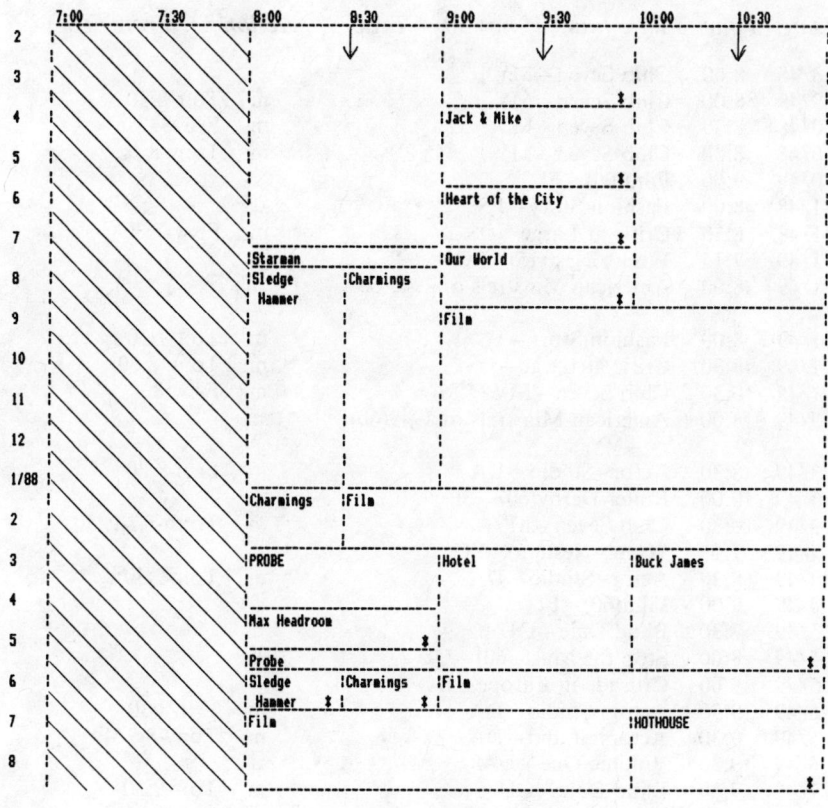

Date	Time	Title (min. if not 30) — Type	Action	From/To
8/48	8:00	Club Seven — MV	d	
9/48	8:00	Club Seven — MV	m	To:r-8:30
10/48	8:30	Club Seven — MV	m	Fr:r-8
10/48	8:30	Club Seven — MV	m	To:w-8
10/48	9:00	Film(60) — FI	s	
11/48	8:00	Fashion Story — FS	d	
11/48	8:30	Critic at Large — DS	m	Fr:w-7:30
1/49	7:15	Wren's Nest(15) — SC	d	
1/49	8:00	American Minstrels of 1949(60) — VY	d	
1/49	8:00	Fashion Story — FS	m	To:t-7:30
1/49	8:30	Critic at Large — DS	m	To:w-8:30
1/49	10:30	Club Seven — MV	m	Fr:w-8
3/49	8:00	American Minstrels of 1949(60) — VY	c	
3/49	8:30	Actors Studio — DA	m	Fr:n-8:30
3/49	10:00	Roller Derby(60) — SP	s	
3/49	10:30	Club Seven — MV	m	To:m-f-7-9/50
4/49	7:15	Wren's Nest(15) — SC	c	
4/49	8:30	Actors Studio — DA	m	To:r-9:30
4/49	9:00	Film(60) — FI	f	
5/49	7:30	Blind Date — QU	d	
5/49	8:00	Stop the Music(60) — QU	d	
5/49	9:00	Crusade in Europe — DO	d	
5/49	9:30	Actors Studio — DA	m	Fr:r-8:30
5/49	9:30	Actors Studio — DA	m	To:w-8-9/49
6/49	9:30	Volume One — DA	d	
7/49	7:30	Blind Date — QU	m	To:r-9:30
7/49	9:30	Blind Date — QU	m	Fr:r-7:30
7/49	9:30	Volume One — DA	c	
9/49	7:30	Lone Ranger — WE	d	
9/49	9:30	Blind Date — QU	m	To:f-8:30
9/49	9:30	Boris Karloff — SA	d	
10/49	9:00	Crusade in Europe — DO	c	
10/49	9:30	Boris Karloff — SA	m	To:r-9
11/49	9:00	Boris Karloff — SA	m	Fr:r-9:30
11/49	9:30	The Ruggles — SC	d	
12/49	9:00	Boris Karloff — SA	c	
12/49	9:00	Wendy Barrie — IV	m	Fr:w-8
12/49	9:30	Author Meets the Critics — DS	m	Fr:w-9
12/49	9:30	The Ruggles — SC	m	To:f-8:30
2/50	9:00	Wendy Barrie — IV	m	To:tr-7:30(n)
3/50	9:00	Blind Date — QU	m	Fr:f-8:30
3/50	9:30	Author Meets the Critics — DS	m	To:w-8:30
3/50	9:30	Holiday Hotel — MV	d	
4/50	7:15	Art Ford on Broadway(15) — IV	d	
6/50	7:15	Art Ford on Broadway(15) — IV	c	
6/50	9:00	ABC Showcase — VS	d	
6/50	9:00	Blind Date — QU	m	To:r-9:30-8/50
6/50	9:30	Holiday Hotel — MV	m	To:r-9-9/50

Date	Time	Title (min. if not 30) — Type	Action	From/To
6/50	9:30	The Ruggles—SC	m	Fr:n-10
7/50	9:00	ABC Showcase—VS	c	
7/50	9:00	Arthur Murray Party—MV	d	
8/50	9:30	Blind Date—QU	m	Fr:r-9-6/50
8/50	9:30	The Ruggles—SC	m	To:m-8:30-1/51
9/50	7:00	Club Seven—MV	m	Fr:r-10:30-3/49
9/50	9:00	Arthur Murray Party—MV	m	To:n-9(d)
9/50	9:00	Holiday Hotel—MV	m	Fr:r-9:30-6/50
10/50	10:00	I Cover Times Square—ND	d	
12/50	7:00	Andy and Della Russell(5)—MU	d	
1/51	10:00	I Cover Times Square—ND	c	
5/51	10:00	Industries for America—DO	d	
5/51	10:00	Roller Derby(60)—SP	f	
5/51	10:30	America in View—TR	d	
6/51	7:00	Andy and Della Russell(5)—MU	c	
7/51	10:00	Industries for America—DO	m	To:n-10
7/51	10:00	Roller Derby(60)—SP	s	
7/51	10:30	America in View—TR	m	To:f-10:30
8/51	7:00	Club Seven—MV	c	
8/51	10:00	Jerry Colonna—CV	m	Fr:f-8
8/51	10:00	Roller Derby(60)—SP	f	
8/51	10:30	Earl Wrightson(15)—MU	m	Fr:w-7:45-6/50(c)
9/51	9:30	Film—FI	s	
9/51	9:30	Blind Date—QU	m	To:s-9-6/52(n)
9/51	10:00	Jerry Colonna—CV	m	To:s-7:30
9/51	10:45	Sports Camera(15)—SH	m	Fr:t-9:30-9/50
9/51	10:45	Sports Camera(15)—SH	m	To:s-8:30-12/51
10/51	9:00	Herb Shriner—CV	d	
10/51	9:00	Holiday Hotel—MV	c	
10/51	10:00	Paul Dixon—VY	s	
10/51	10:45	Carmel Myers Show(15)—IV	m	Fr:t-7:15
12/51	9:30	Film—FI	f	
1/52	9:30	Boxing—SP	s	
1/52	10:00	Paul Dixon—VY	f	
2/52	10:00	America's Health(15)—DO	m	Fr:s-9:30-10/51
2/52	10:15	Industries for America(15)—DO	m	Fr:f-10:30-12/51
2/52	10:30	Earl Wrightson(15)—MU	c	
2/52	10:45	Carmel Myers Show(15)—IV	c	
3/52	10:00	America's Health(15)—DO	c	
3/52	10:15	Industries for America(15)—DO	m	To:r-9:30-7/57
4/52	8:00	The Ruggles—SC	m	Fr:w-9
4/52	8:00	Stop the Music(60)—QU	m	To:t-10:30-9/54
4/52	8:30	Chance of a Lifetime—TA	d	
4/52	9:00	Herb Shriner—CV	c	
5/52	9:00	Mr. Arsenic—PA	d	
6/52	8:00	The Ruggles—SC	c	
6/52	9:00	Mr. Arsenic—PA	c	
6/52	9:30	Boxing—SP	f	
7/52	8:00	A Date with Judy—SC	d	
7/52	9:00	Marshall Plan in Action—DO	m	Fr:t-8

Date	Time	Title (min. if not 30) – Type	Action	From/To
7/52	9:30	Do's and Don'ts – IS	d	
8/52	9:00	Marshall Plan in Action – DO	c	
8/52	9:30	Do's and Don'ts – IS	c	
9/52	9:00	Politics on Trial – DB	d	
9/52	9:30	On Guard – DO	m	Fr:m-9:30
10/52	8:00	A Date with Judy – SC	m	To:w-7:30-1/53
10/52	8:00	News – NW	s	
10/52	9:00	Politics on Trial – DB	c	
11/52	9:00	Perspective – DS	d	
12/52	8:00	Greatest Man on Earth – QU	d	
12/52	8:00	News – NW	f	
12/52	9:30	On Guard – DO	m	To:s-10-12/53
12/52	9:30	Valentino – DR	d	
1/53	9:00	Perspective – DS	m	To:m-9
2/53	8:00	Film – FI	s	
2/53	8:00	Greatest Man on Earth – QU	c	
3/53	9:00	Boxing(60) – SP	s	
3/53	9:30	Valentino – DR	c	
3/53	10:00	Personality Puzzle – QU	d	
3/53	10:30	Quick as a Flash – QU	d	
6/53	9:00	Boxing(60) – SP	f	
6/53	9:00	Madison Square Garden Highlights – ST	d	
6/53	10:00	Personality Puzzle – QU	c	
7/53	8:30	Doorway to Danger – SD	m	Fr:f-9-8/52(n)
7/53	10:30	Film – FI	s	
7/53	10:30	Quick as a Flash – QU	m	To:r-8-9/53
8/53	8:30	Chance of a Lifetime – TA	m	To:f-10(d)
8/53	9:30	Dotty Mack – MU	m	Fr:t-9(d)
9/53	8:00	Film – FI	f	
9/53	8:00	Quick as a Flash – QU	m	Fr:r-10:30-7/53
9/53	9:00	Madison Square Garden Highlights – ST	m	To:s-8:30
9/53	10:00	Gold Seal Playhouse – DA	d	
10/53	8:30	Doorway to Danger – SD	c	
10/53	8:30	Ray Bolger – SC	d	
10/53	9:00	Back That Fact – QU	d	
10/53	9:30	Dotty Mack – MU	m	To:s-7:30-4/54
10/53	9:30	Kraft Television Theater(60) – DA	d	
10/53	10:00	Gold Seal Playhouse – DA	c	
10/53	10:30	Film – FI	f	
11/53	9:00	Back That Fact – QU	c	
12/53	9:00	Doctor I.Q. – QU	m	Fr:w-9:30
1/54	9:00	Doctor I.Q. – QU	m	To:m-8:30
1/54	9:00	Talent Patrol – TA	m	Fr:s-8
2/54	8:00	Quick as a Flash – QU	c	
3/54	8:00	It's About Time – QU	d	
3/54	8:00	It's About Time – QU	m	To:n-7:30
3/54	9:00	Open Hearing – PA	d	
3/54	9:00	Talent Patrol – TA	m	To:r-8

Date	Time	Title (min. if not 30) — Type	Action	From/To
4/54	8:00	Talent Patrol — TA	m	Fr:r-9
7/54	8:00	Melody Tour(60) — MV	d	
7/54	8:00	Talent Patrol — TA	m	To:w-7:30
7/54	8:30	Ray Bolger — SC	m	To:f-8:30-9/54
7/54	9:00	Open Hearing — PA	m	To:n-8:30-2/57
8/54	9:00	Sammy Kaye — MV	m	Fr:s-8-9/53(n)
9/54	7:00	Kukla, Fran & Ollie(15) — KV	m	Fr:m-f-7-6/52(n)
9/54	8:00	Melody Tour(60) — MV	c	
10/54	8:00	The Mail Story — DA	d	
10/54	8:30	Treasury Men in Action — CD	m	Fr:r-8:30-4/54(n)
12/54	8:00	The Mail Story — DA	c	
1/55	8:00	Talent Patrol — TA	m	Fr:m-8
1/55	9:00	Sammy Kaye — MV	m	To:s-10-9/58
1/55	9:30	Kraft Television Theater(60) — DA	c	
1/55	9:30	Ponds Theatre(60) — DA	d	
2/55	9:00	Star Tonight — DA	d	
6/55	8:00	Talent Patrol — TA	m	To:r-8
6/55	8:00	Talent Patrol(60) — TA	m	Fr:r-8
6/55	8:30	Treasury Men in Action — CD	m	To:f-8:30
7/55	7:00	Soupy Sales(15) — KV	d*	
7/55	9:30	Greatest Sports Thrills — SH	m	Fr:s-8:30-9/54
7/55	9:30	Ponds Theatre(60) — DA	c	
7/55	10:00	Let's See — QU	d	
8/55	7:00	Soupy Sales(15) — KV	c*	
8/55	10:00	Let's See — QU	c	
9/55	8:00	Talent Patrol(60) — TA	c	
9/55	9:30	Down You Go — QU	m	Fr:s-9:30(c)
9/55	9:30	Greatest Sports Thrills — SH	m	To:r-10-11/55
9/55	10:00	Outside, USA — DO	d	
10/55	8:00	Life Is Worth Living — RE	m	Fr:t-8-4/55(d)
10/55	8:30	Stop the Music — QU	m	Fr:t-10:30-5/55
10/55	10:00	Outside, USA — DO	m	To:t-10
11/55	10:00	Greatest Sports Thrills — SH	m	Fr:r-9:30-9/55
1/56	10:00	Greatest Sports Thrills — SH	m	To:r-9:30-6/56
1/56	10:00	Music at the Meadowbrook — MV	m	Fr:s-8-12/53
4/56	8:00	Eddy Arnold — MV	d	
4/56	8:00	Life Is Worth Living — RE	m	To:m-9-10/56
4/56	10:00	Dotty Mack — MU	m	Fr:m-9
4/56	10:00	Music at the Meadowbrook — MV	c	
6/56	8:00	Eddy Arnold — MV	m	To:w-9:30
6/56	8:00	Film(60) — FI	s	
6/56	8:30	Stop the Music — QU	c	
6/56	9:30	Down You Go — QU	m	To:s-7:30(n)
6/56	9:30	Greatest Sports Thrills — SH	m	Fr:r-10-1/56
7/56	7:00	Jack Drees Sports Show(15) — SN	d*	
7/56	10:00	Compass — TR	m	Fr:s-10-9/55
7/56	10:00	Dotty Mack — MU	m	To:m-8
8/56	7:00	Jack Drees Sports Show(15) — SN	c*	
8/56	9:00	Star Tonight — DA	c	
9/56	8:00	Film(60) — FI	f	

Date	Time	Title (min. if not 30) – Type	Action	From/To
9/56	9:00	Combat Sergeant – WD	m	Fr:f-8
9/56	9:00	Combat Sergeant – WD	c	
9/56	9:30	Greatest Sports Thrills – SH	c	
9/56	10:00	Compass – TR	m	To:r-9:30-6/57
10/56	8:00	Circus Time(60) – VY	d	
10/56	9:00	Wire Service(60) – ND	d	
10/56	10:00	Ozark Jubilee(60) – MU	m	Fr:s-7:30
12/56	10:00	Air Time '57 – MV	d	
12/56	10:00	Ozark Jubilee(60) – MU	m	To:s-10
2/57	9:00	Danny Thomas Show – SC	m	Fr:m-8
2/57	9:00	Wire Service(60) – ND	m	To:m-7:30
2/57	9:30	Bold Journey – TR	m	Fr:m-7:30
4/57	10:00	Air Time '57 – MV	c	
4/57	10:00	Telephone Time – DA	d	
6/57	7:00	Sports Focus(15) – SN	d*	
6/57	8:00	Circus Time(60) – VY	c	
6/57	9:30	Bold Journey – TR	m	To:m-8:30
6/57	9:30	Compass – TR	m	Fr:r-10-9/56
6/57	10:00	Telephone Time – DA	m	To:t-9:30
7/57	7:00	Sports Focus(15) – SN	m*	To:m-f-7-9/57
7/57	8:00	Big Picture – DO	m	Fr:t-10-10/56
7/57	8:00	Big Picture – DO	m	To:f-10
7/57	8:30	Enterprise – DO	m	Fr:w-9:30-1/55
7/57	8:30	Enterprise – DO	m	To:f-9
7/57	9:00	Danny Thomas Show – SC	m	To:m-9-10/57(c)
7/57	9:00	Theatre Time – DA	d	
7/57	9:30	Compass – TR	m	To:n-9
7/57	9:30	Industries for America – DO	m	Fr:r-10:15-2/52
8/57	7:00	Kukla, Fran & Ollie(15) – KV	c	
8/57	8:00	Cowtown Rodeo(60) – RO	d	
9/57	7:00	Sports Focus(15) – SN	m	Fr:m-f-7
9/57	7:30	Circus Boy – AD	m	Fr:n-7:30(n)
9/57	7:30	Lone Ranger – WE	c	
9/57	8:00	ABC Presents(60) – DO	m	Fr:m-9
9/57	8:00	Cowtown Rodeo(60) – RO	m	To:m-7:30-6/58
9/57	9:00	Theatre Time – DA	c	
9/57	9:30	Industries for America – DO	c	
9/57	9:30	O.S.S. – WD	d	
10/57	8:00	ABC Presents(60) – DO	c	
10/57	8:00	Zorro – AD	d	
10/57	8:30	Real McCoys – SC	d	
10/57	9:00	Pat Boone – MV	d	
10/57	10:00	Navy Log – MR	m	Fr:w-8:30
1/58	9:30	Navy Log – MR	m	Fr:r-10
1/58	9:30	O.S.S. – WD	m	To:m-7:30
1/58	10:00	Modern Science Theater – DO	d	
1/58	10:00	Navy Log – MR	m	To:r-9:30
3/58	10:00	Make Me Laugh – QU	d	
3/58	10:00	Modern Science Theater – DO	c	
6/58	10:00	Confession – IV	d	

Date	Time	Title (min. if not 30) — Type	Action	From/To
6/58	10:00	Make Me Laugh — QU	c	
7/58	9:00	Andy Williams Show — MV	d*	
9/58	7:00	Sports Focus(15) — SN	c	
9/58	7:30	Circus Boy — AD	c	
9/58	9:00	Andy Williams Show — MV	m*	To:t-10-7/59(c)
9/58	9:30	Navy Log — MR	c	
9/58	10:00	Confession — IV	m	To:t-10
9/58	10:00	Stars of Jazz — MU	m	Fr:m-9
10/58	7:30	Leave It to Beaver — SC	m	Fr:w-8(c)
10/58	9:30	Rough Riders — WE	d	
10/58	10:00	Stars of Jazz — MU	m	To:n-9:30
10/58	10:00	Traffic Court — CR	m	Fr:n-9
11/58	10:00	This Is Music — MU	m	Fr:m-10
11/58	10:00	Traffic Court — CR	m	To:m-10
2/59	10:00	Sammy Kaye — MV	m	Fr:s-10
2/59	10:00	This Is Music — MU	m	To:m-9:30
4/59	10:00	Sammy Kaye — MV	m	To:s-10
4/59	10:00	This Is Music — MU	m	Fr:m-9:30
5/59	10:00	This Is Music — MU	c	
5/59	10:00	Your Neighbor the World — DO	m	Fr:n-var-1/59
6/59	7:30	Leave It to Beaver — SC	m	To:r-9
7/59	7:30	Oh Boy — MU	d	
7/59	9:00	Leave It to Beaver — SC	m*	Fr:r-7:30
9/59	7:30	Oh Boy — MU	c	
9/59	8:00	Zorro — AD	c	
9/59	9:00	Leave It to Beaver — SC	m*	To:s-8:30
9/59	9:30	Meet McGraw — CD	m	Fr:n-10:30
9/59	9:30	Rough Riders — WE	c	
10/59	7:30	Gale Storm — SC	m	Fr:s-9-4/59(c)
10/59	8:00	Donna Reed — SC	m	Fr:w-9
10/59	9:30	Meet McGraw — CD	c	
10/59	9:30	Untouchables(60) — CD	d	
10/59	10:00	Your Neighbor the World — DO	c	
10/59	10:30	Take a Good Look — QU	d	
3/60	7:30	Gale Storm — SC	c	
4/60	7:30	Steve Canyon — AD	m	Fr:t-8-9/59(n)
6/60	9:00	Hey Jeannie — SC	m	Fr:s-9:30-5/57(c)
6/60	9:00	Pat Boone — MV	c	
8/60	10:30	Silents Please — VS	d*	
9/60	7:30	Guestward Ho! — SC	d	
9/60	7:30	Steve Canyon — AD	c	
9/60	9:00	Hey Jeannie — SC	c	
9/60	9:00	My Three Sons — SC	d	
10/60	10:30	Silents Please — VS	m*	To:r-10:30-3/61
3/61	10:30	Silents Please — VS	m	Fr:r-10:30-10/60
3/61	10:30	Take a Good Look — QU	c	
9/61	7:30	Adventures of Ozzie & Harriet — SC	m	Fr:w-8:30
9/61	7:30	Guestward Ho! — SC	c	
10/61	9:30	Margie — SC	d	
10/61	9:30	Untouchables(60) — CD	m	To:r-10

Date	Time	Title (min. if not 30) — Type	Action	From/To
10/61	10:00	Untouchables(60) — CD	m	Fr:r-9:30
10/61	10:30	Silents Please — VS	c	
4/62	9:30	The Law & Mr. Jones — LD	m	Fr:f-10:30-9/61
4/62	9:30	Margie — SC	m	To:f-7:30
9/62	8:30	Leave It to Beaver — SC	m	Fr:s-8:30
9/62	8:30	Real McCoys — SC	m	To:n-9(c)
9/62	10:00	Untouchables(60) — CD	m	To:t-9:30
10/62	9:30	The Law & Mr. Jones — LD	c	
10/62	9:30	McHale's Navy — SC	d	
10/62	10:00	Alcoa Premiere(60) — DA	m	Fr:t-10
9/63	7:30	Adventures of Ozzie & Harriet — SC	m	To:w-7:30
9/63	7:30	Flintstones — KV	m	Fr:f-8:30
9/63	8:30	Leave It to Beaver — SC	c	
9/63	8:30	My Three Sons — SC	m	Fr:r-9
9/63	9:00	Jimmy Dean(60) — MV	d	
9/63	9:00	My Three Sons — SC	m	To:r-8:30
9/63	9:30	McHale's Navy — SC	m	To:t-8:30
9/63	10:00	Alcoa Premiere(60) — DA	c	
9/63	10:00	Edie Adams — MV	d	
10/63	10:00	Sid Caesar — CV	d	
1/64	10:30	ABC News Reports — DO	m	Fr:n-10:30
3/64	9:00	Ensign O'Toole — SC	m	Fr:n-7-9/63(n)
3/64	9:00	Jimmy Dean(60) — MV	m	To:r-9:30
3/64	9:30	Jimmy Dean(60) — MV	m	Fr:r-9
3/64	10:00	Edie Adams — MV	c	
3/64	10:00	Sid Caesar — CV	c	
8/64	9:30	Jimmy Dean(60) — MV	m	To:r-10
8/64	10:30	ABC News Reports — DO	c	
9/64	9:00	Bewitched — SC	d	
9/64	9:00	Ensign O'Toole — SC	c	
9/64	9:30	Peyton Place — SL	d	
9/64	10:00	Jimmy Dean(60) — MV	m	Fr:r-9:30
12/64	7:30	Flintstones — KV	m	To:f-7:30
12/64	7:30	Johnny Quest — KV	m	Fr:f-7:30
9/65	7:30	Johnny Quest — KV	c	
9/65	7:30	Shindig — MU	m	Fr:w-8:30
9/65	8:30	My Three Sons — SC	m	To:r-8:30(c)
9/65	8:30	O.K. Crackerby — SC	d	
9/65	10:00	Jimmy Dean(60) — MV	m	To:f-10
9/65	10:00	The Long Hot Summer(60) — DR	d	
1/66	7:30	Batman — AD	d	
1/66	7:30	Shindig — MU	c	
1/66	8:00	Donna Reed — SC	m	To:s-8
1/66	8:00	Gidget — SC	m	Fr:w-8:30
1/66	8:30	Double Life of Henry Phyfe — SC	d	
1/66	8:30	O.K. Crackerby — SC	c	
1/66	10:00	Baron(60) — SD	d	
1/66	10:00	The Long Hot Summer(60) — DR	m	To:w-10
7/66	10:00	Avengers(60) — SD	m	Fr:m-10
7/66	10:00	Baron(60) — SD	c	

Date	Time	Title (min. if not 30) — Type	Action	From/To
8/66	9:30	Peyton Place — SL	m	To:mw-9:30
9/66	8:00	F Troop — SC	m	Fr:t-9
9/66	8:00	Gidget — SC	c	
9/66	8:30	Double Life of Henry Phyfe — SC	c	
9/66	8:30	Tammy Grimes — SC	d	
9/66	8:30	Tammy Grimes — SC	c	
9/66	9:30	That Girl — SC	d	
9/66	10:00	Avengers(60) — SD	m	To:f-10-1/67
9/66	10:00	Hawk(60) — CD	d	
10/66	8:30	Dating Game — QU	d	
12/66	10:00	Hawk(60) — CD	m	To:w-10-4/76(n)
1/67	8:30	Bewitched — SC	m	Fr:r-9
1/67	8:30	Dating Game — QU	m	To:s-7:30
1/67	9:00	Bewitched — SC	m	To:r-8:30
1/67	9:00	Love on a Rooftop — SC	m	Fr:t-9:30
1/67	10:00	ABC Stage 67(60) — VS	m	Fr:w-10
4/67	9:00	Love on a Rooftop — SC	m	To:r-9:30
4/67	9:00	That Girl — SC	m	Fr:r-9:30
4/67	9:30	Love on a Rooftop — SC	m	Fr:r-9
4/67	9:30	That Girl — SC	m	To:r-9
5/67	10:00	ABC Stage 67(60) — VS	c	
5/67	10:00	Summer Focus(60) — DO	d	
8/67	8:00	F Troop — SC	c	
8/67	9:30	Love on a Rooftop — SC	m	To:w-9-5/71
8/67	10:00	Summer Focus(60) — DO	c	
9/67	8:00	Flying Nun — SC	d	
9/67	9:30	Peyton Place — SL	m	Fr:mt-9:30
9/67	10:00	Good Company — IV	d	
12/67	10:00	Good Company — IV	c	
3/68	7:30	Batman — AD	c	
3/68	7:30	Second Hundred Years — SC	m	Fr:w-8:30
9/68	7:30	Second Hundred Years — SC	c	
9/68	7:30	Ugliest Girl in Town — SC	d	
9/68	9:30	Journey to the Unknown(60) — SA	d	
9/68	9:30	Peyton Place — SL	m	To:m-9;w-8:30
1/69	7:30	Ugliest Girl in Town — SC	c	
1/69	8:00	Flying Nun — SC	m	To:r-7:30
1/69	9:00	That Girl — SC	m	To:r-8
1/69	9:30	Journey to the Unknown(60) — SA	c	
2/69	7:30	Flying Nun — SC	m	Fr:r-8
2/69	8:00	That Girl — SC	m	Fr:r-9
2/69	9:00	What's It All About, World?(60) — CV	d	
5/69	9:00	Tom Jones(60) — MV	m	Fr:f-7:30
5/69	9:00	What's It All About, World?(60) — CV	c	
8/69	10:00	It Takes a Thief(60) — SD	m	Fr:t-8:30
9/69	7:30	Flying Nun — SC	m	To:w-7:30
9/69	7:30	Ghost & Mrs. Muir — SC	m	Fr:s-8:30(n)

Date	Time	Title (min. if not 30) – Type	Action	From/To
1/70	7:30	Pat Paulsen's Half a Comedy Hour – CV	d	
1/70	7:30	Ghost & Mrs. Muir – SC	m	To:f-8:30
1/70	10:00	It Takes a Thief(60) – SD	m	To:m-7:30
1/70	10:00	Paris 7000(60) – AD	d	
4/70	7:30	Animal World – WL	m	Fr:r-7:30-9/69(c)
4/70	7:30	Pat Paulsen's Half a Comedy Hour – CV	c	
6/70	10:00	Paris 7000(60) – AD	c	
6/70	10:00	The Survivors(60) – DR	m	Fr:m-9-1/70
9/70	7:30	Animal World – WL	m	To:n-7:30-7/71
9/70	7:30	Matt Lincoln(60) – MD	d	
9/70	8:00	That Girl – SC	m	To:f-9
9/70	9:00	Barefoot in the Park – SC	d	
9/70	9:00	Tom Jones(60) – MV	m	To:f-10
9/70	9:30	Odd Couple – SC	d	
9/70	10:00	Immortal(60) – AD	d	
9/70	10:00	The Survivors(60) – DR	c	
1/71	7:30	Alias Smith and Jones(60) – WE	d	
1/71	7:30	Matt Lincoln(60) – MD	c	
1/71	9:00	Barefoot in the Park – SC	c	
1/71	9:00	Danny Thomas Show – SC	m	Fr:w-8
1/71	9:30	Dan August(60) – CD	m	Fr:w-10
1/71	9:30	Odd Couple – SC	m	To:f-9:30
1/71	10:00	Immortal(60) – AD	m	To:w-9:30-5/71
9/71	7:30	Alias Smith and Jones(60) – WE	m	To:r-8
9/71	8:00	Alias Smith and Jones(60) – WE	m	Fr:r-7:30
9/71	8:30	Bewitched – SC	m	To:w-8
9/71	9:00	Danny Thomas Show – SC	c	
9/71	9:00	Longstreet(60) – CD	d	
9/71	9:30	Dan August(60) – CD	m	To:w-9-5/73(c)
9/71	10:00	Owen Marshall, Counselor at Law (60) – LD	d	
8/72	8:00	Alias Smith and Jones(60) – WE	m	To:s-8
8/72	9:00	Longstreet(60) – CD	c	
9/72	8:00	The Mod Squad(60) – CD	m	Fr:t-7:30
9/72	9:00	Assignment Vienna(60) – SD	d	
9/72	9:00	Jigsaw(60) – CD	d	
10/72	9:00	Delphi Bureau(60) – SD	d	
12/72	9:00	Assignment Vienna(60) – SD	m	To:s-10
12/72	9:00	Jigsaw(60) – CD	m	To:s-10-2/73
1/73	9:00	Delphi Bureau(60) – SD	m	To:s-10-3/73
1/73	9:00	Kung Fu(60) – WE	m	Fr:s-8-11/72
1/73	10:00	Owen Marshall, Counselor at Law (60) – LD	m	To:w-10
1/73	10:00	Streets of San Francisco(60) – CD	m	Fr:s-9
9/73	8:00	Mod Squad(60) – CD	c	
10/73	8:00	Toma(60) – CD	d	
1/74	8:00	Chopper One – CD	d	
1/74	8:00	Toma(60) – CD	m	To:f-10

Date	Time	Title (min. if not 30) — Type	Action	From/To
1/74	8:30	Firehouse — AD	d	
7/74	8:00	Chopper One — CD	c	
7/74	8:00	Temperature's Rising — SC	m	Fr:t-8-1/74
8/74	8:00	Temperature's Rising — SC	c	
8/74	8:30	Firehouse — AD	c	
8/74	9:00	Kung Fu(60) — WE	m	To:s-9
8/74	10:00	Streets of San Francisco(60) — CD	m	To:r-9
9/74	8:00	Odd Couple — SC	m	Fr:r-9:30
9/74	8:30	Paper Moon — SC	d	
9/74	9:00	Streets of San Francisco(60) — CD	m	Fr:r-10
9/74	10:00	Harry-O(60) — CD	d	
1/75	8:00	Barney Miller — SC	d	
1/75	8:00	Odd Couple — SC	m	To:f-9:30
1/75	8:30	Karen — SC	d	
1/75	8:30	Paper Moon — SC	c	
6/75	8:30	Karen — SC	c	
6/75	8:30	Texas Wheelers — SC	m	Fr:f-9:30-10/74
7/75	8:00	Almost Anything Goes(60) — QU	d*	
7/75	8:30	Texas Wheelers — SC	c	
8/75	8:00	Almost Anything Goes(60) — QU	m*	To:s-8-1/76
9/75	8:30	On the Rocks — SC	d	
1/76	8:00	Barney Miller — SC	m	To:r-8:30
1/76	8:00	Welcome Back, Kotter — SC	m	Fr:t-8:30
1/76	8:30	Barney Miller — SC	m	Fr:r-8
1/76	8:30	On the Rocks — SC	m	To:m-8
8/76	8:30	What's Happening — SC	d*	
8/76	8:30	What's Happening — SC	m*	To:s-8:30-11/76
9/76	9:00	Streets of San Francisco(60) — CD	m	To:r-10
9/76	9:00	Tony Randall — SC	d	
9/76	9:30	Nancy Walker Show — SC	d	
9/76	10:00	Harry-O(60) — CD	c	
9/76	10:00	Streets of San Francisco(60) — CD	m	Fr:r-9
12/76	8:30	Barney Miller — SC	m	To:r-9
12/76	8:30	What's Happening — SC	m	Fr:s-8:30
12/76	9:00	Barney Miller — SC	m	Fr:r-8:30
12/76	9:00	Tony Randall — SC	m	To:r-9:30
12/76	9:30	Nancy Walker Show — SC	c	
12/76	9:30	Tony Randall — SC	m	Fr:r-9
3/77	9:30	Three's Company — SC	d	
3/77	9:30	Tony Randall — SC	m	To:s-9:30-9/77(c)
3/77	10:00	Westside Medical(60) — MD	d*	
4/77	10:00	Westside Medical(60) — MD	m*	To:r-10-6/77
5/77	9:30	Three's Company — SC	m	To:r-9:30-8/77
6/77	9:30	Fish — SC	m	Fr:s-8:30
6/77	10:00	Streets of San Francisco(60) — CD	c	
6/77	10:00	Westside Medical(60) — MD	m	Fr:r-10-4/77
8/77	9:30	Fish — SC	m	To:s-8
8/77	9:30	Three's Company — SC	m	Fr:r-9:30-4/77
8/77	10:00	Westside Medical(60) — MD	c	
9/77	9:30	Carter Country — SC	d	

Date	Time	Title (min. if not 30) — Type	Action	From/To
9/77	9:30	Three's Company — SC	m	To:t-9
9/77	10:00	Redd Foxx(60) — CV	d	
1/78	8:30	Fish — SC	m	Fr:s-8-11/77
1/78	8:30	What's Happening — SC	m	To:s-8
1/78	10:00	Redd Foxx(60) — CV	c	
2/78	10:00	Baretta(60) — CD	m	Fr:w-10
3/78	9:30	A.E.S. Hudson Street — SC	d	
3/78	9:30	Carter Country — SC	m	To:t-9:30-5/78
4/78	8:30	Fish — SC	m	To:r-9:30
4/78	8:30	What's Happening — SC	m	Fr:s-8
4/78	9:30	A.E.S. Hudson Street — SC	c	
5/78	8:30	Operation Petticoat — SC	m	Fr:s-8:30
5/78	8:30	What's Happening — SC	m	To:r-8:30
5/78	9:30	Fish — SC	m	Fr:r-8:30
6/78	8:30	Operation Petticoat — SC	m	To:f-8:30
6/78	8:30	What's Happening — SC	m	Fr:r-8:30
6/78	9:30	Fish — SC	c	
6/78	9:30	Film(90) — FI	s	
6/78	10:00	Baretta(60) — CD	c	
8/78	8:00	Welcome Back, Kotter — SC	m	To:m-8
8/78	9:30	Film(90) — FI	f	
9/78	8:00	Mork and Mindy — SC	d	
9/78	9:30	Soap — SC	m	Fr:t-9:30-3/78
9/78	10:00	Family(60) — DR	m	Fr:t-10-5/78
1/79	8:30	Delta House — SC	d	
1/79	8:30	Delta House — SC	m	To:s-8
1/79	8:30	What's Happening — SC	m	To:f-8:30
2/79	8:30	Angie — SC	d	
2/79	8:30	Makin' It — DR	d	
2/79	8:30	Makin' It — DR	m	To:f-8
3/79	9:30	Carter Country — SC	m*	Fr:s-8:30-1/79
3/79	10:00	Family(60) — DR	m	To:f-8
4/79	10:00	Doctors' Private Lives(60) — MD	d	
4/79	10:00	Doctors' Private Lives(60) — MD	c	
5/79	10:00	Family(60) — DR	m	Fr:f-8
5/79	10:00	Family(60) — DR	m	To:m-10-12/79
5/79	10:00	20/20(60) — NM	m	Fr:var
8/79	8:00	Laverne & Shirley — SC	m	Fr:t-8:30
8/79	8:00	Mork and Mindy — SC	m	To:n-8
8/79	8:30	Angie — SC	m	To:t-8:30
8/79	9:30	Carter Country — SC	c*	
9/79	8:30	Benson — SC	d	
12/79	8:00	Laverne & Shirley — SC	m	To:m-8
1/80	8:00	Mork and Mindy — SC	m	Fr:n-8
3/80	9:30	Associates — SC	m	Fr:n-8:30-10/79
3/80	9:30	Soap — SC	m	To:w-9:30-10/80
4/80	9:30	Associates — SC	c	
5/80	9:30	The Ropers — SC	m	Fr:s-8:30-3/80
5/80	9:30	The Ropers — SC	m	
5/80	9:30	Semi-Tough — SC	d	

Date	Time	Title (min. if not 30) — Type	Action	From/To
6/80	9:30	Nobody's Perfect — SC	d	
6/80	9:30	Semi-Tough — SC	c	
7/80	8:30	Angie — SC	m	Fr:s-8-4/80
7/80	8:30	Benson — SC	m	To:f-8
8/80	9:30	Nobody's Perfect — SC	c	
9/80	9:30	It's a Living — SC	d	
10/80	8:30	Angie — SC	c	
11/80	8:30	Bosom Buddies — SC	d	
1/81	9:30	It's a Living — SC	m	To:t-9:30-6/81
2/81	9:30	Taxi — SC	m	Fr:w-9
9/81	8:30	Best of the West — SC	d	
9/81	8:30	Bosom Buddies — SC	m	To:r-9
10/81	9:00	Bosom Buddies — SC	m*	Fr:r-8:30
10/81	9:00	Bosom Buddies — SC	m*	To:f-8:30
1/82	8:30	Best of the West — SC	m	To:f-9
2/82	8:00	Mork and Mindy — SC	m	To:r-8:30-4/82
2/82	8:30	Bosom Buddies — SC	m	Fr:f-8:30
3/82	8:00	Police Squad — SC	d	
3/82	8:00	Police Squad — SC	m	To:r-9:30-7/82
3/82	8:30	Bosom Buddies — SC	m	To:r-8:30-5/82
3/82	9:00	Barney Miller — SC	m	To:f-8:30
3/82	9:00	9 to 5 — SC	d	
4/82	8:00	No Soap, Radio — SC	d	
4/82	8:30	Mork and Mindy — SC	m	Fr:r-8-2/82
4/82	9:00	Barney Miller — SC	m	Fr:f-8:30
4/82	9:00	9 to 5 — SC	m	To:t-9:30-9/82
5/82	8:00	Mork and Mindy — SC	m	Fr:r-8:30
5/82	8:00	No Soap, Radio — SC	c	
5/82	8:30	Bosom Buddies — SC	m	Fr:r-8:30-3/82
5/82	8:30	Mork and Mindy — SC	m	To:r-8
6/82	8:00	Mork and Mindy — SC	c	
6/82	8:30	Bosom Buddies — SC	m	To:s-9-7/84(n)
6/82	9:30	Taxi — SC	m	To:r-9:30-9/82(n)
7/82	8:00	Darkroom(60) — SA	m	Fr:f-9-1/82
7/82	9:30	Police Squad — SC	m	Fr:r-8-3/82
8/82	8:00	Darkroom(60) — SA	c	
9/82	8:00	Joanie Loves Chachi — SC	m	Fr:t-8:30-4/82
9/82	8:30	Star of the Family — SC	d	
9/82	9:00	Barney Miller — SC	c	
9/82	9:00	Too Close for Comfort — SC	m	Fr:t-9:30
9/82	9:30	Police Squad — SC	c	
10/82	9:30	It Takes Two — SC	d	
12/82	8:00	Joanie Loves Chachi — SC	m	To:t-8:30
12/82	8:30	Star of the Family — SC	c	
1/83	8:00	Greatest American Hero(60) — AD	m	Fr:f-9-11/82
2/83	8:00	Condo — SC	d	
2/83	8:00	Greatest American Hero(60) — AD	c	
2/83	8:30	Amanda's — SC	d	
3/83	8:00	Benson — SC	m	Fr:f-8
3/83	8:00	Condo — SC	m	To:r-8:30

Date	Time	Title (min. if not 30) — Type	Action	From/To
3/83	8:30	Amanda's — SC	c	
3/83	8:30	Condo — SC	m	Fr:r-8
4/83	8:00	Benson — SC	m	To:f-8
4/83	8:30	Condo — SC	m	To:r-8
5/83	8:00	Condo — SC	m	Fr:r-8:30
5/83	8:30	New Odd Couple — SC	m	Fr:f-8
6/83	8:00	Condo — SC	c	
6/83	8:00	Film(90) — FI	s	
6/83	8:30	New Odd Couple — SC	c	
6/83	9:00	Too Close for Comfort — SC	m	To:r-8:30-8/83
7/83	8:00	Film(90) — FI	f	
8/83	8:00	Eye on Hollywood — NM	d	
8/83	8:30	Too Close for Comfort — SC	m	Fr:r-9-6/83
8/83	9:00	Reggie — SC	d	
9/83	8:00	Eye on Hollywood — NM	m	To:m-f-12-2/84
9/83	8:00	Trauma Center(60) — MD	d	
9/83	8:30	Too Close for Comfort — SC	c	
9/83	9:00	9 to 5 — SC	m	Fr:t-9:30
9/83	9:00	Reggie — SC	c	
9/83	9:30	It Takes Two — SC	c	
9/83	9:30	It's Not Easy — SC	d	
10/83	8:00	Trauma Center(60) — MD	m	To:r-9
10/83	9:00	9 to 5 — SC	c	
10/83	9:30	It's Not Easy — SC	c	
11/83	9:00	Trauma Center(60) — MD	m	Fr:r-8
12/83	8:00	Automan(60) — SF	d	
12/83	9:00	Masquerade(60) — SD	d	
12/83	9:00	Trauma Center(60) — MD	c	
1/84	8:00	Automan(60) — SF	m	To:m-8-3/84
1/84	9:00	Masquerade(60) — SD	m	To:f-9-3/84
3/84	8:00	Two Marriages(60) — DR	m	Fr:w-9-9/83
3/84	8:00	Two Marriages(60) — DR	c	
3/84	9:00	Lottery(60) — DA	m	Fr:r-9-12/83
3/84	9:00	Lottery(60) — DA	m	To:r-9-6/84
4/84	8:00	Film(120) — FI	s	
6/84	8:00	Happy Days — SC	m	Fr:t-8:30
6/84	8:00	Film(120) — FI	f	
6/84	9:00	Lottery(60) — DA	m	Fr:r-9-3/84
7/84	8:00	Happy Days — SC	c	
7/84	9:00	Lottery(60) — DA	c	
8/84	8:00	People Do the Craziest Things — CY	d	
8/84	8:30	Who's the Boss? — SC	d	
8/84	9:00	Glitter(60) — DR	d	
9/84	8:00	People Do the Craziest Things — CY	m	To:n-10:30-3/85
9/84	8:30	Who's the Boss? — SC	m	To:t-8
9/84	9:00	Glitter(60) — DR	c	
10/84	8:00	Film(120) — FI	s	
3/85	8:00	Wildside(60) — WE	d	
3/85	8:00	Film(120) — FI	f	
3/85	9:00	Eye to Eye(60) — CD	d	

Date	Time	Title (min. if not 30) — Type	Action	From/To
4/85	8:00	Wildside(60) — WE	c	
5/85	8:00	Street Hawk(60) — AD	m	Fr:f-9-3/85
5/85	8:00	Street Hawk(60) — AD	c	
5/85	8:00	Film(120) — FI	s	
5/85	9:00	Eye to Eye(60) — CD	c	
8/85	8:00	Film(120) — FI	f	
9/85	8:00	Fall Guy(60) — AD	m	Fr:w-8-7/85
9/85	9:00	Lady Blue(60) — CD	d	
10/85	8:00	Fall Guy(60) — AD	m	To:s-8
10/85	9:00	Lady Blue(60) — CD	m	To:s-9
11/85	8:00	Shadow Chasers(60) — AD	d	
11/85	9:00	Colbys(60) — SL	d	
1/86	8:00	Ripley's Believe It or Not(60) — VY	m	Fr:n-7
1/86	8:00	Shadow Chasers(60) — AD	c	
8/86	8:00	Ripley's Believe It or Not(60) — VY	c	
9/86	8:00	Our World(60) — NM	d	
3/87	9:00	Colbys(60) — SL	c	
4/87	9:00	Jack and Mike(60) — DR	m	Fr:t-10
5/87	9:00	Jack and Mike(60) — DR	c	
6/87	9:00	Heart of the City(60) — CD	m	Fr:s-9-1/87
7/87	8:00	Starman(60) — SF	m	Fr:s-10
7/87	8:00	Starman(60) — SF	m	To:f-10
7/87	8:00	Our World(60) — NM	m	To:r-9
7/87	9:00	Our World(60) — NM	m	Fr:r-8
7/87	9:00	Heart of the City(60) — CD	c	
8/87	8:00	Sledge Hammer — SC	m	Fr:f-8
8/87	8:30	Charmings — SC	m	Fr:f-8-4/87
8/87	9:00	Our World(60) — NM	c	
8/87	10:00	20/20(60) — NM	m	To:f-10
9/87	9:00	Film(120) — FI	s	
1/88	8:00	Sledge Hammer — SC	m	To:f-9:30
1/88	8:00	Charmings — SC	m	Fr:r-8:30
1/88	8:30	Charmings — SC	m	To:r-8
1/88	8:30	Film(150) — FI	s	
1/88	9:00	Film(120) — FI	f	
2/88	8:00	Charmings — SC	m	To:r-8:30-6/88
2/88	8:30	Film(150) — FI	f	
3/88	8:00	Probe(60) — CD	d	
3/88	9:00	Hotel(60) — DR	m	Fr:s-10-1/88
3/88	10:00	Buck James(60) — DR	m	Fr:n-10-1/88
4/88	8:00	Max Headroom(60) — DR	m	Fr:f-9-10/87
4/88	8:00	Probe(60) — CD	m	To:r-8-5/88
5/88	8:00	Max Headroom(60) — DR	c	
5/88	8:00	Probe(60) — CD	m	Fr:r-8-4/88
5/88	8:00	Probe(60) — CD	m	To:s-8
5/88	9:00	Hotel(60) — DR	m	To:s-10
5/88	10:00	Buck James(60) — DR	c	
6/88	8:00	Sledge Hammer — SC	m	Fr:f-9:30-2/88
6/88	8:00	Sledge Hammer — SC	c	
6/88	8:30	Charmings — SC	m	Fr:r-8-2/88

Date	Time	Title (min. if not 30) — Type	Action	From/To
6/88	8:30	Charmings — SC	c	
6/88	9:00	Film(120) — FI	s	
6/88	9:00	Film(120) — FI	f	
7/88	8:00	Film(120) — FI	s	
7/88	10:00	Hothouse(60) — DR	d	
8/88	8:00	Film(120) — FI	f	
8/88	10:00	Hothouse(60) — DR	c	

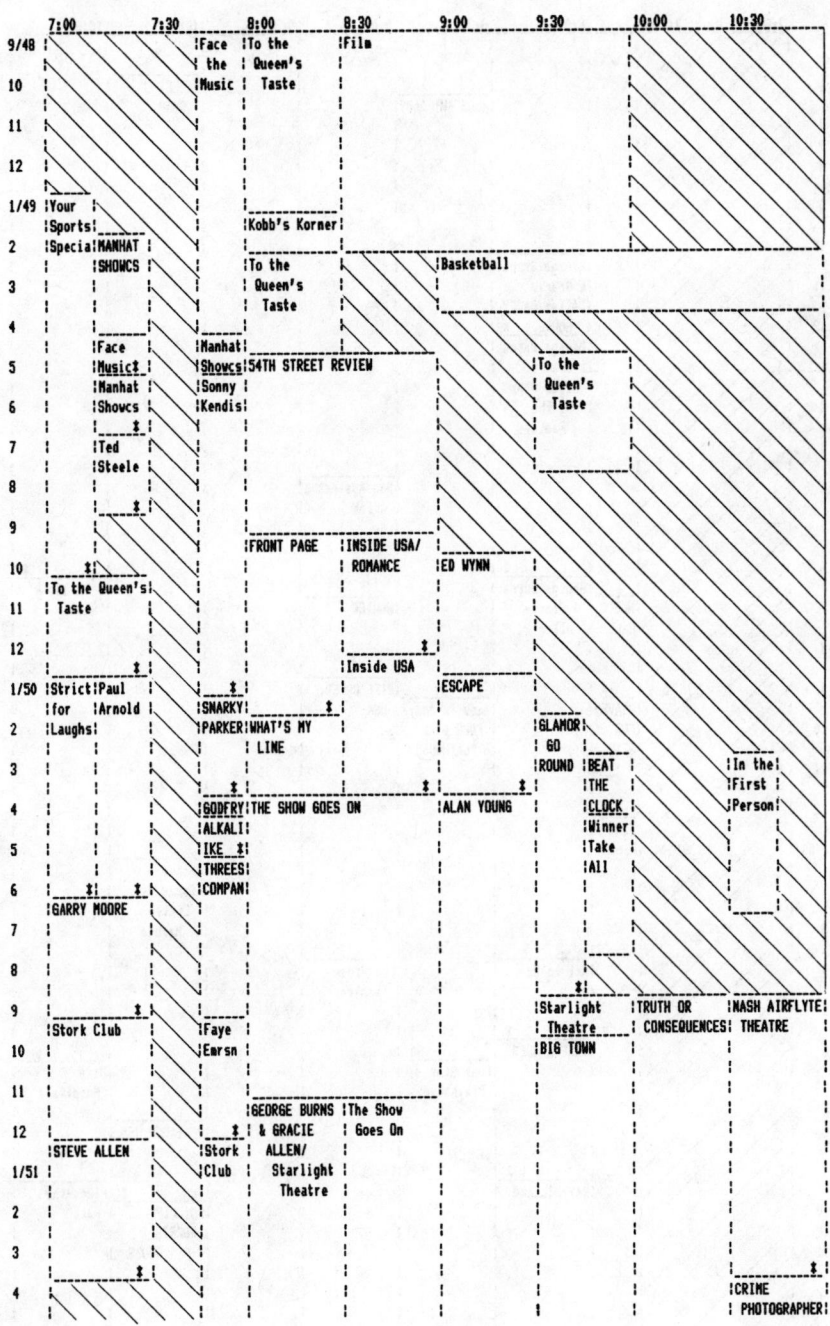

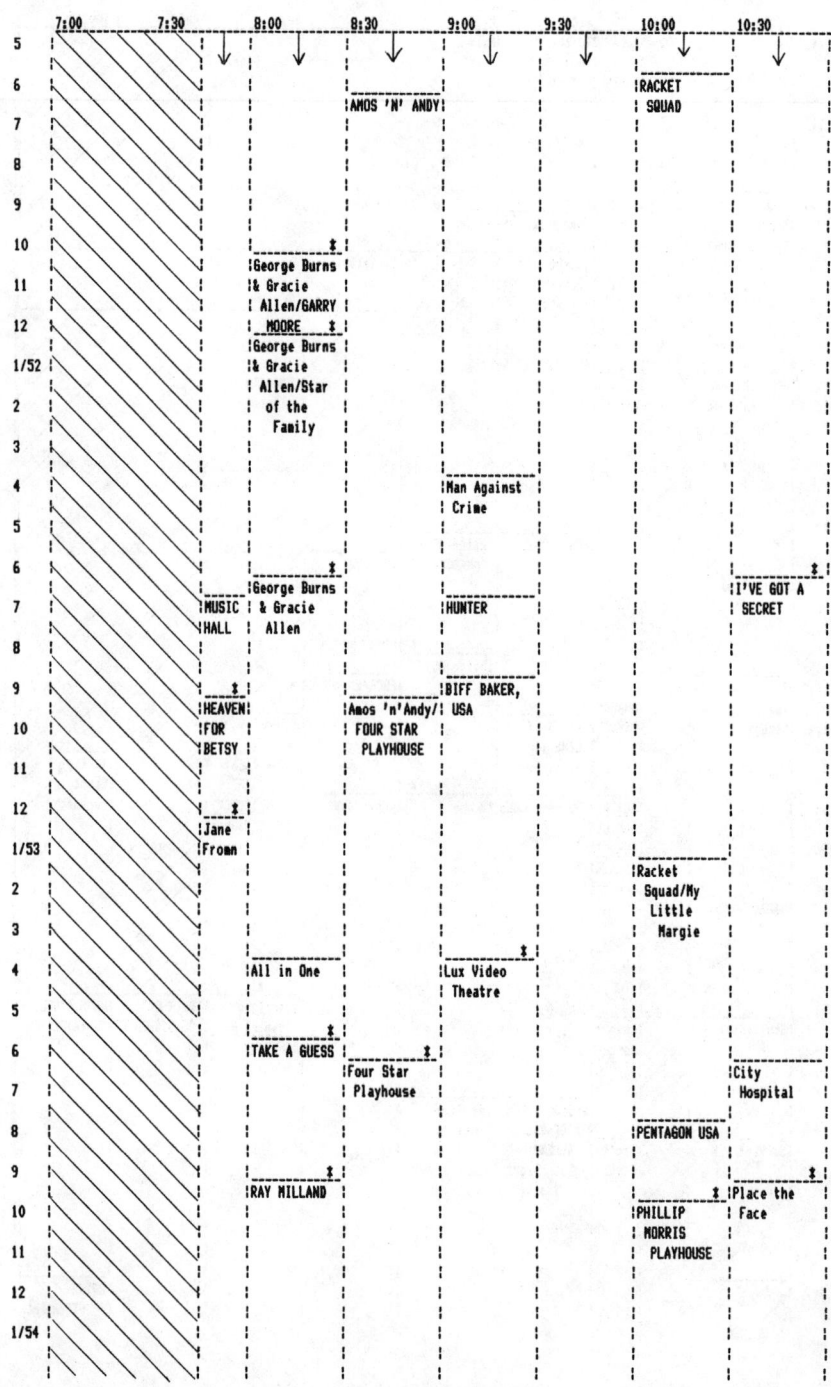

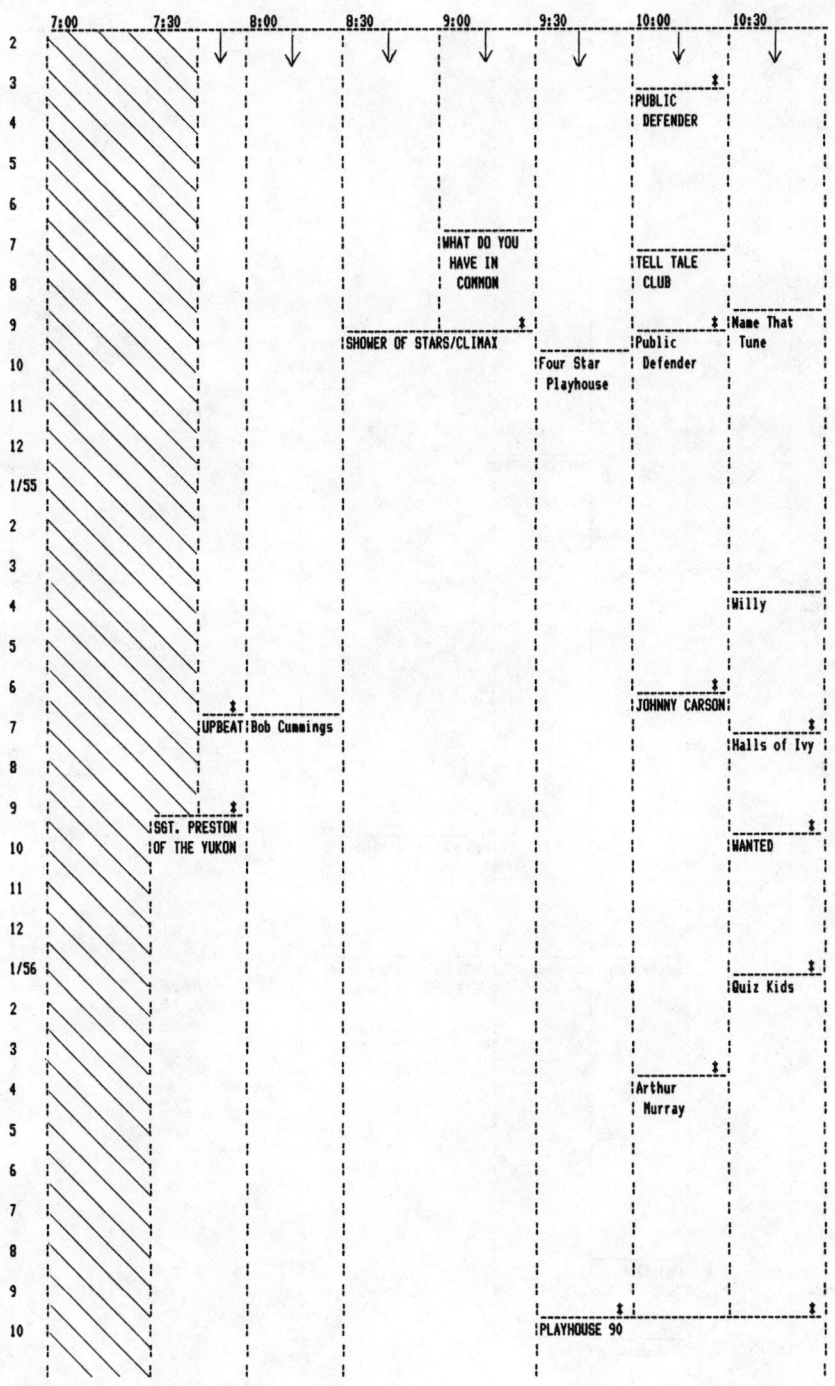

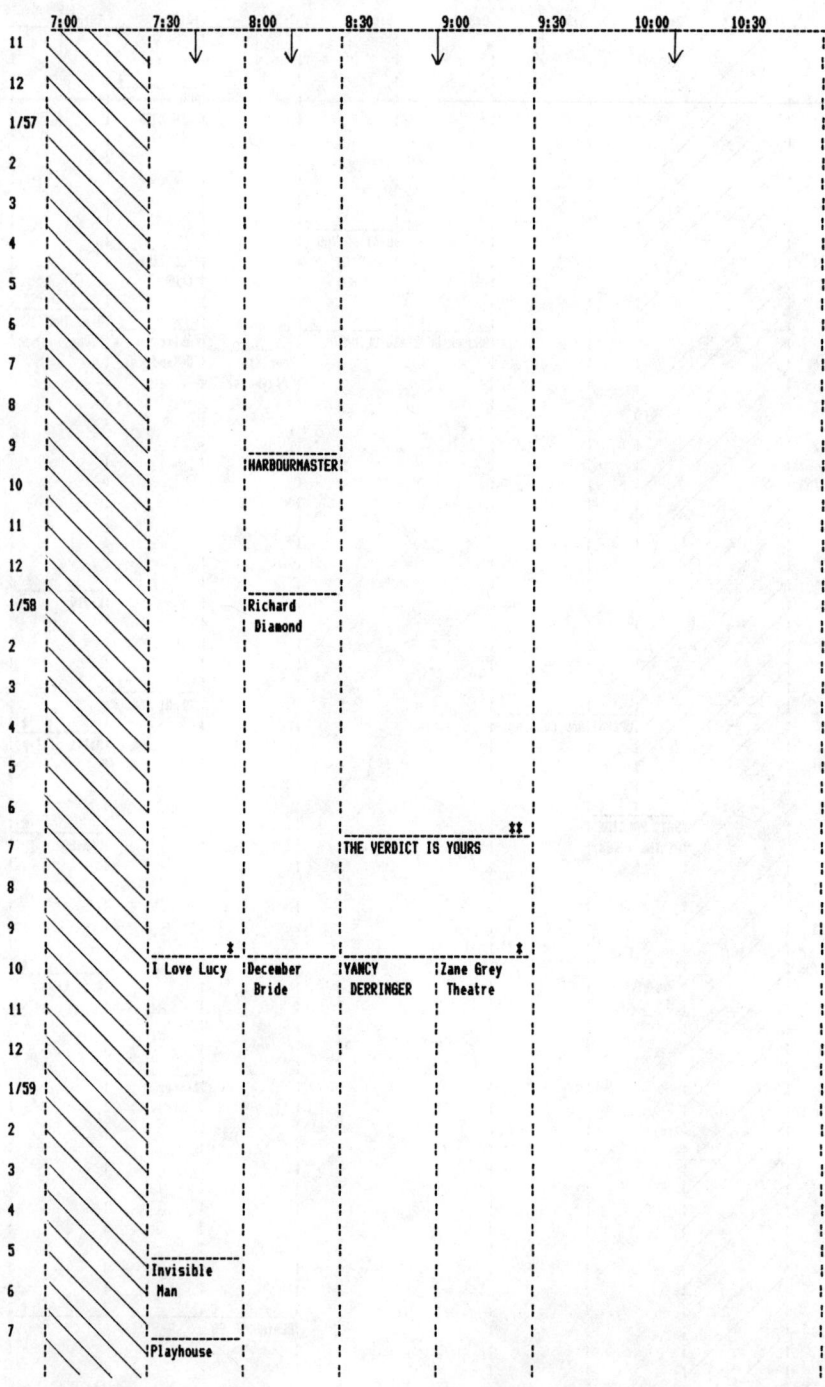

	7:00	7:30	8:00	8:30	9:00	9:30	10:00	10:30
11		↓	↓		↓		↓	
12								
1/57								
2								
3								
4								
5								
6								
7								
8								
9			HARBOURMASTER					
10								
11								
12								
1/58			Richard Diamond					
2								
3								
4								
5								
6								
7				THE VERDICT IS YOURS				
8								
9								
10		I Love Lucy	December Bride	YANCY DERRINGER	Zane Grey Theatre			
11								
12								
1/59								
2								
3								
4								
5		Invisible Man						
6								
7		Playhouse						

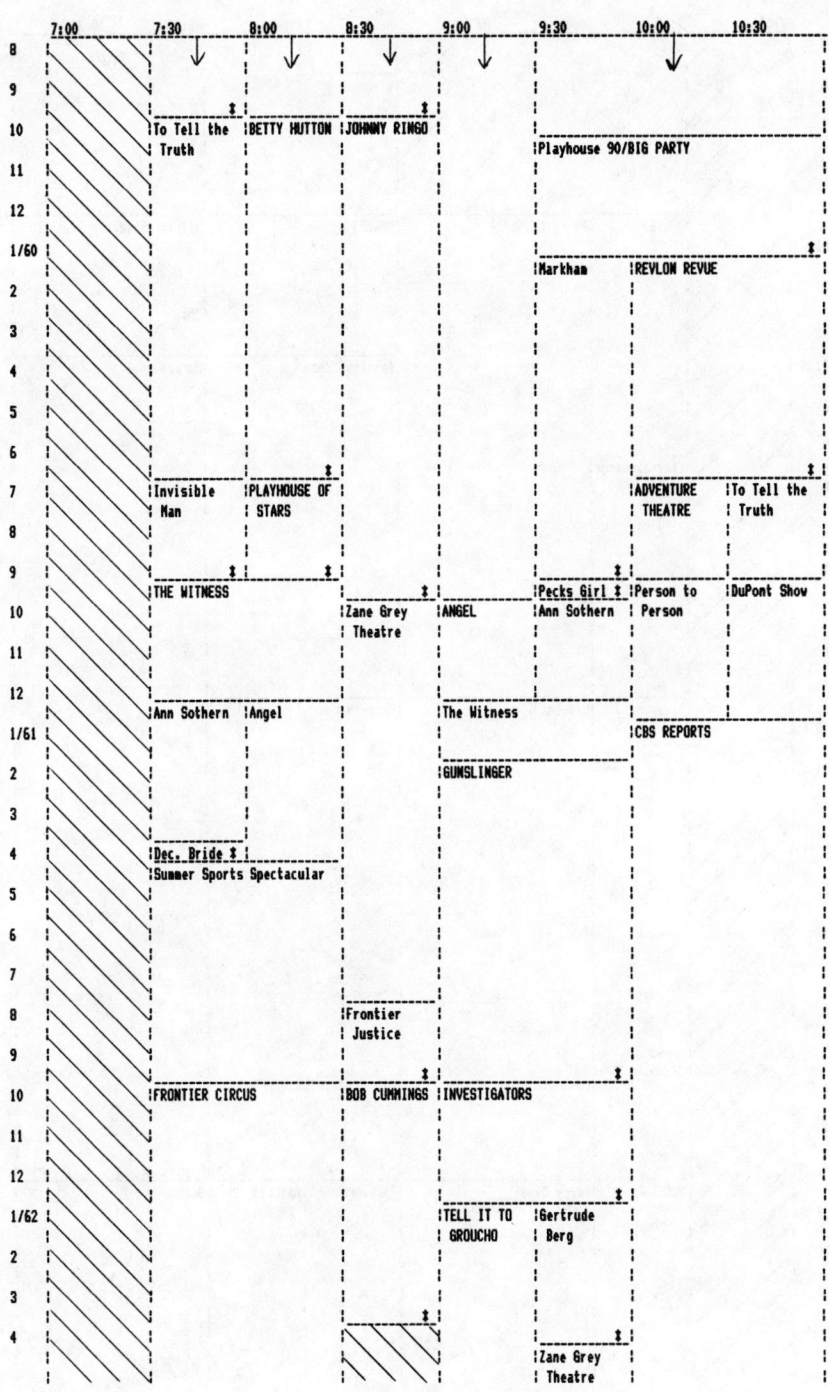

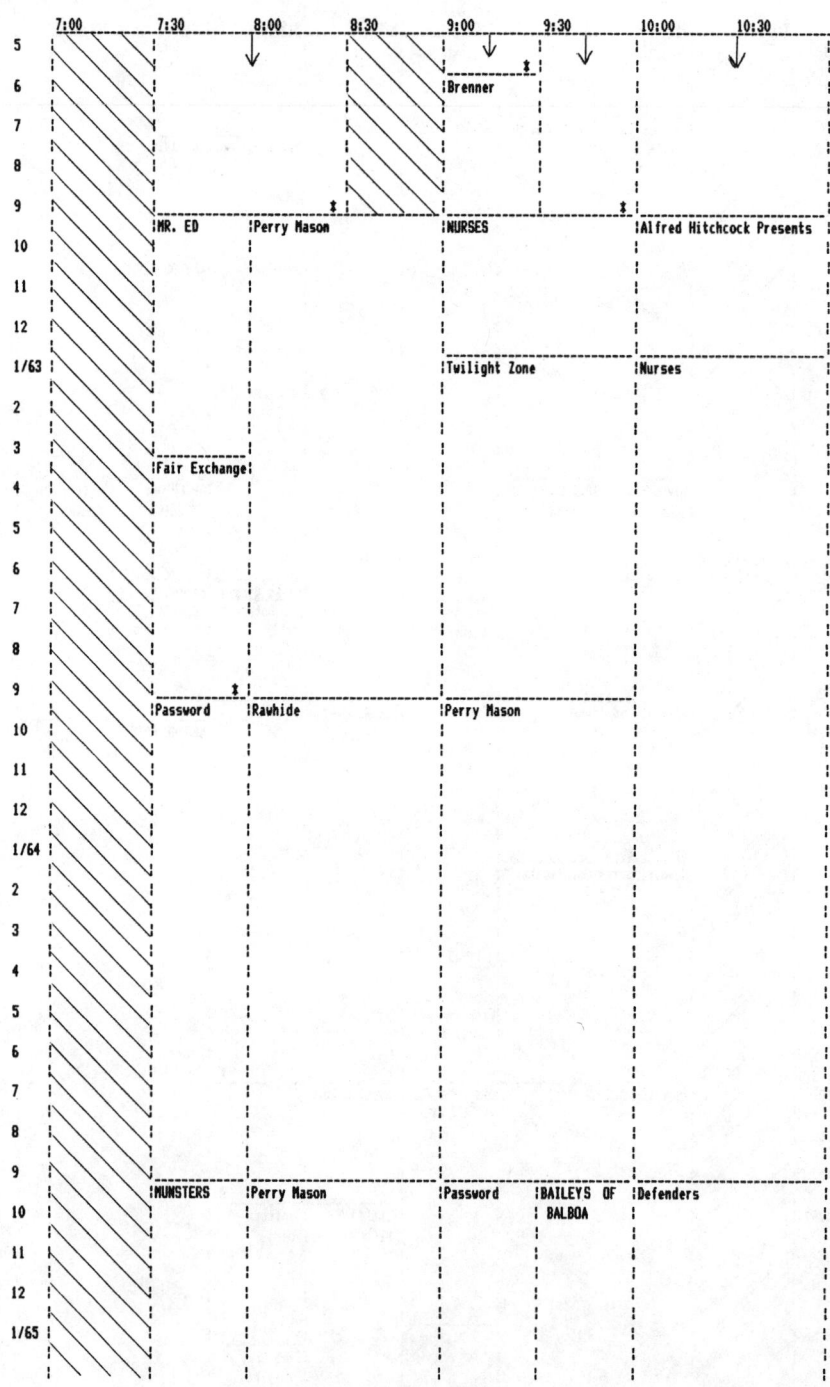

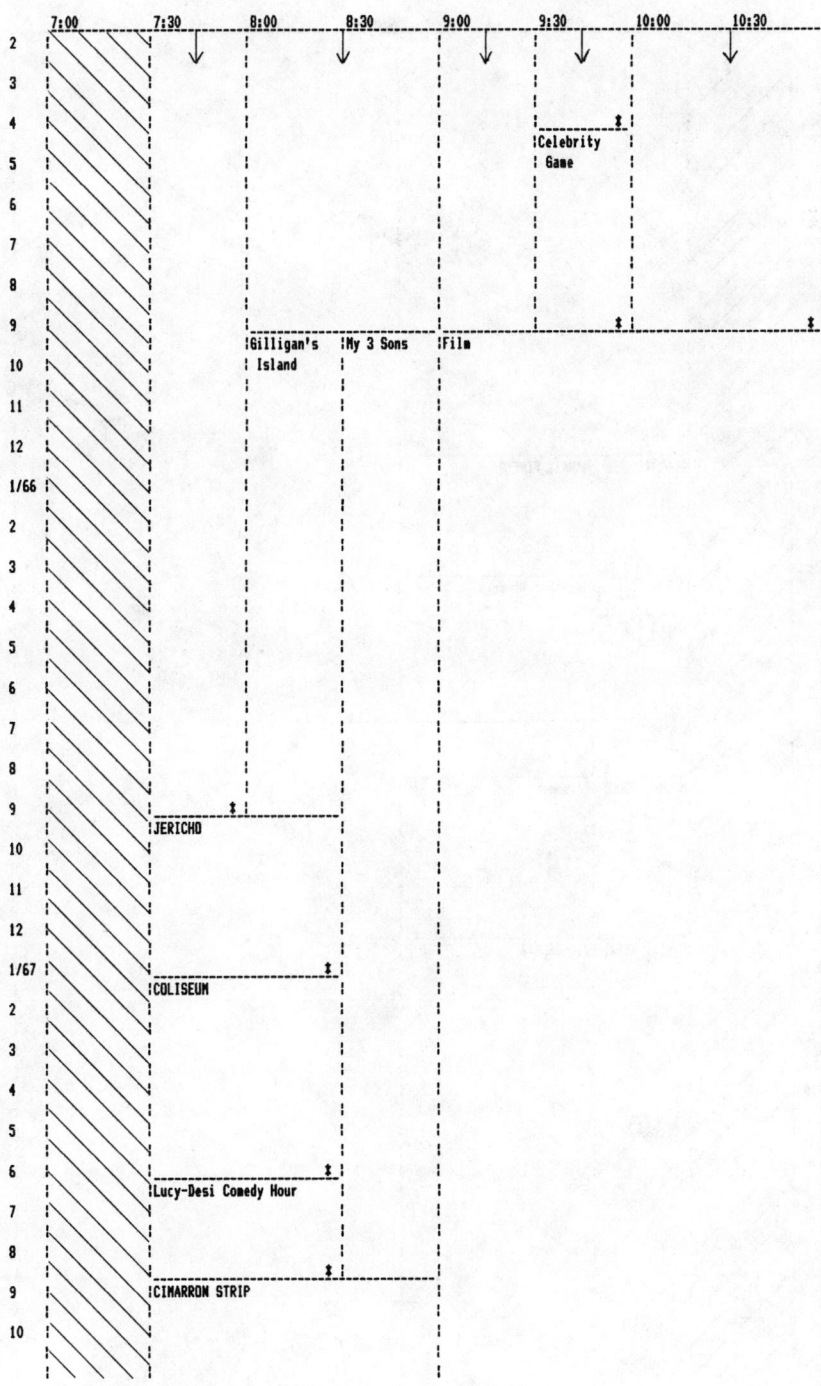

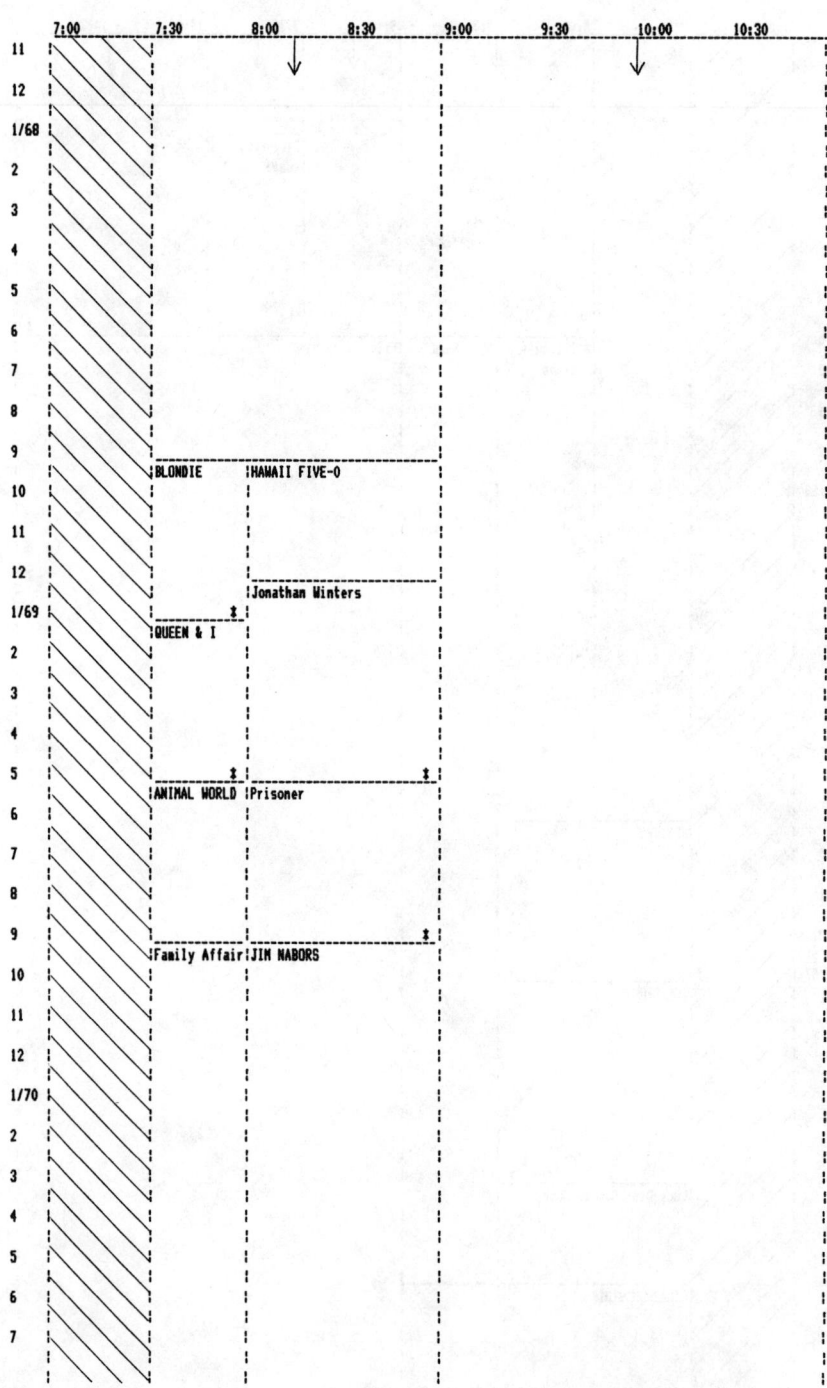

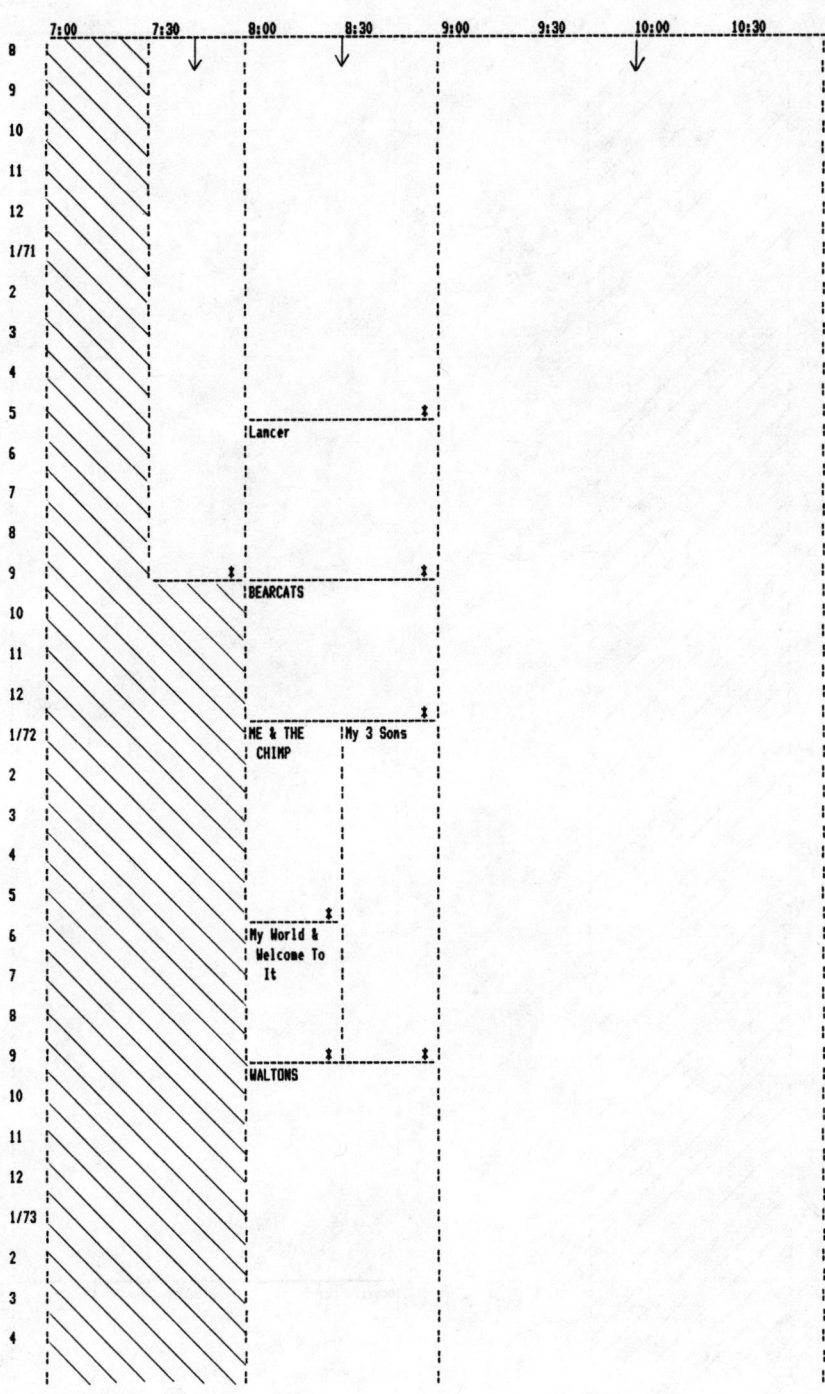

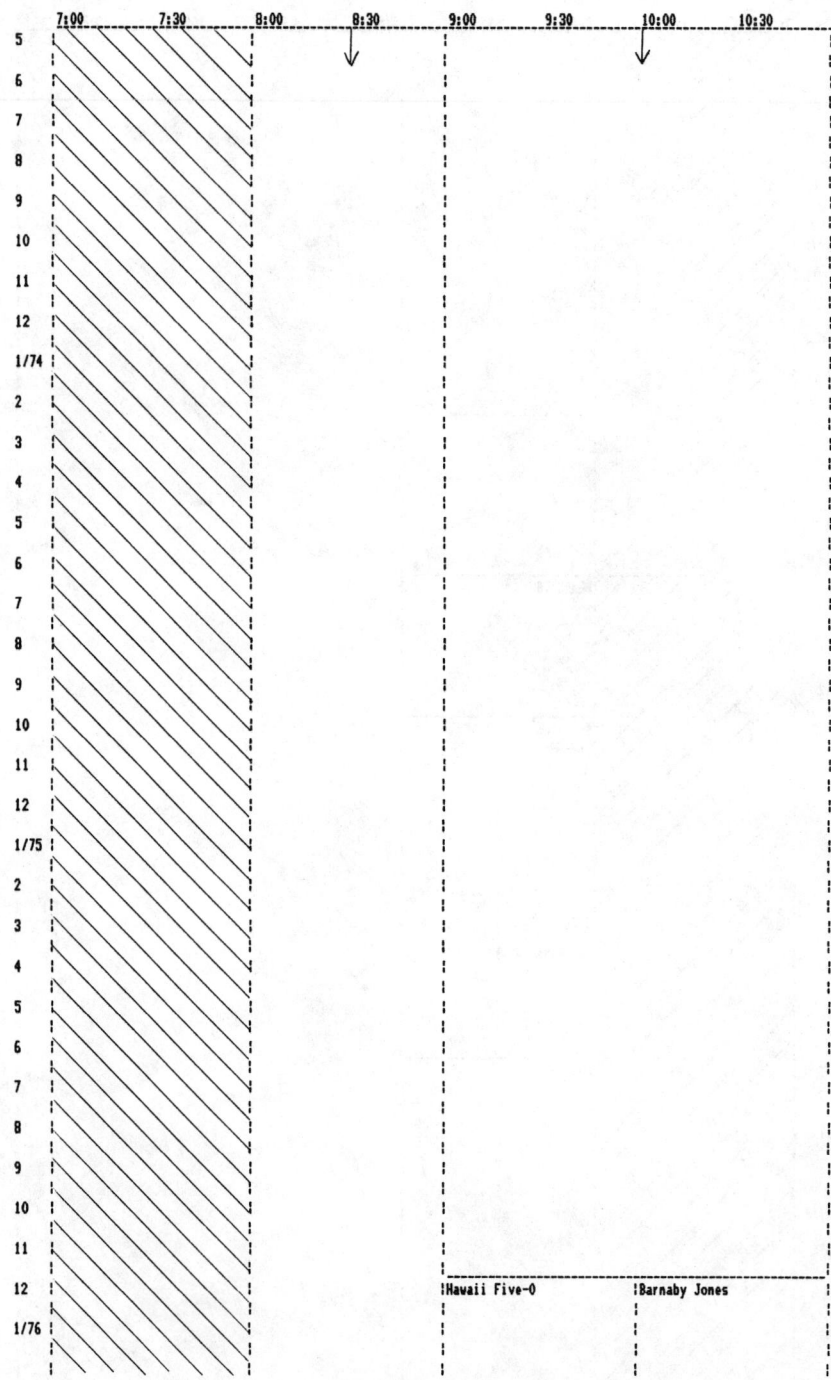

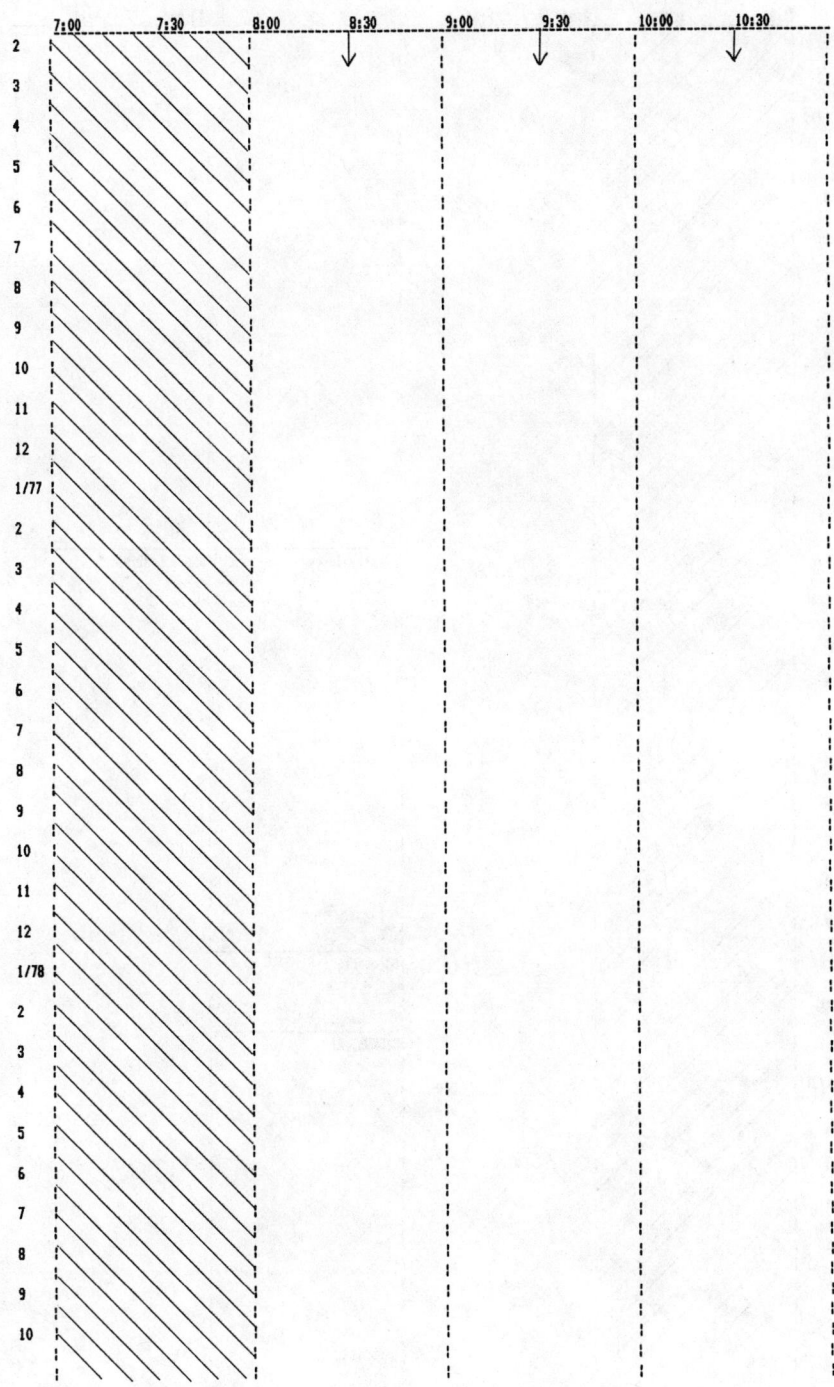

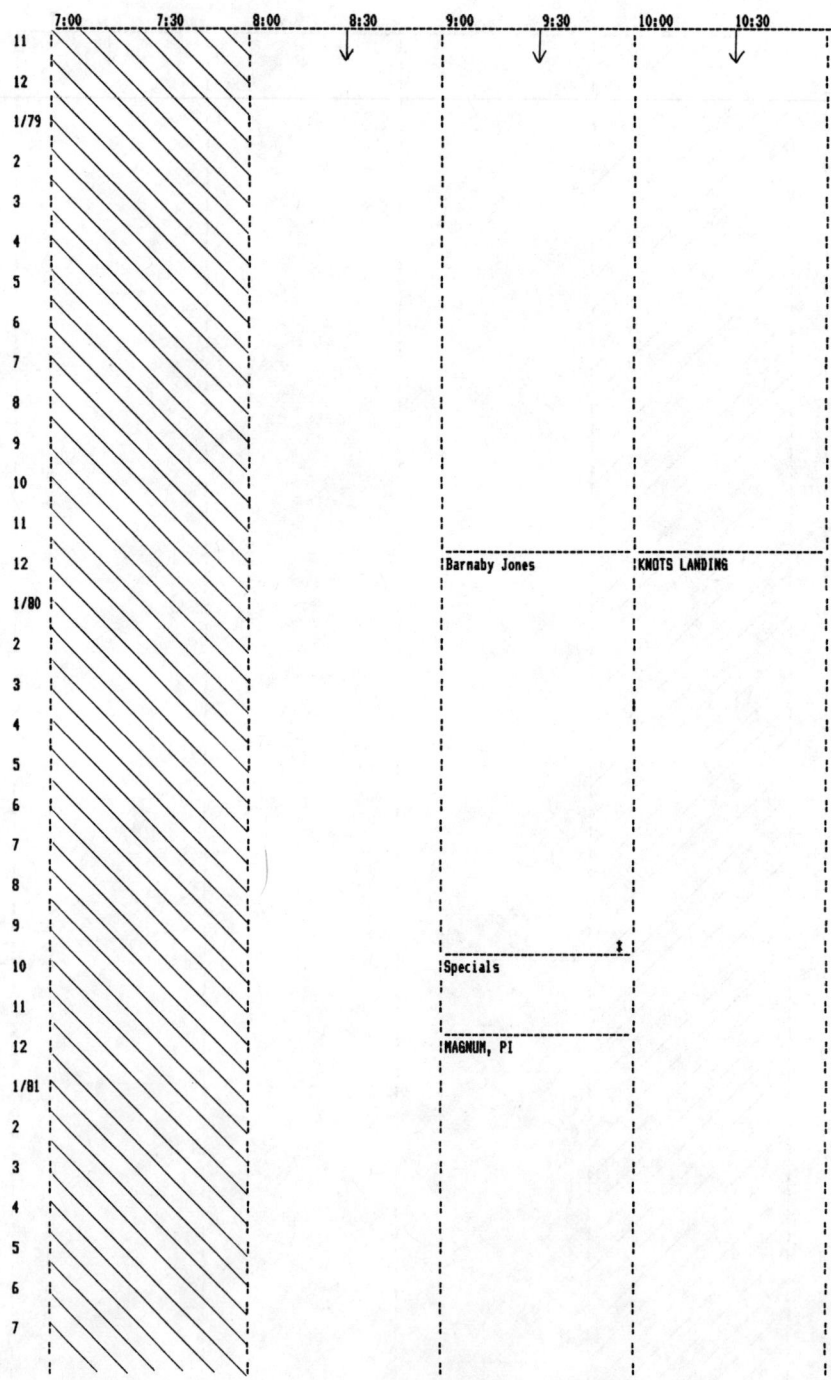

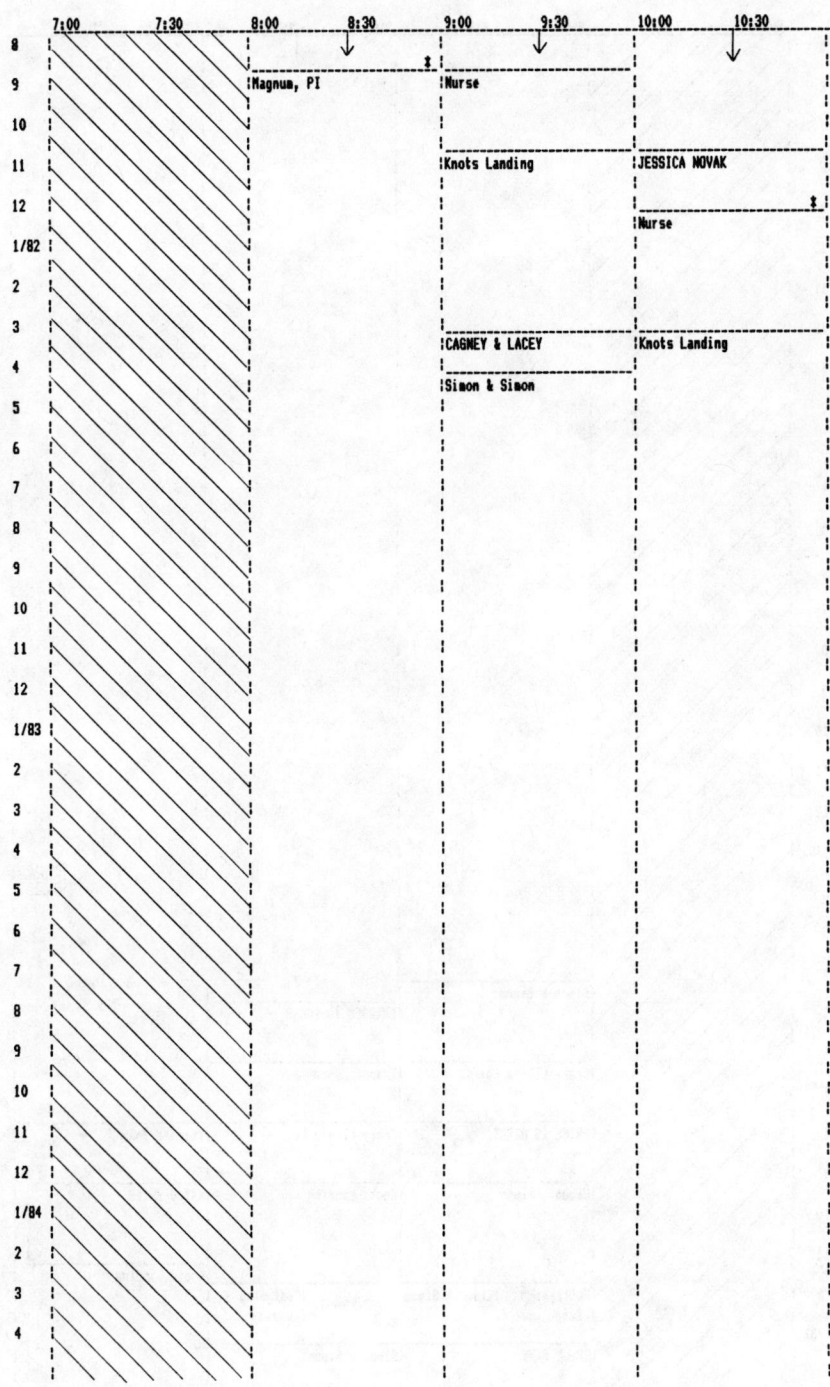

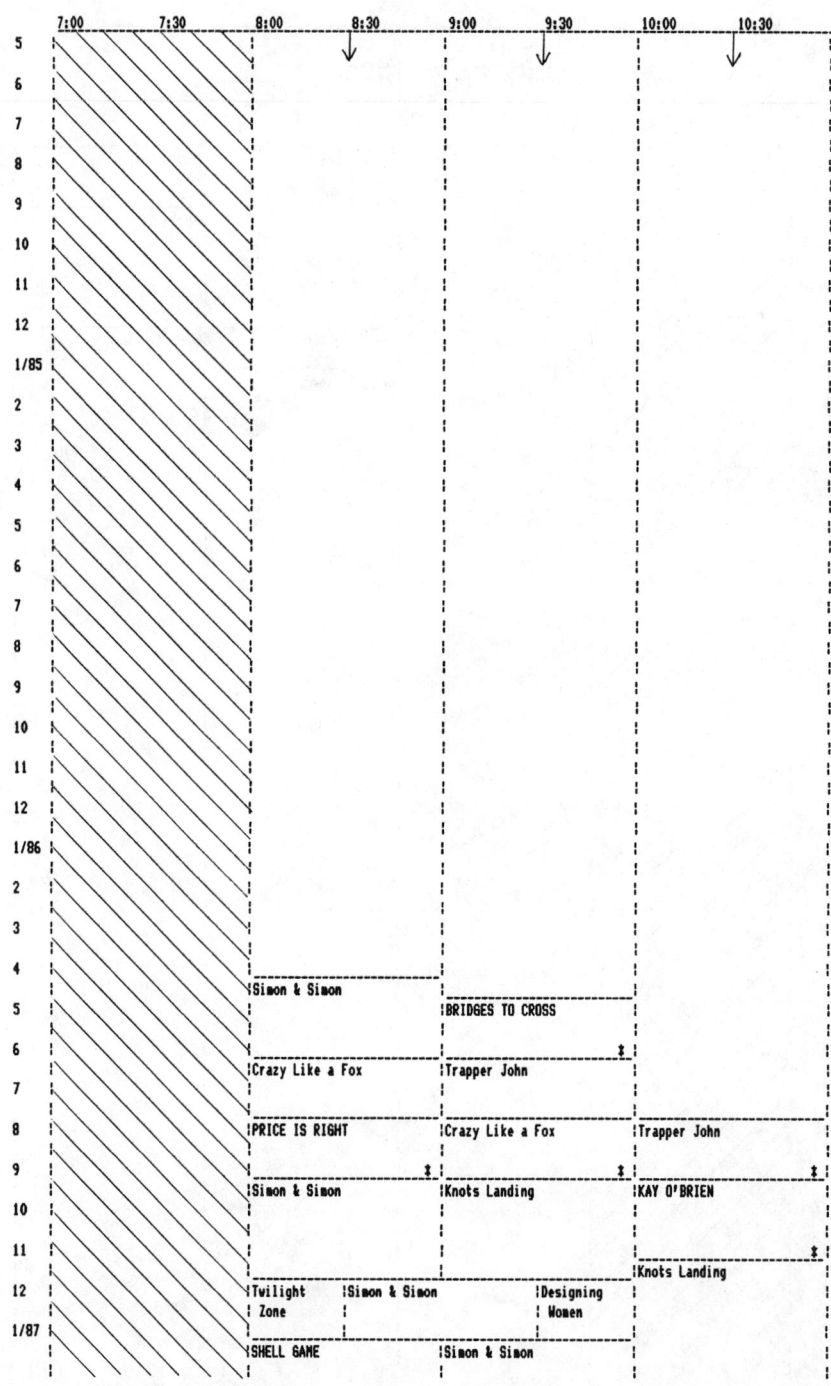

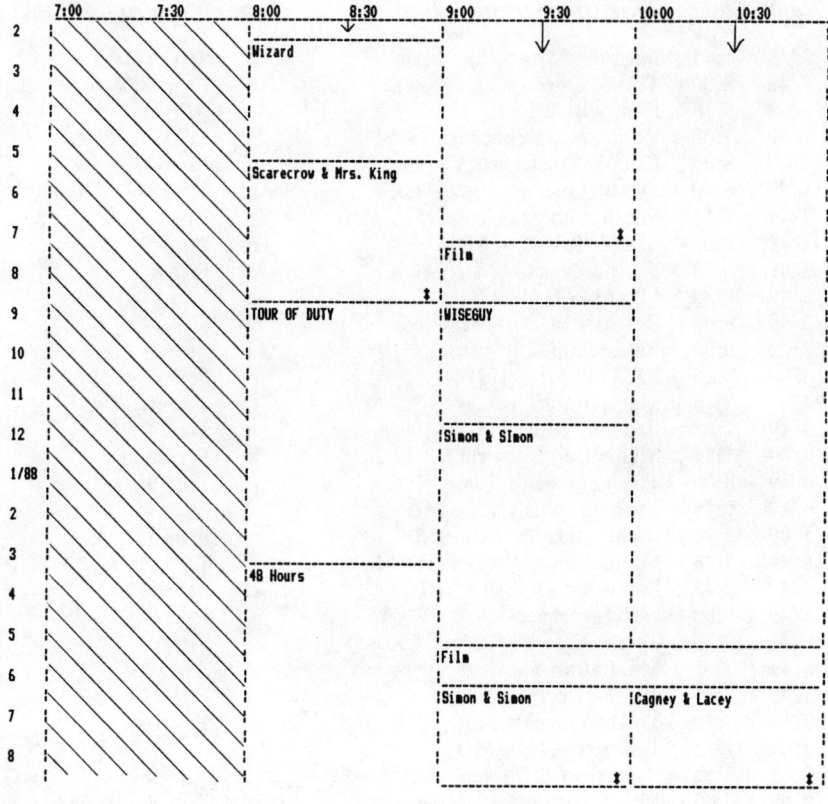

Date	Time	Title (min. if not 30) — Type	Action	From/To
8/48	7:45	Face the Music(15) — MU	m	Fr:m-f-7:15
8/48	8:00	To the Queen's Taste — CK	m	Fr:m-8:05
8/48	8:30	Film(90) — FI	s	
1/49	7:00	Your Sports Special(15) — SN	m	Fr:f-7
1/49	8:00	Kobb's Korner — MV	m	Fr:w-8
1/49	8:00	To the Queen's Taste — CK	m	To:r-8
2/49	7:15	Manhattan Showcase(15) — MV	d	
2/49	8:00	Kobb's Korner — MV	m	To:w-9
2/49	8:00	To the Queen's Taste — CK	m	Fr:r-8
2/49	8:30	Film(90) — FI	f	
2/49	9:00	Basketball(120) — SP	s	
3/49	9:00	Basketball(120) — SP	f	
4/49	7:15	Face the Music(15) — MU	m	Fr:tr-7:45
4/49	7:15	Manhattan Showcase(15) — MV	m	To:mtrf-7:45
4/49	7:45	Face the Music(15) — MU	m	To:tr-7:15
4/49	7:45	Manhattan Showcase(15) — MV	m	Fr:var-7:15
4/49	8:00	To the Queen's Taste — CK	m	To:r-9:30
5/49	7:15	Face the Music(15) — MU	c	
5/49	7:15	Manhattan Showcase(15) — MV	m	Fr:mtrf-7:45
5/49	7:45	Manhattan Showcase(15) — MV	m	To:mwr-7:15
5/49	7:45	Sonny Kendis(10) — MU	m	Fr:mw-7:15
5/49	8:00	54th Street Review(60) — VY	d	
5/49	9:30	To the Queen's Taste — CK	m	Fr:r-8
6/49	7:15	Manhattan Showcase(15) — MV	c	
7/49	7:15	Ted Steele(15) — MU	m	Fr:t-9
7/49	9:30	To the Queen's Taste — CK	m	To:m-8
8/49	7:15	Ted Steele(15) — MU	c	
8/49	7:55	Ruthie on the Telephone(5) — CY	d	
9/49	8:00	54th Street Review(60) — VY	m	To:f-9
9/49	8:00	Front Page — ND	d	
9/49	8:30	Inside U.S.A. with Chevrolet — MV	d	
9/49	8:30	Romance — DA	d	
10/49	7:00	To the Queen's Taste — CK	m	Fr:m-8
10/49	7:00	Your Sports Special(15) — SN	c	
10/49	9:00	Ed Wynn — CV	d	
11/49	7:55	Herb Shriner(5) — CV	d	
11/49	7:55	Ruthie on the Telephone(5) — CY	c	
12/49	7:00	To the Queen's Taste — CK	c	
12/49	8:30	Romance — DA	c	
12/49	9:00	Ed Wynn — CV	m	To:s-9
1/50	7:00	Strictly for Laughs(15) — MU	m	Fr:mtwf-7
1/50	7:15	Paul Arnold(15) — MU	m	Fr:mwf-7:15
1/50	7:45	Life with Snarky Parker(15) — KV	d	
1/50	7:45	Sonny Kendis(10) — MU	c	
1/50	8:00	Front Page — ND	c	
1/50	9:00	Escape — DA	d	
2/50	7:55	Herb Shriner(5) — CV	c	
2/50	8:00	What's My Line — QU	d	
2/50	9:30	Glamour-Go-Round(15) — IV	d	
3/50	7:45	Life with Snarky Parker(15) — KV	c	

Date	Time	Title (min. if not 30) – Type	Action	From/To
3/50	8:00	The Show Goes On(60) – VY	d	
3/50	8:00	What's My Line – QU	m	To:w-9
3/50	8:30	Inside U.S.A. with Chevrolet – MV	c	
3/50	9:00	Escape – DA	c	
3/50	9:45	Beat the Clock(45) – QU	d	
3/50	10:30	In the First Person(15) – IV	m	Fr:s-7:15
4/50	7:45	Alkali Ike(15) – CY	d	
4/50	7:45	Arthur Godfrey and His Ukulele (15) – IS	d	
4/50	7:45	Arthur Godfrey and His Ukulele (15) – IS	m	To:tf-7:45
4/50	9:00	Alan Young – CV	d	
4/50	9:45	Beat the Clock(45) – QU	m	To:s-8
4/50	9:45	Winner Take All(45) – QU	m	Fr:w-8:30-1/49
5/50	7:45	Alkali Ike(15) – CY	c	
5/50	7:45	Three's Company(15) – MU	d	
6/50	7:00	Garry Moore – VY	d	
6/50	7:00	Strictly for Laughs(15) – MU	c	
6/50	7:15	Paul Arnold(15) – MU	c	
6/50	10:30	In the First Person(15) – IV	m	To:n-9:45
7/50	9:00	Starlight Theater – DA	m*	Fr:m-8
7/50	9:45	Winner Take All(45) – QU	m	To:t-9
8/50	9:30	Glamour-Go-Round(15) – IV	c	
9/50	7:00	Garry Moore – VY	c	
9/50	7:00	Stork Club – TK	m	Fr:mwf-7:45
9/50	7:45	Faye Emerson(15) – IV	m	Fr:w-8
9/50	7:45	Three's Company(15) – MU	m	To:mwf-7:45
9/50	9:00	Starlight Theater – DA	m*	To:r-9:30
9/50	9:30	Starlight Theater – DA	m	Fr:r-9
9/50	9:30	Starlight Theater – DA	m	To:r-8
9/50	10:00	Truth or Consequences – QU	d	
9/50	10:30	Nash Airflyte Theatre – DA	d	
10/50	9:30	Big Town – ND	d	
11/50	8:00	George Burns & Gracie Allen – SC	d	
11/50	8:00	The Show Goes On(60) – VY	m	To:r-8:30
11/50	8:00	Starlight Theater – DA	m	Fr:r-8
11/50	8:30	The Show Goes On – VY	m	Fr:r-8
12/50	7:00	Steve Allen – CV	d	
12/50	7:00	Stork Club – TK	m	To:trs-7:45
12/50	7:45	Faye Emerson(15) – IV	c	
12/50	7:45	Stork Club(15) – TK	m	Fr:m-f-7
3/51	7:00	Steve Allen – CV	c	
3/51	10:30	Nash Airflyte Theatre – DA	c	
4/51	10:30	Crime Photographer – ND	d	
5/51	10:00	Truth or Consequences – QU	m	To:t-10-5/54(n)
6/51	8:30	Amos 'n' Andy – SC	d	
6/51	8:30	The Show Goes On – VY	m	To:s-9:30
6/51	10:00	Racket Squad – CD	d	
7/51	9:00	Meet Corliss Archer – SC	d*	
9/51	9:00	Meet Corliss Archer – SC	c*	

Date	Time	Title (min. if not 30) – Type	Action	From/To
10/51	8:00	Garry Moore – VY	d	
10/51	8:00	Starlight Theater – DA	c	
12/51	8:00	Garry Moore – VY	c	
1/52	8:00	Star of the Family – CV	m	Fr:f-10-6/51
3/52	9:00	Alan Young – CV	m	To:n-9:30-2/53
4/52	9:00	Man Against Crime – CD	m	Fr:f-8:30
6/52	7:45	Stork Club(15) – TK	m	To:s-7
6/52	8:00	Star of the Family – CV	c	
6/52	9:00	Man Against Crime – CD	m	To:w-9:30-10/52
6/52	10:30	Crime Photographer – ND	c	
6/52	10:30	I've Got a Secret – QU	d	
7/52	7:45	Music Hall(15) – MU	d	
7/52	8:30	Steve Allen – CV	d*	
7/52	9:00	Hunter – SD	d	
8/52	9:00	Hunter – SD	m	To:w-9:30
9/52	7:45	Heaven for Betsy(15) – SC	d	
9/52	7:45	Music Hall(15) – MU	c	
9/52	8:30	Four Star Playhouse – DA	d	
9/52	8:30	Steve Allen – CV	c*	
9/52	9:00	Biff Baker U.S.A. – AD	d	
12/52	7:45	Heaven for Betsy(15) – SC	c	
12/52	7:45	Jane Froman's U.S.A. Canteen(15) – MV	m	Fr:s-9
1/53	10:00	My Little Margie – SC	m	Fr:s-7:30-11/52(n)
3/53	8:00	George Burns & Gracie Allen – SC	m	To:m-8
3/53	9:00	Biff Baker U.S.A. – AD	c	
4/53	8:00	All in One – CV	m	Fr:s-9-1/53
4/53	9:00	Lux Video Theatre – DA	m	Fr:m-8
5/53	8:00	All in One – CV	c	
6/53	8:00	Take a Guess – QU	d	
6/53	8:30	Amos 'n' Andy – SC	c	
6/53	10:30	City Hospital – MD	m	Fr:t-9
6/53	10:30	I've Got a Secret – QU	m	To:w-9:30
7/53	7:45	Summertime U.S.A.(15) – MU	d*	
7/53	10:00	My Little Margie – SC	m	To:w-8:30-9/53(n)
7/53	10:00	Racket Squad – CD	m	To:m-9
8/53	7:45	Summertime U.S.A.(15) – MU	c*	
8/53	10:00	Pentagon, U.S.A. – DA	d	
9/53	8:00	Ray Milland – SC	d	
9/53	8:00	Take a Guess – QU	c	
9/53	10:00	Pentagon, U.S.A. – DA	c	
9/53	10:30	City Hospital – MD	c	
9/53	10:30	Place the Face – QU	m	Fr:t-8:30(n)
10/53	10:00	Philip Morris Playhouse – DA	d	
3/54	10:00	Philip Morris Playhouse – DA	c	
3/54	10:00	Public Defender – LD	d	
6/54	7:45	Summer Holiday(15) – MU	d*	
6/54	9:00	Lux Video Theatre – DA	m	To:r-10-8/54(n)
7/54	8:00	What's in a Word – QU	d*	

Date	Time	Title (min. if not 30) — Type	Action	From/To
7/54	9:00	What Do You Have in Common? —QU	d	
7/54	10:00	Public Defender — LD	m	To:m-9
7/54	10:00	Telltale Club — CD	d	
8/54	10:30	Place the Face — QU	m	To:s-8(n)
9/54	7:45	Summer Holiday(15) — MU	c*	
9/54	8:00	What's in a Word — QU	c*	
9/54	8:30	Four Star Playhouse — DA	m	To:r-9:30
9/54	8:30	Shower of Stars(60) — MV	d	
9/54	9:00	What Do You Have in Common? —QU	c	
9/54	9:30	Big Town — ND	m	To:w-10:30(n)
9/54	10:00	Public Defender — LD	m	Fr:m-9
9/54	10:00	Telltale Club — CD	c	
9/54	10:30	Name That Tune — QU	m	Fr:m-8-6/54
10/54	8:30	Climax(60) — DA	d	
10/54	9:30	Four Star Playhouse — DA	m	Fr:r-8:30
3/55	10:30	Name That Tune — QU	m	To:t-7:30-9/55
4/55	10:30	Willy — LD	m	Fr:s-10:30
6/55	7:45	Jane Froman's U.S.A. Canteen(15) —MV	c	
6/55	8:00	Ray Milland — SC	m	To:f-9:30
6/55	10:00	Johnny Carson — CV	d	
6/55	10:00	Public Defender — LD	c	
7/55	7:45	Upbeat(15) — MU	d	
7/55	8:00	Bob Cummings — SC	m	Fr:n-10:30(n)
7/55	10:30	Halls of Ivy — SC	m	Fr:t-8:30
7/55	10:30	Willy — LD	c	
9/55	7:30	Sgt. Preston of the Yukon —AD	d	
9/55	7:45	Upbeat(15) — MU	c	
9/55	10:30	Halls of Ivy — SC	c	
10/55	10:30	Wanted — DA	d	
1/56	10:30	Quiz Kids — QU	m	Fr:n-7-11/53
1/56	10:30	Wanted — DA	c	
3/56	10:00	Johnny Carson — CV	c	
4/56	10:00	Arthur Murray Party — MV	m	Fr:t-8:30-9/55(n)
9/56	9:30	Four Star Playhouse — DA	c	
9/56	10:00	Arthur Murray Party — MV	m	To:t-8-4/57(n)
9/56	10:30	Quiz Kids — QU	c	
10/56	9:30	Playhouse 90(90) — DA	d	
9/57	8:00	Bob Cummings — SC	m	To:t-9:30(n)
9/57	8:00	Harbourmaster — AD	d	
12/57	8:00	Harbourmaster — AD	m	To:n-8:30(a)
1/58	8:00	Richard Diamond, Pvt. Detective —CD	m	Fr:m-9:30-9/57
6/58	8:30	Climax(60) — DA	c	
6/58	8:30	Shower of Stars(60) — MV	c	
7/58	8:30	The Verdict Is Yours(60) — CR	d	
9/58	7:30	Sgt. Preston of the Yukon — AD	c	

Date	Time	Title (min. if not 30) — Type	Action	From/To
9/58	8:00	Richard Diamond, Pvt. Detective — CD	m	To:n-10-2/59
9/58	8:30	The Verdict Is Yours(60) — CR	c	
10/58	7:30	I Love Lucy — SC	m	Fr:m-9
10/58	8:00	December Bride — SC	m	Fr:m-9:30-6/58
10/58	8:30	Yancy Derringer — WE	d	
10/58	9:00	Dick Powell's Zane Grey Theatre — WA	m	Fr:f-8:30-7/58
5/59	7:30	I Love Lucy — SC	m	To:f-8:30-7/59
5/59	7:30	Invisible Man — SD	m	Fr:t-8
7/59	7:30	Invisible Man — SD	m	To:r-7:30-7/60
7/59	7:30	The Playhouse — DA	m	Fr:t-10:30-9/57
9/59	7:30	The Playhouse — DA	c	
9/59	8:00	December Bride — SC	m	To:f-9:30-7/60
9/59	8:30	Yancy Derringer — WE	c	
10/59	7:30	To Tell the Truth — QU	m	Fr:t-8:30
10/59	8:00	Betty Hutton Show — SC	d	
10/59	8:30	Johnny Ringo — WE	d	
10/59	9:30	Big Party(90) — VY	d	
1/60	9:30	Big Party(90) — VY	c	
1/60	9:30	Markham — CD	m	Fr:s-10:30
1/60	9:30	Playhouse 90(90) — DA	m	To:t-9:30-7/61
1/60	10:00	Revlon Revue(60) — VY	d	
6/60	7:30	To Tell the Truth — QU	m	To:r-10:30
6/60	8:00	Betty Hutton Show — SC	c	
6/60	10:00	Revlon Revue(60) — VY	c	
7/60	7:30	Invisible Man — SD	m	Fr:r-7:30-7/59
7/60	8:00	Playhouse of Stars — DA	d	
7/60	10:00	Adventure Theatre — AD	d	
7/60	10:30	To Tell the Truth — QU	m	Fr:r-7:30
9/60	7:30	Invisible Man — SD	c	
9/60	7:30	The Witness(60) — CR	d	
9/60	8:00	Playhouse of Stars — DA	c	
9/60	8:30	Johnny Ringo — WE	c	
9/60	9:00	Dick Powell's Zane Grey Theatre — WA	m	To:r-8:30
9/60	9:30	Markham — CD	c	
9/60	9:30	Peck's Bad Girl — SC	m	Fr:t-8
9/60	9:30	Peck's Bad Girl — SC	c	
9/60	10:00	Adventure Theatre — AD	m	To:f-9:30-7/61
9/60	10:00	Person to Person — IV	m	Fr:f-10:30
9/60	10:30	DuPont Show with June Allyson — DA	m	Fr:m-10:30
9/60	10:30	To Tell the Truth — QU	m	To:m-7:30
10/60	8:30	Dick Powell's Zane Grey Theatre — WA	m	Fr:r-9
10/60	9:00	Angel — SC	d	
10/60	9:30	Ann Sothern — SC	m	Fr:m-9:30-7/60
12/60	7:30	The Witness(60) — CR	m	To:r-9
12/60	8:00	Angel — SC	m	Fr:r-9

Date	Time	Title (min. if not 30) — Type	Action	From/To
12/60	9:00	Angel — SC	m	To:r-8
12/60	9:00	The Witness(60) — CR	m	Fr:r-7:30
12/60	10:00	Person to Person — IV	m	To:f-10:30-6/61
12/60	10:30	DuPont Show with June Allyson — DA	m	To:m-10:30
1/61	9:00	The Witness(60) — CR	c	
1/61	10:00	CBS Reports(60) — DO	d	
2/61	9:00	Gunslinger(60) — WE	d	
3/61	7:30	Ann Sothern — SC	m	To:m-9:30-7/61
4/61	7:30	December Bride — SC	m	Fr:f-9:30-9/60
4/61	7:30	December Bride — SC	c	
4/61	7:30	Summer Sports Spectacular(60) — SP	s	
4/61	8:00	Angel — SC	m	To:w-9
7/61	8:30	Dick Powell's Zane Grey Theatre — WA	m	To:r-9:30-4/62
8/61	8:30	Frontier Justice — WA	m	Fr:m-9-9/59
9/61	7:30	Summer Sports Spectacular(60) — SP	f	
9/61	8:30	Frontier Justice — WA	c	
9/61	9:00	Gunslinger(60) — WE	c	
10/61	7:30	Frontier Circus(60) — DR	d	
10/61	8:30	Bob Cummings — CO	d	
10/61	9:00	Investigators(60) — CD	d	
12/61	9:00	Investigators(60) — CD	c	
1/62	9:00	Tell It to Groucho — CY	d	
1/62	9:30	Gertrude Berg — SC	m	Fr:w-9:30
3/62	8:30	Bob Cummings — CO	c	
4/62	9:30	Dick Powell's Zane Grey Theatre — WA	m	Fr:r-8:30-7/61
4/62	9:30	Gertrude Berg — SC	c	
5/62	9:00	Tell It to Groucho — CY	c	
6/62	9:00	Brenner — CD	m	Fr:m-10:30-9/61
9/62	7:30	Frontier Circus(60) — DR	c	
9/62	7:30	Mr. Ed — SC	d	
9/62	8:00	Perry Mason(60) — LD	m	Fr:s-7:30
9/62	9:00	Brenner — CD	m	To:n-9:30-5/64
9/62	9:00	The Nurses(60) — MD	d	
9/62	9:30	Dick Powell's Zane Grey Theatre — WA	c	
9/62	10:00	Alfred Hitchcock Presents(60) — SA	m	Fr:t-8:30(n)
9/62	10:00	CBS Reports(60) — DO	m	To:w-7:30
12/62	9:00	The Nurses(60) — MD	m	To:r-10
12/62	10:00	Alfred Hitchcock Presents(60) — SA	m	To:f-9:30
1/63	9:00	Twilight Zone(60) — FA	m	Fr:f-10-9/62
1/63	10:00	The Nurses(60) — MD	m	Fr:r-9
3/63	7:30	Fair Exchange — SC	m	Fr:f-9:30-12/62
3/63	7:30	Mr. Ed — SC	m	To:w-7:30-12/64
9/63	7:30	Fair Exchange — SC	c	

Date	Time	Title (min. if not 30) — Type	Action	From/To
9/63	7:30	Password — QU	m	Fr:m-10
9/63	8:00	Perry Mason(60) — LD	m	To:r-9
9/63	8:00	Rawhide(60) — WE	m	Fr:f-7:30
9/63	9:00	Perry Mason(60) — LD	m	Fr:r-8
9/63	9:00	Twilight Zone(60) — FA	m	To:f-9:30
9/64	7:30	The Munsters — SC	d	
9/64	7:30	Password — QU	m	To:r-9
9/64	8:00	Perry Mason(60) — LD	m	Fr:r-9
9/64	8:00	Rawhide(60) — WE	m	To:f-7:30
9/64	9:00	Password — QU	m	Fr:r-7:30
9/64	9:00	Perry Mason(60) — LD	m	To:r-8
9/64	9:30	Baileys of Balboa — SC	d	
9/64	10:00	Defenders(60) — LD	m	Fr:s-8:30
9/64	10:00	The Nurses(60) — MD	m	To:t-10
4/65	9:30	Baileys of Balboa — SC	c	
4/65	9:30	Celebrity Game — QU	m	Fr:n-9-9/64
9/65	8:00	Gilligan's Island — SC	m	Fr:s-8:30
9/65	8:00	Perry Mason(60) — LD	m	To:n-9
9/65	8:30	My Three Sons — SC	m	Fr:r-8:30(a)
9/65	9:00	Film(120) — FI	s	
9/65	9:00	Password — QU	m	To:m-10:30-4/67
9/65	9:30	Celebrity Game — QU	c	
9/65	10:00	Defenders(60) — LD	c	
9/66	7:30	Jericho(60) — WD	d	
9/66	7:30	The Munsters — SC	c	
9/66	8:00	Gilligan's Island — SC	m	To:m-7:30
1/67	7:30	Coliseum(60) — VY	d	
1/67	7:30	Jericho(60) — WD	c	
6/67	7:30	Coliseum(60) — VY	c	
6/67	7:30	Lucy-Desi Comedy Hour(60) — SC	m	Fr:w-10-9/65
8/67	7:30	Lucy-Desi Comedy Hour(60) — SC	c	
8/67	8:30	My Three Sons — SC	m	To:s-8:30
9/67	7:30	Cimarron Strip(90) — WE	d	
9/68	7:30	Blondie — SC	d	
9/68	7:30	Cimarron Strip(90) — WE	m	To:t-8:30-7/71
9/68	8:00	Hawaii Five-O(60) — CD	d	
12/68	8:00	Hawaii Five-O(60) — CD	m	To:w-10
12/68	8:00	Jonathan Winters(60) — CV	m	Fr:w-10
1/69	7:30	Blondie — SC	c	
1/69	7:30	The Queen and I — SC	d	
5/69	7:30	Animal World — WL	d	
5/69	7:30	The Queen and I — SC	c	
5/69	8:00	Jonathan Winters(60) — CV	c	
5/69	8:00	The Prisoner(60) — AD	m	Fr:s-7:30-9/68
9/69	7:30	Animal World — WL	m	To:r-7:30-4/70(a)
9/69	7:30	Family Affair — SC	m	Fr:m-9:30
9/69	8:00	Jim Nabors Hour(60) — CV	d	
9/69	8:00	The Prisoner(60) — AD	c	
6/70	8:00	Happy Days(60) — VY	d*	
8/70	8:00	Happy Days(60) — VY	c*	

Date	Time	Title (min. if not 30) – Type	Action	From/To
5/71	8:00	Jim Nabors Hour(60) – CV	c	
5/71	8:00	Lancer(60) – WE	m	Fr:t-7:30-6/70
9/71	7:30	Family Affair – SC	c	
9/71	8:00	Bearcats(60) – AD	d	
9/71	8:00	Lancer(60) – WE	c	
12/71	8:00	Bearcats(60) – AD	c	
1/72	8:00	Me and the Chimp – SC	d	
1/72	8:30	My Three Sons – SC	m	Fr:m-10
5/72	8:00	Me and the Chimp – SC	c	
6/72	8:00	My World and Welcome to It – SC	m	Fr:m-7:30
9/72	8:00	My World and Welcome to It – SC	c	
9/72	8:00	Waltons(60) – DR	d	
9/72	8:30	My Three Sons – SC	c	
11/75	9:00	Film(120) – FI	f	
12/75	9:00	Hawaii Five-O(60) – CD	m	Fr:f-9
12/75	10:00	Barnaby Jones(60) – CD	m	Fr:f-10
3/79	8:00	Chisholms(60) – WE	d*	
4/79	8:00	Chisholms(60) – WE	m*	To:s-8-1/80
4/79	8:00	Time Express(60) – DR	d*	
5/79	8:00	Time Express(60) – DR	c*	
11/79	9:00	Hawaii Five-O(60) – CD	m	To:t-9
11/79	10:00	Barnaby Jones(60) – CD	m	To:r-9
12/79	9:00	Barnaby Jones(60) – CD	m	Fr:r-10
12/79	10:00	Knots Landing(60) – SL	d	
3/80	8:00	Palmerstown, U.S.A.(60) – DR	d*	
4/80	9:00	Hagen(60) – CD	m*	Fr:s-10
4/80	9:00	Hagen(60) – CD	c*	
4/80	10:00	Contender(60) – DR	d*	
5/80	8:00	Palmerstown, U.S.A.(60) – DR	m*	To:t-8-3/81
5/80	10:00	Contender(60) – DR	c*	
9/80	9:00	Barnaby Jones(60) – CD	c	
12/80	9:00	Magnum, P.I.(60) – CD	d	
4/81	8:00	Checking In – SC	d*	
4/81	8:00	Checking In – SC	c*	
4/81	8:30	Park Place – SC	d*	
4/81	8:30	Park Place – SC	c*	
4/81	10:00	Nurse(60) – MD	d*	
5/81	10:00	Nurse(60) – MD	m*	To:r-9-9/81
8/81	8:00	Waltons(60) – DR	c	
8/81	9:00	Magnum, P.I.(60) – CD	m	To:r-8
9/81	8:00	Magnum, P.I.(60) – CD	m	Fr:r-9
9/81	9:00	Nurse(60) – MD	m	Fr:r-10-5/81
10/81	9:00	Nurse(60) – MD	m	To:w-9
10/81	10:00	Knots Landing(60) – SL	m	To:r-9
11/81	9:00	Knots Landing(60) – SL	m	Fr:r-10
11/81	10:00	Jessica Novak(60) – DR	d	
12/81	10:00	Jessica Novak(60) – DR	c	
12/81	10:00	Nurse(60) – MD	m	Fr:w-9
3/82	9:00	Cagney & Lacey(60) – CD	d	
3/82	9:00	Knots Landing(60) – SL	m	To:r-10

Date	Time	Title (min. if not 30) — Type	Action	From/To
3/82	10:00	Knots Landing(60) — SL	m	Fr:r-9
3/82	10:00	Nurse(60) — MD	m	To:f-10
4/82	9:00	Cagney & Lacey(60) — CD	m	To:m-10-10/82
4/82	9:00	Simon & Simon(60) — CD	m	Fr:t-8
3/83	10:00	Tucker's Witch(60) — CD	m*	Fr:w-10-11/82
6/83	10:00	Tucker's Witch(60) — CD	m*	To:m-9
8/84	10:00	Mickey Spillane's Mike Hammer (60) — CD	m*	Fr:s-10-4/84
9/84	10:00	Mickey Spillane's Mike Hammer (60) — CD	m*	To:s-10
8/85	10:00	Hometown(60) — CO	d*	
9/85	10:00	Hometown(60) — CO	m*	To:t-8
4/86	8:00	Magnum, P.I.(60) — CD	m	To:s-10
4/86	8:00	Simon & Simon(60) — CD	m	Fr:r-9
4/86	9:00	Simon & Simon(60) — CD	m	To:r-8
4/86	9:00	Bridges to Cross(60) — DR	d	
6/86	8:00	Simon & Simon(60) — CD	m	To:t-8
6/86	8:00	Crazy Like a Fox(60) — CO	m	Fr:s-8
6/86	9:00	Bridges to Cross(60) — DR	c	
6/86	9:00	Trapper John, MD(60) — MD	m	Fr:t-8-3/86
7/86	8:00	Crazy Like a Fox(60) — CO	m	To:r-9
7/86	9:00	Trapper John, MD(60) — MD	m	To:r-10
7/86	10:00	Knots Landing(60) — SL	m	To:r-9-9/86
8/86	8:00	Price Is Right(60) — QU	d	
8/86	9:00	Crazy Like a Fox(60) — CO	m	Fr:r-8
8/86	10:00	Trapper John, MD(60) — MD	m	Fr:r-9
9/86	8:00	Simon & Simon(60) — CD	m	Fr:t-8
9/86	8:00	Price Is Right(60) — QU	c	
9/86	9:00	Knots Landing(60) — SL	m	Fr:r-10-7/86
9/86	9:00	Crazy Like a Fox(60) — CO	c	
9/86	10:00	Kay O'Brien(60) — LD	d	
9/86	10:00	Trapper John, MD(60) — MD	c	
11/86	8:00	Simon & Simon(60) — CD	m	To:r-8:30
11/86	9:00	Knots Landing(60) — SL	m	To:r-10
11/86	10:00	Knots Landing(60) — SL	m	Fr:r-9
11/86	10:00	Kay O'Brien(60) — LD	c	
12/86	8:00	Twilight Zone — FA	m	Fr:s-10-10/86
12/86	8:30	Simon & Simon(60) — CD	m	Fr:r-8
12/86	9:30	Designing Women — SC	m	Fr:m-9:30
1/87	8:00	Twilight Zone — FA	m	To:f-10-7/87
1/87	8:00	Shell Game(60) — CD	d	
1/87	8:30	Simon & Simon(60) — CD	m	To:r-9
1/87	9:00	Simon & Simon(60) — CD	m	Fr:r-8:30
1/87	9:30	Designing Women — SC	m	To:m-9:30-3/87
2/87	8:00	Wizard(60) — AD	m	Fr:t-8
2/87	8:00	Shell Game(60) — CD	m	To:w-9-6/87
5/87	8:00	Wizard(60) — AD	m	To:t-8
5/87	8:00	Scarecrow & Mrs. King(60) — AD	m	Fr:f-8-2/87
7/87	9:00	Simon & Simon(60) — CD	m	To:r-9-12/87
7/87	9:00	Film(120) — FI	s	

Date	Time	Title (min. if not 30) — Type	Action	From/To
8/87	8:00	Scarecrow & Mrs. King(60) — AD	c	
8/87	9:00	Film(120) — FI	f	
9/87	8:00	Tour of Duty(60) — WD	d	
9/87	9:00	Wiseguy(60) — CD	d	
11/87	9:00	Wiseguy(60) — CD	m	To:m-10-1/88
12/87	9:00	Simon & Simon(60) — CD	m	Fr:t-8-8/87
3/88	8:00	Tour of Duty(60) — WD	m	To:s-9
3/88	8:00	48 Hours(60) — DO	m#	Fr:t-8
5/88	9:00	Simon & Simon(60) — CD	m	To:r-9-6/88
5/88	9:00	Film(120) — FI	s	
5/88	10:00	Knots Landing(60) — SL	m	To:r-10-9/88
6/88	9:00	Simon & Simon(60) — CD	m	Fr:r-9-5/88
6/88	9:00	Film(120) — FI	f	
6/88	10:00	Cagney & Lacey(60) — CD	m	Fr:m-10
8/88	9:00	Simon & Simon(60) — CD	c	
8/88	10:00	Cagney & Lacey(60) — CD	c	

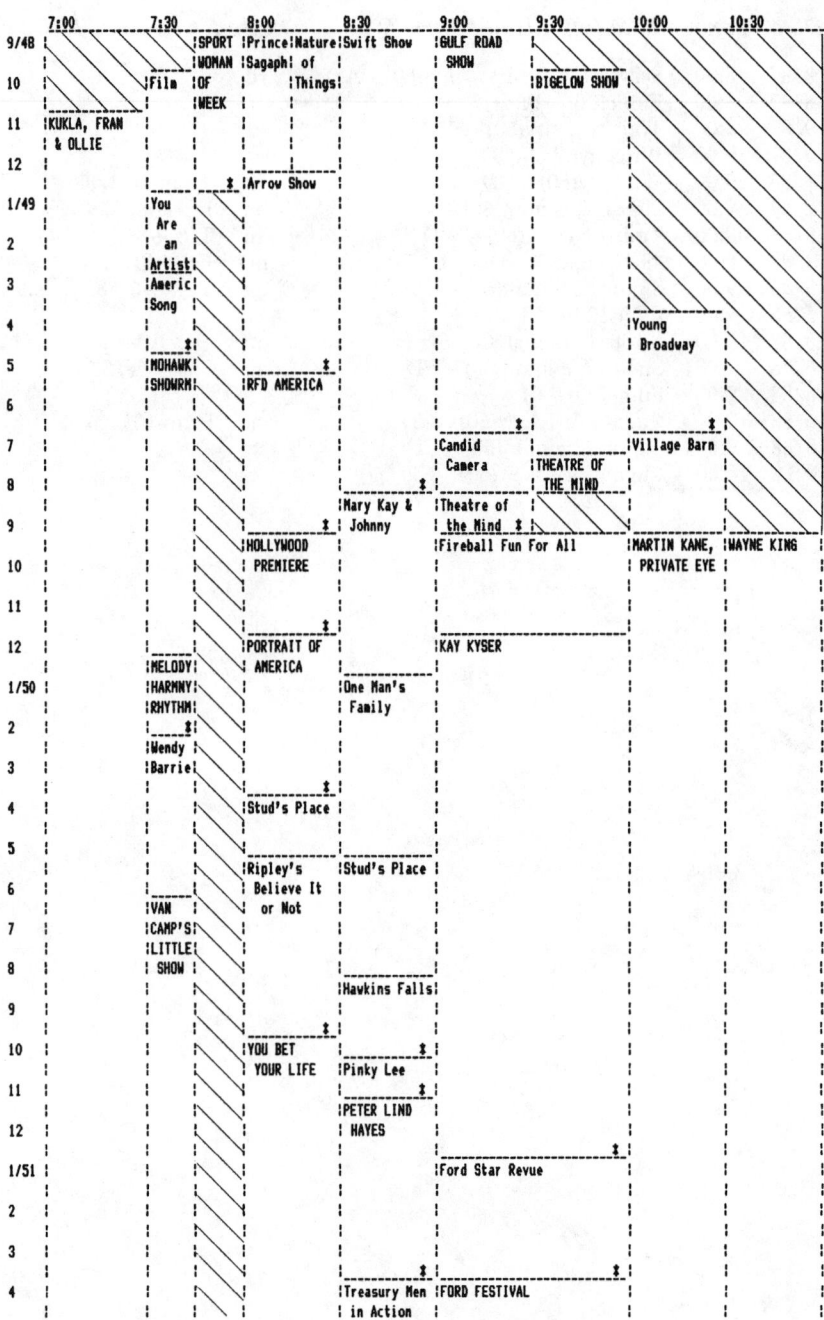

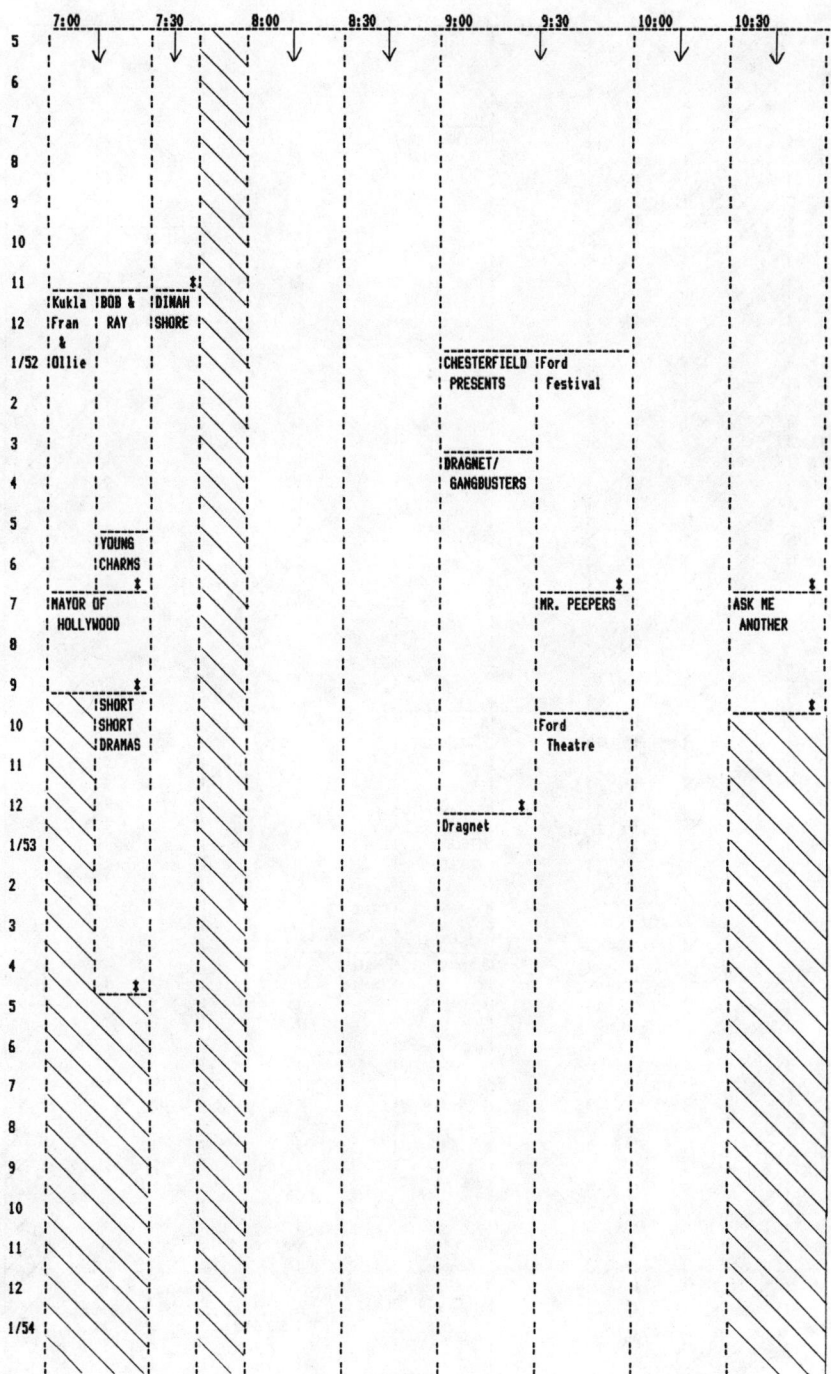

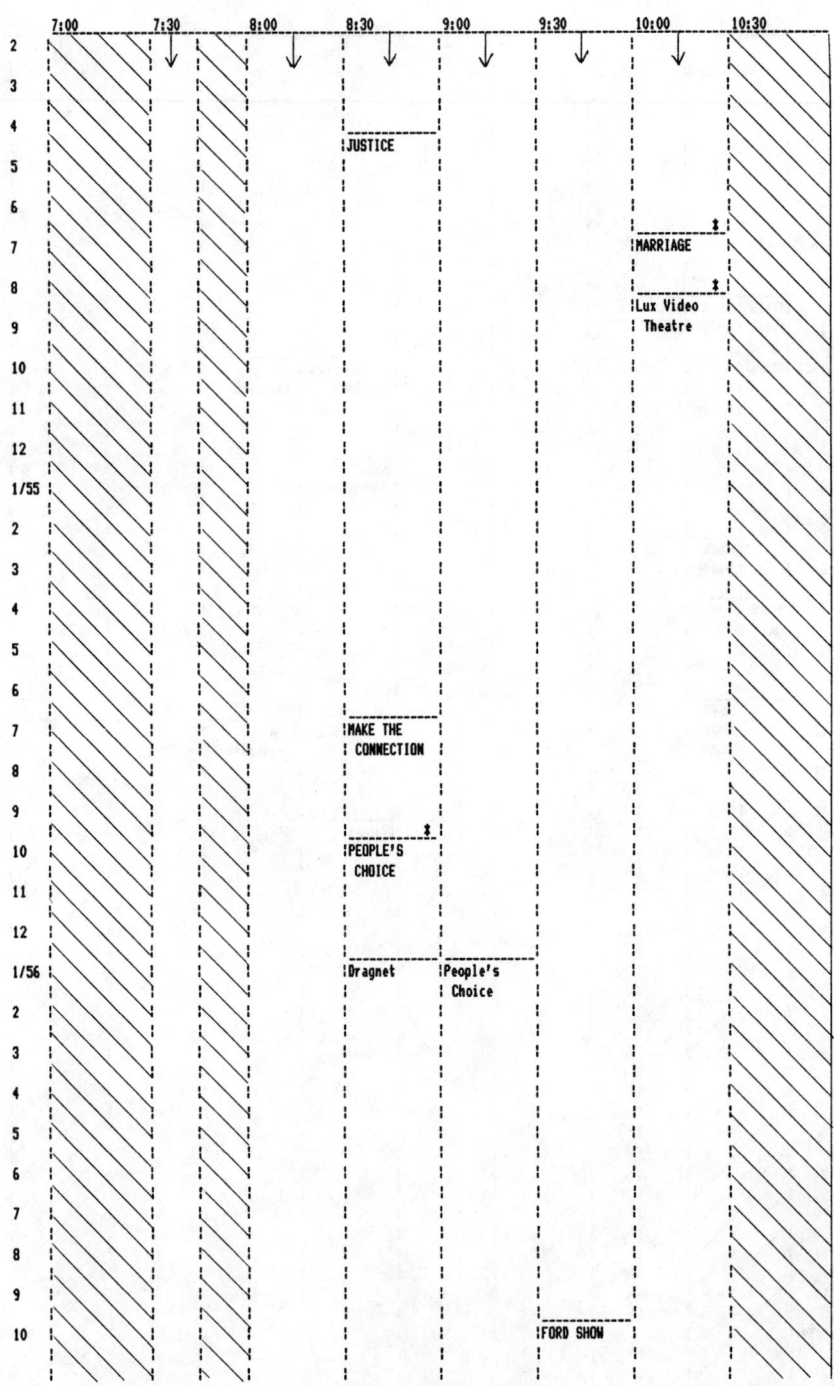

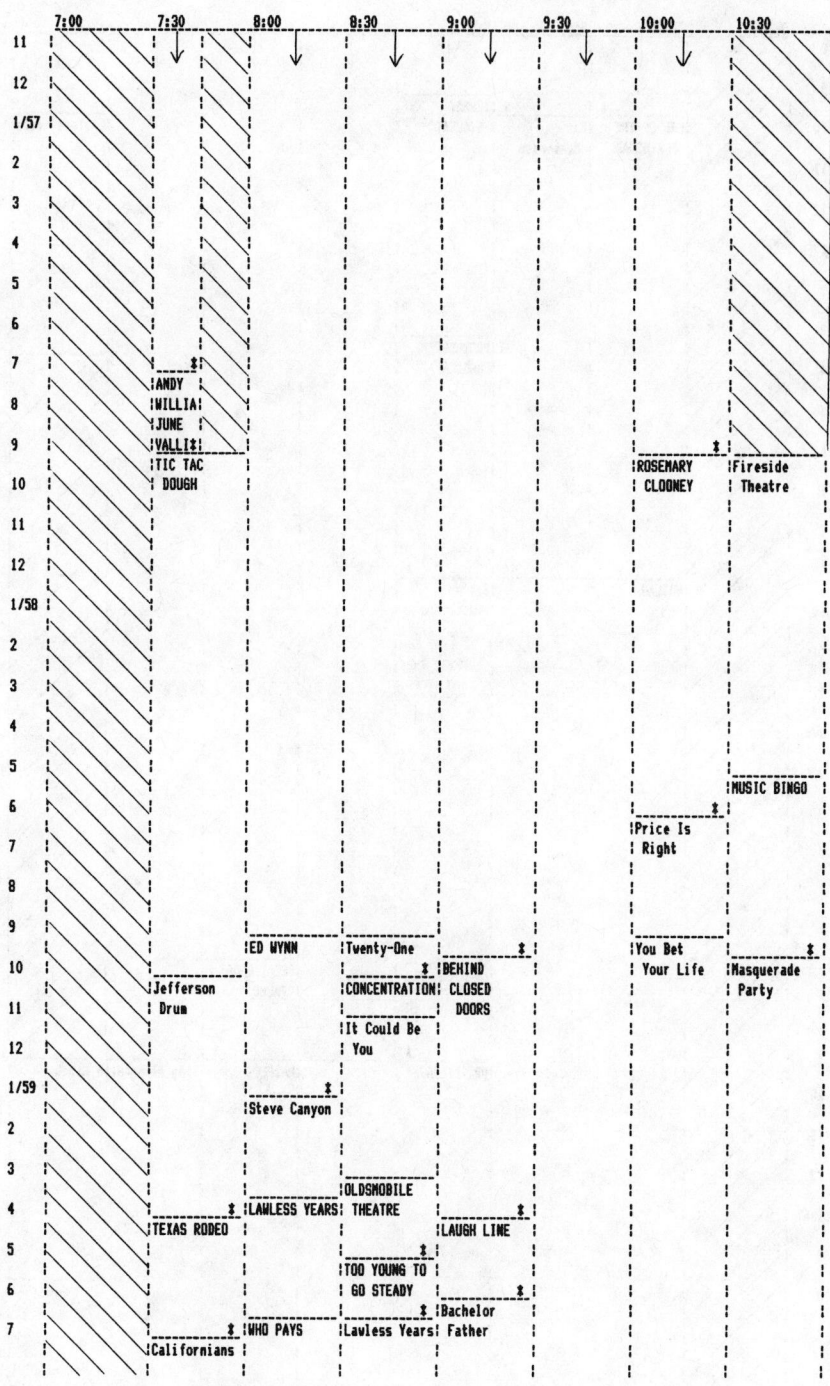

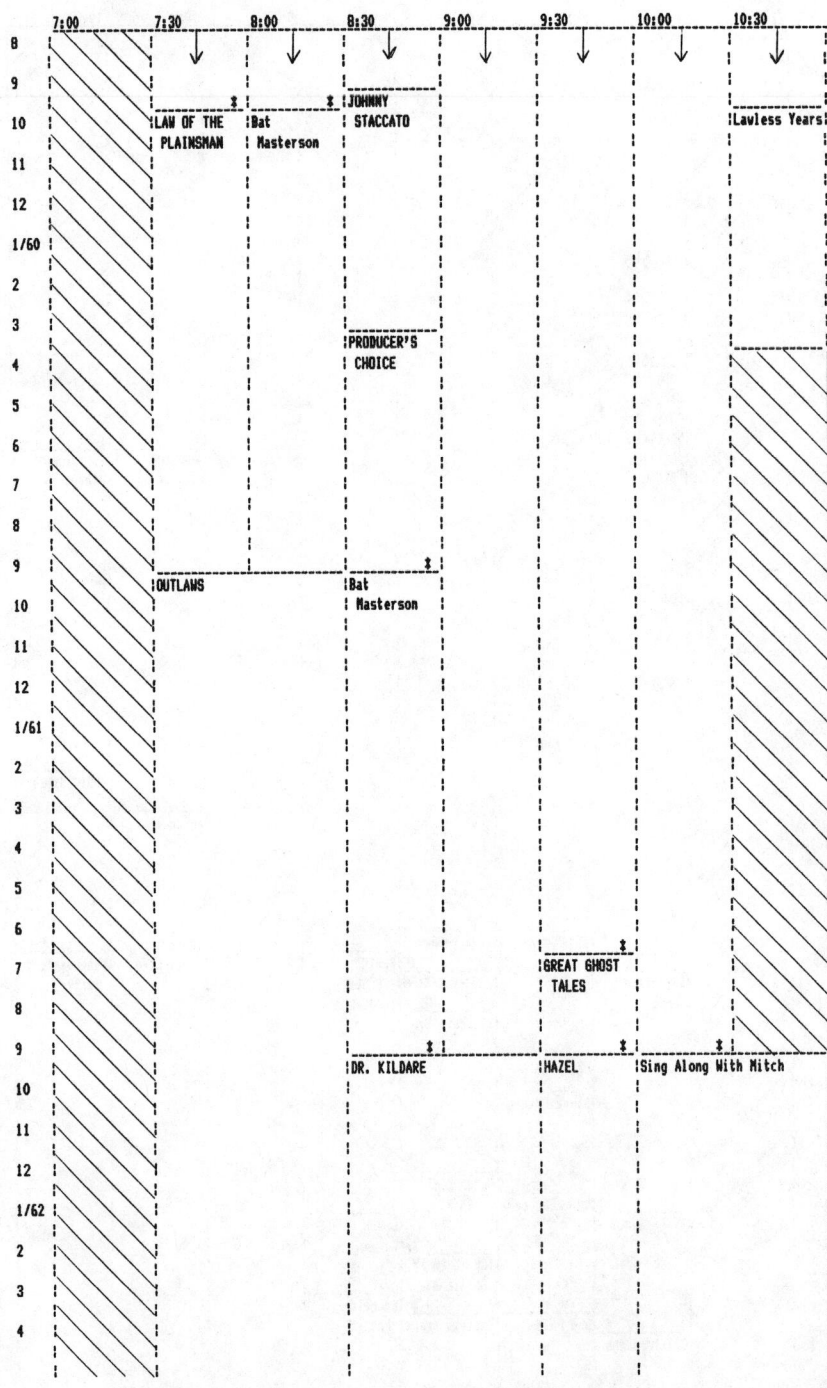

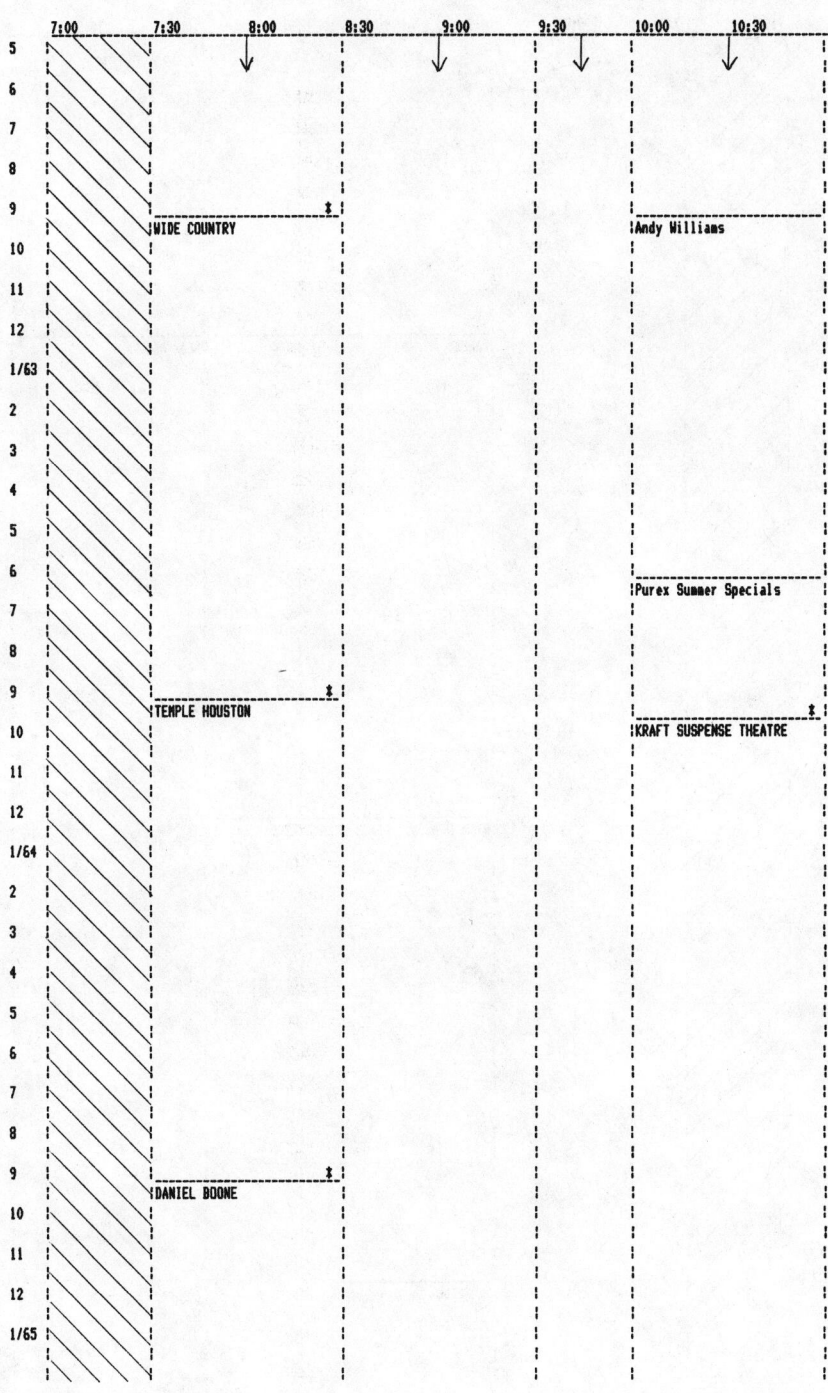

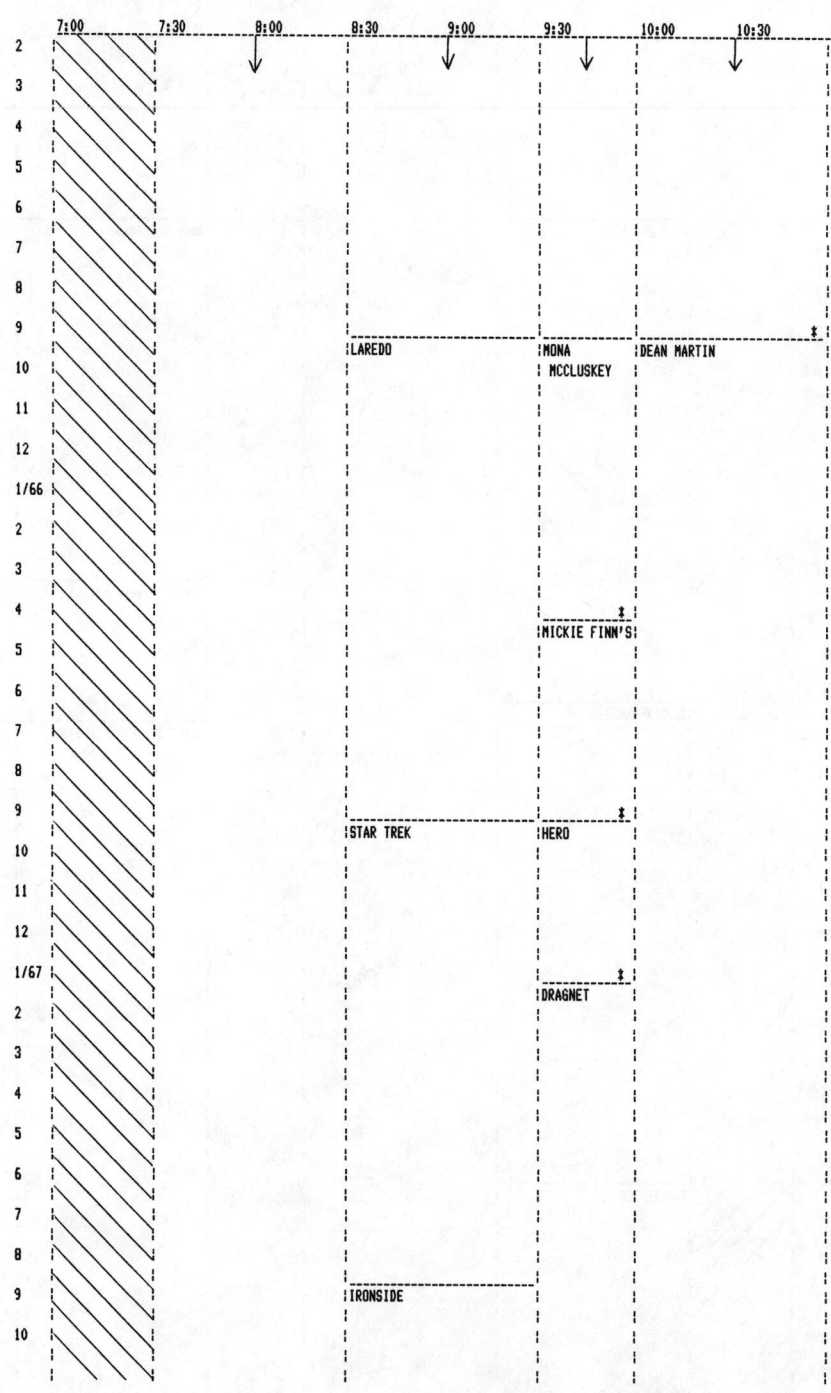

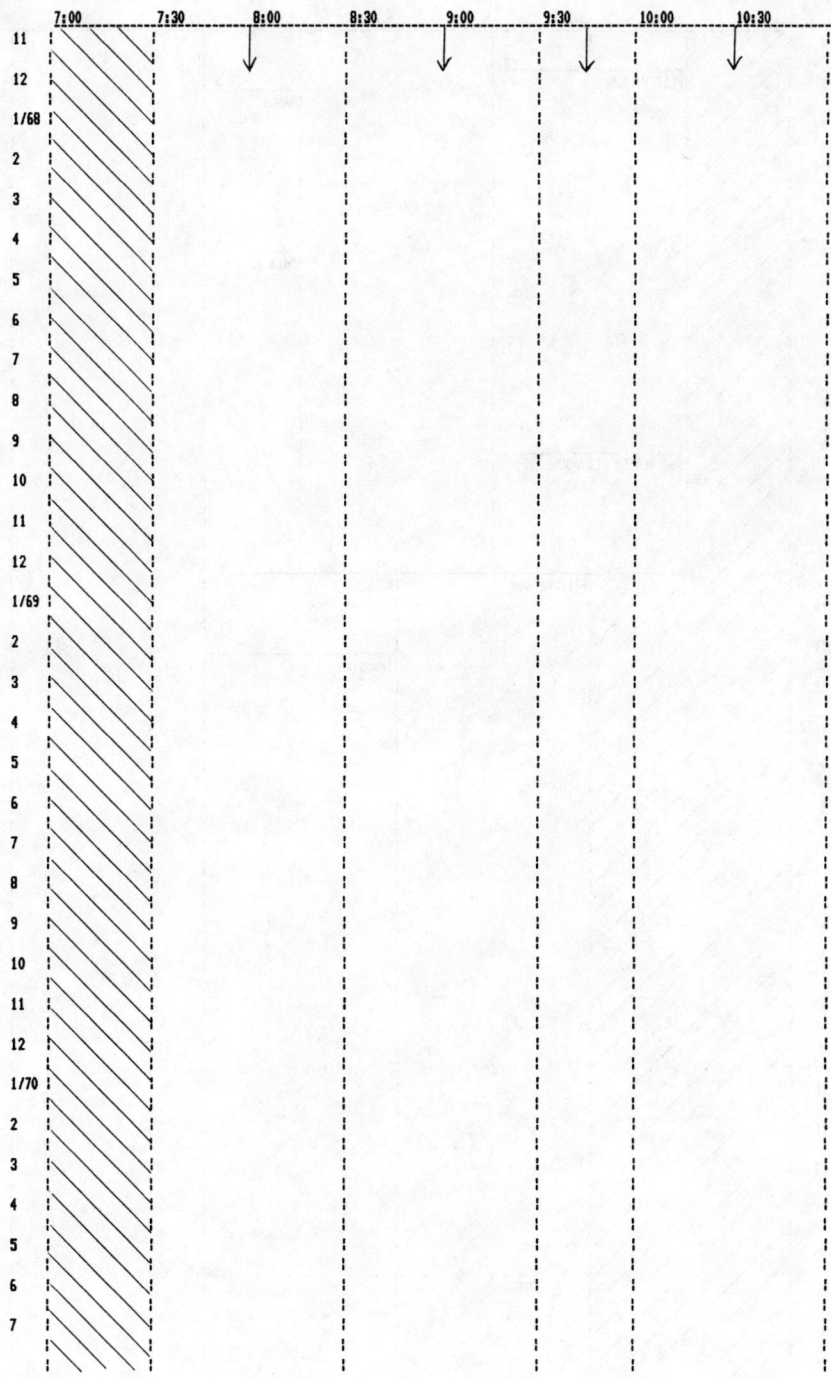

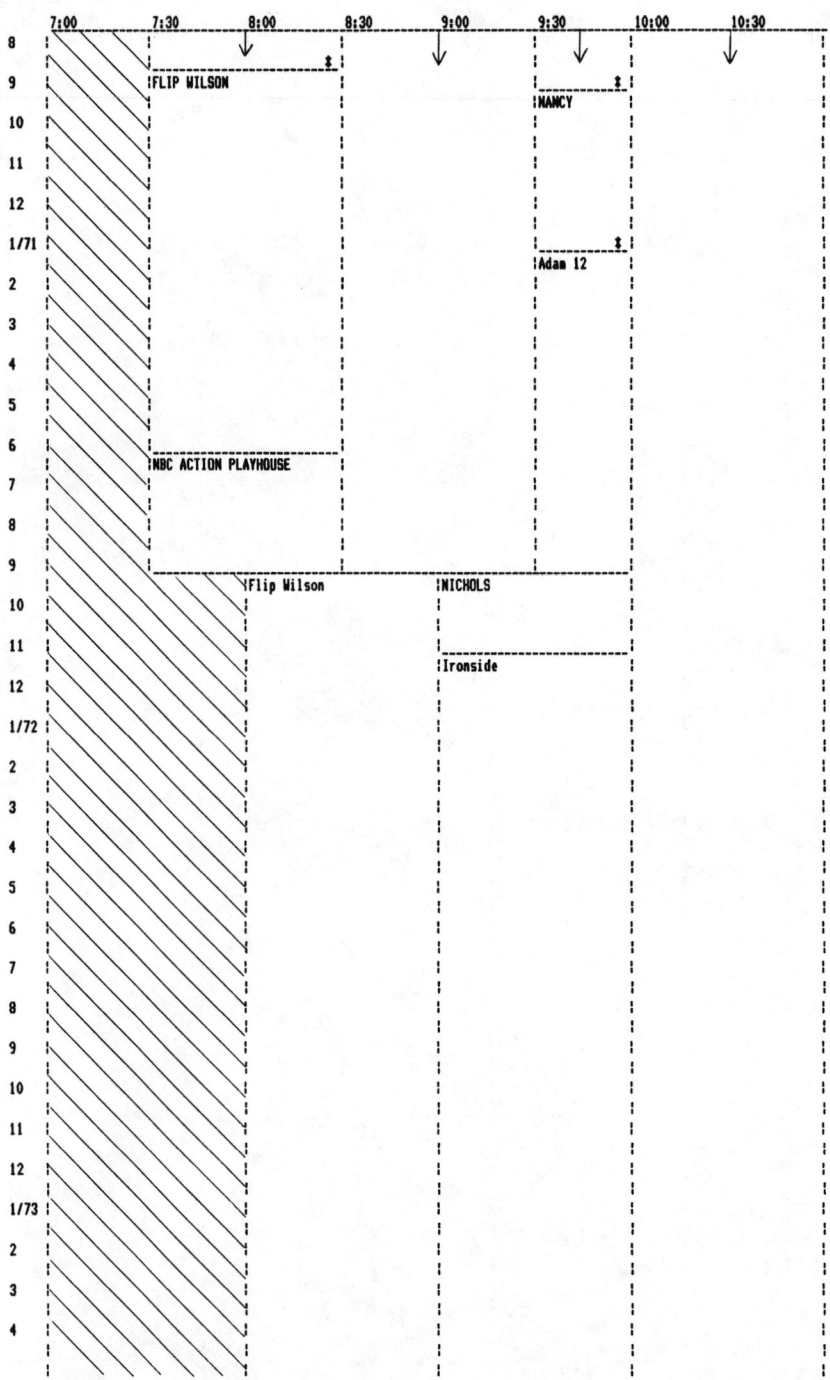

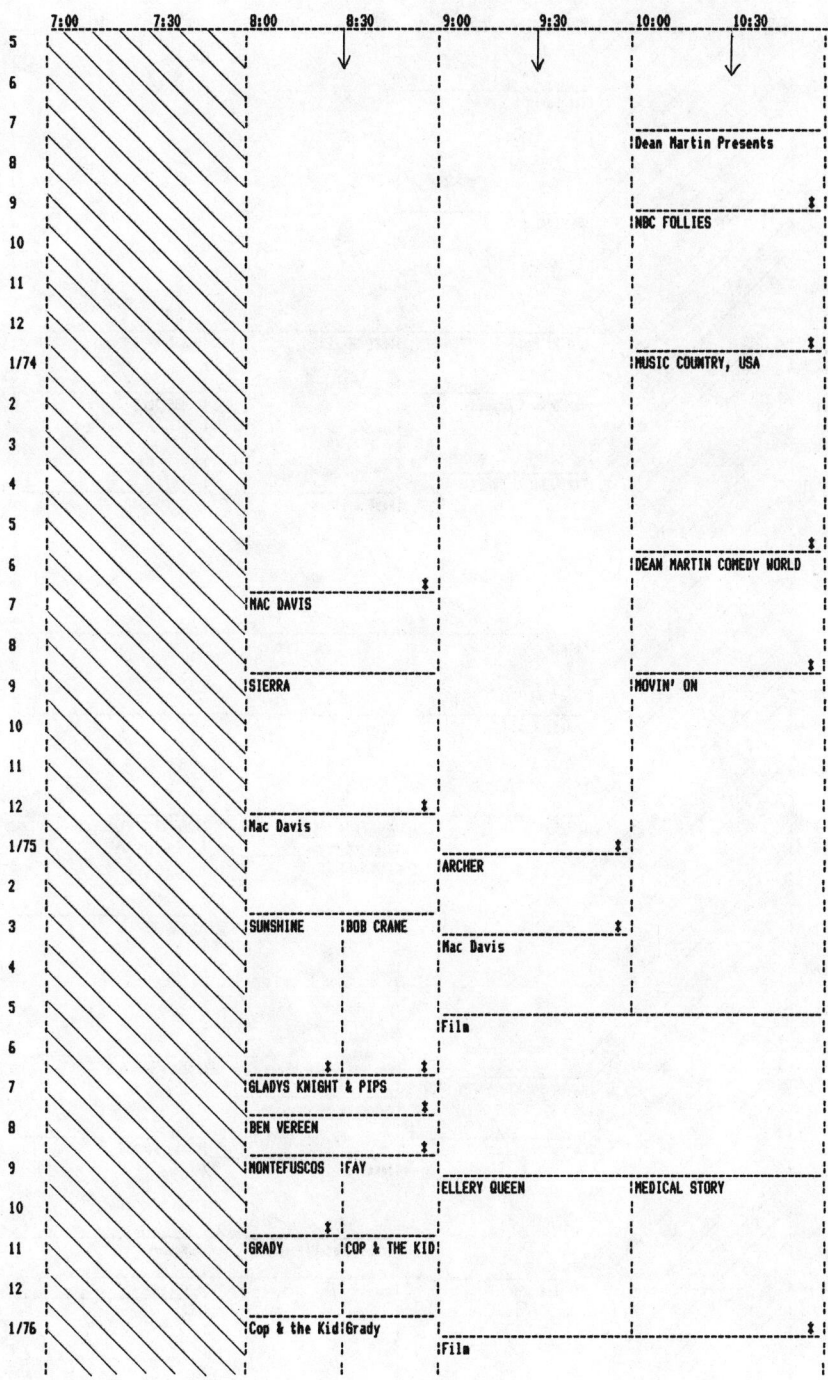

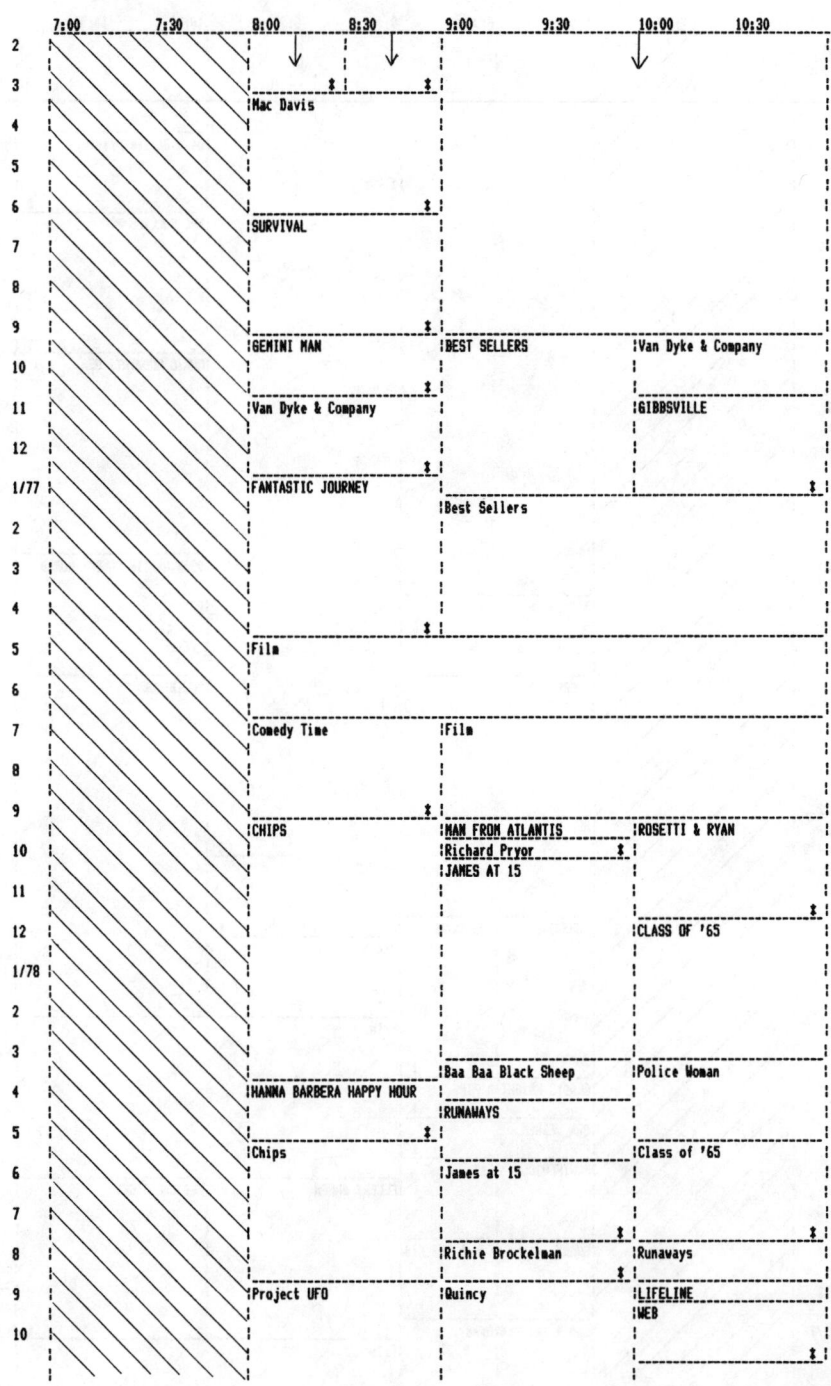

	7:00	7:30	8:00	8:30	9:00	9:30	10:00	10:30
2								
3			Mac Davis					
4								
5								
6			SURVIVAL					
7								
8								
9			GEMINI MAN		BEST SELLERS		Van Dyke & Company	
10								
11			Van Dyke & Company				GIBBSVILLE	
12								
1/77			FANTASTIC JOURNEY					
2					Best Sellers			
3								
4								
5			Film					
6								
7			Comedy Time		Film			
8								
9			CHIPS		MAN FROM ATLANTIS		ROSETTI & RYAN	
10					Richard Pryor			
					JAMES AT 15			
11								
12							CLASS OF '65	
1/78								
2								
3								
4			HANNA BARBERA HAPPY HOUR		Baa Baa Black Sheep		Police Woman	
					RUNAWAYS			
5			Chips				Class of '65	
6					James at 15			
7								
8					Richie Brockelman		Runaways	
9			Project UFO		Quincy		LIFELINE	
							WEB	
10								

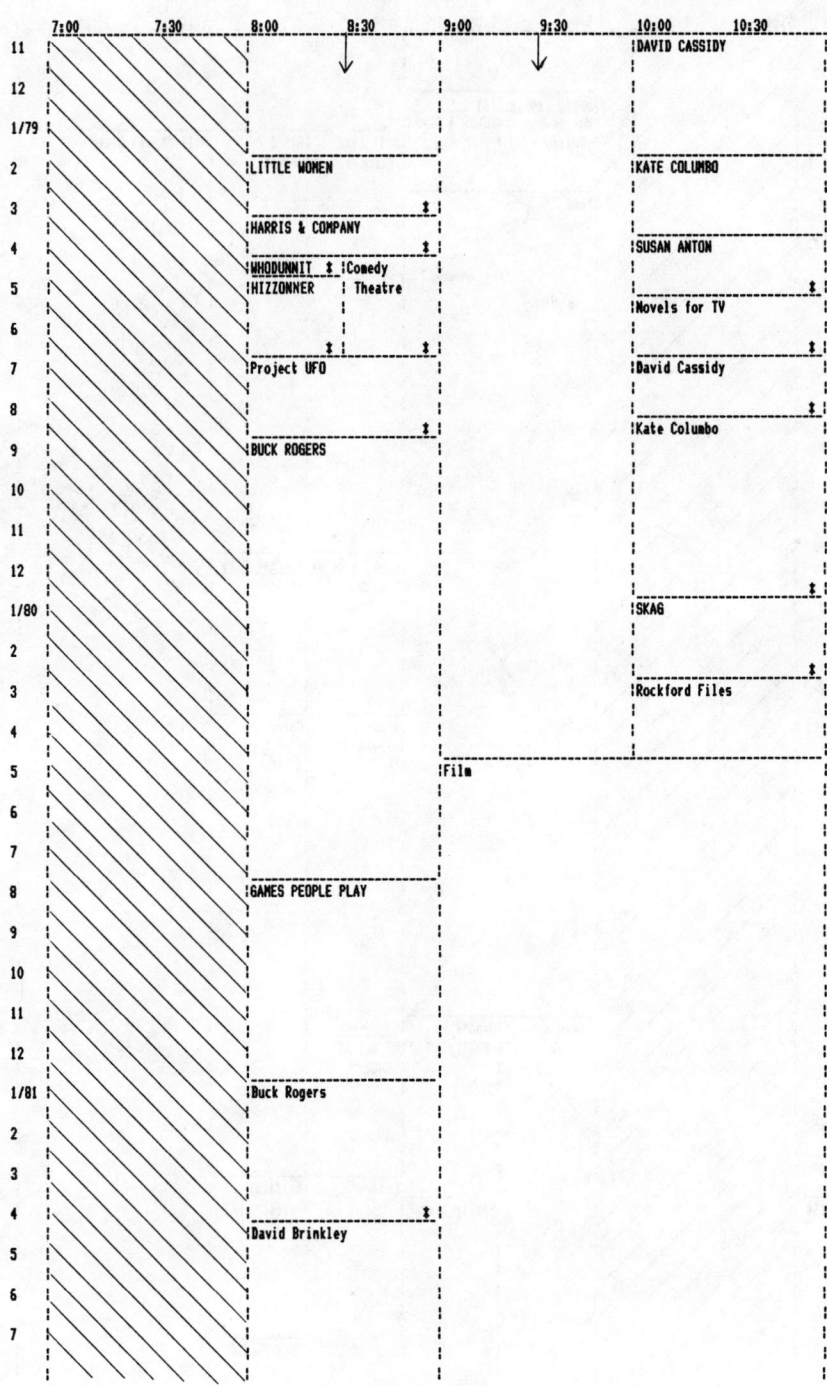

	7:00	7:30	8:00	8:30	9:00	9:30	10:00	10:30
11							DAVID CASSIDY	
12								
1/79								
2			LITTLE WOMEN				KATE COLUMBO	
3			HARRIS & COMPANY					
4							SUSAN ANTON	
5			WHODUNNIT · Comedy					
			HIZZONNER · Theatre				Novels for TV	
6								
7			Project UFO				David Cassidy	
8							Kate Columbo	
9			BUCK ROGERS					
10								
11								
12								
1/80							SKAG	
2								
3							Rockford Files	
4								
5					Film			
6								
7								
8			GAMES PEOPLE PLAY					
9								
10								
11								
12								
1/81			Buck Rogers					
2								
3								
4								
5			David Brinkley					
6								
7								

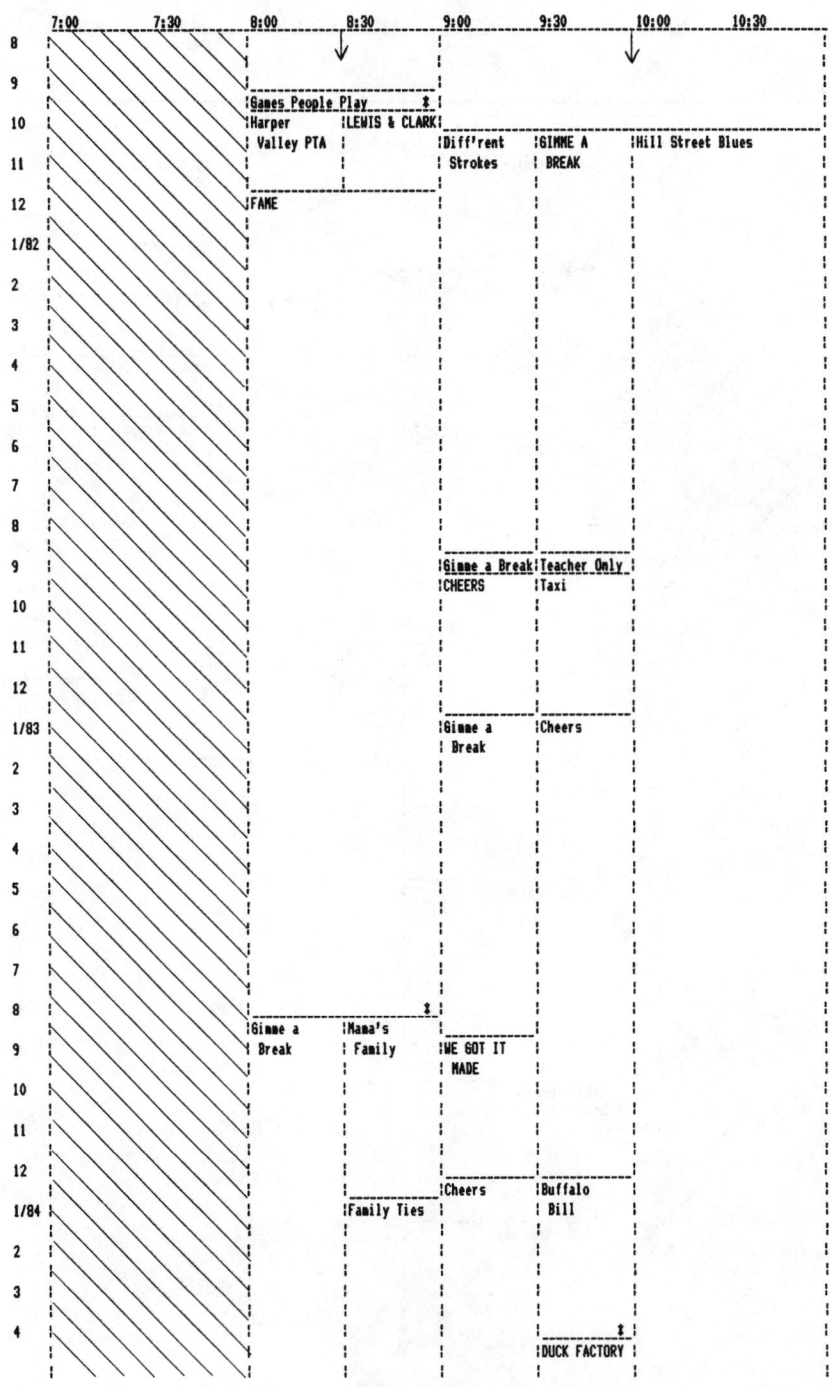

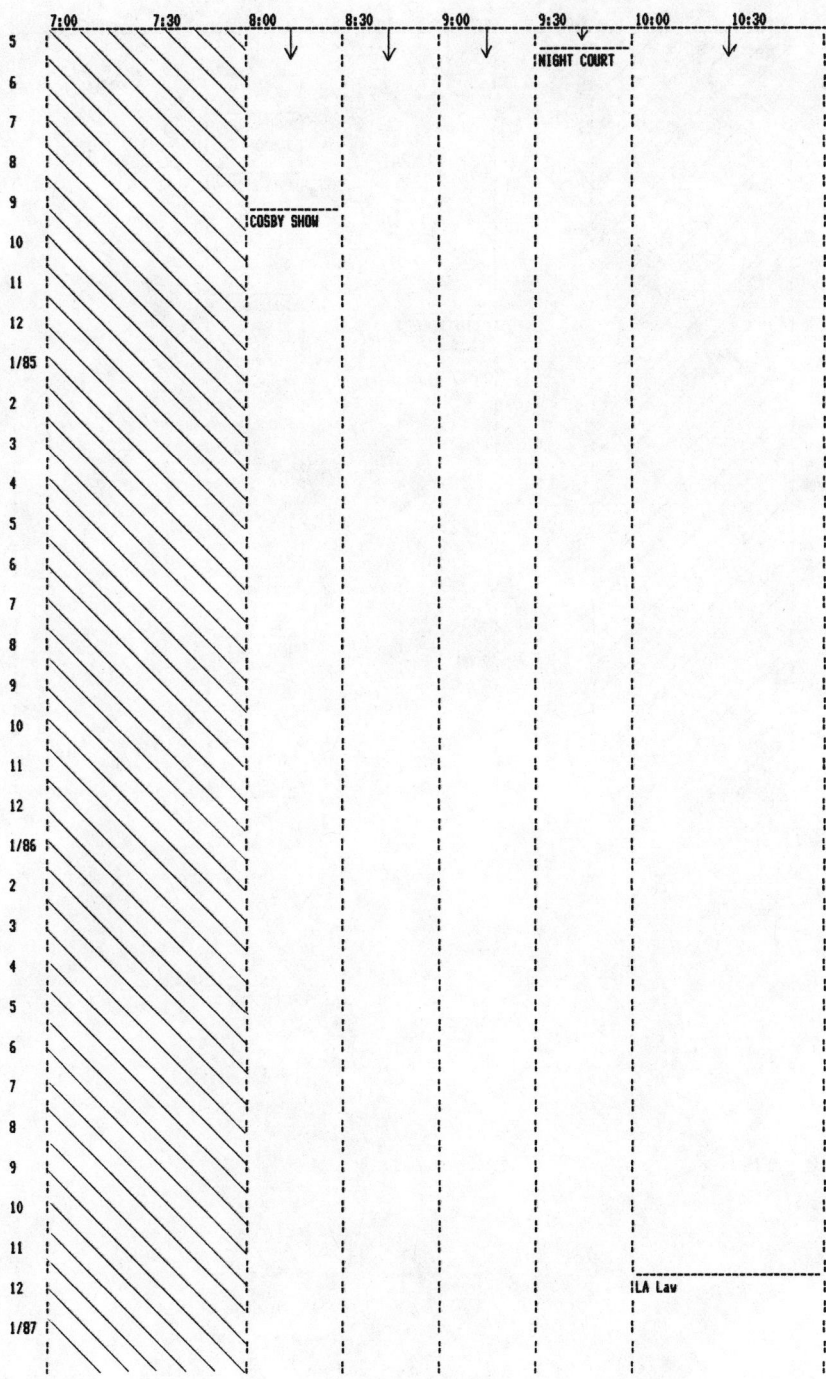

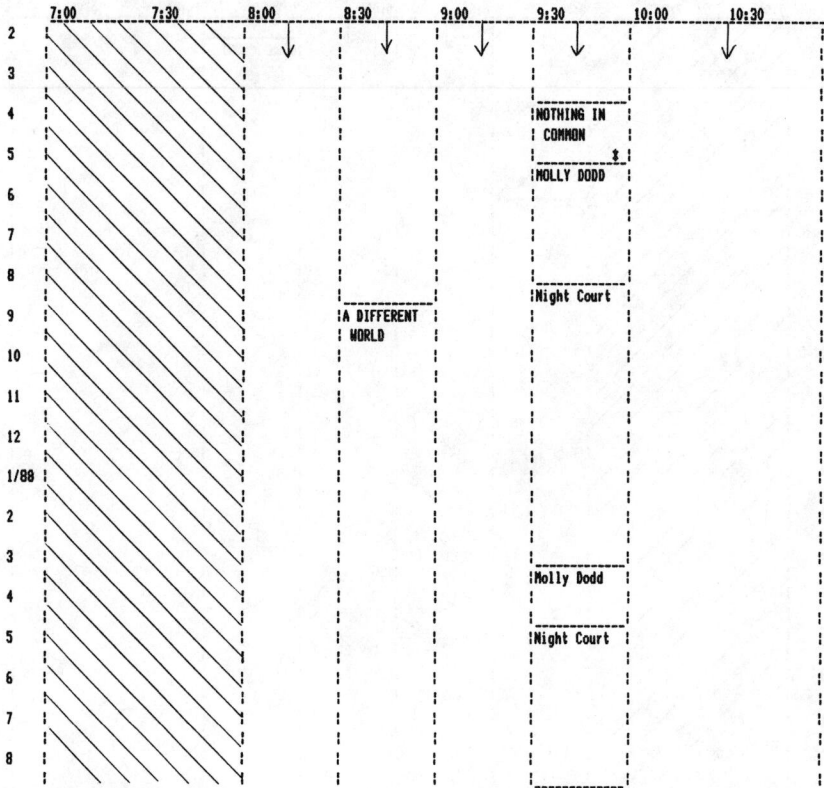

Date	Time	Title (min. if not 30) — Type	Action	From/To
4/48	8:15	Nature of Things(15) — IS	m	Fr:r-9:45
4/48	8:30	Swift Show — MV	d	
9/48	7:45	Sportswoman of the Week(15) — IV	d	
9/48	8:00	Princess Sagaphi(15) — TR	m	Fr:m-8
9/48	9:00	Gulf Road Show Starring Bob Smith — TA	d	
10/48	7:30	Film(15) — FI	s	
10/48	9:30	Bigelow Show — VY	d	
11/48	7:00	Kukla, Fran & Ollie — KV	d	
12/48	7:30	Film(15) — FI	f	
12/48	7:45	Sportswoman of the Week(15) — IV	c	
12/48	8:00	Arrow Show — CV	m	Fr:r-8:30
12/48	8:00	Princess Sagaphi(15) — TR	m	To:m-8:45
12/48	8:15	Nature of Things(15) — IS	m	To:m-var
1/49	7:30	You Are an Artist(15) — IS	m	Fr:w-7:30
2/49	7:30	You Are an Artist(15) — IS	m	To:s-7:30-7/49
3/49	7:30	America Song(15) — MU	m	Fr:m-7:30
4/49	7:30	America Song(15) — MU	c	
4/49	10:00	Young Broadway — MU	m	Fr:w-7:30
5/49	7:30	Mohawk Showroom(15) — MU	d	
5/49	8:00	Arrow Show — CV	c	
5/49	8:00	R.F.D. America — IS	d	
6/49	7:00	Judy Splinters(15) — KV	d*	
6/49	7:15	Mary Kay and Johnny(15) — SC	m	Fr:w-9(c)
6/49	9:00	Gulf Road Show Starring Bob Smith — TA	c	
6/49	10:00	Young Broadway — MU	c	
7/49	9:00	Candid Camera — CY	m	Fr:n-7:30
7/49	9:30	Bigelow Show — VY	m	To:w-9-10/49(c)
7/49	9:30	Theater of the Mind — DS	d	
7/49	10:00	Village Barn — MV	m	Fr:m-10
8/49	7:00	Judy Splinters(15) — KV	c*	
8/49	7:15	Mary Kay and Johnny(15) — SC	m	To:r-8:30
8/49	7:30	Words and Music(15) — MU	d*	
8/49	8:30	Mary Kay and Johnny — SC	m	Fr:m-f-7:15
8/49	8:30	Swift Show — MV	c	
8/49	9:00	Candid Camera — CY	m	To:m-9(c)
8/49	9:00	Theater of the Mind — DS	m	Fr:r-9:30
8/49	9:30	Theater of the Mind — DS	m	To:r-9
9/49	7:30	Words and Music(15) — MU	c*	
9/49	8:00	Hollywood Premiere — VY	d	
9/49	8:00	R.F.D. America — IS	c	
9/49	9:00	Fireball Fun-for-All(60) — CV	m	Fr:t-8
9/49	9:00	Theater of the Mind — DS	c	
9/49	10:00	Martin Kane, Private Eye — CD	d	
9/49	10:00	Village Barn — MV	m	To:m-9:30
9/49	10:30	Wayne King — MU	d	
11/49	8:00	Hollywood Premiere — VY	c	
11/49	9:00	Fireball Fun-for-All(60) — CV	c	

Date	Time	Title (min. if not 30) — Type	Action	From/To
12/49	7:30	Melody, Harmony & Rhythm(15)—MU	d	
12/49	7:30	Mohawk Showroom(15)—MU	m	To:mwf-7:30
12/49	8:00	Portrait of America—IV	d	
12/49	8:30	Mary Kay and Johnny—SC	m	To:s-9
12/49	9:00	Kay Kyser's Kollege of Musical Knowledge(60)—QU	d	
1/50	8:30	One Man's Family—SL	m	Fr:f-8
2/50	7:30	Melody, Harmony & Rhythm(15)—MU	c	
2/50	7:30	Wendy Barrie(15)—IV	m	Fr:r-9(a)
3/50	8:00	Portrait of America—IV	c	
4/50	8:00	Stud's Place—VY	m	Fr:s-8:45
5/50	8:00	Ripley's Believe It or Not—VY	m	Fr:w-8
5/50	8:00	Stud's Place—VY	m	To:r-8:30
5/50	8:30	One Man's Family—SL	m	To:s-7:30-7/50
5/50	8:30	Stud's Place—VY	m	Fr:r-8
6/50	7:30	Van Camp's Little Show(15)—MU	d	
6/50	7:30	Wendy Barrie(15)—IV	m	To:mwf-7:30
6/50	10:00	Harness Racing(60)—SP	s*	
7/50	7:00	Ransom Sherman—CV	d*	
7/50	9:00	Ford Star Revue(60)—CV	d*	
8/50	7:00	Ransom Sherman—CV	c*	
8/50	8:30	Hawkins Falls, Population 6,200—CO	m	Fr:s-8
8/50	8:30	Stud's Place—VY	m	To:f-10:30-10/50(a)
8/50	10:00	Harness Racing(60)—SP	f*	
9/50	8:00	Ripley's Believe It or Not—VY	c	
9/50	9:00	Ford Star Revue(60)—CV	m*	To:r-9-1/51
10/50	8:00	You Bet Your Life—QU	d	
10/50	8:30	Hawkins Falls, Population 6,200—CO	c	
10/50	8:30	Pinky Lee—SC	m	Fr:w-10:30-8/50
11/50	8:30	Peter Lind Hayes—SC	d	
11/50	8:30	Pinky Lee—SC	c	
12/50	9:00	Kay Kyser's Kollege of Musical Knowledge(60)—QU	c	
1/51	9:00	Ford Star Revue(60)—CV	m	Fr:r-9-9/50
3/51	8:30	Peter Lind Hayes—SC	c	
3/51	9:00	Ford Star Revue(60)—CV	c	
4/51	8:30	Treasury Men in Action—CD	m	Fr:m-8-12/50(a)
4/51	9:00	Ford Festival(60)—MV	d	
7/51	7:00	Ernie in Kovacsland—CV	d*	
7/51	7:30	Songs at Twilight(15)—MU	d*	
7/51	8:00	It Pays to Be Ignorant—QU	m*	Fr:m-8:30-9/49(c)
7/51	10:00	Freddy Martin—MV	d*	
7/51	10:30	Short Story Playhouse—DA	d*	
8/51	7:00	Ernie in Kovacsland—CV	c*	
8/51	7:30	Songs at Twilight(15)—MU	c*	
8/51	10:00	Freddy Martin—MV	m*	To:w-10:30

Date	Time	Title (min. if not 30) — Type	Action	From/To
8/51	10:30	Short Story Playhouse — DA	c*	
9/51	8:00	It Pays to Be Ignorant — QU	c*	
11/51	7:00	Kukla, Fran & Ollie — KV	m	To:m-f-7
11/51	7:00	Kukla, Fran & Ollie(15) — KV	m	Fr:m-f-7
11/51	7:15	Bob and Ray(15) — CV	d	
11/51	7:30	Dinah Shore(15) — MU	d	
11/51	7:30	Van Camp's Little Show(15) — MU	c	
12/51	9:00	Ford Festival(60) — MV	m	To:r-9:30
1/52	9:00	Chesterfield Presents — DA	d	
1/52	9:30	Ford Festival — MV	m	Fr:r-9
3/52	9:00	Chesterfield Presents — DA	c	
3/52	9:00	Dragnet — CD	d	
3/52	9:00	Gangbusters — RA	d	
5/52	7:15	Bob and Ray(15) — CV	m	To:m-7:30-4/53
5/52	7:15	Those Endearing Young Charms (15) — SC	d	
6/52	7:00	Kukla, Fran & Ollie(15) — KV	m	To:m-f-7-9/54(a)
6/52	7:15	Those Endearing Young Charms (15) — SC	c	
6/52	9:30	Ford Festival — MV	c	
6/52	10:30	Wayne King — MU	c	
7/52	7:00	Mayor of Hollywood — VY	d	
7/52	7:30	Liberace(15) — MV	d*	
7/52	9:30	Mr. Peepers — SC	d	
7/52	10:30	Ask Me Another — QU	d	
8/52	7:30	Liberace(15) — MV	c*	
8/52	8:30	What Happened — QU	d*	
8/52	8:30	What Happened — QU	c*	
9/52	7:00	Mayor of Hollywood — VY	c	
9/52	7:15	Short Short Dramas(15) — DA	d	
9/52	9:30	Mr. Peepers — SC	m	To:n-7:30
9/52	10:30	Ask Me Another — QU	c	
10/52	9:30	Ford Theatre — DA	m	Fr:f-10-6/51(c)
12/52	9:00	Gangbusters — RA	c	
4/53	7:15	Short Short Dramas(15) — DA	c	
7/53	7:30	Eddy Arnold(15) — MV	m*	Fr:mwf-7:45-8/52(c)
10/53	7:30	Eddy Arnold(15) — MV	c*	
4/54	8:30	Justice — LD	d	
4/54	8:30	Treasury Men in Action — CD	m	To:r-8:30-10/54(a)
6/54	10:00	Martin Kane, Private Eye — CD	c	
7/54	10:00	The Marriage — SC	d	
8/54	7:30	Vaughn Monroe(15) — MV	d*	
8/54	10:00	Lux Video Theatre — DA	m	Fr:r-9-6/54(c)
8/54	10:00	The Marriage — SC	c	
9/54	7:30	Vaughn Monroe(15) — MV	m*	To:tr-7:30-7/55
6/55	8:30	Justice — LD	m	To:n-10:30-10/55
7/55	7:30	Vaughn Monroe(15) — MV	m*	Fr:tr-7:30-9/54
7/55	8:30	Make the Connection — QU	d	
9/55	7:30	Vaughn Monroe(15) — MV	c*	
9/55	8:30	Make the Connection — QU	c	

Date	Time	Title (min. if not 30) — Type	Action	From/To
10/55	8:30	People's Choice — SC	d	
12/55	8:30	People's Choice — SC	m	To:r-9
12/55	9:00	Dragnet — CD	m	To:r-8:30
1/56	8:30	Dragnet — CD	m	Fr:r-9
1/56	9:00	People's Choice — SC	m	Fr:r-8:30
7/56	7:30	Chevrolet on Broadway(15) — MV	d*	
9/56	7:30	Chevrolet on Broadway(15) — MV	c*	
9/56	9:30	Ford Theatre — DA	m	To:w-9:30(a)
10/56	9:30	Ford Show — MV	d	
7/57	7:30	Andy Williams and June Valli(15) — MU	d	
7/57	7:30	Dinah Shore(15) — MU	c	
7/57	9:30	High-Low — QU	d*	
9/57	7:30	Andy Williams and June Valli(15) — MU	c	
9/57	7:30	Tic Tac Dough — QU	d	
9/57	9:30	High-Low — QU	c*	
9/57	10:00	Lux Show Starring Rosemary Clooney — MV	d	
9/57	10:00	Lux Video Theatre — DA	c	
9/57	10:30	Fireside Theater — DA	m	Fr:t-9-6/57
5/58	10:30	Fireside Theater — DA	m	To:n-8-6/63(a)
5/58	10:30	Music Bingo — QU	d	
6/58	10:00	Lux Show Starring Rosemary Clooney — MV	c	
6/58	10:00	The Price Is Right — QU	m	Fr:m-7:30
7/58	9:30	Buckskin — WE	d*	
9/58	8:00	Ed Wynn — SC	d	
9/58	8:00	You Bet Your Life — QU	m	To:r-10
9/58	8:30	Dragnet — CD	m	To:t-7:30
9/58	8:30	Twenty-One — QU	m	Fr:m-9
9/58	9:00	People's Choice — SC	c	
9/58	9:30	Buckskin — WE	m*	To:f-7:30
9/58	10:00	The Price Is Right — QU	m	To:w-8:30
9/58	10:00	You Bet Your Life — QU	m	Fr:r-8
9/58	10:30	Music Bingo — QU	c	
10/58	7:30	Jefferson Drum — WE	m	Fr:f-7:30
10/58	7:30	Tic Tac Dough — QU	m	To:m-7:30
10/58	8:30	Concentration — QU	d	
10/58	8:30	Twenty-One — QU	c	
10/58	9:00	Behind Closed Doors — SD	d	
10/58	10:30	Masquerade Party — QU	m	Fr:m-8:30(c)
11/58	8:30	Concentration — QU	m	To:m-9:30-4/61
11/58	8:30	It Could Be You — QU	m	Fr:w-10-9/58
1/59	8:00	Ed Wynn — SC	c	
1/59	8:00	Steve Canyon — AD	m	Fr:s-9
3/59	8:00	Steve Canyon — AD	m	To:t-8
3/59	8:30	It Could be You — QU	m	To:s-10:30-9/59
3/59	8:30	Oldsmobile Music Theatre — VS	d	
4/59	7:30	Jefferson Drum — WE	c	

Date	Time	Title (min. if not 30) — Type	Action	From/To
4/59	7:30	Texas Rodeo — RO	d	
4/59	8:00	The Lawless Years — CD	d	
4/59	9:00	Behind Closed Doors — SD	c	
4/59	9:00	Laugh Line — QU	d	
5/59	8:30	Oldsmobile Music Theatre — VS	c	
5/59	8:30	Too Young to Go Steady — SC	d	
6/59	8:00	The Lawless Years — CD	m	To:r-8:30
6/59	8:30	Too Young to Go Steady — SC	c	
6/59	9:00	Bachelor Father — SC	m	Fr:n-7:30(c)
6/59	9:00	Laugh Line — QU	c	
7/59	7:30	Californians — WE	m	Fr:t-9
7/59	7:30	Texas Rodeo — RO	c	
7/59	8:00	Who Pays — QU	d	
7/59	8:30	The Lawless Years — CD	m	Fr:r-8
7/59	9:30	21 Beacon Street — CD	d*	
9/59	7:30	Californians — WE	c	
9/59	8:00	Who Pays — QU	c	
9/59	8:30	Johnny Staccato — CD	d	
9/59	8:30	The Lawless Years — CD	m	To:r-10:30
9/59	9:30	21 Beacon Street — CD	m*	To:n-10:30-12/59(a)
9/59	10:30	Masquerade Party — QU	m	To:m-7:30(c)
10/59	7:30	Law of the Plainsman — WE	d	
10/59	8:00	Bat Masterson — WE	m	Fr:w-9:30
10/59	10:30	The Lawless Years — CD	m	Fr:r-8:30
3/60	8:30	Johnny Staccato — CD	m	To:n-10:30(a)
3/60	8:30	Producer's Choice — DA	d	
3/60	10:30	The Lawless Years — CD	m	To:f-9-5/61
8/60	9:30	Wrangler — WE	d*	
9/60	7:30	Law of the Plainsman — WE	m	To:m-8:30-7/62(a)
9/60	7:30	The Outlaws(60) — WE	d	
9/60	8:00	Bat Masterson — WE	m	To:r-8:30
9/60	8:30	Bat Masterson — WE	m	Fr:r-8
9/60	8:30	Producer's Choice — DA	c	
9/60	9:30	Wrangler — WE	c*	
6/61	9:30	Ford Show — MV	c	
7/61	9:30	Great Ghost Tales — OA	d	
9/61	8:30	Bat Masterson — WE	c	
9/61	8:30	Dr. Kildare(60) — MD	d	
9/61	9:00	Bachelor Father — SC	m	To:t-8(a)
9/61	9:30	Great Ghost Tales — OA	c	
9/61	9:30	Hazel — SC	d	
9/61	10:00	Sing Along with Mitch(60) — MV	m	Fr:f-9-4/61
9/61	10:00	You Bet Your Life — QU	c	
7/62	9:30	Lively Ones — MV	d*	
9/62	7:30	The Outlaws(60) — WE	c	
9/62	7:30	Wide Country(60) — WE	d	
9/62	9:30	Lively Ones — MV	m*	To:r-9:30-7/63
9/62	10:00	Andy Williams Show(60) — MV	m	Fr:t-10-9/59(c)
9/62	10:00	Sing Along with Mitch(60) — MV	m	To:f-8:30
6/63	10:00	Andy Williams Show(60) — MV	m	To:t-10-9/63

Date	Time	Title (min. if not 30) — Type	Action	From/To
6/63	10:00	Purex Summer Specials(60) —VY	m	Fr:f-9:30-9/62
7/63	9:30	Lively Ones—MV	m*	Fr:r-9:30-9/62
9/63	7:30	Temple Houston(60)—WE	d	
9/63	7:30	Wide Country(60)—WE	c	
9/63	9:30	Lively Ones—MV	c*	
9/63	10:00	Purex Summer Specials(60)—VS	c	
10/63	10:00	Kraft Suspense Theater(60)—SA	d	
8/64	9:30	New Christy Minstrels—MV	d*	
9/64	7:30	Daniel Boone(60)—WE	d	
9/64	7:30	Temple Houston(60)—WE	c	
9/64	9:30	New Christy Minstrels—MV	c*	
9/65	8:30	Dr. Kildare(60)—MD	m	To:mt-8:30
9/65	8:30	Laredo(60)—WE	d	
9/65	9:30	Hazel—SC	m	To:m-9:30(c)
9/65	9:30	Mona McCluskey—SC	d	
9/65	10:00	Dean Martin(60)—CV	d	
9/65	10:00	Kraft Suspense Theater(60)—SA	c	
4/66	9:30	Mickie Finn's—MV	d	
4/66	9:30	Mona McCluskey—SC	c	
6/66	10:00	Dean Martin Summer Show(60) —VY	d*	
9/66	8:30	Laredo(60)—WE	m	To:f-10
9/66	8:30	Star Trek(60)—SF	d	
9/66	9:30	Hero—SC	d	
9/66	9:30	Mickie Finn's—MV	c	
9/66	10:00	Dean Martin Summer Show(60) —VY	m*	To:r-10-6/67
1/67	9:30	Dragnet—CD	d	
1/67	9:30	Hero—SC	c	
6/67	10:00	Dean Martin Summer Show(60) —VY	m*	Fr:r-10-9/66
8/67	8:30	Star Trek(60)—SF	m	To:f-8:30
9/67	8:30	Ironside(60)—CD	d	
9/67	10:00	Dean Martin Summer Show(60) —VY	m*	To:r-10-7/71
6/68	10:00	Dean Martin Presents(60)—MV	d*	
9/68	10:00	Dean Martin Presents(60)—MV	m*	To:r-10-7/69
7/69	10:00	Dean Martin Presents(60)—MV	m*	Fr:r-10-9/68
9/69	10:00	Dean Martin Presents(60)—MV	m*	To:r-10-7/70
7/70	10:00	Dean Martin Presents(60)—MV	m*	Fr:r-10-9/69
8/70	7:30	Daniel Boone(60)—WE	c	
9/70	7:30	Flip Wilson(60)—CV	d	
9/70	9:30	Dragnet—CD	c	
9/70	9:30	Nancy—SC	d	
9/70	10:00	Dean Martin Presents(60)—MV	m*	To:r-10-7/72
1/71	9:30	Adam 12—CD	m	Fr:s-8:30
1/71	9:30	Nancy—SC	c	
6/71	7:30	Flip Wilson(60)—CV	m	To:r-8-9/71
6/71	7:30	NBC Action Playhouse(60)—DA	d	

Date	Time	Title (min. if not 30) — Type	Action	From/To
7/71	10:00	Dean Martin Summer Show(60) —VY	m*	Fr:r-10-9/67
8/71	10:00	Dean Martin Summer Show(60) —VY	c*	
9/71	7:30	NBC Action Playhouse(60)—DA	m	To:r-9-5/72
9/71	8:00	Flip Wilson(60)—CV	m	Fr:r-7:30-6/71
9/71	8:30	Ironside(60)—CD	m	To:t-7:30
9/71	9:00	Nichols(60)—WE	d	
9/71	9:30	Adam 12—CD	m	To:w-8
11/71	9:00	Ironside(60)—CD	m	Fr:t-7:30
11/71	9:00	Nichols(60)—WE	m	To:t-9:30
5/72	9:00	NBC Action Playhouse(60)—DA	m*	Fr:r-7:30-9/71
6/72	8:00	NBC Adventure Theatre(60)—AA	m*	Fr:s-7:30-9/71
7/72	10:00	Dean Martin Presents(60)—MV	m*	Fr:r-10-9/70
9/72	8:00	NBC Adventure Theatre(60)—AA	c*	
9/72	9:00	NBC Action Playhouse(60)—DA	c*	
9/72	10:00	Dean Martin Presents(60)—MV	m*	To:r-10-7/73
6/73	8:00	Helen Reddy(60)—MV	d*	
7/73	10:00	Dean Martin Presents(60)—MV	m	Fr:r-10-9/72
7/73	10:00	Dean Martin(60)—CV	m	To:f-10-9/73
8/73	8:00	Helen Reddy(60)—MV	c*	
9/73	10:00	Dean Martin Presents(60)—MV	c	
9/73	10:00	NBC Follies(60)—CV	d	
12/73	10:00	NBC Follies(60)—CV	c	
1/74	10:00	Music Country USA(60)—MU	d	
5/74	10:00	Music Country USA(60)—MU	c	
6/74	8:00	Flip Wilson(60)—CV	c	
6/74	10:00	Dean Martin Comedy World(60) —CV	d	
7/74	8:00	Mac Davis(60)—MV	d	
8/74	8:00	Mac Davis(60)—MV	m	To:r-8-12/74
8/74	10:00	Dean Martin Comedy World(60) —CV	c	
9/74	8:00	Sierra(60)—AD	d	
9/74	10:00	Movin' On(60)—AD	d	
12/74	8:00	Mac Davis(60)—MV	m	Fr:r-8-8/74
12/74	8:00	Sierra(60)—AD	c	
1/75	9:00	Archer(60)—CD	d	
1/75	9:00	Ironside(60)—CD	c	
2/75	8:00	Mac Davis(60)—MV	m	To:r-9
3/75	8:00	Sunshine—SC	d	
3/75	8:30	Bob Crane—SC	d	
3/75	9:00	Archer(60)—CD	c	
3/75	9:00	Mac Davis(60)—MV	m	Fr:r-8
5/75	9:00	Mac Davis(60)—MV	m	To:r-8-3/76
5/75	9:00	Film(120)—FI	s	
5/75	10:00	Movin' On(60)—AD	m	To:t-8-9/75
6/75	8:00	Sunshine—SC	c	
6/75	8:30	Bob Crane—SC	c	
7/75	8:00	Gladys Knight & the Pips(60)—MV	d	

Date	Time	Title (min. if not 30) — Type	Action	From/To
7/75	8:00	Gladys Knight & the Pips(60) — MV	c	
8/75	8:00	Ben Vereen...Comin' at Ya(60) — MV	d	
8/75	8:00	Ben Vereen...Comin' at Ya(60) — MV	c	
9/75	8:00	The Montefuscos — SC	d	
9/75	8:30	Fay — SC	d	
9/75	9:00	Adventures of Ellery Queen(60) — CD	d	
9/75	9:00	Film(120) — FI	f	
9/75	10:00	Medical Story(60) — ME	d	
10/75	8:00	The Montefuscos — SC	c	
10/75	8:30	Fay — SC	m	To:w-9:30-5/76
11/75	8:00	Grady — SC	d	
11/75	8:30	Cop and the Kid — SC	d	
12/75	8:00	Grady — SC	m	To:r-8:30
12/75	8:30	Cop and the Kid — SC	m	To:r-8
1/76	8:00	Cop and the Kid — SC	m	Fr:r-8:30
1/76	8:30	Grady — SC	m	Fr:r-8
1/76	9:00	Adventures of Ellery Queen(60) — CD	m	To:n-8
1/76	9:00	Film(120) — FI	s	
1/76	10:00	Medical Story(60) — ME	c	
3/76	8:00	Cop and the Kid — SC	c	
3/76	8:00	Mac Davis(60) — MV	m	Fr:r-9-5/75
3/76	8:30	Grady — SC	c	
6/76	8:00	Mac Davis(60) — MV	c	
6/76	8:00	Survival(60) — WL	d	
9/76	8:00	Gemini Man(60) — AD	d	
9/76	8:00	Survival(60) — WL	c	
9/76	9:00	Film(120) — FI	f	
9/76	9:00	NBC's Best Sellers(60) — DA	d	
9/76	10:00	Van Dyke and Company(60) — CV	m	Fr:m-10
10/76	8:00	Gemini Man(60) — AD	c	
10/76	10:00	Van Dyke and Company(60) — CV	m	To:r-8
11/76	8:00	Van Dyke and Company(60) — CV	m	Fr:r-10
11/76	10:00	Gibbsville(60) — ND	d	
12/76	8:00	Van Dyke and Company(60) — CV	c	
1/77	8:00	Fantastic Journey(60) — SF	d	
1/77	9:00	NBC's Best Sellers(60) — DA	m	To:r-9
1/77	9:00	NBC's Best Sellers(120) — DA	m	Fr:r-9
1/77	10:00	Gibbsville(60) — ND	c	
4/77	8:00	Fantastic Journey(60) — SF	c	
4/77	9:00	NBC's Best Sellers(120) — DA	m	To:m-9
5/77	8:00	Film(180) — FI	s	
6/77	8:00	Film(180) — FI	f	
7/77	8:00	Comedy Time(60) — CA	m	Fr:w-9:30
7/77	9:00	Film(120) — FI	s	
9/77	8:00	Chips(60) — CD	d	
9/77	8:00	Comedy Time(60) — CA	c	

Date	Time	Title (min. if not 30) — Type	Action	From/To
9/77	9:00	Man from Atlantis(60) — AD	d	
9/77	9:00	Man from Atlantis(60) — AD	m	To:t-8
9/77	9:00	Film(120) — FI	f	
9/77	10:00	Rosetti and Ryan(60) — LD	d	
10/77	9:00	James at 15(60) — DR	d	
10/77	9:00	Richard Pryor(60) — CV	m	Fr:t-8
10/77	9:00	Richard Pryor(60) — CV	c	
11/77	10:00	Rosetti and Ryan(60) — LD	c	
12/77	10:00	What Really Happened to the Class of '65?(60) — DA	d	
3/78	8:00	Chips(60) — CD	m	To:s-8
3/78	9:00	Baa Baa Black Sheep(60) — WD	m	Fr:w-9
3/78	9:00	James at 15(60) — DR	m	To:r-9-6/78
3/78	10:00	Police Woman(60) — CD	m	Fr:w-10
3/78	10:00	What Really Happened to the Class of '65?(60) — DA	m	To:r-10-5/78
4/78	8:00	Hanna-Barbera Happy Hour(60) — CV	d	
4/78	9:00	Baa Baa Black Sheep(60) — WD	m	To:w-9-7/78
4/78	9:00	The Runaways(60) — DR	d	
5/78	8:00	Chips(60) — CD	m	Fr:s-8
5/78	8:00	Hanna-Barbera Happy Hour(60) — CV	c	
5/78	9:00	The Runaways(60) — DR	m	To:r-10-8/78
5/78	10:00	Police Woman(60) — CD	m	To:w-10
5/78	10:00	What Really Happened to the Class of '65?(60) — DA	m	Fr:r-10-3/78
6/78	9:00	James at 15(60) — DR	m	Fr:r-9-3/78
7/78	9:00	James at 15(60) — DR	c	
7/78	10:00	What Really Happened to the Class of '65?(60) — DA	c	
8/78	8:00	Chips(60) — CD	m	To:s-8
8/78	9:00	Richie Brockelman, Pvt. Eye(60) — CD	m	Fr:f-9-4/78
8/78	9:00	Richie Brockelman, Pvt. Eye(60) — CD	c	
8/78	10:00	The Runaways(60) — DR	m	Fr:r-9-5/78
8/78	10:00	The Runaways(60) — DR	m	To:t-8-5/79
9/78	8:00	Project UFO(60) — DR	m	Fr:n-8
9/78	9:00	Quincy, M.E.(60) — CD	m	Fr:f-10
9/78	10:00	Lifeline(60) — MO	d	
9/78	10:00	Lifeline(60) — MO	m	To:n-10
9/78	10:00	W.E.B.(60) — DR	d	
10/78	10:00	W.E.B.(60) — DR	c	
11/78	10:00	David Cassidy — Man Undercover (60) — CD	d	
1/79	8:00	Project UFO(60) — DR	m	To:r-8-7/79
1/79	10:00	David Cassidy — Man Undercover (60) — CD	m	To:r-10-7/79
2/79	8:00	Little Women(60) — DR	d	

Date	Time	Title (min. if not 30) — Type	Action	From/To
2/79	10:00	Kate Columbo(60) — CD	d	
3/79	8:00	Harris and Company(60) — DR	d	
3/79	8:00	Little Women(60) — DR	c	
3/79	10:00	Kate Columbo(60) — CD	m	To:r-10-8/79
4/79	8:00	Harris and Company(60) — DR	c	
4/79	8:00	Whodunnit? — QU	d	
4/79	8:00	Whodunnit? — QU	c	
4/79	8:30	Comedy Theatre — CA	m	Fr:m-8-9/76
4/79	10:00	Susan Anton(60) — MV	d	
5/79	8:00	Hizzonner — SC	d	
5/79	10:00	NBC Novels for Television(60) — DA	m	Fr:w-9
5/79	10:00	Susan Anton(60) — MV	c	
6/79	8:00	Hizzonner — SC	c	
6/79	8:30	Comedy Theatre — CA	c	
6/79	10:00	NBC Novels for Television(60) — DA	c	
7/79	8:00	Project UFO(60) — DR	m	Fr:r-8-1/79
7/79	10:00	David Cassidy — Man Undercover (60) — CD	m	Fr:r-10-1/79
8/79	8:00	Project UFO(60) — DR	c	
8/79	10:00	David Cassidy — Man Undercover (60) — CD	c	
8/79	10:00	Kate Columbo(60) — CD	m	Fr:r-10-3/79
9/79	8:00	Buck Rogers in the 25th Century (60) — SF	d	
12/79	10:00	Kate Columbo(60) — CD	c	
1/80	10:00	Skag(60) — DR	d	
2/80	10:00	Skag(60) — DR	c	
3/80	10:00	Rockford Files(60) — CD	m	Fr:f-9-12/79
4/80	9:00	Quincy, M.E.(60) — CD	m	To:w-10
4/80	10:00	Rockford Files(60) — CD	m	To:f-9-6/80
5/80	9:00	Film(120) — FI	s	
7/80	8:00	Buck Rogers in the 25th Century (60) — SF	m	To:s-8
8/80	8:00	Games People Play(60) — QU	d	
12/80	8:00	Games People Play(60) — QU	m	To:s-10-6/81
1/81	8:00	Buck Rogers in the 25th Century (60) — SF	m	Fr:s-8-9/80
4/81	8:00	Buck Rogers in the 25th Century (60) — SF	c	
4/81	8:00	NBC Magazine with David Brinkley (60) — NM	m	Fr:f-10
9/81	8:00	Games People Play(60) — QU	m	Fr:s-10
9/81	8:00	Games People Play(60) — QU	c	
9/81	8:00	NBC Magazine with David Brinkley (60) — NM	m	To:f-8
10/81	8:00	Harper Valley P.T.A. — SC	m	Fr:f-8-8/81
10/81	8:30	Lewis & Clark — SC	d	
10/81	9:00	Diff'rent Strokes — SC	m	Fr:w-9

Date	Time	Title (min. if not 30) – Type	Action	From/To
10/81	9:00	Film(120) – FI	f	
10/81	9:30	Gimme a Break – SC	d	
10/81	10:00	Hill Street Blues(60) – CD	m	Fr:t-9-8/81
11/81	8:00	Harper Valley P.T.A. – SC	m	To:s-8
11/81	8:30	Lewis & Clark – SC	m	To:s-8:30
12/81	8:00	Fame(60) – DR	d	
8/82	9:00	Diff'rent Strokes – SC	m	To:s-8
8/82	9:30	Gimme a Break – SC	m	To:r-9
9/82	9:00	Cheers – SC	d	
9/82	9:00	Gimme a Break – SC	m	Fr:r-9:30
9/82	9:00	Gimme a Break – SC	m	To:s-9
9/82	9:30	Taxi – SC	m	Fr:r-9:30-6/82(a)
9/82	9:30	Teachers Only – SC	m	Fr:w-9:30-6/82
9/82	9:30	Teachers Only – SC	m	To:s-9:30-2/83
12/82	9:00	Cheers – SC	m	To:r-9:30
12/82	9:30	Taxi – SC	m	To:s-9:30
1/83	9:00	Gimme a Break – SC	m	Fr:s-9
1/83	9:30	Cheers – SC	m	Fr:r-9
8/83	8:00	Fame(60) – DR	c	
8/83	8:00	Gimme a Break – SC	m	Fr:r-9
8/83	8:30	Mama's Family – SC	m	Fr:s-9-6/83
8/83	9:00	Gimme a Break – SC	m	To:r-8
9/83	9:00	We Got It Made – SC	d	
12/83	8:30	Mama's Family – SC	m	To:s-9:30
12/83	9:00	Cheers – SC	m#	Fr:r-9:30
12/83	9:00	We Got It Made – SC	m	To:s-9
12/83	9:30	Buffalo Bill – SC	m	Fr:w-9:30-8/83
12/83	9:30	Cheers – SC	m	To:r-9
1/84	8:30	Family Ties – SC	m	Fr:w-9:30
4/84	9:30	Buffalo Bill – SC	c	
4/84	9:30	Duck Factory – SC	d	
5/84	9:30	Duck Factory – SC	m	To:w-9:30
5/84	9:30	Night Court – SC	d	
9/84	8:00	Cosby Show – SC	d#	
9/84	8:00	Gimme a Break – SC	m	To:s-8:30
3/86	9:30	All Is Forgiven – SC	d*	
3/86	9:30	All Is Forgiven – SC	m*	To:s-9:30
5/86	9:30	All Is Forgiven – SC	m*	Fr:s-9:30
6/86	9:30	All Is Forgiven – SC	m*	To:s-9:30-8/86
11/86	10:00	Hill Street Blues(60) – CD	m	To:t-9
12/86	10:00	L.A. Law(60) – LD	m#	Fr:f-10
3/87	9:30	Night Court – SC	m	To:w-9
4/87	9:30	Nothing in Common – SC	d	
5/87	9:30	Days & Nights of Molly Dodd – SC	d	
5/87	9:30	Nothing in Common – SC	c	
8/87	8:30	Family Ties – SC	m	To:n-8
8/87	9:30	Night Court – SC	m	Fr:w-9
8/87	9:30	Days & Nights of Molly Dodd – SC	m	To:r-9:30-3/88
9/87	8:30	A Different World – SC	d#	
3/88	9:30	Night Court – SC	m	To:f-9

Date	Time	Title (min. if not 30) — Type	Action	From/To
3/88	9:30	Days & Nights of Molly Dodd — SC	m	Fr:r-9:30-8/87
4/88	9:30	Days & Nights of Molly Dodd — SC	c	
5/88	9:30	Night Court — SC	m	Fr:f-9
8/88	9:30	Night Court — SC	m	To:w-9

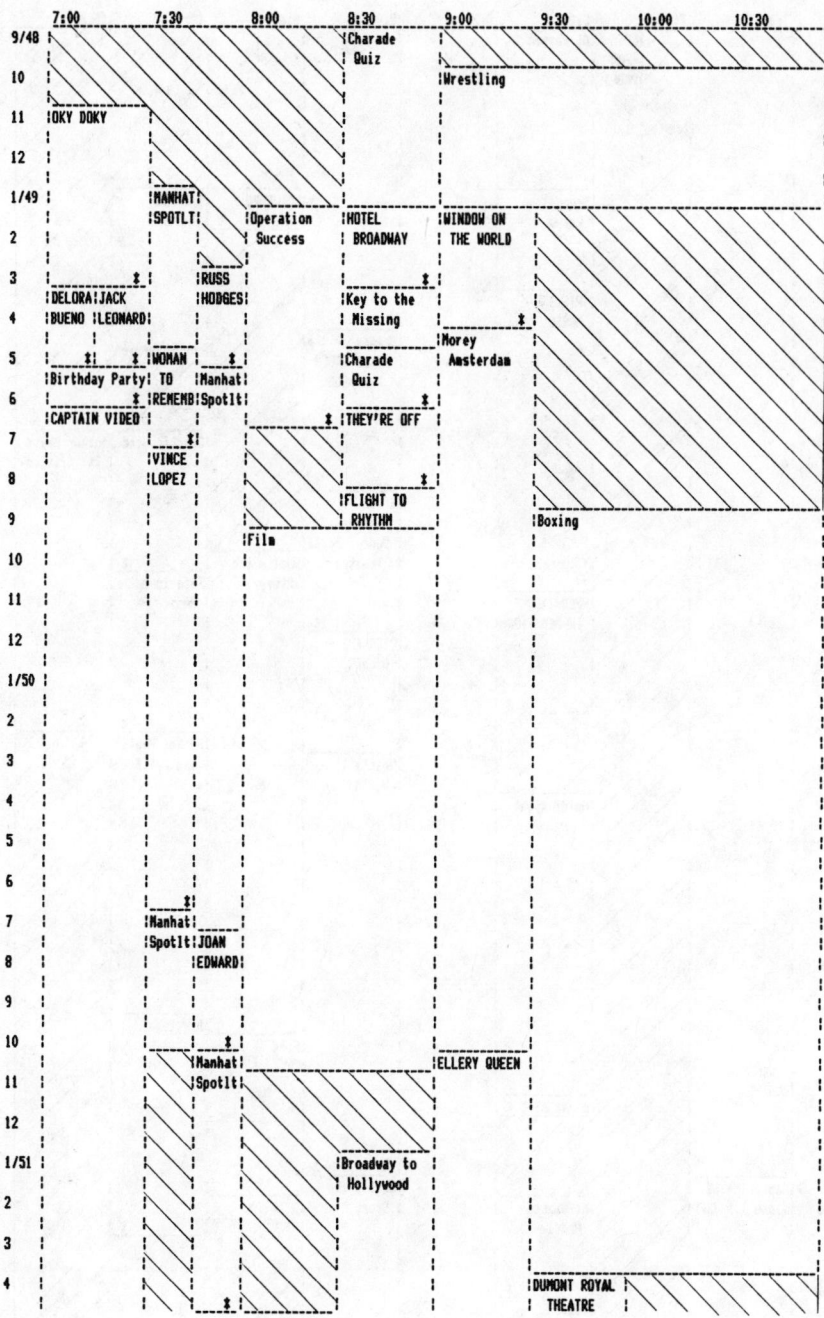

	7:00	7:30	8:00	8:30	9:00	9:30	10:00	10:30
9/48				Charade Quiz				
10					Wrestling			
11	OKY DOKY							
12								
1/49		MANHAT SPOTLT	Operation	HOTEL	WINDOW ON			
2			Success	BROADWAY	THE WORLD			
3		RUSS						
	DELORA JACK	HODGES		Key to the				
4	BUENO LEONARD			Missing				
					Morey			
5	WOMAN		Charade	Amsterdam				
	Birthday Party TO	Manhat	Quiz					
6	REMEMB Spotlt							
	CAPTAIN VIDEO		THEY'RE OFF					
7	VINCE							
8	LOPEZ							
			FLIGHT TO					
9		Film	RHYTHM	Boxing				
10								
11								
12								
1/50								
2								
3								
4								
5								
6								
7	Manhat							
	Spotlt JOAN							
8	EDWARD							
9								
10	Manhat	ELLERY QUEEN						
11	Spotlt							
12								
1/51		Broadway to						
2		Hollywood						
3								
4				DUMONT ROYAL THEATRE				

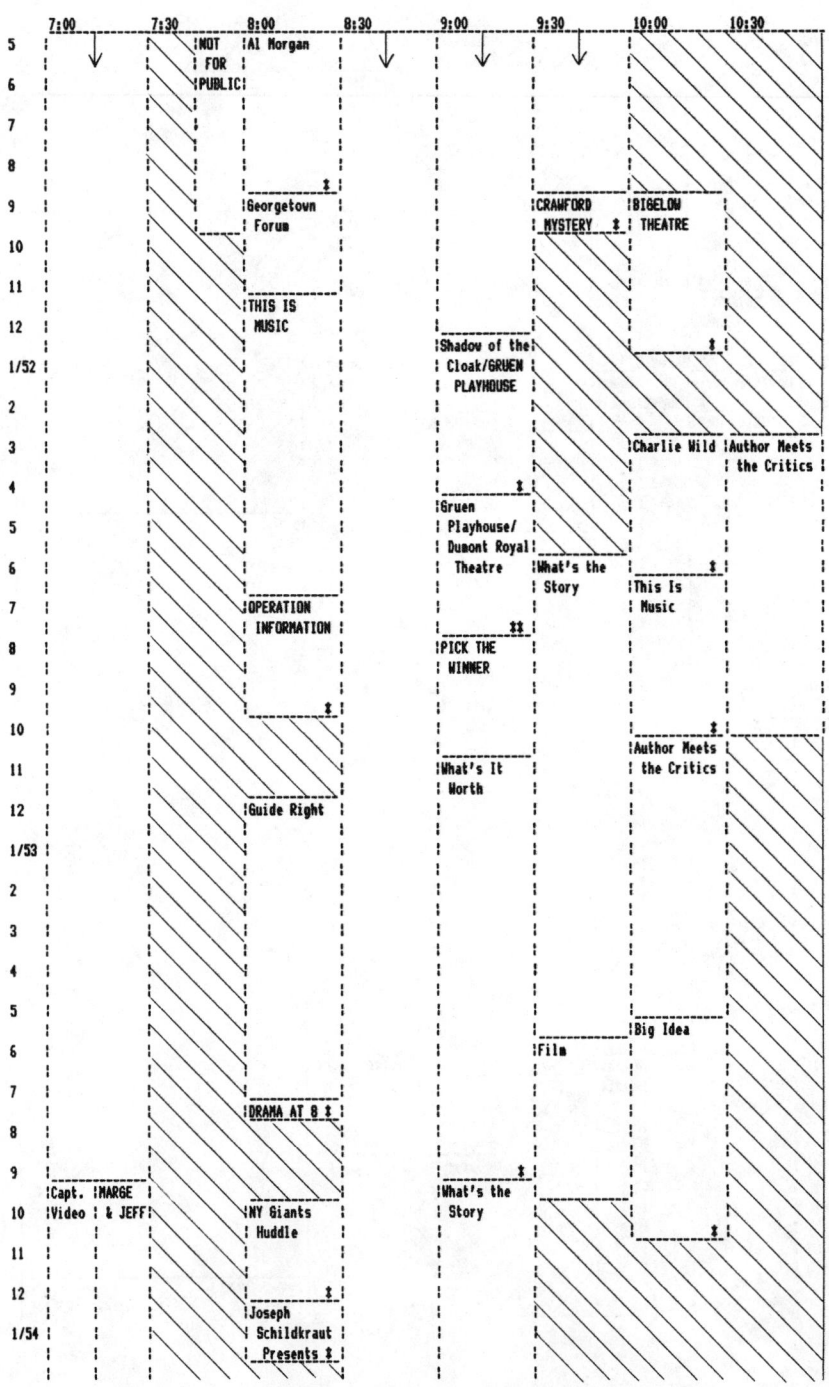

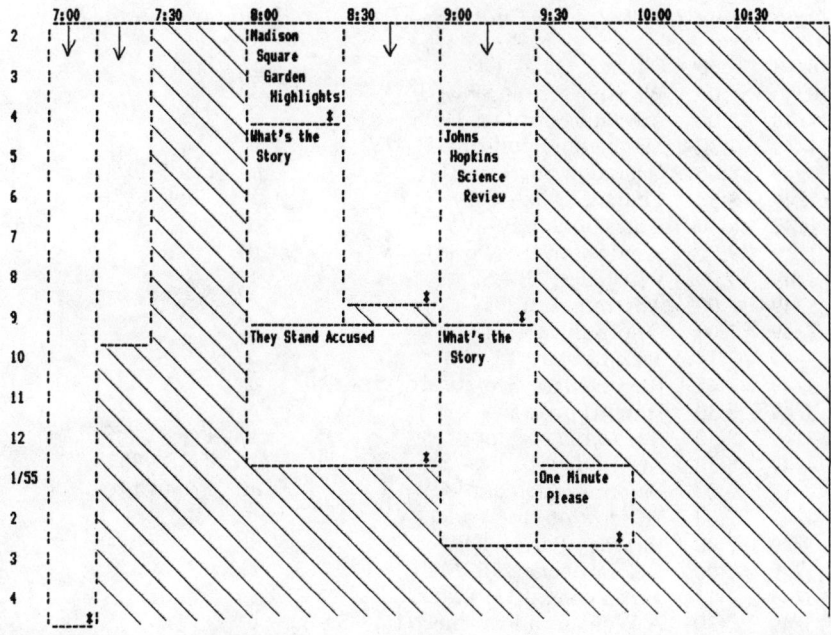

Date	Time	Title (min. if not 30) — Type	Action	From/To
8/48	8:30	Charade Quiz—QU	m	Fr:r-8
10/48	9:00	Wrestling(120)—SP	s	
11/48	7:00	Adventures of Oky Doky—KV	d	
1/49	7:30	Manhattan Spotlight(15)—IV	d	
1/49	8:00	Operation Success—IF	m	Fr:t-8-10/48
1/49	8:30	Charade Quiz—QU	m	To:w-8
1/49	8:30	Hotel Broadway—VY	d	
1/49	9:00	Window on the World—VY	d	
1/49	9:00	Wrestling(120)—SP	f	
3/49	7:00	Adventures of Oky Doky—KV	c	
3/49	7:00	Delora Bueno(15)—MU	d	
3/49	7:15	Jack Leonard(15)—MU	d	
3/49	7:45	Russ Hodges' Scoreboard(15)—SN	d	
3/49	8:30	Hotel Broadway—VY	c	
3/49	8:30	Key to the Missing—IV	m	Fr:f-7
4/49	8:30	Key to the Missing—IV	m	To:f-9:30
4/49	9:00	Morey Amsterdam—CV	m	Fr:m-var(c)
4/49	9:00	Window on the World—VY	c	
5/49	7:00	Birthday Party—KV	m	Fr:w-7-3/49
5/49	7:00	Delora Bueno(15)—MU	c	
5/49	7:15	Jack Leonard(15)—MU	c	
5/49	7:30	A Woman to Remember(15)—SL	d	
5/49	7:30	Manhattan Spotlight(15)—IV	m	To:r-7:45
5/49	7:45	Russ Hodges' Scoreboard(15)—SN	c	
5/49	7:45	Manhattan Spotlight(15)—IV	m	Fr:r-7:30
5/49	8:30	Charade Quiz—QU	m	Fr:w-8
6/49	7:00	Birthday Party—KV	c	
6/49	7:00	Captain Video & His Video Rangers —KV	d	
6/49	8:00	Operation Success—IF	c	
6/49	8:30	Charade Quiz—QU	c	
6/49	8:30	They're Off—QU	d	
7/49	7:30	Vincent Lopez(15)—MV	d	
7/49	7:30	A Woman to Remember(15)—SL	c	
8/49	8:00	Flight to Rhythm—MU	d	
8/49	8:30	They're Off—QU	c	
8/49	9:30	Boxing(90)—SP	s	
9/49	8:00	Flight to Rhythm—MU	c	
9/49	8:00	Film(60)—FI	s	
6/50	7:30	Vincent Lopez(15)—MV	c	
7/50	7:30	Manhattan Spotlight(15)—IV	m	Fr:r-7:45
7/50	7:45	Joan Edwards(15)—MU	d	
7/50	7:45	Manhattan Spotlight(15)—IV	m	To:r-7:30
10/50	7:30	Manhattan Spotlight(15)—IV	m	To:r-7:45
10/50	7:45	Joan Edwards(15)—MU	c	
10/50	7:45	Manhattan Spotlight(15)—IV	m	Fr:r-7:30
10/50	8:00	Film(60)—FI	f	
10/50	9:00	Adventures of Ellery Queen —CD	d	
10/50	9:00	Morey Amsterdam—CV	c	

Date	Time	Title (min. if not 30) — Type	Action	From/To
1/51	8:30	Broadway to Hollywood — Headline Club — QU	m	Fr:w-10
3/51	9:30	Boxing(90) — SP	f	
4/51	7:45	Manhattan Spotlight(15) — IV	c	
4/51	9:30	DuMont Royal Theatre — DA	d	
5/51	7:45	Not for Publication(15) — ND	d	
5/51	8:00	Al Morgan — MU	m	Fr:m-8:30-2/51
7/51	9:00	Down You Go — QU	m*	Fr:w-9
7/51	9:30	DuMont Royal Theatre — DA	m	To:r-9-4/52
8/51	8:00	Al Morgan — MU	c	
9/51	7:45	Not for Publication(15) — ND	m	To:f-8:30-12/51
9/51	8:00	Georgetown University Forum — DS	m	Fr:t-8
9/51	9:00	Down You Go — QU	m*	To:f-9
9/51	9:30	Crawford Mystery Theatre — QU	d	
9/51	9:30	Crawford Mystery Theatre — QU	c	
9/51	10:00	Bigelow Theatre — DA	d	
10/51	10:45	Football This Week(15) — SN	d	
11/51	8:00	Georgetown University Forum — DS	m	To:n-7-3/52
11/51	8:00	This Is Music — MU	d	
12/51	9:00	Adventures of Ellery Queen — CD	m	To:n-7:30(a)
12/51	9:00	Shadow of the Cloak — SD	m	Fr:w-9:30
12/51	10:00	Bigelow Theatre — DA	c	
12/51	10:45	Football This Week(15) — SN	c	
1/52	9:00	Gruen Playhouse — DA	d	
3/52	10:00	Charlie Wild, Private Detective — CD	m	Fr:t-8(a)
3/52	10:30	Author Meets the Critics — DS	m	Fr:w-8:30-9/50(a)
4/52	9:00	DuMont Royal Theatre — DA	m	Fr:r-9:30-7/51
4/52	9:00	Shadow of the Cloak — SD	c	
6/52	8:00	This Is Music — MU	m	To:r-10
6/52	9:00	DuMont Royal Theatre — DA	c	
6/52	9:30	What's the Story? — QU	m	Fr:t-10:30
6/52	10:00	Charlie Wild, Private Detective — CD	c	
6/52	10:00	This Is Music — MU	m	Fr:r-8
7/52	8:00	Operation Information — IS	d	
7/52	9:00	Gruen Playhouse — DA	c	
8/52	9:00	Pick the Winner — PO	d	
9/52	8:00	Operation Information — IS	c	
10/52	9:00	Pick the Winner — PO	m	To:m-10
10/52	10:00	Author Meets the Critics — DS	m	Fr:r-10:30
10/52	10:00	This Is Music — MU	c	
10/52	10:30	Author Meets the Critics — DS	m	To:r-10
11/52	9:00	What's It Worth? — QU	m	Fr:w-8:30
12/52	8:00	Guide Right — VY	m	Fr:m-9
5/53	9:30	What's the Story? — QU	m	To:w-7:30
5/53	10:00	Author Meets the Critics — DS	m	To:w-9:30
5/53	10:00	Big Idea — IN	m	Fr:m-9
6/53	9:30	Film — FI	s	
7/53	8:00	Drama at Eight — DA	d	

Date	Time	Title (min. if not 30) – Type	Action	From/To
7/53	8:00	Drama at Eight – DA	c	
7/53	8:00	Guide Right – VY	m	To:f-8:30
9/53	7:00	Captain Video & His Video Rangers – KV	m	To:m-f-7
9/53	7:00	Captain Video & His Video Rangers (15) – KV	m	Fr:m-f-7
9/53	7:15	Marge and Jeff(15) – SC	d	
9/53	9:00	What's It Worth? – QU	c	
9/53	9:00	What's the Story? – QU	m	Fr:n-10
9/53	9:30	Film – FI	f	
10/53	8:00	N.Y. Giants Quarterback Huddle – ST	m	Fr:w-7:30-12/52
10/53	10:00	Big Idea – IN	c	
12/53	8:00	Joseph Schildkraut Presents – DA	m	Fr:w-8:30
12/53	8:00	N.Y. Giants Quarterback Huddle – ST	c	
1/54	8:00	Joseph Schildkraut Presents – DA	c	
2/54	8:00	Madison Square Garden Highlights – ST	m	Fr:s-8:30(a)
4/54	8:00	Madison Square Garden Highlights – ST	c	
4/54	8:00	What's the Story? – QU	m	Fr:r-9
4/54	9:00	Johns Hopkins Science Review – IF	m	Fr:w-8
4/54	9:00	What's the Story? – QU	m	To:r-8
8/54	8:30	Broadway to Hollywood – Headline Club – QU	c	
9/54	7:15	Marge and Jeff(15) – SC	c	
9/54	8:00	They Stand Accused(60) – CR	m	Fr:n-10-10/52
9/54	8:00	What's the Story? – QU	m	To:r-9
9/54	9:00	Johns Hopkins Science Review – IF	c	
9/54	9:00	What's the Story? – QU	m	Fr:r-8
12/54	8:00	They Stand Accused(60) – CR	c	
1/55	9:30	One Minute Please – QU	m	Fr:f-9:30
2/55	9:00	What's the Story? – QU	m	To:w-8
2/55	9:30	One Minute Please – QU	c	
4/55	7:00	Captain Video & His Video Rangers (15) – KV	c	

Thursday Programming
Moves Summary

1948-49

ABC. *Series Premieres:* American Minstrels of 1949; Blind Date; Crusade in Europe; Fashion Story; Stop the Music; Volume One; Wren's Nest. *Key Programming Moves:* STOP THE MUSIC debuts on ABC; this quiz series was one of the more successful series on ABC during its early years; it stayed on the air until 6/56.

CBS. *Series Premieres:* 54th Street Revue; Manhattan Showcase.

NBC. *Series Premieres:* Bigelow Show; Gulf Road Show; Kukla, Fran & Ollie; Mohawk Showroom; R.F.D. America; Sportswoman of the Week; Theatre of the Mind.

DuMont. *Series Premieres:* Captain Video & His Video Rangers; Delora Bueno; Flight to Rhythm; Hotel Broadway; Jackie Leonard; Manhattan Spotlight; Oky Doky; Russ Hodges; They're Off; Vincent Lopez; Window on the World; A Woman to Remember. *Key Programming Moves:* In April, THE MOREY AMSTERDAM SHOW is moved to Thursday, 9–9:30; it stays in this slot until 10/50.

1949-50

ABC. *Series Premieres:* ABC Showcase; Art Ford; Arthur Murray Party; Boris Karloff; Holiday Hotel; Lone Ranger; The Ruggles. *Key Programming Moves:* THE LONE RANGER debuts in the 7:30–8 slot, where it stays for the next seven years; this highly successful series was one of the first westerns on television and many of the followers were patterned after THE LONE RANGER's simple formula of good vs. evil; prior to its debut it had been a successful radio series for over 15 years.

CBS. *Series Premieres:* Alan Young Show; Alkali Ike; Arthur Godfrey and His Ukulele; Beat the Clock; Ed Wynn Show; Escape; The Front Page;

Garry Moore Show; Glamour Go Round; Inside U.S.A.; Life with Snarky Parker; Romance; The Show Goes On; Three's Company; What's My Line. *Key Programming Moves:* WHAT'S MY LINE debuts in February, the beginning of a 17 year run on CBS; in April, it is moved to Wednesday; In April, THE ALAN YOUNG SHOW debuts in the 9–9:30 slot; this comedy variety series stayed in this slot until 3/52.

NBC. *Series Premieres:* Hollywood Premiere; Kay Kyser; Martin Kane, Private Eye; Melody, Harmony & Rhythm; Portrait of America; Van Camp's Little Show; Wayne King. *Key Programming Moves:* MARTIN KANE, PRIVATE EYE debuts in the 10–10:30 slot, where it stayed for its entire five year run; WAYNE KING debuts in the 10:30–11 slot; it stays on the air until 6/52.

DuMont. *Series Premieres:* Joan Edwards. *Key Programming Moves:* DuMont airs boxing in the 9:30–11 slot.

1950–51

ABC. *Series Premieres:* America in View; I Cover Times Square; Industries for America.

CBS. *Series Premieres:* Amos 'n' Andy; Big Town; Crime Photographer; George Burns & Gracie Allen Show; Nash Airflyte Theatre; Racket Squad; Steve Allen; Truth or Consequences. *Key Programming Moves:* GEORGE BURNS & GRACIE ALLEN SHOW debuts in November; seen every other week, it occupied the 8–8:30 time slot until 3/53; it was then moved to Monday where it lasted another five years; AMOS 'N' ANDY debuts; this highly successful radio series came to television in June; the series became the focal point of black groups that claimed it was demeaning to black people; responding to the pressure, CBS took the series off the air in 6/53; BIG TOWN debuts in the 9:30–10 slot, where it stays until 9/54; RACKET SQUAD debuts in June in the 10–10:30 time slot, which it occupied until 7/53.

NBC. *Series Premieres:* Ford Festival; Peter Lind Hayes; You Bet Your Life. *Key Programming Moves:* YOU BET YOUR LIFE debuts; this quiz program, hosted by Groucho Marx, began as a radio series and made the transition to television successfully; it occupied the 8–8:30 slot until 9/58, then it lasted another three years in the 10–10:30 slot.

DuMont. *Series Premieres:* Adventures of Ellery Queen; DuMont Royal Theatre; Not for Publication. *Key Programming Moves:* THE ADVENTURES OF ELLERY QUEEN debuts; it is fairly successful and lasts on DuMont until 12/51, when ABC acquired it; DuMont stopped airing boxing in 3/51; BROADWAY TO HOLLYWOOD is moved into the 8:30–9 slot in January; it stays in this slot until its cancellation in 8/54.

1951-52

ABC. *Series Premieres:* Chance of a Lifetime; A Date with Judy; Do's
& Don'ts; Herb Shriner; Mr. Arsenic. *Key Programming Moves:* In April,
STOP THE MUSIC is taken off the air; it will return in 9/54 on Tuesdays; In
April, ABC stops programming the 10-11 hour.

CBS. *Series Premieres:* Garry Moore Show; Hunter; I've Got a Secret;
Music Hall. *Key Programming Moves:* In March, THE ALAN YOUNG SHOW
is taken off the air; it will return in 2/53 on Sundays; In June, I'VE GOT A
SECRET debuts in the 10:30-11 slot, where it stays for one year, then moves
to Wednesday.

NBC. *Series Premieres:* Ask Me Another; Bob & Ray; Chesterfield
Presents; Dragnet; Gangbusters; Mayor of Hollywood; Mr. Peepers;
Young Charms. *Key Programming Moves:* DRAGNET debuts in 3/52; this
series was one of the most successful police shows ever; it was based on ac-
tual crimes from the Los Angeles Police Department's files; it stayed on
Thursday until 9/58, when it was moved to Tuesday; WAYNE KING is
cancelled in 6/52.

DuMont. *Series Premieres:* Bigelow Theatre; Crawford Mystery;
Gruen Playhouse; Operation Information; Pick the Winner; This Is
Music.

1952-53

ABC. *Series Premieres:* Greatest Man on Earth; Madison Square
Garden Highlights; Personality Puzzle; Perspective; Politics on Trial;
Quick as a Flash; Valentino. *Key Programming Moves:* In March, ABC
resumed programming the 10-11 slot.

CBS. *Series Premieres:* Biff Baker, U.S.A.; Four Star Playhouse;
Heaven for Betsy; Pentagon, U.S.A.; Take a Guess. *Key Programming
Moves:* In March, GEORGE BURNS & GRACIE ALLEN SHOW is moved to
Monday; In June, amid viewer protests, AMOS 'N' ANDY is cancelled; In
June, I'VE GOT A SECRET is moved to Wednesday; In July, RACKET SQUAD
is moved to Monday.

NBC. *Series Premieres:* Short, Short Dramas. *Key Programming
Moves:* NBC discontinues programming the 10:30-11 slot; it doesn't resume
programming this slot until 9/57.

DuMont. *Series Premieres:* Drama at 8. *Key Programming Moves:* By
the end of the season, DuMont had reduced its programming to 2½ hours
on Thursday.

1953–54

ABC. *Series Premieres:* Back That Fact; Gold Seal Playhouse; It's About Time; Kraft TV Theatre; Melody Tour; Open Hearing; Ray Bolger Show; Sammy Kaye. *Key Programming Moves:* In November, ABC discontinues programming the 10:30–11 slot; it doesn't resume programming this slot until 10/59.

CBS. *Series Premieres:* Philip Morris Playhouse; Public Defender; Ray Milland Show; Tell Tale Club; What Do You Have in Common?. *Key Programming Moves:* BIG TOWN is picked up by NBC at the end of the season and is moved to Wednesday.

NBC. *Series Premieres:* Justice; Marriage. *Key Programming Moves:* NBC's Thursday lineup is dominant, with three programs ranked in the top ten, DRAGNET (#2), YOU BET YOUR LIFE (#4), and FORD THEATRE (#8); MARTIN KANE, PRIVATE EYE is cancelled in 6/54 after a five year run.

DuMont. *Series Premieres:* Marge and Jeff. *Key Programming Moves:* DuMont stops programming after 9:30, leaving it with only two hours of Thursday night programming; BROADWAY TO HOLLYWOOD is cancelled at the end of the season.

1954–55

ABC. *Series Premieres:* Let's See; Mail Story; Pond's Theatre; Star Tonight.

CBS. *Series Premieres:* Climax; Johnny Carson Show; Shower of Stars; Upbeat. *Key Programming Moves:* CLIMAX debuts in the 8:30–9:30 slot; this successful dramatic anthology series stayed in this slot until its cancellation in 6/58; In July, THE BOB CUMMINGS SHOW is moved to Thursday in the 8–8:30 slot.

NBC. *Series Premieres:* Make the Connection. *Key Programming Moves:* LUX VIDEO THEATRE is moved to Thursday in the 10–10:30 slot, where it stayed until its cancellation in 9/57; NBC is still the leader on Thursday with DRAGNET and YOU BET YOUR LIFE among the four highest rated series on television.

DuMont. *Key Programming Moves:* In April, DuMont stops offering Thursday night programming.

1955–56

ABC. *Series Premieres:* Eddy Arnold; Outside, USA.

CBS. *Series Premieres:* Sgt. Preston of the Yukon; Wanted. *Key*

Programming Moves: SGT. PRESTON OF THE YUKON debuts; it occupies the 7:30–8 slot until its cancellation in 9/58; THE QUIZ KIDS is moved to Thursday in 1/56; it is cancelled at the end of the season.

NBC. *Series Premieres:* The People's Choice. *Key Programming Moves:* THE PEOPLE'S CHOICE debuts; the series lasts until 9/58; FORD THEATRE is moved to Wednesday at the end of the season; YOU BET YOUR LIFE (#7) and DRAGNET (#8) are ranked among the top ten rated series on television.

1956–57

ABC. *Series Premieres:* Air Time '57; Circus Time; Cowtown Rodeo; Telephone Time; Theatre Time; Wire Service. *Key Programming Moves:* After eight years, THE LONE RANGER is cancelled at the end of the season.

CBS. *Series Premieres:* Playhouse 90. *Key Programming Moves:* PLAYHOUSE 90 debuts; this 90 minute dramatic anthology series was the most respected of all the dramatic anthology series of the 1950s; it occupied the 9:30–11 slot until 1/60; THE BOB CUMMINGS SHOW is picked up by NBC and moved to Tuesday at the end of the season.

NBC. *Series Premieres:* Andy Williams & June Valli Show; Ford Show. *Key Programming Moves:* THE FORD SHOW debuts in the 9:30–10 slot, replacing FORD THEATRE; it lasts until 7/61; LUX VIDEO THEATRE is cancelled at the end of the season.

1957–58

ABC. *Series Premieres:* Confession; Make Me Laugh; Modern Science Theatre; O.S.S.; Pat Boone; The Real McCoys; Zorro. *Key Programming Moves:* ABC resumes programming from 10–10:30; THE REAL MCCOYS debuts in the 8:30–9 time slot, which it occupied until 9/62; PAT BOONE debuts in the 9–9:30 slot, where it stayed until its cancellation in 6/60.

CBS. *Series Premieres:* Harbourmaster; The Verdict Is Yours. *Key Programming Moves:* CLIMAX is cancelled in 6/58; SGT. PRESTON OF THE YUKON is cancelled at the end of the season.

NBC. *Series Premieres:* Music Bingo; Rosemary Clooney; Tic Tac Dough. *Key Programming Moves:* NBC resumes programming the 10:30–11 slot; THE PEOPLE'S CHOICE is cancelled and DRAGNET is moved to Tuesday at the end of the season.

1958-59

ABC. *Series Premieres:* Oh Boy; Rough Riders. *Key Programming Moves:* THE REAL McCOYS was the #8 rated series on television.

CBS. *Series Premieres:* Yancy Derringer. *Key Programming Moves:* After four years on Monday, DECEMBER BRIDE is moved to Thursday; it is taken off the air at the end of the season.

NBC. *Series Premieres:* Behind Closed Doors; Concentration; Ed Wynn; Laugh Line; The Lawless Years; Oldsmobile Theatre; Texas Rodeo; Too Young to Go Steady; Who Pays. *Key Programming Moves:* After six relatively stable years, NBC is constantly shuffling it's Thursday night lineup in 1958-59; none of the new combinations seems to work; YOU BET YOUR LIFE is moved into the 10-10:30 slot, where it stays until its cancellation in 9/61.

1959-60

ABC. *Series Premieres:* Take a Good Look; The Untouchables. *Key Programming Moves:* ABC resumes programming the 10:30-11 slot; THE UNTOUCHABLES debuts in the 9:30-10:30 slot; it lasts until 9/63; THE DONNA REED SHOW is moved to Thursday in the 8-8:30 slot; it stayed in this slot until 1/66; PAT BOONE is cancelled in June.

CBS. *Series Premieres:* Adventure Theatre; Betty Hutton Show; Big Party; Johnny Ringo; Playhouse of Stars; Revlon Revue. *Key Programming Moves:* In January, PLAYHOUSE 90 is taken off the air; it returned in the summer of 1961 on Tuesday.

NBC. *Series Premieres:* Johnny Staccato; Law of the Plainsman; Producer's Choice. *Key Programming Moves:* BAT MASTERSON is moved to Thursday; In April, NBC again discontinues programming the 10:30-11 slot.

1960-61

ABC. *Series Premieres:* Guestward Ho; My Three Sons. *Key Programming Moves:* ABC wins the night as THE REAL McCOYS (#5) and THE UNTOUCHABLES (#8) are both among the highest rated series on television; MY THREE SONS debuts; it stays on ABC's Thursday night schedule for five years.

CBS. *Series Premieres:* Angel; CBS Reports; Gunslinger; The Witness. *Key Programming Moves:* CBS REPORTS debuts in prime time, in the 10-11 slot.

NBC. *Series Premieres:* Great Ghost Tales; The Outlaws. *Key Programming Moves:* THE FORD SHOW, YOU BET YOUR LIFE and BAT MASTERSON are cancelled at the end of the season.

1961–62

ABC. *Series Premieres:* Margie. *Key Programming Moves:* THE ADVENTURES OF OZZIE & HARRIET is moved to Thursday, 7:30–8; this move, along with the debut of MARGIE, gave ABC a 2½ hour block of situation comedies; it continued to keep this block for two years; THE REAL MCCOYS is picked up by CBS at the end of the season; THE UNTOUCHABLES is moved to Tuesday at the end of the season.

CBS. *Series Premieres:* Bob Cummings; Frontier Circus; Investigators; Tell It to Groucho. *Key Programming Moves:* After NBC's cancellation of Groucho Marx's YOU BET YOUR LIFE, CBS tried another series with Groucho as the host, TELL IT TO GROUCHO; it lasted only five months; CBS REPORTS is moved to Wednesday at the end of the season.

NBC. *Series Premieres:* Dr. Kildare; Hazel. *Key Programming Moves:* NBC resumes programming the 10:30–11 slot; DR. KILDARE and HAZEL debut in the 8:30–10 time period; both series stayed in this period until 9/65.

1962–63

ABC. *Series Premieres:* McHale's Navy. *Key Programming Moves:* LEAVE IT TO BEAVER is moved to Thursday, 8:30–9; it is cancelled at the end of the season; MCHALE'S NAVY debuts in the 9:30–10 slot; at the end of the season, it is moved to Wednesday; THE ADVENTURES OF OZZIE & HARRIET is moved to Wednesday at the end of the season.

CBS. *Series Premieres:* Mr. Ed; The Nurses. *Key Programming Moves:* After five years on Saturday, PERRY MASON is moved to Thursday.

NBC. *Series Premieres:* Wide Country.

1963–64

ABC. *Series Premieres:* Edie Adams; Jimmy Dean Show; Sid Caesar Show.

CBS. *Key Programming Moves:* After four years on Friday,

RAWHIDE is moved to Thursday; at the end of the season it is returned to Friday.

NBC. *Series Premieres:* Kraft Suspense Theatre; Temple Houston.

1964–65

ABC. *Series Premieres:* Bewitched; Peyton Place. *Key Programming Moves:* BEWITCHED debuts; this sitcom becomes the second highest rated series on television; it stays on ABC's Thursday night schedule until 9/71; MY THREE SONS is picked up by CBS at the end of the season.

CBS. *Series Premieres:* Baileys of Balboa; The Munsters. *Key Programming Moves:* THE DEFENDERS is moved to Thursday, 10–11; it is cancelled at the end of the season; PERRY MASON moves to Sunday at the end of the season.

NBC. *Series Premieres:* Daniel Boone. *Key Programming Moves:* DANIEL BOONE debuts in the 7:30–8:30 slot; it occupied this slot until its cancellation in 9/70; DR. KILDARE is shortened to 30 minutes and is moved to Monday and Tuesday at the end of the season; HAZEL is picked up by CBS at the end of the season.

1965–66

ABC. *Series Premieres:* Baron; Batman; Double Life of Henry Phyfe; The Long Hot Summer; OK Crackerby. *Key Programming Moves:* THE DONNA REED SHOW is moved to Saturday in January; BATMAN (#5) and BEWITCHED (#7) were among the highest rated series on television.

CBS. *Key Programming Moves:* GILLIGAN'S ISLAND is moved to Thursday; at the end of the season it is moved to Monday; After five years on ABC, MY THREE SONS is picked up by CBS; it continued on CBS until 8/72; CBS airs films in the 9–11 slot, a practice it continued until 12/75.

NBC. *Series Premieres:* Dean Martin Show; Laredo; Mickie Finn's; Mona McCluskey. *Key Programming Moves:* THE DEAN MARTIN SHOW debuts in the 10–11 slot, which it occupied until 7/73.

1966–67

ABC. *Series Premieres:* Dating Game; Hawk; Tammy Grimes Show; That Girl. *Key Programming Moves:* THAT GIRL debuts; it lasts on ABC until 9/71.

CBS. *Series Premieres:* Coliseum; Jericho. *Key Programming Moves:* MY THREE SONS is moved to Saturday at the end of the season.

NBC. *Series Premieres:* Dragnet; Hero; Star Trek. *Key Programming Moves:* In January, NBC introduces a new DRAGNET; similar in format to the original, and also starring Jack Webb, this version had a fairly successful run for almost four years.

1967–68

ABC. *Series Premieres:* The Flying Nun; Good Company. *Key Programming Moves:* ABC discontinues programming the 10:30–11 slot; in January they also stopped programming from 10–10:30.

CBS. *Series Premieres:* Cimarron Strip. *Key Programming Moves:* CIMARRON STRIP debuts; this 90 minute western was an attempt to imitate the success of NBC's THE VIRGINIAN; is didn't achieve the success it hoped for, and was taken off the air at the end of the season.

NBC. *Series Premieres:* Ironside. *Key Programming Moves:* IRONSIDE debuts; this detective series brought Raymond Burr (formerly of the successful series, PERRY MASON) back to weekly television; the series maintained a place on NBC's Thursday night schedule until its cancellation in 1/75.

1968–69

ABC. *Series Premieres:* Journey to the Unknown; Ugliest Girl in Town; What's It All About, World?. *Key Programming Moves:* ABC resumes programming until 10:30; in February, they once again cut back to 7:30–10.

CBS. *Series Premieres:* Animal World; Blondie; Hawaii Five-O; The Queen & I. *Key Programming Moves:* HAWAII FIVE-O debuts, beginning a highly successful 12 year run; in December, it is moved to Wednesday night.

1969–70

ABC. *Series Premieres:* Paris 7000; Pat Paulsen. *Key Programming Moves:* THAT GIRL is moved to Friday at the end of the season.

CBS. *Series Premieres:* Jim Nabors Show. *Key Programming Moves:* After three successful years on Monday, FAMILY AFFAIR is moved into the lead-off slot on Thursday.

NBC. *Key Programming Moves:* DANIEL BOONE and DRAGNET are cancelled at the end of the season.

1970-71

ABC. *Series Premieres:* Alias Smith and Jones; Barefoot in the Park; The Immortal; Matt Lincoln; The Odd Couple. *Key Programming Moves:* ABC brought Neil Simon to prime time television by adapting two of his plays into weekly series, BAREFOOT IN THE PARK and THE ODD COUPLE; BAREFOOT IN THE PARK lasted only four months, while THE ODD COUPLE lasted for five years; After seven years on Thursday, ABC moved BE-WITCHED to Wednesday at the end of the season.

CBS. *Key Programming Moves:* FAMILY AFFAIR is cancelled at the end of the season.

NBC. *Series Premieres:* Flip Wilson Show; NBC Action Playhouse; Nancy. *Key Programming Moves:* THE FLIP WILSON SHOW debuts; it becomes the second highest rated series on television; IRONSIDE, helped by the enormous lead-in audience from THE FLIP WILSON SHOW becomes the fourth highest rated series on television.

1971-72

ABC. *Series Premieres:* Longstreet; Owen Marshall, Counselor at Law. *Key Programming Moves:* In compliance with the FCC's new Prime Time Access Rule, limiting networks to three hours of prime time programming, all three networks cut back to three hours (8-11) of prime time programming.

CBS. *Series Premieres:* Bearcats; Me and the Chimp. *Key Programming Moves:* In January, MY THREE SONS is moved to Thursday; it is cancelled at the end of the season, ending a 12 year run.

NBC. *Series Premieres:* Nichols. *Key Programming Moves:* THE FLIP WILSON SHOW is again the #2 rated series on television.

1972-73

ABC. *Series Premieres:* Assignment Vienna; Delphi Bureau; Jigsaw. *Key Programming Moves:* THE MOD SQUAD is moved to Thursday and is placed in the lead-off slot; it is cancelled at the end of the season; In January, THE STREETS OF SAN FRANCISCO is moved to Thursday; it continues on Thursday until its cancellation in 6/77.

CBS. *Series Premieres:* The Waltons. *Key Programming Moves:* THE WALTONS debuts in the 8-9 slot; this series competed successfully with NBC's highly rated FLIP WILSON SHOW and surpassed it in the ratings; THE WALTONS would occupy this time slot until 9/81, proving to be a strong lead-in for CBS' Thursday night lineup for almost eight years.

NBC. *Key Programming Moves:* After eight years on Thursday, THE DEAN MARTIN SHOW is moved to Friday at the end of the season.

1973–74

ABC. *Series Premieres:* Chopper One; Firehouse; Toma.

CBS. *Key Programming Moves:* THE WALTONS becomes the #2 rated series on television.

NBC. *Series Premieres:* Dean Martin Comedy World; Mac Davis Show; Music Country, USA; NBC Follies. *Key Programming Moves:* THE FLIP WILSON SHOW is cancelled at the end of the season.

1974–75

ABC. *Series Premieres:* Almost Anything Goes; Barney Miller; Harry-O; Karen; Paper Moon. *Key Programming Moves:* BARNEY MILLER debuts in January; it stays on ABC's Thursday night schedule until 9/82.

NBC. *Series Premieres:* Archer; Ben Vereen; Bob Crane Show; Gladys Knight & the Pips; Movin' On; Sierra; Sunshine. *Key Programming Moves:* NBC constantly shuffled its Thursday night lineup in an attempt to find the right combination; nothing clicked for them.

1975–76

ABC. *Series Premieres:* On the Rocks. *Key Programming Moves:* In January, WELCOME BACK, KOTTER is moved to Thursday, 8–8:30.

CBS. *Key Programming Moves:* In December, CBS stops airing films and begins airing weekly series; HAWAII FIVE-O and BARNABY JONES are moved into the 9–10 and 10–11 slots, respectively; CBS' Thursday lineup will stay intact for the next four years.

NBC. *Series Premieres:* Cop and the Kid; Ellery Queen; Fay; Grady; Medical Story; Montefuscos; Survival. *Key Programming Moves:* NBC's Thursday lineup is constantly changing; again, nothing works.

1976–77

ABC. *Series Premieres:* Nancy Walker Show; Three's Company; Tony Randall Show. *Key Programming Moves:* ABC airs two hour (8–10) block of sitcoms; it is fairly successful, finishing in a strong second place to CBS;

THREE'S COMPANY debuts in March; at the end of the season, it is moved to Tuesday where it stayed for seven successful years; THE STREETS OF SAN FRANCISCO is cancelled in 6/77.

NBC. *Series Premieres:* Best Sellers; Fantastic Journey; Gemini Man; Gibbsville. *Key Programming Moves:* For the third consecutive year NBC continually searched for a stable lineup without much success.

1977–78

ABC. *Series Premieres:* A.E.S. Hudson Street; Carter Country; Redd Foxx.

NBC. *Series Premieres:* Chips; Class of '65; Hanna Barbera Happy Hour; James at 15; Man from Atlantis; Rosetti and Ryan; Runaways. *Key Programming Moves:* For the fourth consecutive year, NBC constantly juggled its lineup; nothing seems to work for them.

1978–79

ABC. *Series Premieres:* Angie; Delta House; Doctor's Private Lives; Makin' It; Mork and Mindy. *Key Programming Moves:* MORK AND MINDY debuts; this comedy, starring the hip comedian Robin Williams, became the third highest rated series on television; it is moved to Sunday at the end of the season; ANGIE debuts in February; this sitcom became the #5 series on television; at the end of the season, it is moved to Tuesday; In May, 20/20 is moved to Thursday in the 10–11 slot, which it occupied until 9/87.

NBC. *Series Premieres:* David Cassidy; Harris and Company; Hizzonner; Kate Columbo; Lifeline; Little Women; Susan Anton; W.E.B; Whodunnit. *Key Programming Moves:* NBC shuffled its lineup for the fifth year in a row, though there was some stability with the placement of QUINCY in the 9–10 slot.

1979–80

ABC. *Series Premieres:* Benson; Nobody's Perfect; Semi-Tough. *Key Programming Moves:* As part of ABC's strategy of placing one of its successful series in the lead-off slot each night, LAVERNE & SHIRLEY was moved to Thursday, replacing MORK AND MINDY, which was moved to Sunday; the experiment failed, and by January LAVERNE & SHIRLEY was returned to its Tuesday slot and MORK AND MINDY was returned to its 8–8:30

slot on Thursday; neither series regained their large audiences; BENSON debuts; beginning a successful six year run; in July it was moved to Friday.

CBS. *Series Premieres:* Knot's Landing. *Key Programming Moves:* In December, HAWAII FIVE-O was moved to Tuesday; In December, KNOT'S LANDING debuts; this spin-off from the highly successful series DALLAS, became a fixture in CBS' Thursday lineup, where it still airs; BARNABY JONES was cancelled at the end of the season.

NBC. *Series Premieres:* Buck Rogers in the 25th Century; Games People Play; Skag. *Key Programming Moves:* In May, NBC replaces weekly series with films in the 9–11 slot.

1980–81

ABC. *Series Premieres:* Bosom Buddies; It's a Living. *Key Programming Moves:* In February, TAXI is moved to Thursday in the 9:30–10 slot; it stays there until 6/82 when it was dropped by ABC, only to be picked up by NBC the following season.

CBS. *Series Premieres:* Magnum, P.I. *Key Programming Moves:* MAGNUM, P.I. debuts, beginning a very successful seven year run on CBS.

1981–82

ABC. *Series Premieres:* Best of the West; 9 to 5; No Soap Radio; Police Squad. *Key Programming Moves:* MORK & MINDY and TAXI are cancelled in June, and BARNEY MILLER is cancelled at the end of the season; TAXI is picked up by NBC for the following season.

CBS. *Series Premieres:* Cagney & Lacey; Jessica Novak. *Key Programming Moves:* CAGNEY & LACEY debuts in March in a limited run; it returns the following season on Monday; In April, SIMON & SIMON is moved to Thursday 9–10, forming (with MAGNUM, P.I. and KNOT'S LANDING) a lineup that would continue for the next four years.

NBC. *Series Premieres:* Fame; Gimme a Break; Lewis & Clark. *Key Programming Moves:* DIFF'RENT STROKES (9–9:30) and HILL STREET BLUES (10–11) are moved to Thursday; DIFF'RENT STROKES is moved to Saturday at the end of the season, but HILL STREET BLUES stayed in the 10–11 slot until 12/87.

1982–83

ABC. *Series Premieres:* Amanda's; Condo; Eye on Hollywood; It Takes Two; Reggie; Star of the Family. *Key Programming Moves:* ABC constantly juggled the programming in the 8–9 slot; nothing worked well.

NBC. *Series Premieres:* Cheers. *Key Programming Moves:* CHEERS debuts; along with HILL STREET BLUES, it provided a strong foundation for NBC's Thursday night schedule.

1983–84

ABC. *Series Premieres:* Automan; It's Not Easy; Masquerade; Trauma Center. *Key Programming Moves:* ABC's 8–10 slots are in disarray, as the network constantly switches series and time slots; nothing catches on.

NBC. *Series Premieres:* Duck Factory; Night Court; We Got It Made. *Key Programming Moves:* In January, FAMILY TIES is moved to Thursday 8:30–9, and in May, NIGHT COURT debuts; NBC's Thursday night lineup is taking shape, and the following season it will finally overtake CBS.

1984–85

ABC. *Series Premieres:* Eye to Eye; Glitter; People Do the Craziest Things; Wildside; Who's the Boss. *Key Programming Moves:* WHO'S THE BOSS debuts; in October it is moved to Tuesday; In October, ABC abandons weekly series in favor of films in the 8–10 slot; they try weekly series again in April, but by June they are back to airing films.

NBC. *Series Premieres:* The Cosby Show. *Key Programming Moves:* THE COSBY SHOW debuts in the 8–8:30 slot; this series became the most successful series of the 1980s and one of the most successful of all time; it carried NBC from last place to being the top rated network; it completed a Thursday night lineup that will remain as one of the strongest in the history of prime time television.

1985–86

ABC. *Series Premieres:* Colbys; Lady Blue; Shadow Chasers.

CBS. *Series Premieres:* Bridges to Cross; The Price Is Right. *Key Programming Moves:* The success of NBC's lineup caused CBS to dismantle its own longstanding lineup; in April, MAGNUM, P.I. is moved to Saturday;

in June, SIMON & SIMON is moved to Tuesday; TRAPPER JOHN, MD is moved to Thursday in August and is cancelled at the end of the season.

NBC. *Key Programming Moves:* THE COSBY SHOW is the highest rated series on television; the rest of NBC's Thursday night lineup is also in the top ten.

1986–87

ABC. *Series Premieres:* Our World. *Key Programming Moves:* 20/20 is moved to Friday at the end of the season.

CBS. *Series Premieres:* Kay O'Brien; The Shell Game.

NBC. *Series Premieres:* Days & Nights of Molly Dodd; Nothing in Common. *Key Programming Moves:* NBC's four sitcoms, led by THE COSBY SHOW (#1) are again among the ten highest rated series on television; In December, HILL STREET BLUES is moved to Tuesday, and L.A. LAW is moved into the 10–11 slot; FAMILY TIES is moved to Sunday at the end of the season.

1987–88

ABC. *Series Premieres:* Hothouse; Probe.

CBS. *Series Premieres:* Tour of Duty; Wiseguy. *Key Programming Moves:* SIMON & SIMON is cancelled at the end of the season; CAGNEY & LACEY is moved to Thursday in July; it is cancelled at the end of the season.

NBC. *Series Premieres:* A Different World. *Key Programming Moves:* A DIFFERENT WORLD (a spin-off from THE COSBY SHOW) debuts in the slot following THE COSBY SHOW; the series is not received well by the critics, but because of its time slot it is a ratings success (the #2 rated series on television); THE COSBY SHOW is the #1 rated series on television for the third consecutive year; NIGHT COURT is moved to Wednesday at the end of the season.

Friday Night
September 1948 — August 1988

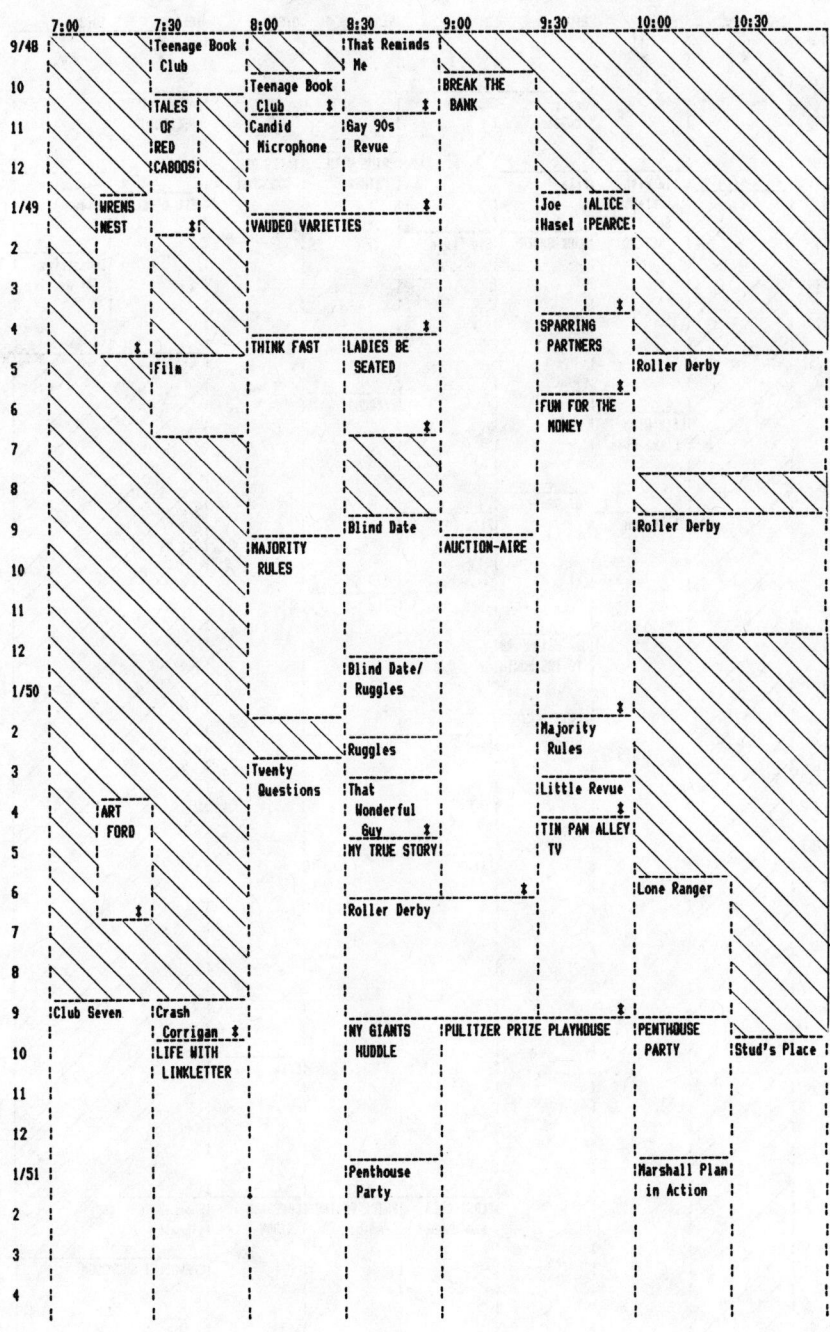

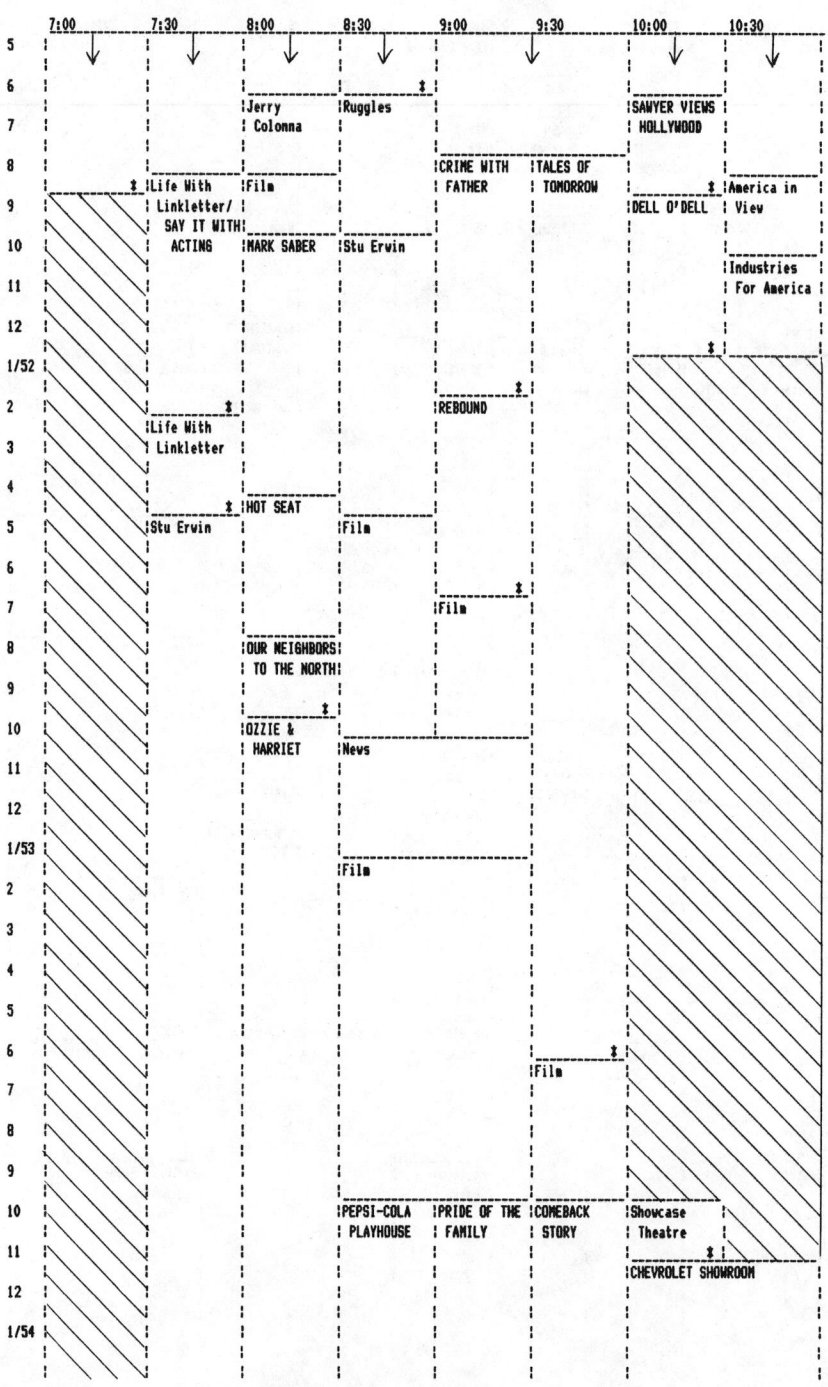

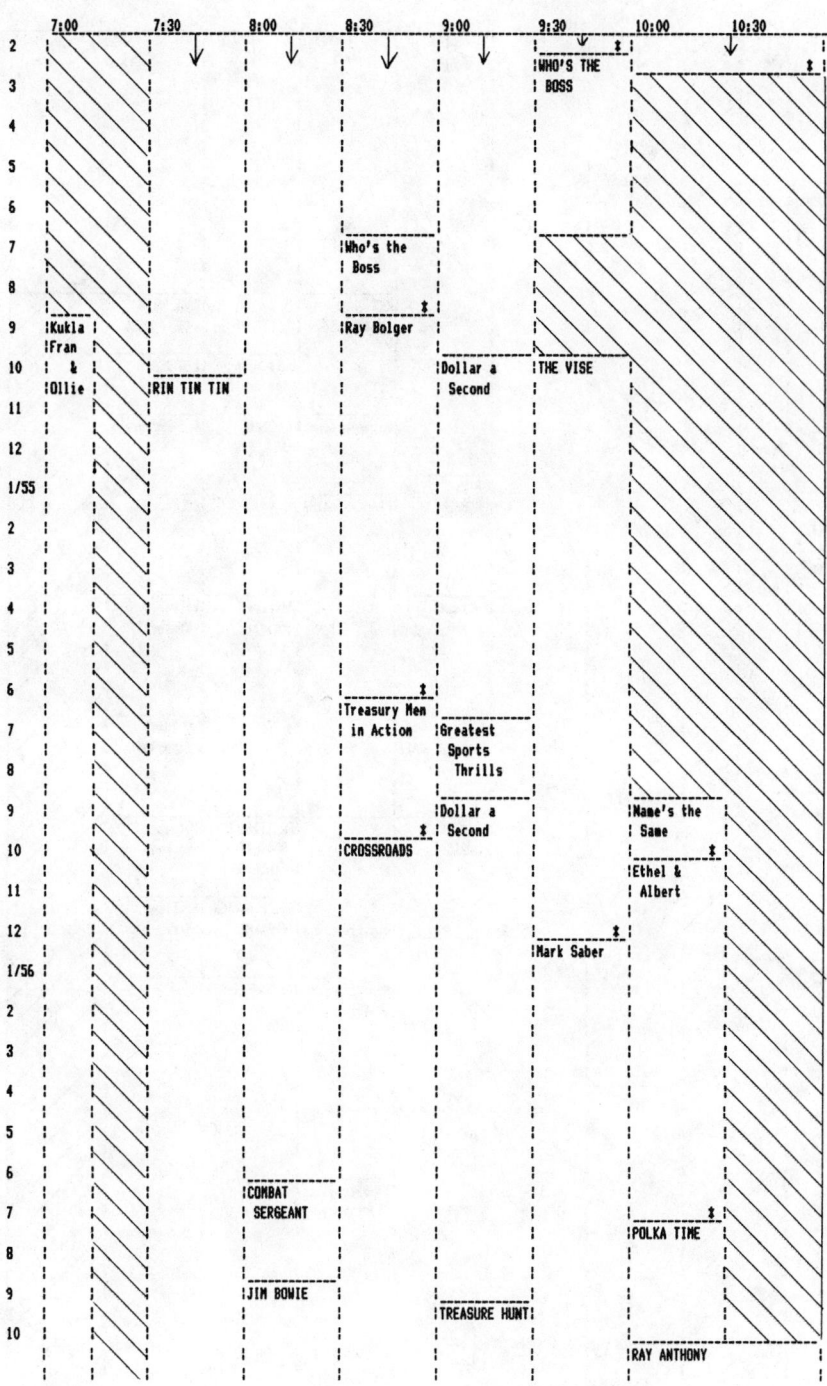

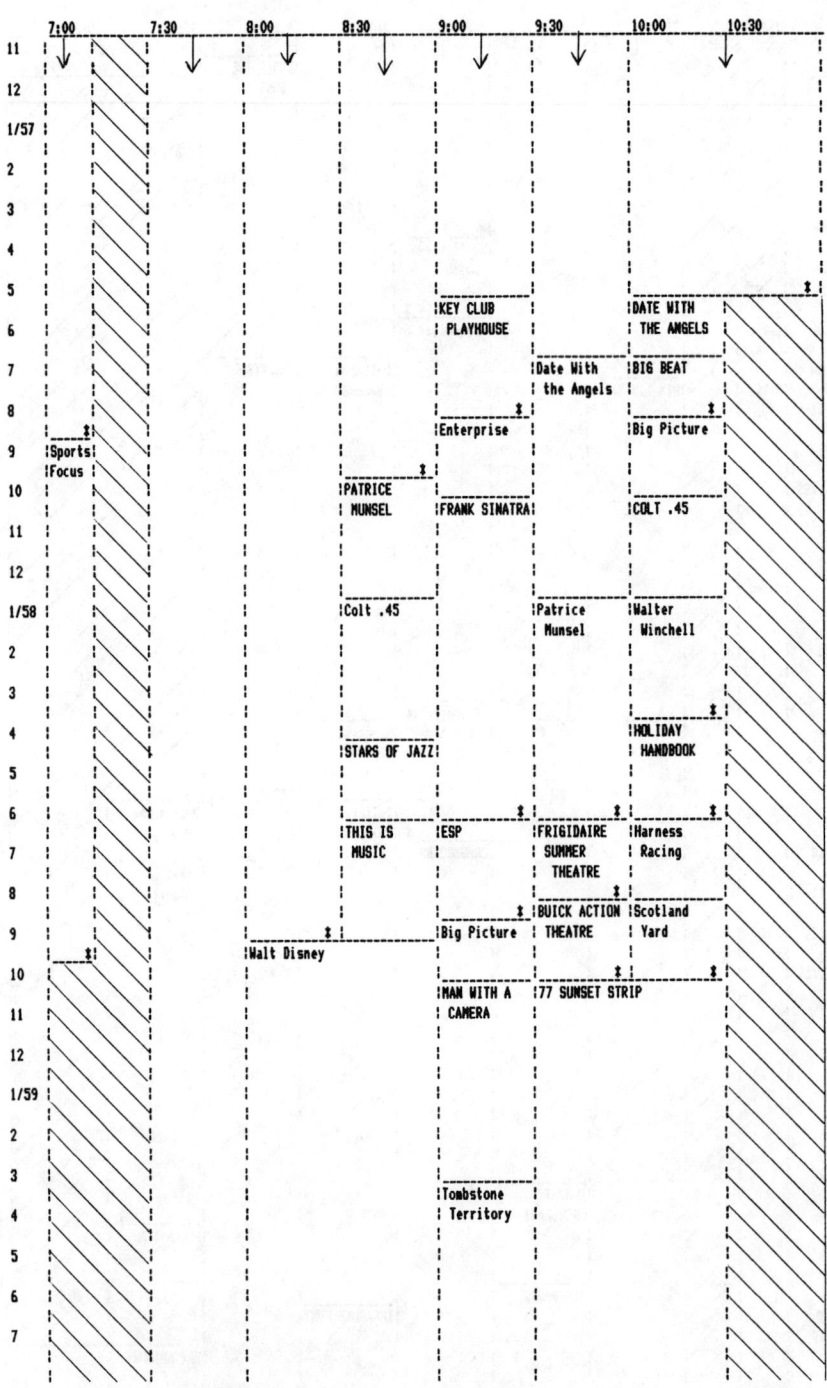

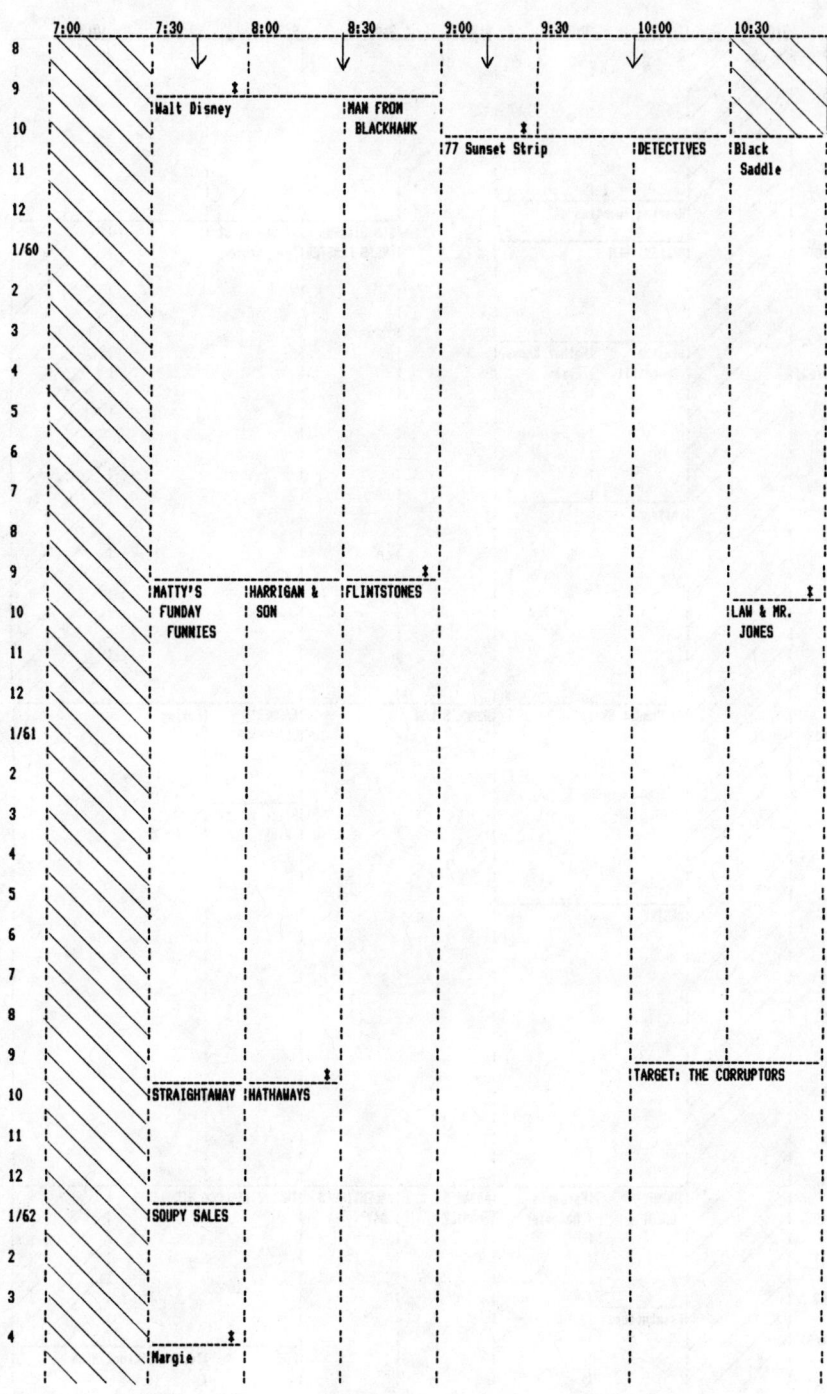

	7:00	7:30	8:00	8:30	9:00	9:30	10:00	10:30
8		↓		↓		↓		↓
9		Walt Disney		MAN FROM				
10				BLACKHAWK	77 Sunset Strip		DETECTIVES	Black
11								Saddle
12								
1/60								
2								
3								
4								
5								
6								
7								
8								
9		MATTY'S	HARRIGAN &	FLINTSTONES				
10		FUNDAY	SON					LAW & MR.
11		FUNNIES						JONES
12								
1/61								
2								
3								
4								
5								
6								
7								
8								
9							TARGET: THE CORRUPTORS	
10		STRAIGHTAWAY	HATHAWAYS					
11								
12								
1/62		SOUPY SALES						
2								
3								
4		Margie						

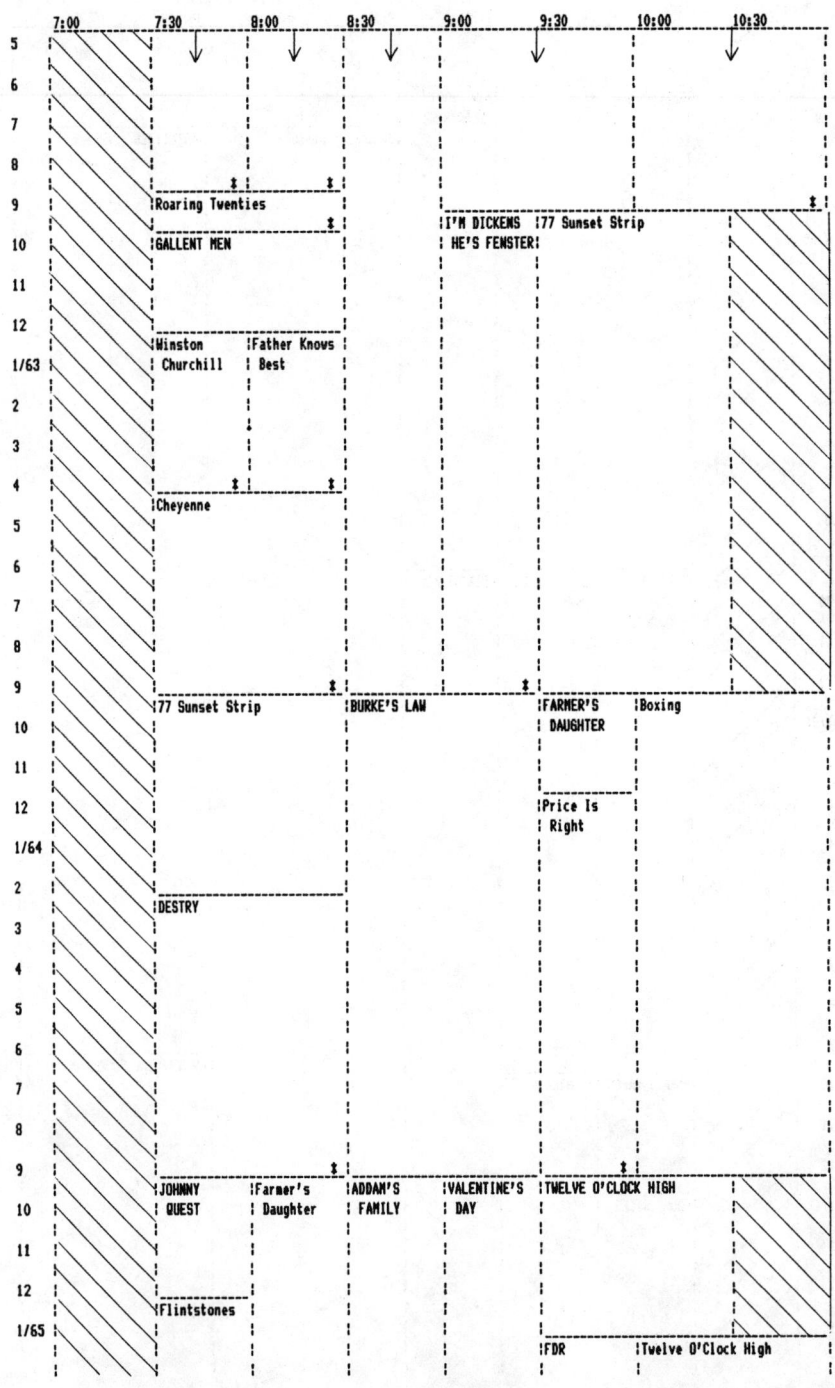

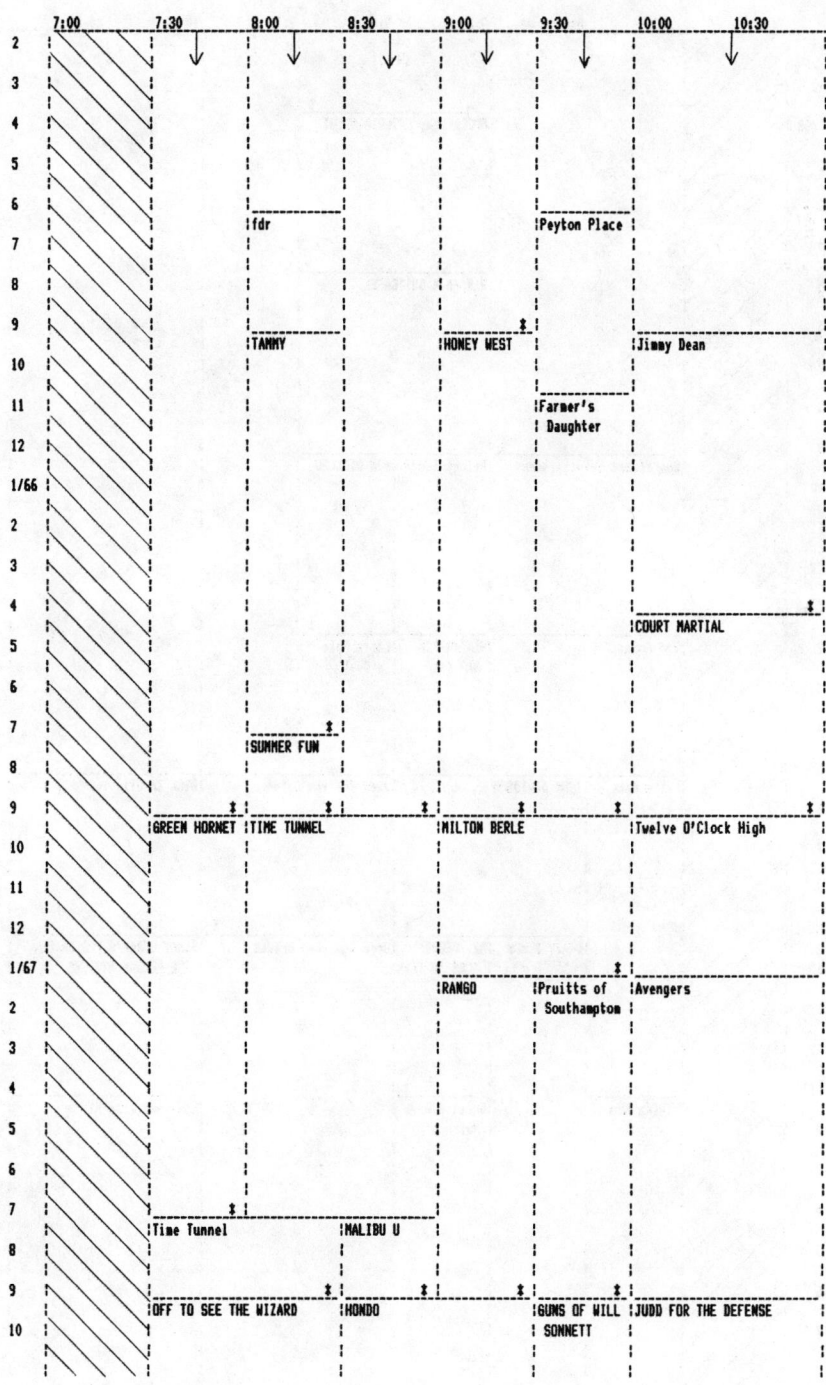

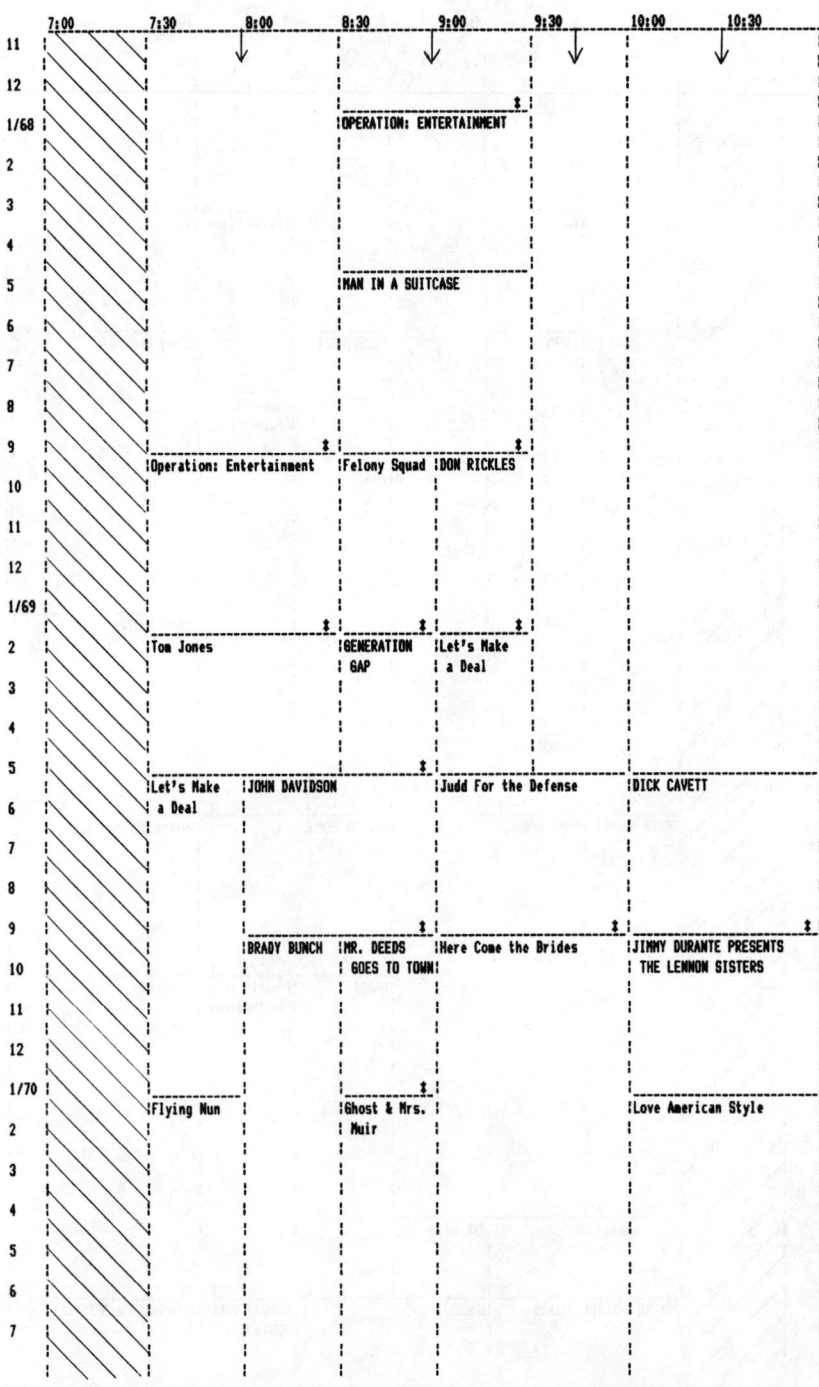

	7:00	7:30	8:00	8:30	9:00	9:30	10:00	10:30
8		↓	↓	↓		↓		↓
9		Brady Bunch	Nanny & the Professor	PARTRIDGE FAMILY	That Girl	Love American Style	Tom Jones	
10								
11								
12								
1/71						Odd Couple	Love American Style	
2								
9		Brady Bunch			Room 222			

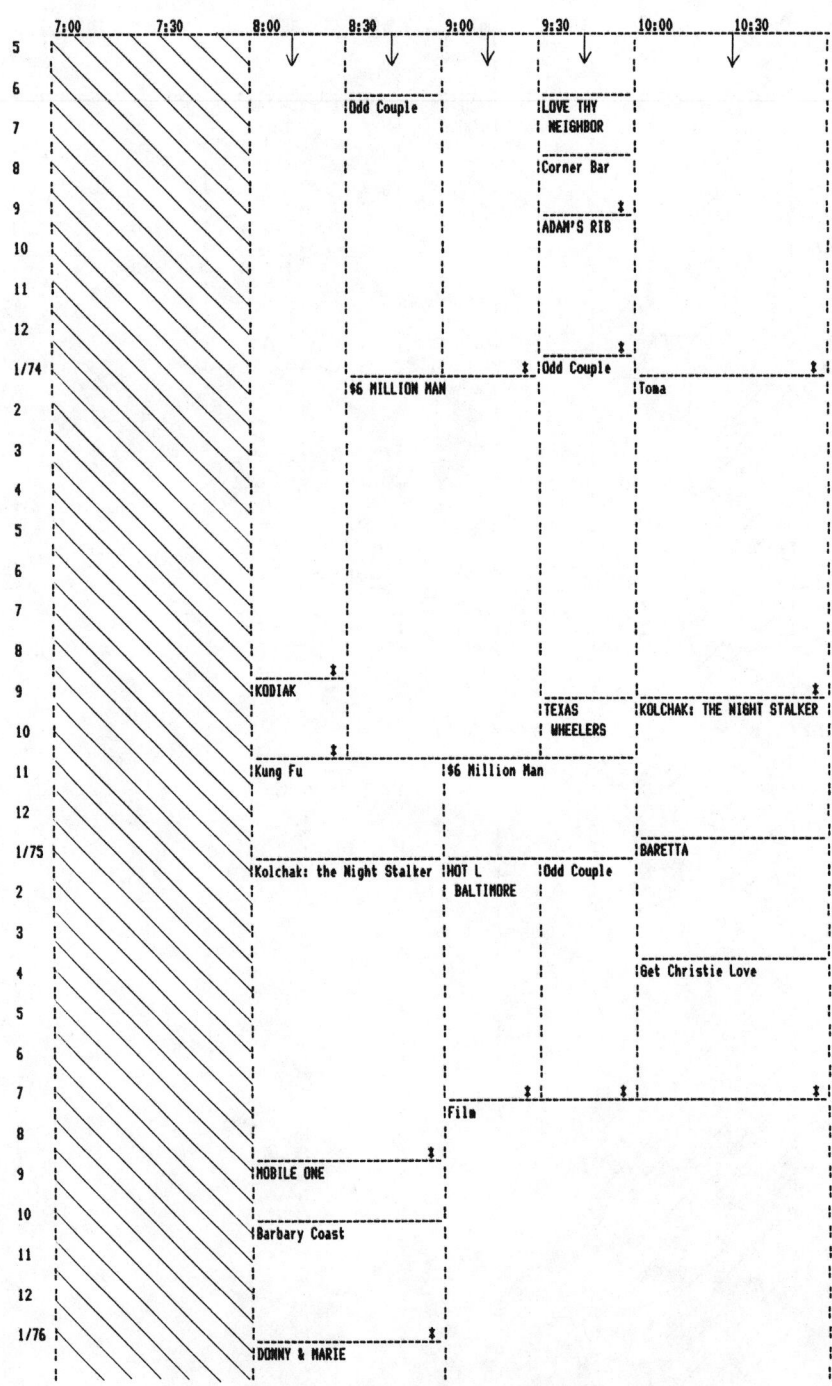

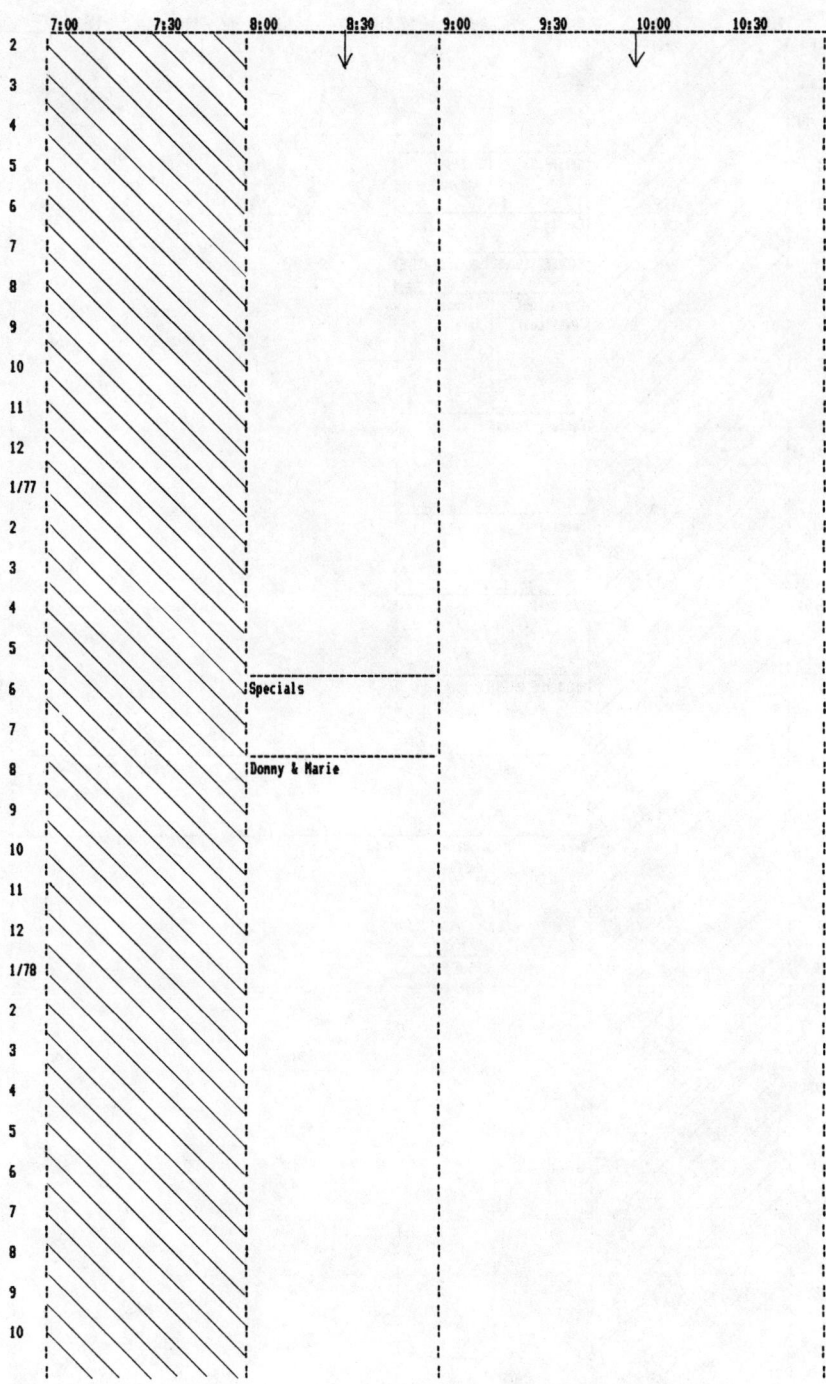

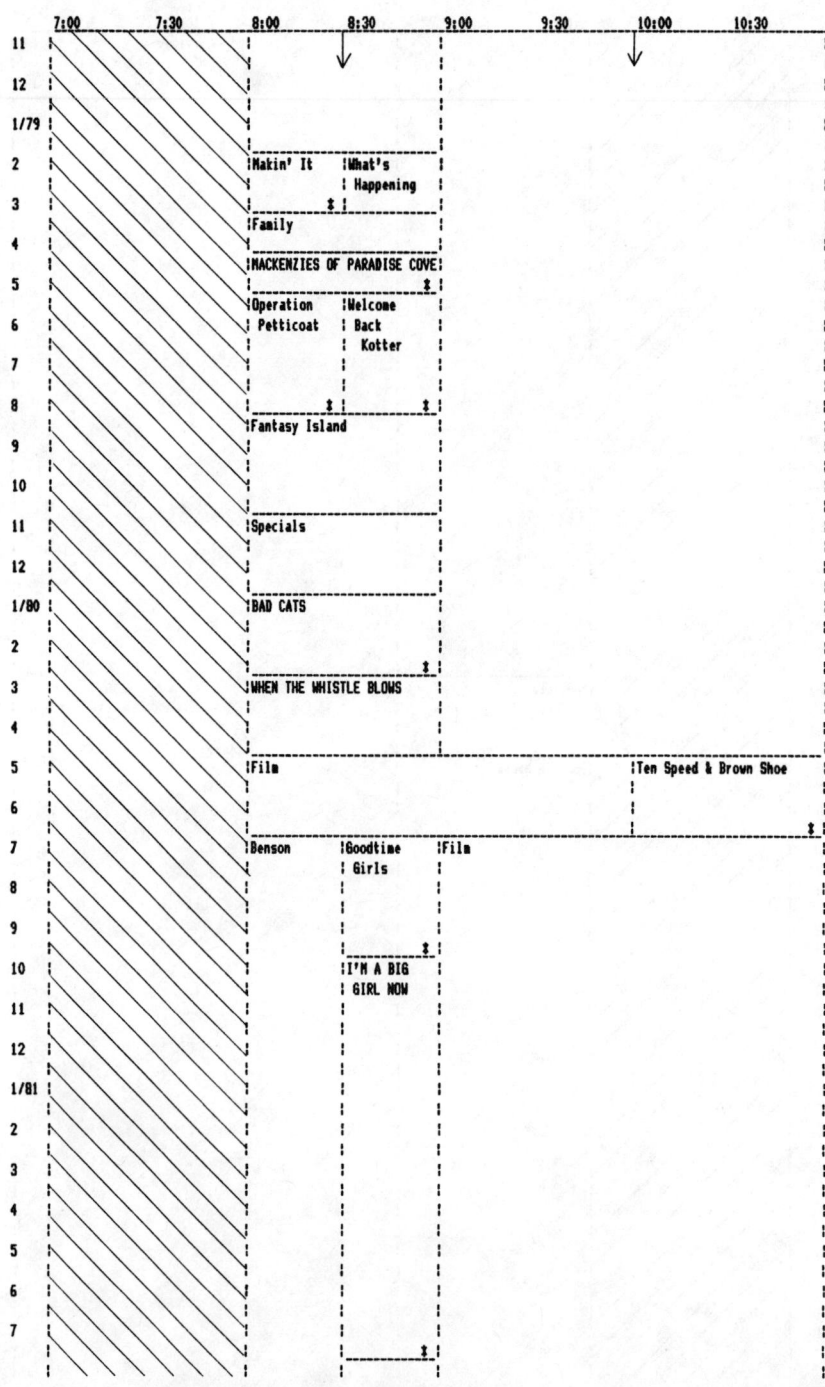

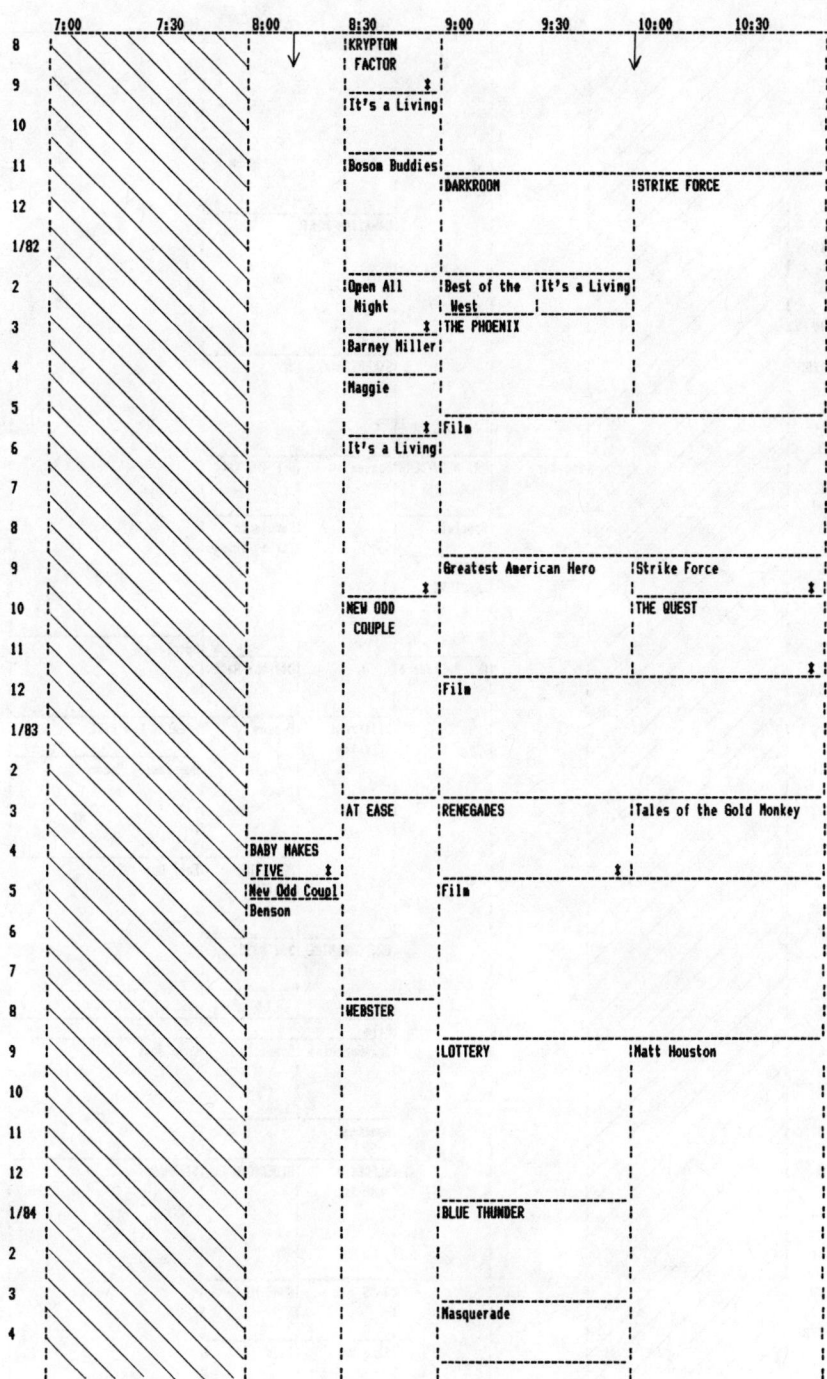

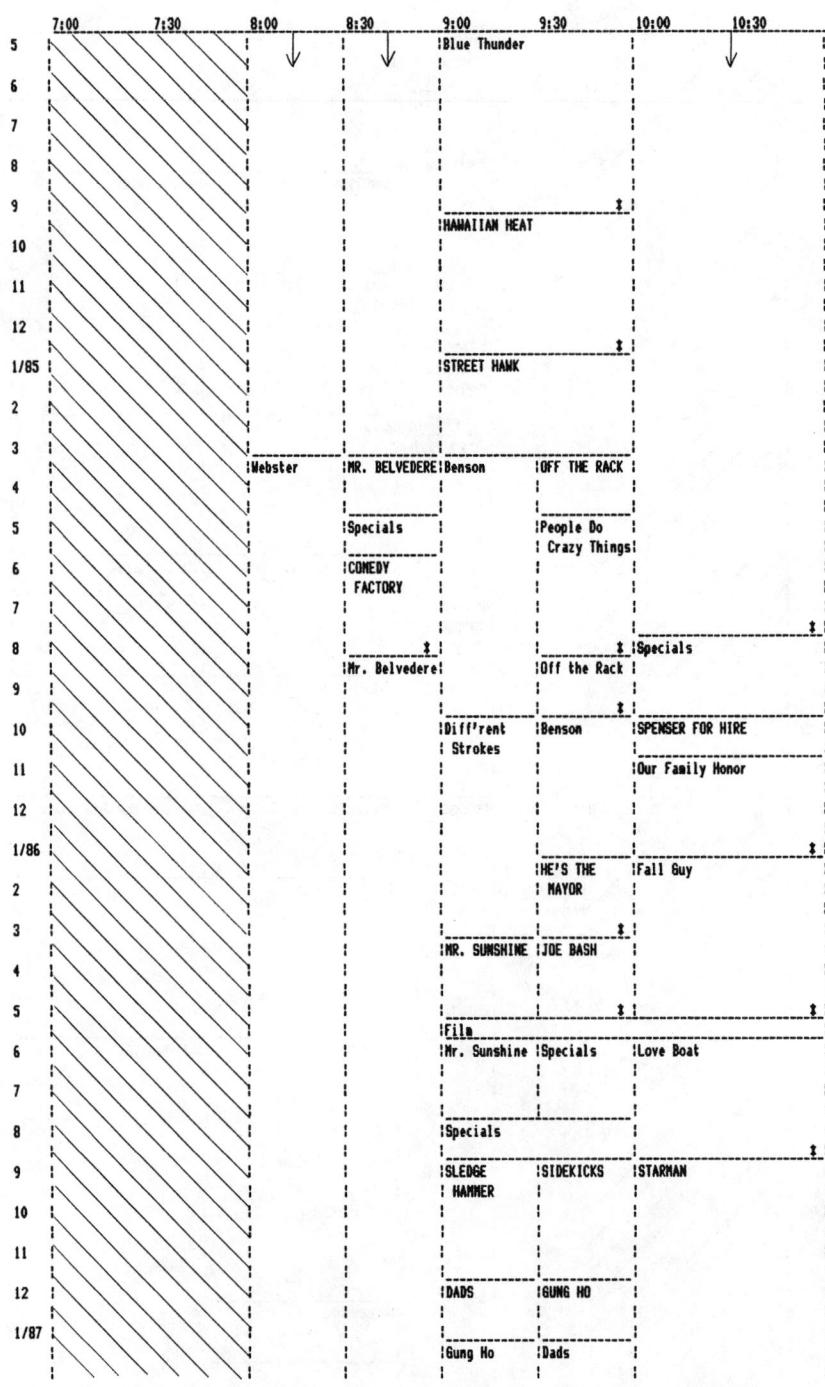

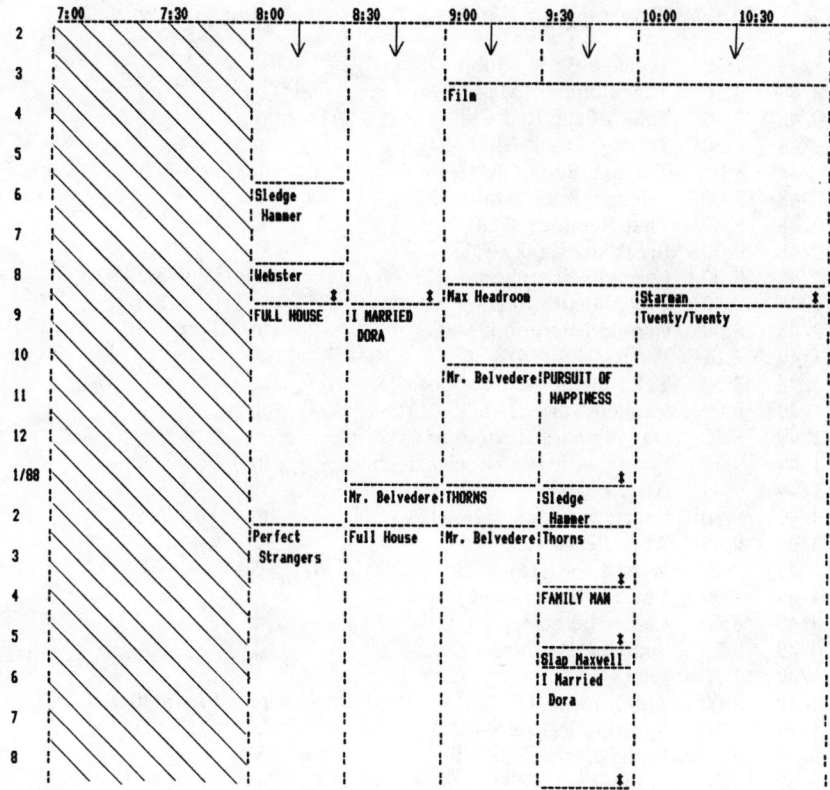

Date	Time	Title (min. if not 30) – Type	Action	From/To
8/48	7:30	Teenage Book Club – DS	d	
8/48	8:30	That Reminds Me – DS	d	
10/48	7:30	Tales of the Red Caboose(15) – AD	d	
10/48	7:30	Teenage Book Club – DS	m	To:f-8
10/48	8:00	Teenage Book Club – DS	m	Fr:f-7:30
10/48	8:00	Teenage Book Club – DS	c	
10/48	8:30	That Reminds Me – DS	c	
10/48	9:00	Break the Bank – QU	d	
11/48	8:00	Candid Microphone – CY	m	Fr:w-8:30
11/48	8:30	Gay Nineties Revue – MV	m	Fr:w-8
12/48	8:00	Candid Microphone – CY	m	To:n-7:30-5/49(n)
1/49	7:15	Wren's Nest(15) – SC	d	
1/49	7:30	Tales of the Red Caboose(15) – AD	c	
1/49	8:00	Vaudeo Varieties(60) – VY	d	
1/49	8:30	Gay Nineties Revue – MV	c	
1/49	9:30	Sports with Joe Hasel(15) – SN	m	Fr:s-7:30
1/49	9:45	Alice Pearce(15) – MV	d	
3/49	9:30	Sports with Joe Hasel(15) – SN	m	To:t-7:15
3/49	9:45	Alice Pearce(15) – MV	c	
4/49	7:15	Wren's Nest(15) – SC	c	
4/49	8:00	Vaudeo Varieties(60) – VY	c	
4/49	8:30	Ladies Be Seated – QU	d	
4/49	9:30	Sparring Partners – QU	d	
5/49	7:30	Film – FI	s	
5/49	8:00	Think Fast – QU	m	Fr:s-8:30
5/49	9:30	Sparring Partners – QU	c	
5/49	10:00	Roller Derby(60) – SP	s	
6/49	7:30	Film – FI	f	
6/49	8:30	Ladies Be Seated – QU	c	
6/49	9:30	Fun for the Money – QU	d	
7/49	10:00	Roller Derby(60) – SP	f	
9/49	8:00	Majority Rules – QU	d	
9/49	8:00	Think Fast – QU	m	To:n-8
9/49	8:30	Blind Date – QU	m	Fr:r-9:30
9/49	9:00	Auction-Aire – HS	d	
9/49	9:00	Break the Bank – QU	m	To:w-10(n)
9/49	10:00	Roller Derby(60) – SP	s	
11/49	10:00	Roller Derby(60) – SP	f	
12/49	8:30	The Ruggles – SC	m	Fr:r-9:30
1/50	8:00	Majority Rules – QU	m	To:f-9:30
1/50	9:30	Fun for the Money – QU	c	
2/50	8:30	Blind Date – QU	m	To:r-9
2/50	9:30	Majority Rules – QU	m	Fr:f-8
3/50	8:00	Twenty Questions – QU	m	Fr:s-8-12/49(n)
3/50	8:30	The Ruggles – SC	m	To:n-10
3/50	8:30	That Wonderful Guy – SC	m	Fr:w-9
3/50	9:30	Little Revue – MU	m	Fr:n-8:30
3/50	9:30	Majority Rules – QU	m	To:n-8:30
4/50	7:15	Art Ford on Broadway(15) – IV	d	
4/50	8:30	That Wonderful Guy – SC	c	

Date	Time	Title (min. if not 30) — Type	Action	From/To
4/50	9:30	Little Revue — MU	c	
4/50	9:30	Tin Pan Alley TV — MV	d	
5/50	8:30	My True Story — DA	d	
6/50	7:15	Art Ford on Broadway(15) — IV	c	
6/50	8:00	My True Story — DA	m*	Fr:f-8:30
6/50	8:30	My True Story — DA	m	To:f-8
6/50	8:30	Roller Derby(60) — SP	s	
6/50	9:00	Auction-Aire — HS	c	
6/50	10:00	Lone Ranger — WE	s	
9/50	7:00	Club Seven — MV	m	Fr:r-10:30-3/49
9/50	7:30	Crash Corrigan's Ranch — KV	m*	Fr:s-7
9/50	7:30	Crash Corrigan's Ranch — KV	c*	
9/50	8:00	My True Story — DA	c*	
9/50	8:30	N.Y. Giants Quarterback Huddle — ST	d	
9/50	8:30	Roller Derby(60) — SP	f	
9/50	9:00	Pulitzer Prize Playhouse(60) — DA	d	
9/50	9:30	Tin Pan Alley TV — MV	c	
9/50	10:00	Lone Ranger — WE	f	
9/50	10:00	Penthouse Party — VY	d	
10/50	7:30	Life with Linkletter — QU	d	
10/50	10:30	Stud's Place — VY	m	Fr:r-8:30-8/50(n)
12/50	7:00	Andy and Della Russell(5) — MU	d	
12/50	8:30	N.Y. Giants Quarterback Huddle — ST	m	To:w-7:30-9/52(d)
12/50	10:00	Penthouse Party — VY	m	To:f-8:30
1/51	8:30	Penthouse Party — VY	m	Fr:f-10
1/51	10:00	Marshall Plan in Action — DO	s	
6/51	7:00	Andy and Della Russell(5) — MU	c	
6/51	8:00	Jerry Colonna — CV	m	Fr:m-8
6/51	8:00	Twenty Questions — QU	m	To:f-8(d)
6/51	8:30	Penthouse Party — VY	c	
6/51	8:30	The Ruggles — SC	m	Fr:w-8
6/51	10:00	Marshall Plan in Action — DO	f	
6/51	10:00	Sawyer Views Hollywood — MV	d	
7/51	9:00	Pulitzer Prize Playhouse(60) — DA	m	To:w-10-12/51
8/51	7:00	Club Seven — MV	c	
8/51	7:30	Say It with Acting — QU	d	
8/51	8:00	Film — FI	s	
8/51	8:00	Jerry Colonna — CV	m	To:r-10
8/51	9:00	Crime with Father — CD	d	
8/51	9:30	Tales of Tomorrow — FA	d	
8/51	10:00	Sawyer Views Hollywood — MV	c	
8/51	10:30	America in View — TR	m	Fr:r-10:30
8/51	10:30	Stud's Place — VY	m	To:m-10:30
9/51	8:00	Film — FI	f	
9/51	8:30	The Ruggles — SC	m	To:w-9-1/52
9/51	10:00	Dell O'Dell — VY	d	
10/51	8:00	Mark Saber — CD	d	
10/51	8:30	Stu Erwin — SC	m	Fr:s-7:30

Date	Time	Title (min. if not 30)—Type	Action	From/To
10/51	10:30	America in View—TR	m	To:s-10:45-1/52
10/51	10:30	Industries for America—DO	m	Fr:n-10
12/51	10:00	Dell O'Dell—VY	c	
12/51	10:30	Industries for America—DO	m	To:r-10:15-2/52
1/52	9:00	Crime with Father—CD	c	
2/52	7:30	Say It with Acting—QU	c	
2/52	9:00	Rebound—DA	d	
4/52	7:30	Life with Linkletter—QU	c	
4/52	8:00	The Hot Seat—IV	d	
4/52	8:00	Mark Saber—CD	m	To:w-9:30
4/52	8:30	Stu Erwin—SC	m	To:f-7:30
5/52	7:30	Stu Erwin—SC	m	Fr:f-8:30
5/52	8:30	Film—FI	s	
6/52	9:00	Rebound—DA	c	
7/52	8:00	The Hot Seat—IV	m	To:n-7:30-10/52
7/52	9:00	Film—FI	s	
8/52	8:00	Our Neighbors to the North—DO	d	
9/52	8:00	Our Neighbors to the North—DO	c	
10/52	8:00	Adventures of Ozzie & Harriet—SC	d	
10/52	8:30	Film—FI	f	
10/52	8:30	News(60)—NW	s	
10/52	9:00	Film—FI	f	
1/53	8:30	Film(60)—FI	s	
1/53	8:30	News(60)—NW	f	
6/53	9:30	Film—FI	s	
6/53	9:30	Tales of Tomorrow—FA	c	
7/53	8:00	Summer Theatre—DA	d*	
9/53	8:00	Summer Theatre—DA	c*	
9/53	8:30	Film(60)—FI	f	
9/53	9:30	Film—FI	f	
10/53	8:30	Pepsi-Cola Playhouse—DA	d	
10/53	9:00	Pride of the Family—SC	d	
10/53	9:30	Comeback Story—IV	d	
10/53	10:00	Showcase Theater—DA	m	Fr:s-8
11/53	10:00	Showcase Theater—DA	c	
11/53	10:00	Your Chevrolet Showroom(60)—VY	d	
2/54	9:30	Comeback Story—IV	c	
2/54	9:30	Who's the Boss?—QU	d	
2/54	10:00	Your Chevrolet Showroom(60)—VY	c	
6/54	8:30	Pepsi-Cola Playhouse—DA	m	To:n-7:30
6/54	9:30	Who's the Boss?—QU	m	To:f-8:30
7/54	8:30	Who's the Boss?—QU	m	Fr:f-9:30
8/54	8:30	Who's the Boss?—QU	c	
9/54	7:00	Kukla, Fran & Ollie(15)—KV	m	Fr:m-f-7-6/52(n)
9/54	8:30	Ray Bolger—SC	m	Fr:r-8:30-7/54
9/54	9:00	Pride of the Family—SC	m	To:n-7-6/55(c)
10/54	7:30	Adventures of Rin Tin Tin—WE	d	
10/54	7:30	Stu Erwin—SC	m	To:w-8:30
10/54	9:00	Dollar a Second—QU	m	Fr:n-10-8/54(n)
10/54	9:30	The Vise—SA	d	

Date	Time	Title (min. if not 30) — Type	Action	From/To
6/55	8:30	Ray Bolger — SC	c	
6/55	8:30	Treasury Men in Action — CD	m	Fr:r-8:30
6/55	9:00	Dollar a Second — QU	m	To:t-9:30(n)
7/55	7:00	Soupy Sales(15) — KV	d*	
7/55	8:00	Greatest Sports Thrills — SH	m*	Fr:s-8:30-9/54
7/55	9:00	Greatest Sports Thrills — SH	m	Fr:s-8:30-9/54
8/55	7:00	Soupy Sales(15) — KV	c*	
8/55	9:00	Greatest Sports Thrills — SH	m	To:r-10-11/55
9/55	8:00	Greatest Sports Thrills — SH	m*	To:r-10-11/55
9/55	8:30	Treasury Men in Action — CD	c	
9/55	9:00	Dollar a Second — QU	m	Fr:t-9:30(n)
9/55	10:00	The Name's the Same — QU	m	Fr:t-10
10/55	8:30	Crossroads — DA	d	
10/55	10:00	Ethel and Albert — SC	m	Fr:m-9:30
10/55	10:00	The Name's the Same — QU	c	
12/55	9:30	Mark Saber — CD	m	Fr:w-7:30-6/54
12/55	9:30	The Vise — SA	c	
6/56	8:00	Adventures of Ozzie & Harriet — SC	m	To:w-9-10/56
6/56	8:00	Combat Sergeant — WD	d	
7/56	7:00	Jack Drees(15) — SN	d*	
7/56	10:00	Ethel and Albert — SC	c	
7/56	10:00	Polka Time — MU	d	
8/56	7:00	Jack Drees(15) — SN	c*	
8/56	8:00	Combat Sergeant — WD	m	To:r-9
9/56	8:00	Adventures of Jim Bowie — WE	d	
9/56	9:00	Dollar a Second — QU	m	To:s-9:30-6/57(n)
9/56	9:00	Treasure Hunt — QU	d	
10/56	10:00	Polka Time — MU	m	To:t-10
10/56	10:00	Ray Anthony(60) — MV	d	
5/57	9:00	Key Club Playhouse — DA	d	
5/57	9:00	Treasure Hunt — QU	m	To:t-7:30-12/57(n)
5/57	10:00	Date with the Angels — SC	d	
5/57	10:00	Ray Anthony — MV	c	
6/57	7:00	Sports Focus(15) — SN	d*	
6/57	9:30	Mark Saber — CD	m	To:f-7:30-9/57(n)
6/57	10:00	Date with the Angels — SC	m	To:f-9:30
7/57	7:00	Sports Focus(15) — SN	m*	To:m-f-7-9/57
7/57	9:30	Date with the Angels — SC	m	Fr:f-10
7/57	10:00	Big Beat — MU	d	
8/57	7:00	Kukla, Fran & Ollie(15) — KV	c	
8/57	9:00	Enterprise — DO	m	Fr:r-8:30
8/57	9:00	Key Club Playhouse — DA	c	
8/57	10:00	Big Beat — MU	c	
8/57	10:00	Big Picture — DO	m	Fr:r-8
9/57	7:00	Sports Focus(15) — SN	m	Fr:m-f-7-7/57
9/57	8:30	Crossroads — DA	c	
10/57	8:30	Patrice Munsel — MV	d	
10/57	9:00	Enterprise — DO	m	To:n-7-3/58
10/57	9:00	Frank Sinatra — VS	d	
10/57	10:00	Big Picture — DO	m	To:f-9-9/58

Date	Time	Title (min. if not 30) – Type	Action	From/To
10/57	10:00	Colt .45 – WE	d	
12/57	8:30	Patrice Munsel – MV	m	To:f-9:30
12/57	9:30	Date with the Angels – SC	m	To:w-9:30
12/57	10:00	Colt .45 – WE	m	To:f-8:30
1/58	8:30	Colt .45 – WE	m	Fr:f-10
1/58	9:30	Patrice Munsel – MV	m	Fr:f-8:30
1/58	10:00	Walter Winchell File – RA	m	Fr:w-9:30
3/58	10:00	Walter Winchell File – RA	c	
4/58	8:30	Colt .45 – WE	m	To:n-9-10/58
4/58	8:30	Stars of Jazz – MU	d	
4/58	10:00	Holiday Handbook – TR	d	
6/58	8:30	Stars of Jazz – MU	m	To:m-9
6/58	8:30	This Is Music – MU	d	
6/58	9:00	Frank Sinatra – VS	c	
6/58	9:30	Frigidaire Summer Theatre – DA	d	
6/58	9:30	Patrice Munsel – MV	c	
6/58	10:00	Harness Racing – SP	s	
6/58	10:00	Holiday Handbook – TR	c	
7/58	9:00	E.S.P. – QU	d	
8/58	8:00	Adventures of Jim Bowie – WE	c	
8/58	9:00	E.S.P. – QU	c	
8/58	9:30	Buick Action Theatre – DA	d	
8/58	9:30	Frigidaire Summer Theatre – DA	c	
8/58	10:00	Harness Racing – SP	f	
8/58	10:00	Scotland Yard – RA	m	Fr:w-9:30-6/58
9/58	7:00	Sports Focus(15) – SN	c	
9/58	8:00	Walt Disney(60) – KV	m	Fr:w-7:30
9/58	8:30	This Is Music – MU	m	To:m-7:30
9/58	9:00	Big Picture – DO	m	Fr:f-10-10/57
9/58	10:30	News(15) – NW	s	
10/58	9:00	Big Picture – DO	m	To:s-10-6/59
10/58	9:00	Man with a Camera – DR	d	
10/58	9:30	Buick Action Theatre – DA	c	
10/58	9:30	77 Sunset Strip(60) – CD	d	
10/58	10:00	Scotland Yard – RA	c	
3/59	9:00	Man with a Camera – DR	m	To:m-10:30
3/59	9:00	Tombstone Territory – WE	m	Fr:w-8:30-9/58
5/59	10:30	News(15) – NW	f	
9/59	7:30	Adventures of Rin Tin Tin – WE	c	
9/59	7:30	Walt Disney(60) – KV	m	Fr:f-8
9/59	8:00	Walt Disney(60) – KV	m	To:f-7:30
9/59	8:30	Man from Blackhawk – WE	d	
10/59	9:00	77 Sunset Strip(60) – CD	m	Fr:f-9:30
10/59	9:00	Tombstone Territory – WE	c	
10/59	9:30	77 Sunset Strip(60) – CD	m	To:f-9
10/59	10:00	The Detectives – CD	d	
10/59	10:30	Black Saddle – WE	m	Fr:s-9(n)
9/60	7:30	Matty's Funday Funnies – KV	d	
9/60	7:30	Walt Disney(60) – KV	m	To:n-6:30
9/60	8:00	Harrigan and Son – SC	d	

Date	Time	Title (min. if not 30) — Type	Action	From/To
9/60	8:30	Flintstones — KV	d	
9/60	8:30	Man from Blackhawk — WE	c	
9/60	10:30	Black Saddle — WE	c	
10/60	10:30	The Law and Mr. Jones — LD	d	
9/61	7:30	Matty's Funday Funnies — KV	m	To:s-7
9/61	8:00	Harrigan and Son — SC	c	
9/61	10:00	The Detectives — CD	m	To:f-8:30(n)
9/61	10:00	Target: The Corruptors(60) — ND	d	
9/61	10:30	The Law and Mr. Jones — LD	m	To:r-9:30-4/62
10/61	7:30	Straightaway — AD	d	
10/61	8:00	Hathaways — SC	d	
12/61	7:30	Straightaway — AD	m	To:w-8
1/62	7:30	Soupy Sales — KV	d	
4/62	7:30	Margie — SC	m	Fr:r-9:30
4/62	7:30	Soupy Sales — KV	c	
8/62	7:30	Margie — SC	c	
8/62	8:00	Hathaways — SC	c	
9/62	7:30	Roaring Twenties(60) — ND	m	Fr:s-7:30-1/62
9/62	7:30	Roaring Twenties(60) — ND	c	
9/62	9:00	I'm Dickens — He's Fenster — SC	d	
9/62	9:00	77 Sunset Strip(60) — CD	m	To:f-9:30
9/62	9:30	77 Sunset Strip(60) — CD	m	Fr:f-9
9/62	10:00	Target: The Corruptors(60) — ND	c	
10/62	7:30	Gallant Men(60) — WD	d	
12/62	7:30	Gallant Men(60) — WD	m	To:s-7:30
12/62	7:30	Winston Churchill — DO	m	Fr:n-10:30-6/61
12/62	8:00	Father Knows Best — SC	m	Fr:n-7
4/63	7:30	Cheyenne(60) — WE	m	Fr:m-7:30-12/62
4/63	7:30	Winston Churchill — DO	c	
4/63	8:00	Father Knows Best — SC	c	
9/63	7:30	Cheyenne(60) — WE	c	
9/63	7:30	77 Sunset Strip(60) — CD	m	Fr:f-9:30
9/63	8:30	Burke's Law(60) — CD	d	
9/63	8:30	Flintstones — KV	m	To:r-7:30
9/63	9:00	I'm Dickens — He's Fenster — SC	c	
9/63	9:30	Farmer's Daughter — SC	d	
9/63	9:30	77 Sunset Strip(60) — CD	m	To:f-7:30
9/63	10:00	Boxing(45) — SP	s	
9/63	10:45	Make That Spare(15) — QU	m	Fr:s-10:45
11/63	9:30	Farmer's Daughter — SC	m	To:w-8:30
12/63	9:30	Price Is Right — QU	m	Fr:w-8:30
2/64	7:30	Destry(60) — WE	d	
2/64	7:30	77 Sunset Strip(60) — CD	m	To:w-10-4/64
9/64	7:30	Destry(60) — WE	c	
9/64	7:30	Johnny Quest — KV	d	
9/64	8:00	Farmer's Daughter — SC	m	Fr:w-8:30
9/64	8:30	Addam's Family — SC	d	
9/64	8:30	Burke's Law(60) — CD	m	To:w-9:30
9/64	9:00	Valentine's Day — SC	d	
9/64	9:30	Price Is Right — QU	c	

Date	*Time*	*Title (min. if not 30) — Type*	*Action*	*From/To*
9/64	9:30	Twelve O'Clock High(60) — WD	d	
9/64	10:00	Boxing(45) — SP	f	
9/64	10:45	Make That Spare(15) — QU	c	
12/64	7:30	Flintstones — KV	m	Fr:r-7:30
12/64	7:30	Johnny Quest — KV	m	To:r-7:30
1/65	9:30	F.D.R. — DO	d	
1/65	9:30	Twelve O'Clock High(60) — WD	m	To:f-10
1/65	10:00	Twelve O'Clock High(60) — WD	m	Fr:f-9:30
6/65	8:00	F.D.R. — DO	m	Fr:f-9:30
6/65	8:00	Farmer's Daughter — SC	m	To:m-9:30
6/65	9:30	F.D.R. — DO	m	To:f-8
6/65	9:30	Peyton Place — SL	m	Fr:tr-9:30
9/65	8:00	F.D.R. — DO	c	
9/65	8:00	Tammy — SC	d	
9/65	9:00	Honey West — CD	d	
9/65	9:00	Valentine's Day — SC	c	
9/65	10:00	Jimmy Dean(60) — MV	m	Fr:r-10
9/65	10:00	Twelve O'Clock High(60) — WD	m	To:m-7:30
10/65	9:30	Peyton Place — SL	m	To:mtr-9:30
11/65	9:30	Farmer's Daughter — SC	m	Fr:m-9:30
4/66	10:00	Court-Martial(50) — WD	d	
4/66	10:00	Jimmy Dean(60) — MV	c	
7/66	8:00	Summer Fun — CA	d	
7/66	8:00	Tammy — SC	c	
9/66	7:30	Flintstones — KV	c	
9/66	7:30	Green Hornet — CD	d	
9/66	8:00	Summer Fun — CA	c	
9/66	8:00	Time Tunnel(60) — SF	d	
9/66	8:30	Addam's Family — SC	c	
9/66	9:00	Honey West — CD	c	
9/66	9:00	Milton Berle(60) — CV	d	
9/66	9:30	Farmer's Daughter — SC	c	
9/66	10:00	Court-Martial(50) — WD	c	
9/66	10:00	Twelve O'Clock High(60) — WD	m	Fr:m-7:30
1/67	9:00	Milton Berle(60) — CV	c	
1/67	9:00	Rango — SC	d	
1/67	9:30	Pruitts of Southampton — SC	m	Fr:t-9
1/67	10:00	Avengers(60) — SD	m	Fr:r-10-9/66
1/67	10:00	Twelve O'Clock High(60) — WD	c	
7/67	7:30	Green Hornet — CD	c	
7/67	7:30	Time Tunnel(60) — SF	m	Fr:f-8
7/67	8:00	Time Tunnel(60) — SF	m	To:f-7:30
7/67	8:30	Malibu U — MU	d	
9/67	7:30	Off to See the Wizard(60) — KV	d	
9/67	7:30	Time Tunnel(60) — SF	c	
9/67	8:30	Hondo(60) — WE	d	
9/67	8:30	Malibu U — MU	c	
9/67	9:00	Rango — SC	c	
9/67	9:30	Guns of Will Sonnett — WE	d	
9/67	9:30	Pruitts of Southampton — SC	c	

Date	Time	Title (min. if not 30) — Type	Action	From/To
9/67	10:00	Avengers(60) — SD	m	To:w-7:30-1/68
9/67	10:00	Judd, for the Defense(60) — LD	d	
12/67	8:30	Hondo(60) — WE	c	
1/68	8:30	Operation: Entertainment(60) — VY	d	
4/68	8:30	Operation: Entertainment(60) — VY	m	To:f-7:30-9/68
5/68	8:30	Man in a Suitcase(60) — CD	d	
9/68	7:30	Off to See the Wizard(60) — KV	c	
9/68	7:30	Operation: Entertainment(60) — VY	m	Fr:f-8:30-4/68
9/68	8:30	Felony Squad — CD	m	Fr:m-9
9/68	8:30	Man in a Suitcase(60) — CD	c	
9/68	9:00	Don Rickles — CV	d	
1/69	7:30	Operation: Entertainment(60) — VY	c	
1/69	8:30	Felony Squad — CD	c	
1/69	9:00	Don Rickles — CV	c	
2/69	7:30	This Is Tom Jones(60) — MV	d	
2/69	8:30	Generation Gap — QU	d	
2/69	9:00	Let's Make a Deal — QU	m	Fr:n-8:30-9/67
5/69	7:30	Let's Make a Deal — QU	m	Fr:f-9
5/69	7:30	This Is Tom Jones(60) — MV	m	To:r-9
5/69	8:00	John Davidson(60) — MV	d	
5/69	8:30	Generation Gap — QU	c	
5/69	9:00	Judd, for the Defense(60) — LD	m	Fr:f-10
5/69	9:00	Let's Make a Deal — QU	m	To:f-7:30
5/69	9:30	Guns of Will Sonnett — WE	m	To:m-8:30
5/69	10:00	Dick Cavett(60) — TK	d	
5/69	10:00	Judd, for the Defense(60) — LD	m	To:f-9
9/69	8:00	Brady Bunch — SC	d	
9/69	8:00	John Davidson(60) — MV	c	
9/69	8:30	Mr. Deeds Goes to Town — SC	d	
9/69	9:00	Here Come the Brides(60) — CO	m	Fr:w-7:30
9/69	9:00	Judd, for the Defense(60) — LD	c	
9/69	10:00	Dick Cavett(60) — TK	c	
9/69	10:00	Jimmy Durante Presents Lennon Sisters(60) — MV	d	
1/70	7:30	Flying Nun — SC	m	Fr:w-7:30
1/70	7:30	Let's Make a Deal — QU	m	To:s-7:30
1/70	8:30	Ghost and Mrs. Muir — SC	m	Fr:s-8:30(n)
1/70	8:30	Mr. Deeds Goes to Town — SC	c	
1/70	10:00	Jimmy Durante Presents Lennon Sisters(60) — MV	m	To:s-9:30
1/70	10:00	Love, American Style(60) — CA	m	Fr:m-10
9/70	7:30	Brady Bunch — SC	m	Fr:f-8
9/70	7:30	Flying Nun — SC	c	
9/70	8:00	Brady Bunch — SC	m	To:f-7:30
9/70	8:00	Nanny and the Professor — SC	m	Fr:w-7:30
9/70	8:30	Ghost and Mrs. Muir — SC	c	
9/70	8:30	Partridge Family — SC	d	
9/70	9:00	Here Come the Brides(60) — CO	c	
9/70	9:00	That Girl — SC	m	Fr:r-8
9/70	9:30	Love, American Style — CA	m	Fr:f-10

Date	Time	Title (min. if not 30) — Type	Action	From/To
9/70	10:00	Love, American Style(60) — CA	m	To:f-9:30
9/70	10:00	This Is Tom Jones(60) — MV	m	Fr:r-9
1/71	9:30	Love, American Style — CA	m	To:f-10
1/71	9:30	Odd Couple — SC	m	Fr:r-9:30
1/71	10:00	Love, American Style(60) — CA	m	Fr:f-9:30
1/71	10:00	This Is Tom Jones(60) — MV	c	
9/71	7:30	Brady Bunch — SC	m	To:f-8
9/71	8:00	Brady Bunch — SC	m	Fr:f-7:30
9/71	8:00	Nanny and the Professor — SC	m	To:m-8
9/71	9:00	Room 222 — SC	m	Fr:w-8
9/71	9:00	That Girl — SC	c	
6/73	8:30	Odd Couple — SC	m	Fr:f-9:30
6/73	8:30	Partridge Family — SC	m	To:s-8
6/73	9:30	Love Thy Neighbor — SC	d	
6/73	9:30	Odd Couple — SC	m	To:f-8:30
7/73	9:30	Love Thy Neighbor — SC	m	To:w-8
8/73	9:30	Corner Bar — SC	m	Fr:w-8:30-8/72
9/73	9:30	Adam's Rib — SC	d	
9/73	9:30	Corner Bar — SC	c	
12/73	9:30	Adam's Rib — SC	c	
1/74	8:30	Odd Couple — SC	m	To:f-9:30
1/74	8:30	Six Million Dollar Man(60) — AD	d	
1/74	9:00	Room 222 — SC	c	
1/74	9:30	Odd Couple — SC	m	Fr:f-8:30
1/74	10:00	Love, American Style(60) — CA	c	
1/74	10:00	Toma(60) — CD	m	Fr:r-8
8/74	8:00	Brady Bunch — SC	c	
9/74	8:00	Kodiak — CD	d	
9/74	9:30	Odd Couple — SC	m	To:r-8
9/74	9:30	Texas Wheelers — SC	d	
9/74	10:00	Kolchak: The Night Stalker(60) — DR	d	
9/74	10:00	Toma(60) — CD	c	
10/74	8:00	Kodiak — CD	c	
10/74	8:30	Six Million Dollar Man(60) — AD	m	To:f-9
10/74	9:30	Texas Wheelers — SC	m	To:r-8:30-6/75
11/74	8:00	Kung Fu(60) — WE	m	Fr:s-9
11/74	9:00	Six Million Dollar Man(60) — AD	m	Fr:f-8:30
12/74	10:00	Kolchak: The Night Stalker(60) — DR	m	To:f-8
1/75	8:00	Kolchak: The Night Stalker(60) — DR	m	Fr:f-10
1/75	8:00	Kung Fu(60) — WE	m	To:s-8
1/75	9:00	Hot L Baltimore — SC	d	
1/75	9:00	Six Million Dollar Man(60) — AD	m	To:n-7:30
1/75	9:30	Odd Couple — SC	m	Fr:r-8
1/75	10:00	Baretta(60) — CD	d	
3/75	10:00	Baretta(60) — CD	m	To:w-10
4/75	10:00	Get Christie Love(60) — CD	m	Fr:w-10
7/75	9:00	Hot L Baltimore — SC	c	

Date	Time	Title (min. if not 30) — Type	Action	From/To
7/75	9:00	Film(120) — FI	s	
7/75	9:30	Odd Couple — SC	c	
7/75	10:00	Get Christie Love(60) — CD	c	
8/75	8:00	Kolchak: The Night Stalker(60) — DR	c	
9/75	8:00	Mobile One(60) — AD	d	
10/75	8:00	Barbary Coast(60) — WE	m	Fr:m-8
10/75	8:00	Mobile One(60) — AD	m	To:m-8
1/76	8:00	Barbary Coast(60) — WE	c	
1/76	8:00	Donny and Marie(60) — MV	d	
5/77	8:00	Donny and Marie(60) — MV	m	To:w-8
8/77	8:00	Donny and Marie(60) — MV	m	Fr:w-8
6/78	8:00	Tabitha — SC	m*	Fr:s-8-1/78
6/78	8:30	Operation Petticoat — SC	m*	Fr:r-8:30
8/78	8:00	Tabitha — SC	c*	
8/78	8:30	Operation Petticoat — SC	m*	To:m-8:30
1/79	8:00	Donny and Marie(60) — MV	m	To:n-7
2/79	8:00	Makin' It — AD	m	Fr:r-8:30
2/79	8:30	What's Happening — SC	m	Fr:r-8:30
3/79	8:00	Family(60) — DR	m	Fr:r-10
3/79	8:00	Makin' It — AD	c	
3/79	8:30	What's Happening — SC	m	To:s-8
4/79	8:00	Family(60) — DR	m	To:r-10
4/79	8:00	Mackenzies of Paradise Cove(60) — AD	d	
5/79	8:00	Mackenzies of Paradise Cove(60) — AD	c	
5/79	8:00	Operation Petticoat — SC	m	Fr:m-8:30-10/78
5/79	8:30	Welcome Back Kotter — SC	m	Fr:s-8:30-3/79
8/79	8:00	Fantasy Island(60) — DR	m	Fr:s-10
8/79	8:00	Operation Petticoat — SC	c	
8/79	8:30	Welcome Back Kotter — SC	c	
10/79	8:00	Fantasy Island(60) — DR	m	To:s-10
1/80	8:00	B.A.D. Cats(60) — CD	d	
2/80	8:00	B.A.D. Cats(60) — CD	c	
3/80	8:00	When the Whistle Blows(60) — SC	d	
4/80	8:00	When the Whistle Blows(60) — SC	m	To:s-10-6/80
4/80	9:00	Film(120) — FI	f	
5/80	8:00	Film(120) — FI	s	
5/80	10:00	Tenspeed and Brown Shoe(60) — CD	m	Fr:n-8-3/80
6/80	8:00	Film(120) — FI	f	
6/80	10:00	Tenspeed and Brown Shoe(60) — CD	c	
7/80	8:00	Benson — SC	m	Fr:r-8:30
7/80	8:30	Goodtime Girls — SC	m	Fr:s-8:30-4/80
7/80	9:00	Film(120) — FI	s	
9/80	8:30	Goodtime Girls — SC	c	
10/80	8:30	I'm a Big Girl Now — SC	d	
7/81	8:30	I'm a Big Girl Now — SC	c	
8/81	8:30	Krypton Factor — QU	d	
9/81	8:30	It's a Living — SC	m	Fr:t-9:30

Date	Time	Title (min. if not 30) — Type	Action	From/To
9/81	8:30	Krypton Factor — QU	c	
10/81	8:30	It's a Living — SC	m	To:s-8:30
11/81	8:30	Bosom Buddies — SC	m	Fr:r-9
11/81	9:00	Darkroom(60) — OA	d	
11/81	9:00	Film(120) — FI	f	
11/81	10:00	Strike Force(60) — CD	d	
1/82	8:30	Bosom Buddies — SC	m	To:r-8:30
1/82	9:00	Darkroom(60) — OA	m	To:r-8-7/82
2/82	8:30	Open All Night — SC	m	Fr:s-8
2/82	9:00	Best of the West — SC	m	Fr:r-8:30
2/82	9:00	Best of the West — SC	m	To:m-8-6/82
2/82	9:30	It's a Living — SC	m	Fr:s-8:30
2/82	9:30	It's a Living — SC	m	To:f-8:30-6/82
3/82	8:30	Barney Miller — SC	m	Fr:r-9
3/82	8:30	Open All Night — SC	c	
3/82	9:00	The Phoenix(60) — SF	d	
4/82	8:30	Barney Miller — SC	m	To:r-9
4/82	8:30	Maggie — SC	m	Fr:s-8-11/81
5/82	8:30	Maggie — SC	c	
5/82	9:00	Film(120) — FI	s	
5/82	9:00	The Phoenix(60) — SF	m	To:w-8-8/82
5/82	10:00	Strike Force(60) — CD	m	To:f-10-9/82
6/82	8:30	It's a Living — SC	m	Fr:f-9:30-2/82
8/82	9:00	Film(120) — FI	f	
9/82	8:30	It's a Living — SC	c	
9/82	9:00	Greatest American Hero(60) — AD	m	Fr:w-8
9/82	10:00	Strike Force(60) — CD	m	Fr:f-10-5/82
9/82	10:00	Strike Force(60) — CD	c	
10/82	8:30	New Odd Couple — SC	d	
10/82	10:00	The Quest(60) — AD	d	
11/82	9:00	Greatest American Hero(60) — AD	m	To:r-8-1/83
11/82	10:00	The Quest(60) — AD	c	
12/82	9:00	Film(120) — FI	s	
2/83	8:30	New Odd Couple — SC	m	To:f-8-5/83
2/83	9:00	Film(120) — FI	f	
3/83	8:00	Benson — SC	m	To:r-8
3/83	8:30	At Ease — SC	d	
3/83	9:00	Renegades(60) — CD	d	
3/83	10:00	Tales of the Gold Monkey(60) — AD	m	Fr:w-8
4/83	8:00	Baby Makes Five — SC	d	
4/83	8:00	Baby Makes Five — SC	c	
4/83	9:00	Renegades(60) — CD	c	
4/83	10:00	Tales of the Gold Monkey(60) — AD	m	To:w-9-6/83
5/83	8:00	Benson — SC	m	Fr:r-8
5/83	8:00	New Odd Couple — SC	m	Fr:f-8:30
5/83	8:00	New Odd Couple — SC	m	To:r-8:30
5/83	9:00	Film(120) — FI	s	
7/83	8:30	At Ease — SC	c	
8/83	8:30	Webster — SC	d	
8/83	9:00	Film(120) — FI	f	

Date	Time	Title (min. if not 30) – Type	Action	From/To
9/83	9:00	Lottery(60) – DA	d	
9/83	10:00	Matt Houston(60) – CD	m	Fr:n-8
12/83	9:00	Lottery(60) – DA	m	To:r-9-3/84
1/84	9:00	Blue Thunder(60) – CD	d	
3/84	9:00	Blue Thunder(60) – CD	m	To:m-8
3/84	9:00	Masquerade(60) – SD	m	Fr:r-9-1/84
4/84	9:00	Masquerade(60) – SD	c	
5/84	9:00	Blue Thunder(60) – CD	m	Fr:m-8
9/84	9:00	Blue Thunder(60) – CD	c	
9/84	9:00	Hawaiian Heat(60) – CD	d	
12/84	9:00	Hawaiian Heat(60) – CD	c	
1/85	9:00	Street Hawk(60) – AD	d	
3/85	8:00	Webster – SC	m	Fr:f-8:30
3/85	8:00	Benson – SC	m	To:f-9
3/85	8:30	Webster – SC	m	To:f-8
3/85	8:30	Mr. Belvedere – SC	d	
3/85	9:00	Street Hawk(60) – AD	m	To:r-8-5/85
3/85	9:30	Off the Rack – SC	d	
4/85	8:30	Mr. Belvedere – SC	m	To:f-8:30-8/85
4/85	9:00	Benson – SC	m	Fr:f-8
4/85	9:30	Off the Rack – SC	m	To:f-9:30-8/85
4/85	10:00	Me & Mom(60) – CD	d*	
5/85	9:30	People Do the Craziest Things – CY	m	Fr:n-10:30
5/85	10:00	Me & Mom(60) – CD	c*	
7/85	10:00	Matt Houston(60) – CD	c	
8/85	8:30	Mr. Belvedere – SC	m	Fr:f-8:30-4/85
8/85	9:30	People Do the Craziest Things – CY	c	
8/85	9:30	Off the Rack – SC	m	Fr:f-9:30-4/85
9/85	9:00	Benson – SC	m	To:f-9:30
9/85	9:30	Off the Rack – SC	c	
10/85	9:00	Diff'rent Strokes – SC	m	Fr:s-8(n)
10/85	9:30	Benson – SC	m	Fr:f-9
10/85	10:00	Spenser for Hire(60) – CD	d	
10/85	10:00	Spenser for Hire(60) – CD	m	To:t-10
11/85	10:00	Our Family Honor(60) – DR	m	Fr:t-10
1/86	9:30	Benson – SC	m	To:s-8:30
1/86	9:30	He's the Mayor – SC	d	
1/86	10:00	Fall Guy(60) – AD	m	Fr:s-8
1/86	10:00	Our Family Honor(60) – DR	c	
3/86	9:00	Diff'rent Strokes – SC	m	To:s-8-6/86
3/86	9:00	Mr. Sunshine – SC	d	
3/86	9:30	He's the Mayor – SC	c	
3/86	9:30	Joe Bash – SC	d	
5/86	8:30	Ripley's Believe It or Not – VY	s*	
5/86	9:00	Mr. Sunshine – SC	m	To:s-8
5/86	9:00	Film(120) – FI	s	
5/86	9:00	Film(120) – FI	f	
5/86	9:30	Joe Bash – SC	c	
5/86	10:00	Fall Guy(60) – AD	c	
6/86	8:30	Ripley's Believe It or Not – VY	f*	

Date	Time	Title (min. if not 30) — Type	Action	From/To
6/86	8:30	Comedy Factory — CV	d	
6/86	9:00	Mr. Sunshine — SC	m	Fr:s-8
6/86	10:00	Love Boat(60) — CO	m	Fr:s-9
7/86	9:00	Mr. Sunshine — SC	m	To:w-8:30
8/86	8:30	Comedy Factory — CV	c	
8/86	10:00	Love Boat(60) — CO	c	
9/86	9:00	Sledge Hammer — SC	d	
9/86	9:30	Sidekicks — SC	d	
9/86	10:00	Starman(60) — SF	d	
11/86	9:00	Sledge Hammer — SC	m	To:s-8:30
11/86	9:30	Sidekicks — SC	m	To:s-8
12/86	9:00	Dads — SC	d	
12/86	9:30	Gung Ho — SC	d	
1/87	9:00	Dads — SC	m	To:f-9:30
1/87	9:00	Gung Ho — SC	m	Fr:f-9:30
1/87	9:30	Dads — SC	m	Fr:f-9
1/87	9:30	Gung Ho — SC	m	To:f-9
2/87	9:00	Gung Ho — SC	m	To:s-9-6/87
2/87	9:30	Dads — SC	m	To:s-9:30-6/87
3/87	8:00	Webster — SC	m	To:f-8:30
3/87	8:30	Webster — SC	m*	Fr:f-8
3/87	9:00	Film(120) — FI	s	
3/87	10:00	Starman(60) — SF	m	To:s-8
4/87	8:00	Webster — SC	m	Fr:f-8:30
4/87	8:30	Webster — SC	m*	To:f-8
5/87	8:00	Webster — SC	m	To:s-8
6/87	8:00	Sledge Hammer — SC	m	Fr:s-8:30-3/87
7/87	8:00	Sledge Hammer — SC	m	To:r-8
8/87	8:00	Webster — SC	m	Fr:s-8
8/87	8:00	Webster — SC	c	
8/87	8:30	Mr. Belvedere — SC	m	To:f-9-10/87
8/87	9:00	Max Headroom(60) — DR	m	Fr:t-10-5/87
8/87	9:00	Film(120) — FI	f	
8/87	10:00	Starman(60) — SF	m	Fr:r-8
8/87	10:00	Starman(60) — SF	c	
9/87	8:00	Full House — SC	d	
9/87	8:30	I Married Dora — SC	d	
9/87	10:00	20/20(60) — NM	m#	Fr:r-10
10/87	9:00	Max Headroom(60) — DR	m	To:r-8-4/88
10/87	9:00	Mr. Belvedere — SC	m	Fr:f-8:30-8/87
10/87	9:30	Pursuit of Happiness — SC	d	
1/88	8:30	Mr. Belvedere — SC	m	Fr:f-9
1/88	8:30	I Married Dora — SC	m	To:f-9:30-6/88
1/88	9:00	Mr. Belvedere — SC	m	To:f-8:30
1/88	9:00	Thorns — SC	d	
1/88	9:30	Sledge Hammer — SC	m	Fr:r-8
1/88	9:30	Pursuit of Happiness — SC	c	
2/88	8:00	Full House — SC	m	To:f-8:30
2/88	8:00	Perfect Strangers — SC	m#	Fr:w-8
2/88	8:30	Mr. Belvedere — SC	m	To:f-9

Date	Time	Title (min. if not 30) — Type	Action	From/To
2/88	8:30	Full House — SC	m#	Fr:f-8
2/88	9:00	Mr. Belvedere — SC	m#	Fr:f-8:30
2/88	9:00	Thorns — SC	m	To:f-9:30
2/88	9:30	Thorns — SC	m	Fr:f-9
2/88	9:30	Sledge Hammer — SC	m	To:r-8-6/88
3/88	9:30	Thorns — SC	c	
4/88	9:30	Family Man — SC	d	
5/88	9:30	Slap Maxwell — SC	m	Fr:w-9:30-3/88
5/88	9:30	Slap Maxwell — SC	m	To:w-9:30
5/88	9:30	Family Man — SC	c	
6/88	9:30	I Married Dora — SC	m	Fr:f-8:30-1/88
8/88	9:30	I Married Dora — SC	c	

	7:00	7:30	8:00	8:30	9:00	9:30	10:00	10:30
9/48		Places Please	Face the Music	What's It Worth				
10	YOUR SPORTS SPECIA			CAPTAIN BILLY				
11								
12				MOREY AMSTERDAM	JOHNS HOPKINS SCIENCE REVIEW			
1/49								
2		MANHAT SHOWCS	ADVENTURES IN JAZZ					
3						Film		
4			CAMPUS CORNR / MANHAT SHOWCS					
5								
6			CLIFF EDWARD		THIS IS SHOW BUSINESS			
7				MAMA				
8								
9			POLGAR		54th Street Revue/FORD THEATRE			
10	PAUL ARNOLD		Sonny Kendis	MAN AGAINST CRIME			People's Platform	CAPITOL CLOAK ROOM
11	STRICT FOR LAUGHS		Kendis					
12								
1/50			SNARKY PARKER		Ford Theatre/Actor's Studio			
2								
3								
4			ALKALI IKE					
5								
6	GARRY MOORE		Arthur Godfry		Ford Theatre			
7			STORK CLUB					
8								
9							By Popular Demand	
10	Stork Club		3s Co / Perry Como		Ford Theatre/MAGNAVOX THEATRE		STAR OF THE FAMILY	Beat the Clock
11								
12								
1/51	STEVE ALLEN				CHARLIE WILD PRIVATE DETECTIVE	LIVE LIKE A MILLIONAIRE		
2								
3								
4					Live Like a Millionaire	We Take Your Word		

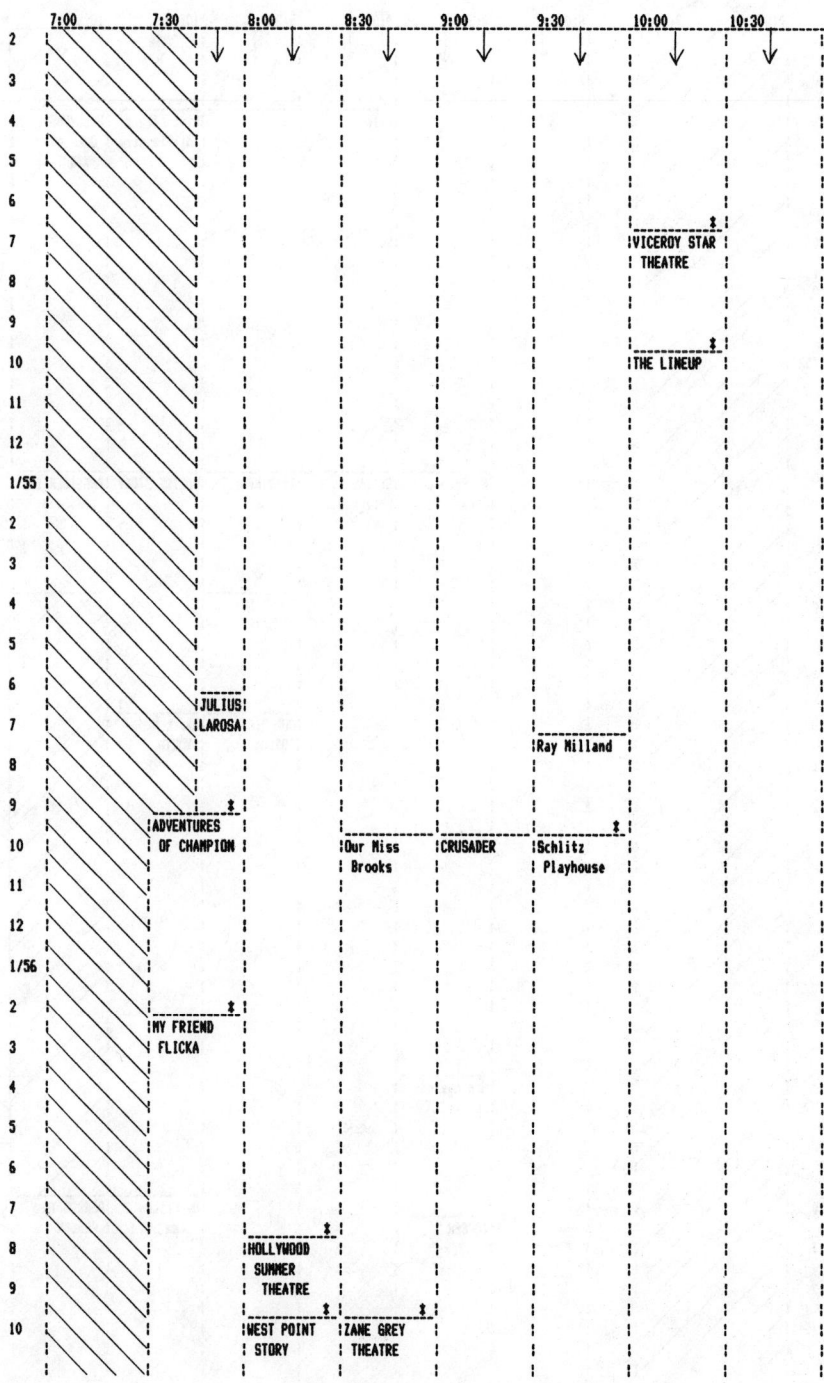

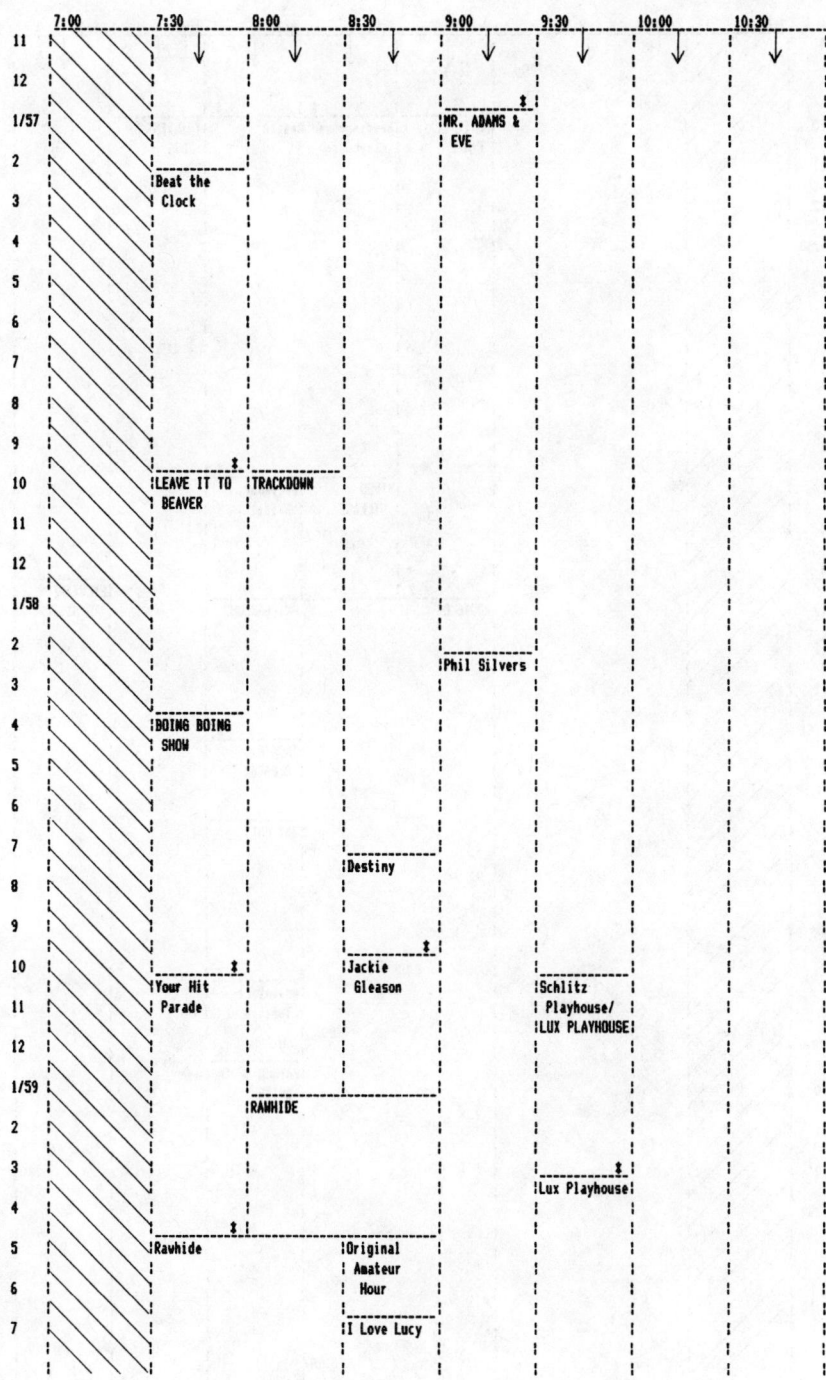

	7:00	7:30	8:00	8:30	9:00	9:30	10:00	10:30
11								
12								
1/57					MR. ADAMS & EVE			
2		Beat the Clock						
3								
4								
5								
6								
7								
8								
9								
10		LEAVE IT TO BEAVER	TRACKDOWN					
11								
12								
1/58								
2					Phil Silvers			
3								
4		BOING BOING SHOW						
5								
6								
7				Destiny				
8								
9								
10		Your Hit Parade		Jackie Gleason		Schlitz Playhouse/ LUX PLAYHOUSE		
11								
12								
1/59			RAWHIDE					
2								
3						Lux Playhouse		
4								
5		Rawhide		Original Amateur Hour				
6								
7				I Love Lucy				

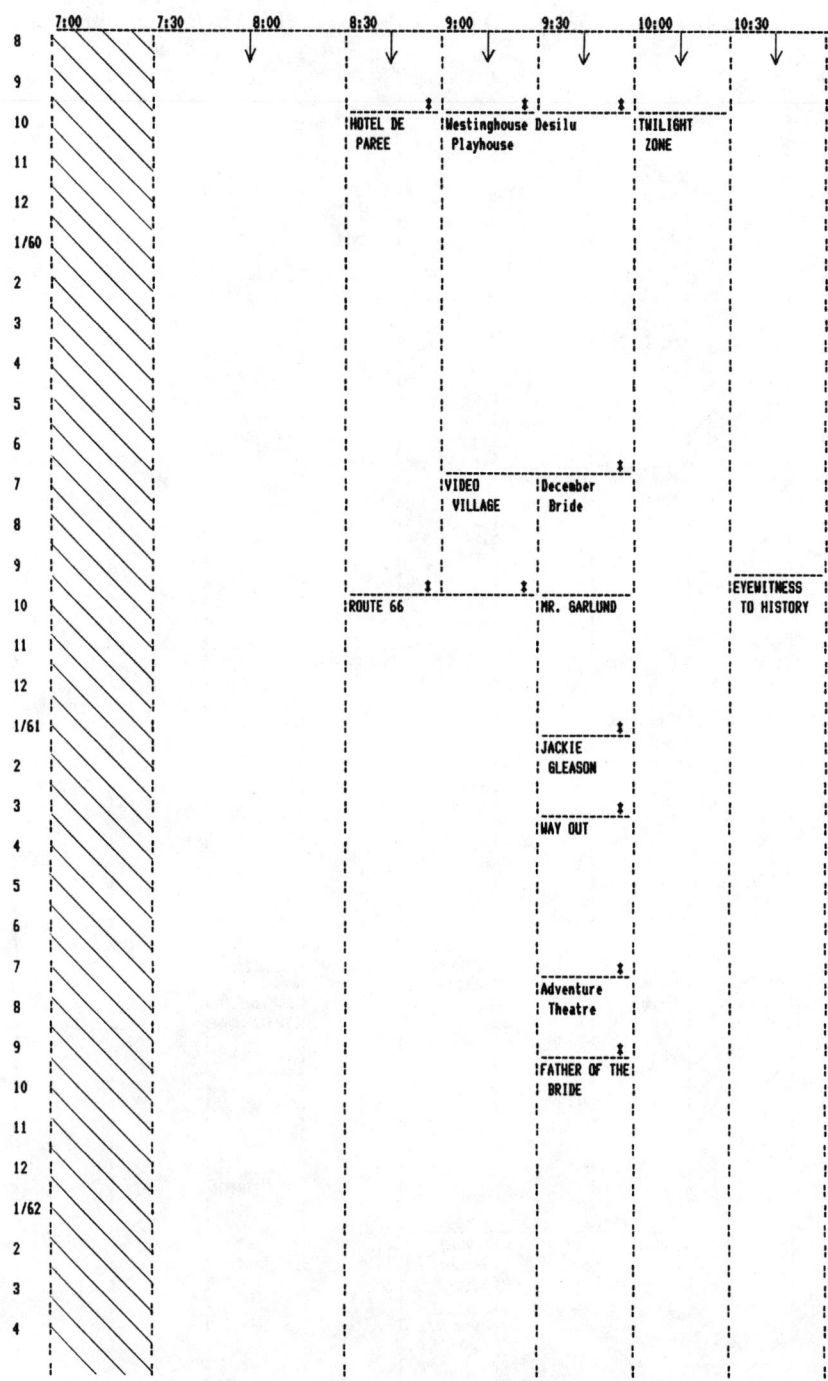

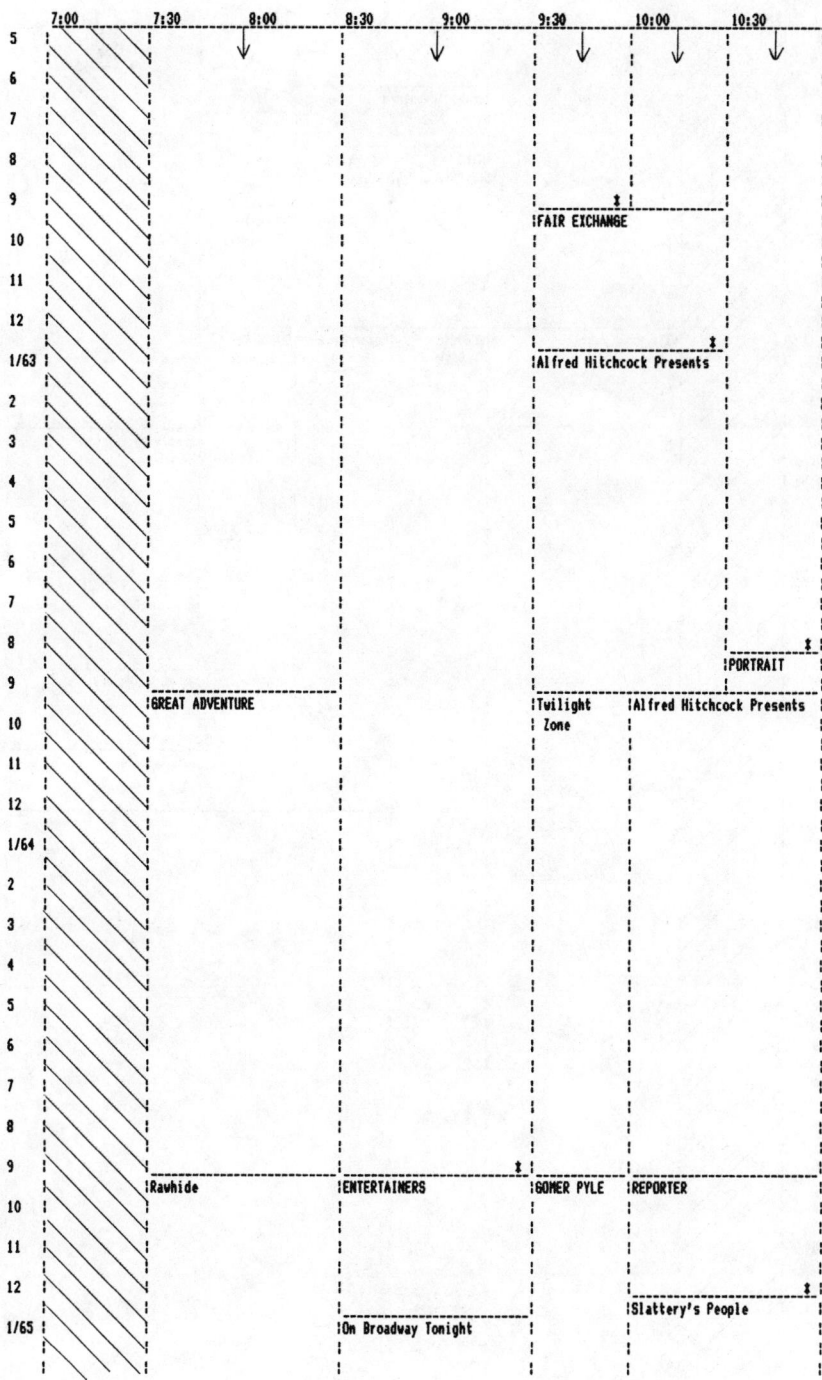

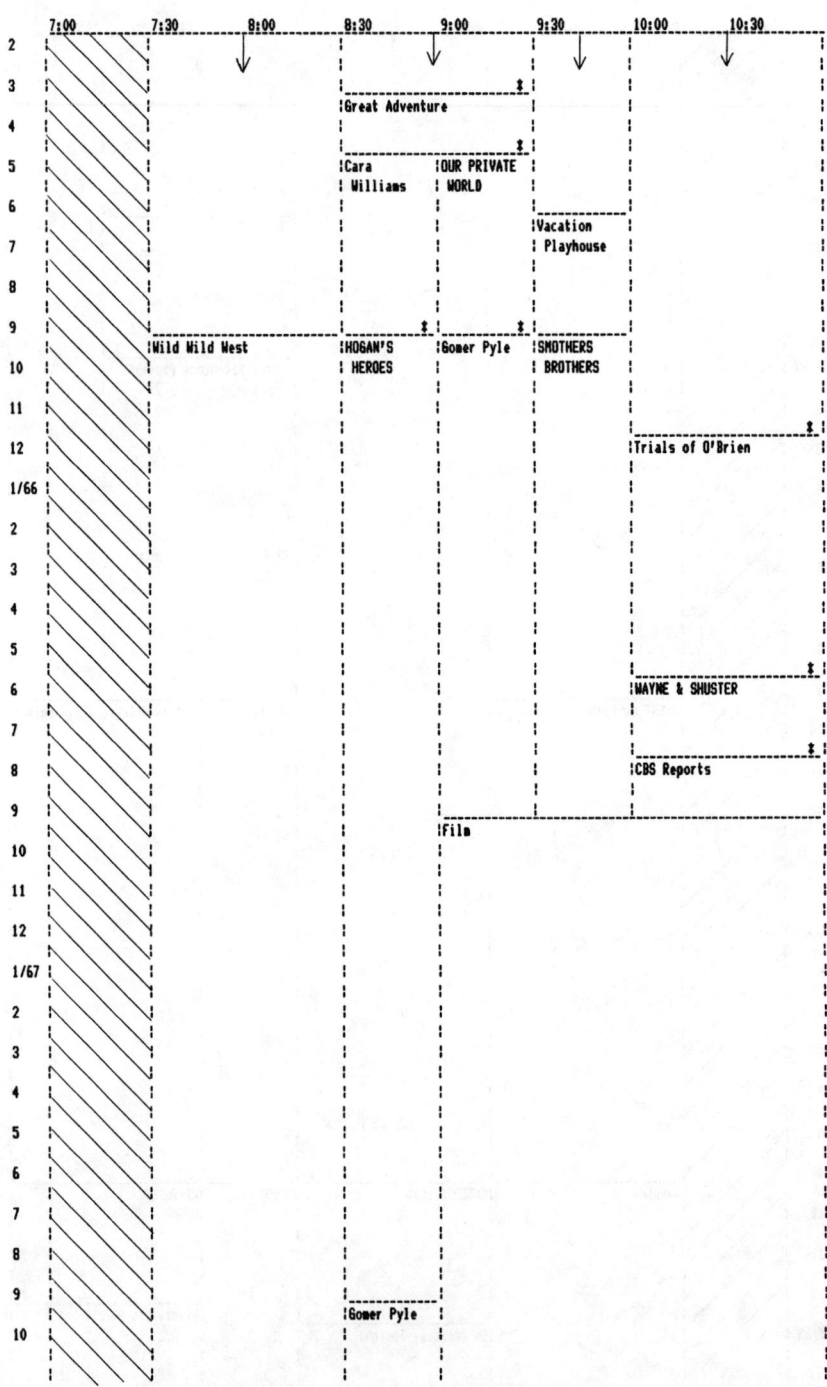

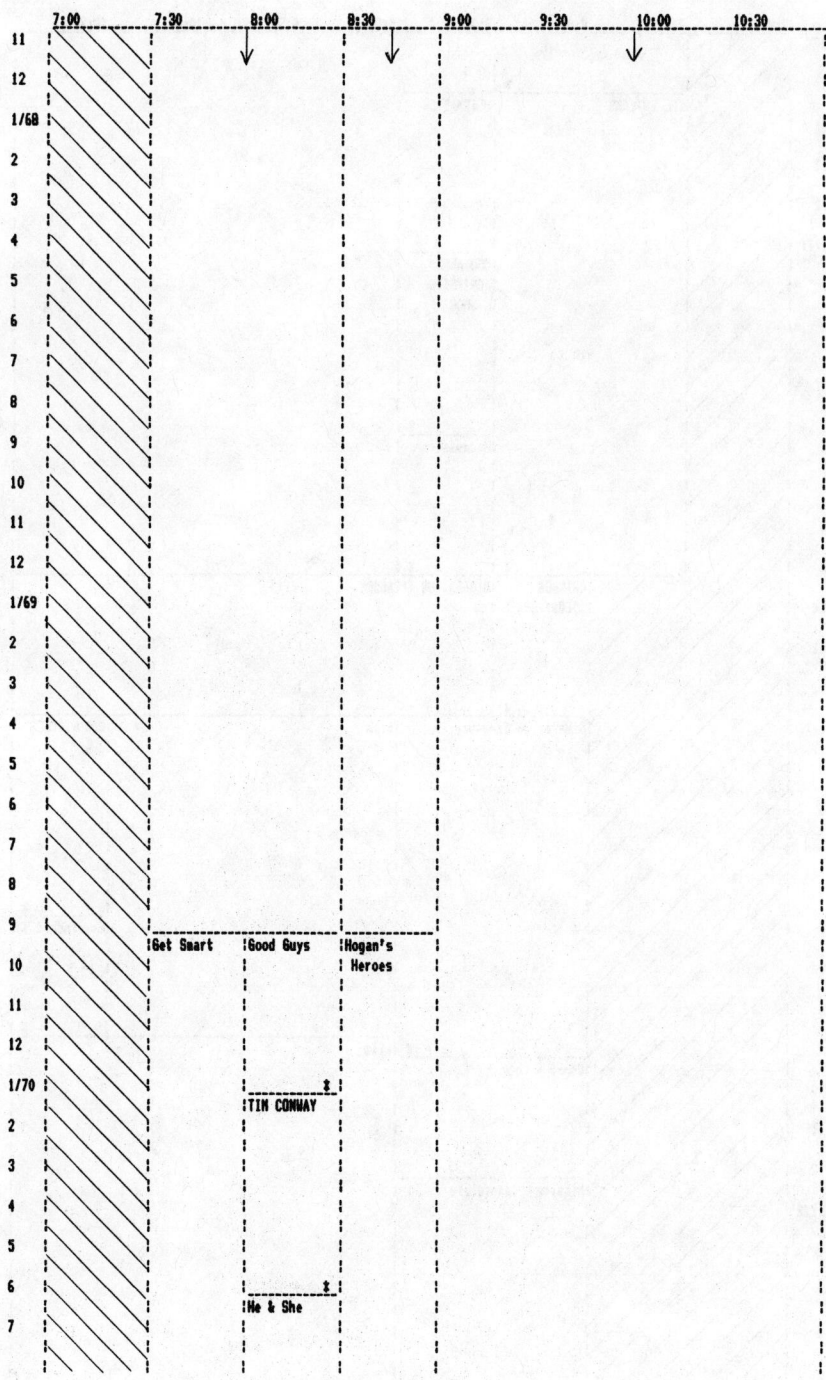

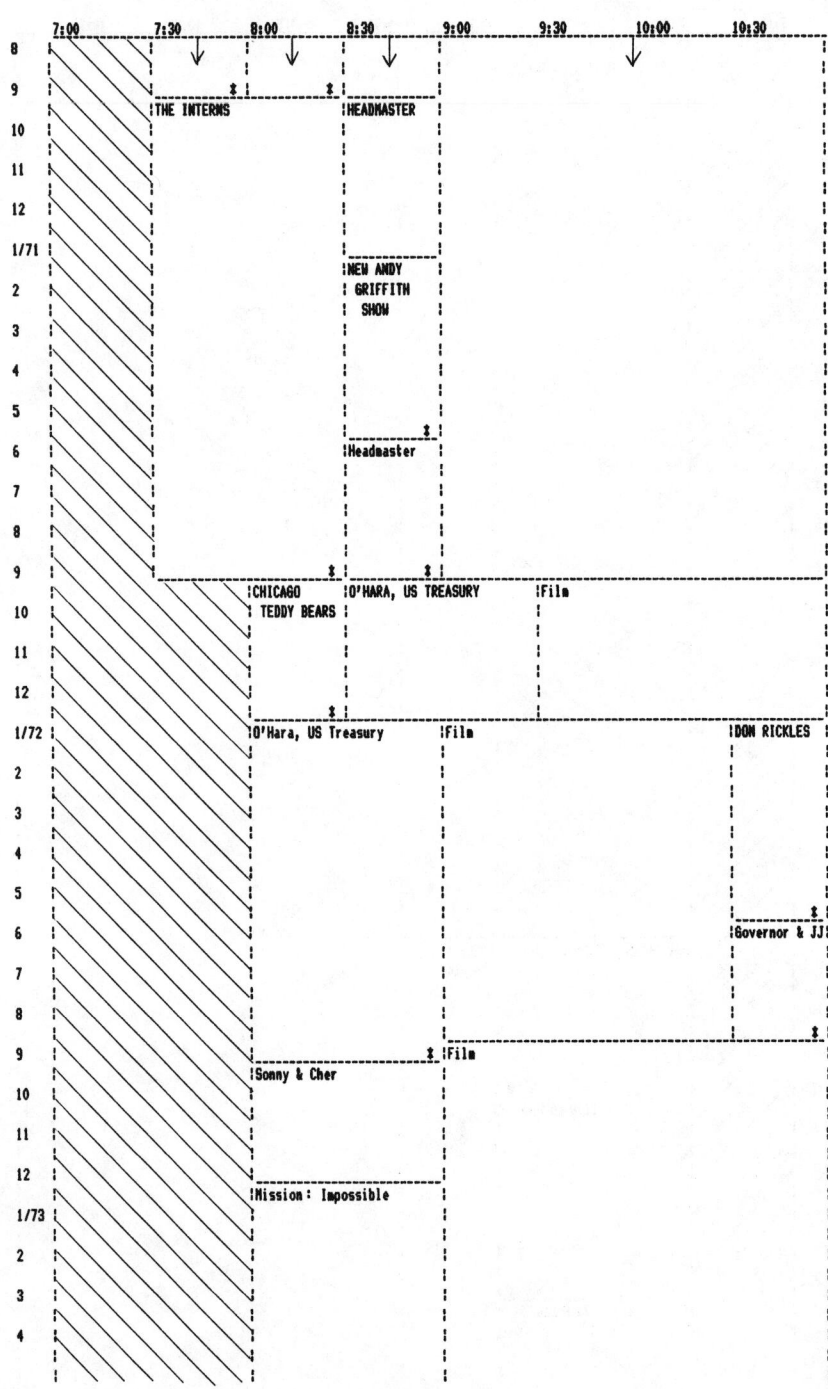

	7:00	7:30	8:00	8:30	9:00	9:30	10:00	10:30

THE INTERNS

HEADMASTER

NEW ANDY GRIFFITH SHOW

Headmaster

CHICAGO TEDDY BEARS

O'HARA, US TREASURY

Film

O'Hara, US Treasury

Film

DON RICKLES

Governor & JJ

Film

Sonny & Cher

Mission: Impossible

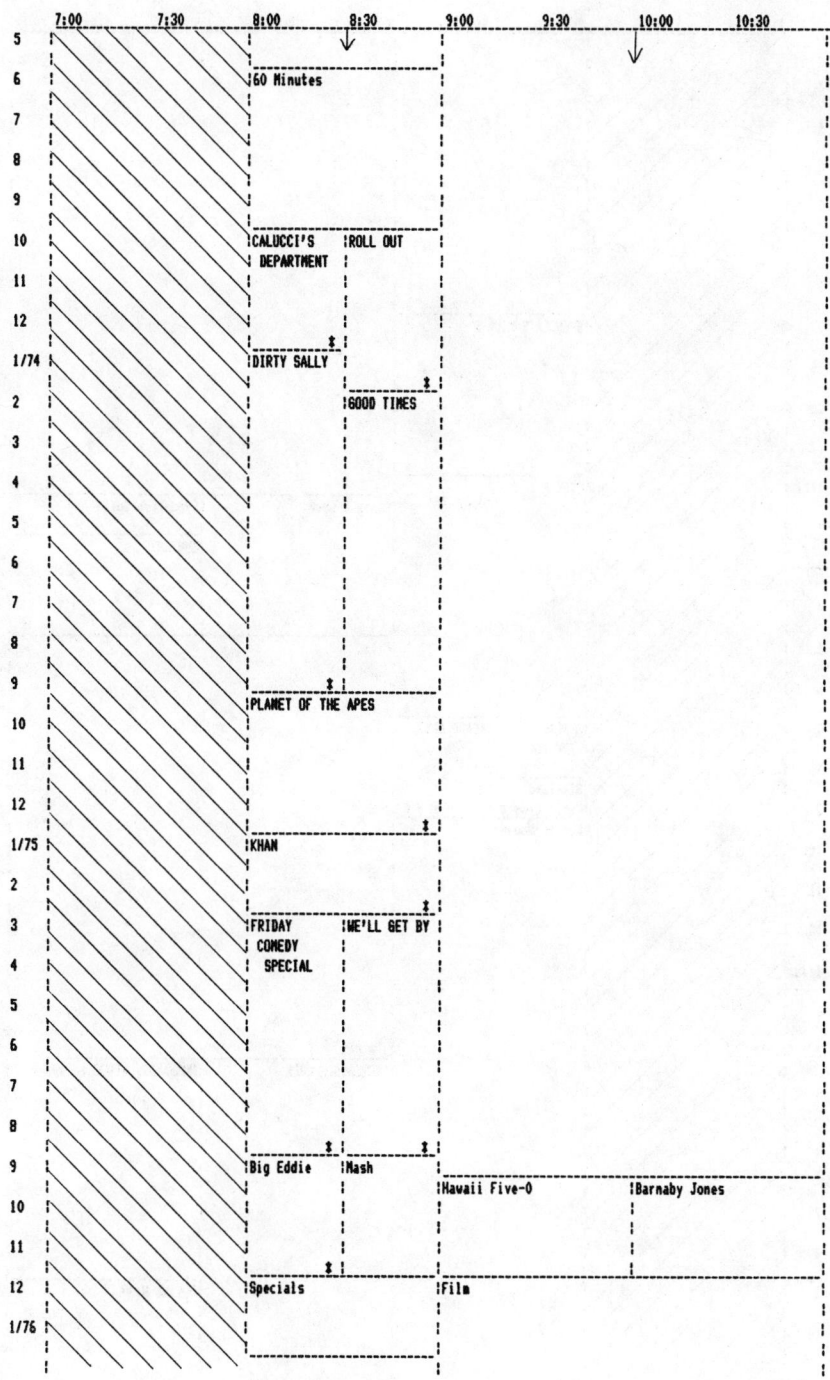

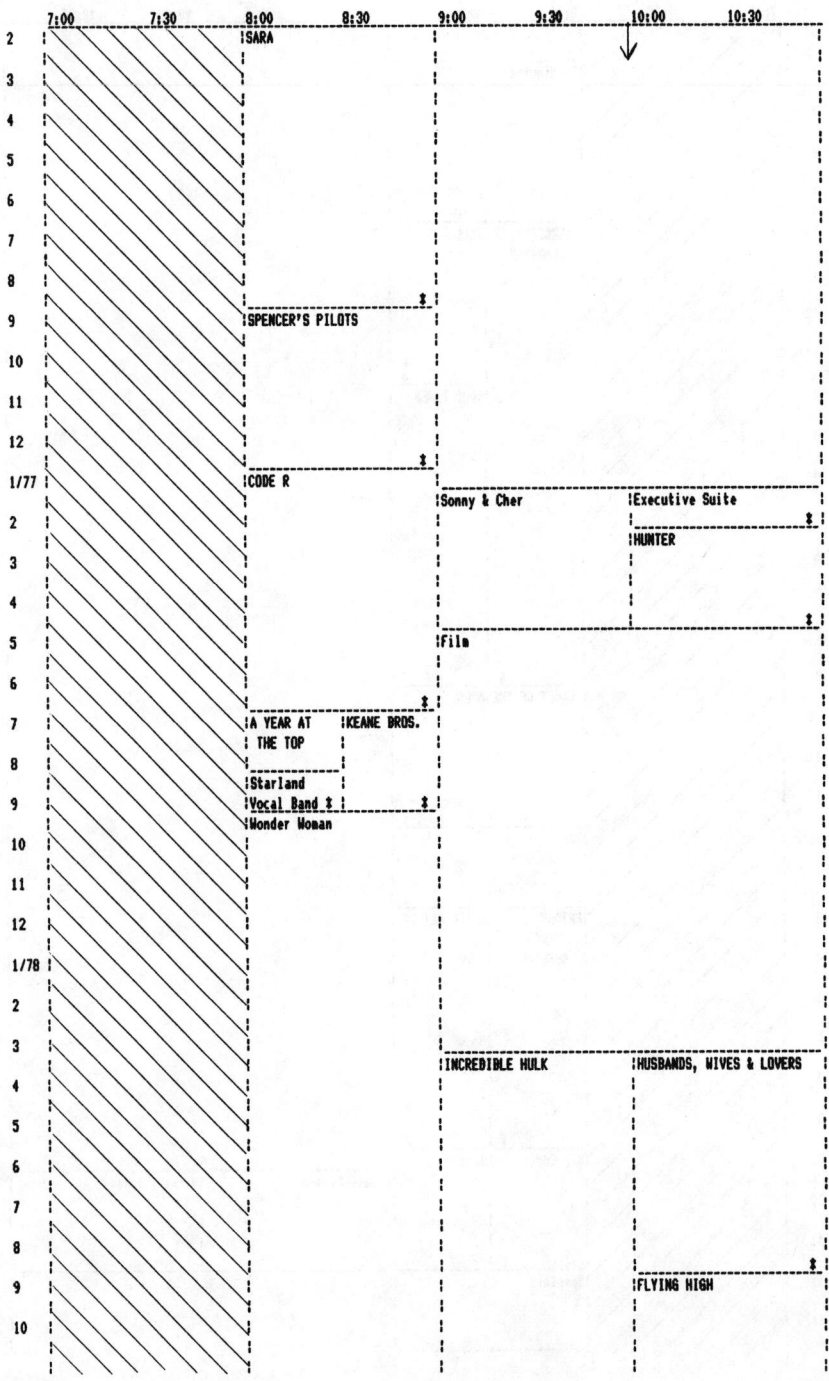

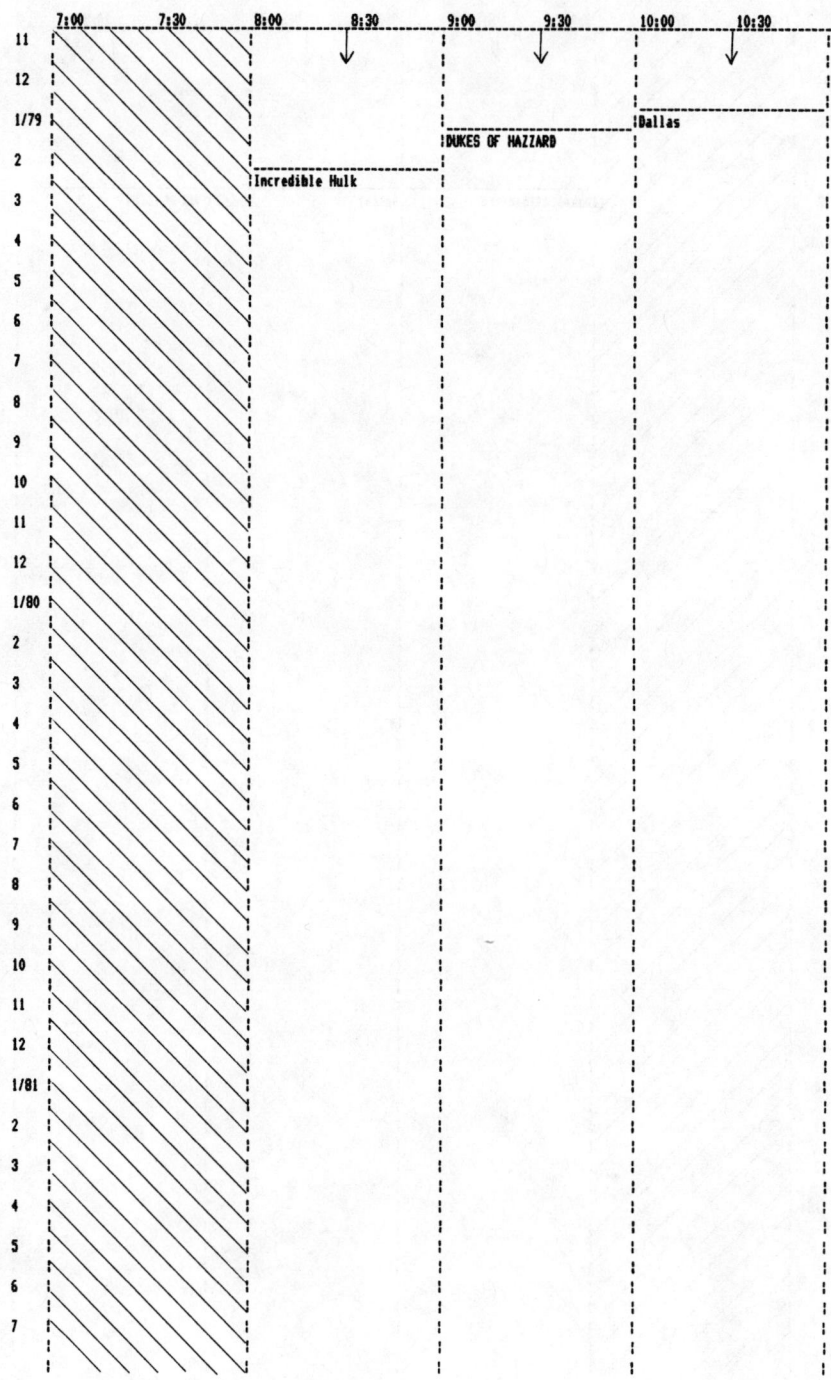

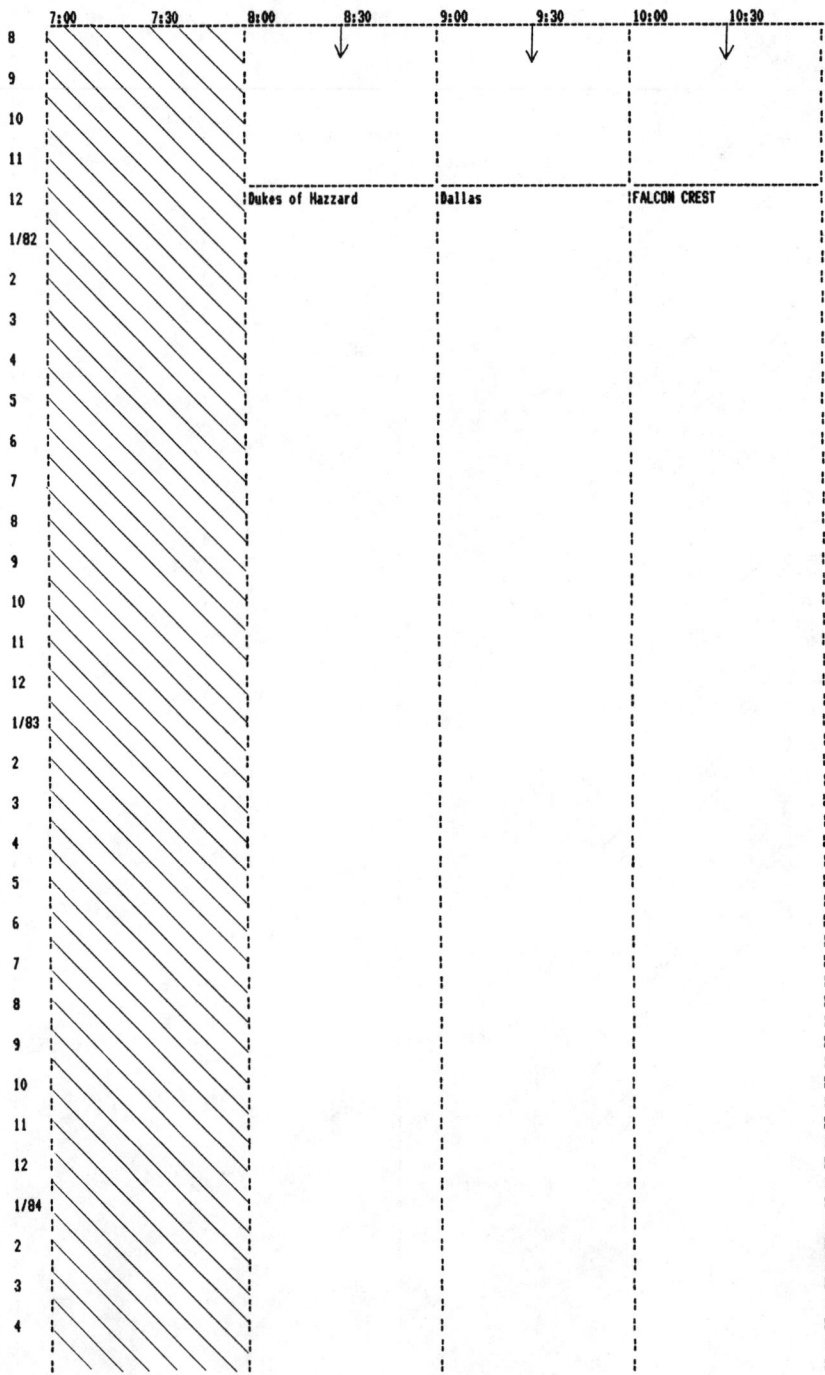

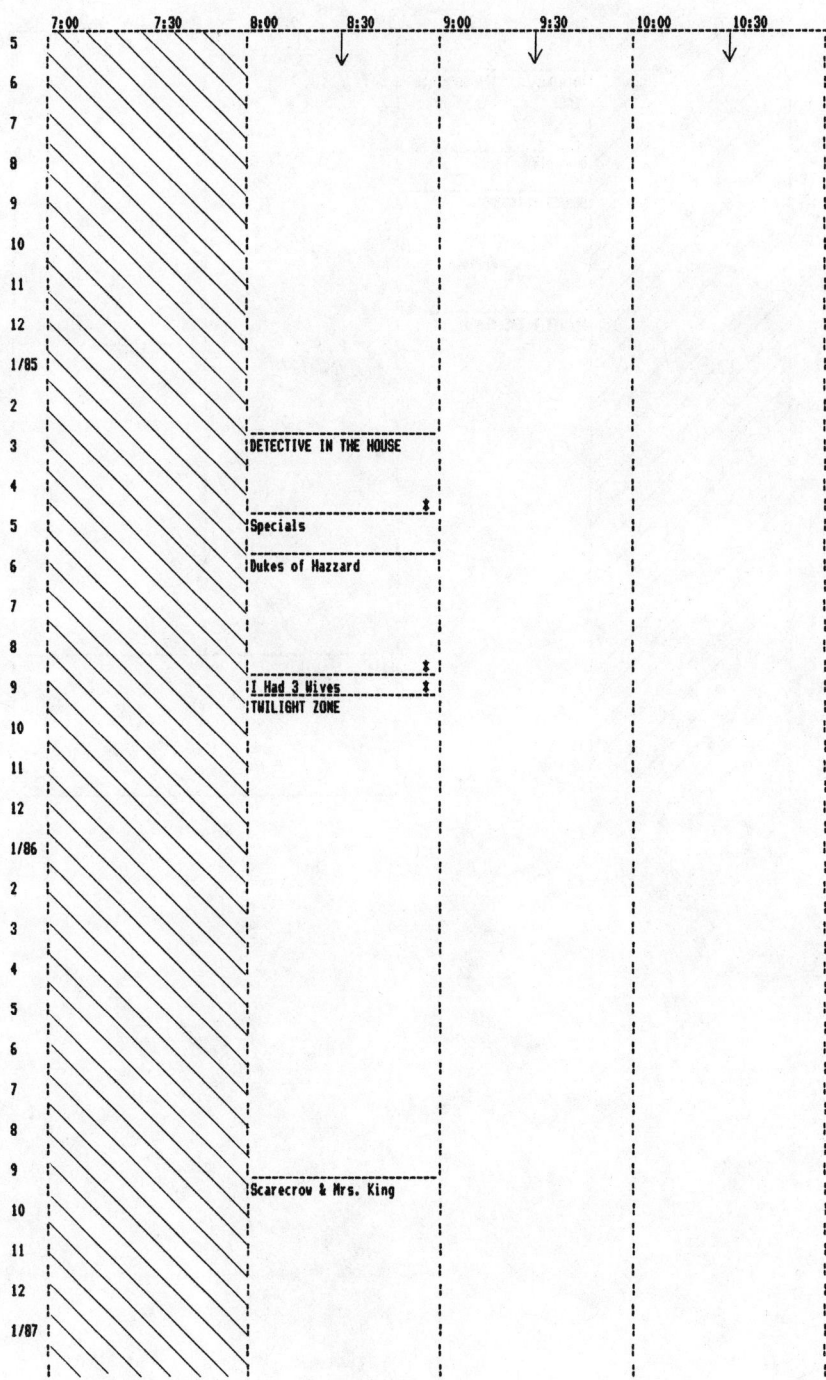

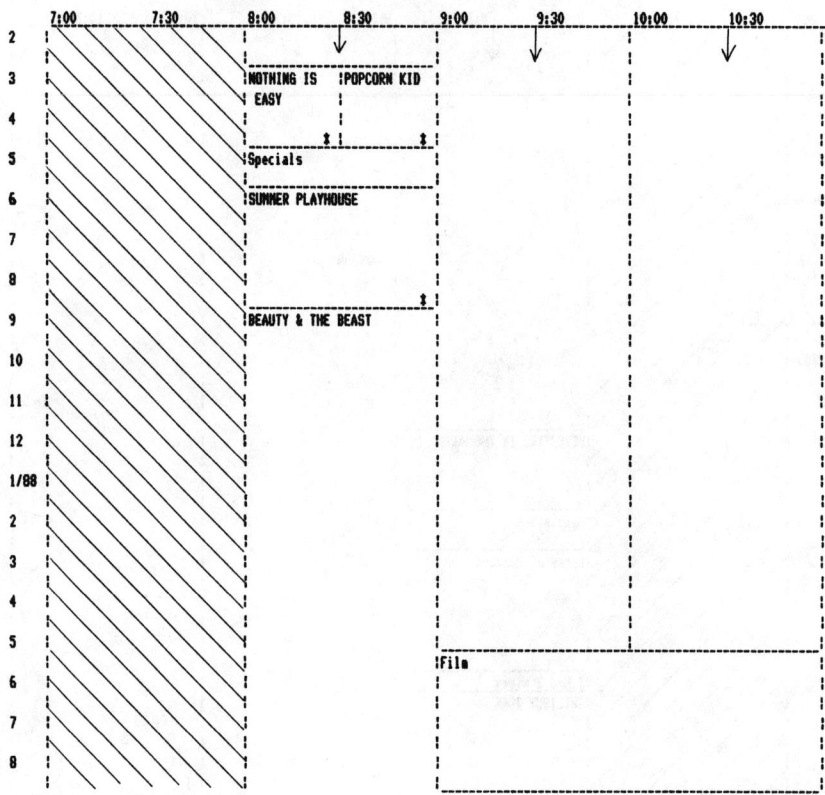

Date	Time	Title (min. if not 30) — Type	Action	From/To
7/48	8:05	What's It Worth?(25) — QU	m	Fr:f-9
8/48	7:15	Places Please(15) — TA	d	
8/48	7:45	Face the Music(15) — MU	m	Fr:m-f-7:15
8/48	8:00	Sportsman's Quiz(5) — QU	m	Fr:m-8
10/48	7:00	Your Sports Special(15) — SN	d	
10/48	8:30	Capt. Billy's Mississippi Music Hall — VY	d	
11/48	8:30	Capt. Billy's Mississippi Music Hall — VY	c	
12/48	8:30	Morey Amsterdam — CV	d	
12/48	9:00	Johns Hopkins Science Review — IF	d	
1/49	8:00	Adventures in Jazz — MU	d	
1/49	8:00	Sportsman's Quiz(5) — QU	c	
1/49	8:05	What's It Worth?(25) — QU	m	To:t-9:30
1/49	8:30	Morey Amsterdam — CV	m	To:m-var
2/49	7:15	Manhattan Showcase(15) — MV	d	
2/49	7:15	Places Please(15) — TA	c	
3/49	7:45	Campus Corner(15) — MU	d	
3/49	7:45	Face the Music(15) — MU	m	To:tr-7:45
3/49	9:30	Film(75) — FI	s	
4/49	7:15	Manhattan Showcase(15) — MV	m	To:mtrf-7:45
4/49	7:45	Campus Corner(15) — MU	c	
4/49	7:45	Manhattan Showcase(15) — MV	m	Fr:var-7:15
5/49	7:45	Cliff Edwards(15) — MU	d	
5/49	7:45	Manhattan Showcase(15) — MV	m	To:mwr-7:15
5/49	9:00	Johns Hopkins Science Review — IF	m	To:t-8:30-10/50(d)
6/49	8:00	Adventures in Jazz — MU	c	
6/49	9:00	This Is Show Business(60) — VY	d	
7/49	8:00	Mama — SC	d	
7/49	9:30	Film(75) — FI	f	
9/49	7:45	Amazing Polgar(15) — IF	d	
9/49	7:45	Cliff Edwards(15) — MU	m	To:m-7:45
9/49	9:00	Fifty-Fourth Street Revue(60) — VY	m	Fr:r-8
9/49	9:00	This Is Show Business(60) — VY	m	To:n-7:30
10/49	7:15	Paul Arnold(15) — MU	d	
10/49	7:45	Amazing Polgar(15) — IF	c	
10/49	7:45	Sonny Kendis(15) — MU	m	Fr:tr-7:45
10/49	8:30	Man Against Crime — CD	d	
10/49	9:00	Ford Theatre(60) — DA	d	
10/49	10:00	People's Platform — DS	m	Fr:m-var
10/49	10:30	Capitol Cloak Room — PA	d	
11/49	7:00	Strictly for Laughs(15) — MU	d	
11/49	7:00	Your Sports Special(15) — SN	c	
11/49	7:55	Herb Shriner(5) — CV	d	
1/50	7:45	Life with Snarky Parker(15) — KV	d	
1/50	7:45	Sonny Kendis(15) — MU	c	
1/50	9:00	Fifty-Fourth Street Revue(60) — VY	m	To:s-8
2/50	7:55	Herb Shriner(5) — CV	c	
2/50	9:00	Actors Studio(60) — DA	m	Fr:t-9
3/50	7:45	Life with Snarky Parker(15) — KV	c	

Date	Time	Title (min. if not 30) – Type	Action	From/To
4/50	7:45	Alkali Ike(15) – CY	d	
5/50	7:45	Alkali Ike(15) – CY	c	
5/50	7:45	Arthur Godfrey and His Ukulele (15) – IS	m	Fr:tr-7:45
6/50	7:00	Garry Moore – VY	d	
6/50	7:00	Strictly for Laughs(15) – MU	c	
6/50	7:15	Paul Arnold(15) – MU	c	
6/50	7:45	Arthur Godfrey and His Ukulele (15) – IS	c	
6/50	8:00	We Take Your Word – QU	m*	Fr:s-9-4/50
6/50	9:00	Actors Studio(60) – DA	c	
7/50	7:45	Stork Club(15) – TK	d	
7/50	8:00	We Take Your Word – QU	m*	To:m-9:30
7/50	8:30	Detective's Wife – SC	d*	
7/50	9:00	Songs for Sale(60) – MU	d*	
8/50	10:00	By Popular Demand – VY	m	Fr:n-7:30
8/50	10:00	People's Platform – DS	c	
9/50	7:00	Garry Moore – VY	c	
9/50	7:00	Stork Club – TK	m	Fr:mwf-7:45
9/50	7:45	Stork Club(15) – TK	m	To:m-f-7
9/50	7:45	Three's Company(15) – MU	m	Fr:tr-7:45
9/50	7:45	Three's Company(15) – MU	c	
9/50	8:30	Detective's Wife – SC	c*	
9/50	9:00	Magnavox Theater(60) – DA	d	
9/50	9:00	Songs for Sale(60) – MU	m*	To:s-7:30-2/51
9/50	10:00	By Popular Demand – VY	c	
9/50	10:00	Star of the Family – CV	d	
9/50	10:30	Beat the Clock – QU	m	Fr:s-8
9/50	10:30	Capitol Cloak Room – PA	c	
10/50	7:45	Perry Como(15) – MV	m	Fr:n-8-6/50(n)
12/50	7:00	Steve Allen – CV	d	
12/50	7:00	Stork Club – TK	m	To:trs-7:45
12/50	9:00	Charlie Wild, Pvt. Detective – CD	d	
12/50	9:00	Ford Theatre(60) – DA	m	To:r-9:30-10/52(n)
12/50	9:00	Magnavox Theater(60) – DA	c	
12/50	9:30	Live Like a Millionaire – TA	d	
3/51	7:00	Steve Allen – CV	c	
3/51	9:00	Charlie Wild, Pvt. Detective – CD	m	To:w-9
3/51	9:00	Live Like a Millionaire – TA	m	Fr:f-9:30
3/51	9:30	Live Like a Millionaire – TA	m	To:f-9
3/51	10:30	Beat the Clock – QU	m	To:s-7:30
3/51	10:30	We Take Your Word – QU	m	Fr:t-10:30-1/51
6/51	9:00	Live Like a Millionaire – TA	m	To:f-10
6/51	10:00	Star of the Family – CV	m	To:r-8-1/52
6/51	10:30	We Take Your Word – QU	c	
7/51	7:45	TV's Top Tunes(15) – MU	d*	
7/51	9:00	Film(60) – FI	s	
7/51	10:00	Live Like a Millionaire – TA	m	Fr:f-9
7/51	10:30	Hollywood Opening Night – DA	d	
8/51	7:45	TV's Top Tunes(15) – MU	m*	To:mwf-7:45-6/53

Date	Time	Title (min. if not 30) – Type	Action	From/To
8/51	8:00	Ad Libbers – VY	d*	
8/51	8:00	Ad Libbers – VY	c*	
9/51	9:00	Film(60) – FI	f	
10/51	9:00	Schlitz Playhouse of Stars(60) – DA	d	
3/52	8:30	Man Against Crime – CD	m	To:r-9
3/52	9:00	Schlitz Playhouse of Stars(60) – DA	m	To:f-9
3/52	10:00	Live Like a Millionaire – TA	m	To:s-7:30-10/52(a)
3/52	10:30	Hollywood Opening Night – DA	m	To:m-9-10/52
4/52	8:30	My Friend Irma – SC	m	Fr:t-10:30
4/52	9:00	Schlitz Playhouse of Stars – DA	m	Fr:f-9
4/52	9:30	It's News to Me – QU	m	Fr:m-9:30
4/52	10:00	Police Story – RA	d	
4/52	10:30	Presidential Timber – PA	m	Fr:r-9-7/48
6/52	9:30	It's News to Me – QU	m	To:n-6:30
6/52	10:30	Presidential Timber – PA	c	
7/52	7:45	Eddy Arnold(15) – MV	d*	
7/52	8:00	Arthur Murray Party – MV	m*	Fr:n-9-5/52(a)
7/52	8:30	Pantomime Quiz – QU	m*	Fr:w-10-3/52(n)
7/52	9:30	Footlight Theatre – DA	d	
8/52	7:45	Eddy Arnold(15) – MV	m*	To:tr-7:30-7/53(n)
8/52	8:00	Arthur Murray Party – MV	m*	To:n-10-10/52(d)
9/52	8:30	Pantomime Quiz – QU	m*	To:f-8-7/53
9/52	9:30	Footlight Theatre – DA	m	To:f-9:30-7/53
9/52	10:00	Police Story – RA	c	
10/52	9:30	Our Miss Brooks – SC	d	
10/52	10:00	Mr. & Mrs. North – CO	d	
6/53	7:45	TV's Top Tunes(15) – MU	m*	Fr:mwf-7:45-8/51
6/53	8:30	My Friend Irma – SC	m	To:f-10-10/53
7/53	8:00	Pantomime Quiz – QU	m*	Fr:f-8:30-9/52
7/53	8:30	Man Against Crime – CD	m	Fr:w-9:30
7/53	9:30	Footlight Theatre – DA	m*	Fr:f-9:30-9/52
8/53	7:45	TV's Top Tunes(15) – MU	m*	To:mwf-7:45-6/54
8/53	8:00	Pantomime Quiz – QU	m*	To:t-8:30-10/53(d)
9/53	9:30	Footlight Theatre – DA	c*	
9/53	10:00	Mr. & Mrs. North – CO	m	To:t-10:30-1/54(n)
10/53	8:30	Man Against Crime – CD	m	To:n-10:30(d)
10/53	8:30	Topper – SC	d	
10/53	10:00	My Friend Irma – SC	m	Fr:f-8:30-6/53
10/53	10:30	Person to Person – IV	d	
6/54	7:45	TV's Top Tunes(15) – MU	m*	Fr:mwf-7:45-8/53
6/54	10:00	My Friend Irma – SC	c	
7/54	8:00	Pantomime Quiz – QU	m*	Fr:t-8:30-4/54(d)
7/54	10:00	Viceroy Star Theatre – DA	d	
7/54	10:30	It's News to Me – QU	m*	Fr:s-10:30-9/53
8/54	7:45	TV's Top Tunes(15) – MU	m*	To:s-10-7/55
8/54	8:00	Pantomime Quiz – QU	m*	To:n-9:30-1/55(a)
8/54	10:30	It's News to Me – QU	c*	
9/54	10:00	Viceroy Star Theatre – DA	c	
10/54	10:00	The Lineup – CD	d	
6/55	7:45	Julius LaRosa(15) – MU	d	

Date	Time	Title (min. if not 30) – Type	Action	From/To
6/55	7:45	Perry Como(15) – MV	m	To:s-8-9/55(n)
6/55	9:30	Our Miss Brooks – SC	m	To:f-8:30-10/55
6/55	10:00	Undercurrent – DA	d*	
7/55	8:00	Pantomime Quiz – QU	m*	Fr:n-9:30-3/55(a)
7/55	9:30	Ray Milland – SC	m	Fr:r-8
7/55	10:30	Windows – DA	d*	
8/55	10:00	Undercurrent – DA	m*	To:f-10-6/56
8/55	10:30	Windows – DA	c*	
9/55	7:30	Adventures of Champion – WE	d	
9/55	7:45	Julius LaRosa(15) – MU	c	
9/55	8:00	Pantomime Quiz – QU	m*	To:f-10:30-7/56
9/55	8:30	Topper – SC	m	To:m-7:30(a)
9/55	9:00	Schlitz Playhouse of Stars – DA	m	To:f-9:30
9/55	9:30	Ray Milland – SC	c	
10/55	8:30	Our Miss Brooks – SC	m	Fr:f-9:30-6/55
10/55	9:00	Crusader – SD	d	
10/55	9:30	Schlitz Playhouse of Stars – DA	m	Fr:f-9
2/56	7:30	Adventures of Champion – WE	c	
2/56	7:30	My Friend Flicka – WE	d	
6/56	10:00	Undercurrent – DA	m*	Fr:f-10-8/55
7/56	8:00	Mama – SC	c	
7/56	10:30	Pantomime Quiz – QU	m*	Fr:f-8-9/55
8/56	8:00	Hollywood Summer Theatre – DA	d	
8/56	10:00	Undercurrent – DA	m*	To:f-10-6/57
9/56	8:00	Hollywood Summer Theatre – DA	c	
9/56	8:30	Our Miss Brooks – SC	c	
9/56	10:30	Pantomime Quiz – QU	m*	To:f-10:30-7/57
10/56	8:00	West Point Story – DA	d	
10/56	8:30	Dick Powell's Zane Grey Theatre – WA	d	
12/56	9:00	Crusader – SD	c	
1/57	9:00	Mr. Adams and Eve – SC	d	
2/57	7:30	Beat the Clock – QU	m	Fr:s-7
2/57	7:30	My Friend Flicka – WE	m	To:s-7
6/57	10:00	Undercurrent – DA	m*	Fr:f-10-8/56
7/57	8:30	Destiny – DA	d*	
7/57	10:30	Pantomime Quiz – QU	m*	Fr:f-10:30-9/56
8/57	10:00	Undercurrent – DA	m*	To:f-10-6/58
9/57	7:30	Beat the Clock – QU	c	
9/57	8:00	West Point Story – DA	m	To:t-10(a)
9/57	8:30	Destiny – DA	m*	To:f-8:30-7/58
9/57	10:30	Pantomime Quiz – QU	m*	To:t-9:30-4/58(a)
10/57	7:30	Leave It to Beaver – SC	d	
10/57	8:00	Trackdown – WE	d	
2/58	9:00	Mr. Adams and Eve – SC	m	To:t-8
2/58	9:00	Phil Silvers – SC	m	Fr:t-8
3/58	7:30	Leave It to Beaver – SC	m	To:w-8
3/58	8:30	Dick and the Duchess – CO	m*	Fr:s-8:30
4/58	7:30	Boing Boing Show – KV	d	
5/58	8:30	Dick and the Duchess – CO	c*	

Date	Time	Title (min. if not 30) — Type	Action	From/To
6/58	10:00	Undercurrent — DA	m*	Fr:f-10-8/57
7/58	8:30	Destiny — DA	m	Fr:f-8:30-9/57
7/58	8:30	Dick Powell's Zane Grey Theatre — WA	m	To:r-9-10/58
7/58	10:30	Personal Appearance — DA	d*	
9/58	8:30	Destiny — DA	c	
9/58	10:00	Undercurrent — DA	c*	
9/58	10:30	Personal Appearance — DA	c*	
10/58	7:30	Boing Boing Show — KV	c	
10/58	7:30	Your Hit Parade — MU	m	Fr:s-10:30-6/58(n)
10/58	8:30	Jackie Gleason — CV	m	Fr:s-8-6/57
10/58	9:30	Lux Playhouse — DA	d	
1/59	8:00	Rawhide(60) — WE	d	
1/59	8:00	Trackdown — WE	m	To:w-8:30
1/59	8:30	Jackie Gleason — CV	m	To:s-7:30-9/62
3/59	9:30	Schlitz Playhouse of Stars — DA	c	
4/59	7:30	Your Hit Parade — MU	c	
4/59	8:00	Rawhide(60) — WE	m	To:f-7:30
5/59	7:30	Rawhide(60) — WE	m	Fr:f-8
5/59	8:30	Original Amateur Hour — TA	m	Fr:s-10-10/58(n)
6/59	8:30	Original Amateur Hour — TA	m	To:f-10:30
7/59	8:30	I Love Lucy — SC	m	Fr:r-7:30-5/59
7/59	10:30	Original Amateur Hour — TA	m*	Fr:f-8:30
9/59	8:30	I Love Lucy — SC	c	
9/59	9:00	Phil Silvers — SC	c	
9/59	9:30	Lux Playhouse — DA	c	
9/59	10:00	The Lineup — CD	m	To:w-7:30
10/59	8:30	Hotel de Paree — WE	d	
10/59	9:00	Westinghouse Desilu Playhouse(60) — DA	m	Fr:m-10
10/59	10:00	Twilight Zone — FA	d	
10/59	10:30	Original Amateur Hour — TA	m*	To:m-10:30-3/60(a)
6/60	9:00	Westinghouse Desilu Playhouse(60) — DA	c	
7/60	9:00	Video Village — QU	d	
7/60	9:30	December Bride — SC	m	Fr:r-8-9/59
9/60	8:30	Hotel de Paree — WE	c	
9/60	9:00	Video Village — QU	c	
9/60	9:30	December Bride — SC	m	To:r-7:30-4/61
9/60	10:30	Eyewitness to History — NA	d	
9/60	10:30	Person to Person — IV	m	To:r-10
10/60	8:30	Route 66(60) — AD	d	
10/60	9:30	Mr. Garlund — AD	d	
1/61	9:30	Jackie Gleason — TK	d	
1/61	9:30	Mr. Garlund — AD	c	
3/61	9:30	Jackie Gleason — TK	c	
3/61	9:30	Way Out — DA	d	
6/61	10:30	Person to Person — IV	m*	Fr:r-10-12/60
7/61	9:30	Adventure Theater — AA	m	Fr:r-10-9/60
7/61	9:30	Way Out — DA	c	

Date	Time	Title (min. if not 30) — Type	Action	From/To
9/61	9:30	Adventure Theater — AA	c	
9/61	9:30	Father of the Bride — SC	d	
9/61	10:30	Person to Person — IV	c*	
9/62	9:30	Fair Exchange(60) — SC	d	
9/62	9:30	Father of the Bride — SC	c	
9/62	10:00	Twilight Zone — FA	m	To:r-9-1/63
12/62	9:30	Fair Exchange(60) — SC	m	To:r-7:30-3/63
1/63	9:30	Alfred Hitchcock Presents(60) — SA	m	Fr:r-10
8/63	10:00	Eyewitness to History — NA	c	
8/63	10:30	Portrait — IV	d	
9/63	7:30	Great Adventure(60) — AA	d	
9/63	7:30	Rawhide(60) — WE	m	To:r-8
9/63	9:30	Alfred Hitchcock Presents(60) — SA	m	To:f-10
9/63	9:30	Twilight Zone — FA	m	Fr:r-9
9/63	10:00	Alfred Hitchcock Presents(60) — SA	m	Fr:f-9:30
9/63	10:30	Portrait — IV	c	
9/64	7:30	Great Adventure(60) — AA	m	To:f-8:30-3/65
9/64	7:30	Rawhide(60) — WE	m	Fr:r-8
9/64	8:30	The Entertainers(60) — VY	d	
9/64	8:30	Route 66(60) — AD	c	
9/64	9:30	Gomer Pyle, U.S.M.C. — SC	d	
9/64	9:30	Twilight Zone — FA	m	To:n-9-5/65
9/64	10:00	Alfred Hitchcock Presents(60) — SA	m	To:m-10(n)
9/64	10:00	The Reporter(60) — ND	d	
12/64	8:30	The Entertainers(60) — VY	m	To:s-9
12/64	10:00	The Reporter(60) — ND	c	
12/64	10:00	Slattery's People(60) — DR	m	Fr:m-10
1/65	8:30	On Broadway Tonight(60) — TA	m	Fr:w-10-9/64
3/65	8:30	Great Adventure(60) — AA	m	Fr:f-7:30-9/64
3/65	8:30	On Broadway Tonight(60) — TA	c	
4/65	8:30	Great Adventure(60) — AA	c	
5/65	8:30	Cara Williams — SC	m	Fr:w-9:30
5/65	9:00	Our Private World — SL	d	
6/65	9:30	Gomer Pyle, U.S.M.C. — SC	m	To:f-9-9/65
6/65	9:30	Vacation Playhouse — VS	m	Fr:m-8:30-9/64
9/65	7:30	Rawhide(60) — WE	m	To:t-7:30
9/65	7:30	Wild Wild West(60) — WE	d	
9/65	8:30	Cara Williams — SC	c	
9/65	8:30	Hogan's Heroes — SC	d	
9/65	9:00	Gomer Pyle, U.S.M.C. — SC	m	Fr:f-9:30-6/65
9/65	9:00	Our Private World — SL	c	
9/65	9:30	Smothers Brothers — SC	d	
9/65	9:30	Vacation Playhouse — VS	m	To:m-8:30-7/66
11/65	10:00	Slattery's People(60) — DR	c	
12/65	10:00	Trials of O'Brien(60) — LD	m	Fr:s-8:30
5/66	10:00	Trials of O'Brien(60) — LD	c	
6/66	10:00	Wayne and Shuster(60) — CY	d	
7/66	10:00	Wayne and Shuster(60) — CY	c	
8/66	10:00	CBS Reports(60) — DO	s	
9/66	9:00	Gomer Pyle, U.S.M.C. — SC	m	To:w-9:30

Date	Time	Title (min. if not 30) — Type	Action	From/To
9/66	9:00	Film(120) — FI	s	
9/66	9:30	Smothers Brothers — SC	c	
9/66	10:00	CBS Reports(60) — DO	f	
9/67	8:30	Gomer Pyle, U.S.M.C. — SC	m	Fr:w-9:30
9/67	8:30	Hogan's Heroes — SC	m	To:s-9
9/69	7:30	Get Smart — SC	m	Fr:s-8(n)
9/69	7:30	Wild Wild West(60) — WE	m	To:m-10-7/70
9/69	8:00	Good Guys — SC	m	Fr:w-8:30
9/69	8:30	Gomer Pyle, U.S.M.C. — SC	m	To:w-8-7/70
9/69	8:30	Hogan's Heroes — SC	m	Fr:s-9
1/70	8:00	Good Guys — SC	c	
1/70	8:00	Tim Conway — SC	d	
3/70	7:30	CBS Adventure — DO	d*	
4/70	7:30	CBS Adventure — DO	c*	
6/70	8:00	He & She — SC	m	Fr:w-9:30-9/68
6/70	8:00	Tim Conway — SC	c	
9/70	7:30	Get Smart — SC	c	
9/70	7:30	The Interns(60) — MD	d	
9/70	8:00	He & She — SC	c	
9/70	8:30	The Headmaster — DR	d	
9/70	8:30	Hogan's Heroes — SC	m	To:n-7:30
1/71	8:30	The Headmaster — DR	m	To:f-8:30-6/71
1/71	8:30	New Andy Griffith Show — SC	d	
5/71	8:30	New Andy Griffith Show — SC	c	
6/71	8:30	The Headmaster — DR	m	Fr:f-8:30-1/71
9/71	7:30	The Interns(60) — MD	c	
9/71	8:00	Chicago Teddy Bears — SC	d	
9/71	8:30	The Headmaster — DR	c	
9/71	8:30	O'Hara, U.S. Treasury(60) — CD	d	
12/71	8:00	Chicago Teddy Bears — SC	c	
12/71	8:30	O'Hara, U.S. Treasury(60) — CD	m	To:f-8
1/72	8:00	O'Hara, U.S. Treasury(60) — CD	m	Fr:f-8:30
1/72	10:30	Don Rickles — SC	d	
5/72	10:30	Don Rickles — SC	c	
6/72	10:30	Governor & J.J. — SC	m	Fr:w-8:30-12/70
8/72	10:30	Governor & J.J. — SC	c	
9/72	8:00	O'Hara, U.S. Treasury(60) — CD	c	
9/72	8:00	Sonny and Cher Comedy Hour(60) — MV	m	Fr:m-10-6/72
12/72	8:00	Mission: Impossible(60) — SD	m	Fr:s-10
12/72	8:00	Sonny and Cher Comedy Hour(60) — MV	m	To:w-8
5/73	8:00	Mission: Impossible(60) — SD	m	To:s-10
6/73	8:00	60 Minutes(60) — NM	m	Fr:t-10-6/71
9/73	8:00	60 Minutes(60) — NM	m	To:n-9:30-7/74
10/73	8:00	Calucci's Department — SC	d	
10/73	8:30	Roll Out — SC	d	
12/73	8:00	Calucci's Department — SC	c	
1/74	8:00	Dirty Sally — WE	d	
1/74	8:30	Roll Out — SC	c	

Date	Time	Title (min. if not 30) – Type	Action	From/To
2/74	8:30	Good Times – SC	d	
9/74	8:00	Dirty Sally – WE	c	
9/74	8:00	Planet of the Apes(60) – SF	d	
9/74	8:30	Good Times – SC	m	To:t-8
12/74	8:00	Planet of the Apes(60) – SF	c	
1/75	8:00	Khan(60) – CD	d	
2/75	8:00	Khan(60) – CD	c	
3/75	8:00	Friday Comedy Special – CA	d	
3/75	8:30	We'll Get By – SC	d	
8/75	8:00	Friday Comedy Special – CA	c	
8/75	8:30	We'll Get By – SC	c	
9/75	8:00	Big Eddie – SC	m	Fr:s-8:30
9/75	8:30	M*A*S*H – SC	m	Fr:t-8:30
9/75	9:00	Hawaii Five-O(60) – CD	m	Fr:t-9
9/75	9:00	Film(120) – FI	f	
9/75	10:00	Barnaby Jones(60) – CD	m	Fr:t-10
11/75	8:00	Big Eddie – SC	c	
11/75	8:30	M*A*S*H – SC	m	To:t-9
11/75	9:00	Hawaii Five-O(60) – CD	m	To:r-9
11/75	10:00	Barnaby Jones(60) – CD	m	To:r-10
12/75	9:00	Film(120) – FI	s	
2/76	8:00	Sara(60) – WE	d	
8/76	8:00	Sara(60) – WE	c	
9/76	8:00	Spencer's Pilots(60) – AD	d	
12/76	8:00	Spencer's Pilots(60) – AD	c	
1/77	8:00	Code R(60) – AD	d	
1/77	9:00	Film(120) – FI	f	
1/77	9:00	Sonny and Cher Comedy Hour(60) – MV	m	Fr:n-8
1/77	10:00	Executive Suite(60) – DR	m	Fr:m-10
2/77	10:00	Executive Suite(60) – DR	c	
2/77	10:00	Hunter(60) – SD	d	
4/77	9:00	Sonny and Cher Comedy Hour(60) – MV	m	To:m-10
4/77	10:00	Hunter(60) – SD	c	
5/77	9:00	Film(120) – FI	s	
6/77	8:00	Code R(60) – AD	c	
7/77	8:00	A Year at the Top – SC	d	
7/77	8:30	Keane Brothers – MV	d	
8/77	8:00	Starland Vocal Band – VY	m	Fr:n-8:30
8/77	8:00	A Year at the Top – SC	m	To:n-8:30
9/77	8:00	Wonder Woman(60) – AD	m	Fr:s-8-7/77(a)
9/77	8:30	Keane Brothers – MV	c	
9/77	8:30	Starland Vocal Band – VY	c	
3/78	9:00	Incredible Hulk(60) – AD	d	
3/78	9:00	Film(120) – FI	f	
3/78	10:00	Husbands, Wives & Lovers(60) – SC	d	
8/78	10:00	Husbands, Wives & Lovers(60) – SC	c	
9/78	10:00	Flying High(60) – DR	d	
12/78	10:00	Flying High(60) – DR	c	

Date	Time	Title (min. if not 30) — Type	Action	From/To
1/79	9:00	Dukes of Hazzard(60) — CO	d	
1/79	9:00	Incredible Hulk(60) — AD	m	To:w-8
1/79	10:00	Dallas(60) — SL	m	Fr:n-10
2/79	8:00	Incredible Hulk(60) — AD	m	Fr:w-8
2/79	8:00	Wonder Woman(60) — AD	m	To:t-8-8/79
11/81	8:00	Incredible Hulk(60) — AD	m	To:w-8-3/82
11/81	9:00	Dukes of Hazzard(60) — CO	m	To:f-8
11/81	10:00	Dallas(60) — SL	m	To:f-9
12/81	8:00	Dukes of Hazzard(60) — CO	m	Fr:f-9
12/81	9:00	Dallas(60) — SL	m	Fr:f-10
12/81	10:00	Falcon Crest(60) — SL	d	
4/82	10:00	Nurse(60) — MD	m*	Fr:r-10
5/82	10:00	Nurse(60) — MD	c*	
3/83	10:00	The Mississippi(60) — LD	d*	
5/83	10:00	The Mississippi(60) — LD	m*	To:t-8-9/83
8/84	8:00	Comedy Zone(60) — CY	d*	
9/84	8:00	Comedy Zone(60) — CY	c*	
2/85	8:00	Dukes of Hazzard(60) — CO	m	To:f-8-6/85
3/85	8:00	Detective of the House(60) — CD	d	
4/85	8:00	Detective of the House(60) — CD	c	
5/85	9:00	Film(120) — FI	s*	
6/85	8:00	Dukes of Hazzard(60) — CO	m	Fr:f-8-2/85
8/85	8:00	Dukes of Hazzard(60) — CO	c	
9/85	8:00	I Had Three Wives(60) — CD	m	Fr:w-8
9/85	8:00	I Had Three Wives(60) — CD	c	
9/85	8:00	Twilight Zone(60) — FA	d	
9/85	9:00	Film(120) — FI	f*	
4/86	8:00	Charlie & Company — SC	m*	Fr:t-8:30-2/86
4/86	8:30	Leo & Liz in Beverly Hills — SC	d*	
5/86	9:00	Film(120) — FI	s*	
6/86	8:00	Charlie & Company — SC	m*	To:w-8:30
6/86	8:30	Leo & Liz in Beverly Hills — SC	c*	
9/86	8:00	Twilight Zone(60) — FA	m	To:s-10
9/86	8:00	Scarecrow & Mrs. King(60) — AD	m	Fr:m-8
9/86	9:00	Film(120) — FI	f*	
2/87	8:00	Scarecrow & Mrs. King(60) — AD	m	To:r-8-5/87
3/87	8:00	Nothing Is Easy — SC	d	
3/87	8:30	Popcorn Kid — SC	d	
4/87	8:00	Nothing Is Easy — SC	c	
4/87	8:30	Popcorn Kid — SC	c	
6/87	8:00	Summer Playhouse(60) — VS	d	
6/87	10:00	Hard Copy(60) — ND	d*	
7/87	10:00	Hard Copy(60) — ND	c*	
7/87	10:00	Twilight Zone(60) — FA	m	Fr:r-8-1/87
7/87	10:00	Twilight Zone(60) — FA	c	
8/87	8:00	Summer Playhouse(60) — VS	c	
8/87	10:00	Adderly(60) — CD	d*	
8/87	10:00	Adderly(60) — CD	c*	

Date	Time	Title (min. if not 30) – Type	Action	From/To
9/87	8:00	Beauty & the Beast(60) – DR	d#	
5/88	9:00	Dallas(60) – SL	m	To:f-9-9/88
5/88	9:00	Film(120) – FI	s	
5/88	10:00	Falcon Crest(60) – SL	m	To:f-10-9/88
8/88	9:00	Film(120) – FI	f	

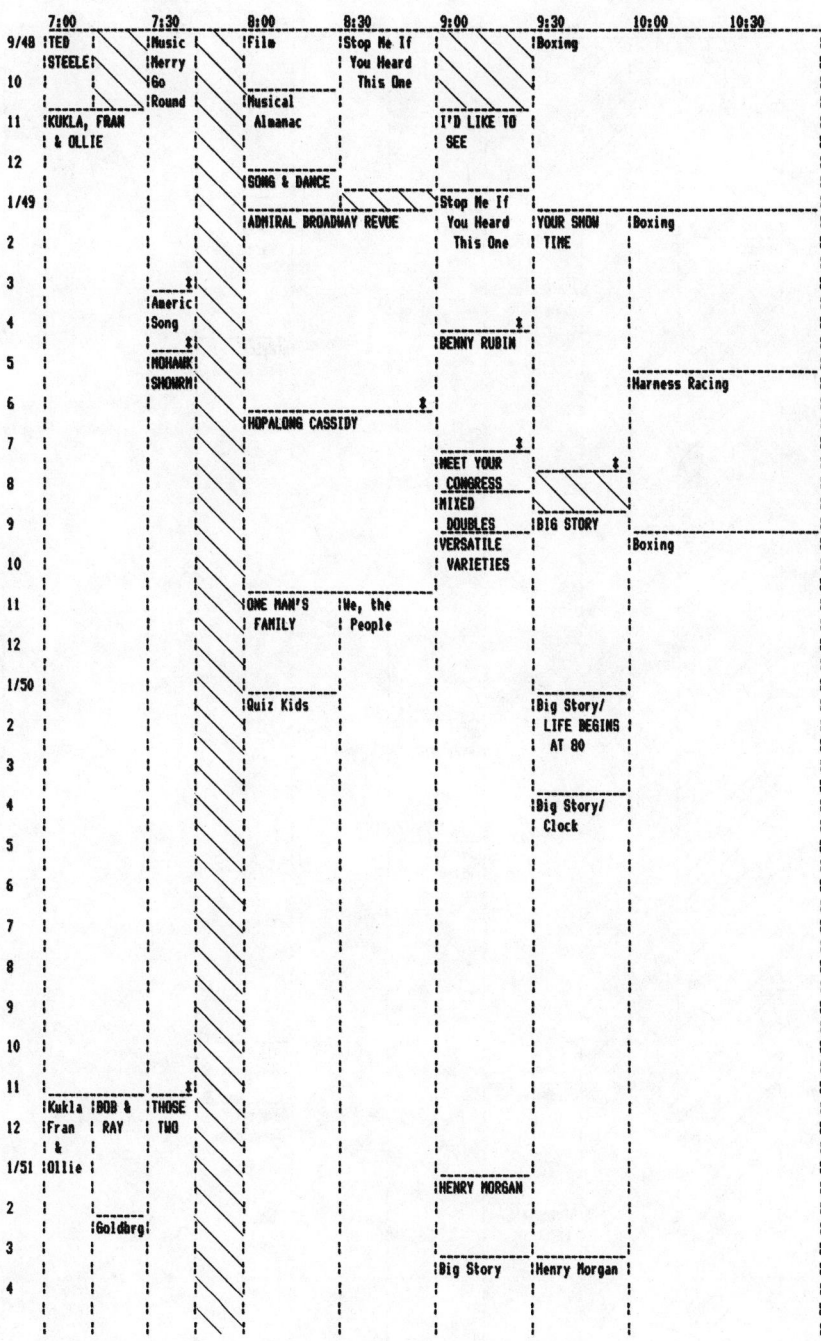

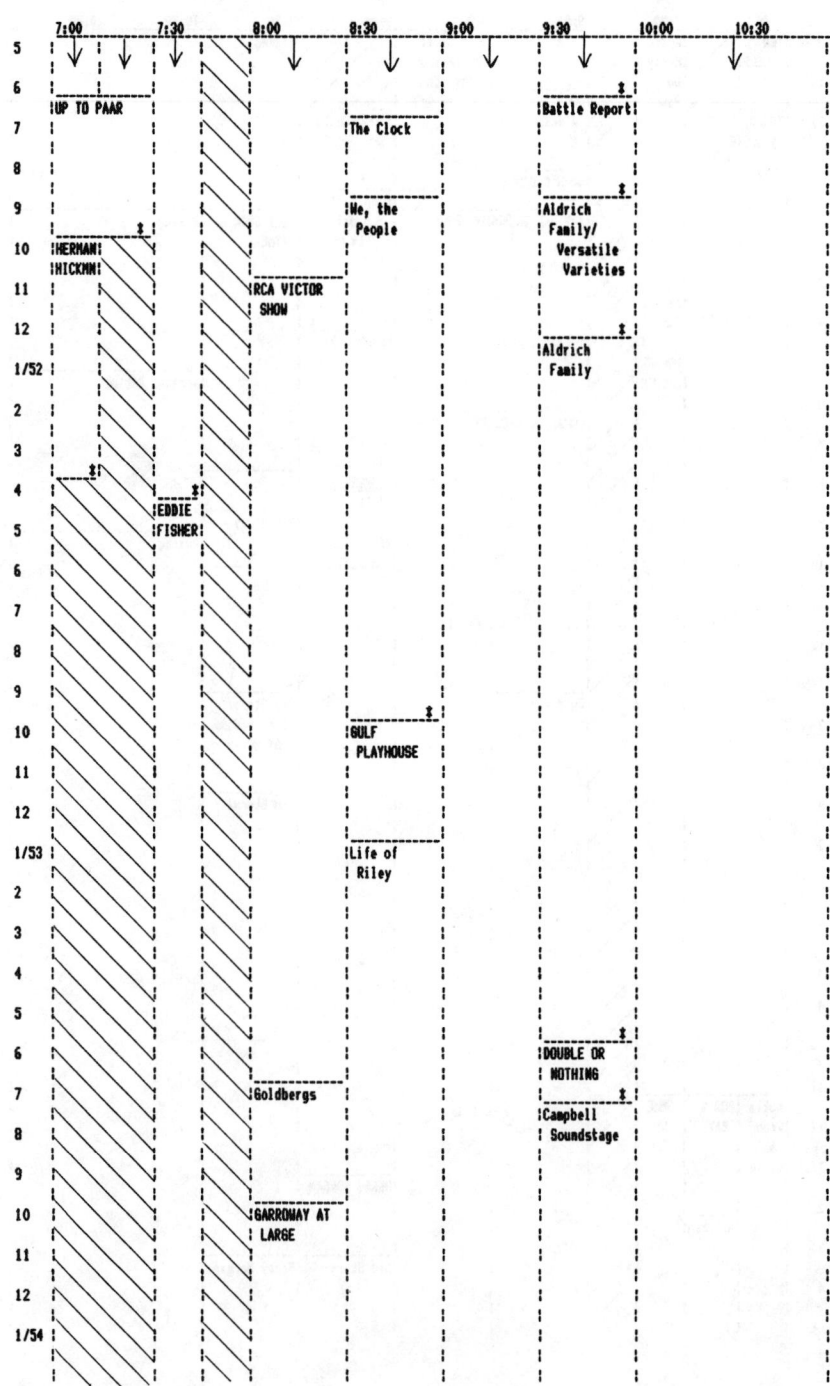

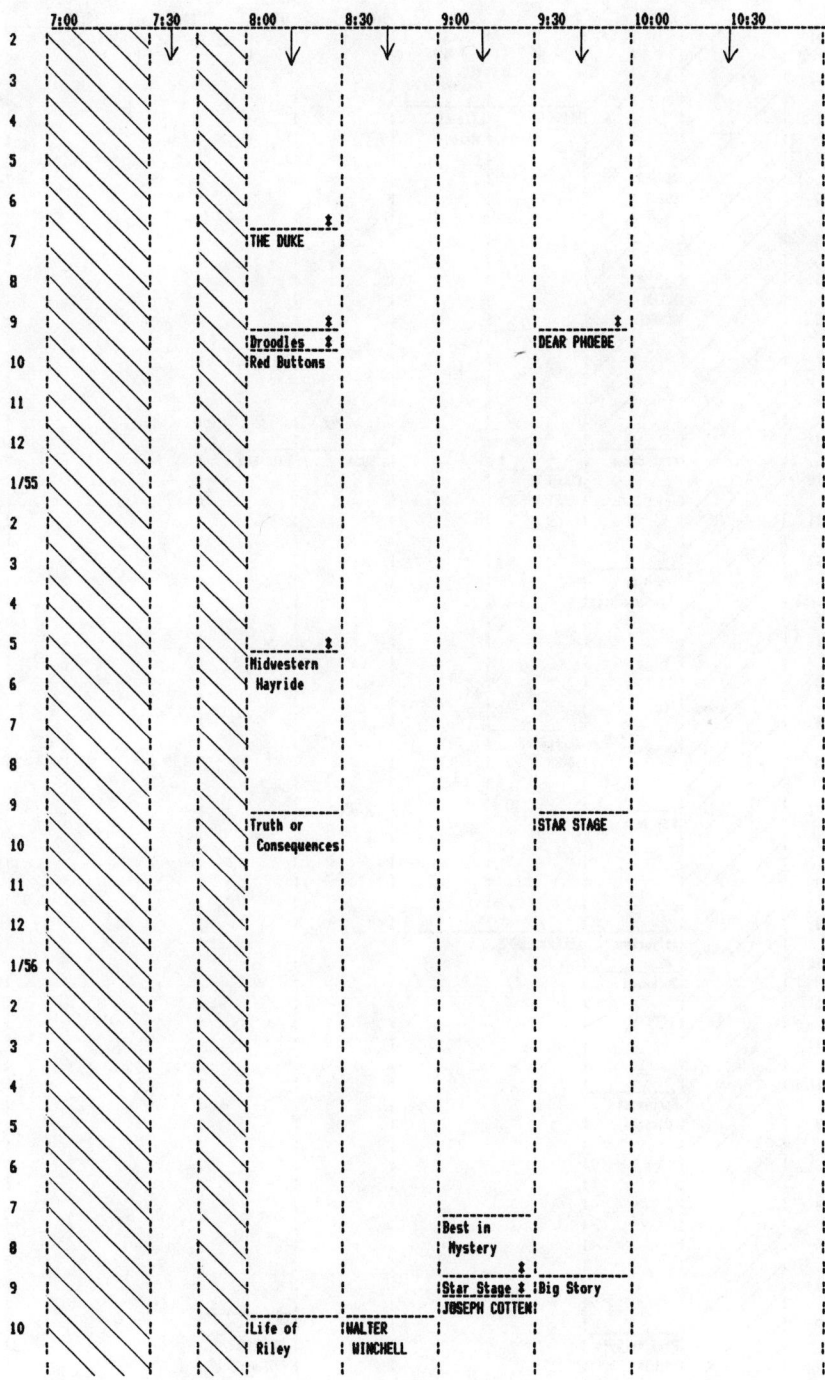

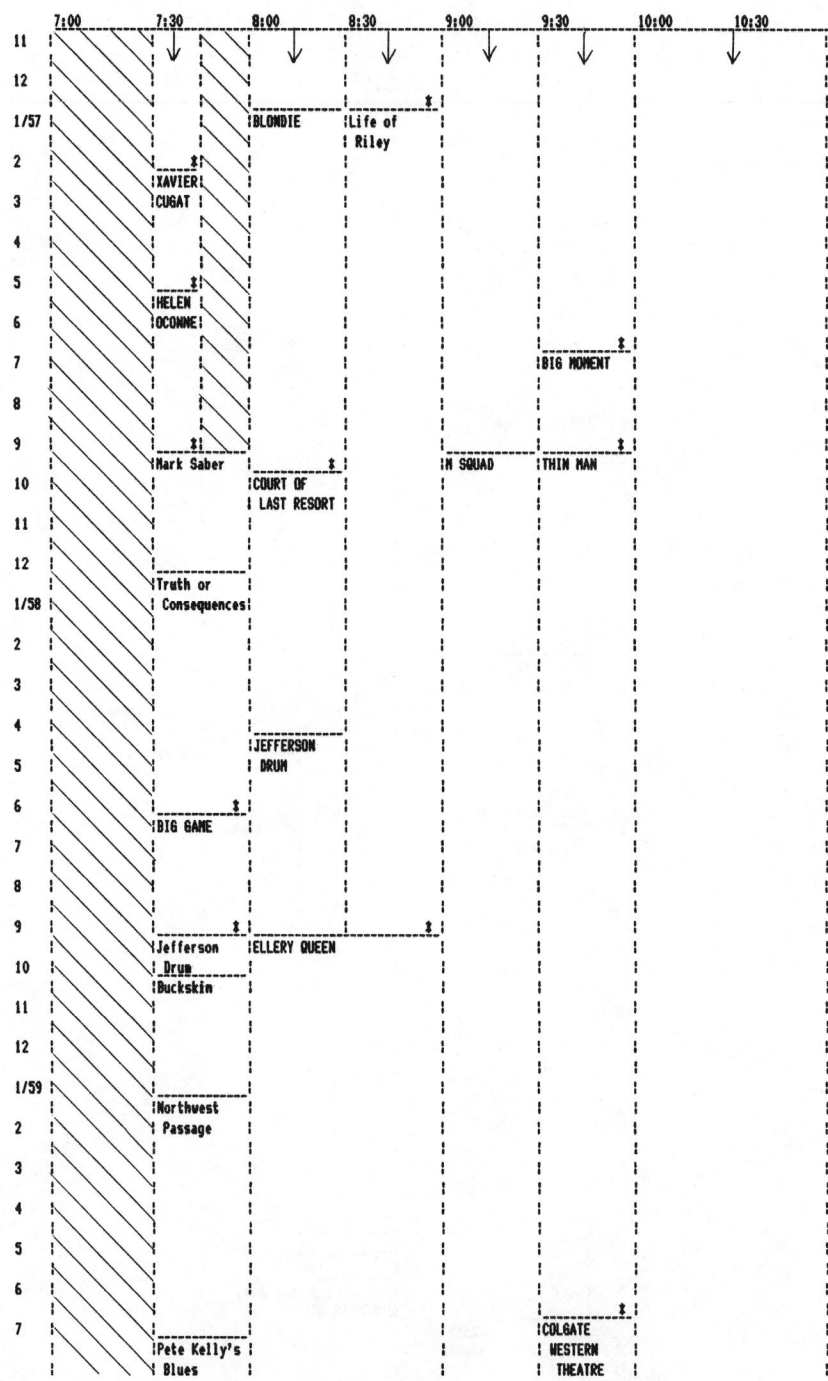

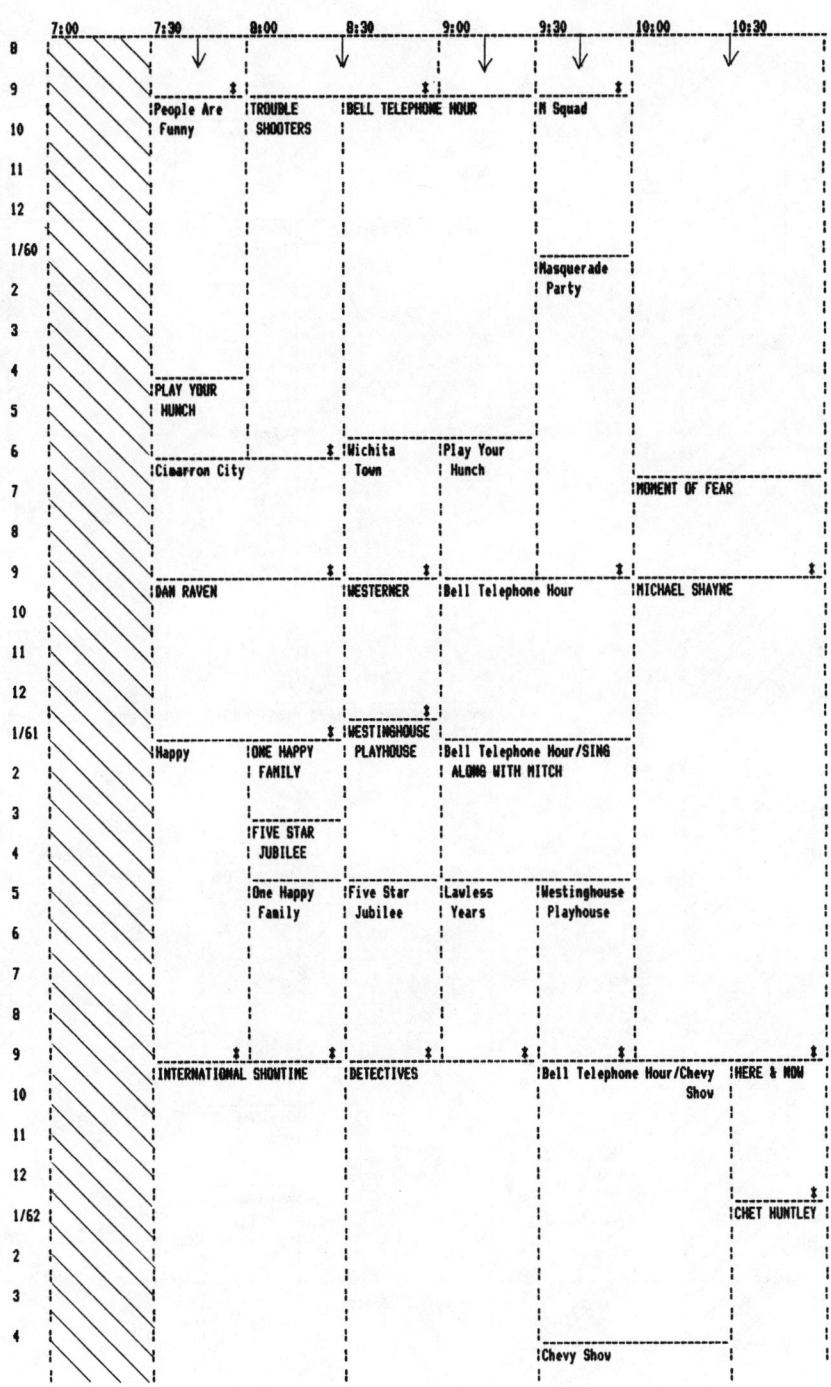

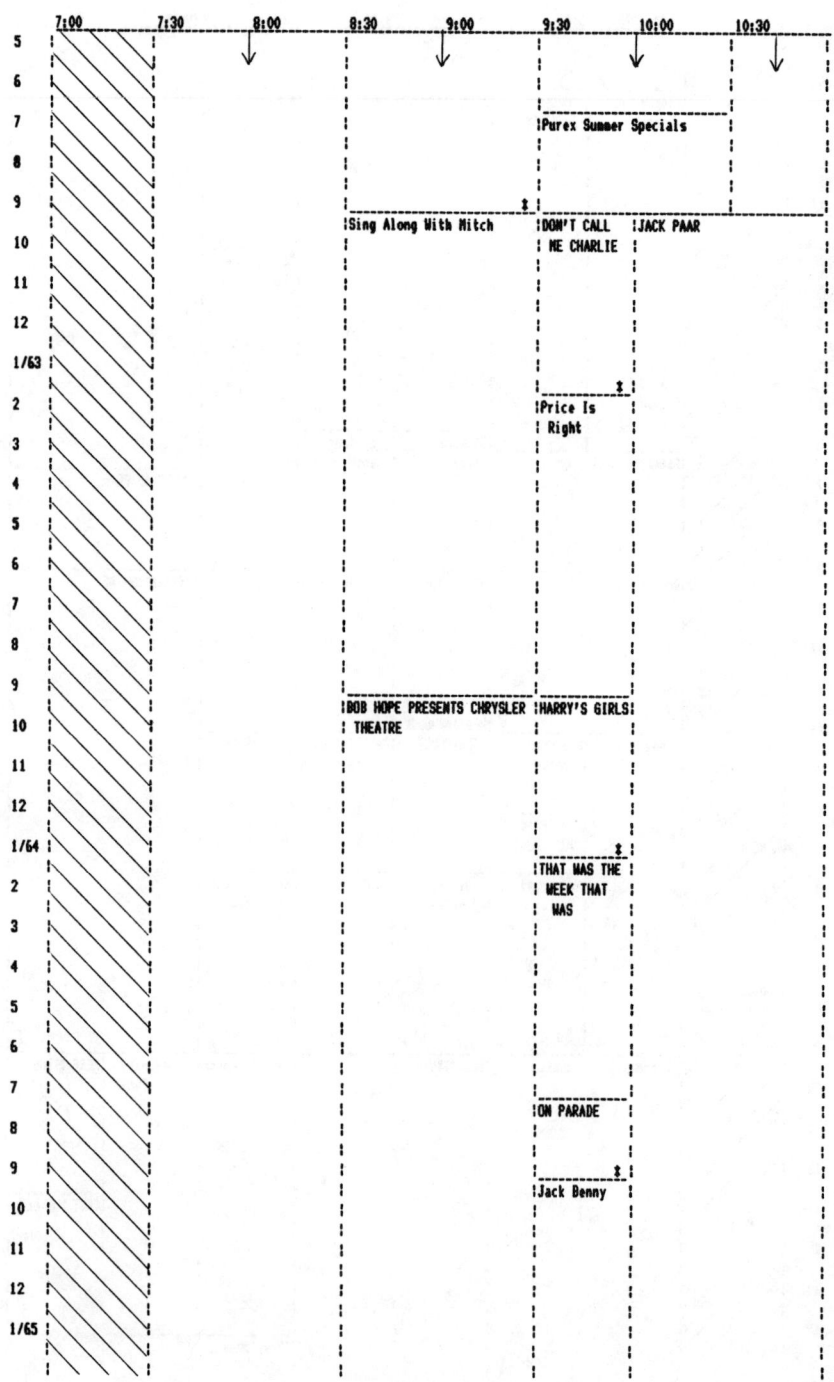

	7:00	7:30	8:00	8:30	9:00	9:30	10:00	10:30

Purex Summer Specials

Sing Along With Mitch

DON'T CALL ME CHARLIE

JACK PAAR

Price Is Right

BOB HOPE PRESENTS CHRYSLER THEATRE

HARRY'S GIRLS

THAT WAS THE WEEK THAT WAS

ON PARADE

Jack Benny

5
6
7
8
9
10
11
12
1/63
2
3
4
5
6
7
8
9
10
11
12
1/64
2
3
4
5
6
7
8
9
10
11
12
1/65

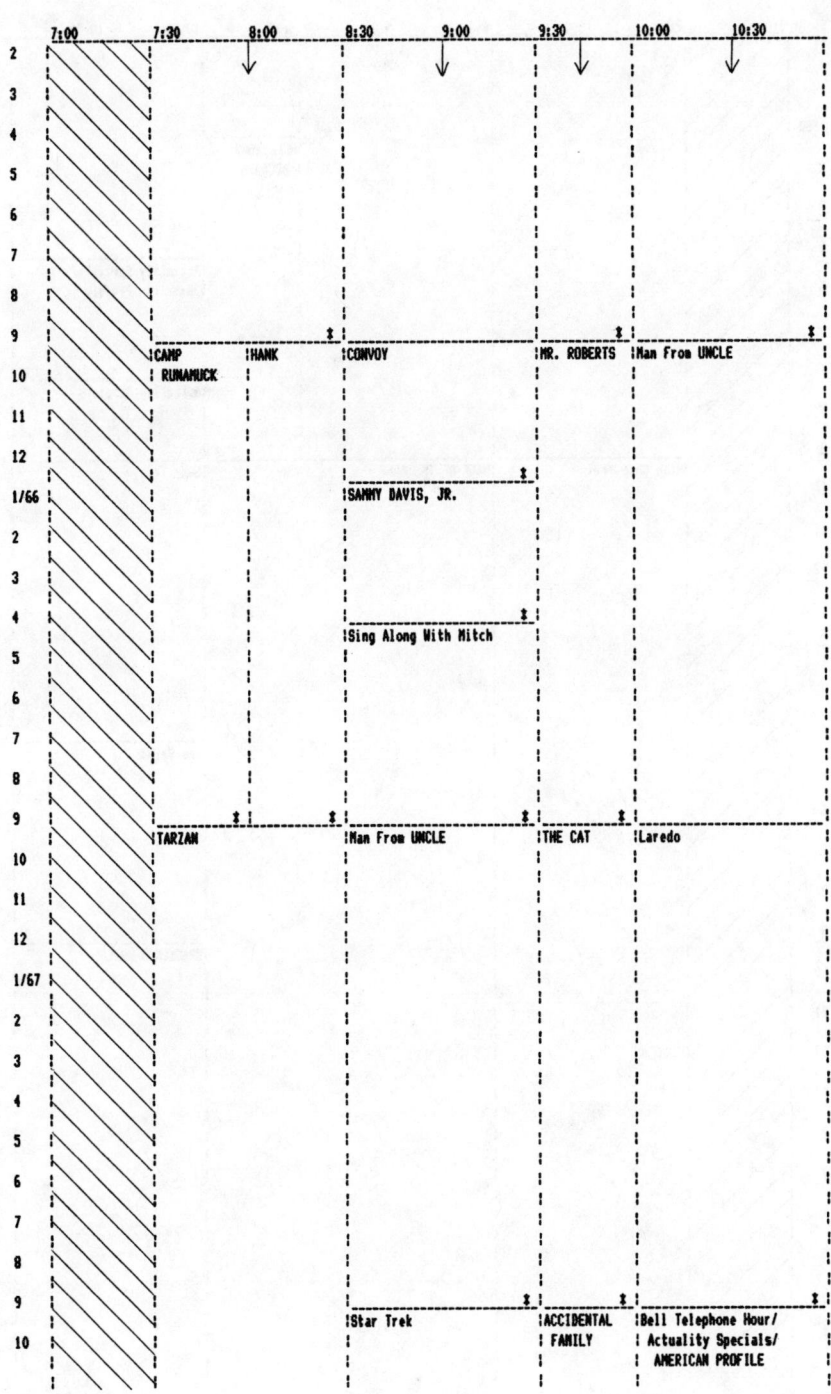

	7:00	7:30	8:00	8:30	9:00	9:30	10:00	10:30
2								
3								
4								
5								
6								
7								
8								
9								
10		CAMP RUNAMUCK	HANK	CONVOY		MR. ROBERTS	Man From UNCLE	
11								
12								
1/66				SAMMY DAVIS, JR.				
2								
3								
4				Sing Along With Mitch				
5								
6								
7								
8								
9								
		TARZAN		Man From UNCLE		THE CAT	Laredo	
10								
11								
12								
1/67								
2								
3								
4								
5								
6								
7								
8								
9								
				Star Trek		ACCIDENTAL FAMILY	Bell Telephone Hour/ Actuality Specials/ AMERICAN PROFILE	
10								

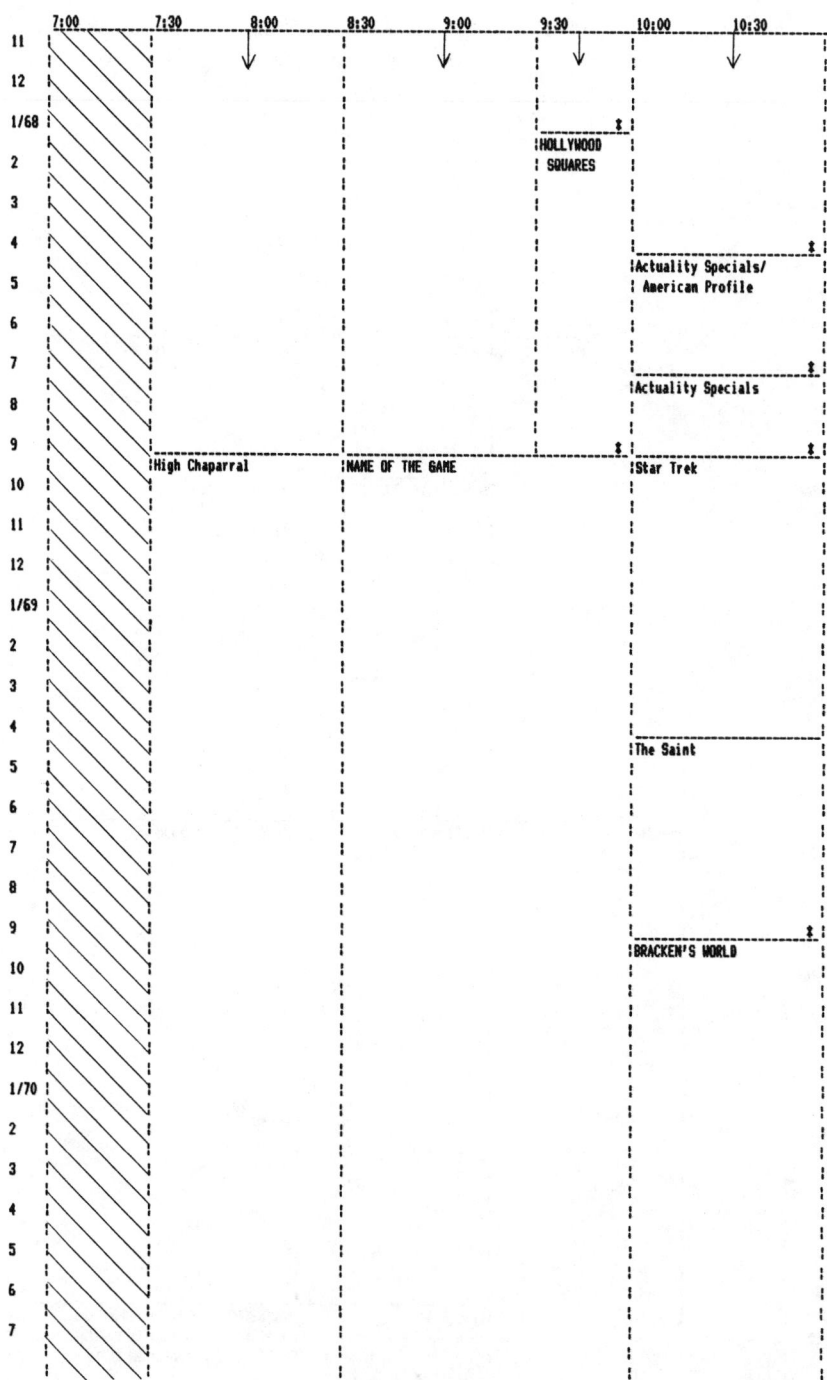

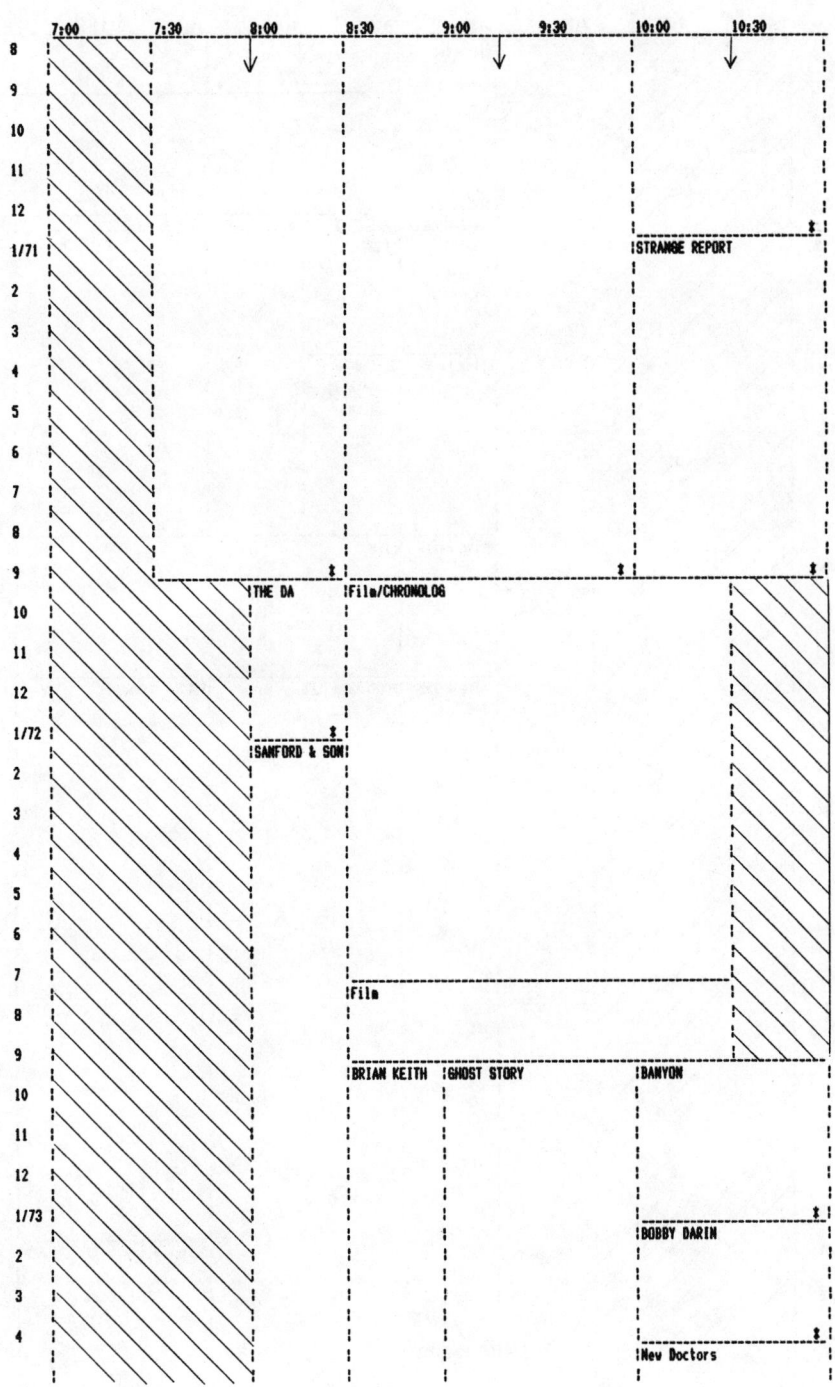

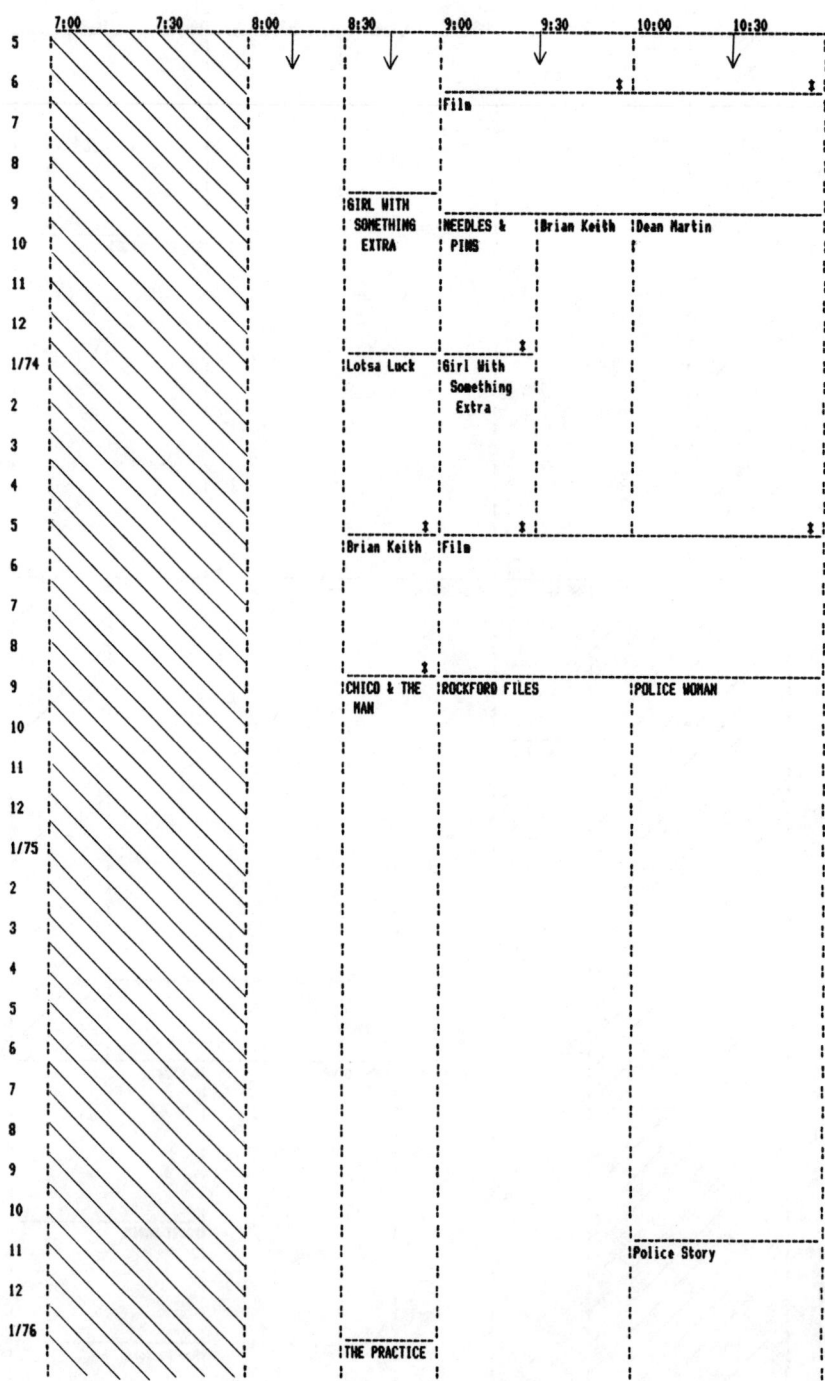

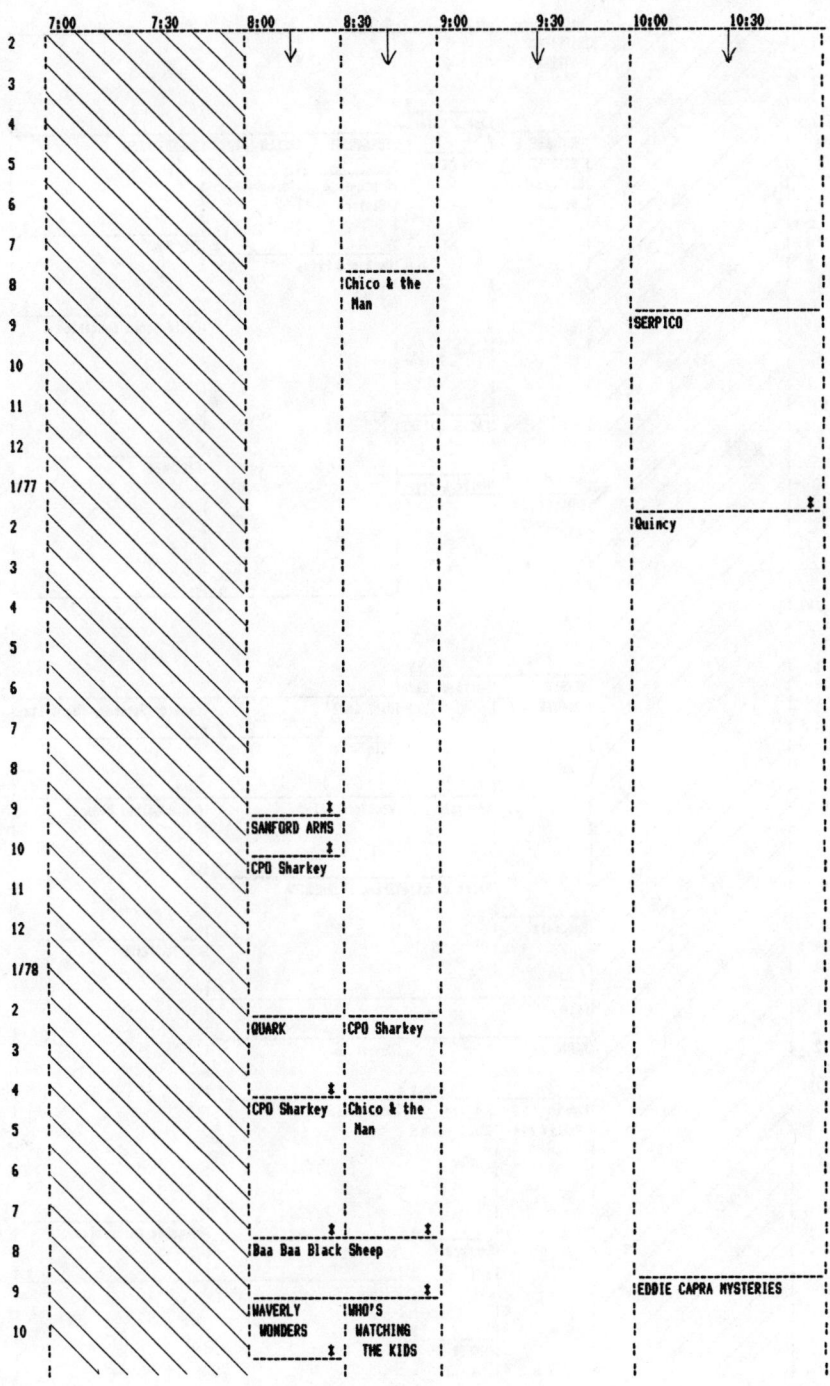

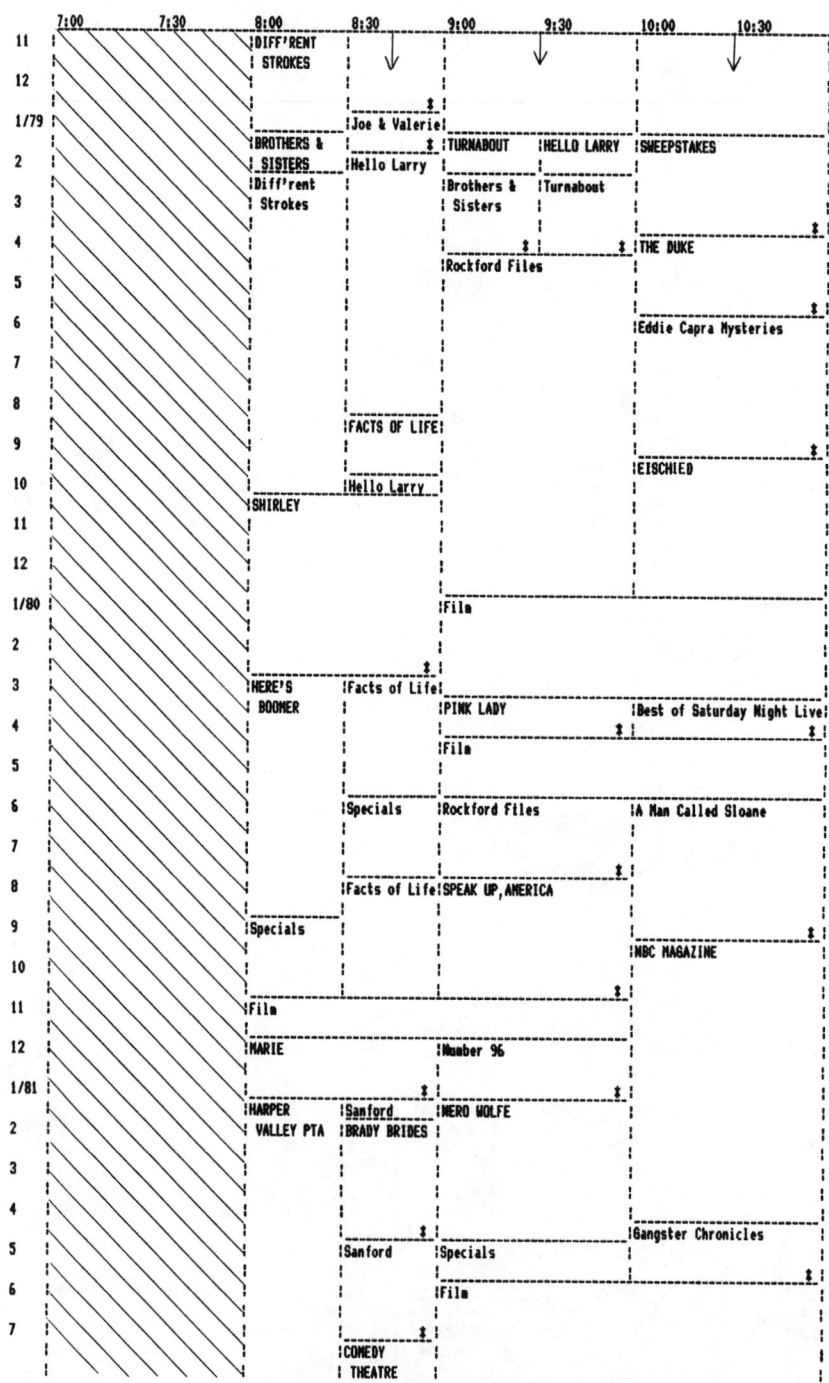

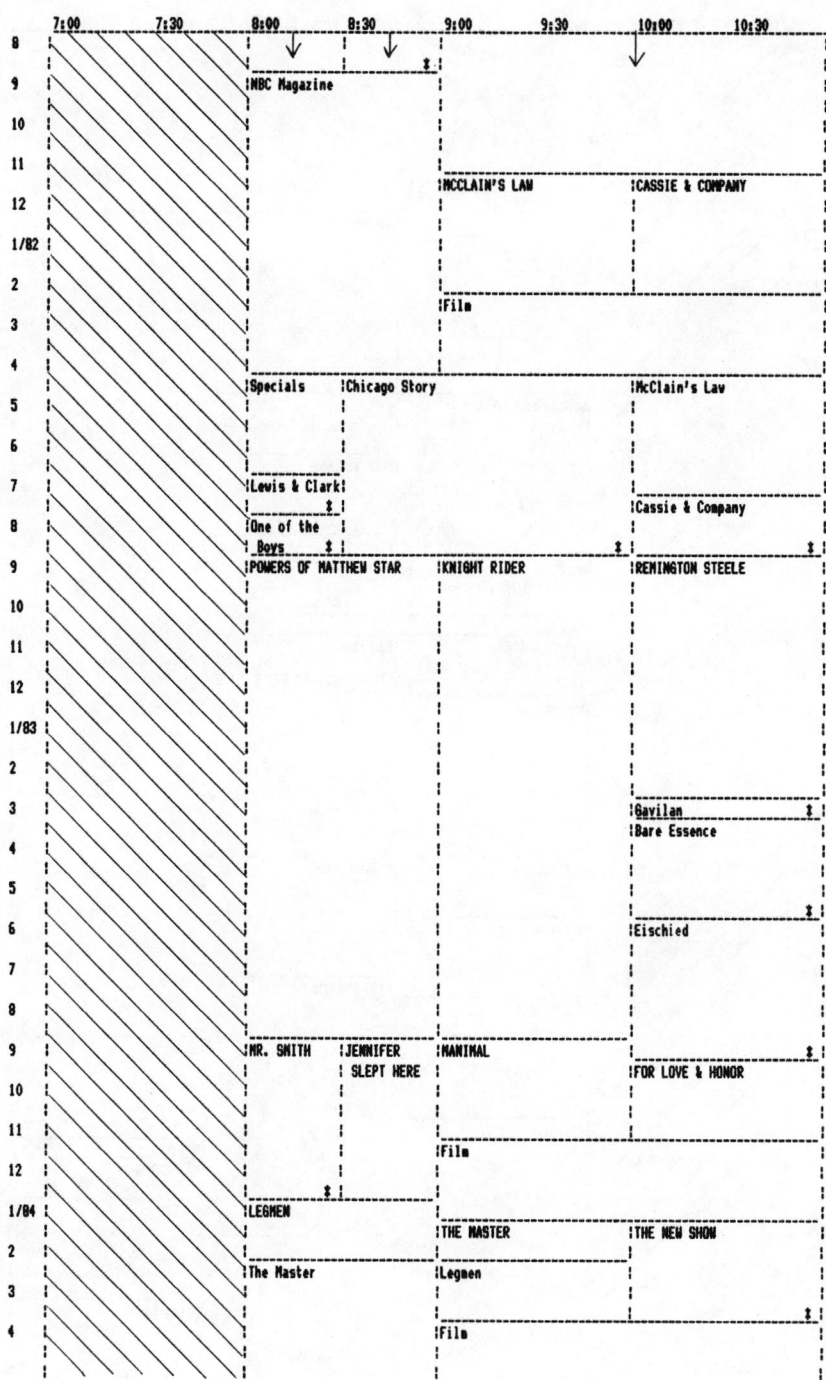

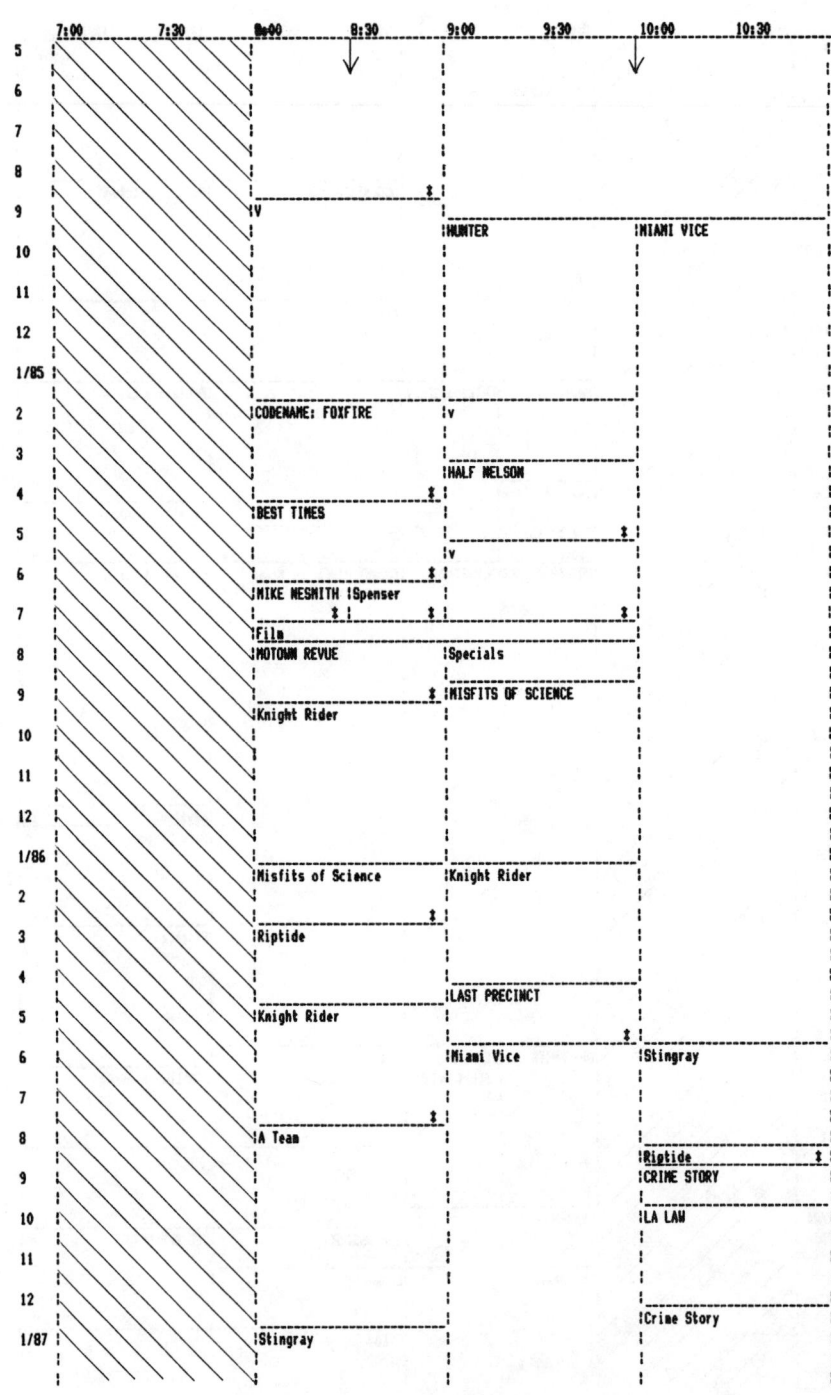

	7:00	7:30	8:00	8:30	9:00	9:30	10:00	10:30
5								
6								
7								
8								
9			V					
10					HUNTER		MIAMI VICE	
11								
12								
1/85								
2			CODENAME: FOXFIRE		V			
3								
4					HALF NELSON			
5			BEST TIMES					
6					V			
7			MIKE NESMITH	Spenser				
8			Film					
			MOTOWN REVUE		Specials			
9			Knight Rider		MISFITS OF SCIENCE			
10								
11								
12								
1/86								
2			Misfits of Science		Knight Rider			
3			Riptide					
4					LAST PRECINCT			
5			Knight Rider					
6					Miami Vice		Stingray	
7								
8			A Team					
9							Riptide	
							CRIME STORY	
10							LA LAW	
11								
12							Crime Story	
1/87			Stingray					

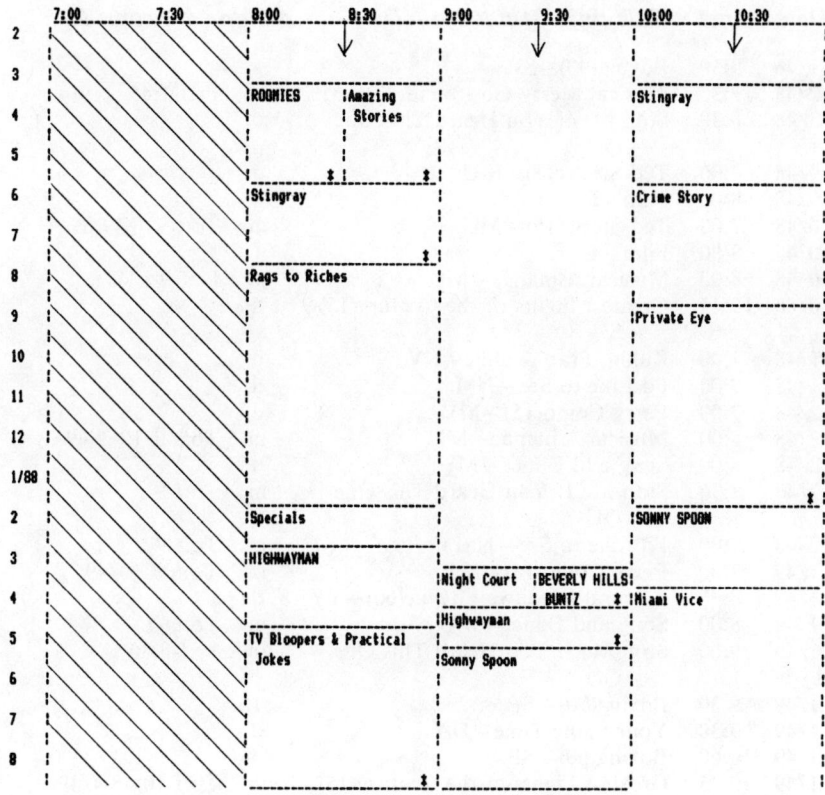

	7:00	7:30	8:00	8:30	9:00	9:30	10:00	10:30
2				↓		↓		↓
3			ROOMIES	Amazing			Stingray	
4				Stories				
5								
6			Stingray				Crime Story	
7								
8			Rags to Riches					
9							Private Eye	
10								
11								
12								
1/88								
2			Specials				SONNY SPOON	
3			HIGHWAYMAN					
4					Night Court	BEVERLY HILLS		
						BUNTZ	Miami Vice	
5			TV Bloopers & Practical		Highwayman			
6			Jokes		Sonny Spoon			
7								
8								

Date	Time	Title (min. if not 30) — Type	Action	From/To
11/46	9:30	Boxing(90) — SP	s	
2/48	7:30	Musical Merry-Go-Round(20) — MU	m	Fr:f-7:45
3/48	8:30	Stop Me If You Heard This One — QU	d	
9/48	7:00	Ted Steele(15) — MU	d	
9/48	8:00	Film — FI	s	
10/48	7:00	Ted Steele(15) — MU	m	To:t-9-4/49(d)
10/48	8:00	Film — FI	f	
10/48	8:00	Musical Almanac — MU	m	Fr:f-9-8/48
10/48	10:45	Greatest Fights of the Century(15) — SH	d	
11/48	7:00	Kukla, Fran & Ollie — KV	d	
11/48	9:00	I'd Like to See — NM	d	
12/48	7:00	Perry Como(15) — MV	d	
12/48	8:00	Musical Almanac — MU	m	To:var-10-2/49
12/48	8:00	Song and Dance — MU	d	
12/48	8:30	Stop Me If You Heard This One — QU	m	To:f-9
12/48	9:00	I'd Like to See — NM	m	To:t-9
1/49	7:00	Perry Como(15) — MV	m	To:n-8-10/49
1/49	8:00	Admiral Broadway Revue(60) — VY	d	
1/49	8:00	Song and Dance — MU	m	To:m-8
1/49	9:00	Stop Me If You Heard This One — QU	m	Fr:f-8:30
1/49	9:30	Boxing(90) — SP	f	
1/49	9:30	Your Show Time — DA	d	
1/49	10:00	Boxing(60) — SP	s	
1/49	10:45	Greatest Fights of the Century(15) — SH	m	To:f-10:45-4/49
3/49	7:30	America Song(15) — MU	m	Fr:m-7:30
3/49	7:30	Musical Merry-Go-Round(20) — MU	c	
4/49	7:30	America Song(15) — MU	c	
4/49	9:00	Benny Rubin — CV	d	
4/49	9:00	Stop Me If You Heard This One — QU	c	
4/49	10:45	Greatest Fights of the Century(15) — SH	m	Fr:f-10:45-1/49
5/49	7:30	Mohawk Showroom(15) — MU	d	
5/49	10:00	Boxing(60) — SP	f	
5/49	10:00	Harness Racing(45) — SP	s	
6/49	7:00	Judy Splinters(15) — KV	d*	
6/49	7:15	Mary Kay and Johnny(15) — SC	m*	Fr:w-9(c)
6/49	8:00	Admiral Broadway Revue(60) — VY	c	
6/49	8:00	Hopalong Cassidy(60) — WE	d	
6/49	9:00	Benny Rubin — CV	c	
7/49	9:00	Meet Your Congress — DB	d	
7/49	9:30	Your Show Time — DA	c	
8/49	7:00	Judy Splinters(15) — KV	c*	
8/49	7:15	Mary Kay and Johnny(15) — SC	m*	To:r-8:30
8/49	7:30	Practice Tee(15) — IS	d*	

Date	Time	Title (min. if not 30) — Type	Action	From/To
8/49	9:00	Meet Your Congress — DB	m	To:s-8
8/49	9:00	Mixed Doubles — DR	d	
9/49	7:30	Practice Tee(15) — IS	c*	
9/49	9:00	Mixed Doubles — DR	m	To:s-8:30
9/49	9:00	Versatile Varieties — KV	d	
9/49	9:30	Big Story — DD	d	
9/49	10:00	Boxing(45) — SP	s	
9/49	10:00	Harness Racing(45) — SP	f	
10/49	8:00	Hopalong Cassidy(60) — WE	c	
11/49	8:00	One Man's Family — SL	d	
11/49	8:30	We, the People — IV	m	Fr:t-9(c)
1/50	8:00	One Man's Family — SL	m	To:r-8:30
1/50	8:00	Quiz Kids — QU	m	Fr:m-10
1/50	9:30	Life Begins at Eighty — DS	d	
3/50	9:30	Life Begins at Eighty — DS	m	To:s-7:30
4/50	9:30	The Clock — SA	m	Fr:w-8:30
6/50	8:00	Magic Slate — KV	d*	
6/50	10:00	Gillette Summer Sports Reel(45) — SH	d*	
7/50	7:00	Ransom Sherman — CV	d*	
7/50	7:30	Wendy Barrie(15) — IV	m*	Fr:tr-7:30
7/50	9:00	Life Begins at Eighty — DS	m*	Fr:s-7:30
8/50	7:00	Ransom Sherman — CV	c*	
8/50	7:30	Wendy Barrie(15) — IV	m*	To:w-8:15
8/50	8:00	Magic Slate — KV	c*	
8/50	9:00	Life Begins at Eighty — DS	m*	To:t-10-10/50
8/50	10:00	Gillette Summer Sports Reel(45) SH	m*	To:f-10-6/51
1/51	9:00	Henry Morgan's Great Talent Hunt — CV	d	
1/51	9:00	Versatile Varieties — KV	m	To:f-9:30-9/51
2/51	9:30	The Clock — SA	m	To:f-8:30-7/51
3/51	9:00	Big Story — DD	m	Fr:f-9:30
3/51	9:00	Henry Morgan's Great Talent Hunt — CV	m	To:f-9:30
3/51	9:30	Big Story — DD	m	To:f-9
3/51	9:30	Henry Morgan's Great Talent Hunt — CV	m	Fr:f-9
6/51	8:30	We, the People — IV	m	To:f-8:30-9/51
6/51	9:30	Battle Report — DO	m	Fr:n-8-9/50
6/51	9:30	Henry Morgan's Great Talent Hunt — CV	c	
6/51	10:00	Gillette Summer Sports Reel(45) — SH	m*	Fr:f-10-8/50
6/51	10:45	Nature of Things(15) — IS	m*	Fr:w-8:15-9/50
7/51	7:00	Ernie in Kovacsland — CV	d*	
7/51	7:30	Songs at Twilight(15) — MU	d*	
7/51	8:30	The Clock — SA	m	Fr:f-9:30-2/51
7/51	9:00	Doorway to Danger — SD	d*	
8/51	7:00	Ernie in Kovacsland — CV	c*	

Date	Time	Title (min. if not 30) — Type	Action	From/To
8/51	7:30	Songs at Twilight(15) — MU	c*	
8/51	8:30	The Clock — SA	m	To:w-9:30-10/51(a)
8/51	9:00	Doorway to Danger — SD	m*	To:f-9-7/52
8/51	9:30	Battle Report — DO	c	
8/51	10:00	Gillette Summer Sports Reel(45) — SH	m*	To:f-10-6/52
8/51	10:45	Nature of Things(15) — IS	m*	To:f-10:45-7/52
9/51	8:30	We, the People — IV	m	Fr:f-8:30-6/51
9/51	9:30	Aldrich Family — SC	m	Fr:n-7:30-6/51
9/51	9:30	Versatile Varieties — KV	m	Fr:f-9-1/51
10/51	8:00	Quiz Kids — QU	m	To:m-8-7/52
11/51	7:00	Kukla, Fran & Ollie — KV	m	To:m-f-7
11/51	7:00	Kukla, Fran & Ollie(15) — KV	m	Fr:m-f-7
11/51	7:15	Bob and Ray(15) — CV	d	
11/51	7:30	Mohawk Showroom(15) — MU	c	
11/51	7:30	Those Two(15) — SC	d	
11/51	8:00	RCA Victor Show — VS	d	
12/51	9:30	Versatile Varieties — KV	c	
2/52	7:15	Bob and Ray(15) — CV	m	To:tr-7:15
2/52	7:15	Goldbergs(15) — SC	m	Fr:m-9:30-6/51(c)
4/52	7:30	Coke Time with Eddie Fisher(15) — MU	d	
6/52	8:00	Curtain Call — DA	d*	
6/52	9:30	Campbell Soundstage — DA	d*	
6/52	10:00	Gillette Summer Sports Reel(45) — SH	m*	Fr:f-10-8/51
7/52	7:00	Kukla, Fran & Ollie(15) — KV	m	To:m-f-7-9/54(a)
7/52	7:00	Up to Paar — QU	d	
7/52	7:15	Goldbergs(15) — SC	m	To:f-8-7/53
7/52	9:00	Doorway to Danger — SD	m*	Fr:f-9-8/51
7/52	10:45	Nature of Things(15) — IS	m*	Fr:f-10:45-8/51
8/52	9:00	Doorway to Danger — SD	m*	To:r-8:30-7/53(a)
8/52	9:30	Campbell Soundstage — DA	m*	To:f-9:30-7/53
8/52	10:00	Gillette Summer Sports Reel(45) — SH	m*	To:f-10-6/53
8/52	10:45	Nature of Things(15) — IS	c*	
9/52	7:00	Up to Paar — QU	c	
9/52	8:00	Curtain Call — DA	c*	
9/52	8:30	We, the People — IV	c	
10/52	7:00	Herman Hickman(15) — ST	d	
10/52	8:30	Gulf Playhouse — DA	d	
12/52	8:30	Gulf Playhouse — DA	m	To:f-8:30-7/53
1/53	8:30	Life of Riley — SC	m	Fr:t-9:30-3/50
3/53	7:00	Herman Hickman(15) — ST	c	
4/53	7:30	Those Two(15) — SC	c	
5/53	9:30	Aldrich Family — SC	c	
6/53	8:00	RCA Victor Show — VS	m	To:m-9-10/53
6/53	9:30	Double or Nothing — QU	d	
6/53	10:00	Gillette Summer Sports Reel(45) — SH	m*	Fr:f-10-8/52

Date	Time	Title (min. if not 30) — Type	Action	From/To
7/53	8:00	Goldbergs — SC	m	Fr:mwf-7:15
7/53	8:30	Gulf Playhouse — DA	m*	Fr:f-8:30-12/52
7/53	9:30	Campbell Soundstage — DA	m	Fr:f-9:30-8/52
7/53	9:30	Double or Nothing — QU	c	
7/53	10:45	It Happened in Sports(15) — ST	d*	
8/53	10:00	Gillette Summer Sports Reel(45) — SH	m*	To:f-10-6/54
8/53	10:45	It Happened in Sports (15) — ST	m*	To:t-10:45
9/53	8:00	Goldbergs — SC	m	To:t-8-4/54(d)
9/53	8:30	Gulf Playhouse — DA	c*	
10/53	8:00	Garroway at Large — VY	d	
6/54	7:30	World of Mr. Sweeney(15) — SC	d*	
6/54	8:00	Garroway at Large — VY	c	
6/54	10:00	Gillette Summer Sports Reel — SH	m*	Fr:f-10-8/53
6/54	10:30	Greatest Moments in Sports(15) — ST	d*	
7/54	8:00	The Duke — SC	d	
7/54	9:00	Best in Mystery — MA	d*	
8/54	7:30	World of Mr. Sweeney(15) — SC	c*	
8/54	10:00	Gillette Summer Sports Reel — SH	m*	To:f-10-6/55
8/54	10:30	Greatest Moments in Sports(15) — ST	m*	To:f-10:45
8/54	10:45	Greatest Fights of the Century(15) — SH	c	
9/54	8:00	Droodles — QU	m	Fr:m-8
9/54	8:00	Droodles — QU	c	
9/54	8:00	The Duke — SC	c	
9/54	9:00	Best in Mystery — MA	m*	To:f-9-7/55
9/54	9:30	Campbell Soundstage — DA	c	
9/54	9:30	Dear Phoebe — SC	d	
9/54	10:45	Greatest Moments in Sports(15) — ST	m	Fr:f-10:30
10/54	8:00	Red Buttons — CV	m	Fr:m-9:30-6/54(c)
2/55	10:45	Greatest Moments in Sports(15) — ST	c	
2/55	10:45	Jan Murray Time(15) — VY	d	
5/55	8:00	Midwestern Hayride — MV	m	Fr:t-8-9/54
5/55	8:00	Red Buttons — CV	c	
5/55	10:45	Jan Murray Time(15) — VY	c	
5/55	10:45	Red Barber's Corner(15) — ST	m	Fr:w-10:45(c)
6/55	7:30	Matt Dennis(15) — MU	d*	
6/55	10:00	Gillette Summer Sports Reel — SH	m*	Fr:f-10-8/54
6/55	10:30	So This Is Hollywood — SC	m*	Fr:s-8:30
7/55	9:00	Best in Mystery — MA	m*	Fr:f-9-9/54
8/55	7:30	Matt Dennis(15) — MU	c*	
8/55	10:00	Gillette Summer Sports Reel — SH	c*	
8/55	10:30	So This Is Hollywood — SC	c*	
9/55	8:00	Midwestern Hayride — MV	m	To:w-10
9/55	8:00	Truth or Consequences — QU	m	Fr:t-10
9/55	9:00	Best in Mystery — MA	m*	To:f-9-7/56

Date	Time	Title (min. if not 30) — Type	Action	From/To
9/55	9:30	Dear Phoebe — SC	m	To:t-8-6/56
9/55	9:30	Star Stage — DA	d	
6/56	7:30	Jaye P. Morgan(15) — MU	d*	
7/56	9:00	Best in Mystery — MA	m	Fr:f-9-9/55
7/56	9:00	Big Story — DD	m	To:f-9:30-9/56
8/56	7:30	Jaye P. Morgan(15) — MU	c*	
8/56	9:00	Best in Mystery — MA	c	
8/56	9:30	Star Stage — DA	m	To:f-9
9/56	8:00	Truth or Consequences — QU	m	To:f-7:30-12/57
9/56	8:30	Life of Riley — SC	m	To:f-8
9/56	9:00	Joseph Cotten — DA	d	
9/56	9:00	Star Stage — DA	m	Fr:f-9:30
9/56	9:00	Star Stage — DA	c	
9/56	9:30	Big Story — DD	m	Fr:f-9-7/56
10/56	8:00	Life of Riley — SC	m	Fr:f-8:30
10/56	8:30	Walter Winchell — VY	d	
12/56	8:00	Life of Riley — SC	m	To:f-8:30
12/56	8:30	Walter Winchell — VY	c	
1/57	8:00	Blondie — SC	d	
1/57	8:30	Life of Riley — SC	m	Fr:f-8
2/57	7:30	Coke Time with Eddie Fisher(15) — MU	c	
2/57	7:30	Xavier Cugat(15) — MU	d	
5/57	7:30	Helen O'Connell(15) — MU	d	
5/57	7:30	Xavier Cugat(15) — MU	c	
6/57	9:30	Big Story — DD	c	
7/57	9:30	Big Moment — SH	d	
9/57	7:30	Helen O'Connell(15) — MU	c	
9/57	7:30	Mark Saber — CD	m	Fr:f-9:30-6/57(a)
9/57	8:00	Blondie — SC	c	
9/57	9:00	Joseph Cotten — DA	m	To:s-10:30-6/58
9/57	9:00	M Squad — CD	d	
9/57	9:30	Big Moment — SH	c	
9/57	9:30	The Thin Man — CO	d	
10/57	8:00	Court of Last Resort — CD	d	
12/57	7:30	Mark Saber — CD	m	To:n-7-10/58
12/57	7:30	Truth or Consequences — QU	m	Fr:f-8-9/56
1/58	10:45	Comment(15) — PA	m	Fr:m-8:30-8/54
1/58	10:45	Red Barber's Corner(15) — ST	c	
4/58	8:00	Court of Last Resort — CD	m	To:w-8-8/59(a)
4/58	8:00	Jefferson Drum — WE	d	
6/58	7:30	Big Game — QU	d	
6/58	7:30	Truth or Consequences — QU	c	
8/58	10:45	Comment(15) — PA	c	
9/58	7:30	Big Game — QU	c	
9/58	7:30	Jefferson Drum — WE	m	Fr:f-8
9/58	8:00	Adventures of Ellery Queen(60) — CD	d	
9/58	8:00	Jefferson Drum — WE	m	To:f-7:30

Date	Time	Title (min. if not 30)—Type	Action	From/To
9/58	8:30	Life of Riley—SC	c	
10/58	7:30	Buckskin—WE	m	Fr:r-9:30
10/58	7:30	Jefferson Drum—WE	m	To:r-7:30
1/59	7:30	Buckskin—WE	m	To:m-7:30
1/59	7:30	Northwest Passage—AD	m	Fr:n-7:30
1/59	10:45	Jackpot Bowling w/ Milton Berle (15)—QU	d	
6/59	9:30	The Thin Man—CO	c	
7/59	7:30	Northwest Passage—AD	m	To:t-7:30
7/59	7:30	Pete Kelly's Blues—DR	m	Fr:n-8:30
7/59	9:30	Colgate Western Theatre—WA	d	
9/59	7:30	People Are Funny—QU	m	Fr:s-7:30
9/59	7:30	Pete Kelly's Blues—DR	c	
9/59	8:00	Adventures of Ellery Queen(60)—CD	c	
9/59	8:00	Troubleshooters—AD	d	
9/59	8:30	Bell Telephone Hour(60)—MU	d	
9/59	9:00	M Squad—CD	m	To:f-9:30
9/59	9:30	Colgate Western Theatre—WA	c	
9/59	9:30	M Squad—CD	m	Fr:f-9
1/60	9:30	M Squad—CD	m	To:t-10
1/60	9:30	Masquerade Party—QU	m	Fr:m-7:30(c)
4/60	7:30	People Are Funny—QU	m	To:w-10:30
4/60	7:30	Play Your Hunch—QU	d	
5/60	8:30	Bell Telephone Hour(60)—MU	m	To:f-9-9/60
6/60	7:30	Cimarron City(60)—WE	m	Fr:s-9:30-9/59
6/60	7:30	Play Your Hunch—QU	m	To:f-9
6/60	8:00	Troubleshooters—AD	c	
6/60	8:30	Wichita Town—WE	m	Fr:w-10:30-4/60
6/60	9:00	Play Your Hunch—QU	m	Fr:f-7:30
6/60	10:00	Boxing(45)—SP	f	
6/60	10:45	Jackpot Bowling w/ Milton Berle (15)—QU	m	To:m-10:30-9/60
7/60	10:00	Moment of Fear(60)—DA	d	
9/60	7:30	Cimarron City(60)—WE	c	
9/60	7:30	Dan Raven(60)—CD	d	
9/60	8:30	The Westerner—WE	d	
9/60	8:30	Wichita Town—WE	c	
9/60	9:00	Bell Telephone Hour(60)—MU	m	Fr:f-8:30-5/60
9/60	9:00	Play Your Hunch—QU	m	To:w-10-6/62
9/60	9:30	Masquerade Party—QU	c	
9/60	10:00	Michael Shayne(60)—CD	d	
9/60	10:00	Moment of Fear(60)—DA	c	
12/60	8:30	The Westerner—WE	c	
1/61	7:30	Dan Raven(60)—CD	c	
1/61	7:30	Happy—SC	m	Fr:w-9-9/60
1/61	8:00	One Happy Family—SC	d	
1/61	8:30	Westinghouse Playhouse—SC	d	
1/61	9:00	Sing Along with Mitch(60)—MV	d	
3/61	8:00	Five Star Jubilee—MV	d	

Date	Time	Title (min. if not 30) — Type	Action	From/To
3/61	8:00	One Happy Family — SC	m	To:f-8-5/61
4/61	8:00	Five Star Jubilee — MV	m	To:f-8:30
4/61	8:30	Westinghouse Playhouse — SC	m	To:f-9:30
4/61	9:00	Bell Telephone Hour(60) — MU	m	To:f-9:30-9/61
4/61	9:00	Sing Along with Mitch(60) — MV	m	To:r-10-9/61
5/61	8:00	One Happy Family — SC	m	Fr:f-8-3/61
5/61	8:30	Five Star Jubilee — MV	m	Fr:f-8
5/61	9:00	The Lawless Years — CD	m	Fr:r-10:30-3/60
5/61	9:30	Westinghouse Playhouse — SC	m	Fr:f-8:30
9/61	7:30	Happy — SC	c	
9/61	7:30	International Showtime(60) — VY	d	
9/61	8:00	One Happy Family — SC	c	
9/61	8:30	The Detectives(60) — CD	m	Fr:f-10(a)
9/61	8:30	Five Star Jubilee — MV	c	
9/61	9:00	The Lawless Years — CD	c	
9/61	9:30	Bell Telephone Hour(60) — MU	m	Fr:f-9-4/61
9/61	9:30	Westinghouse Playhouse — SC	c	
9/61	10:00	Michael Shayne(60) — CD	c	
9/61	10:30	Here and Now — DO	d	
10/61	9:30	Chevy Show(60) — MV	m	Fr:n-9-6/61
12/61	10:30	Here and Now — DO	c	
1/62	10:30	Chet Huntley Reporting — DO	d	
4/62	9:30	Bell Telephone Hour(60) — MU	m	To:t-10-10/63
6/62	9:30	Chevy Show(60) — MV	m	To:n-10-12/62
7/62	9:30	Purex Summer Specials(60) — VS	m	Fr:t-10-9/61
9/62	8:30	The Detectives(60) — CD	c	
9/62	8:30	Sing Along with Mitch(60) — MV	m	Fr:r-10
9/62	9:30	Don't Call Me Charlie — SC	d	
9/62	9:30	Purex Summer Specials(60) — VS	m	To:r-10-6/63
9/62	10:00	Jack Paar(60) — VY	d	
9/62	10:30	Chet Huntley Reporting — DO	m	To:t-10:30
1/63	9:30	Don't Call Me Charlie — SC	c	
2/63	9:30	Price Is Right — QU	m	Fr:m-9:30
9/63	8:30	Bob Hope Presents Chrysler Theater(60) — DA	d	
9/63	8:30	Sing Along with Mitch(60) — MV	m	To:m-10
9/63	9:30	Harry's Girls — SC	d	
9/63	9:30	Price Is Right — QU	m	To:w-8:30(a)
1/64	9:30	Harry's Girls — SC	c	
1/64	9:30	That Was the Week That Was — CY	d	
7/64	9:30	On Parade — MV	d	
7/64	9:30	That Was the Week That Was — CY	m	To:t-9:30-9/64
9/64	9:30	Jack Benny — CY	m	Fr:t-9:30(c)
9/64	9:30	On Parade — MV	c	
9/65	7:30	Camp Runamuck — SC	d	
9/65	7:30	International Showtime(60) — VY	c	
9/65	8:00	Hank — SC	d	
9/65	8:30	Bob Hope Presents Chrysler Theater(60) — DA	m	To:w-9
9/65	8:30	Convoy(60) — WD	d	

Date	Time	Title (min. if not 30) – Type	Action	From/To
9/65	9:30	Jack Benny – CY	c	
9/65	9:30	Mr. Roberts – SC	d	
9/65	10:00	Jack Paar(60) – VY	c	
9/65	10:00	Man from U.N.C.L.E.(60) – SD	m	Fr:m-8
12/65	8:30	Convoy(60) – WD	c	
1/66	8:30	Sammy Davis, Jr.(60) – MV	d	
4/66	8:30	Sammy Davis, Jr.(60) – MV	c	
4/66	8:30	Sing Along with Mitch(60) – MV	m	Fr:m-10-9/64
9/66	7:30	Camp Runamuck – SC	c	
9/66	7:30	Tarzan(60) – AD	d	
9/66	8:00	Hank – SC	c	
9/66	8:30	Man from U.N.C.L.E.(60) – SD	m	Fr:f-10
9/66	8:30	Sing Along with Mitch(60) – MV	c	
9/66	9:30	Mr. Roberts – SC	c	
9/66	9:30	T.H.E. Cat – AD	d	
9/66	10:00	Laredo(60) – WE	m	Fr:r-8:30
9/66	10:00	Man from U.N.C.L.E.(60) – SD	m	To:f-8:30
9/67	8:30	Man from U.N.C.L.E.(60) – SD	m	To:m-8
9/67	8:30	Star Trek(60) – SF	m	Fr:r-8:30
9/67	9:30	Accidental Family – SC	d	
9/67	9:30	T.H.E. Cat – AD	c	
9/67	10:00	Actuality Specials(60) – DO	m	Fr:n-6:30-6/67
9/67	10:00	American Profile(60) – DO	d	
9/67	10:00	Bell Telephone Hour(60) – MU	m	Fr:n-6:30-4/67
9/67	10:00	Laredo(60) – WE	c	
1/68	9:30	Accidental Family – SC	c	
1/68	9:30	Hollywood Squares – QU	d	
4/68	10:00	Bell Telephone Hour(60) – MU	c	
7/68	10:00	American Profile(60) – DO	c	
9/68	7:30	High Chaparral(60) – WE	m	Fr:n-10
9/68	7:30	Tarzan(60) – AD	m	To:w-7:30-6/69
9/68	8:30	Name of the Game(90) – AD	d	
9/68	8:30	Star Trek(60) – SF	m	To:f-10
9/68	9:30	Hollywood Squares – QU	c	
9/68	10:00	Actuality Specials(60) – DO	c	
9/68	10:00	Star Trek(60) – SF	m	Fr:f-8:30
4/69	10:00	The Saint(60) – MY	m	Fr:s-7:30-9/68
4/69	10:00	Star Trek(60) – SF	m	To:t-7:30-6/69
9/69	10:00	Bracken's World(60) – DR	d	
9/69	10:00	The Saint(60) – MY	c	
12/70	10:00	Bracken's World(60) – DR	c	
1/71	10:00	Strange Report(60) – CD	d	
9/71	7:30	High Chaparral(60) – WE	c	
9/71	8:00	The D.A. – LD	d	
9/71	8:30	Film(120) – FI	s	
9/71	8:30	Name of the Game(90) – AD	c	
9/71	10:00	Strange Report(60) – CD	c	
10/71	9:00	Chronolog(120) – NM	d	
1/72	8:00	The D.A. – LD	c	
1/72	8:00	Sanford and Son – SC	d	

Date	Time	Title (min. if not 30) – Type	Action	From/To
7/72	8:00	The Partners – SC	m*	Fr:s-8-1/72
7/72	9:00	Chronolog(120) – NM	c	
9/72	8:00	The Partners – SC	c*	
9/72	8:30	Brian Keith – SC	d	
9/72	8:30	Film(120) – FI	f	
9/72	9:00	Ghost Story(60) – OA	d	
9/72	10:00	Banyon(60) – CD	d	
1/73	10:00	Banyon(60) – CD	c	
1/73	10:00	Bobby Darin(60) – MV	d	
4/73	10:00	Bobby Darin(60) – MV	c	
5/73	10:00	The New Doctors(60) – MD	m	Fr:t-9-1/73
6/73	9:00	Ghost Story(60) – OA	c	
6/73	9:00	Film(120) – FI	s	
6/73	10:00	The New Doctors(60) – MD	c	
8/73	8:30	Brian Keith – SC	m	To:f-9:30
9/73	8:30	Girl with Something Extra – SC	d	
9/73	9:00	Film(120) – FI	f	
9/73	9:00	Needles and Pins – SC	d	
9/73	9:30	Brian Keith – SC	m	Fr:f-8:30
9/73	10:00	Dean Martin(60) – CV	m	Fr:r-10-7/73
12/73	8:30	Girl with Something Extra – SC	m	To:f-9
12/73	9:00	Needles and Pins – SC	c	
1/74	8:30	Lotsa Luck – SC	m	Fr:m-8
1/74	9:00	Girl with Something Extra – SC	m	Fr:f-8:30
5/74	8:30	Brian Keith – SC	m	Fr:f-9:30
5/74	8:30	Lotsa Luck – SC	c	
5/74	9:00	Girl with Something Extra – SC	c	
5/74	9:00	Film(120) – FI	s	
5/74	9:30	Brian Keith – SC	m	To:f-8:30
5/74	10:00	Dean Martin(60) – CV	c	
8/74	8:30	Brian Keith – SC	c	
8/74	9:00	Film(120) – FI	f	
9/74	8:30	Chico and the Man – SC	d	
9/74	9:00	Rockford Files(60) – CD	d	
9/74	10:00	Police Woman(60) – CD	d	
10/75	10:00	Police Woman(60) – CD	m	To:t-9
11/75	10:00	Police Story(60) – RA	m	Fr:t-9
1/76	8:30	Chico and the Man – SC	m	To:w-9
1/76	8:30	The Practice – SC	d	
7/76	8:30	The Practice – SC	m	To:w-8-10/76
8/76	8:30	Chico and the Man – SC	m	Fr:w-9:30
8/76	10:00	Police Story(60) – RA	m	To:t-10
9/76	10:00	Serpico(60) – CD	d	
1/77	10:00	Serpico(60) – CD	c	
2/77	10:00	Quincy, M.D.(60) – CD	m	Fr:n-9:30-11/76
9/77	8:00	Sanford and Son – SC	c	
9/77	8:00	Sanford Arms – SC	d	
10/77	8:00	C.P.O. Sharkey – SC	m	Fr:w-9-8/77
10/77	8:00	Sanford Arms – SC	c	
2/78	8:00	Quark – SC	d	

Date	*Time*	*Title (min. if not 30) — Type*	*Action*	*From/To*
2/78	8:00	C.P.O. Sharkey — SC	m	To:f-8:30
2/78	8:30	Chico and the Man — SC	m	To:f-8:30-4/78
2/78	8:30	C.P.O. Sharkey — SC	m	Fr:f-8
3/78	9:00	Richie Brockelman, Pvt. Eye(60) — CD	d*	
4/78	8:00	C.P.O. Sharkey — SC	m	Fr:f-8:30
4/78	8:00	Quark — SC	c	
4/78	8:30	C.P.O. Sharkey — SC	m	To:f-8
4/78	8:30	Chico and the Man — SC	m	Fr:f-8:30-2/78
4/78	9:00	Richie Brockelman, Pvt. Eye(60) — CD	m*	To:r-9-8/78
7/78	8:00	C.P.O. Sharkey — SC	c	
7/78	8:30	Chico and the Man — SC	c	
8/78	8:00	Baa Baa Black Sheep(60) — WD	m	Fr:w-9
8/78	10:00	Quincy, M.E.(60) — CD	m	To:r-9
9/78	8:00	Baa Baa Black Sheep(60) — WD	c	
9/78	8:00	Waverly Wonders — SC	d	
9/78	8:30	Who's Watching the Kids — SC	d	
9/78	10:00	Eddie Capra Mysteries(60) — CD	d	
10/78	8:00	Waverly Wonders — SC	c	
11/78	8:00	Diff'rent Strokes — SC	d	
12/78	8:30	Who's Watching the Kids — SC	c	
1/79	8:00	Brothers and Sisters — SC	d	
1/79	8:00	Diff'rent Strokes — SC	m	To:f-8
1/79	8:30	Joe & Valerie — SC	m	Fr:w-8:30-5/78
1/79	9:00	Rockford Files — (60) — CD	m	To:s-10
1/79	9:00	Turnabout — SC	d	
1/79	9:30	Hello Larry — SC	d	
1/79	10:00	Eddie Capra Mysteries(60) — CD	m	To:f-10-6/79
1/79	10:00	Sweepstakes(60) — DA	d	
2/79	8:00	Brothers and Sisters — SC	m	To:f-9
2/79	8:00	Diff'rent Strokes — SC	m	Fr:f-8
2/79	8:30	Hello Larry — SC	m	Fr:f-9:30
2/79	8:30	Joe & Valerie — SC	c	
2/79	9:00	Brothers and Sisters — SC	m	Fr:f-8
2/79	9:00	Turnabout — SC	m	To:f-9:30
2/79	9:30	Hello Larry — SC	m	To:f-8:30
2/79	9:30	Turnabout — SC	m	Fr:f-9
3/79	10:00	Sweepstakes(60) — DA	c	
4/79	9:00	Brothers and Sisters — SC	c	
4/79	9:00	Rockford Files(60) — CD	m	Fr:s-10
4/79	9:30	Turnabout — SC	c	
4/79	10:00	The Duke(60) — CD	d	
5/79	10:00	The Duke(60) — CD	c	
6/79	10:00	Eddie Capra Mysteries(60) — CD	m	Fr:f-10-1/79
8/79	8:30	Facts of Life — SC	d	
8/79	8:30	Hello Larry — SC	m	To:f-8:30-10/79
9/79	8:30	Facts of Life — SC	m	To:f-8:30-3/80
9/79	10:00	Eddie Capra Mysteries(60) — CD	c	
9/79	10:00	Eischied(60) — CD	d	

Date	Time	Title (min. if not 30) — Type	Action	From/To
10/79	8:00	Diff'rent Strokes — SC	m	To:w-9
10/79	8:00	Shirley(60) — CO	d	
10/79	8:30	Hello Larry — SC	m	Fr:f-8:30-8/79
10/79	8:30	Hello Larry — SC	m	To:w-9:30
12/79	9:00	Rockford Files(60) — CD	m	To:r-10-3/80
12/79	10:00	Eischied(60) — CD	m	To:n-10
1/80	9:00	Film(120) — FI	s	
2/80	8:00	Shirley(60) — CO	c	
3/80	8:00	Here's Boomer — AD	d	
3/80	8:30	Facts of Life — SC	m	Fr:f-8:30-9/79
3/80	9:00	Pink Lady(60) — CV	d	
3/80	9:00	Film(120) — FI	f	
3/80	10:00	Best of Saturday Night Live(60) — CV	m	Fr:w-10
4/80	9:00	Pink Lady(60) — CV	c	
4/80	9:00	Film(120) — FI	s	
4/80	10:00	Best of Saturday Night Live(60) — CV	c	
5/80	8:30	Facts of Life — SC	m	To:w-9:30
5/80	9:00	Film(120) — FI	f	
6/80	9:00	Rockford Files(60) — CD	m	Fr:r-10-4/80
6/80	10:00	A Man Called Sloane(60) — SD	m	Fr:s-10-12/79
7/80	9:00	Rockford Files(60) — CD	c	
8/80	8:00	Here's Boomer — AD	m	To:n-7:30-9/81
8/80	8:30	Facts of Life — SC	m	Fr:w-9:30
8/80	9:00	Speak Up, America(60) — QU	d	
9/80	10:00	A Man Called Sloane(60) — SD	c	
9/80	10:00	NBC Magazine(60) — NM	d	
10/80	8:30	Facts of Life — SC	m	To:w-9:30
10/80	9:00	Speak Up, America(60) — QU	c	
11/80	8:00	Film(120) — FI	s	
11/80	8:00	Film(120) — FI	f	
12/80	8:00	Marie(60) — MV	d	
12/80	9:00	Number 96(60) — DR	m	Fr:r-10
1/81	8:00	Harper Valley P.T.A. — SC	d	
1/81	8:00	Marie(60) — MV	c	
1/81	8:30	Sanford — SC	m	Fr:w-9:30-9/80
1/81	8:30	Sanford — SC	m	To:f-8:30-5/81
1/81	9:00	Nero Wolfe(60) — CD	d	
1/81	9:00	Number 96(60) — DR	c	
2/81	8:30	Brady Brides — SC	d	
4/81	8:30	Brady Brides — SC	c	
4/81	9:00	Nero Wolfe(60) — CD	m	To:t-10
4/81	10:00	Gangster Chronicles(60) — CD	m	Fr:s-9
4/81	10:00	NBC Magazine(60) — NM	m	To:r-8
5/81	8:30	Sanford — SC	m	Fr:f-8:30-1/81
5/81	10:00	Gangster Chronicles(60) — CD	c	
6/81	9:00	Film(120) — FI	s	
7/81	8:30	Comedy Theatre — CA	d	
7/81	8:30	Sanford — SC	c	

Date	Time	Title (min. if not 30) — Type	Action	From/To
8/81	8:00	Harper Valley P.T.A.—SC	m	To:r-8-10/81
8/81	8:30	Comedy Theatre—CA	c	
9/81	8:00	NBC Magazine(60)—NM	m	Fr:r-8
11/81	9:00	McClain's Law(60)—CD	d	
11/81	9:00	Film(120)—FI	f	
1/82	10:00	Cassie & Company(60)—CD	d	
2/82	9:00	McClain's Law(60)—CD	m	To:s-10
2/82	9:00	Film(120)—FI	s	
2/82	10:00	Cassie & Company(60)—CD	m	To:t-10-6/82
4/82	8:00	NBC Magazine(60)—NM	m	To:s-10
4/82	8:30	Chicago Story(90)—DR	m	Fr:s-8:30
4/82	9:00	Film(120)—FI	f	
4/82	10:00	McClain's Law(60)—CD	m	Fr:s-10
7/82	8:00	Lewis & Clark—SC	m	Fr:s-8:30-1/82
7/82	8:00	Lewis & Clark—SC	c	
7/82	10:00	Cassie & Company(60)—CD	m	Fr:t-10
7/82	10:00	McClain's Law(60)—CD	m	To:t-10
8/82	8:00	One of the Boys—SC	m	Fr:s-8:30-6/82
8/82	8:00	One of the Boys—SC	c	
8/82	8:30	Chicago Story(90)—DR	c	
8/82	10:00	Cassie & Company(60)—CD	c	
9/82	8:00	Powers of Matthew Star(60)—SF	d	
9/82	9:00	Knight Rider(60)—AD	d	
9/82	10:00	Remington Steele(60)—CD	d	
2/83	10:00	Remington Steele(60)—CD	m	To:t-9
3/83	10:00	Bare Essence(60)—SL	m	Fr:t-9
3/83	10:00	Gavilan(60)—AD	m	Fr:t-9-12/82
3/83	10:00	Gavilan(60)—AD	c	
5/83	10:00	Bare Essence(60)—SL	c	
6/83	10:00	Eischied(60)—CD	m	Fr:n-10-1/80
8/83	8:00	Powers of Matthew Star(60)—SF	m	To:n-7
8/83	9:00	Knight Rider(60)—AD	m	To:n-8
9/83	8:00	Mr. Smith—SC	d	
9/83	8:30	Jennifer Slept Here—SC	d	
9/83	9:00	Manimal(60)—AD	d	
9/83	10:00	Eischied(60)—CD	c	
9/83	10:00	For Love and Honor(60)—SL	d	
11/83	9:00	Manimal(60)—AD	m	To:s-9
11/83	9:00	Film(120)—FI	s	
11/83	10:00	For Love and Honor(60)—SL	m	To:t-10
12/83	8:00	Mr. Smith—SC	c	
12/83	8:30	Jennifer Slept Here—SC	m	To:s-8:30-4/84
1/84	8:00	Legmen(60)—CD	d	
1/84	9:00	The Master(60)—AD	d	
1/84	9:00	Film(120)—FI	f	
1/84	10:00	The New Show(60)—CV	d	
2/84	8:00	Legmen(60)—CD	m	To:f-9
2/84	8:00	The Master(60)—AD	m	Fr:f-9
2/84	9:00	Legmen(60)—CD	m	Fr:f-8
2/84	9:00	The Master(60)—AD	m	To:f-8

Date	*Time*	*Title (min. if not 30) — Type*	*Action*	*From/To*
3/84	9:00	Legmen(60) — CD	c	
3/84	10:00	The New Show(60) — CV	c	
4/84	9:00	Film(120) — FI	s	
8/84	8:00	The Master(60) — AD	c	
9/84	8:00	V(60) — SF	d	
9/84	9:00	Hunter(60) — CD	d	
9/84	9:00	Film(120) — FI	f	
9/84	10:00	Miami Vice(60) — CD	d	
12/84	10:00	Hot Pursuit(60) — DR	m*	Fr:s-10
12/84	10:00	Hot Pursuit(60) — DR	c*	
1/85	8:00	V(60) — SF	m	To:f-9
1/85	9:00	Hunter(60) — CD	m	To:s-10
2/85	8:00	Codename: Foxfire(60) — AD	d	
2/85	9:00	V(60) — SF	m	Fr:f-8
3/85	9:00	V(60) — SF	m	To:f-9-5/85
3/85	9:00	Half Nelson(60) — CD	d	
4/85	8:00	Best Times(60) — CO	d	
4/85	8:00	Codename: Foxfire(60) — AD	c	
5/85	9:00	V(60) — SF	m	Fr:f-9-3/85
5/85	9:00	Half Nelson(60) — CD	c	
6/85	8:00	Best Times(60) — CO	c	
6/85	8:00	Mike Nesmith — CY	d	
6/85	8:30	Spencer — SC	m	Fr:s-9:30-1/85
7/85	8:00	Mike Nesmith — CY	c	
7/85	8:00	Film(120) — FI	s	
7/85	8:00	Film(120) — FI	f	
7/85	8:30	Spencer — SC	c	
7/85	9:00	V(60) — SF	c	
8/85	9:00	Motown Revue(60) — MU	d	
9/85	8:00	Knight Rider(60) — AD	m	Fr:n-8
9/85	9:00	Misfits of Science(60) — CD	d	
9/85	9:00	Motown Revue(60) — MU	c	
1/86	8:00	Misfits of Science(60) — CD	m	Fr:f-9
1/86	8:00	Knight Rider(60) — AD	m	To:f-9
1/86	9:00	Misfits of Science(60) — CD	m	To:f-8
1/86	9:00	Knight Rider(60) — AD	m	Fr:f-8
2/86	8:00	Misfits of Science(60) — CD	c	
3/86	8:00	Riptide(60) — CD	m	Fr:t-9
4/86	8:00	Riptide(60) — CD	m	To:f-10-8/86
4/86	9:00	Knight Rider(60) — AD	m	To:f-8
4/86	9:00	Last Precinct(60) — CD	d	
5/86	8:00	Knight Rider(60) — AD	m	Fr:f-9
5/86	9:00	Last Precinct(60) — CD	c	
5/86	10:00	Miami Vice(60) — CD	m	To:f-9
6/86	9:00	Miami Vice(60) — CD	m	Fr:f-10
6/86	10:00	Stingray(60) — CD	m	Fr:t-10
8/86	8:00	A-Team(60) — AD	m	Fr:t-8
8/86	8:00	Knight Rider(60) — AD	c	
8/86	10:00	Stingray(60) — CD	m	To:f-8-1/87
8/86	10:00	Riptide(60) — CD	m	Fr:f-8-4/86

Date	Time	Title (min. if not 30) — Type	Action	From/To
8/86	10:00	Riptide(60)—CD	c	
9/86	10:00	Crime Story(60)—CD	d	
9/86	10:00	Crime Story(60)—CD	m	To:t-9
10/86	10:00	L.A. Law(60)—LD	d	
12/86	8:00	A-Team(60)—AD	m	To:n-7-5/87
12/86	10:00	Crime Story(60)—CD	m	Fr:t-9
12/86	10:00	L.A. Law(60)—LD	m	To:r-10
1/87	8:00	Stingray(60)—CD	m	Fr:f-10-8/86
3/87	8:00	Stingray(60)—CD	m	To:f-10
3/87	8:00	Roomies—SC	d	
3/87	8:30	Amazing Stories—DA	m	Fr:m-8:30
3/87	10:00	Stingray(60)—CD	m	Fr:f-8
3/87	10:00	Crime Story(60)—CD	m	To:f-10-6/87
5/87	8:00	Roomies—SC	c	
5/87	8:30	Amazing Stories—DA	c	
5/87	10:00	Stingray(60)—CD	m	To:f-8
6/87	8:00	Stingray(60)—CD	m	Fr:f-10
6/87	10:00	Crime Story(60)—CD	m	Fr:f-10-3/87
7/87	8:00	Stingray(60)—CD	c	
8/87	8:00	Rags to Riches(60)—CO	m	Fr:n-8
8/87	10:00	Crime Story(60)—CD	m	To:t-10
9/87	10:00	Private Eye(60)—CD	d	
1/88	8:00	Rags to Riches(60)—CO	m	To:n-7-7/88
1/88	10:00	Private Eye(60)—CD	c	
2/88	10:00	Sonny Spoon(60)—CD	d	
3/88	8:00	Highwayman(60)—AD	d	
3/88	9:00	Night Court—SC	m	Fr:r-9:30
3/88	9:00	Miami Vice(60)—CD	m	To:f-10
3/88	9:30	Beverly Hills Buntz—SC	d	
3/88	10:00	Sonny Spoon(60)—CD	m	To:f-9-5/88
4/88	8:00	Highwayman(60)—AD	m	To:f-9
4/88	9:00	Night Court—SC	m	To:r-9:30
4/88	9:00	Highwayman(60)—AD	m	Fr:f-8
4/88	9:30	Beverly Hills Buntz—SC	c	
4/88	10:00	Miami Vice(60)—CD	m#	Fr:f-9
5/88	8:00	TV Bloopers & Practical Jokes(60)—CY	m	Fr:m-8-2/86
5/88	9:00	Sonny Spoon(60)—CD	m	Fr:f-10-3/88
5/88	9:00	Highwayman(60)—AD	c	
8/88	8:00	TV Bloopers & Practical Jokes(60)—CY	c	
8/88	9:00	Sonny Spoon(60)—CD	m	To:f-8

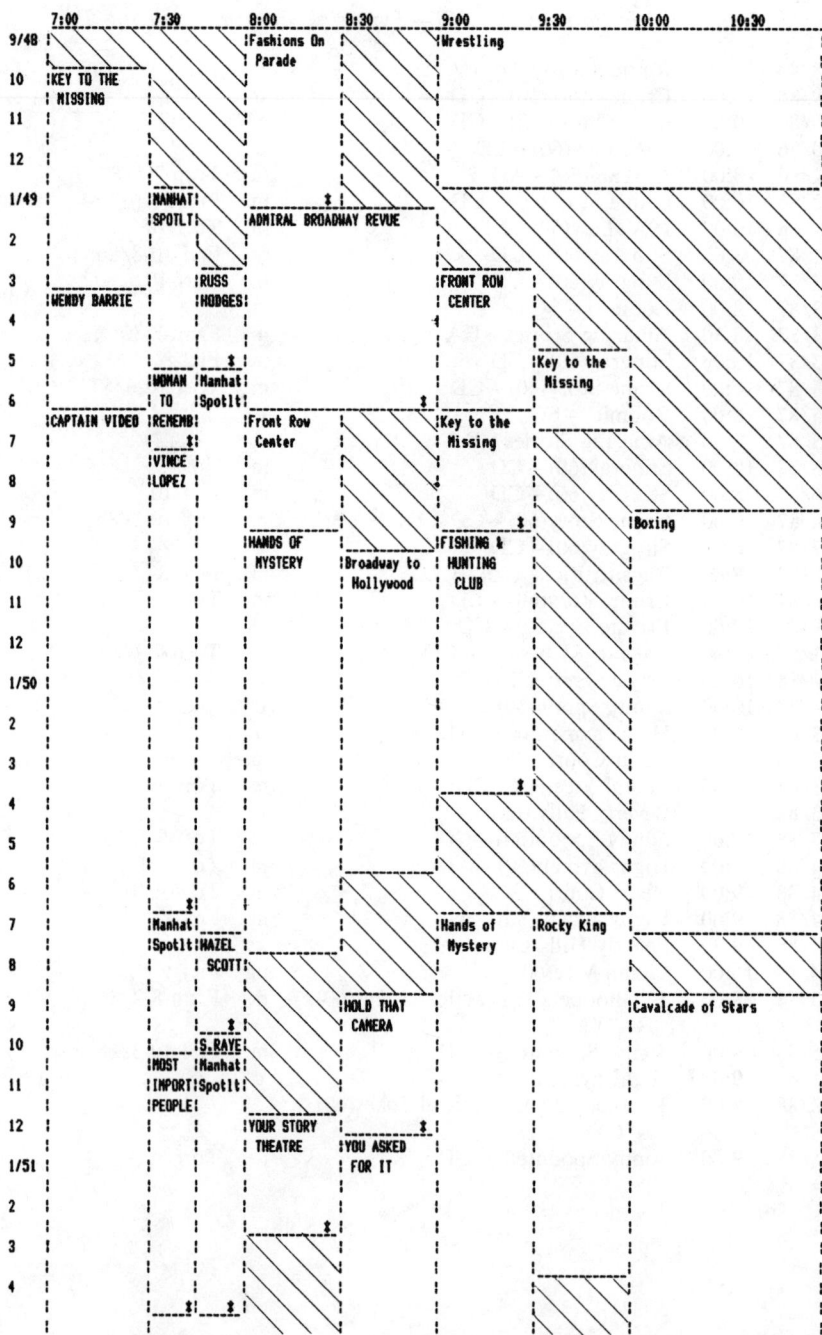

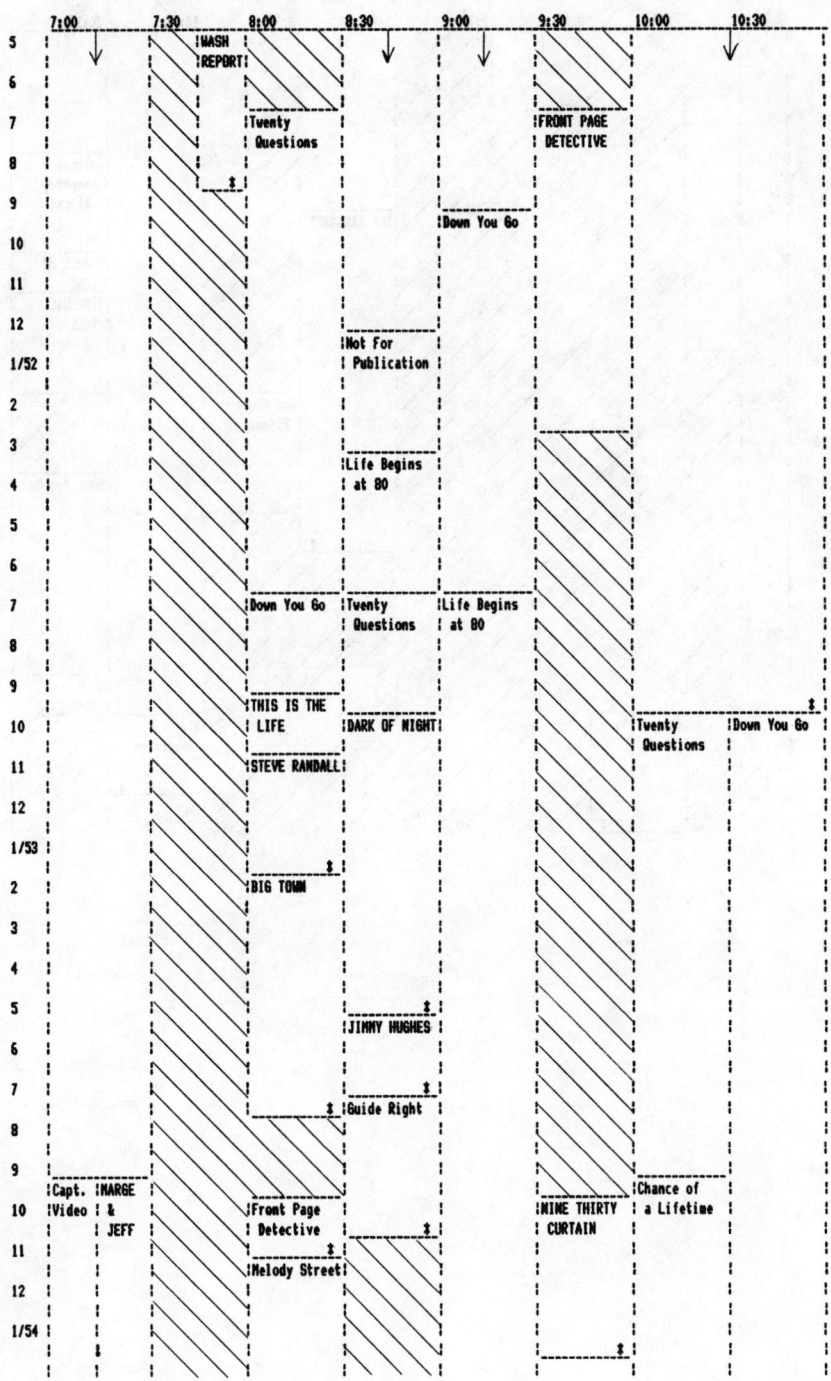

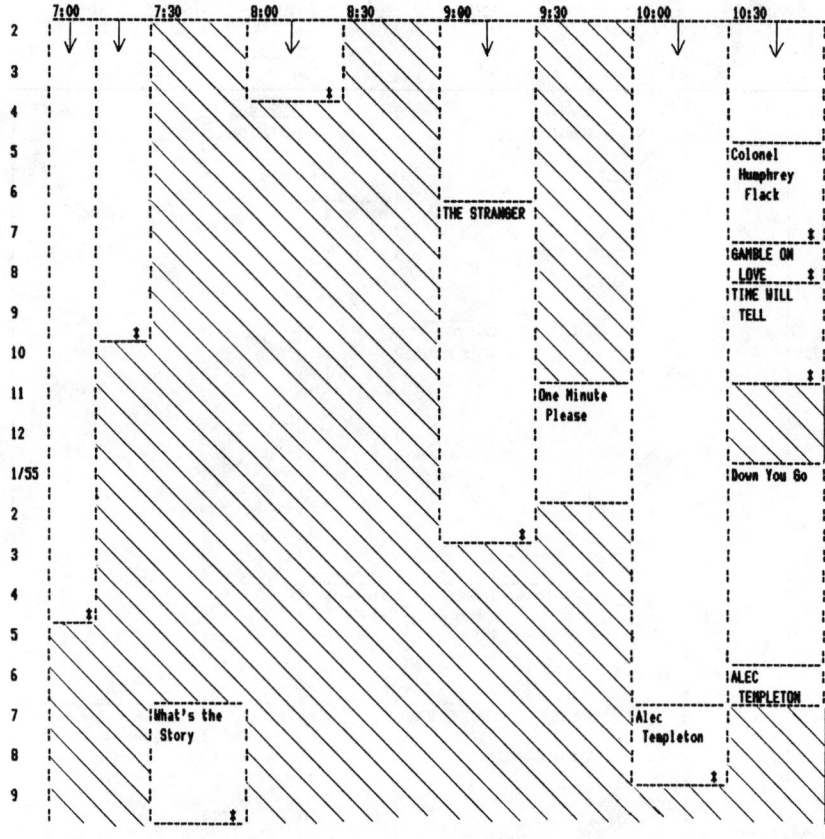

Date	Time	Title (min. if not 30) — Type	Action	From/To
7/48	9:00	Wrestling(120) — SP	s	
8/48	8:00	Fashions on Parade — FS	d	
10/48	7:00	Key to the Missing — IV	d	
12/48	9:00	Wrestling(120) — SP	f	
1/49	7:30	Manhattan Spotlight(15) — IV	d	
1/49	8:00	Fashions on Parade — FS	c	
1/49	8:00	Admiral Broadway Revue(60) — VY	d	
3/49	7:00	Key to the Missing — IV	m	To:r-8:30
3/49	7:00	Wendy Barrie — IV	d	
3/49	7:45	Russ Hodges' Scoreboard(15) — SN	d	
3/49	9:00	Front Row Center — MV	d	
5/49	7:30	A Woman to Remember(15) — SL	d	
5/49	7:30	Manhattan Spotlight(15) — IV	m	To:f-7:45
5/49	7:45	Russ Hodges' Scoreboard(15) — SN	c	
5/49	7:45	Manhattan Spotlight(15) — IV	m	Fr:f-7:30
5/49	9:30	Key to the Missing — IV	m	Fr:r-8:30
6/49	7:00	Captain Video & His Video Rangers — KV	d	
6/49	7:00	Wendy Barrie — IV	m	To:w-7
6/49	8:00	Front Row Center — MV	m	Fr:f-9
6/49	8:00	Admiral Broadway Revue(60) — VY	c	
6/49	9:00	Front Row Center — MV	m	To:f-8
6/49	9:00	Key to the Missing — IV	m	Fr:f-9:30
6/49	9:30	Key to the Missing — IV	m	To:f-9
7/49	7:30	Vincent Lopez(15) — MV	d	
7/49	7:30	A Woman to Remember(15) — SL	c	
9/49	8:00	Front Row Center — MV	m	To:n-7
9/49	8:00	Hands of Mystery — MA	d	
9/49	9:00	Fishing and Hunting Club — ST	d	
9/49	9:00	Key to the Missing — IV	c	
9/49	10:00	Boxing(60) — SP	s	
10/49	8:30	Broadway to Hollywood — Headline Clues — QU	m	Fr:w-8:30
3/50	9:00	Fishing and Hunting Club — ST	c	
5/50	8:30	Broadway to Hollywood — Headline Clues — QU	m	To:w-10
6/50	7:30	Vincent Lopez(15) — MV	c	
7/50	7:30	Manhattan Spotlight(15) — IV	m	Fr:f-7:45
7/50	7:45	Hazel Scott(15) — MU	d	
7/50	7:45	Manhattan Spotlight(15) — IV	m	To:f-7:30
7/50	8:00	Hands of Mystery — MA	m	To:f-9
7/50	9:00	Hands of Mystery — MA	m	Fr:f-8
7/50	9:30	Rocky King, Inside Detective — CD	m	Fr:s-8:30
7/50	10:00	Boxing(60) — SP	f	
9/50	7:45	Hazel Scott(15) — MU	c	
9/50	8:30	Hold That Camera — QU	d	
9/50	10:00	Cavalcade of Stars(60) — CV	m	Fr:s-9
10/50	7:30	Most Important People(15) — MV	d	
10/50	7:30	Manhattan Spotlight(15) — IV	m	To:f-7:45
10/50	7:45	Susan Raye(15) — MU	d	

Date	Time	Title (min. if not 30) — Type	Action	From/To
10/50	7:45	Susan Raye(15) — MU	m	To:m-7:30
11/50	7:45	Manhattan Spotlight(15) — IV	m	Fr:f-7:30
12/50	8:00	Your Story Theater — DA	d	
12/50	8:30	Hold That Camera — QU	c	
12/50	8:30	You Asked for It — NM	d	
2/51	8:00	Your Story Theater — DA	c	
3/51	9:30	Rocky King, Inside Detective — CD	m	To:n-9
4/51	7:30	Most Important People(15) — MV	c	
4/51	7:45	Manhattan Spotlight(15) — IV	c	
5/51	7:45	Washington Report(15) — DS	d	
7/51	8:00	Twenty Questions — QU	m	Fr:f-8(a)
7/51	9:30	Front Page Detective — ND	d	
8/51	7:45	Washington Report(15) — DS	c	
9/51	9:00	Down You Go — QU	m	Fr:r-9
9/51	9:00	Hands of Mystery — MA	m	To:t-10
12/51	8:30	Not for Publication — ND	m	Fr:mr-7:45-9/51
12/51	8:30	You Asked for It — NM	m	To:m-9(a)
2/52	9:30	Front Page Detective — ND	m	To:f-8-10/53
3/52	8:30	Life Begins at Eighty — DS	m	Fr:m-8:30(a)
3/52	8:30	Not for Publication — ND	m	To:t-10
6/52	8:00	Twenty Questions — QU	m	To:f-8:30
6/52	8:30	Life Begins at Eighty — DS	m	To:f-9
6/52	9:00	Down You Go — QU	m	To:f-8
7/52	8:00	Down You Go — QU	m	Fr:f-9
7/52	8:30	Twenty Questions — QU	m	Fr:f-8
7/52	9:00	Life Begins at Eighty — DS	m	Fr:f-8:30
9/52	8:00	Down You Go — QU	m	To:f-10:30
9/52	8:00	This Is the Life — RD	d	
9/52	8:30	Twenty Questions — QU	m	To:f-10
9/52	10:00	Cavalcade of Stars(60) — CV	c	
10/52	8:00	This Is the Life — RD	m	To:n-9:30
10/52	8:30	Dark of Night — DA	d	
10/52	10:00	Twenty Questions — QU	m	Fr:f-8:30
10/52	10:30	Down You Go — QU	m	Fr:f-8
11/52	8:00	Steve Randall — CD	d	
1/53	8:00	Steve Randall — CD	c	
2/53	8:00	Big Town — ND	d	
5/53	8:30	Dark of Night — DA	c	
5/53	8:30	Jimmy Hughes, Rookie Cop — CD	d	
7/53	8:00	Big Town — ND	c	
7/53	8:30	Guide Right — VY	m	Fr:r-8
7/53	8:30	Jimmy Hughes, Rookie Cop — CD	c	
9/53	7:00	Captain Video & His Video Rangers — KV	m	To:m-f-7
9/53	7:00	Captain Video & His Video Rangers (15) — KV	m	Fr:m-f-7
9/53	7:15	Marge and Jeff(15) — SC	d	
9/53	10:00	Chance of a Lifetime — TA	m	Fr:r-8:30(a)
9/53	10:00	Twenty Questions — QU	m	To:m-8
10/53	8:00	Front Page Detective — ND	m	Fr:f-9:30-2/52

Date	Time	Title (min. if not 30) — Type	Action	From/To
10/53	8:30	Guide Right — VY	c	
10/53	9:30	Nine Thirty Curtain — DA	d	
11/53	8:00	Front Page Detective — ND	c	
11/53	8:30	Melody Street — MU	m	Fr:w-8:30
1/54	9:30	Nine Thirty Curtain — DA	c	
2/54	8:30	Melody Street — MU	c	
4/54	10:30	Down You Go — QU	m	To:w-9:30
5/54	10:30	Colonel Humphrey Flack — SC	m	Fr:s-10
6/54	9:00	Life Begins at Eighty — DS	m	To:n-9:30-9/54
6/54	9:00	The Stranger — CD	d	
7/54	10:30	Colonel Humphrey Flack — SC	c	
7/54	10:30	Gamble on Love — QU	d	
8/54	10:30	Gamble on Love — QU	c	
8/54	10:30	Time Will Tell — QU	d	
9/54	7:15	Marge and Jeff(15) — SC	c	
10/54	10:30	Time Will Tell — QU	c	
11/54	9:30	One Minute Please — QU	m	Fr:t-8:30
1/55	9:30	One Minute Please — QU	m	To:r-9:30
1/55	10:30	Down You Go — QU	m	Fr:w-10
2/55	9:00	The Stranger — CD	c	
4/55	7:00	Captain Video & His Video Rangers (15) — KV	c	
5/55	10:30	Down You Go — QU	m	To:s-9:30(c)
6/55	10:00	Chance of a Lifetime — TA	m	To:n-9(a)
6/55	10:30	It's Alec Templeton Time — MU	d	
6/55	10:30	It's Alec Templeton Time — MU	m	To:f-10
7/55	7:00	What's the Story — QU	m	Fr:w-8
7/55	10:00	It's Alec Templeton Time — MU	m	Fr:f-10:30
8/55	10:00	It's Alec Templeton Time — MU	c	
9/55	7:30	What's the Story — QU	c	

Friday Programming
Moves Summary

1948–49

ABC. *Series Premieres:* Alice Pearce; Break the Bank; Fun for the Money; Ladies Be Seated; Sparring Partners; Tales of the Red Caboose; Think Fast; Vaudeo Varieties; Wren's Nest. *Key Programming Moves:* BREAK THE BANK debuts; it moves to NBC at the end of the season; the series had runs on all three major networks prior to leaving the air in 1/57.

CBS. *Series Premieres:* Adventures in Jazz; Campus Corner; Captain Billy; Cliff Edwards; Johns Hopkins Science Review; Mama; Manhattan Showcase; Morey Amsterdam; This Is Show Business; Your Sports Special. *Key Programming Moves:* MAMA debuts in the 8–8:30 slot, which it occupied for its entire run, until 7/56.

NBC. *Series Premieres:* Admiral Broadway Revue; Benny Rubin; Hopalong Cassidy; I'd Like to See; Kukla, Fran & Ollie; Meet Your Congress; Mixed Doubles; Mohawk Showroom; Song and Dance; Ted Steele; Your Show Time. *Key Programming Moves:* ADMIRAL BROADWAY REVUE debuts in 1/49; it is simulcast on NBC and DuMont; it is cancelled in 6/49; NBC begins airing boxing in the 9:30–11 slot (10–11, in 1/49); it continued this practice until 6/60.

DuMont. *Series Premieres:* Admiral Broadway Revue; Captain Video & His Video Rangers; Front Row Center; Key to the Missing; Manhattan Spotlight; Russ Hodges; Vincent Lopez; Wendy Barrie; A Woman to Remember. *Key Programming Moves:* ADMIRAL BROADWAY REVUE debuts in 1/49; it is simulcast on DuMont and NBC; it is cancelled in 6/49.

1949–50

ABC. *Series Premieres:* Art Ford on Broadway; Auction-Aire; Majority Rules; My True Story; Tin Pan Alley TV.

CBS. *Series Premieres:* Alkali Ike; Amazing Polgar; Capitol Cloak Room; Ford Theatre; Garry Moore Show; Life with Snarky Parker; Man Against Crime; Paul Arnold Show; The Stork Club; Strictly for Laughs. *Key Programming Moves:* MAN AGAINST CRIME debuts in the 8:30-9 slot; the series lasted on CBS until 10/53.

NBC. *Series Premieres:* Big Story; Life Begins at Eighty; One Man's Family; Versatile Varieties. *Key Programming Moves:* BIG STORY debuts; this dramatic anthology series continued on NBC's Friday night schedule until its cancellation in 6/57. In January, THE QUIZ KIDS is moved to Friday, 8-8:30; it stayed in this slot until 10/51.

DuMont. *Series Premieres:* Fishing and Hunting Club; Hands of Mystery; Hazel Scott.

1950-51

ABC. *Series Premieres:* Crime with Father; Life with Linkletter; N.Y. Giants Quarterback Huddle; Penthouse Party; Pulitzer Prize Playhouse; Sawyer Views Hollywood; Tales of Tomorrow. *Key Programming Moves:* TALES OF TOMORROW debuts in 8/51; it lasts until 6/53.

CBS. *Series Premieres:* Charlie Wild, Pvt. Detective; Hollywood Opening Night; Live Like a Millionaire; Magnavox Theatre; Star of the Family; Steve Allen Show. *Key Programming Moves:* MAMA is the #10 rated series on television; it helps CBS win the night.

NBC. *Series Premieres:* Bob and Ray; Henry Morgan Show; Those Two; Up to Paar.

DuMont. *Series Premieres:* Front Page Detective; Hold That Camera; Most Important People; Susan Raye Show; Washington Report; You Asked for It; Your Story Theatre. *Key Programming Moves:* CAVALCADE OF STARS is moved to Friday, 10-11; it stays in this slot until its cancellation in 9/52. YOU ASKED FOR IT debuts in 12/50; it runs on DuMont for one year and it is then picked up by ABC, where it lasts until 9/59; this series was the forerunner to the "info-tainment" genre (REAL PEOPLE, THAT'S IN-CREDIBLE, etc.) popular in the 1980s.

1951-52

ABC. *Series Premieres:* Dell O'Dell; Hot Seat; Mark Saber; Our Neighbors to the North; Rebound; Say It with Acting. *Key Programming Moves:* THE STU ERWIN SHOW is moved to Friday; it continues as part of ABC's Friday night lineup for the next three years; ABC discontinues programming the 10-11 slot in 1/52.

CBS. *Series Premieres:* Footlight Theatre; Police Story; Presidential Timber; Schlitz Playhouse of Stars. *Key Programming Moves:* SCHLITZ PLAYHOUSE OF STARS debuts; this 60 minute dramatic anthology series is cut back to 30 minutes in 4/52; it remains on CBS' Friday night schedule until 3/59; In April, MY FRIEND IRMA is moved to Friday.

NBC. *Series Premieres:* Coke Time with Eddie Fisher; Herman Hickman; RCA Victor Show. *Key Programming Moves:* THE ALDRICH FAMILY is moved to Friday, 9:30–10; it stays in this slot until its cancellation in 5/53.

DuMont. *Key Programming Moves:* CAVALCADE OF STARS is cancelled at the end of the season.

1952–53

ABC. *Series Premieres:* Adventures of Ozzie & Harriet. *Key Programming Moves:* THE ADVENTURES OF OZZIE & HARRIET debuts in the 8–8:30 slot, beginning a very successful 14 year run on ABC; it occupies this time slot until 6/56.

CBS. *Series Premieres:* Mr. & Mrs. North; Our Miss Brooks. *Key Programming Moves:* OUR MISS BROOKS debuts; this series stays part of CBS' Friday night lineup until its cancellation in 9/56; CBS' Friday night lineup is the clear ratings leader during 1952–53.

NBC. *Series Premieres:* Double or Nothing; Gulf Playhouse. *Key Programming Moves:* In January, LIFE OF RILEY is moved to Friday, 8:30–9; it stays in this slot, almost exclusively, until 9/58; THE ALDRICH FAMILY is cancelled in 5/53.

DuMont. *Series Premieres:* Big Town; Dark of Night; Jimmy Hughes Show; Steve Randall; This Is the Life.

1953–54

ABC. *Series Premieres:* Chevrolet Showroom; Comeback Story; Pepsi-Cola Playhouse; Pride of the Family; Who's the Boss?. *Key Programming Moves:* ABC resumes programming in the 10–11 slot, with SHOWCASE THEATRE, the CHEVROLET SHOWROOM; they discontinue programming this slot again in March; THE STU ERWIN SHOW is moved to Wednesday at the end of the season.

CBS. *Series Premieres:* Person to Person; Topper; Viceroy Star Theatre. *Key Programming Moves:* TOPPER debuts in the 8:30–9 slot; it stays in this slot until 9/55, when it is picked up by ABC; PERSON TO PERSON debuts; this interview series, hosted by Edward Murrow and later by

Charles Collingwood, stayed in the 10:30–11 slot until 12/60; MY FRIEND IRMA is cancelled in 6/54.

NBC. *Series Premieres:* The Duke; Garroway at Large.

DuMont. *Series Premieres:* Gamble on Love; Marge and Jeff; Nine Thirty Curtain; The Stranger; Time Will Tell. *Key Programming Moves:* CHANCE OF A LIFETIME is moved to Friday, 10–10:30; it stays in this slot until 6/55; By April, DuMont has cut back to two hours of programming on Friday night (7–7:30, 9–9:30 and 10–11).

1954–55

ABC. *Series Premieres:* Adventures of Rin Tin Tin; The Vise. *Key Programming Moves:* ADVENTURES OF RIN TIN TIN debuts in the 7:30–8 slot, which it occupies until its cancellation in 9/59.

CBS. *Series Premieres:* Julius LaRosa; The Lineup. *Key Programming Moves:* THE LINEUP debuts in the 10–10:30 slot, which it occupies until 9/59; TOPPER is dropped by CBS at the end of the season.

NBC. *Series Premieres:* Dear Phoebe.

DuMont. *Series Premieres:* Alec Templeton. *Key Programming Moves:* DuMont ceases Friday night programming at the end of the season.

1955–56

ABC. *Series Premieres:* Combat Sergeant; Crossroads; Polka Time. *Key Programming Moves:* ABC resumes programming in the 10–10:30 slot; THE ADVENTURES OF OZZIE & HARRIET is moved to Wednesday at the end of the season.

CBS. *Series Premieres:* Adventures of Champion; Crusader; Hollywood Summer Theatre; My Friend Flicka. *Key Programming Moves:* After seven years, MAMA is cancelled in 7/56; OUR MISS BROOKS is cancelled at the end of the season.

NBC. *Series Premieres:* Star Stage. *Key Programming Moves:* TRUTH OR CONSEQUENCES is moved to Friday; it is taken off the air at the end of the season, only to return in 12/57.

1956–57

ABC. *Series Premieres:* Adventures of Jim Bowie; Big Beat; A Date with the Angels; Key Club Playhouse; Ray Anthony; Treasure Hunt. *Key*

Programming Moves: THE ADVENTURES OF JIM BOWIE debuts in the 8–8:30 slot; it is a moderate success in the beginning; its appeal wanes and it lasts for only two years; ABC resumes programming in the 10–11 slot; in May, they again cut back to 10:30.

CBS. *Series Premieres:* Mr. Adams and Eve; West Point Story; Zane Grey Theatre. *Key Programming Moves:* ZANE GREY THEATRE debuts; this western anthology series lasts on CBS until 9/62.

NBC. *Series Premieres:* Big Moment; Blondie; Helen O'Connell Show; Joseph Cotten Show; Walter Winchell; Xavier Cugat. *Key Programming Moves:* After eight seasons, THE BIG STORY is cancelled in 6/57.

1957–58

ABC. *Series Premieres:* Buick Action Theatre; Colt .45; E.S.P.; Frank Sinatra; Frigidaire Summer Theatre; Holiday Handbook; Patrice Munsel; Stars of Jazz; This Is Music. *Key Programming Moves:* Frank Sinatra is brought back to weekly television by ABC with THE FRANK SINATRA SHOW; it fared poorly, lasting only one season; ABC's Friday night lineup is constantly being changed; during the season 14 different series are shuffled in and out of the 8:30–10:30 time period; nothing catches on.

CBS. *Series Premieres:* Boing Boing Show; Leave It to Beaver; Trackdown. *Key Programming Moves:* LEAVE IT TO BEAVER debuts; in March it is moved to Wednesday; the series will last only one season on CBS before being picked up by ABC, where it will run for another five years; In February, THE PHIL SILVERS SHOW is moved to Friday, 9–9:30, where it stayed until its cancellation in 9/59; In July, ZANE GREY THEATRE is moved to Thursday.

NBC. *Series Premieres:* Big Game; Court of Last Resort; Jefferson Drum; M Squad; The Thin Man. *Key Programming Moves:* M SQUAD and THE THIN MAN debut in the 9–9:30 and 9:30–10 slots, respectively; LIFE OF RILEY is cancelled at the end of the season.

1958–59

ABC. *Series Premieres:* Man with a Camera; 77 Sunset Strip. *Key Programming Moves:* 77 SUNSET STRIP debuts; it will stay on ABC's Friday night schedule until 9/63; After four years on Wednesday, DISNEYLAND is moved to Friday, where it stays until 9/60; THE ADVENTURES OF RIN TIN TIN is cancelled at the end of the season.

CBS. *Series Premieres:* Lux Playhouse; Rawhide. *Key Programming*

Moves: RAWHIDE, starring a young Clint Eastwood, debuts in 1/59; in May it is moved into the 7:30–8:30 slot, which it occupied until 9/63; YOUR HIT PARADE is moved to Friday; it is cancelled in 4/59; SCHLITZ PLAY-HOUSE OF STARS is cancelled in 3/59, after almost eight years on CBS; THE PHIL SILVERS SHOW is cancelled at the end of the season; THE LINEUP is moved to Wednesday at the end of the season.

NBC. *Series Premieres:* Colgate Western Theatre; Adventures of Ellery Queen.

1959–60

ABC. *Series Premieres:* The Detecitves; Man from Blackhawk. *Key Programming Moves:* DISNEYLAND moves to Sunday at the end of the season; ABC resumes programming the 10:30–11 slot.

CBS. *Series Premieres:* Hotel de Paree; Twilight Zone; Video Village. *Key Programming Moves:* TWILIGHT ZONE debuts, beginning a successful six year run on CBS; After seven years on Friday, PERSON TO PERSON is moved to Thursday at the end of the season.

NBC. *Series Premieres:* Bell Telephone Hour; Moment of Fear; Play Your Hunch; Troubleshooters. *Key Programming Moves:* BELL TELEPHONE HOUR debuts; it stays on NBC's schedule, off and on, until 4/68; After three years on Friday, M SQUAD is moved to Tuesday in 1/60; NBC, which had been airing boxing on Friday nights since 1948, stops air-ing it in 6/60.

1960–61

ABC. *Series Premieres:* Flintstones; Harrigan & Son; The Law and Mr. Jones; Matty's Funday Funnies. *Key Programming Moves:* THE FLINTSTONES debuts; this animated series was a prehistoric take-off on THE HONEYMOONERS; it was highly successful, attracting many adults, as well as children; it lasts for six years.

CBS. *Series Premieres:* Eyewitness to History; Jackie Gleason Show; Mr. Garlund; Route 66; Way Out. *Key Programming Moves:* ROUTE 66 debuts in the 8:30–9:30 slot, where it stays until its cancellation in 9/64; RAWHIDE is the #6 rated series on television.

NBC. *Series Premieres:* Dan Raven; Five Star Jubilee; Michael Shayne; One Happy Family; Sing Along with Mitch; Westerner; Westinghouse Playhouse. *Key Programming Moves:* NBC constantly shuffles its Friday lineup; nothing seems to work as NBC cancels the entire lineup at the end of the season.

1961-62

ABC. *Series Premieres:* Hathaways; Soupy Sales Show; Straightaway; Target: The Corruptors.
CBS. *Series Premieres:* Father of the Bride. *Key Programming Moves:* CBS is the clear ratings leader on Friday night; TWILIGHT ZONE is taken off the air at the end of the season; it will be brought back in an expanded 60 minute format on Thursday in 1/63.
NBC. *Series Premieres:* Chet Huntley; The Detectives; Here and Now; International Showtime. *Key Programming Moves:* INTERNATIONAL SHOWTIME debuts; this variety series is a moderate success and continues in the 7:30-8:30 slot until 9/65.

1962-63

ABC. *Series Premieres:* Gallant Men; I'm Dickens—He's Fenster. *Key Programming Moves:* ABC cuts programming back to three hours on Friday nights (7:30-10:30); In April, CHEYENNE is moved to Friday; it is cancelled at the end of the season; THE FLINTSTONES is moved to Thursday at the end of the season.
CBS. *Series Premieres:* Fair Exchange; Portrait. *Key Programming Moves:* In January, ALFRED HITCHCOCK PRESENTS is moved to Friday; RAWHIDE is moved to Thursday at the end of the season.
NBC. *Series Premieres:* Don't Call Me Charlie; Jack Paar Show. *Key Programming Moves:* After his successful run as host of a late night talk show, NBC moves Jack Paar to prime time in THE JACK PAAR SHOW; the series is a moderate success and lasts for three years.

1963-64

ABC. *Series Premieres:* Burke's Law; Destry; Farmer's Daughter. *Key Programming Moves:* ABC resumes programming the 10:30-11 slot on Friday; 77 SUNSET STRIP is moved to the lead-off slot at the beginning of the season; in February, it is moved to Wednesday; ABC brings boxing back to Friday nights, scheduling it in the 10-11 slot; it is stopped at the end of the season; In December, THE PRICE IS RIGHT is moved to Friday; it is cancelled at the end of the season, ending a seven year prime time run.
CBS. *Series Premieres:* Great Adventure. *Key Programming Moves:* TWILIGHT ZONE is returned to Friday, in its original 30 minute format; it is scheduled in the 9:30-10 slot, followed by ALFRED HITCHCOCK PRESENTS, forming a solid 90 minute block; ROUTE 66 is cancelled at the end of the season.

NBC. *Series Premieres:* Bob Hope Presents the Chrysler Theatre; Harry's Girls; On Parade; That Was the Week That Was. *Key Programming Moves:* THAT WAS THE WEEK THAT WAS debuts in 1/64; this series was a satiric look at the week's news headlines (a forerunner to the highly popular "Weekend Update" feature of NBC's SATURDAY NIGHT LIVE of the 1970s and 1980s); it is moved to Tuesday for the following season.

1964–65

ABC. *Series Premieres:* Addam's Family; F.D.R.; Johnny Quest; Twelve O'Clock High; Valentine's Day. *Key Programming Moves:* ABC offers an entirely different lineup of Friday night programming; THE ADDAM'S FAMILY debuts; this sitcom was a spoof of the monster genre; it was a moderate hit, but like most "gimmick" shows, its popularity faded quickly; In December, THE FLINTSTONES is returned to Friday, where it stays until its cancellation in 9/66.

CBS. *Series Premieres:* The Entertainers; Gomer Pyle, U.S.M.C.; Our Private World; The Reporter. *Key Programming Moves:* Like ABC, CBS offers an entirely different Friday night lineup this season; RAWHIDE is returned to Friday; it is moved again at the end of the season; GOMER PYLE, U.S.M.C. debuts; this series was a spin-off from the highly successful ANDY GRIFFITH SHOW; it is a smash success in its own right, becoming the third highest rated series on television.

NBC. *Key Programming Moves:* THE JACK BENNY SHOW is picked up by NBC after 14 years on CBS; it doesn't have much steam left, and is cancelled at the end of the season. INTERNATIONAL SHOWTIME and THE JACK PAAR SHOW are cancelled at the end of the season.

1965–66

ABC. *Series Premieres:* Court Martial; Honey West; Summer Fun; Tammy. *Key Programming Moves:* At the end of the season, ABC cancels its entire Friday night lineup.

CBS. *Series Premieres:* Hogan's Heroes; The Smothers Brothers Show; Wayne and Shuster. *Key Programming Moves:* HOGAN'S HEROES debuts and becomes the #9 rated series on television; along with the #3 rated GOMER PYLE, U.S.M.C., CBS has one of the most successful hours (8:30–9:30) on television; it is short-lived because at the end of the season, GOMER PYLE, U.S.M.C. is moved to Wednesday.

NBC. *Series Premieres:* Camp Runamuck; Convoy; Hank; Mr. Roberts; Sammy Davis, Jr. Show. *Key Programming Moves:* NBC offers an entirely different Friday night lineup; NBC's five new series are all cancelled by season's end.

1966–67

ABC. *Series Premieres:* Green Hornet; Malibu U; Milton Berle Show; Rango; Time Tunnel. *Key Programming Moves:* ABC offers an entirely different Friday lineup; nothing takes hold.

CBS. *Key Programming Moves:* CBS begins airing films in the 9–11 slot; it continues this practice for most of the next 11 years; HOGAN'S HEROES is moved to Saturday at the end of the season.

NBC. *Series Premieres:* T.H.E. Cat; Tarzan. *Key Programming Moves:* TARZAN debuts in the 7:30–8:30 slot; THE MAN FROM U.N.C.L.E. is cancelled at the end of the season.

1967–68

ABC. *Series Premieres:* Guns of Will Sonnett; Hondo; Judd for the Defense; Man in a Suitcase; Off to See the Wizard; Operation: Entertainment. *Key Programming Moves:* ABC offers a lineup of all new series; none really catch on with the audience.

CBS. *Key Programming Moves:* GOMER PYLE, U.S.M.C. is returned to Friday; it again becomes the #3 rated series on television.

NBC. *Series Premieres:* Accidental Family; American Profile; Hollywood Squares.

1968–69

ABC. *Series Premieres:* Dick Cavett; Don Rickles; Generation Gap; John Davidson. *Key Programming Moves:* For the fourth consecutive year, ABC is shuffling its lineup in an attempt to find a winning combination; nothing works.

CBS. *Key Programming Moves:* GOMER PYLE, U.S.M.C. is the #2 rated series on television; at the end of the season it is taken off the air because the star wanted to do other projects.

NBC. *Series Premieres:* Name of the Game. *Key Programming Moves:* THE NAME OF THE GAME debuts; this 90 minute dramatic series has a rotating cast; it lasts for three years.

1969-70

ABC. *Series Premieres:* Brady Bunch; Jimmy Durante Presents the Lennon Sisters; Mr. Deeds Goes to Town. *Key Programming Moves:* THE BRADY BUNCH debuts; this series lasts for five years, all on ABC.

CBS. *Series Premieres:* Tim Conway Show. *Key Programming Moves:* HOGAN'S HEROES is returned to Friday, 8:30-9; at the end of the season, it is again moved, this time to Sunday; GET SMART is moved to Friday; it is cancelled at the end of the season.

NBC. *Series Premieres:* Bracken's World.

1970-71

ABC. *Series Premieres:* Partridge Family. *Key Programming Moves:* THE PARTRIDGE FAMILY debuts, beginning a fairly successful four year run; After five years of searching for a lineup that would work on Friday, ABC finally found one—a 2½ hour block of sitcoms; THAT GIRL is moved to Friday; it is cancelled at the end of the season.

CBS. *Series Premieres:* Headmaster; The Interns; The New Andy Griffith Show. *Key Programming Moves:* CBS brings Andy Griffith back to prime time television, first in THE HEADMASTER, then in THE NEW ANDY GRIFFITH SHOW; neither works, as both are cancelled by season's end.

NBC. *Series Premieres:* Strange Report. *Key Programming Moves:* NBC cancels its entire lineup at the end of the season.

1971-72

ABC. *Key Programming Moves:* All three networks cut back to three hours of prime time programming, in accordance with the FCC's new Prime Time Access Rule; ABC's Friday night lineup of comedies continues to work, winning the night.

CBS. *Series Premieres:* Chicago Teddy Bears; Don Rickles; O'Hara, U.S. Treasury.

NBC. *Series Premieres:* Chronolog; The D.A.; Sanford and Son. *Key Programming Moves:* SANFORD AND SON debuts in January; this series starring Redd Foxx becomes an enormous hit for NBC; it will occupy the 8-8:30 slot until 9/77; this year it is the sixth highest rated series on television.

1972-73

ABC. *Series Premieres:* Love Thy Neighbor. *Key Programming Moves:* THE PARTRIDGE FAMILY is moved to Saturday in 6/73.

NBC. *Series Premieres:* Banyon; Bobby Darin; Brian Keith Show; Ghost Story. *Key Programming Moves:* SANFORD AND SON becomes the #2 rated series on television.

1973-74

ABC. *Series Premieres:* Adam's Rib; $6 Million Man. *Key Programming Moves:* $6 MILLION MAN debuts in 1/74, becoming an instant hit; it lasts on ABC's schedule until 3/78; ROOM 222 and LOVE AMERICAN STYLE are cancelled in 1/74; THE BRADY BUNCH is cancelled and THE ODD COUPLE is moved to Thursday at the end of the season.

CBS. *Series Premieres:* Calucci's Department; Dirty Sally; Good Times; Roll Out. *Key Programming Moves:* GOOD TIMES debuts in 2/74; this spin-off from MAUDE, which was itself a spin-off from ALL IN THE FAMILY, was moved to Tuesday at the end of the season; it lasts on CBS' schedule until 8/79.

NBC. *Series Premieres:* The Girl with Something Extra; Needles and Pins. *Key Programming Moves:* SANFORD AND SON is the #3 rated series on television.

1974-75

ABC. *Series Premieres:* Baretta; Hot L Baltimore; Kodiak; Kolchak: The Night Stalker; Texas Wheelers. *Key Programming Moves:* BARETTA debuts in 1/75, beginning a three year run; in 3/75 it is moved to Wednesday; In July, ABC begins airing films in the 9–11 slot, a practice it will continue until 11/81.

CBS. *Series Premieres:* Friday Comedy Special; Khan; Planet of the Apes; We'll Get By.

NBC. *Series Premieres:* Chico and the Man; Police Woman; Rockford Files. *Key Programming Moves:* NBC introduces three new series, CHICO AND THE MAN, THE ROCKFORD FILES, and POLICE WOMAN; all three become big hits for NBC; NBC wins Friday night in a landslide as SANFORD AND SON and CHICO AND THE MAN are the #2 and #3 rated series on television.

1975-76

ABC. *Series Premieres:* Donny and Marie; Mobile One. *Key Programming Moves:* In January, DONNY AND MARIE debuts in the 8-9 slot; the debut of this series coincided with NBC's moving of CHICO AND THE MAN to Wednesday, and it scored fairly well with the audience; it occupied this slot until 1/79.

CBS. *Series Premieres:* Sara. *Key Programming Moves:* At the beginning of the season, CBS attempted to seriously challenge NBC for Friday night supremacy by moving three of its successful series to Friday (M∗A∗S∗H, HAWAII FIVE-O, and BARNABY JONES); unable to make much of a dent in NBC's audience, they moved all three to other nights by December.

NBC. *Series Premieres:* The Practice. *Key Programming Moves:* SANFORD AND SON is the #7 rated series on television; In January, NBC moved CHICO AND THE MAN to Wednesday; it didn't fare well and was returned to its original Friday slot in August; it never recaptured its audience.

1976-77

CBS. *Series Premieres:* Code R; Hunter; Keane Brothers; Spencer's Pilots; A Year at the Top.

NBC. *Series Premieres:* Serpico. *Key Programming Moves:* In February, QUINCY is moved to Friday, 10-11; SANFORD AND SON is cancelled at the end of the season.

1977-78

CBS. *Series Premieres:* Husbands, Wives & Lovers; Incredible Hulk. *Key Programming Moves:* THE INCREDIBLE HULK debuts in 3/78; it lasts until 6/82.

NBC. *Series Premieres:* Quark; Sanford Arms. *Key Programming Moves:* In an attempt to recapture some of the departed SANFORD AND SON's audience, NBC introduces a situational spin-off, SANFORD ARMS; the series lasts only one month; CHICO AND THE MAN is cancelled in 7/78.

1978-79

ABC. *Series Premieres:* Mackenzies of Paradise Cove. *Key Programming Moves:* In January, DONNY AND MARIE is moved to Sunday.

CBS. *Series Premieres:* Dukes of Hazzard; Flying High. *Key Programming Moves:* DUKES OF HAZZARD debuts in 1/79; it will be part of CBS' Friday night lineup until 9/85; In January, DALLAS is moved to Friday; this series remains part of CBS' Friday night lineup to the present time.

NBC. *Series Premieres:* Diff'rent Strokes; The Duke; Eddie Capra Mysteries; The Facts of Life; Hello Larry; Sweepstakes; Turnabout; Waverly Wonders; Who's Watching the Kids. *Key Programming Moves:* NBC's Friday schedule is in a constant state of disarray; through all the turmoil, two series debut which will become major hits for the network in subsequent years — DIFF'RENT STROKES and THE FACTS OF LIFE, the latter being a spin-off from the former.

1979–80

ABC. *Series Premieres:* B.A.D. Cats; When the Whistle Blows. *Key Programming Moves:* As part of ABC's strategy of leading-off every night with one of its hit series, FANTASY ISLAND is moved into the 8–9 slot on Friday; by October it was returned to its original Saturday night position; In July, BENSON is moved to Friday, 8–8:30; it occupied this slot, almost exclusively, until 3/85.

CBS. *Key Programming Moves:* DALLAS becomes the #6 and THE DUKES OF HAZZARD becomes the #9 rated series on television, catapulting CBS to a lopsided ratings victory on Friday night.

NBC. *Series Premieres:* Eischied; Here's Boomer; Pink Lady; Shirley; Speak Up, America. *Key Programming Moves:* NBC's Friday lineup is still in constant turmoil, with nothing staying in one place long enough to catch on.

1980–81

ABC. *Series Premieres:* I'm a Big Girl Now; The Krypton Factor.

CBS. *Key Programming Moves:* DALLAS becomes the #1 rated series on television, followed by THE DUKES OF HAZZARD (#2); CBS is again the ratings leader on Friday.

NBC. *Series Premieres:* Brady Brides; Comedy Theatre; Harper Valley P.T.A.; Marie; NBC Magazine; Nero Wolfe. *Key Programming Moves:* For the third year in a row NBC is constantly changing its Friday night lineup; still nothing works.

1981–82

ABC. *Series Premieres:* Darkroom; The Phoenix; Strike Force.

CBS. *Series Premieres:* Falcon Crest. *Key Programming Moves:* In December, THE INCREDIBLE HULK is taken off the air; Also in December, FALCON CREST debuts in the 10–11 slot, where it continues to the present time; DALLAS is the #1 rated series on television for the second consecutive year; THE DUKES OF HAZZARD is rated #6.

NBC. *Series Premieres:* Cassie & Company; McClain's Law.

1982–83

ABC. *Series Premieres:* At Ease; Baby Makes Five; The New Odd Couple; The Quest; Renegades; Webster. *Key Programming Moves:* WEBSTER debuts in 8/83; it stays part of ABC's Friday lineup until 8/87.

CBS. *Key Programming Moves:* DALLAS slips to #2 in the ratings; FALCON CREST moves up to #8.

NBC. *Series Premieres:* Knight Rider; Powers of Matthew Star; Remington Steele. *Key Programming Moves:* KNIGHT RIDER and REMINGTON STEELE debut; both series are moved to different nights by season's end, where they become modest successes for NBC.

1983–84

ABC. *Series Premieres:* Blue Thunder; Lottery.

CBS. *Key Programming Moves:* DALLAS is the #1 rated series on television for the third time in the past four years; FALCON CREST is #7.

NBC. *Series Premieres:* For Love and Honor; Jennifer Slept Here; Leg Men; Manimal; The Master; Mr. Smith; The New Show.

1984–85

ABC. *Series Premieres:* Comedy Factory; Hawaiian Heat; Mr. Belvedere; Off the Rack; Street Hawk.

CBS. *Series Premieres:* Detective in the House. *Key Programming Moves:* THE DUKES OF HAZZARD is cancelled at the end of the season; DALLAS is again the #1 rated series on television.

NBC. *Series Premieres:* Best Times; Codename: Foxfire; Half Nelson; Hunter; Miami Vice; Mike Nesmith; Motown Revue; V. *Key Programming*

Moves: MIAMI VICE debuts; this series combines elements of the new music video style (ala MTV) and the traditional crime drama form; it becomes a hit for NBC.

1985–86

ABC. *Series Premieres:* He's the Mayor; Joe Bash; Mr. Sunshine; Spenser for Hire. *Key Programming Moves:* THE FALL GUY and THE LOVE BOAT are moved to Friday; both of these long-running series are cancelled by season's end.

CBS. *Series Premieres:* Twilight Zone. *Key Programming Moves:* CBS introduces a new version of THE TWILIGHT ZONE; it does not perform as well as CBS hoped it would; DALLAS is again among the top 10 rated series on television.

NBC. *Series Premieres:* Last Precinct; Misfits of Science. *Key Programming Moves:* In June, MIAMI VICE is moved into the 9–10 slot, opposite CBS' DALLAS; MIAMI VICE's ratings suffer as it loses to DALLAS, though DALLAS' ratings are also hurt by the move.

1986–87

ABC. *Series Premieres:* Dads; Gung Ho; Sidekicks; Sledge Hammer; Starman. *Key Programming Moves:* WEBSTER is cancelled at the end of the season.

CBS. *Series Premieres:* Nothing Is Easy; Popcorn Kid; Summer Playhouse.

NBC. *Series Premieres:* Crime Story; L.A. Law; Roomies. *Key Programming Moves:* L.A. LAW debuts; in December it is moved to Thursday.

1987–88

ABC. *Series Premieres:* Family Man; Full House; I Married Dora; Pursuit of Happiness; The Thorns. *Key Programming Moves:* 20/20 is moved to Friday, 10–11, after eight years on Thursday; In February, PERFECT STRANGERS is moved to Friday, 8–8:30.

CBS. *Series Premieres:* Beauty & the Beast.

NBC. *Series Premieres:* Beverly Hills Buntz; The Highwayman; Sonny Spoon. *Key Programming Moves:* In April, MIAMI VICE is moved back to its original 10–11 slot; the ratings improve.

Saturday Night

September 1948 — August 1988

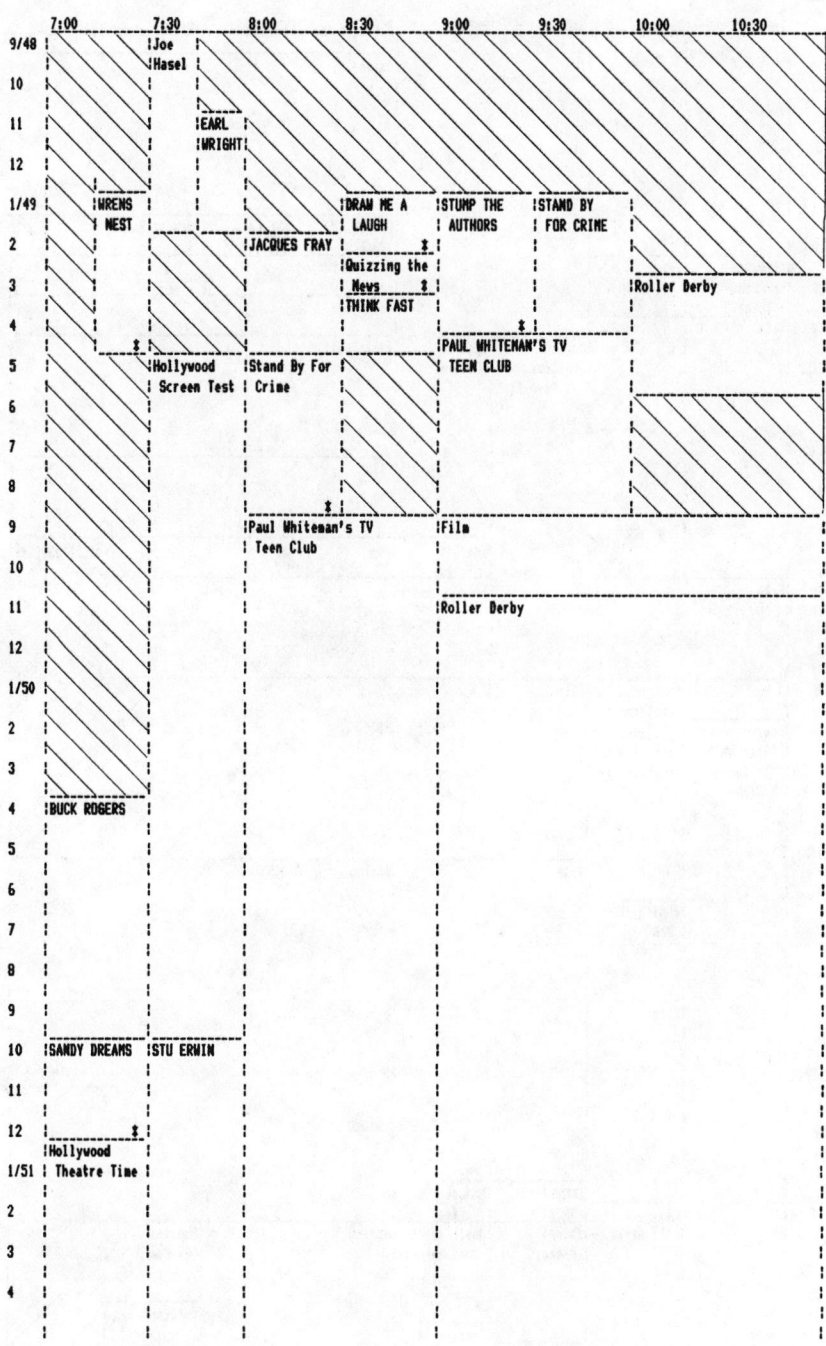

	7:00	7:30	8:00	8:30	9:00	9:30	10:00	10:30
5					Baseball			
6								
7								
8								
9					LESSON IN	America's	Harness Racing	
10	PERSONAL	Jerry			_SAFETY_ | Health	Harness Racing	
11	APPEARANCE	Colonna			Film			
12	_THEATRE_ | Film		Paul	Sports	Basketball			
1/52			Whiteman's	Camera				
2			TV Teen Club					
3					Film			
4								
5				Baseball				Sprts Camera
6	Film			Film				
7								
8								
9		Paul	Film					
10	Paul	Whiteman's						
	Whiteman's	_TV Teen Club_						
11	TV Teen	Live Like a						
	Club	Millionaire						
12								
1/53								
2			Film	Boxing				
		WHAT'S YOUR						
3		BID						
4								
5		Film						
6								
7								
8								
9			SHOWCASE	Madison Sq.				
10		Leave It to	_THEATRE_	_Garden_				
11		the Girls	Talent	Music at	Boxing		Madison Sq.	
			Patrol	Meadowbrook			Garden	
12							On Guard	
1/54	On Your Way			Madison Sq.				
			Enterprise	_Garden_				

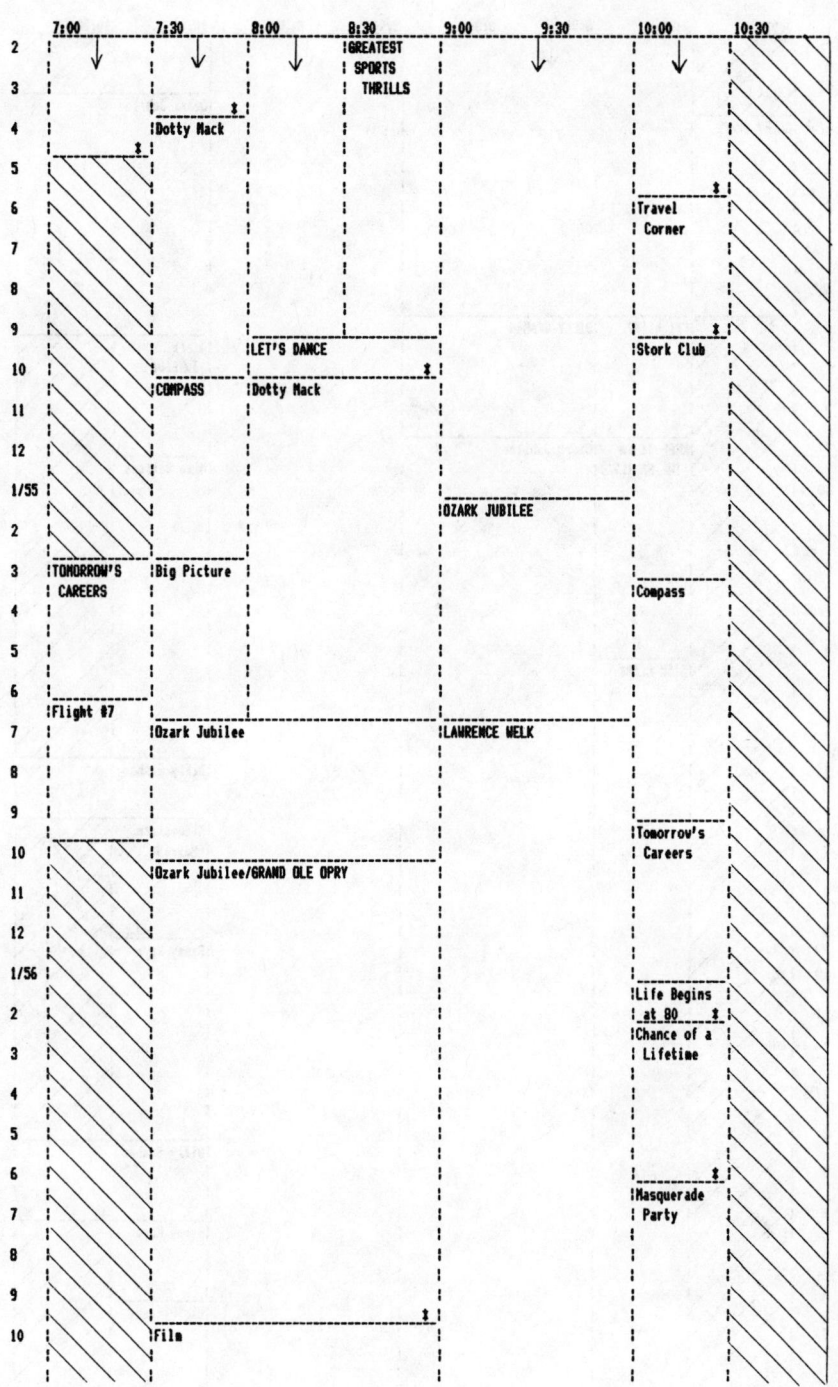

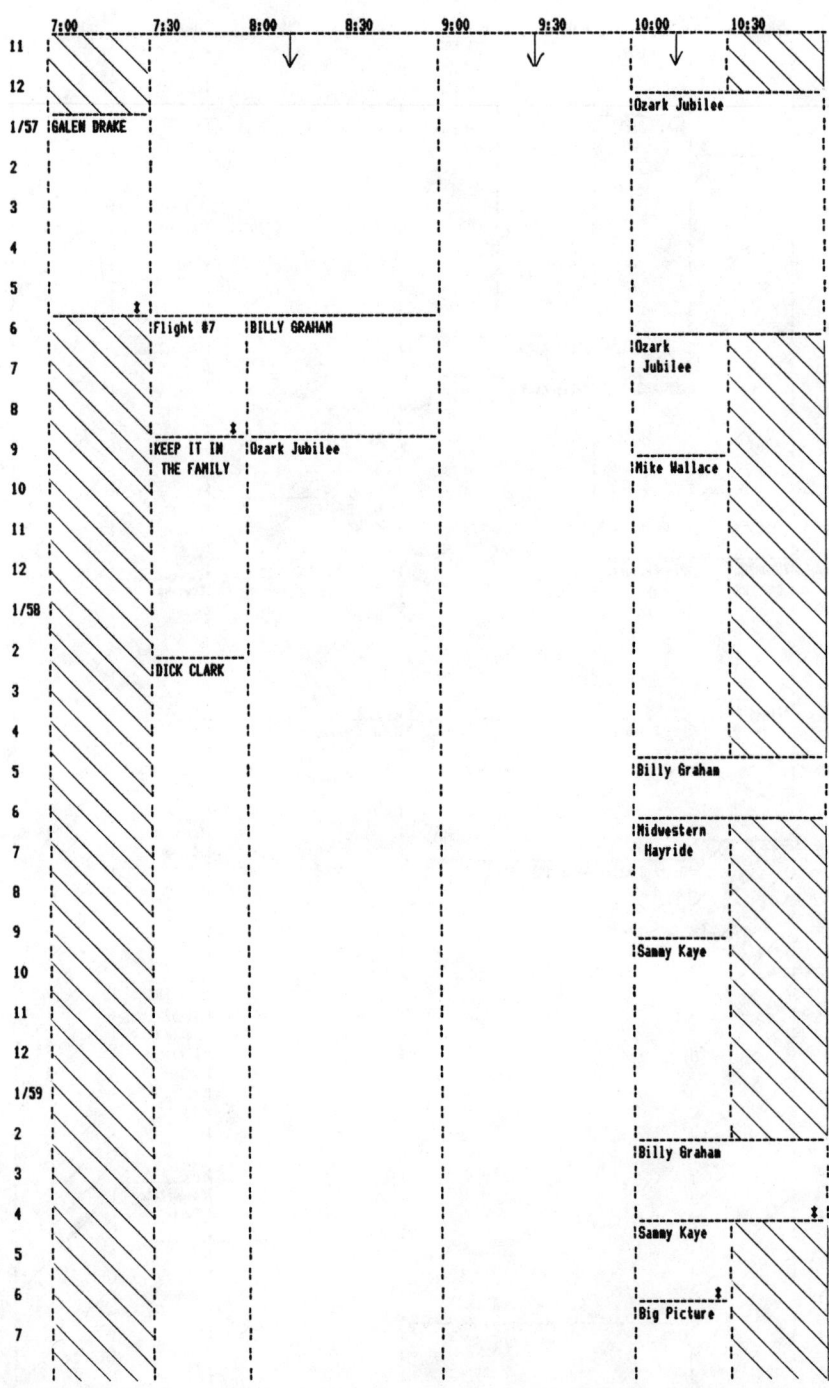

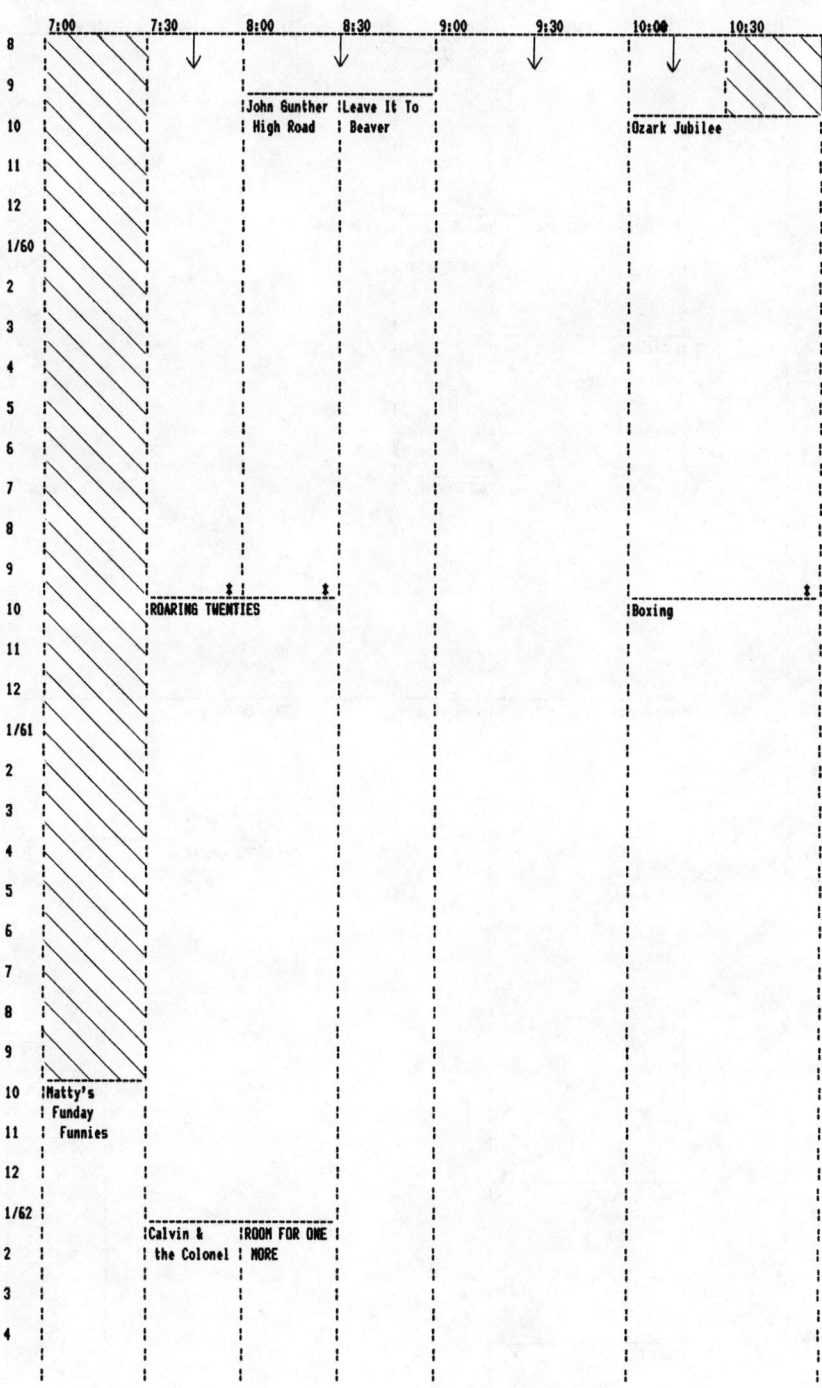

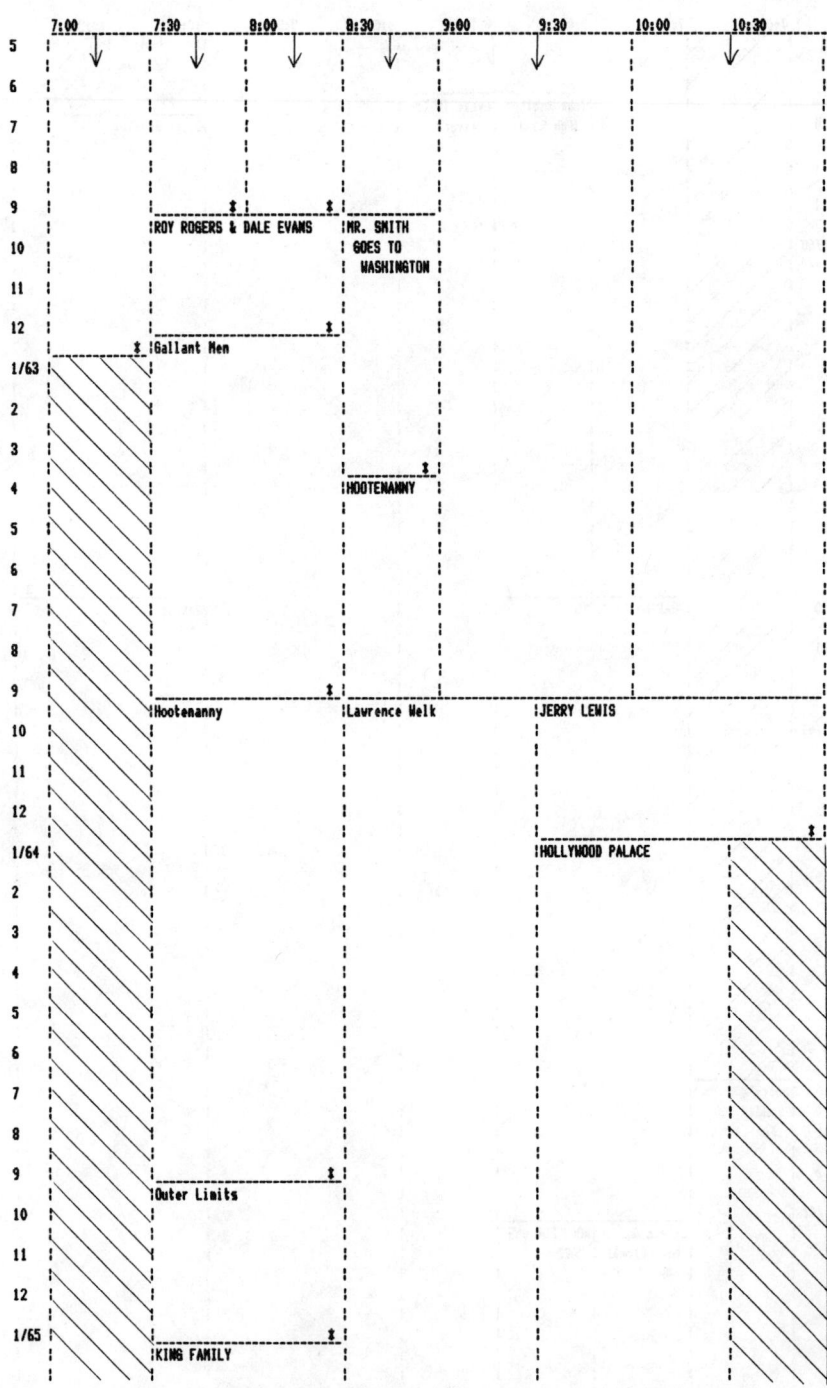

	7:00	7:30	8:00	8:30	9:00	9:30	10:00	10:30

ROY ROGERS & DALE EVANS

MR. SMITH GOES TO WASHINGTON

Gallant Men

HOOTENANNY

Hootenanny

Lawrence Welk

JERRY LEWIS

HOLLYWOOD PALACE

Outer Limits

KING FAMILY

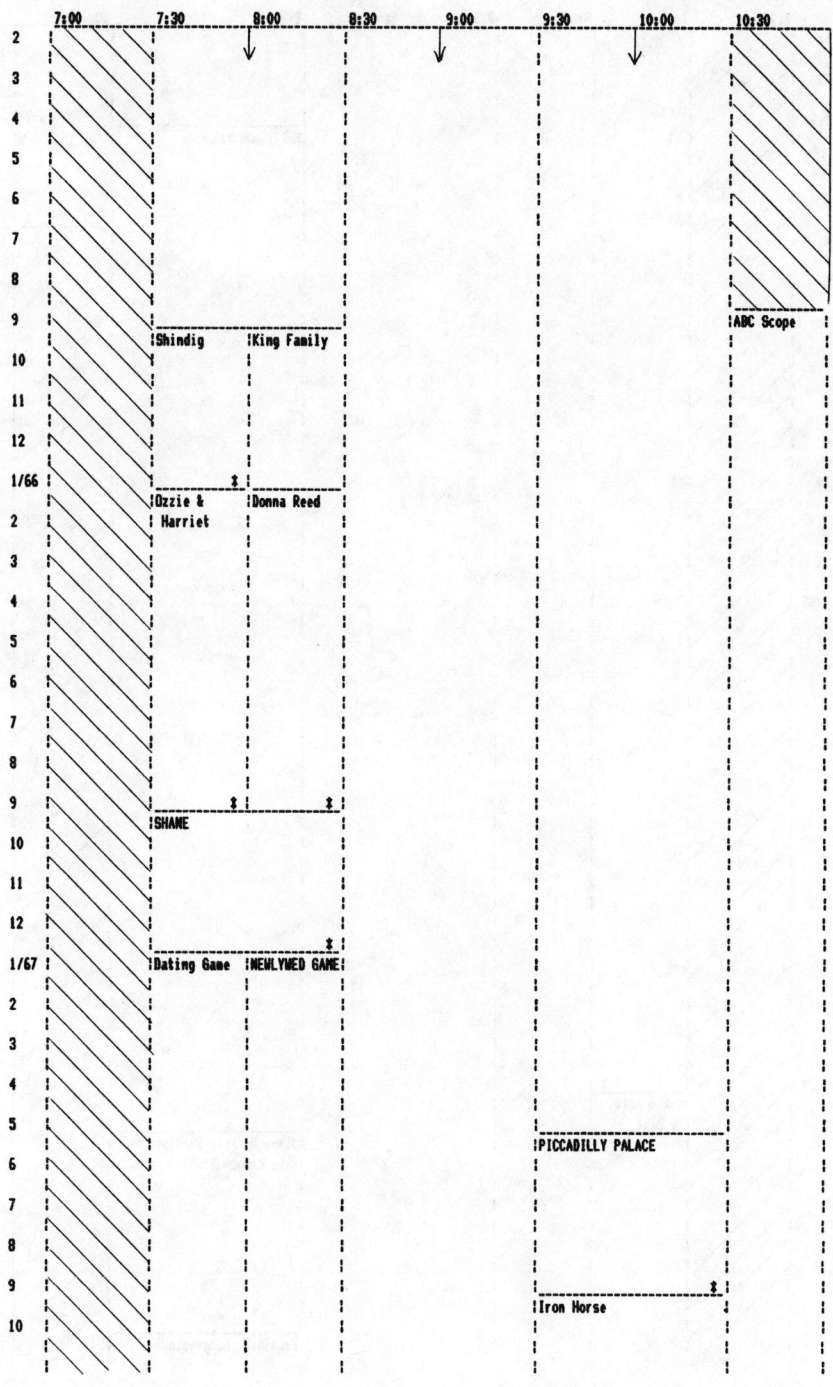

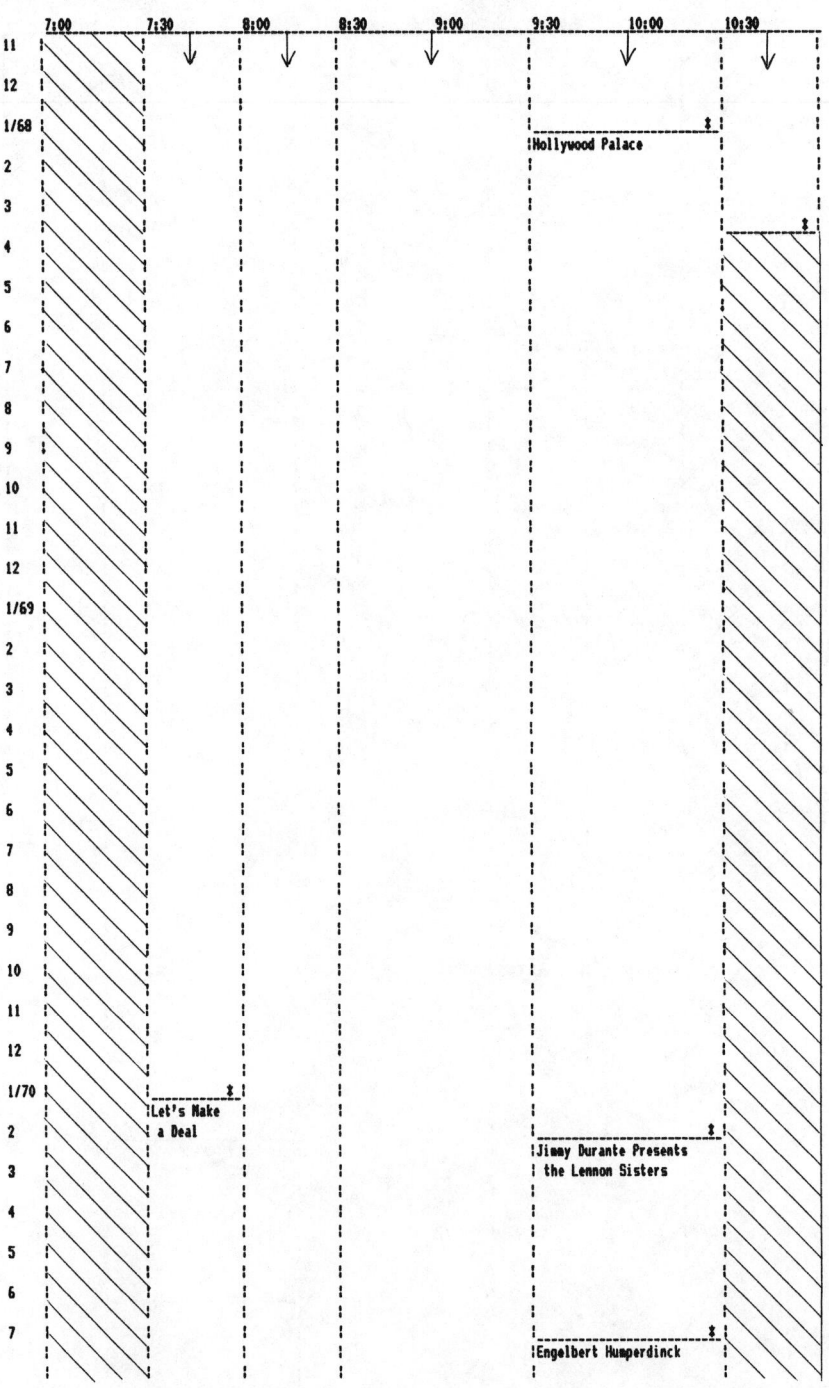

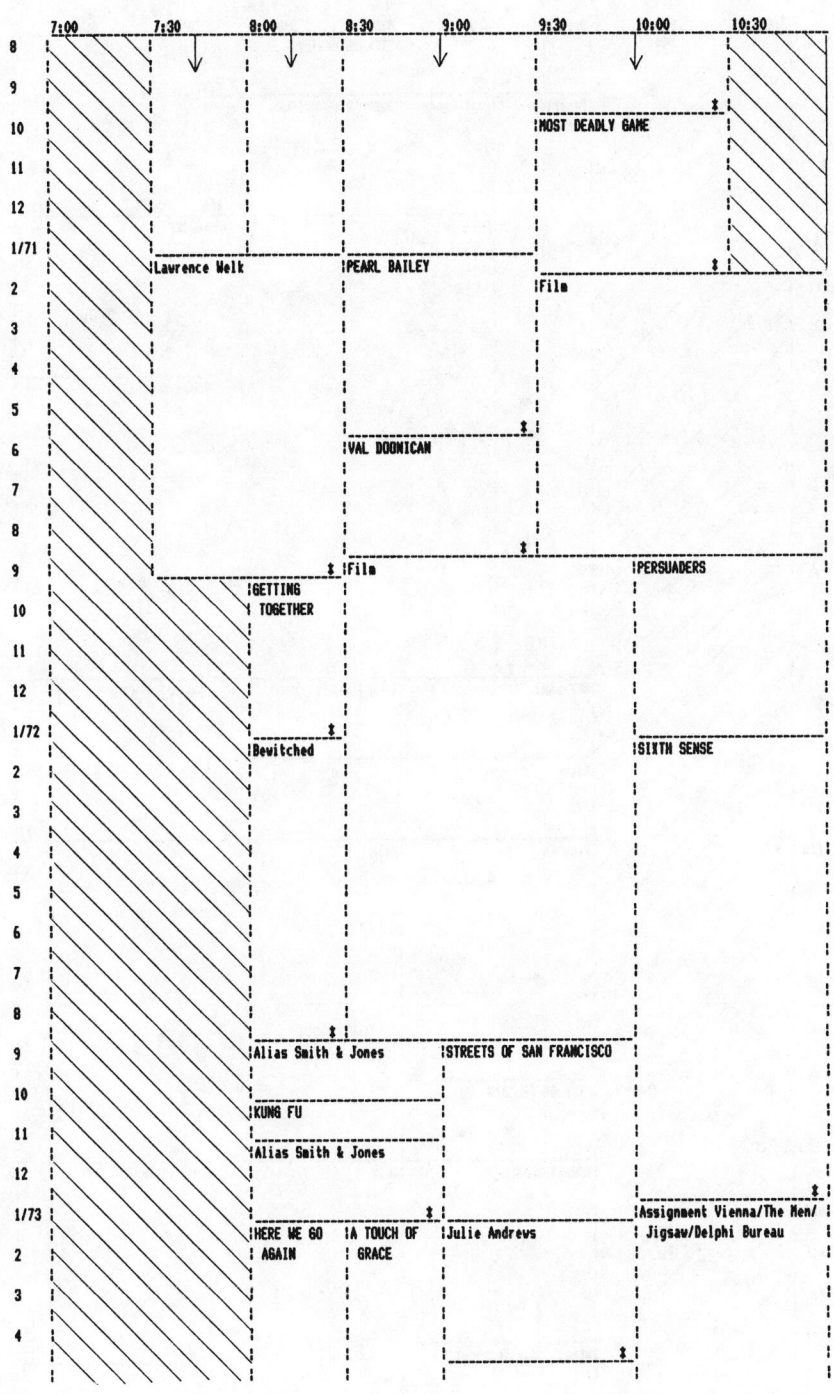

	7:00	7:30	8:00	8:30	9:00	9:30	10:00	10:30
8		↓		↓		↓		↓	
9								
10						MOST DEADLY GAME		
11								
12								
1/71		Lawrence Welk		PEARL BAILEY				
2						Film		
3								
4								
5								
6				VAL DOONICAN				
7								
8								
9			GETTING	Film		PERSUADERS		
10			TOGETHER					
11								
12								
1/72			Bewitched			SIXTH SENSE		
2								
3								
4								
5								
6								
7								
8								
9			Alias Smith & Jones	STREETS OF SAN FRANCISCO			
10			KUNG FU					
11			Alias Smith & Jones					
12								
1/73			HERE WE GO	A TOUCH OF	Julie Andrews	Assignment Vienna/The Men/	
2			AGAIN	GRACE		Jigsaw/Delphi Bureau	
3								
4								

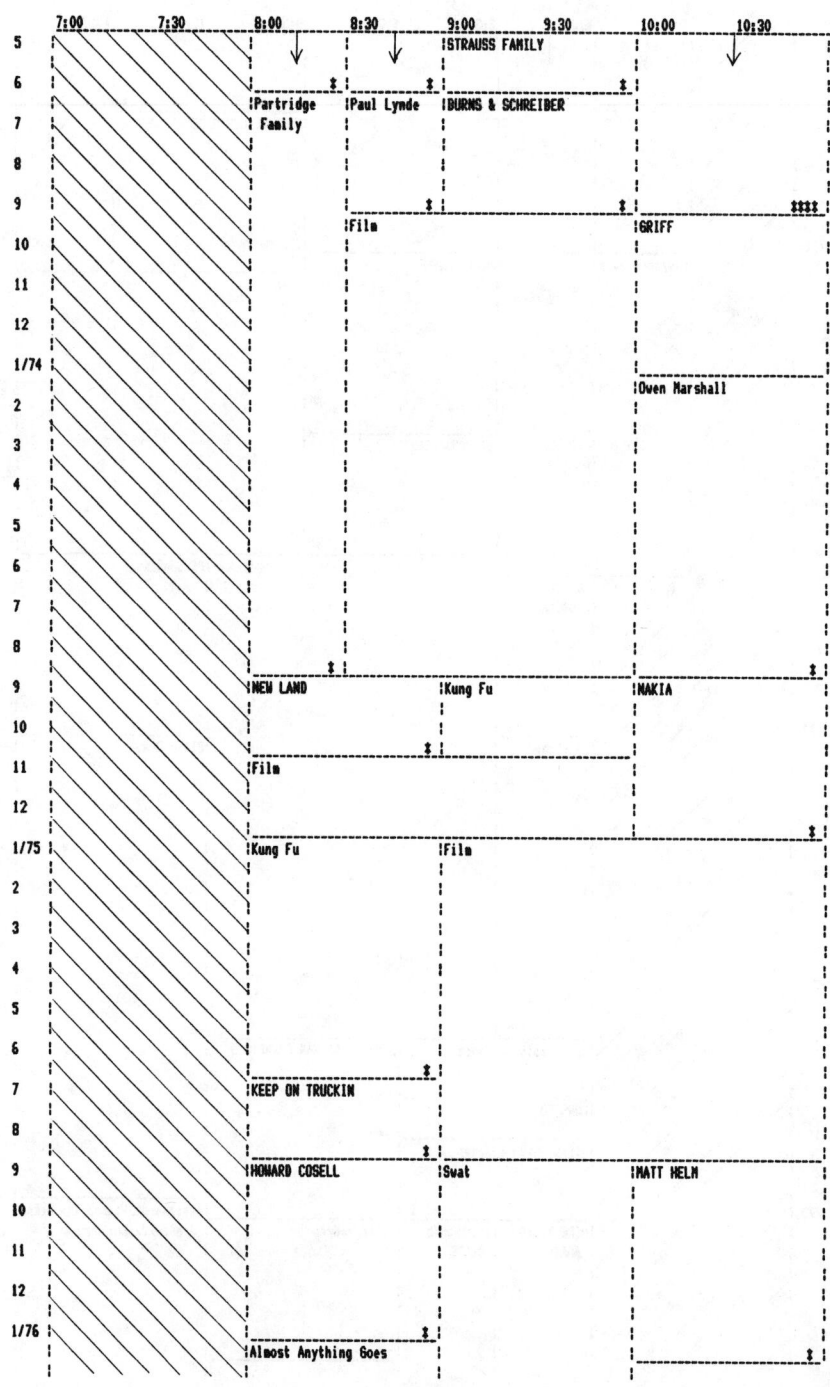

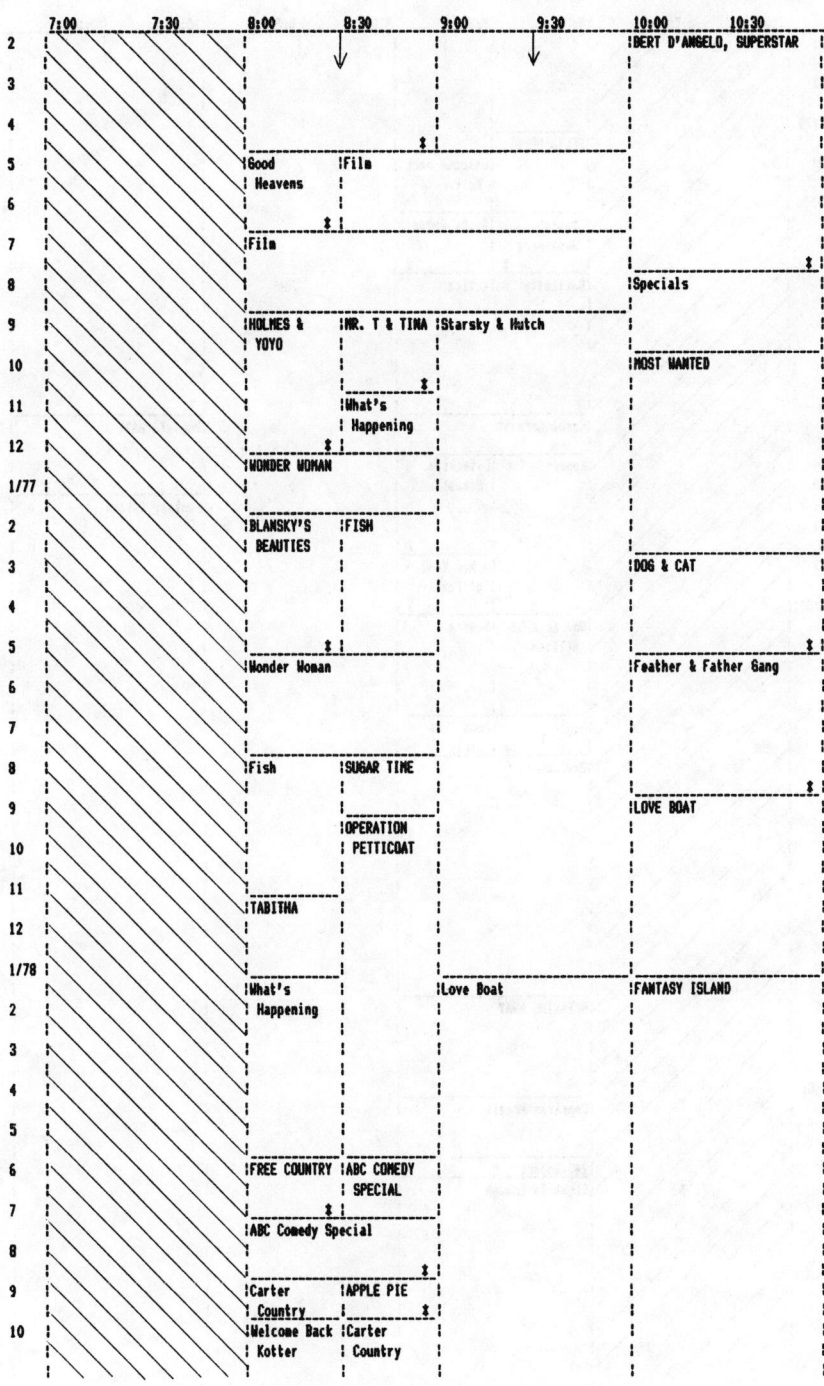

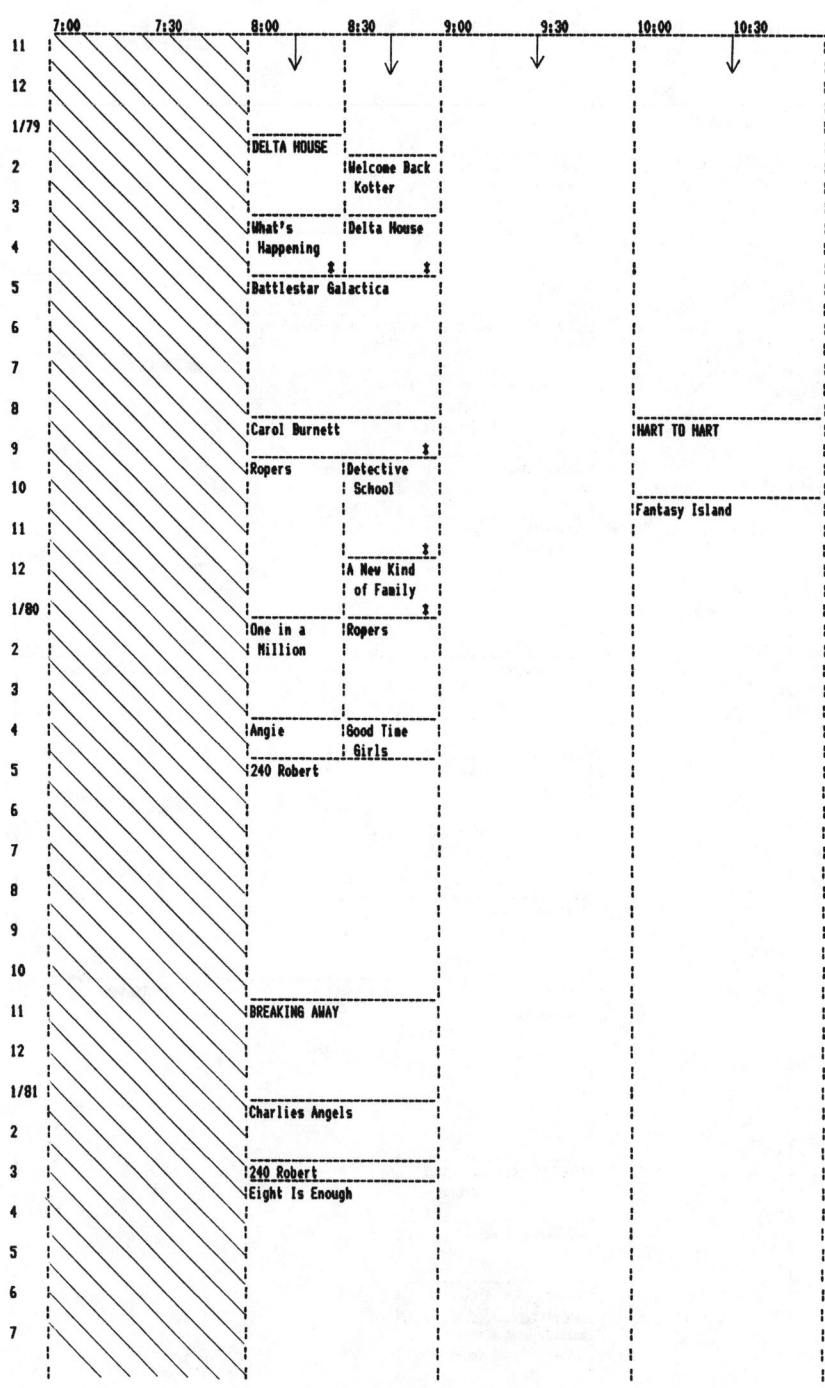

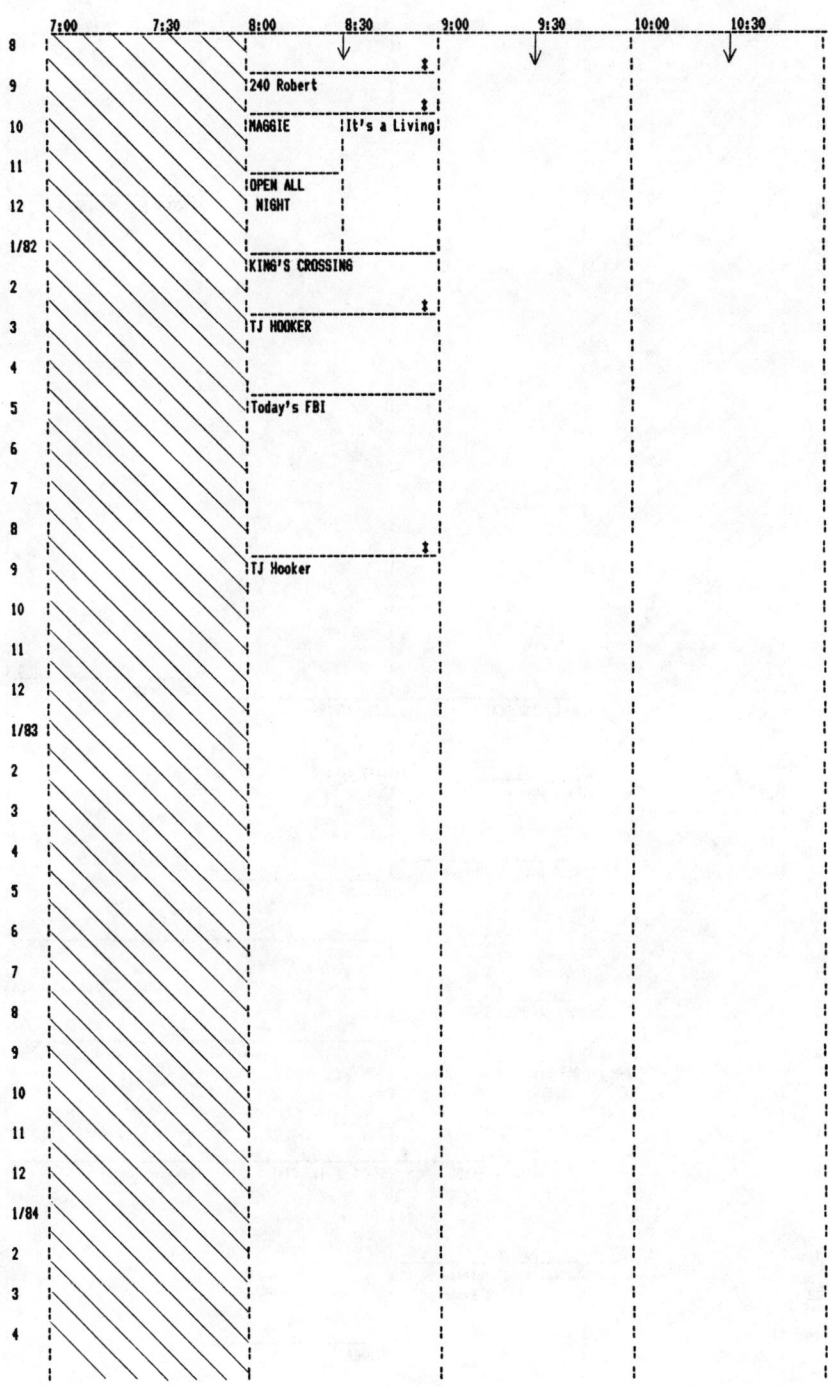

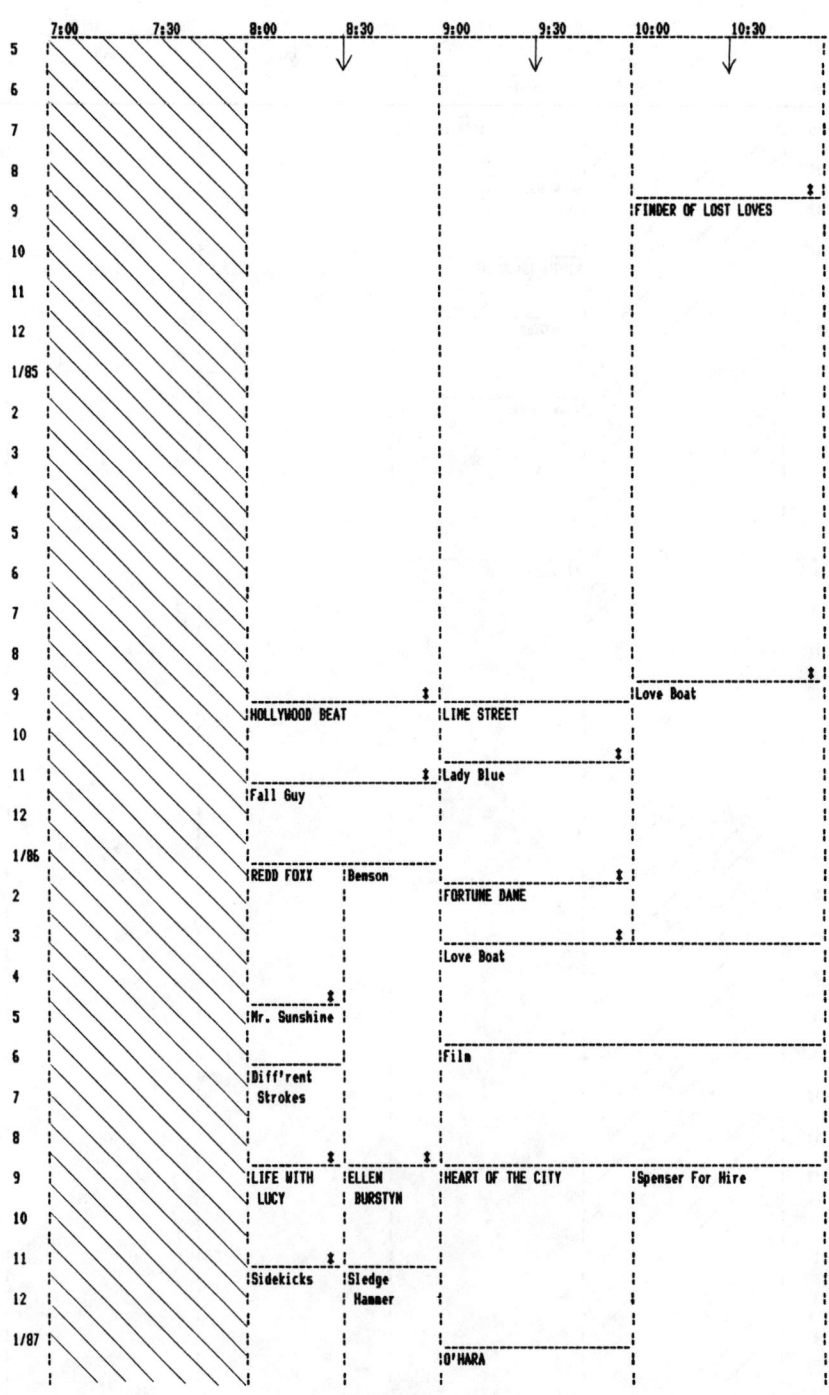

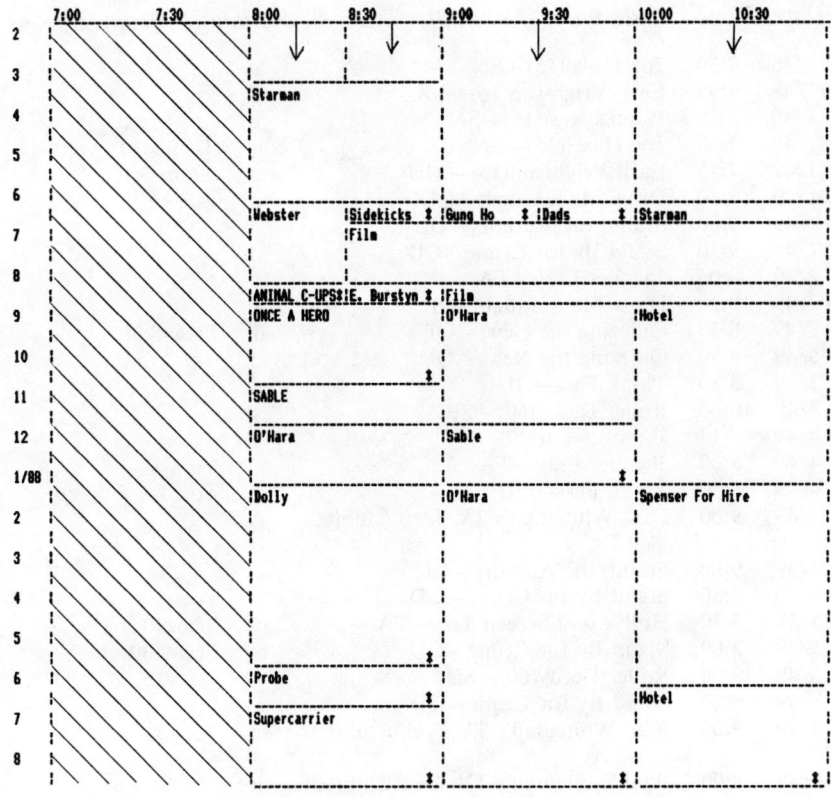

	7:00	7:30	8:00	8:30	9:00	9:30	10:00	10:30
2								
3			Starman					
4								
5								
6								
7			Webster	Sidekicks / Film	Gung Ho	Dads	Starman	
8			ANIMAL C-UPS/E. Burstyn / Film					
9			ONCE A HERO		O'Hara		Hotel	
10								
11			SABLE					
12			O'Hara		Sable			
1/88			Dolly		O'Hara		Spenser For Hire	
2								
3								
4								
5								
6			Probe				Hotel	
7			Supercarrier					
8								

Date	*Time*	*Title (min. if not 30) — Type*	*Action*	*From/To*
8/48	7:30	Joe Hasel(15) — SN	d	
11/48	7:45	Earl Wrightson(15) — MU	d	
1/49	7:15	Wren's Nest(15) — SN	d	
1/49	7:30	Joe Hasel(15) — SN	m	To:f-9:30
1/49	7:45	Earl Wrightson(15) — MU	m	To:m-7:15
1/49	8:30	Draw Me a Laugh — QU	d	
1/49	9:00	Stump the Authors — QU	d	
1/49	9:30	Stand By for Crime — CD	d	
2/49	8:00	Jacques Fray — TA	d	
2/49	8:30	Draw Me a Laugh — QU	c	
2/49	8:30	Quizzing the News — QU	m	Fr:w-8:30
3/49	8:30	Quizzing the News — QU	c	
3/49	8:30	Think Fast — QU	d	
3/49	10:00	Roller Derby(60) — SP	s	
4/49	7:15	Wren's Nest(15) — SC	c	
4/49	8:00	Jacques Fray — TA	m	To:n-8
4/49	8:30	Think Fast — QU	m	To:f-8
4/49	9:00	Paul Whiteman's TV Teen Club(60) — TA	d	
4/49	9:00	Stump the Authors — QU	c	
4/49	9:30	Stand By for Crime — CD	m	To:s-8
5/49	7:30	Hollywood Screen Test — TA	m	Fr:n-8
5/49	8:00	Stand By for Crime — CD	m	Fr:s-9:30
5/49	10:00	Roller Derby(60) — SP	f	
8/49	8:00	Stand By for Crime — CD	c	
8/49	9:00	Paul Whiteman's TV Teen Club(60) — TA	m	To:s-8
9/49	8:00	Paul Whiteman's TV Teen Club(60) — TA	m	Fr:s-9
9/49	9:00	Film(120) — FI	s	
10/49	9:00	Film(120) — FI	f	
11/49	9:00	Roller Derby(120) — SP	s	
4/50	7:00	Buck Rogers — SF	d	
6/50	9:00	Marshall Plan in Action — DO	d*	
7/50	7:00	Crash Corrigan's Ranch — KV	d*	
7/50	9:00	Marshall Plan in Action — DO	m*	To:n-10
8/50	7:00	Crash Corrigan's Ranch — KV	m*	To:f-7:30
9/50	7:00	Buck Rogers — SF	m	To:t-8:30
9/50	7:30	Hollywood Screen Test — TA	m	To:m-7:30
10/50	7:00	Sandy Dreams — KV	d	
10/50	7:30	Stu Erwin — SC	d	
12/50	7:00	Hollywood Theatre Time — VS	m	Fr:n-8
12/50	7:00	Sandy Dreams — KV	c	
5/51	9:00	Baseball(120) — SP	s	
5/51	9:00	Roller Derby(120) — SP	f	
9/51	7:30	Stu Erwin — SC	m	To:f-8:30
9/51	9:00	Baseball(120) — SP	f	
9/51	9:00	Lesson in Safety — IS	d	
9/51	9:30	America's Health — DO	m	Fr:m-10
9/51	10:00	Harness Racing(60) — SP	s	

Date	Time	Title (min. if not 30) – Type	Action	From/To
10/51	7:00	Hollywood Theatre Time – VS	c	
10/51	7:00	Personal Appearance Theater – DA	d	
10/51	7:30	Jerry Colonna – CV	m	Fr:r-10
10/51	9:00	Lesson in Safety – IS	c	
10/51	9:00	Harness Racing(120) – SP	s	
10/51	9:30	America's Health – DO	m	To:r-10-2/52
10/51	10:00	Harness Racing(60) – SP	f	
11/51	7:00	Personal Appearance Theater – DA	c	
11/51	7:30	Jerry Colonna – CV	c	
11/51	9:00	Harness Racing(120) – SP	f	
11/51	9:00	Film(60) – FI	s	
12/51	7:00	Film – FI	s	
12/51	8:00	Paul Whiteman's TV Teen Club(60) – TA	m	To:s-8
12/51	8:00	Paul Whiteman's TV Teen Club – TA	m	Fr:s-8
12/51	8:30	Sports Camera – SH	m	Fr:r-10:45-9/51
12/51	9:00	Basketball(120) – SP	s	
12/51	9:00	Film(60) – FI	f	
1/52	10:45	America in View(15) – TR	m	Fr:f-10:30-10/51
3/52	9:00	Basketball(120) – SP	f	
3/52	9:00	Film(120) – FI	s	
3/52	10:45	America in View(15) – TR	m	To:n-9-6/52
5/52	8:30	Baseball(120) – SP	s	
5/52	8:30	Sports Camera – SH	m	To:s-10:30
5/52	9:00	Film(120) – FI	f	
5/52	10:30	Sports Camera – SH	m	Fr:s-8:30
5/52	10:30	Sports Camera – SH	c	
6/52	7:00	Film – FI	f	
6/52	7:00	Film(60) – FI	s	
6/52	8:30	Baseball(120) – SP	f	
6/52	8:30	Film(120) – FI	s	
8/52	7:00	Film(60) – FI	f	
8/52	8:00	Paul Whiteman's TV Teen Club	m	To:s-7:30
8/52	8:30	Film(120) – FI	f	
9/52	7:30	Paul Whiteman's TV Teen Club – TA	m	Fi:s-8
9/52	8:00	Film(120) – FI	s	
10/52	7:00	Paul Whiteman's TV Teen Club – TA	m	Fr:s-7:30
10/52	7:30	Live Like a Millionaire – TA	m	Fr:f-10-3/52(c)
10/52	7:30	Paul Whiteman's TV Teen Club – TA	m	To:s-7
1/53	8:00	Film(120) – FI	f	
1/53	8:00	Film(60) – FI	s	
1/53	9:00	Boxing(120) – SP	s	
2/53	7:30	Live Like a Millionaire – TA	c	
2/53	7:30	What's Your Bid – HS	d	
4/53	7:30	What's Your Bid – HS	m	To:n-10(d)
5/53	7:00	Music at the Meadowbrook(60) – MV	d*	

Date	Time	Title (min. if not 30) — Type	Action	From/To
5/53	7:30	Film — FI	s	
9/53	7:00	Music at the Meadowbrook(60) — MV	m*	To:s-8:30
9/53	7:30	Film — FI	f	
9/53	8:00	Film(60) — FI	f	
9/53	8:00	Showcase Theater — DA	d	
9/53	8:30	Madison Square Garden Highlights — SH	m	Fr:r-9
10/53	7:30	Leave It to the Girls — DS	m	Fr:n-10:30-12/51(n)
10/53	8:00	Showcase Theater — DA	m	To:f-10
10/53	8:00	Talent Patrol — TA	m	Fr:w-8
10/53	8:30	Madison Square Garden Highlights — SH	m	To:s-10
10/53	8:30	Music at the Meadowbrook — MV	m	Fr:s-7
10/53	9:00	Boxing(120) — SP	f	
10/53	9:00	Boxing(60) — SP	s	
10/53	10:00	Madison Square Garden Highlights — SH	m	Fr:s-8:30
12/53	7:00	Paul Whiteman's TV Teen Club — TA	m	To:n-7:30
12/53	8:30	Music at the Meadowbrook — MV	m	To:r-10-1/56
12/53	10:00	Madison Square Garden Highlights — SH	m	To:s-8:30
12/53	10:00	On Guard — DO	m	Fr:r-9:30-12/52
1/54	7:00	On Your Way — QU	m	Fr:w-9:30(d)
1/54	8:00	Enterprise — DO	m	Fr:n-10:30-3/53
1/54	8:00	Talent Patrol — TA	m	To:r-9
1/54	8:30	Madison Square Garden Highlights — SH	m	Fr:s-10
1/54	8:30	Madison Square Garden Highlights — SH	m	To:r-8(d)
2/54	8:30	Greatest Sports Thrills — SH	d	
3/54	7:30	Leave It to the Girls — DS	c	
4/54	7:00	On Your Way — QU	c	
4/54	7:30	Dotty Mack — MU	m	Fr:r-9:30-10/53
5/54	10:00	On Guard — DO	c	
6/54	10:00	Travel Corner — TR	m	Fr:m-9:30
9/54	8:00	Enterprise — DO	m	To:w-9:30
9/54	8:00	Let's Dance(60) — MU	d	
9/54	8:30	Greatest Sports Thrills — SH	m	To:m-7:30-6/55
9/54	10:00	Stork Club — TK	m	Fr:s-7-10/53(c)
9/54	10:00	Travel Corner — TR	c	
10/54	7:30	Compass — TR	d	
10/54	7:30	Dotty Mack — MU	m	To:s-8
10/54	8:00	Dotty Mack(60) — MU	m	Fr:s-7:30
10/54	8:00	Let's Dance(60) — MU	c	
1/55	9:00	Boxing(60) — SP	f	
1/55	9:00	Ozark Jubilee(60) — MU	d	
2/55	7:30	Compass — TR	m	To:s-10
3/55	7:00	Tomorrow's Careers — IF	d	

Date	Time	Title (min. if not 30) — Type	Action	From/To
3/55	7:30	Big Picture — DO	m	Fr:n-8:30
3/55	10:00	Compass — TR	m	Fr:s-7:30
3/55	10:00	Stork Club — TK	m	To:n-9:15
6/55	7:00	Flight #7 — TR	m	Fr:n-8-2/55
6/55	7:00	Tomorrow's Careers — IF	m	To:s-10-9/55
6/55	7:30	Big Picture — DO	m	To:t-8:30-8/55
6/55	8:00	Dotty Mack(60) — MU	m	To:t-9:30
6/55	9:00	Ozark Jubilee(60) — MU	m	To:s-7:30
7/55	7:30	Ozark Jubilee(90) — MU	m	Fr:s-9
7/55	9:00	Lawrence Welk(60) — MU	d	
9/55	7:00	Flight #7 — TR	m	To:s-7:30-6/57
9/55	10:00	Compass — TR	m	To:r-10-7/56
9/55	10:00	Tomorrow's Careers — IF	m	Fr:s-7-6/55
10/55	8:00	Grand Ole Opry(90) — MU	d	
1/56	10:00	Life Begins at Eighty — DS	m	Fr:n-10
1/56	10:00	Tomorrow's Careers — IF	m	To:t-10
2/56	10:00	Life Begins at Eighty — DS	c	
3/56	10:00	Chance of a Lifetime — TA	m	Fr:n-9
6/56	10:00	Chance of a Lifetime — TA	c	
6/56	10:00	Masquerade Party — QU	m	Fr:w-9
9/56	7:30	Ozark Jubilee(90) — MU	m	To:r-10
9/56	8:00	Grand Ole Opry(90) — MU	c	
10/56	7:30	Film(90) — FI	s	
12/56	10:00	Masquerade Party — QU	m	To:w-8-3/57(n)
12/56	10:00	Ozark Jubilee(60) — MU	m	Fr:r-10
1/57	7:00	Galen Drake — KV	d	
5/57	7:00	Galen Drake — KV	c	
5/57	7:30	Film(90) — FI	f	
6/57	7:30	Flight #7 — TR	m	Fr:s-7-9/55
6/57	8:00	Billy Graham Crusade(60) — RE	d	
6/57	10:00	Ozark Jubilee(60) — MU	m	To:s-10
6/57	10:00	Ozark Jubilee — MU	m	Fr:s-10
8/57	7:30	Flight #7 — TR	c	
8/57	8:00	Billy Graham Crusade(60) — RE	m	To:s-10-5/58
9/57	7:30	Keep It in the Family — QU	d	
9/57	8:00	Ozark Jubilee(60) — MU	m	Fr:s-10
9/57	10:00	Mike Wallace Interviews — IV	m	Fr:n-10
9/57	10:00	Ozark Jubilee — MU	m	To:s-8
2/58	7:30	Dick Clark — MU	d	
2/58	7:30	Keep It in the Family — QU	c	
4/58	10:00	Mike Wallace Interviews — IV	m	To:n-10
5/58	10:00	Billy Graham Crusade(60) — RE	m	Fr:s-8-8/57
6/58	10:00	Billy Graham Crusade(60) — RE	m	To:s-8-9/58
6/58	10:00	Midwestern Hayride — MV	m	Fr:n-9:30-10/57
9/58	8:00	Billy Graham Crusade(60) — RE	m*	Fr:s-10-6/58
9/58	10:00	Midwestern Hayride — MV	m	To:n-7-5/59
9/58	10:00	Sammy Kaye — MV	m	Fr:r-9-1/55
10/58	8:00	Billy Graham Crusade(60) — RE	m*	To:s-10-2/59
2/59	10:00	Billy Graham Crusade(60) — RE	m	Fr:s-8-10/58
2/59	10:00	Sammy Kaye — MV	m	To:r-10

Date	Time	Title (min. if not 30) — Type	Action	From/To
4/59	10:00	Billy Graham Crusade(60) — RE	c	
4/59	10:00	Sammy Kaye — MV	m	Fr:r-10
6/59	10:00	Big Picture — DO	m	Fr:f-9-10/58
6/59	10:00	Sammy Kaye — MV	c	
9/59	8:00	John Gunther's High Road — TR	m	Fr:m-8:30
9/59	8:00	Ozark Jubilee(60) — MU	m	To:s-10
9/59	8:30	Leave It to Beaver — SC	m	Fr:r-9
9/59	10:00	Big Picture — DO	m	To:w-7:30
10/59	10:00	Ozark Jubilee(60) — MU	m	Fr:s-8
9/60	7:30	Dick Clark — MU	c	
9/60	8:00	John Gunther's High Road — TR	c	
9/60	10:00	Ozark Jubilee(60) — MU	c	
10/60	7:30	Roaring Twenties(60) — ND	d	
10/60	10:00	Boxing(45) — SP	s	
10/60	10:45	Make That Spare(15) — QU	d	
10/61	7:00	Matty's Funday Funnies — KV	m	Fr:f-7:30
1/62	7:30	Calvin and the Colonel — KV	m	Fr:t-8:30-11/61
1/62	7:30	Roaring Twenties(60) — ND	m	To:f-7:30-9/62
1/62	8:00	Room for One More — SC	d	
7/62	10:45	Saturday Sports Final(15) — SN	d*	
9/62	7:30	Calvin and the Colonel — KV	c	
9/62	7:30	Roy Rogers & Dale Evans(60) — MV	d	
9/62	8:00	Room for One More — SC	c	
9/62	8:30	Leave It to Beaver — SC	m	To:r-8:30
9/62	8:30	Mr. Smith Goes to Washington — SC	d	
10/62	10:45	Saturday Sports Final(15) — SN	c*	
12/62	7:00	Matty's Funday Funnies — KV	c	
12/62	7:30	Gallant Men(60) — WD	m	Fr:f-7:30
12/62	7:30	Roy Rogers & Dale Evans(60) — MV	c	
3/63	8:30	Mr. Smith Goes to Washington — SC	c	
4/63	8:30	Hootenanny — MU	d	
9/63	7:30	Gallant Men(60) — WD	c	
9/63	7:30	Hootenanny(60) — MU	m	Fr:s-8:30
9/63	8:30	Hootenanny — MU	m	To:s-7:30
9/63	8:30	Lawrence Welk(60) — MU	m	Fr:s-9
9/63	9:00	Lawrence Welk(60) — MU	m	To:s-8:30
9/63	9:30	Jerry Lewis(90) — TK	d	
9/63	10:00	Boxing(60) — SP	f	
9/63	10:45	Make That Spare(15) — QU	m	To:f-10:45
12/63	9:30	Jerry Lewis(90) — TK	c	
1/64	9:30	Hollywood Palace(60) — VY	d	
9/64	7:30	Hootenanny(60) — MU	c	
9/64	7:30	Outer Limits(60) — FA	m	Fr:m-7:30
1/65	7:30	King Family(60) — MV	d	
1/65	7:30	Outer Limits(60) — FA	c	
9/65	7:30	King Family(60) — MV	m	To:s-8
9/65	7:30	Shindig — MU	m	Fr:w-8:30
9/65	8:00	King Family — MV	m	Fr:s-7:30

Date	Time	Title (min. if not 30) — Type	Action	From/To
9/65	10:30	ABC Scope — DO	m	Fr:w-10:30
1/66	7:30	Adventures of Ozzie & Harriet — SC	m	Fr:w-7:30
1/66	7:30	Shindig — MU	c	
1/66	8:00	Donna Reed — SC	m	Fr:r-8
1/66	8:00	King Family — MV	m	To:w-8:30-2/69
9/66	7:30	Adventures of Ozzie & Harriet — SC	c	
9/66	7:30	Shane(60) — WE	d	
9/66	8:00	Donna Reed — SC	c	
12/66	7:30	Shane(60) — WE	c	
1/67	7:30	Dating Game — QU	m	Fr:r-8:30
1/67	8:00	Newlywed Game — QU	d	
5/67	9:30	Hollywood Palace(60) — VY	m	To:m-10-9/67
5/67	9:30	Piccadilly Palace(60) — MV	d	
9/67	9:30	Iron Horse(60) — WE	m	Fr:m-7:30
9/67	9:30	Piccadilly Palace(60) — MV	c	
1/68	9:30	Hollywood Palace(60) — VY	m	Fr:m-10
1/68	9:30	Iron Horse(60) — WE	c	
3/68	10:30	ABC Scope — DO	c	
6/69	9:30	Johnny Cash(60) — MV	d*	
9/69	9:30	Johnny Cash(60) — MV	m*	To:w-9-1/70
1/70	7:30	Dating Game — QU	c	
1/70	7:30	Let's Make a Deal — QU	m	Fr:f-7:30
2/70	9:30	Hollywood Palace(60) — VY	c	
2/70	9:30	Jimmy Durante Presents the Lennon Sisters(60) — MV	m	Fr:f-10
7/70	9:30	Engelbert Humperdinck(60) — MV	m	Fr:w-10
7/70	9:30	Jimmy Durante Presents the Lennon Sisters(60) — MV	c	
9/70	9:30	Engelbert Humperdinck(60) — MV	c	
10/70	9:30	The Most Deadly Game(60) — CD	d	
1/71	7:30	Lawrence Welk(60) — MU	m	Fr:s-8:30
1/71	7:30	Let's Make a Deal — QU	m	To:m-7:30
1/71	8:00	Newlywed Game — QU	m	To:m-8
1/71	8:30	Lawrence Welk(60) — MU	m	To:s-7:30
1/71	8:30	Pearl Bailey(60) — MV	d	
1/71	9:30	The Most Deadly Game(60) — CD	c	
2/71	9:30	Film(90) — FI	s	
5/71	8:30	Pearl Bailey(60) — MV	c	
6/71	8:30	Val Doonican(60) — MV	d	
8/71	8:30	Val Doonican(60) — MV	c	
8/71	9:30	Film(90) — FI	f	
9/71	7:30	Lawrence Welk(60) — MU	c	
9/71	8:00	Getting Together — SC	d	
9/71	8:30	Film(90) — FI	s	
9/71	10:00	Persuaders(60) — AD	d	
1/72	8:00	Bewitched — SC	m	Fr:w-8
1/72	8:00	Getting Together — SC	c	
1/72	10:00	Persuaders(60) — AD	m	To:w-9:30
1/72	10:00	Sixth Sense(60) — DR	d	
7/72	10:00	Ken Berry Wow Show(60) — MV	d*	

Date	Time	Title (min. if not 30) – Type	Action	From/To
8/72	8:00	Bewitched – SC	c	
8/72	8:30	Film(90) – FI	f	
8/72	10:00	Ken Berry Wow Show(60) – MV	c*	
9/72	8:00	Alias Smith and Jones(60) – WE	m	Fr:r-8
9/72	9:00	Streets of San Francisco(60) – CD	d	
10/72	8:00	Kung Fu(60) – WE	d	
10/72	8:00	Alias Smith and Jones(60) – WE	m	To:s-8
11/72	8:00	Kung Fu(60) – WE	m	To:r-9-1/73
11/72	8:00	Alias Smith and Jones(60) – WE	m	Fr:s-8
12/72	10:00	Sixth Sense(60) – DR	c	
1/73	8:00	Alias Smith and Jones(60) – WE	c	
1/73	8:00	Here We Go Again – SC	d	
1/73	8:30	A Touch of Grace – SC	d	
1/73	9:00	Julie Andrews Hour(60) – MV	m	Fr:w-10
1/73	9:00	Streets of San Francisco(60) – CD	m	To:r-10
1/73	10:00	Assignment Vienna(60) – SD	m	Fr:r-9
1/73	10:00	The Men(60) – AD	m	Fr:r-9
2/73	10:00	Jigsaw(60) – CD	m	Fr:r-9-12/72
3/73	10:00	Delphi Bureau(60) – SD	m	Fr:r-9-1/73
4/73	9:00	Julie Andrews Hour(60) – MV	c	
5/73	9:00	Strauss Family(60) – DR	d	
6/73	8:00	Here We Go Again – SC	c	
6/73	8:00	Partridge Family – SC	m	Fr:f-8:30
6/73	8:30	Paul Lynde – SC	m	Fr:w-8
6/73	8:30	A Touch of Grace – SC	c	
6/73	9:00	Burns and Schreiber(60) – CV	d	
6/73	9:00	Strauss Family(60) – DR	c	
6/73	10:00	Assignment Vienna(60) – SD	c	
8/73	10:00	Jigsaw(60) – CD	c	
9/73	8:30	Paul Lynde – SC	c	
9/73	8:30	Film(90) – FI	s	
9/73	9:00	Burns and Schreiber(60) – CV	c	
9/73	10:00	Delphi Bureau(60) – SD	c	
9/73	10:00	Griff(60) – CD	d	
9/73	10:00	The Men(60) – AD	c	
1/74	10:00	Griff(60) – CD	c	
1/74	10:00	Owen Marshall, Counselor at Law (60) – LD	m	Fr:w-10
8/74	8:00	Partridge Family – SC	c	
8/74	8:30	Film(90) – FI	f	
8/74	10:00	Owen Marshall, Counselor at Law (60) – LD	c	
9/74	8:00	The New Land(60) – AD	d	
9/74	9:00	Kung Fu(60) – WE	m	Fr:r-9
9/74	10:00	Nakia(60) – CD	d	
10/74	8:00	The New Land(60) – AD	c	
10/74	9:00	Kung Fu(60) – WE	m	To:f-8
11/74	8:00	Film(120) – FI	s	
12/74	8:00	Film(120) – FI	f	
12/74	10:00	Nakia(60) – CD	c	

Date	Time	Title (min. if not 30) — Type	Action	From/To
1/75	8:00	Kung Fu(60) — WE	m	Fr:f-8
1/75	9:00	Film(120) — FI	s	
6/75	8:00	Kung Fu(60) — WE	c	
7/75	8:00	Keep on Truckin'(60) — CV	d	
8/75	8:00	Keep on Truckin'(60) — CV	c	
8/75	9:00	Film(120) — FI	f	
8/75	10:00	Matt Helm(60) — CD	d	
9/75	8:00	Saturday Night Live with Howard Cosell(60) — VY	d	
9/75	9:00	S.W.A.T.(60) — CD	m	Fr:m-9
1/76	8:00	Almost Anything Goes(60) — QU	m	Fr:t-8-8/75
1/76	8:00	Saturday Night Live with Howard Cosell(60) — VY	c	c
1/76	10:00	Matt Helm(60) — CD	c	
2/76	10:00	Bert D'Angelo, Superstar(60) — CD	d	
4/76	8:00	Almost Anything Goes(60) — QU	c	
4/76	9:00	S.W.A.T.(60) — CD	m	To:t-9
5/76	8:00	Good Heavens — SC	m	Fr:m-8:30
5/76	8:30	Film(90) — FI	s	
6/76	8:00	Good Heavens — SC	c	
6/76	8:30	Film(90) — FI	f	
7/76	8:00	Film(120) — FI	s	
7/76	10:00	Bert D'Angelo, Superstar(60) — CD	c	
8/76	8:00	Film(120) — FI	f	
9/76	8:00	Holmes and Yoyo — SC	d	
9/76	8:30	Mr. T and Tina — SC	d	
9/76	9:00	Starsky and Hutch(60) — CD	m	Fr:w-10
10/76	8:30	Mr. T and Tina — SC	c	
10/76	10:00	Most Wanted(60) — CD	d	
11/76	8:30	What's Happening — SC	m	Fr:r-8:30-8/76
12/76	8:00	Holmes and Yoyo — SC	c	
12/76	8:00	Wonder Woman(60) — AD	d	
12/76	8:30	What's Happening — SC	m	To:r-8:30
1/77	8:00	Wonder Woman(60) — AD	m	To:s-8-5/77
2/77	8:00	Blansky's Beauties — SC	d	
2/77	8:30	Fish — SC	d	
2/77	10:00	Most Wanted(60) — CD	m	To:m-9
3/77	10:00	Dog and Cat(60) — CD	d	
5/77	8:00	Blansky's Beauties — SC	c	
5/77	8:00	Wonder Woman(60) — AD	m	Fr:s-8-1/77
5/77	8:30	Fish — SC	m	To:r-9:30
5/77	10:00	Dog and Cat(60) — CD	c	
5/77	10:00	Feather and Father Gang(60) — CD	m	Fr:m-10
7/77	8:00	Wonder Woman(60) — AD	m	To:f-8-9/77(c)
8/77	8:00	Fish — SC	m	Fr:r-9:30
8/77	8:30	Sugar Time — SC	d	
8/77	10:00	Feather and Father Gang(60) — CD	c	
9/77	8:30	Operation Petticoat — SC	d	
9/77	8:30	Sugar Time — SC	m	To:m-8-4/78
9/77	10:00	Love Boat(60) — CO	d	

Date	Time	Title (min. if not 30) – Type	Action	From/To
11/77	8:00	Fish – SC	m	To:r-8:30-1/78
11/77	8:00	Tabitha – SC	d	
1/78	8:00	Tabitha – SC	m	To:f-8-6/78
1/78	8:00	What's Happening – SC	m	Fr:r-8:30
1/78	9:00	Love Boat(60) – CO	m	Fr:s-10
1/78	9:00	Starsky and Hutch(60) – CD	m	To:w-10
1/78	10:00	Fantasy Island(60) – DR	d	
1/78	10:00	Love Boat(60) – CO	m	To:s-9
5/78	8:00	What's Happening – SC	m	To:r-8:30
5/78	8:30	Operation Petticoat – SC	m	To:r-8:30
6/78	8:00	Free Country – SC	d	
6/78	8:30	ABC Saturday Comedy Special – CA	d	
7/78	8:00	ABC Saturday Comedy Special (60) – CA	m	Fr:s-8:30
7/78	8:00	Free Country – SC	c	
7/78	8:30	ABC Saturday Comedy Special – CA	m	To:s-8
8/78	8:00	ABC Saturday Comedy Special (60) – CA	c	
9/78	8:00	Carter Country – SC	m	Fr:t-9:30
9/78	8:00	Carter Country – SC	m	To:s-8:30
9/78	8:30	Apple Pie – SC	d	
9/78	8:30	Apple Pie – SC	c	
10/78	8:00	Welcome Back, Kotter – SC	m	Fr:m-8
10/78	8:30	Carter Country – SC	m	Fr:s-8
1/79	8:00	Delta House – SC	d	
1/79	8:00	Welcome Back, Kotter – SC	m	To:s-8:30
1/79	8:30	Carter Country – SC	m	To:r-9:30-3/79
2/79	8:30	Welcome Back, Kotter – SC	m	Fr:s-8
3/79	8:00	Delta House – SC	m	To:s-8:30
3/79	8:00	What's Happening – SC	m	Fr:f-8:30
3/79	8:30	Delta House – SC	m	Fr:s-8
3/79	8:30	Welcome Back, Kotter – SC	m	To:f-8:30-5/79
4/79	8:00	What's Happening – SC	c	
4/79	8:30	Delta House – SC	c	
5/79	8:00	Battlestar Gallactica(60) – SF	m	Fr:n-8
8/79	8:00	Battlestar Gallactica(60) – SF	m	To:n-7-1/80
8/79	8:00	Carol Burnett(60) – CV	m	Fr:w-8-8/78
8/79	10:00	Fantasy Island(60) – DR	m	To:f-8
8/79	10:00	Hart to Hart(60) – AD	d	
9/79	8:00	Carol Burnett(60) – CV	c	
9/79	8:00	Ropers – SC	m	Fr:n-8:30
9/79	8:30	Detective School – SC	m	Fr:t-8:30
10/79	10:00	Fantasy Island(60) – DR	m	Fr:f-8
10/79	10:00	Hart to Hart(60) – AD	m	To:t-10
11/79	8:30	Detective School – SC	c	
12/79	8:30	A New Kind of Family – SC	m	Fr:n-7:30-10/79
1/80	8:00	One in a Million – SC	m	Fr:t-8:30
1/80	8:00	Ropers – SC	m	To:s-8:30

Date	Time	Title (min. if not 30) — Type	Action	From/To
1/80	8:30	A New Kind of Family — SC	c	
1/80	8:30	Ropers — SC	m	Fr:s-8
3/80	8:00	One in a Million — SC	c	
3/80	8:30	Ropers — SC	m	To:r-9:30-5/80
4/80	8:00	Angie — SC	m	Fr:m-8:30-2/80
4/80	8:00	Angie — SC	m	To:r-8:30-7/80
4/80	8:30	Goodtime Girls — SC	m	Fr:t-8:30-2/80
4/80	8:30	Goodtime Girls — SC	m	To:f-8:30-8/80
5/80	8:00	240-Robert(60) — AD	m	Fr:m-8-12/79
6/80	10:00	When the Whistle Blows(60) — SC	m	Fr:f-8-4/80
6/80	10:00	When the Whistle Blows(60) — SC	m	To:n-8
10/80	8:00	240-Robert(60) — AD	m	To:s-8-3/81
11/80	8:00	Breaking Away(60) — AD	d	
1/81	8:00	Breaking Away(60) — AD	m	To:m-8-6/81
1/81	8:00	Charlie's Angels(60) — CD	m	Fr:n-8
2/81	8:00	Charlie's Angels(60) — CD	m	To:w-8-6/81
3/81	8:00	Eight Is Enough(60) — CO	m	Fr:w-8
3/81	8:00	240-Robert(60) — AD	m	Fr:s-8-10/80
3/81	8:00	240-Robert(60) — AD	m	To:s-8-9/81
8/81	8:00	Eight Is Enough(60) — CO	c	
9/81	8:00	240-Robert(60) — AD	m	Fr:s-8-3/81
9/81	8:00	240-Robert(60) — AD	c	
10/81	8:00	Maggie — SC	d	
10/81	8:30	It's a Living — SC	m	Fr:f-8:30
11/81	8:00	Maggie — SC	m	To:f-8:30-4/82
11/81	8:00	Open All Night — SC	d	
1/82	8:00	King's Crossing(60) — SL	d	
1/82	8:00	Open All Night — SC	m	To:f-8:30
1/82	8:30	It's a Living — SC	m	To:f-9:30
2/82	8:00	King's Crossing(60) — SL	c	
3/82	8:00	T.J. Hooker(60) — CD	d	
4/82	8:00	T.J. Hooker(60) — CD	m	To:s-8-9/82
5/82	8:00	Today's FBI(60) — CD	m	Fr:m-8
8/82	8:00	Today's FBI(60) — CD	c	
9/82	8:00	T.J. Hooker(60) — CD	m	Fr:s-8-4/82
8/84	10:00	Fantasy Island(60) — DR	c	
9/84	10:00	Finder of Lost Loves(60) — DR	d	
8/85	10:00	Finder of Lost Loves(60) — DR	c	
9/85	8:00	T.J. Hooker(60) — CD	c	
9/85	8:00	Hollywood Beat(60) — CD	d	
9/85	9:00	Love Boat(60) — CO	m	To:s-10
9/85	9:00	Lime Street(60) — AD	d	
9/85	10:00	Love Boat(60) — CO	m	Fr:s-9
10/85	9:00	Lime Street(60) — AD	c	
11/85	8:00	Hollywood Beat(60) — CD	c	
11/85	8:00	Fall Guy(60) — AD	m	Fr:r-8
11/85	9:00	Lady Blue(60) — CD	m	Fr:r-9
1/86	8:00	Redd Foxx — SC	d	
1/86	8:00	Fall Guy(60) — AD	m	To:f-10
1/86	8:30	Benson — SC	m	Fr:f-9:30

Date	Time	Title (min. if not 30) — Type	Action	From/To
1/86	9:00	Lady Blue(60) — CD	c	
2/86	9:00	Fortune Dane(60) — CD	d	
3/86	9:00	Love Boat(60) — CO	m	Fr:s-10
3/86	9:00	Fortune Dane(60) — CD	c	
3/86	10:00	Love Boat(60) — CO	m	To:s-9
4/86	8:00	Redd Foxx — SC	c	
5/86	8:00	Mr. Sunshine — SC	m	Fr:f-9
5/86	9:00	Love Boat(60) — CO	m	To:f-10
6/86	8:00	Diff'rent Strokes — SC	m	Fr:f-9-3/86
6/86	8:00	Mr. Sunshine — SC	m	To:f-9
6/86	9:00	Film(120) — FI	s	
8/86	8:00	Diff'rent Strokes — SC	c	
8/86	8:30	Benson — SC	c	
8/86	9:00	Film(120) — FI	f	
9/86	8:00	Life with Lucy — SC	d	
9/86	8:30	Ellen Burstyn — SC	d	
9/86	9:00	Heart of the City(60) — CD	d	
9/86	10:00	Spenser for Hire(60) — CD	m	Fr:t-10
11/86	8:00	Life with Lucy — SC	c	
11/86	8:00	Sidekicks — SC	m	Fr:f-9:30
11/86	8:30	Ellen Burstyn — SC	m	To:s-8:30-8/87
11/86	8:30	Sledge Hammer — SC	m	Fr:f-9
1/87	9:00	Heart of the City(60) — CD	m	To:r-9-6/87
1/87	9:00	O'Hara(60) — CD	d	
3/87	8:00	Starman(60) — SF	m	Fr:f-10
3/87	8:00	Sidekicks — SC	m	To:s-8:30-6/87
3/87	8:30	Sledge Hammer — SC	m	To:f-8-6/87
6/87	8:00	Webster — SC	m	Fr:f-8
6/87	8:00	Starman(60) — SF	m	To:s-10
6/87	8:30	Sidekicks — SC	m	Fr:s-8-3/87
6/87	8:30	Sidekicks — SC	c	
6/87	9:00	Gung Ho — SC	m	Fr:f-9-2/87
6/87	9:00	Gung Ho — SC	c	
6/87	9:00	O'Hara(60) — CD	m	To:s-9-9/87
6/87	9:30	Dads — SC	m	Fr:f-9:30-2/87
6/87	9:30	Dads — SC	c	
6/87	10:00	Starman(60) — SF	m	Fr:s-8
6/87	10:00	Starman(60) — SF	m	To:r-8
6/87	10:00	Spenser for Hire(60) — CD	m	To:t-10
7/87	8:30	Film(150) — FI	s	
8/87	8:00	Animal Crack-Ups — WL	d	
8/87	8:00	Animal Crack-Ups — WL	c	
8/87	8:00	Webster — SC	m	To:f-8
8/87	8:30	Ellen Burstyn — SC	m	Fr:s-8:30-11/86
8/87	8:30	Ellen Burstyn — SC	c	
8/87	8:30	Film(150) — FI	f	
8/87	9:00	Film(120) — FI	s	
8/87	9:00	Film(120) — FI	f	
9/87	8:00	Once a Hero(60) — FY	d	
9/87	9:00	O'Hara(60) — CD	m	Fr:s-9-6/87

Date	Time	Title (min. if not 30) — Type	Action	From/To
9/87	10:00	Hotel(60) — DR	m	Fr:w-10
10/87	8:00	Once a Hero(60) — FY	c	
11/87	8:00	Sable(60) — AD	d	
11/87	8:00	Sable(60) — AD	m	To:s-9
11/87	9:00	O'Hara(60) — CD	m	To:s-8
12/87	8:00	O'Hara(60) — CD	m	Fr:s-9
12/87	9:00	Sable(60) — AD	m	Fr:s-8
1/88	8:00	Dolly(60) — VY	m	Fr:n-9
1/88	8:00	O'Hara(60) — CD	m	To:s-9
1/88	9:00	O'Hara(60) — CD	m	Fr:s-8
1/88	9:00	Sable(60) — AD	c	
1/88	10:00	Spenser for Hire(60) — CD	m	Fr:n-8
1/88	10:00	Hotel(60) — DR	m	To:r-9-3/88
5/88	8:00	Dolly(60) — VY	c	
6/88	8:00	Probe(60) — CD	m	Fr:r-8
6/88	8:00	Probe(60) — CD	c	
6/88	10:00	Spenser for Hire(60) — CD	m	To:w-10
6/88	10:00	Hotel(60) — DR	m	Fr:r-9
7/88	8:00	Supercarrier(60) — AD	m	Fr:n-8-4/88
8/88	8:00	Supercarrier(60) — AD	c	
8/88	9:00	O'Hara(60) — CD	c	
8/88	10:00	Hotel(60) — DR	c	

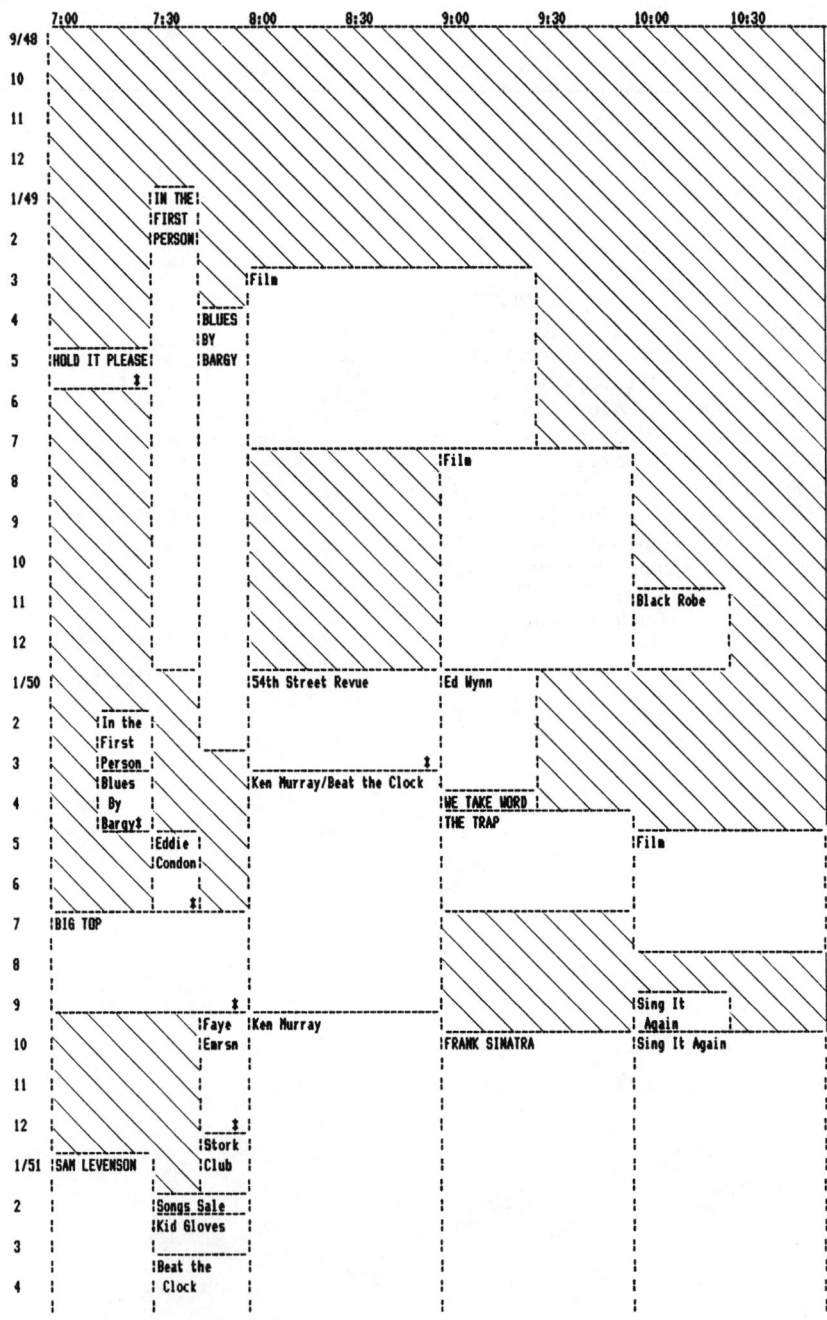

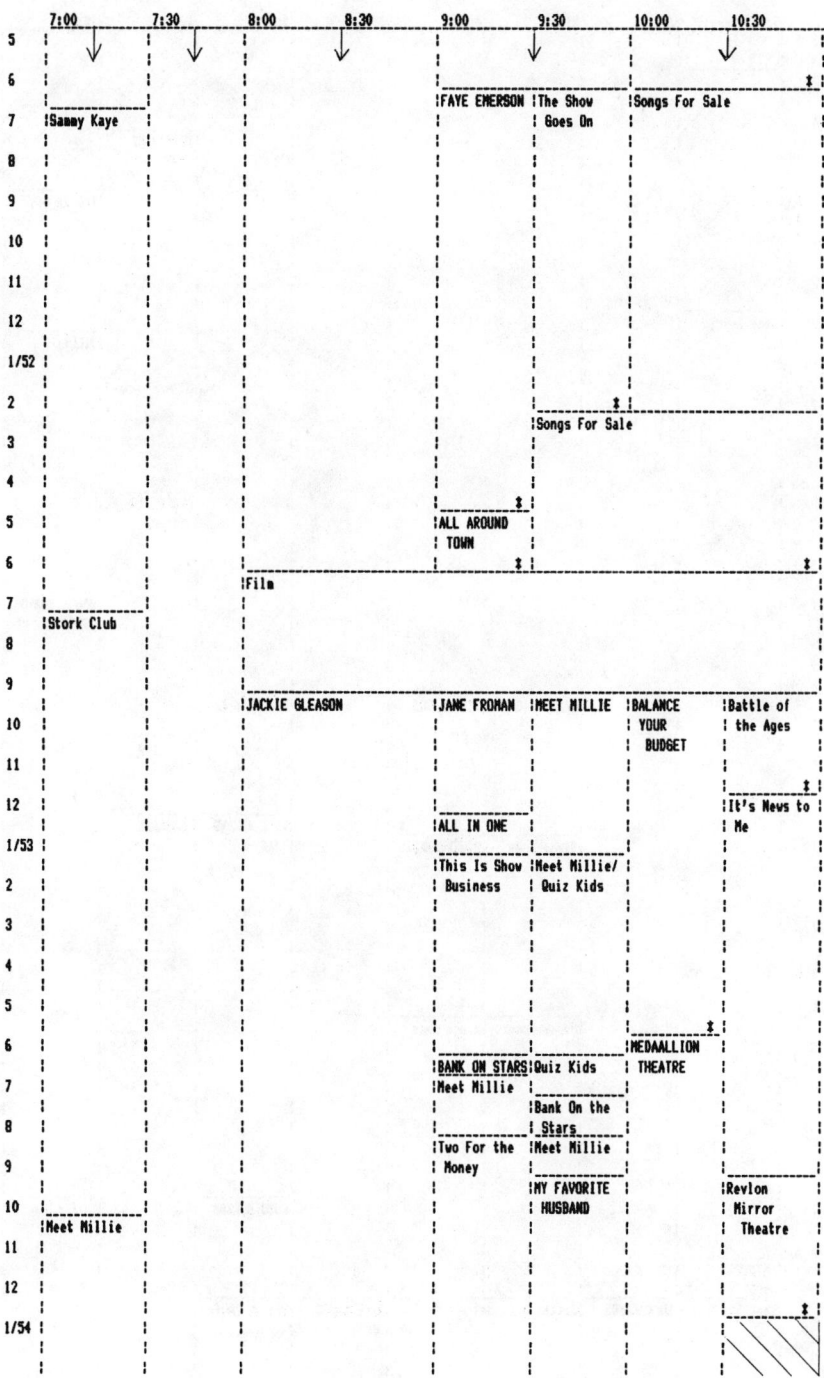

	7:00	7:30	8:00	8:30	9:00	9:30	10:00	10:30
2								
3								
4							THAT'S MY	
5							BOY	
6								TWO IN LOVE
7								
8								
9	Gene Autry							WILLY
10								
11								
12								
1/55							PROFESSIONAL	
2							FATHER	
3								
4								DAMON RUNYON
5								THEATRE
6								
7			AMERICA'S GREATEST BANDS			Down You Go	TV's Top	
8							Tunes	
9						IT'S ALWAYS	GUNSMOKE	
10			Stage Show	HONEYMOONERS		JAN		
11								
12								
1/56								
2			Honeymooners	Stage Show				
3								
4								
5								
6								
7						RUSS MORGAN		HIGH FINANCE
8								
9	SATURDAY SPORTS							
	Beat the Clock	BUCCANEERS	Jackie Gleason		GALE STORM	HEY JEANNIE		
10								

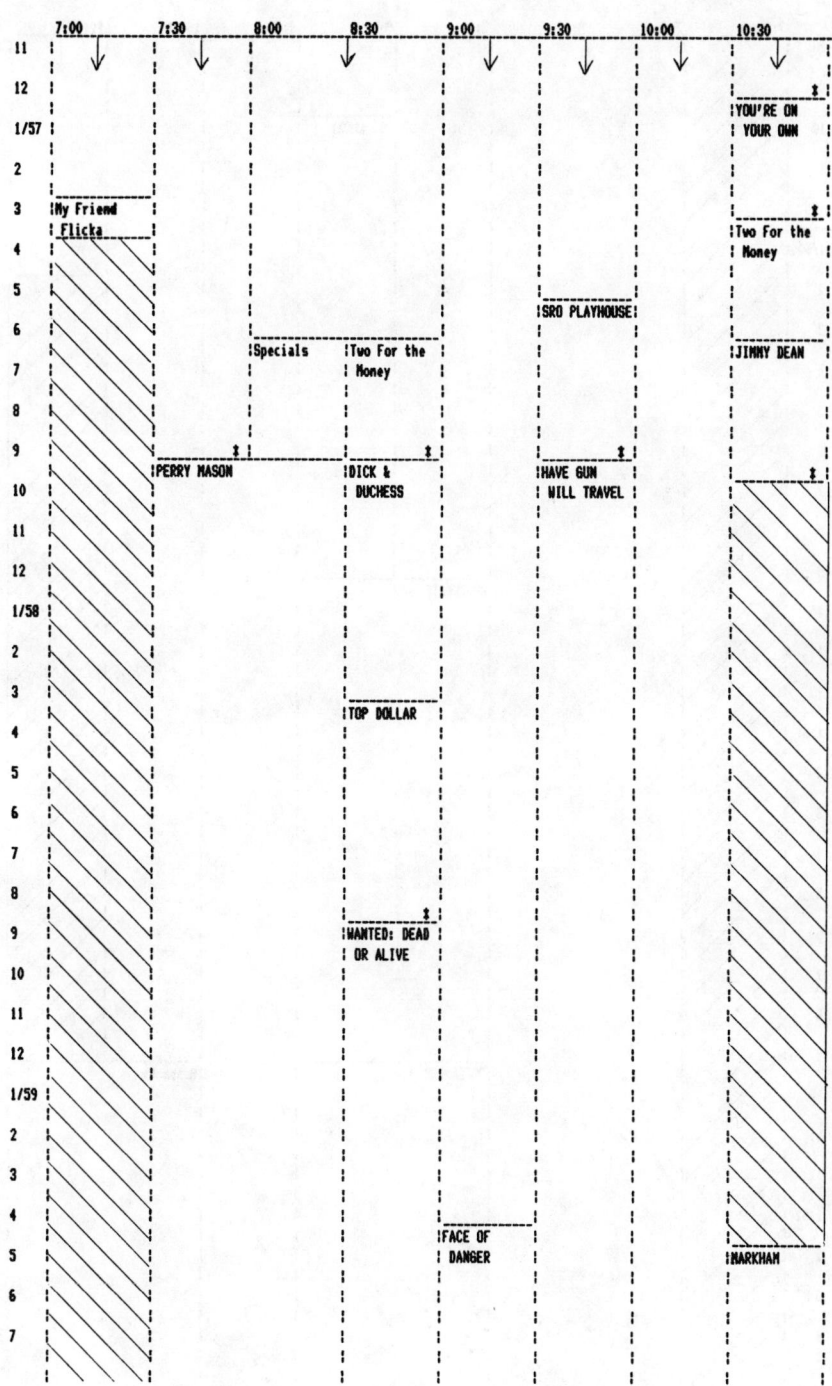

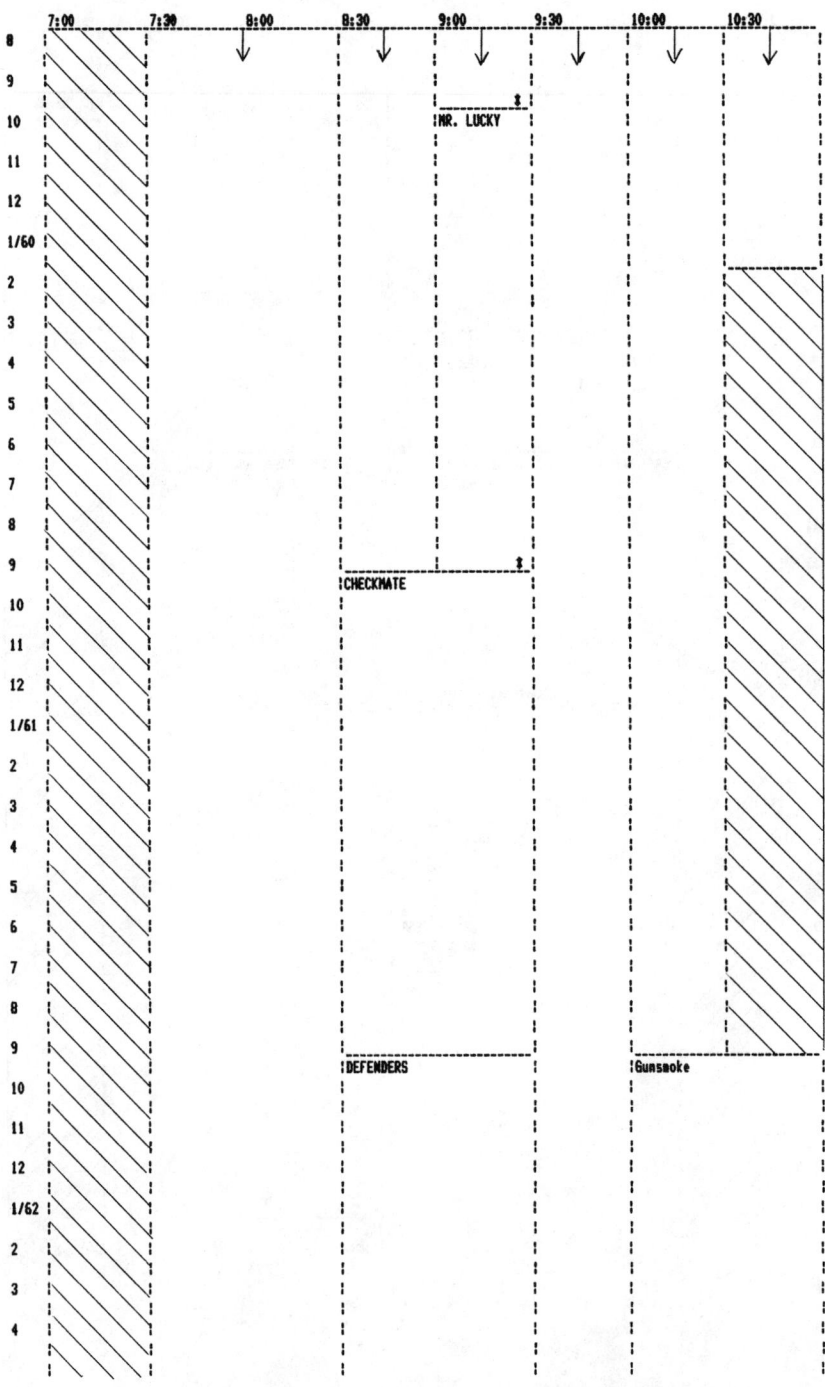

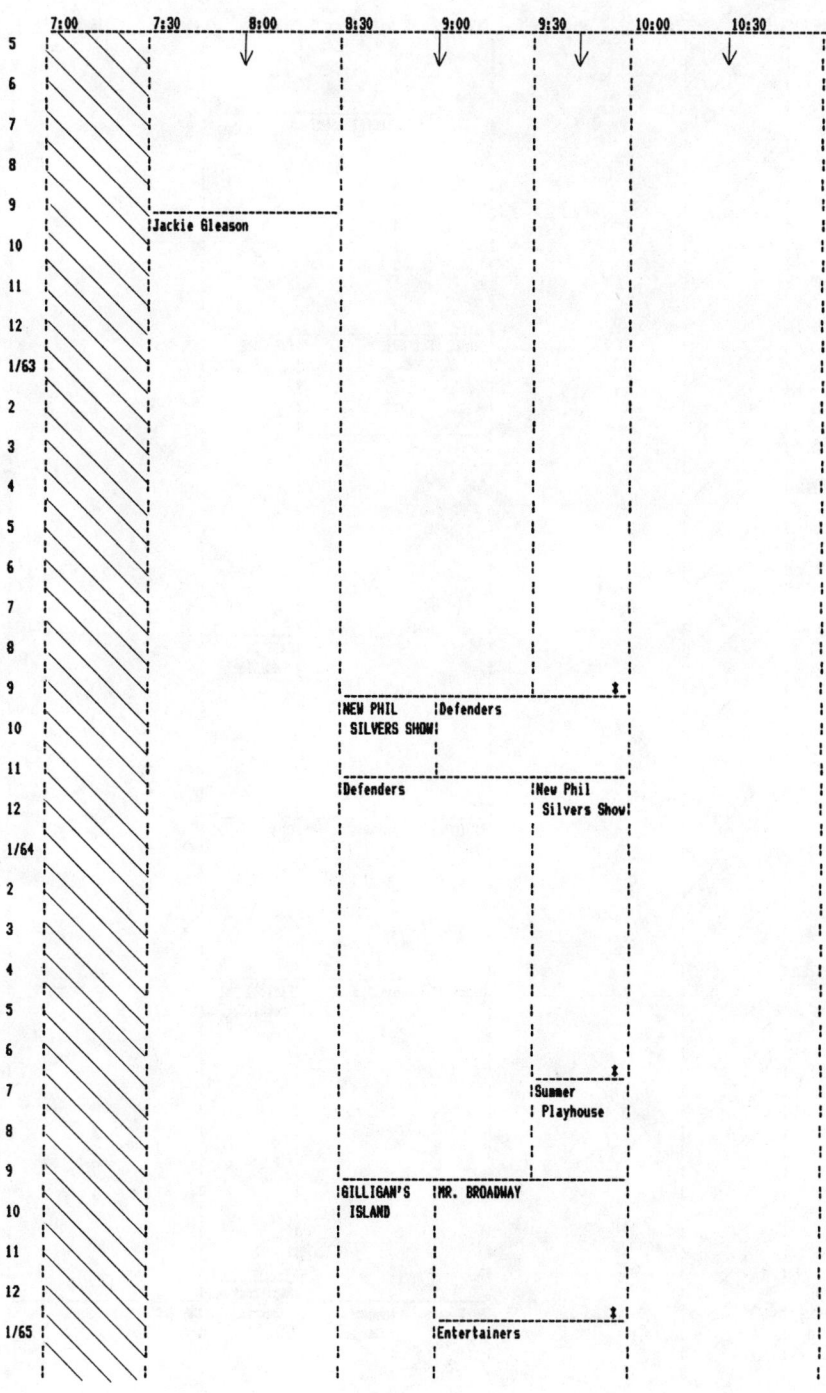

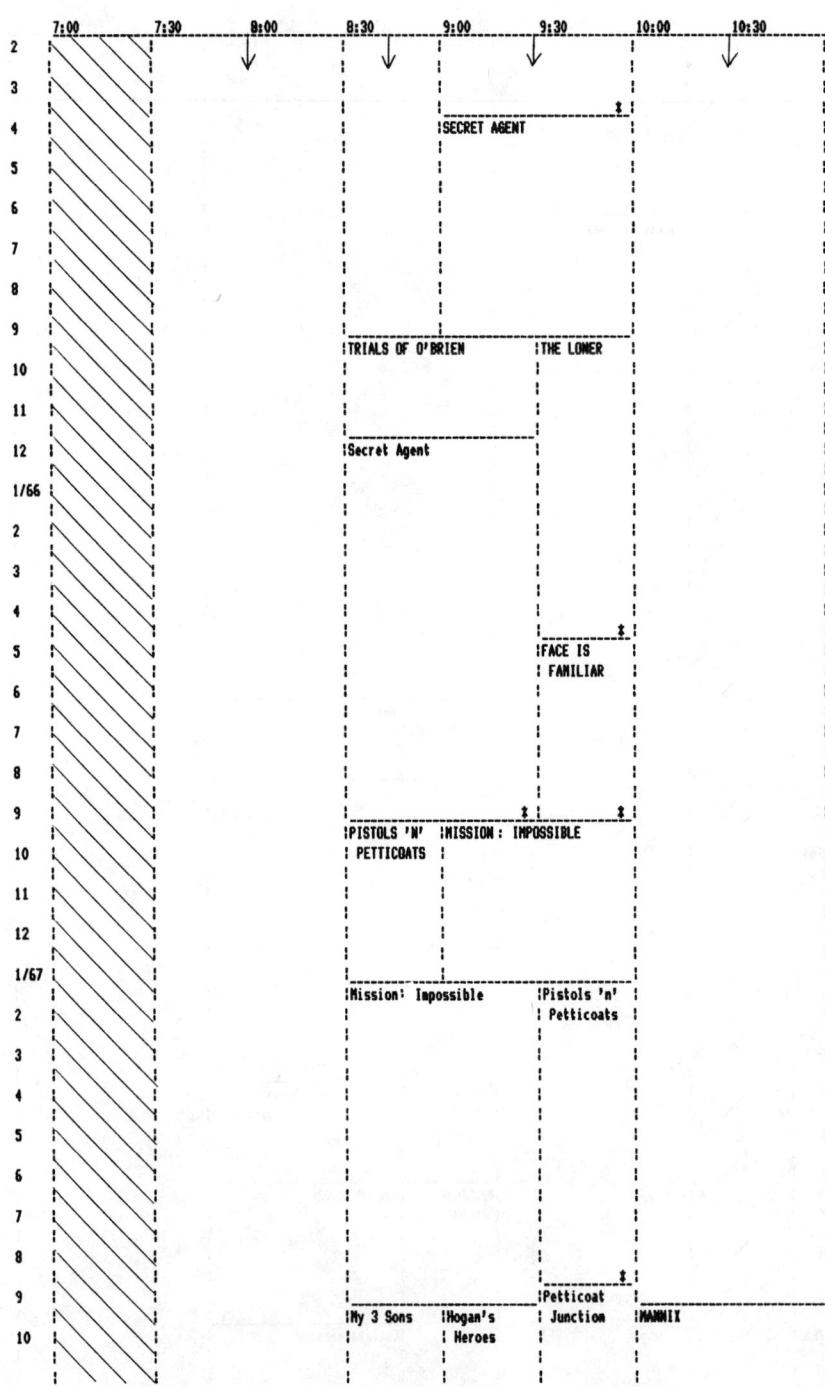

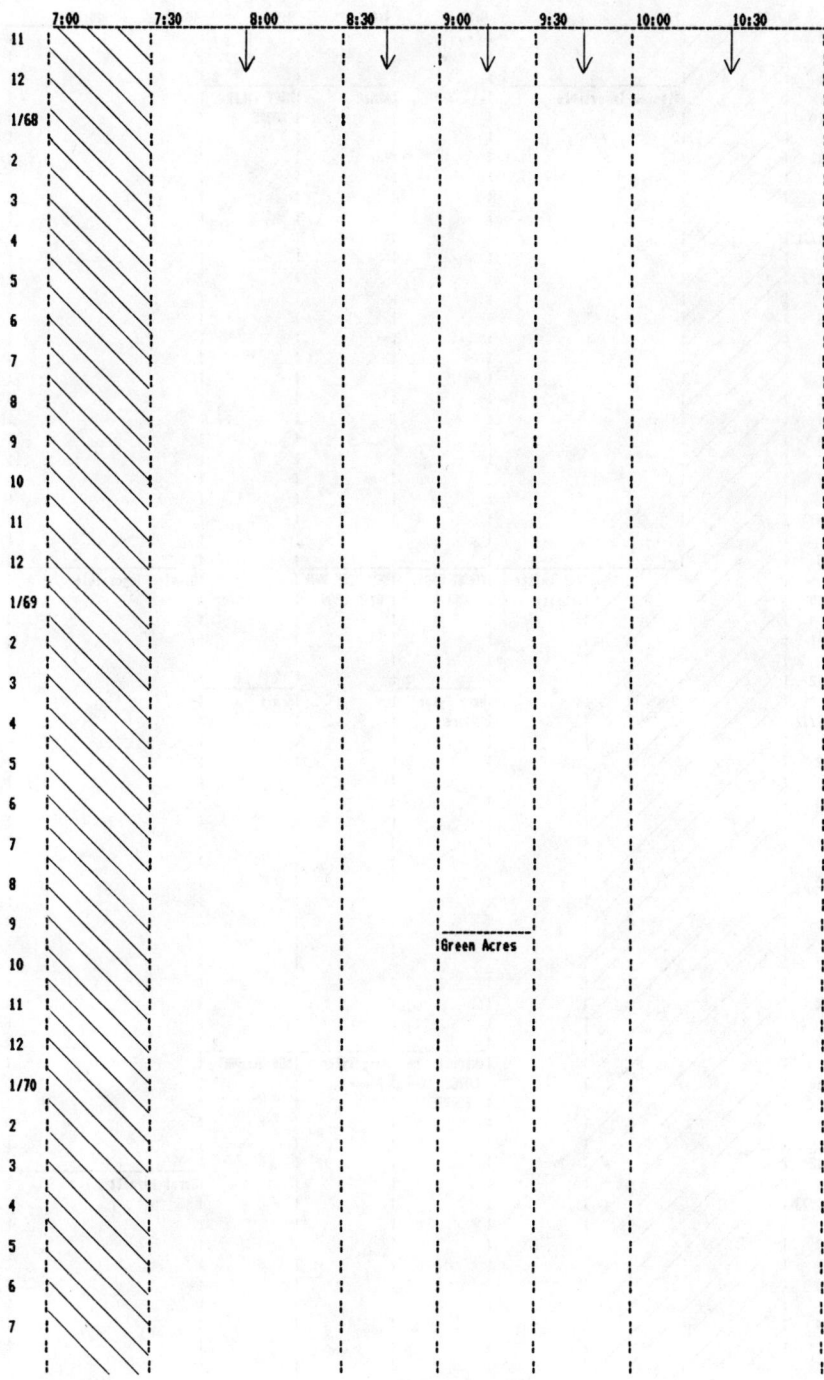

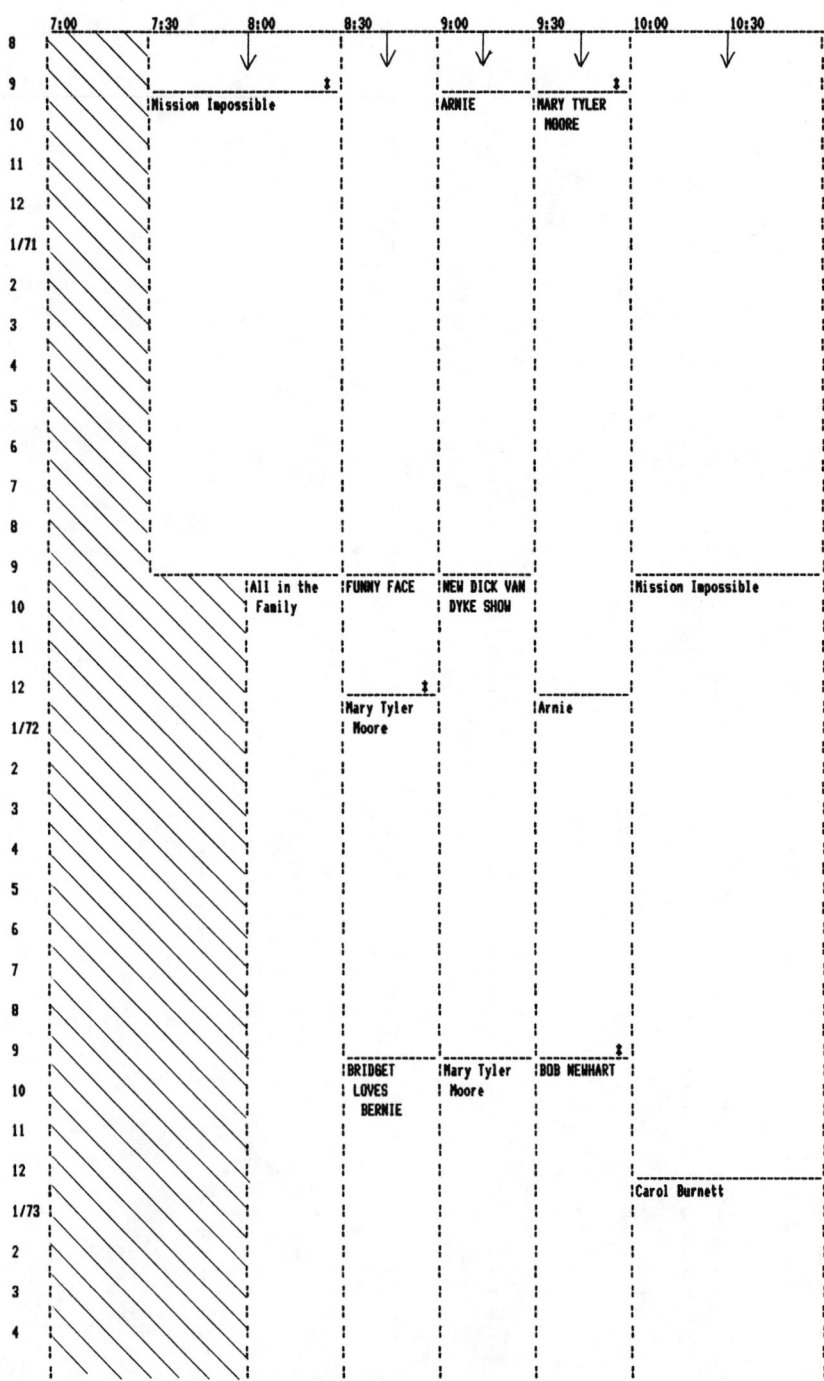

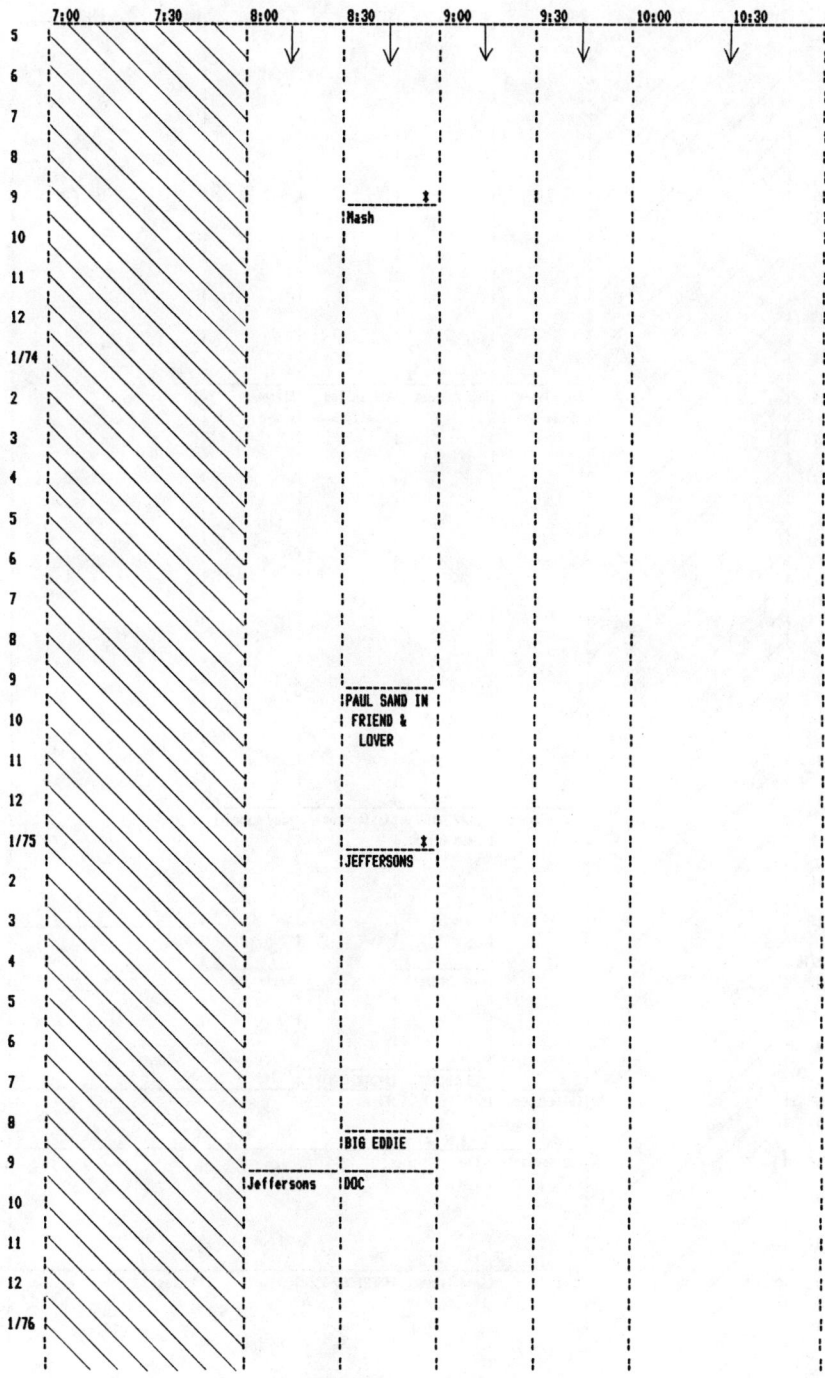

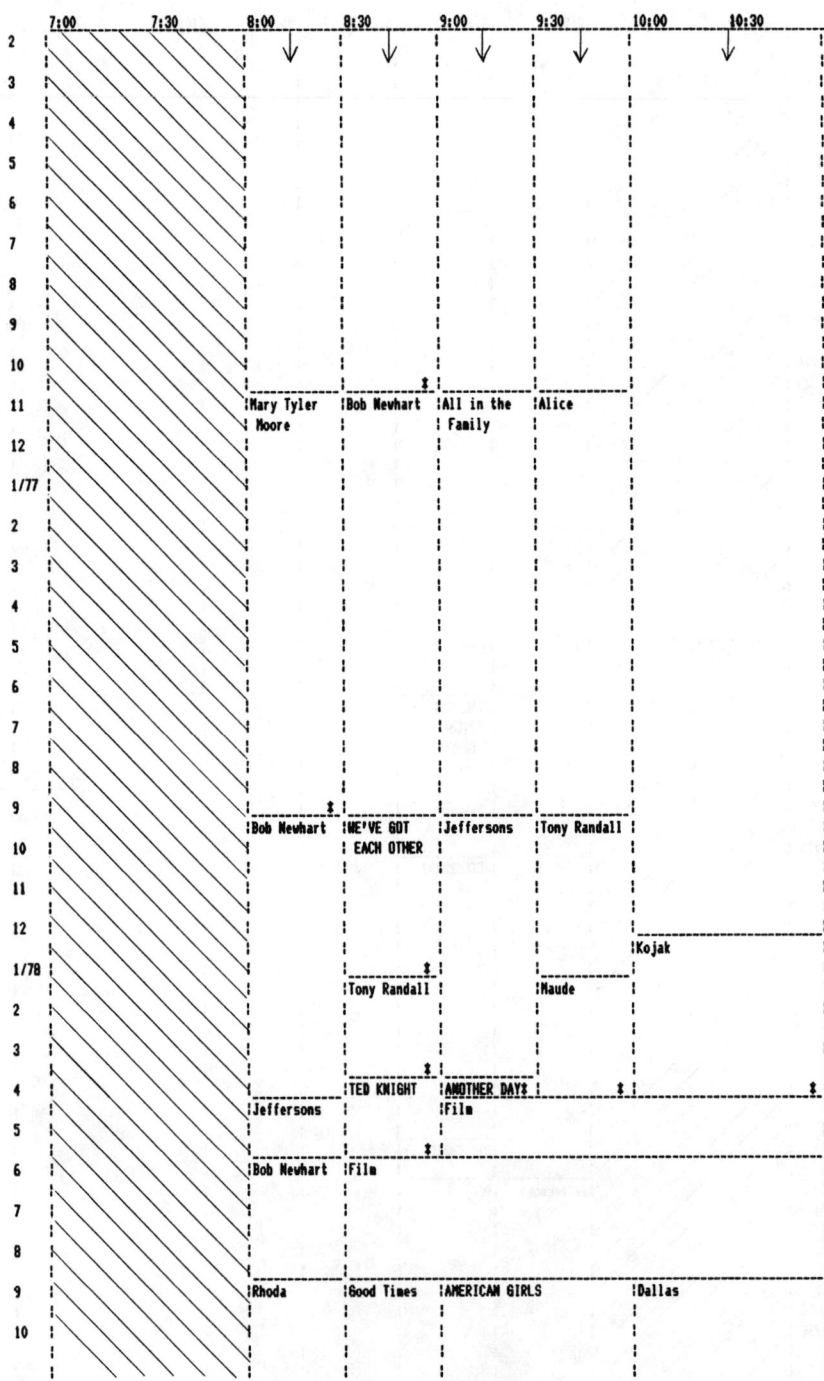

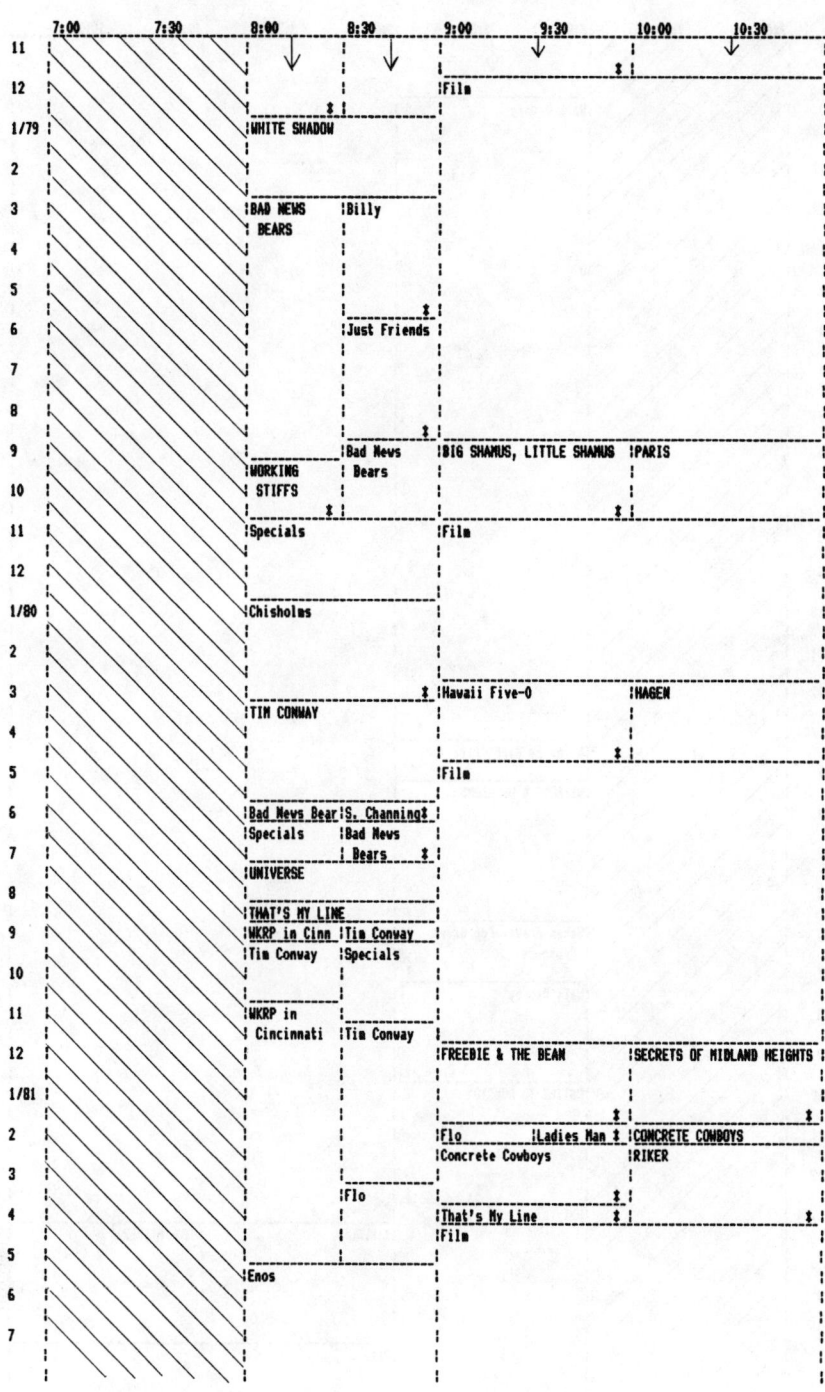

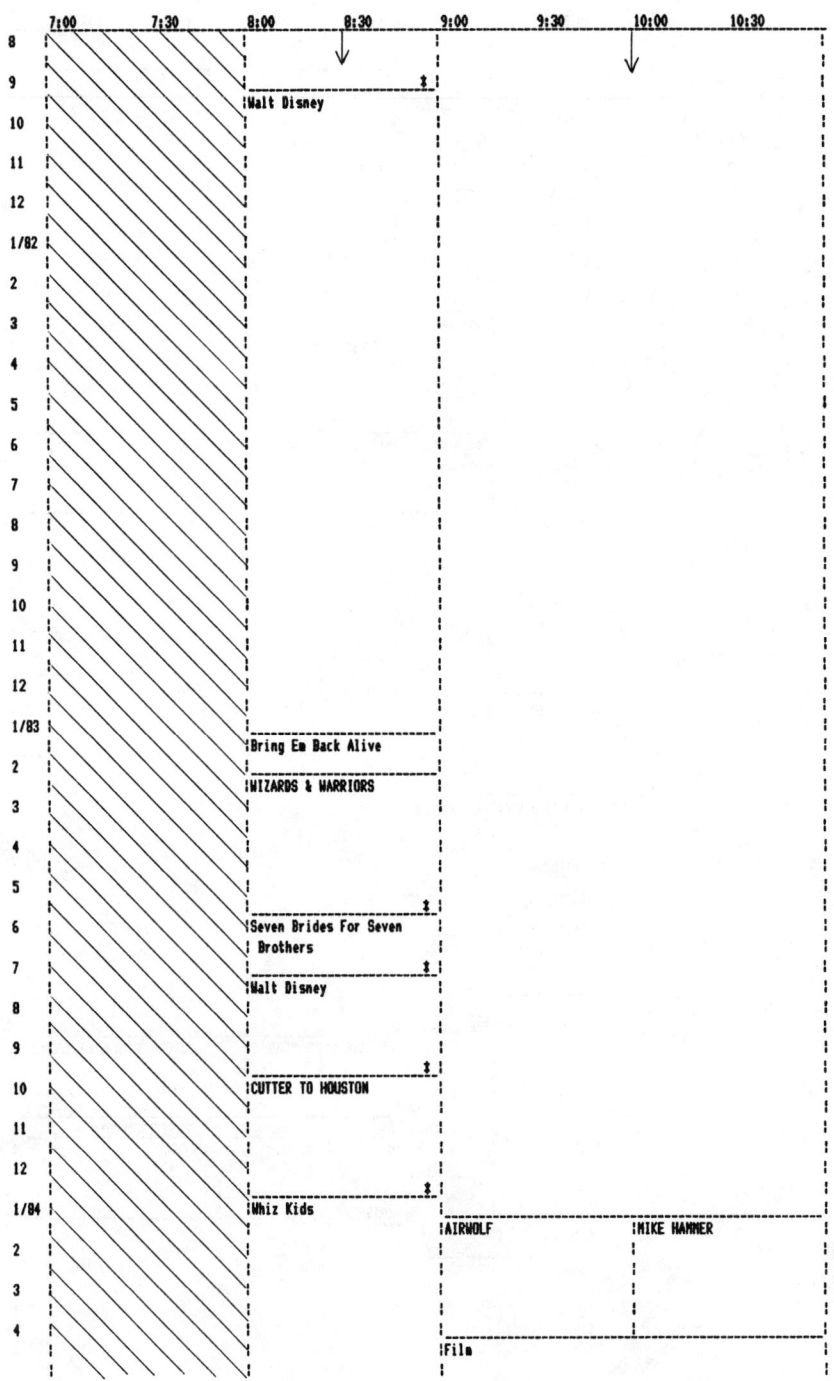

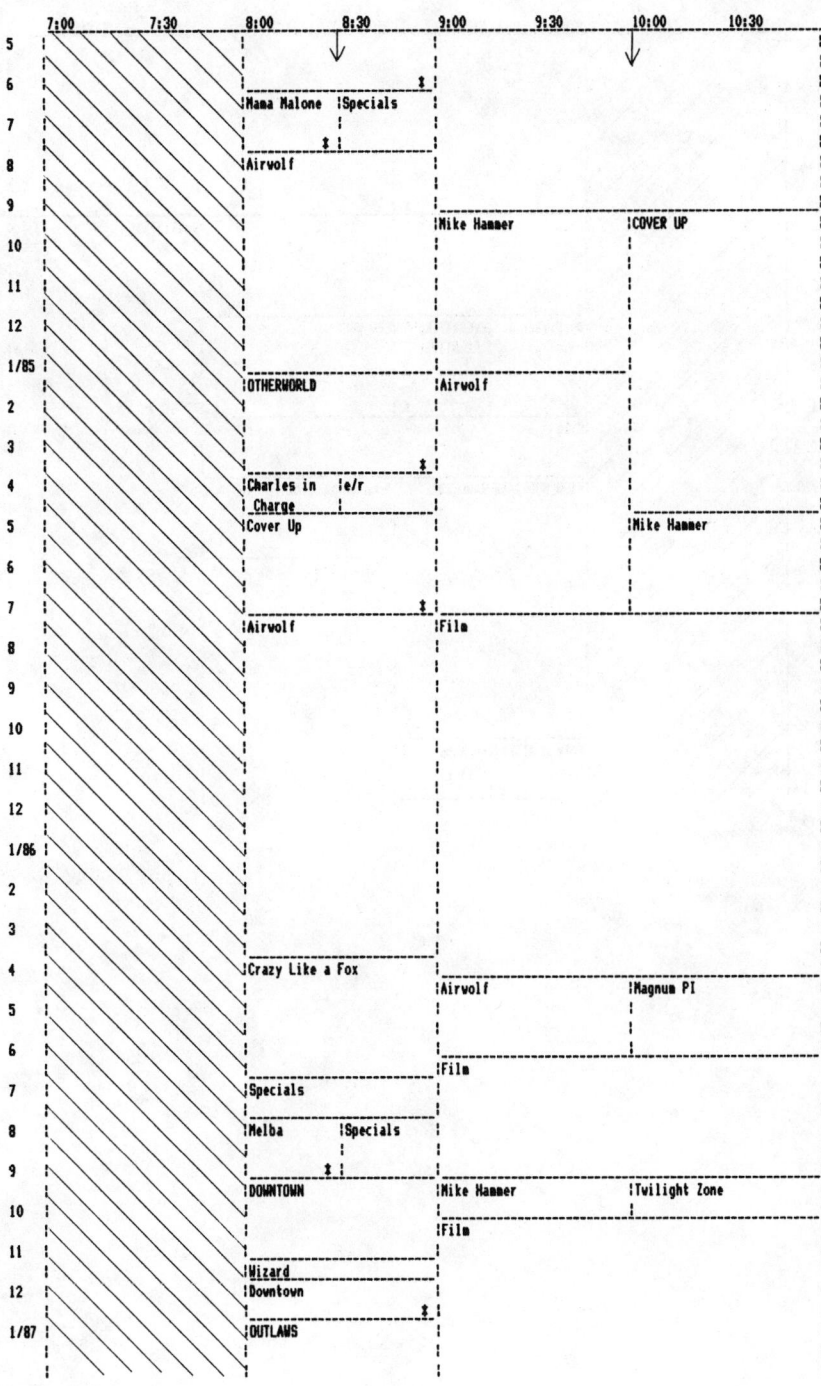

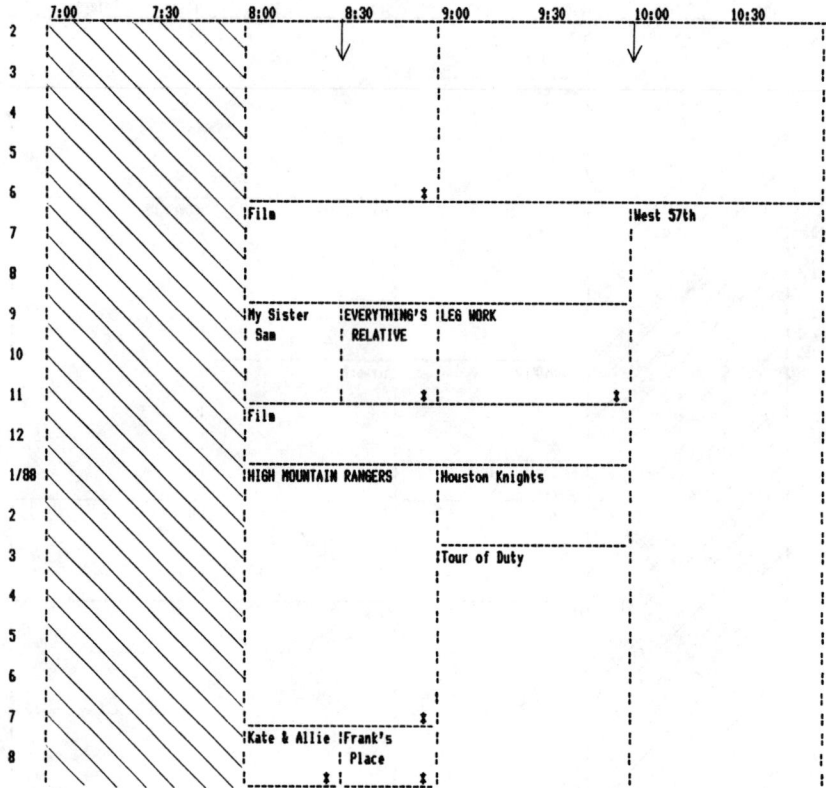

Date	Time	Title (min. if not 30) — Type	Action	From/To
1/49	7:30	In the First Person(15) — IV	d	
3/49	8:00	Film(90) — FI	s	
4/49	7:45	Blues by Bargy(15) — MU	d	
5/49	7:00	Hold It Please — QU	d	
5/49	7:00	Hold It Please — QU	c	
7/49	8:00	Film(90) — FI	f	
7/49	9:00	Film(60) — FI	s	
8/49	7:45	Blues by Bargy(15) — MU	m	To:s-7:45
8/49	7:45	Blues by Bargy(10) — MU	m	Fr:s-7:45
8/49	7:55	Ruthie on the Telephone(5) — CY	d	
11/49	7:55	Herb Shriner(5) — CV	d	
11/49	7:55	Ruthie on the Telephone(5) — CY	c	
11/49	10:00	Black Robe — CR	m	Fr:m-var
12/49	7:30	In the First Person(15) — IV	m	To:s-7:15-2/50
12/49	9:00	Film(60) — FI	f	
12/49	10:00	Black Robe — CR	m	To:r-8
1/50	8:00	Fifty-Fourth Street Revue(60) — VY	m	Fr:f-9
1/50	8:00	Ken Murray(60) — VY	d	
1/50	9:00	Ed Wynn — CV	m	Fr:r-9
2/50	7:15	In the First Person(15) — IV	m	Fr:s-7:30-12/49
2/50	7:45	Blues by Bargy(10) — MU	m	To:s-7:15
2/50	7:55	Herb Shriner(5) — CV	m	To:r-9-10/51(a)
3/50	7:15	Blues by Bargy(15) — MU	m	Fr:s-7:45
3/50	7:15	In the First Person(15) — IV	m	To:r-10:30
3/50	8:00	Fifty-Fourth Street Revue(60) — VY	c	
3/50	9:00	Ed Wynn — CV	m	To:t-9
4/50	7:15	Blues by Bargy(15) — MU	c	
4/50	8:00	Beat the Clock(60) — QU	m	Fr:r-9:45
4/50	9:00	The Trap(60) — DA	d	
4/50	9:00	We Take Your Word — QU	d	
4/50	9:00	We Take Your Word — QU	m	To:f-8-6/50
5/50	7:30	Eddie Condon — MU	m	Fr:s-9:30-9/49(n)
5/50	10:00	Film(60) — FI	s	
6/50	7:30	Eddie Condon — MU	c	
6/50	9:00	The Trap(60) — DA	c	
7/50	7:00	Big Top(60) — VY	d	
7/50	10:00	Film(60) — FI	f	
9/50	7:00	Big Top(60) — VY	c	
9/50	7:45	Faye Emerson(15) — IV	m	Fr:w-8(n)
9/50	8:00	Beat the Clock(60) — QU	m	To:f-10:30
9/50	10:00	Sing It Again — QU	d	
9/50	10:00	Sing It Again — QU	m	To:s-10
10/50	9:00	Frank Sinatra(60) — MV	d	
10/50	10:00	Sing It Again(60) — QU	m	Fr:s-10
12/50	7:45	Faye Emerson(15) — IV	c	
12/50	7:45	Stork Club(15) — TK	m	Fr:m-f-7
1/51	7:00	Sam Levenson — CY	d	
1/51	7:45	Stork Club(15) — TK	m	To:tr-7:45
2/51	7:30	Kid Gloves — SP	s	
2/51	7:30	Songs for Sale — MU	m	Fr:f-9-9/50

Date	Time	Title (min. if not 30) — Type	Action	From/To
2/51	7:30	Songs for Sale — MU	m	To:s-10-6/51
3/51	7:30	Beat the Clock — QU	m	Fr:f-10:30
3/51	7:30	Kid Gloves — SP	f	
6/51	7:00	Sam Levenson — CY	m	To:t-8-4/52
6/51	8:00	Film(60) — FI	s*	
6/51	9:00	Faye Emerson's Wonderful Town — VY	d	
6/51	9:00	Frank Sinatra(60) — MV	m	To:t-8-10/51
6/51	9:30	The Show Goes On — VY	m	Fr:r-8:30
6/51	10:00	Sing It Again(60) — QU	c	
6/51	10:00	Songs for Sale(60) — MU	m	Fr:s-7:30-2/51
7/51	7:00	Sammy Kaye — MV	m	Fr:n-8-7/50(n)
9/51	8:00	Film(60) — FI	f*	
2/52	9:30	The Show Goes On — VY	c	
2/52	10:00	Songs for Sale(60) — MU	m	To:s-9:30
3/52	9:30	Songs for Sale(90) — MU	m	Fr:s-10
4/52	9:00	Faye Emerson's Wonderful Town — VY	c	
5/52	9:00	All Around Town — IV	d	
6/52	8:00	Ken Murray(60) — VY	m	To:n-9:30-2/53
6/52	8:00	Film(180) — FI	s	
6/52	9:00	All Around Town — IV	c	
6/52	9:30	Songs for Sale(90) — MU	c	
7/52	7:00	Sammy Kaye — MV	m	To:s-8-8/53(n)
7/52	7:00	Stork Club — TK	m	Fr:tr-7:45
9/52	8:00	Jackie Gleason(60) — CV	d	
9/52	8:00	Film(180) — FI	f	
9/52	9:00	Jane Froman's USA Canteen — MV	d	
9/52	9:30	Meet Millie — SC	d	
9/52	10:00	Balance Your Budget — QU	d	
9/52	10:30	Battle of the Ages — TA	m	Fr:t-9-6/52(d)
11/52	10:30	Battle of the Ages — TA	c	
12/52	9:00	All in One — CV	d	
12/52	9:00	Jane Froman's USA Canteen — MV	m	To:tr-7:45
12/52	10:30	It's News to Me — QU	m	Fr:f-10:30-9/52
1/53	9:00	All in One — CV	m	To:r-8-4/53
1/53	9:00	This Is Show Business — VY	m	Fr:n-7:30
1/53	10:00	Quiz Kids — QU	m	Fr:m-8-9/52(n)
5/53	10:00	Balance Your Budget — QU	c	
6/53	9:00	Bank on the Stars — QU	d	
6/53	9:00	Bank on the Stars — QU	m	To:s-9:30
6/53	9:00	This Is Show Business — VY	m	To:t-9-9/53
6/53	9:30	Meet Millie — SC	m	To:s-9
6/53	10:00	Medallion Theatre — DA	d	
7/53	8:00	Larry Storch(60) — CV	d*	
7/53	9:00	Meet Millie — SC	m	Fr:s-9:30
7/53	9:30	Bank on the Stars — QU	m	Fr:s-9
7/53	10:00	Quiz Kids — QU	m	To:n-7
8/53	9:00	Meet Millie — SC	m	To:s-9:30
8/53	9:00	Two for the Money — QU	m	Fr:t-10(n)

Date	Time	Title (min. if not 30) – Type	Action	From/To
8/53	9:30	Bank on the Stars – QU	m	To:s-8-5/54(n)
8/53	9:30	Meet Millie – SC	m	Fr:s-9
9/53	8:00	Larry Storch(60) – CV	c*	
9/53	9:30	Meet Millie – SC	m	To:s-7
9/53	9:30	My Favorite Husband – SC	d	
9/53	10:30	It's News to Me – QU	m	To:f-10:30-7/54
9/53	10:30	Revlon Mirror Theatre – DA	m	Fr:t-8(n)
10/53	7:00	Meet Millie – SC	m	Fr:s-9:30
10/53	7:00	Stork Club – TK	m	To:s-10-9/54(a)
12/53	10:30	Revlon Mirror Theatre – DA	c	
2/54	7:00	Meet Millie – SC	m	To:t-9
4/54	10:00	Medallion Theatre – DA	c	
4/54	10:00	That's My Boy – SC	d	
6/54	10:30	Two in Love – QU	d	
7/54	8:00	Stage Show(60) – MV	d*	
7/54	9:30	Jack Paar – VY	d*	
9/54	7:00	Gene Autry – WE	m	Fr:t-8
9/54	8:00	Stage Show(60) – MV	m*	To:s-8-10/55
9/54	9:30	Jack Paar – VY	c*	
9/54	10:30	Two in Love – QU	c	
9/54	10:30	Willy – LD	d	
1/55	10:00	Professional Father – SC	d	
1/55	10:00	That's My Boy – SC	m	To:n-7:30-6/59
3/55	10:30	Willy – LD	m	To:r-10:30
4/55	10:30	Damon Runyon Theatre – DA	d	
6/55	8:00	America's Greatest Bands(60) – MU	d	
6/55	8:00	Jackie Gleason(60) – CV	m	To:s-8-9/56
6/55	9:30	Down You Go – QU	m	Fr:f-10:30(d)
6/55	9:30	My Favorite Husband – SC	m	To:t-10:30-10/55
7/55	10:00	Professional Father – SC	c	
7/55	10:00	TV's Top Tunes – MU	m	Fr:mwf-7:45-8/54
9/55	8:00	America's Greatest Bands(60) – MU	c	
9/55	9:30	Down You Go – QU	m	To:r-9:30(a)
9/55	9:30	It's Always Jan – SC	d	
9/55	10:00	Gunsmoke – WE	d	
9/55	10:00	TV's Top Tunes – MU	c	
10/55	8:00	Stage Show – MV	m	Fr:s-8-9/54
10/55	8:30	Honeymooners – SC	d	
2/56	8:00	Honeymooners – SC	m	Fr:s-8:30
2/56	8:00	Stage Show – MV	m	To:s-8:30
2/56	8:30	Honeymooners – SC	m	To:s-8
2/56	8:30	Stage Show – MV	m	Fr:s-8
6/56	9:30	It's Always Jan – SC	c	
6/56	10:30	Damon Runyon Theatre – DA	c	
7/56	9:30	Russ Morgan – MU	d	
7/56	10:30	High Finance – QU	d	
8/56	7:00	Gene Autry – WE	c	
8/56	7:00	Saturday Sports Mirror – SN	d	
9/56	7:00	Beat the Clock – QU	m	Fr:s-7:30
9/56	7:00	Saturday Sports Mirror – SN	c	

Date	Time	Title (min. if not 30) — Type	Action	From/To
9/56	7:30	Beat the Clock — QU	m	To:s-7
9/56	7:30	Buccaneers — AD	d	
9/56	8:00	Honeymooners — SC	c	
9/56	8:00	Jackie Gleason(60) — CV	m	Fr:s-8-6/55
9/56	8:30	Stage Show — MV	c	
9/56	9:00	Gale Storm — SC	d	
9/56	9:00	Two for the Money — QU	m	To:s-10:30-3/57
9/56	9:30	Hey Jeannie — SC	d	
9/56	9:30	Russ Morgan — MU	c	
12/56	10:30	High Finance — QU	c	
12/56	10:30	You're on Your Own — QU	d	
2/57	7:00	Beat the Clock — QU	m	To:f-7:30
3/57	7:00	My Friend Flicka — WE	m	Fr:f-7:30
3/57	7:00	My Friend Flicka — WE	m	To:w-7:30-6/57
3/57	10:30	Two for the Money — QU	m	Fr:s-9-9/56
3/57	10:30	You're on Your Own — QU	c	
5/57	9:30	Hey Jeannie — SC	m	To:r-9-6/60(a)
5/57	9:30	S.R.O. Playhouse — DA	d	
6/57	8:00	Jackie Gleason(60) — CV	m	To:f-8:30-10/58
6/57	8:30	Two for the Money — QU	m	Fr:s-10:30
6/57	10:30	Jimmy Dean — MV	d	
6/57	10:30	Two for the Money — QU	m	To:s-8:30
9/57	7:30	Buccaneers — AD	c	
9/57	7:30	Perry Mason(60) — LD	d	
9/57	8:30	Dick and the Duchess — SC	d	
9/57	8:30	Two for the Money — QU	c	
9/57	9:30	Have Gun Will Travel — WE	d	
9/57	9:30	S.R.O. Playhouse — DA	c	
9/57	10:30	Jimmy Dean — MV	c	
3/58	8:30	Dick and the Duchess — SC	m	To:f-7:30
3/58	8:30	Top Dollar — QU	d	
8/58	8:30	Top Dollar — QU	c	
9/58	8:30	Wanted: Dead or Alive — WE	d	
4/59	9:00	Face of Danger — DA	d	
4/59	9:00	Gale Storm — SC	m	To:r-7:30-10/59(a)
5/59	10:30	Markham — CD	d	
7/59	7:30	Reckoning(60) — DA	d*	
9/59	7:30	Reckoning(60) — DA	m*	To:w-7:30-6/60
9/59	9:00	Face of Danger — DA	c	
10/59	9:00	Mr. Lucky — AD	d	
1/60	10:30	Markham — CD	m	To:r-9:30
9/60	8:30	Checkmate(60) — CD	d	
9/60	8:30	Wanted: Dead or Alive — WE	m	To:w-8:30
9/60	9:00	Mr. Lucky — AD	c	
9/61	8:30	Checkmate(60) — CD	m	To:w-8:30
9/61	9:00	Defenders(60) — LD	d	
9/61	10:00	Gunsmoke — WE	m	To:s-10
9/61	10:00	Gunsmoke(60) — WE	m	Fr:s-10
9/62	7:30	Jackie Gleason(60) — CV	m	Fr:f-8:30-1/59
9/62	7:30	Perry Mason(60) — LD	m	To:r-8

Date	Time	Title (min. if not 30) — Type	Action	From/To
6/63	7:30	Lucy-Desi Comedy Hour(60) — CV	m*	Fr:m-9-9/62
9/63	7:30	Lucy-Desi Comedy Hour(60) — CV	m*	To:s-7:30-6/64
9/63	8:30	Defenders(60) — LD	m	To:s-9
9/63	8:30	New Phil Silvers Show — SC	d	
9/63	9:00	Defenders(60) — LD	m	Fr:s-8:30
9/63	9:30	Have Gun Will Travel — WE	c	
11/63	8:30	Defenders(60) — LD	m	Fr:s-9
11/63	8:30	New Phil Silvers Show — SC	m	To:s-9:30
11/63	9:00	Defenders(60) — LD	m	To:s-8:30
11/63	9:30	New Phil Silvers Show — SC	m	Fr:s-8:30
6/64	7:30	Lucy-Desi Comedy Hour(60) — CV	m*	Fr:s-7:30-9/63
6/64	9:30	New Phil Silvers Show — SC	c	
7/64	9:30	Summer Playhouse — VS	m	Fr:t-9:30-9/57(n)
9/64	7:30	Lucy-Desi Comedy Hour(60) — CV	m*	To:w-10-6/65
9/64	8:30	Defenders(60) — LD	m	To:r-10
9/64	8:30	Gilligan's Island — SC	d	
9/64	9:00	Mr. Broadway(60) — DR	d	
9/64	9:30	Summer Playhouse — VS	m	To:m-8:30-6/65
12/64	9:00	Mr. Broadway(60) — DR	c	
1/65	9:00	The Entertainers(60) — VY	m	Fr:f-8:30
3/65	9:00	The Entertainers(60) — VY	c	
4/65	9:00	Secret Agent(60) — SD	d	
6/65	7:30	Fanfare(60) — MV	d*	
9/65	7:30	Fanfare(60) — MV	c*	
9/65	8:30	Gilligan's Island — SC	m	To:r-8
9/65	8:30	Trials of O'Brien(60) — LD	d	
9/65	9:00	Secret Agent(60) — SD	m	To:s-8:30-12/65
9/65	9:30	The Loner — WE	d	
11/65	8:30	Trials of O'Brien(60) — LD	m	To:f-10
12/65	8:30	Secret Agent(60) — SD	m	Fr:s-9-9/65
4/66	9:30	The Loner — WE	c	
5/66	9:30	The Face Is Familiar — QU	d	
6/66	7:30	Continental Showcase(60) — VY	d*	
9/66	7:30	Continental Showcase(60) — VY	c*	
9/66	8:30	Pistols 'n' Petticoats — SC	d	
9/66	8:30	Secret Agent(60) — SD	c	
9/66	9:00	Mission: Impossible(60) — SD	d	
9/66	9:30	The Face Is Familiar — QU	c	
1/67	8:30	Mission: Impossible(60) — SD	m	Fr:s-9
1/67	8:30	Pistols 'n' Petticoats — SC	m	To:s-9:30
1/67	9:00	Mission: Impossible(60) — SD	m	To:s-8:30
1/67	9:30	Pistols 'n' Petticoats — SC	m	Fr:s-8:30
6/67	7:30	Away We Go(60) — MV	d*	
8/67	9:30	Pistols 'n' Petticoats — SC	c	
9/67	7:30	Away We Go(60) — MV	c*	
9/67	8:30	Mission: Impossible(60) — SD	m	To:n-10
9/67	8:30	My Three Sons — SC	m	Fr:r-8:30
9/67	9:00	Hogan's Heroes — SC	m	Fr:f-8:30
9/67	9:30	Petticoat Junction — SC	m	Fr:t-9:30
9/67	10:00	Gunsmoke(60) — WE	m	To:m-7:30

Date	Time	Title (min. if not 30) – Type	Action	From/To
9/67	10:00	Mannix(60) – CD	d	
6/68	7:30	The Prisoner(60) – AD	d*	
9/68	7:30	The Prisoner(60) – AD	m*	To:r-8-5/69
9/69	9:00	Green Acres – SC	m	Fr:w-9:30
9/69	9:00	Hogan's Heroes – SC	m	To:f-8:30
9/70	7:30	Jackie Gleason(60) – CV	c	
9/70	7:30	Mission: Impossible(60) – SD	m	Fr:n-10
9/70	9:00	Arnie – SC	d	
9/70	9:00	Green Acres – SC	m	To:t-8
9/70	9:30	Mary Tyler Moore – SC	d	
9/70	9:30	Petticoat Junction – SC	c	
9/71	7:30	Mission: Impossible(60) – SD	m	To:s-10
9/71	8:00	All in the Family – SC	m	Fr:t-9:30-7/71
9/71	8:30	Funny Face – SC	d	
9/71	8:30	My Three Sons – SC	m	To:m-10
9/71	9:00	Arnie – SC	m	To:m-10:30
9/71	9:00	New Dick Van Dyke Show – SC	d	
9/71	10:00	Mannix(60) – CD	m	To:w-10
9/71	10:00	Mission: Impossible(60) – SD	m	Fr:s-7:30
12/71	8:30	Funny Face – SC	c	
12/71	8:30	Mary Tyler Moore – SC	m	Fr:s-9:30
12/71	9:30	Arnie – SC	m	Fr:m-10:30
12/71	9:30	Mary Tyler Moore – SC	m	To:s-8:30
9/72	8:30	Bridget Loves Bernie – SC	d	
9/72	8:30	Mary Tyler Moore – SC	m	To:s-9
9/72	9:00	Mary Tyler Moore – SC	m	Fr:s-8:30
9/72	9:00	New Dick Van Dyke Show – SC	m	To:n-9
9/72	9:30	Arnie – SC	c	
9/72	9:30	Bob Newhart – SC	d	
12/72	10:00	Carol Burnett(60) – CV	m	Fr:w-8
12/72	10:00	Mission: Impossible(60) – SD	m	To:f-8
5/73	10:00	Mission: Impossible(60) – SD	m*	Fr:f-8
9/73	8:30	Bridget Loves Bernie – SC	c	
9/73	8:30	M*A*S*H – SC	m	Fr:n-8
9/73	10:00	Mission: Impossible(60) – SD	c*	
7/74	10:00	Barnaby Jones(60) – CD	m	Fr:t-10
9/74	8:30	M*A*S*H – SC	m	To:t-8:30
9/74	8:30	Paul Sand in Friends and Lovers – SC	d	
9/74	10:00	Barnaby Jones(60) – CD	m	To:t-10
1/75	8:30	Jeffersons – SC	d	
1/75	8:30	Paul Sand in Friends and Lovers – SC	c	
6/75	10:00	Moses – the Lawgiver(60) – RD	d*	
8/75	8:30	Big Eddie – SC	d	
8/75	8:30	Jeffersons – SC	m	To:s-8
8/75	10:00	Dick Cavett(60) – VY	d*	
8/75	10:00	Moses – the Lawgiver(60) – RD	m*	To:n-10-6/79
9/75	8:00	All in the Family – SC	m	To:m-9
9/75	8:00	Jeffersons – SC	m	Fr:s-8:30

Date	Time	Title (min. if not 30) — Type	Action	From/To
9/75	8:30	Big Eddie — SC	m	To:f-8
9/75	8:30	Doc — SC	d	
9/75	10:00	Dick Cavett(60) — VY	c*	
6/76	10:00	Dinah and Her New Best Friends (60) — MV	d*	
7/76	10:00	Dinah and Her New Best Friends (60) — MV	c*	
8/76	8:30	Ivan the Terrible — SC	d*	
8/76	10:00	Diahann Carroll(60) — MV	d*	
9/76	8:30	Ivan the Terrible — SC	c*	
9/76	10:00	Diahann Carroll(60) — MV	c*	
10/76	8:00	Jeffersons — SC	m	To:w-8:30
10/76	8:30	Doc — SC	c	
10/76	9:00	Mary Tyler Moore — SC	m	To:s-8
10/76	9:30	Bob Newhart — SC	m	To:s-8:30
11/76	8:00	Mary Tyler Moore — SC	m	Fr:s-9
11/76	8:30	Bob Newhart — SC	m	Fr:s-9:30
11/76	9:00	All in the Family — SC	m	Fr:w-9
11/76	9:30	Alice — SC	m	Fr:w-9:30
7/77	10:00	Andros Targets(60) — ND	m*	Fr:m-10-5/77
7/77	10:00	Andros Targets(60) — ND	c*	
9/77	8:00	Bob Newhart — SC	m	Fr:s-8:30
9/77	8:00	Mary Tyler Moore — SC	c	
9/77	8:30	Bob Newhart — SC	m	To:s-8
9/77	9:00	All in the Family — SC	m	To:n-9
9/77	9:00	Jeffersons — SC	m	Fr:m-8
9/77	9:30	Alice — SC	m	To:n-9:30
9/77	9:30	Tony Randall — SC	m	Fr:r-9:30-3/77(a)
10/77	8:30	We've Got Each Other — SC	d	
12/77	10:00	Carol Burnett(60) — CV	m	To:n-10
12/77	10:00	Kojak(60) — CD	m	Fr:n-10
1/78	8:30	Tony Randall — SC	m	To:s-8:30
1/78	8:30	Tony Randall — SC	m	Fr:s-9:30
1/78	8:30	We've Got Each Other — SC	c	
1/78	9:30	Maude — SC	m	Fr:m-9
3/78	8:30	Tony Randall — SC	c	
3/78	9:00	Jeffersons — SC	m	To:s-8
4/78	8:00	Bob Newhart — SC	m	To:s-8-6/78
4/78	8:00	Jeffersons — SC	m	Fr:s-9
4/78	8:30	Ted Knight — SC	d	
4/78	9:00	Another Day — SC	d	
4/78	9:00	Another Day — SC	c	
4/78	9:30	Maude — SC	c	
4/78	10:00	Kojak(60) — CD	c	
5/78	8:00	Jeffersons — SC	m	To:m-8
5/78	8:30	Ted Knight — SC	c	
5/78	9:00	Film(120) — FI	s	
6/78	8:00	Bob Newhart — SC	m	Fr:s-8-4/78
6/78	8:30	Film(150) — FI	s	
6/78	9:00	Film(120) — FI	f	

Date	Time	Title (min. if not 30) — Type	Action	From/To
8/78	8:00	Bob Newhart — SC	c	
8/78	8:30	Film(150) — FI	f	
9/78	8:00	Rhoda — SC	m	Fr:n-8
9/78	8:30	Good Times — SC	m	Fr:m-8:30
9/78	9:00	The American Girls(60) — AD	d	
9/78	10:00	Dallas(60) — SL	m	Fr:n-10-4/78
11/78	9:00	The American Girls(60) — AD	c	
11/78	10:00	Dallas(60) — SL	m	To:n-10
12/78	8:00	Rhoda — SC	c	
12/78	8:30	Good Times — SC	m	To:w-8:30-5/79
12/78	9:00	Film(120) — FI	s	
1/79	8:00	White Shadow(60) — DR	m	Fr:m-8
2/79	8:00	White Shadow(60) — DR	m	To:m-8
3/79	8:00	Bad News Bears — SC	d	
3/79	8:30	Billy — SC	m	Fr:m-8
5/79	8:30	Billy — SC	c	
6/79	8:30	Stockard Channing in Just Friends — SC	m	Fr:n-9:30
8/79	8:30	Stockard Channing in Just Friends — SC	c	
8/79	9:00	Film(120) — FI	f	
9/79	8:00	Bad News Bears — SC	m	To:s-8:30
9/79	8:00	Working Stiffs — SC	d	
9/79	8:30	Bad News Bears — SC	m	Fr:s-8
9/79	9:00	Big Shamus, Little Shamus(60) — CD	d	
9/79	10:00	Paris(60) — CD	d	
10/79	8:00	Working Stiffs — SC	c	
10/79	8:30	Bad News Bears — SC	m	To:s-8-6/80
10/79	9:00	Big Shamus, Little Shamus(60) CD	c	
10/79	10:00	Paris(60) — CD	m	To:t-10-12/79
11/79	9:00	Film(120) — FI	s	
1/80	8:00	Chisholms(60) — WE	m	Fr:r-8-4/79
2/80	9:00	Film(120) — FI	f	
3/80	8:00	Chisholms(60) — WE	c	
3/80	8:00	Tim Conway(60) — CV	d	
3/80	9:00	Hawaii Five-O(60) — CD	m	Fr:t-9-1/80
3/80	10:00	Hagen(60) — CD	d	
4/80	9:00	Hawaii Five-O(60) — CD	c	
4/80	10:00	Hagen(60) — CD	m	To:r-10
5/80	8:00	Tim Conway(60) — CV	m	To:s-8:30-8/80
5/80	9:00	Film(120) — FI	s	
6/80	8:00	Bad News Bears — SC	m	Fr:s-8:30-10/79
6/80	8:00	Bad News Bears — SC	m	To:s-8:30
6/80	8:30	Stockard Channing — SC	m	Fr:m-8:30-4/80
6/80	8:30	Stockard Channing — SC	c	
7/80	8:00	Universe(60) — SI	d	
7/80	8:30	Bad News Bears — SC	m	Fr:s-8
7/80	8:30	Bad News Bears — SC	c	

Date	Time	Title (min. if not 30) — Type	Action	From/To
8/80	8:00	That's My Line(60) — CV	d	
8/80	8:00	That's My Line(60) — CV	m	To:t-8-2/81
8/80	8:00	Universe(60) — SI	m	To:t-8:30-6/81
8/80	8:00	WKRP in Cincinnati — SC	m	Fr:m-8:30
8/80	8:30	Tim Conway — CV	m	Fr:s-8-5/80
9/80	8:00	Tim Conway — CV	m	Fr:s-8:30
9/80	8:00	WKRP in Cincinnati — SC	m	To:m-9:30
9/80	8:30	Tim Conway — CV	m	To:s-8
10/80	8:00	Tim Conway — CV	m	To:s-8:30
11/80	8:00	WKRP in Cincinnati — SC	m	Fr:m-8:30
11/80	8:30	Tim Conway — CV	m	Fr:s-8
11/80	9:00	Film(120) — FI	f	
12/80	9:00	Freebie and the Bean(60) — CD	d	
12/80	10:00	Secrets of Midland Heights(60) — SL	d	
1/81	9:00	Freebie and the Bean(60) — CD	c	
1/81	10:00	Secrets of Midland Heights(60) — SL	c	
2/81	9:00	Concrete Cowboys(60) — AD	m	Fr:s-10
2/81	9:00	Flo — SC	m	Fr:m-8
2/81	9:00	Flo — SC	m	To:s-8:30
2/81	9:30	Ladies Man — SC	m	Fr:m-8:30
2/81	9:30	Ladies Man — SC	c	
2/81	10:00	Concrete Cowboys(60) — AD	d	
2/81	10:00	Concrete Cowboys(60) — AD	m	To:s-9
2/81	10:00	Riker(60) — CD	d	
3/81	8:30	Flo — SC	m	Fr:s-9
3/81	8:30	Tim Conway — CV	m	To:m-8:30-6/81
3/81	9:00	Concrete Cowboys(60) — AD	c	
4/81	9:00	That's My Line(60) — CV	m	Fr:t-8
4/81	9:00	That's My Line(60) — CV	c	
4/81	9:00	Film(120) — FI	s	
4/81	10:00	Riker(60) — CD	c	
5/81	8:00	Enos(60) — CO	m	Fr:w-8
5/81	8:00	WKRP in Cincinnati — SC	m	To:m-8
5/81	8:30	Flo — SC	m	To:t-8:30
9/81	8:00	Enos(60) — CO	c	
9/81	8:00	Walt Disney(60) — KV	m	Fr:n-7(n)
1/83	8:00	Bring 'Em Back Alive(60) — AD	m	Fr:t-8
1/83	8:00	Walt Disney(60) — KV	m	To:t-8
2/83	8:00	Bring 'Em Back Alive(60) — AD	m	To:t-8-5/83
2/83	8:00	Wizards and Warriors(60) — AD	d	
5/83	8:00	Wizards and Warriors(60) — AD	c	
6/83	8:00	Seven Brides for Seven Brothers (60) — AD	m	Fr:w-8-3/83
7/83	8:00	Seven Brides for Seven Brothers (60) — AD	c	
7/83	8:00	Walt Disney(60) — KV	m	Fr:t-8-2/83
9/83	8:00	Walt Disney(60) — KV	c	
10/83	8:00	Cutter to Houston(60) — MD	d	
12/83	8:00	Cutter to Houston(60) — MD	c	
1/84	8:00	Whiz Kids(60) — AD	m	Fr:w-8

Date	Time	Title (min. if not 30) — Type	Action	From/To
1/84	9:00	Airwolf(60) — SD	d	
1/84	9:00	Film(120) — FI	f	
1/84	10:00	Mickey Spillane's Mike Hammer(60) — CD	d	
4/84	9:00	Airwolf(60) — SD	m	To:s-8-8/84
4/84	9:00	Film(120) — FI	s	
4/84	10:00	Mickey Spillane's Mike Hammer(60) — CD	m	To:r-10-8/84
6/84	8:00	Mama Malone — SC	m	Fr:w-8:30-4/84
6/84	8:00	Whiz Kids(60) — AD	c	
7/84	8:00	Mama Malone — SC	c	
8/84	8:00	Airwolf(60) — SD	m	Fr:s-9
9/84	9:00	Mickey Spillane's Mike Hammer(60) — CD	m	Fr:r-10
9/84	9:00	Film(120) — FI	f	
9/84	10:00	Cover Up(60) — SD	d	
1/85	8:00	Airwolf(60) — SD	m	To:s-9
1/85	8:00	Otherworld(60) — SF	d	
1/85	9:00	Airwolf(60) — SD	m	Fr:s-8
1/85	9:00	Mickey Spillane's Mike Hammer(60) — CD	m	To:s-10-5/85
3/85	8:00	Otherworld(60) — SF	c	
4/85	8:00	Charles in Charge — SC	m	Fr:w-8
4/85	8:00	Charles in Charge — SC	m	To:w-8-6/85
4/85	8:30	E/R — SC	m	Fr:w-8:30
4/85	8:30	E/R — SC	m	To:w-8:30-6/85
4/85	10:00	Cover Up(60) — SD	m	To:s-8
5/85	8:00	Cover Up(60) — SD	m	Fr:s-10
5/85	10:00	Mickey Spillane's Mike Hammer(60) — CD	m	Fr:s-9-1/85
7/85	8:00	Airwolf(60) — SD	m	Fr:s-9
7/85	8:00	Cover Up(60) — SD	c	
7/85	9:00	Airwolf(60) — SD	m	To:s-8
7/85	9:00	Film(120) — FI	s	
7/85	10:00	Mickey Spillane's Mike Hammer(60) — CD	m	To:t-9-4/86
3/86	8:00	Airwolf(60) — SD	m	To:s-9
4/86	8:00	Crazy Like a Fox(60) — CO	m	Fr:w-9
4/86	9:00	Airwolf(60) — SD	m	Fr:s-8
4/86	9:00	Film(120) — FI	f	
4/86	10:00	Magnum, P.I.(60) — CD	m	Fr:r-8
6/86	8:00	Crazy Like a Fox(60) — CO	m	To:r-8
6/86	9:00	Airwolf(60) — SD	m	To:w-9
6/86	9:00	Film(120) — FI	s	
6/86	10:00	Magnum, P.I.(60) — CD	m	To:t-9
8/86	8:00	Melba — SC	m	Fr:t-8-2/86
9/86	8:00	Melba — SC	c	
9/86	8:00	Downtown(60) — CD	d	
9/86	9:00	Mickey Spillane's Mike Hammer(60) — CD	m	Fr:t-9-5/86

Date	Time	Title (min. if not 30) — Type	Action	From/To
9/86	9:00	Film(120) — FI	f	
9/86	10:00	Twilight Zone(60) — FA	m	Fr:f-8
10/86	9:00	Mickey Spillane's Mike Hammer(60) — CD	m	To:w-8
10/86	9:00	Film(120) — FI	s	
10/86	10:00	Twilight Zone(60) — FA	m	To:r-8-12/86
11/86	8:00	Downtown(60) — CD	m	To:t-8
11/86	8:00	Downtown(60) — CD	m	Fr:t-8
11/86	8:00	Wizard(60) — AD	m	Fr:t-8
11/86	8:00	Wizard(60) — AD	m	To:t-8
12/86	8:00	Downtown(60) — CD	c	
1/87	8:00	Outlaws(60) — CD	d	
4/87	8:00	Mickey Spillane's Mike Hammer(60) — CD	m*	Fr:w-8
4/87	8:00	Mickey Spillane's Mike Hammer(60) — CD	m*	To:w-8
5/87	8:00	Outlaws(60) — CD	c	
6/87	8:00	Film(120) — FI	s	
6/87	9:00	Film(120) — FI	f	
6/87	10:00	West 57th(60) — NM	m#	Fr:t-8
8/87	8:00	Film(120) — FI	f	
9/87	8:00	My Sister Sam — SC	m	Fr:m-8:30
9/87	8:30	Everything's Relative — SC	d	
9/87	9:00	Leg Work(60) — CD	d	
11/87	8:00	Film(120) — FI	s	
11/87	8:00	My Sister Sam — SC	m	To:t-8:30-3/88
11/87	8:30	Everything's Relative — SC	c	
11/87	9:00	Leg Work(60) — CD	c	
12/87	8:00	Film(120) — FI	f	
1/88	8:00	High Mountain Rangers(60) — AD	d	
1/88	9:00	Houston Knights(60) — CD	m	Fr:t-8
2/88	9:00	Houston Knights(60) — CD	m	To:t-8-4/88
3/88	9:00	Tour of Duty(60) — WD	m#	Fr:r-8
7/88	8:00	Kate & Allie — SC	m	Fr:m-8
7/88	8:00	High Mountain Rangers(60) — AD	c	
7/88	8:30	Frank's Place — SC	m	Fr:t-9:30-4/88
8/88	8:00	Kate & Allie — SC	c	
8/88	8:30	Frank's Place — SC	c	

	7:00	7:30	8:00	8:30	9:00	9:30	10:00	10:30
9/48								
10				TV Screen Magazine				
11			THE EYES HAVE IT		Basketball			
12		TV Screen Magazine						
1/49				SATURDAY NT JAMBOREE				
2			Saturday Night Jamboree	EDDIE CONDON				
3								
4					Who Said That	Saturday Night Jamboree	GARROWAY AT LARGE	
5		Maggie Privat Wire	TV Screen Magazine					
6								
7								
8		You Are An Artist	US MARINE BAND / Meet Your Congress	For Your Pleasure		Eddie Condon	3 Flames	
9		Nature of Things	Meet Your Congress	Mixed Doubles		Meet the Press		
10								
11			TWENTY QUESTIONS	CHICAG JAZZ / STUDS PLACE				
12								
1/50	CHILDREN'S SKETCH BOOK		SATURDAY SQUARE		Mary Kay & Johnny	AROUND THE TOWN	Meet the Press	
2	AMERICAN FORUM OF THE AIR	Mary Kay & Johnny	JACK CARTER		YOUR SHOW OF SHOWS			
3		WAITING FOR THE BREAK						
4		Life Begins at 80					FAYE EMERSN	
5								
6							Harness Racing	
7								
8		One Man's Family						
9								
10	HANK MCCUNE						Your Hit Parade	
11								
12								
1/51	VICTOR BORGE							
2								
3								
4								

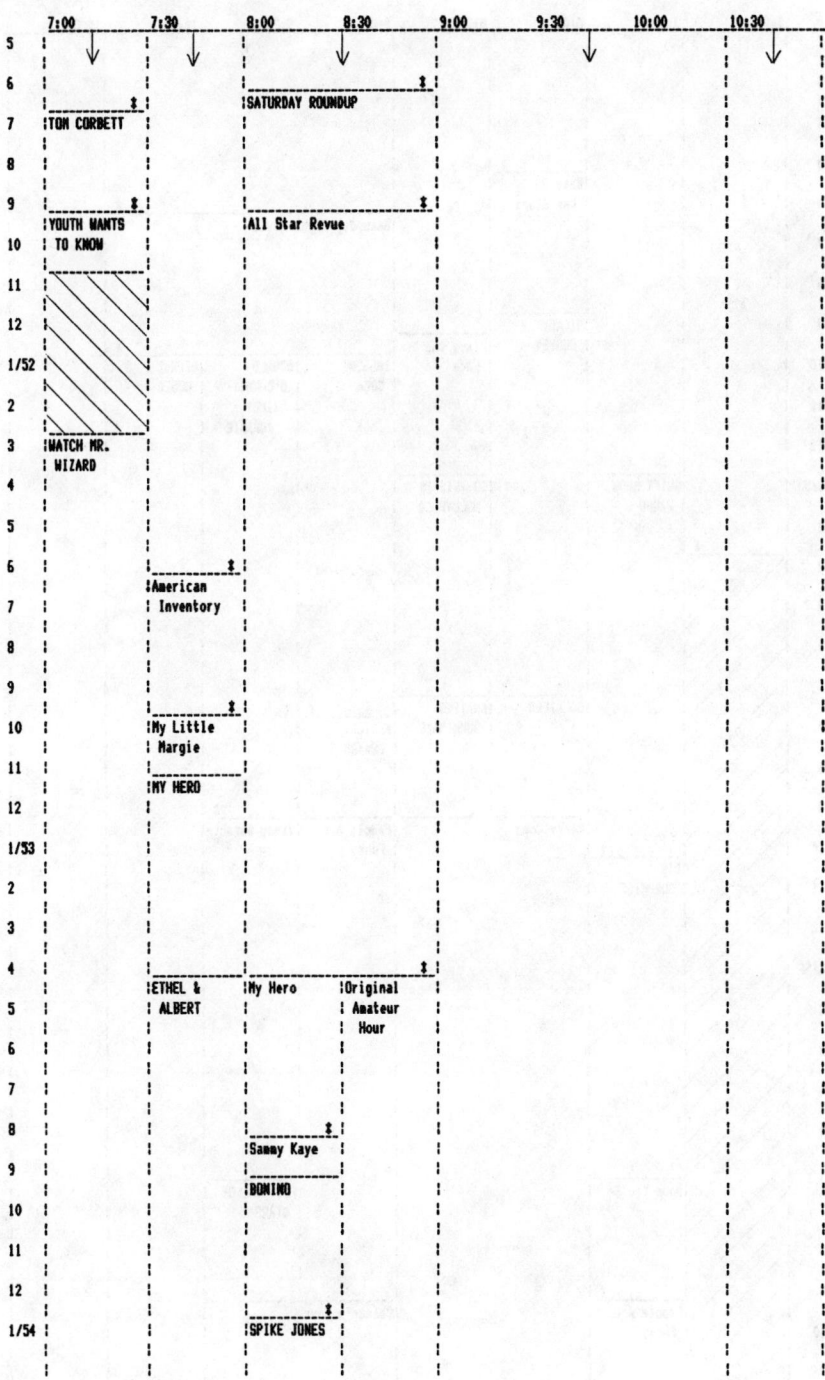

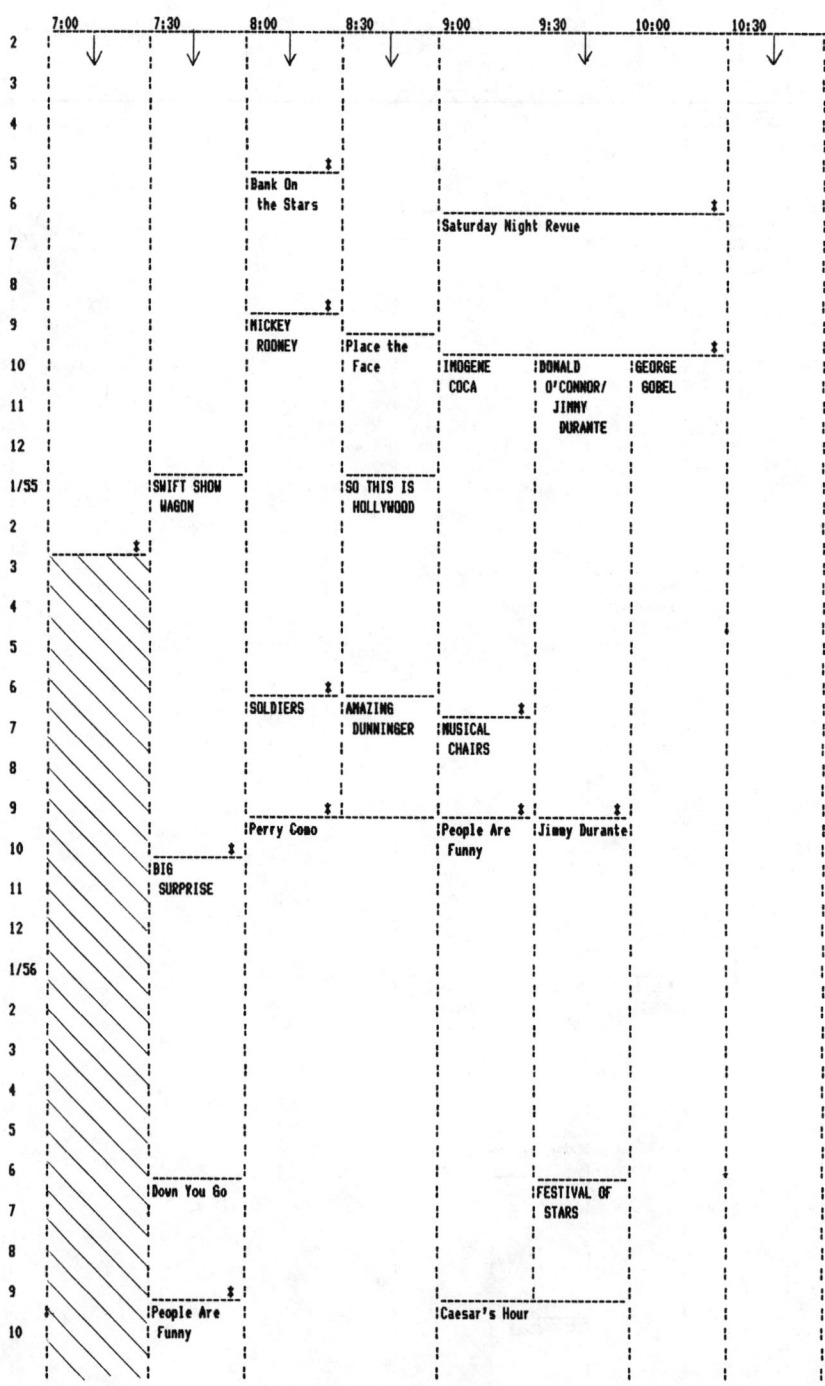

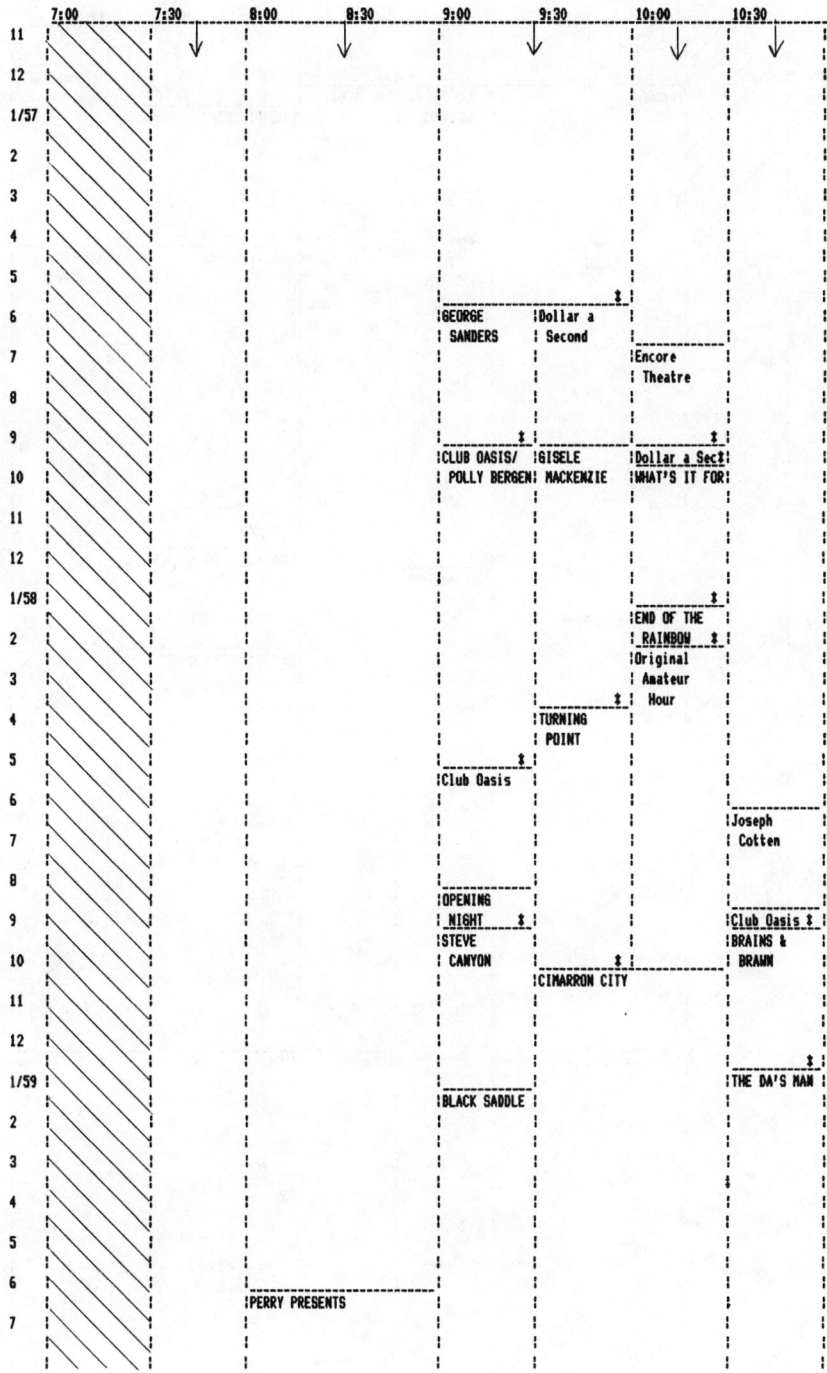

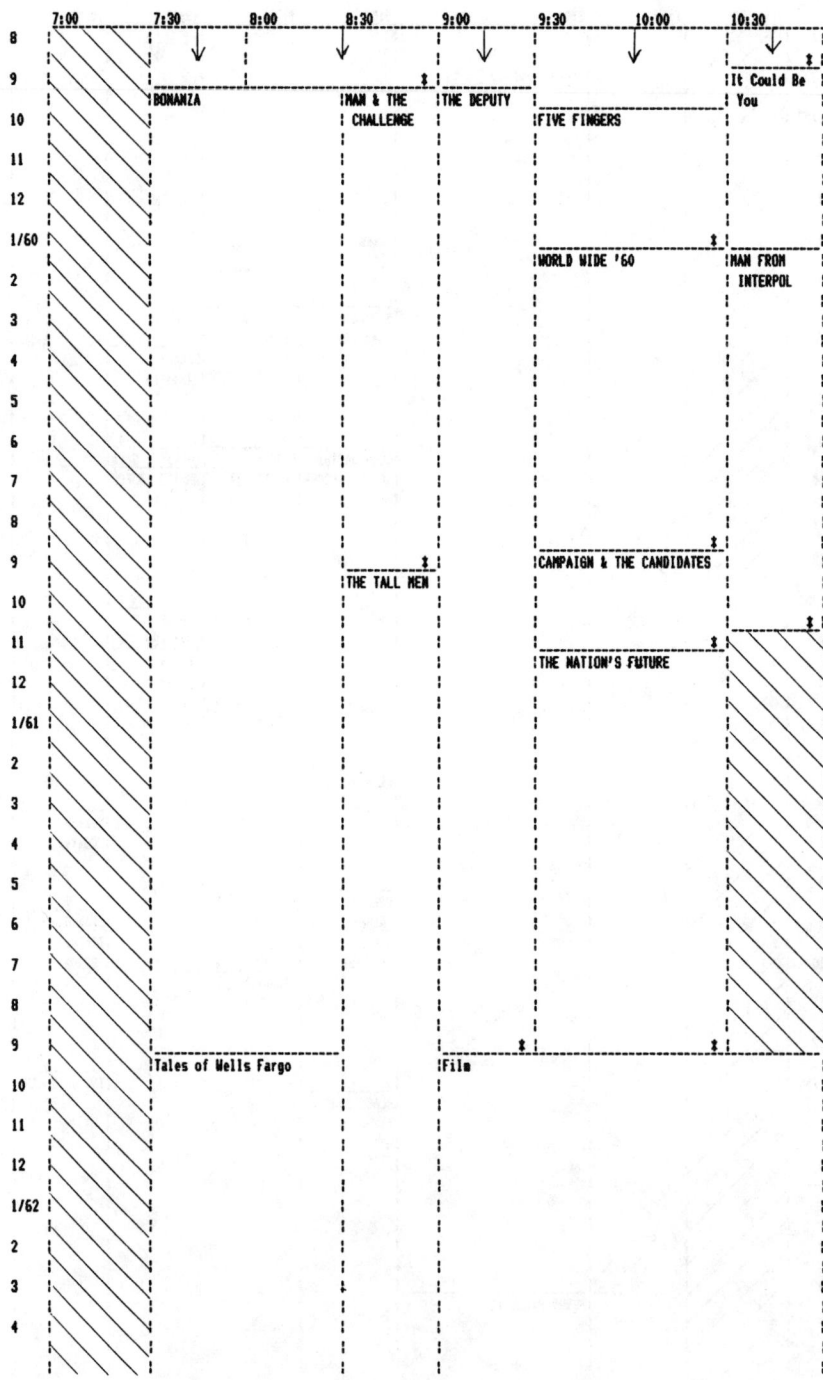

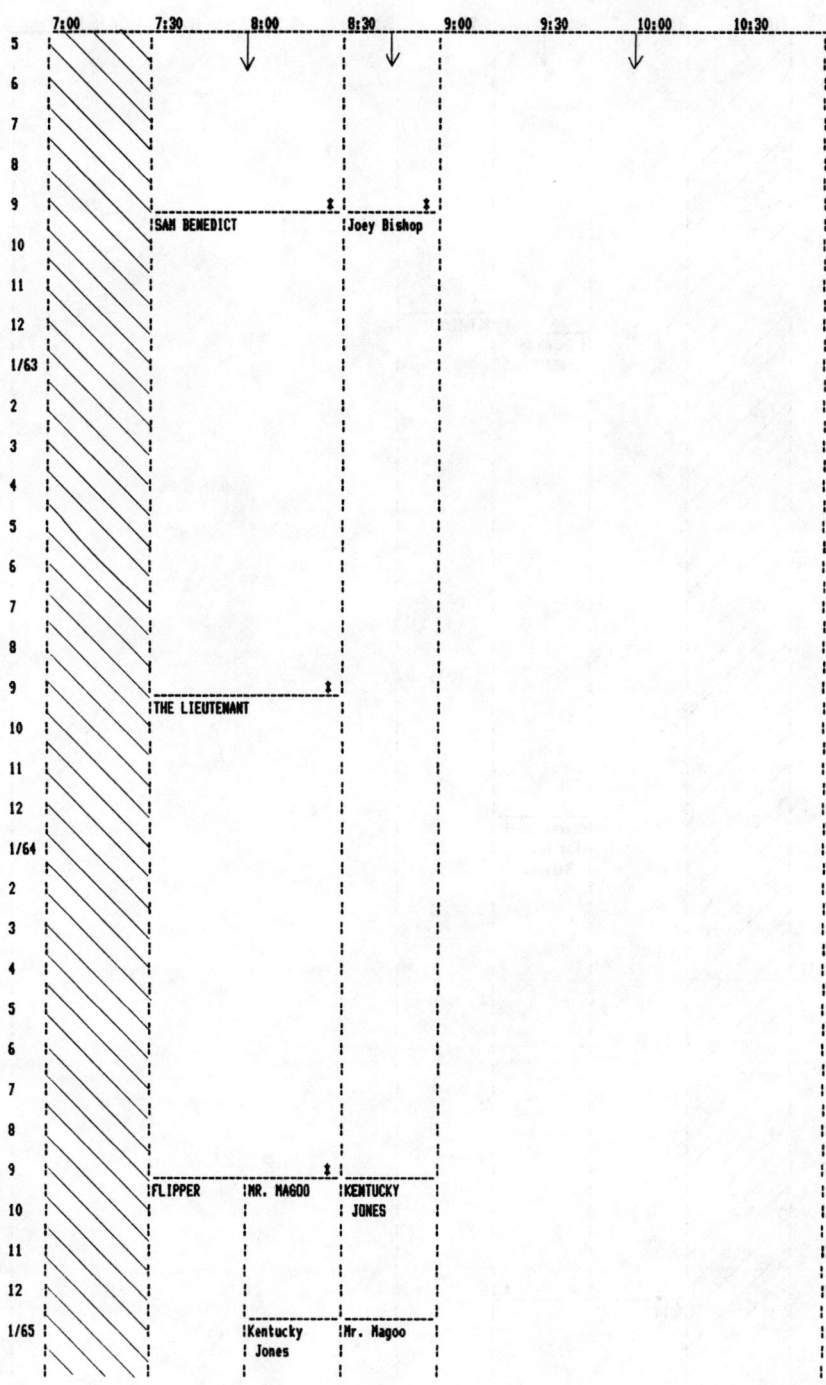

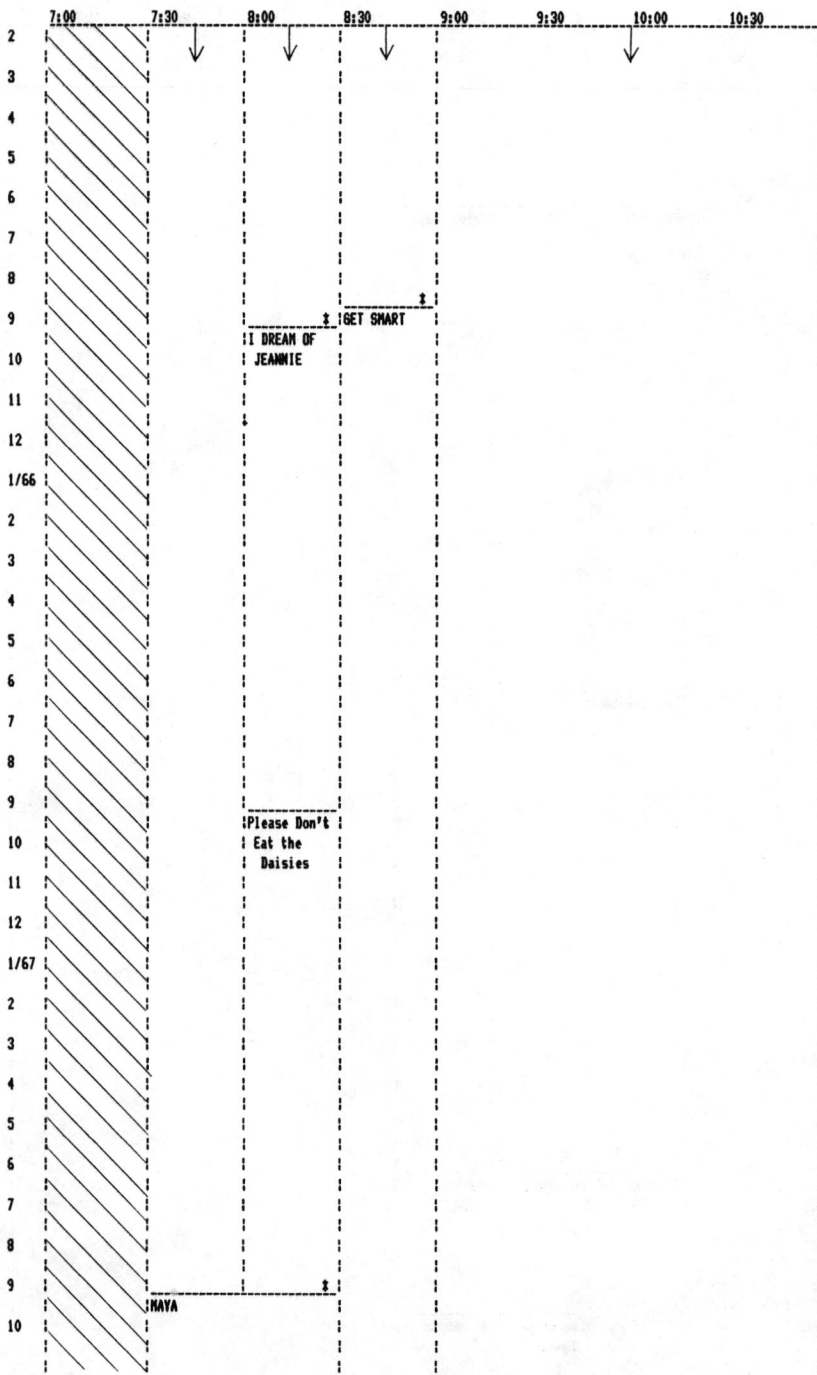

I DREAM OF
JEANNIE

GET SMART

Please Don't
Eat the
Daisies

MAYA

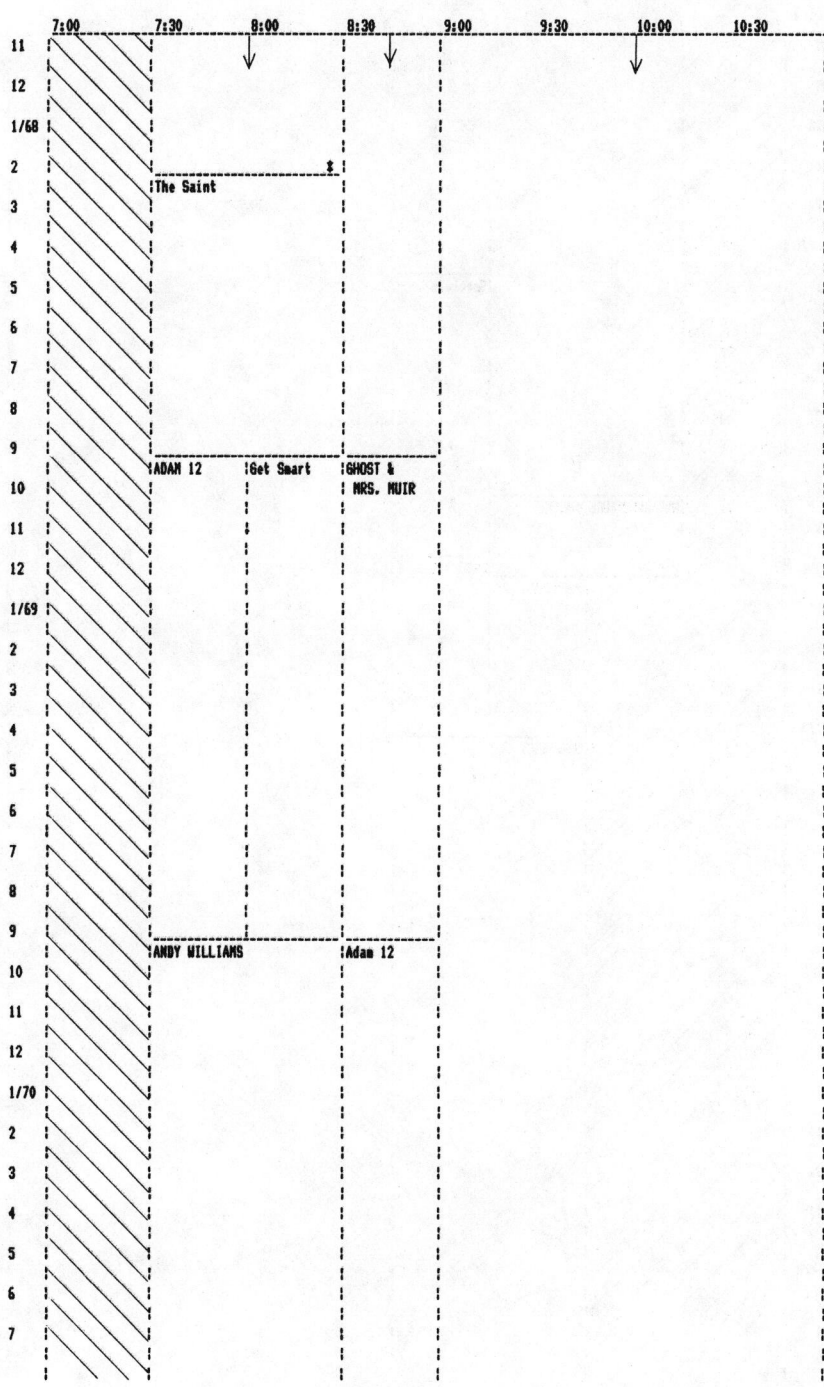

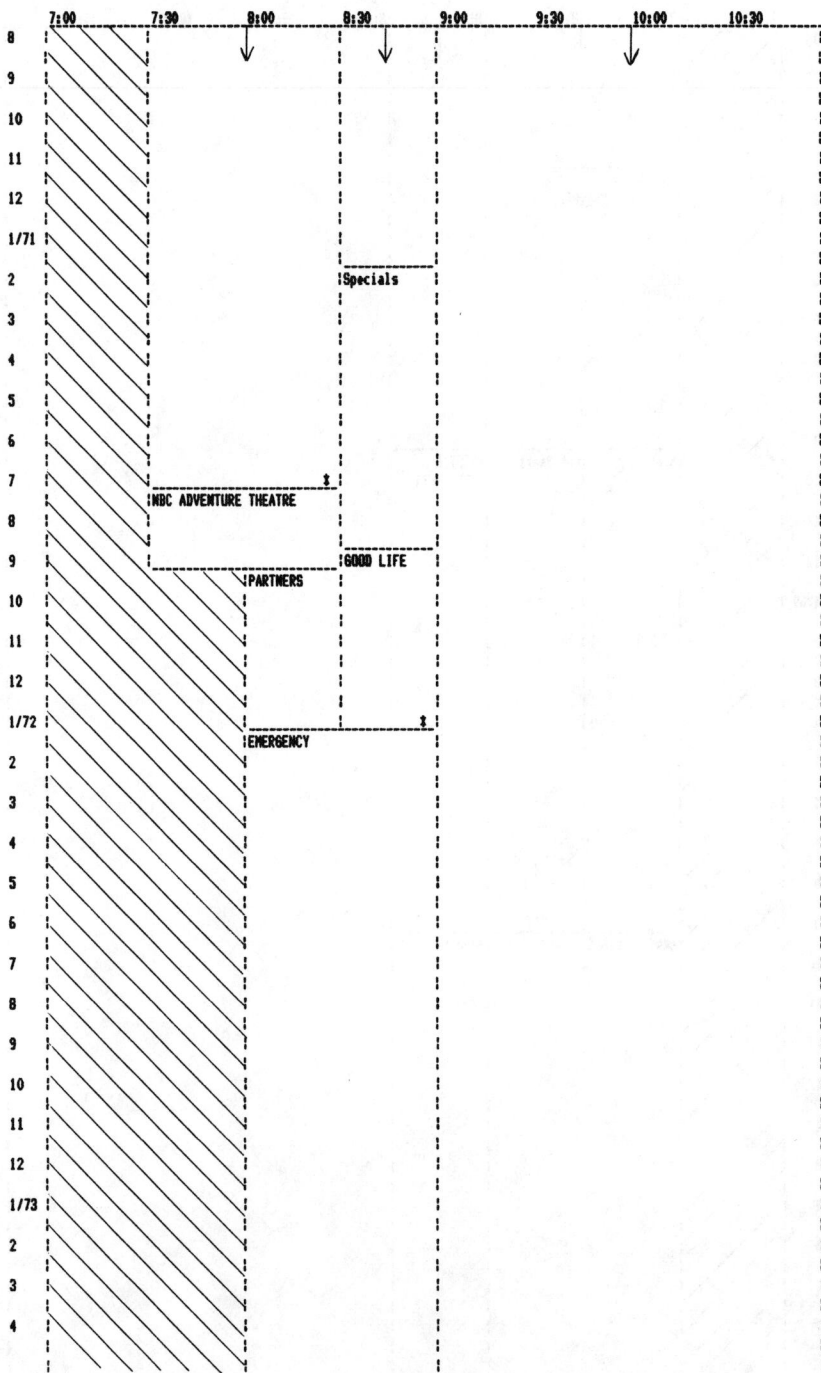

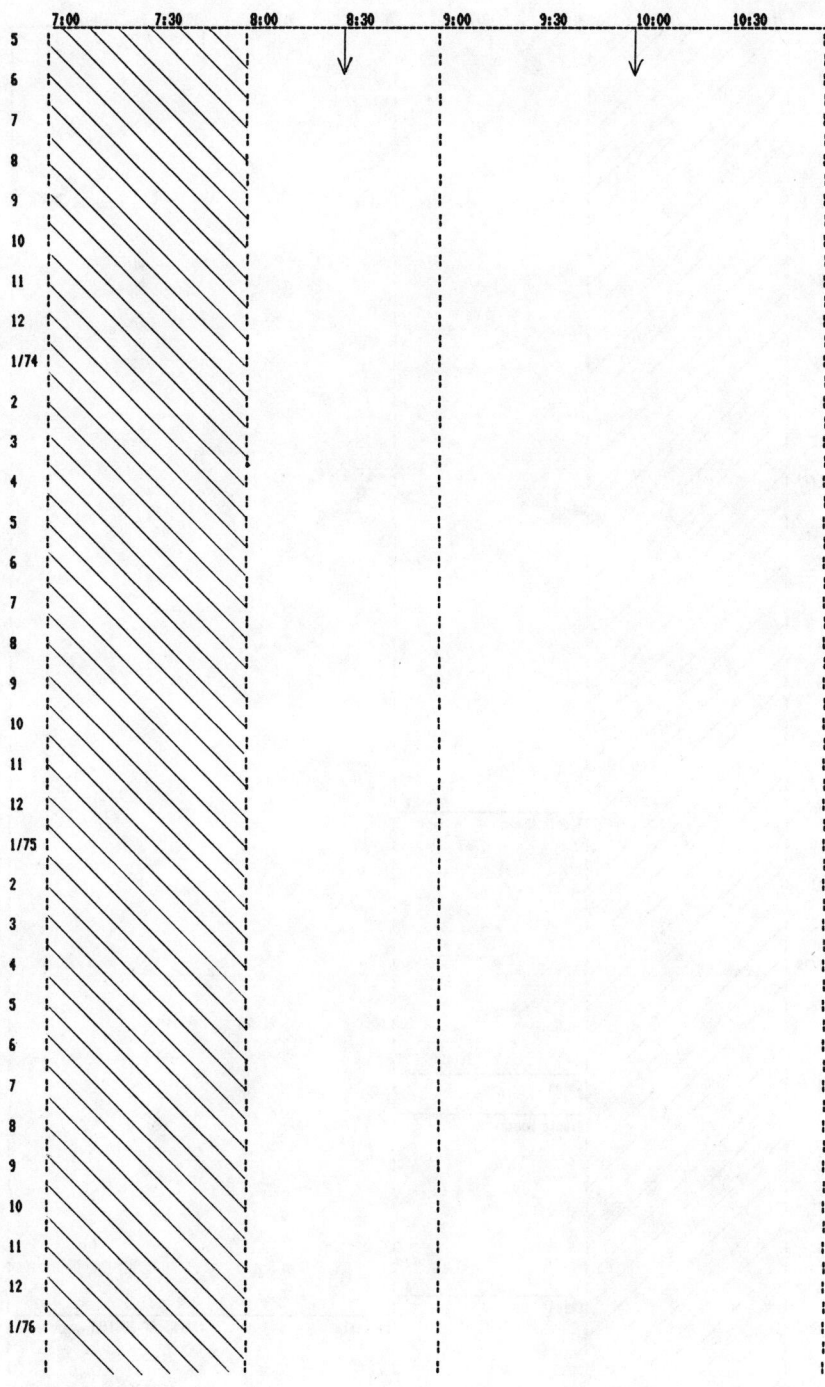

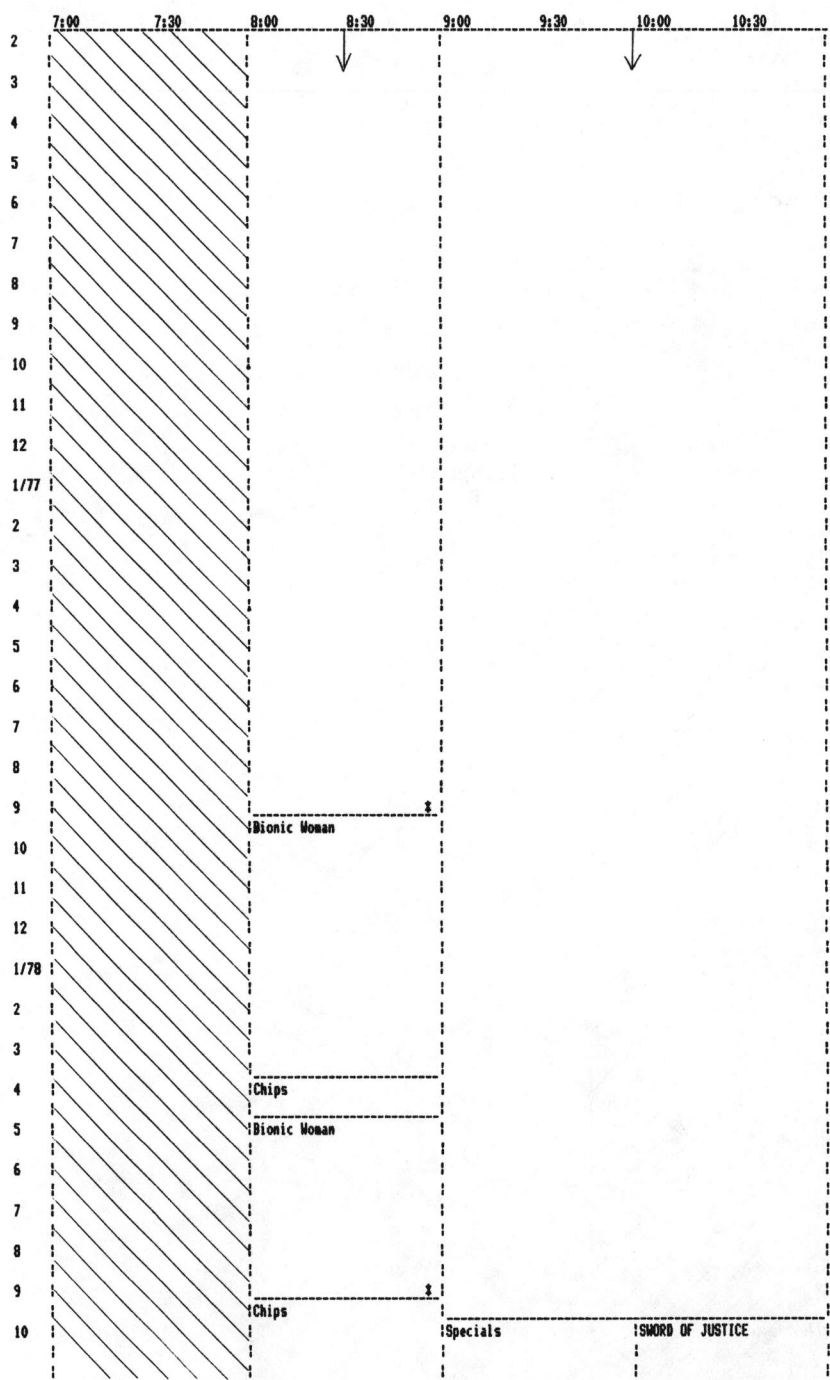

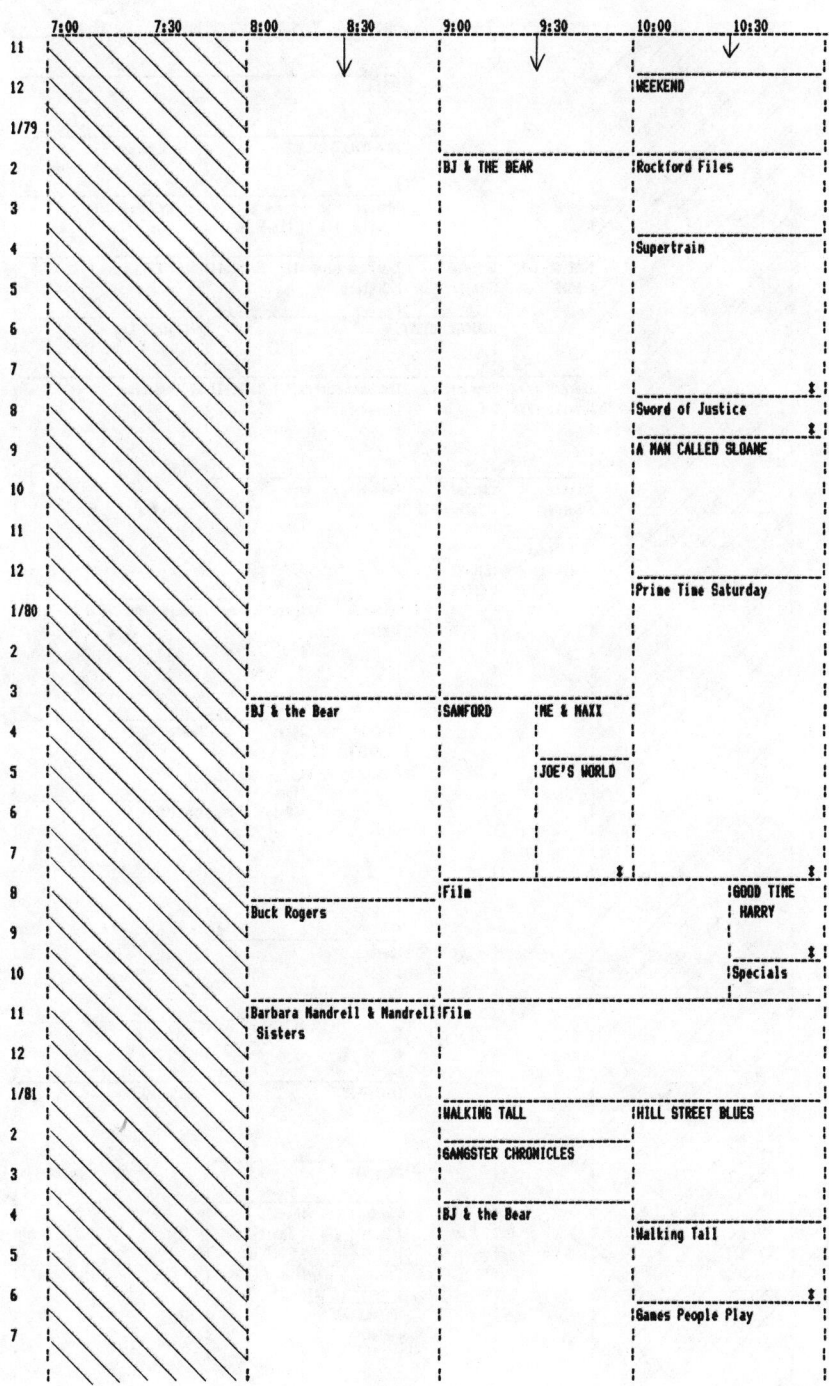

	7:00	7:30	8:00	8:30	9:00	9:30	10:00	10:30
11				↓		↓		↓
12							WEEKEND	
1/79								
2					BJ & THE BEAR		Rockford Files	
3								
4							Supertrain	
5								
6								
7								
8							Sword of Justice	
9							A MAN CALLED SLOANE	
10								
11								
12							Prime Time Saturday	
1/80								
2								
3								
			BJ & the Bear		SANFORD	ME & MAXX		
4								
5						JOE'S WORLD		
6								
7								
8					Film			GOOD TIME
			Buck Rogers					HARRY
9								
10								Specials
11			Barbara Mandrell & Mandrell Sisters		Film			
12								
1/81								
					WALKING TALL		HILL STREET BLUES	
2								
					GANGSTER CHRONICLES			
3								
					BJ & the Bear			
4							Walking Tall	
5								
6								
							Games People Play	
7								

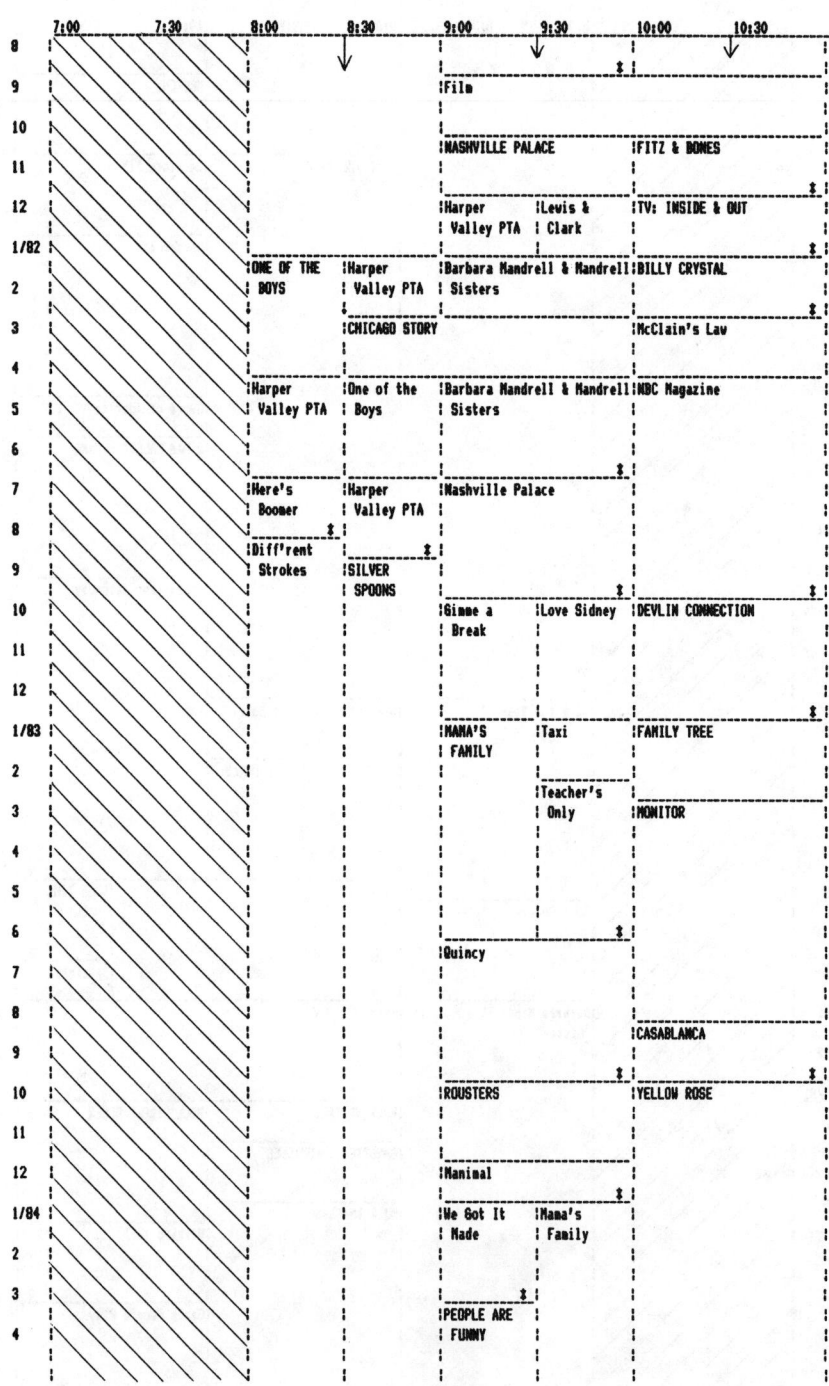

	7:00	7:30	8:00	8:30	9:00	9:30	10:00	10:30
8								
9					Film			
10					NASHVILLE PALACE		FITZ & BONES	
11								
12					Harper	Lewis &	TV: INSIDE & OUT	
					Valley PTA	Clark		
1/82			ONE OF THE	Harper	Barbara Mandrell & Mandrell		BILLY CRYSTAL	
2			BOYS	Valley PTA	Sisters			
3				CHICAGO STORY			McClain's Law	
4								
			Harper	One of the	Barbara Mandrell & Mandrell		NBC Magazine	
5			Valley PTA	Boys	Sisters			
6								
7			Here's	Harper	Nashville Palace			
			Boomer	Valley PTA				
8								
			Diff'rent					
9			Strokes	SILVER				
				SPOONS				
10					Gimme a	Love Sidney	DEVLIN CONNECTION	
					Break			
11								
12								
1/83					MAMA'S	Taxi	FAMILY TREE	
					FAMILY			
2						Teacher's		
3						Only	MONITOR	
4								
5								
6								
7					Quincy			
8							CASABLANCA	
9								
10					ROUSTERS		YELLOW ROSE	
11								
12					Manimal			
1/84					We Got It	Mama's		
2					Made	Family		
3								
4					PEOPLE ARE			
					FUNNY			

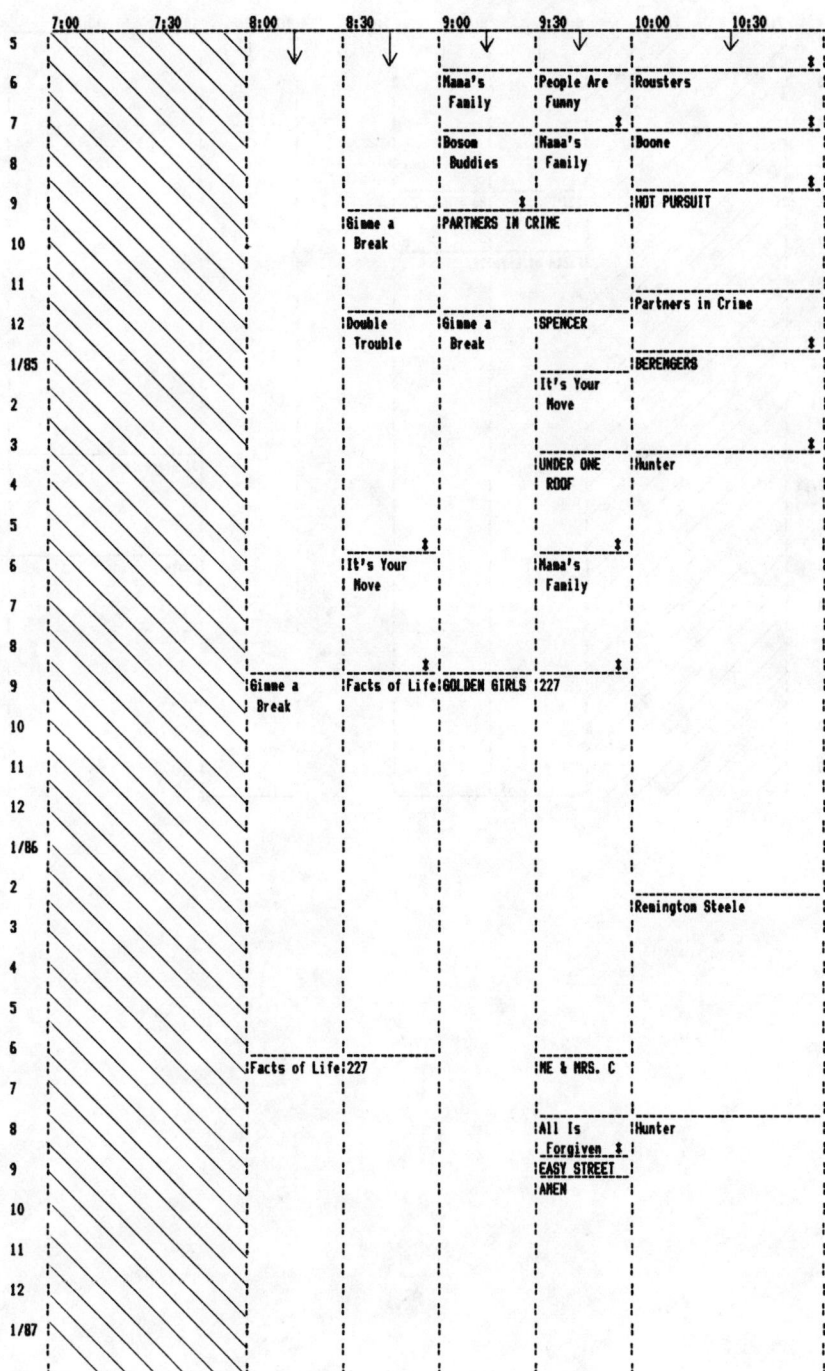

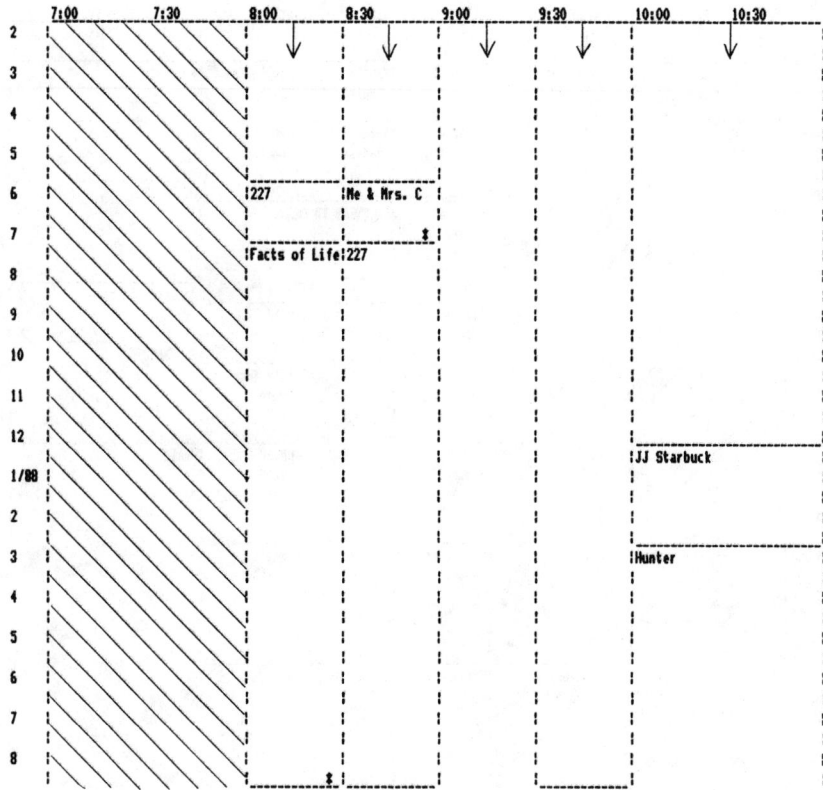

Date	Time	Title (min. if not 30) — Type	Action	From/To
10/48	8:30	Television Screen Magazine — VS	m	Fr:t-var
11/48	8:00	The Eyes Have It — QU	d	
11/48	9:00	Basketball(120) — SP	s	
12/48	7:30	Television Screen Magazine — VS	m	Fr:s-8:30
12/48	8:30	Saturday Night Jamboree — MU	d	
12/48	8:30	Television Screen Magazine — VS	m	To:s-7:30
1/49	8:00	The Eyes Have It — QU	c	
1/49	8:00	Saturday Night Jamboree — MU	m	Fr:s-8
1/49	8:30	Eddie Condon — MU	d	
1/49	8:30	Saturday Night Jamboree — MU	m	To:s-8
3/49	9:00	Basketball(120) — SP	f	
4/49	7:30	Television Screen Magazine — VS	m	To:s-8
4/49	8:00	Saturday Night Jamboree — MU	m	To:s-9:30
4/49	9:00	Who Said That? — QU	m	Fr:n-10:30
4/49	9:30	Saturday Night Jamboree — MU	m	Fr:s-8
4/49	10:00	Garroway at Large — VY	d	
5/49	7:30	Maggi's Private Wire(15) — IV	d	
5/49	8:00	Television Screen Magazine — VS	m	Fr:s-7:30
7/49	7:30	Maggi's Private Wire(15) — IV	c	
7/49	7:30	You Are an Artist(15) — IS	m	Fr:r-7:30-4/49
7/49	8:00	Television Screen Magazine — VS	c	
7/49	8:00	U.S. Marine Band — MU	d	
7/49	8:30	Eddie Condon — MU	m	To:s-9:30
7/49	8:30	For Your Pleasure — MU	m	Fr:w-8-9/48
7/49	9:30	Eddie Condon — MU	m	Fr:s-8:30
7/49	9:30	Saturday Night Jamboree — MU	c	
7/49	10:00	Garroway at Large — VY	m	To:n-10
7/49	10:00	Three Flames — MU	m	Fr:m-10
8/49	8:00	Meet Your Congress — DB	m	Fr:f-9
8/49	8:00	U.S. Marine Band — MU	c	
8/49	10:00	Three Flames — MU	c	
9/49	7:30	Nature of Things(15) — IS	m	Fr:m-9:30
9/49	7:30	You Are an Artist(15) — IS	c	
9/49	8:30	For Your Pleasure — MU	c	
9/49	8:30	Mixed Doubles — DR	m	Fr:f-9
9/49	9:30	Eddie Condon — MU	m	To:s-7:30-5/50(c)
9/49	9:30	Meet the Press — IV	m	Fr:m-10
10/49	8:00	Meet Your Congress — DB	c	
10/49	8:30	Mixed Doubles — DR	c	
11/49	8:00	Twenty Questions — QU	d	
11/49	8:30	Chicago Jazz(15) — MU	d	
11/49	8:45	Stud's Place(15) — VY	d	
12/49	8:00	Twenty Questions — QU	m	To:f-8-3/50(a)
12/49	8:30	Chicago Jazz(15) — MU	c	
12/49	8:45	Stud's Place(15) — VY	m	To:r-8-4/50
12/49	9:00	Who Said That? — QU	m	To:m-10:30
12/49	9:30	Meet the Press — IV	m	To:s-10
1/50	7:00	Children's Sketch Book — KV	d	
1/50	8:00	Saturday Square(60) — VY	d	
1/50	9:00	Mary Kay and Johnny — SC	m	Fr:r-8:30

Date	Time	Title (min. if not 30) – Type	Action	From/To
1/50	9:30	Around the Town – DO	d	
1/50	10:00	Meet the Press – IV	m	Fr:s-9:30
2/50	7:00	American Forum of the Air – DS	d	
2/50	7:00	Children's Sketch Book – KV	c	
2/50	7:30	Mary Kay and Johnny – SC	m	Fr:s-9
2/50	7:30	Nature of Things(15) – IS	m	To:w-8:15-6/50
2/50	8:00	Jack Carter(60) – VY	d	
2/50	8:00	Saturday Square(60) – VY	c	
2/50	9:00	Mary Kay and Johnny – SC	m	To:s-7:30
2/50	9:00	Your Show of Shows(90) – CV	d	
2/50	9:30	Around the Town – DO	c	
2/50	10:00	Meet the Press – IV	m	To:n-var-10/50
3/50	7:30	Mary Kay and Johnny – SC	c	
3/50	7:30	Waiting for the Break – VY	d	
4/50	7:30	Life Begins at Eighty – DS	m	Fr:f-9:30
4/50	7:30	Waiting for the Break – VY	c	
4/50	10:30	Faye Emerson(15) – IV	d	
5/50	10:30	Faye Emerson(15) – IV	m	To:w-8
6/50	8:00	Hawkins Falls, Population 6200(60) – CO	d*	
6/50	10:30	Harness Racing – SP	s	
7/50	7:30	Life Begins at Eighty – DS	m	To:f-9
7/50	7:30	One Man's Family – SL	m	Fr:r-8:30-5/50
8/50	8:00	Hawkins Falls, Population 6200(60) – CO	m*	To:r-8:30
9/50	7:00	American Forum of the Air – DS	m	To:n-10-7/51
9/50	7:00	Hank McCune – SC	d	
9/50	10:30	Harness Racing – SP	f	
10/50	10:30	Your Hit Parade – MU	m	Fr:m-9-8/50
12/50	7:00	Hank McCune – SC	c	
1/51	7:00	Victor Borge – CV	d	
6/51	7:00	Victor Borge – CV	c	
6/51	8:00	Jack Carter(60) – VY	c	
6/51	8:00	Saturday Roundup(60) – WA	d	
6/51	9:00	Midwestern Hayride(60) – MV	d*	
6/51	10:00	Doodles Weaver – CV	d*	
7/51	7:00	Tom Corbett, Space Cadet – KV	d	
7/51	7:30	Art Ford – QU	d*	
7/51	10:30	Manhunt – DA	d*	
9/51	7:00	Tom Corbett, Space Cadet – KV	c	
9/51	7:00	Youth Wants to Know – DS	d	
9/51	7:30	Art Ford – QU	c*	
9/51	8:00	All Star Revue(60) – CV	m	Fr:w-8-7/51
9/51	8:00	Saturday Roundup(60) – WA	c	
9/51	9:00	Midwestern Hayride(60) – MV	m*	To:t-8-6/52
9/51	10:00	Doodles Weaver – CV	c*	
9/51	10:30	Manhunt – DA	m*	To:s-10:30-7/52
10/51	7:00	Youth Wants to Know – DS	m	To:w-8:30-6/52
3/52	7:00	Watch Mr. Wizard – IS	d	
6/52	7:30	American Inventory – DD	m	Fr:n-8-8/51

Date	Time	Title (min. if not 30) — Type	Action	From/To
6/52	7:30	One Man's Family — SL	c	
6/52	9:00	Blind Date — QU	m*	Fr:r-9:30-9/51(a)
6/52	9:30	Saturday Night Dance Party(60) — VY	d*	
7/52	9:00	Blind Date — QU	m*	To:t-8-5/53(d)
7/52	9:00	Saturday Night Dance Party(90) — VY	m*	Fr:s-9:30
7/52	9:30	Saturday Night Dance Party(60) — VY	m*	To:s-9
7/52	10:30	Manhunt — DA	m*	Fr:s-10:30-9/51
8/52	9:00	Saturday Night Dance Party(90) — VY	c*	
8/52	10:30	Manhunt — DA	c*	
9/52	7:30	American Inventory — DD	c	
10/52	7:30	My Little Margie — SC	m	Fr:m-9(c)
11/52	7:30	My Hero — SC	d	
11/52	7:30	My Little Margie — SC	m	To:r-10-1/53(c)
4/53	7:30	Ethel and Albert — SC	d	
4/53	7:30	My Hero — SC	m	To:s-8
4/53	8:00	All Star Revue(60) — CV	c	
4/53	8:00	My Hero — SC	m	Fr:s-7:30
4/53	8:30	Original Amateur Hour — TA	m	Fr:t-10-9/52
6/53	9:00	Saturday Night Revue(90) — VY	d*	
6/53	10:30	Private Secretary — SC	m*	Fr:n-7:30(c)
7/53	7:30	My Son Jeep — SC	d*	
8/53	7:30	My Son Jeep — SC	c*	
8/53	8:00	My Hero — SC	c	
8/53	8:00	Sammy Kaye — MV	m	Fr:s-7-7/52(c)
9/53	8:00	Bonino — SC	d	
9/53	8:00	Sammy Kaye — MV	m	To:r-9-8/54(a)
9/53	9:00	Saturday Night Revue(90) — VY	m*	To:s-9-6/54
9/53	10:30	Private Secretary — SC	m*	To:n-7:30(c)
12/53	8:00	Bonino — SC	c	
1/54	8:00	Spike Jones — CV	d	
5/54	8:00	Bank on the Stars — QU	m	Fr:s-9:30-8/53(c)
5/54	8:00	Spike Jones — CV	c	
6/54	9:00	Saturday Night Revue(90) — VY	m	Fr:s-9-9/53
6/54	9:00	Your Show of Shows(90) — CV	c	
6/54	10:30	Private Secretary — SC	m*	Fr:n-7:30(c)
7/54	7:30	Youth Wants to Know — DS	m*	Fr:w-8:30-9/52
8/54	7:30	Youth Wants to Know — DS	c*	
8/54	8:00	Bank on the Stars — QU	c	
9/54	8:00	Mickey Rooney — SC	d	
9/54	8:30	Original Amateur Hour — TA	m	To:n-9:30-10/55(a)
9/54	8:30	Place the Face — QU	m	Fr:r-10:30(c)
9/54	9:00	Saturday Night Revue(90) — VY	c	
9/54	10:30	Private Secretary — SC	m*	To:n-7:30(c)
10/54	9:00	Imogene Coca — CV	d	
10/54	9:30	Donald O'Connor — SC	d	
10/54	9:30	Jimmy Durante — CV	d	

Date	*Time*	*Title (min. if not 30) — Type*	*Action*	*From/To*
10/54	10:00	George Gobel — CV	d	
12/54	7:30	Ethel and Albert — SC	m	To:m-9:30-6/55(c)
12/54	8:30	Place the Face — QU	m	To:t-8-6/55
1/55	8:30	So This Is Hollywood — SC	d	
1/55	7:30	Swift Show Wagon — VY	d	
2/55	7:00	Watch Mr. Wizard — IS	c	
6/55	8:00	Mickey Rooney — SC	c	
6/55	8:00	The Soldiers — SC	d	
6/55	8:30	Amazing Dunninger — QU	d	
6/55	8:30	So This Is Hollywood — SC	m	To:f-10:30
6/55	9:00	Imogene Coca — CV	c	
6/55	10:30	Your Play Time — DA	m*	Fr:n-7:30-9/54(c)
7/55	9:00	Musical Chairs — QU	d	
7/55	10:00	And Here's the Show — CV	d*	
9/55	8:00	The Soldiers — SC	c	
9/55	8:30	Amazing Dunninger — QU	m	To:w-8:30-5/56(a)
9/55	9:00	Musical Chairs — QU	c	
9/55	9:00	People Are Funny — QU	m	Fr:n-7
9/55	9:30	Donald O'Connor — SC	c	
9/55	10:00	And Here's the Show — CV	c*	
9/55	10:30	Your Play Time — DA	c*	
10/55	7:30	Big Surprise — QU	d	
10/55	7:30	Swift Show Wagon — VY	c	
6/56	7:30	Big Surprise — QU	m	To:t-8-9/56
6/56	7:30	Down You Go — QU	m	Fr:r-9:30(a)
6/56	8:00	Patti Page(60) — MV	d*	
6/56	9:30	Festival of Stars — DA	d	
6/56	9:30	Jimmy Durante — CV	c	
6/56	10:30	Adventure Theatre — AA	d*	
7/56	8:00	Julius LaRosa(60) — MV	d*	
7/56	8:00	Patti Page(60) — MV	c*	
7/56	10:00	Encore Theatre — DA	d*	
8/56	8:00	Julius LaRosa(60) — MV	m*	To:s-8-6/57
8/56	8:00	Tony Bennett(60) — MV	d*	
9/56	7:30	Down You Go — QU	c	
9/56	7:30	People Are Funny — QU	m	Fr:s-9
9/56	8:00	Tony Bennett(60) — MV	c*	
9/56	9:00	Caesar's Hour(60) — CV	m	Fr:m-8-6/56
9/56	9:00	People Are Funny — QU	m	To:s-7:30
9/56	9:30	Festival of Stars — DA	m	To:t-8-7/57
9/56	10:00	Encore Theatre — DA	m*	To:s-10-7/57
9/56	10:30	Adventure Theatre — AA	m*	To:s-10:30-6/57
5/57	9:00	Caesar's Hour(60) — CV	c	
6/57	8:00	Julius LaRosa(60) — MV	m*	Fr:s-8-8/56
6/57	9:00	George Sanders Mystery Theatre — MA	d	
6/57	9:30	Dollar a Second — QU	m	Fr:f-9-9/56(a)
6/57	10:00	George Gobel — CV	m	To:t-8-9/57
6/57	10:30	Adventure Theatre — AA	m*	Fr:s-10:30-9/56
7/57	10:00	Encore Theatre — DA	m	Fr:s-10-9/56

Date	Time	Title (min. if not 30) — Type	Action	From/To
8/57	10:30	Adventure Theatre — AA	c*	
9/57	8:00	Julius LaRosa(60) — MV	c*	
9/57	9:00	Club Oasis — VY	d	
9/57	9:00	George Sanders Mystery Theatre — MA	c	
9/57	9:00	Polly Bergen — MV	d	
9/57	9:30	Dollar a Second — QU	m	To:s-10
9/57	9:30	Gisele Mackenzie — MV	d	
9/57	10:00	Dollar a Second — QU	m	Fr:s-9:30
9/57	10:00	Dollar a Second — QU	c	
9/57	10:00	Encore Theatre — DA	c	
10/57	10:00	What's It For — QU	d	
1/58	10:00	End of the Rainbow — QU	d	
1/58	10:00	What's It For — QU	c	
2/58	10:00	End of the Rainbow — QU	c	
2/58	10:00	Original Amateur Hour — TA	m	Fr:n-7-12/57
3/58	9:30	Gisele Mackenzie — MV	c	
4/58	9:30	Turning Point — DA	d	
5/58	9:00	Polly Bergen — MV	c	
6/58	8:00	Bob Crosby(60) — MV	d*	
6/58	10:30	Joseph Cotten — DA	m	Fr:t-9-9/57
6/58	10:30	Your Hit Parade — MU	m	To:f-7:30-10/58(c)
8/58	9:00	Club Oasis — VY	m	To:s-10:30
8/58	9:00	Opening Night — DA	d	
8/58	10:30	Joseph Cotten — DA	m	To:m-9:30-7/59(c)
9/58	8:00	Bob Crosby(60) — MV	c*	
9/58	9:00	Opening Night — DA	c	
9/58	9:00	Steve Canyon — AD	d	
9/58	10:30	Brains and Brawn — QU	d	
9/58	10:30	Club Oasis — VY	m	Fr:s-9
9/58	10:30	Club Oasis — VY	c	
10/58	9:30	Cimarron City(60) — WE	d	
10/58	9:30	Turning Point — DA	c	
10/58	10:00	Original Amateur Hour — TA	m	To:f-8:30-5/59(c)
12/58	10:30	Brains and Brawn — QU	c	
1/59	9:00	Black Saddle — WE	d	
1/59	9:00	Steve Canyon — AD	m	To:r-8
1/59	10:30	The D.A.'s Man — CD	d	
6/59	8:00	Perry Presents(60) — MV	d	
8/59	10:30	The D.A.'s Man — CD	c	
9/59	7:30	Bonanza(60) — WE	d	
9/59	7:30	People Are Funny — QU	m	To:f-7:30
9/59	8:00	Perry Presents(60) — MV	c	
9/59	8:30	Man and the Challenge — AD	d	
9/59	9:00	Black Saddle — WE	m	To:f-10:30
9/59	9:00	The Deputy — WE	d	
9/59	9:30	Cimarron City(60) — WE	m	To:f-7:30-6/60
9/59	10:30	It Could Be You — QU	m	Fr:r-8:30-3/59
10/59	9:30	Five Fingers(60) — SD	d	
1/60	9:30	Five Fingers(60) — SD	c	

Date	Time	Title (min. if not 30) — Type	Action	From/To
1/60	9:30	World Wide '60(60) — DO	d	
1/60	10:30	It Could Be You — QU	m	To:w-10-6/61
1/60	10:30	Man from Interpol — CD	d	
8/60	9:30	World Wide '60(60) — DO	c	
9/60	8:30	Man and the Challenge — AD	c	
9/60	8:30	The Tall Man — WE	d	
9/60	9:30	The Campaign and the Candidates (60) — NA	d	
10/60	10:30	Man from Interpol — CD	c	
11/60	9:30	The Campaign and the Candidates (60) — NA	c	
11/60	9:30	The Nation's Future(60) — DB	d	
9/61	7:30	Bonanza(60) — WE	m	To:n-9
9/61	7:30	Tales of Wells Fargo(60) — WE	m	Fr:m-8:30
9/61	9:00	The Deputy — WE	c	
9/61	9:00	Film(120) — FI	s	
9/61	9:30	The Nation's Future(60) — DB	c	
9/62	7:30	Sam Benedict(60) — LD	d	
9/62	7:30	Tales of Wells Fargo(60) — WE	c	
9/62	8:30	Joey Bishop — SC	m	Fr:w-8:30-6/62
9/62	8:30	The Tall Man — WE	c	
9/63	7:30	The Lieutenant(60) — DR	d	
9/63	7:30	Sam Benedict(60) — LD	c	
9/64	7:30	Flipper — AD	d	
9/64	7:30	The Lieutenant(60) — DR	c	
9/64	8:00	Mr. Magoo — KV	d	
9/64	8:30	Joey Bishop — SC	m	To:n-9:30
9/64	8:30	Kentucky Jones — SC	d	
12/64	8:00	Mr. Magoo — KV	m	To:s-8:30
12/64	8:30	Kentucky Jones — SC	m	To:s-8
1/65	8:00	Kentucky Jones — SC	m	Fr:s-8:30
1/65	8:30	Mr. Magoo — KV	m	Fr:s-8
8/65	8:30	Mr. Magoo — KV	c	
9/65	8:00	I Dream of Jeannie — SC	d	
9/65	8:00	Kentucky Jones — SC	c	
9/65	8:30	Get Smart — SC	d	
9/66	8:00	I Dream of Jeannie — SC	m	To:m-8
9/66	8:00	Please Don't Eat the Daisies — SC	m	Fr:t-8
9/67	7:30	Flipper — AD	m	To:n-7-6/88
9/67	7:30	Maya(60) — AD	d	
9/67	8:00	Please Don't Eat the Daisies — SC	c	
2/68	7:30	Maya(60) — AD	c	
2/68	7:30	The Saint(60) — MY	m	Fr:n-10-9/67
9/68	7:30	Adam 12 — CD	d	
9/68	8:00	The Saint(60) — MY	m	To:f-10-4/69
9/68	8:00	Get Smart — SC	m	Fr:s-8:30
9/68	8:30	Get Smart — SC	m	To:s-8
9/68	8:30	Ghost and Mrs. Muir — SC	d	
9/69	7:30	Adam 12 — CD	m	To:s-8:30
9/69	7:30	Andy Williams(60) — MV	m	Fr:n-10-5/67

Date	Time	Title (min. if not 30) — Type	Action	From/To
9/69	8:00	Get Smart — SC	m	To:f-7:30(c)
9/69	8:30	Adam 12 — CD	m	Fr:s-7:30
9/69	8:30	Ghost and Mrs. Muir — SC	m	To:f-8:30(a)
6/70	7:30	Ray Stevens(60) — CV	d*	
8/70	7:30	Ray Stevens(60) — CV	c*	
8/70	7:30	NBC Comedy Playhouse(60) — CA	m*	Fr:m-9-9/68
9/70	7:30	NBC Comedy Playhouse(60) — CA	c*	
1/71	8:30	Adam 12 — CD	m	To:r-9:30
7/71	7:30	Andy Williams(60) — MV	c	
7/71	7:30	NBC Adventure Theatre(60) — AA	d	
9/71	7:30	NBC Adventure Theatre(60) — AA	m	To:r-8-6/72
9/71	8:00	The Partners — SC	d	
9/71	8:30	The Good Life — SC	d	
1/72	8:00	Emergency(60) — MD	d	
1/72	8:00	The Partners — SC	m	To:f-8-7/72
1/72	8:30	The Good Life — SC	c	
7/72	8:00	NBC Comedy Theatre(60) — CA	m*	Fr:m-8-8/71
9/72	8:00	NBC Comedy Theatre(60) — CA	c*	
9/77	8:00	Bionic Woman(60) — AD	m	Fr:w-8-5/77(a)
9/77	8:00	Emergency(60) — MD	c	
3/78	8:00	Bionic Woman(60) — AD	m	To:s-8-5/78
4/78	8:00	Chips(60) — CD	m	Fr:r-8
4/78	8:00	Chips(60) — CD	m	To:r-8
5/78	8:00	Bionic Woman(60) — AD	m	Fr:s-8-3/78
9/78	8:00	Bionic Woman(60) — AD	c	
9/78	8:00	Chips(60) — CD	m	Fr:r-8
9/78	9:00	Film(120) — FI	f	
10/78	10:00	Sword of Justice(60) — AD	d	
11/78	10:00	Sword of Justice(60) — AD	m	To:n-10
12/78	10:00	Weekend(60) — NM	d	
1/79	10:00	Weekend(60) — NM	m	To:n-10
2/79	9:00	B.J. and the Bear(60) — CO	d	
2/79	10:00	Rockford Files(60) — CD	m	Fr:f-9
3/79	10:00	Rockford Files(60) — CD	m	To:f-9
4/79	10:00	Supertrain(60) — DA	m	Fr:w-8
7/79	9:00	Sword of Justice(60) — AD	m*	Fr:n-10-12/78
7/79	9:00	Sword of Justice(60) — AD	m*	To:s-10
7/79	10:00	Supertrain(60) — DA	c	
8/79	10:00	Sword of Justice(60) — AD	m	Fr:s-9
8/79	10:00	Sword of Justice(60) — AD	c	
9/79	10:00	A Man Called Sloane(60) — SD	d	
12/79	10:00	A Man Called Sloane(60) — SD	m	To:f-10-6/80
12/79	10:00	Prime Time Saturday(60) — NM	m	Fr:n-10
3/80	8:00	B.J. and the Bear(60) — CO	m	Fr:s-9
3/80	8:00	Chips(60) — CD	m	To:n-8
3/80	9:00	B.J. and the Bear(60) — CO	m	To:s-8
3/80	9:00	Sanford — SC	d	
3/80	9:30	Me and Maxx — SC	d	
4/80	9:30	Me and Maxx — SC	m	To:f-8:30
5/80	9:30	Joe's World — SC	d	

Date	Time	Title (min. if not 30) – Type	Action	From/To
7/80	9:00	Sanford – SC	m	To:w-9:30
7/80	9:30	Joe's World – SC	c	
7/80	10:00	Prime Time Saturday(60) – NM	c	
8/80	8:00	B.J. and the Bear(60) – CO	m	To:t-9-1/81
8/80	8:00	Buck Rogers in the 25th Century (60) – SF	m	Fr:r-8
8/80	9:00	Film(90) – FI	s	
8/80	10:30	Good Time Harry – SC	d	
9/80	10:30	Good Time Harry – SC	c	
10/80	8:00	Buck Rogers in the 25th Century (60) – SF	m	To:r-8-1/81
10/80	9:00	Film(90) – FI	f	
11/80	8:00	Barbara Mandrell & Mandrell Sisters(60) – MV	m	Fr:t-10
11/80	9:00	Film(120) – FI	s	
1/81	9:00	Walking Tall(60) – CD	d	
1/81	9:00	Film(120) – FI	f	
1/81	10:00	Hill Street Blues(60) – CD	d	
2/81	9:00	Gangster Chronicles(60) – CD	d	
2/81	9:00	Walking Tall(60) – CD	m	To:t-10
3/81	9:00	Gangster Chronicles(60) – CD	m	To:f-10
4/81	9:00	B.J. and the Bear(60) – CO	m	Fr:t-9
4/81	10:00	Hill Street Blues(60) – CD	m	To:t-9
4/81	10:00	Walking Tall(60) – CD	m	Fr:t-10
6/81	10:00	Games People Play(60) – QU	m	Fr:r-8-12/80
6/81	10:00	Walking Tall(60) – CD	c	
8/81	9:00	B.J. and the Bear(60) – CO	c	
8/81	10:00	Games People Play(60) – QU	m	To:r-8
9/81	9:00	Film(120) – FI	s	
10/81	9:00	Nashville Palace(60) – MV	d	
10/81	9:00	Film(120) – FI	f	
10/81	10:00	Fitz and Bones(60) – CO	d	
11/81	9:00	Nashville Palace(60) – MV	m	To:s-9-7/82
11/81	10:00	Fitz and Bones(60) – CO	c	
12/81	9:00	Harper Valley P.T.A. – SC	m	Fr:r-8
12/81	9:30	Lewis & Clark – SC	m	Fr:r-8:30
12/81	10:00	Television: Inside and Out(60) – NM	d	
1/82	8:00	Barbara Mandrell & Mandrell Sisters(60) – MV	m	To:s-9
1/82	8:00	One of the Boys – SC	d	
1/82	8:30	Harper Valley P.T.A. – SC	m	Fr:s-8
1/82	9:00	Barbara Mandrell & Mandrell Sisters(60) – MV	m	Fr:s-8
1/82	9:00	Harper Valley P.T.A. – SC	m	To:s-8:30
1/82	9:30	Lewis & Clark – SC	m	To:f-8-7/82
1/82	10:00	Billy Crystal(60) – CV	d	
1/82	10:00	Television: Inside and Out(60) – NM	c	
2/82	8:30	Harper Valley P.T.A. – SC	m	To:s-8-4/82
2/82	9:00	Barbara Mandrell & Mandrell Sisters(60) – MV	m	To:s-9-4/82

Date	Time	Title (min. if not 30) – Type	Action	From/To
2/82	10:00	Billy Crystal(60) – CV	c	
3/82	8:30	Chicago Story(90) – DR	d	
3/82	10:00	McClain's Law(60) – CD	m	Fr:f-9
4/82	8:00	Harper Valley P.T.A. – SC	m	Fr:s-8:30-2/82
4/82	8:00	One of the Boys – SC	m	To:s-8:30
4/82	8:30	Chicago Story(90) – DR	m	To:f-8:30
4/82	8:30	One of the Boys – SC	m	Fr:s-8
4/82	9:00	Barbara Mandrell & Mandrell Sisters(60) – MV	m	Fr:s-9-2/82
4/82	10:00	McClain's Law(60) – CD	m	To:f-10
4/82	10:00	NBC Magazine(60) – NM	m	Fr:f-8
6/82	8:00	Harper Valley P.T.A. – SC	m	To:s-8:30
6/82	8:30	One of the Boys – SC	m	To:f-8-8/82
6/82	9:00	Barbara Mandrell & Mandrell Sisters(60) – MV	c	
7/82	8:00	Here's Boomer – AD	m	Fr:n-7:30-11/81
7/82	8:30	Harper Valley P.T.A. – SC	m	Fr:s-8
7/82	9:00	Nashville Palace(60) – MV	m	Fr:s-9-11/81
8/82	8:00	Diff'rent Strokes – SC	m	Fr:r-9
8/82	8:00	Here's Boomer – AD	c	
8/82	8:30	Harper Valley P.T.A. – SC	c	
9/82	8:30	Silver Spoons – SC	d	
9/82	9:00	Nashville Palace(60) – MV	c	
9/82	10:00	NBC Magazine(60) – NM	c	
10/82	9:00	Gimme a Break – SC	m	Fr:r-9
10/82	9:30	Love, Sidney – SC	m	Fr:w-9:30
10/82	10:00	Devlin Connection(60) – CD	d	
12/82	9:00	Gimme a Break – SC	m	To:r-9
12/82	9:30	Love, Sidney – SC	m	To:m-8-3/83
12/82	10:00	Devlin Connection(60) – CD	c	
1/83	9:00	Mama's Family – SC	d	
1/83	9:30	Taxi – SC	m	Fr:r-9:30
1/83	10:00	Family Tree(60) – DR	d	
2/83	9:30	Taxi – SC	m	To:w-9:30
2/83	9:30	Teachers Only – SC	m	Fr:r-9:30-9/82
2/83	10:00	Family Tree(60) – DR	m	To:w-10-7/83
3/83	10:00	Monitor(60) – NM	d	
6/83	9:00	Mama's Family – SC	m	To:r-8:30-8/83
6/83	9:00	Quincy, M.E.(60) – CD	m	Fr:w-10
6/83	9:30	Teachers Only – SC	c	
8/83	10:00	Casablanca(60) – SD	d	
8/83	10:00	Monitor(60) – NM	m	To:n-7
9/83	9:00	Quincy, M.E.(60) – CD	c	
9/83	10:00	Casablanca(60) – SD	c	
10/83	9:00	Rousters(60) – AD	d	
10/83	10:00	Yellow Rose(60) – SL	d	
11/83	9:00	Rousters(60) – AD	m	To:s-10-6/84
12/83	9:00	Manimal(60) – AD	m	Fr:f-9
12/83	9:00	Manimal(60) – AD	c	
1/84	9:00	We Got It Made – SC	m	Fr:r-9

Date	Time	Title (min. if not 30) — Type	Action	From/To
1/84	9:30	Mama's Family—SC	m	Fr:r-8:30
3/84	9:00	People Are Funny—QU	d	
3/84	9:00	We Got It Made—SC	c	
4/84	8:30	Jennifer Slept Here—SC	m*	Fr:f-8:30-12/83
5/84	8:30	Jennifer Slept Here—SC	m*	To:w-8:30-7/84
5/84	9:00	People Are Funny—QU	m	To:s-9:30
5/84	9:30	Mama's Family—SC	m	To:s-9
5/84	10:00	Yellow Rose(60)—SL	c	
6/84	9:00	Mama's Family—SC	m	Fr:s-9:30
6/84	9:30	People Are Funny—QU	m	Fr:s-9
6/84	10:00	Rousters(60)—AD	m	Fr:s-9-11/83
7/84	9:00	Bosom Buddies—SC	m	Fr:r-8:30-6/82(a)
7/84	9:00	Mama's Family—SC	m	To:s-9:30
7/84	9:30	Mama's Family—SC	m	Fr:s-9
7/84	9:30	People Are Funny—QU	c	
7/84	10:00	Boone(60)—DR	m	Fr:m-8-12/83
7/84	10:00	Rousters(60)—AD	c	
8/84	10:00	Boone(60)—DR	c	
9/84	8:30	Gimme a Break—SC	m	Fr:r-8
9/84	8:30	Silver Spoons—SC	m	To:n-7
9/84	9:00	Bosom Buddies—SC	c	
9/84	9:00	Partners in Crime(60)—CD	d	
9/84	9:30	Mama's Family—SC	m	To:s-9:30-6/85
9/84	10:00	Hot Pursuit(60)—DR	d	
11/84	8:30	Gimme a Break—SC	m	To:s-9
11/84	9:00	Partners in Crime(60)—CD	m	To:s-10
11/84	10:00	Hot Pursuit(60)—DR	m	To:f-10
11/84	10:00	Partners in Crime(60)—CD	m	Fr:s-9
12/84	8:30	Double Trouble—SC	m	Fr:w-8-9/84
12/84	9:00	Gimme a Break—SC	m	Fr:s-8:30
12/84	9:30	Spencer—SC	d	
12/84	10:00	Partners in Crime(60)—CD	c	
1/85	9:30	Spencer—SC	m	To:f-8:30-6/85
1/85	9:30	It's Your Move—SC	m	Fr:w-9:30
1/85	10:00	Berengers(60)—SL	d	
3/85	9:30	Under One Roof—SC	d	
3/85	9:30	It's Your Move—SC	m	To:s-8:30-6/85
3/85	10:00	Hunter(60)—CD	m	Fr:f-9-1/85
3/85	10:00	Berengers(60)—SL	c	
5/85	8:30	Double Trouble—SC	c	
5/85	9:30	Under One Roof—SC	c	
6/85	8:30	It's Your Move—SC	m	Fr:s-9:30-3/85
6/85	9:30	Mama's Family—SC	m	Fr:s-9:30-9/84
8/85	8:00	Diff'rent Strokes—SC	m	To:f-9(a)
8/85	8:30	It's Your Move—SC	c	
8/85	9:00	Gimme a Break—SC	m	To:s-8
8/85	9:30	Mama's Family—SC	c	
9/85	8:00	Gimme a Break—SC	m	Fr:s-9
9/85	8:30	Facts of Life—SC	m	Fr:w-9
9/85	9:00	Golden Girls—SC	d#	

Date	Time	Title (min. if not 30) — Type	Action	From/To
9/85	9:30	227 — SC	d	
2/86	10:00	Hunter(60) — CD	m	To:t-9
2/86	10:00	Remington Steele(60) — CD	m	Fr:t-10
3/86	9:30	All Is Forgiven — SC	m*	Fr:r-9:30
4/86	9:30	All Is Forgiven — SC	m*	To:r-9:30
6/86	8:00	Gimme a Break — SC	m	To:w-9
6/86	8:00	Facts of Life — SC	m	Fr:s-8:30
6/86	8:30	Facts of Life — SC	m	To:s-8
6/86	8:30	227 — SC	m	Fr:s-9:30
6/86	9:30	Me & Mrs. C — SC	d	
6/86	9:30	227 — SC	m	To:s-8:30
7/86	9:30	Me & Mrs. C — SC	m	To:s-9:30-4/87
7/86	10:00	Remington Steele(60) — CD	m	To:t-10-2/87
8/86	9:30	All Is Forgiven — SC	m	Fr:r-9:30
8/86	9:30	All Is Forgiven — SC	c	
8/86	10:00	Hunter(60) — CD	m	Fr:t-9
9/86	9:30	Easy Street — SC	d	
9/86	9:30	Easy Street — SC	m	To:n-8
9/86	9:30	Amen — SC	d	
4/87	8:30	Sweet Surrender — SC	d*	
4/87	9:30	Me & Mrs. C — SC	m*	Fr:s-9:30-7/86
5/87	8:00	Facts of Life — SC	m	To:w-9
5/87	8:30	Sweet Surrender — SC	m*	To:w-9:30-7/87
5/87	8:30	227 — SC	m	To:s-8
5/87	9:30	Me & Mrs. C — SC	m*	To:s-8:30
6/87	8:00	227 — SC	m	Fr:s-8:30
6/87	8:30	Me & Mrs. C — SC	m	Fr:s-9:30
7/87	8:00	Facts of Life — SC	m	Fr:w-9
7/87	8:00	227 — SC	m	To:s-8:30
7/87	8:30	Me & Mrs. C — SC	c	
7/87	8:30	227 — SC	m	Fr:s-8
12/87	10:00	Hunter(60) — CD	m	To:t-9
12/87	10:00	JJ Starbuck(60) — CD	m	Fr:t-9
2/88	10:00	JJ Starbuck(60) — CD	m	To:t-9-6/88
3/88	10:00	Hunter(60) — CD	m#	Fr:t-9
8/88	8:00	Facts of Life — SC	c	
8/88	8:30	227 — SC	m	To:s-8
8/88	9:30	Amen — SC	m	To:s-8:30

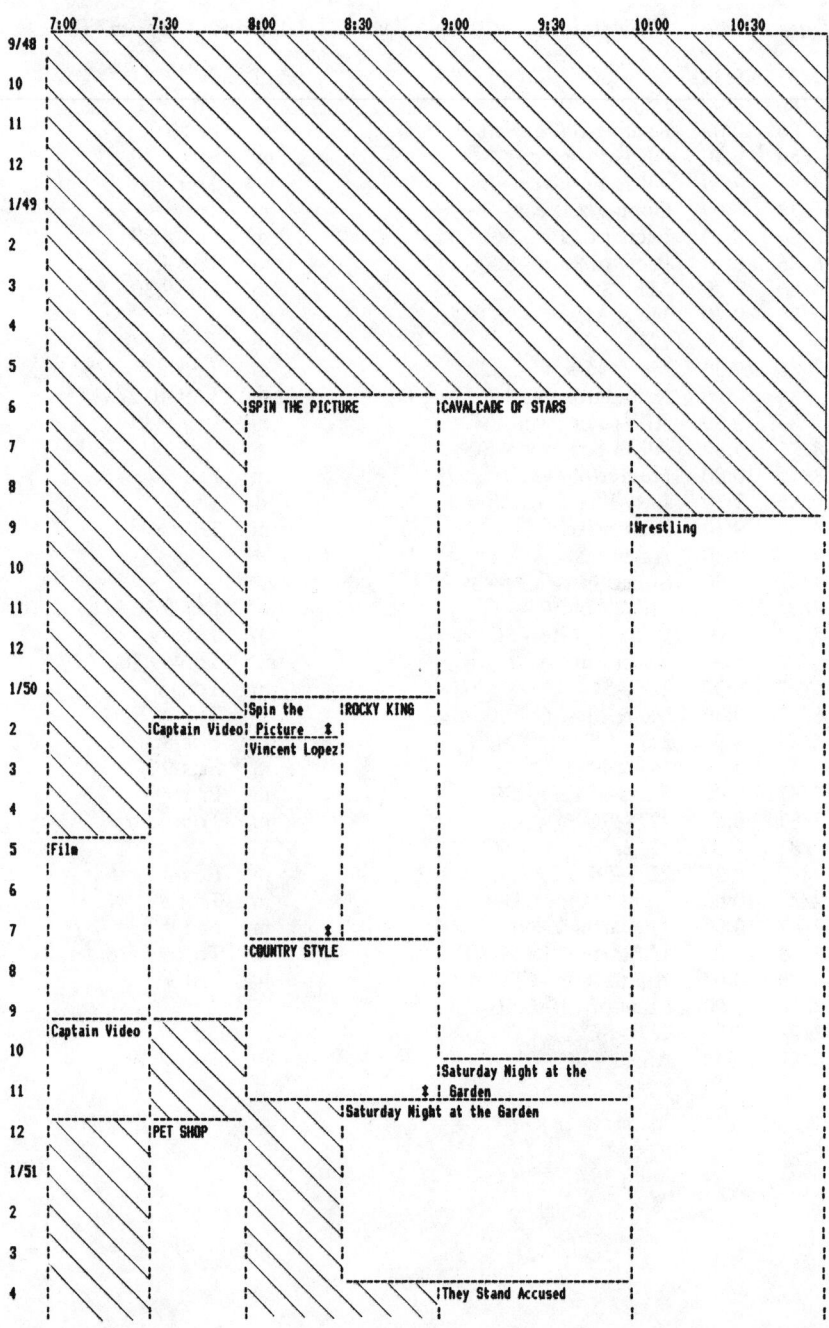

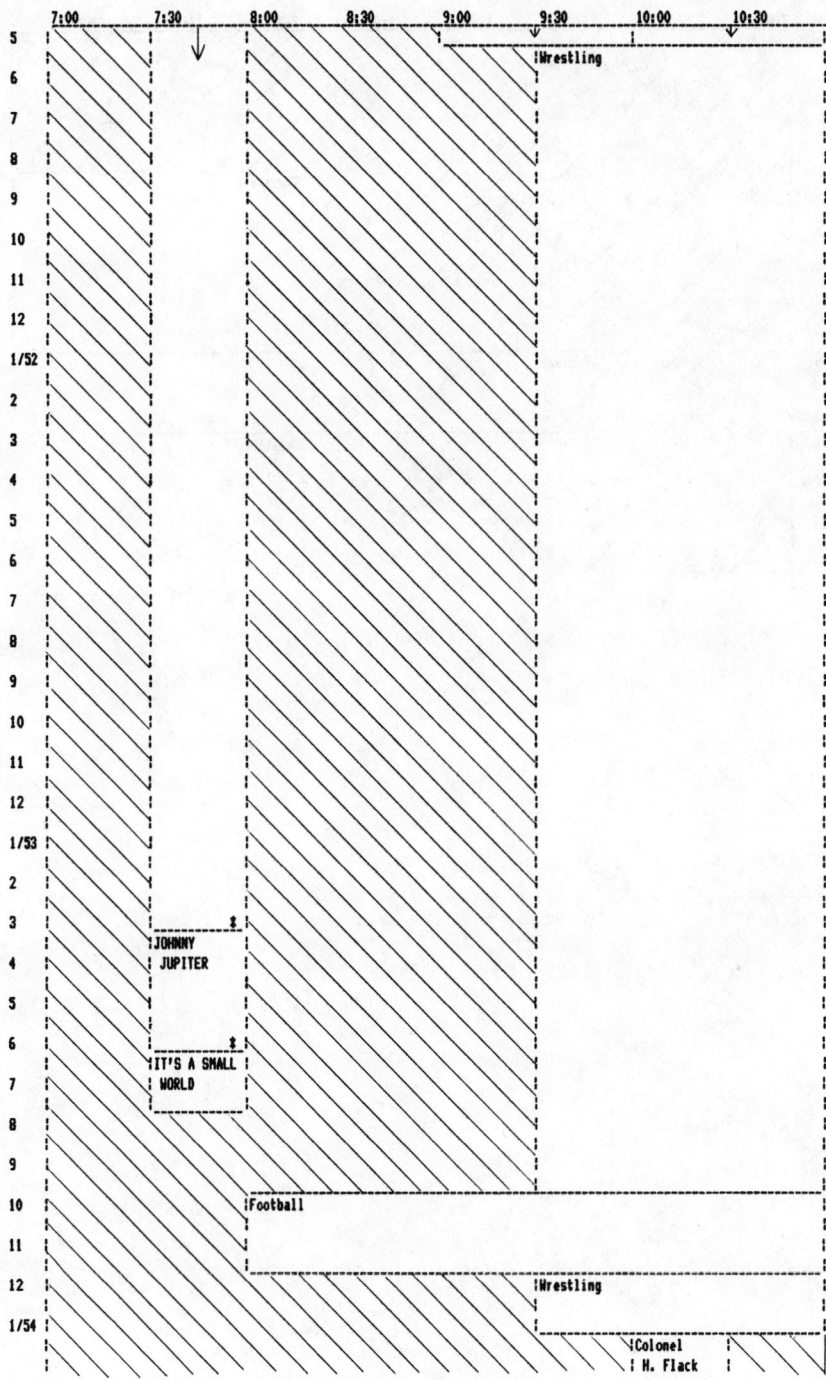

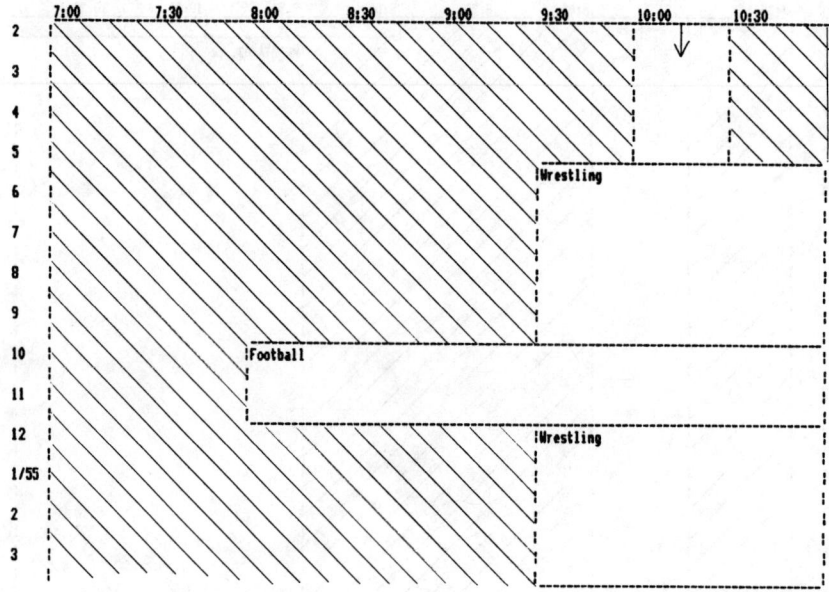

Date	Time	Title (min. if not 30) — Type	Action	From/To
6/49	8:00	Spin the Picture(60) — QU	d	
6/49	9:00	Cavalcade of Stars(60) — CV	d	
9/49	10:00	Wrestling(60) — SP	s	
1/50	8:00	Spin the Picture(60) — QU	m	To:s-8
1/50	8:00	Spin the Picture — QU	m	Fr:s-8
1/50	8:30	Rocky King, Inside Detective — CD	d	
2/50	7:30	Captain Video & Video Rangers — KV	s	
2/50	8:00	Spin the Picture — QU	c	
2/50	8:00	Vincent Lopez — MV	m	Fr:m-f-7:30
5/50	7:00	Film — FI	s	
7/50	8:00	Country Style(60) — MV	d	
7/50	8:00	Vincent Lopez — MV	c	
7/50	8:30	Rocky King, Inside Detective — CD	m	To:f-9:30
9/50	7:00	Captain Video & Video Rangers — KV	m	Fr:s-7:30
9/50	7:00	Film — FI	f	
9/50	7:30	Captain Video & Video Rangers — KV	m	To:s-7
9/50	9:00	Cavalcade of Stars(60) — CV	m	To:f-10
10/50	9:00	Saturday Night at the Garden(60) — SP	s	
11/50	7:00	Captain Video & Video Rangers — KV	f	
11/50	8:00	Country Style(60) — MV	c	
11/50	8:30	Saturday Night at the Garden(90) — SP	s	
11/50	9:00	Saturday Night at the Garden(60) — SP	f	
3/51	8:30	Saturday Night at the Garden(90) — SP	f	
4/51	9:00	They Stand Accused(60) — CR	m	Fr:n-10
5/51	9:00	They Stand Accused(60) — CR	m	To:t-10
5/51	9:30	Wrestling(90) — SP	s	
5/51	10:00	Wrestling(60) — SP	f	
12/51	7:30	Pet Shop — DS	d	
3/53	7:30	Johnny Jupiter — KV	d	
3/53	7:30	Pet Shop — DS	c	
6/53	7:30	It's a Small World — TR	d	
6/53	7:30	Johnny Jupiter — KV	c	
7/53	7:30	It's a Small World — TR	m	To:m-8
9/53	9:30	Wrestling(90) — SP	f	
10/53	8:00	Football(180) — SP	s	
11/53	8:00	Football(180) — SP	f	
12/53	9:30	Wrestling(90) — SP	s	
1/54	9:30	Wrestling(90) — SP	f	
1/54	10:00	Colonel Humphrey Flack — SC	m	Fr:w-9
5/54	9:30	Wrestling(90) — SP	s	

Date	Time	Title (min. if not 30) — Type	Action	From/To
5/54	10:00	Colonel Humphrey Flack — SC	m	To:f-10:30
9/54	9:30	Wrestling(90) — SP	f	
10/54	8:00	Football(180) — SP	s	
11/54	8:00	Football(180) — SP	f	
12/54	9:30	Wrestling(90) — SP	s	
3/55	9:30	Wrestling(90) — SP	f	

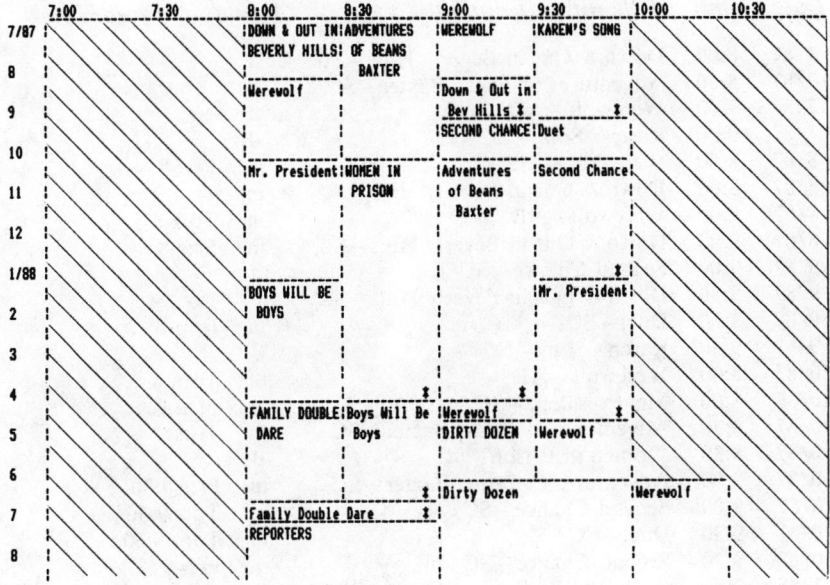

Date	Time	Title (min. if not 30) — Type	Action	From/To
7/87	8:00	Down & Out in Beverly Hills — SC	d	
7/87	8:30	Adventures of Beans Baxter — SC	d	
7/87	9:00	Werewolf — AD	d	
7/87	9:30	Karen's Song — SC	d	
8/87	8:00	Werewolf — AD	m	Fr:s-9
8/87	8:00	Down & Out in Beverly Hills — SC	m	To:s-9
8/87	9:00	Werewolf — AD	m	To:s-8
8/87	9:00	Down & Out in Beverly Hills — SC	m	Fr:s-8
9/87	9:00	Second Chance — SC	d	
9/87	9:00	Down & Out in Beverly Hills — SC	c	
9/87	9:30	Duet — SC	m	Fr:n-8:30
9/87	9:30	Karen's Song — SC	c	
10/87	8:00	Werewolf — AD	m	To:n-8
10/87	8:00	Mr. President — SC	m	Fr:n-9
10/87	8:30	Adventures of Beans Baxter — SC	m	To:s-9
10/87	8:30	Women in Prison — SC	d	
10/87	9:00	Adventures of Beans Baxter — SC	m	Fr:s-8:30
10/87	9:00	Second Chance — SC	m	To:s-9:30
10/87	9:30	Duet — SC	m	To:n-9:30
10/87	9:30	Second Chance — SC	m	Fr:s-9
1/88	8:00	Boys Will Be Boys — SC	d	
1/88	8:00	Mr. President — SC	m	To:s-9:30
1/88	9:30	Mr. President — SC	m	Fr:s-8
1/88	9:30	Second Chance — SC	c	
4/88	8:00	Family Double Dare — QU	d	
4/88	8:00	Boys Will Be Boys — SC	m	To:s-8:30
4/88	8:30	Boys Will Be Boys — SC	m	Fr:s-8
4/88	8:30	Women in Prison — SC	c	
4/88	9:00	Werewolf — AD	m	Fr:n-8
4/88	9:00	Werewolf — AD	m	To:s-9:30
4/88	9:00	Adventures of Beans Baxter — SC	c	
4/88	9:30	Werewolf — AD	m	Fr:s-9
4/88	9:30	Mr. President — SC	c	
5/88	9:00	Dirty Dozen — WD	d	
6/88	9:00	Dirty Dozen — WD	m	To:s-9
6/88	9:00	Dirty Dozen(60) — WD	m#	Fr:s-9
6/88	9:30	Werewolf — AD	m	To:s-10
6/88	10:00	Werewolf — AD	m#	Fr:s-9:30
7/88	8:00	Family Double Dare — QU	m	To:s-8
7/88	8:00	Family Double Dare(60) — QU	m	Fr:s-8
7/88	8:00	Family Double Dare(60) — QU	c	
7/88	8:00	Reporters(60) — AD	d#	
7/88	8:30	Boys Will Be Boys — SC	c	

Saturday Programming
Moves Summary

1948–49

ABC. *Series Premieres:* Draw Me a Laugh; Earl Wrightson; Jacques Fray; Paul Whiteman's TV Teen Club; Stand By for Crime; Stump the Authors; Think Fast; Wren's Nest. *Key Programming Moves:* By March, ABC offered a full lineup of programming on Saturday; PAUL WHITE-MAN'S TV TEEN CLUB debuts in 4/49; it continues on ABC's Saturday lineup until 12/53.

CBS. *Series Premieres:* Blues by Bargy; Hold It Please; In the First Person. *Key Programming Moves:* CBS starts slowly on Saturday, offering only minimal programming during 1948–49.

NBC. *Series Premieres:* Eddie Condon; The Eyes Have It; Garroway at Large; Saturday Night Jamboree; U.S. Marine Band. *Key Programming Moves:* NBC offers the most ambitious slate of Saturday night programming of the networks; even so, none of the series they air makes any lasting impression.

DuMont. *Series Premieres:* Cavalcade of Stars; Spin the Picture. *Key Programming Moves:* DuMont doesn't begin offering programming on Saturday until 6/49; CAVALCADE OF STARS debuts in 6/49.

1949–50

ABC. *Series Premieres:* Buck Rogers. *Key Programming Moves:* In November, ABC schedules Roller Derby in the 9–11 slot; it lasts until 5/51.

CBS. *Series Premieres:* Big Top; The Trap; We Take Your Word. *Key Programming Moves:* THE KEN MURRAY SHOW is moved to Saturday in 3/50; it occupied the 8–9 slot until 6/52.

NBC. *Series Premieres:* American Forum of the Air; Around the

Town; Chicagoland Jazz; Children's Sketch Book; Faye Emerson; Jack Carter Show; Saturday Square; Stud's Place; Twenty Questions; Waiting for the Break; Your Show of Shows. *Key Programming Moves:* YOUR SHOW OF SHOWS debuts in 2/50; this 90 minute comedy variety series, starring Sid Caesar, becomes one of the classics; it is highly popular with the audience, lasting until 6/54.

DuMont. *Series Premieres:* Country Style; Rocky King Show. *Key Programming Moves:* DuMont offers professional wrestling in the 10–11 slot; wrestling would be a mainstay on DuMont's Saturday night lineup throughout its history.

1950-51

ABC. *Series Premieres:* Sandy Dreams; Stu Erwin Show. *Key Programming Moves:* THE STU ERWIN SHOW debuts; at the end of the season it is moved to Friday.

CBS. *Series Premieres:* Faye Emerson; Frank Sinatra; Sam Levenson. *Key Programming Moves:* CBS brings Frank Sinatra to prime time television as THE FRANK SINATRA SHOW debuts; it is not the hit CBS had hoped it would be and it is moved to Tuesday at the end of the season; BEAT THE CLOCK is moved into the 7:30–8 slot in 3/51; it occupied this time period until 9/56.

NBC. *Series Premieres:* Hank McCune; Saturday Roundup; Tom Corbett; Victor Borge. *Key Programming Moves:* YOUR HIT PARADE is moved to Saturday in the 10:30–11 slot, following YOUR SHOW OF SHOWS; it occupied this slot until 6/58; YOUR SHOW OF SHOWS is the #4 rated series on television.

DuMont. *Series Premieres:* Pet Shop. *Key Programming Moves:* By 5/51, DuMont has cut back its Saturday night programming to two hours (7:30–8 and 9:30–11); wrestling is expanded to 90 minutes.

1951-52

ABC. *Series Premieres:* Lesson in Safety; Personal Appearance Theatre. *Key Programming Moves:* In December, PAUL WHITEMAN'S TV TEEN CLUB is cut back to 30 minutes.

CBS. *Series Premieres:* All Around Town. *Key Programming Moves:* THE KEN MURRAY SHOW is taken off the air in 6/52; a 30 minute version returns in 2/53 on Sunday.

NBC. *Series Premieres:* Watch Mr. Wizard; Youth Wants to Know. *Key Programming Moves:* ALL STAR REVUE is moved to Saturday, 8–9; it continues in this slot until its cancellation in 4/53. YOUR SHOW OF SHOWS is the #8 rated series on television.

1952-53

ABC. *Series Premieres:* What's Your Bid.

CBS. *Series Premieres:* All in One; Balance Your Budget; Bank on the Stars; Jackie Gleason Show; Jane Froman; Medallion Theatre; Meet Millie. *Key Programming Moves:* THE JACKIE GLEASON SHOW debuts; this comedy variety series becomes a feature on CBS' Saturday night lineup over the next 18 years.

NBC. *Series Premieres:* Ethel and Albert; My Hero. *Key Programming Moves:* ALL STAR REVUE is cancelled in 4/53.

DuMont. *Series Premieres:* It's a Small World; Johnny Jupiter. *Key Programming Moves:* DuMont ceases programming in the 7:30-8 slot in 7/53, leaving the network with only 90 minutes of Saturday night programming.

1953-54

ABC. *Series Premieres:* Greatest Sports Thrills; Showcase Theatre.

CBS. *Series Premieres:* My Favorite Husband; That's My Boy; Two in Love. *Key Programming Moves:* TWO FOR THE MONEY is moved to Saturday, 9-9:30; MY FAVORITE HUSBAND debuts; series stays on CBS' schedule until 9/57; THE JACKIE GLEASON SHOW is the #8 rated series on television.

NBC. *Series Premieres:* Bonino; Spike Jones. *Key Programming Moves:* YOUR SHOW OF SHOWS is cancelled in 6/54.

DuMont. *Key Programming Moves:* DuMont airs professional football live, in the 8-11 slot.

1954-55

ABC. *Series Premieres:* Compass; Lawrence Welk Show; Let's Dance; Ozark Jubilee; Tomorrow's Careers. *Key Programming Moves:* THE LAWRENCE WELK SHOW debuts in 7/55 in the 9-10 slot; this series stays on ABC's Saturday night schedule until its cancellation in 9/71; it then went into syndication and continued into the 1980s.

CBS. *Series Premieres:* America's Greatest Bands; Damon Runyon Theatre; Professional Father; Willy. *Key Programming Moves:* THE GENE

AUTRY SHOW is moved to Saturday, 7–7:30, where it stayed until its cancellation in 8/56; THE JACKIE GLEASON SHOW leaves the air at the end of the season, even though it was the #2 rated series on television; Mr. Gleason returned the following season in THE HONEYMOONERS; MY FAVORITE HUSBAND is moved to Tuesday at the end of the season.

NBC. *Series Premieres:* Amazing Dunninger; Donald O'Connor; George Gobel Show; Imogene Coca Show; Jimmy Durante Show; Mickey Rooney Show; Musical Chairs; So This Is Hollywood; The Soldiers; Swift Show Wagon. *Key Programming Moves:* THE GEORGE GOBEL SHOW debuts; it becomes the #8 rated series on television; it goes on to a highly successful five year run on NBC.

DuMont. *Key Programming Moves:* DuMont ceases programming on Saturday in 3/55.

1955–56

ABC. *Series Premieres:* Grand Ole Opry.

CBS. *Series Premieres:* Gunsmoke; High Finance; The Honeymooners; It's Always Jan; Russ Morgan; Saturday Sports. *Key Programming Moves:* GUNSMOKE debuts; this western series occupied the 10–10:30 slot; it would become one of the most successful series in the history of television, lasting 21 years, all on CBS; THE HONEYMOONERS debuts; although this series starring Jackie Gleason was a modest hit, CBS dropped it at the end of the season and brought Jackie Gleason back in a 60 minute variety series the following year.

NBC. *Series Premieres:* Big Surprise; Festival of Stars. *Key Programming Moves:* THE PERRY COMO SHOW is moved to Saturday, 8–9; it occupied this slot until 6/59.

1956–57

ABC. *Series Premieres:* Billy Graham; Galen Drake.

CBS. *Series Premieres:* Buccaneers; Gale Strom Show; Hey Jeannie; Jimmy Dean Show; S.R.O. Playhouse; You're on Your Own. *Key Programming Moves:* GUNSMOKE becomes the #8 rated series on television; TWO FOR THE MONEY is cancelled at the end of the season.

NBC. *Series Premieres:* George Sanders. *Key Programming Moves:* PEOPLE ARE FUNNY is moved to Saturday, 7:30–8; it stays in this time slot until 9/59; THE PERRY COMO SHOW becomes the #9 rated series on television.

1957–58

ABC. *Series Premieres:* Dick Clark; Keep It in the Family. *Key Programming Moves:* THE DICK CLARK SHOW debuts; this was a prime time version of his successful daytime series; it lasted three years in prime time.

CBS. *Series Premieres:* Dick and the Duchess; Have Gun Will Travel; Perry Mason; Top Dollar. *Key Programming Moves:* PERRY MASON debuts in the 7:30–8:30 slot, which it occupied until 9/62; this courtroom drama was to become the prototype for all lawyer series to follow; HAVE GUN WILL TRAVEL debuts in the 9:30–10 slot, leading-in to GUNSMOKE; it occupied this slot until its cancellation in 9/63; GUNSMOKE becomes the #1 rated series on television; HAVE GUN WILL TRAVEL is #4; this marked the beginning of a wave of westerns on all three networks, each tryng to capitalize and duplicate the success and appeal of GUNSMOKE.

NBC. *Series Premieres:* Club Oasis; End of the Rainbow; Gisele MacKenzie; Opening Night; Polly Bergen; Turning Point; What's It For. *Key Programming Moves:* YOUR HIT PARADE is dropped at the end of the season; it is picked up by CBS and moved to Friday the following season.

1958–59

CBS. *Series Premieres:* Face of Danger; Markham; Wanted Dead or Alive. *Key Programming Moves:* Riding the popularity of the western wave, WANTED DEAD OR ALIVE debuts; it lasts until 3/61; GUNSMOKE is again the #1 rated series on television; HAVE GUN WILL TRAVEL is #3, as CBS wins Saturday night handily; six of the top seven series on television are westerns.

NBC. *Series Premieres:* Black Saddle; Brains and Brawn; Cimarron City; The D.A.'s Man; Perry Presents; Steve Canyon. *Key Programming Moves:* THE PERRY COMO SHOW is moved to Wednesday at the end of the season.

1959–60

ABC. *Key Programming Moves:* LEAVE IT TO BEAVER is moved to Saturday, 8:30–9, where it stays for the next three years; THE DICK CLARK SHOW is cancelled at the end of the season.

CBS. *Series Premieres:* Mr. Lucky. *Key Programming Moves:* CBS is again the clear ratings winner on Saturday, with GUNSMOKE being the

#1 rated series for the third consecutive year and HAVE GUN WILL TRAVEL #3.

NBC. *Series Premieres:* Bonanza; The Deputy; Five Fingers; Man and the Challenge; Man from Interpol; World Wide '60. *Key Programming Moves:* BONANZA debuts; this western series will go on to become one of the most successful series in television history once it is moved to Sunday in 9/61.

1960–61

ABC. *Series Premieres:* The Roaring Twenties. *Key Programming Moves:* ABC brings back boxing to Saturday night (in the 10–11 slot); it stays with it for the next three years.

CBS. *Series Premieres:* Checkmate. *Key Programming Moves:* CBS wins Saturday night again; GUNSMOKE extends its reign as television's #1 series to four years; HAVE GUN WILL TRAVEL is #3 for the third consecutive year.

NBC. *Series Premieres:* The Campaign and the Candidates; The Nation's Future; The Tall Men. *Key Programming Moves:* NBC concedes the 9:30– 10:30 slot to CBS by scheduling public affairs programming during this time period; BONANZA is moved to Sunday at the end of the season.

1961–62

ABC. *Series Premieres:* Room for One More. *Key Programming Moves:* LEAVE IT TO BEAVER is moved to Thursday at the end of the season.

CBS. *Series Premieres:* The Defenders. *Key Programming Moves:* GUNSMOKE is expanded to 60 minutes; it is still highly popular (rated #3); PERRY MASON becomes the #5 rated series on television; it is moved to Thursday at the end of the season; THE DEFENDERS debuts in the 8:30–9:30 slot, following PERRY MASON; this series, which lasted for five years, became one of the most critically acclaimed series in the history of television.

NBC. *Key Programming Moves:* TALES OF WELLS FARGO is moved to Saturday; it is cancelled at the end of the season; NBC begins airing films in the 9–11 slot; it continues this practice until 9/78.

1962-63

ABC. *Series Premieres:* Hootenanny; Mr. Smith Goes to Washington; Roy Rogers & Dale Evans. *Key Programming Moves:* ABC discontinues airing boxing at the end of the season.

CBS. *Key Programming Moves:* THE JACKIE GLEASON SHOW is returned to Saturday night and placed in the 7:30-8:30 slot; it stays in this slot until its cancellation in 9/70; GUNSMOKE, while still popular, drops to #10 in the ratings; HAVE GUN WILL TRAVEL is cancelled at the end of the season.

NBC. *Series Premieres:* Sam Benedict.

1963-64

ABC. *Series Premieres:* Hollywood Palace; Jerry Lewis Show. *Key Programming Moves:* ABC introduces THE JERRY LEWIS SHOW, a 90 minute talk show; it is cancelled after three months; HOLLYWOOD PALACE debuts; this variety series, featuring different talent each week, stayed on ABC's schedule until 2/70.

CBS. *Series Premieres:* New Phil Silvers Show. *Key Programming Moves:* THE DEFENDERS is moved to Thursday at the end of the season.

NBC. *Series Premieres:* The Lieutenant.

1964-65

ABC. *Series Premieres:* King Family. *Key Programming Moves:* THE KING FAMILY debuts in 1/65, giving ABC a three hour block of variety programs on Saturday night.

CBS. *Series Premieres:* Gilligan's Island; Mr. Broadway; Secret Agent. *Key Programming Moves:* GILLIGAN'S ISLAND debuts; this series is a modest success and is moved to Thursday at the end of the season.

NBC. *Series Premieres:* Flipper; Kentucky Jones; Mr. Magoo.

1965-66

ABC. *Key Programming Moves:* In January, ABC moved two of its long-running situation comedies to Saturday, THE ADVENTURES OF OZZIE & HARRIET and THE DONNA REED SHOW; both are cancelled at the end of the season.

CBS. *Series Premieres:* The Face Is Familiar; The Loner; Trials of O'Brien.

NBC. *Series Premieres:* Get Smart; I Dream of Jeannie. *Key Programming Moves:* I DREAM OF JEANNIE and GET SMART debut; both of these series will have long, successful runs on NBC; at the end of the season I DREAM OF JEANNIE is moved to Monday.

1966–67

ABC. *Series Premieres:* Newlywed Game; Piccadilly Palace; Shane. *Key Programming Moves:* In 1/67, THE DATING GAME is moved into the 7:30-8 slot and THE NEWLYWED GAME debuts in the 8-8:30 slot, forming a one hour block of quiz shows; this block continues for the next four years.

CBS. *Series Premieres:* Mission: Impossible; Pistols 'n' Petticoats. *Key Programming Moves:* MISSION: IMPOSSIBLE debuts; this series will stay on CBS' schedule for the next seven years; THE JACKIE GLEASON SHOW becomes the #5 rated series on television; GUNSMOKE is moved to Monday at the end of the season.

1967–68

CBS. *Series Premieres:* Mannix. *Key Programming Moves:* MANNIX debuts in the 10-11 slot, which it occupies until 9/71; CBS moves MY THREE SONS, HOGAN'S HEROES and PETTICOAT JUNCTION to Saturday, establishing a 90 minute sitcom block from 8:30-10; THE JACKIE GLEASON SHOW is the #9 rated series on television.

NBC. *Series Premieres:* Maya.

1968–69

CBS. *Key Programming Moves:* HOGAN'S HEROES is moved to Friday at the end of the season.

NBC. *Series Premieres:* Adam 12; The Ghost and Mrs. Muir. *Key Programming Moves:* ADAM 12 debuts; this series will continue on NBC's schedule for the next seven years; GET SMART is moved to Friday at the end of the season.

1969-70

ABC. *Key Programming Moves:* In January, THE DATING GAME is cancelled and replaced by LET'S MAKE A DEAL; HOLLYWOOD PALACE is cancelled in 2/70.

CBS. *Key Programming Moves:* GREEN ACRES is moved to Saturday; at the end of the season it is moved to Tuesday; THE JACKIE GLEASON SHOW and PETTICOAT JUNCTION are both cancelled at the end of the season.

NBC. *Series Premieres:* Andy Williams Show.

1970-71

ABC. *Series Premieres:* Most Deadly Game; Pearl Bailey Show; Val Doonican Show. *Key Programming Moves:* ABC moves LET'S MAKE A DEAL and THE NEWLYWED GAME to Monday in 1/71; THE LAWRENCE WELK SHOW is cancelled at the end of the season; it will continue in syndication into the 1980s.

CBS. *Series Premieres:* Arnie; Mary Tyler Moore Show. *Key Programming Moves:* THE MARY TYLER MOORE SHOW debuts; this highly successful series will be an integral part of CBS' Saturday schedule until its cancellation in 9/77; MY THREE SONS is moved to Monday and MANNIX is moved to Wednesday at the end of the season.

NBC. *Series Premieres:* NBC Adventure Theatre.

1971-72

ABC. *Series Premieres:* Getting Together; The Persuaders; Sixth Sense. *Key Programming Moves:* All three networks cut back to three hours of prime time programming in compliance with the FCC's new Prime Time Access Rule; BEWITCHED is moved to Saturday in 1/72; it is cancelled at the end of the season.

CBS. *Series Premieres:* Funny Face; The New Dick Van Dyke Show. *Key Programming Moves:* ALL IN THE FAMILY is moved to Saturday and placed in the 8-8:30 slot; in this slot, it becomes the highest rated series on television and becomes a very strong lead-in and anchor for CBS' Saturday night lineup; THE MARY TYLER MOORE SHOW is the #10 rated series on television.

NBC. *Series Premieres:* Emergency; The Good Life; Partners. *Key Programming Moves:* EMERGENCY debuts in 1/72; this series occupies the 8-9 slot for its entire five year run.

1972–73

ABC. *Series Premieres:* Burns and Schreiber; Here We Go Again; Kung Fu; Strauss Family; Streets of San Francisco; A Touch of Grace. *Key Programming Moves:* THE STREETS OF SAN FRANCISCO debuts; in 1/73 it is moved to Thursday, where it runs for over four years.

CBS. *Series Premieres:* Bob Newhart Show; Bridget Loves Bernie. *Key Programming Moves:* BRIDGET LOVES BERNIE debuts; although it is the #5 rated series on television (due primarily to the audience provided by ALL IN THE FAMILY, again the #1 series), it is cancelled at the end of the season; THE BOB NEWHART SHOW debuts, beginning a highly successful six year run on CBS; THE CAROL BURNETT SHOW is moved to Saturday, 10–11, in 12/72; along with THE MARY TYLER MOORE SHOW (#7 rated series), CBS' Saturday lineup is one of the strongest in the history of television.

1973–74

ABC. *Series Premieres:* Griff.

CBS. *Key Programming Moves:* M*A*S*H is moved into the 8:30–9 slot; it stays for one season and is then moved to Tuesday; CBS' Saturday lineup is again the runaway ratings winner, with ALL IN THE FAMILY (#1), M*A*S*H (#4), and THE MARY TYLER MOORE SHOW (#9) all among the top ten rated series.

1974–75

ABC. *Series Premieres:* Keep on Truckin'; Nakia; The New Land.

CBS. *Series Premieres:* Big Eddie; The Jeffersons; Paul Sand in Friends and Lovers. *Key Programming Moves:* THE JEFFERSONS debuts in 1/75; this is the third spin-off from ALL IN THE FAMILY; it is an immediate hit (#4 rated series) and helps continue CBS' dominance on Saturday; ALL IN THE FAMILY is the #1 rated series for the fourth consecutive year; at the end of the season it is moved to Monday.

1975–76

ABC. *Series Premieres:* Bert D'Angelo, Superstar; Howard Cosell Live; Matt Helm. *Key Programming Moves:* ABC tries a live variety series hosted by Howard Cosell; the series, HOWARD COSELL LIVE, lasts only four months.

CBS. *Series Premieres:* Doc. *Key Programming Moves:* CBS continues its dominance on Saturday, though it is showing signs of slippage (none of its series were rated in the top 10); THE JEFFERSONS is moved to Wednesday at the end of the season.

1976–77

ABC. *Series Premieres:* Blansky's Beauties; Dog and Cat; Fish; Holmes and YoYo; Most Wanted; Mr. T and Tina; Sugar Time; Wonder Woman. *Key Programming Moves:* ABC is constantly shuffling its lineup; nothing catches on.

CBS. *Key Programming Moves:* ALL IN THE FAMILY is returned to Saturday; ALICE is also moved to Saturday, continuing CBS' two-hour block of sitcoms; THE MARY TYLER MOORE SHOW is cancelled and ALL IN THE FAMILY and ALICE are moved to Sunday at the end of the season.

NBC. *Key Programming Moves:* EMERGENCY is cancelled at the end of the season.

1977–78

ABC. *Series Premieres:* ABC Comedy Special; Fantasy Island; Free Country; The Love Boat; Operation Petticoat; Tabitha. *Key Programming Moves:* THE LOVE BOAT debuts; this successful series lasts until 8/86; FANTASY ISLAND debuts in 1/78; it continues on ABC until 8/84.

CBS. *Series Premieres:* Another Day; Ted Knight Show; We've Got Each Other. *Key Programming Moves:* CBS is constantly shuffling its lineup; THE CAROL BURNETT SHOW is moved to Sunday in 12/77; Long-running CBS series, KOJAK and MAUDE are moved to Saturday and then they are cancelled in 4/78; THE BOB NEWHART SHOW is cancelled at the end of the season.

NBC. *Key Programming Moves:* NBC picks up THE BIONIC WOMAN after ABC dropped it and placed it on Saturday; it is cancelled at the end of the season; NBC discontinues airing films in the 9–11 slot at the end of the season.

1978–79

ABC. *Series Premieres:* Apple Pie; Delta House; Hart to Hart. *Key Programming Moves:* ABC is constantly shuffling its 8–9 slot; nothing catches on.

CBS. *Series Premieres:* American Girls; Bad News Bears; White Shadow. *Key Programming Moves:* RHODA is moved to Saturday; it is cancelled in 12/78; CBS begins airing films in the 9–11 slot in 12/78; they continue this practice for most of the next eight years.

NBC. *Series Premieres:* B.J. and the Bear; Sword of Justice; Weekend. *Key Programming Moves:* CHIPS is moved to Saturday, 8–9; it stays in this slot until 3/80.

1979–80

CBS. *Series Premieres:* Big Shamus, Little Shamus; Hagen; Paris; That's My Line; Tim Conway Show; Universe; Working Stiffs. *Key Programming Moves:* CBS is looking for a lineup that works; nothing does; HAWAII FIVE-O is moved to Saturday in 3/80; it is cancelled in 5/80.

NBC. *Series Premieres:* Good Time Harry; Joe's World; A Man Called Sloane; Me and Maxx; Sanford. *Key Programming Moves:* CHIPS is moved to Sunday in 3/80.

1980–81

ABC. *Series Premieres:* Breaking Away. *Key Programming Moves:* THE LOVE BOAT becomes the #5 rated series on television, as ABC becomes the ratings leader on Saturday.

CBS. *Series Premieres:* Concrete Cowboys; Freebie and the Bean; Riker; Secrets of Midland Heights.

NBC. *Series Premieres:* Gangster Chronicles; Hill Street Blues; Walking Tall. *Key Programming Moves:* HILL STREET BLUES debuts in 1/81; this series breaks new ground in the crime drama genre — it is more realistic than previous crime dramas and has several storylines within each episode, some of which trail on for weeks; this series is not a ratings success but is highly praised by critics and NBC stays with it.

1981–82

ABC. *Series Premieres:* King's Crossing; Maggie; Open All Night; T.J. Hooker.

NBC. *Series Premieres:* Billy Crystal; Chicago Story; Fitz and Bones; Nashville Palace; One of the Boys; Television: Inside and Out. *Key Programming Moves:* NBC is continually changing its lineup; nothing catches on.

1982–83

ABC. *Key Programming Moves:* THE LOVE BOAT is the #9 rated series on television.

CBS. *Series Premieres:* Wizards and Warriors.

NBC. *Series Premieres:* Devlin Connection; Family Tree; Mama's Family; Monitor; Silver Spoons. *Key Programming Moves:* DIFF'RENT STROKES is moved to Saturday, 8–8:30; it stays in this time slot until 8/85.

1983–84

ABC. *Key Programming Moves:* FANTASY ISLAND is cancelled at the end of the season.

CBS. *Series Premieres:* Airwolf; Cutter to Houston; Mike Hammer.

NBC. *Series Premieres:* People Are Funny; The Rousters; Yellow Rose.

1984–85

ABC. *Series Premieres:* Finder of Lost Loves.

CBS. *Series Premieres:* Cover Up; Otherworld.

NBC. *Series Premieres:* Berengers; Hot Pursuit; Partners in Crime; Spencer; Under One Roof. *Key Programming Moves:* NBC schedules a two-hour block of situation comedies from 8–10; it begins to attract an audience.

1985–86

ABC. *Series Premieres:* Fortune Dane; Hollywood Beat; Lime Street; Redd Foxx Show. *Key Programming Moves:* THE LOVE BOAT has finally run its course, after nine years on Saturday night; DIFF'RENT STROKES is moved to Saturday in 6/86; it is cancelled at the end of the season, as is BENSON.

CBS. *Key Programming Moves:* For the sixth consecutive year, CBS has not made any significant programming moves on Saturday night.

NBC. *Series Premieres:* Golden Girls; Me & Mrs. C; 227. *Key Programming Moves:* THE GOLDEN GIRLS debuts; this series forms a strong anchor for NBC's lineup, which is now the ratings leader on Saturday.

1986-87

ABC. *Series Premieres:* Animal Crack-Ups; Ellen Burstyn Show; Heart of the City; Life with Lucy; O'Hara. *Key Programming Moves:* ABC brings back Lucille Ball to weekly television in LIFE WITH LUCY; it does not do well and is cancelled after two months.

CBS. *Series Premieres:* Downtown; The Outlaws.

NBC. *Series Premieres:* Amen; Easy Street. *Key Programming Moves:* NBC strengthens its leading position on Saturday with a new series, AMEN; it becomes a modest hit.

Fox. *Series Premieres:* Adventures of Beans Baxter; Down & Out in Beverly Hills; Karen's Song; Werewolf. *Key Programming Moves:* Fox introduces its second night of programming in 7/87, with two hours (8–10) of offerings; none of their entries makes a significant impact.

1987-88

ABC. *Series Premieres:* Once a Hero; Sable. *Key Programming Moves:* DOLLY and HOTEL are moved to Saturday and subsequently cancelled.

CBS. *Series Premieres:* Everything's Relative; High Mountain Rangers; Leg Work. *Key Programming Moves:* With the move of TOUR OF DUTY to Saturday in 3/88 CBS appears to finally have some stability in its Saturday lineup; KATE & ALLIE is moved to Saturday in 7/88, and is cancelled at the end of the season.

NBC. *Key Programming Moves:* NBC is the ratings leader on Saturday again; THE FACTS OF LIFE is cancelled at the end of the season.

Fox. *Series Premieres:* Boys Will Be Boys; Dirty Dozen; Family Double Dare; The Reporters; Second Chance; Women in Prison. *Key Programming Moves:* Fox expands its Saturday lineup to 2½ hours (8–10:30) in 7/88.

Index

H

Midwestern Hayride 6, 23, 55, 70, 71, 263, 264, 351, 366, 561, 577, 614, 629, 680
Mike Nesmith 572, 586, 607
Mike Wallace Interviews 6, 23, 24, 86, 614, 629
The Millionaire 325–327, 339, 341, 383, 385
Milton Berle Show **(1948–56)** 247–249, 262, 264, 279; **(1958–59)** 352, 367, 384; **(1966–67)** 511, 526, 602
Misadventures of Sheriff Lobo 258–259, 270, 291
Misfits of Science 572, 586, 608
Miss Winslow and Son 334, 345, 392
Mission: Impossible 35–37, 47, 89, 542–543, 555, 644, 646, 657, 658, 704
The Mississippi 232, 244, 557
Mr. Adams and Eve 223, 239, 537, 552, 598
Mr. & Mrs. North 248–249, 264, 535, 551, 596
Mr. Arsenic 400, 415, 489
Mr. Belvedere 518–519, 531, 532, 533, 607
Mr. Black 99, 114, 180
Mr. Broadway 643, 657, 703
Mr. Citizen 299, 315, 383
Mr. Deeds Goes to Town 512, 527, 603
Mr. District Attorney 100, 115, 116, 181
Mr. Ed 328–329, 342, 387, 434, 449, 493
Mr. Garlund 538, 553, 599
Mr. I Magination 29, 44, 83
Mr. Lucky 642, 656, 701
Mr. Magoo 669–670, 684, 703
Mr. Merlin 137, 148, 335, 345, 346, 393
Mr. Novak 252–253, 267, 286
Mr. Peepers 53–54, 68, 69, 85, 455, 471, 489
Mr. President 82, 94, 695, 696
Mr. Roberts 565, 581, 601
Mr. Smith 571, 585, 607
Mr. Smith Goes to Washington 616, 630, 703
Mr. Sunshine 310, 322, 518, 531, 532, 608, 624, 636
Mr. T and Tina 621, 633, 707
Mr. Terrific 131, 145, 187
Mixed Doubles 559, 575, 594, 664, 679
Mobile One 108, 122, 514, 529, 605
The Mod Squad 204–205, 216, 217, 287, 288, 407–408, 422, 496
Modern Science Theater 402, 418, 491
Mohawk Showroom 151–152, 166, 167, 180, 247, 262, 279, 349–350, 364, 365, 380, 454, 469, 470, 487, 559, 574, 576, 594
Moment of Decision 300, 315, 383

Moment of Fear **(1960)** 563, 579, 599; **(1964–65)** 252, 253, 267, 286
Moments of Music 198, 212, 280
Mona McCluskey 460, 474, 494
Monday Night Special 107, 121, 189
Monday Theatre 171, 172
Monitor 64, 75, 93, 676, 687, 709
The Monkees 157–158, 171, 187, 188
The Monroes 303, 318, 387
The Montefuscos 463, 476, 497
Moonlighting 210–211, 219, 293
Morey Amsterdam 125, 140, 481, 484, 487, 534, 549, 594
Mork and Mindy 14, 26, 27, 92, 409–411, 424, 425, 498, 499
Morning Star/Evening Star 233, 245, 293
Moses – the Lawgiver 40, 50, 658
The Most Deadly Game 619, 631, 705
Most Important People 374, 378, 381, 588, 591, 592, 595
Most Wanted **(1976–77)** 109, 122, 621, 633, 707; **(1987–88)** 82, 95
Mothers-in-Law 58–59, 72, 89
Motorola TV Theater 198–199, 213, 282
Motown Revue 572, 586, 607
Movieland Quiz 197, 212
Movin' On 256–257, 269, 463, 475, 497
Mulligan's Stew 257, 269, 291
The Munsters 434–435, 450, 494
Murder, She Wrote 42–43, 51, 94
Music at the Meadowbrook 401, 417, 612, 627, 628
Music Bingo 457, 472, 491
Music Country USA 463, 475, 497
Music 55 222, 238, 282
Music for a Summer Night 300–301, 316, 384
Music from Chicago 77–78, 80, 84
Music Hall 221, 237, 281, 430, 446, 489
Music in Velvet 3, 4, 18, 20, 83
Music on Ice 56, 71, 87
The Music Scene 121, 160, 188
Music Shop 55, 70, 87
The Music Show 274, 277, 278, 281, 375–376, 379
Musical Almanac 151, 166, 247, 262, 559, 574
Musical Chairs 666, 682, 700
Musical Merry-Go-Round 559, 574
My Favorite Husband 45, 46, 222, 238, 639–640, 655, 699, 700
My Favorite Martian 34–35, 46, 47, 88
My Friend Flicka 55, 70, 326, 340, 536–537, 552, 597, 641, 656
My Friend Irma 221, 237, 281, 535–536, 551, 596, 597
My Friend Tony 59, 72, 89

Q